T5-CQD-417

North Island

	AUCKLAND	BULLS	DANNEVIRKE	GISBORNE	HAMILTON	HASTINGS	KAITAIA	LEVIN	MASTERTON	NAPIER	NEW PLYMOUTH	PALMERSTON NTH	ROTORUA	TAUMARUNUI	TAUPO	TAURANGA	THAMES	WAIOURU	WANGANUI	WELLINGTON	WHAKATANE
BULLS	498																				
DANNEVIRKE	548	84																			
GISBORNE	509	421	337																		
HAMILTON	126	372	422	400																	
HASTINGS	447	187	103	236	321																
KAITAIA	325	823	873	834	451	772															
LEVIN	554	56	104	441	428	207	879														
MASTERTON	637	139	109	446	511	212	962	159													
NAPIER	426	206	122	215	300	21	751	226	231												
NEW PLYMOUTH	368	207	291	609	242	322	693	263	346	413											
PALMERSTON NTH	528	30	54	391	402	157	853	50	109	176	237										
ROTORUA	235	311	351	291	109	250	560	367	450	229	318	341									
TAUMARUNUI	318	210	294	468	162	285	613	266	349	264	183	240	177								
TAUPO	279	229	269	334	153	168	604	285	368	147	300	259	82	117							
TAURANGA	210	394	434	299	108	333	535	450	533	312	350	424	83	260	165						
THAMES	115	440	480	413	106	447	440	496	579	358	348	470	167	268	211	114					
WAIOURU	423	115	199	478	267	282	748	171	254	261	288	145	196	105	114	279	325				
WANGANUI	454	44	128	465	328	231	779	100	183	250	163	74	307	166	225	390	434	127			
WELLINGTON	647	149	197	534	521	300	972	93	99	319	356	143	460	359	378	543	589	264	193		
WHAKATANE	304	391	437	205	195	336	629	447	530	315	404	421	86	263	168	94	208	282	393	546	
WHANGAREI	171	669	719	680	297	618	154	725	808	597	539	699	406	489	450	381	286	594	625	818	475

Travel Distances

South Island

	ALEXANDRA	ASHBURTON	BLENHEIM	CHRISTCHURCH	DUNEDIN	GORE	GREYMOUTH	HAAST	HOKITIKA	INVERCARGILL	KAIKOURA	MILFORD	MT COOK	NELSON	OAMARU	PICTON	QUEENSTOWN	REEFTON	TE ANAU	TIMARU	WANAKA
ASHBURTON	371																				
BLENHEIM	778	407																			
CHRISTCHURCH	457	86	321																		
DUNEDIN	189	275	683	361																	
GORE	139	427	834	513	152																
GREYMOUTH	570	295	331	255	565	709															
HAAST	235	490	666	554	424	374	335														
HOKITIKA	529	300	372	260	570	668	41	294													
INVERCARGILL	204	492	899	578	217	65	731	396	690												
KAIKOURA	646	275	132	189	547	702	338	673	379	767											
MILFORD	387	685	1092	771	410	258	849	514	808	280	960										
MT COOK	241	244	651	330	319	380	524	360	529	445	519	578									
NELSON	866	503	117	417	799	951	296	631	337	1016	249	1145	747								
OAMARU	227	161	568	247	114	266	451	383	456	331	436	524	215	685							
PICTON	807	436	29	350	711	863	360	695	401	928	161	1121	680	113	597						
QUEENSTOWN	92	401	808	487	281	167	554	219	513	189	676	307	271	850	294	837					
REEFTON	649	339	252	253	609	781	79	414	120	826	259	928	603	217	495	281	633				
TE ANAU	266	564	971	650	289	137	728	393	687	159	839	121	426	1024	403	1000	166	807			
TIMARU	312	76	483	162	199	351	366	426	371	416	351	609	209	600	85	512	337	410	488		
WANAKA	87	347	749	428	276	226	483	148	442	248	617	366	212	779	235	778	71	562	245	278	
WESTPORT	675	400	265	336	670	814	105	440	146	836	342	954	629	230	556	294	659	83	823	471	588

Travel Distances

Reed
New Zealand Atlas

Reed
New Zealand Atlas

General Editor
D.W. McKenzie

Reed
in association with the
Department of Survey and Land Information

Contents

Published by Reed Books, a division of Reed Publishing (NZ) Ltd, 39 Rawene Road, Birkenhead, Auckland 10. Associated companies, branches and representatives throughout the world. **www.reed.co.nz**

This book is copyright. Except for the purpose of fair reviewing, no part of this publication may be reproduced, or transmitted in any form or by any means, electronic or mechanical, including photocopying, recording, or any information storage and retrieval system, without permission in writing from the publisher. Infringers of copyright render themselves liable to prosecution.

ISBN 0 7900 0400 3

Copyright © Department of Survey and Land Information (maps) and Reed Publishing (NZ) Ltd (text) 1987

First published by Heinemann Publishers Ltd 1987
Reprinted 1990, 1993
This edition 1995
Reprinted 1997, 1999

Design by Sally Hollis-McLeod/Moscow
Printed in China

General Editor

D.W. McKenzie, M.Sc.
Professor Emeritus
Department of Geography
Victoria University of Wellington
Founding President and Life Member
New Zealand Cartographic Society

Contributing Writers

David G. Rankin, B.A., Ph.D.
Senior Lecturer
Department of Geography
University of Auckland

Neil Rennie, B.A.
Former Editor
NZ Farmer

Graeme R. Stevens, M.Sc., Ph. D.
Chief Palæontologist
New Zealand Geological Survey
Department of Scientific and Industrial Research

Consultants

R.C. Cooper, B.Com., M.A., Ph. D.
Botanist

R.C. Green, B.A., B.Sc., Ph. D., F.R.S.N.Z., M.A.N.A.S.
Professor in Prehistory
Department of Anthropology
University of Auckland

P.L. Hosking, B.A., M.A., Ph. D.
Senior Lecturer
Department of Geography
University of Auckland

Michael King, D. Phil.
Historian

Neville Lapthorne
Cartographer
Department of Survey and Land Information

Preface

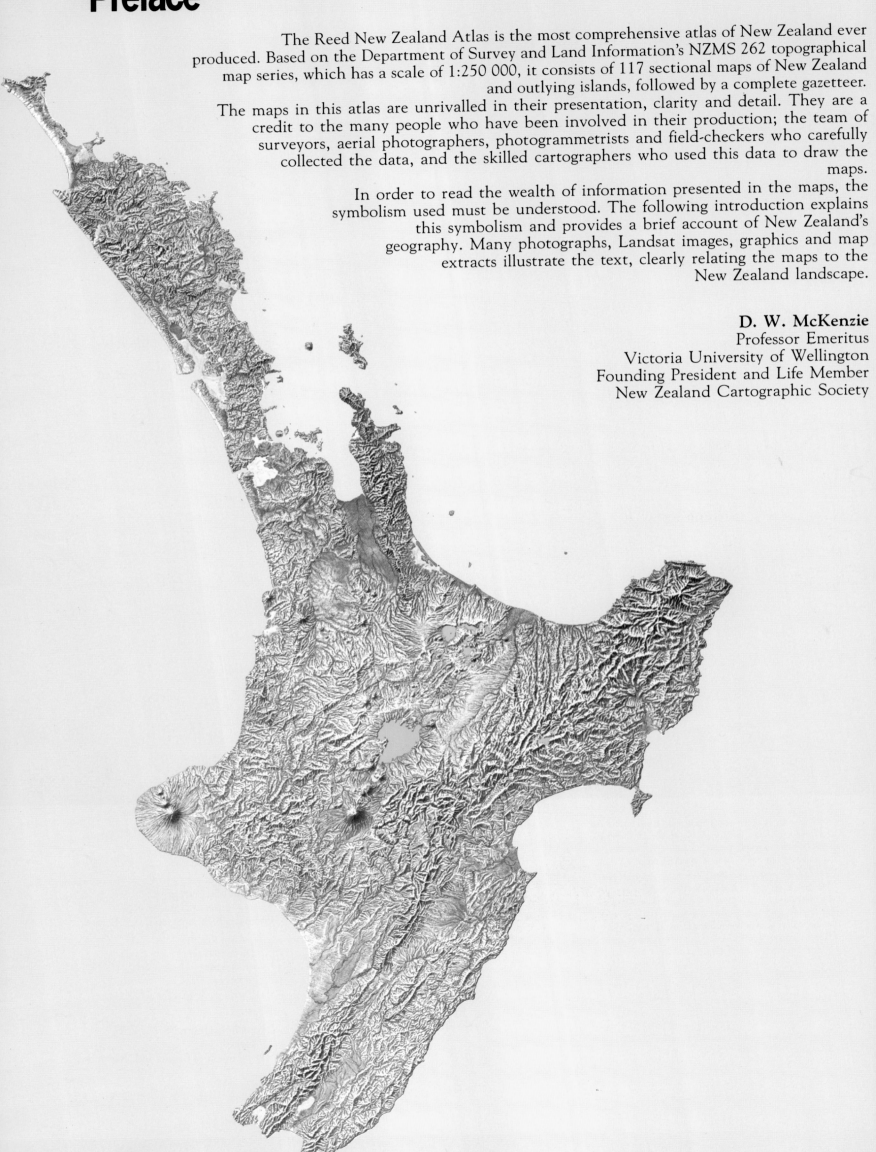

The Reed New Zealand Atlas is the most comprehensive atlas of New Zealand ever produced. Based on the Department of Survey and Land Information's NZMS 262 topographical map series, which has a scale of 1:250 000, it consists of 117 sectional maps of New Zealand and outlying islands, followed by a complete gazetteer.

The maps in this atlas are unrivalled in their presentation, clarity and detail. They are a credit to the many people who have been involved in their production; the team of surveyors, aerial photographers, photogrammetrists and field-checkers who carefully collected the data, and the skilled cartographers who used this data to draw the maps.

In order to read the wealth of information presented in the maps, the symbolism used must be understood. The following introduction explains this symbolism and provides a brief account of New Zealand's geography. Many photographs, Landsat images, graphics and map extracts illustrate the text, clearly relating the maps to the New Zealand landscape.

D. W. McKenzie
Professor Emeritus
Victoria University of Wellington
Founding President and Life Member
New Zealand Cartographic Society

Introduction

An atlas is more than a book of maps; it is an invitation to explore both the past and the present. It provides the basic detail of mountains, plains, lakes, fiords, rivers, beaches and many other features—over which are draped the signs of human occupation. In New Zealand these signs include large cities; tiny, isolated communities; unsealed roads winding deep into the hills; and major highways linking the main centres.

Maps are one way of learning about the landscape. We can become familiar with an area by walking or driving around it, or by climbing to the top of a local vantage point, but we are limited by what our eyes can scan. However, looking at a map of the same area for the first time changes our perception. Maps can show us the positions of both natural and constructed features as well as the relationships between them.

The scale of a map determines the amount of detail. In this atlas, for example, the 1:250 000 scale shows major roads but not very short ones—these have been omitted to make the maps clearer. City map directories, on the other hand, obviously have to show and name every street. Each map therefore includes only those features that are important for its purposes.

Maps encourage us to ask questions: Why is New Zealand where it is? When were the urban centres developed? How was the country colonised and populated? What effect does the climate have on landforms and patterns of human occupation?

Although maps alone cannot answer such questions, they are an essential tool for finding the answers and understanding other aspects of the landscape —its history, its present form and its potential. However, before this tool can be used effectively, we must know something about it. The purpose of the following pages is to explain what the maps in this atlas show and how they relate to the real world.

Map by J. Petro, Department of Survey and Land Information.

Geological Time Scale			
Years (millions)	Era	Period	Epoch
0 ■	Cenozoic	Quaternary	HOLOCENE / PLEISTOCENE
		Tertiary	PLIOCENE / MIOCENE / OLIGOCENE / EOCENE / PALEOCENE
50 ■			
100 ■	Mesozoic	Cretaceous	Upper / Lower
150 ■		Jurassic	Upper / Middle / Lower
200 ■		Triassic	Upper / Middle / Lower
250 ■	Paleozoic	Permian	Upper / Lower
300 ■		Carboniferous	
350 ■			
400 ■		Devonian	Upper / Middle / Lower
		Silurian	
450 ■		Ordovician	Upper / Middle / Lower
500 ■			
		Cambrian	Upper / Middle / Lower
550 ■			
600 ■		Precambrian	

Fig. 1

How New Zealand was shaped

New Zealand's geological and geomorphological history began in the Precambrian era, which ended 570 million years ago (fig. 1). At this time New Zealand's ancestral landmass was in the mid-latitudes of the Northern Hemisphere. New Zealand and other countries now in the Southern Hemisphere, along with India, formed a super-continent known today as Gondwana. Australia and New Zealand were close to Asiatic USSR, China and Indo-China.

A slow rotation of Gondwana swung Australia and New Zealand progressively southwards so that by the Silurian period New Zealand was positioned at about 30°S latitude (fig. 2). Southerly drift continued in the Devonian period, when contact was lost with Asia.

In the Permian period (fig. 3) New Zealand was close to the South Pole and felt the effects of ice-caps that built up on Australia, Antarctica, Africa, India and South America. Cold-tolerant shellfish inhabited the seas around New Zealand, and the land vegetation was dominated by a hardy seed fern (*Glossopteris*).

In the succeeding Triassic and Jurassic periods (figs. 4 and 5) eastern Gondwana was gradually rotated away from the South Pole, and New Zealand returned to mid-latitudes. At this time an equable climate and the availability of land links facilitated the movement of a variety of Gondwana plants and animals into New Zealand, including the ancestors of many of the native and endemic elements in our flora and fauna—the kauri, podocarps, ferns, tuataras, insects, native frogs, moas and kiwis.

In the Cretaceous period (fig. 6) splitting movements along the future sites of the Indian and South Atlantic Oceans separated eastern from western Gondwana and again swung New Zealand into a position close to the South Pole. Various plants and animals used Antarctica as a stepping stone to move from South America into Australia and New Zealand at about this time. The plants included the ancestors of the southern beech (*Nothofagus*) and the New Zealand Proteaceae (rewarewa and toru).

The Tasman Sea opened up between 80 and 60 million years ago, and similar movements also took place to the south of New Zealand between the Campbell Plateau and Antarctica. The opening up of oceanic areas around New Zealand left the ancient Gondwana elements (podocarps, tuataras, moas, kiwis, etc.) as the endemic flora and fauna. Later arrivals had to either float or fly across vast distances of ocean, or rely on human transportation, accompanying Maori and European settlement.

430-400 MILLION YEARS (MIDDLE SILURIAN)

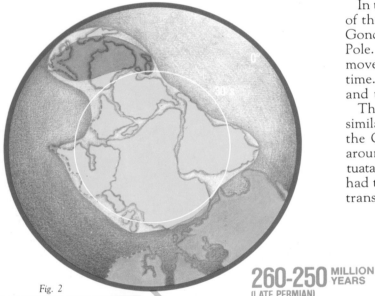

Fig. 2

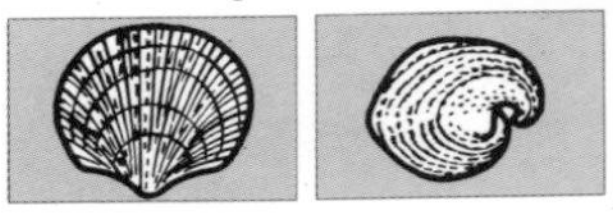

260-250 MILLION YEARS (LATE PERMIAN)

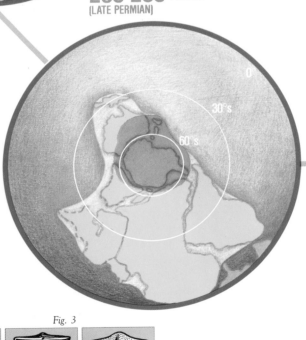

Fig. 3

208-192 MILLION YEARS (LATE TRIASSIC)

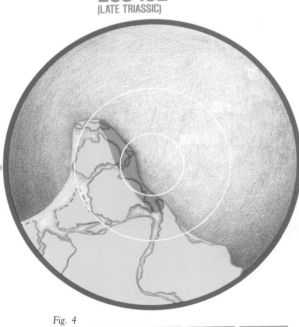

Fig. 4

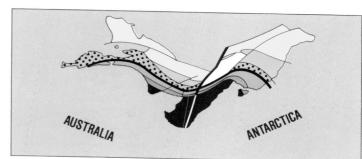

Fig. 9

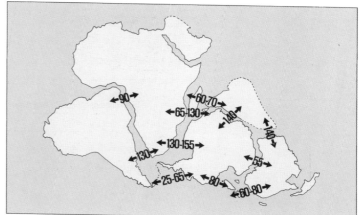

Fig. 8

As the infant oceans opened up around New Zealand, some groups of flying animals successfully colonised the country, presumably by overflying the steadily widening oceanic gaps. These included the New Zealand wrens and thrushes, the wattlebirds and the New Zealand bat (fig. 7).

The super-continent of Gondwana began to show the first signs of breaking up between 155 and 130 million years ago. As splitting movements occurred between the individual continental masses, sea flooded in to form oceans that eventually developed into the major oceans of today. Figure 8 shows the times, expressed as millions of years from the present, at which the various continents began to separate from Gondwana. The Tasman Sea opened up between 80 and 60 million years ago; the segment of the Southern Ocean between the Campbell Plateau and Antarctica began to open up about 80 million years ago; and Australia began to separate from Antarctica about 55 million years ago.

New Zealand's current shape is a very recent feature in geological terms, having come into existence during the past 100 000 years. Although opinions differ regarding details, it is generally agreed that for long periods of geological time ancient New Zealand lay along the eastern margin of Gondwana, sometimes having the form of an archipelago but more often forming part of the sea-floor adjacent to Australia and Antarctica. Between 140 and 120 million years ago earth movements began to shape an ancestral New Zealand landmass, and, somewhat later, between 110 and 80 million years ago, the same movements shifted this away from Gondwana.

Figure 9 shows how ancestral New Zealand may have looked some 130 million years ago, before the opening up of the Tasman Sea. The patterns indicate various bands of rock, which at that time were continuous but have now been disrupted by movements along fault lines.

The earth's crust is composed of a gigantic patchwork of interlocking slabs (plates), all moving independently in response to underlying global stresses and strains (fig. 10). Like enormous ice-floes, the plates jostle one another—sometimes colliding head on and overriding each other, sometimes scraping past sideways, and sometimes pulling apart.

The plate margins are the focus of most of the active phenomena of the earth: mountain-building, earthquakes and volcanic eruptions. New Zealand's active environment of mountains, earthquakes and volcanoes stems directly from its position astride the boundary between the Indian-Australian and Pacific Plates.

65-53 MILLION YEARS (PALEOCENE)

Fig. 7

175-135 MILLION YEARS (MIDDLE AND LATE JURASSIC)

110-95 MILLION YEARS (MIDDLE CRETACEOUS)

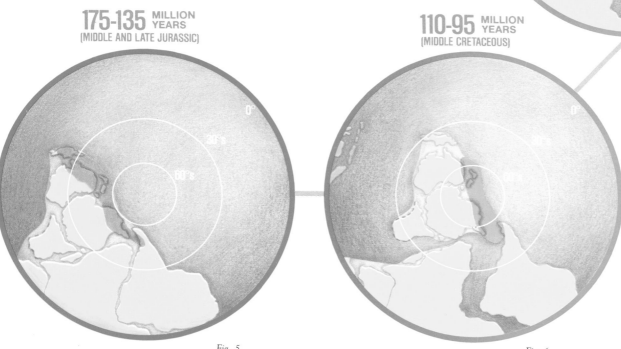

Fig. 5

Fig. 6

Below figures 2 to 7 are examples of the animals and plants that came to New Zealand at the time specified. The red patterns give an indication of the areas of past distribution and the migration routes that were available.

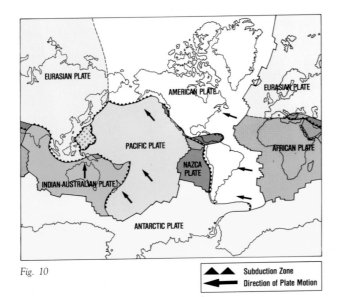

Fig. 10

Subduction Zone
Direction of Plate Motion

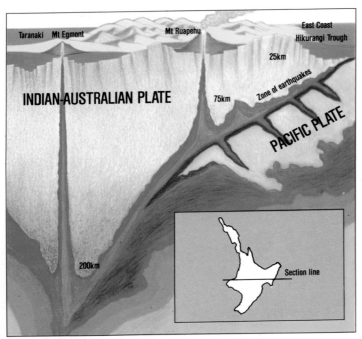

Fig. 11

Glaciers are the remnants of ice-sheets that covered large parts of the earth during the ice ages. The Tasman Glacier, pictured here, is fed by snow brought to the Southern Alps by the prevailing winds off the Tasman Sea. (Air Logistics)

The modern form of New Zealand has largely been shaped by the interactions between these two enormous plates. Offshore from the east coast of the North Island the Pacific Plate plunges beneath the edge of the Indian-Australian Plate (fig. 11). Along the plate boundary the earth's crust is buckled downwards, forming a deep furrow in the sea-floor—the Hikurangi Trough. As the Pacific Plate descends, sea-floor sediments are scraped off its upper surface by the hard rocks of the continental edge of the Indian-Australian Plate, acting like a giant bulldozer blade. The scraping-off process has created along the east coast, and in a zone immediately offshore, an extensive area of intensely folded and faulted sands and muds. The piled-up sediments offshore will in time emerge from the sea, adding a new strip of land to New Zealand.

The leading edge of the Indian-Australian Plate has been warped upwards to form an extensive area of broken country comprising the axial mountain ranges and associated foothill areas. Behind the axial ranges stretching and cracking of the crust has occurred, providing routes for molten material to rise to the earth's surface, thus forming the Taupo-Rotorua and Taranaki volcanic regions. This molten material (magma) has been derived from the melting of the Pacific Plate where it descends deeply under the North Island and encounters progressively hotter temperatures.

Glaciers and volcanoes

Glaciers, floods, volcanoes, winds and the sea have formed and sculptured New Zealand's surface. Climatic fluctuations, which produced a succession of glacial and inter-glacial periods, also caused sea-levels to rise and fall and brought about changes in the distribution and intensity of erosion.

The effects of glaciation during the Quaternary period were confined mainly to the South Island. In a succession of advances and retreats, the glaciers carved out U-shaped valleys and deposited vast tracts of sediment and debris. The major glaciers, such as the Tasman, Franz Josef, Fox, Godley and Murchison, are shown on map 74. In areas where glacial moraine blocked the U-shaped valleys, ribbon lakes, such as Tekapo, Ohau and Pukaki, have been formed.

The Canterbury Plains were created mainly by the merging of outwash fans from the Waimakariri, Rakaia and Rangitata Valleys. Rocks were carried forward in the ice-sheet; then, as the climate changed and the ice-sheet receded, these rocks were dumped to form terminal moraines. The outwash plains that formed in front of the ice are the alluvial fans of sand and gravel deposited by streams flowing from the glaciers.

On map 85 the area between the broad, braided Rakaia and Waimakariri Rivers is a mixture of outwash and alluvium. During the early glacial period the outwash plains were covered in a fine, light loam. This dust was then picked up by the predominantly westerly winds and deposited over much of the South Island.

The Quaternary period in the North Island was characterised by volcanic processes. Mounts Ruapehu, Tongariro and Ngauruhoe were formed as magma welled up through the fault lines in a series of violent eruptions. Layer upon layer of cinder, ash and lava built up to form the classical conical stratovolcano shape. Part of Lake Taupo was formed when a huge bubble of gas and rock burst in a shattering blast. The land collapsed and the ash settled to depths of 200 metres.

Earthquakes and explosions occurred right across the Volcanic Plateau through to the Bay of Plenty, leaving in their wake volcanoes such as Mounts Tarawera, Putauaki, Maunganui, and White Island. At this time much of the rest of the North Island was also in a state of volcanic ferment, with a series of eruptions in Taranaki, the Waikato, Auckland and Northland.

The Auckland isthmus is densely marked with explosion craters such as the Orakei Basin and volcanic cones such as Mount Eden and Mount Wellington. These volcanoes were formed from a fluid lava that seeped upwards and outwards. The lava formed scoria cones and produced more gentle domelike structures, the youngest of which, Rangitoto Island in the Hauraki Gulf, was probably still being formed 300 years ago.

Climate

New Zealand's three main islands extend from latitude 34°S to 47°S, and the altitude ranges from sea-level to 3764 metres at Mount Cook. The country is long—1600 kilometres—and narrow, being only 400 kilometres at its maximum breadth. Surrounded by the Tasman Sea and the Pacific Ocean, with the Southern Ocean to the south, and with the nearest landmass—Australia—1600 kilometres to the west, New Zealand has a climate with a marked maritime influence.

Warm air rises at the equator and cools. As it cools, it descends, compresses and warms up. At about latitude 30°S this descending air forms a belt called the subtropical high-pressure zone. Some of this air flows south to produce the westerly wind belt. During the summer months the subtropical high tends to move south to surround the North Island.

An anticyclone is a body of moving air of higher pressure than the surrounding air in which the pressure decreases away from the centre. Anticyclones that form over the southern Indian Ocean move eastwards, spinning anticlockwise over Australia and across the Tasman Sea into the Pacific Ocean. Warm air and cold air do not readily mix, so when air originating in the tropics comes up against colder air from the polar regions, a front is formed. Since the two air masses are moving in different directions, there is friction between them. The warmer air tends to override the cold air, and any reduction in air pressure may give rise to a depression. A depression spins clockwise and is a relatively low-pressure system. As these fronts and depressions move across New Zealand, they bring cloudy conditions and, frequently, rain. Although dense cloud cover is a regular occurrence, it tends to be short-lived.

New Zealand's weather is therefore a mixture of anticyclones bringing warm, clear skies in summer and a cold clarity in winter; frontal rainfall from the west and south-west; and, at times, cyclones moving down onto the country from the north. This mixture of anticyclones and depressions produces a variable weather pattern modified by the topography and aspect of any particular location.

Warm, wet air moving onto the west coast of the South Island, for example, hits the Alps and rises. It cools, expands, and condensed moisture falls as rain or snow. This is called orographic rain, and in the Alps it exceeds 8000 millimetres per year. To the east this creates an area of rain shadow because the dried air has shed most of its load. Parts of Central Otago are semi-arid, with a mean annual rainfall of 300 millimetres. In the North Island this effect is far less pronounced, but two of the driest areas are southern Hawke's Bay and Wairarapa. Most of New Zealand gets between 600 and 1500 millimetres of rain per year.

The mean annual sea-level temperature varies from 15°C in the north to 9°C in the south. The annual temperature range (the difference between the highest and lowest temperature) varies from 8°C in Northland and the west coast of the North Island, through 9–10°C over the remainder of the North Island and the east coast of the South Island, to 14°C in Central Otago.

Much of the country receives over 2000 hours of sunshine per year. The sunniest locations are those sheltered from the west and south. Blenheim, Nelson and Whakatane each receive more than 2350 hours annually. The cloudiest areas are Southland and coastal Otago, which generally receive fewer than 1700 hours annually.

Climate's importance to the economy is incalculable. Agriculture, horticulture, viticulture, silviculture, market gardening and tourism all depend, at least in part, on the climate. Our reaction to seasonal weather patterns depends on our livelihood. A prolonged spell of high temperatures makes for pleasant days at the beach for some, but can mean drought and economic ruin for the farmer. Meteorologists forecasting the weather or predicting long-term climatic trends are, in effect, economic consultants. They operate in the realm of uncertainty, where events have only a certain probability of occurring. There are, of course, unpredictable events, such as highly localised frosts, hail storms and tornadoes that can wipe out seasonal crops.

The constraints climate imposes are to be seen all around—in the distribution of native vegetation, crops and even population.

Although lowland farms, such as this one near Masterton, are often highly productive, they can be severely damaged by flooding during prolonged periods of heavy rain. (Photobank)

Natural hazards

Within a human life-span, the natural processes shaping the landscape are so slow that they usually pass unnoticed. But they can occur suddenly and violently: earthquakes, volcanic eruptions, floods and fires. These natural hazards can kill people and animals, damage farmland, smash buildings, and even devastate towns and cities. People cannot control such powerful forces; they can only try to limit their impact.

Earthquakes and floods are the major hazards in New Zealand. High-rise buildings must therefore be built to comply with stringent earthquake regulations, and most of the major rivers incorporate a variety of flood-control measures.

However, no human precautions could have prevented the mud-flow or lahar that burst from the crater of Mount Ruapehu on Christmas Eve, 1953. With tragic suddenness, the mass of mud and water swept away the Tangiwai Bridge, and the overnight express train from Wellington to Auckland plunged into the Whangaehu River, with the loss of 151 lives.

In 1840, during the early months of settlement, Europeans in Wellington experienced their first earthquake. Eight years later an earthquake destroyed about half of the small settlement, causing many to abandon it, and in 1855 the most severe earthquake in New Zealand's history took place there.

In 1886 Mount Tarawera literally blew off its top in one of the most violent explosions ever experienced by New Zealanders. Thick layers of ash coated thousands of square kilometres of surrounding land, and 153 people died. The villages of Te Wairoa, Te Ariki and Moura were buried, the famous Pink and White Terraces were destroyed, and Lake Rotomahana sank and emptied. Seven years later it gradually refilled to produce a lake twenty times its former size.

In 1929 the Murchison-Karamea earthquake, followed by a fortnight of severe tremors, caused widespread structural damage to the landscape and buildings in Nelson, Westport and Greymouth.

Soon after, in 1931, another earthquake, this time in Hawke's Bay, reduced Napier and Hastings to ruins, and 255 lives were lost. The bed of Ahuriri Lagoon was lifted, creating 3650 hectares of new land. The effects were felt from Wairoa to northern Wairarapa, with slips and cracks, realignment of water courses, and severe damage to bridges and communications.

In 1942 a series of earthquakes hit Wellington, the Hutt Valley, Wairarapa and Manawatu, causing widespread damage over the area—including the settlements of Carterton, Masterton, Eketahuna and Pahiatua.

Earthquakes are an ever-present hazard in New Zealand, where the earthquake belt is well defined. The only uncertainty is not if but when the next major earthquake will occur.

When Mount Tarawera erupted in 1886 this 19-kilometre rift opened up. The explosion could be heard as far away as Auckland. Until this eruption Tarawera had lain dormant for about 900 years. (Lloyd Homer/New Zealand Geological Survey)

Mountain-building today

The Alpine Fault has torn the South Island apart. Over millions of years the area in the north-west of the Landsat satellite image has been moved 450 kilometres away from similar rocks in Otago and Southland. In this region the Alpine Fault has split into active parallel faults running north-eastward, producing tilted blocks including the Kaikoura Range. This period of mountain-building, called the Kaikoura Orogeny, continues today.

The Kaikoura Orogeny was preceded by another great period of mountain-building some 140 to 110 million years ago. The mountains built up then were worn down to a peneplain, remnants of which are evident in many parts of New Zealand. In Otago the peneplain surface is well preserved, as shown in the accompanying photograph of the area near Middlemarch.

Landsat: Nelson and Marlborough. The satellite images that appear in this atlas were taken by Landsat satellites operated by the National Aeronautics and Space Administration (NASA), USA, and supplied by the Department of Survey and Land Information and the Remote Sensing Section, DSIR. The images are derived from multi-spectral scanning equipment operating during the satellite's almost north-south orbit every eight days at an altitude of 900 kilometres. The scanned data are returned in spectral bands, which can be combined to produce the type of image reproduced here. Green vegetation appears red, water, rocks and settlements appear blue, and so on. Thus variation in colouring provides useful information on land use, seasonal changes and other matters.

Floods occur more frequently than earthquakes, and they are often severe. For example, in the North Island, the Waikato, Waipara, Manawatu, Ruamahanga and Hutt Rivers are susceptible to flooding. In the South Island, such rivers as the Rangitata and Waimakariri in Canterbury, the Taieri and Clutha in Otago, and the Mataura in Southland can submerge the plains, causing extensive damage.

It is an unfortunate fact that although the lowlands and plains are the most productive agricultural land, heavily stocked and intensively farmed, they are also vulnerable to the consequences of heavy rains falling in the catchment areas of the rivers that wind through them.

Flood-control measures are expensive, and even the more comprehensive systems cannot guarantee protection in times of heavy, sustained downpours, such as the 400 millimetres that fell in 24 hours onto the Tangoio catchment of Hawke's Bay in 1963.

Floods in the lower valley of the Ruamahanga in the Wairarapa covered 3500 hectares in August 1977. Extensive erosion in the hill country followed, and slips bared over 1000 hectares. Steady rain until October destroyed fencing, overflowed stock dams, eroded access roads, and lowered both lambing percentages and milk production.

In 1978, over a period of 24 hours, the lower stretches of the Clutha flooded. Some 70 000 hectares of the Waimea Plain were also submerged, resulting in heavy stock losses, damage to roads and bridges, and severe scouring and silting of farmland. Further south, Mataura's 4500 inhabitants had to be evacuated.

The eastern Bay of Plenty was struck by a severe earthquake in March 1987. This photograph of Edgecumbe railway station, with tracks bent in opposite directions and an overturned locomotive, shows the magnitude of the forces that were unleashed. (Ross Land)

Kaikoura Range. (Lloyd Homer/New Zealand Geological Survey)

Peneplain near Middlemarch. (Lloyd Homer/New Zealand Geological Survey)

According to Maori tradition, New Zealand's first settlers came from 'Hawaiki'. They crossed great expanses of ocean in canoes, with the help of the sun, moon, wind and stars. The wakataua (war canoe) prow pictured here was carved in the mid-nineteenth century, and has been attributed to Rakaruhi Rukupo. (Athol McCredie)

Fire has been responsible for the destruction of much of New Zealand's native forest cover. This aerial photograph taken near Riverhead illustrates the destructive effects of a burn-off that has got out of control. (Air Logistics)

The human impact

Since the first human settlement in New Zealand, the basic landform structure of the country has barely altered. During this period, the large-scale effects of weathering and erosion would have been negligible. Human impact, however, has changed the vegetation cover of the country, which has in turn increased erosion and modified local landscapes.

Before the arrival of the early Polynesian voyagers 800 to 1200 years ago, forest covered roughly 80 per cent of New Zealand. The climate was milder than it is today. Thus, in areas where rainfall was sufficient for tree growth, forest cover was probably at a maximum. Perhaps, even in the drier areas, if relief and aspect were favourable, small pockets of tree cover would have been established.

The first migrants may have arrived as early as the sixth century. They are thought to have come from the Southern Cooks or the Society Islands — the Hawaiki of the legends. One theory is that they chanced upon the North Island after being blown off their original course by a storm, to be carried west, then south, by the winds and currents. Others argue that the voyages were planned. Archaeological evidence suggests that Northland was their first point of contact with New Zealand. After a short time, they began moving south along the rivers and coast by canoe. Some of the early Polynesian colonists lived on the seaward fringes of Southland and Otago, and by 1100 were established along the Waitaki, Taieri and Clutha Valleys.

The immediate coastal areas yielded fish, seals, sea-birds and shellfish, and pigeons living in trees such as totara and rimu in the podocarp forests were captured. Various species of moa — large flightless birds that lived on the fringe of the forest — were also eaten.

Moa-hunting was particularly important in parts of the southern South Island, but seal remains predominate in many archaeological sites in the North Island. In some areas the colonists practised agriculture from the beginning and there is no evidence of moa-hunting at all.

Gradually, humans began to transform the native vegetation. In the North Island, bush was deliberately burnt to make way for agriculture.

By the time of European colonisation, forest cover had been reduced to about 50 per cent of New Zealand's land area. Now the process of destruction was accelerated. Burn-offs, the milling of native timber, the application of fertiliser, and the introduction of new plants, cattle, sheep, deer, opossums and rabbits all helped to modify the biological environment. Red deer, for instance, are now widespread through the tussock and forests of the South Island, as well as along the North Island mountain backbone extending into the Urewera and Kaimai Ranges. But establishing permanent pasture to support the emerging sheep- and cattle-based economy brought the greatest changes. The continued effect has been to reduce forest cover to about 23 per cent of the land area.

The following example illustrates the dramatic change that has taken place within the last 150 years (a fraction of a second in geological time). In the early nineteenth century bush covered two-thirds of the North Island: Northland, King Country, Urewera and Taranaki, through the Rangitikei and Manawatu, to southern Hawke's Bay and the Wairarapa. By the middle of the century this had probably shrunk to half through firing for timber extraction. Forests such as those in Northland were destroyed to extract a relatively small number of usable trees. This huge area remained waste land until the 1870s. Once the lowland and coastal areas had been occupied for sheep and cattle farming, settlement could only expand into the bush-covered hills. An exception to this was expansion up the Hutt Valley as early as the 1840s.

In the 1870s settlers began to open up the area between Hawke's Bay and Wellington. They introduced dairying in the 1880s around Palmerston North (established in 1870) and the Manawatu Plains. Norsewood and Dannevirke are a permanent reminder of the Scandinavian settlers who played such an important role in clearing the bush in southern Hawke's Bay and the Wairarapa.

It was virtually a subsistence existence, but in time cereals were grown on the cleared land, grasses were introduced, and small dairy farms were established.

The first shipment of frozen meat to Britain in 1882 is a landmark in New Zealand's economic history. Refrigeration opened up a guaranteed market in Great Britain for meat and dairy products, laying the foundations of a pastoral economy.

However, clearing bush to establish pasture also brought problems. In many areas the change in vegetation cover from forest to pasture has been a major factor in accelerating the erosion of the land. The main mistake was land-use practices that took no account of the potential dangers associated with removing forest cover from steep slopes with unstable soils. By the time the dangers were understood, erosion was occurring on a scale beyond the control of the individual farmer. The instability of the landscape was consequently matched by fluctuations in farming profitability, which have had a marked effect on small rural communities. Settlements do not usually prosper in areas that are economically unstable or declining.

But the history of resource development in New Zealand is as much about the coast as it is about the land, from sustaining the early Polynesian settlers to the recent development of recreational areas. New Zealand has a lengthy and varied coastline – from the long, golden sweep of Ninety Mile Beach to the deep, cliffed sounds of Fiordland – yet in some areas the pressure on the coastline for competing uses produces conflict.

The Bay of Islands is such a case. Here the mixture of land and sea provides a natural landscape of great beauty that deserves to be conserved and enjoyed. Today, however, parts of the Bay of Islands are draped with colonies of retirement and holiday homes. In these areas there is a conflict between the demand for land for further development and the preservation of the region's scenic assets – which are the mainstay of its tourist economy.

It has been estimated that 80 per cent of the Bay of Islands' 700 kilometres of coastline is unsuitable for residential development because of its rugged terrain, inaccessibility or low-lying nature. Pressure for development has therefore been concentrated within the remaining 20 per cent. Severe problems are now becoming evident as a result of waste disposal and storm-water run-off from built-up areas. Land-clearing operations and land-use intensification in the rural areas close to the coastal zone have led to further conflict.

The Bay of Islands is also a major oyster-farming centre. Again, there are potential conflicts of interests between the type of land use allowed near the marine farms and the need to maintain a high water quality.

Coastal management issues in the Bay of Islands illustrate an important lesson to be learned from New Zealand's economic history: urban, rural and marine development usually bring costs and disadvantages as well as benefits.

Russell, in the Bay of Islands, was New Zealand's largest European settlement before 1840 and was briefly the capital. It subsequently became a backwater until its emergence as a tourist resort early this century. (Photobank)

Native forests

The current distribution of native forest reflects the impact of people and fire and the expansion of areas that are no longer able to sustain a rich forest cover because of environmental changes. Within each forest the distribution of species is determined by their climatic tolerance – that is, by aspect, distance from the coast, altitude, latitude, wind, rainfall and temperature.

The kauri (*Agathis australis*) is supreme among New Zealand's native trees. Rising to heights of over 30 metres, with a massive cylindrical trunk, it is free of branches for the greater part of its height. Colonists quickly realised its value for timber and felled large numbers for milling. Sadly, vast tracts of forest were fired simply to provide access to prime trees.

The southern limit of kauri is from the Bay of Plenty westwards to Kawhia Harbour. Sizeable stands of kauri now survive only in pockets of Northland, Auckland, Great Barrier Island and the Coromandel Peninsula. It commonly grows with other native species. On the Maungataniwha, Waitakere and Hunua Ranges, for instance, kauri can be found alongside rimu (*Dacrydium cupressinum*), totara (*Podocarpus totara*), miro (*Prumnopitys ferrugineas*) and rewarewa (*Knightia excelsa*). In suitable areas this complex is joined by lowland trees such as tawa (*Beilschmiedia tawa*), taraire (*Beilschmiedia taraire*), matai (*Prumnopitys taxifolia*) and kahikatea (*Dacrycarpus dacrydioides*).

Forest in the Raukumara Range is predominantly mixed evergreen conifer/broadleaf, giving way to a dominance of beech (*Nothofagus* spp.) in the Huiarau Range and an area westwards to the Kaimanawa Mountains with a long finger extending south along the Ruahine Range. The southern tip of the Ruahines and the northern tip of the Tararuas, separated by Palmerston North in the centre, contain a wide variety of forest types, tawa and miro being dominant.

As the Tararuas wind south to link up with the Rimutakas, beech forest is dominant, with other species mixing in. The lower western slopes of the ranges carry trees such as rimu, tawa, taraire, matai, totara and kahikatea.

A similar combination is present in a belt swinging down along the west coast, from the vicinity of Hamilton, through the Pirongia Forest Park, and following the ranges into the King Country. The same type of forest also occurs in the Rangitoto Range and extends south along the Hauhungaroa Range. Following the ranges south from the Mokau River mouth, this pattern is replaced by mixed evergreen conifer/broadleaf forest, with species such as rimu, tawa, miro, southern rata (*Metrosideros umbellata*) and beech, terminating north of Wanganui.

Te Matua Ngahere, located in the Waipoua Forest Sanctuary, is the second largest kauri in New Zealand. Thousands of these magnificent trees have been felled over the last 150 years, much of the valuable timber being wasted. (Photobank)

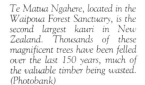

In pre-European times beech trees dominated huge areas of forest throughout the South Island and the lower part of the North Island. Large specimens reach more than 50 metres in height with gnarled and often buttressed trunks. (Photobank)

The South Island has an extensive, though less complex, cover of native forest. On Stewart Island mixed evergreen conifer/broadleaf forest is dominant. This gives way to forests featuring rimu and matai on the Maclennan and Forest Ranges in the south-east of the South Island.

Northward from Fiordland, extending along the western side of the Main Divide as far as the Strachan Range, are the great beech forests, with rimu, tawa, miro, kamahi (*Weinmannia racemosa*) and southern rata emerging on the coastal fringe and the lower slopes of the fiords. From Westland National Park north to Greymouth, and extending inland from the coast, is a mixture of rimu and matai and a mixed evergreen conifer/broadleaf complex, yielding with increased elevation to forest dominated by tawa.

The northernmost section of the West Coast to Cape Farewell and spreading eastwards along the Richmond Ranges features tawa, rimu, miro, southern rata and beech, giving way, with elevation, to beech as the major type.

Farming the land

Pastoral farming has dominated New Zealand's economy for the past century. However, its development has involved much more than farmers simply capitalising on the excellent growing conditions provided by abundant rainfall and sunshine. The complex techniques of pastoral-farm management have had to be learned, often at substantial cost to the farmer. Many of New Zealand's early settlers had no farming experience or knowledge of the variety of soils that had evolved under a forest cover.

In the first decades of European settlement the Maori provided much of the food required by the new towns' inhabitants. Taught by the missionaries, they enthusiastically adopted European farming methods and crops, growing a variety of grains and fruit for sale (and even for export).

In the mid-nineteenth century most European farmers grew crops mainly for their own consumption, as the population was not large enough to sustain a home market. Many foodstuffs could not be imported, and local methods of processing and preserving were primitive. The influx of settlers caused by the gold rushes increased the demand for food, and many miners grew their own. In the South Island merino sheep were raised for their wool and

Above: Kaingaroa Forest and village. (J. H. Johns/New Zealand Forest Service)

Right: Kaimanawa State Forest Park. (J. H. Johns/New Zealand Forest Service)

Mapping vegetation patterns

In this atlas native forest (including subalpine vegetation above the bush line in mountain areas) is distinguished from exotic forest. The former is represented by a green colour, and the latter by a green colour with overprinted pine tree symbols.

Map 21, part of which is reproduced here, illustrates this distinction for large areas of adjacent native and exotic forest near Rotorua. The accompanying photographs show the contrasting appearance of these two types of vegetation. One of the characteristic topographical features of exotic plantations is a dense roading network, which is partly determined by the relief of the landscape.

grazed among the high-country tussock, while wheat was grown on the plains.

In the 1870s wool and wheat were the principal farm products and, with gold, were the main exports. The South Island dominated the economy at this time.

Sheep numbers increased from 1.5 million in 1858 to 13 million by 1878. Overstocking led to overgrazing of both the grasses growing in association with the tussock and the new tussock shoots. Burn-offs produced new shoots, but repeated fires destroyed the tussock, depleted the soil fertility and accelerated soil erosion. An increasing rabbit population then exacerbated the problem. Exports of rabbit skins rose from 33 000 in 1873 to 17 million in 1893, reflecting the magnitude of the increase.

Refrigerated shipping, which began in 1882, signalled the start of a major change in the types of farming practised in New Zealand. This technological breakthrough made possible the pasture-based economy that characterised the next century. Refrigeration meant that New Zealand could produce perishable goods like meat and dairy products for export (mainly to the United Kingdom) instead of being limited to non-perishable products like wheat and wool.

The predominant breed of sheep changed from the single-purpose (wool-producing) merino to the dual-purpose (wool- and meat-producing) Romney. Cattle could be farmed in large numbers, encouraging the development of sheep/beef farming, where the two breeds complemented each other well in an all-grass farming system.

Dairying for export became possible, making small holdings economic. The climate and flat lands of Taranaki and Waikato were ideally suited to dairying. This, combined with the fact that a far greater area of hill country in the North Island was suited to sheep/beef farming than in the South Island, meant that the balance of economic dominance began slowly shifting from the South Island to the North Island as more and more land was brought into pasture in the latter.

During the first decade after refrigeration, improved internal communications, resulting from Vogel's public works scheme, helped to accelerate the process of change. Sheep numbers grew from 13 million in 1881 to 20 million by 1893. Sown pasture, principally in the North Island, increased from 1.4 million hectares in 1881 to 4 million in 1895.

In the early 1900s farming continued to expand. Top-dressing pasture with artificial fertilisers greatly increased production levels and the types of country that could be farmed successfully. The internal-combustion engine in cars and, later, tractors improved both communications and farming productivity. Further expansion was encouraged by the World War I demand for wool, meat, butter and cheese.

This aerial photograph taken near Karaka, south of Auckland, shows the typically intensive land use of farms on flat and gently sloping lowlands. (Air Logistics)

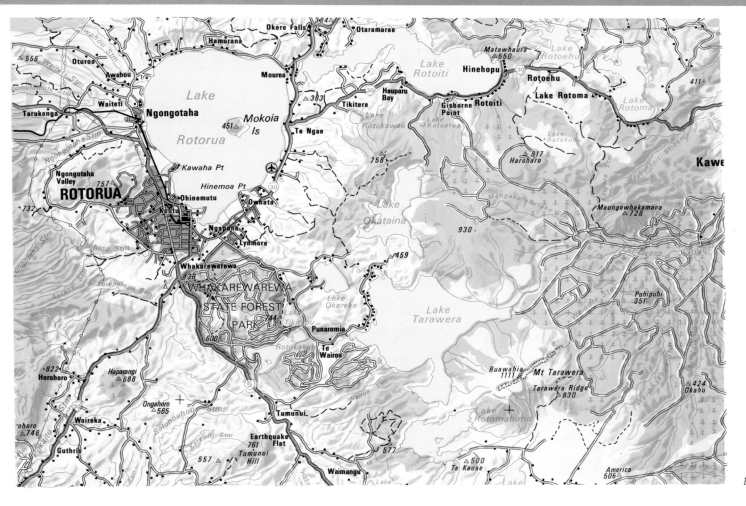

Extract from map 21.

After World War I a large number of returned soldiers were settled in government-sponsored farm-settlement schemes. In the 1920s and 1930s, however, particularly during the Depression, many of these schemes failed, and would-be farmers were forced to walk off their land. The reasons for these failures were that most of the farms were too small to make economic units and, especially on steeper hill country, once the natural fertility of the soil had been exhausted, there was no economic way of applying fertiliser. Furthermore, in many areas rabbits reached plague proportions, eating the pastures bare.

There were, on the other hand, several advances during this period. Rural electrification schemes — which grew rapidly in the 1930s — made living more comfortable and farming more efficient. New grass strains, suited to specific regional requirements, were introduced. On the Volcanic Plateau scientists discovered the cause of the 'bush sickness' that had prevented large areas from being farmed. The problem was cobalt deficiency, and it was solved by adding the trace element to fertiliser.

On dairy farms cows were grazed in just a few large paddocks, with hay and root crops used as winter feed. Half of the herds were still hand-milked, and stock diseases were a persistent problem.

In the typical sheep/beef farming pattern, sheep were grazed on the lower-quality hill pastures before being brought down and sold to fat-lamb farms on the more fertile lowlands. Flocks averaged about 1000 sheep, but the carrying capacity of the land varied considerably between regions.

The next 50 years brought many changes. After World War II aerial top-dressing began. This major technological advance allowed fertiliser — especially superphosphate, slag and lime — to be applied economically to hill-country pastures for the first time, encouraging the establishment of white clover and other grass species to improve pasture quality.

The other great advances were the development of hormone herbicides, which could economically kill woody weeds like gorse, manuka and blackberry, and organophosphate insecticides, which destroyed a wide range of insect pests affecting both animals and pastures.

Penicillin and broad-spectrum drenches dramatically improved animal health. Artificial insemination raised the genetic quality of dairy herds. Genetic-selection techniques were used to improve the productivity of sheep and cattle. New sheep breeds, especially the Coopworth and Perendale, intended for specific farming landscapes, contributed to general increases in the production of meat and wool.

The development of electric fences and rotational grazing — first on dairy farms but later on hill country — allowed the healthier, more productive animals to make much better use of the greater quantities of higher-quality pasture grown.

Other improvements were better tracks, better vehicles to drive on them,

Poor access and unstable soils create management problems on hill-country farms such as this one near Kaukapakapa, north of Auckland. (Air Logistics)

Farming patterns

The contrast between hill-country and lowland farming is very conspicuous in the area around Methven and the Rakaia River. As the accompanying extract from map 80, aerial photograph and Landsat satellite image illustrate, the flat landscape of the plains lends itself to a patchwork of small, intensely farmed holdings linked by a grid pattern of straight roads. In the sparsely settled hill and mountain country, on the other hand, extensive farming takes place on very large, often remote, runs.

The Canterbury Plains lie in a rain-shadow area in the lee of the Southern Alps, which act as a barrier to the moisture-laden westerly winds. Productive farming in this region is dependent on a large-scale system of irrigation fed from the Rakaia River by the Rangitata Diversion Race.

Above: Landsat: The Canterbury Plains and part of the Southern Alps. (NASA)

Right: Methven and the Rakaia River. (New Zealand Aerial Mapping Ltd)

and the almost complete replacement of horses by tractors—all resulting in far greater farming efficiency. These advances led to a steady increase in average stocking levels for sheep, cows and cattle, a trend that is continuing.

By the 1980s the average dairy farm had 123 cows, each giving a higher yield than cows half a century earlier. Farm size had increased through amalgamation and new land being broken in, but the actual number of farms had decreased.

The 1970s and 1980s have been a period of major change. The climate has been less favourable, with a number of drought years adversely affecting productivity and production in some regions. Britain's entry into the European Economic Community began to close off the assured export market of the previous 90 years, and rises in oil and phosphate prices markedly increased farming expenses.

This time of change and instability led some to question the entrenched use of pasture. Forest farming, which had been experimented with in the 1960s, expanded. This involves planting *Pinus radiata* at a low density on good pasture land and allowing cattle to graze among the trees. Multi-tier management systems similar to this are being tried out in places as widespread as Canterbury, Otago, the Pouto Peninsula near Dargaville, and the Glengarry Station outside Napier.

New livestock species are also becoming important. Goats, formerly considered pests, are being farmed for fibre, milk and meat. Angora goats are being raised for mohair, cashmere goats for cashmere, and New Zealand has even developed a new fibre breed called 'cashgora'.

In 1970 permission was given for deer to be farmed. Deer had been established in the wild in the 1850s, but after causing extensive damage to the forests they were classified as noxious animals. By 1986 there were about 3000 deer farms. Deer management and breeding techniques have been steadily developed, and today deer (like goats) are farmed using the same techniques as sheep and cattle, with modifications to suit the peculiarities of the species. The impetus behind deer farming was originally the Asian markets, where high prices for velvet could be obtained. Now the main emphasis is on the expanding venison market.

The greatest diversification in the agricultural sector has been in horticulture. Tree and vine fruits are concentrated in areas with favourable microclimates and soil types, and, usually, a history of development and entrepreneurial vigour.

Long-established fruits such as apples, peaches and nectarines predominate in Hawke's Bay; citrus from the East Coast northwards, especially in the Bay of Islands and the Bay of Plenty; cherries in Marlborough; and apricots in Central Otago. The growing of wine grapes has spread from the Auckland region to Poverty Bay, Hawke's Bay, Marlborough and Nelson. New exotic

Goat farming became established in New Zealand during the 1970s, many animals being imported from Tasmania. By the mid-1980s approximately 10000 were being milked commercially, and over 5000 were being farmed for mohair. (Photobank)

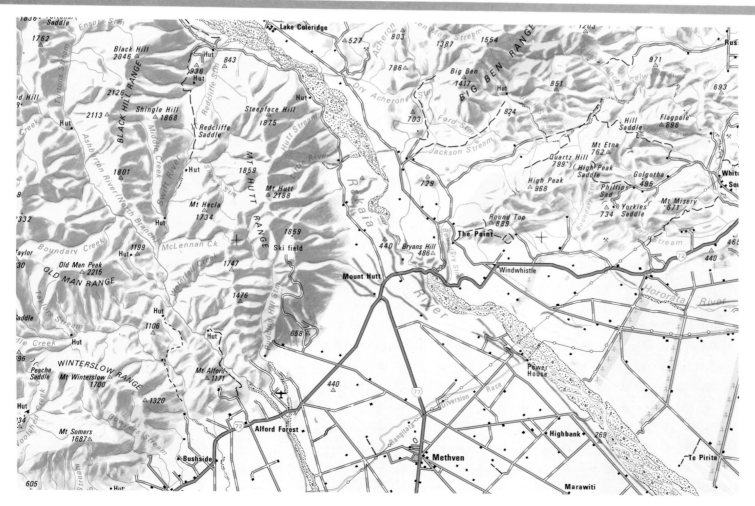

Extract from map 80.

In 1963 there were about 75 hectares of kiwifruit in commercial production; by the mid-1980s this figure had risen to almost 20000 hectares. Most kiwifruit orchards are family-owned, and a large number of them are found in the area surrounding Te Puke, pictured here. (Photobank)

fruits such as tamarillo and feijoa have emerged in the northern part of the North Island. But the fruit that has attracted the greatest attention—and the one that fuelled the boom in horticulture—is kiwifruit. Over half of the land in kiwifruit is concentrated in Tauranga County, having displaced dairying in the process.

Despite these changes, traditional pastoral farming still earns a large proportion of New Zealand's export income. Dairy farms remain concentrated in the North Island, especially in South Auckland, Taranaki and the Bay of Plenty, although they are found in combination with intensive sheep and beef farming over much of lowland and hill-country North Island, in areas near Christchurch and Dunedin, and in sporadic zones dotted along the length of Westland.

Sheep predominate in Canterbury, Otago and Southland. The role they play in the farming system depends very much on the specific nature of the area as well as the different management plans adopted by individual farms. Intensive sheep farming, sometimes combined with beef, is typical of the Volcanic Plateau, the lowlands south of Hastings and Masterton, the Nelson-Tasman Bay lowlands, Southland and the Otago interior.

Semi-extensive sheep farming is traditionally suited to the hill country of both islands. In the South Island it runs back into the high country, where extensive sheep farming predominates. A similar pattern is evident in parts of the North Island such as the King Country, the ranges from East Cape to the Wairarapa, and inland Wanganui.

New Zealand exporters of agricultural products are largely price-takers rather than price-makers on world markets. Off-farm costs as well as export dollars earned determine the economic viability of any particular agricultural or horticultural enterprise. Expenditure beyond the farm gate—freezing works charges, transport expenses and all input costs—have risen faster than farm earnings since 1974, steadily reducing farm profitability, especially in traditional sheep, beef and dairy farming. The inevitable result has been a reduction in capital inputs into the farming system. Farmers apply less fertiliser, stocking rates drop, pasture quality falls, and good management practice is reluctantly compromised. Since 1985, however, major restructuring of both the farming and the national economy has begun, which may reverse this trend.

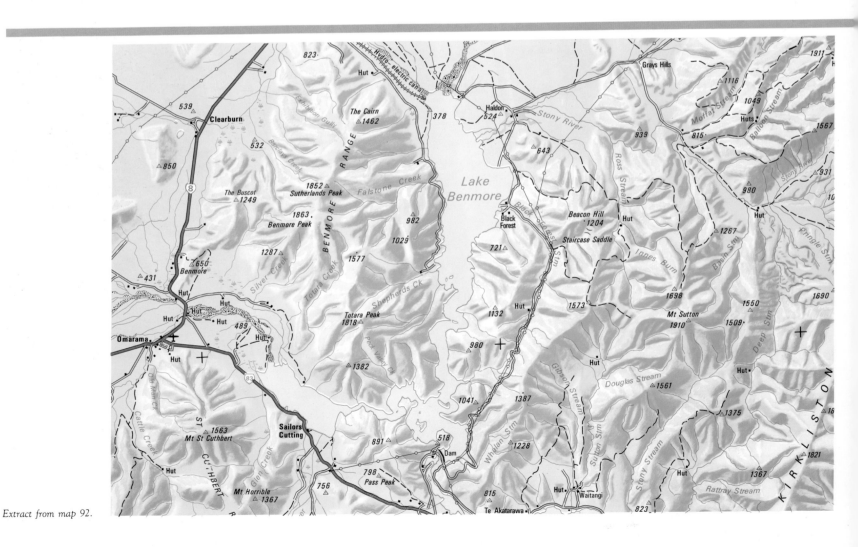

Extract from map 92.

Exotic forests and national parks

In the same way as native forest has been replaced by sown pasture, many marginal areas have been planted in exotic conifers. The first major planting came in a burst from the mid-1920s to the mid-1930s. This was mainly concentrated on the scrubland of the Volcanic Plateau, especially in the Kaingaroa area. At that time the land was unsuitable for cattle because of the prevalence of bush sickness. The conifers, a mixture of Douglas fir and lodgepole, Corsican, ponderosa and radiata pines, were to eventually supply the domestic market.

The second phase of extensive plantings began in 1965. This time the impetus came from the expanding exotic-timber industry, which aimed at supplying export markets with logs, sawn timber, pulp and paper.

Plantings were on hill-country farmland that had either reverted to scrub or had severe erosion problems, as in Poverty Bay. The areas planted had to be extensive enough to support the timber industry and preferably not too remote from a port.

The favoured species is *Pinus radiata*, which takes only 25 to 30 years to reach maturity. This species accounts for approximately 90 per cent of the more than one million hectares of state and private exotic forests.

Every region now has some exotic forests. The greatest concentration is still in the central North Island, with secondary concentrations in Northland, the East Coast-Poverty Bay region, Hawke's Bay, Nelson-Marlborough and Otago.

The remote mountain areas of both islands have been subject to very little modification by humans. These areas comprise a large part of over 2 million hectares that have been designated National Parks. The purpose of the parks is to preserve native flora and fauna, to conserve water, soil and forest, and to provide recreation areas for the public of New Zealand.

In the North Island there is the Urewera National Park — a series of remote, misty valleys covered with dense bush. The area includes Lake Waikaremoana and is the ancestral home of the Tuhoe tribe. Tongariro National Park, the first National Park, designated in 1887, contains Mounts Ruapehu, Tongariro and Ngauruhoe. Ruapehu and Ngauruhoe are still active volcanoes, the former rising to over 2700 metres. Egmont National Park is dominated by the stratovolcano of Mount Taranaki or Mount Egmont (2500 metres). Whanganui National Park was gazetted in 1986. Finally, the Bay of Islands and Hauraki Gulf Maritime Parks encompass many kilometres of coastline and numerous islands.

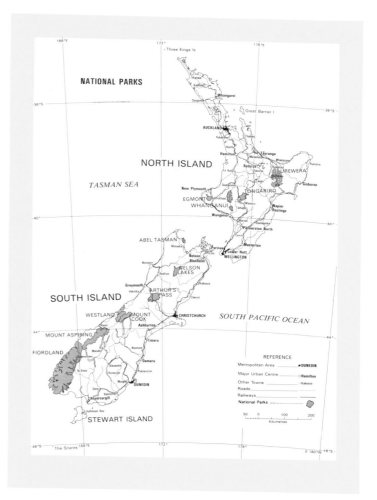

Mapping relief

In earlier atlases attempts were made to depict relief by means of rather crude pictures of hills and mountains. This technique was eventually replaced by layer colouring, where different colours represented different elevations, or the use of contour lines.

A clearer and more realistic technique is used in this atlas. Relief is depicted by obliquely lit shadows that fall towards the observer and to the right. Lit slopes are highlighted in pale yellow, and frequent spot heights provide a guide to altitude differences.

Part of map 92 is reproduced here. This shows, among other things, that the height of Benmore Peak is 1863 metres. By comparing the map with the Landsat satellite image of the same region and the oblique aerial photograph of Lake Benmore, we can see how realistically the map depicts the relief of the real landscape.

Above: Landsat: South Canterbury and North Otago. (NASA)

Left: Lake Benmore. (Lloyd Homer/New Zealand Geological Survey)

The South Island's parks range from the headlands, islands, bays, beaches and lagoons of Abel Tasman National Park to Lakes Rotoiti and Rotorua in Nelson Lakes National Park. Fiordland National Park is one of the largest in the world, including Lakes Te Anau and Manapouri as well as Doubtful, Dusky and Milford Sounds. Two extremely rare species of flightless bird—the takahe and the kakapo—are hidden in its remote areas.

Westland, Arthur's Pass, Mount Aspiring and Mount Cook National Parks are laid out along the backbone of the Southern Alps. Mount Cook National Park contains the Tasman, Murchison, Hooker and Mueller Glaciers, and numerous peaks such as Mounts Tasman, Hicks and Haast. It is dominated by 3764-metre Mount Cook itself. On the eastern side of the divide is Arthur's Pass National Park, a mixture of mountains and glaciers, forests and river flats. On the west lies Westland National Park, descending from the mountains to rain forest, the Franz Josef and Fox Glaciers, and finally to the coast, sole resting place, near the Okarito Lagoon, of the kotuku or white heron.

Marlborough Sounds Maritime Park was established in 1979. Made up of more than 100 separate reserves, it comprises a labyrinth of waterways, islands and high peninsulas.

Despite the National Parks' remoteness, their native flora and fauna have not always been successfully protected from human interference. Heather was planted in the Tongariro National Park during 1914 in a misguided attempt to reproduce the Scottish Highlands; the Abel Tasman National Park's forests were burned down, leaving only two areas of virgin rain forest; and exotic shrubs and trees have been introduced on many occasions. All of the parks have problems with introduced opossums, deer, pigs, goats, stoats, rats and cats.

European settlement

In 1769 Captain James Cook circumnavigated New Zealand. For the first time, the physical limits of the country were defined and mapped, though Abel Tasman had charted the west coast of both islands in 1642. Cook's chart of the coastline was remarkably accurate, given the time and conditions under which it was constructed. Banks Peninsula was incorrectly recorded as an island, and there was some doubt as to whether Stewart Island was in fact an island or part of the mainland. However, these are relatively minor inaccuracies. Cook's cartography put an end to the widespread European belief in Terra Australis, showing that New Zealand was not the edge of a large, unknown continent but a series of islands.

The first European settlers after Cook were sealers, who arrived in the 1790s. Based on the southern coast of the South Island, they slaughtered seals until, by 1810, the population was reduced to an uneconomic level.

In the 1820s it was the turn of the whalers, who established bases in the Tory Channel, Preservation Inlet and, later, Otago.

At this time, timber began to be seriously exploited, especially the kauri forests of Northland, and settlers also recognised the commercial importance of kauri gum.

Permanent European settlement in New Zealand dates from the establishment of mission stations in the early nineteenth century. In 1840 New Zealand was annexed as a colony of Great Britain. At this time the European population numbered 2000, the Maori population perhaps 50 000.

In the 1840s the first wave of planned migration from Britain began under the auspices of Edward Gibbon Wakefield's New Zealand Company, and by the mid-1850s 12 000 had arrived under this scheme.

During the early years of European settlement most of the population was distributed around the coast. By the 1850s the European population had risen to 40 000 and the major centres of Wellington, Auckland, New Plymouth, Wanganui, Nelson, Christchurch and Dunedin had been established.

Moving people and produce

To a large extent these early settlements were independent of each other, and each sought to develop its own hinterland. The thick vegetation cover and the rugged relief of the interior made land-based communications extremely difficult and led to the emergence of a multitude of small coastal ports. With the gradual development of the interior and the expansion of broken-in areas, the larger settlements captured the trade of the smaller ports. This, along with the development of internal communications, especially rail, led to the irreversible decline of many small coastal settlements.

The railway system was important in developing the Waikato, and by 1887 the line extended as far south as Te Kuiti in the King Country. Settlers needed transport to get onto the land, to bring in their requirements and, in time, to bring out their produce—eventually for export, but initially to supply the growing Auckland market. It is not surprising, therefore, that the population distribution was closely aligned to the rail network, and by 1906 the Waikato rail system was virtually the same as it is today. Between 1900 and 1920 several developments in the agricultural economy of the Waikato were aided by the rail network, especially after the opening of the North Island trunk line linking Auckland and Wellington in 1908. Refrigerated rolling stock was important in transporting produce from the freezing works and dairy factories to the ports. The rail system also transported livestock and brought in the phosphate and lime that were essential for pasture improvement. This eventually led to the development of a more intensive farming system based on dairying and fat-lamb farming.

The Coromandel Peninsula, with its industries based on the exploitation of timber, gold and kauri gum, developed without the benefit of rail and was connected to Auckland by coastal shipping. In the Bay of Plenty lowlands, the absence of early railway links restricted the development of settlement.

The two most important features of railway construction between 1921 and 1936 were the linking of the Whangarei-Kaikohe line with the main line from Auckland and the extension of the branch line from Waihi to Taneatua. Since their completion, both lines have played a great part in aiding the development of both Northland and the Bay of Plenty.

Rail was equally important to the development of Canterbury. Lyttelton Harbour was encircled by a volcanic crater rim up to 500 metres high, which provided excellent shelter but inhibited access to Christchurch and the plains. For Christchurch to develop, this natural barrier had to be overcome. Eventually it was decided to tunnel under the Port Hills, an enormous project that was started in July 1861. Six years later, the first Lyttelton-Christchurch passenger train steamed through the tunnel. By 1875 Christchurch was linked to Oxford and Rangiora, Ashburton and Southbridge, Malvern and Lyttelton. Rail bound the hinterland to the emerging city and, in time, contributed to Christchurch's dominant role as the commercial and industrial centre of the Canterbury region.

By the mid-1930s rail's dominance was waning as road transport developed. The development of an effective transportation network—coastal shipping, rail and road—was essential for New Zealand's regional development, acting as a lifeline from the hinterland to the metropolitan centres by providing a means whereby raw materials and finished products could circulate.

Lyttelton Harbour is Canterbury's main port. A railway tunnel linked it with Christchurch in 1867, but it was not until 1964 that a road tunnel was opened — the longest one in New Zealand. (Photobank)

In 1900 Burnetts Face, near Westport, was a thriving coal-mining centre employing many people. Today mining has ceased and the town is deserted. (Alexander Turnbull Library)

Population changes

The opening up of new areas during this period led to major shifts in the distribution of the population. As pastoral farming developed, the migrants began to spread inland from the coast onto the South Island plains and into the Wairarapa and Hawke's Bay. The movement into Central Otago and the West Coast was made by a new type of migrant: single men after gold.

Early Otago's history is one of resource development and resource exploitation, of fortunes made and fortunes lost—boom and bust. It began with Johnny Jones, who reared sheep and grew grain at Waikouaiti. Then, in 1848, Charles Suisted established his Goodwood homestead near Pleasant River, growing wheat, oats and potatoes. By 1855 the Taieri Plains were being drained and reclaimed, and land was occupied as far south as the Clutha. The tussock of the Waitaki Basin was ideal for extensive sheep farming, and by 1860 Central Otago was occupied for grazing. There were nearly 300 000 sheep, and many of the large runholders made fortunes.

Then came the gold. In 1861 Gabriel Read struck gold in Tuapeka, and later that year gold was found at Waitahuna. The rush was on. The provincial population, largely composed of single men, increased from 12 000 to over 30 000. In 1862 work began at the Dunstan diggings near the confluence of the Clutha and Kawarau Rivers; then Clyde, the Carrick Range, Bannockburn, Cardrona, the Arrow, the Shotover—speculation, migration and false rumour were rife. In 1863–64 the Manuherikia, Maniototo, St Bathans, Garibaldi, Kyeburn, the Taieri River, Hyde and Hinton followed. Cash flowed into the local economy, which fed and supplied the miners.

The European population in Central Otago, which had leaped from 300 to 24 000 between 1861 and 1863, just as rapidly declined, to leave only 7000 people and a trail of deserted diggings by 1865. Yet the small towns that had emerged as service centres lived on, and some even grew—for example, Mosgiel, Naseby, Queenstown, Lawrence, Ranfurly, Oamaru and Balclutha.

Between 1858 and 1871 there was rapid growth in Otago and Southland and, to a lesser extent, in Canterbury, Hawke's Bay and the West Coast. In the next three decades Taranaki emerged as the region of most rapid growth, with Wellington, Manawatu and Wairarapa joining the areas of above-average growth. The West Coast had begun its relative decline.

By 1901 the North Island contained over half of the population, with rapid expansion in Northland, Auckland, Waikato, the Bay of Plenty, the Volcanic Plateau, East Cape and Poverty Bay, and above-average growth in the southern half of the North Island. During this period, the South Island's population was still expanding, albeit slowly. Up to the 1970s, rapid growth occurred in the Bay of Plenty and the Volcanic Plateau, and above-

Transport systems

In order to make the maps as clear as possible, roads in this atlas are represented by casings or parallel lines with a band of colour between them. The width of this band is standardised, although the width of the road it represents may vary. Different types of road are distinguished by the use of different colours. Railways appear as solid black lines, and airports are marked by aeroplane symbols.

This Landsat satellite image and extract from map 52 illustrate how Wellington's transport system is constrained by its geography. Wellington owes its existence to the presence of a sheltered harbour. This lies on a fault line, as does the main access route to the Hutt Valley. This route contains a state highway and a railway line, by which people and produce are channelled to and from the capital. Since Wellington is surrounded by hills, it was not easy to find a suitable location for an airport. This now runs across the isthmus between Lyall Bay and Evans Bay.

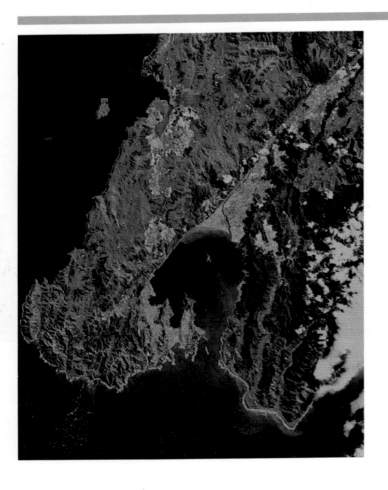

Landsat: Wellington. (NASA)

average growth continued in the Auckland, Whangarei, Hawke's Bay, Wellington and Nelson regions. A slow growth rate was evident over much of the remainder of the country.

Pockets of decline had become evident throughout the country: Hokianga in the north; the East Cape; a zone containing Dannevirke, Woodville and Pahiatua; Wanganui; Buller and the eastern edge of Marlborough; inland from Dunedin and Waimate; Bruce County; and Stewart Island.

If a rural area has good communications and easy access to larger towns, it may be possible to maintain the intensity of farm production in the face of population decrease. Southland's declining population has had an adverse effect on small rural service centres, but there is no evidence to suggest that farm productivity has suffered. The situation is much more serious in those areas remote from large towns or main lines of communication, where the viability of farming and the small rural townships are closely interconnected.

Rural population change is, in part, a reflection of the demographic and economic rhythms that sweep through the regions, quickly in some areas, slowly in others. Between 1981 and 1986 growth was evident in some of the remote counties, such as Lake and Vincent in the South Island, Hokianga and Mangonui in the North, as well as those counties adjacent to major cities, such as Rodney and Franklin, which lie to the immediate north and south of Auckland, and Rangiora, north of Christchurch. Some population increases are temporary and are associated with the influx of construction workers, as in Whangarei and Vincent Counties. The outcome, in time, is a decline in population, as has occurred in Mackenzie County with the winding down of the water-resource development programme centred on Twizel. In other areas population growth is not truly rural but is the outcome of urban overspill or tourist development projects in areas adjacent to major tourist centres, the area around Queenstown being a good example.

The main trends in the distribution of New Zealand's population over the last 150 years have been a drift from the South Island to the North and from the southern to the northern part of the North Island; the dominance of urban growth, both relatively and absolutely; and migration from rural to urban areas. Population growth in the early decades of European colonisation was fuelled largely by successive waves of immigration in which single males predominated, but since the late 1870s the major component of growth has been a natural increase in population, boosted periodically by periods of high inward migration.

Great Britain has always been the main source of immigrants, but the population is also composed of people of Chinese, Dalmatian, Dutch, German, Greek, Indian, Italian and Polish stock. Since the end of World

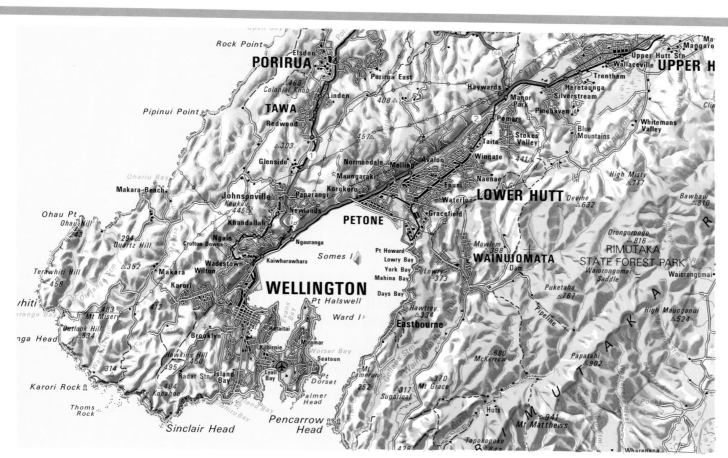

Extract from map 52.

War II there has been a substantial influx of Polynesian Pacific Islanders from Samoa, the Cook Islands and, to a lesser degree, Niue, Tokelau and Tonga. More recently New Zealand has accepted considerable numbers of new settlers from South-east Asia under a refugee resettlement programme.

The most significant contribution to population growth has come from the Maori people. By the late 1800s contact with European diseases, from which they had little immunity, had reduced the Maori population to about 40 000. Since then there has been a dramatic revival, and now more than one in ten New Zealanders are of Maori descent.

The growth of towns and cities

Although farming has dominated New Zealand's economy for over 100 years, the country is almost 80 per cent urban.

Small-town New Zealand is part of the rural landscape. Settlements set up to service the rural economy typically consist of a church, chapel, school, stock and station agent, post office, bank, hotel, dairy, and other stores strung out along a main street backed by a huddle of houses. Wherever land is farmed, small towns develop as the focus of the community and are the first link in the chain that ends with the big cities.

There are many settlements whose sole reason for existing is resource development—for example, Kaingaroa (forestry), Huntly (coal), Wairakei (geothermal steam), Meremere (electricity) and Roxburgh (hydro-electricity).

The history of most hydro towns is not unlike that of the gold-strike settlements: a rapid influx of construction workers, mostly single and male, then an equally speedy decline as the construction side of the project is wound down, leaving a residual population of maintenance employees and their families. Karapiro, Arapuni, Waipapa, Maraetai, Whakamaru, Mangakino, Atiamuri and Ohakuri illustrate the intensity of use of the Waikato River as a hydro resource. Kaitawa and Piripaua on the Waikaretaheke River, which flows south-east out of Lake Waikaremoana, are two small hydro settlements in the Hawke's Bay region. Other schemes are associated with the lakes and rivers of the South Island: Lake Coleridge and Highbank; Benmore, Aviemore and Waitaki on the upper reaches of the Waitaki River; Roxburgh Hydro and Waipori in Otago; and Manapouri and Monowai in the south-west.

The timber towns are a contrast. Permanent and often growing settlements, they are all located in the central North Island: Kaingaroa for planting, tending, thinning and pruning; Murupara for its railhead; and Kawerau for pulp and paper. The most spectacular growth town has been Tokoroa, with its pulp and paper mill located 7 kilometres to the south at Kinleith.

The growth of other settlements has been associated with the commercial exploitation of methanol. In 1983 a methanol plant was opened at Waitara, in Taranaki, using natural gas from the offshore Maui Field. Methanol can be used in the manufacture of many products, including dyes, resins, textiles, fibres and artificial rubber. Here it is also used in the production of fertiliser at the nearby ammonia-urea plant. In 1986 a synthetic fuel plant was opened at Motunui. The plant employs a catalytic process to transform the methanol obtained from natural gas into gasoline.

Several processes have underlain rural development. There have been changes in numbers of farm holdings and on-farm workers, with developments in pastoral farming and the agricultural diversification programmes that have resulted from increased irrigation. Rural services have become increasingly centralised, as has rural residential development, and these have implications for the larger settlements.

The secondary urban centres, most of which have a specialised role, have tended to fare better than small rural communities. Whangarei has oil refining; Tauranga has the timber industries of the central Volcanic Plateau, as well as kiwifruit; Gisborne's fishing port supplies the local food freezing plant and draws on the intensive cropping of the Poverty Bay flats; Napier and Timaru function as outlets for wool and for the produce from freezing works in either the actual cities or in their hinterlands; New Plymouth is an export port for dairy produce and has an additional role related to natural gas and associated development.

The commercial areas of the secondary urban centres, originally along a single main street, have grown in size. Whangarei has expanded in the area adjacent to the original wharf; Tauranga along the waterfront; Rotorua

The discovery of the Kapuni gas-condensate field in 1959 and the enormous offshore Maui field 10 years later led to the establishment of several large petrochemical plants in Taranaki. This photograph shows the gas-treatment plant at Oaonui. (Photobank)

northward from its original nucleus around the railway station; and Timaru from its Caroline Bay harbour. Hamilton is the home of the University of Waikato and the agricultural research centre at Ruakura; Palmerston North has Massey University, several research centres, and military camps nearby at Linton and Ohakea; and Nelson is the site of the Cawthron Institute for biological and agricultural research. There is an aluminium smelter at Bluff and viticulture around Hastings, and a variety of thermal and scenic attractions in and around Rotorua make it a centre for both domestic and international tourism. What all these secondary centres have in common are close ties with their surrounding rural areas. The prosperity of the cities is very much allied to the economic fortunes of their rural sectors.

This hierarchy of settlements is crowned by the long-established metropolitan centres of Auckland, Wellington, Christchurch and Dunedin. It is not surprising that the four major metropolitan centres have ports. The colonial settlers came by sea, it was the sea that provided the communications between the early settlements, and it is by sea that the bulk of New Zealand's international trade is exported or imported.

Dunedin, founded in 1848, was the site of the first university. It has a safe harbour, and land was reclaimed early in its history. The inner suburbs, such as Mornington, Belleknowes, Roslyn and North Dunedin, form the core that spreads south over the narrow peninsula to St Kilda, exposed to southerlies from the sea. Further development has occurred inland, with suburbs such as Green Island, Abbotsford, Fairfield and, further still, Mosgiel strung out along the roads leading south-west to the Taieri Plains. On the seaward side there is a sequence of development hugging the north harbour shore through Ravensbourne, St Leonards and Roseneath to the heavy industry and deep waters of Port Chalmers. The southern banks of the harbour are dotted with marine suburbs.

Further north is Christchurch, through which flow the rivers Avon and Heathcote. Industry was established in the late nineteenth century at Woolston, Addington and Sydenham, with early suburbanisation at New Brighton, Opawa, Linwood, Mount Pleasant, Merivale and Fendalton. Christchurch is a relatively compact city, with a central gridiron street pattern. The central suburbs run one into the other before struggling irregularly north to Belfast and Kaiapoi, east to New Brighton on Pegasus Bay, west to Hornby and Islington, or winding eastwards again along the estuary to Clifton, Sumner and the port of Lyttelton.

At the southern tip of the North Island, bounded by the Tararuas to the north and Cook Strait to the south, lies Wellington, settled in 1840 and capital city since 1865. The central city is oriented towards Lambton Harbour, and much of it is built on land reclaimed from the 1850s onwards. The introduction of a tramway system in 1878 enabled suburban development to occur further from the original nucleus, at Oriental Bay and Island Bay, Miramar, Karori and Seatoun, Lyall Bay and Wadestown. Lower Hutt was linked by rail as early as 1874 and in time the Hutt Valley developed, first as a series of residential suburbs then subsequently as a centre for industry. Road and rail have encouraged development to the north through Johnsonville, Tawa, Porirua and Titahi Bay, then stringing out through Plimmerton and Pukerua Bay to Paekakariki, Paraparaumu and Waikanae. Around the harbour itself, development curves through a series of bays to Eastbourne.

Auckland was established in 1840 and is the most populous metropolitan area. Its nucleus emerged around the port at Commercial Bay on the Waitemata Harbour and struck south along Queen Street, still the centre for retailing and commerce. During the 1850s Onehunga developed, along with little village settlements at Epsom and Newmarket. By the 1880s the main area of growth was along the southern coast of the isthmus at Onehunga and Otahuhu. However, as the tram routes expanded through the early 1900s, population and industry began to spread over the isthmus. Beyond the core of inner suburbs, mainly residential suburbs developed throughout the inter-war period: Orakei through to St Heliers in the east and a curving belt running from Point Chevalier to Three Kings, Royal Oak and the industrial area of Penrose.

After 1945 the city formed an almost continuous belt from Papakura in the south to Torbay in the north, although, apart from the early settlements of Northcote, Devonport and Takapuna, the housing boom on the North Shore dates from the opening of the harbour bridge in 1959.

Auckland, Christchurch, Dunedin and Wellington—so different in character and each occupying a highly distinctive site—have certain aspects of their development in common: a sheltered port location, extensive areas of reclamation, scattered settlement in the early days, consolidation as farmed land was turned over to urban uses, tramways and railways pushing the suburban frontier further outwards from the core, and, with the advent of the motor car, a low-density suburban sprawl based on the quarter-acre section.

Auckland's landscape is punctuated with volcanic cones. These made ideal defence sites, and early Maori settlements were clustered around them. The resulting artificial terraces are clearly visible in this aerial photograph of Mount Wellington. (Air Logistics)

Scale and style

Cartographers must ask themselves two questions before producing a map: What is the map intended to represent? And what is the most appropriate scale for the map?

This atlas is a topographical one; that is, it shows both natural and cultural features, as well as the height and shape of the terrain. Its scale is 1:250 000, which imposes limits on what symbols can be used, how large they should be, and how much detail of the landscape must be omitted for the sake of clarity.

The six illustrations in this section show how maps are derived from the reality of the landscape.

The first colour photograph is a low-altitude oblique view of Iona College in Havelock North. Although this is a 'realistic' view (similar to what could be seen from the top of a high tower), it does not depict the relationships between features as clearly as the second photograph, which is a vertical view of a larger area. The third image is actually a series of standard black-and-white aerial photographs that have been assembled into a mosaic, with names and a grid added. Some map characteristics are appearing.

By placing pairs of overlapping vertical photographs in stereo-plotting machines, photogrammetrists can obtain a three-dimensional view of the land. This is then adjusted to tie in with control points established on the ground by surveyors, and distortions in the photographs (which result from the tip and tilt of the aircraft and variations in the height of the ground beneath the camera) are corrected. Aerial photographs that have been modified in this way are known as 'orthophotographs', and the mosaics they form are termed 'orthophotomaps'. Using these and other data, cartographers draw the maps and prepare them for printing.

Examples of three finished maps are given here. These show vividly how different scales dramatically affect what can be learned from each map. Although many details that appeared in the photographs can no longer be seen, the relationship of Havelock North to the surrounding region becomes increasingly apparent.

The first map, which has a scale of 1:25 000, has a part of an aerial photograph printed on top to show how features of the landscape are converted into symbols. This demonstrates the selectivity of mapping. Although many individual buildings (such as Iona College) can still be seen, trees are represented by scattered symbols (sometimes with a green background) rather than individual trees. The roads have had to be enlarged and made uniform in size, and different types of road are represented by different colours. The relief is depicted by contours.

The map, through its use of symbols, has taken a definite step away from photographic representation.

In the next map, which has a scale of 1:50 000, a major step has been taken in the representation of relief. An oblique shadow, as though a light were falling from the north-west, is used with contours, and the relief of the landscape seems to come to life. The use of symbols and the degree of selectivity has also increased. Larger buildings, such as Iona College, still appear, but groups of smaller buildings are represented by a black screen (a pattern of black dots). Havelock North is now placed in its local setting.

The next step to the 1:250 000 scale of this atlas is significant, and it is essential to understand the changes involved in order to grasp how the maps depict a real landscape. The scale is one fifth that of the previous map, and corresponding changes in both the use of symbols and the degree of selectivity are equally drastic. The much broader view now obtained is extremely valuable.

Contours have now been omitted, and the relief of the landscape is instead represented by oblique shading, with frequent spot heights showing actual altitudes. The smaller scale means that roads must appear wider than their actual size (or else they would not be clearly visible), intricate curving must be smoothed, and many small roading patterns must be eliminated. The building symbol (a black square) now represents a group of buildings—usually four or five, though this may vary to a certain extent. The map has become simpler and clearer.

Low-altitude oblique aerial photograph.

Vertical aerial photograph. (New Zealand Aerial Mapping Ltd)

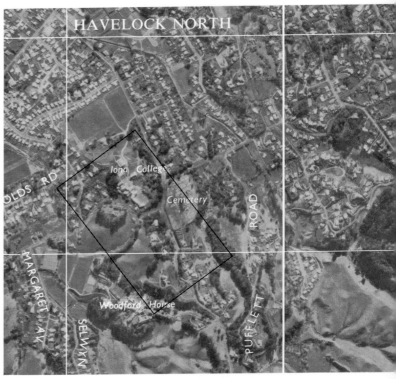

Photographic mosaic. (Department of Survey and Land Information)

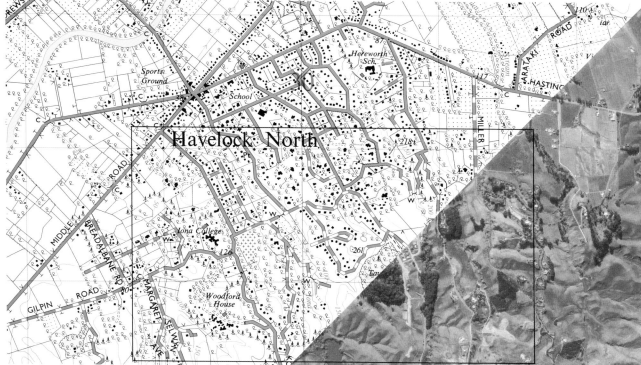

Map extract from NZMS 2 series (1:25 000) combined with vertical aerial photograph. (Department of Survey and Land Information)

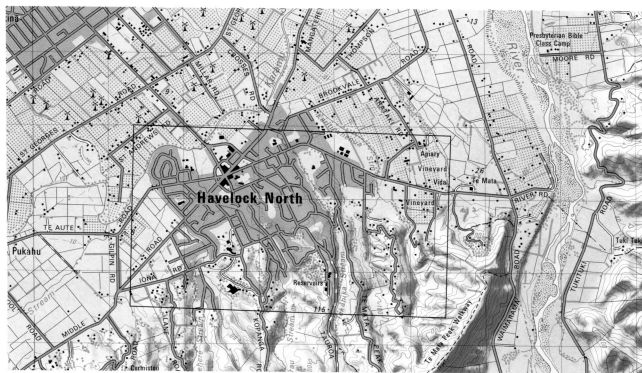

Map extract from NZMS 260 series (1:50 000). (Department of Survey and Land Information)

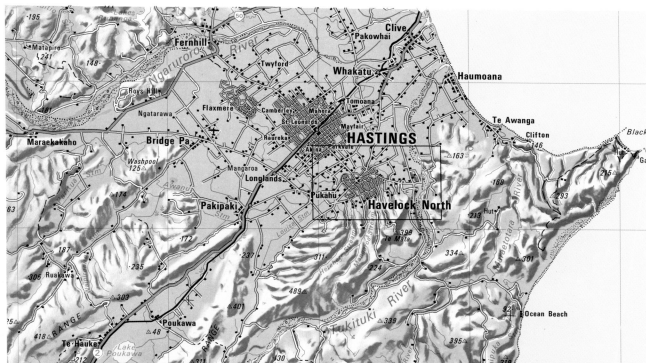

Extract from map 43 (1:250 000).

Conventional signs

Many of the map symbols used in this atlas are pictorial. The view may be horizontal, as in the symbols for lighthouse, radio mast and exotic forest, or it may be vertical, as in the symbols for aerodrome and airport. As far as possible, the colours used approximate those appearing in nature: blue for water, green for forest and black for rock. All these symbols are intended to be easily recognisable.

The symbols for road transport are more complex and more artificial. They must show the different types of surface as well as the controlling authorities, indicating if each road is a National or Provincial State Highway and giving its official number on a coloured shield.

Roads are shown as parallel lines. The distance between the lines is dependent on the scale of the maps and does not show the actual width of the road on the ground. This can be seen by comparing the maps and vertical photographs of Otaki and Levin, and the two maps of Paeroa, shown here.

As the map scale changes, not only must the size of the road symbol be changed but road winding must sometimes be simplified. This is also true of natural features, as can be seen in the streams north of Paeroa. Simplification and some generalisation are inevitable in map-making.

The map symbol for built-up areas, including shopping or business areas, is a black screen. However, a problem is posed by the mapping of detached buildings. Three examples are given on these pages. Two maps of part of the Hauraki Plains near Paeroa show the standard solution: a single black square representing a number of buildings, nominally three to five, the placement of which depends on cartographic judgement. A black square can also indicate a single isolated homestead, which is normally named.

When, as in the example shown here of the area south of Levin, the farming pattern is more intensive, with some market gardening, appropriate placement of the black squares becomes more difficult. A comparison of the map with the oblique and vertical photographs shows how the atlas has simplified reality and how the map must be interpreted.

Reference

ROADS

National State Highway	
Provincial State Highway	
Other roads	
Vehicle track	
Foot track	
Road Surface { sealed	
metalled	
unmetalled	
Tunnel	

NATURAL FEATURES

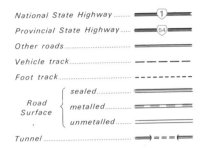

Stream or watercourse
Sand & mud
Sand & shingle
Swamp
Mangroves
Coastal rocks
Sandhills
Waterfall
Glacier
Cliff
Rock outcrop
Cave
Saddle
Native forest
Exotic forest
National Park or
State Forest Park boundary

RAILWAYS

Railway	
Railway station	
Level crossing	
Road over railway	
Railway over road	
Tramway	

OTHER CULTURAL FEATURES

Built-up area	
Building or group of buildings	•
Isolated homestead	Titirangi
Radio mast; TV Mast	
Main electric power line	
International Airport	
Airport	
Aerodrome	
Lighthouse	
Mine or quarry	
Racecourse	

HEIGHT INFORMATION

Elevation in metres	721
Trig station	

Left: extract from map 48.

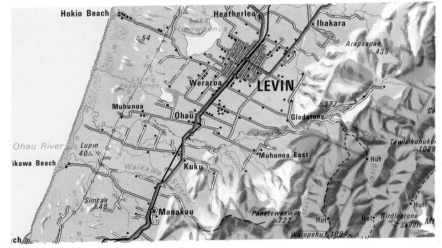

Oblique aerial photograph of Levin. (J. H. Johns/Department of Survey and Land Information)

Vertical aerial photograph. (Department of Survey and Land Information)

A related problem in mapping settlement is brought out by the example of Otaki shown here. The built-up part of Otaki is shown by the standard black screen, a few black squares representing houses in some open areas, and different-shaped black symbols indicating detached buildings to the north. The difficulties involved in mapping a group of houses with the scale used in this atlas are illustrated by the settlement near the mouth of the Otaki River. The only possible solution is a grouping of black square symbols. As the vertical and oblique photographs show, this is a generalised and simplified representation of a more varied and complicated reality.

Extract from map 48.

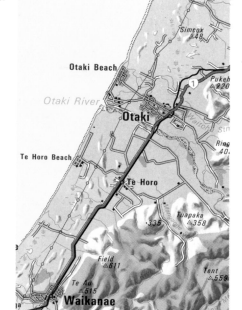

Vertical aerial photograph. (New Zealand Aerial Mapping Ltd)

Oblique aerial photograph of Otaki, taken from near the mouth of the Otaki River. (J. H. Johns/Department of Survey and Land Information)

Map extract from NZMS 260 series (1:50 000). (Department of Survey and Land Information)

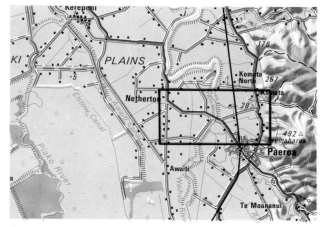

Extract from map 15.

Index to maps

New Zealand is a country with two dominant directional trends: one north-east from Stewart Island to the Bay of Plenty and another north-west from the Waikato to North Cape. This makes a simple grid break-up of the maps almost impossible. Consequently, the maps have been divided with the user's convenience in mind, and in some cases quite large overlaps exist (for example, map 38). Cook Strait is covered by a special double-page map (54/55).

Maps 116–18 cover New Zealand's outlying islands. These do not appear on this grid but on the map facing map 118.

At the bottom of each map (except maps 116–18) is a small inset showing its location in New Zealand and a grid showing its relationship to adjacent maps.

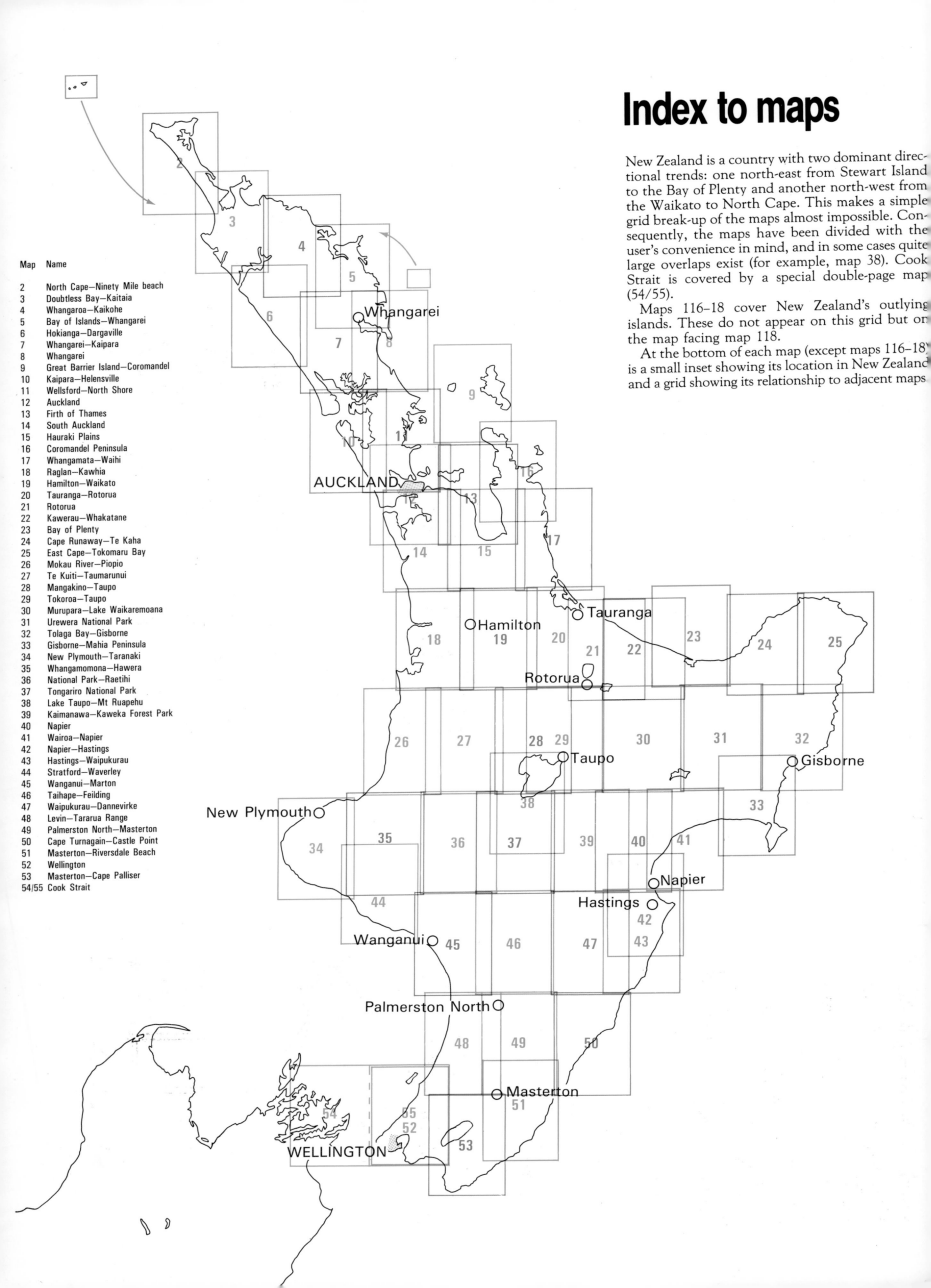

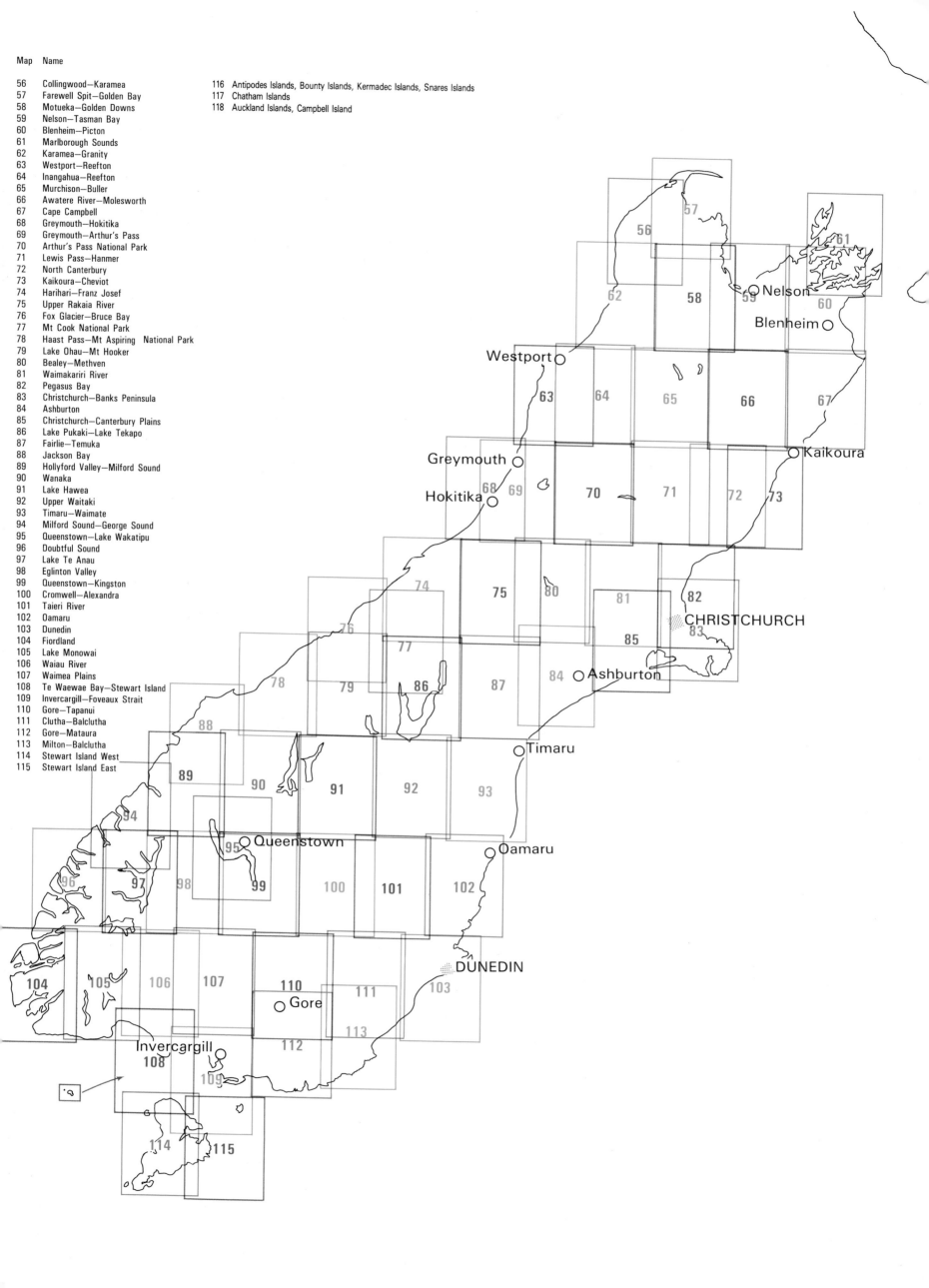

Map Name

56 Collingwood—Karamea
57 Farewell Spit—Golden Bay
58 Motueka—Golden Downs
59 Nelson—Tasman Bay
60 Blenheim—Picton
61 Marlborough Sounds
62 Karamea—Granity
63 Westport—Reefton
64 Inangahua—Reefton
65 Murchison—Buller
66 Awatere River—Molesworth
67 Cape Campbell
68 Greymouth—Hokitika
69 Greymouth—Arthur's Pass
70 Arthur's Pass National Park
71 Lewis Pass—Hanmer
72 North Canterbury
73 Kaikoura—Cheviot
74 Harihari—Franz Josef
75 Upper Rakaia River
76 Fox Glacier—Bruce Bay
77 Mt Cook National Park
78 Haast Pass—Mt Aspiring National Park
79 Lake Ohau—Mt Hooker
80 Bealey—Methven
81 Waimakariri River
82 Pegasus Bay
83 Christchurch—Banks Peninsula
84 Ashburton
85 Christchurch—Canterbury Plains
86 Lake Pukaki—Lake Tekapo
87 Fairlie—Temuka
88 Jackson Bay
89 Hollyford Valley—Milford Sound
90 Wanaka
91 Lake Hawea
92 Upper Waitaki
93 Timaru—Waimate
94 Milford Sound—George Sound
95 Queenstown—Lake Wakatipu
96 Doubtful Sound
97 Lake Te Anau
98 Eglinton Valley
99 Queenstown—Kingston
100 Cromwell—Alexandra
101 Taieri River
102 Oamaru
103 Dunedin
104 Fiordland
105 Lake Monowai
106 Waiau River
107 Waimea Plains
108 Te Waewae Bay—Stewart Island
109 Invercargill—Foveaux Strait
110 Gore—Tapanui
111 Clutha—Balclutha
112 Gore—Mataura
113 Milton—Balclutha
114 Stewart Island West
115 Stewart Island East

116 Antipodes Islands, Bounty Islands, Kermadec Islands, Snares Islands
117 Chatham Islands
118 Auckland Islands, Campbell Island

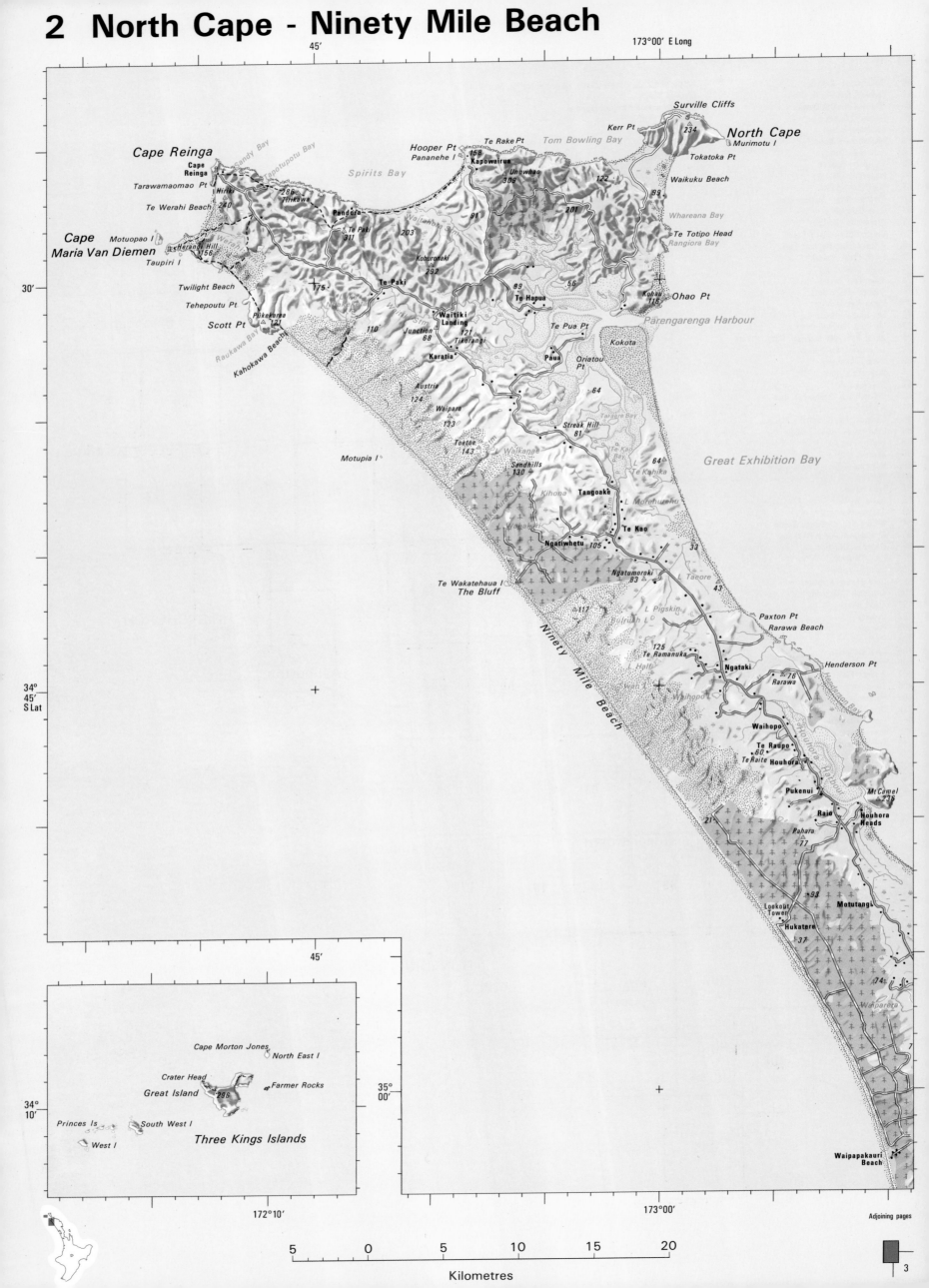

North Cape

Surville Cliffs
Kerr Pt
234
Murimotu I
Tom Bowling Bay
Tokatoka Pt
Te Rake Pt
Hooper Pt
Pananehe I · 158
Waikuku Beach
Kapowairua
Unuwhao
309
122
99
Whareana Bay

Cape Reinga
Sandy Bay
Tapotupotu Bay
Spirits Bay
Cape Reinga
Tarawamaomao Pt
Te Werahi Beach 240
Hiriki
286
Tirikawa
Pandora
Te Paki 311
203
91
201
Te Totipo Head
Rangiora Bay

Cape
Maria Van Diemen
Motuopao I
Herangi Hill 156
Taupiri I
Twilight Beach
Tehepoutu Pt
Scott Pt
Pukekaroa 121
Kahokawa Beach
Raukawa Bay

Kohuronaki
292
Te Paki
175
110
89
56
Waitiki Landing
Junction 68
121
Tikorangi
Karatia
Te Pua Pt
Paua
Oriatou Pt
Kokota
Te Hapua
Kohau 115
Ohao Pt
Parengarenga Harbour

Austria 124
Waipara 133
64
Toetoe 143
Waikanae
Streak Hill 81
64
Te Kahika
Te Kao Bay
Great Exhibition Bay

Motupia I
Sandhills 130
Kihona
Tangoake
L Morehurehu

Te Kao
Ngatiwhetu 105
33

Te Wakatehaua I
The Bluff
Ngatumoroki 83
L Taeore
43
117
L Pigskin
Bulrush L
Paxton Pt
Rarawa Beach
125
Te Ramanuka
L Heath
Ngataki
76
Rarawa
Henderson Pt
Waihopo
Waihopo
Te Raupo 60
Te Raite
Houhora
Houhora Harbour
Pukenui
Mt Camel 236
Raio
Houhora Heads
21
Pahara 77

Ninety Mile Beach

Lookout Tower
93
Motutangi
Hukatere 37
74
Waiparera

Waipapakauri Beach

34°45' S Lat

34°45'
S Lat

Cape Morton Jones
North East I
Crater Head
Farmer Rocks
Great Island
296
35°00'
Princes Is
South West I
West I
Three Kings Islands
34°10'

172°10'
45'
173°00' E Long
173°00'

5   0   5   10   15   20
Kilometres

Adjoining pages

173°00' E Long

173°15' E Long

30'

45'

Doubtless Bay

Rangaunu Bay

Cape Karikari

Moturoa Islands

Moturoa I

Sugarloaf I

Staffa Rock

Whale I

Taumatara Pt

Maraewhiti Pt

Matawherohia Pt

Pihakoa Pt

Matai Bay

158

Merita

Koware

142

Knuckle Pt

Whangatupere Bay

Karikari

Peninsula

183

Brodies Ck

Whatuwhiwhi

Simmonds Is

Grenville Pt

Kowhai Beach

Perforated Pt

Farmer Pt

Waihopo

Te Raupo

60

Te Raite

Houhora

Pukenui

Mt Camel

236

Stanley Pt

Perpendicular Pt

Raie

Houhora Heads

Pahara

77

21

Houhora Harbour

Motutara Bay

Raupo Bay

46

Puheke

132

Rotokawau

Rangiputa

28

Tokerau Beach

East Beach

17

11

Motutangi Swamp

93

Motutangi

Lookout Tower

Hukatere

37

Waihuahua Swamps

L Waikaramu

Kuaka Pt

Kawakawa

Kaimaumau

74

36

Waiparera Creek

L Waiparera

Waiharara

76

Rangaunu Harbour

Kaikino Stm

28

Tokerau Beach

Berghan Pt

170

Puketakahia Pt

Te Reinga Bay

Tekura Rocks

Otonga

Taemaro

Whakaangi

334

177

Kaiwhetu

203

Puketutu

353

Hihi

Tokomata

164

Osprey Head

Mangonui Harbour

Awapoko R

Puketutu I

Aurere Stm

Omaia I

Prices Pt

Okatakata Islands

64

Lake Ohia

L Ohia

Aurere

Taipa

Cable Bay

Coopers Beach

Mangonui

Oruaiti

35°00' S Lat

Paparore

Unahi

Pekerau

115

Pararake

Parapara

470

203

141

Back River

166

Aputerewa

Kenana

141

Paranaui

266

Nakepua

89

Waipapakauri

Sweetwater

Waimanoni

Kaingaroa

Te Ahoponga

142

Hikurangi

179

Toatoa

Oruru

Oruru

262

Omatai

265

Waipapakauri Beach

L Ngatu

67

Karaponia

Taumata

236

165

Tuanaki

186

Kohumaru

238

Awanui

98

Kapuokai

315

Te Korihi

80

Peria

Puhangatohoraka

289

Fern Flat

Te Arai

359

Oturu

Taware

145

Fairburn

183

Kaiaka

Mangatoetoe

Honeymoon Valley

Okahautaumanga

406

Kaitaia

Otepo

11

Rangitihi

Pamapuria

Te Puhi

Victoria Valley

RANGE

Ahipara Bay

L Waimimiha

92

Ruaroa

Mangataiore

MAUNGATANIWHA

Maungataniwha

567

Okahu

Puketutu

420

138

Kotipu

Te Rore

537

277

Tauroa Point

Ahipara

Pukepoto

Maungaheremona

305

293

Mangamuka

Shipwreck Bay

207

Wainui Junction

Diggers Valley

136

Raetea

751

445

Umaumakaroro

Pautouto

Omahuta

Tauroa

201

Tauroa Peninsula

558

Taumatamahoe

296

Takahue

630

Kumetewhiwhia

Mangataipa

139

Mangamuka Bridge

Waitaha Stm

329

Kaipaua

462

596

Waitawa

413

Titaha

476

Paihikokuri

333

418

Otainga

202

325

Manukau

Orowhano

507

Waiotehue

Broadwood

Orawau

Mohuiti

Tutekehua

Oturia

200

Hunahuna Stm

360

Herekareao

177

Pukemiro

202

Te Karae

Umawera

Kahikatoa

Hereking

Awaroa

Pareokawa

235

Te Wharangi

256

Paponga

194

Mata

Urungaio

Whakaoma

152

Orira

Rawhia

Herekino Harbour

Puhata

Owhata

280

Pauanui

226

Kohe

Runaruna

Waiwakaruku

228

236

84

Te Huahua

221

Kohukohu

Mangungu

Ivydale

Horeke

216

Pukewhao

Whangape

Rotokakahi

Opango

482

Pawarenga

268

Tapuwae

132

Panguru

183

Motuti

160

Motukauri

Kohukohu

Rangiora

Motukataka

Matawhera

186

Wairere

Haponga

125

Motukiore

Papua

193

Te Umakuri Pt

Whangape Harbour

Otoi Rock

654

655

Tauwhara

600

Waireia

530

Mitimiti

Matihetihe

Reena

Punehu

Te Karaka

Onoke

152

Opara

Ohuri

173°00'

15'

15'

30'

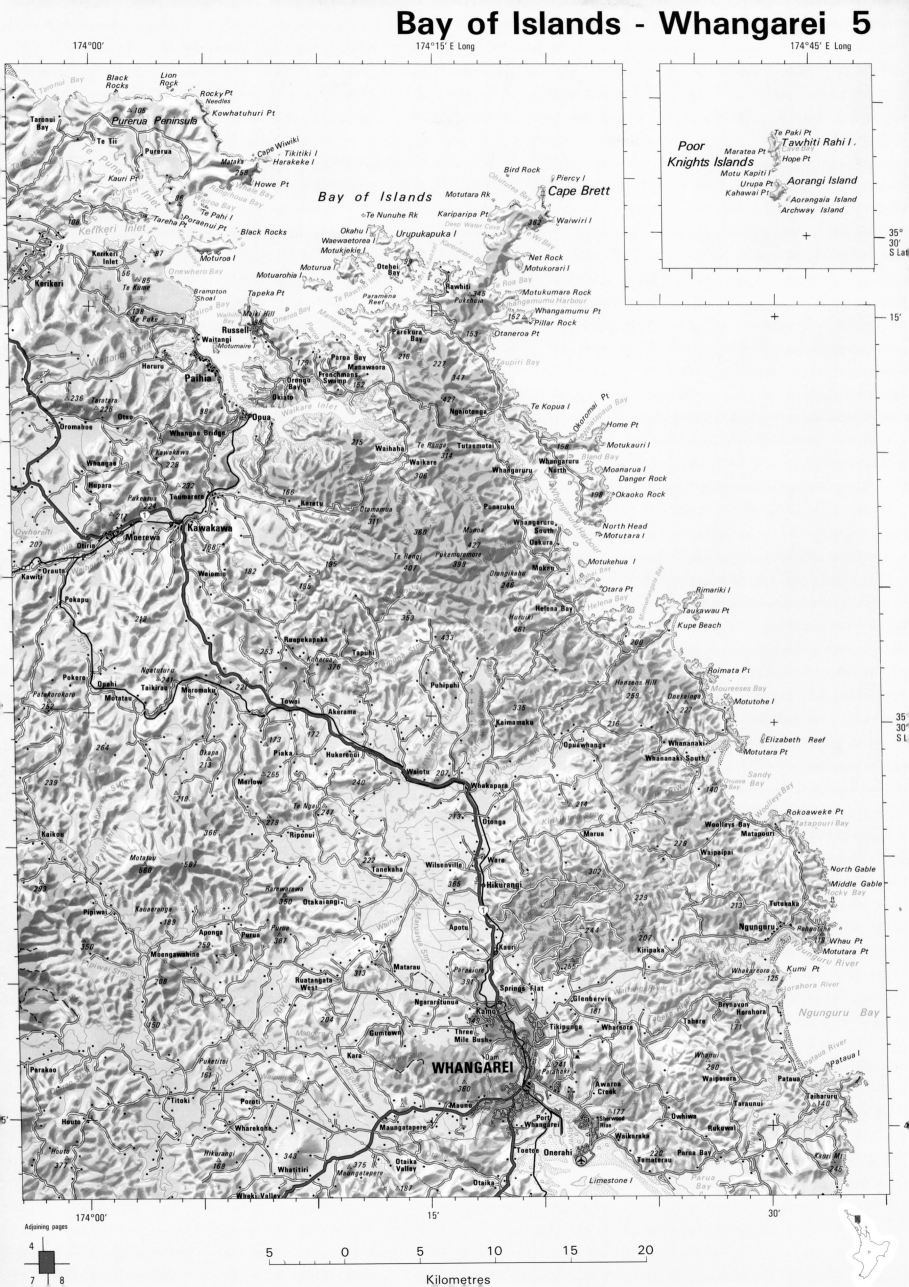

6 Hokianga - Dargaville

173°30' E Long

45'

173°30'

45'

Kilometres

5   0   5   10   15   20

Adjoining pages
4
7

174°00' E Long

15'

35° 45'

36° 00' S

174°00'

15'

8 Whangarei

174°30' E Long

45'

15'

High Peak Rocks

Sugarloaf Rock

Rokoaweke Pt
Matapouri Bay
Woolleys Bay
Matapouri
Marua
Waipaipai
214
279
North Gable
213
Middle Gable
Rocky Bay
Tutukaka
302
Tutukaka Head
229
Tutukaka Harbour
244
Kiripaka
207
Ngunguru
Rehuotane
Rauhomaumau I
119 Whau Pt
Motutara Pt
Ngunguru River
255
Whakareoro
Kumi Pt
125
Horahora River
Springs Flat
Glenbervie
181
Brynavon
Horahora
Ngunguru Bay
Kamo
Tikipunga
Whareora
Tahere
171
Gumtown
Three Mile Bush
Pataua River
Whanui
290
Waiparera
Pataua I
Kara
Dam
WHANGAREI
241
Parahaki
Awaroa Creek
Taraunui
Pataua
Taiharuru River
Taiharuru Head
Moturewa I
Maunu
360
177
Sherwood Rise
Owhiwa
Taiharuru
Port Whangarei
Waikaraka
Rukuwai
140
Taiharuru Bay
Onerahi
Parua Bay
Kauri Mt
Wahoa Bay
Toetoe
Tamaterau
220
245
Maungatapere
Limestone I
Awarua Rock
Otaika Valley
375
Parua Bay
162
Maungatapere
187
Otaika
Mangawhati Pt
McLeod Bay
Ocean Beach
Puwera
161
Portland
Whangarei Harbour
Whangarei Heads
411
Bream Islands
199
Tikorangi
Hewlett Pt
One Tree Point
Manaia
Oakleigh
Reotahi Bay
420
Taurikura
Takahiwai
Marsden Bay
Urquharts
Bream Head
Maungakaramea
Mata
185
Marsden Point
Bay
383
Bream Head
491
Bream Head
Mangapai
Frenchman I
Busby Head
Smugglers Bay
Peach Cove
Moewhare
163
Springfield
Marotere Islands
Tauraroa
Coppermine I
Parahaka
Ngatoka
262
Ruakaka
Mauitahi I
Lady Alice I
Whatupuke I
Waikiekie
176
Kukunui
262
Hen & Chickens Group
Waiotira
Ruarangi
244
Waipu Caves
Waikiekie
239
North River
Bream Bay
Taranga Island
183
Pukekohe
201
Waipu
Waipu River
Sail Rock
Taipuha
Braigh
Marereti
360
338
Waipu Cove
McKenzie Cove
Andersons Cove
Bream Tail
McGregor Rock
Snapper Knoll
Bunker Hill
238
257
Langs Beach
167
Pahi
Weirere
Pilbrow Hill
292
326
Sentinel Rock
Paparoa
174
Cattlemount
397
281
431
Mangawhai Heads
Maungaturoto
Brynderwyn
Molesworth
Mangawhai Harbour
Huarau
Bald Rock
238
Tara
Pukekaroro
Mangawhai
Bickerstaffe
159
Pukekaroro
301
Marohemo
Hakaru
Pahi
Whakapirau
Te Arai Pt
Arapaoa
133
Kaiwaka Stn
85
Kaiwaka
Te Arai Point
168
Tanoa
Batley
165
199
Te Arai
137
Ngaupiko Pt
Topuni
192
Fairy Hill
154
134
Rocky Pt
Coates Bay
Mohinui
167
Tomarata

35°
45'

36°
00'
S Lat

5   0   5   10   15   20
Kilometres
174°30'
45'

Adjoining pages
5
7
10 11

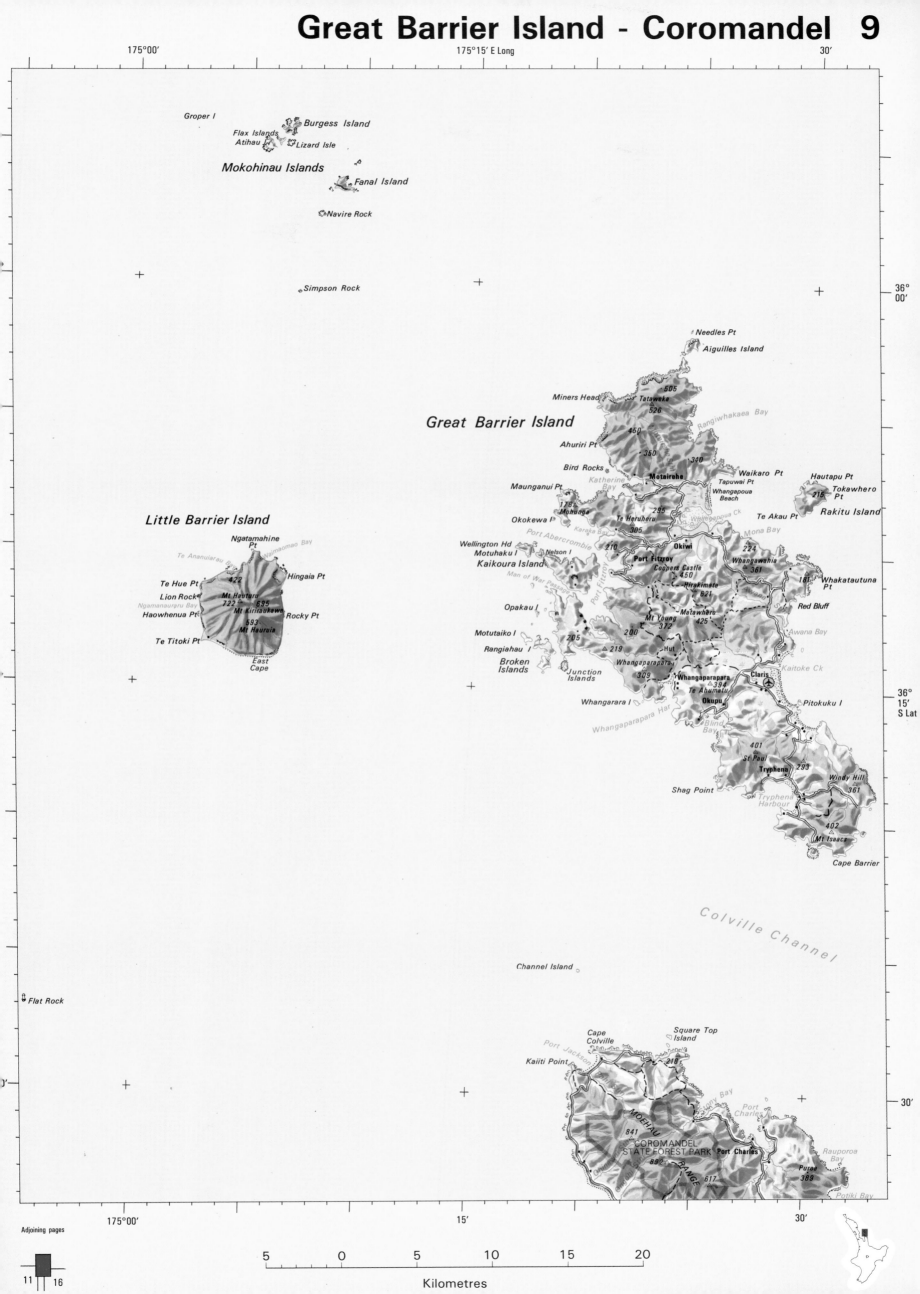

175°00' 175°15' E Long 30'

Groper I
Burgess Island
Flax Islands
Atihau Lizard Isle
Mokohinau Islands
Fanal Island
Navire Rock

Simpson Rock

36° 00'

Needles Pt
Aiguilles Island

Miners Head
Tataweka
505
526
Great Barrier Island
450
Rangiwhakaea Bay
Ahuriri Pt
350
340
Bird Rocks
Motairehe
Waikaro Pt
Tapuwai Pt
Hautapu Pt
Maunganui Pt
Katherine Bay
Whangapoua Beach
215
Tokawhero Pt
178
Mohunga
295
Te Akau Pt
Rakitu Island
Okokewa I
Te Heruheru
305
Whangapoua Ck
Mona Bay
Port Abercrombie
Karaka Bay
Wellington Hd
210
Okiwi
Motuhaku I
Nelson I
Port Fitzroy
224
Kaikoura Island
Coopers Castle
Whangawahia
450
361
Man of War Passage
Hirakimata
181
Whakatautuna Pt
621
Opakau I
Mt Young
Matawhero
Red Bluff
372
425
Motutaiko I
200
Awana Bay
205
219
Hut
Rangiahau I
Whangaparapara
Broken Islands
309
Kaitoke Ck
394
Claris
Junction Islands
Whangaparapara
Te Ahumata
Pitokuku I
Whangarara I
Okupu
36° 15' S Lat
Whangaparapara Har
Blind Bay
401
St Paul
Tryphena
293
Windy Hill
Shag Point
361
Tryphena Harbour
402
Mt Isaacs
Cape Barrier

Colville Channel

Little Barrier Island
Ngatamahine Pt
Te Ananuiarau Bay
Waimaomao Bay
Hingaia Pt
Te Hue Pt
422
Lion Rock
Mt Hauturu
Ngamanaurgru Bay
722
695
Mt Kiritaukawe
Haowhenua Pt
593
Rocky Pt
Mt Hauruia
Te Titoki Pt
East Cape

Channel Island

Flat Rock

Cape Colville
Square Top Island
Kaiiti Point
218
Port Jackson
Sandy Bay
Port Charles

841
MOEHAU
Port Charles
COROMANDEL
STATE FOREST PARK
892
RANGE
389
Purea
617
Rauporoa Bay

30'

Adjoining pages

11 | 16

5   0   5   10   15   20

Kilometres

174°00' 174° 15' E Long 30'

15'

Mohinui
187
Rototuna
Kellys Bay
Kaiwhitu I
Tinopai
Matihe Pt
The Bluff
119
Mohinui
122
Te Hana
80
Hargreaves Run
176
Oruawharo
Port Albert
1
214
Maarangi
Moturoa
Island
Pen
Oneriri
Wellsford
Toetoe Pt
Okaro Creek
Wharehine
120
Hoteo
North
Lake
Karaka
Lake
Rotootuauriri
Humuhumu
156
107
126
Puketaratara
Kikitangeo
Wayby
255
Lake
Mokena
Lake
Rotokawau
Lady
Franklin
Bank
Tapora
Reserve
165
Lake
Waingata
Lake
Kanono
Pouto
Okahukura
Peninsula
44
Tauhoa
Hoteo
129
North Head
Kaipara Head
Te Ngaio
Point
Orongo
59
Karaka
Point
Mt Harriet
229
Mangakura
Orongo Pt
Moturemu I
16
Atuanui
305
293
Kaipara
Entrance
Papakanui Spit
South Head
106
Te Kawau
Point
Kakaraia
Flats
Woodcocks
Glorit
268
300
259
Tataraki
Komokoriki
South
Head
Harbour
100
Kaipara Flats
Araparera
207
36°
30'
S Lat
163
Te Rakataia
91
Tuhirangi
215
Kakanui
Omokoiti Flats
Kakanui Pt
Makarau
Lake
Otaha
Waioneke
Lake
Kuwakata
160
Mairetahi Ck
Waitangi
179
Rangitira
Shelly
Beach
Oyster
Point
110
Kanohi
252
Riteakawatau
Lake
Kereta
191
Opahekeheke
Island
Kaukapakapa
Lake
Karaki
38
158
Beach
Lake
Pouto
Auahine
179
Parkhurst
117
Patukuri
Loch
Norrie
112
Parakai
141
158
Pureora
167
Te Pua
Helensville
75
Puketutu
182
Paehoka
45'
Lookout
Tower
135
Wharepapa
16
169
Woodhill
Waikoukou
Valley
Rewiti
Muriwai
165
Kopuakai
Waimauku
Huapai
202
166
222
Muriwai
Beach
Oaia I
207
Puketotara
180
259
Waitakere
Raetahinga
Point
Taumata
Te Henga
Te Hana
Dam
Kuataika
265
337
123
Simla
Hutt
Anawhata

174°00' 15' 30'

Adjoining pages

7	8
11	
12	

5 0 5 10 15 20

Kilometres

174° 45' E Long

Kilometres

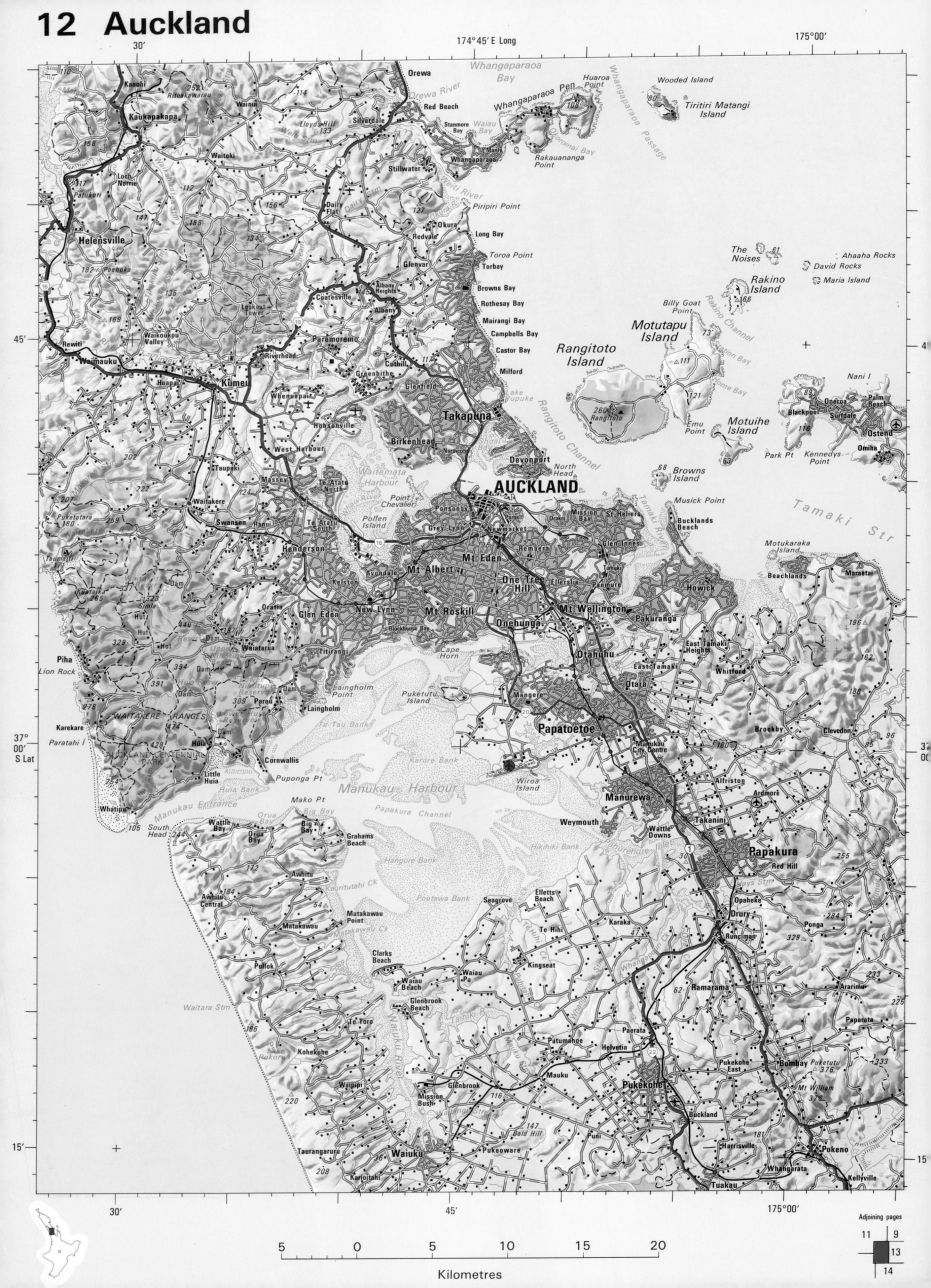

174°45′ E Long   175°00′

30′

Whangaparaoa Bay

Orewa
Red Beach
Wooded Island
Huaroa Point
Whangaparaoa Pen
Tiritiri Matangi Island

Kanohi
Kaukapakapa
Wainui
Silverdale
Stanmore Bay
Waiau Bay
Whangaparaoa Passage

Riteakawarau
Waitoki
Stillwater
Whangaparaoa
Rakauananga Point

Loch Norrie
Patukori
Dairy Flat
Piripiri Point
The Noises
Ahaaha Rocks
David Rocks
Maria Island

Helensville
Paehoka
Lookout Tower
Okura
Redvale
Toroa Point
Torbay
Rakino Island

45′

Rewiti
Waikoukou Valley
Coatesville
Glenvar
Albany Heights
Browns Bay
Rothesay Bay
Mairangi Bay
Campbells Bay
Billy Goat Point
Motutapu Island
Station Bay
Nani I

Waimauku
Kumeu
Paremoremo
Albany
Castor Bay
Milford
Rangitoto Island
Home Bay
Blackpool
Oneroa
Palm Beach

Huapai
Riverhead
Cuthill
Lake Pupuke
Surfdale
Ostend

Whenuapai
Greenhithe
Glenfield
Takapuna
Omiha

Hobsonville
Glenorie
Waitemata Harbour
Birkenhead
Northcote
Devonport
North Head
Rangitoto Channel
Emu Point
Motuihe Island
Park Pt
Kennedys Point

West Harbour
Massey
Te Atatu North
Point Chevalier
AUCKLAND
Browns Island
Tamaki Str

Taupaki
Waitakere
Swanson
Ranui
Te Atatu South
Pollen Island
Ponsonby
Parnell
Mission Bay
St Heliers
Musick Point

Puketotara
Henderson
Grey Lynn
Newmarket
Orakei
Bucklands Beach
Motukaraka Island

Kuataika
Oratia
Kelston
Avondale
Mt Albert
Mt Eden
Remuera
Glen Innes
Tamaki
Beachlands
Maraetai

Simla Hut
Glen Eden
New Lynn
One Tree Hill
Ellerslie
Panmure
Howick

Piha
Lion Rock
Waiatarua
Titirangi
Mt Roskill
Onehunga
Mt Wellington
Pakuranga
East Tamaki Heights

Karekare
Paratahi I
Parau
Laingholm
Eaingholm Point
Puketutu Island
Cape Horn
Otahuhu
East Tamaki
Whitford

Whatipu
Huia
Cornwallis
Little Huia
Puponga Pt
Te Tau Banks
Mangere
Otara

AUCKLAND CENTENNIAL PARK
WAITAKERE RANGES
Karore Bank
Wiroa Island
Papatoetoe
Manukau City Centre
Brookby
Clevedon

South Head
Wattle Bay
Orua Bay
Mako Pt
Big Bay
Grahams Beach
Manukau Harbour
Papakura Channel
Manurewa
Alfriston
Ardmore

Awhitu
Hangore Bank
Hikihiki Bank
Weymouth
Wattle Downs
Takanini
Papakura
Red Hill

Awhitu Central
Poutawa Bank
Seagrove
Elletts Beach
Opaheke
Ponga

Matakawau Point
Matakawau
Karaka
Te Hihi
Drury
Runciman

37° 00′ S Lat

Clarks Beach
Waiau Pa
Kingseat
Ramarama
Ararimu

Pollok
Waiau Beach
Glenbrook Beach
Paerata
Paparata

Waitara Stm
Te Toro
Mauku
Patumahoe
Helvetia
Pukekohe East
Bombay
Mt William

Kohekohe
Waipipi
Glenbrook
Mission Bush
Puni
Pukekohe
Buckland

Taurangaruru
Waiuku
Pukeoware
Bald Hill
Harrisville
Pokeno

15′

Karioitahi
Mauku
Whangarata
Kellyville

Tuakau

175°00'

175°15' E Long

30'

Hauraki Gulf

Ahaaha Rocks
David Rocks
Maria Island

D'Urville Rocks

Horuhoru Rock

Thumb Point

Hooks Bay

Waiheke Island

Nani I
Thompsons Point
Owhiti Bay
Stony Batter
220

Oneroa
Palm Beach
Blackpool
Surfdale
Onetangi Bay
Onetangi
229

116
Ostend
Tarahiki Island

Kennedys Point
154
231
Maunganui
Cowes
Pakatoa Island

Omiha
136
66
Rotoroa Island

Tamaki Strait
Awaawaroa Bay
Waiheke Channel
728
Scully Reef

Kauri Pt
Ponui Island
173
Ponui

Beachlands
Maraetai
Umupuia Beach
Whakakaiwhara Point
Pakihi Island

196
Koherurahi Point
Karamuramu Island

162
Wairoa Bay
Raukura Point

188
199
Orere Point
Clevedon
Kawakawa Bay
Wakakawa Bay
Orere Point
96
85
Mataikokako
355
Orere
Papapakanga Stm

373
Waimangu Stm
127
Waimangu Point

393
477
197
Matingarahi
Matingarahi Point

428
564
HUNUA RANGES
Kohukohunui
688

255
535
405
Wharekawa

Hunua
399
374
473
480
Whakatiwai Stm
145
Whakatiwai

Dam
Moumoukai
Mangatangi Reservoir
Kaiaua

Ponga
284
470
Pukapuka
Workman
425

329
Dam

445
487
Mangatangi
160
Vining
63
Rangipo

233
351
254

Ararimu
225
Paparimu
127

Paparata
One Tree Hill
270
Happy Valley
168
Miranda

Bombay
Puketutu
376
333
271
Mangatangi
Hotsprings
1.5

Mt William
376
Kopuku Stm

Mangatawhiri
23
Ratoroa
329
Waitakaruru
Pipiroa
Kopuarahi
Turua

Pokeno
Maramarua

Kellyville
Kopuku
Maramarua Mill

238
Waiaro
314
Waikawau
Waikawau Bay
Waikawau R

Whangaahei

Colville Bay
Te Whau Pt
Colville
312
Whanake
305
COROMANDEL S.F.P
Tuateawa
Tuateawa Stm

Motukawao Group
Motupotaka
Motukahaua
524
284
Kennedy Bay
212
Kahutara
171
Amodeo Bay
Kennedy Bay

Motuwi
Motukaramarama
541
Pukenui
364
Hapapawera

Moturua
Papaaroha
515

Motuoruhi
169
507
Kaipawa
586
Hikutawatawa

Waimate Island
126
Motukopake Island
Coromandel

Motutapere Island
131
568
Preece Point

Whanganui Island
196
Castle Rock
521
Te Kouma
227
Waimate Channel
Coromandel Harbour

Rangipukea Island
Waiau
509
Metutere
532
Wekarua I

Deadmans Pt
Manaia
532
Tawhitirahi
Manaia Harbour
Pukewharareke

Kirita Bay
Pukewhakataratara
395
564
728
Kakatarahae

Hauturu
537
393
Fog Hill

Kereta
463
760
Papakai

418

Waikawau
819
Maumaupaki
COROMANDEL RANGE
Five Mile Stm

Te Mata
577
Te Kaka
642

Tapu
Tapu River

Ruamahanga
720

Waiomu

Te Puru
646
683

Thornton Bay
Ngarimu Bay

Tararu
695
Whakatete Bay
351
665
447

Tararu
400

Thames
295
Karaka
Parawai
Kauaeranga

Totara
200

Kopu
Orongo
Matatoki
258

Waihou River
Piako River
Puriri R

Firth of Thames

175°00'
Adjoining pages

11 | 16
14 | 15 | 17

5   0   5   10   15   20

Kilometres

45' 175°00' E Long

37°00'

37°15' S Lat

30'

45' 175°00'

Kilometres

5 0 5 10 15 20

Adjoining pages

12	13
15	
18	

175°30′ E Long

Umupuia Beach
Whakakaiwhara Point
Koherurahi Point
Pakihi Island
Karamuramu Island
Raukura Point
Wairoa Bay
199
Orere Point
Kawakawa Bay
Orere Point
Matakokako 355
Orere
127
Waimangu Point
Matingarahi
Matingarahi Point
Hunua
428
393
477
197
HUNUA RANGES
564
Kohukohunui 688
Dam
399 374
Moumoukai
535
405
473 480
Wharekawa
Mangatangi Reservoir
470 Pukepuka
Workman 425
145
Whakatiwai
Dam
Paparimu
487 Mangatangi
Kaiaua
160 Vining
63 Rangipo
225
One Tree Hill 270
Happy Valley
445
351
254
Mangatawhiri
127
Miranda
Mangatangi
168
Hotsprings
Maramarua
Rataroa 329
Waitakaruru
Kopuku
Maramarua Mill
Meremere
Island Block
Otumaika 123
Mangatarata
Puketoka 186
191
276 Pukekamaka
Okaeria
Whangamarino
126 Whataroa
Waerenga
Pukerua 91
Taniwha
375 455
461 Ratawera
Te Kauwhata
Ratamaroke 390
Waiterimu
535 Maungakawa
Ruakaka
220
Matahuru
282
Rangiriri West
Motunuia Island
Mangapiko Valley
Ohinewai
Pororua 265
505
365
Te Hoe 515
Pukekapia
Rakaumanga
282 Pukemore
Mangawara
Kimihia
207
Huntly
Mahuta
Orini
Westmere
Weavers Crossing
Te Kauri
Te Piringa
Hangawera 302

Firth of Thames

Hauturu 564
537
Kakatarahae
728
277
Mill Creek
463
393
Fog Hill
Kereta
416
760
Papakai
205
Coroglen
819 Maumaupaki
Five Mile Stm
Waikawau
542
Te Mata
577
Tapu
Te Kaka
642
Ruamahanga
782
COROMANDEL
Waiomu
716
Hut
720
Te Puru
646
Hut 795 Mt Rowe 846
Thornton Bay
683
Ngarimu Bay
STATE FOREST PARK
Taruru 695
Whakatete Bay
351
665
447
Hihi 718
Tararu
400
Motutapere 829
Thames
295 Karaka
Te Puke 400
Parawai
Kauaeranga
Kaitarakihi 882
Totara
200
Kopu
556
Pakirarahi 787
Orongo
Matatoki 258
Pipiroa
Kopuarahi
664
Waitakaruru
Turua
Puriri R
Puriri
Ngatea
5
Omahu 544
Kerepehi
Wharepoa
HAURAKI
PLAINS
Hikutaia
Torehape
Komata North 267
Netherton
Komata 28
Kaihere
492 Taumaharua
Patetonga
Awaiti
Paeroa
56
Te Moananui
Waiti
Tahuna
Tirohia 278 544
Hoe-O-Tainui
Otway
Mangaiti
10
Springdale
Elstow
Te Aroha
Te Piringa

Adjoining pages

12	13	16
14		17
18	19	

5   0   5   10   15   20

Kilometres

37°00'

37°15' S Lat

Bay of Plenty

Mayor Island

The Aldermen Islands

COROMANDEL STATE FOREST PARK

COROMANDEL RANGE

KAIMAI MAMAKU STATE FOREST PARK

45'

176°00'

15'

Adjoining pages

16	
15	
19	20

5   0   5   10   15   20

Kilometres

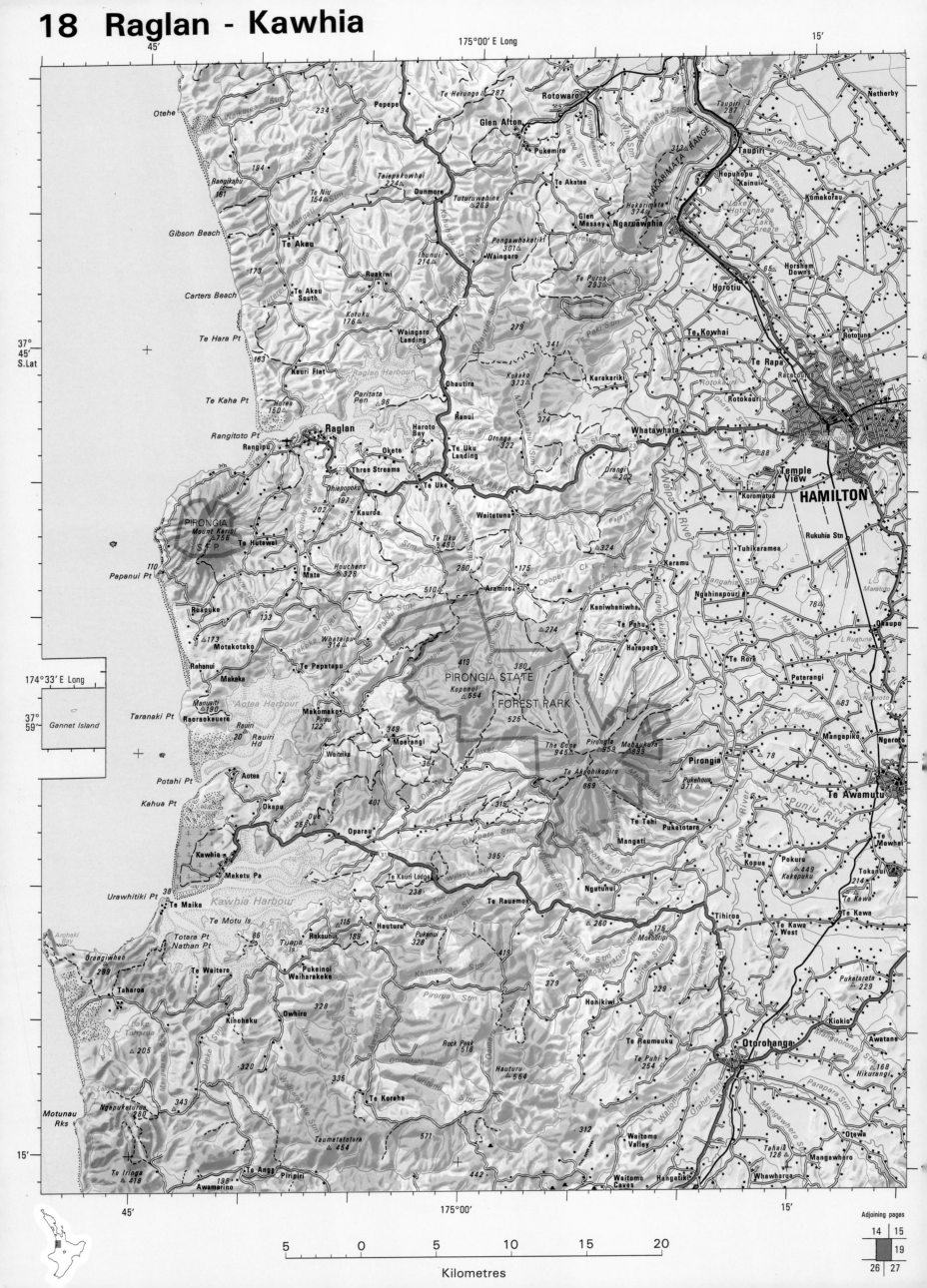

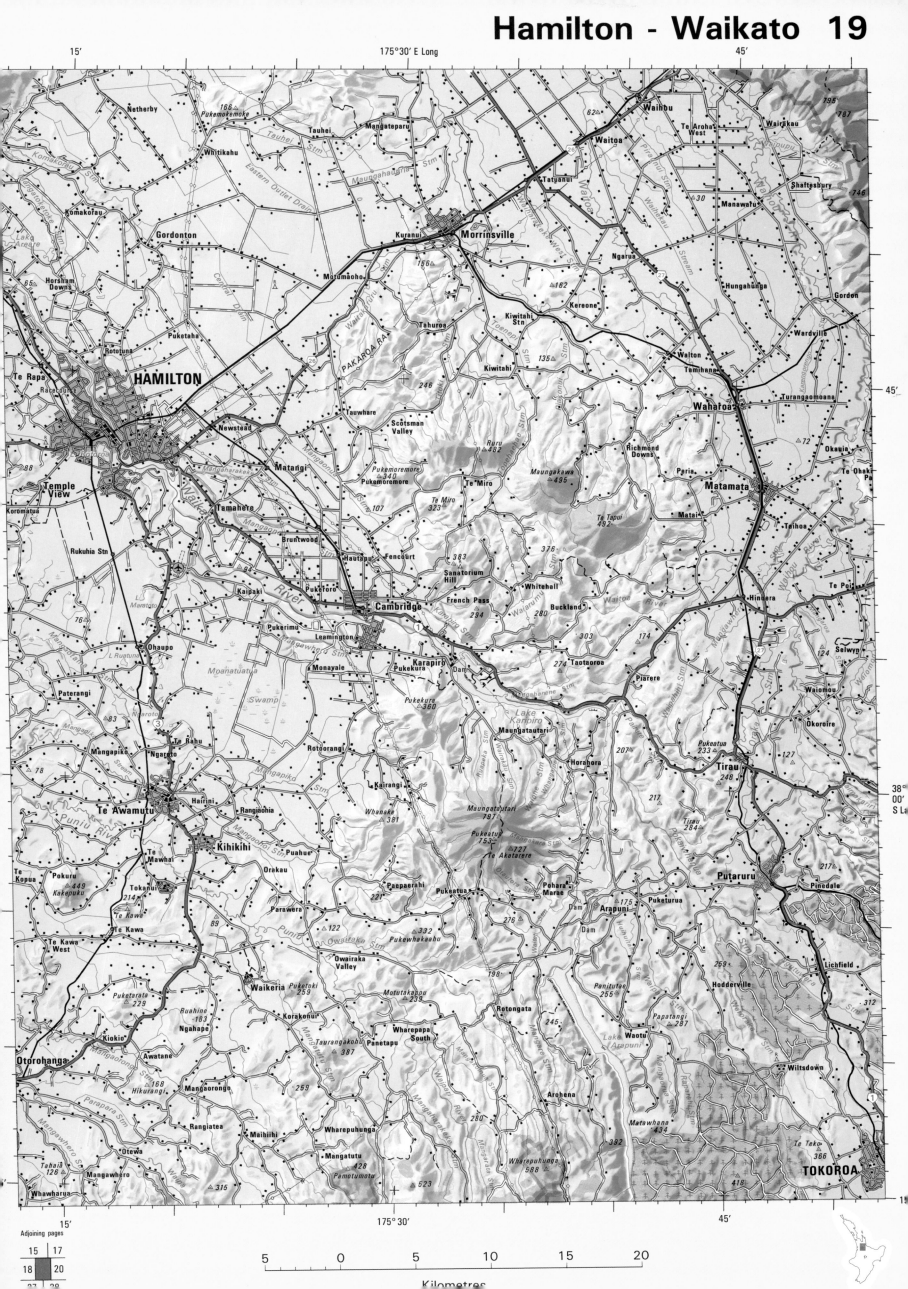

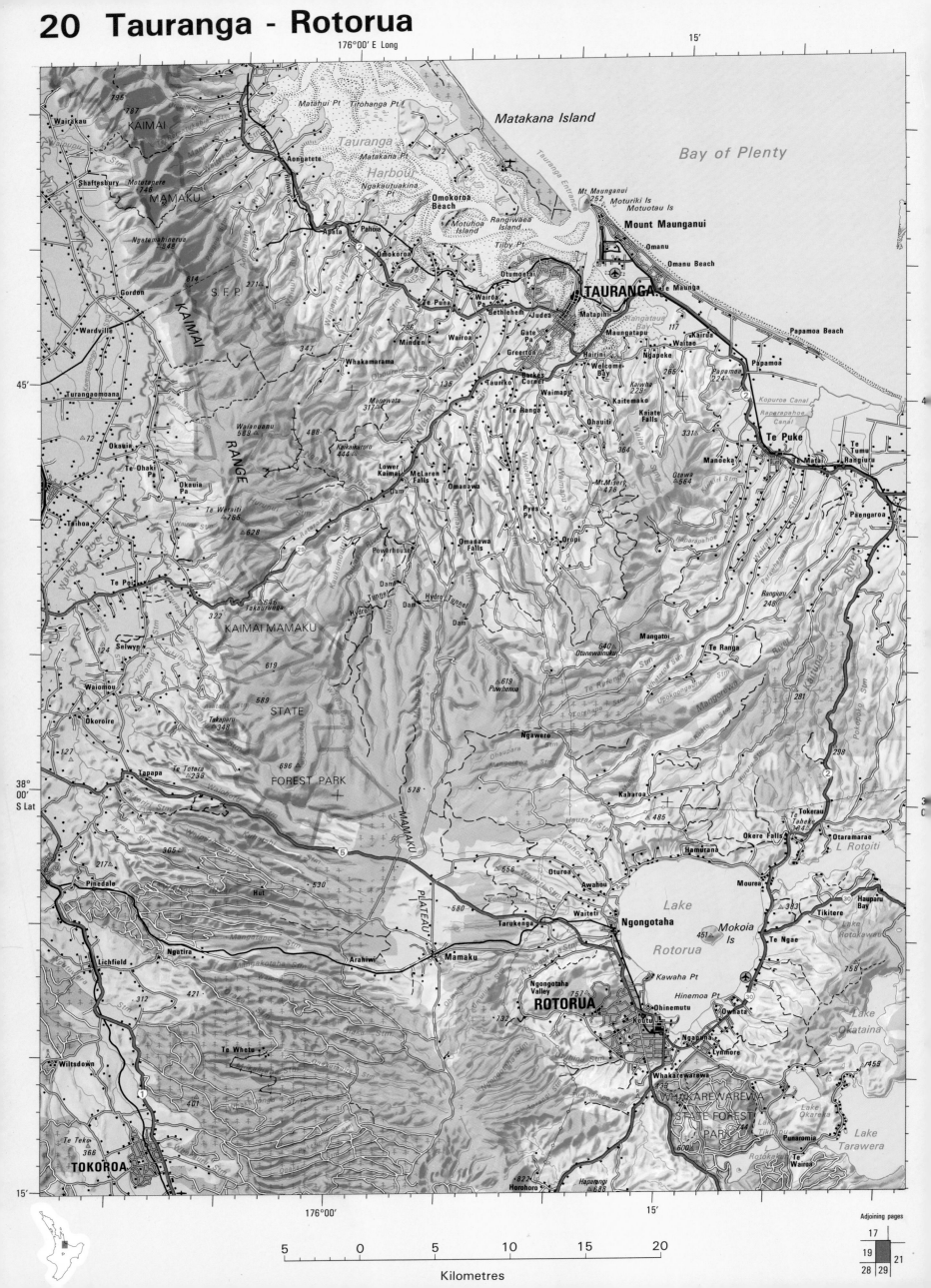

20 Tauranga - Rotorua

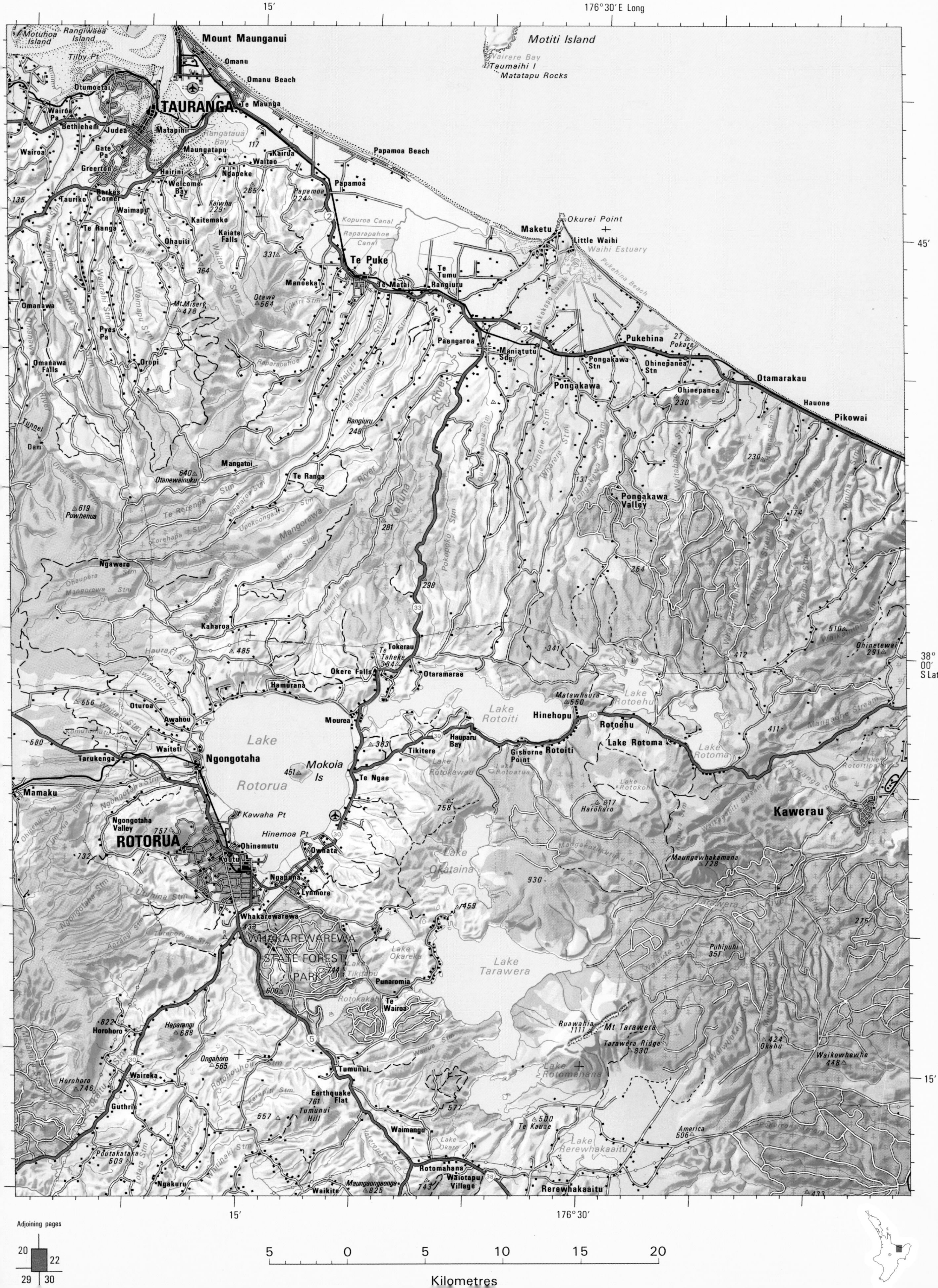

15'
176°30'E Long
45'
38° 00' S Lat
15'

Motiti Island
Wairere Bay
Taumaihi I
Matatapu Rocks

Motuhoa Island
Rangiwāea Island
Tilby Pt
Mount Maunganui
Omanu
Omanu Beach
Otumoetai
Te Maunga
TAURANGA
Wairoa Pa
Bethlehem
Judea
Matapihi
Mangataua Bay
117
Maungatapu
Papamoa Beach
Wairoa
Gate Pa
Hairini
Kairua
Papamoa
Greerton
Barkes Corner
Welcome Bay
Waitao
Ngapeke
135
Tauriko
Waimapu
Kaiwha 229
265
Papamoa 224
Te Ranga
Ohauiti
Kaitemako
Kaiate Falls
2
Kopuroa Canal
Maketu
Okurei Point
Little Waihi
Waihi Estuary
Omanawa
Mt Misery 478
331
Raparapahoe Canal
Te Puke
Te Matai
Te Tumu
Pukehina Beach
Pyes Pa
364
Manoeka
Rangiuru
Pukehina
Omanawa Falls
Oropi
Otawa 564
Kaituna River
21 Pokere
Omanawa
Paengaroa
Maniatutu Sdgn
Pongakawa Stn
Ohinepanea Stn
Otamarakau
Pongakawa
Ohinepanea
Hauone
230
Pikowai
Rangiuru 248
131
Pongakawa Valley
174
Mangatoi
Otanewainuku 640
Te Ranga
619 Puwhenua
281
264
230
Ngawero
298
510
Ohinetewai 291
412
Kaharoa
33
341
485
Tokerau
Te Taheke 344
Lake Rotoehu
411
Okere Falls
Otaramarae
556
Hamurana
Matawhaura 550
Oturoa
Lake Rotoiti
Hinehopu
30
Rotoehu
Awahou
Mourea
Lake Rotoma
580
Waiteti
Lake Rotorua
383
Hauparu Bay
Tikitere
Gisborne Point
Rotoiti
Lake Rotoma
Tarukenga
Ngongotaha
451
Mokoia Is
Te Ngae
Lake Rotokawau
Lake Rotoatua
Lake Rotokohu
Mamaku
Kawaha Pt
758
817 Haroharo
Kawerau
Ngongotaha Valley 757
Hinemoa Pt
732
ROTORUA
Koutu
Ohinemutu
Owhata
Lake Okataina
Maungawhakamana 728
Nganuma
Lynmore
930
459
Whakarewarewa
275
WHAKAREWAREWA STATE FOREST PARK
Lake Okareka
Lake Tarawera
744
Punaromia
Puhipuhi 351
600
Te Wairoa
Lake Rotokakahi
822
Horohoro
Haparangi 688
Ruawahia 1111
Mt Tarawera
424 Okahu
Ongahoro 565
Tumunui
Tarawera Ridge 830
Waikowhewhe 448
Horohoro 746
Waireka
Earthquake Flat 761
Lake Rotomahana
577
Guthrie
557
Tumunui Hill
500 Te Kauae
America 506
Poutakataka 509
Waimangu
Lake Okaro
Lake Rerewhakaaitu
Ngakuru
Waikite
Maungaongaonga 825
143
Rotomahana
Waiotapu Village
38
Rerewhakaaitu
433

Adjoining pages
20 | 22
29 | 30
5 0 5 10 15 20
Kilometres
15' 176°30'

22 Kawerau - Whakatane

177°00' E Long

15'

30'

Mt Gisborne
321
White Island
Club Rocks (Whakaari)

37°
45'
S Lat

Bay   of   Plenty

Tokata Island
Rurima Island
Moutoki Island
353 Motuhora Island

Rangitaiki River
8 Wahieroa
2
Thornton
Piripai
Kohi Point
Paroa
Kopeopeo
Kopeopeo Canal
183 Otarawairere Bay
Poroporo
Ohope
WHAKATANE
Port Ohope
White Pine Bush
Pahou
Ohiwa
Waioeka River
Waiaua River
Haurere Point
Awakeri
Awakeri Springs
Ohakana I
Uretara I
Waiotahi Beach
Hikuwai Beach
Opape
35
Whakatane West
207
Ohiwa Harbour
Waiotahi Beach
386
Oroi
293
370
Wainui
Cheddar Valley
Kukumoa
Hospital Hill
49 Tablelands
Lower Waiaua
Omarumutu
38°
00'
Pekatahi
Waiotahi
Paerata Ridge
Opotiki
Tirohanga
229
351
Taneatua
Waingarara
Kererutahi
Kutarere
Waiotahi Pa
Woodlands
Te Rere Pa
Waiaua
Pukemoremore
349
287
Te Ruauhi
Apanui
2
Otara
Te Kapuaarangi
471
Upper Waiaua
196
208
Waiputatawa
552
Waiotahi Valley
419
Waioeka Pa
326
481
632
Opouriao
Matahapa
686
Ruatoki North
Nukuhou North
Matahanea
808
Waimana
355
Pukenuioraho
729
Te Ahitahutahu
678
Taumaihi
696
670
Taumatamiere
478
Tataiahapi Pa
814
Maungawhiorangi
Okiore
808
Waikirikiri
Raroa Pa
Tanatena
Hut
208
564
472
610
869
808
655

5   0   5   10   15   20

Kilometres

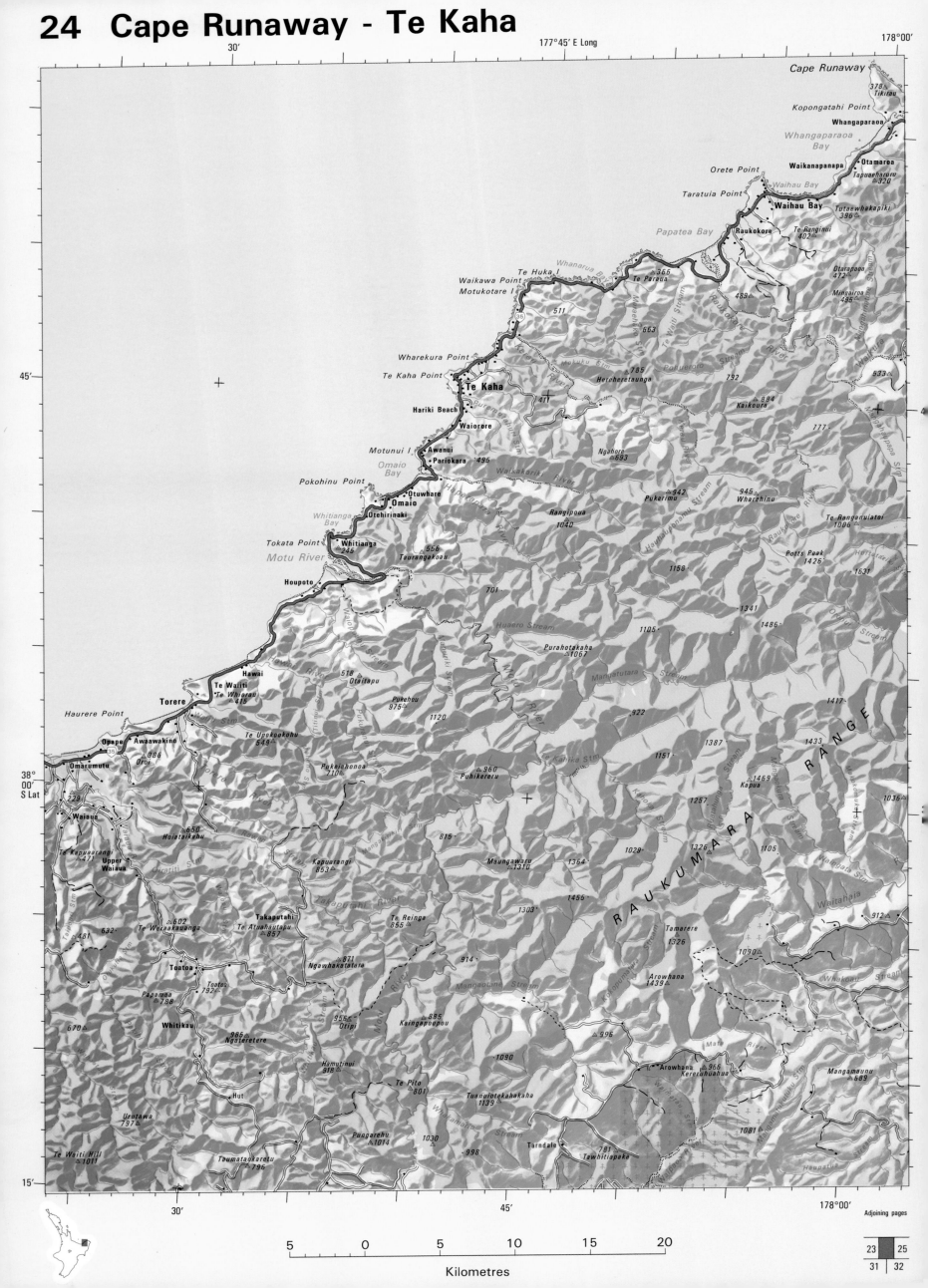

Cape Runaway

378 Tikirau
Kopongatahi Point
Whangaparaoa
Whangaparaoa Bay
Orete Point
Waikanapanapa
Otamaroa
Tapuaeharuru 320
Taratuia Point
Waihau Bay
Waihau Bay
Te Ranginui 402
Raukokore
Tutaewhakapiki 396
Papatea Bay
Otarapaoa 472
Mingairoa 495
Te Huka I.
Whanarua Bay
366
Te Paraua
489
533
Waikawa Point
Motukotare I.
511
Pohueroro
792
777
Wharekura Point
663
Te Kaha Point
Te Kaha
Heteheretaunga
785
411
Kaikoura 884
Hariki Beach
Waiorore
Ngahore 693
Rangipoua 1040
Pukerimu 942
945 Wharehinu
Motunui I.
Awanui
Pariokara 495
Te Ranganuiatoi 1006
Omaio Bay
Pokohinu Point
Potts Peak 1426
1631
Otuwhare
Omaio
Otehirinaki
1158
Whitianga Bay
1341
1486
Tokata Point
Whitianga 245
556
Taurangakoau
701
Motu River
Huaero Stream
1105
Houpoto
Purahotakaha 1067
Mangatutara Stream
1417
518
Otaitapu
Pukehou 975
1120
922
1387
1433
Hawai
Te Waiti
'Te Whiorau' 415
Torere
Te Upokookohu 549
1151
1257
1469
Kapua
Haurere Point
Opape
Awaawakino 386
Oror
Pukeiahonoa 710
960
Puhikereru
1326
1105
Omarumutu
229
Waiaua
815
Maungawaru 1310
1029
1364
1036
Te Kapuaarangi 471
Upper Waiaua
Hoiataikahu 650
Kapuarangi 853
1455
1303
1326
Tamarere 1326
1090
602
Te Weraakauanga
632
481
Takaputahi
Te Atuahautapu 857
Te Reinga 855
914
Arowhana 1439
Toatoa
Toatoa 792
Ngawhakatatara 871
912
Papamoa 788
Whitikau
965 Ngateretere
Otipi 956
Kaingapoupou 885
996
Arowhana 966
Kereruhuahua
Mangamaunu 689
670
Hamutinui 918
1090
Urutawa 797
Hut
Te Pito 801
Tuanuiotekahakaha 1139
1081
Te Waiti Hill 1011
Taumataokaretu 796
Pungarehu 1014
1030
998
Tarndale
781
Tawhitiapaka

RAUKUMARA RANGE

Adjoining pages

| 23 | 25 |
| 31 | 32 |

178°00'
178°15'E Long
30'
30'

Cape Runaway
Otarawhata I
Tahurua Point
Lottin Point
Midway Point

378 Tikirau
Ruahakoakoa 474
440

Kopongatahi Point
466 Hakaonga
Matakaoa Point

Whangaparaoa
Potaka
Wharekahika River
Hicks Bay

Whangaparaoa Bay
Te Pekaoterangihekeiho 240
Haupara Point

Otamaroa
Waikanapanapa
Tapuaeharuru 320
152
Hovells Watching Dog 673

Tutaewhakapiki 396
343

Otarapaoa 472
480
Waikura
511
Pukeamaru 990
Paoneone 268
Te Araroa
384 Kakanui
309 Maungakaka
Horoera Point

Mingairoa 495
274 Ngawhakatatara
686
Pukeamaru
253 Mataipuku
Awatere
Taumataorei 317
313
Kokomukataranga
269
East Cape
East Cape

533
411
Te Kumi
762 Te Kokomuka
Tapatu
Ngatohuahira 393
Tarakengarara 368
Pukeotarumai 329
129
Whangaokeno Is (East I)

777
Te Kapua 861
Oruataiaka 666
Te Hue
Taumataomiro 382

Taumaoteawhengaiao 1166
539 Whakaangiangi
Maraehara
37° 45' S Lat

Aoparauri 1242
Raukumara 1413
Mangatutaekuri 232
Rangitukia

Ahiapurua 1173
Peroporo River
Tikitiki
Te Horo
Waiapu River
131

Te Ranganuiatoi 1006
Komapara 1006
Waiorongomai River
472
Te – Whakaumuatangihia
Tutara 313
Kakariki
Te Pohue
339

1013 Pungarehunui
473 Tutumatai
Whakawhitira
297
Port Awanui
Te Upokoohinepaki Point

1631
Ohinepoutea
Pakihiroa
Tapuaeroa River
Waiorongomai
Takamore
Rotokautuku
297 Pukeatua
Reporua

Wharekia 1013
Taitai 678
374 Otapokura
Whakapourangi
Ruatoria
Manutahi
267
Koutuamoa Point

Hut
Hikurangi 1752
Aorangi 1273
484 Whakamu
Hiruharama
Tuparoa

1417
Aria 899
575 Karewa
Aorangi
Makarika
Otuauri 507
244
Kaimoho Point

Te Umuotamaihu 1036
427 Tokiameha
506 Tutuwhinau
Waikahawai Point
Whareponga

3° 3'
491
Hakurangi 420
Ohineakai

754
710 Rangikohua
Tawhana
Waipiro
Waipiro Bay
38° 00'

912
Ihungia
Wahingamuku 537
373 Pukemanuka
Te Puia Springs
Koutunui Head

Huiarua
728 Pirauau
533
Wharekiri 473
Tawhiti 520
Moutahiauru I
Motuaiuri I

684 Pukeraki
Mangatarata
539 Maungaroa
Hautanoa
Mangahauini
Tuatini
Koutunui Point

Mangamaunu 689
610
Whakaumu 557
486 Toiroa
Tokomaru Bay
Ongaruru
Tokomaru Bay

594
Hikuwai
Mawhai Point

625
533
579

178°00'
Adjoining pages
15'
30'

Kilometres

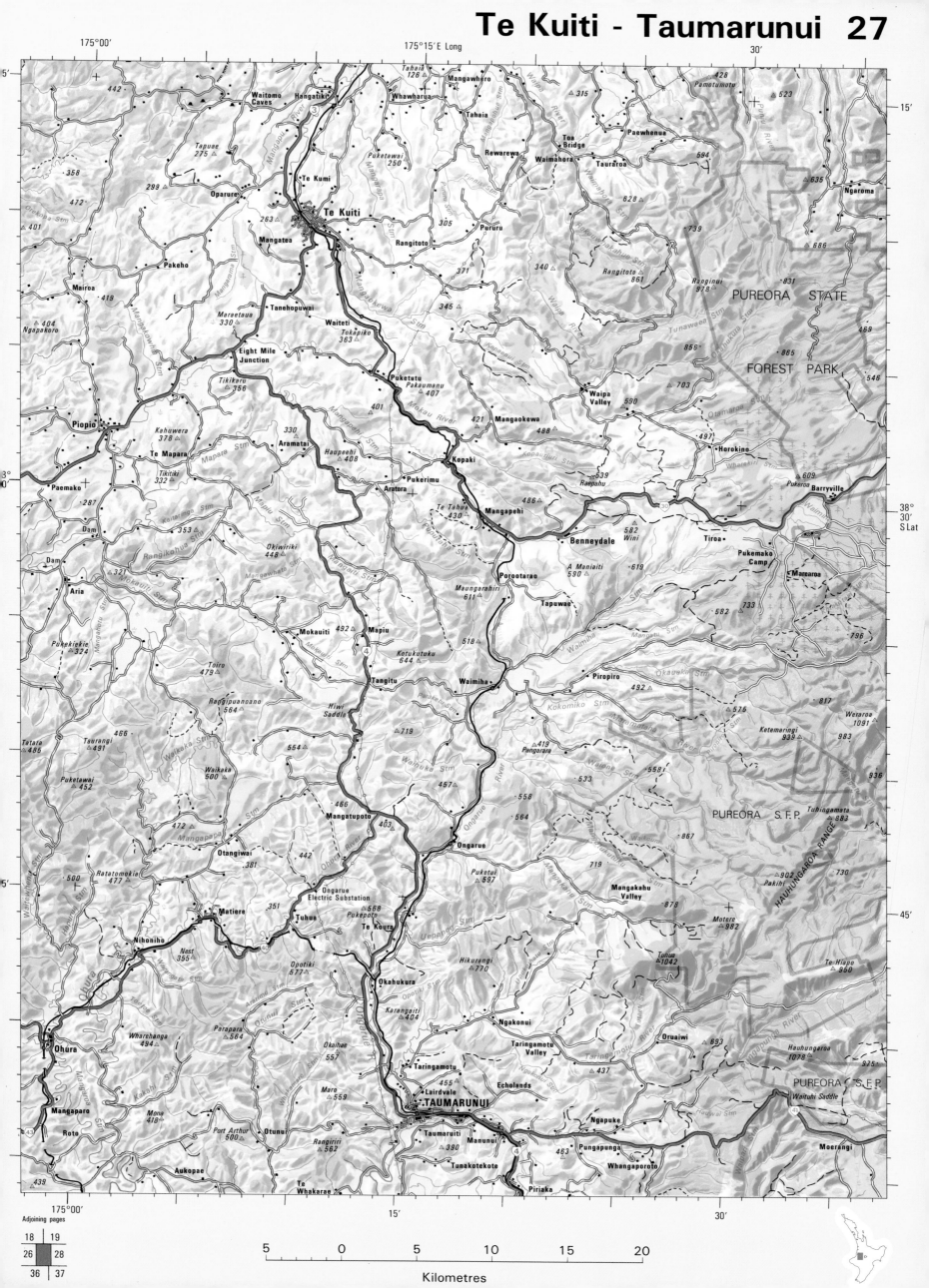

175°00' 175°15'E Long 30'

15'

38°
30'
S Lat

45'

175°00' 15' 30'

Adjoining pages

18	19
26	28
36	37

5   0   5   10   15   20

Kilometres

Place names and features

Waitomo Caves, Hangatiki, Tahaia 126, Mangawhero, Whawharua, Tahaia, Pamotumotu 428, 523, Ngaroma

442, Waipa River, 315, Paewhenua, 635

Tapuae 275, Puketawai 250, Rewarewa, Toa Bridge, Waimahora, Tauraroa, 594, 628, 739

358, 472, 299, Oparure, Te Kumi, Finnis Stm, Pururu, 340, Rangitoto 861, Rekeu Pakahue Stm, 686

401, Te Kuiti, 263, Mangatea, Rangitoto, 305, 371, Ranginui 978, 831, PUREORA STATE

Pakeho, 419, 345, 856, 865, 469

Mairoa, 404 Ngapakoro, Maraetaua 330, Tanehopuwai, Waiteti, Tokapiko 363, 401, Puketutu, Pakaumanu 407, 421, Mangaokewa, Waipa Valley 590, 703, FOREST PARK, 546

Piopio, Kahuwera 378, Tikikaru 356, Aramatai, 330, Haupeehi 408, 486, Mangapehi, 497, Horokino, 609

Te Mapara, Mapara Stm, Pukerimu, Kopaki, Raepahu, Pukeroa Barryville

Paemako, 287, Tikitiki 332, Aratora, Te Tahua 430, 582 Wini, Tiroa, Pukemako Camp

Dam, 353, Okiwiriki 448, 488, 486, Mangapehi, A Maniaiti 590, 619, Marearoa

Aria, 321, Mangawhata Stm, Porootarao, Tapuwae, 582, 733, 796

Pukekiekie 324, Mokauiti 492, Mapiu, Maungarahiri 611, 518, Piropiro 492, 575, 817, Weraroa 1091, 983

Toiro 479, Kotukutuku 644, Waimiha, Ketemaringi 939, 936

Taurangi 491, Tangitu, Hiwi Saddle, 719, Pangarara 419, 558, Tuhingamata 883

466, Waikaka 500, 554, Waihuka Stm, 457, 533, 867, PUREORA S.F.P.

Puketawai 452, 472, 466, Mangatupoto, 403, 558, 564, 719, 902, 730

Ratatomokia 477, Otangiwai, 381, 442, Ongarue, Puketui 597, Mangakahu Valley, 878, Pakihi, HAUHUNGAROA RANGE

500, Ongarue Electric Substation, Matiere, 351, 568, Pukepoto, Te Koura, Motere 982, Te Hiapo 950

Nihoniho, Nest 355, Opotiki 577, Hikurangi 770, Tuhua 1042

Wharehanga 494, Parapara 564, Okahukura, Karangaiti 404, Ngakonui, Taringamotu Valley, Oruaiwi 693, Hauhungaroa 1078, 975

Ohura, Okaihae 557, 437, Echolands, PUREORA S.F.P., Waituhi Saddle

Mangaparo, Mona 418, Maro 559, Taringamotu, Lairdvale, TAUMARUNUI, Ngapuke, Moerangi

Roto, Port Arthur 500, Otunui, Rangiriri 562, 455, Taumaruiti, Manunui, 463, Pungapunga, Whangaporoto

439, Aukopae, Te Whakarae, Tunakotekote, 390, Piriaka

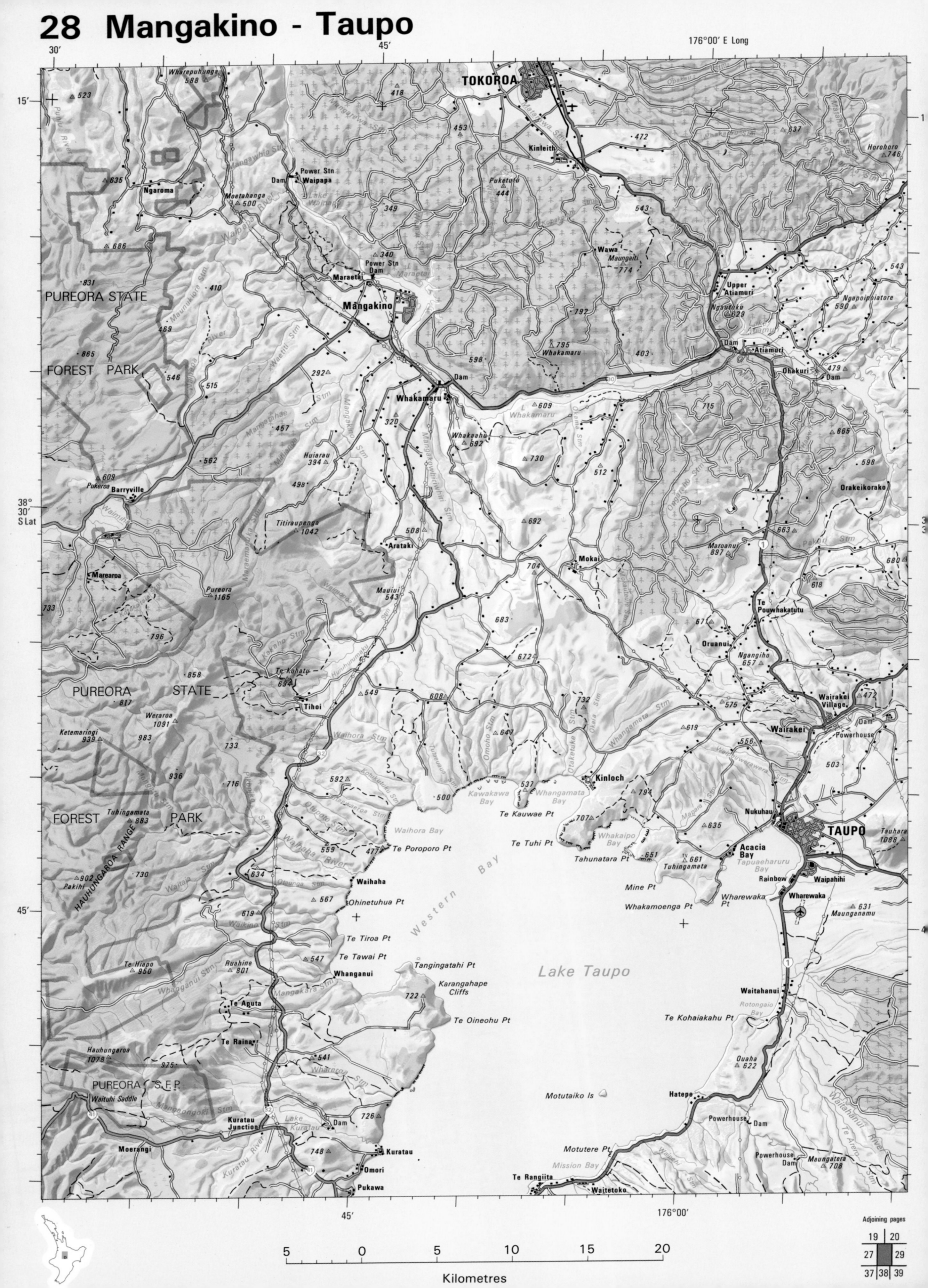

30'   45'   176°00' E Long

15'

TOKOROA

△ 523
Wharepuhunga 588
418
453
△ 837
Horohoro
△ 746

△ 635
Ngaroma
Moetahanga △ 500
Power Stn
Waipapa
Dam
Kinleith
△ 472
Kinleith

PUREORA STATE
△ 686
Power Stn
Dam
Maraetai
349
Puketutu
444
543·
Wawa
Maungaiti
774
Upper
Atiamuri
Ngapoipoiatore
590
△ 543

·831
410
Mangakino
△ 340
792
Ngautoku
629

FOREST PARK
·865
459
Dam
Whakamaru
598
☆795
Whakamaru
403
Dam
Atiamuri
Ohakuri
△ 479
Dam

546
515
292
320
△ 609
L
Whakamaru
715
665

△609
Pukeoa Barryville
457
Huiarau
394 △
498
Whakaahu
△ 692
730
512
△ 598
Orakeikorako

38°
30'
S Lat
·562
Titiraupenga
△ 1042
508 △
Arataki
△ 692
663
680
△

·858
Pureora
1165
Mauiui
543
704
Mokai
618
Te
Pouwhakatutu

Marearoa
817
796
683
671
Oruanui
Ngangiho
657

PUREORA   STATE
733
Te Kohatu
694
549
608
672
732
Wairakei
Village
△ 472

Weraroa
1091
Tihoi
647
575
Dam

Ketemaringi
939
983
733
592
△ 500
537
Whangamata
Bay
△ 619
Wairakei
Powerhouse
556·

936
716
Kawakawa
Bay
794
Kinloch
503

FOREST   PARK
Tuhingamata
883
559
Te Poroporo Pt
Te Kauwae Pt
707
635
Nukuhau
TAUPO
Tauhara
1068

·902
730
634
477
Waihaha
Te Tuhi Pt
Tahunatara Pt
651
661
Tuhingamata
Acacia
Bay
Tapuaeharuru
Bay

Pakihi
567
Ohinetuhua Pt
Mine Pt
Rainbow
Waipahihi
△ 631
Maunganamu

619
Te Tiroa Pt
Whakamoenga Pt
Wharewaka
Pt
Wharewaka

45'
547
Te Tawai Pt
Western   Bay
Lake Taupo

Te Hiapo
△ 950
Ruahine
801
Whanganui
Tangingatahi Pt
Waitahanui
Rotongaio
Bay

Te Aputa
722 △
Karangahape
Cliffs
Te Oineohu Pt
Te Kohaiakahu Pt

Hauhungaroa
1078
975
541
Ouaha
622

PUREORA S.F.P.
726
Motutaiko Is
Hatepe
Waitahanui
River

Waituhi Saddle
748 △
Kuratau
Powerhouse
Dam

Kuratau
Junction
Dam
Motutere Pt
Powerhouse
Dam
Maungatara
708

Moerangi
Omori
Mission Bay
Te Rangiita

Pukawa
Waitetoko

5   0   5   10   15   20
Kilometres

176°00'

Adjoining pages
19 | 20
27 | 29
37 | 38 | 39

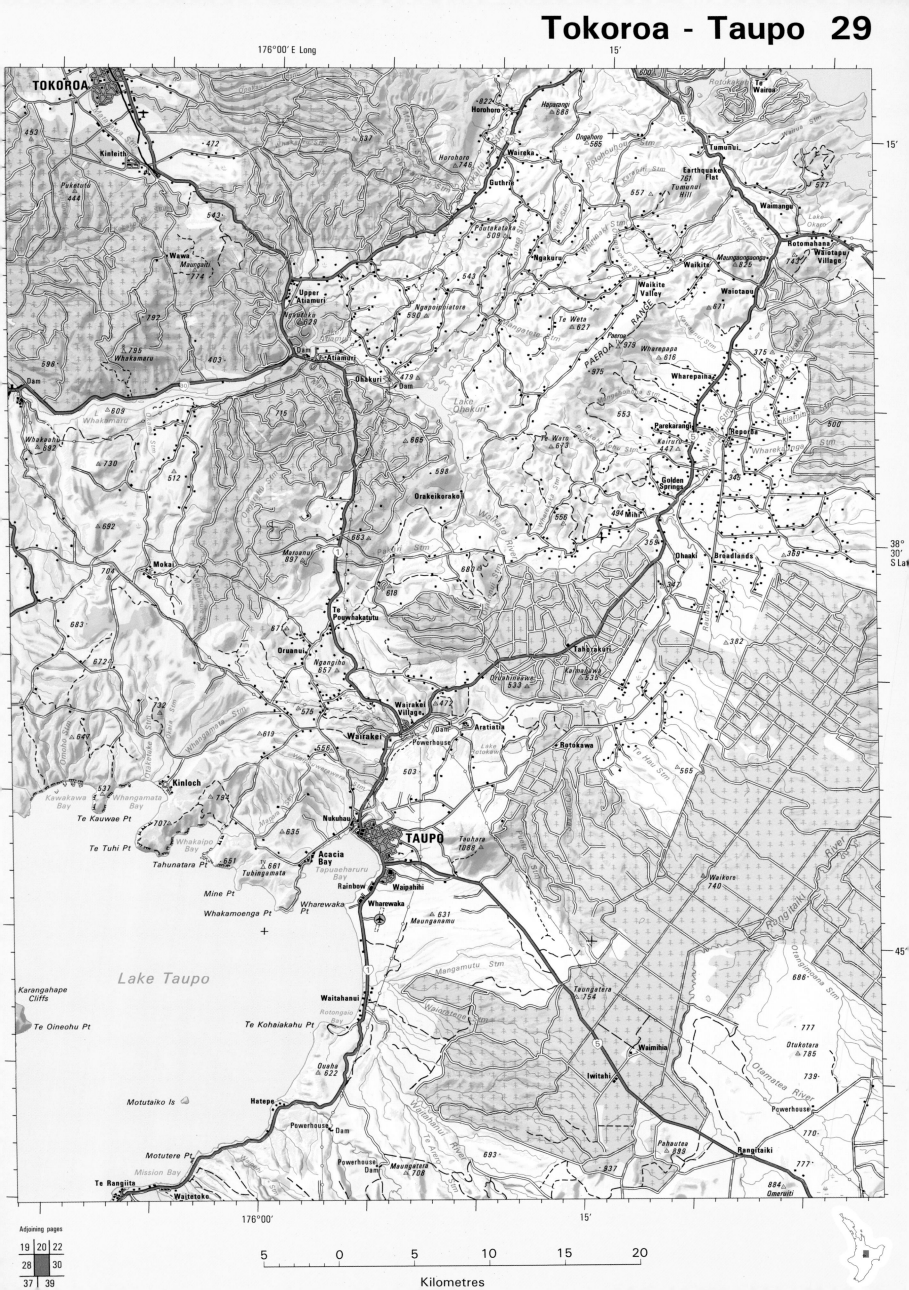

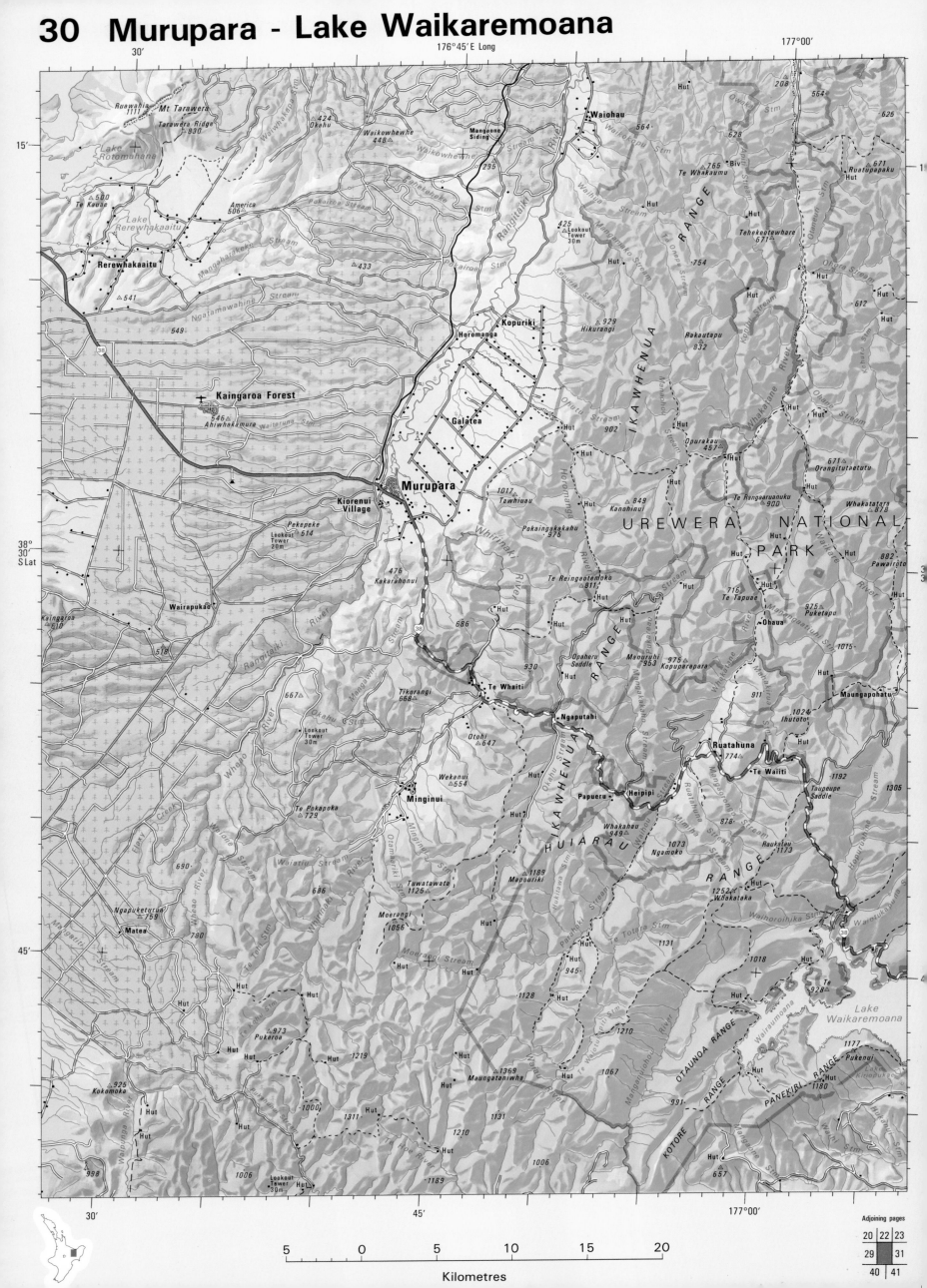

30 Murupara - Lake Waikaremoana

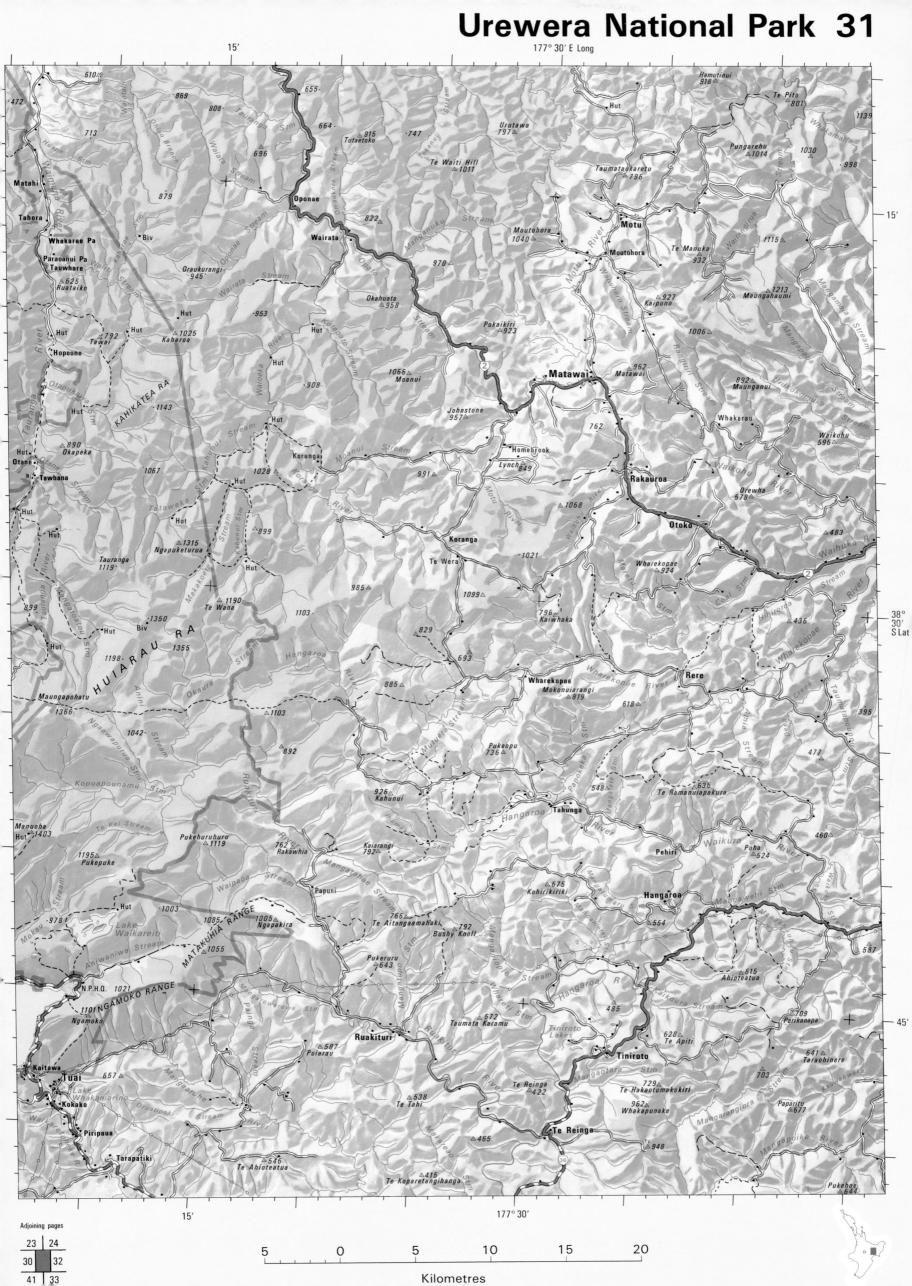

177° 30' E Long

15'

177° 30'

Kilometres

Adjoining pages

23	24
30	32
41	33

178°00' E Long

45'

15'

-1090
Tuanuiotekahakaha 1139
Arowhana 966
Kereruhuahua
Mangamaunu 689
Mangamaunu
610
Whakaumu 557
15'
Tokomaru Bay
Ongaruru

Tarndale
781 Tawhitiapaka
1081
625
594
579
Hikuwai
486 Toiroa
533

15'
951
Waihirau Stm
838
846
Tutamoe 998
617
Haupatua
Stream
Noumarua Stm
Puakato 675
Arero
489
Anaura Bay
15'

Mangatu Stream
433
529 Wheturau
Waipaoa
Mangaorongo Stream
683
Panikau Stream
Huanui
Tauwharepare Tirohanga
555
Mangatokerau
The Three Bridges
325
Motuoroi Is

799
777
718
447
Waitangi
Parabeka 596
Huanui
Te Kaho 461
Mangatuna
Marau 277
Marau Point
Tokatea Rocks

Whatatutu
351
391
Waihora River
Waingaromia River
Arakihi 613
701
Hokoroa
The Five Bridges
309
Wharekaka
Paerau Point
Karaka Bay

Waikohu
Puha
428
303
505 Ahioteatua
511
Kanakanaia
Motumate Stm
430
Manga
Takapau
Mangaheia
Tolaga Bay
Hauiti
Tolaga Bay
Mitre Rocks
Pourewa I

Te Karaka
Te Kapua 299
Mangaoai Stm
366
Ngauotekaka 610
472
Paremata
343 Titirangi
Whareopaia 301

38° 30' S Lat
365
395
316 Tangihanga
504 Kaiwinika
Waimata
388
Wharekiri
Tatuaotemaumu 412
277
264 Nuinuikai
Rototahi
Waihau Bay

Waipaoa
Kaitaratahi
361
Kopaatuaki
306
251
Waiharehare Bay

Ngatapa
Ormond
137
Waiohika 342 Waipura
Pukeakura 497
Whangara
Gable End Foreland
Gable Islet
Te Ikaarongamai Bay

Waituhi
Waihirere
Lake Repongaere
Pouawa
Pariokonohi Point

Waerengaahika
Hexton
428 Motukeo
Turihaua
Pouawa River

Patutahi
514
Makauri
Rimuroa 290
Tatapouri 239
Turihaua Point

Makaraka
Matawhero
Makorori
Tatapouri Point

Waerengaokuri
Papatu 379
Manutuke
Matawhero Stn
GISBORNE
Okitu
Makorori Point

Te Aroha Stream
Wainui
Tuaheni Point

Te Haranga 229
Tuamotu I
Poverty Bay

45'
Pakowhai
270 Takarangi
Muriwai
Waipaoa River
Young Nicks Head
Ariel Rock

Rerepi 481
Te Arai River
Maraetaha River

518
683
221

Maraetaha
Bartletts

178°00'
15'

Adjoining pages

24 | 25
31
33

177°45' E Long

178°00'

GISBORNE

Hexton
Patutahi
Makauri
Makaraka
Matawhero
Matawhero Stn
Manutuke

Poverty Bay

Tahunga
Pehiri
Poha △524
460
514
Te Aroha
Kaiarangi 792
Kohirikiriki △675
Hangaroa
554
Waerengaokuri
Papatu △379
Rimuhau △587
Te Aitangaamahaki 766
Bushy Knoll 792
Te Haranga 229
Pakowhai
Young Nicks Head
Pukeruru 643
△485
Ahioteatua △515
Takarangi △270
Muriwai
45'
Ruakituri
Taumata Katamu △572
Te Apiti 628
Parikanapa △709
703
Taraohinere △641
Rerepi 481
Maraetaha River
Tiniroto Lakes
Tiniroto
Whakapunake 962
Paparitu △677
518△
Maraetaha
Te Reinga △422
Te Tahi △538
948
Mangepoike River
683
2 221
Te Reinga
Pukehoe △644
290
Whareongaonga
△465
Te Koparetangihanga △415
405
Pukaroronui 740
497△
Tarewa 579
Bartletts
Kotare
Pukeronui △588
Whareotamanui
396
"Puninga"
375
△332
Marumaru
Tukemokihi
△329
Te Kaihekiapanui △734
△657
406
Otirangi
Te Hiwera △340
Taungaruawahine △458
Tangihanga △627
582△
369
442
Ohinemaemae △211
Whakaumu 449
Pukeorara 677△
Moumoukai △611
407
Kohitane △184
Puketapu 390
252
460
376
Hot Springs Reserve
302
Morere
Taumataoriaki
354
Mahanga △345
Kahuitara △149
Nth Clyde
Tuhara
180
△341
△308
418
198
△318
Paokuhukura
220
291
Mahanga 236
Lake Rotopounamu
Wairoa
129
154
Opurua
Whakaki
Nuhaka
249△
Kopuawhara Stn
Pukenui Beach
Whakaki Lagoon
Ohuia Lagoon
Ngamotu Lagoon
Wairau Lagoon
Te Paeroa Lagoon
Nuhaka River
Opoutama
Maungawhio Lagoon
Oraka Beach
Waikokopu
Mahia Beach
Mahia △238
Auroa Point
Whakatakahe Head
201
Table Cape
Te Heruotaraia Point
Te Kapu 366
185
163
Long Point
Taupiri 370
Mahia Peninsula
Rahuimokairoa △403
233
△360
Tawapata
Hekerangi Point
△227
Ahuriri Point
Portland Island

39°00' S Lat

15'

30'
45'
178°00'

Adjoining pages

31 | 32
41

Kilometres
5   0   5   10   15   20

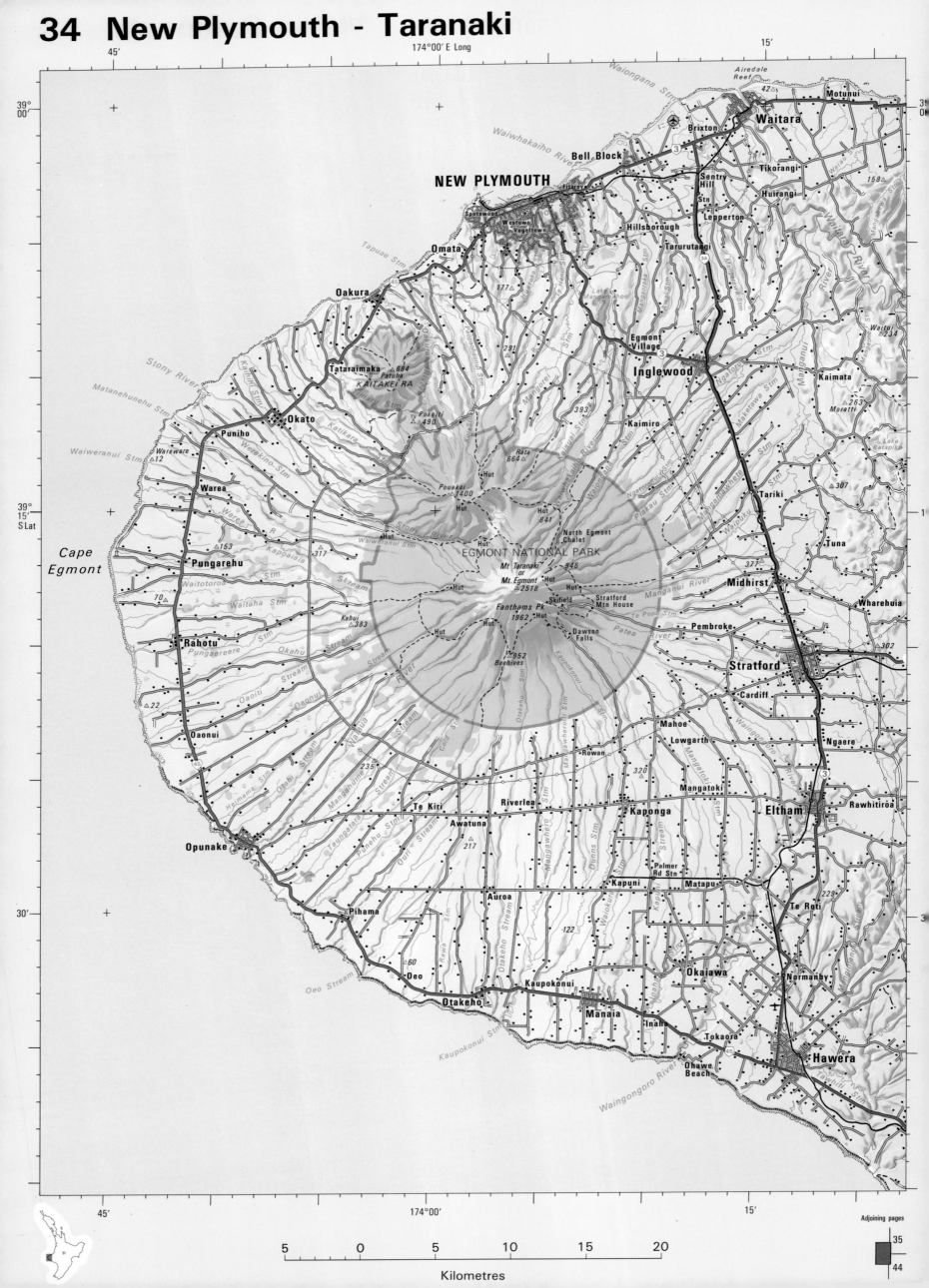

34 New Plymouth - Taranaki

39°00'

NEW PLYMOUTH

Airedale Reef
42 △
Motunui
Waitara
Brixton
Tikorangi
Bell Block   Huirangi
Sentry Hill   158 △
Fitzroy   Stn
Spotswood   Lepperton
Westown   Hillsborough
Vogeltown
Omata   Tarurutangi

Oakura   177 △   Egmont Village   Waitui
234 △
Lake Mangamahoe   Inglewood
291   Kaimata
Tataraimaka   684 △   Kaimiro   263 △
Patuha   Moratti
KAITAKE RA   393
Pukeiti   Rata
490 △   664 △   307 △
Okato
Puniho   Tariki
Wareware   Pouakai   Hut   Tuna
12 △   1400   841
Warea   North Egmont   Midhirst
Hut   Chalet   377 △
153 △   EGMONT NATIONAL PARK   Wharehuia
Pungarehu   317   Mt Taranaki   946
or   Hut
Hut   Mt Egmont   Stratford
70 △   Kahui   2518   Mtn House
383 △   Skifield   Pembroke
Rahotu   Fanthams Pk   Dawson   Stratford
Pungaereere   1962   Falls   302 △
Hut   Hut   Cardiff
22 △   952   Mahoe
Beehives   Lowgarth
Oaonui   Rowan   Ngaere
320   Mangatoki
235   Eltham
Te Kiri   Riverlea   Rawhitiroa
Awatuna   Kaponga   Palmer
217   Rd Stn
Opunake   Kapuni   Matapu
Auroa   Te Roti
229 △
Pihama
122   Okaiawa   Normanby
60   Oeo
Kaupokonui
Otakeho   Manaia   Tokaora
Inaha
Hawera
Ohawe
Beach

39°15' S Lat

39° 15'

30'

Cape Egmont

45'   174°00'   15'

Adjoining pages

5   0   5   10   15   20
Kilometres

35
44

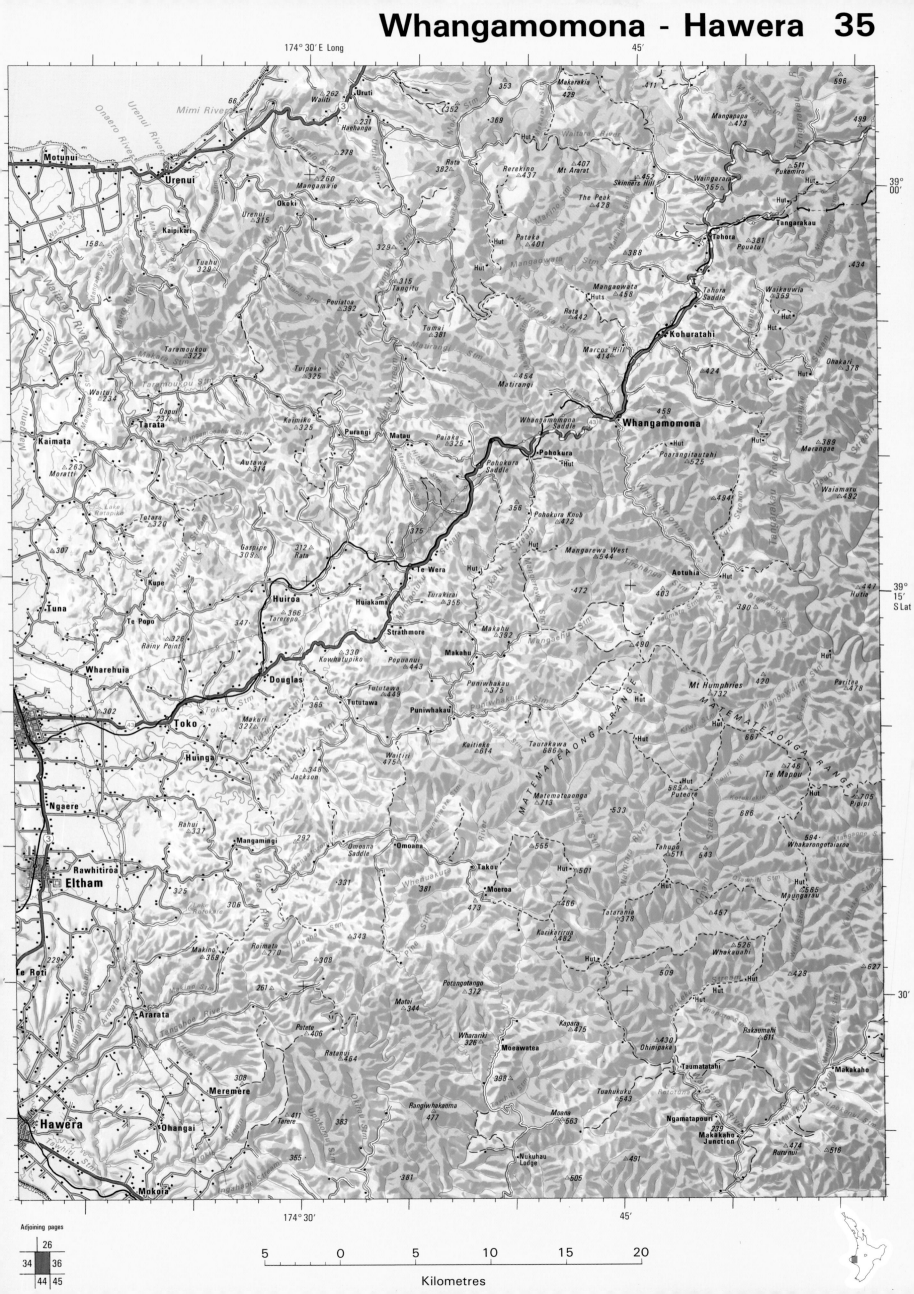

174° 30' E Long
45'

39°
00'

Onaero River
Urenui River
Mimi River
Motunui
Urenui
Waiad Stm
Mangaoapa Stm
66
Waiiti
262
Uruti
231
Haehanga
278
352
353
369
Makarakia
429
411
Waitara River
595
499
Mangapapa
473
511
Pukemiro
Kaipikari
Mangaoue
Okoki
Mangamaio
260
Urenui
315
329
Rata
382
Rerekino
437
Mt Ararat
407
Skinners Hill
452
The Peak
428
Waingarara
355
Hut
Tahora
381
Pouatu
Tangarakau
158
Tuahu
329
Makara Stm
Taranaki Stm
Tangitu
315
Mangaowata Stm
Pataka
401
Hut
388
434
Pouiatoa
392
Ohui River
Tumai
381
Mangapaka Stm
Rata
442
Mangaowata
458
Huts
Tahora Saddle
Waikauwia
359
Hut
Taramoukou
322
Tuipake
325
Matirangi
Marcos' Hill
414
Kohuratahi
Hut
Waitui
234
Taramoukou Stm
454
Matirangi
459
424
Ohakari
378
Hut
Oapui
237
Tarata
Kaimiko
325
Purangi
Matau
Paiaka
325
Whangamomona Saddle
(43)
Whangamomona
389
Marangae
Kaimata
Mangaoeanui Stm
Autawa
314
Pohokura
Hut
Poarangitautahi
525
Hut
Moratti
263
Makino Stream
356
494
Waiamaru
492
Lake Ratapiko
Totara
320
Gaspipe
309
312
Rata
375
Te Wera
Hut
Pohokura Saddle
Pohokura Knob
472
Haao
Kupe
Mangaotutu Stm
Turakirai
356
Mangahu Stream
Mangarewa West
544
Aotuhia
Hut
447
Hutia
307
Te Popo
326
Huiroa
366
Tarerepo
347
Huiakama
Strathmore
Makahu
392
472
403
390
Tuna
Rainy Point
Kowhatupiko
330
Popuanui
443
Makahu
Puniwhakau
375
Mangaehu River
490
Mt Humphries
732
420
Paritea
478
Wharehuia
302
Douglas
Tututawa
449
Tututawa
Puniwhakau
Puniwhakau Stm
Waingamemena Stm
Hut
MATEMATEAONGA RANGE
667
Toko
43
Makuri
327
365
Kaitieke
614
Taurakawa
686
Hut
Te Mapou
746
Huinga
Mangaehu Stm
Waitiri
475
Matemateaonga
713
589
Puteore
Hut
705
Pipipi
Jackson
348
533
686
Rahui
337
Mangamingi
292
Omoana Saddle
Omoana
555
Tahupo
511
543
594
Whakarongotaiaroa
Ngaere
Rawhitiroa
Eltham
325
331
Whenuakura
381
Takou
Moeroa
473
501
Hut
466
Maungarau
565
Hut
Te Roti
229
Lake Rotokare
306
343
Tatarania
378
457
Whakauahi
526
Makino
369
Roimata
270
308
Pine Stm
509
Hut
429
627
261
Potangotango
372
Hut
Pohokura Stream
Ararata
Matai
344
Kapara
475
Rakaumahi
611
Meremere
Patete
406
Wharariki
326
Moeawatea
430
Ohinipaka
308
398
Taumatatahi
Makakaho
Hawera
Ohangai
411
Tarere
383
Ratanui
464
Rangiwhakaoma
477
Tuahukuku
543
Ngamatapouri
239
Makakaho Junction
474
Rurumui
516
Mokoia
355
381
Nukuhau Lodge
491
Moana
563
505

174° 30'
45'

39°
15'
S Lat

39°
15'

30'

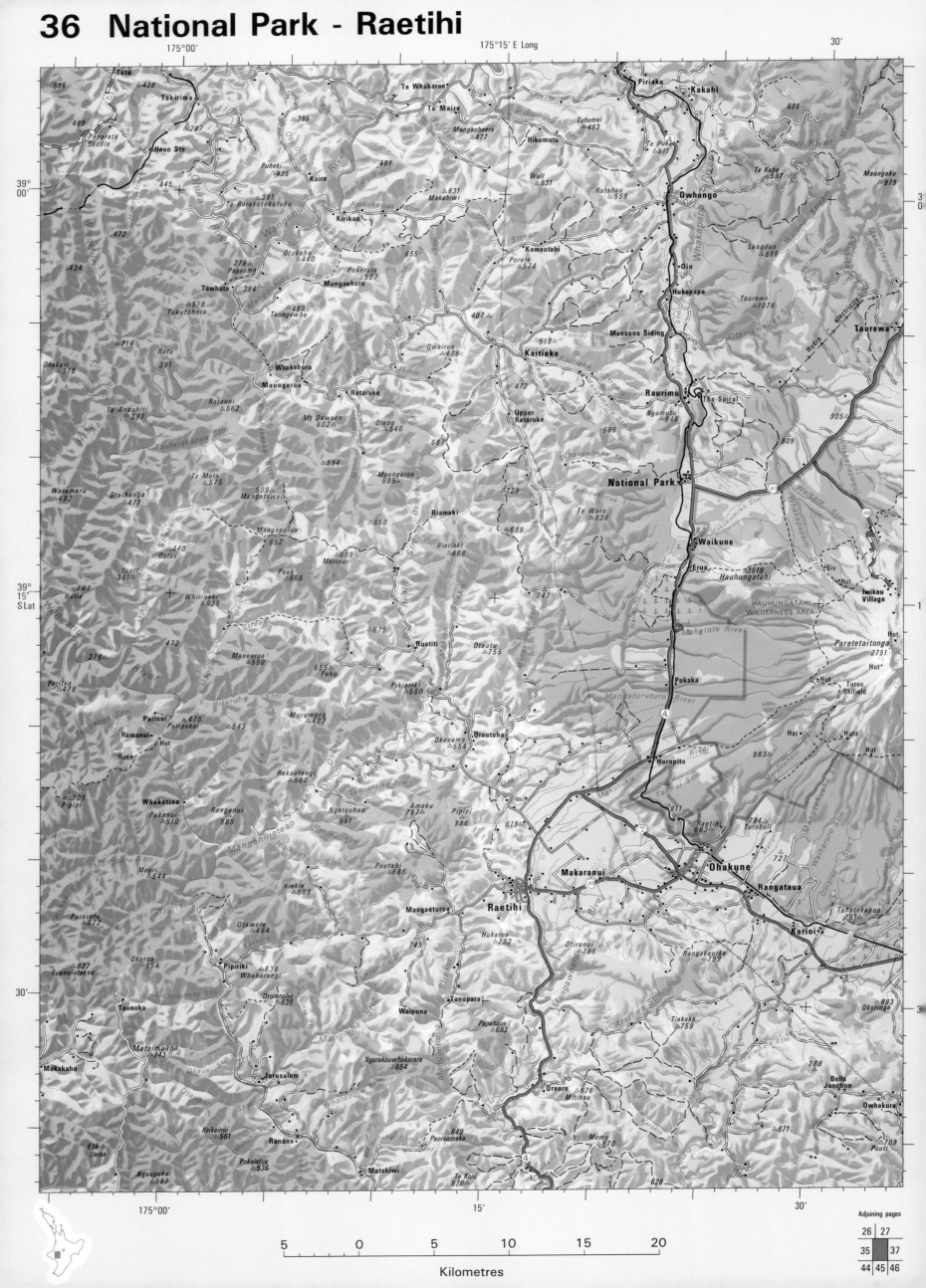

175°00'
175°15' E Long
30'

39°00'

30'

Tatu
596
439
43
287
Tokirima
499
Paparata Saddle
Heao Stn
445
434
472

Puheki
435
Koiro
491
Makahiwi
631
Te Rerekotukutuku
391
279 Papauma
Otukehu
440
Tawhata
394
Pukerata
587
Mangaohutu
518
Tukutahora
Taungawha
489
655
214
407

Whakahoro
Maungaroa
Retaruke
Owairua
476
518
Kaitieke
472

Te Maire
Mangaohaere
477
Hikumutu
Te Whakarae
Kawautahi
Porere
574

Piriaka
Kakahi
686
Tutumai
463
Te Puke
511
Wall
631
Ratahau
559
Owhango
Oio
Hukapapa
Taurewa
1076
Mansons Siding
Langdon
866
Maungaku
979
Taurewa
Te Kaha
597

Wanganui River

Rata
391
Ohakari
378
Ratanui
562
Te Anaohiti
397
Mt Dawson
602
Oteppa
546
687
Upper Retaruke
Ngamutu
846
Raurimu
The Spiral
905
809

Te Mata
575
509
Mangatawai
Otaihanga
477
Waiamaru
492
594
Maungaroa
699
650
Riamaki
729
689
National Park
Te Waro
836
Waikune
47
48

Scott
381
Oates
440
Whirinaki
635
Mangapurua
652
Morinui
699
Peak
666
Riariaki
668
675
747
Erua
1519
Hauhungatahi
Biv
Hut
Iwikau Village
HAUHUNGATAHI WILDERNESS AREA
Paretetaitonga
2751
Hut

447
Hatia
472
376
Manearoa
590
655 Pehu
Ruatiti
Otautu
755
Pokaka
Makotote River
Hut
Turoa Skifield

Paritea
478
Piriki
478
Pikiariki
580
Murumuru
482
543
Parinui
475
Paripakai
Ramanui
Hut
Rakautangi
560
Okauamo
554
Orautoha
Horopito
Mangaturuturu River
983
Hut
Huts
Hut
811

705
Pipipi
Whakatina
Pukenui
510
Ranganui
585
Ngatauhao
551
Ameku
757
Pipipi
786
619
Raetihi
893
Turnbull
794
Ohakune
727

Mauri
544
Kiekie
589
Poutahi
686
Makaranui
49
Rangataua
Tahatekapua
751

Puraroto
572
Okoroa
654
Otamore
464
Mangaeturoa
749
Raetihi
Hukaroa
792
Otiranui
795
Rangakauika
799
Karioi

627
Tuaniotakou
Pipiriki
636
Whaharangi
Otoranoho
636
Tanupara
Waipuna
893
Okotinga

Taunoko
Mataimoana
743
Jerusalem
Ngarakauwhakarara
654
Papahaua
683
788
Bells Junction

Makakaho
Keikeinui
551
Ranana
Pokaiatua
536
Matahiwi
Paoraameka
649
Te Koni
676
Oreore
676
Mitihau
Momo
670
628
671
709
Pouti
Owhakura

616
Ueroa
Ngaupoko
557

175°00'
15'
30'

Adjoining pages
26 27
35 37
44 45 46

5   0   5   10   15   20
Kilometres

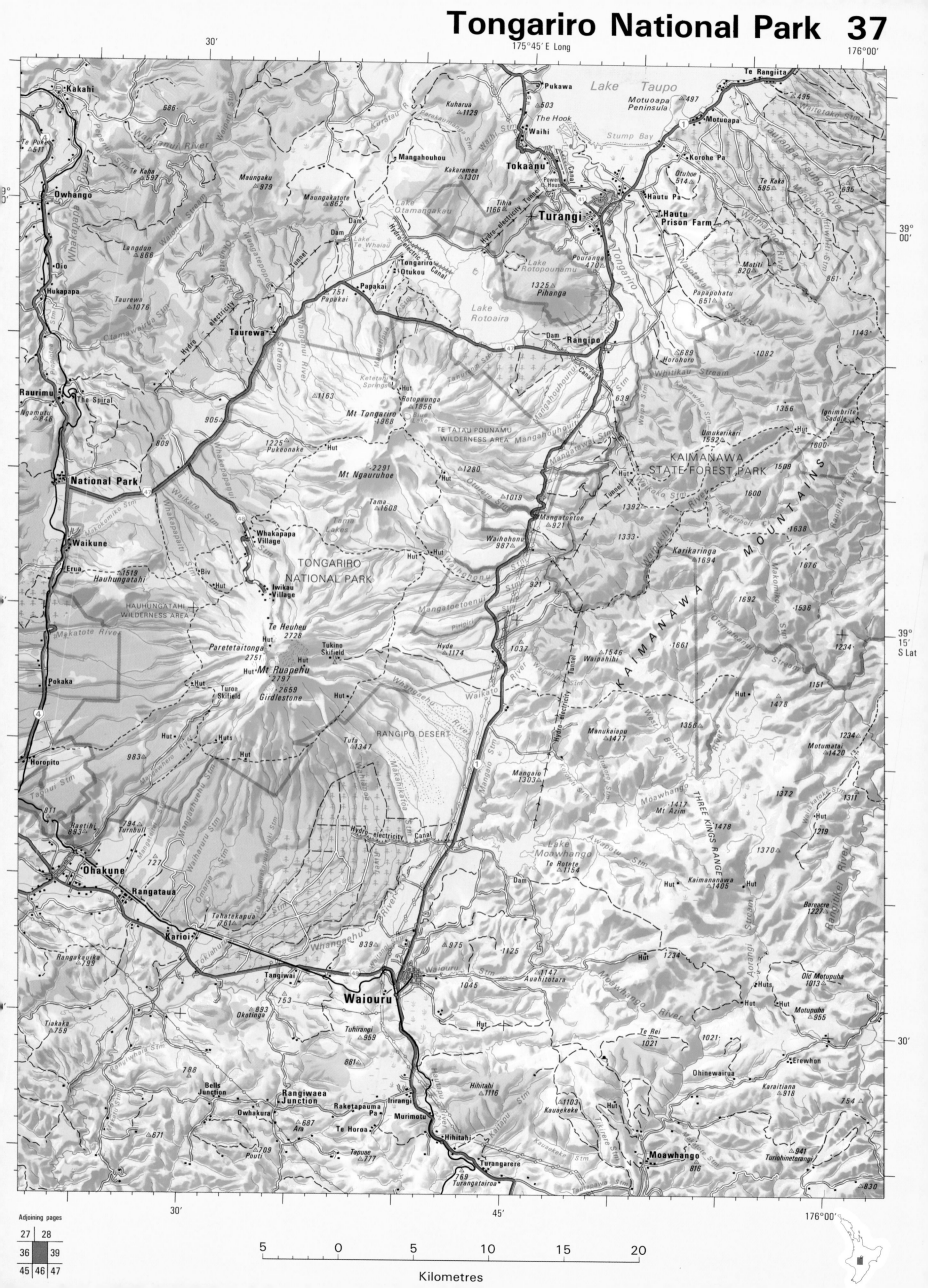

Kakahi

Te Puke △511

Owhango

Oio

Hukapapa

Raurimu

The Spiral

Ngamutu △846

National Park

Waikune

Erua

Hauhungatahi △1519

Pokaka

Horopito

811

Raetihi 693

Turnbull

Ohakune

Rangataua

Karioi

Rangakauika △799

Tiakaka △759

Bells Junction

Owhakura

Rangiwaea Junction

Raketapauma Pa

Te Horoa

Tapuae 777

Pouti 709

788

893 Okotinga

753

Tuhirangi △959

881

Irirangi

Murimotu

Hihitahi

769 Turangatairoa

Turangarere

Lake Taupo

Pukawa

Motuoapa Peninsula

The Hook

Waihi

Kuharua △1129

Kakaramea △1301

Mangahouhou

Tihia △1166

Tokaanu

Maungaku △979

Maungakatote △862

Turangi

Otamangakau

Tongariro

Otukou

751 Papakai

Papakai

Taurewa

Ketetahi Springs

Mt Tongariro 1968

1163

Rotopaunga △1856

Blue Lake

Pukeonake △1225

Mt Ngauruhoe △2291

1280

Tama △1608

Tama Lakes

Whakapapa Village

Biv

TONGARIRO NATIONAL PARK

Iwikau Village

HAUHUNGATAHI WILDERNESS AREA

Te Heuheu 2728

Paretetaitonga 2751

Tukino Skifield

Mt Ruapehu 2797

Girdlestone 2659

Turoa Skifield

983

RANGIPO DESERT

Tufa △1347

Te Rangiita

△495

△497

Motuoapa

Korohe Pa

Otuhoe 514

Te Kaka △595

△835

Hautu Pa

Hautu Prison Farm

861

Motiti B20

Papapohatu 651△

Pouranga △470

Pihanga △1325

Rangipo

△689 Horohoro

·1082

1143

Lake Rotopounamu

Lake Rotoaira

TE TATAU POUNAMU WILDERNESS AREA

1019

Whitikau Stream

1356

Ignimbrite Saddle

1600

KAIMANAWA STATE FOREST PARK

Umukarikari △1592

△1509

Hut

Mangatoetoe △921

Waihohonu 987

921

639

1392

1333

Karikaringa △1694

1676

1638

1600

Hyde ·1174

1037

△1546 Waipahihi

1661

1356

Manukaiapu △1477

Mangaio 1303

Moawhango

△1417 Mt Azim

Lake Moawhango

Te Rotete △1154

Dam

1692

·1536

1151

1478

1234

1234△

Motumatai △1420

1372

1370△

1478

THREE KINGS RANGE

KAIMANAWA MOUNTAINS

1311

Hut

1219

Hut

Kaimananawa △1405

Bareacre 1227

Old Motupuha 1013△

Motupuha △955

839

△975

·1125

△1147 Auahitotara

1045

Tahatekapua △761

Tangiwai

Waiouru

1234

Hut

Huts

△1103 Kauaekeke

Hihitahi △1116

Moawhango 816

941△

754 △

Erewhon

Ohinewairua

Te Rei 1021

1021·

Karaitiana △918

Turiohineterangi

△830

5 0 5 10 15 20

Kilometres

38 Lake Taupo - Mt Ruapehu

Kilometres

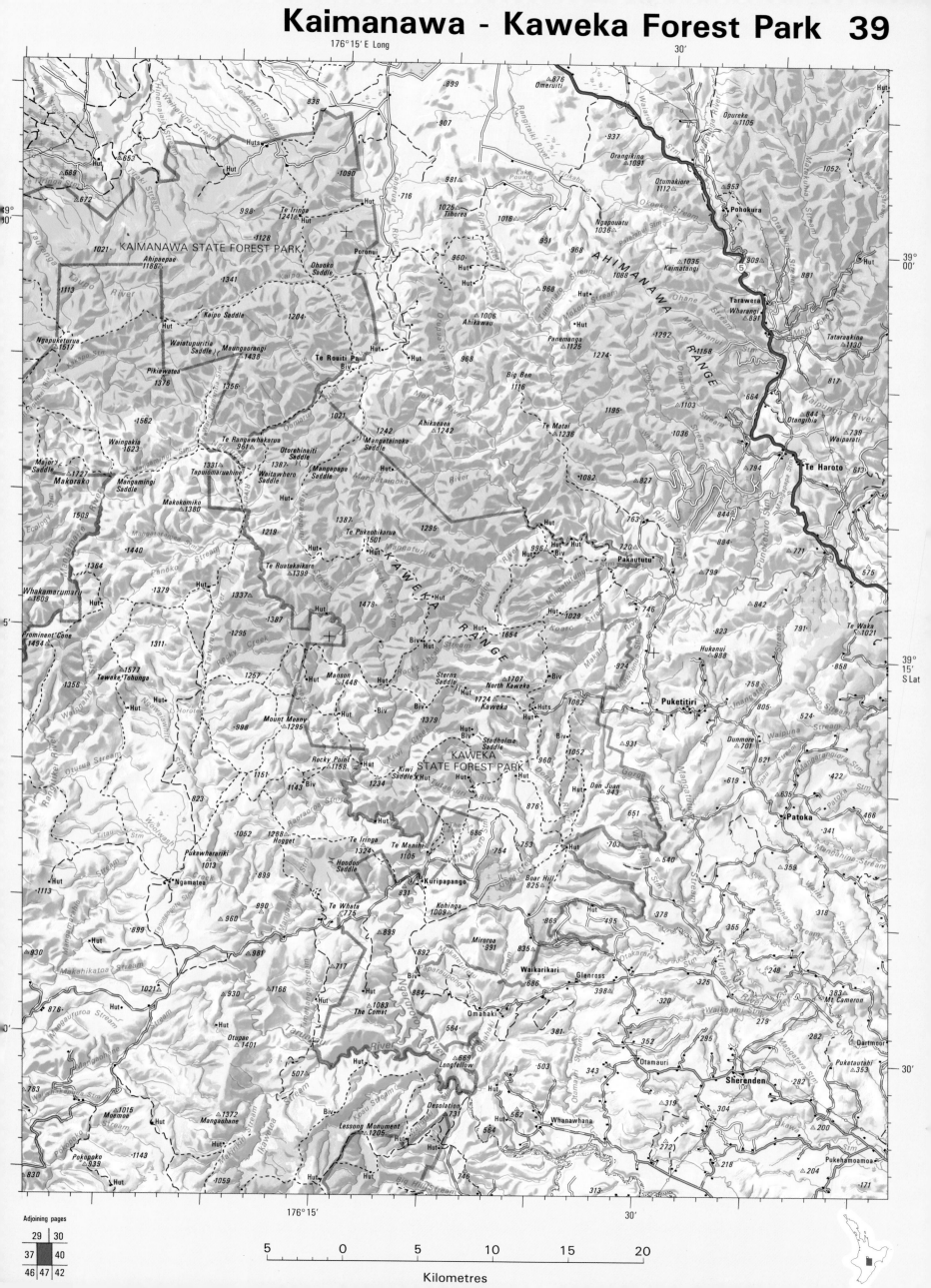

5   0   5   10   15   20

Kilometres

30' 176° 45' E Long 177°00'

876 Omeruiti
937
Opureke 1105
Wharerangiora 1234
983
Matai River 418
Maungataniwha

39°00'
Orangikino 1091
Otumakiore 1112
953
Pohokura 1383
991
Upokokahara 555
755
Te Ihuorurumaioterangi 763

1016
Ngapouatu 1036
Okoeke Stream
Pohokura
1052
1295
1186
930
869
625
612 Waitore

AHIMANAWA
968 1035
909
881
1061
1173
637
Te Kooti's Lookout 733
678
Willowflat 477
Kokohitoa 690

1088 Kaimatangi
1006
968 Hut
Tarawera
Wharangi 891
Tataraakina 1130
1000
Te Hoe 390
Te Heruotureia 809
534
601

Panemanga 1125
1292
1158 RANGE
1274
817
887
681
911
404
Patuwahine 776
558
363 Kotoko
308

Big Ben 1116
Te Matai 1236
1195
1103
664
844
Otangihia
739 Waiparati
597
Taraponui 1308
979
823
Mokara
539
Lake Opouahi
726
407

1082
827
1036
794
Te Haroto 613
664
MAUNGAHARURU RANGE
1013
Muori Stream
412
Kahika
292

Hut Hut Biv
763
884
Kopua 1073
Patikaikai 724
786
323
Tutira
424
517

996 Hut
720 Pakaututu
799
771
575
Wakaateo 1095
975
Lake Tutira 494
384
390

Hut 1029
842
823
791
Te Waka 1021
498
Waikoau
632
500
480
295
Lachlan 221
Aropaoanui

39°15' S Lat
1654
924
Hukanui 988
758
Ohurakura 568
378
314
367
280
223
161 Waipatiki Beach

1707 Biv
North Kaweka
Puketitiri
805
524
Te Pohue 858
Deep
396 Kaiwaka Stm
339
341
98

1724 Kaweka
Huts 1082
931
Dunmore 701
621
442
379
273
Tangoio
95
Tangoio Bluff

Studholme Saddle
960 1052
619
Patoka
466
317
259
308
244

876 Don Juan 943
651
Patoka
341
Mangahina Stream
328
204
Eskdale
319
202

753 754
703
540
359
Rissington
Puketapu 371
190
Bay View

869 495
378
355
318
McNeill 350
224
Wharerangi 105
Westshore
Bluff Hill
Hospital Hill

Miroroa 991
835
248
383 Mt Cameron
279
208 Apley
Poraiti
NAPIER

Waikarikari 686
Glenross
325
Dartmoor
282
187
Puketapu
Tamatea Onekawa Marewa

398
320
295
Puketautahi 353
182
Moteo
Taradale 141 Otatara
Maraenui

503
343
304
Sherenden 282
110
Waiohiki
Awatoto
Awatoto Stn

Hut 562
Whanawhana
319
200
Pukehamoamoa
112
Meeanee

564
272
218
204
171
195
313

30' 45' 177°00'

5   0   5   10   15   20
Kilometres

177°00' E Long

15'

983
Maungataniwha
930
Upokokahara
△555
Te Ihuorurumaioterangi
△763
Lake Rotonui
Lake Rotoiti
Willowflat
477
Kokohitoa
690
678
Waitore
612
565
Puketikitiki
437
Tirotirowhetu
404
301

571
543
487
410
511
418
625
755
Otoi
426
433
329
534
601
363
Kotoko
308
△329
Tirohanga
282
253
194
163
517
424
384
323
295
221
Lachlan
161
223

554
455
Matauraura
390
Tukutapa
449
131
322
Ruapapa
Cricklewood
410
Pihanui Wahanui
324
289
259
305
240
196
208
307
258
265
205
233

386
429
342
281
375
△332
Rangiahua
Whakamai
244
240
Frasertown
Ohinepaka
186
211
Wairoa

39°00'

Kotemaori
307
Raupunga
Waihua
Mohaka
Putorino
Kahika
Tutira
359
494
480
390
632△
500
Waikoau
Tareha
367
280
341
308
244
98
202
190
Wharerangi
106
Poraiti
Westshore
Eskdale
Bay View

Te Kooti's Lookout
△733
637△
Te Hoe
△390
Te Heruotureia
△809
Patuwahine
776
△911
△404
△558
△979
726
823
539
Mokara
412
292
407

Hawke   Bay

39°15'
S Lat

Tangoio
Tangoio Bluff
Waipatiki Beach
Aropaoanui
Aropaoanui River
Waipatiki Stream

NAPIER
Bluff Hill
Hospital Hill
Taradale
Otatara
Tamatea Onekawa Marewa
Pirimai Maraenui
Meeanee
Waiohiki
Awatoto
Awatoto Stn

Wairoa River
Ngamotu Lagoon

177°00'

15'

30'

5   0   5   10   15   20

Kilometres

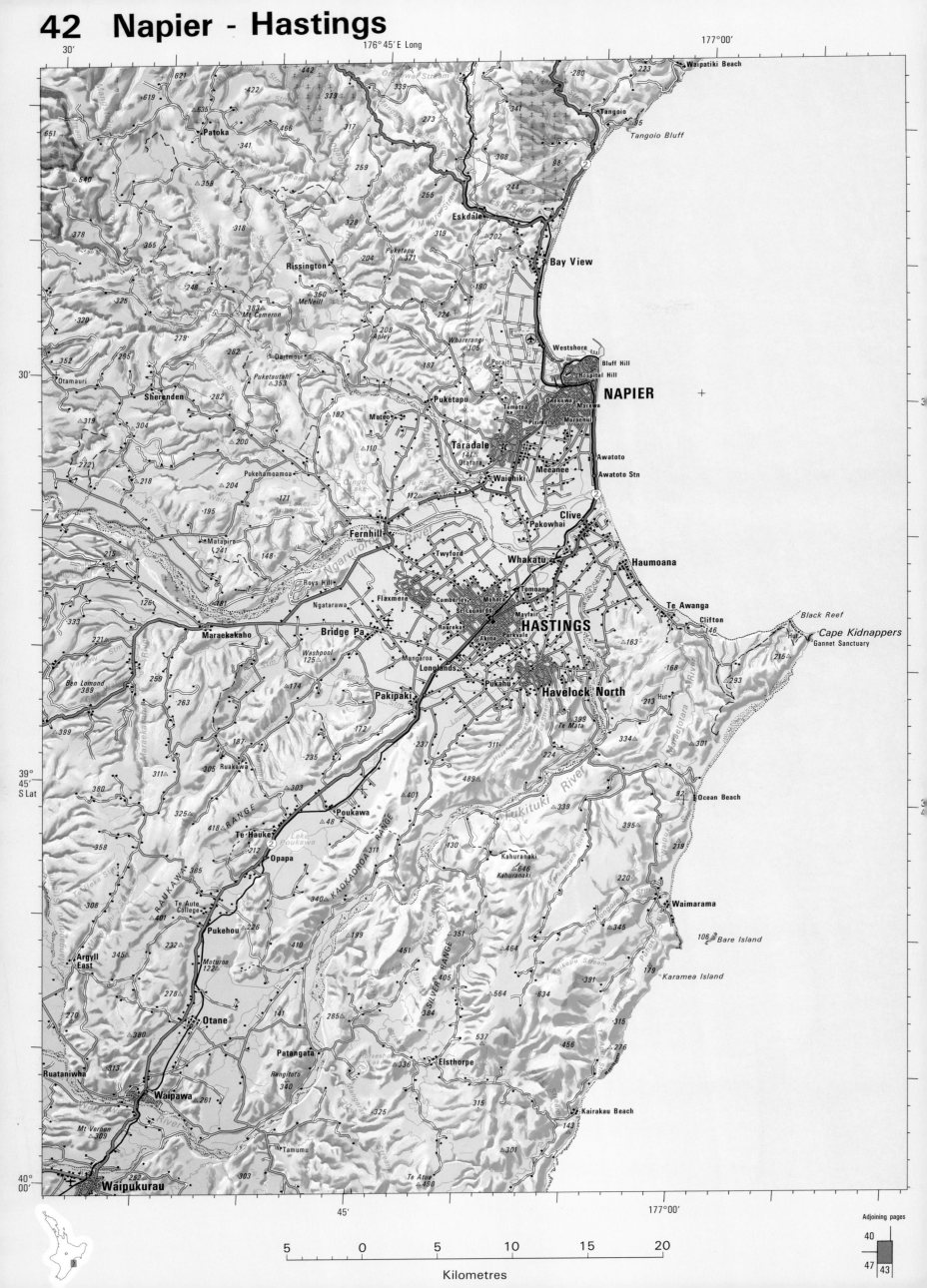

176° 45' E Long
177°00'

621
·619
·442
339
·280
223
Waipatiki Beach
·635
·422
319
317
273
341
Tangoio
·466
·540
651
·359
Patoka
·341
·359
·248
259
328
Tangoio Bluff
95
·378
·318
255
308
98
244
·355
·320
204
Eskdale
319
202
Rissington
371
Puketapu
McNeill
350
383
Mt Cameron
204
190
Bay View
·279
·282
Dartmoor
208
Apley
·325
·352
295
Whareangi
105
·319
·248
Sherenden
282
Poraiti
Westshore
Otamauri
272
·218
182
Moteo
110
187
Bluff Hill
Hospital Hill
NAPIER
304
Puketautahi
353
Puketapu
Tamatea
Onekawa
Marewa
Pukehamoamoa
204
171
112
Taradale
141
Pirimai
Maraenui
·195
Otatara
·215
148
Oingo Lake
Te Rotal
Waiohiki
Meeanee
Awatoto
·241
Fernhill
Awatoto Stn
Matapiro
126
Roys Hill
Twyford
Clive
Pakowhai
·181
Ngatarawa
Whakatu
Haumoana
·333
221
Flaxmere
Camberley
Mahora
Tomoana
Te Awanga
Maraekakaho
Bridge Pa
St Leonards
Mayfair
Clifton
Black Reef
259
Washpool
Raureka
Akina
HASTINGS
146
Cape Kidnappers
Ben Lomond
125
Mangaroa
Parkvale
163
Gannet Sanctuary
389
174
Longlands
Pakipaki
Pukahu
168
215
·263
305
Ruakawa
Havelock North
213
Hut
399
293
311
172
237
311
334
301
·399
187
235
401
489
224
Te Mata
·380
325
311
305
303
92
Ocean Beach
Ruakawa
339
395
Poukawa
130
219
418
Te Hauke
48
RANGE
Kahuranaki
220
358
212
Opapa
646
Kahuranaki
·308
385
Te Aute College
RAUKAWA
340
KAOKAOROA RANGE
Waimarama
401
Pukehou
226
199
351
345
Argyll East
232
345
410
451
464
106
Bare Island
278
Moturoa
122
405
179
Karamea Island
270
141
285
384
·391
Otane
·380
537
564
634
313
Patangata
456
315
Ruataniwha
Rangitoto
336
Elsthorpe
276
Waipawa
340
261
325
315
Kairakau Beach
Mt Vernon
309
143
252
303
Tamumu
301
Te Atua
450
Waipukurau

39°45' S Lat

40°00'

45'
177°00'

Adjoining pages
40
47 43

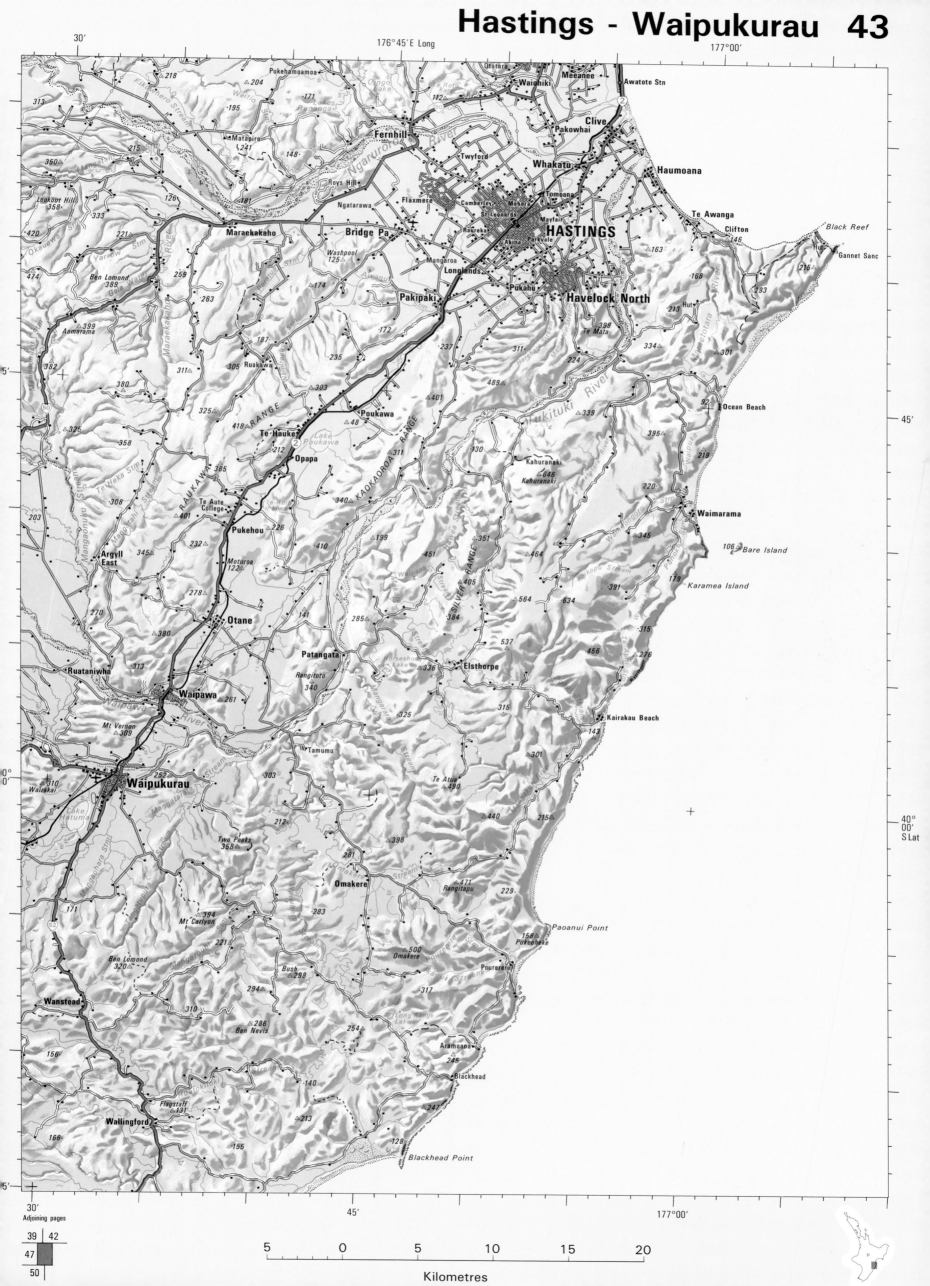

30'
176°45'E Long
177°00'

Pukehamoamoa
204
Otatora
Waiohiki
Meeanee
Awatoto Stn
218
313
Waitio
112
112
Clive
2
Oingo Lake
Roto Runanga
Pakowhai
195
171
Fernhill
Matapiro
241
148
Twyford
Whakatu
Haumoana
350
Roys Hill
Ngatarawa
126
181
Flaxmere
Camberley
Tomoana
Te Awanga
Lookout Hill
358
333
Ngataroa
St Leonards
Mahora
Clifton
Black Reef
420
221
Maraekakaho
Bridge Pa
Raureka
HASTINGS
146
Gannet Sanc
474
Ben Lomond
389
259
Washpool
125
Mangaroa
Akina Parkvale
163
Yarrow Stm
Longlands
Mayfair
168
Okauewa Stm
263
174
Pakipaki
Pukahu
Havelock North
293
382
Aomarama
399
305 Ruakawa
172
237
311
Te Mata
399
334
301
380
311
303
401
489
224
325
418 RANGE
48
Poukawa
130
339
Ocean Beach
92
325
Te Hauke
212
311
KAOKAOROA RANGE
Kahuranaki
646
395
219
358
385
Opapa
340
Kahuranaki
220
385
Te Aute College
401
Te Roto Nui
199
351
Waimarama
232
226 Pukehou
410
451
464
345
106 Bare Island
Argyll East
345
Moturoa
122
405
179 Karamea Island
270
278
141
285
384
564
634
315
380 Otane
537
456
276
313
Patangata
Rangitoto
340
Horseshoe Lake
336
Elsthorpe
315
Ruataniwha
Mt Vernon
309
261
Tamumu
325
315
Kairakau Beach
143
Waipawa
303
301
252
212
Te Atua
490
310
Wairakei
Two Peaks
358
398
440
215
Lake Hatuma
Waipukurau
281
Omakere
471
Rangitapu
229
171
283
Paoanui Point
158
Pukeoheke
394
Mt Carlyon
221
500
Omakere
Pourerere
Ben Lomond
320
Bush
298
317
Wanstead
294
310
286
Ben Nevis
254
Aramoana
245
156
140
Blackhead
52
Flagstaff
131
213
Wallingford
247
166
155
128
Blackhead Point

45'
45'

40°00'S Lat

45'
177°00'

Kilometres
5 0 5 10 15 20

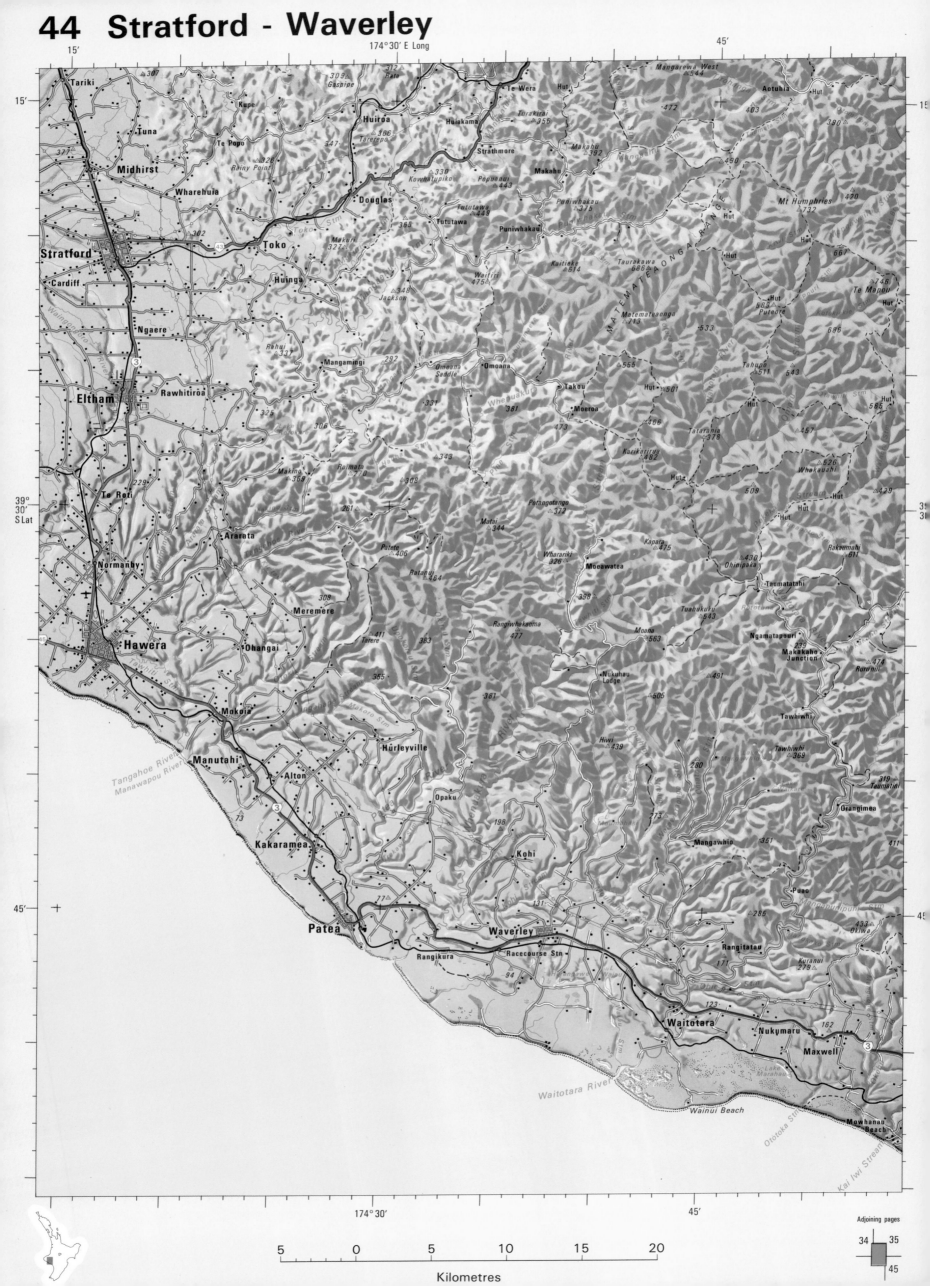

44 Stratford - Waverley

15′

Tariki
Kupe
△307
309△ Gaslpipe
312 Rato
Te Wera
Hut
Mangarewa West △544
Aotuhia
Hut
15′

Tuna
Huiroa
Huiakama
Turakirai △355
−472
403
△390

Midhirst
Te Popo
366 Tarerepo
347
Huiakama
Strathmore
Makahu △392
−490
Mt Humphries △732
420

Wharehuia
△326
Rainy Point
Douglas
330 Kowhatupiko
Popuanui △443
Makahu
Puniwhakau △375
Hut
Hut
667

Stratford
302
Toko
△365
Tututawa △449
Tututawa
Puniwhakau
△533
Hut
748 Te Mapou

Cardiff
45
Huinga
△348 Jackson
Waitiri △475
Kaitieke △614
Taurakawa △686
MATEMATEAONGA RANGE
Matemateaonga △713
Hut
589 Puteore
Hut

Ngaere
Rahui △337
Mangamingi
292
Omoana Saddle
Omoana
Takou
−555
−533
Hut ·501
Tahupo △511
543
686

Eltham
Rawhitiroa
△326
−331
△381
Moeroa
473
△466
Karikarirua △482
Tatarania △378
△457
Hut △565

Te Roti
326
306
Makino △369
Roimata △270
△343
△308
Hut
△526 Whakauahi
509
△429

Ararata
229△
261△
Patete △406
Matai △344
Potangotango △372
Kapara △475
△430 Ohinipaka
Rakaumahi △611
Hut

Normanby
Meremere
△308
Ratapui △464
Wharariki △326
Moeawatea
398
Tuahukuku △543
Taumatatahi

Hawera
Ohangai
411 Tarere
383
Rangiwhakaoma △477
Moana △563
△491
Ngamatapouri
239
Makakaho Junction
△474 Rurunui

Mokoia
355
△381
Nukuhau Lodge
505
Hiwi △439
280
Tawhiwhi
Tawhiwhi △369

Manutahi
Hurleyville
319 Taumatini

Alton
Opaku
198
273
Mangawhio
351
411

Kakaramea
73
Kohi
131
△285
Puao

Patea
77
94
Waverley
Racecourse Stn
433 Okiwa
Rangitatau
171
Kuranui
279△

Rangikura
123
Waitotara
Nukumaru
162
Maxwell

Waitotara River
Wainui Beach
Mowhanau Beach

5 0 5 10 15 20

Kilometres

Adjoining pages
34 35
45

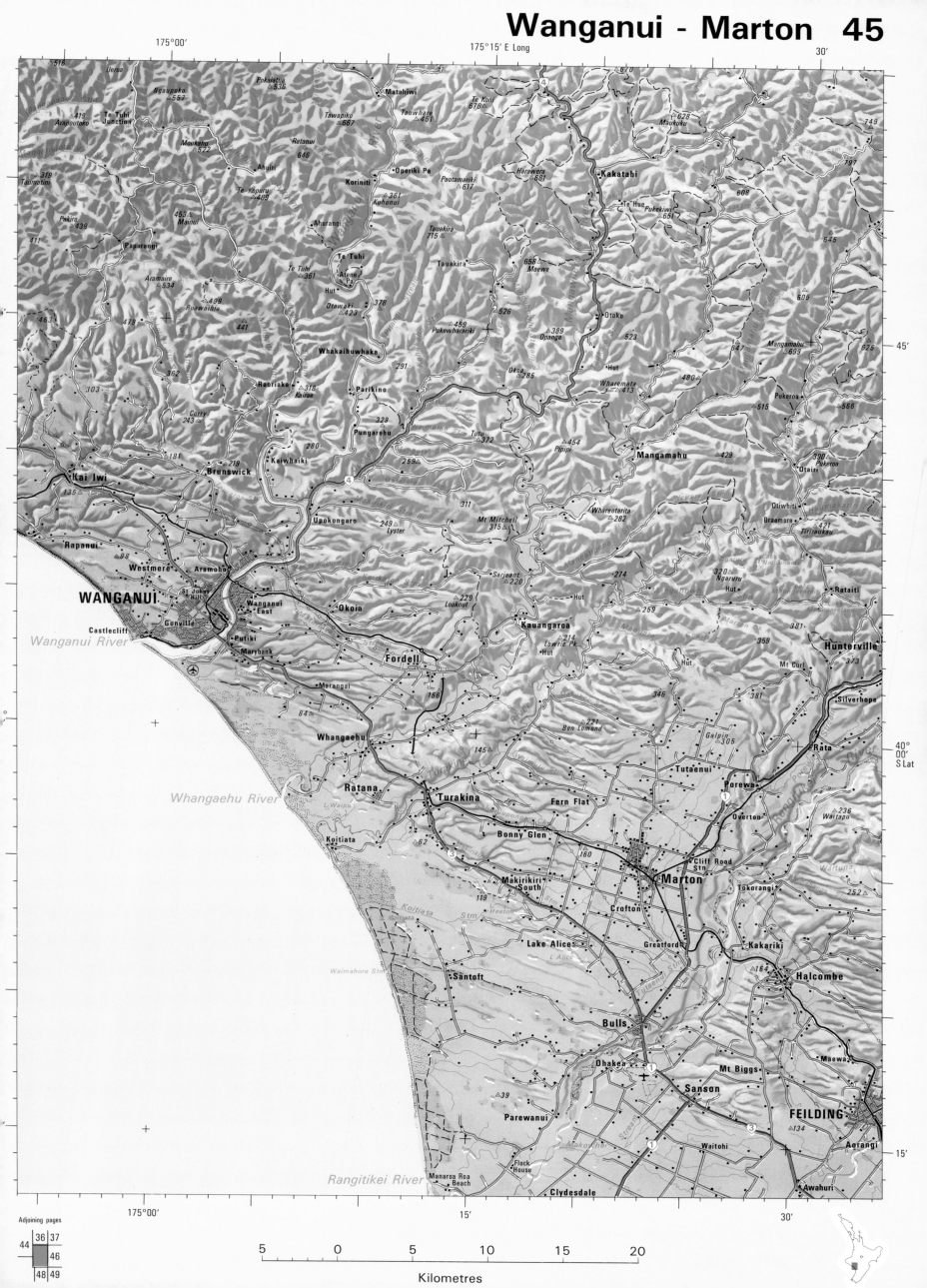

WANGANUI

Kai Iwi
Brunswick
Rapanui
Westmere
Aramoho
St Johns Hill
Gonville
Castlecliff
Putiki
Marybank

Wanganui River

Upokongaro
Okoia
Fordell

Kaiwhaiki
Parikino
Pungarehu
Kairae
Raoriaka

Marangai
Whangaehu

Whangaehu River

Ratana
Koitiata
Turakina
Fern Flat
Bonny Glen

Makirikiri South
Heaton

Lake Alice
L Alice

Santoft

Waimahora Stm

Parewanui
Flock House

Bulls
Ohakea

Clydesdale
Manaroa Roa Beach

Rangitikei River

Whangaehu
Kauangaroa
Lowrie Pk
Hut

Sarjeant
Lookout

Mt Mitchell
Mt Curl

Ben Lomond

Galpin
Tutaenui
Porewa
Overton

Marton
Cliff Road Stn
Crofton
Greatford
Kakariki
Halcombe

Tokorangi
Mt Biggs
Sanson
Maewa
Waitohi
Aorangi

FEILDING

Hunterville
Silverhope
Rata
Waitapu

Tiraukau
Braemore
Otiwhiti
Ngaruru
Rataiti
Pukeroa
Otairi

Mangamahu
Pukeroa
Pukeiwi
Wharemata
Opanga
Okoa
Otoko
Te Hue
Pipipi

Kakatahi
Maukuku
Matahiwi
Te Koni
Tauwhare
Harawera
Maewe
Tauakira

Operiki Pa
Paotamariki
Korinti
Kuhunui
Pukewharariki
Tutu

Matahiwi
Tawapiko
Ratanui
Ahuiti
Te Kopuru
Ahurangi

Ngaupoko
Pokaiatua
Meukahu
Mainui

Ueroa
Te Tuhi Junction
Arapoutoko
Taumatini
Pakira
Paparangi

Aramaire
Ruawaihia
Te Tuhi
Atene Pa
Hut
Otawaki
Whakaihuwhaka

Carry
Corry
Lyster

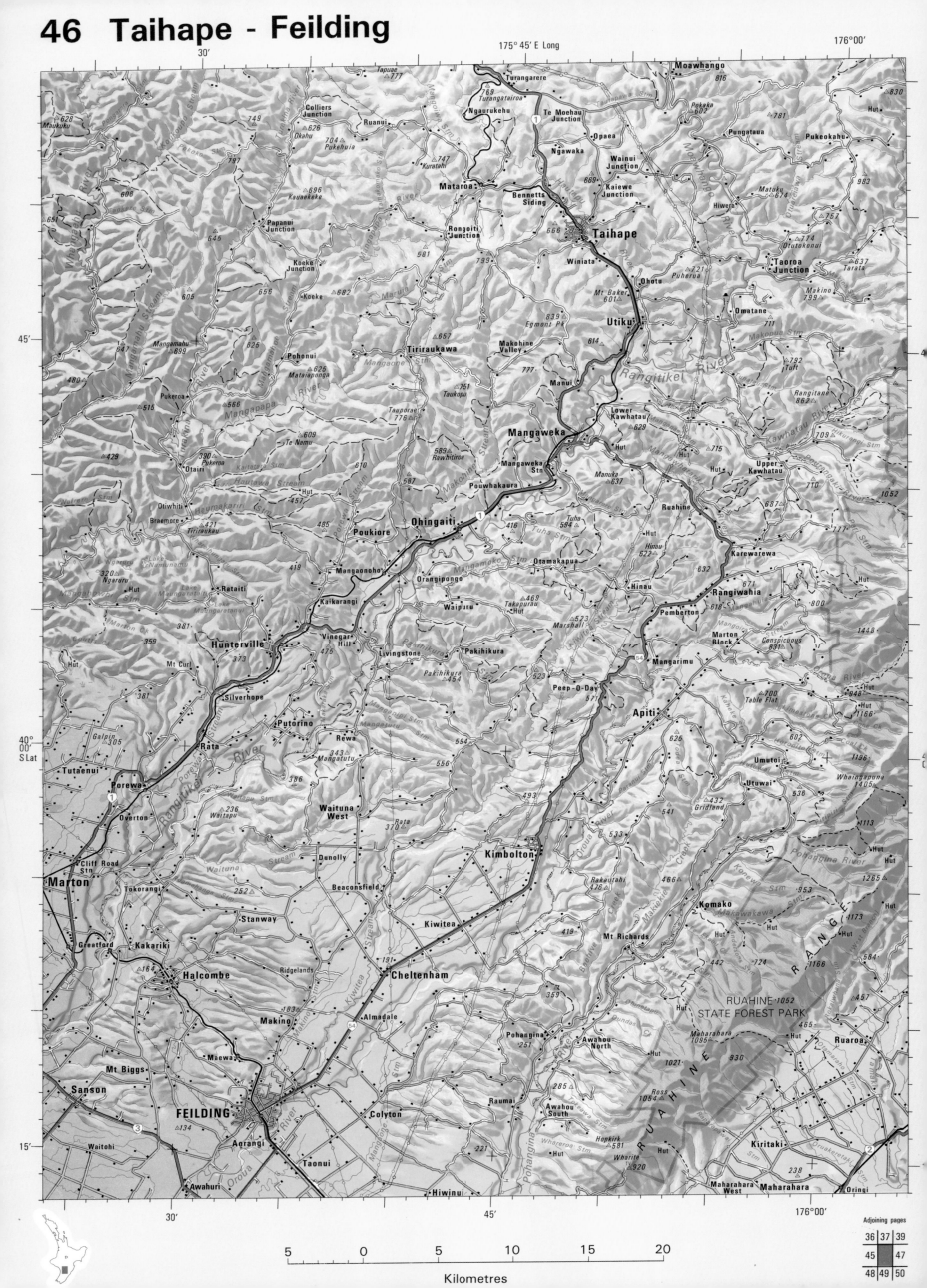

175° 45' E Long
30'
176°00'

Moawhango

Tapuae △777
Turangarere
△769
Turangatairoa
Ngaurukehu
Te Moehau Junction
Opaea
Ngawaka
Wainui Junction
816
△830
Pakaka 602
△781
Pungataua
Pukeokahu
Hut

Colliers Junction
Ruanui
749
Okahu △626
704 △ Pukehuia
△747 Kuratahi
Mataroa
Bennetts Siding
669△
Kaiewe Junction
Matuku △674
Hiwera
△757
983

△628 Maukuku
651△
797
608
△696 Kauaekeke
Papanui Junction
645
Rongoiti Junction
666
Taihape
Winiata
Puherua
721△
Ohotu
Otutokonui
△774
Taoroa Junction
637 △ Tarata

45'
656
Koeke Junction
△682 Koeke
605
Tiriraukawa
581
799
Makohine Valley
Mt Baker 601△
839△
Egmont Pk
614△
Utiku
Omatane
711
Makino 799 △

647△ Mangamahu △699
625
480△
Pohonui
△625 Mataiaponga
657△
Mangaone Stm
777
Manui
Rangitikei River
△792 Tuft

566△ Pukeroa
515
△609 Te Namu
751 Taukopu
Tauporae 776△
589△ Rawhitiroa
Lower Kawhatau
629
△715
Hut
Upper Kawhatau
709△ Hikurangi Stm
Rangitane 862△

△429
390△ Pukeroa
Otairi
610
587
Mangaweka
Mangaweka Stn
Pouwhakaura
Manuka △637
Hut
710
687△
1052

Heumakariri Stm
△421 Tiriraukau
Braemore
485
Ohingaiti
416△
Tuha 594△
Tuha Stm
Ruahine
632
Hut
777△
Karewarewa

320△ Ngaruru
419
Mangaonoho
Orangiponge
Mangameko Stm
Otamakapua
Hinau 622△
671△
Hut
Rangiwahia

Lake Maunganuiototo
381
Kaikarangi
Waipuru
△469 Takapurau Hut
Hinau
618△
Pemberton
800△
Marton Block
Conspicuous 831△
1448

359
Hunterville
Vinegar Hill
475
373
Livingstone
Pakihikura
Pakihikura △454
523 Marshall
523
Mangarimu
54
△700 Table Flat
948△
Hut
1166

Mt Curl
381
Silverhope
Peep-O-Day
571
Apiti
625△
602△
Umutoi
1196

Galpin 305
Putorino
Rewa
594
Rata 370△
493
541
432△ Gridland
Utuwai
536
Whaingapuna 1405△
1113

40°00' S Lat
Rata
236△ Waitapu
343 Mangatutu
556
533
Komako
953△
1265△

Tutaenui
Porewa
1
Overton
386
Waituna West
Kimbolton
Rakautahi 476△
466△
Mt Richards
Hut
1173

Cliff Road Stn
Marton
Tokorangi
252 △
Dunolly
Beaconsfield
419
442△
724△
1166
584

Greatford
Kakariki
164△
Stanway
Ridgelands
Kiwitea
359
Ruahine 1052
State Forest Park
465△
△457

Halcombe
183△
Cheltenham
191
Almadale
Pohangina 251
Awahou North
Maharahara 1095△
Ruaroa

Mt Biggs
Making
54
285△
Awahou South
1021
930
Maharahara West
Maharahara
Oringi

Sanson
Maewa
Raumai
Hopkirk 581
Wharite △920
238△
Kiritaki

FEILDING
3
134△
Agrangi
Colyton
221
Hut
2

Waitohi
Taonui
Hiwinui
Awahuri

40°00' S Lat
45'
176°00'

Adjoining pages

36	37	39
45	49	47
48	49	50

5   0   5   10   15   20
Kilometres

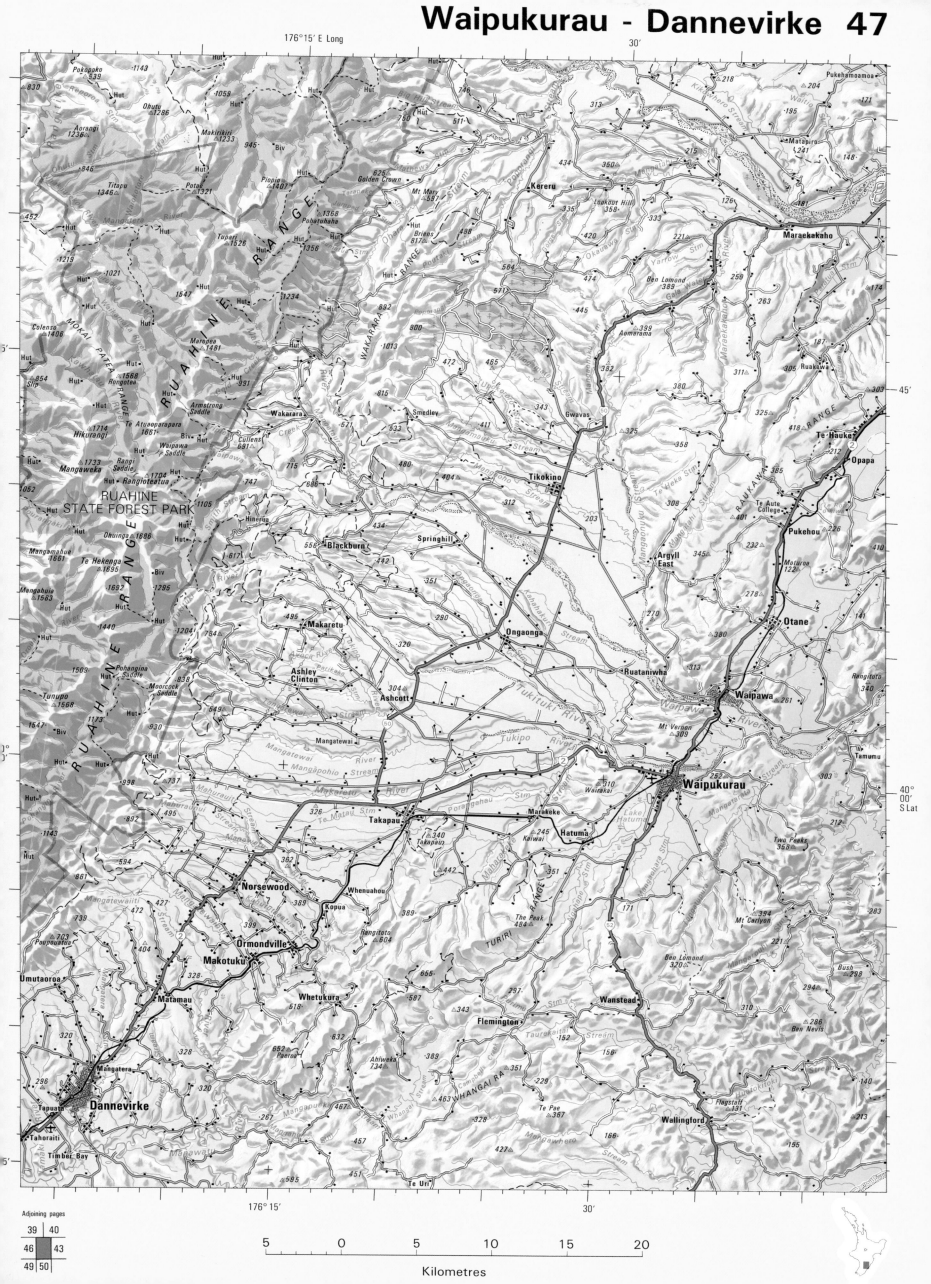

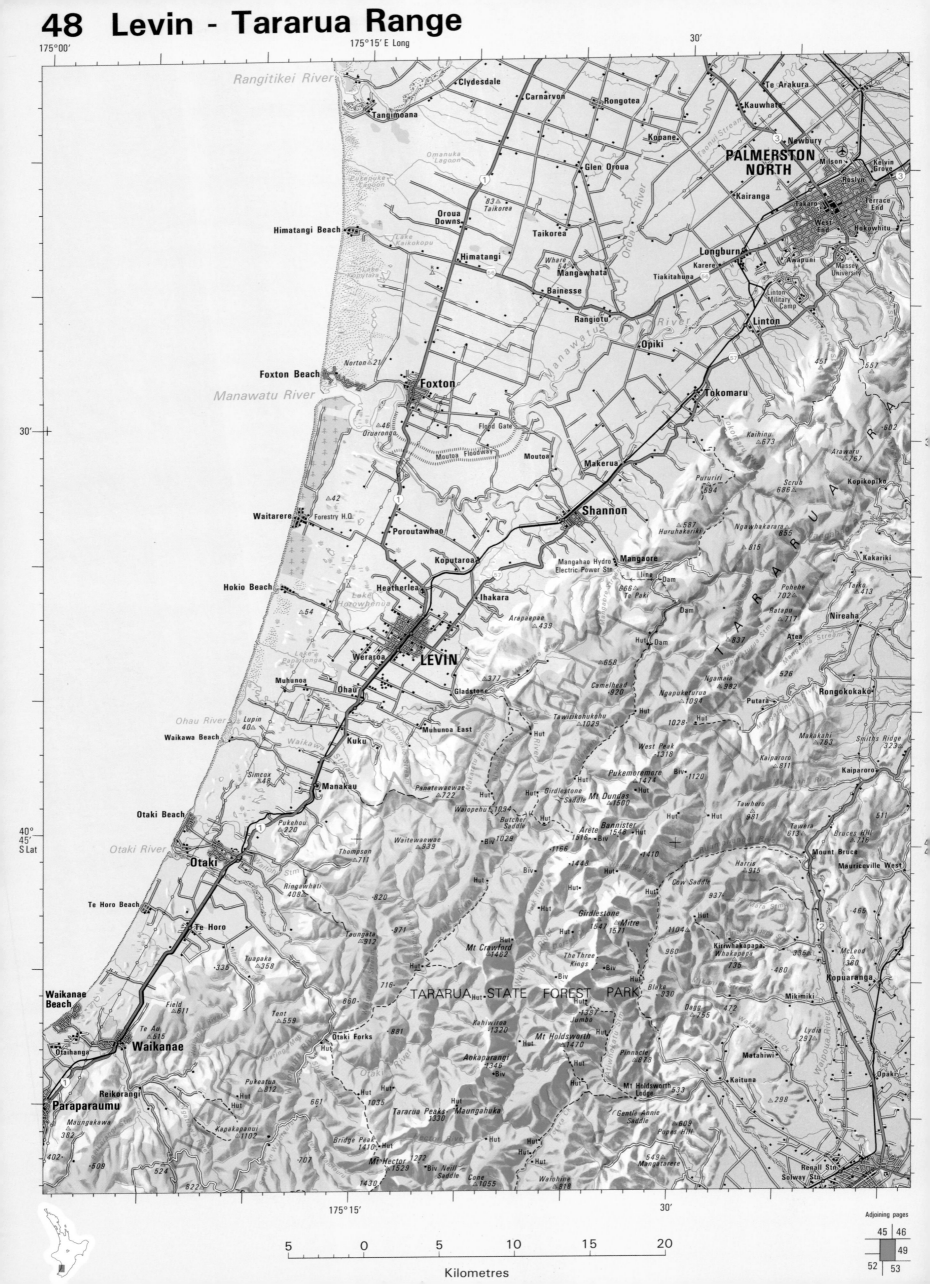

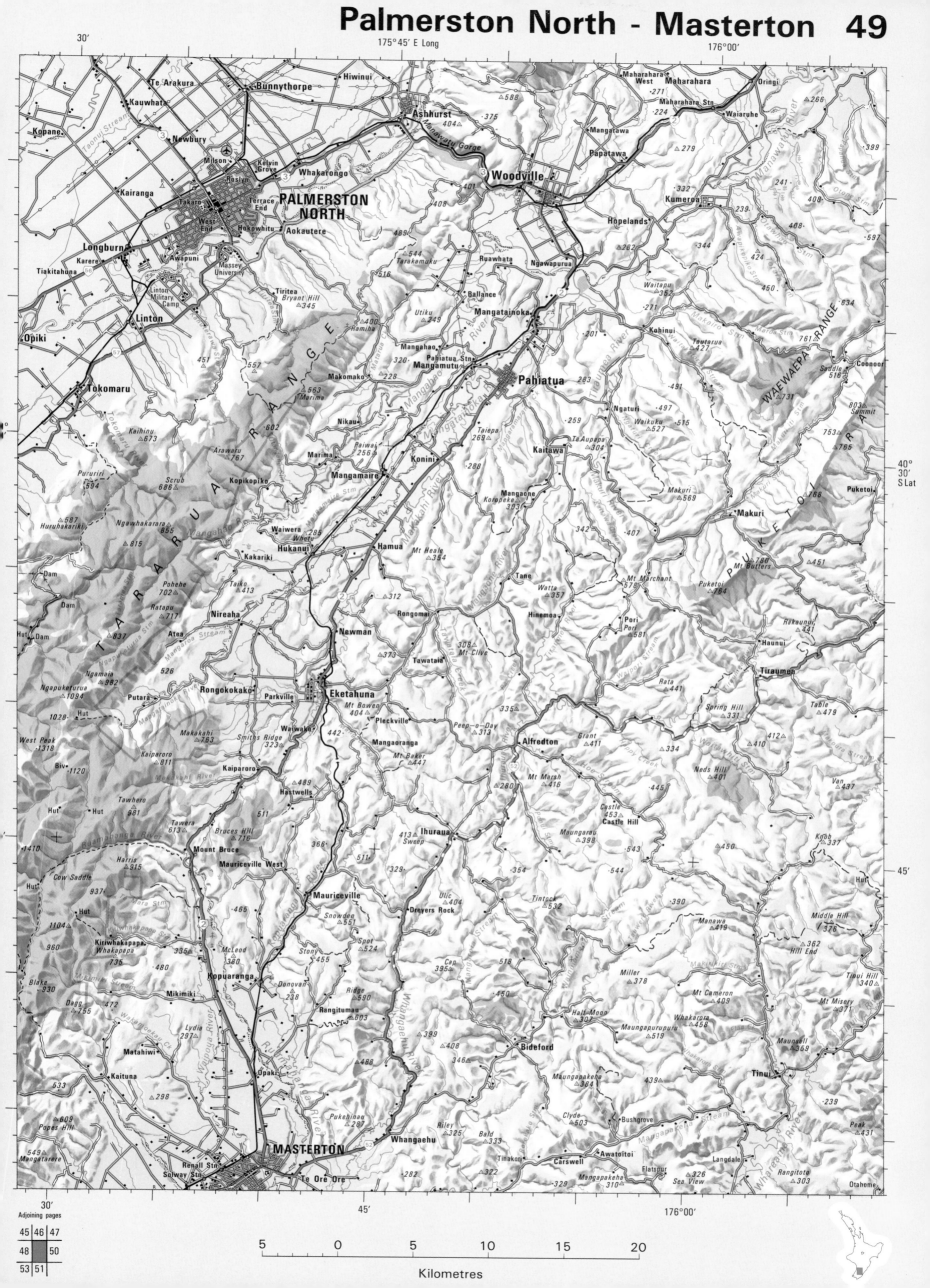

175°45' E Long

176°00'

30'

Te Arakura
Kauwhata
Kopane
Bunnythorpe
Hiwinui
Maharahara West · 271 · Maharahara · 266 Oringi
Newbury
Milson
Kelvin Grove
Roslyn
Takaro
Ashhurst · 404 △ · 375 · 588
Maharahara Stn · 224 · 279 Waiaruhe
Kairanga
West End
Terrace End
PALMERSTON NORTH
Whakarongo
Manawatu Gorge
Papatawa
· 2
· 399
Longburn
Karere
Awapuni
Massey University
Hokowhitu
Aokautere
· 401
Woodville · 3
· 332 Kumeroa
· 239 · 408
· 597
Tiakitahuna
Linton Military Camp
· 489
· 408
· 424
· 344
· 450
Opiki
Linton
Tiritea Bryant Hill △ 345
· 544 Tarakamuku
Ruawhata
Ngawapurua
· 262
· 761
· 634
· 400 Ramiha
· 516
Utiku △ 249
Ballance
Mangatainoka
· 271
· 201
Kohinui
Waitapu · 352
Makairo Stn
Marda Stn
Tokomaru
· 451
· 557
· 563 Marima
Makomako · 228
· 320 Mangahao
Pahiatua Stn
Mangamutu
· 283
Waikuku △ 527
Tautarua △ 427
· 491
WAEWAEPA RANGE △ 731
Saddle 516 Coonoor
Kaihinu △ 673
· 602
Nikau
Marima
Paiwai △ 256
Koninî
Pahiatua
· 259
Ngaturi · 497
· 515
· 803 Summit
· 753 △ 765
Pururiri · 594
Scrub 686 △
Arawaru △ 767
Kopikopiko
Mangamaire
· 288
Taiepa 269
Kaitawa
Te Aupapa △ 304
Makuri △ 569
· 768 Puketoi
Huruhakariki △ 587
Ngawhakarara △ 855
△ 815
Waiwera · 285 Whetu
Hukanui
Hamua
Mangaone Koropeke 303
· 342
· 407
Makuri · 451
Kakariki
Mt Heale △ 354
Tane
Watta △ 357
Mt Marchant · 578
· 780 Mt Butters
Rakaunui △ 441
Pohehe 702 △
Ratapu △ 717
Taiko △ 413
Nireaha
Rongomai
· 312
Hinemoa
Puketoi △ 764
Haunui
Atea
△ 837
Newman
· 373
· 308 Mt Clive
Tawataia
Pori Pori △ 581
Tiraumea
Ngamaia △ 982
· 526
Rongokokako
Parkville
Eketahuna
Mt Bowen △ 404
Peep-o-Day △ 313
· 335 △
Rata △ 441
Spring Hill △ 331
Table △ 479
Ngapuketurua △ 1094
Putara
· 1028 Hut
Makakahi △ 783
Smiths Ridge △ 323
Waiwaka
· 442
Pleckville
Mangaoranga
Alfredton
Grant △ 411
· 334
· 410
· 412 △
Neds Hill △ 401
Van △ 437
West Peak · 1318
Kaiparoro △ 811
Kaiparoro
△ 489
Hastwells
Mt Baker △ 447
Mt Marsh △ 416
· 280
· 445
Castle △ 453 Castle Hill
· 543
Knob △ 337
· 450
Biv · 1120
Tawhero △ 981
· 511
Ihuraua Sweep · 413
· 329
· 354
Maungarau △ 398
· 544
Hut
Hut
Hut
Tawera 613 △
Bruces Hill △ 716
· 366 △
· 511
· 1410
Harris △ 915
Mount Bruce
Mauriceville West
Ulic · 404
Dreyers Rock
Tintock · 532
· 390
Manawa △ 419
Middle Hill · 376
Cow Saddle 937 △
· 465
Mauriceville
Snowden · 551
Hill End △ 362
· 1104 △
Hut
Kiriwhakapapa Whakapapa 735
McLeod 380 △
· 335 △
Spot △ 524
Cap 395 △
· 518
Miller △ 378
Tinui Hill 340 △
· 960
· 480
Kopuaranga
Donovan △ 238
Stony · 455
· 450
Mt Cameron △ 409
Mt Misery △ 371
Blake 930
Mikimiki
Ridge △ 590
Rangitumau △ 603
Half Moon △ 307
Whakarora △ 458
Maunsell △ 359
Dagg △ 755
· 472
Lydia 297 △
· 399
· 408
Bideford
Maungapurupuru △ 519
Matahiwi
· 298
· 346
Maungapakeha △ 384
· 439 △
Tinui
Kaituna
Opaki
Pukehinau △ 287
Riley △ 325
Bald △ 333
Clyde △ 503
Bushgrove
Peak △ 431
· 533
· 609 Popes Hill
Whangaehu
· 282
Tinakori △ 322
· 329
Carswell
Awatoitoi
Maungapakeha 310 △
· 326 Sea View
Rangitoto △ 303
· 549 Mangatarere
Renall Stn
Solway Stn
MASTERTON
Te Ore Ore
· 52
Tinakori △
Flatspur
Langdale
Otahome

30'

45'

176°00'

Adjoining pages

45	46	47
48		50
53	51	

5   0   5   10   15   20

Kilometres

176° 30' E Long

Ngapaeruru
·595
·451
Te Uri
Wilder Sett.
405·
Kaiparahoura Stm
·288
Bird Island
Porangahau River
Mangatoro
·369
404·
·428
192
·422
441·
433·
·525
Howe
·286
·399
Koroponui
424·
Mangatuna
Porangahau
·603
Motea
Whangai 632
·555
Waitahora
307
305 Taumatawhakatangihangakoauauotamateapokaiwhenuakitanatahu
·153
·596
Toi Flat
460
Mangaorapa
·597
·539
Homebush
·402
Mount Pleasant
·337
Oporae 754
Waipatiki
·117
·634
412
484
Te Awaputahi 582
Wahatuara 736
Weber
315
154
355
669
Mahoe
Iris 432
Towai
Oporae
432
Coonoor
721
Mt McCartle
425
52
354
Pukepoto
210
·249
Horoeka
343
Ti Tree Point
Waimiro
Wimbledon
803
Summit
Pukewhinau 377
Waione
372
·765
222
530
Taumataoteatua 443
Korora
209
Mt Bovis 204
209
Puketoi
386
Mt Alta 230
238
Herbertville
285
Cape Turnagain
Beehive 330
348
Mangatiti
425
Pongaroa
Huiru 224
Ranui 415
Akaroa
248
Mangatiti 352
286
Mt Cadmus 284
Kohiku
309
271
Mt Attile 353
Kereru 343
Rakaunui
440
Akitio
Waihoki
290
312
Benvorlich
Waihoki
Valley
Rakauhau 373
Razorback
530
241
226
Mara
Owahanga Hill
Rara 405
Owahanga
Wig 415
Van 437
442
384 Scrub
Pukeamuku 503
Tanewa 448
Hut
300
Omaruapakihau
429
Mataikona
392
Mt Percy 472
357
Tinui Hill 340
Mt Misery 371
397
289
Okau
Haldon 411
Whakataki
Windy 381
Castlepoint
Peak 431
Castle Point
Otahome

40°
30'
S Lat

45'

Kilometres
5 0 5 10 15 20

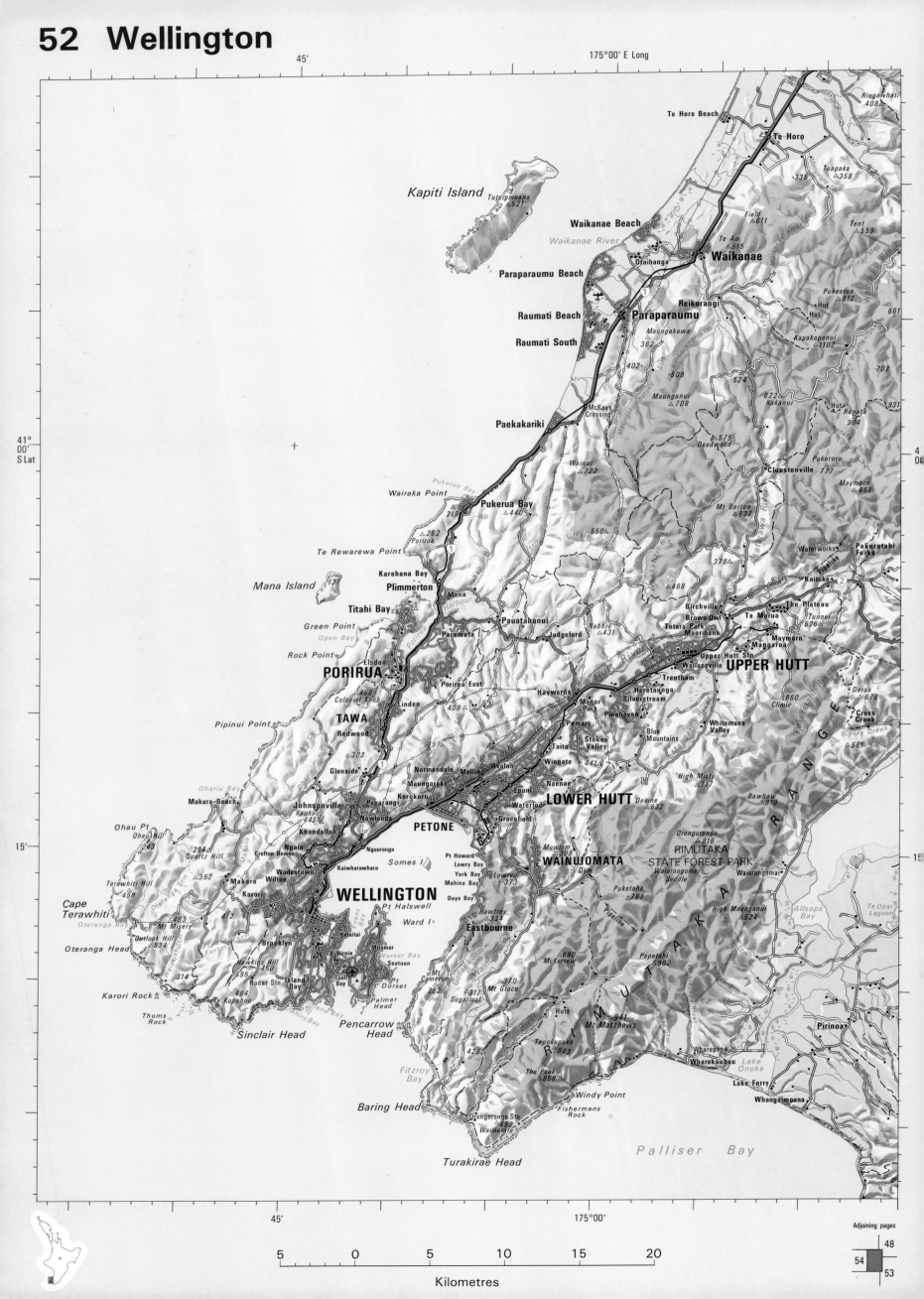

45'

175°00' E Long

Ringawhati
△408

Te Horo Beach

Te Horo

Tuapaka
△358
·335

Kapiti Island
Tuteremoana
△521

Field
△611

Tent
△559

Waikanae Beach

Waikanae River

Te Au
△515

Waikanae

Otaihanga

Pukeatua
△812

Hut

Parapaumu Beach

Reikorangi

Hut
661

Raumati Beach

Parapaumu

Maungakawa
△382

Kapakapanui
△1102

Raumati South

402·

·509

524

Maungakawa
△708

822
Kakanui

Hut
931

Hut △ Renata
904

McKays
Crossing

Paekakariki

Wainui
△722

·575
Deadwood

Pukeruru
△777

-707

Cloustonville

41°
00'
S Lat

Pukerua Bay

Maymorn
△851

Wairaka Point

Pukerua Bay
△440

Mt Barton
△627

△219
Porirua

550
△

Waterworks

Pakuratahi
Forks

Te Rewarewa Point

1

△468

378△

Pipeline

Kaitoke

2

Mana Island △121

Karehana Bay
Plimmerton

Mana
Harbour

Birchville
Brown Owl
Totara Park
Maoribank

The Plateau

Titahi Bay

Paremata

Nabhra
△431

Tunnel
626△

Green Point
Open Bay

Pauatahanui

Upper Hutt Stn

Maymorn

Rock Point

Judgeford

Maungaroa

Elsdon

Wallaceville

UPPER HUTT

PORIRUA

△468
Colonial Knob

Porirua East

Trentham

Heretaunga

860
Climie

Deraa
△678

Pipinui Point

TAWA

Linden

408 △

Silverstream

Cross
Creek

Redwood

Haywards

Manor
Park

Pinehaven

Whitemans
Valley

·561

457△

△303

Pomare

2

1

Glenside

Normandale Melling

Taita

Stokes
Valley

Blue
Mountains

Ohariu Bay

Maungaraki

Avalon

Wingate
△441

High Misty
△717

Makara Beach

Paparangi

Korokoro

Naenae

Johnsonville
Kaukau
△445

Newlands

Epuni

Bawbaw
△810

Waterloo

LOWER HUTT

Devine
△632

Orongorongo
△816

Khandallah

PETONE

Gracefield

Ohau Pt
Ohau Hill
△243

Ngaio

Ngauranga

294
Quartz Hill

Crofton Downs

Somes I.

Pt Howard
Lowry Bay

WAINUIOMATA

RIMUTAKA
STATE FOREST PARK

Waiorongomai
Saddle

Waiorongomai

Terawhiti Hill
△458

Makara

△352

Wadestown
Wilton

Kaiwharawhara

York Bay
Lowry
△373

Dam

Puketaha
△767

Cape
Terawhiti
Oteranga Bay

Karori

△483
Mt Misery

412△

Mahina Bay
Days Bay

High Maunganui
△524

Te Opai
Lagoon

WELLINGTON

Hawtrey
△334

Allsops
Bay

Outlook Hill
△534

Brooklyn

Pt Halswell

Oteranga Head

314

Hataitai

Kilbirnie

Miramar

Evans Bay

Ward I.

Eastbourne

Mowlem
△398

Papatahi
△902

Hawkins Hill
△450

△495

Seatoun
Vorser Bay

McKerrow
△690

Karori Rock

△484

Radar Stn

Island
Bay

Lyall Bay

Pt Dorset

Mt
Cameron
252

△370
Mt Grace

Pirinoa

Te Kopahau

Island Bay

317
Sugarloaf

Palmer
Head

Thoms Rock

Pencarrow
Head

Mt Matthews
△941

Wharepapa

Sinclair Head

Fitzroy
Bay

428·

Tapokopoko
△843

Wharekauhau

Lake
Onoke

Lake Ferry

Baring Head

Orongorongo Stn

The Peak
△858

Windy Point

Whangaimoana

Waimatara

Fishermans
Rock

Turakirae Head

Palliser Bay

45'

175°00'

5   0   5   10   15   20

Kilometres

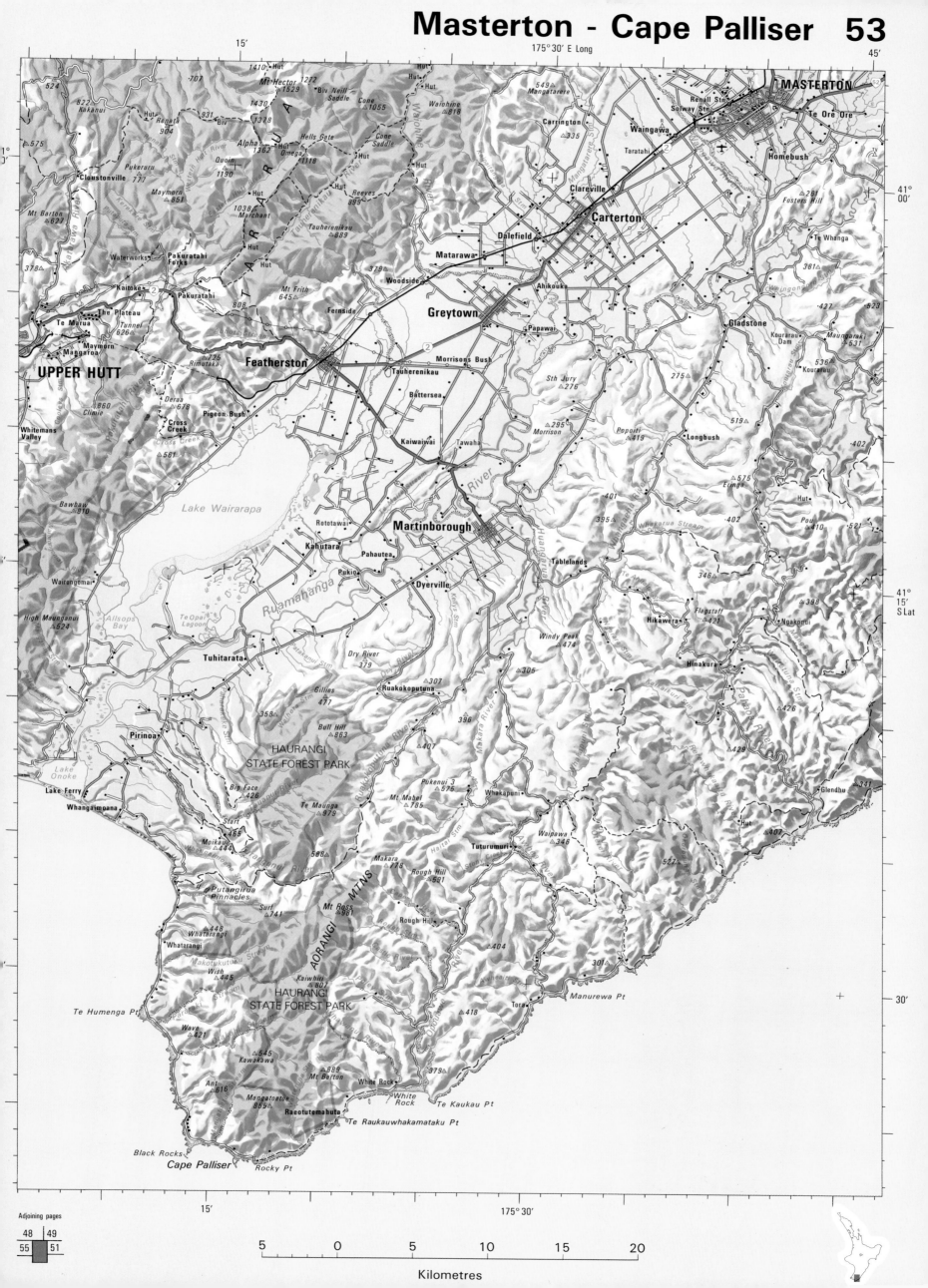

175°30' E Long

15'

45'

MASTERTON

Renall Stn
Solway Stn
Te Ore Ore

Waingawa

549△
Mangatarere

Carrington
△335

Taratahi

Homebush

△261
Fosters Hill

Clareville

Carterton

Te Whanga

Dalefield

Matarawa

Ahikouka

△361

Waiohine
△818

379△

Woodside

Greytown

Papawai

Waingongoro River

Gladstone

Kourarau
Dam

Maungaraki
△531

536△
Kourarau

Fernside

·427

·523

Mt Hector 1272
△1529

1410· Hut

Hut

Hut

Hut

Cone
△1055

Biv Neill
Saddle

1430·

·707

822△
Kakanui

·524

Regata
904

931

Biv

1378·

Alpha
△1362

Quoin
△1190

Hells Gate

Hut Omega
△1118

Cone
Saddle

Hut

Hut

Reeves
895·

Hut

1038·
Marchant

Tauherenikau
△889

Hut

Mt Barton
△627

Maymorn
△851

·575

1°
0'

41°
00'

Cloustonville 777
Pukeruru

Morrisons Bush

Tauherenikau

Sth Jury
△276

275△

519△

Popoiti
△419

Longbush

·402

Waterworks
Pakuratahi
Forks

Mt Frith
645△

808·

Battersea

Morrison

Kaitoke
Pakuratahi

295△

·401

·575
Eringa

The Plateau
Te Marua
Tunnel
626△

·725
Rimutaka

Featherston

Kaiwaiwai

Tawaha

395△

·402

Pou
△410

·521

Hut

Maymorn
Mangaroa

△860
Climie

Deraa
△678

Pigeon Bush

53

UPPER HUTT

Cross
Creek

Cross Creek

△561

Rototawai

Whangarua River

Whakarua Stream

Hut

41°
15'
S Lat

Bawbaw
△810

Lake Wairarapa

Martinborough

△346

Flagstaff
△421

398△

Hikawera

Ngakonui

High Maunganui
△524

Allsops
Bay

Te Opai
Lagoon

Kahutara

Pahautea

Pukio

Tablelands

305△

△426

Waitongomai

Ruamahanga

Dyerville

Kelly's Stm

Windy Peak
△474

Hinakura

Tuhitarata

Dry River
379

Gillies
477

△307

Ruakokoputuna

396

Pirinoa

358△

Bull Hill
△863

·407

△429

Lake
Onoke

HAURANGI
STATE FOREST PARK

Big Face
·426

Te Maunga
△979

Pukenui 3
△575

Mt Mabel
△785

Whakapuni

527△

Glendhu

△341

Lake Ferry

Whangaimoana

Start
·465

Moikau
△444

588·

Makara
△778

Rough Hill
591

Tuturumuri

Waipawa
△346

Hut

·407

Putangirua
Pinnacles

Surf
△741

Mt Ross
△961

Rough Hill

△404

AORANGI MTNS

301△

Whatarangi
·448
△445

Wish

Kaiwhiti
△807

△418

Tora

Manurewa Pt

30'

Te Humenga Pt

HAURANGI
STATE FOREST PARK

Wave
·421

△545
Kawakawa

Ant
·616

Mangatoetoe
855·

Mt Barton
△889

White Rock

379△

White
Rock

Te Kaukau Pt

Raeotutemahuta

Te Raukauwhakamataku Pt

Black Rocks

Rocky Pt

Cape Palliser

15'

175° 30'

S T R A I T

Kapiti Island
Tuteremoana △521

Te Horo Beach

Otaki

△408

Te Horo

△335 △358 *Tuapaka*

Pukeatua
Field △812
△611 *Hui Hut*

Waikanae Beach
Waikanae River
Te Au
Otaihanga △515 Waikanae

Tent △559

Kapakapanui △1102

66

Paraparaumu Beach

Reikorangi

Raumati Beach Paraparaumu
Maungakawa △382

Raumati South
402· ·509 524 822 *Kokanui*
Maunganui △708 Hut· *Reneta* △904

McKays Crossing ·575 *Deadwood*

Paekakariki *Wainui* △722 *Pukeruru*
Cloustonville 777
550· *Maymorn* △851

Pukerua Bay
Wairaka Point △262 Pukerua Bay △440
Te Rewarewa Point △219 *Porirua* Mt Barton △627
Porirua 378△ Waterworks Pakuratahi Forks

Mana Island △121
Karehana Bay
Plimmerton
Mana *Harbour* Kaitoke
468△ Birchville The Plateau
2
Titahi Bay Paremata Pauatahanui *Nabira* Brown Owi Te Marua *Tunnel*
Green Point Paremata Judgeford △431 Totara Park 626△
Open Bay Maoribank Maymorn
Rock Point *Elsdon* Mangaroa
Upper Hutt Stn
PORIRUA Porirua East Wallaceville UPPER HUTT
Deraa △678
·468 Haywards Heretaunga Trentham 860 Cross
Colonial Knob Manor Silverstream *Climie* Creek
Pipinui Point Linden Park Pinehaven
TAWA 408△ Pomare △561
Redwood Taita Stokes Blue
*Whitemans
Valley*
△303 457△ Wingate Valley Mountains
Glenside 441·
1 Normandale Melling *High Misty*
Oharlu Bay Maungaraki Avalon △717 *Bawbaw* △810
Makara Beach Paparangi Korokoro Naenae
Johnsonville Waterloo Epuni LOWER HUTT *Devine* △632
Kaukau △445 Newlands Gracefield
Khandallah PETONE *Orongorongo* △816
Ohau Pt Ngaio Ngauranga *Mowlem* △398
Ohau Hill △243 Crofton Downs Pt Howard WAINUIOMATA *Wairongomai Saddle*
968△ Wadestown Lowry Bay RIMUTAKA Wairongomai
Quartz Hill Wilton Kaiwharawhara *Somes I.* York Bay STATE FOREST PARK
·352 Makara *Lowry* △373 *Puketaha* △767
Karori Mahina Bay *Pipeline* *High Maunganui* △524
Terawhiti Hill WELLINGTON Days Bay *Allsops Bay*
△458 *412* Pt Halswell *Hawtrey* △334
Cape Terawhiti Brooklyn Ward I. Eastbourne *Puketaha*
Oteranga Bay △483 Hataitai
Mt Misery Kilbirnie Miramar △690
Outlook Hill Hawkins Hill Worser Bay *McKerrow*
△534 △450 Seatoun *Papatahi* △902
Oteranga Head 314 495△ Radar Stn Pt Dorset Mt Cameron △370 *Mt Grace*
△484 Island Bay 252 *Sugarloaf* Huts
Karori Rock ♠ Lyall Bay *Te Kopahou* Pirinoa
Thoms Rock *Palmer Head* 317· 428· *Tapokopoko* △843 *Mt Matthews* △941

Sinclair Head Pencarrow *Wharepapa*
Head *Wharekauhau* Lake Onoke

Fitzroy Bay *The Peak* △858 *R I M U T A K A*
Baring Head *Windy Point* Lake Ferry
Orongorongo Stn △492 *Fishermans Rock*
Turakirae Head *Waimatea* Whangaimoana

P a l l i s e r B a y

45' 175°00'E Long 41°00'S Lat 15'

Adjoining pages

61 | 48
60 | 53

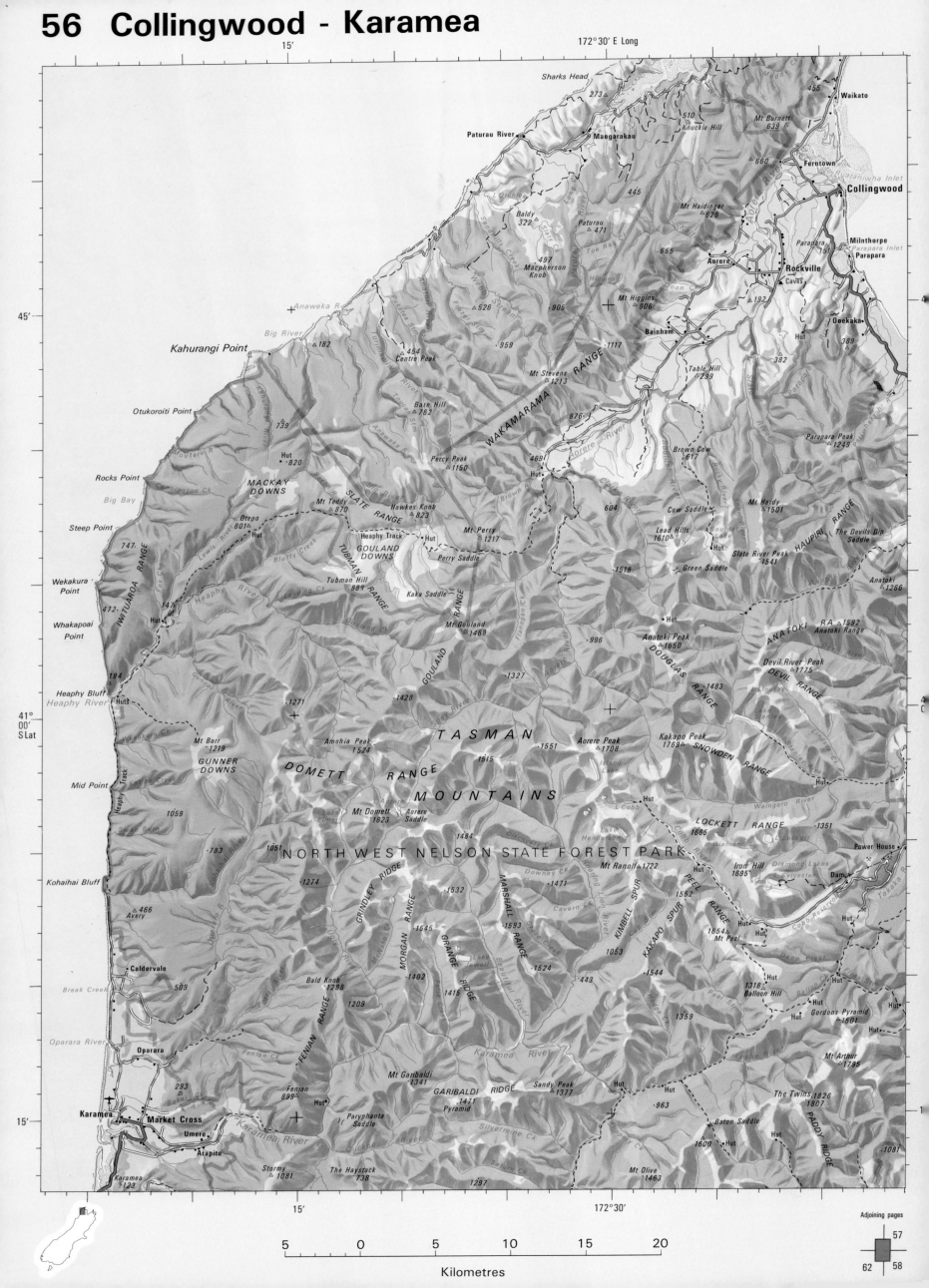

172°30' E Long

Sharks Head
273 △
455
Waikato
510
Knuckle Hill
Mt Burnett 639
Paturau River
Mangarakau
· 445
Mt Haidinger 626
· 660
Ferntown
Ruataniwha Inlet
Collingwood
L Otuhie
Baldy 322
Starry C
Paturau 471
· 655
Parapara
Milnthorpe 151
Aorere
Rockville
Parapara Inlet
Parapara
497 Macpherson Knob
· 192
Caves
Mt Higgins △ 906
Onekaka
· 905
Bainham
· 389
45'
Anaweka R
· 526
· 959
RANGE 1117
Hut
· 382
Big River
· 182
Baldy
Table Hill △ 299
Kahurangi Point
· 454 Centre Peak
Mt Stevens 1213
WAKAMARAMA
876 ·
Parapara Peak · 1249
Otukoroiti Point
· 139
Bare Hill 762
· 469
Brown Cow 617
Mt Hardy △ 1501
· 820
Percy Peak · 1150
Hut
· 604
Cow Saddle
Slate River Peak 1541
The Devils Dip Saddle
Rocks Point
MACKAY DOWNS
SLATE RANGE
Mt Teddy △ 870
Hawkes Knob △ 823
Lead Hills 1610 ·
Boulder Lake
HAUPIRI RANGE
Big Bay
Otepo 801 △
Hut
Heaphy Track
Mt Perry · 1217
Green Saddle
Hut
Anatoki △ 1266
Steep Point
747 ·
GOULAND DOWNS
Hut
· 1518
ANATOKI RA △ 1592 Anatoki Range
Wekakura Point
472 △
Tubman Hill 889
Perry Saddle
Kaka Saddle
Anatoki Peak △ 1650
Devil River Peak · 1775
DEVIL RANGE
Whakapoai Point
147 ·
TUBMAN RANGE
GOULAND RANGE
Mt Gouland · 1468
· 996
DOUGLAS RANGE
· 1483
41° 00' S Lat
Hut
· 1327
· 1428
· 1271
TASMAN
· 1551
Kakapo Peak △ 1769
SNOWDEN RANGE
Heaphy Bluff
194 ·
Heaphy River
Huts
Mt Barr · 1219
Amohia Peak · 1524
DOMETT RANGE
· 1515
Aorere Peak · 1708
Hut
GUNNER DOWNS
MOUNTAINS
Mid Point
1059 ·
L Cobb
LOCKETT RANGE 1666
· 1351
Mt Domett · 1623
Aorere Saddle
Lake Henderson
L Lockett
Power House
· 783
· 1484
NORTH WEST NELSON STATE FOREST PARK
Mt Ranolf 1722
Iron Hill 1695
Kohaihai Bluff
· 1274
GRINDLEY RIDGE
· 1532
MARSHALL RANGE
PEEL RANGE 1552
Dam
· 466 Avery
Hut
MORGAN RANGE
· 1471
Hut
· 1053
Mt Peel 1654 △
Hut
Caldervale
509 ·
Bald Knob · 1288
· 1545
GRANGE RIDGE
· 1593
· 1544
1318 · Balloon Hill
Hut
Break Creek
FENIAN RANGE
1209
· 1402
· 1415
· 1524
· 443
· 1359
Gordons Pyramid · 1501
Oparara River
Oparara
· 293
Mt Garibaldi · 1341
GARIBALDI RIDGE
Sandy Peak · 1377
Hut
Mt Arthur · 1795
Hut
Karamea
Market Cross
Fenian 899 ·
Hut
Paryphanta Saddle
1471 Pyramid
Hut
· 963
The Twins 1826 1807
15'
Umere
Stormy 1081
The Haystack 738
· 1297
Mt Olive 1463
· 1600
Hut
Baton Saddle
Hut
PADDY RIDGE
Atapito
Karamea · 123
Karamea River
1600
· 1081

Adjoining pages
57
62 | 58

5 0 5 10 15 20
Kilometres

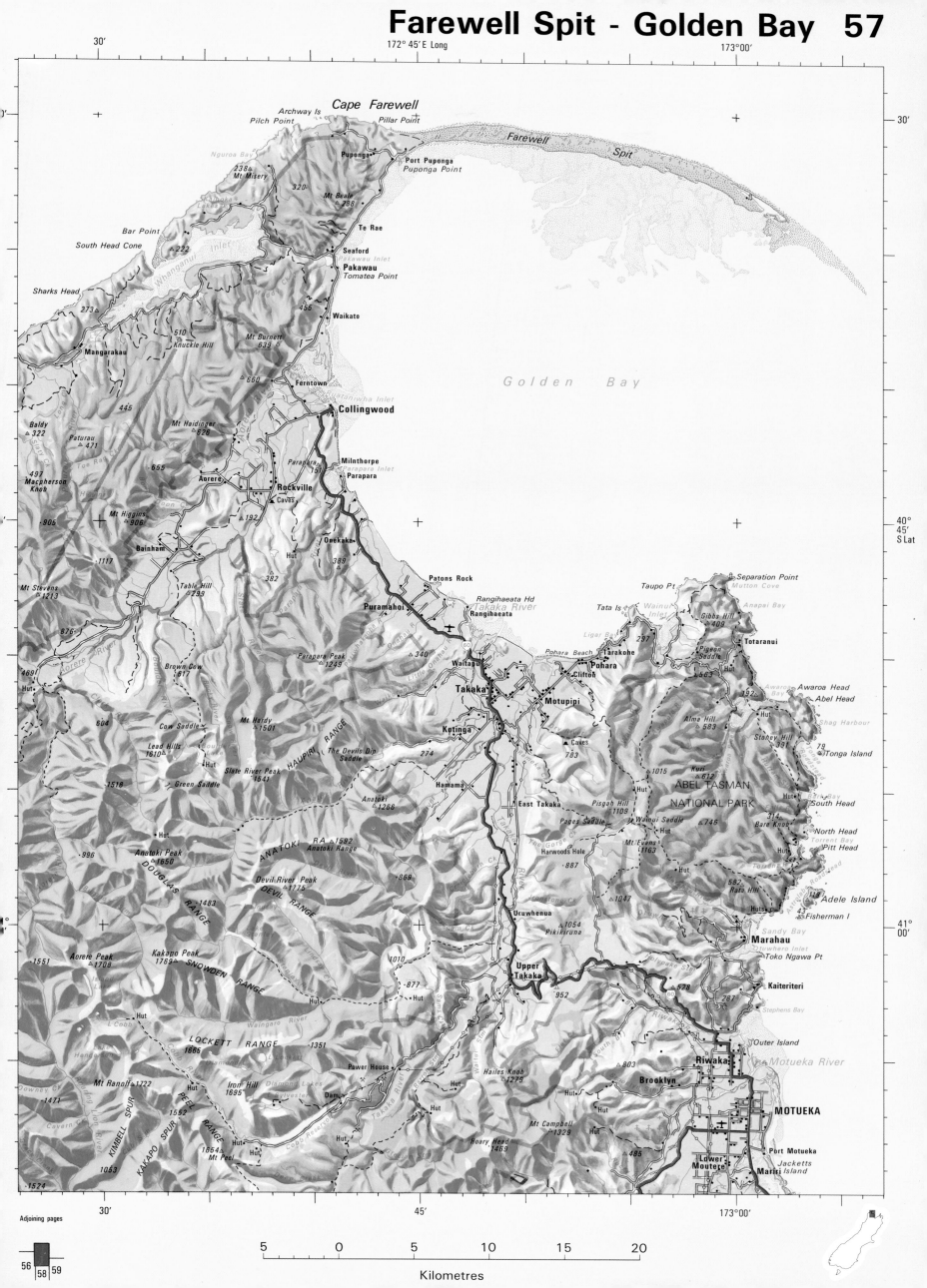

172° 45' E Long

173°00'

Cape Farewell

Archway Is
Pilch Point

Pillar Point

Farewell   *Spit*

Nguroa Bay

Puponga

Port Puponga
Puponga Point

238▲
Mt Misery
320

Mt Beale
▲ 288

Te Rae

Bar Point

Seaford
South Head Cone   △222

Pakawau
Tomatea Point

Sharks Head

273 △

Waikato

510

Mt Burnett
639 ▲

Mangarakau

Knuckle Hill

Golden   Bay

△ 660

Ferntown

445

Ruataniwha Inlet

Baldy
△ 322

Mt Haidinger
△ 626

Collingwood

Paturau
△ 471

· 655

Milnthorpe
Parapara
Parapara Inlet

497
Macpherson
Knob

Aorere

Rockville

· 905

Mt Higgins
▲ 906

△ 192

Caves

Bainham

Onekaka

Separation Point
Mutton Cove

· 1117

· 382

▲ 389

Taupo Pt

Wainu Inlet

Anapai Bay

Mt Stevens
△ 1213

Table Hill
△ 299

Patons Rock

Tata Is

Gibbs Hill
△ 409

· 876

Rangihaeata Hd
Takaka River
Rangihaeata

Ligar Bay 297

Pigeon
Saddle

Totaranui

Brown Cow
· 617

Parapara Peak
▲ 1249

· 340

60

Pohara Beach
Tarakohe

· 563

·469
Hut

Puramahoi

Waitapu

Pohara
Clifton

192

Awaroa   Awaroa Head
Bay   Abel Head

· 604

Mt Hardy
▲ 1501

Cow Saddle

HAUPIRI RANGE

The Devils Dip
Saddle

Takaka

Motupipi

274

Alma Hill
△ 583

Shag Harbour

Stoney Hill
△ 391   79

Lead Hills
1610△

Hut

Kotinga

Caves
783

ABEL TASMAN

△ 1015

Kuri
△ 612

314▲
Bare Knob

Tonga Island

Green Saddle

Slate River Peak
▲ 1541

Hamama

NATIONAL PARK

South Head

· 1518

Anatoki
△ 1266

East Takaka

Pisgah Hill
△ 1109

△ 746

North Head
Torrent Bay

Hut

ANATOKI RA △ 1592
Anatoki Range

· 869

Pages Saddle

Wainui Saddle

Pitt Head

· 996

Anatoki Peak
△ 1650

Harwoods Hole
· 887

Mt Evans
△ 1163

Hut

582·
Rata Hill

·19 Adele Island
·43 Fisherman I

DOUGLAS RANGE

Devil River Peak
△ 1775

DEVIL RANGE

· 1047

Huts

· 1483

Uruwhenua

Sandy Bay

Aorere Peak
△ 1708

Kakapo Peak
1769△

SNOWDEN RANGE

△ 1054
Pikikiruna

Marahau
Otuwhero Inlet
Toko Ngawa Pt

· 1551

1010

Upper
Takaka

· 877

· 952

60

528

287

Kaiteriteri

Stephens Bay

LOCKETT RANGE
1665

· 1351

Power House

Hailes Knob
△ 1279

· 803

Outer Island

Riwaka

Motueka River

Mt Ranolf △ 1722

Iron Hill
1695

Hut

Brooklyn

·1471

KIMBELL SPUR

KAKAPO SPUR

· 1552

PEEL RANGE

Dam

Hut

Mt Campbell
△ 1329

MOTUEKA

Port Motueka

1854△
Mt Peel

Hut

Hoary Head
1469

· 485

Jacketts
Island

· 1053

Lower
Moutere

Mariri

·1524

Adjoining pages

5   0   5   10   15   20
Kilometres

56
58 | 59

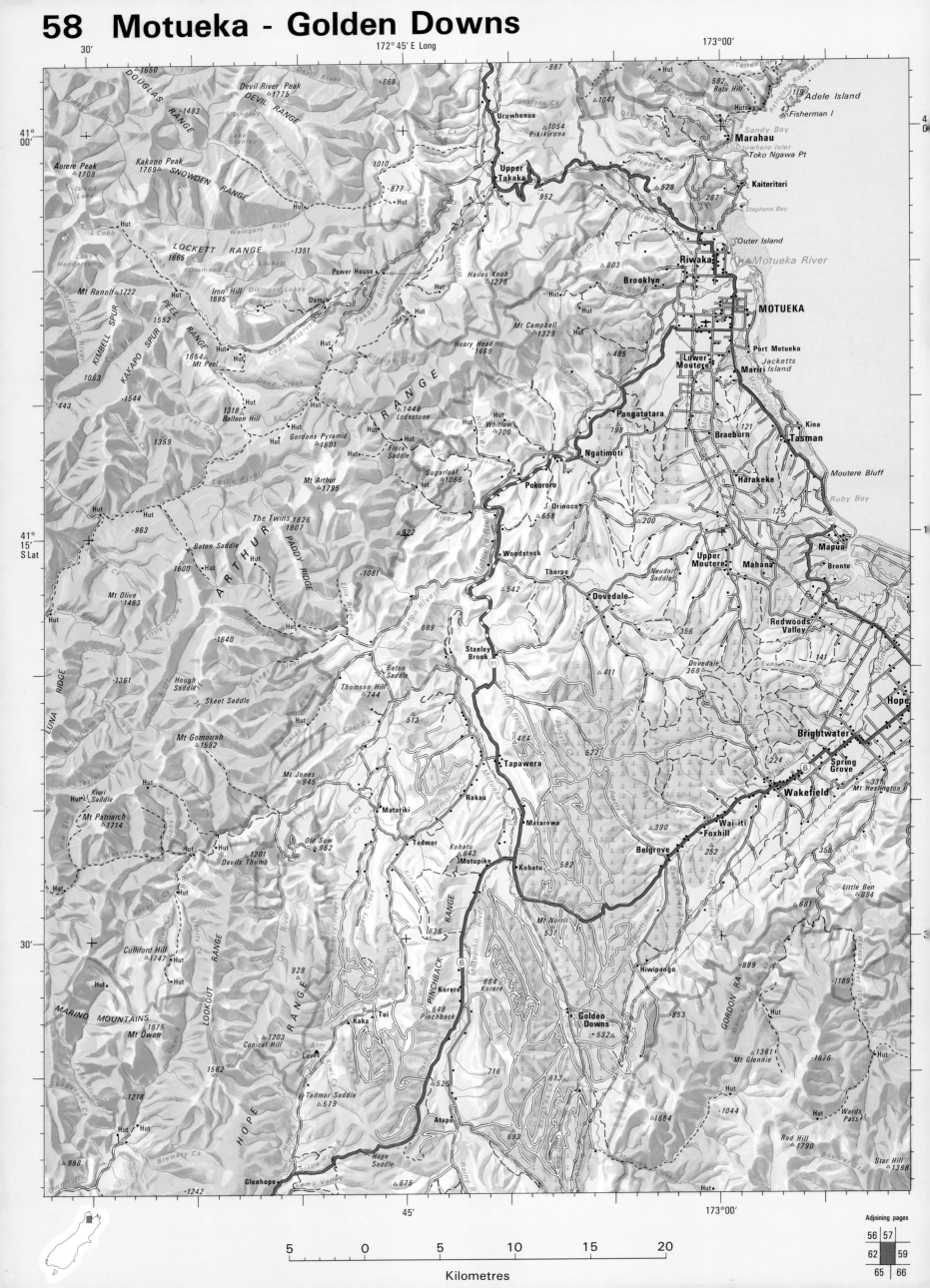

172° 45' E Long
173° 00'

30'

41° 00'

DOUGLAS RANGE
Buller Stm
·1650
Aorere Peak 1708
Island Lake
L Lindsay
Devil River Peak 1775
DEVIL RANGE
Devil River
·869
·887
Torrent River
582 Rata Hill
·119
Adele Island
43
Fisherman I

Kakapo Peak 1769
SNOWDEN RANGE
·1483
Ironstone Ck
·1047
Huts
Astrolabe Roadstead
Uruwhenua
·1054 Pikikiruna
Sam Ck
Upper Takaka
952
·877
·1010
Hut
Hut
Sandy Bay
Marahau
Otuwhero Inlet
Toko Ngawa Pt
Kaiteriteri
528
287
Stephens Bay

L Cobb
Lake Henderson
LOCKETT RANGE 1665
·1351
Diamond L
L Lockett
Iron Hill 1695
Diamond Lakes
L Sylvester
Power House
Dam
·803
Hailes Knob 1279
Outer Island
Riwaka
Brooklyn
MOTUEKA
Motueka River

Mt Ranolf 1722
PEEL SPUR 1552
Mt Peel 1654
Gordons Pyramid 1501
·1318 Balloon Hill
Grecian Stm
Hoary Head 1469
·485
Mt Campbell 1329
Port Motueka
Jacketts Island
Lower Moutere
Mariri
Pangatotara
198
Braeburn
·121
Kina
Tasman
Moutere Bluff

41° 15' S Lat
Hut
·1544
·1359
·1053
·443
KAKAPO SPUR
KIMBELL SPUR
Deep Creek
Ballon Ck
Flora Stm
RANGE
·1448 Lodestone
Flora Saddle
Hut Whitlow ·700
North Br
Ngatimoti
Pokororo
·658 Orinoco
Harakeke
125
Ruby Bay

·963
Mt Arthur 1795
The Twins 1826 1807
ARTHUR RANGE
PADDY RIDGE
Sugarloaf 1066
·922
Woodstock
Thorpe
·200
Upper Moutere
Mahana
Mapua
Bronte

Baton Saddle
·1600
Mt Olive ·1463
·1640
Leslie River
Ellis River
·1081
Baton River
689
Dove River
·542
Dovedale
Neudorf Saddle
·356
Redwoods Valley
141

Hut
·1361
Hough Saddle
Skeet Saddle
Thomson Hill 744
Baton Saddle
Stanley Brook
81
·411
Twin Valley Stm
Dovedale 368
Eves Valley Stm
Hope

Mt Gomorrah 1592
513
484
·522
Brightwater
·224
Spring Grove
6
Mt Heslington 331

Mt Jones 945
Kiwi Saddle
Mt Patriarch 1714
Matariki
Tapawera
Rakau
Mararewa
·390
Wai-iti
Foxhill
252
Belgrove
Wakefield
358
Wairoa River

·1201 Devils Thumb
Old Sow 962
Tadmor
Kohatu 643
Motupiko
Kohatu
582
·681
Little Ben 884

LOOKOUT RANGE
Culliford Hill 1747
Hut
·636
Mt Norris 531
Hiwipango
·899
·1189

MARINO MOUNTAINS
Mt Owen 1875
928
·1203 Conical Hill
Caves
PINCHBACK RANGE
Korere
664 Korere
·648 Pinchback
Tui
Kaka
Golden Downs
·532
·853
GORDON RA
·1361 Mt Glennie
·1676

HOPE RANGE
·1562
·1218
Tadmor Saddle ·579
Atapo
716
613
·1664
·1044
Red Hill 1790
Wards Pass
Star Hill 1368

·998
Hope Saddle
Glenhope
Lamb Valley
·675
693
·526
·1242

30'

45'
173° 00'

5   0   5   10   15   20

Kilometres

173°00' 173°15'E Long 30'

Tasman   Bay

Torrent Inf.
Hut
582
Rata Hill
119 *Adele Island*
Huts
43 *Fisherman I*
Sandy Bay
41°00'
Marahau
Otuwhero Inlet
Toko Ngawa Pt
Kaiteriteri
528
287
Stephens Bay

Cape Soucis
Pukerau Pt
Grahams P
Croisilles Hill
694
Whangamoa Head
409
Whangamoa Hd
Maunganui 549
Ronga Saddle
Sth Castor Peak
863

Outer Island
Motueka River
Riwaka

Pepin Island
Puketi Pt
Delaware Bay
Cable Bay
Ataata Point
401
McKay Bluff
Drumduan 657
Glenduan
Blue Hill 609
490
Gentle Annie
Whangamoa
Rai Saddle 247
Lookout 485

MOTUEKA
Port Motueka
Jacketts Island
Lower Moutere
Mariri
121
Kina
Tasman
Braeburn
Harakeke
125
Moutere Bluff
Ruby Bay

Wakapuaka
Hira
Whangamoa Saddle
506
Marybank
Atawhai
Dodsons Valley
Tui Glen
Port Nelson
Bay View
Kaka Hill 458
400
Saddle Hill 1214
Mt Duppa 1133
Smith 662
Rai Valley
Mt Rimu 625
Carluke
586
41°15'S Lat

Mapua
Bronte
Upper Moutere
Mahana
356
Rabbit Island
Bells Island
Bests Island
Waimea Inlet
Haulashore
NELSON
Tahunanui
Bishopdale
Enner Glynn
Stoke
693
652
Hut
Pelorus Bridge
Hut

Redwoods Valley
141
Dovedale 368
Hope
RICHMOND
Jenkins Hill 775
Maungatapu 1014
Little Twin 1151
Coppermine Saddle
Dun Saddle
640
792
988
Mt Bradley 602
Benbown 1043
Hut

Brightwater
224
571
Mt Malita Hut 959
939
The Rocks
1335
Banks Creek
Johnson Creek
Hut
Hut

Spring Grove
Wakefield
6
Mt Heslington 331
Goat Hill 549
Hackett Riv.
Serpentine River
Miner R
Totara Saddle
Huts
Roebuck Ck
811
Conical Knob 1204
Mt Fishtail 1643
1306 Mt Baldy
1366
Quartz Ck
Hut

Wai-iti
Foxhill
390
252
358
Hut
1283
Mt Stewart
Weka Saddle
942
Serpentine
Mt Gale 1433
Lower Saddle
1053
Mt Fell 1606
Hut
Mt Bryant
1760
Hut
1201

Belgrove
681
Little Ben 884
Hut
Waterfall Ck
Slaty Peak 1551
1414
RICHMOND
Mt Richmond
1064
956
Hut

MT RICHMOND STATE FOREST PARK
908
1128
Bishops Cap 1425
Mt Rintoul 1731
Hut
448
429
30'
899
Hut
Wairoa River
853
Hut
1189
1676
1530
860
586
441
Te Rou
Wairau Valley

1361
Mt Glennie
Hut
1044
Hut
1489
Mt Edelweiss
Lake Chalice
1387
1015
Lansdowne 452
473

1684
Hut
Wards Pass Stm
Hut
Goulter River
Mt Patriarch 1656
Hut
Wairau   River
Hillersden
Wantwood 562
832
Hut

Red Hill 1790
Patriarch
Mt Olympus 944
Sweets Saddle
Star Hill 1368
Hut

173°00' 15' 30'

5   0   5   10   15   20
Kilometres

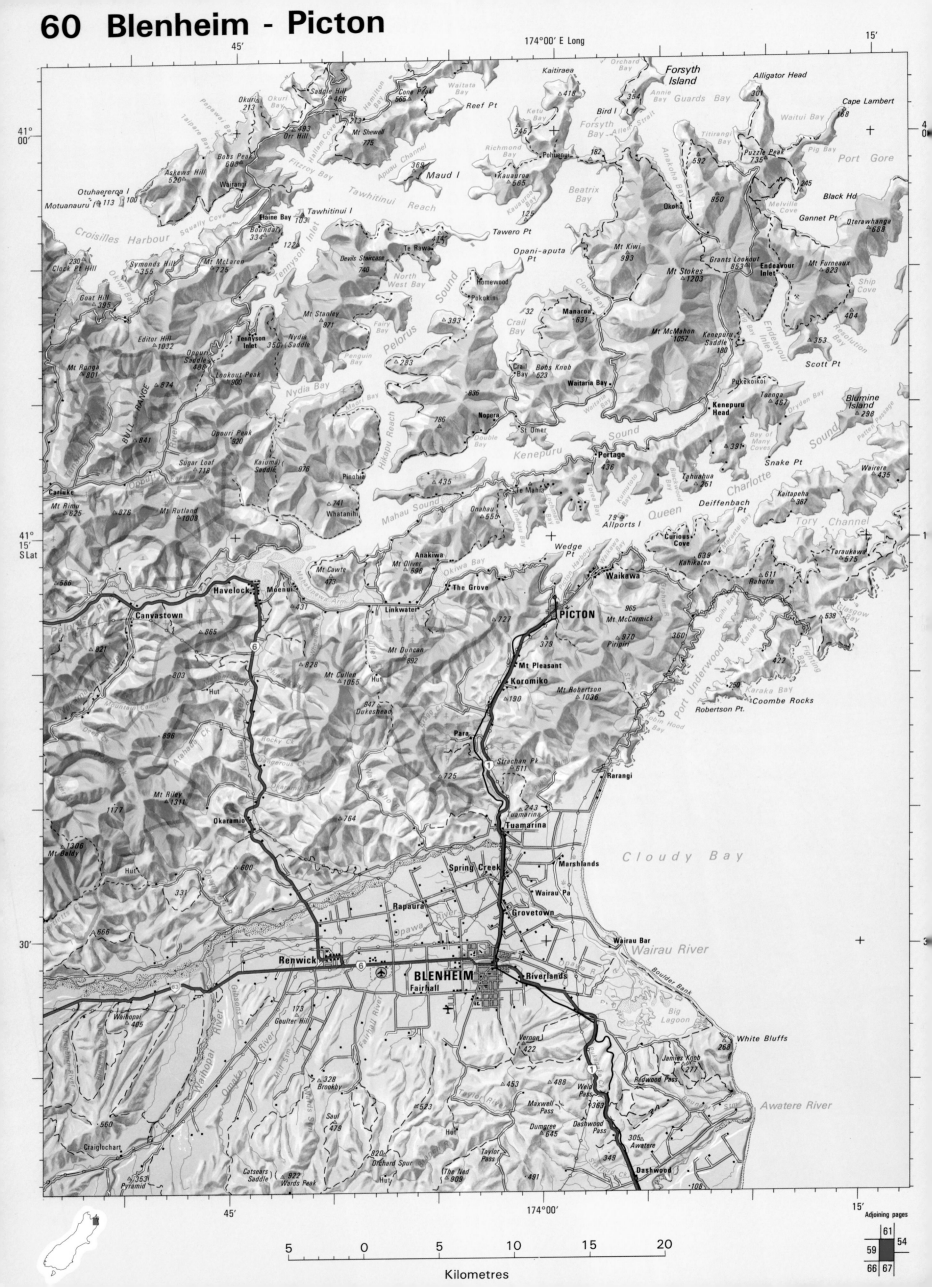

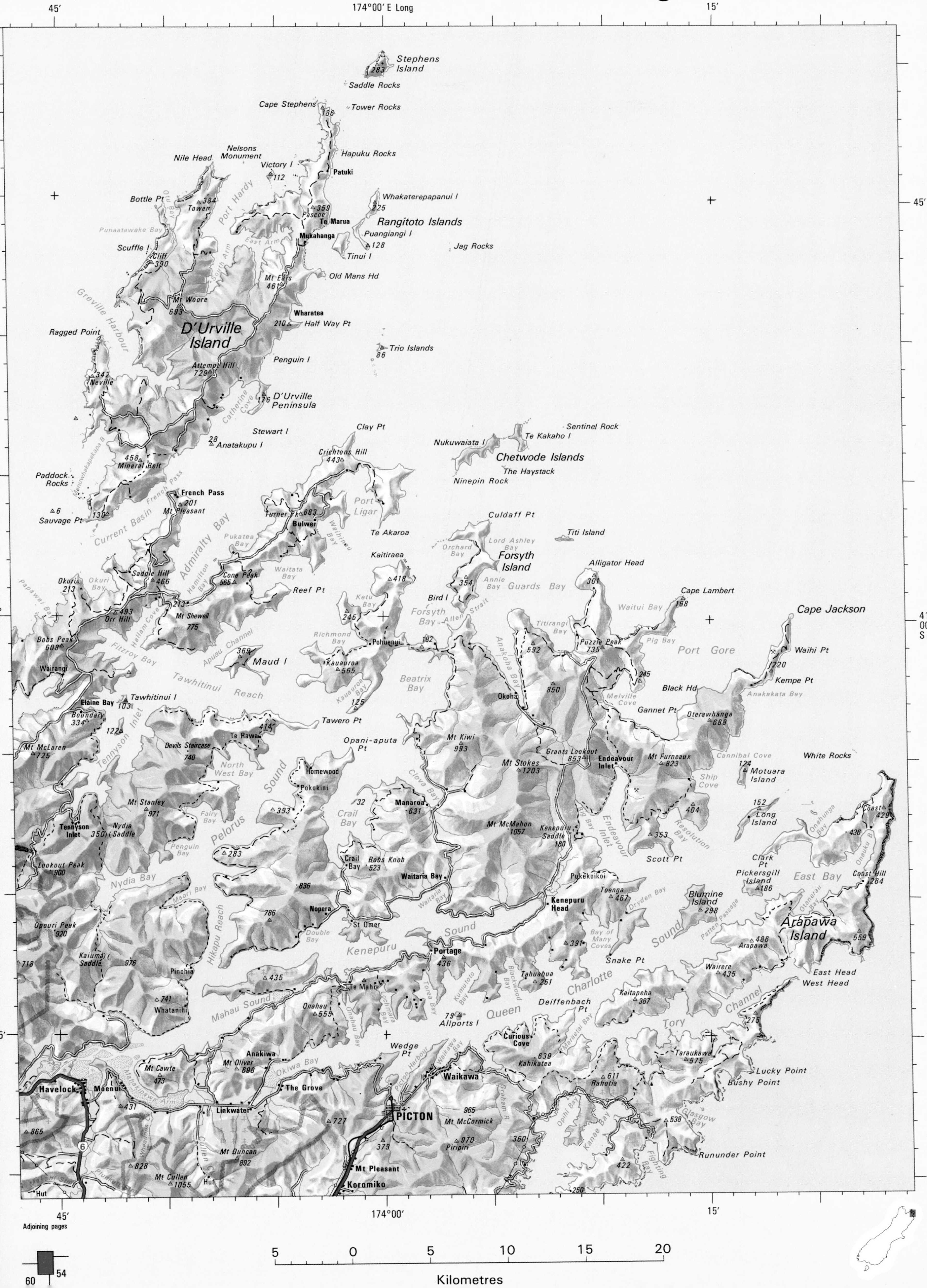

45' 174°00' E Long 15'

Stephens Island
283
Saddle Rocks
Cape Stephens
Tower Rocks
186
Hapuku Rocks
Nile Head
Nelsons Monument
Victory I
112
Patuki
Whakaterepapanui I
225
Bottle Pt
384
Tower
Port Hardy
359
Pascoe
Te Marua
Rangitoto Islands
Puangiangi I
128
Scuffle I
Cliff
390
Mukahanga
Tinui I
Jag Rocks
East Arm
Punaatawake Bay
South Arm
Mt Ears
461
Old Mans Hd
Greville Harbour
Mt Woore
693
Wharatea
210
Half Way Pt
Ragged Point
D'Urville Island
342
Neville
Attempt Hill
729
Penguin I
Trio Islands
86
D'Urville Peninsula
176
Catherine Cove
Stewart I
Clay Pt
Sentinel Rock
Te Kakaho I
Nukuwaiata I
458
Mineral Belt
28
Anatakupu I
Crichtons Hill
443
Chetwode Islands
The Haystack
Paddock Rocks
French Pass
201
Mt Pleasant
Port Ligar
Ninepin Rock
French Pass
6
Sauvage Pt
130
Current Basin
Turner Pk
683
Bulwer
Waihinau
Te Akaroa
Culdaff Pt
Titi Island
Pukatea Bay
Admiralty Bay
Kaitiraea
Orchard Bay
Lord Ashley Bay
Forsyth Island
354
Alligator Head
301
Okuria
213
Okuri Bay
Saddle Hill
466
Cone Peak
565
Waitata Bay
Reef Pt
418
Ketu Bay
Annie Bay
Guards Bay
Cape Lambert
168
Waitui Bay
Cape Jackson
493
Orr Hill
213
Mt Shewell
775
Hamilton Cove
Apuau Channel
369
Maud I
245
Bird I
Richmond Bay
Forsyth Bay
Pohuenui
182
Titirangi Bay
592
Puzzle Peak
735
Pig Bay
Port Gore
Waihi Pt
1220
Bobs Peak
608
Fitzroy Bay
Kauauroa
565
Beatrix Bay
Anakoha Bay
850
245
Black Hd
Kempe Pt
Anakakata Bay
Wairangi
Tawhitinui Reach
Kauauroa Bay
125
Okoha
Melville Cove
Gannet Pt
Oterawhanga
688
White Rocks
Elaine Bay
103
Tawhitinui I
Tawero Pt
Opani-aputa Pt
Mt Kiwi
993
Grants Lookout
853
Endeavour Inlet
Mt Furneaux
823
124
Motuara Island
Cannibal Cove
Boundary
334
122
Te Rawa
414
Devils Staircase
740
North West Bay
Homewood
Pokokini
Clova Bay
Mt Stokes
1203
Ship Cove
152
Long Island
404
Coast
429
Mt McLaren
725
Pelorus Sound
32
393
Manaroa
631
Crail Bay
Mt McMahon
1057
Kenepuru Saddle
180
353
Resolution Bay
Clark Pt
Pickersgill Island
186
Coast Hill
264
Mt Stanley
971
Fairy Bay
Crail Bay
Bobs Knob
523
Waitaria Bay
Scott Pt
Zig Zag Bay
Tennyson Inlet
350
Nydia Saddle
Penguin Bay
283
836
Waitaria Bay
Pukekoikoi
Toenga
467
Dryden Bay
Blumine Island
298
East Bay
559
Lookout Peak
900
Nydia Bay
786
Nopera
St Omer
Double Bay
Kenepuru Sound
Kenepuru Head
Bay of Many Coves
Snake Pt
Arapawa
486
Wairere
435
Arapawa Island
Opouri Peak
920
Maori Bay
Portage
436
391
Charlotte Sound
Kaiuma Saddle
976
Pinohia
435
Te Mahia
Tahuahua
251
Kaitapeha
387
East Head
West Head
718
741
Whatanihi
Mahau Sound
Onahau
555
Onahau Bay
Lochmara Bay
Torea Bay
794
Allports I
Kumutoto Bay
Deiffenbach Pt
Blackwood Bay
Queen
Tory Channel
275
5'
Anakiwa
Mt Cawte
473
Mt Oliver
598
Okiwa Bay
Wedge Pt
Curious Cove
Kahikatea
639
Taraukawa
575
Lucky Point
Bushy Point
Havelock
Moenui
The Grove
Waikawa
611
Rahotia
Glasgow Bay
865
6
431
Linkwater
727
Picton
Mt McCormick
965
970
Piripiri
360
538
Kanae Bay
Rununder Point
Mt Duncan
892
Mt Pleasant
Koromiko
379
422
Fighting Bay
Hut
Mt Cullen
1055
Hut
250

5 0 5 10 15 20

Kilometres

41°00' S Lat

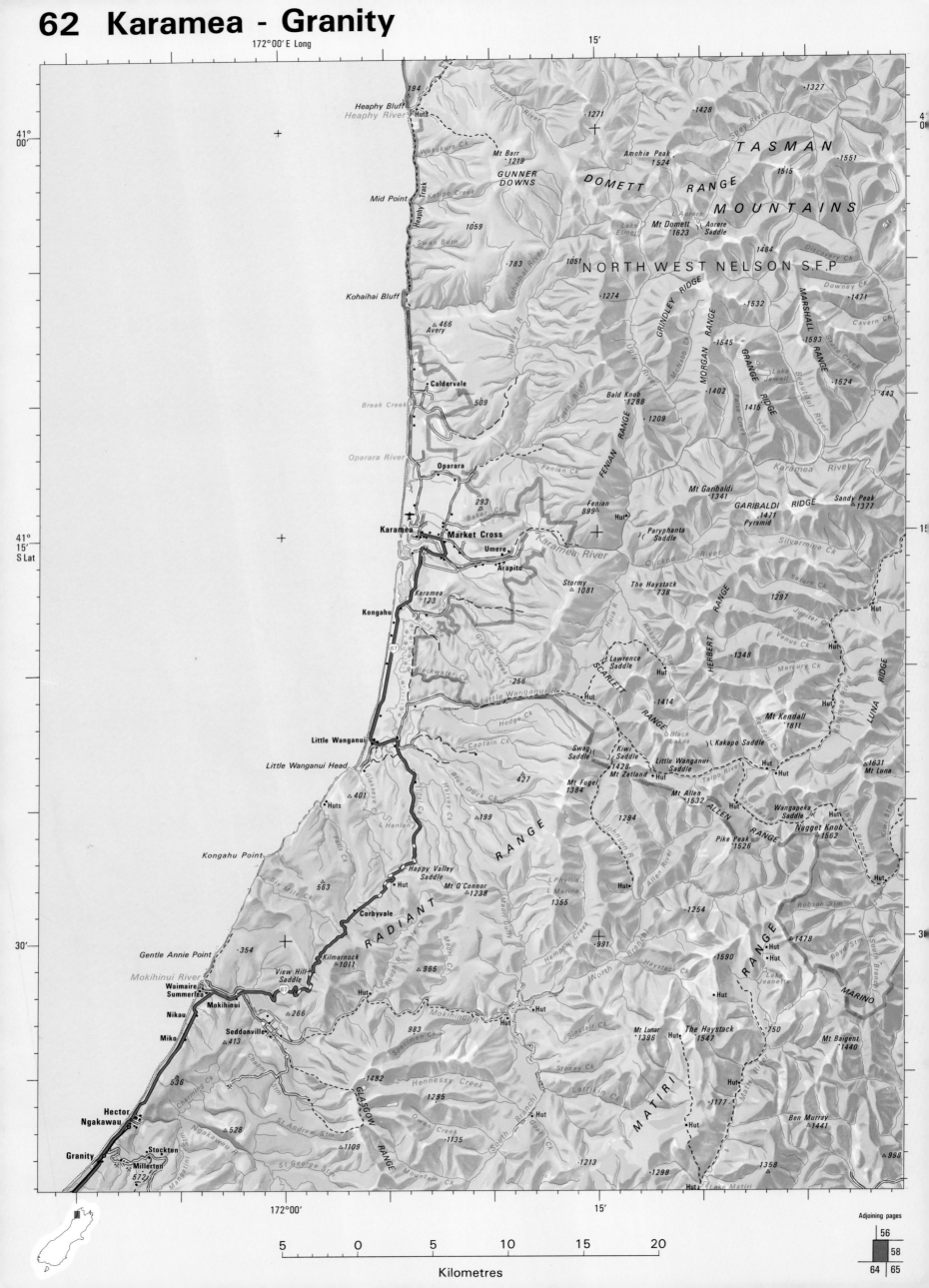

172°00'E Long

TASMAN

DOMETT RANGE MOUNTAINS

GUNNER DOWNS

NORTH WEST NELSON S.F.P

Heaphy Bluff
Heaphy River
·194
Huts

Mid Point
Heaphy Track

Wekakura Ck
Katipo Creek
Swan Burn

Gunner River
Spey River
·1327
·1271
·1428
·1551
·1515
Amohia Peak
·1524
L Aorere
Mt Domett
·1623
Aorere Saddle
·1484
Discovery Ck
Downey Ck
·1471
Cavern Ck

Mt Barr
·1219

·1059

·783
·1051

·1274

Grindley Ridge
McNabb Ck
Morgan Range
·1545
·1532
Grange Ridge
·1593
Marshall Range
·1524
False Creek
Beautiful River
·443

Kohaihai Bluff

Kohaihai River
Oparara R

△466 Avery

Caldervale

Break Creek

Oparara River

·509

Oparara

·293

Baker Ck

Fenian Ck
Fenian Range

Bald Knob
·1288
·1209
·1402
·1415

·1341
Mt Garibaldi

Karamea River

GARIBALDI RIDGE
·1471 Pyramid
Sandy Peak
△1377

Silvermine Ck

Karamea
Market Cross
Umere
Arapito

Fenian
899 △

Hut

Karamea River

Paryphanta Saddle

Cuckoo River

Saturn Ck

·1297

Hut

Jupiter Ck

Karamea
·123

Stony Ck

Kongahu

·1081 Stormy

The Haystack
738

Herbert Range

·1348

Venus Ck
Mercury Ck

Hut

Hut

Luna Ridge

Little Wanganui R

·256

Grenille Creek

Blackwater Ck

Hodge Ck

Captain Ck

Lawrence Saddle

Scarlett Range

Hula R

Katapu River

Hut

Hut

·1414

·1811 Mt Kendall

Hut

Little Wanganui

Little Wanganui Head

Glasseye Ck

△401

Huts

Blue Duck Ck

Harvey Ck

△199

427

Swag Saddle
Kiwi Saddle
·1428
Mt Zetland
Hut
Black Lakes
Kakapo Saddle
Little Wanganui Saddle
Taipo River

Hut

·1631 Mt Luna

Kongahu Point

Tidal Ck

Falls Ck

△401

L Hanlan
Six Mile Ck

△563

Happy Valley Saddle
Hut

Mt O'Connor
·1238

RADIANT RANGE

Maori Ck

1294

·199

Mt Fugel
·1384
Mt Allen
·1532

L Phyllis
L Marina
1355

ALLEN RANGE

Pike Peak
·1526

Wangapeka Saddle
Hut
Nugget Knob
△1562

Hut

Corbyvale

Gentle Annie Point

Mokihinui River

Waimaire
Summerlea

Nikau

Miko

Kilmarnock
△1011

View Hill Saddle

△354

67

△266

△965

Rough & Tumble Ck

Johnson R

Allen River

Robson Strm

·1254

△1478

Hut

Seddonville
△413

△528

·536

Maori Gully

Hempies Creek

Owen Creek

·991

Haystack Ck

North Branch

L Jeanette

·1590

·1177

MATIRI RANGE

MARINO

△1358

Mokihinui R

Specimen Ck

983

1482

1295

Hennessy Creek

Chasm Ck

St Andrew Strm

△1109

Mountain Ck

St George Strm

Stoney Ck

Sinclair Ck

Larrikin Ck

South Branch

Goat Ck

Mt Lunar
·1396

The Haystack
1547

·750

Hut

Hut

Mt Baigent
△1440

Hector
Ngakawau

Granity

Stockton

Millerton
△572

Manganui

Ngakawau River

·1213

·1135

·1298

Matiri River

Ben Murray
△1441

△998

Hut

L Matiri

GLASGOW RANGE

15'

41°00'

41°15' S Lat

41°00'

15'

30'

Adjoining pages
56
58
64 65

171° 30'E Long

45'

Karamea Bight

Buller River

Three Steeples

Black Reef

Buller Bay

Carters Beach

Westport

Fairdown

Cape Foulwind

Cape Foulwind

Tauranga Bay

Sergeants Hill

Gillows Dam

Reservoir

Power House

Lake Rochfort

Birchfield

1010 Mt Augustus

748 Mt Stockton

1106 Mt Frederick

824

407

Dam

Hut

Waimangaroa

Conns Creek

Denniston

869

Burnetts Face

1062 Mt William

Hut

512

Huts

Blue Duck Ck

ADDISONS FLAT

55

Dam

53

Organs

Coal Creek

796

Te Kuha

1038 Mt Rochfort

Cascade

MT WILLIAM RANGE

786

Mt Waller 198

Mt Courtney 373

VIRGIN FLAT

155

Waimea Ck

Island Creek

Omanu Creek

1004

1023

587

Sinclairs Castle

Mt Cassin 706

Lower Buller Gorge

Hawk's Crag

639

644

Tiroroa

Rahui

340 Mt Burley

Berlins

Berlins Bluff 741

Rocklands 401

Inangahua Junction

Oweka

465

Okari River

Okari Lagoon

Nine Mile Beach

Totara River

Mountain Creek

Hut

665

Needle 1288

Buckland Ck

Ohikanui River

960

Ayesha Stm

Jess Ck

Hard Creek

Inangahua Landing

239

135

Charleston

233

289

Hut Ananui Caves

Little Totara River

Tailings Creek

O'Keefe Ck

Mt Kelvin 1434

Beta Creek

Gamma Creek

Delta Creek

Mt Galileo 1265

564

1135

983

387

Rotokohu 312

Needle Point

253

312

457

401

Madmans Ck

Awakari River

Waitakere River

Aranui Creek

Mt Euclid 1440

1410

Three Sisters 1372

Morgan Tops

Denis Creek

Eta Creek

1050

1204

1257

1076

1227

Mt Copernicus

1149

McMurray Ck

Fletcher Ck

Cells Creek

282

Larrys Creek

198

42° 00' S Lat

Woodpecker Bay

Seal Island

Kaipakati Point

Tiromoana

373

419

Atbara Creek

Sirdar Creek

RANGE

Mt Einstein 1349

Iota Ck

1525 Mt Uriah

1333

Bird Ck

Te Wharau

255

Cronadun

329

Pahautane

Fox River

Bessons Dam

472

Cave Creek North

Wagon Ck

Mt Curie 1349

1485 Mt Faraday

1486 Mt Micawber

Mt Steele 1303

1425 Mt Stevenson

Giles Creek

Miamai Creek

Capleston

Waitahu

401

713

Hatters Bay

Meybille Bay

Te Miko

Perpendicular Point

Porarari

Fossil Creek

328

Dilemma Creek

Mt Priestly 1394

1394

Morrison Ck

Mills Ck

Mt Epping 1454

1362 Mt Raoulia

427

Reefton

Taipoiti

465

Reefton Saddle

Blacks Point

Crushington 716

Punakaiki

Dolomite Point

Blowholes, Pancake Rocks

Razorback Point

368

Bullock Ck

Pororari River

831

1252 Mt Bovis

1257

Mt Dewar 1433

Mt Ramsay 1410

1455 Mt Lodge

PAPAROA

Gordon Creek

1288 Mt Wise

1281

Rough River

MAIMAI PLAINS

Maimai

Tawhai

Stony Creek

Bell Creek

569

357

Mawheraiti River

Slab Hut Creek

Antonios Ck

Progress Junction

556

663

Lawson Ck

259

659

953

Tindale Creek

Mt Johnston 1250

Mt Pecksniff 1295

1280 Mt Marshall

Mirfin Creek

Hinau

379

Merrijigs

772

213

White Knight 1227

1190 Hawera

Pike Stream

564

Craigieburn Creek

Mawheraiti

Mawheraiti

Waimaunga

Blackwater R.

586

881

Big River 838

1021

1065

1135

Slaty Ck

442

Burton Ck

Hukarere

Blackwater

Hut

621

Deep Ck

Barrytown

82

1070 Mt Anderson

1104

Big River

Hatpin Creek

Doolan Ck

198

Mossy Ck

Snowy River

Seventeen Mile Bluff

1220 Mt Ryall

1074

Deadmans Ck

Ikamatua

IKAMATUA PLAIN

Hukawai

Bald Hill 1191

Ten Mile Ck

1212 Croesus Knob

Mt St Patrick 1082

358

Craigieburn

Mullighi Creek

Grey River

Totara Flat

336

Duffers

Granville 419

Waipuna

Waiuta

569

Greigs

Raupo

Slaty Creek

Nobles

171° 30'

45'

15'

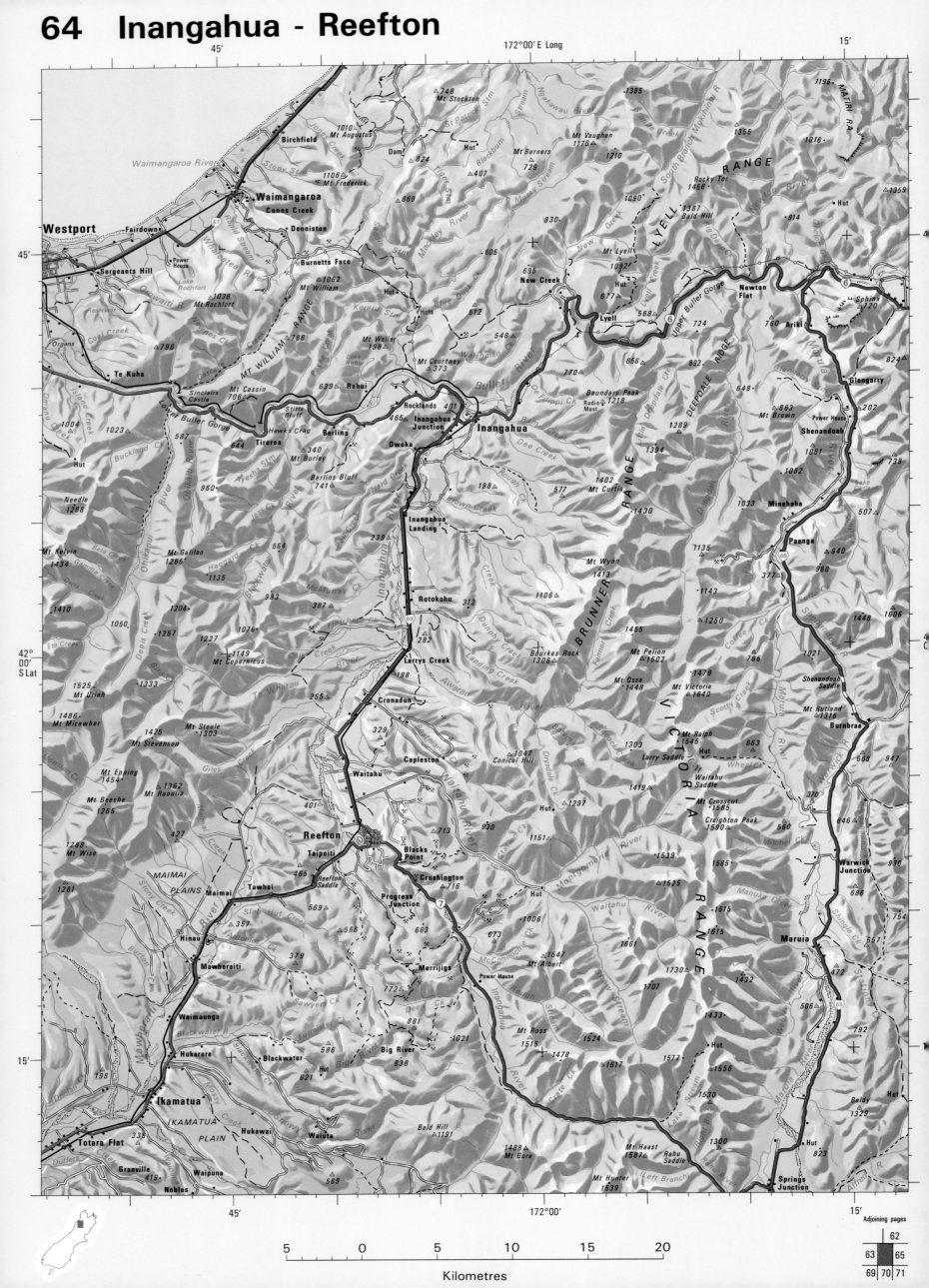

64 Inangahua - Reefton

172°00'E Long

45'

15'

Westport

Waimangaroa

Conns Creek

Birchfield

Fairdown

Denniston

Sergeants Hill

Burnetts Face

Te Kuha

Mt William

Mt Rochfort

LYELL RANGE

MATIRI RA

Mt Stockton △748

Mt Augustus 1010

Dam

Hut

Blackburn

Mt Berners 729

Mt Vaughan 1176

Mt Frederick 1106

△824

△407

△869

Mt Lyell 1092

New Creek

Rocky Tor 1456

Bald Hill 1387

Hut

△1359

Lyell

Newton Flat

Upper Buller Gorge

Ariki

Sphinx 720

Sinclairs Castle

Mt Cassin 706

Rahui 639

Rocklands 401

Inangahua Junction

Inangahua

Boundary Peak 1218

Mt Brown △863

Glengarry

△202

Berlins

Oweka

Tiroroa

Hawk's Bluff

Stitts Bluff

Mt Burley 340

Shenandoah

△1051

Minehaha

Mt Galileo 1265

Berlins Bluff 741

△239

Inangahua Landing

△198

△577

Mt Curtis 1402

△1430

△1033

Paenga △940

Rotokohu △312

Mt Wynn 1413

△1135

△1250

△1606

△1448

△1021

Larrys Creek △282

△198

Bourkes Rock 1306

Mt Pelion 1502

Mt Ossa 1448

Mt Victoria 1640

Shenandoah Saddle

Cronadun △255

Conical Hill 1047

Mt Ralph 1545

Hut

Mt Rutland 1315

Burnbrae

Capleston

△329

Waitahu

Larry Saddle

△663

△668

△947

Reefton

Taipoiti

Blacks Point

Crushington

△930

Hut

Waitahu Saddle

Mt Crosscut 1585

Creighton Peak 1590

△560

△646

Warwick Junction

△930

△686

Tawhai

Maimai

Progress Junction

△663

△673

△1006

△1539

△1585

△1615

Maruia

△754

△657

Hinau

Mawheraiti

Merrijigs △772

Power House

Mt Albert 1547

△1661

△1730

△1707

△1432

△1433

△472

Waimaunga

Big River △838

Bald Hill 1191

△1021

Mt Ross 1516

△1524

△1577

△1556

△1617

Hukarere

Blackwater

Waiuta

Mt Gore 1488

Mt Haast 1587

Rahu Saddle

△1300

△823

Ikamatua

Hukawai

Mt Hunter 1539

Springs Junction

Totara Flat

Granville

Waipuna

Nobles

Adjoining pages

	62	
63	70	65
69	70	71

Kilometres

5   0   5   10   15   20

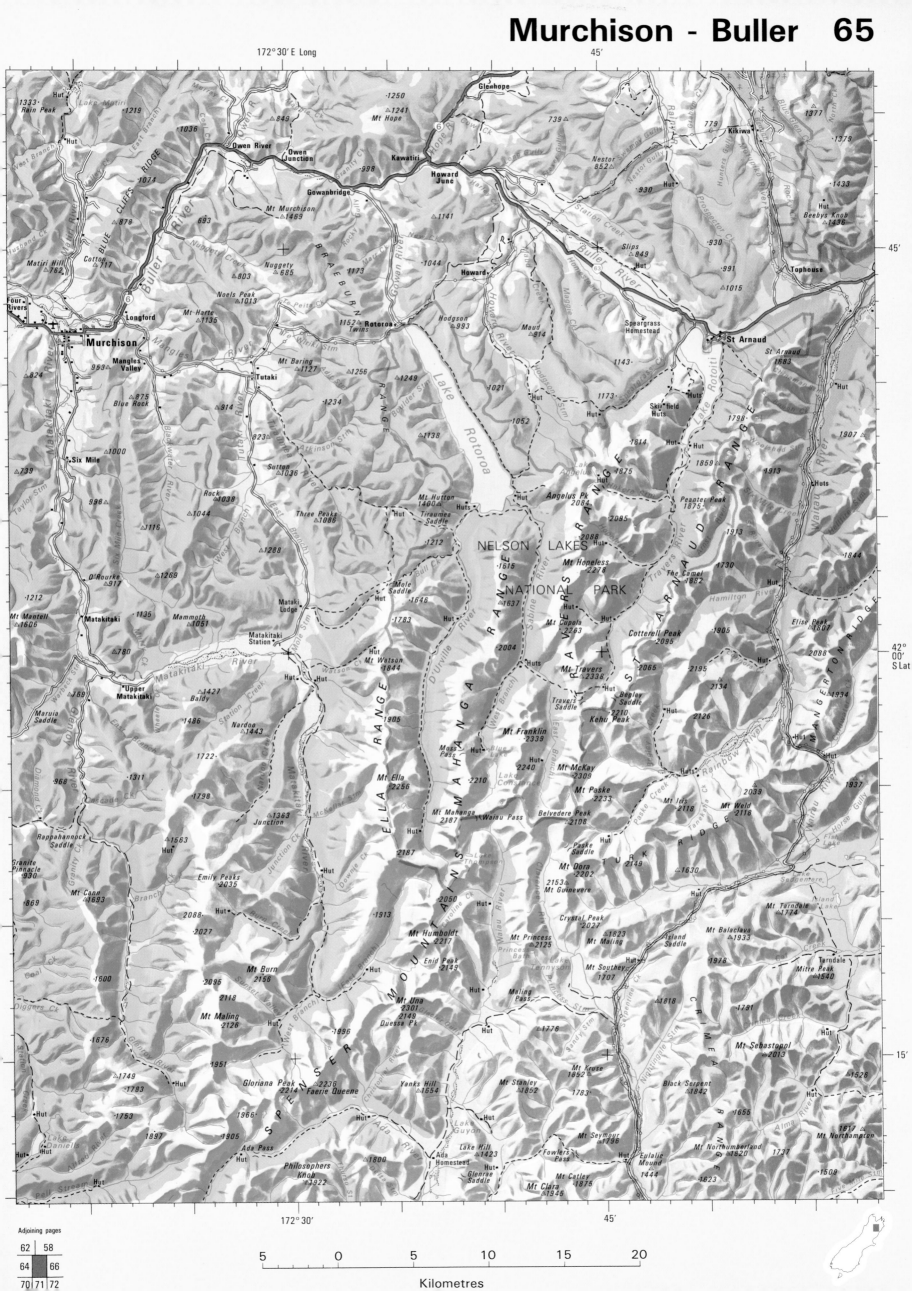

172°30' E Long
45'

1333 Rain Peak
Hut
·1219
Lake Matiri
Murray Creek
·1250
·1241 Mt Hope
Glenhope
739 △
Kikiwa
1377
·1379

Coal Ck
Owen River (East Branch)
·849
998·
Kawatiri
·1036
Nestor 852
Hut
·930
779
·1433

BLUE CLIFFS RIDGE
·1074
·878
693
Owen River
Owen Junction
Gowanbridge
Howard Junc
Station Creek
930·
·991
·1436 Beebys Knob
Hut

Husband Ck
West Branch
·117 Cotton
Mt Murchison ·1469
·1173
·1141
Howard
Buller River
·1015
Tophouse

Matiri Hill △762
Nuggety 685·
△803 Noels Peak ·1013
·1044
Maud Ck
Hamilton Ck
Speargrass Homestead
St Arnaud

Four Rivers
Longford
Mt Harte △1135
Te Peits Ck
1152△ Rotoroa Twins
Hodgson △993
·1143
Hut
·1173
Ski field Huts
St Arnaud 1683

Murchison
953·
Mangles Valley
·1256
△1249
Gowan River
Howard River
·1021
Hut
·1798
Hut
Hut

△824
△875 Blue Rock
△914
·1234
Mt Baring ·1127
Adit Stm
·1052
Lake Angelus
·1814
·1859
·1913
·1907

·739
·1000 Six Mile
·823
Sutton ·1036
·1138
△1875
Huttinkere Stm

·998
Rock △1038
Three Peaks ·1086
Mt Hutton 1400
Tiraumea Saddle
Hut
Angelus Pk 2084
·2095
Peanter Peak 1875
·1913
·1844

△1116
△1044
·1288
·1212
Hut
Bull Ck
·1615
·1637
·2088
Mt Hopeless 2278
NELSON LAKES NATIONAL PARK
The Camel 1882
Hamilton River
·1730
Hut
Elise Peak △1807

Mt Mantell △1606
Matakitaki
·1135
Mammoth ·1051
Mataki Lodge
Mole Saddle
·1646
·1783
Mt Cupola ·2263
Huts
Cotterell Peak 2095
·1905
·2195
·2088
·2134
△1934

△780
Matakitaki Station
Mt Watson ·1844
·2004
Huts
Mt Travers ·2338
·2065
·2126
·2039
·1937

·769 Upper Matakitaki
△1427 Baldy
·1905
Travers Saddle
Begley Saddle
Kehu Peak
Huts

Maruia Saddle
·1486
Nardoo △1443
Mt Franklin 2339
Moss Pass
Mt McKay ·2309
Mt Iris 2118
Mt Weld 2118

·968
·1722
·1311
·1798
Mt Ella 2256
·2210
Blue Lake
·2240
Mt Paske ·2233
Belvedere Peak 2108
Huts

Rappahannock Saddle
·1563
Junction ·1363
Mt Mahanga 2187
Waiau Pass
Lake Constance
Paske Saddle
Mt Dora ·2202
·2149
·1630

Granite Pinnacle ·930
Emily Peaks 2035
·2187
Lake Thompson
·2153 Mt Guinevere
TURK RIDGE
Mt Tarndale 1774

Mt Cann △1693
·869
·2088
·2027
·1913
Crystal Peak ·2027
△1823 Mt Maling
Island Saddle
Mt Balaclava △1933

·1600
Mt Burn 2156
·2095
Mt Humboldt 2217
Enid Peak 2149
Mt Princess 2125
·1978
Tarndale Mitre Peak △1540

·1676
·2118
·2050
Mt Una 2301
2149 Duessa Pk
Princess Bath
Lake Tennyson
Mt Southey 1707
△1818
·1791

SPENSER MOUNTAINS
Mt Maling ·2126
·1996
Maling Pass
·1776
Mt Sebastopol ·2013

·1749
·1951
Gloriana Peak 2236 Faerie Queene
Yanks Hill 1654
Mt Kruse 1852
·1783
Black Serpent △1842
·1526

·1783
·1753
·1966
·1905
Ada Pass
Mt Stanley 1852
·1655
·1617 Mt Northampton

Lake Daniells
Hut
·1897
Philosophers Knob ·1922
·1800
Lake Hill △1423
Ada Homestead
Glenrae Saddle
Fowlers Pass
Mt Seymour 1796
Eulalie Mound 1444
Mt Northumberland △1820
1737
·1509

Mt Clara 1945
Mt Catley 1875
·1623

172°30'
45'
15'
42°00' S Lat
45'

Adjoining pages

62	58
64	66
70	71	72

5   0   5   10   15   20
Kilometres

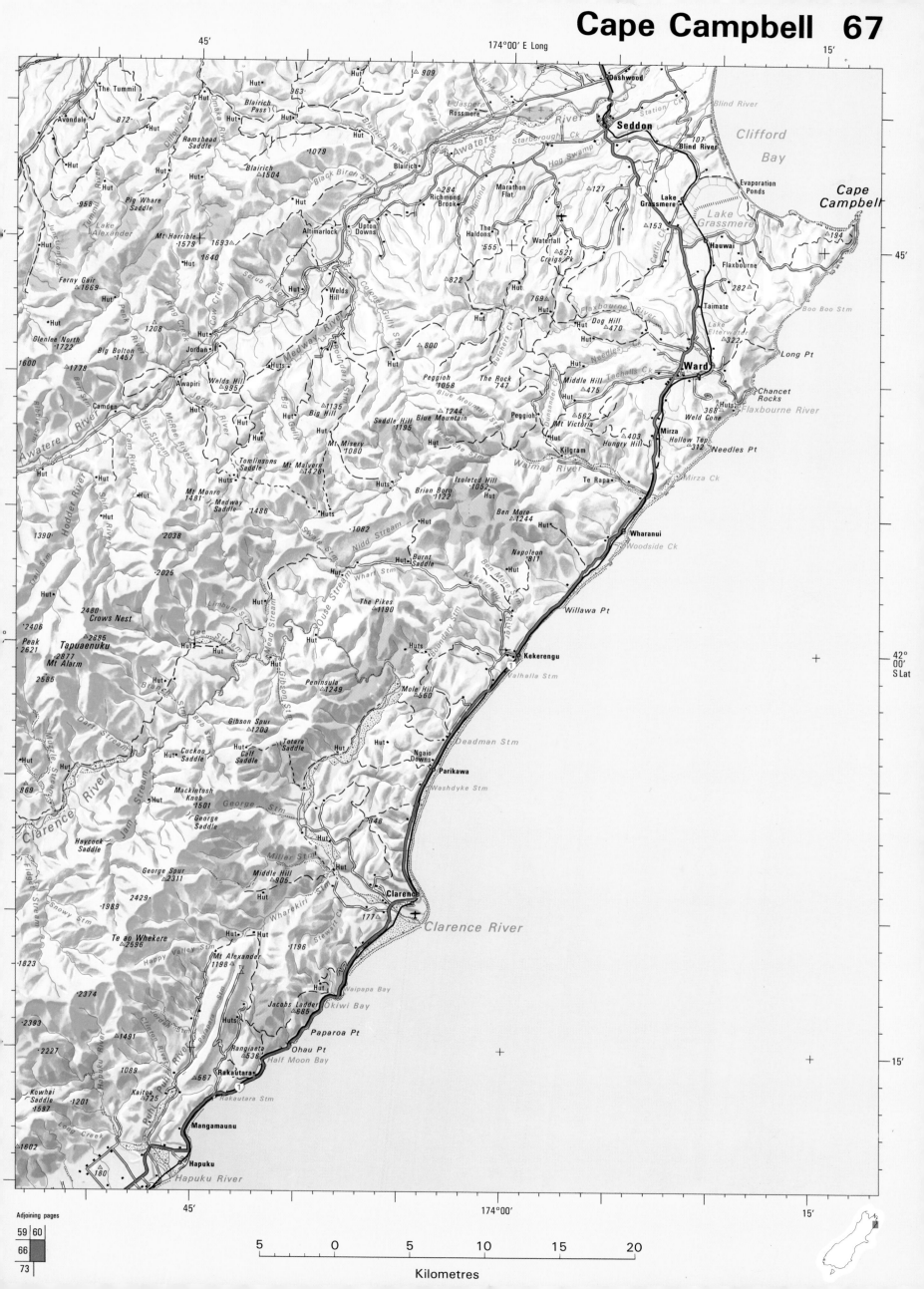

Cape Campbell

Clifford Bay

Blind River

Dashwood

Seddon

Blind River

107

Clifford Bay

Evaporation Ponds

Lake Grassmere

Lake Grassmere

Hauwai

194

Flaxbourne

282

Boo Boo Stm

The Tummil

Avondale

872

The Tummil

Hut

Hut

Blairich Pass

Hut

563

Hut

909

Nine Brook

I. Jaspers

Rossmore

Awatere River

Station Ck

Ramshead Saddle

Hut

1079

Blairich

1504

Black Birch Stm

Blairich River

Blairich

Richmond Brook

Richmond Brook

284

Marathon Flat

Marathon Flat

Hog Swamp Ck

Starborough Ck

127

Lake Grassmere

153

Cattle Ck

Pig Whare Saddle

958

Lake Alexander

Mt Horrible

1579

1693

1640

Altimarlock

Upton Downs

Hut

Hut

822

The Haldons

555

Waterfall

521

Craigs Pk

769

Hut

Dog Hill

470

Hut

Flaxbourne River

322

Lake Elterwater

Taimate

Long Pt

Ferny Gair

1669

Hut

Cow Creek

Scrub Road

Welds Hill

Hut

Ring Creek

1208

Jordan

Medway River

Boundary Stm

Hut

800

Butchers Ck

Hut

Hut

Needles Stm

Ward

Chancet Rocks

Weld Cone

368

Flaxbourne River

Glenlee North

1722

Big Bolton

1457

1600

1778

Awapiri

Welds Hill

995

Jordan River

Big Hut Gully

1135

Big Hill

Saddle Hill

1195

Peggioh

1058

The Rock

747

Blue Mountain Stm

1244

Blue Mountain

Peggioh

Middle Hill

475

Mt Victoria

562

Dunsandel Ck

Tachells Ck

Mirza

Hollow Top

312

Needles Pt

Camden

McRae River

Cam River

Isis Stream

Hut

Shin River

Hut

1390

Hodder River

Tail Stm

Welds Hill

Hut

Huts

Mt Misery

1080

Hut

Ferngule Stm

Kilgram

Hungry Hill

403

Te Rapa

Mirza Ck

Tomlinsons Saddle

Mt Malvern

1426

Huts

Brian Boru

1122

Isolated Hill

1052

Hut

Waima River

Mt Monro

1481

Medway Saddle

1486

Swale Stm

Nidd Stream

1082

Hut

Ben More

1244

Hut

Wharanui

Woodside Ck

2038

2025

Burnt Saddle

Hut

Wharf Stm

Napoleon

811

Hut

Ben More Stm

Kekerengu River

Crows Nest

2480

Limburn Stm

Mead Stream

Ouse Stream

Hut

The Pikes

1190

Hut

Huts

Boundary Stm

Willawa Pt

2406

Peak

2621

Tapuaenuku

2895

2877

Mt Alarm

2585

Dee Stream

Hut

Hut

Gibson Stm

Huts

Kekerengu

1

Valhalla Stm

Snow Bob Stm

Peninsula

1249

Mole Hill

560

Hut

Deadman Stm

Dart Stream

Branch

Hut

Hut

Gibson Spur

1203

Hut

Calf Saddle

Totara Saddle

Hut

Ngaio Downs

Parikawa

869

Hut

Hut

Cuckoo Saddle

Hut

George Stm

Hut

Washdyke Stm

Clarence River

Mackintosh Knob

1501

George Saddle

948

Hut

Jam Stream

Haycock Saddle

George Spur

2311

Middle Hill

905

Miller Stm

Hut

Wharekiri

Clarence

171

Clarence River

Snowy Stm

1989

2429

1196

Stewart Ck

Te ao Whekere

2596

Hut

Hut

1823

Happy Valley Stm

Mt Alexander

1198

TV

2374

Waipapa Bay

Hut

2393

1491

Jacobs Ladder

685

Okiwi Bay

Jordan River

Paraewa Stm

2227

Rangiaeta

536

Ohau Pt

Paparoa Pt

1089

Rakautara

567

Half Moon Bay

Puhi Puhi River

Kowhai Saddle

1597

1201

Kaitoa

725

Rakautara Stm

1

1602

Mangamaunu

Hapuku

180

Hapuku River

Long Creek

Clinton River

Hapuku River

171°00'E Long

Fourteen Mile Bluff

Greigs
Motukiekie Rocks
320
564
Nine Mile Bluff
637
Rapahoe
Point Elizabeth
343
Dunollie
493
Runanga
297
Coal Creek
Batty Ck
Bridge Creek
Cobden
Taylorville
Grey River
62
Blaketown
Greymouth
Omoto
Dobson
Karoro
Kaiata
Boddytown
343
343
South Beach
KAIATA RANGE
Paroa
Kakawau
447
Rutherglen
Gladstone
Shanty Town
Welshmans
Camerons
Marsden
Taramakau River
Kumara Junction
Greenstone River
Foleys Ck
226
Chesterfield
40
Racecourse
Kumara
Greenstone
Waimea Creek
Power House
320
Awatuna
Power House
Dillmanstown
Taramakau
Arahura River
Callaghans
Dam
73
Hohonu
Kaihinu
Arahura Stn
Stafford
270
Kapitea Resvr
Houhou
Goldsborough
Seaview
Arahura
390
Kumara Reservoir
Blue Spur
Kawhaka
Lake Mudgie
Hokitika
Okuku Reservoir
Turiwhate
Hokitika River
Humphreys
351
1369
Mt Turiwhate
Takutai
Kennedy Ck
Arthurstown
Kaniere
366
Island Hill
989
Mananui
Woodstock
Kanieri
Power House
Kawhaka Pass
Lake Tarleton
Rimu
396
427
Milltown
Sandstone Ck
Blue Bottle Ck
Hut
Waitihinihi Creek
20
L Mahinapua
Butchers Ck
Hans
1125
Huts
Frosty Ck
Tuhua
1059
Ruatapu
770
Biv
Groves Swamp
829
Mt Graham
Lake Kaniere
Hut
Ogilvie Lagoon
Kokatahi
Hut
1059
Slip Bay
Mt Brown
Huts
Hut
Camp Creek
Duck Creek
NEWTON RANGE
Hut
Kowhitirangi
229
1318
Biv
Mt Camelback
561
Styx River
Huts
Donoghues
Mt Harry
351
Hut
BROWNING RA
Mt Lathrop
Ross
617
Hut
1859
1905
Mikonui River
229
One Tree Saddle
Cairn Peak
366
777 Round Top
1242
Genoa Pk Biv
Hut
Biv
1509
808
Wilson Saddle
716
686
Doctor Hill
922
Mt Diedrich
1084
1608
Mt Reeves
1783
Mt Griffiths
2057
Waitaha River
168
Mt Greenland
905
Hut
Biv
Mt Misery
1615
Biv
Zit Saddle
Mt Camsell
2118
Griffiths Saddle
Kakapotahi
Fergusons
Murray Saddle
Biv

171°00'

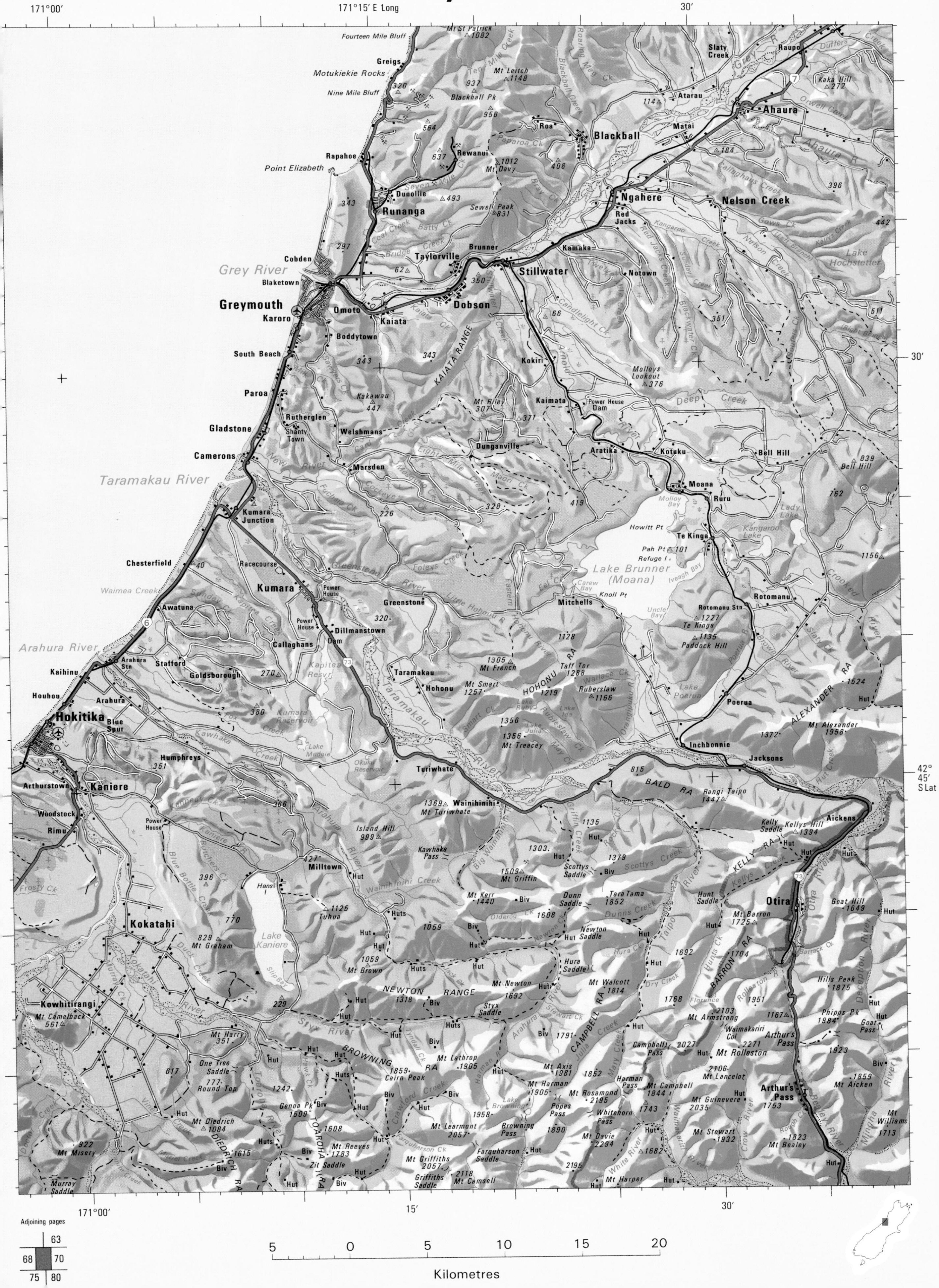

171°00' 171°15' E Long 30'

Fourteen Mile Bluff
Mt St Patrick △1082
Greigs
Motukiekie Rocks
Nine Mile Bluff 320
Ten Mile Creek
Mt Leitch △1148
937
Blackhall Pk Roaring Meg Ck
Blackball Creek
956
564 Roa 114△
Atarau
Slaty Creek
Raupo Duffers Creek
Grey R
Kaka Hill △272
Ahaura
Rapahoe 637 Rewanui 1012 Mt Davy 408 Paparoa Range Blackball Matai 184
Point Elizabeth
343 Dunollie △493
Runanga Seven Mile Sewell Peak △831
Ngahere Nelson Creek 396
Bray Ck
Red Jacks Red Jacks Creek Kangaroo Creek 442
Grey River Cobden 297 Coal Creek Batty Ck Brunner
Taylorville 62 Stillwater Kamaka Notown Twelve Mile Ck 511
Blaketown 350 Dobson Candlelight Ck Sunday Ck Blackwater Ck Lake Hochstetter
Greymouth Omoto 66
Karoro Kaiata Kokiri 351
Boddytown Arnold River Molloys Lookout △376 30'
South Beach 343 343 Kaimata Power House Dam Deep Creek
Paroa Mt Riley 307 Kakawau △447 371 Aratika Kotuku Bell Hill 839 Bell Hill
Rutherglen Shanty Town Welshmans Eight Mile Creek Dunganville Moana 762
Gladstone Cameroons Marsden Maori Ck Ruru Lady Lake Kangaroo Lake
Taramakau River 226 328 419 Howitt Pt Te Kinga Refuge I Pah Pt △101 1156
Kumara Junction Greenstone River Little Hohonu R Mitchells Iveagh Bay Lake Brunner (Moana) Carew Bay Knoll Pt Uncle Bay Rotomanu Crooked River
Chesterfield 40 Racecourse Foleys Creek Eastern Hohonu River 1128 Rotomanu Stn △1227 Paddock Hill △1135
Waimea Creek Kumara Power House Greenstone 320 Taff Top 1288 Te Kinga Poerua
Awatuna Power House Dillmanstown Dam Taramakau 1305 Mt French HOHONU RA Ruberslaw △1166 Wallace Ck Lake Poerua
6 Callaghans Hohonu Mt Smart 1257 1219 Poerua ALEXANDER RA 1524
Arahura River Stafford 270 Goldsborough 380 Lake Ruby Lake Ida Lake Julia 1372 Mt Alexander 1958 Hut
Kaihinu Arahura Stn Kumara Reservoir 1356 1356 Mt Treacey Inchbonnie Jacksons 42° 45' S Lat
Houhou Blue Spur Kawhaka Creek Lake Mahinapua Okuku Reservoir 815 BALD RA Rangi Taipo △1447 Aickens
Hokitika Humphreys 351 Turiwhate Griffin Creek 1135 Hut Kelly Saddle Kellys Hill △1394
Arthurstown Kaniere 366 1369△ Wainihinihi Mt Turiwhate 1303. Scottys Saddle 1379 Scottys Creek KELLY RA Hut 73
Woodstock Campbell Ck Island Hill 999△ Kawhaka Pass 1509△ Mt Griffin Biv Dunn Saddle Tara Tama 1852 Hunt Saddle Otira Goat Hill 1649
Rimu Kaniere River 427' Milltown Hut Wainihinihi Creek Mt Kerr 1440 Biv Oldeng Ck 1608 Dunns Creek Mt Barron 1725 Hut
Frosty Ck 396 Hans I Butchers Ck 1059 Newton Hut Saddle 1692 BARRON RA 1704 Barrack Ck Deception River
Kokatahi 770 1125 Tuhua Hut Huts Biv Hura Saddle 1768 Rolleston Hills Peak 1875
829 Mt Graham Lake Kaniere Hut Mt Walcott 1814 2103 Mt Armstrong 1951 1167△ Phipps Pk 1984
Kowhitirangi Slab Bay 1059 Mt Brown Huts NEWTON RANGE Mt Newton 1692 Styx Saddle Stewart Ck Waimakariri Col 2271 Arthur's Pass Goat Pass
Mt Camelback △561 Okarito River Duck Creek 229 Biv 1318 Biv 1791 CAMPBELL RA 2027 Campbell Pass 2106 Mt Rolleston 1923
Mt Harry 351 Hut Mt Lathrop 1905 Mt Axis 1981 1852 Harman Pass Mt Campbell 1844 Mt Guinevere 2035 Arthur's Pass 1753 Mt Aicken 1859
One Tree Saddle BROWNING RA 1859 Cairn Peak Biv Mt Harman 1905 Mt Rosamond 2195 2271 Mt Lancelot Mt Stewart 1932 Mt Williams 1713
777- Round Top 617 1242 Biv Lake Browning Popes Pass Whitehorn Pass 1743 Mt Bealey 1823
Genoa Pk 1509 Biv Hut Browning Pass 1890 Mt Davie 2294 White River 1682 2195
Mt Diedrich △1084 DIEDRICH RA 1608 Mt Learmont 2057 Farquharson Saddle 1958 2195 Mt Harper
922 Mt Misery OTEHAKE RA 1615 Mt Reeves 1783 Mt Griffiths 2057 Zit Saddle 2118 Mt Camsell Mt Griffiths Saddle
Murray Saddle Griffiths Saddle

171°00' 15' 30'

Adjoining pages
63
68 | 70
75 | 80

5 0 5 10 15 20
Kilometres

172°00' E Long

45'

15'

Kilometres

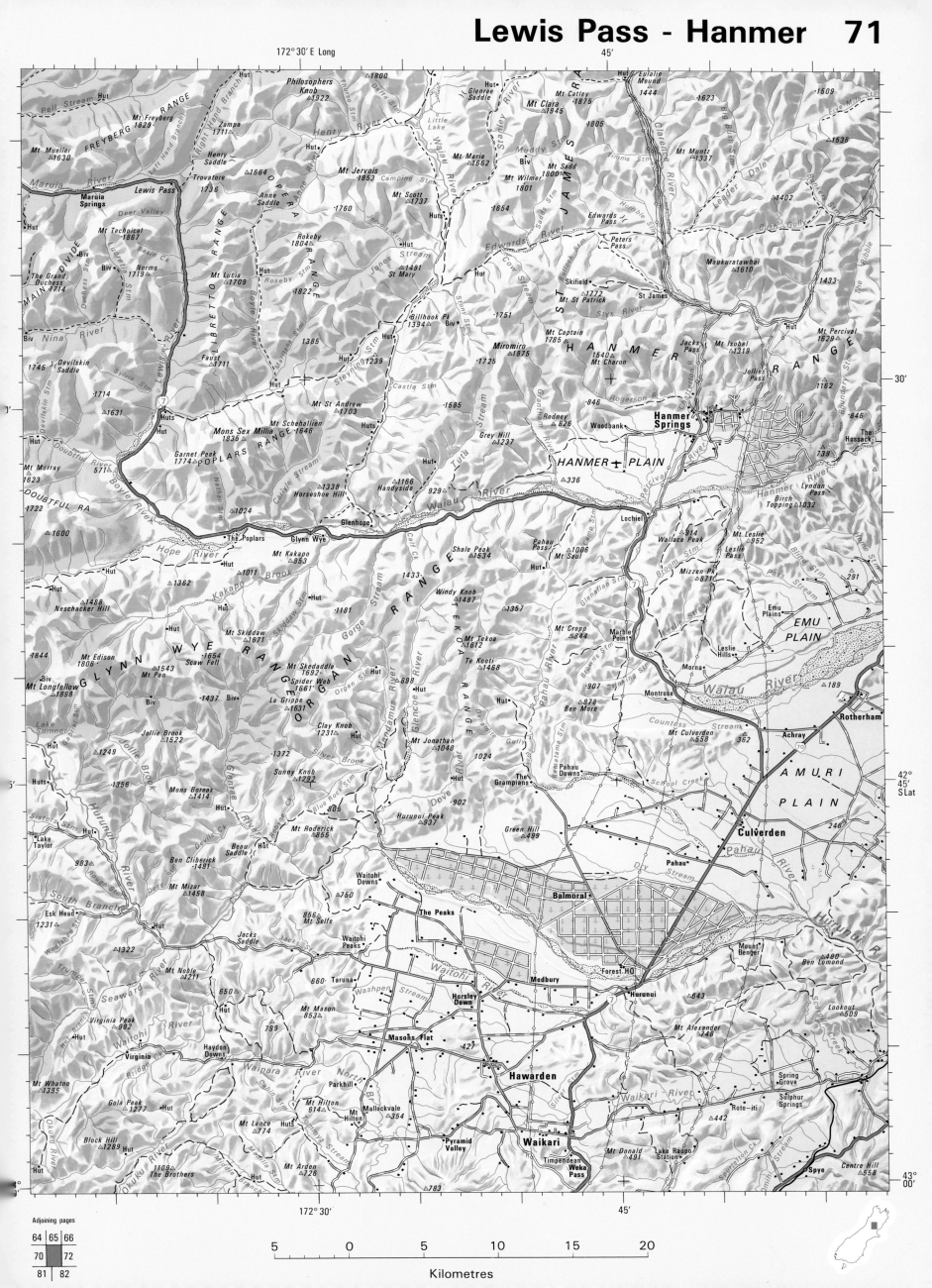

Kilometres

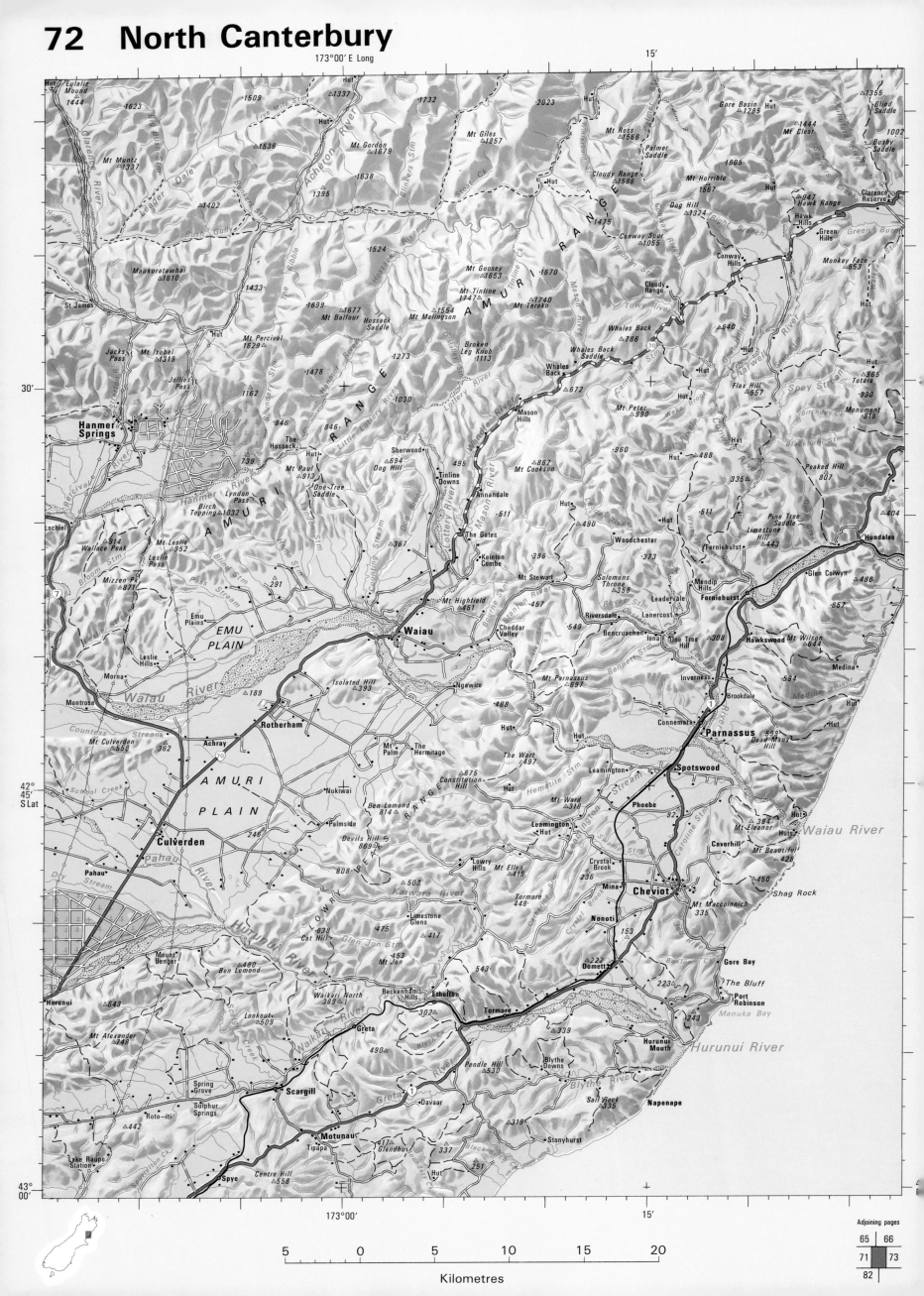

173°00' E Long

15'

30'

42°
45'
S Lat

43°
00'

173°00'

15'

Kilometres

5   0   5   10   15   20

Adjoining pages

65	66
71	73
82	

173° 30'E Long

Hapuku
·1721
△1602
Hut
△1355   △1569   Blind Saddle   Hapuku River
Gore Basin   Sandy Saddle   180
·1285   Hut   Swyncombe   Harnetts Ck
Mt Ross   △1444   1002   △824   Middle Ck
△1566   Mt Clear   Bushy Saddle   Swyncombe   Mt Fyffe
Palmer Saddle   Rangamahoe   326
·2023   Hut   ·1605   Clarence Reserve   Mt Furneaux   Kaikoura
Mt Horrible   ·947   Lynton Downs   134   TV Mast Kaikoura
Cloudy Range   1567   Hawk Range   The Lakes
△1586   Dog Hill   Hawk Hills   ·244   Kowhai
△1324   Green Hills   South Bay
·1475   Green Burn   ·190   Point Kean
Conway Spur   Puketa   Kaikoura Peninsula
△1055   Conway Hills   Monkey Face   753   Atia Pt   East Head
Hut   ·653   914△   622   South Bay
·1670   Cloudy Range   Hut
Mt Terako   Towy River   ·959   Goose Bay
△1740   △640   Goose Bay
Whales Back   Hut   Oaro
△786   Hut   Hut   Flax Hill   Hut
Whales Back Saddle   557   △965   Hut
Whales Back   Charwell River   Totara   Pukaroro Rock
△672   Spey Stream   ·930
Mason Hills   Mt Peter   Monument   Spy Glass Pt
△990   Hut   ·818   Haumuri Bluffs
·867   ·960   Hut
Mt Cookson   △488   335·   Peaked Hill   △404
Hut   807   Mt Guardian   Claverley
·511   ·511   Pine Tree Saddle   Conway River
△490   Hut   Limestone Hill   Hundalee   Conway Flat
Woodchester   Ferniehurst   △443
·396   ·373   Glen Colwyn   △486
Solomons Throne   Mendip Hills   ·657
Mt Stewart   △358   Ferniehurst   Big Bush Gully
·457   Leadervale   Mt Wilson
Riversdale   Lanercost   Hawkswood   △644
Cheddar Valley   ·549   Bencruachan   Iona   One Tree Hill   △308   Medina
Inverness   ·594
·488   Mt Parnassus   Medina River   Hut
△697   Brookdale   Hut
Hut   Connemara
The Wart   Parnassus   599·
△497   Leamington   Dead Mans Hill
Spotswood   Waiau River
Hut   Mt Ward
△318   Phoebe   ·92   Hut
Leamington Hut   Mt Eleanor   Huts
△364
Caverhill
Crystal Brook   Mt Beautiful
Mt Ellen   ·236   △428
△419   Mina   ·450
Tormore   Cheviot   Shag Rock
448·   Mt Maccoinnich   335
Nonoti   153
△222   Gore Bay
Domett   The Bluff
·223   Port Robinson
Tormore   ·243   Manuka Bay
△339   Hurunui Mouth
Blythe Downs   Hurunui River
·319   Sail Rock   ·335   Napenape
Stonyhurst

15'   173° 30'   45'

5   0   5   10   15   20
Kilometres

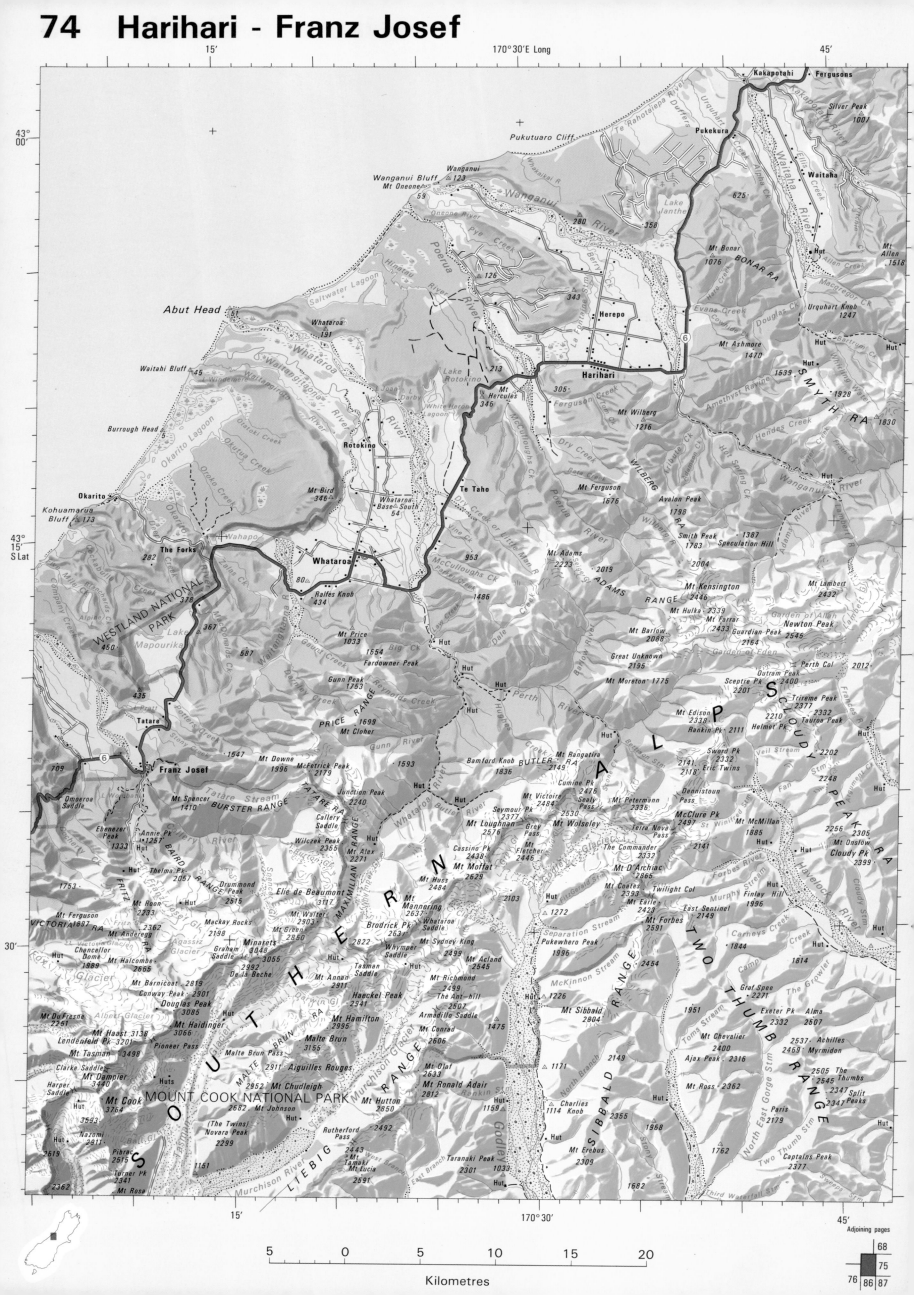

Kilometres

Adjoining pages

169°45' E Long

170°00'

15'

15'

Three Mile Lagoon

Blanchards Bluff

Five Mile Lagoon

Waiho R

78

Company Creek

Omoeroa Bluff 45

30' 69

450

Omoeroa Hill 682

709

434

Galway Point

Gillespies Point

22 142

107 351

389

L Gibbs

Lake Mueller

Waitangi Creek
Waihapi Creek
Gibbs Creek
Docherty Stream
Waikukupa River

Gillespies Beach

Whelan Creek

Lake Lyttle

Lake Skiffington

Swamp

495

Otorokua Point 25

190

Cook River

Waiowhai Stream

Lake Matheson

Lake Gault

389

457

Cook Saddle

Clearwater River

Cook Bluff
Malcolms Knob 130

Boyds Ck

Fox Glacier

Mt Mitchell 1631

195

Bullock Creek

Stony Ck

Fox River

Hut

Hut

250

450

1433

Sam Peak 1827

5

327

Hut

Craig Pk 1914

FOX RA

43° 30' S Lat

Nicholson Ck

Saltwater Ck

Havelock Ck

Karangarua

WESTLAND N.P.

Manakaiaua River

Gordon Ck

Karangarua River

1494

Balfour River

Balfour Gl

BALFOUR RANGE

La Perouse Glacier

Harper Saddle

Jacobs Bluff 76

Makawhio Point

12

6

Ryan Peak 1943

COPLAND RANGE

Mt Myers 1699

Architect Creek

Lyttle Peak 2251

Mt Copland 2345

La Perouse 3079

Baker Saddle

Ngataus Knob
Hut 1204

Shiels Peak 2042

NAVIGATOR RANGE

Hut

Jacobs River

Heretaniwha

90

Bruce Bay

549

Karangarua 1386

Copland River

Price Peak 1913

Strauchon R

Dilemma Peak 2619

Hut

Heretaniwha Point

Lake

Rough Ck

Misty Peak 1593

KARANGARUA RA

Mt Glorious 2233

Lean Pk 2362

Copland Pass

Hut

Hanata I
Otitia Rock

Buttress Pt

Mt Arthur 427

42

Mt Jacob 1364

Mt Richie 1760

Regina Creek

THE SIERRA RA

Scott Peak 2545

Du Faur Peak 2332

The Footstool 2765

Mt Gates 318

Huts

Mahitahi

Bannock Brae 1244

Mt McDonald 1995

Hut

1234 Conical Hill

Douglas River

Blizzard Peak 2408

3157 Mt Sefton

Paringa Hill 517

Hunt Hill 792

Flagstaff Creek

Mt Hermann 1821

Mt Gloin Peak 2073

Mt Peculiar 1913

Hut

Mt Brunner 2667

Paringa River

Mt Douglas 1198

Mt Kinihi 1722

1974

BARE ROCKY RANGE

Jagged Spur 1737

Hut

Gladiator 2126

Mt Thompson 2636

Hut Mt Ollivier 1917

Jacobs River

BANNOCK BRAE RANGE

Mt Howitt 1966

Karangarua Saddle

Twain Col

Lake Paringa

Ward Hill 533

Mt Reynolds 1600

Argentum 1237

Mt Butzbach 2073

Query Peak 1966

Mt Townsend 2035

HOOKER RANGE

Mt Isabel 2545

Mount Cook

Sebastopol 1468

45

Mt Kinnaird 1226

Hut

STRACHAN RANGE

Morgan River

Fettes Pk 2454

Mueller Pass

Mt Burns 2738

Fyfe Pass 2335

Mt Sealy 2637

1478

Hut

Mt Hawkins 2377

Mt Paterson 1951

Tekoa 2027

Mt Montgomery

Mt Spence 2438

Mt Egar Thompson 2379

The Valley of Darkness

Mt Millington 1905

1463

Mathers Peak 2286

Mt Strachan 2545

Mt Elliot 2339

Mt McKerrow 2629

Mt Hopkins 2682

Mt Hodgkinson 1486

Power Knob 1509

Mt Dechen 2630

Mt Sinclair 2240

2240 Prudence Peak

Hut

Mt Lloyd 2195

Tunnel Ck

Mt Jack 2362

Mt Humphries 2446

Richardson Gl

Freds Stream

Hut

Rainytop 1608

Plover Crag 1753

Eureka 1829

Mt McCullaugh 2286

Mt Hooker 2652

Lower Otoko Pass

Mt Gow 1852

Mt Percy Smith 2469

Mt Williams 2536

Mt Browning 2416

2430

Mt Brown 2179

Round Hill 1318

Clarke Pass

Byron Creek

Hut

Bush Stream

Monro Peak 2050

Rough Ridge 1821

The Outpost 1676

1333

Mt Clarke 2454

2355

2536

Mt Dark 2469

Shattered Pk 2088

Clarke River

Hut

Mt Solution 1699

SOLUTION RANGE

Mt Ward 2644

Baker Peak 2200

2484

Low Spur 1867

Clarkes Mound 1070

Landsborough River

Mt Hickson 2300

Mt Jackson 2454

Barron Peak 2260

Fraser Creek

Huts

Hut Peak

Hut

2263

Twin Stream

Mt Dobson 2271

Hut

45'

30'

45'

170°00'

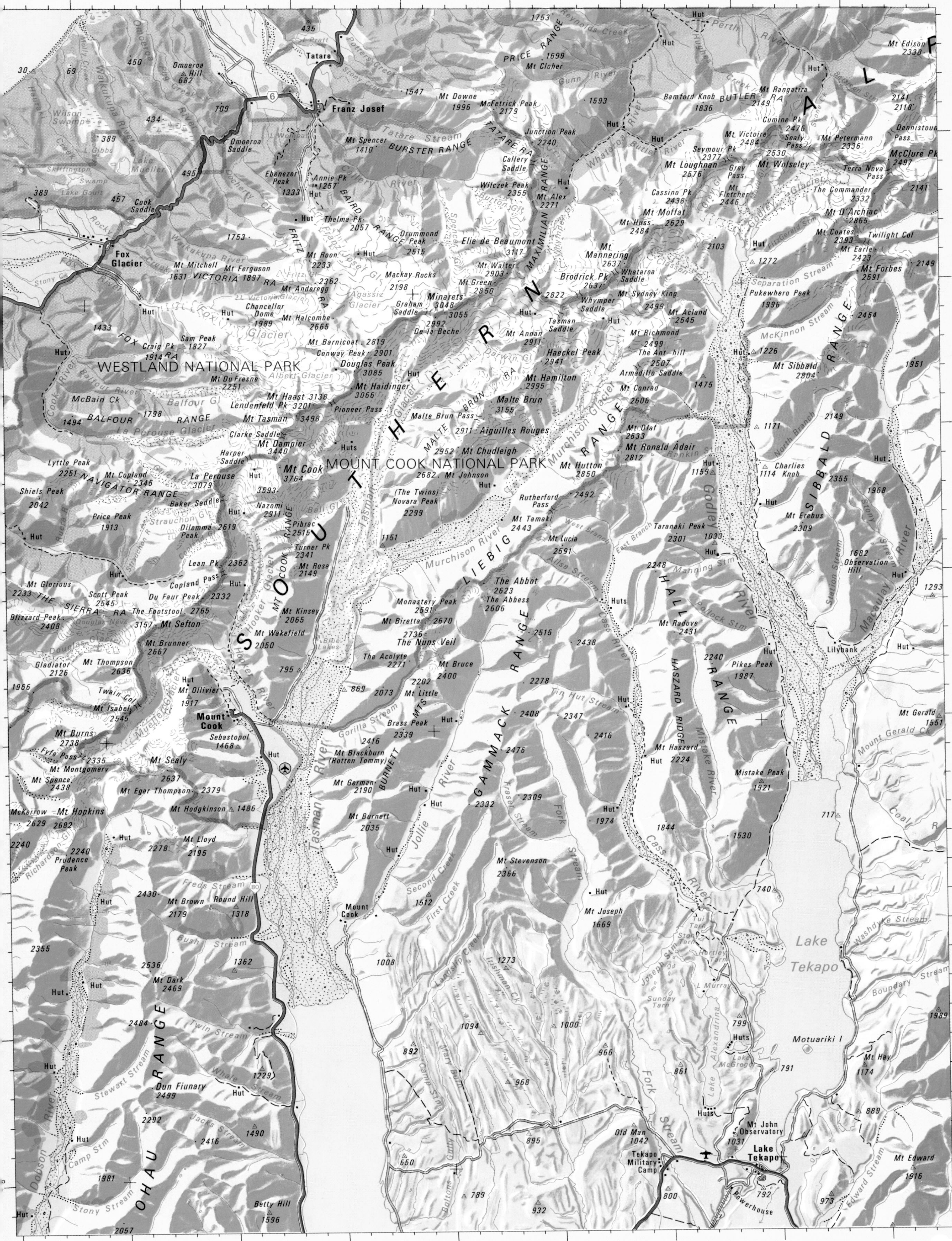

170°00′ 170°15′ E Long 30′

WESTLAND NATIONAL PARK

MOUNT COOK NATIONAL PARK

Ranges: SOUTHERN ALPS, BURSTER RANGE, BAIRD RANGE, FRITZ RANGE, VICTORIA RA, FOX RA, BALFOUR RANGE, NAVIGATOR RANGE, THE SIERRA RA, MALTE BRUN RA, DARWIN RA, LIEBIG RANGE, GAMMACK RANGE, BURNETT MTS, HALL RANGE, HASZARD RIDGE, SIBBALD RANGE, MAXIMILIAN RANGE, COOK RANGE, OHAU RANGE, PRICE RANGE, BUTLER RA, TATARE RA

Towns / places: Franz Josef, Fox Glacier, Mount Cook, Tatare, Lake Tekapo, Lilybank

Peaks (selected):
Mt Cook 3764, Mt Tasman 3498, Mt Dampier 3440, Mt Haast 3138, Lendenfeld Pk 3201, Mt Haidinger 3066, Douglas Peak 3085, La Perouse 3079, Elie de Beaumont 3117, Malte Brun 3155, Minarets 3048, De la Beche 2992, Graham Saddle 3055, Mt Sefton 3157, 3.593 (Mt Cook), Mt Chudleigh 2952, Aiguilles Rouges 2911, Mt Hutton 2850, Mt Hamilton 2995, Mt Walter 2903, Mt Green 2850, Mt Annan 2911, Haeckel Peak 2941, The Ant-hill 2507, Mt Johnson 2682, Novara Peak 2299, Rutherford Pass 2492, Mt Tamaki 2443, Mt Lucia 2591, The Abbot 2623, The Abbess 2606, Monastery Peak 2591, Mt Biretta 2670, The Nuns Veil 2736, The Acolyte 2271, Mt Bruce 2400, Mt Little 2202, Brass Peak 2339, Mt German 2190, Mt Burnett 2035, Mt Stevenson 2366, Mt Joseph 1669

Mt Edison 2330, Mt Rangatira 2149, Mt Petermann 2336, McClure Pk 2497, Terra Nova Pass, Dennistoun Pass, Mt D'Archiac 2865, Mt Coates 2393, Mt Earles 2423, Mt Forbes 2591, Twilight Col, Mt Sibbald 2804, Mt Sealy, Mt Erebus 2309, Observation Hill 1682, Pikes Peak 1987, Mt Haszard 2224, Mistake Peak 1921, Mt Gerald 1551, Mt Hay 1174, Mt Edward 1916

Mt Victoire 2484, Seymour Pk 2377, Mt Loughnan 2576, Cassino Pk 2438, Mt Moffat 2629, Mt Huss 2484, Mt Fletcher 2445, Mt Wolseley, Grey Pass, Sealy Pass, Cumine Pk 2475, Bamford Knob 1836, Junction Peak 2240, Mt Mannering 2637, Mt Richmond 2499, Mt Conrad 2606, Mt Acland 2545, Mt Sydney King 2499, Mt Olaf 2633, Mt Ronald Adair 2812, Taranaki Peak 2301, Mt Radove 2431, Armadillo Saddle, Whymper Saddle, Brodrick Pk 2631, Whataroa Saddle, Tasman Saddle, Pukewhero Peak 1996, Charlies Knoh 1114, Separation Stream

Westland side peaks: Omoeroa Hill 682, Ebenezer Peak 1333, Annie Pk 1257, Mt Spencer 1410, Thelma Pk 2057, Mt Roon 2233, Mt Ferguson 2362, Mt Mitchell 1631, Mt Anderegg, Chancellor Dome 1989, Mt Halcombe 2665, Sam Peak 1827, Craig Pk 1914, Mt Du Fresne 2251, Mt Barnicoat 2819, Conway Peak 2901, Orummond Peak 2515, Mackay Rocks 2198, McFetrick Peak 2179, Mt Downe 1996, Mt Cloher, Mt Alex 2271, Wilczek Peak 2355, Callery Saddle

Lyttle Peak 2251, Mt Copland 2345, Shiels Peak 2042, Price Peak 1913, Baker Saddle, Nazomi 2911, Pibrac 2515, Turner Pk 2341, Mt Rosa 2149, Lean Pk 2362, Mt Kinsey 2065, Mt Wakefield 2050, Harper Saddle, Clarke Saddle, Pioneer Pass, Malte Brun Pass, Mt Glorious 2233, Scott Peak 2545, Du Faur Peak 2332, The Footstool 2765, Blizzard Pk 2408, Mt Brunner 2667, Gladiator 2126, Mt Thompson 2636, Twain Col, Mt Ollivier 1917, Mt Isabel 2545, Mt Burns 2738, Fyfe Pass 2335, Mt Montgomery, Mt Spence 2438, Mt Sealy 2637, Mt Egar Thompson 2379, Mt Hodgkinson 1486, Mt Lloyd 2195, Mt Brown 2179, Round Hill 1318, Mt Dark 2469, Dun Fiunary 2499, Betty Hill 1596, Mckerrow 2629, Mt Hopkins 2682, Prudence Peak 2240, Sebastopol 1468, Copland Pass, Dilemma Peak 2619

Glaciers: Fox Glacier, Franz Josef Glacier, Victoria Glacier, Agassiz Glacier, Albert Glacier, Balfour G, La Perouse Glacier, Tasman Glacier, Murchison Glacier, Godley Glacier, Hooker Glacier, Mueller Glacier, Strauchon R Gl, Douglas Névé

Rivers / streams: Omoeroa River, Waikukupa River, Waiho River, Cook River, Balfour River, Karangarua River, Copland River, Dobson River, Tasman River, Hooker River, Murchison River, Jollie River, Cass River, Macaulay River, Godley River, Reynolds Creek, Gunn River, Whataroa River, Butler River, Perth River, Maerewhenua, Stewart River, Twin Stream, Freds Stream, Boundary Stream, Coal Stream

Lake Tekapo, Lake Mueller, Lake Gault, Wilson Swamp, Motuariki I, Mt John Observatory, Tekapo Military Camp, Powerhouse

Spot heights (selected): 435, 450, 682, 709, 495, 457, 389, 1753, 1433, 1494, 1798, 1914, 1966, 2240, 2355, 2484, 2536, 2292, 2416, 1981, 2057, 1490, 1362, 1318, 1229, 869, 795, 1008, 1094, 892, 968, 966, 932, 789, 650, 895, 800, 792, 973, 861, 791, 799, 740, 717, 1033, 1159, 1226, 1272, 1475, 1951, 2149, 2454, 1968, 2355, 1989, 1293, 1530, 1844, 2240, 2347, 2408, 2416, 2438, 2515, 2278, 1512, 1273, 1000

43°30′ 43°45′ S Lat 44°

Haast Pass - Mt Aspiring National Park

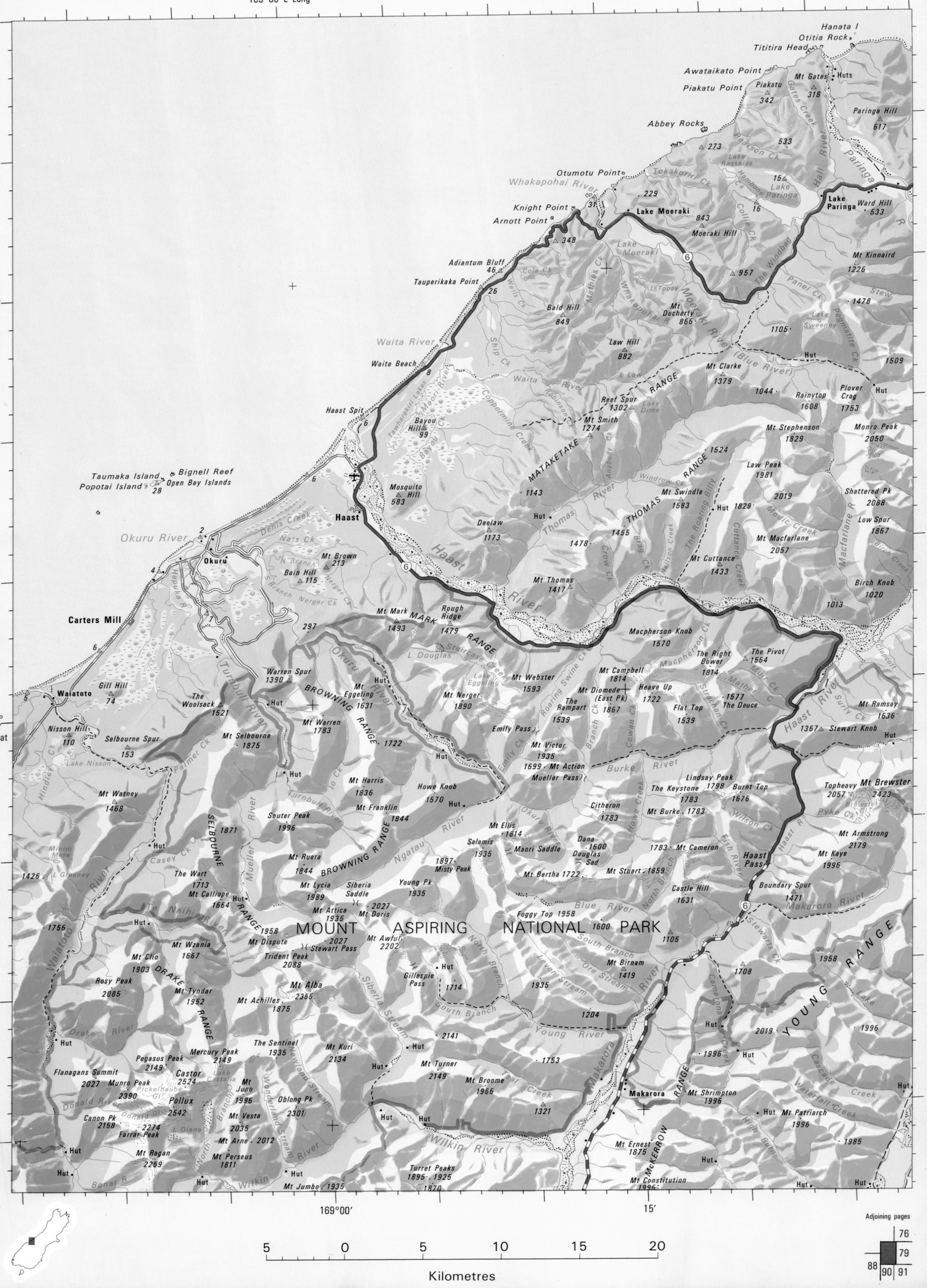
169°00′ E Long
15′
45′
44° 00′ S Lat
15′
169°00′
Hanata I
Otitia Rock
Tititira Head
Awataikato Point
Piakatu Point
Piakatu 342
Mt Gates 318
Huts
Gates Creek
Paringa Hill 617
Abbey Rocks
273
533
Pearson Ck
Lake Rasselas
Tokakoriri Ck
Hall River
Paringa
Otumotu Points
Whakapohai River
229
15
Lake Paringa
16
Collie Ck
Lake Paringa
Ward Hill 533
Knight Point
31
Lake Moeraki
843
Moeraki Hill
Arnott Point
348
Lake Moeraki
The Windbag
Mt Kinnaird 1226
Adiantum Bluff 46
Cole Ck
957
Panel Ck
Tauperikaka Point 26
Wells Ck
Mathias Ck
L Topsy
Moeraki River
1478
Stew
Bald Hill 849
Mt Docherty 866
Whakapohai R
Lake Sweeney
Pegmatite Ck
1105
Waita River
Ship Ck
Law Hill 882
(Blue River)
Hut
1509
Waita Beach
8
Waita
River
L Law
Mt Clarke 1379
RANGE
1044
Rainytop 1608
Plover Crag 1753
Hut
Maori River
Robinson Ck
Reef Spur 1302
Lake Dime
Haast Spit
Tawharekiri Lakes
Bayou Hill 99
Bayou Ck
Coppermine Creek
Mt Smith 1274
Mt Stephenson 1829
Monro Peak 2050
6
MATAKETAKE
1524
Anybody Ck
Taumaka Island
Bignell Reef
Popotai Island
Open Bay Islands
28
6
Law Peak 1981
Mosquito Hill 583
1143
Windrow Ck
RANGE
Mt Swindle 1583
THOMAS
The Roaring Billy
Shattered Pk 2088
Hut
1829
2019
Haast
Hut
Thomas
River
Moolic Creek
Low Spur 1867
Deelaw 1173
1455
Brag Ck
Wilson Creek
Cuttance Creek
Mt Macfarlane 2057
Macfarlane R
Okuru River
Denis Creek
2
Nats Ck
1478
Crow Ck
Birch Creek
Okuru
Mt Brown 213
N Branch
Haast
Mt Cuttance 1433
Bain Hill 115
6
4
Hapuka R
S Branch
Nerger Ck
River
Mt Thomas 1417
Birch Knob 1020
Carters Mill
7
Mt Mark 1493
Rough Ridge 1479
1013
MARK
297
Macpherson Knob 1570
6
RANGE
L Douglas
Staircase Creek
The Right Bower 1814
The Pivot 1564
Okuru
Macpherson Ck
Clapcott
Warren Spur 1390
Mt Campbell 1814
Roaring Swine Ck
Muir Ck
Waiatoto
Gill Hill 74
Hut
Lake Eggeling
Mt Webster 1593
Mather C
5
River
Mt Eggeling 1631
Mt Diomede (East Pk) 1867
Heave Up 1722
1577 The Deuce
Surly Ck
Turnbull River
The Woolsack 1521
Hut
BROWNING
Mt Nerger 1890
The Rampart 1539
Flat Top 1539
Strachan Ck
Mt Ramsay 1636
Haast River
Nisson Hill 110
Mt Warren 1783
RANGE
Emily Pass
Branch Ck
Cowan Ck
1367 Stewart Knob
Selbourne Spur 153
Mt Selbourne 1875
1722
Hut
Hindley
Lake Nisson
Palmer Ck
Hut
Emily Ck
Mt Victor 1935
Burke
River
Hut
1699 Mt Action
Mueller Pass
Lindsay Peak 1798
Burnt Top 1676
Topheavy 2057
Mt Brewster 2423
Mt Watney 1468
Io Ck
Mt Harris 1836
Howe Knob 1570
The Keystone 1783
Brewster
Turnbull River
Hut
Citheron 1783
Howe Creek
Mt Burke 1783
Pyke Ck
Mt Franklin 1844
Wilson Ck
Haast R
SELBOURNE
Souter Peak 1996
Okuru River
Mt Armstrong 2179
1871
Mueller River
Mt Ellis 1814
Minim Mere
Hut
Dana 1600
Mt Kaye 1996
Salamis 1935
Maori Saddle
Douglas Sad
1783
Mt Cameron
Fish River
Haast Pass
Mt Ruera 1844
Ngatau River
1426
L Greaney
Casey Ck
BROWNING RANGE
1897 Misty Peak
Mt Bertha 1722
Mt Stuart 1859
The Wart 1713
River
Mt Lycia 1989
Siberia Saddle
Young Pk 1935
North Branch
Castle Hill 1631
Boundary Spur 1471
Mt Calliope 1664
Hut
Mt Attica 1935
2027 Mt Doris
Foggy Top 1958
Blue River
Makarora River
Te Naihi River
RANGE
6
Hut
1756
1958
MOUNT ASPIRING NATIONAL PARK
1600
1105
Waiatoto
Mt Dispute
2027
Mt Awful 2202
South Branch
YOUNG RANGE
Mt Wzania 1667
Stewart Pass
Stewarts Ck
1958
Mt Chio 1903
Trident Peak 2088
Mt Birnam 1419
1708
DRAKE
Hut
Ore Stream
Gillespie Pass
North Branch
Leven Stream
Rosy Peak 2085
Mt Tyndar 1952
Mt Alba 2355
1714
1935
Camerons
Lake
RANGE
Mt Achilles 1875
Siberia Stream
South Branch
1204
River
Hut
2019
1996
Drake River
Young River
Hut
The Sentinel 1935
2141
Hut
Pegasus Peak 2149
Mercury Peak 2149
Mt Kuri 2134
Hut
1996
Hut
Flanagans Summit 2027
Castor 2524
Lake Castalia
Mt Juno 1996
Hut
Mt Turner 2149
1753
Cascade
Creek
Munro Peak 2390
Pickelhaube
Oblong Pk 2301
Mt Broome 1966
Makarora
Makarora
RANGE
Mt Shrimpton 1996
Hut
Donald River
Pollux 2542
Newland Stream
Creek
1321
Waterfall Creek
Canon Pk 2158
Donald Gl
Mt Vesta 2035
Hut
Hut
Hut
Mt Patriarch 1996
2274 Farrar Peak
L Diana
Wonderland Stream
High Burn
Hut
Mt Arne 2012
Wilkin River
Mt Ernest 1875
1985
Mt Ragan 2259
North Branch
Mt Perseus 1811
River
McKERROW
Hut
Hut
Hut
Hut
Bonar R
Hut
Wilkin
Mt Jumbo 1935
Turret Peaks 1895 1925 1870
Mt Constitution 1996
Hut
Hut
5 0 5 10 15 20
Kilometres
Adjoining pages
76
79
88
90
91

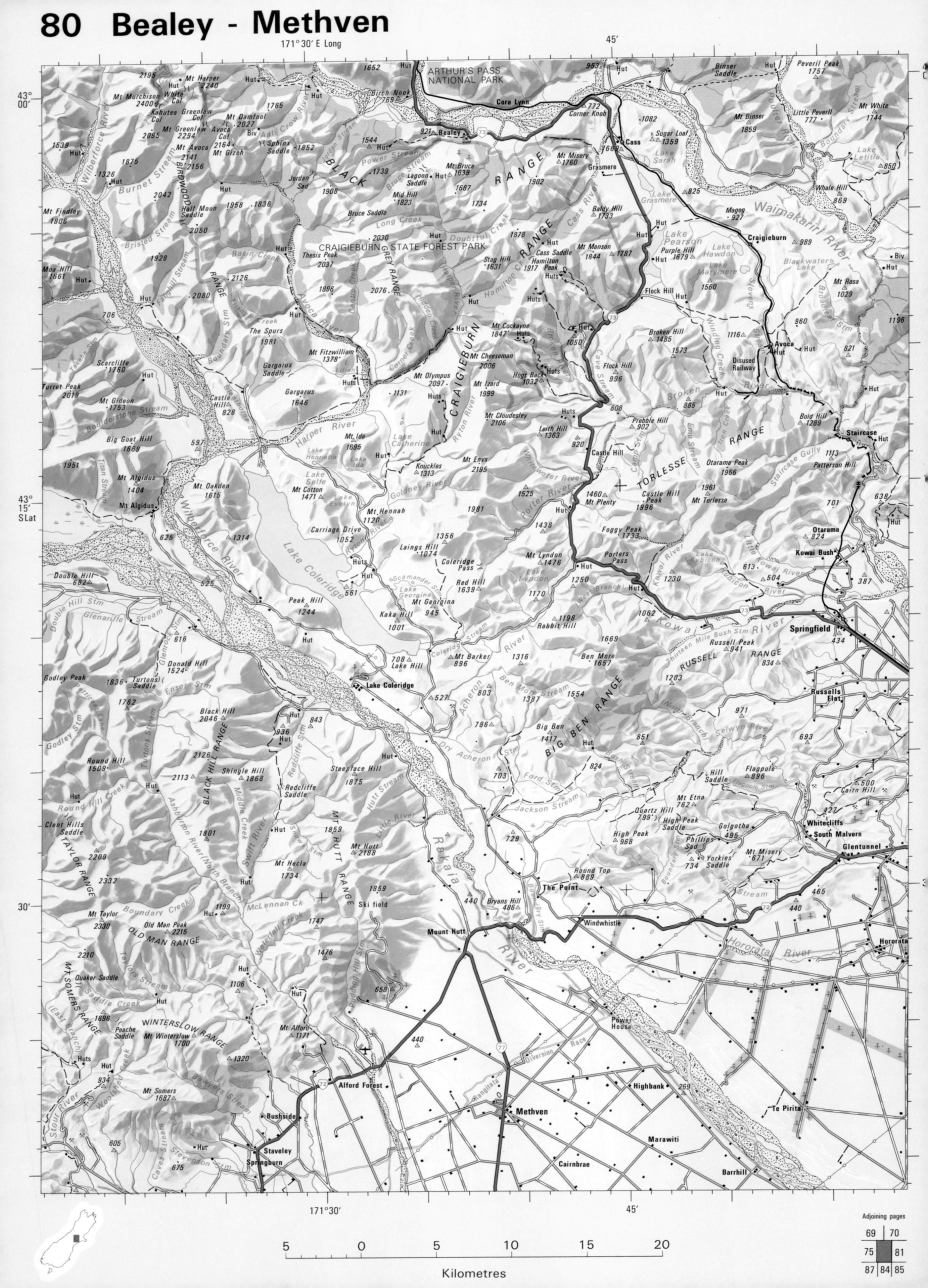

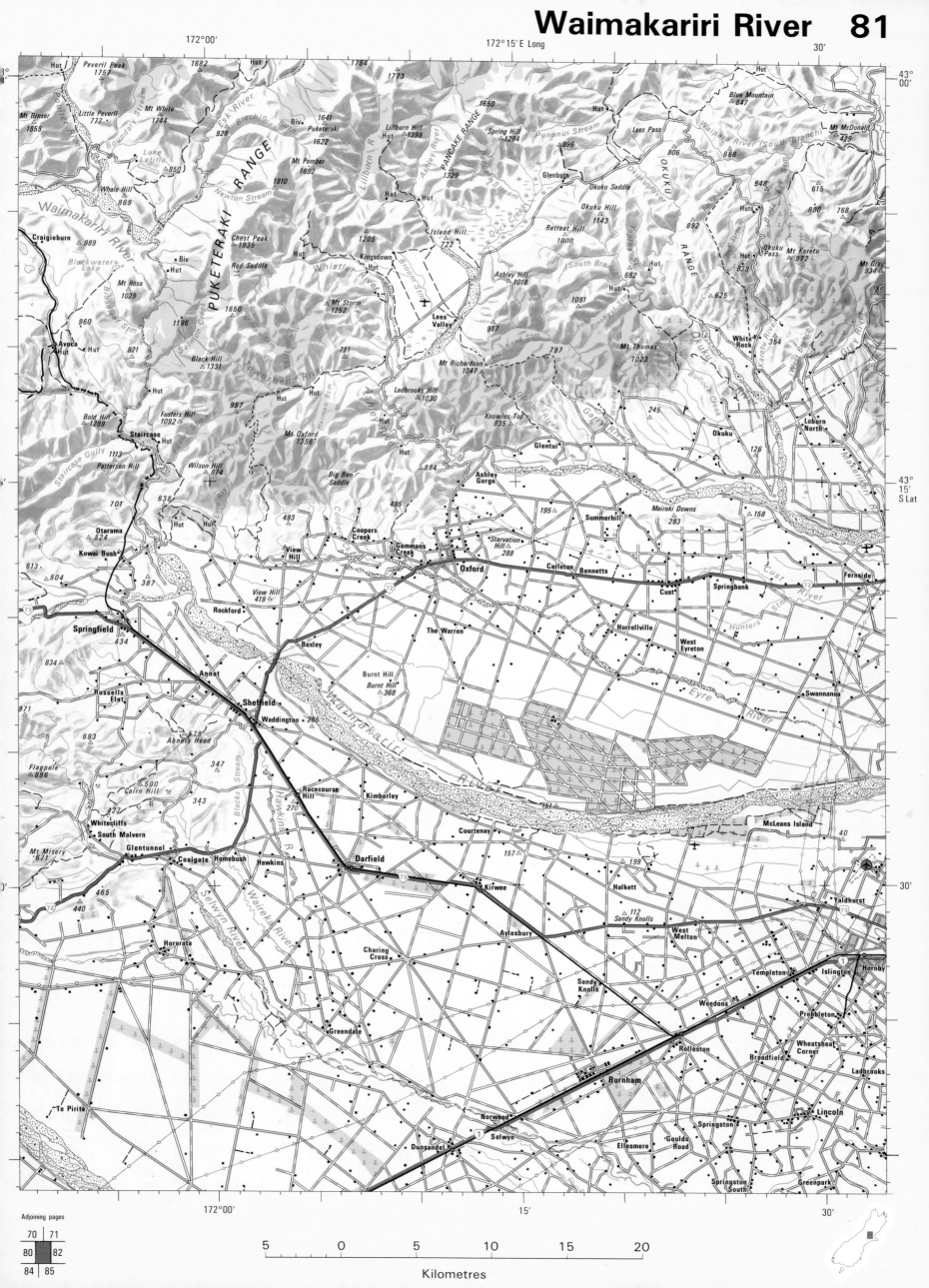

172°00' 172°15'E Long 30'

43°00'

Peveril Peak 1757
Hut
Little Peverll 777
Mt White 1744
1682
Hut
1754
1773
Blue Mountain △847
Hut
Mt Binser 1859
Boundary Stream
Lake Letitia △850
Esk River
Brechin Burn
928
1641 Puketeraki 1622
1650
Spring Hill △1284
Lees Pass
806
666
Mt McDonald 429
Whale Hill 869
PUKETERAKI RANGE
Mt Pember 1692
1810
Lillburn Hill △1398
Hut
PANCAKE RANGE
Punanui Stream
896
548
615
Waiau River (South Branch)
Craigieburn △989
Blackwater Lake
Red Saddle
Newton Stream
1205
Kingsdown
Hut
Hut
Island Hill 722
1329
Glenburn
Okuku Saddle
OKUKU RANGE
892
800 768
Waimakariri River
Hut
Mt Rosa 1029
1650
Hut
Chest Peak 1935
Mt Storm 1252
Whistler River
Hut
Lees Valley
Ashley Hill △1018
Okuku Hill △1143
Retreat Hill 1000
1081
652
Hut
625
Hut
838
Okuku Pass
Mt Karetu △972
Mt Grey 934
960
1196
Black Hill △1331
711
917
797
Mt Thomas 1023
Fox Creek
White Rock
354
Avoca Hut
Hut
821
Townshend River
Ashley River
Mt Richardson 1047
Garry River
Glenthui River
245
Okuku
126
Makerikeri R
Bold Hill 1289
Fosters Hill 1092
957
Ladbrooks Hill 1030
Knowles Top 835
Glentui
Loburn North
Staircase
Hut
Hut
Wilson Hill 874
Hut
884
Ashley Gorge
Summerhill
Mairaki Downs 283
158
43°15' S Lat
Staircase Gully 1113
Patterson Hill
638
Eyre River
493
495
Coopers Creek
Starvation Hill 288
195
Carleton
Bennetts
Cust
Springbank
Cust River
Fernside
701
Otarama 824
Hut
Hut
387
View Hill
Gammans Creek
Oxford
72
Kowai Bush
613
504
Rockford
View Hill 419
The Warren
Horrellville
West Eyreton
Hunters Stm
72
Springfield 434
Bexley
Burnt Hill
Eyre River
Swannanoa
834
Annat
Burnt Hill 368
Russells Flat
971
Sheffield
Waddington 266
579 Abners Head
Waimakariri River
693
347
Racecourse Hill
Kimberley
161
McLeans Island
40
Flagpole 896
500 Cairn Hill
343
Blacks Stream
270
Courtenay
157
199
421
Whitecliffs
South Malvern
Glentunnel
Hawkins River
Darfield
Kirwee
Halkett
Yaldhurst
1
Mt Misery 671
Coalgate
Homebush
Hawkins
73
112 Sandy Knolls
West Melton
465 440
72
Aylesbury
Templeton
Islington
Hornby
Hororata
Selwyn River
Wairiki River
Charing Cross
Sandy Knolls
Weedons
Prebbleton
Greendale
Rolleston
Wheatsheaf Corner
Broadfield
Ladbrooks
Burnham
30'
Te Pirita
Norwood
1
Selwyn
Springston
Lincoln
Goulds Road
Dunsandel
Ellesmere
Springston South
Greenpark

172°00' 15' 30'

5   0   5   10   15   20

Kilometres

172°45'E Long
173°00'

43°00'
30'

Spye
Happy Valley
Glenmark
Omihi
Burnt Hut Hill 369
78
Omihi S
290
Vulcan 409
Motunau Beach
Motunau Island

Hut
Mt McDonald 429
North Dean 573
South Dean 571
642
280
Oldnam 496
Montserrat 458
1
783
Waipara
107
Mt Cass 526
Totara 557
548
615
Mt Brown 490
190
800 768
Glasnevin
Okuku Pass
Mt Karetu 972
Washbell Ck
365
Ella 346
Glengarry 146
Mt Grey 934
185
Woolshed 34

Waipara River

Karetu River
West Branch
Grey
354
265
Seadown 185
Amberley

Loburn North
Kowai River
182
Amberley Beach

416
Leithfield
126
Balcairn
Leithfield Beach
Loburn
168
Stony Ck
5
Sefton
1
Saltwater Creek

43°15'S Lat
158
Ashley
Ashley River
Waikuku
Waikuku Beach

Cust River
72
Coldstream
Fernside
Rangiora
Woodend

Southbrook
Tuahiwi
Woodend Beach

Ohoka
Flaxton
Pegasus Bay
Mandeville North
Wetheral
Wilsons Siding
Kaiapoi
The Pines Beach
Swannanoa
Ohapuku
Kairaki

Waimakariri River
Brooklands
Clarkville
Stewarts Gully
Eyreton
Coutts Island
Kainga
Spencerville
Chaneys
Belfast
Ouruhia

McLeans Island
40
Styx
Marshland
Harewood
Northcote
Waimairi Beach

Papanui
Burwood

30'
Shirley
Bryndwr
St Albans
New Brighton
Fendalton
Richmond
Yaldhurst
Riccarton
Linwood
Aranui
75
Addington
CHRISTCHURCH
Islington
Sockburn
Southshore
1
Hornby
Spreydon
Opawa
Woolston
Templeton
Redcliffs
Hoon Hay
Sumner Head
Oaklands
Cashmere
281
Mt Pleasant
Taylors Mistake
Prebbleton
Heathcote
Sumner
75
Halswell
Mt Pleasant
Taylors Mistake
Godley Head 246
Wheatsheaf Corner
Dyers Pass
Rapaki
Mt Evans 299
Evans Pass
Broadfield
Sugarloaf 496
Lyttelton
Adderley Head
Marleys Hill 502
Purau Bay
Lyttelton Harbour
184
Lansdowne
Governors Bay
Diamond Harbour
252
Wakaroa Point
Ladbrooks
323
Quail Island
407
Port Levy
356
Otohuao Head
Lincoln
Ohinetahi
255
Charteris Bay
Mt Evans 703
Port Levy
466
Pigeon Bay
141
Allandale
372
Purau
Zigzag 318
Graeme 446
Long Lookout Point
Taitapu
Coopers Knob 573
300
Wild Cattle Hill 500
Haytor 594
100
Chorlton
West Head
148
315
Teddington
211
Raupo Bay
Greenpark
East Head

30'
45'
173°00'

Adjoining pages
71 | 72
81 |
85 | 83

5   0   5   10   15   20
Kilometres

171°45'E Long   172°00'

30'

WINTERSLOW RANGE
1696
Peache Saddle
Hut
Mt Winterslow 1700
Mt Alford △1171
1320
Hut
934
605
Woolshed Creek
Mt Somers 1687
Caves Stream
Stevenson Stm
675
Bowyers Stream
Gawler Stm
The Brothers 423
Cavendish
Gawler Downs 640
580
Montalto
347
372△

Alford Forest
Bushside
Staveley
Springburn
Buccleuch
Mt Somers
Ashburton River (South Branch)
Valetta
Anama
Mayfield
Ruapuna
Lismore
Carew
201
128
Ealing
79
Rangitata
Belfield
Rangitata Island
Orari
Ohapi
Orton
Winchester
Clandeboye
Temuka
Milford

72
440△
Rangitata
Diversion Race
Power House
Highbank
269
Te Pirita

Methven
Marawiti
Cairnbrae
Barrhill
Lyndhurst
Urrall
Lauriston
Rokeby
Sherwood
Mitcham
Somerton
Hadfield
Overdale
Chertsey

Ashburton River (North Branch)
Ashburton Forks
Punawai
Hackthorne
Greenstreet
Westerfield
Winchmore
77
Dromore
Fairfield
Fairton
Newland
Pendarves

Mt Harding Ck
Lagmhor
Marpnan
Hinds River
ASHBURTON
Allenton
Netherby
Hampstead
Tinwald
Seafield
Winslow
Wakanui
Windermere
Willowby
Huntingdon
Hinds
Wheatstone
Flemington
Riverside
Eiffelton
Ashton
Waterton
Hakatere
Ashburton River
Longbeach
Lowcliffe
Hinds River
Coldstream
Coopers Creek
(Middle Channel)
South Channel
Kapurutiki Creek
Rangitata River
Orari River

45'

44°00' S Lat

15'

30'   171°45'

5   0   5   10   15   20

Kilometres

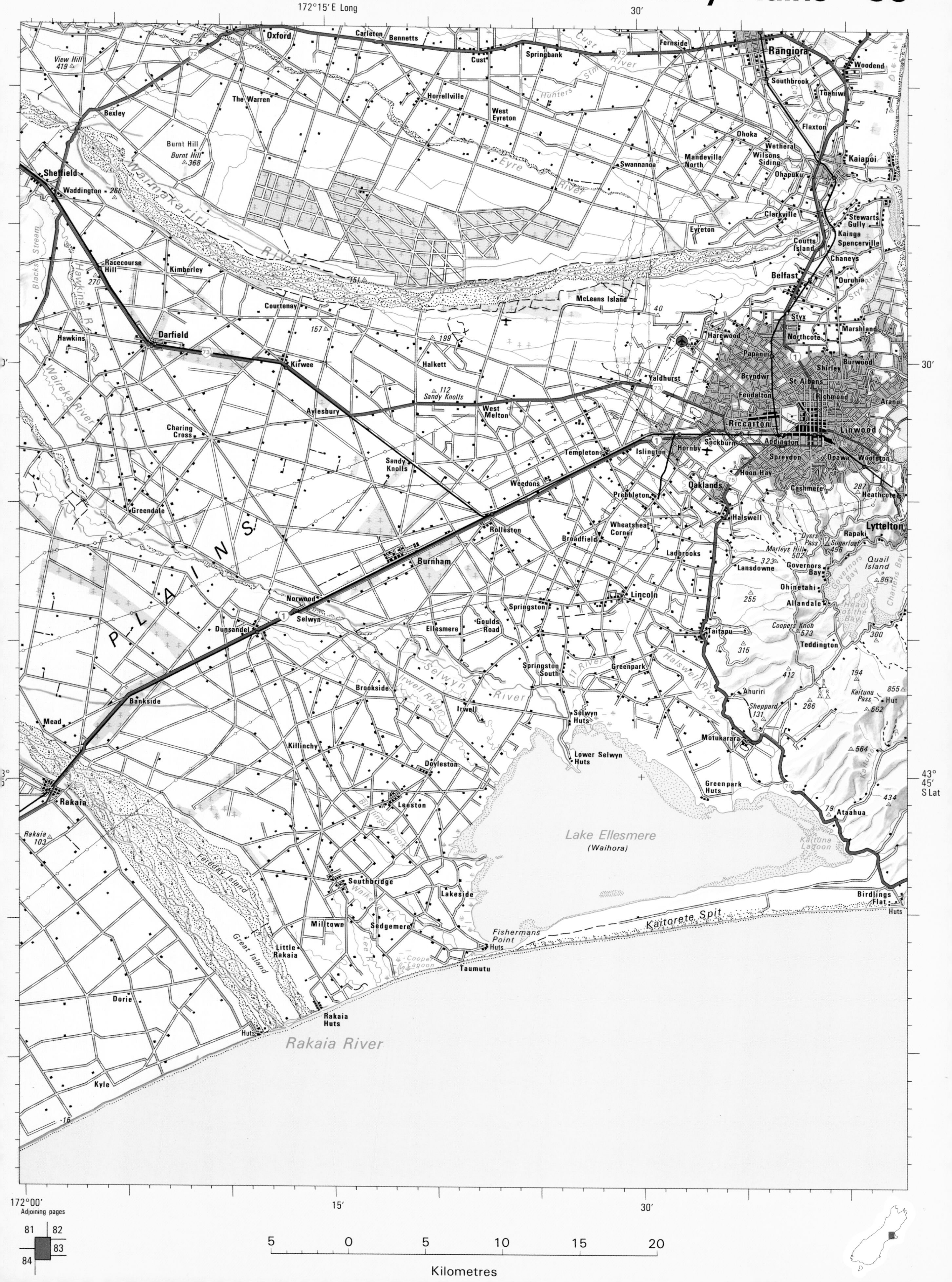

172°15' E Long

30'

Oxford • Carleton • Bennetts • Fernside • Rangiora
View Hill 419 • Cust • Springbank • Southbrook • Woodend
Bexley • The Warren • West Eyreton • Horrellville • Tuahiwi
Burnt Hill 368 • Flaxton
Sheffield • Eyre River • Ohoka • Wetheral • Kaiapoi
Waddington 266 • Swannanoa • Mandeville North • Wilsons Siding • Ohapuku
Racecourse Hill 270 • Kimberley • Clarkville • Stewarts Gully
Hawkins • Eyreton • Coutts Island • Kainga Spencerville • Chaneys
Courtenay • 161 • McLeans Island • 40 • Belfast • Ouruhia • Styx River
Darfield • 157 • 199 • Styx • Marshland
Kirwee • Halkett • Harewood • Northcote
Yaldhurst • Papanui • Bryndwr • St Albans • Burwood
Aylesbury • 112 Sandy Knolls • West Melton • Riccarton • Fendalton • Richmond • Shirley • Aranui
Charing Cross • Templeton • Islington • Hornby • Sockburn • Addington • Linwood
Greendale • Sandy Knolls • Weedons • Oaklands • Hoon Hay • Spreydon • Opawa • Woolston
Rolleston • Broadfield • Prebbleton • Wheatsheaf Corner • Cashmere 287 • Heathcote
Burnham • Ladbrooks • Halswell • Dyers Pass • Rapaki • Lyttelton
Norwood • Lincoln • Springston • Lansdowne 323 • Marleys Hill 502 • Sugarloaf 496 • Quail Island 863
Selwyn • Ellesmere • Goulds Road • 255 • Governors Bay • Ohinetahi • Allandale • Head of the Bay
Dunsandel • Brookside • Irwell • Springston South • Greenpark • Coopers Knob 573 • Teddington 300
Bankside • Killinchy • L11 River • Selwyn Huts • Taitapu 315 • 412 • 194
Mead • Doyleston • Lower Selwyn Huts • Ahuriri • Sheppard 131 • 266 • Kaituna Pass 562 • 855
Rakaia • Leeston • Motukarara • 564
Rakaia 103 • Southbridge • Lakeside • Greenpark Huts • 79 Ataahua • 434
Milltown • Sedgemere • Fishermans Point Huts • Lake Ellesmere (Waihora) • Kaituna Lagoon • Birdlings Flat
Little Rakaia • Taumutu • Cooper Lagoon
Dorie • Kaitorete Spit
Rakaia Huts
Kyle • Rakaia River

PLAINS

Waimakariri River
Hawkins R.
Waireka River
Blacks Stream
Hunters Stream
Cust River
North Brook
Styx River
Selwyn River
Irwell River
Halswell River
L11 River
Foleday Island
Great Island
Little Island
Billings Brook
Kaitorete Spit

43° 30'
43° 45' S Lat

172°00'
Adjoining pages

81 | 82
83
84

5 0 5 10 15 20
Kilometres

15' 30'

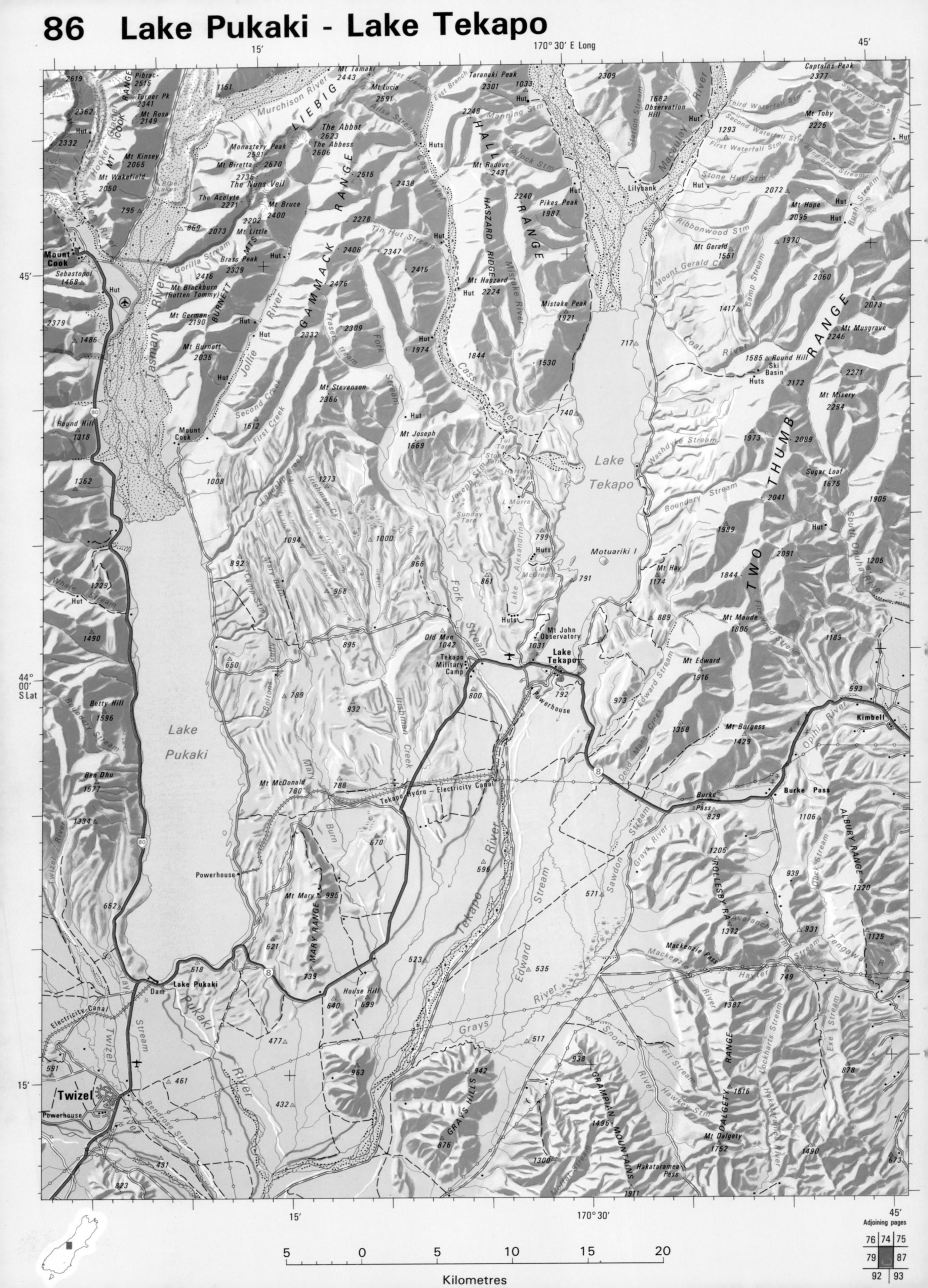

170° 30′ E Long

15′

45′

Kilometres

5   0   5   10   15   20

Adjoining pages

76	74	75
79		87
92	93	

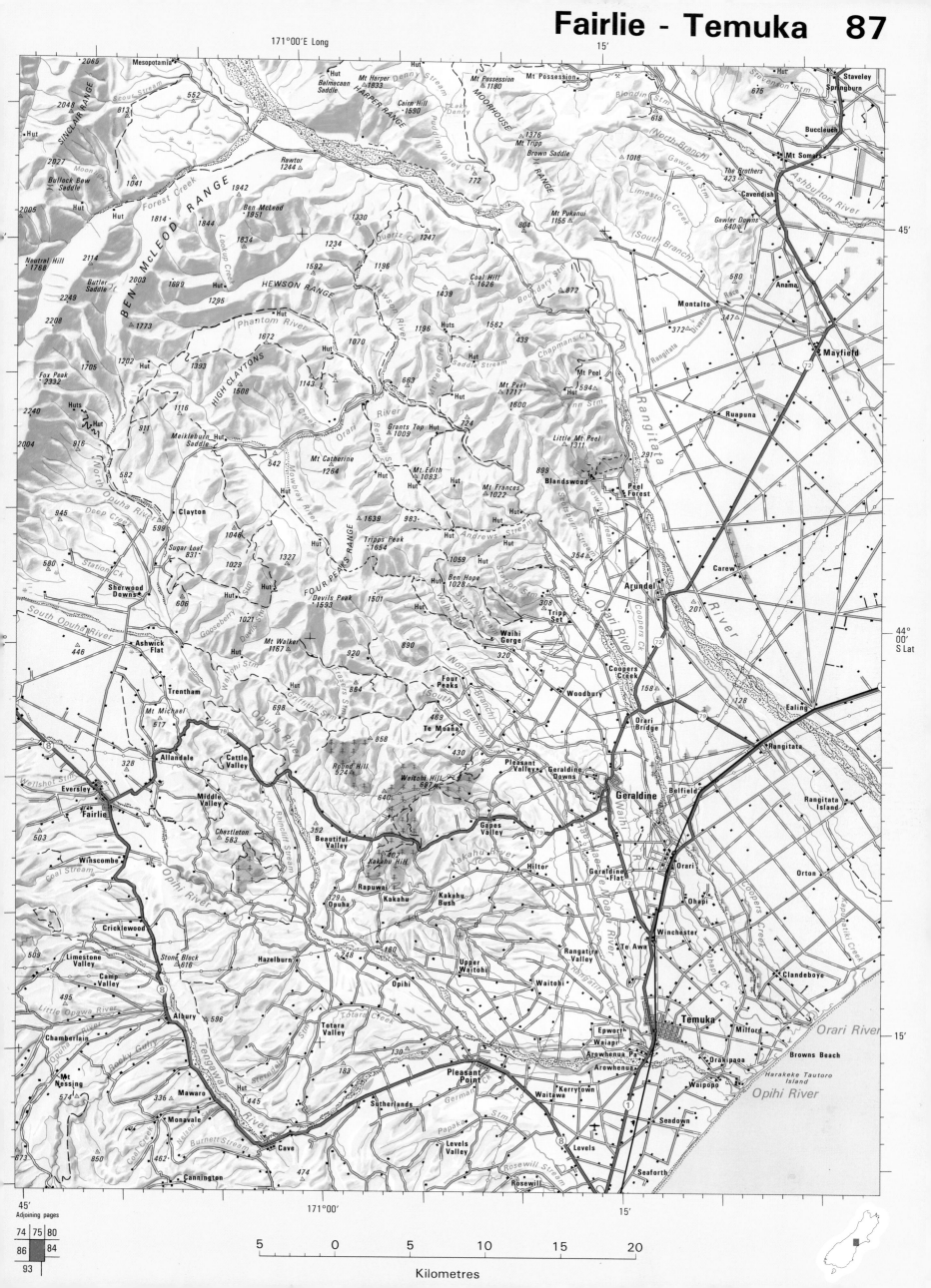

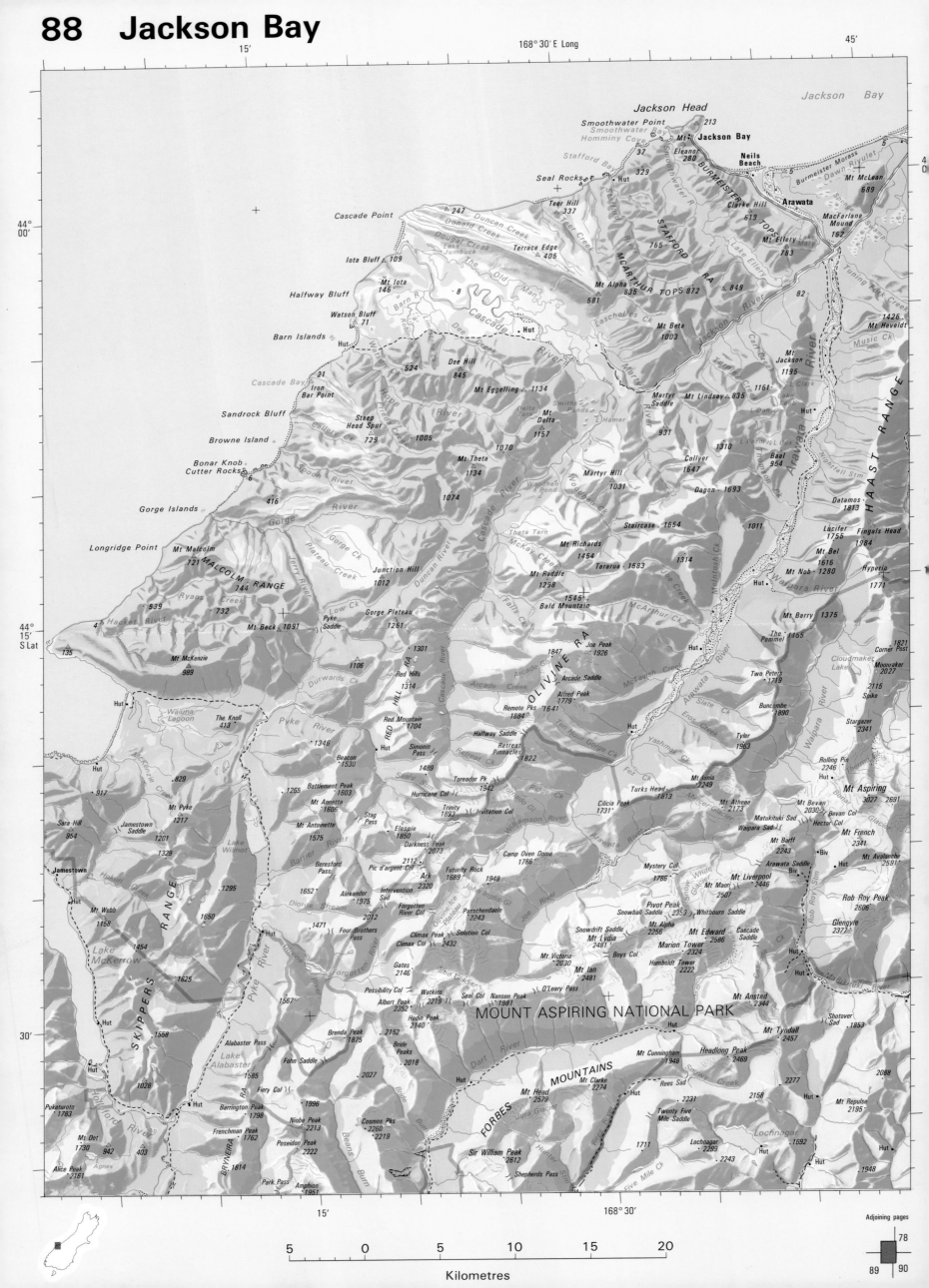

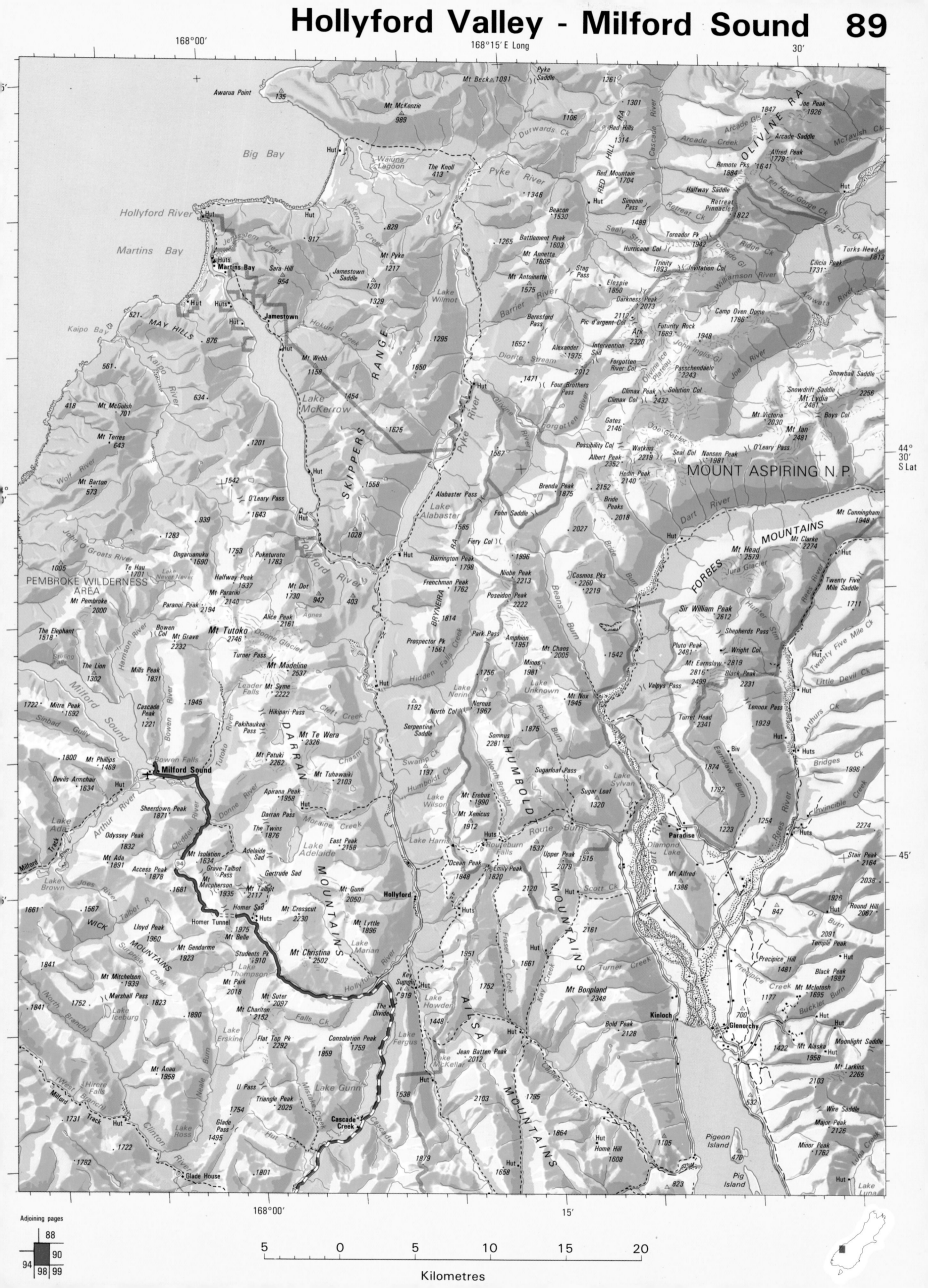

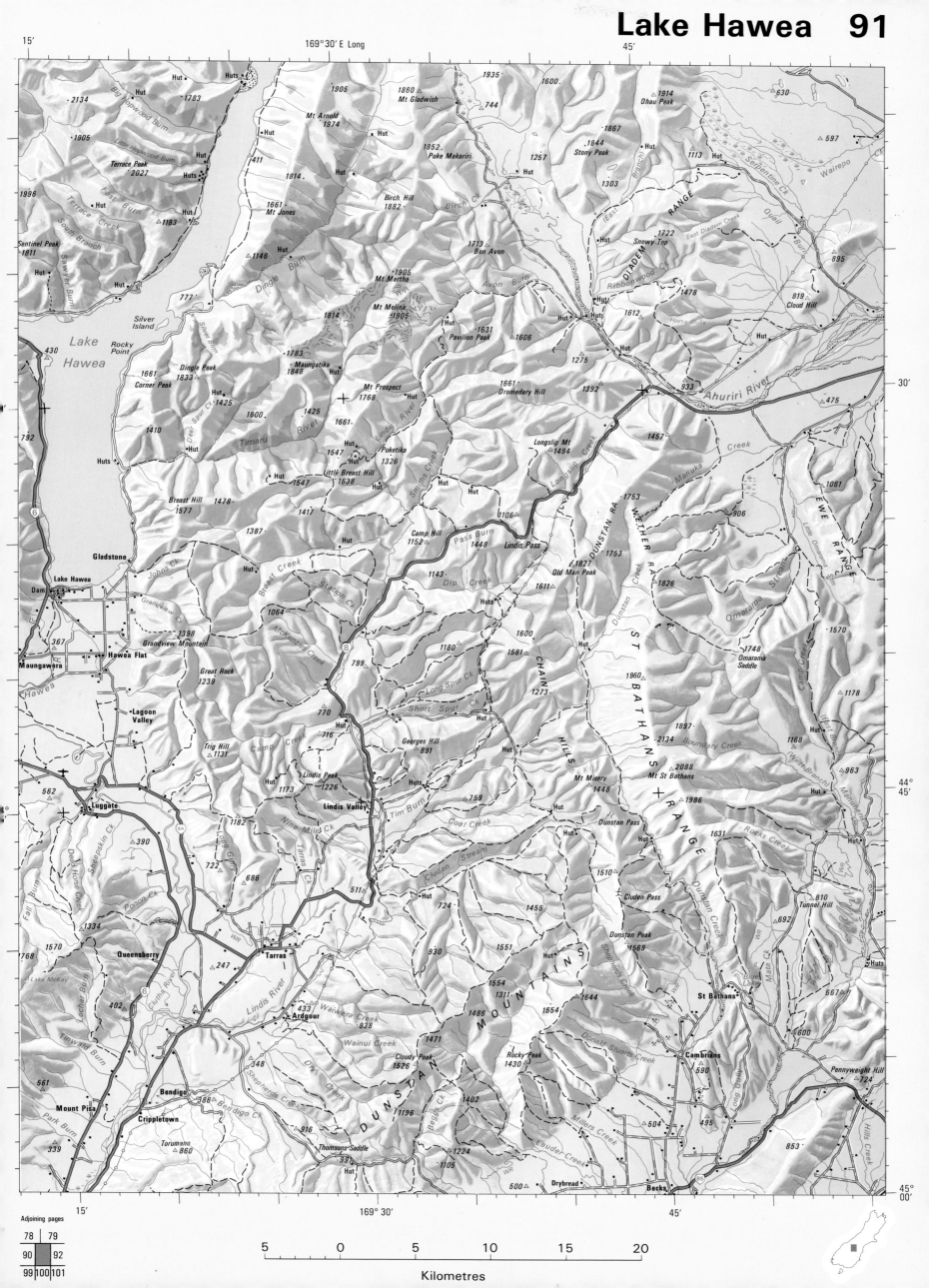

Adjoining pages

78	79
90	100/101	92
99	101

Kilometres

170°00'

170° 15' E Long

30'

823

Hydro-electric canal

Hut

Grays Hills

1911

Hut

539

Clearburn

The Cairn
1462

378

Haldon

524

Stony River

1115

1049

Moffat Stream

1721

Hut

Hut

Mt MacGregor
1016

532

Evanburn Gully

Barclays Creek

Huts

815

1567

868

850

The Buscot
1249

1852
Sutherlands Peak

Falstone Creek

Lake
Benmore

643

939

980

931

1021

721

BENMORE RANGE

1863
Benmore Peak

982

Black
Forest

Beacon Hill
1204

Hut

1267

Round Hill
817

1287

1029

721

Staircase Saddle

Innes Burn

1550

1690

1709

1467

1577

Totara Creek

Shepherds Ck

1132

1573

1698

Mt Sutton
1910

1509

Deep Stm

1808

Omarama

Totara Peak
1818

Peak Valley Ck

980

Hut

Douglas Stream
1561

Hut

Basin Stm

1375

557

30'

489

Hut

1382

1041

1387

Whalen Stm
1228

Gibson Stream

Sutton Stm

Hut

1864

1821

558

650
Benmore

431

St CUTHBERT RA

Mt St Cuthbert
1563

Sailors
Cutting

891

518
Dam

815

Waitangi

823

Stony Stream

1367

Rattray Stream

556

McKays St

Poplar Stm

Hut

Glen Creek

798
Pass Peak

Te Akatarawa

Hakataramea

Maungatiro

Mt Horrible
1367

756

Otamatapaio River

Otematata

844

Aviemore

562

Lake
Aviemore

994

422

Deep Stm

Hut
Dam

967

461

Balmoral
362

Alfred Ck

Hut

Aviemore

Lake
Waitaki

922
Mt Dryburgh

Wharua

1779

1195

931

1295

1239

1486

Fern Gully Ck

Lake Waitaki
Wharekuri

Dam

438

Gorge Hill
637

Victoria
787

1833

1440

1182

893

Mt Weta
1432

Parsons Ck

Rock Stm

1698

Wharekun Ck

1216

708

Hakataramea
494
Fettercairn

864

1021

1836

Hut

Huts

Hut

1929
Mt Bitterness

Hut
1254

820

Kurow
Kurow Hill

Station Peak
885

1847

1871

1417

Clear Stream

Huts

Hut

Rocky Top
1935

Hut

591

Strachans

165

1852

1487

1410

1316

1443

Kohurau
2010

Hut

Otiake

Meyer
799

Hut

1509

1517

Hut

1289

Big Ben
1361

1720

Waikaura
374

Otekaieke

1516

Hut

1242

Hut

Green Gully

Mt Domet
1935

1172

Otekaieke Hill

358

Campbell
Park

1674

Hut

Hut

Grayson Peak
1661

Mt David
1412

539

Huts
Falls Dam

1622

1539

1333

Cone

Otekaieke River

993
Lower Ben
Lomond

Maerewhenua

991

1454

Boundary Creek

Gullies Creek

Blue Duck Creek

Hut

1720

Cone
1291

Ben Lomond
1052

Mt Ida
1692

Mt Buster

Mt Kyeburn
1636

Cone

822

Livingstone
444

724

Hills Creek

1018

1570

1333

Little Kye Burn

933
Diggings Peak

1009

Danseys Pass

591

610

Seagull Hill
729

970

767

Kyeburn
Diggings

Kye Burn

Mt Alexander
1357

593

Idaburn

West Eweburn Dam

170°00'

15'

30'

Adjoining pages

79	86
91	93
101	102

45'   171°00' E Long   15'

Hut · Hut
· 827
Mt Nessing
1597
1436

687
934   Dam
· 343   474
Taiko   194
Washdyke
Puhuka
Washdyke Lagoon

THE
868
1591
Te Huruhuru
1525
Mt Nimrod
1442
1063
917

Cannington
347
309
Motukaika R
Motukaika
Cave Hill
542
135
285
Hadlow
Smithfield
Gleniti
Claremont
Caroline Bay
TIMARU

721
Hakataramea Downs
Francis Stm
432
Pratt Stm
382
Patiti Point

500   719
Round Hill
817

HUNTERS
722
Mt Airini
1248 1373
Peter Stream
Anderson Stm
Scour Stm
Two Legged Stm
Two Mile Stm

Elder Stm
(South Branch)
369
380
317
242
Holme Station
388
96
Fairview
Adair Redruth
Scarborough
Mutu Mutu Point
Tuhawaiki Point

557 · Cattle Creek
Cattle Creek
Gorman Stm

377
358
Gordons Stm
170
Maungati
Gordons Valley
Southburn
Pareora West
Otipua
52
Normanby
Kingsdown
Pig Hunting Creek

HILLS
867
1079
709
Otaio Gorge
Otaio River
Blue Cliffs
231
Esk Valley
82
Lyalldale
Springbrook
48
Pareora
Pareora River

Kowhatu
· 567
Kinbrace
Mt Blyth
1006
Kohika
153
117 67
St Andrews
Otaio River

Struan
Hut · Florence
867
Aitken
1063
Mt Cecil
1005
Kohika
Otaio

Mt Sydney
625
· 1036
863
802
153
Kohika Stm

728
· 1021
Hunter
Makikihi River

Stony Creek
410
Bluestone
Mt Studholme
1085 Hut TV
Hook Bush
Gunns Bush
Waiariari
Makikihi

Balmoral
· 362
· 885
Pentland Hill
667
555
Mt Shrives
958
Lansdown
Hook R
Hook
Wainono Lagoon

471
769
919
Pentland Hills
766
Kelceys Bush
Waituna
Norton Reserve
Deep Creek
Studholme
Waimate Creek
Nukuroa

860
832
Tara 908
479
Maytown
82
20

1021
Mt Orr
· 448
Waihaorunga
Waimate
· 408
341
Uretane
44
Willowbridge
Waihao River
44°45' S Lat

Meyer
799
Kelchers
Round Hill
246
Douglas
Waihao Forks
Kapua
Arno
344
McLeans

Mt Parker
660 · Hut
Waihao Downs
319
Elephant Hill
510
Elephant Hill
McLeans
Gum Tree Flat
Green Hills
Morven
230

Elephant Hill Stream
313
Mt Harris
284
279
Broad Gully

82
Takiroa
506
Waikakahi
204
161
Dog Kennel
Grays Corner

Duntroon
232
Bortons
Ikawai
Tawai

Kokoamo
Black Point
WR
WR

Georgetown
Awamoka
Waitaki
48
Glenavy

Ngapara
Awamoka Stream
Waikoura Ck
Waitaki
Waitaki River

Tokarahi
1385
Queens Flat
Stony Ridge
286
Papakaio
18

· 444
287
Corriedale
Peebles
Big Hill
318

Rakis Table
325
Windsor
Windsor Park
Spring Gully
203
Airedale
Hilderthorpe
Richmond

5   0   5   10   15   20

Kilometres

Kilometres

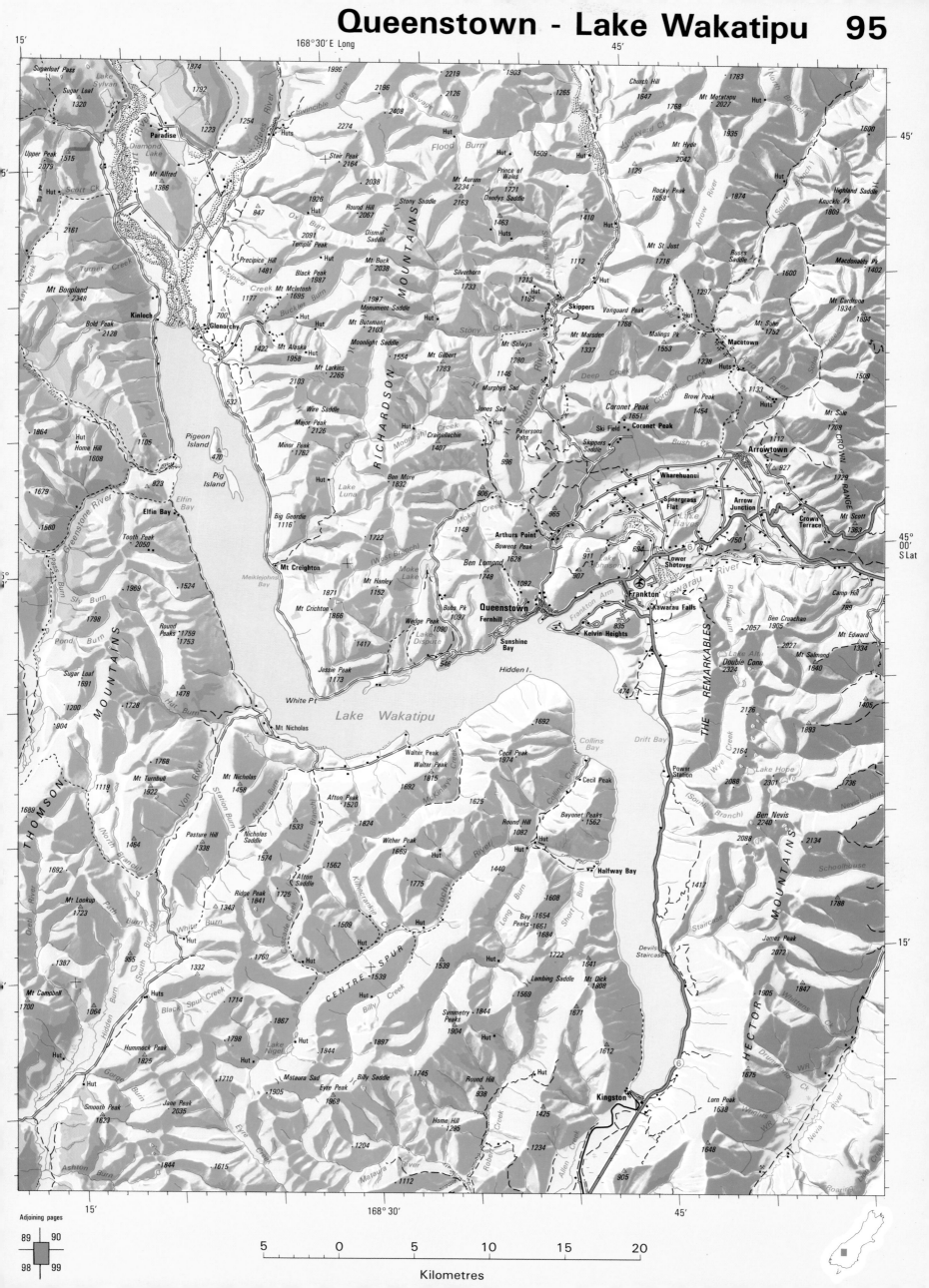

Sugarloaf Pass
Lake Sylvan
Sugar Loaf 1320
1874
1792
1996
2219 2196
2126
1903
Church Hill 1647
Mt Metatapu 2027
1783
Hut

Upper Peak 2079
Mt Alfred 1386
Paradise
1223 1254
Invincible Creek
2408
2274
Flood Burn
1265
1509
1768
Mt Hyde 2042
1129
1935
1600

Scott Ck
Hut
2161
847
Ox Burn
Round Hill 2067
Stony Saddle
Mt Aurum 2234
2163
Prince of Wales 1721
Dandys Saddle
1410
1116
Mt St Just 1716
Rocky Peak 1658
Roses Saddle
1874
Highland Saddle
Knuckle Pk 1809

Mt Bonpland 2348
Precipice Hill 1481
2091
Temple Peak
1926
2038
Dismal Saddle
1463
Huts
Silverhorn 1733
1213
1195
Hut
1112
1600
1297
Macdonalds Pk 1402
Mt Cardrona 1934

Kinloch
Glenorchy
700
1422
Black Peak 1987
Mt McIntosh 1695
1177
Buckler Creek
1987
Monument Saddle
Mt Butement 2103
Hut
Hut
Silverhorn
Skippers
Vanguard Peak 1768
Mt Marsden 1337
Malings Pk 1553
1238
Huts
Macetown
Mt Soho 1752
1894
1509

Bold Peak 2128
Mt Alaska 1958
Hut
Moonlight Saddle
Mt Larkins 2265
Mt Gilbert 1783
Mt Selwyn 1280
1146
Murphys Sad
Deep Creek
Coronet Peak 1651
Brow Peak 1454
1133
Huts
Mt Sale 1709

1864
Hut
Home Hill 1608
1105
Pigeon Island
470
2103
Wire Saddle
Major Peak 2126
Minor Peak 1762
1554
Craigellachie 1407
Jones Sad
996
Patersons Pass
Ski Field
Coronet Peak
Skippers Saddle
1112
1729
Arrowtown
927

1679
823
Pig Island
Elfin Bay
Big Geordie 1116
Ben More 1832
Lake Luna
906
965
Wharehuanui
Speargrass Flat
Lake Hayes
Arrow Junction
750
Crown Terrace
Mt Scott 1363

1580
Elfin Bay
Tooth Peak 2050
1524
1722
Moke Creek
1149
Arthurs Point
Bowens Peak 1628
911
Lake Johnson
907
Lower Shotover
694
6

1969
Mt Creighton
1871
Mt Hanley 1152
Moke Lake
Ben Lompond 1748
1082
Frankton
Frankton Arm
835
Kawarau Falls
Kelvin Heights
Camp Hill 789
Ben Cruachan 1905
2057
Mt Edward

1798
Round Peaks 1759 1753
Mt Crichton 1866
1417
Wedge Peak 1090
Lake Dispute
546
Queenstown
Fernhill
Sunshine Bay
Hidden I.
474
2027
Mt Salmond 1640
1334
1405

Sugar Loaf 1691
1478
1728
Jessie Peak 1173
White Pt
Lake Wakatipu
Hidden I.
Double Cone 2324
2126
2164

1200
904
Mt Nicholas
Walter Peak
Walter Peak 1815
Cecil Peak 1974
Collins Bay
Drift Bay
Power Station
Lake Alta
Lake Hope
2301
736

1768
Mt Turnbull 1922
Mt Nicholas 1458
1692
McKinlays Creek
1692
1625
Cecil Peak
2088
2088
Ben Nevis 2240
1893

1689
1119
1464
Afton Burn
Pasture Hill 1338
Afton Peak 1520
1824
Wither Peak 1669
Hut
Round Hill 1082
Hut
Bayonet Peaks 1562
Halfway Bay
1417
2134
1788

1692
Nicholas Saddle
1533
1574
1562
1775
Hut
1440
Long Burn
1608
Staircase Creek

Mt Lookup 1723
Ridge Peak 1841
1343
1725
1509
Lochy River
Hut
Bay Peaks 1654 1651
1684
Devils Staircase

1387
1332
1760
Hut
1539
1722
Lambing Saddle
Mt Dick 1808
James Peak 2072

Mt Campbell 1700
1064
Huts
1714
Centre Spur
Hut
1539
Billy Creek
Symmetry Peaks 1844 1904
1569
1671
1612
1905

1867
1798
Lake Nigel
1844
1897
Hut
Hut
Hut
1675
1847

Hummock Peak 1825
1710
Mataura Sad
Eyre Peak 1968
Billy Saddle
1745
Round Hill 938
Hut
Kingston
1648

Smooth Peak 1623
Jane Peak 2035
1905
1204
Home Hill 1295
1425
1234
Lorn Peak 1638
905

1844
1615
1112

RICHARDSON MOUNTAINS
THOMSON MOUNTAINS
THE REMARKABLES
HECTOR MOUNTAINS
CROWN RANGE

Adjoining pages

89	90
98	99

Kilometres
5   0   5   10   15   20

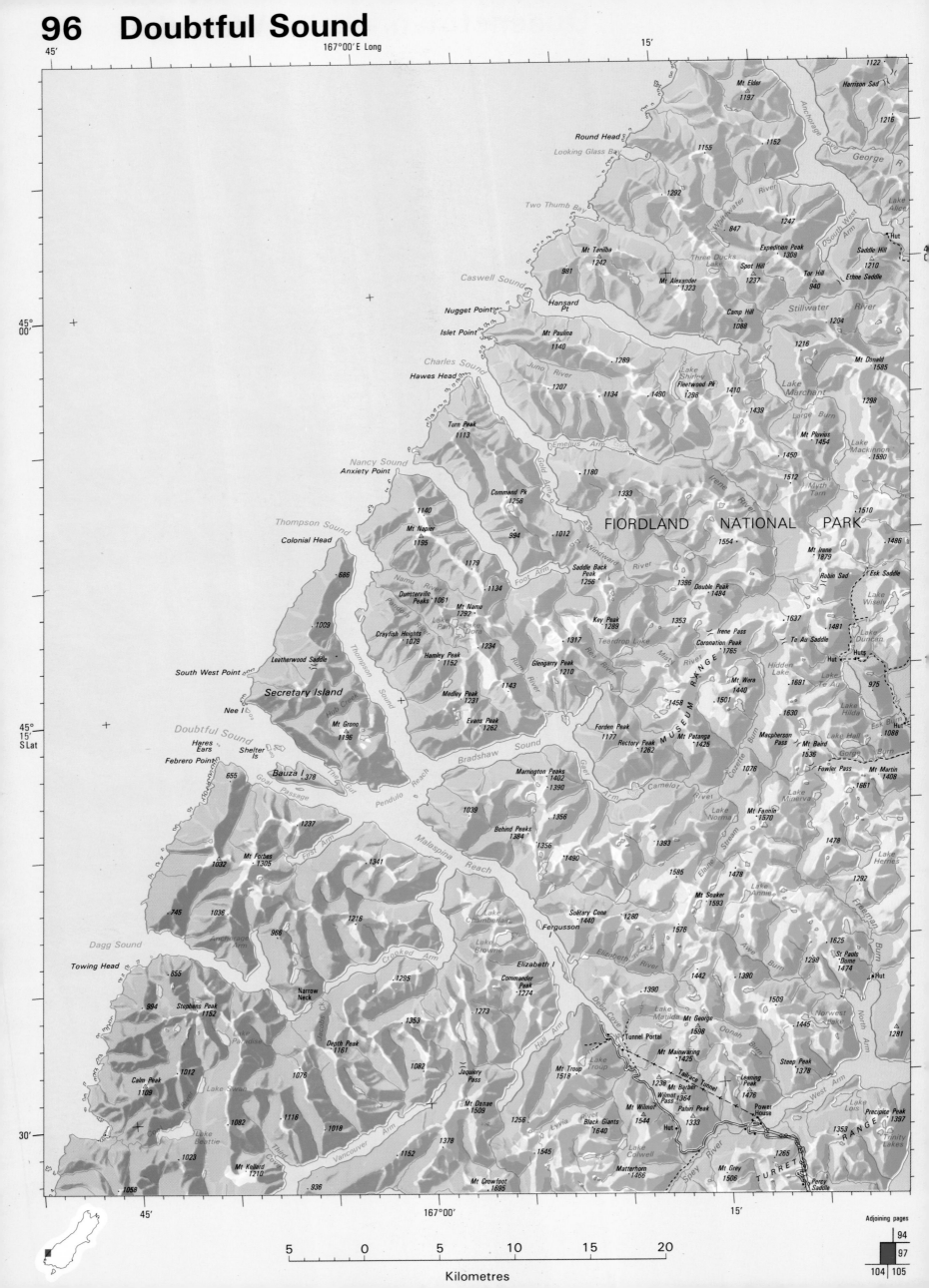

167°00' E Long

45'

15'

45°
00'

45°
15'
S Lat

30'

45'

167°00'

FIORDLAND   NATIONAL   PARK

Places, features and spot heights (selected readings):

Mt Elder 1197 · Harrison Sad · 1122 · 1216 · George R · Lake Alice · Hut · Round Head · Looking Glass Bay · 1155 · 1152 · 1292 · Whitewater River · 1247 · O'South West Arm · Saddle Hill · Two Thumb Bay · 847 · Expedition Peak 1308 · Spot Hill 1237 · Tor Hill 940 · Ethne Saddle 1210 · Mt Tanilba 1242 · Three Ducks Lake · Mt Alexander 1323 · Stillwater River · Caswell Sound · 981 · Hansard Pt · Camp Hill 1088 · 1204 · Nugget Point · Mt Paulina 1140 · 1216 · Islet Point · 1289 · Mt Donald 1585 · Charles Sound · Juno River · Lake Shirley · Fleetwood Pk 1298 · 1410 · Lake Marchant · 1298 · Hawes Head · 1207 · 1134 · 1490 · 1439 · Large Burn · Turn Peak 1113 · Emelius Arm · 1450 · Mt Pluvius 1454 · Lake Mackinnon 1590 · Nancy Sound · Gold Arm · 1180 · 1512 · Myth Tarn · 1510 · Anxiety Point · Command Pk 1256 · 1333 · Mt Irene 1879 · 1486 · 1140 · Thompson Sound · Mt Napier 1195 · 994 · 1012 · Windward River · 1554 · Robin Sad · Esk Saddle · Colonial Head · 1179 · Saddle Back Peak 1256 · 1396 · Double Peak 1484 · Te Au Saddle · 1481 · Lake Wisely · 686 · Namu River · 1134 · 1637 · Lake Duncan · Huts · Dunsterville Peaks 1061 · Mt Namu 1292 · Key Peak 1289 · 1353 · Irene Pass · Coronation Peak 1765 · Hidden Lake · 1691 · Lake Te Au · 975 · 1009 · Pandora Pass · Lake Pam · Lake Dora · Teardrop Lake · Red River · Misty River · 1630 · Lake Hilda · Crayfish Heights 1079 · 1234 · 1317 · 1458 · Mt Wera 1440 · 1501 · MUSEUM RANGE · Hamley Peak 1152 · 1143 · Glengarry Peak 1210 · Forden Peak 1177 · Rectory Peak 1262 · Mt Patanga 1425 · Macpherson Pass · Lake Hall · Esk Burn · Hut 1088 · Leatherwood Saddle · South West Point · Medley Peak 1231 · Evans Peak 1262 · Gael Arm · Cozette Burn · Mt Baird 1536 · Gorge Burn · Nee I · Mt Grono 1196 · Hub Creek · Thompson Sound · Camelot River · 1076 · Fowler Pass · Mt Martin 1408 · Hares Ears · Shelter Is · Bradshaw Sound · Marrington Peaks 1402 · 1390 · Lake Minerva · 1661 · Febrero Point · 655 · Bauza I 378 · Goal Passage · Pendulo Reach · 1039 · 1356 · Lake Norma · Mt Fannin 1570 · 1478 · 1237 · Behind Peaks 1384 · 1356 · 1393 · Lake Herries · Mt Forbes 1305 · 1032 · 1341 · 1490 · 1585 · Elaine Stream · 1478 · Lake Annie · 1292 · First Arm · Malaspina Reach · 1356 · Mt Soaker 1593 · 745 · 1036 · 1216 · Lake Chamberlain · Solitary Cone 1440 · 1280 · 1576 · 1625 · 966 · Anchorage Arm · Lake Browne · Fergusson · St Pauls Dome 1474 · Dagg Sound · Crooked Arm · 1442 · 1390 · 1298 · Hut · Towing Head · 855 · 1295 · Elizabeth I · Elizabeth River · 1390 · 1509 · 994 · Stephens Peak 1152 · Narrow Neck · Commander Peak 1274 · 1273 · Lake Matilda · Mt George 1598 · 1445 · Norwest Lake · North Arm · 1353 · Depth Peak 1161 · 1353 · Deep Cove · Tunnel Portal · Mt Mainwaring 1425 · Oonah Burn · Awe Burn · 1281 · Calm Peak 1109 · 1012 · Jacobs Ck · 1076 · 1082 · Jaquiery Pass · Mt Troup 1518 · Lake Troup · 1238 · Tailrace Tunnel · Leaning Peak 1476 · Steep Peak 1378 · West Arm · Lake Lois · Precipice Peak 1397 · Lake Paradise · 1116 · 1018 · Hall Arm · Mt Danae 1509 · 1256 · Mt Barber 1364 · Pahiri Peak 1333 · Power House · 1353 · Spey River · TURRET RANGE · Trinity Lakes · 1082 · Lake Swan · Triad Cove · Vancouver Arm · 1378 · R Lywia · Mt Wilmot 1544 · Wilmot Pass · Hut · Lake Beattie · 1023 · 1152 · Black Giants 1640 · Lake Colwell · 1265 · Mt Kellard 1210 · 936 · Mt Crowfoot 1695 · 1545 · Matterhorn 1466 · Mt Grey 1506 · Percy Saddle · 1058

Kilometres

5   0   5   10   15   20

Adjoining pages

94
97
104 | 105

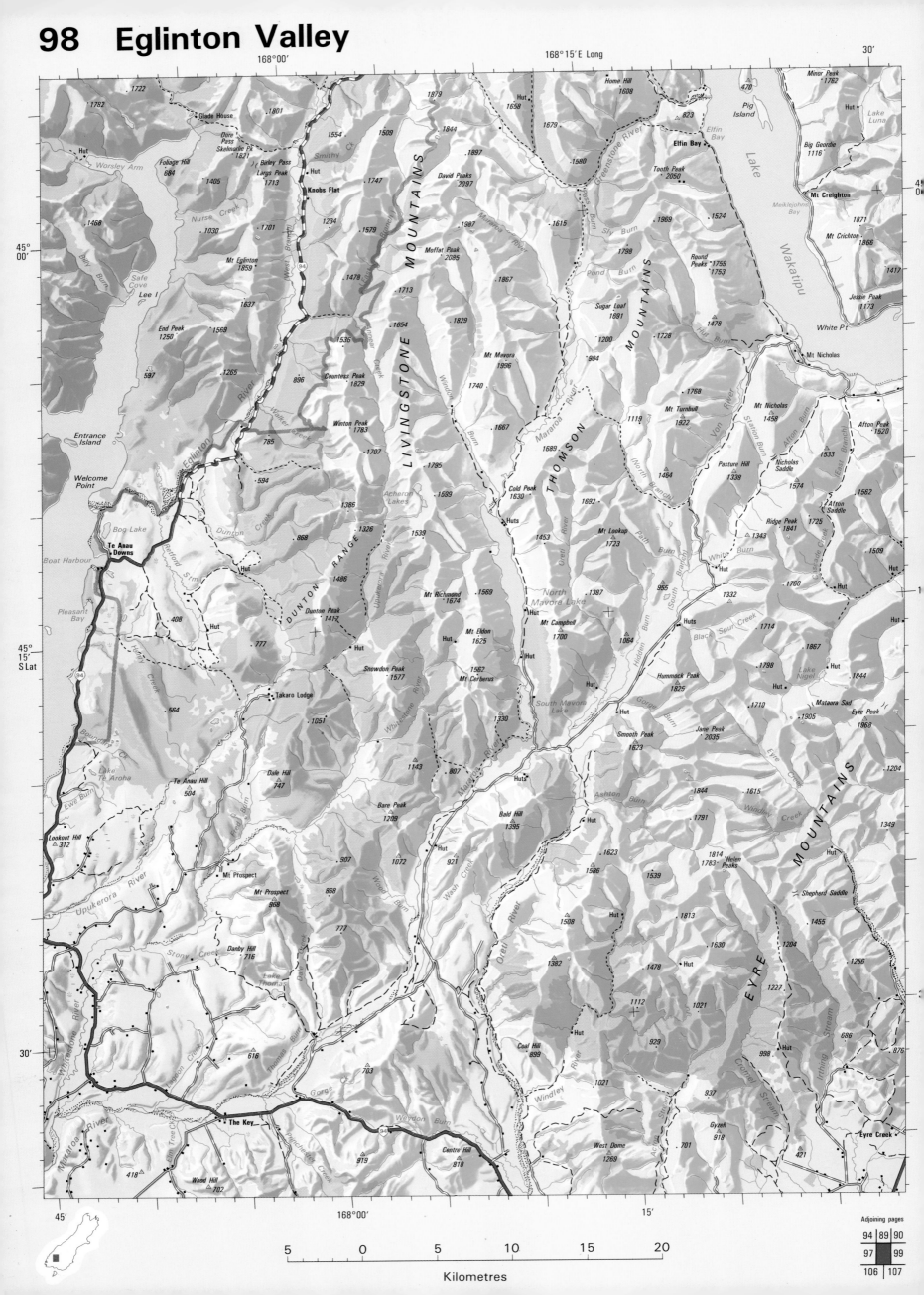

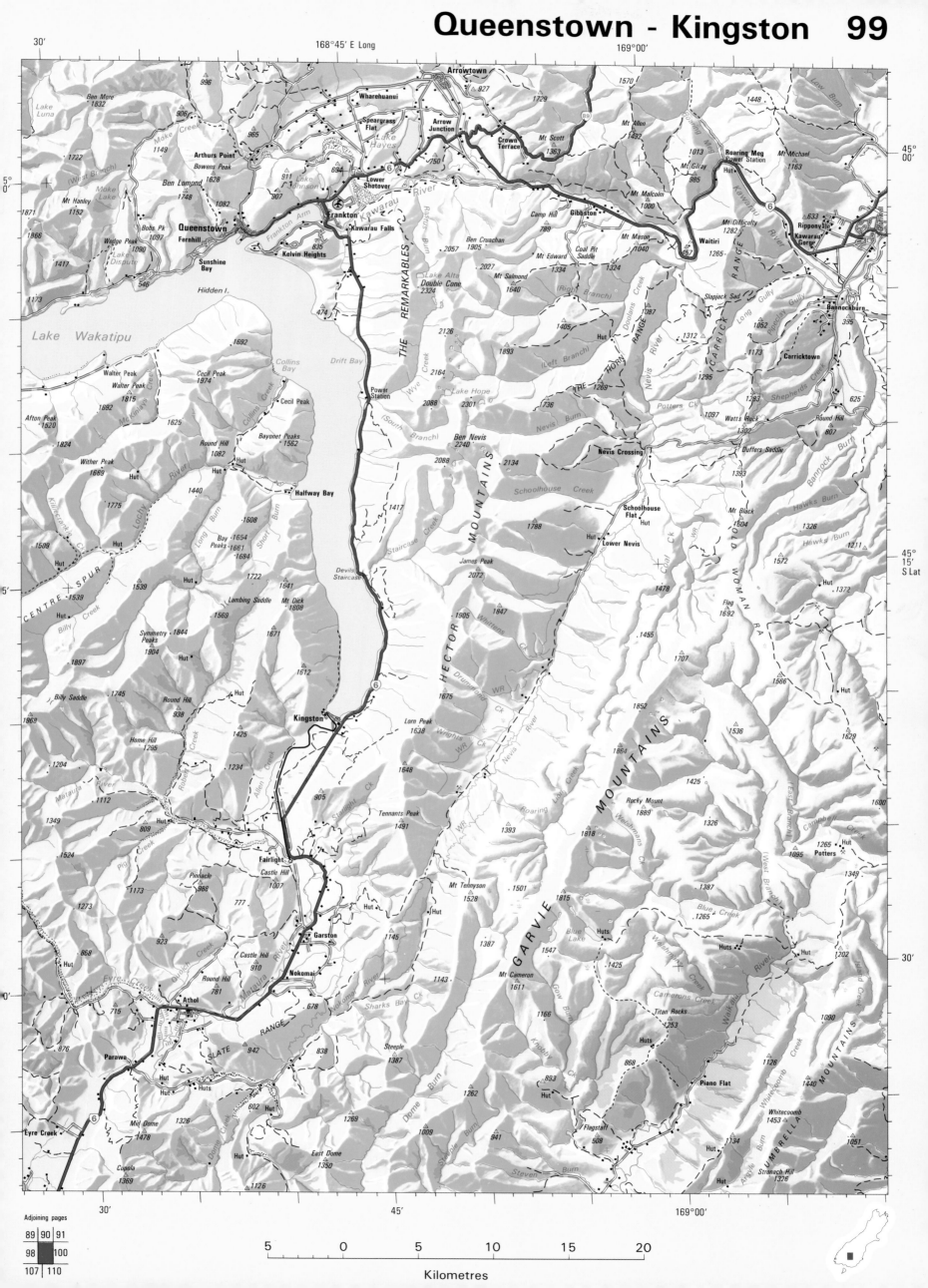

Adjoining pages

89	90	91
98		100
107	110	

5   0   5   10   15   20

Kilometres

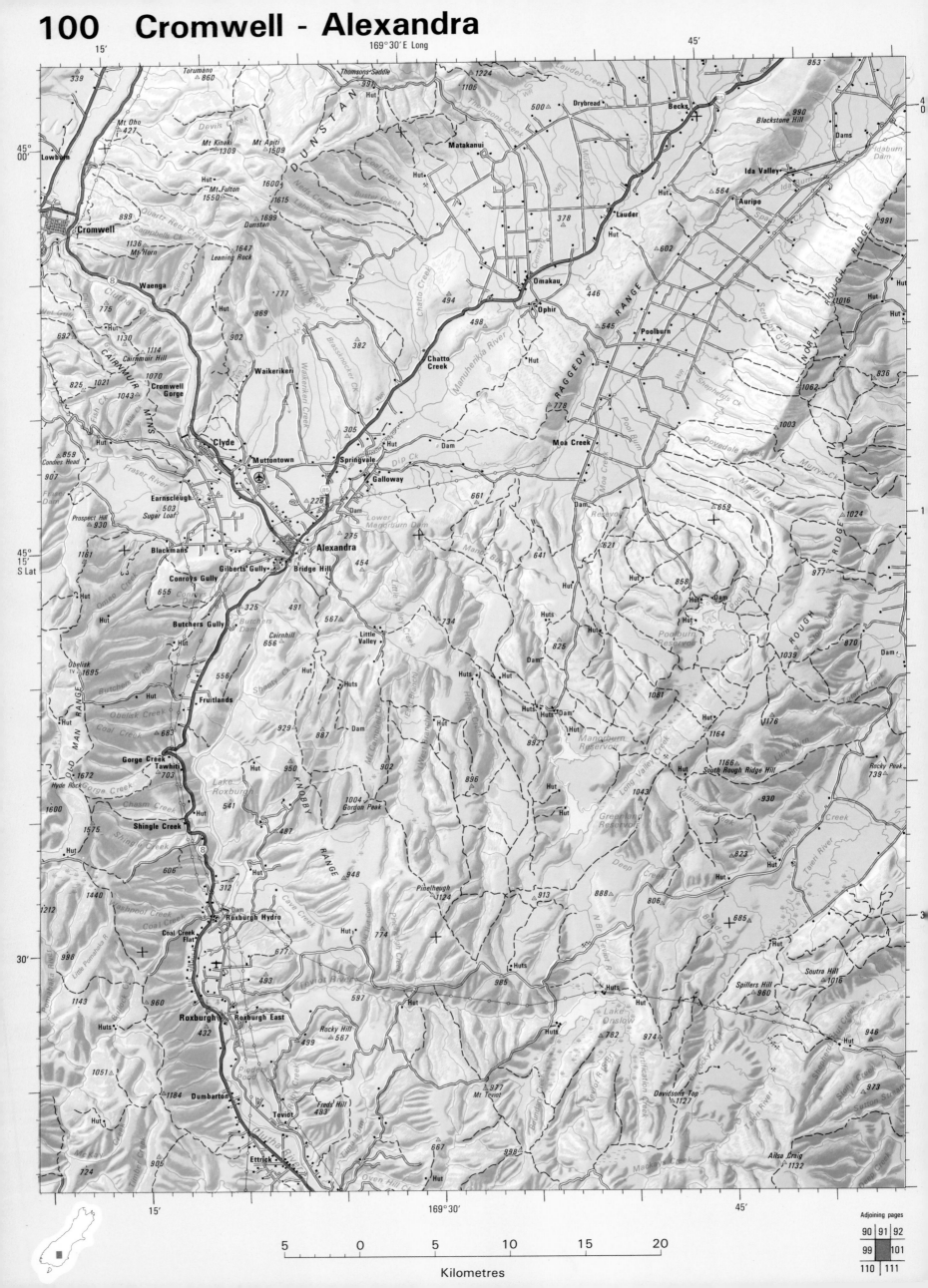

Kilometres

Adjoining pages

90	91	92
99		101
110	111	

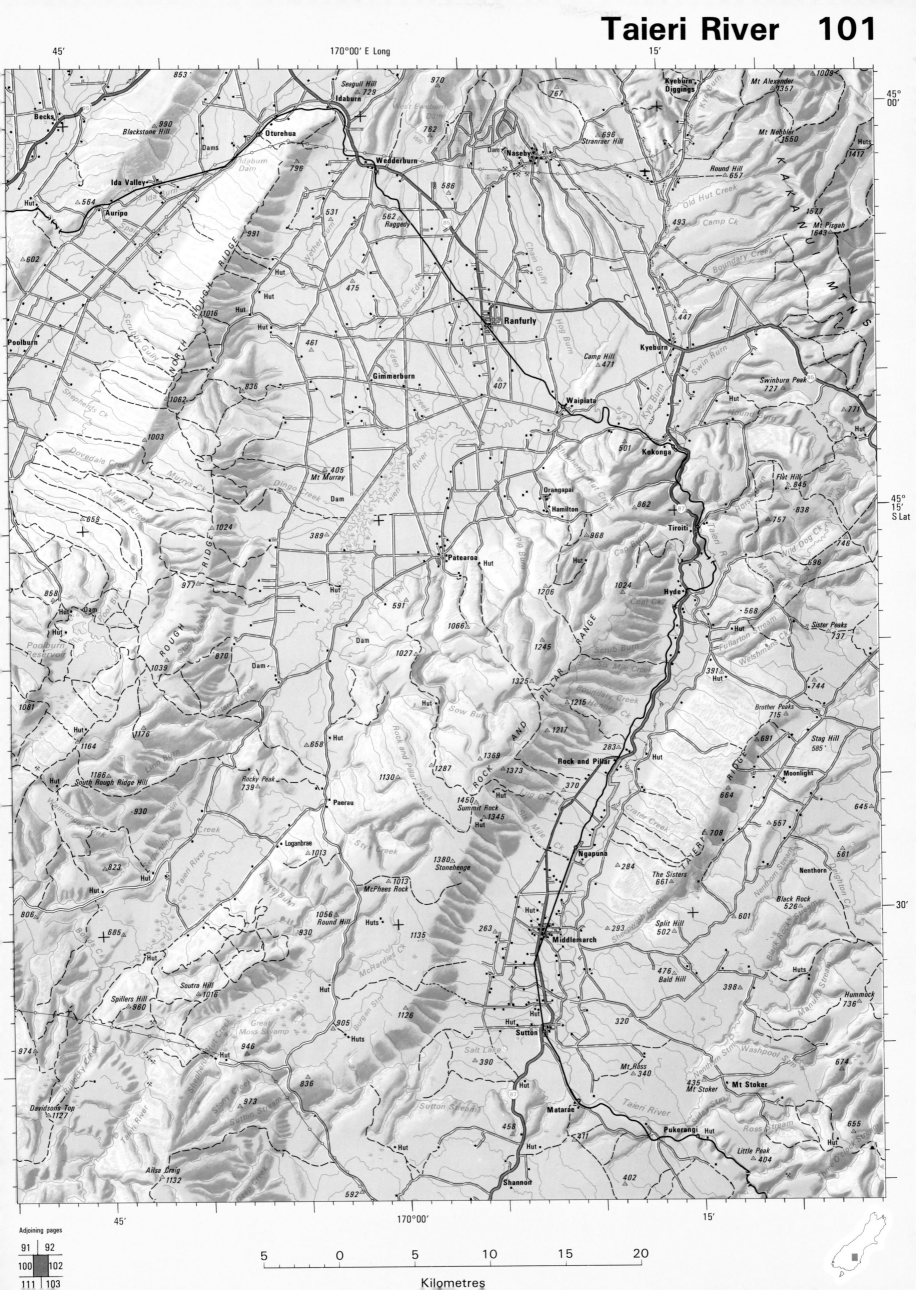

170°45'E Long

171°00'

△1009
Hilderthorpe
WR
Richmond
45° 00'
Rakis Table
△325
Airedale
Windsor Park
△203
83
Pukeuri
1389
1417
Huts 1180
Windsor
Roseberry
△254
△158
123
593
Tapui
△140
Round Hill
△236
Huts
Hut
Maruakoa
Elderslie
Enfield
△137
△229
908
(North Branch)
Mole Hill
△616
725
Marakerake
Five Forks
Whitstone
Hut
Stony Creek
Fuchsia Ck
Kia Ora
Cormacks
Ardgowan
△461
Fuchsia Creek
Weston
Whitecraig
△163
Waiareka Junction
960
△899
686
Kauru Hill
△461
△94
Deborah
Hut 924
892
Kauru Hill
OAMARU
Mt Evelyn
△1399
555
△98
Alma
△133
Cape Wanbrow
Mt Dasher
△1304
Hut
Hut
Incholme
Totara
Hectors Strm △351
Island Stream
Reidston
Teschemakers
Kakanui Peak
△1528
Mt Difficulty
△774
Mt Maheno
△55
1295
Kattothyrst
△1293
Obelisk
△578
Waianui
Whitecraig
2514
Trig Island
△895
656
Kakanui
△75
Kakanui River
Kakanui Point
△771
△491
Taranui
All Day Bay
Hut 987
Hut
Orere Point
△860
Hut
Round Hill
△743
Hut 939
△474
Herbert
763
Hut
932
966
877
△592
Otepopo
△704
Waianakarua River
(North Branch)
Hut △594
The Bluff △116
Lookout Bluff
Morrisons
828
Table Hill
Waianakarua
△518
753
Conical Peak △937
Bells Saddle 885
△679
△463
Kakaho Creek
Green Valley
(Middle Branch)
Highlay Hill △820
593
440
Waihemo
366
789
Mount Fortune
△604
△562
Hampden
Sister Peaks △137
Shag Valley
621
△604
Hut
Moeraki
Tikoraki Point
Deepdell Creek
559
△449
Hillgrove
△155
Kaik
Tawhiroko Point
△744
Waynes
△594
Moeraki
Okahau Point
Macraes Flat
569
Makareao
329
△401
Katiki
Katiki Point
Stag Hill △585
Dunback
Hut
Trotters Gorge
594
Dunback Hill △598
Inch Valley
229
599
Stoneburn
238
Hut
645
Glenpark
Pukehiwitahi 227
Shag Point
561
714 Lots Wife
Meadowbank
390
Bushey
140
Shag Point
Shag River
Little Hummock 732
695
Palmerston △343
Puketapu
581
Pleasant Valley
Mt Royal △319
Stony Creek
Swampy Hill △733
593 Mt Trotter
△418 Mt Pleasant
Wairunga
528
Bobbys Head 102
710 Mt Royal
238
Goodwood
Hummock 736
Hut
Flag Swamp
674
616
Hawksbury Bush
Tumai
Pleasant River
Mt Watkin
Derdan Hill △443
660
469
Waikouaiti
Mt Scott △680
165
Bucklands Crossing
123
Cornish Head
Mt Paul △549
351
Waikouaiti River
598
655
Merton
1
Karitane
Huts
Puketeraki
535
402
Green Head
714
518
413
338
343
Seacliff
Brinns Head

30'
45'
171°00'

5   0   5   10   15   20
Kilometres

Adjoining pages
92 | 93
101
103

170°30' E Long

15'
45'

△402
376
△508
510
△496
355
Deep Stream
Deep Stream
732
△670
413△
△401
Omimi
Warrington
△559
Hindon Stn
Christmas Creek
Little Mt Allan
△365
Evansdale
Blueskin Bay
Te Purakanui Bay
148
Potato Point
185
Purakanui
Heywood Point
Hindon
Hindon
Mt Allan
Mt Allan
715
777
Silver Peak
760
Waitati
Osborne
201
Heywood
Point
Aramoana
Taiaroa Head
△515
△477
△447
△399
△443
Mt Hyde
505△
△517
423
Double Hill
Upper Waitati
1
Mihiwaka
Mihiwaka
561
Te Ngaru
Harington Point
Te Rauone Beach
Pipikaretu
Point
Round Ridge Hill
452△
348
Parera
Duck Point
Taioma
△557
Boulder Hill
△525
Powder Hill
739
Swampy
Summit
666
Swampy
Spur
Pigeon
Flat
Mt
Cargill
680
Mt Cargill
Harwood
Otakou
McArthny Hill
△254
Wickliffe Bay
Lee Stream
306
Salisbury
Whare
Flat
TV
Sawyers
Bay
Port
Chalmers
Harveys Flat
North
Taieri
Glenleith
Glenleith
△393
Quarantine
Island
91
Broad
Bay
Portobello
Hoopers Inlet
Papanui Inlet
△644
Wyllies
Crossing
28
North
East Valley
St
Leonards
315
Mt Charles
△408
Papanui Beach
Woodside
Outram
Riverside
7
Waikati
DUNEDIN
North
Dunedin
Ravensbourne
Macandrew
Bay
Sandymount
Pukehiki
Cape
Saunders
Maungatua
△895
Mosgiel
Wingatui
361
Abbotts
Hill
203
Mornington
Waverley
Highcliff
381
69
320
Sandymount
121
West Taieri
Fairfield
Green
Island
Caversham
St
Kilda
Andersons
Bay
Ocean Grove
Harakehe Head
△105
Owhiro
East
Taieri
△473
159
St Clair
Bird Island
Maori Head
Momona
Scroggs
Hill
355
Scroggs Hill
Waldronville
Black Head
White Island
Otago Peninsula
Berwick
Otokia
218
Gledknowe
303
Westwood
Ocean View
Green Island
Kaikorai Stream
△174
Otokia Hill
Brighton
Bruce Rocks
Henley
△140
Reids Stream
46°
00'
S Lat
Waihola
Hill
184
216
Ferry Hill
1
Waihola
267
Kuri Bush
Clarendon
△319
△307
Taieri Mouth
31
Taieri Island
Taieri River
Gorge Hill
△404
Taieri Beach
△440
Akatore
Akatore Creek
△406
77
Quoin Point
Glenledi
Bull Creek
Chrystalls Beach
81
Glenledi Stream
Tokomairiro River
Toko Mouth

170°30'
15'
15'

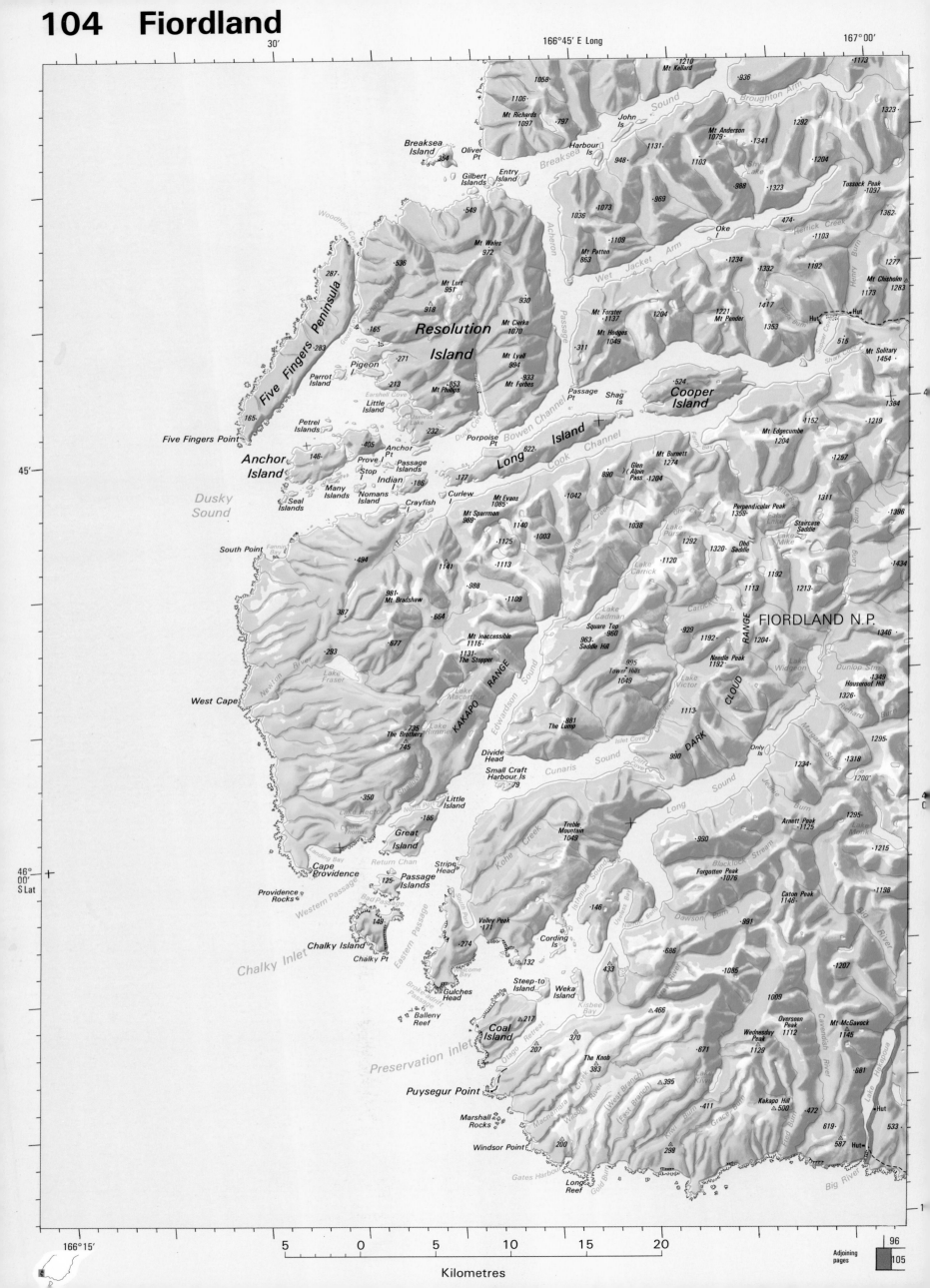

166°15'

166°45' E Long

167°00'

30'

·1173

·1210 Mt Kellard

·1058

·936

Broughton Arm

·1323

·1106

·797

·1292

Mt Richards 1097

John Is

Sound

·1341

Mt Anderson 1079

·1204

·1131

1103

Shy Lake

·1073

·988 ·1323

Tussock Peak ·1097

·1204

Breaksea Island

·354

Oliver Pt

Harbour Is

Breaksea

948

·969

Oke I

474·

Herrick Creek

·1103

·1362

Gilbert Islands

Entry Island

·549

·1036

·1109

Mt Patten 863

1234·

·1332

1192

·1277

Mt Chisholm 1283

Mt Wales 972

·536

930

Acheron

·1234

·1221 Mt Pender

·1417

1353

Henry Burn

1173

Mt Solitary 1454

Mt Lort 951

918

·1137

Mt Clerke 1070

·1204

Mt Forster

Passage

515

·165

·853 Mt Philips

Mt Lyall 994

·933 Mt Forbes

Mt Hodges 1049

·311

·524·

Cooper Island

1152

·1219

Pigeon I

·271

Parrot Island

·213

Little Island

Useless Lake

Passage Pt

Shag Is

Mt Edgecumbe 1204

·1384

Petrel Islands

·232

Porpoise Pt

Bowen Channel

Long Island

Cook

Channel

Fanny Bay

·1257

Five Fingers Point

165

·405

Anchor Pt

·177

622·

Mt Burnett 1274

Perpendicular Peak 1359

1311

·1396

146·

Prove I

Passage Islands

·186

890

Glen Alpin Pass ·1204

Oho Ck

Lake Purser

Staircase Saddle

Anchor Island

Stop I

Curlew I

Mt Evans 1085·

·1042

1038

1292

Oho Saddle

Seal Islands

Many Islands

Nomans Island

Crayfish I

Mt Sparrman 969·

1140

·1003

1320·

1192

·1434

Dusky Sound

1141

·1125

·1113

Lake Carrick

Carrick R

1113

·1213

South Point

·494

·988

·1120

·929

1346

Mt Bradshaw

981·

·1109

Lake Cadman

1192

RANGE

1204

387

·664

Square Top ·960 Saddle Hill 963·

FIORDLAND N.P.

West Cape

·293

·677

Mt Inaccessible 1116·

KAKAPO

995 Tower Hills 1049

Needle Peak 1192

CLOUD

Dunlop Stm

·1349 Houseroof Hill

1326

1131· The Stopper

Edwardson

Lake Victor

1113·

DARK

Richard

The Brothers

735

Lake Kirmiss

·1295

745

861 The Lump

990

Only Is

1234·

·1318

Divide Head

Islet Cove

·1200

West Cape

Small Craft Harbour Is

79

Cunaris

Cliff Cove

Sound

Margaret Stm

·350

Little Island

·186

Treble Mountain 1049

Long

Sound

Arnett Peak ·1125

·1295

·1215

Great Island

·990

Kohe Creek

Forgotten Peak ·1076

Cape Providence

·125

Stripe Head

Isthmus Sound

Useless Bay

Nancy Bend

Caton Peak 1146·

·1198

Passage Islands

·146

Blacklock Stream

Providence Rocks

South Port

433

·686

·991

·1085

·1207

149·

Valley Peak 171

Cording Is

132

Chalky Island

·274

Dawson Burn

1009

Chalky Pt

Steep-to Island

Weka Island

Overseen Peak 1112

Mt McGavock 1145

Gulches Head

△217

Kisbee Bay

△466

Wednesday Peak 1129

·671

·681

Balleny Reef

370

△207

△395

·411

619·

533

Coal Island

The Knob 383

Kakapo Hill △500

·472

·587 Hut

Puysegur Point

298

Preservation Inlet

Marshall Rocks

200

Windsor Point

Long Reef

Big River

45'

45'

46° 00' S Lat

167° 45' E Long
168° 00'
30'

30'

45'

46° 00' S Lat

45'

30'
45'
168° 00'

Te Waewae Bay

LONGWOOD RA

Adjoining pages

97	98
105	107
108	109

5   0   5   10   15   20

Kilometres

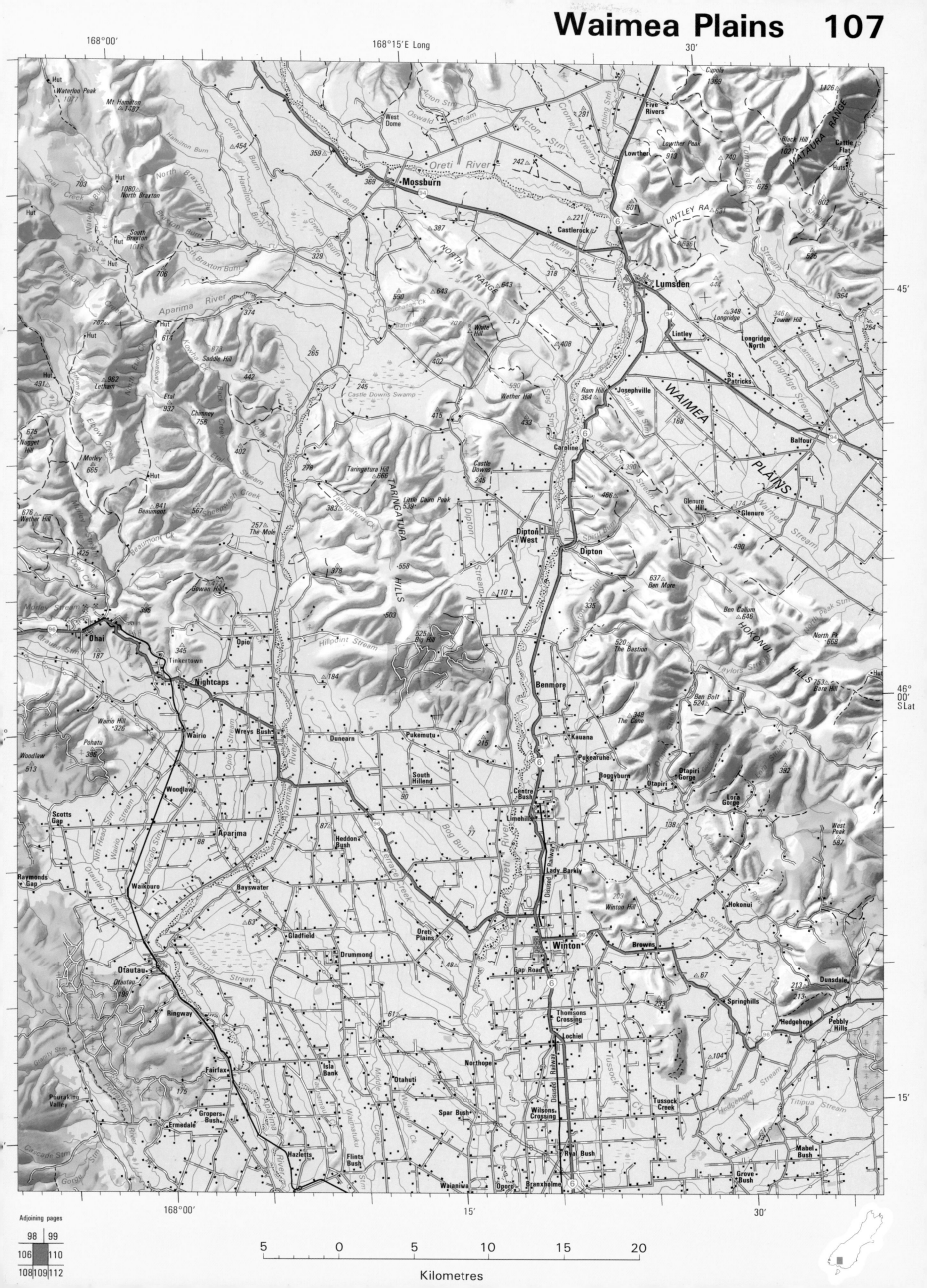

168°00'
168°15'E Long
30'

Hut
Waterloo Peak
1077
Mt Hamilton
1487
West
Dome
Acton Stm
Oswald
Acton Stm
Cromel Stream
Cupola
1369
1126
Five
Rivers
Black Hill
1021
MATAURA RANGE
Cattle
Flat
Centre Burn
△454
359△
Oreti River
242△
Lowther
Lowther Peak
913
740
675
Huts
802
North Braxton Burn
Hamilton Burn
369
Mossburn
94
291
601
LINTLEY RA
631
636
525
Coal Creek
Hut
703
Hut
1080
North Braxton
South Braxton
1018
706
△387
Castlerock
6
45'
Hut
Braxton Burn
Aparima River
△221
Murray Creek
318
Lumsden
444
Hut
787
614
374
329
590
Buchanan Ck
643
707
Roe Burn
Scew Burn
94
348
Longridge
346
Tower Hill
254
Sth Braxton Burn
Kowhai Ck
673
Saddle Hill
442
265
Barnhill St
White
Hill
408
Lintley
Longridge
North
St
Patricks
Longridge Stream
Tomachs Stream
Hut
491
Letham
962
Kangaroo Ck
Etal
932
Chimney
758
402
Flaxy Stream
Stony Ck
245
402
415
Wether Hill
590
433
Ram Hill
364
Josephville
Ram Hill Stm
WAIMEA
168
Balfour
94
676
Wether Hill
841
Beaumont
567
Sheepwash Creek
257
The Mole
278
Taringatura Hill
666
Taringatura Ck
383
Little Cairn Peak
539
Castle
Downs
245
Caroline
6
Okaihana Stream
390
466△
Glenure
Hill
174
Glenure
490
PLAINS
425
Elbow Creek
Morley
665
Beaumont Ck
Gowan Hill
547
378
558
503
Dipton Stream
10
Dipton
West
Dipton
637
Ben More
Salt Burn
335
Ben Callum
646
North Pk
668
HOKONUI
Waimea Stream
Morley Stream
395
Ohai
96
345
187
Tinkertown
Opio
Kelpy Ck
Hillpoint Stream
184
525
Big Hill
Benmore
520
The Bastion
348
The Cone
Ben Bolt
524
HILLS
753
Bare Hill
Hut
Wairio Hill
326
Nightcaps
Wairio
Wreys Bush
Opio Stream
Dunearn
Pukemutu
215
Kauana
Pukearuhe
Taylors Stream
392
Pohatu
386
Woodlaw
513
Aparima River
South
Hillend
90
Boggyburn
Otapiri
Gorge
Otapiri
Long Stream
138
West
Peak
587
Woodlaw
Nth Head Stm
Wairio Stm
Centre
Bush
Scotts
Gap
Aparima
877
88
96
Heddon
Bush
Bog Burn
Oreti River
77
Limehills
Mataura River
Raymonds
Gap
Waikouro
63
Bayswater
Terrace Creek
Lady Barkly
Disused Railway
209
Winton Hill
Hokonui
Otautau
Otautau
199
Gladfield
Drummond
Oreti
Plains
643
48
Disused Railway
Winton
Browns
67
213
Dunsdale
Ringway
61
Gap Road
6
233
Springhills
Hedgehope
Pebbly
Hills
Fairfax
175
Isla
Bank
Otahuti
Spar Bush
Thomsons
Crossing
Lochiel
Northope
104
Tussock Ck
Tussock
Creek
Pourakino
Valley
Gropers
Bush
Ermedale
Hazletts
Flints
Bush
Waimatuku Creek
Waianiwa
Oporo
Wilsons
Crossing
Ryal Bush
Branxholme
Disused Railway
6
Mabel
Bush
Grove
Bush
Cascade Stm
Gorge
168°00'
15'
30'

46°
00'
SLat

15'

5   0   5   10   15   20

Kilometres

167°45' E Long

168°00'

30'

Pukemaori

132

Raymonds Gap

Waikouro

416

Helmet Hill
△606

259

△213

268

283

Orauea River

Otautau Stream

Waimatuku Stm

White Hill
241

134

197

Pikopiko

104

Boundary Ck.

Otautau

Otautau
199

213

233

Tuatapere

Happy Valley

Clunie Stm

Ringway

250 △
Masons Hill

Papatotara
Te Tua

138

Camp Ck.

804

Fairfax

164

△268

Pouraking Valley

175

Waikoau River

167

Te Waewae

Keegan Ck.

Granity Stm

Ermedale

Waimeamea River

378

Deep Stm

Gropers Bush

46°
15'
S Lat

△578

774
·774

Port Craig
Hut

Sand Hill Point

Waiau River

99

Waihoaka

Stucks
Hill
139

△147

Pouttu's Ck.

LONGWOOD

764

Cascade Stm

RANGE

Gorge

Gummies Bush

Orepuki

Taunoa Stream

Waipango

260
Round Hill

Round Hill

Taylors Ck.

Waikawa

Monkey I

Pahia Point

Pahia Hill
227

99

Longwood

Jacobs River Estuary

Pahia

Round Hill

Ruahine

Colac Bay

Riverton

Wakapatu

Lake George

171

122
Riverton

141

Old Man Rock

·118

Oraka
163

Pig Island

Kawakaputa Bay

114 △

Oraka Point

Wakaputa Point

Raratoka Island

Centre Island

Hapuka Rock

Escape Reefs

166° 50'

46°
35'

Little Solander
Island

Solander Island
300

Pt. F.N.P.

Bishops and Clerks Islands

Cave Pt

Black Rock Point

44

Hut

White Rock Point

159

360

Hut

Lucky Point

Rugged Islands

530

Saddle Point

Hut

750

Mt Anglem
888

980

Hut

North Red Head

Red Head Peak
490

607

Little Mt Anglem
738

The Knobbies

North West Bay

Roger Head
Sealers Bay

27

190

30'

167° 45'

168°00'

5   0   5   10   15   20

Kilometres

Pouraking Valley
Gropers Bush
Ermedale
Cascade Stm
Gorge
Moa Creek
Spook Stm
Taylors Ck
Gummies Bush
Hazletts
Flints Bush
Spar Bush
Wilsons Crossing
Tussock Creek
Titipua Stream
Aparima River
Waimatuku Stream
Waianiwa Ck
Rya Bush
Mabel Bush
Grove Bush
Waipango
Thornbury
Wrights Bush
Waimatuku
Waianiwa
Oporo
Branxholme
Makarewa Junction
Rakahouka
47
Otaitai Bush
Wallacetown
Underwood
Makarewa
Waikiwi Stm
Longwood
Taramoa
Lornville
Roslyn Bush
Jacobs River Estuary
Linds Bridge
West Plains
Grasmere
Myross Bush
Longbush
Woodlands
Colac Bay
Riverton
171 122 Riverton
The Rocks
Howells Point
Waikiwi
Gladstone
Glengarry
Kennington
Rimu
Oraka 163
Oraka Point
Pig Island
Colac Bay
Oreti River
Murihiku
Otatara
INVERCARGILL
Heidelberg
45
Centre Island
Halfway Rocks
Oreti Beach
Bushy Pt
Waimatua
Timpanys
Tisbury
Mokotua
Escape Reefs
Clifton
Woodend
Motu Rimu
Waimatua Creek
46° 30' S Lat
Mokomuto Inlet
Sandy Point
New River Estuary
Awarua
Mokoia Stream
Awarua Plains
Waituna Creek
Bombay Rk
Omaui Island
Steep Head
Omaui
13
Muddy Creek
Three Sisters 173
Greenhills
Duck Ck
Barracouta Point
Colyers I
Bluff Harbour
Joeys I
Awarua Bay
Flat Hill 125
Tikore I
Shag Rock
Greenpoint
Ocean Beach
Aluminium Smelter
Bluff 265 The Bluff
Tiwai Point
Stirling Point
Lookout Point
Dog Island
Foveaux
North Head 63
Black Rock Point
44
Hut
White Rock Point
Lucky Point
Caroline
45
Saddle Point
Strait
Bird Island
West Point 65
Ruapuke Island
Lagoon Bay
Mt Anglem 888 980
Christmas Village Bay
Hut
Henrietta Bay
Little Mt Anglem 738
607
Garden Point
Fife Rock
South Islets 43
South Point
Murray River
Gull Rock Pt 38
Newton Rock
376
606 The Paps 610
Hut
North Island 36
Half Passage Rock
Hazelburgh Group
Freshwater River
L Sheila
430
302
Hut
Port William
Womens Island
Edwards Island
Jacky Lee Island
Muttonbird Islands
Bunker Islets
Kanetetoe Island
THOMSON RIDGE 219
Rocky Mt 549
305
511
Peters Pt Bobs Point
43 Mamaku Point
Herekopare Island 42
183
96
Hut
127
Native Island
Bench Island 63
267
Hut
93
Halfmoon Bay
68
Ackers Point
223
258
Dynamite Point
110
Prices Pt
Paterson Inlet
Tolson R
Horseshoe Bay
Halfmoon Bay
Abbott Passage

Adjoining pages

107
108 | 112
114 | 115

168°00' 15' 30'

5 0 5 10 15 20
Kilometres

169°00' E Long

45'

15'

Matheson R

1018

995

Hut

776 Station Burn

Flat Hill

Steeple Burn

857 Craigie Hill

Dome Burn

321

1244 Crown Rock

977

689

498

Hut

Huts

Gore Creek

Hut

Argyle Hill 787

1156

Hut

Sandy Creek

735

608

BLACK UMBRELLA RANGE

Parasol Creek

Thomsons Creek

Bedrog Burn

Rob Roy Creek (West Br)

Round Hill 710

458

1090

922

Black Hill 723

Argyle Burn

Winding Ck

Black Umbrella 1107

45'

Waikaia

259

Leithen Burn

596 Mole Hill

Dunrobin

Edievale

Waikaia River

Round Down 633

744

657

502

Spylaw

Dusky Hill 612

Park Hill

Anguilla Stream

Mathesons Corner

90

254

Waiparu 451

Mount Wendon 845

634

Heriot

Waipounamu

500

Wendon Stream

297

Pomahaka River (East Br)

Greenvale

Crookston

Ardlussa

151

Mataura River

Longridge

McKellar Stream

Waikaia Hill 393

Waikaka Stream

246

Crossans Corner

167

Kelso

Black Gully

Riversdale

181 Sandstone

Pyramid

273 Pyramid

Chatton North

Waikaka

Te Kiteroa

Waikaka Stream (East Br)

236

Tapanui

922

Kaweku

Sandstone Stream

258

252

Otama

East Chatton

166 Maitland

Merino Downs

166

180

218

Glenkenich

689

351

183

Chatton

204

Waikoikoi

Pomahaka

475

Waimea Hill 571

152

Knapdale

166

281

216

Mandeville

Okapuia Ck

Willowbank

159

Waikaka Valley

320

Otamita

94

358

Croydon

82

66

Benio

164

Conical Hill

The Cone 313

342

Otamita Stream

552 Mt. Peel

HOKONUI

Kelvin Peak 639

Whiterigg

McNab

Otikerama

209

Pukerau 210

Arthurton

Waipahi

482

HILLS

564

GORE

East Gore

Waipahi Stream

Beacon Hill 201

Pukemaire 624

645

213

Waimumu

408 Waikaka

288

Kaiwera Stream

Wairuna Peak 481

Dunsdale 549

133

Charlton

146

66

Kaiwera

295

Wairuna

378

Dunsdale Stream

Hedgehope Stream

Te Tipua

Mataura River

Ferndale

325

Otaraia

366 Otaraia Hill

500 Stony Peak

96

Waitane

Pebbly Hill 154

Mataura

377

Waikana

464

522

Titipua Stream

Brydone

Tuturau

42

Mataura 311

Ota Ck

296

346

516

485 Kuriwao

261

444

377

Mimihau Stream

Waiarikiki

430

The Cairn 658

462

515

Ota Creek

177

271

Edendale

83

Mimihau

Oware

C.S.F.P

CATLINS S.F

1

46°00' S Lat

15'

45'

169°00'

15'

Adjoining pages

99	100
107	111
109	112	113

5   0   5   10   15   20

Kilometres

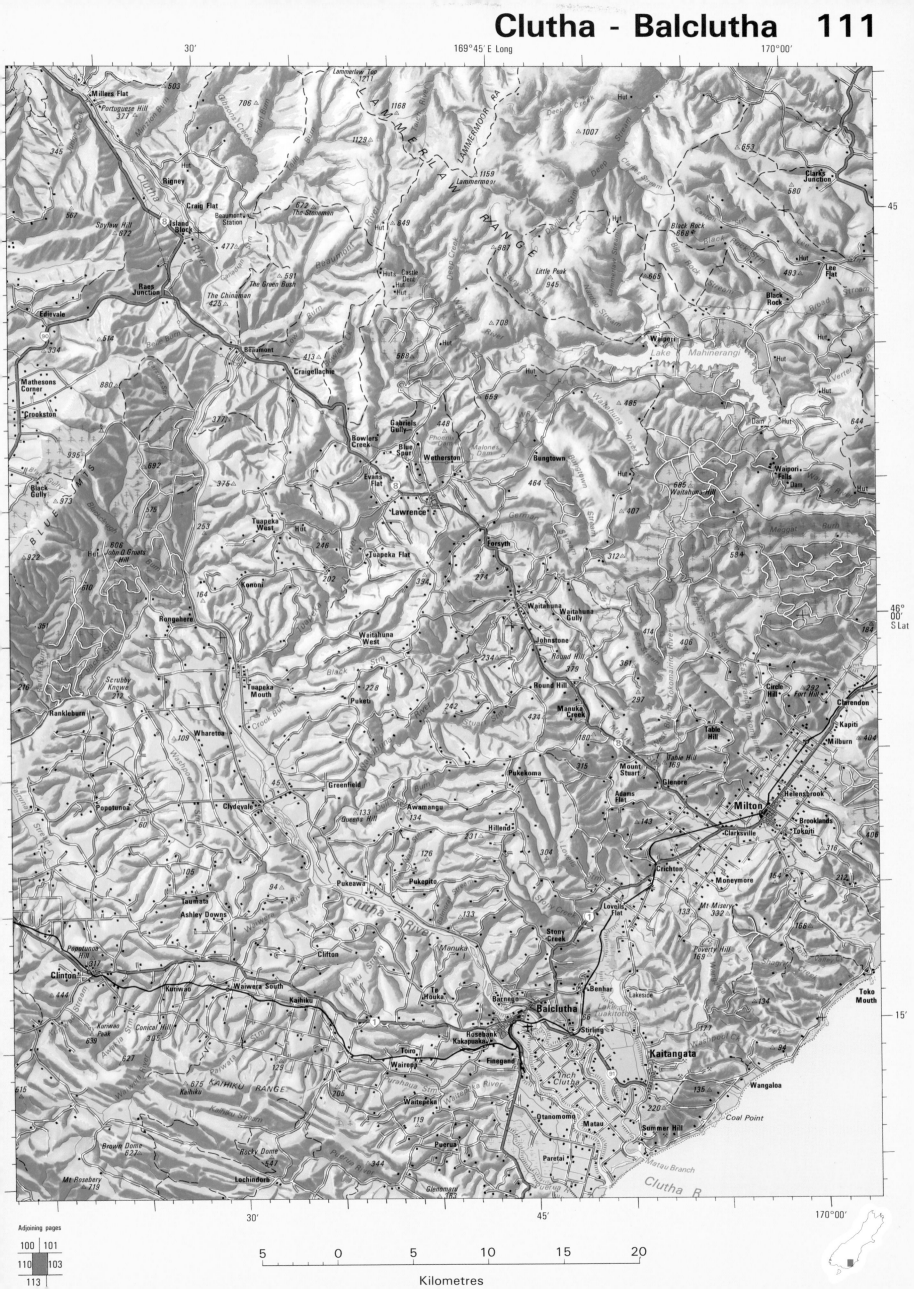

169°45' E Long
170°00'

30'

45'

Millers Flat
503
Portuguese Hill 377
345
706
Gibbons Creek
Munzion Burn
LAMMERLAW
Lammerlaw Top 1211
1168
1129
1159
Lammermoor
1007
653
Clark's Junction 580
Rigney
Hut
Craig Flat
567
Spylaw Hill 672
8 Island Block
Beaumont Station
The Stoneman 672
477
The Chinaman 425
591
The Green Bush
Hut 849
Castle Dent Hut
987
Little Peak 945
RANGE
Black Rock 668
Hut
Lee Flat 493
Black Rock
Raes Junction
708
Edievale
90
334
514
Belle Burn
Beaumont
413
Craigellachie
588
Hut
Waipori
Lake Mahinerangi
Hut
Matheson's Corner
880
3771
Gabriels Gully
448
Phoenix Dam
Malones Dam
659
Wetherston
Bungtown
Hut
Waitahuna Hill 685
Waipori Falls Dam
644
Crookston
Bowlers Creek
Blue Spur
995
692
375
Evans Flat
464
407
312
Black Gully 973
575
253
Lawrence 8
Tuapeka West Hut
246
Forsyth
German
584
922
John O Groats Hill 606
Hut
202
Tuapeka Flat
274
Meggat Burn
610
164
Kononi
394
312
406
184
Rongahere
351
Waitahuna West
Waitahuna
Waitahuna Gully
414
216
Scrubby Knowe 212
Tuapeka Mouth
228
Puketi
242
Johnstone
Round Hill 379
361
297
Circle Hill
292 Fort Hill
Clarendon
Rankleburn
Wharetoa 109
45
Greenfield
434
Round Hill
Manuka Creek
180
Table Hill
Kapiti
Milburn 404
Popotunoa
60
Queens Hill 133
Awamangu 134
Hillend
315
Table Hill 169
Mount Stuart
Glenore
Helensbrook
105
Clydevale
231
304
Adams Flat
143
Milton
Brooklands Tokoiti
94
Pukeawa
126
Pukepito
133
Clarksville
316
Taumata
Ashley Downs
Crichton
Moneymore
154
212
Clifton
Lovells Flat
Mt Misery 332
133
166
Clinton 444
Kuriwao
Waiwera South
Kaihiku
Te Houka
Stony Creek
1
Poverty Hill 169
Kuriwao Peak 639
Conical Hill 305
Barnego
Benhar
Lakeside
134
Toko Mouth
615
Brown Dome 627
675 Kaihiku
KAIHIKU RANGE
Toiro
Wairepo
Rosebank
Kakapuaka
Finegand
Balclutha
Stirling
Lake Tuakitoto
Kaitangata
91
Wangaloa
Mt Rosebery 719
Rocky Dome 547
205
119
Waitepeka
Puerua
Otanomomo
Matau
Summer Hill
135
220
Coal Point
Lochindorb
344
Paretai
Inch Clutha
Glenomaru 363
Clutha R
Puerua River
Matau Branch

46°00' S Lat

45

15'

30'
45'
170°00'

5 0 5 10 15 20
Kilometres

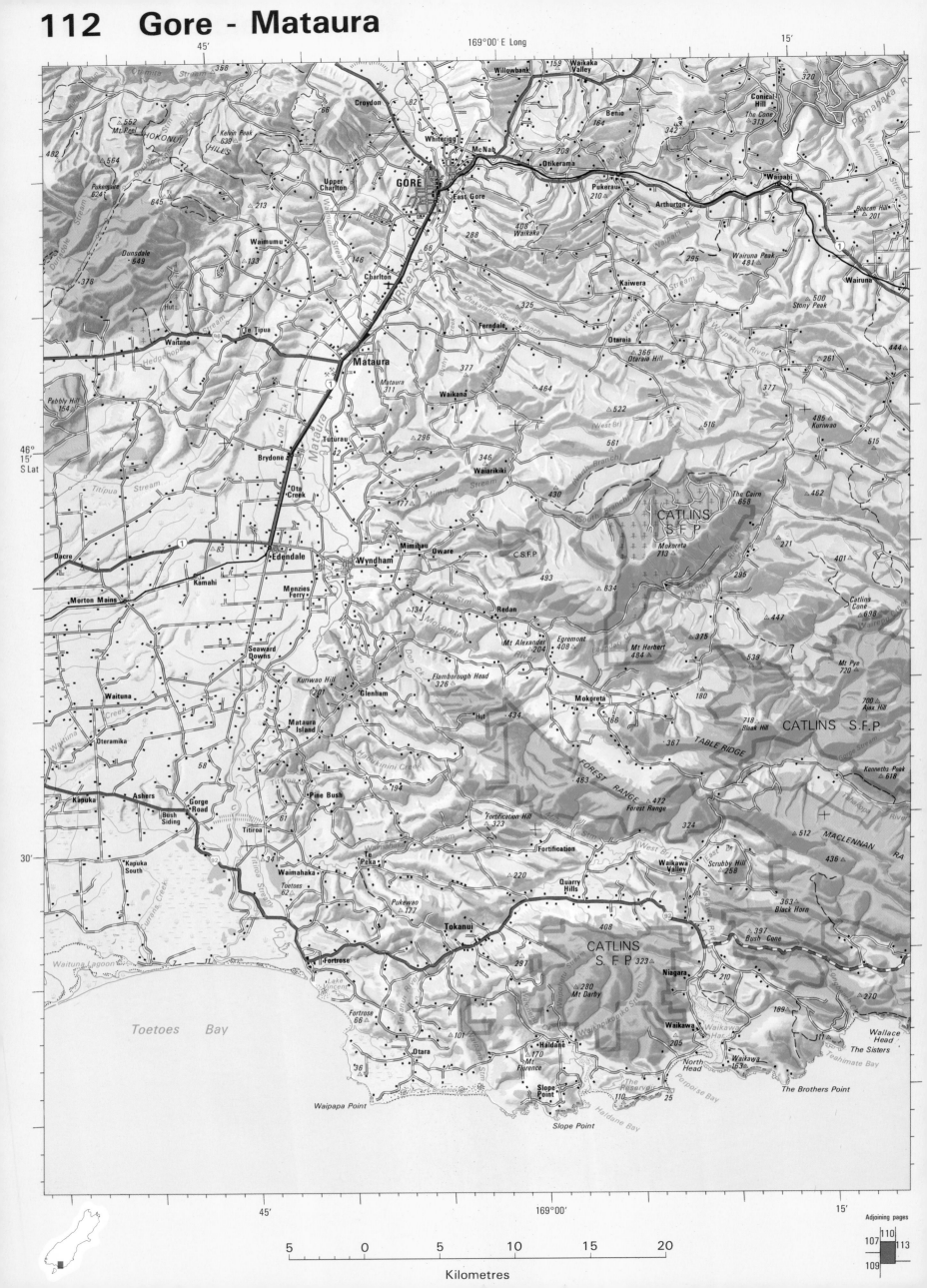

Kilometres

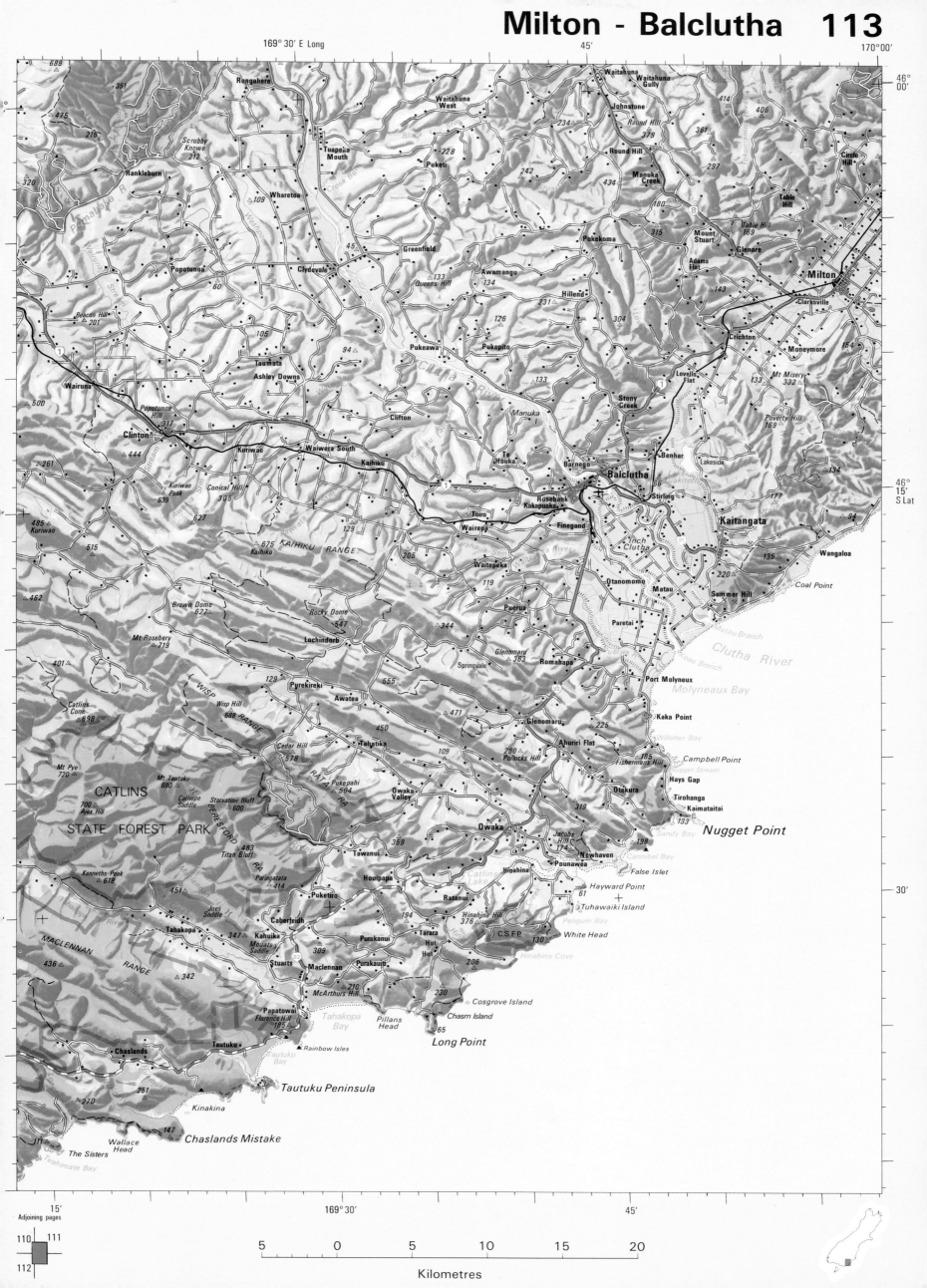

169° 30' E Long

45'

170° 00'

46° 00'

689
351
Rongahere
Waitahuna
Waitahuna Gully
475
216
Scrubby Knowe 212
Tuapeka Mouth
Waitahuna West
Johnstone
Round Hill 379
234
361
414
406
Circle Hill
320
Rankleburn
Puketi
242
434
Manuka Creek
297
Table Hill
Wharetoa
109
45
Round Hill
180
8
Table Hill 169
Popotunoa
Clydevale
Greenfield
Queens Hill 133
Awamangu 134
Pukekoma
315
Mount Stuart
Glenore
Milton
60
Hillend
231
304
Adams Flat
Clarksville
94
Pukeawa
126
Pukepito
143
Crichton
Beacon Hill 201
105
133
Manuka
Moneymore
154
Taumata
Ashley Downs
Clifton
1
Lovells Flat
Mt Misery 332
Wairuna
133
Stony Creek
133
Poverty Hill 169
500
Te Houka
Popotunoa Hill 317
Clinton
444
Kuriwao
Waiwera South
Kaihiku
Barnego
Benhar
Lakeside
134
261
Conical Hill 305
Balclutha
Stirling
66
177
Kuriwao Peak 639
Rosebank
Kakapuaka
Kaitangata
627
Toiro
Finegand
Inch Clutha
485 Kuriwao
129
KAIHIKU RANGE
Wairepa
94
515
675 Kaihiku
205
Waitepeka
Otanomomo
Matau
Summer Hill
220
135
Wangaloa
Coal Point
462
Brown Dome 627
Rocky Dome 547
119
Puerua
Paretai
Mt Rosebery 719
Lochindorb
344
Glenomaru 363
Romahapa
Clutha River
401
129
Pyrekireki
555
Springvale
Port Molyneux
Molyneaux Bay
Catlins Cone 698
WISP RANGE
Wisp Hill 688
Awatea
471
Glenomaru
225
Kaka Point
Willsher Bay
Mt Pye 720
Cedar Hill 578
450
Tahatika
109
280
Pollocks Hill
Ahuriri Flat
Fishermans Hill 185
Campbell Point
Nugget Stream
Hays Gap
CATLINS
Mt Tautuku 690
RATA RA
Pukepahi 504
Owaka Valley
Otekura
Tirohanga
Kaimataitai
700 Ajax Hill
Calliope Saddle
Starvation Bluff 600
319
133
Nugget Point
STATE FOREST PARK
BERESFORD RA
Owaka
359
Jacobs Hill 174
198
Sandy Bay
Mt Pye 720
483 Titan Bluff
Tawanui
Newhaven
Cannibal Bay
Kenneths Peak 618
Paringatata 414
Houipapa
Hinahina
Pounawea
False Islet
451
Joes Saddle
Puketiro
Ratanui
61
Hayward Point
Tahakopa
347
Kahuika
Caberfeidh
194
Hinahina Hill 376
Tuhawaiki Island
309
Mouats Saddle
Purakanui
Tarara Hut Hut
C.S.F.P.
White Head
436
Stuarts
Maclennan
Purakaujp
206
130
342
210
McArthurs Hill
230
Cosgrove Island
MACLENNAN RANGE
Papatowai
Florence Hill 185
Tahakopa Bay
Pillans Head
Chasm Island
65
Long Point
270
251
Tautuku
Rainbow Isles
Tautuku Peninsula
Kinakina
111
The Sisters
Wallace Head
147
Chaslands Mistake
Chaslands
Teahimate Bay

46° 15' S Lat

30'

15'

169° 30'

45'

Adjoining pages
110 | 111
112

Kilometres

5   0   5   10   15   20

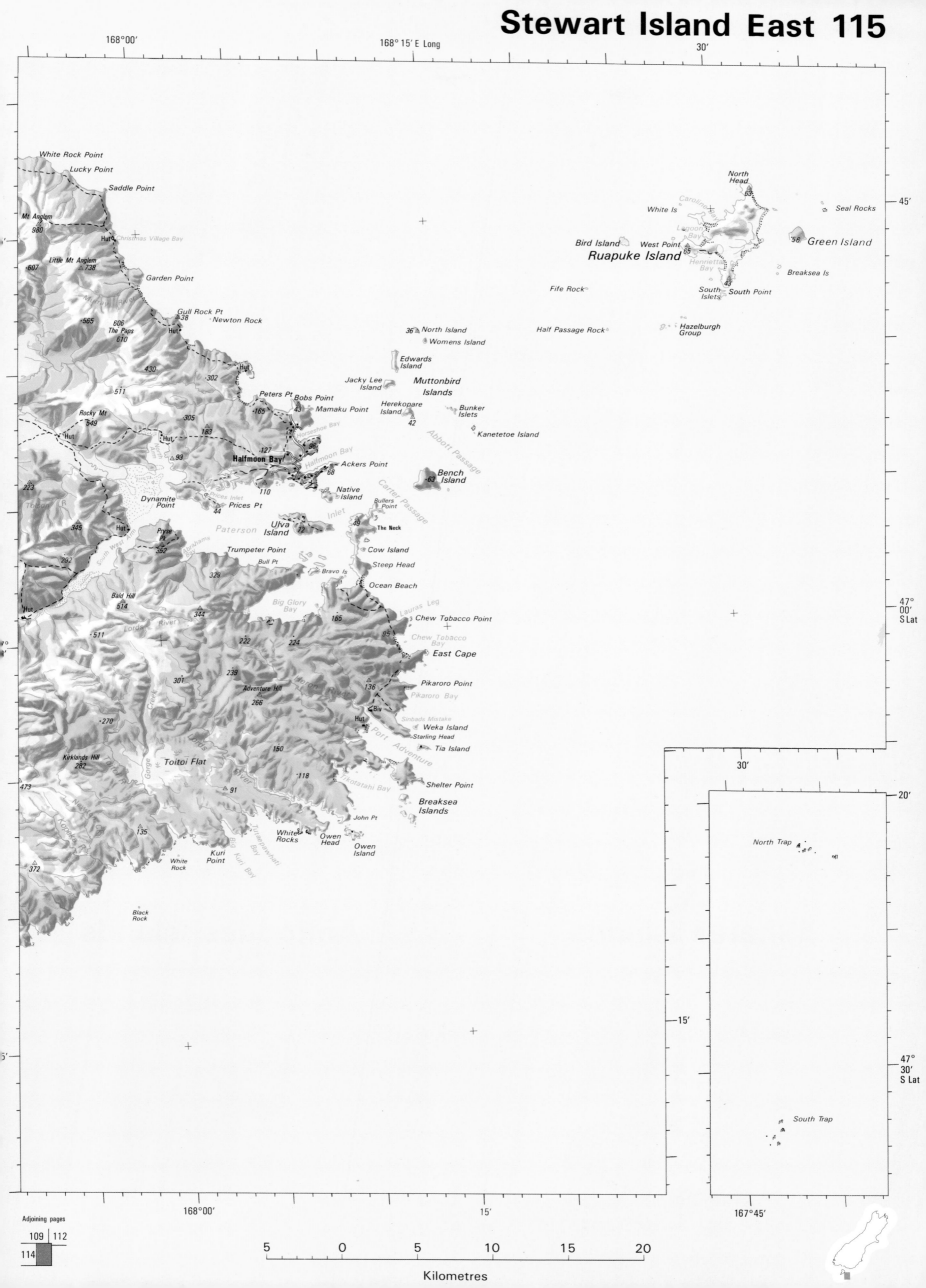

168°00'

168°15' E Long

30'

45'

White Rock Point

Lucky Point

Saddle Point

Mt Anglem
·980

Little Mt Anglem △738

·607

Garden Point

·565

606
The Paps
610

Hut

Gull Rock Pt
Newton Rock

430

·302

511

Hut

Rocky Mt
549

305

183

Hut

△93

Hut

Peters Pt *Bobs Point*
·165
43 *Mamaku Point*

127

96

Halfmoon Bay

Horseshoe Bay

Halfmoon Bay

68

Ackers Point

223

Tolson R

Dynamite Point

44 *Prices Pt*

Prices Inlet

110

Native Island

Paterson

Inlet

Bullers Point
5

Ulva Island
72

49

The Neck

345

Hut

Pryse Pk
·352

292

Trumpeter Point

Bull Pt

Bravo Is

Cow Island

Steep Head

Hut

Bald Hill
514

329

Lords River

344

·511

222

224

Ocean Beach

165

95

Lauras Leg

Chew Tobacco Point

Chew Tobacco Bay

East Cape

239

301

Adventure Hill
266

136

Biv

Pikaroro Point
Pikaroro Bay

Heron River

Hut

·270

150

Sinbads Mistake

Weka Island
Starling Head

Tia Island

Port Adventure

Kirklands Hill
282

Gorge

Toitoi Flat

·118

Tikotatahi Bay

Shelter Point

473

△91

Breaksea Islands

135

John Pt

△372

White Rocks

Owen Head

Owen Island

Kuri Point

Big Kuri Bay

Tutaemawhati Bay

Black Rock

North Head

White Is

Caroline

·63

Seal Rocks

Bird Island

West Point

Lagoon Bay

·56 *Green Island*

65

Ruapuke Island

Henrietta Bay

Breaksea Is

43

South Islets

South Point

Fife Rock

Hazelburgh Group

36 *North Island*

Womens Island

Half Passage Rock

Edwards Island

Jacky Lee Island

Muttonbird Islands

Abbott Passage

Herekopare Island
42

Bunker Islets

Kanetetoe Island

·63 *Bench Island*

Carter Passage

47°00' S Lat

30'

20'

North Trap

15'

47°30' S Lat

South Trap

167°45'

Adjoining pages

109 | 112
114

5   0   5   10   15   20

Kilometres

Kermadec Islands

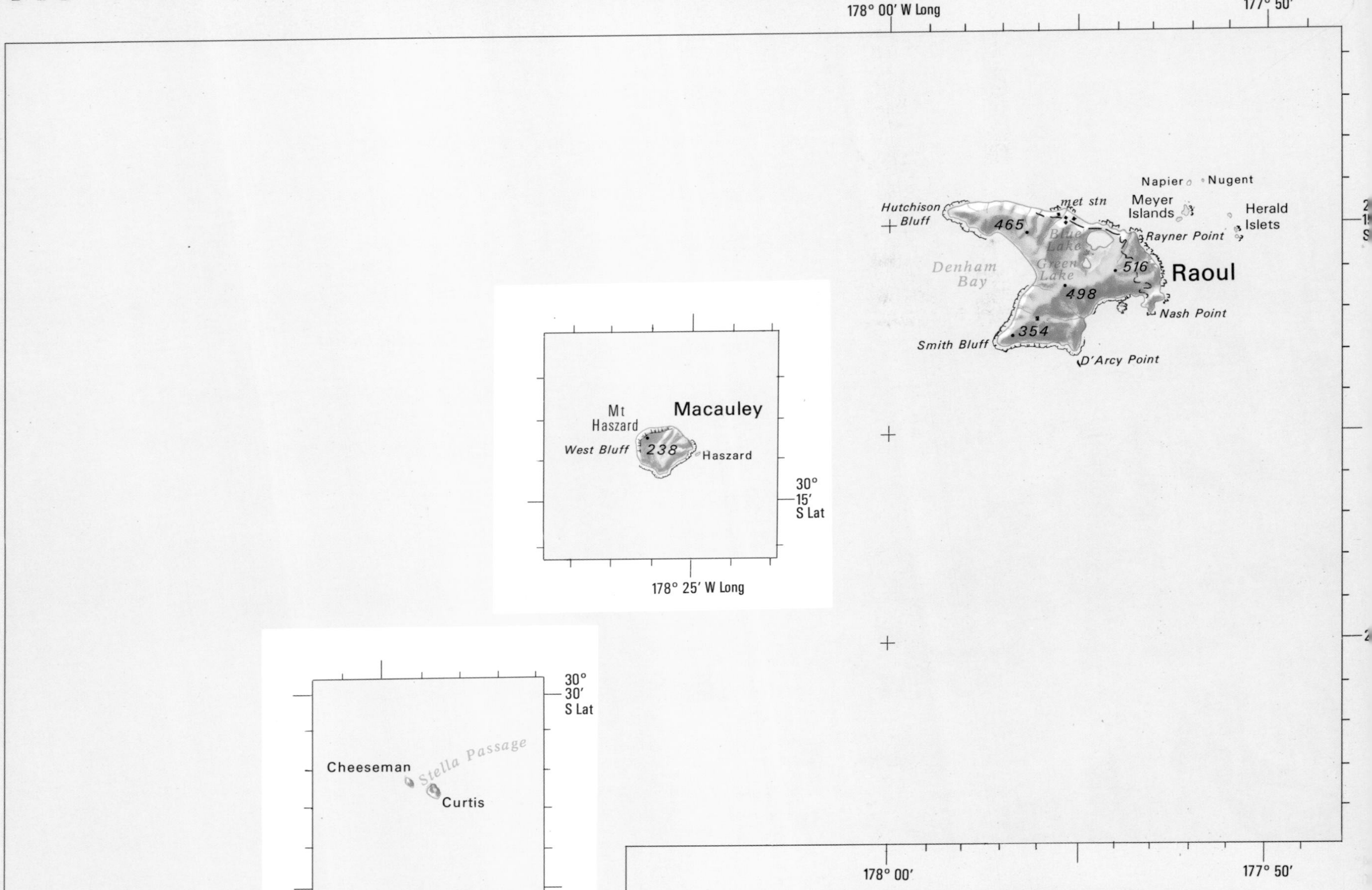

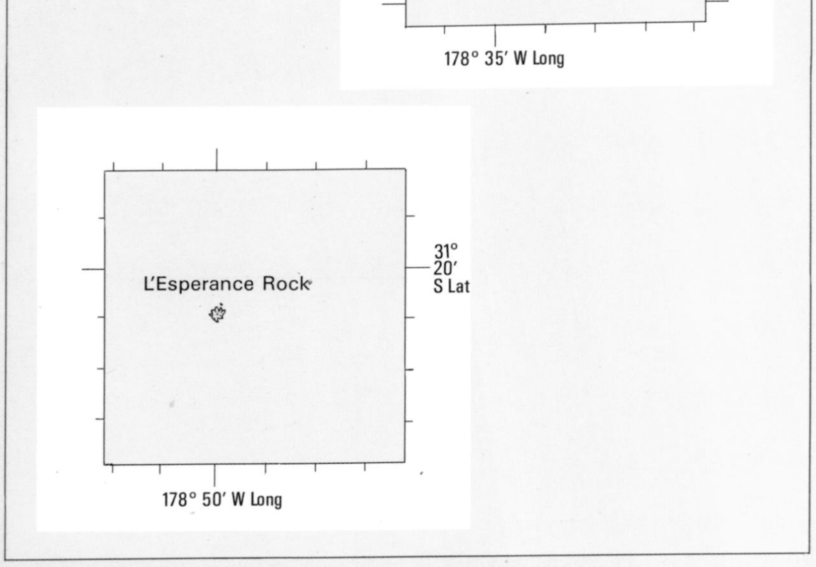

178° 00' W Long

177° 50'

Napier • Nugent

Hutchison
Bluff

met stn

Meyer
Islands

Herald
Islets

465

Rayner Point

Denham
Bay

Blue
Lake
Green
Lake

•516

Raoul

•498

Smith Bluff

•354

Nash Point

D'Arcy Point

Mt
Haszard

Macauley

West Bluff 238

Haszard

30°
15'
S Lat

178° 25' W Long

30°
30'
S Lat

Cheeseman

Stella Passage

Curtis

178° 35' W Long

L'Esperance Rock

31°
20'
S Lat

178° 50' W Long

Bounty Islands

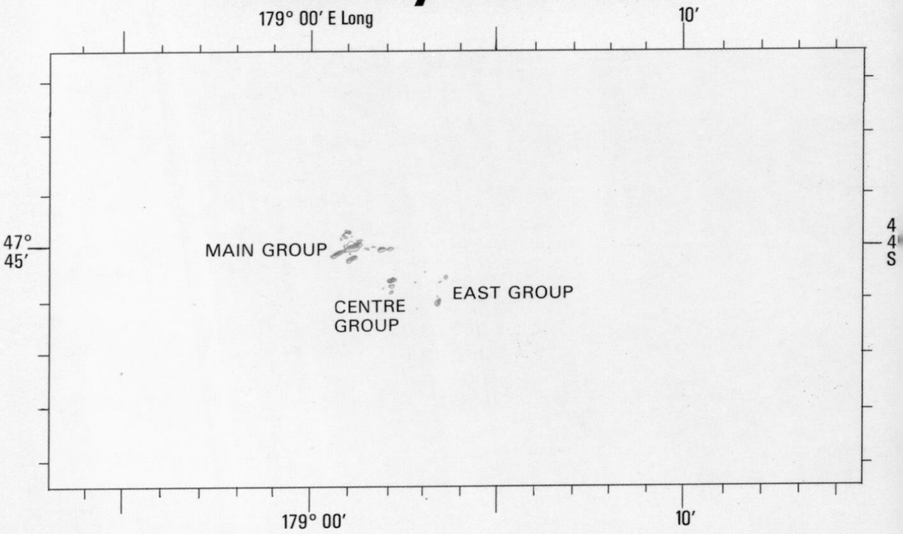

178° 00'

177° 50'

179° 00' E Long

10'

47°
45'

MAIN GROUP

EAST GROUP

CENTRE
GROUP

179° 00'

10'

Snares Islands

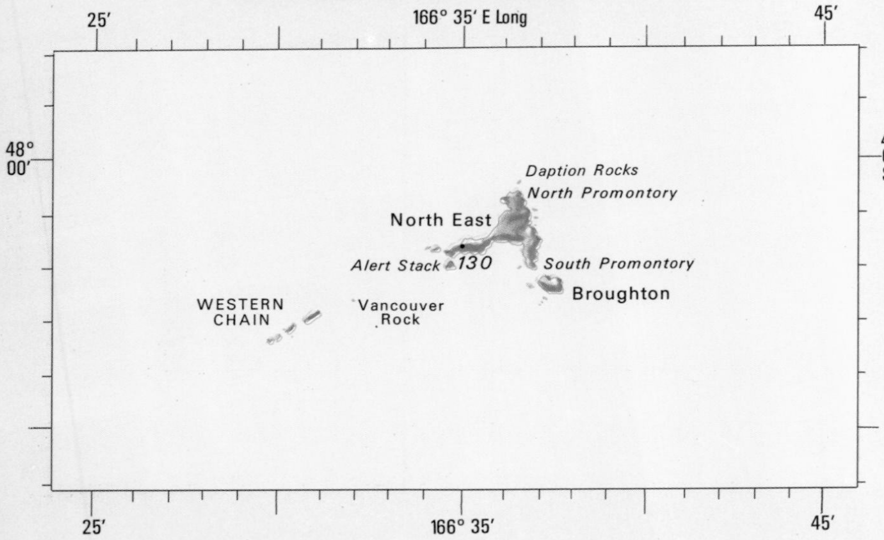

166° 35' E Long

45'

48°
00'

Daption Rocks

North Promontory

North East

Alert Stack •130

South Promontory

WESTERN
CHAIN

Vancouver
Rock

Broughton

25'

166° 35'

45'

Antipodes Islands

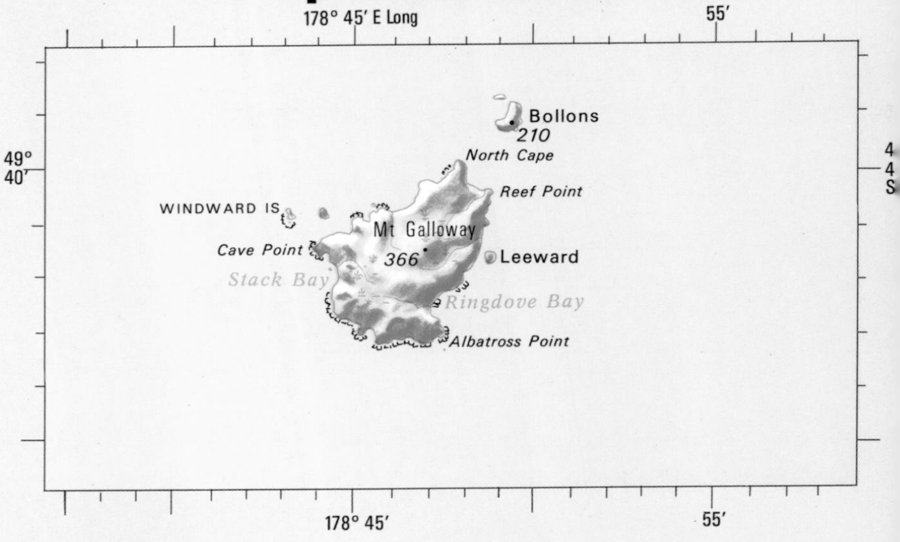

178° 45' E Long

55'

Bollons
210

North Cape

48°
00'
S Lat

49°
40'

WINDWARD IS

Reef Point

Cave Point

Mt Galloway
366

Leeward

Stack Bay

Ringdove Bay

Albatross Point

178° 45'

55'

5   0   5   10   15   20

Kilometres

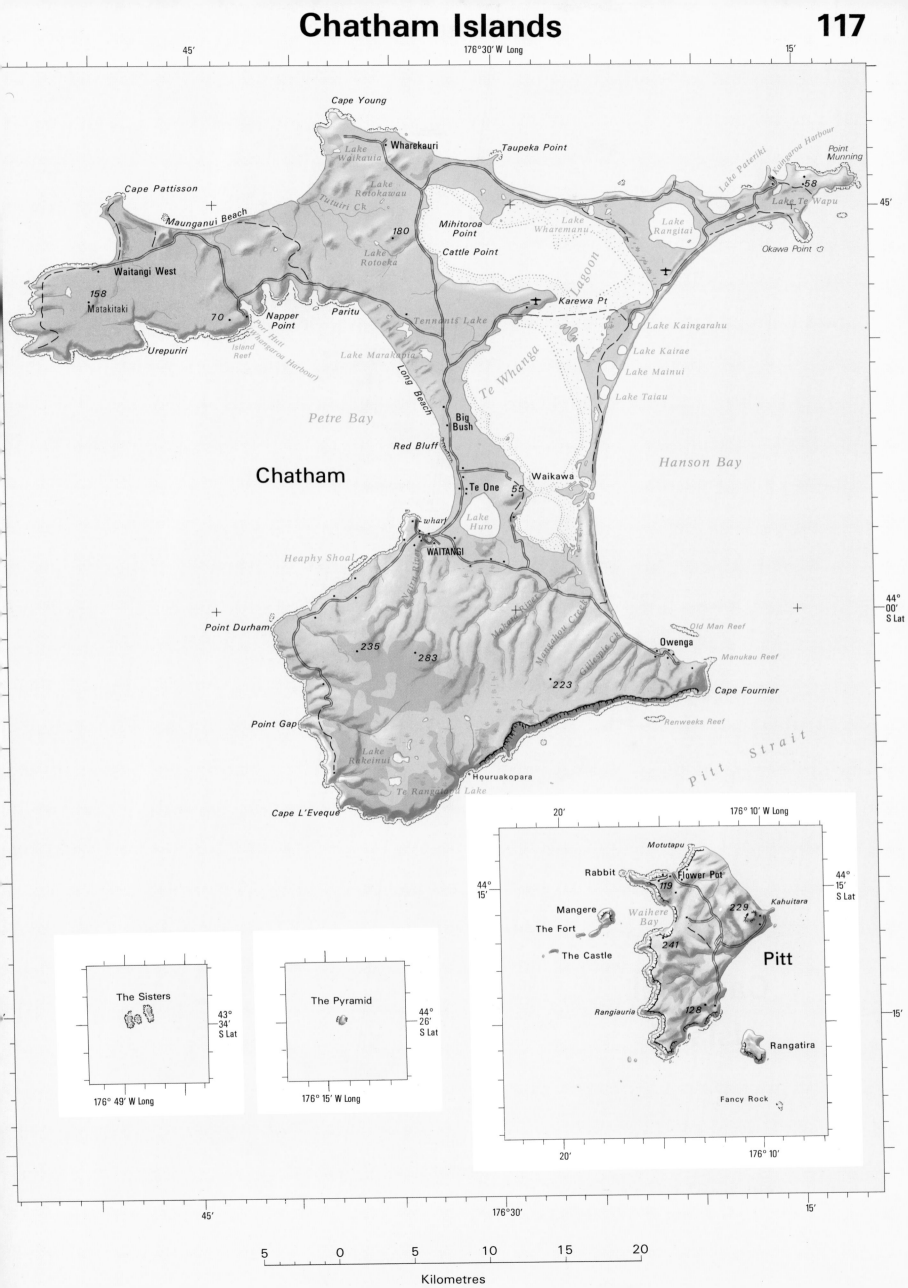

Cape Young

Wharekauri

Taupeka Point

Point Munning

Lake Waikauia

Lake Pateriki

Kaingaroa Harbour

Cape Pattisson

Maunganui Beach

Lake Rotokawau

Tutuiri Ck

•58

Lake Te Wapu

·180

Mihitoroa Point

Lake Wharemanu

Lake Rangitai

Okawa Point

Waitangi West

Lake Rotoeka

Cattle Point

158
Matakitaki

70

Napper Point

Paritu

Lake Kaingarahu

Urepuriri

Port Hutt
(Whangaroa Harbour)

Island Reef

Tennants Lake

Karewa Pt

Lake Kairae

Lake Marakapia

Lake Mainui

Lake Taiau

Long Beach

Te Whanga

Petre Bay

Big Bush

Lagoon

Hanson Bay

Red Bluff

Chatham

Te One

Waikawa

55

Lake Huro

wharf

WAITANGI

Heaphy Shoal

Point Durham

235

·283

Old Man Reef

Owenga

Manukau Reef

223

Cape Fournier

Point Gap

Renweeks Reef

Lake Rakeinui

Pitt Strait

Houruakopara

Te Rangatapu Lake

Cape L'Eveque

The Sisters

43°
34'
S Lat

The Pyramid

44°
26'
S Lat

176° 49' W Long

176° 15' W Long

176° 10' W Long

Motutapu

Rabbit

Flower Pot

44°
15'
S Lat

·119

229

Kahuitara

Mangere

Waihere Bay

The Fort

·241

The Castle

Pitt

Rangiauria

·128

Rangatira

Fancy Rock

5   0   5   10   15   20

Kilometres

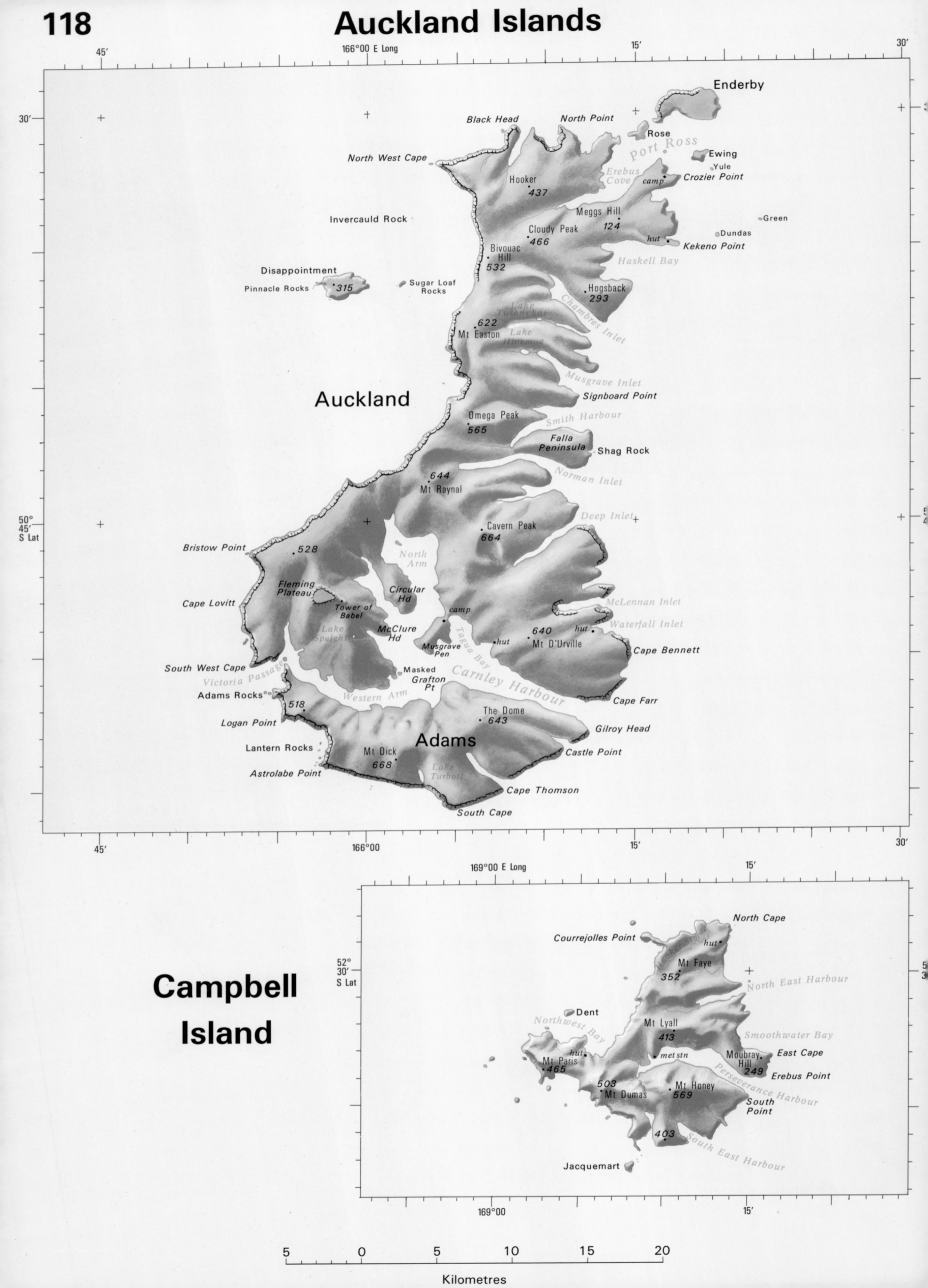

Auckland Islands

Enderby

Black Head   North Point

North West Cape

Rose

Port Ross

Ewing

Yule

Erebus Cove

Crozier Point

Hooker
437

camp

Meggs Hill
124

hut

Green

Kekeno Point

Dundas

Invercauld Rock

Cloudy Peak
466

Bivouac
Hill
532

Haskell Bay

Disappointment
315

Hogsback
293

Pinnacle Rocks

Sugar Loaf
Rocks

Chambres Inlet

Mt Easton
622

*Lake
Tutanekai*

*Lake
Hinemoa*

Musgrave Inlet

Signboard Point

Auckland

Omega Peak
565

Smith Harbour

Falla
Peninsula

Shag Rock

644
Mt Raynal

Norman Inlet

Cavern Peak
664

Deep Inlet

Bristow Point

528

*North
Arm*

Fleming
Plateau

Circular
Hd

McLennan Inlet

Cape Lovitt

Tower of
Babel

camp

Waterfall Inlet

McClure
Hd

640
Mt D'Urville

hut

Cape Bennett

*Lake
Speight*

Musgrave
Pen

hut

South West Cape

Victoria Passage

Masked
Grafton
Pt

Toe ua Bay

Carnley Harbour

Cape Farr

Adams Rocks

Western Arm

518

The Dome
643

Gilroy Head

Logan Point

Adams

Castle Point

Lantern Rocks

Mt Dick
668

*Lake
Turbott*

Cape Thomson

Astrolabe Point

South Cape

**Campbell
Island**

North Cape

Courrejolles Point

hut

Mt Faye
352

North East Harbour

Dent

Mt Lyall
413

Northwest Bay

Smoothwater Bay

hut

Mt Paris
465

met stn

Moubray
Hill
249

East Cape

Erebus Point

503
Mt Dumas

Mt Honey
569

Perseverance Harbour

South
Point

403

South East Harbour

Jacquemart

5   0   5   10   15   20

Kilometres

New Zealand and Outlying Islands

100   0   100   200   300
Kilometres

Raoul
Macauley
Cheeseman *Curtis*
KERMADEC ISLANDS
l'Esperance Rk

THREE KINGS IS
Cape Reinga *North Cape*
Cape Karikari
Kaitaia
Bay of Islands *Cape Brett*
Kaikohe
Whangarei
Dargaville
Little Barrier
Great Barrier
Kaipara Harbour *Hauraki Gulf*
MERCURY IS
AUCKLAND
COROMANDEL PENINSULA
Thames
Mayor *White*
Waikato R. **Tauranga** *Cape Runaway*
Huntly Morrinsville *Bay of* *East Cape*
HAMILTON Cambridge *Plenty*
North I **Rotorua** Whakatane
Te Kuiti Tokoroa Kawerau
Taupo **Gisborne**
Taumarunui
Wairoa
New Plymouth Ruapehu *Mahia Peninsula*
Mt Taranaki or Mt Egmont 2797 *Hawke*
Cape Egmont 2518 *Bay*
Hawera **Hastings** **Napier**
Taihape *C Kidnappers*
Wanganui
Palmerston Dannevirke
North
Levin *C Turnagain*
Cape Farewell *Farewell Spit* **Porirua** Masterton
Collingwood *Tasman* **Lower Hutt**
Bay *Cook* **WELLINGTON**
Picton *Strait* *C Palliser*
Nelson Blenheim
Cape Foulwind 2885
Westport
South I
Greymouth Kaikoura
Hokitika
Hurunui R.
3764 *Mt Cook*
Haast **CHRISTCHURCH**
Jackson Head Ashburton *BANKS PENINSULA*
Canterbury
Timaru *Bight*
Milford Sd 3027
Waitaki R.
Queenstown Oamaru
Doubtful Sd Alexandra
Resolution **DUNEDIN**
Dusky Sd
Gore Balclutha
Puysegur Point *Clutha R.*
Solander **Invercargill**
Ruapuke
Halfmoon Bay
Southwest Cape Stewart

TASMAN SEA

The Sisters
CHATHAM Chatham
ISLANDS
Pitt

SOUTH PACIFIC OCEAN

BOUNTY IS

SNARES IS

ANTIPODES IS

AUCKLAND ISLANDS

Campbell Island

How to use the gazetteer

The following gazetteer is an alphabetical list of all the names that appear in the atlas, together with their designations, positions and map numbers. There is a separate gazetteer for outlying islands at the end.

The first column gives the name of the place or feature. Features are listed under their proper names rather than the actual features—for example, Mount Owen is under 'Owen', not 'Mount'. However, where a locality is named after a feature, it is listed under the feature—for example, Lake Coleridge is under 'Lake'. Note that where a place or feature appears on more than one map there is a separate entry for each of these maps in the gazetteer.

The second column gives the designation of the place or feature in the form of a code-word. 'ISLD', for example, stands for 'island', and 'BDGE' for 'bridge' (see the list of abbreviations opposite).

The third column gives the position of the place or feature in latitude and longitude, to the nearest minute, latitude appearing first. This means that the gazetteer is applicable to many New Zealand maps—not just those in this atlas. In New Zealand (excluding the Chathams and Kermadecs), longitudes are east of the internationally recognised prime meridian, which passes through Greenwich in England. Our longitude numbers therefore read from left to right on maps. Our latitudes, however,

read from top to bottom since we are in the Southern Hemisphere. One degree of latitude or longitude comprises 60 minutes, each of which comprises 60 seconds. Latitude and longitude are marked around the margin of each map, as in the extract from map 38 below.

The fourth column (bold type) gives the map number.

HATEPE	LOC	38 51 176 01	**38**
TAUPO	TOWN	38 42 176 05	**38**
TAUPO, LAKE	LAKE	38 55 175 49	**38**
TAURANGA-TAUPO RIVER	STRM	38 55 175 54	**38**
TOKAANU	POPL	38 58 175 46	**38**
TURANGI	TOWN	39 00 175 48	**38**

The places and features listed in this extract from the gazetteer are also marked on the extract from map 38. This shows how a long river like the Tauranga-Taupo River must have a standard place of reference—in this case the river mouth. A major feature like Lake Taupo, easily located on a map of this scale, does not need a very precise position: the position given is usually near the centre of the feature.

Note that, because of the curvature of the earth, the lines representing latitude and longitude on the map are not quite parallel to the sides of the map.

This atlas and gazetteer employ a system for the mapping of settlements that has been in use for some time by the Department of Survey and Land Information (formerly the Department of Lands and Survey). New Zealanders often use the word city, even officially, for settlements that would not be so described in many other parts of the world. The designations used in the gazetteer (combined with the varied lettering used on the maps) are more precise, however. A distinction is drawn between metropolitan areas (METR)—Auckland, Wellington, Christchurch and Dunedin—and urban satellites (USAT), as well as between the suburbs (SBRB) of each. In descending order of size, there are also references to towns (TOWN), populated places (POPL), and localities (LOC). In the extract from map 38, Taupo and Turangi are towns, Nukuhau is a suburb, Tokaanu is a populated place, Acacia Bay is an urban satellite and Hatepe is a locality. These distinctions are also indicated by different types of lettering.

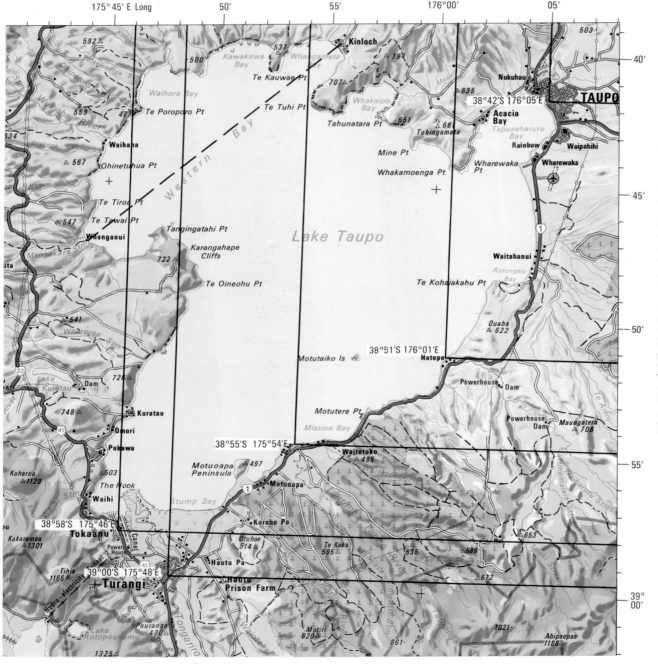

Kilometres

Gazetteer

Abbreviations

AIR	Aerodrome		FLAT	Flat
	Airport		FORD	Ford
	International airport		FRST	Bush
ANCH	Anchorage			Forest
	Roads (coastal)		GLCR	Glacier
	Roadstead			Icefall
BATH	Bath			Ice plateau
BAY	Arm			Snowfield
	Bay		GLKS	Golf course
	Bight			Golf links
	Cove		GLLY	Gully
	Firth		GORG	Canyon
	Inlet			Chasm
BCH	Beach			Gorge
	Slope			Gulch
BDGE	Bridge			Ravine
	Viaduct		GULF	Gulf
BGND	Burial ground		GYSR	Fumarole
	Grave			Geyser
	Urupa (Maori burial ground)		HARB	Harbour
BIVY	Bivouac			Haven
BLDG	Building			Port
	Cabin		HEAD	Head
	Factory			Heads
	Freezing works			Headland
	Hall			Promontory
	Hut		HILL	Brae
	Prison			Hill(s) (under 1000 m)
	Sawmill			Mountain (under 1000 m)
	Shelter			Range (under 1000 m)
	Workshop		HIST	Historic site
BNK	Bank			Redoubt
	Bar		HOSP	Asylum
BSN	Basin			Convalescent home
BSNS	Basins			Hospital
CANL	Canal		HSTD	Farm
CAPE	Cape			Homestead
	Foreland			Station
CAVE	Cave			Station (sheep/cattle)
CEM	Cemetery		ISLD	Island
CGND	Camping ground			Islet
CHAN	Channel		ISLS	Islands
	Entrance (harbour)			Islets
CLIFF	Bluff		ISTH	Isthmus
	Cliff			Neck
CLRG	Clearing		LAGN	Lagoon (coastal)
CRTR	Crater		LAKE	Cauldron
CULV	Culvert			Lagoon (inland)
DAM	Dam			Lake
DRN	Drain			Lakes
	Outfall			Pond
ESTY	Estuary			Pool
FALL	Cascade			Reservoir
	Fall			Tarn
	Falls			Weir
	Waterfall		LTH	Lighthouse
	Waterfalls		LOC	Corner (road corner)
FARM	Farm (school/college)			Fork (river/stream)
FIOR	Fiord			Junction

	Kainga		REEF	Reef
	Landing		ROCK	Crag
	Locality			Rock
	Lookout			Rocks
	Marae		RPDS	Rapids
	Road bend		RSTN	Railway station
	River crossing		RSDG	Railway siding
MBNK	Mudbank			Siding
MEM	Memorial		SAD	Col
	Monument			Saddle
METR	Metropolitan area		SBNK	Sandbank
MINE	Coalmine		SBRB	Suburb
	Coalfield		SCH	College
	Gold mine			High school
	Mine			School
MRFM	Blow hole (coastal)		SEA	Sea
	Marine rock formation		SHL	Shoal
MTN	Mount		SKI	Ski field
	Mountain		SLIP	Slip
	Hill (1000 m plus)		SND	Sound
MTNS	Mountains		SNDS	Sounds
	Peaks (1000 m plus)		SPIT	Spit
	Range (1000 m plus)		SPR	Spring
NLT	Beacon		STRA	Gut
	Navigation Light			Pass (hydro)
PA	Pa			Passage
PARK	Domain			Reach (coastal)
	Forest park			Strait
	Glen (reserve like)		STRM	Brae
	National Park			Brook
	Park			Burn
	Recreation Ground			Cascade
	Reserve			Creek
	Scenic Reserve			Gully (stream)
	Sports Ground			Reach (river)
PASS	Gap			River
	Pass (land)			River diversion
PEAK	Cone			Stream
	Knob			Torrent
	Peak(s)		SWMP	Swamp
PEN	Peninsula		TCE	Terrace
PHSE	Power house		TOWN	Town
PLAT	Down		TREE	Kauri tree
	Plateau		TRCK	Track
PLN	Desert			Walkway
	Plain		TRIG	Trig station
PLTN	Plantation		TUNL	Tunnel
PNT	Point		TWAY	Tramway
PO	Post Office		UNIV	University
POPL	Populated place		USAT	Urban satellite
PPLN	Aqueduct		VLY	Glen (narrow)
	Pipeline			Valley
QURY	Quarry		WELL	Well (gas/oil/water)
RC	Race course		WHF	Jetty
	Trotting course			Quay
RDGE	Brow			Wharf
	Main Divide		WILD	Wilderness area
	Ridge		WRCE	Water race
	Spur		WRK	Wreck

A

Name	Type	Coordinates	Page
A MANIAITI (TRIG)	HILL	38 33 175 23	27
AAN RIVER	STRM	46 14 166 59	105
ABBESS, THE	MTN	43 40 170 18	77
ABBESS, THE	MTN	43 40 170 18	86
ABBEY ROCKS	ROCK	43 40 169 20	78
ABBOT, THE	MTN	43 40 170 18	77
ABBOT, THE	MTN	43 40 170 18	86
ABBOTS STREAM	STRM	41 06 175 17	53
ABBOTT PASSAGE	PASS	46 53 168 15	109
ABBOTT PASSAGE	PASS	46 53 168 15	115
ABBOTTS HILL (TRIG)	HILL	45 52 170 25	103
ABEL HEAD	HEAD	40 51 173 03	57
ABEL TASMAN NATIONAL PARK	PARK	40 55 172 57	57
ABNERS HEAD (TRIG)	HILL	43 24 171 59	81
ABRAHAMS BAY	BAY	46 57 168 02	115
ABRUPT, MOUNT	MTN	41 50 173 33	66
ABUT HEAD	HEAD	43 07 170 15	74
ACACIA BAY	USAT	38 42 176 02	28
ACACIA BAY	USAT	38 42 176 02	38
ACCESS PEAK	PEAK	44 44 167 55	89
ACCESS PEAK	PEAK	44 44 167 55	94
ACHERON LAKES	LAKE	45 10 168 06	97
ACHERON LAKES	LAKE	45 10 168 06	98
ACHERON PASSAGE	STRA	45 40 166 43	104
ACHERON RIVER	STRM	42 24 172 58	72
ACHERON RIVER	STRM	43 24 171 34	80
ACHERON SADDLE	SAD	41 55 173 19	66
ACHILLES	MTN	43 34 170 43	74
ACHILLES, MOUNT	MTN	44 11 168 58	78
ACHRAY	LOC	42 43 172 53	71
ACHRAY	LOC	42 43 172 53	72
ACKERS POINT	PNT	46 54 168 10	109
ACKERS POINT	PNT	46 54 168 10	115
ACLAND, MOUNT	MTN	43 31 170 27	74
ACLAND, MOUNT	MTN	43 31 170 27	77
ACOLYTE, THE	MTN	43 43 170 14	77
ACOLYTE, THE	MTN	43 43 170 14	86
ACTION, MOUNT	MTN	44 03 169 11	78
ACTON STREAM	STRM	45 42 168 25	107
ADA HOMESTEAD	HSTD	42 19 172 37	65
ADA, LAKE	LAKE	44 43 167 52	89
ADA, LAKE	LAKE	44 43 167 52	94
ADA, MOUNT	MTN	44 44 167 53	89
ADA, MOUNT	MTN	44 44 167 53	94
ADA PASS	PASS	42 18 172 28	65
ADA RIVER	STRM	42 20 172 36	65
ADAIR	LOC	44 25 171 11	93
ADAMS FLAT	LOC	46 07 169 50	111
ADAMS FLAT	LOC	46 07 169 50	113
ADAMS HILL (TRIG)	HILL	47 00 167 43	114
ADAMS, MOUNT	MTN	43 16 170 32	74
ADAMS, MOUNT (TRIG)	PEAK	41 19 175 46	51
ADAMS RANGE	MTNS	43 18 170 35	74
ADAMS RIVER	STRM	43 14 170 45	74
ADAMSON CREEK	STRM	43 11 170 38	74
ADDERLEY HEAD	HEAD	43 36 172 50	82
ADDERLEY HEAD	HEAD	43 36 172 50	83
ADDINGTON	SBRB	43 33 172 37	82
ADDINGTON	SBRB	43 33 172 37	83
ADDINGTON	SBRB	43 33 172 37	85
ADDISONS FLAT	FLAT	41 49 171 31	63
ADELAIDE, LAKE	LAKE	44 43 168 02	89
ADELE ISLAND	ISLD	40 59 173 04	57
ADELE ISLAND	ISLD	40 59 173 04	58
ADIANTUM BLUFF (TRIG)	HILL	43 45 169 10	78
ADIT STREAM	STRM	43 14 170 45	74
ADMIRALTY BAY	BAY	40 58 173 51	54
ADMIRALTY BAY	BAY	40 58 173 51	61
ADVENTURE HILL (TRIG)	HILL	47 02 168 05	115
AFTON BURN	STRM	45 07 168 28	95
AFTON BURN (EAST BRANCH)	STRM	45 08 168 28	95
AFTON BURN (EAST BRANCH)	STRM	45 08 168 28	98
AFTON PEAK	PEAK	45 09 168 29	95
AFTON PEAK	PEAK	45 09 168 29	98
AFTON PEAK	PEAK	45 09 168 29	99
AFTON SADDLE	SAD	45 12 168 26	95
AFTON SADDLE	SAD	45 12 168 26	98
AGASSIZ GLACIER	GLCR	43 30 170 13	74
AGASSIZ GLACIER	GLCR	43 30 170 13	77
AGNES, LAKE	LAKE	44 35 168 04	88
AGNES, LAKE	LAKE	44 35 168 04	89
AHAAHA ROCKS	ROCK	36 42 175 01	12
AHAAHA ROCKS	ROCK	36 42 175 01	13
AHAURA	LOC	42 21 171 32	69
AHAURA, LAKE	LAKE	42 33 171 44	70
AHAURA RIVER	STRM	42 21 171 32	69
AHIAPURUA (TRIG)	MTN	37 47 178 03	25
AHIKAEAEA (TRIG)	PEAK	39 07 176 19	39
AHIKAWAU (TRIG)	PEAK	39 03 176 21	39
AHIKIWI	LOC	35 48 173 43	6
AHIKOUKA	LOC	41 04 175 30	53
AHIMANAWA RANGE	MTNS	39 02 176 30	39
AHIMANAWA RANGE	MTNS	39 02 176 30	40
AHIOTEATUA (TRIG)	HILL	38 44 177 40	31
AHIOTEATUA (TRIG)	HILL	38 26 177 58	32
AHIOTEATUA (TRIG)	HILL	38 44 177 40	33
AHIPAEPAE (TRIG)	PEAK	39 02 176 06	38
AHIPAEPAE (TRIG)	PEAK	39 02 176 06	39
AHIPARA	LOC	35 10 173 09	3
AHIPARA BAY	BAY	35 08 173 08	3
AHITITI	LOC	38 52 174 36	26
AHIWEKA (TRIG)	HILL	40 11 176 21	47
AHIWHAKAMURA (TRIG)	HILL	38 25 176 35	30
AHUAHU STREAM	STRM	39 42 175 08	45
AHUAHUITI (TRIG)	HILL	37 34 174 46	14
AHUAPUNGA (TRIG)	HILL	37 34 174 46	14
AHUITI	HSTD	39 39 175 06	45
AHURANGI	HSTD	39 41 175 07	45
AHURIRI	HSTD	43 12 172 34	83
AHURIRI	HSTD	43 12 172 34	85
AHURIRI FLAT	LOC	46 24 169 42	113
AHURIRI POINT	PNT	36 06 175 20	9
AHURIRI RIVER	STRM	44 18 169 37	91
AHURIRI RIVER (EAST BRANCH)	STRM	44 27 169 42	91
AHUROA	LOC	36 29 174 34	11
AHUROA RIVER	STRM	36 00 174 25	7
AHUROA RIVER	STRM	36 00 174 25	8
AHUROA (TRIG)	HILL	37 31 174 53	14
AICKEN, MOUNT	MTN	42 56 171 36	69
AICKEN, MOUNT	MTN	42 56 171 36	70
AICKEN RANGE	MTNS	42 49 171 39	70
AICKENS	LOC	42 47 171 37	69
AICKENS	LOC	42 47 171 37	70
AIGUILLES ISLAND	ISLD	36 02 175 25	9
AIGUILLES ROUGES	MTN	43 35 170 18	74
AIGUILLES ROUGES	MTN	43 35 170 18	77
AILSA CRAIG (TRIG)	MTN	45 39 169 47	100
AILSA CRAIG (TRIG)	MTN	45 39 169 47	101
AILSA MOUNTAINS	MTNS	44 52 168 12	89
AILSA STREAM	STRM	43 41 170 23	77
AILSA STREAM	STRM	43 41 170 23	86
AIREDALE	LOC	45 00 170 56	93
AIREDALE	LOC	45 00 170 56	102
AIREDALE REEF	REEF	38 59 174 15	34
AIRINI, MOUNT	MTN	44 30 170 49	93
AITKEN, MOUNT (TRIG)	MTN	46 08 167 00	105
AITKEN (TRIG)	MTN	44 35 170 46	93
AJAX HILL (TRIG)	HILL	46 26 169 18	112
AJAX HILL (TRIG)	HILL	46 26 169 18	113
AJAX, MOUNT (TRIG)	MTN	42 35 172 04	70
AJAX PEAK	PEAK	42 35 172 04	70
AKA AKA	LOC	37 18 174 48	14
AKA AKA STREAM	STRM	37 19 174 46	14
AKAROA	LOC	40 33 176 15	50
AKAROA	LOC	43 49 172 58	83
AKAROA HARBOUR	HARB	43 50 172 56	83
AKATARAWA RIVER	STRM	41 06 175 06	52
AKATARAWA RIVER	STRM	41 06 175 06	55
AKATERE	LOC	34 59 173 39	4
AKATERE (TRIG)	HILL	35 00 173 40	4
AKATORE	LOC	46 07 170 11	103
AKATORE CREEK	STRM	46 07 170 11	103
AKEAKE STREAM	STRM	36 48 175 44	16
AKERAMA	LOC	35 30 174 10	5

AKINA	SBRB	39 39 176 51	42
AKINA	SBRB	39 39 176 51	43
AKITIO	LOC	40 36 176 25	50
AKITIO RIVER	STRM	40 36 176 25	50
ALABASTER, LAKE	LAKE	44 31 168 10	88
ALABASTER, LAKE	LAKE	44 31 168 10	89
ALABASTER PASS	PASS	44 31 168 13	88
ALABASTER PASS	PASS	44 31 168 13	89
ALAN STREAM	STRM	41 48 173 07	66
ALARM, MOUNT	MTN	42 01 173 38	67
ALASKA, MOUNT	MTN	44 52 168 28	89
ALASKA, MOUNT	MTN	44 52 168 28	95
ALBA, MOUNT	MTN	44 10 168 59	78
ALBANY	LOC	36 44 174 41	11
ALBANY	LOC	36 44 174 41	12
ALBANY HEIGHTS	LOC	36 43 174 41	11
ALBANY HEIGHTS	LOC	36 43 174 41	12
ALBATROSS POINT	PNT	38 07 174 41	18
ALBERT BURN	STRM	44 22 169 08	90
ALBERT BURN SADDLE	SAD	44 24 168 53	90
ALBERT CHANNEL	CHAN	35 14 174 15	5
ALBERT EDWARD PEAK	MTN	45 59 167 15	105
ALBERT GLACIER	GLCR	43 33 170 10	74
ALBERT GLACIER	GLCR	43 33 170 10	77
ALBERT, MOUNT	MTN	44 20 169 05	90
ALBERT, MOUNT (TRIG)	MTN	42 11 172 00	64
ALBERT PEAK	MTN	44 30 168 20	88
ALBERT PEAK	MTN	44 30 168 20	89
ALBERT TOWN	LOC	44 41 169 11	90
ALBURY	LOC	44 14 170 52	87
ALBURY RANGE	MTNS	44 07 170 43	86
ALDERMEN ISLANDS, THE	ISLS	36 58 176 05	17
ALEX, MOUNT	MTN	43 27 170 21	74
ALEX, MOUNT	MTN	43 27 170 21	77
ALEXANDER	MTN	44 26 168 17	88
ALEXANDER	MTN	44 26 168 17	89
ALEXANDER, LAKE	LAKE	41 45 173 40	67
ALEXANDER, MOUNT	MTN	42 43 171 36	69
ALEXANDER, MOUNT	MTN	42 43 171 36	70
ALEXANDER, MOUNT	MTN	42 21 172 07	70
ALEXANDER, MOUNT	MTN	45 00 167 15	96
ALEXANDER, MOUNT (TRIG)	MTN	42 12 173 47	67
ALEXANDER, MOUNT (TRIG)	MTN	42 54 172 49	71
ALEXANDER, MOUNT (TRIG)	MTN	42 54 172 49	72
ALEXANDER, MOUNT (TRIG)	MTN	44 59 170 21	92
ALEXANDER, MOUNT (TRIG)	MTN	44 59 170 21	101
ALEXANDER, MOUNT (TRIG)	HILL	46 23 169 00	112
ALEXANDER PEAK	MTN	46 00 167 16	105
ALEXANDER RANGE	MTNS	42 42 171 36	69
ALEXANDER RIVER	STRM	42 21 171 53	70
ALEXANDRA	POPL	45 15 169 23	100
ALEXANDRINA, LAKE	LAKE	43 56 170 27	77
ALEXANDRINA, LAKE	LAKE	43 56 170 27	86
ALFORD FOREST	LOC	43 37 171 30	80
ALFORD FOREST	LOC	43 37 171 30	84
ALFORD, MOUNT (TRIG)	MTN	43 35 171 28	80
ALFORD, MOUNT (TRIG)	MTN	43 35 171 28	84
ALFRED CREEK	STRM	44 38 170 00	92
ALFRED PEAK	PEAK	44 19 168 29	88
ALFRED PEAK	PEAK	44 19 168 29	89
ALFRED RIVER	STRM	42 21 172 14	70
ALFRED STREAM	STRM	42 17 173 19	66
ALFRED, MOUNT (TRIG)	MTN	44 46 168 22	89
ALFRED, MOUNT (TRIG)	MTN	44 46 168 22	95
ALFREDTON	LOC	40 41 175 51	49
ALFRISTON	SBRB	37 01 174 56	12
ALFRISTON	SBRB	37 01 174 56	14
ALGIDUS, MOUNT (TRIG)	MTN	43 14 171 21	75
ALGIDUS, MOUNT (TRIG)	MTN	43 14 171 21	80
ALGIES BAY	BAY	36 26 174 45	11
ALICE, LAKE	LAKE	44 58 167 28	94
ALICE, LAKE	LAKE	44 58 167 28	97
ALICE, LAKE	LAKE	40 08 175 20	45
ALICE PEAK	PEAK	44 35 168 02	88
ALICE PEAK	PEAK	44 35 168 02	89
ALICE PEAKS	PEAK	46 00 167 12	105
ALL DAY BAY	BAY	45 12 170 53	102
ALLAN, MOUNT (TRIG)	HILL	45 45 170 25	103
ALLAN WATER	STRM	42 22 171 48	70
ALLANDALE	LOC	43 39 172 39	82
ALLANDALE	LOC	43 39 172 39	83
ALLANDALE	LOC	43 39 172 39	85
ALLANDALE	LOC	44 04 170 53	87
ALLANTON	POPL	45 55 170 16	103
ALLEN CREEK	STRM	43 05 170 44	74
ALLEN CREEK	STRM	45 25 168 39	99
ALLEN, MOUNT	MTN	43 06 170 48	74
ALLEN, MOUNT	MTN	43 06 170 48	75
ALLEN, MOUNT	MTN	41 25 172 19	62
ALLEN, MOUNT	MTN	43 06 170 48	75
ALLEN, MOUNT (TRIG)	HILL	47 05 167 48	114
ALLEN, MOUNT (TRIG)	MTN	44 59 169 00	90
ALLEN RANGE	MTNS	41 26 172 21	62
ALLEN RIVER	STRM	41 29 172 17	62
ALLEN STRAIT	STRA	41 00 174 03	54
ALLEN STRAIT	STRA	41 00 174 03	60
ALLEN STRAIT	STRA	41 00 174 03	61
ALLENTON	SBRB	43 53 171 45	84
ALLIGATOR HEAD	HEAD	40 58 174 09	54
ALLIGATOR HEAD	HEAD	40 58 174 09	60
ALLIGATOR HEAD	HEAD	40 58 174 09	61
ALLPORTS ISLAND (TRIG)	ISLD	41 14 174 03	54
ALLPORTS ISLAND (TRIG)	ISLD	41 14 174 03	60
ALLPORTS ISLAND (TRIG)	ISLD	41 14 174 03	61
ALLSOPS BAY	BAY	41 17 175 10	52
ALLSOPS BAY	BAY	41 17 175 10	53
ALLSOPS BAY	BAY	41 17 175 10	55
ALMA	MTN	43 33 170 44	74
ALMA	LOC	45 07 170 55	102
ALMA HILL (TRIG)	HILL	40 52 172 58	57
ALMA PEAK (TRIG)	PEAK	42 09 172 58	66
ALMA RIVER	STRM	42 10 173 05	66
ALMADALE	LOC	40 10 175 39	46
ALPHA CREEK	STRM	43 01 170 41	74
ALPHA, MOUNT	MTN	44 28 168 32	88
ALPHA, MOUNT	MTN	44 28 168 32	90
ALPHA, MOUNT (TRIG)	MTN	44 43 169 04	90
ALPHA, MOUNT (TRIG)	HILL	44 04 168 32	88
ALPHA (TRIG)	PEAK	40 59 175 16	53
ALPINE LAKE	LAKE	43 17 170 08	74
ALTA, LAKE	LAKE	45 04 168 49	95
ALTA, LAKE	LAKE	45 04 168 49	99
ALTA, MOUNT	MTN	44 30 168 58	90
ALTA, MOUNT (TRIG)	HILL	40 30 176 22	50
ALTIMARLOCK	HSTD	41 44 173 51	67
ALTON	LOC	39 40 174 25	44
ALTON BURN	STRM	46 07 167 41	106
ALTON BURN	STRM	46 07 167 41	108
ALUMINIUM SMELTER	BLDG	46 35 168 23	109
AMAZON PEAK	PEAK	43 21 170 50	75
AMBERLEY	POPL	43 10 172 44	82
AMBERLEY BEACH	LOC	43 11 172 46	82
AMBROSE, MOUNT	MTN	43 00 171 14	75
AMBROSE SADDLE	SAD	43 20 170 55	75
AMEKU (TRIG)	HILL	39 23 175 12	36
AMERICA (TRIG)	HILL	38 17 176 35	21
AMERICA (TRIG)	HILL	38 17 176 35	22
AMERICA (TRIG)	HILL	38 17 176 35	30
AMETHYST RAVINE	STRM	43 10 170 38	74
AMIA STREAM	STRM	38 33 177 40	31
AMODEO BAY	LOC	36 41 175 26	13
AMODEO BAY	LOC	36 41 175 26	16
AMOHIA PEAK	HILL	41 01 172 19	56
AMOHIA PEAK	HILL	41 01 172 19	62
AMOKURA STATION	RSTN	37 19 175 04	14
AMOKURA STATION	RSTN	37 19 175 04	15
AMPHION	MTN	44 36 168 14	88
AMPHION	MTN	44 36 168 14	89
AMURI PASS	PASS	42 31 172 11	70
AMURI PLAIN	PLN	42 45 172 55	71
AMURI PLAIN	PLN	42 45 172 55	72
AMURI RANGE	MTNS	42 27 173 04	72
ANAKAKATA BAY	BAY	41 03 174 17	54
ANAKAKATA BAY	BAY	41 03 174 17	61
ANAKIWA	LOC	41 16 173 55	54
ANAKIWA	LOC	41 16 173 55	60
ANAKIWA	LOC	41 16 173 55	61
ANAKOHA BAY	BAY	41 02 174 06	54
ANAKOHA BAY	BAY	41 02 174 06	60
ANAKOHA BAY	BAY	41 02 174 06	61
ANAMA	LOC	43 47 171 23	84
ANAMA	LOC	43 47 171 23	87
ANANUI CAVES	CAVE	41 56 171 29	63
ANAPAI BAY	BAY	40 48 173 00	57
ANARAKE POINT	PNT	36 41 175 36	16
ANATAKUPU ISLAND	TRIG	40 54 173 52	54
ANATAKUPU ISLAND	TRIG	40 54 173 52	61
ANATOKI PEAK (TRIG)	HILL	40 57 172 32	56
ANATOKI PEAK (TRIG)	HILL	40 57 172 32	57
ANATOKI RANGE	MTNS	40 57 172 39	56
ANATOKI RANGE	MTNS	40 57 172 39	57
ANATOKI RANGE (TRIG)	HILL	40 57 172 41	56
ANATOKI RANGE (TRIG)	HILL	40 57 172 41	57
ANATOKI RIVER	STRM	40 51 172 48	57
ANATOKI (TRIG)	HILL	40 55 172 43	56
ANATOKI (TRIG)	HILL	40 55 172 43	57
ANATORI RIVER	STRM	40 42 172 22	56
ANAU, MOUNT	MTN	44 52 167 55	89
ANAU, MOUNT	MTN	44 52 167 55	94
ANAURA BAY	BAY	38 14 178 19	32
ANAURA STREAM	STRM	39 07 176 59	40
ANAURA STREAM	STRM	39 07 176 59	41
ANAWEKA RIVER	STRM	40 45 172 17	56
ANAWHATA	LOC	36 55 174 27	10
ANAWHATA	LOC	36 55 174 27	11
ANAWHENUA STREAM	STRM	39 14 176 29	39
ANAWHENUA STREAM	STRM	39 14 176 29	40
ANCHOR ISLAND	ISLD	45 46 166 31	104
ANCHOR POINT	PNT	45 45 166 34	104
ANCHORAGE ARM	BAY	45 25 166 52	96
ANCHORAGE COVE	BAY	44 56 167 24	94
ANCHORAGE COVE	BAY	44 56 167 24	96
ANCHORAGE ISLAND	ISLD	47 12 167 40	114
ANDEREGG, MOUNT	MTN	43 30 170 10	74
ANDEREGG, MOUNT	MTN	43 30 170 10	77
ANDERSON, MOUNT	MTN	45 35 166 52	104
ANDERSON, MOUNT (TRIG)	MTN	42 14 171 26	63
ANDERSON STREAM	STRM	42 54 172 09	70
ANDERSON STREAM	STRM	44 25 170 41	93
ANDERSONS BAY	SBRB	45 54 170 32	103
ANDERSONS COVE	BAY	36 03 174 34	8
ANDERSONS STREAM	STRM	40 06 175 56	46
ANDREWS STREAM	STRM	43 00 171 48	70
ANDREWS STREAM	STRM	43 55 171 11	87
ANGELUS PEAK	PEAK	41 54 172 45	65
ANGELUS, LAKE	LAKE	41 53 172 45	65
ANGLEM, MOUNT (TRIG)	MTN	46 44 167 55	108
ANGLEM, MOUNT (TRIG)	MTN	46 44 167 55	109
ANGLEM, MOUNT (TRIG)	MTN	46 44 167 55	114
ANGLEM, MOUNT (TRIG)	MTN	46 44 167 55	115
ANGUILLA STREAM	STRM	45 53 169 12	110
ANGUS BURN	STRM	46 15 167 08	105
ANINI STREAM	STRM	38 37 177 15	31
ANITA BAY	BAY	44 35 167 48	94
ANIWANIWA STREAM	STRM	38 45 177 09	31
ANNA, LAKE	LAKE	42 53 171 39	70
ANNA STREAM	STRM	42 57 172 07	70
ANNAN, MOUNT	MTN	43 32 170 21	74
ANNAN, MOUNT	MTN	43 32 170 21	77
ANNANDALE	HSTD	42 34 173 07	72
ANNAT	LOC	43 22 172 00	81
ANNE RIVER	STRM	42 21 172 31	71
ANNE SADDLE	SAD	42 24 172 28	71
ANNEAR CREEK	STRM	45 03 168 03	97
ANNEAR CREEK	STRM	45 03 168 03	98
ANNETTA, MOUNT	MTN	44 22 168 16	88
ANNETTA, MOUNT	MTN	44 22 168 16	89
ANNIE BAY	BAY	40 59 174 05	54
ANNIE BAY	BAY	40 59 174 05	60
ANNIE BAY	BAY	40 59 174 05	61
ANNIE, LAKE	LAKE	45 23 167 17	96
ANNIE PEAK	PEAK	43 26 170 12	74
ANNIE PEAK	PEAK	43 26 170 12	77
ANSTEAD, MOUNT	MTN	44 30 168 37	88
ANSTEAD, MOUNT	MTN	44 30 168 37	90
ANSTEY STREAM	STRM	42 41 173 08	72
ANSTEY STREAM	STRM	42 41 173 08	73
ANT STREAM	STRM	42 57 172 07	70
ANT (TRIG)	HILL	41 34 175 15	53
ANT-HILL, THE	MTN	43 33 170 26	74
ANT-HILL, THE	MTN	43 33 170 26	77
ANTI CROW RIVER	STRM	43 00 171 31	80
ANTIONETTE, MOUNT (TRIG)	MTN	44 23 168 16	88
ANTIONETTE, MOUNT (TRIG)	MTN	44 23 168 16	89
ANTONIOS CREEK	STRM	42 11 171 44	63
ANTONIOS CREEK	STRM	42 11 171 44	64
ANXIETY POINT	PNT	45 06 167 01	96
ANYBODY CREEK	STRM	43 53 169 15	78
AOKAPARANGI	PEAK	40 53 175 21	48
AOKAUTERE	LOC	40 22 175 40	49
AOMARAMA (TRIG)	HILL	39 43 176 31	42
AOMARAMA (TRIG)	HILL	39 43 176 31	43
AOMARAMA (TRIG)	HILL	39 43 176 31	47
AONGATETE	LOC	37 36 175 56	20
AONGATETE RIVER	STRM	37 36 175 58	20
AOPARAURI (TRIG)	MTN	37 46 178 05	25
AORANGAIA ISLAND	ISLD	35 29 174 44	5
AORANGI	LOC	37 57 178 13	25
AORANGI	LOC	40 15 175 35	45
AORANGI	LOC	40 15 175 35	46
AORANGI ISLAND	ISLD	35 28 174 44	5
AORANGI MOUNTAINS	MTNS	41 26 175 21	53
AORANGI STREAM	STRM	38 10 176 12	20
AORANGI STREAM	STRM	38 10 176 12	21
AORANGI STREAM	STRM	39 30 175 54	37
AORANGI (TRIG)	MTN	37 55 178 08	25
AORANGI (TRIG)	PEAK	39 37 176 05	47
AORANGIWAI RIVER	STRM	37 56 178 13	25
AORERE	LOC	40 43 172 36	56
AORERE	LOC	40 43 172 36	57
AORERE, LAKE	LAKE	41 03 172 20	56
AORERE, LAKE	LAKE	41 03 172 20	62
AORERE PEAK (TRIG)	HILL	41 01 172 29	56
AORERE PEAK (TRIG)	HILL	41 01 172 29	57
AORERE PEAK (TRIG)	HILL	41 01 172 29	58
AORERE RIVER	STRM	40 40 172 40	56
AORERE RIVER	STRM	40 40 172 40	57
AORERE SADDLE	SAD	41 04 172 20	56
AORERE SADDLE	SAD	41 04 172 20	62
AOROA	LOC	35 59 173 53	6
AOROA	LOC	35 59 173 53	7
AOTEA	LOC	38 01 174 49	18
AOTEA HARBOUR	HARB	37 59 174 51	18
AOTUHIA	LOC	39 14 174 48	35
AOTUHIA	LOC	39 14 174 48	44
APAKURA STREAM	STRM	37 13 175 39	15
APAKURA STREAM	STRM	37 13 175 39	17
APANUI	LOC	38 03 177 17	23
APARIMA	LOC	46 03 168 04	106
APARIMA	LOC	46 03 168 04	107
APARIMA RIVER	STRM	45 40 167 56	106
APARIMA RIVER	STRM	45 40 167 56	107
APARIMA RIVER	STRM	46 20 168 01	109
APATA	LOC	37 39 175 59	20
APAU CHANNEL	CHAN	41 01 173 53	54
APIRANA PEAK	PEAK	44 42 168 02	89
APITI	POPL	39 59 175 52	46
APITI, MOUNT (TRIG)	MTN	45 00 169 23	100
APITI STREAM	STRM	38 20 176 59	30
APLEY (TRIG)	HILL	39 28 176 45	40
APLEY (TRIG)	HILL	39 28 176 45	42
APONGA	LOC	35 38 174 05	5
APONGA	LOC	35 38 174 05	7
APONGA STREAM	STRM	35 42 174 02	5
APONGA STREAM	STRM	35 42 174 02	7
APOTU	LOC	35 38 174 17	5
APOTU	LOC	35 38 174 17	7
APOTU	LOC	35 38 174 17	8
APUAU CHANNEL	CHAN	41 01 173 53	60
APUAU CHANNEL	CHAN	41 01 173 53	61
APUTEREWA	LOC	35 03 173 31	3
ARA (TRIG)	HILL	39 34 175 36	37
ARAHIWI	LOC	38 06 176 01	20
ARAHURA	LOC	42 42 171 02	68
ARAHURA	LOC	42 42 171 02	69
ARAHURA RIVER	STRM	42 40 171 01	68
ARAHURA RIVER	STRM	42 40 171 01	69
ARAHURA STATION	RSTN	42 40 171 02	68
ARAHURA STATION	RSTN	42 40 171 02	69
ARAKIHI (TRIG)	HILL	38 21 178 03	32
ARAMAIRE STREAM	STRM	39 38 175 10	45
ARAMAIRE (TRIG)	HILL	39 44 175 00	45
ARAMATAI	LOC	38 29 175 10	27
ARAMIRO	LOC	37 54 175 02	18
ARAMOANA	HSTD	40 09 176 50	43
ARAMOANA	LOC	45 47 170 42	103
ARAMOHO	SBRB	39 54 175 03	45
ARANGA	LOC	35 45 173 37	6
ARANGA BEACH	LOC	35 46 173 34	6
ARANUI	SBRB	43 31 172 42	82
ARANUI	SBRB	43 31 172 42	83
ARANUI	SBRB	43 31 172 42	85
ARANUI CREEK	STRM	41 56 171 29	63
ARAPAEPAE (TRIG)	HILL	40 37 175 23	48
ARAPAOA	LOC	36 12 174 13	7
ARAPAOA	LOC	36 12 174 13	8
ARAPAOA RIVER	STRM	36 15 174 18	7
ARAPAOA RIVER	STRM	36 15 174 18	8
ARAPAOA RIVER	STRM	36 15 174 18	10
ARAPARERA	LOC	36 31 174 27	10
ARAPARERA	LOC	36 31 174 27	11
ARAPARERA RIVER	STRM	36 30 174 27	10
ARAPARERA RIVER	STRM	36 30 174 27	11
ARAPAWA ISLAND	ISLD	41 11 174 19	54
ARAPAWA ISLAND	ISLD	41 11 174 19	61
ARAPAWA (TRIG)	HILL	41 12 174 17	54
ARAPAWA (TRIG)	HILL	41 12 174 17	61
ARAPITO	LOC	41 16 172 10	56
ARAPITO	LOC	41 16 172 10	62
ARAPOHUE	LOC	35 59 173 58	7
ARAPOUTOKO (TRIG)	HILL	39 38 174 55	45
ARAPUNI	POPL	38 05 175 39	19
ARAPUNI, LAKE	LAKE	38 10 175 39	19
ARARAT, MOUNT (TRIG)	MTN	38 59 174 42	35
ARARATA	LOC	39 31 174 22	35
ARARATA	LOC	39 31 174 22	44
ARARATA STREAM	STRM	39 32 174 20	35
ARARATA STREAM	STRM	39 32 174 20	44
ARARAWA STREAM	STRM	39 33 175 18	36
ARARIMU	LOC	37 09 175 02	12
ARARIMU	LOC	37 09 175 02	13
ARARIMU	LOC	37 09 175 02	14
ARARIMU STREAM	STRM	36 44 174 31	10
ARARIMU STREAM	STRM	36 44 174 31	11
ARARIMU STREAM	STRM	36 44 174 31	12
ARARIMU STREAM	STRM	38 50 175 08	27
ARARIMU STREAM	STRM	39 29 175 09	36
ARARUA	LOC	36 03 174 11	7
ARATAHA STREAM	STRM	37 56 175 53	20
ARATAKI	LOC	38 31 175 46	28
ARATAPU	LOC	36 01 173 54	6
ARATAPU	LOC	36 01 173 54	7
ARATAUA (TRIG)	HILL	38 48 174 57	26
ARATIATIA	LOC	38 37 176 09	29
ARATIKA	LOC	42 33 171 26	69
ARATORA	LOC	38 30 175 13	27
ARAWARU (TRIG)	HILL	40 31 175 37	48
ARAWARU (TRIG)	HILL	40 31 175 37	49
ARAWATA	LOC	44 01 168 41	88
ARAWATA RIVER	STRM	44 00 168 40	88
ARAWATA SADDLE	SAD	44 26 168 38	88
ARAWATA SADDLE	SAD	44 26 168 38	90
ARCADE CREEK	STRM	44 18 168 23	88
ARCADE CREEK	STRM	44 18 168 23	89
ARCADE GLACIERS	GLCR	44 18 168 27	88
ARCADE GLACIERS	GLCR	44 18 168 27	89
ARCADE SADDLE	SAD	44 18 168 28	88
ARCADE SADDLE	SAD	44 18 168 28	89
ARCHITECT CREEK	STRM	43 37 169 54	76
ARCHWAY ISLAND	ISLD	35 29 174 44	5
ARCHWAY ISLAND	ISLD	40 30 172 41	57
ARDEER BURN	STRM	46 00 167 29	105
ARDEER BURN	STRM	46 00 167 29	106
ARDEN, MOUNT (TRIG)	MTN	43 00 172 29	71
ARDGOUR	LOC	44 53 169 26	91
ARDGOWAN	LOC	45 05 170 57	102
ARDLUSSA	LOC	45 48 168 38	110
ARDMORE	LOC	37 02 174 58	12
ARDMORE	LOC	37 02 174 58	14
AREARE LAKE	LAKE	37 40 175 12	18
AREARE LAKE	LAKE	37 40 175 12	19
ARERO	LOC	38 13 178 15	32
ARETE	PEAK	40 45 175 26	48
ARGENTUM (TRIG)	MTN	43 44 169 33	76
ARGENTUM (TRIG)	MTN	43 44 169 33	79
ARGUMENT CREEK	STRM	43 24 170 47	74
ARGYLE BURN	STRM	45 45 168 55	110
ARGYLE HILL (TRIG)	HILL	45 41 168 57	110
ARGYLL EAST	LOC	39 52 176 32	42
ARGYLL EAST	LOC	39 52 176 32	43
ARGYLL EAST	LOC	39 52 176 32	47
ARIA	LOC	38 34 174 59	26
ARIA	LOC	38 34 174 59	27
ARIA (TRIG)	HILL	37 57 178 08	25
ARIEL ROCK	ROCK	38 44 178 18	32
ARIKI	LOC	41 48 172 13	64
ARIMAWHAI POINT	PNT	36 35 175 47	16
ARK	MTN	44 25 168 21	88
ARK	MTN	44 25 168 21	89
ARMADILLO SADDLE	SAD	43 33 170 25	74
ARMADILLO SADDLE	SAD	43 33 170 25	77
ARMCHAIR STREAM	STRM	41 33 173 25	59
ARMSTRONG, MOUNT	MTN	44 06 169 26	78
ARMSTRONG, MOUNT	MTN	44 06 169 26	79
ARMSTRONG, MOUNT	MTN	42 54 171 30	69
ARMSTRONG SADDLE	SAD	39 47 176 10	47
ARNE, MOUNT	MTN	44 15 168 56	78
ARNETT PEAK	PEAK	46 01 166 54	104
ARNETT PEAK	PEAK	46 01 166 54	105
ARNO	LOC	44 47 170 59	93
ARNOLD, MOUNT	MTN	44 20 169 29	91
ARNOLD RIVER	STRM	42 26 171 22	69
ARNOTT POINT	PNT	43 43 169 12	78
ARNST RIVER	STRM	41 56 172 48	65
AROARO STREAM	STRM	36 58 175 05	13
AROARO STREAM	STRM	36 58 175 05	14
AROARO STREAM	STRM	36 58 175 05	15
AROHAKI BAY	BAY	38 07 174 42	18
AROHENA	LOC	38 12 175 37	19
AROPAOANUI	HSTD	39 16 177 00	40
AROPAOANUI	HSTD	39 16 177 00	41
AROPAOANUI RIVER	STRM	39 17 177 00	40
AROPAOANUI RIVER	STRM	39 17 177 00	41
AROWHANA	HSTD	38 10 177 52	24
AROWHANA	HSTD	38 10 177 52	32
AROWHANA (TRIG)	MTN	38 07 177 52	24
AROWHENUA	LOC	44 16 171 16	87
AROWHENUA PA	LOC	44 16 171 16	87
ARRAN ISLAND	ISLD	45 10 167 38	94
ARRAN ISLAND	ISLD	45 10 167 38	97
ARROW JUNCTION	LOC	44 59 168 51	95
ARROW JUNCTION	LOC	44 59 168 51	99
ARROW RIVER	STRM	45 00 168 53	90
ARROW RIVER	STRM	45 00 168 53	95
ARROW RIVER	STRM	45 00 168 53	99
ARROWSMITH, MOUNT	MTN	43 21 170 59	75
ARROWSMITH RANGE	MTNS	43 22 170 59	75
ARROWTOWN	LOC	44 57 168 50	90
ARROWTOWN	LOC	44 57 168 50	95
ARROWTOWN	LOC	44 57 168 50	99
ARTHUR CREEK	STRM	46 11 167 39	106
ARTHUR CREEK	STRM	46 11 167 39	108
ARTHUR GLACIER	GLCR	43 47 169 55	76
ARTHUR GLACIER	GLCR	43 47 169 55	79
ARTHUR, MOUNT	HILL	43 37 169 34	76
ARTHUR, MOUNT	HILL	43 37 169 34	79
ARTHUR, MOUNT (TRIG)	MTN	41 13 172 41	56
ARTHUR, MOUNT (TRIG)	MTN	41 13 172 41	58
ARTHUR RANGE	MTNS	41 13 172 41	58
ARTHUR RIVER	STRM	44 41 167 55	89
ARTHUR RIVER	STRM	44 41 167 55	94
ARTHURS CREEK	STRM	44 41 168 28	89
ARTHUR'S PASS	LOC	42 57 171 34	69
ARTHUR'S PASS	PASS	42 55 171 34	69
ARTHUR'S PASS NATIONAL PARK	PARK	42 54 171 41	70
ARTHURS POINT	LOC	44 59 168 40	95
ARTHURS POINT	LOC	44 59 168 40	99
ARTHURSTOWN	LOC	42 45 171 00	68
ARTHURSTOWN	LOC	42 45 171 00	69
ARTHURTON	LOC	46 07 169 09	110
ARTHURTON	LOC	46 07 169 09	112
ARTIST DOME	MTN	43 10 170 53	75
ARUNDEL	LOC	43 58 171 17	87
ASHBURTON	TOWN	43 54 171 45	84
ASHBURTON FORKS	LOC	43 44 171 32	84
ASHBURTON GORGE	GORG	43 38 171 12	75
ASHBURTON PEAK	PEAK	43 22 170 58	75
ASHBURTON RIVER	STRM	44 03 171 49	84
ASHBURTON RIVER (NORTH BRANCH)	STRM	43 53 171 43	84
ASHBURTON RIVER (SOUTH BRANCH)	STRM	43 53 171 42	84
ASHCOTT	LOC	39 58 176 20	47
ASHERS	LOC	46 28 168 39	112
ASHHURST	POPL	40 17 175 45	49
ASHLEY	LOC	43 17 172 36	82
ASHLEY	LOC	43 17 172 36	83
ASHLEY CLINTON	LOC	39 57 176 15	47
ASHLEY DOWNS	LOC	46 10 169 29	111
ASHLEY DOWNS	LOC	46 10 169 29	113
ASHLEY GORGE	LOC	43 15 172 12	81
ASHLEY HILL (TRIG)	HILL	43 08 172 14	81
ASHLEY RIVER	STRM	43 07 172 13	81
ASHLEY RIVER	STRM	43 17 172 43	82
ASHLEY RIVER	STRM	43 17 172 43	83
ASHMORE, MOUNT	MTN	43 09 170 41	74
ASHTON	LOC	44 02 171 46	84
ASHTON BURN	STRM	45 22 168 13	95
ASHTON BURN	STRM	45 22 168 13	98
ASHWICK FLAT	LOC	44 00 170 51	87
ASKEWS HILL (TRIG)	HILL	41 02 173 42	60
ASPINALL PEAK	PEAK	44 19 168 53	90
ASPIRING, MOUNT	MTN	44 23 168 44	88
ASPIRING, MOUNT	MTN	44 23 168 44	90
ASPIRING, MOUNT	HSTD	44 30 168 50	90
ASTROLABE ROADSTEAD	ANCH	40 59 173 03	57
ASTROLABE ROADSTEAD	ANCH	40 59 173 03	58
ASTROLABE ROADSTEAD	ANCH	40 59 173 03	59
ATAAHUA	LOC	43 47 172 39	83
ATAAHUA	LOC	43 47 172 39	85
ATAATA POINT	PNT	41 09 173 24	59
ATAHAUA CREEK	STRM	41 22 173 46	60

ATAPO	LOC	41 37 172 47	58
ATARAU	LOC	42 20 171 29	69
ATAWHAI	SBRB	41 14 173 19	59
ATBARA CREEK	STRM	41 59 171 30	63
ATEA	LOC	40 37 175 36	48
ATEA	LOC	40 37 175 36	49
ATENE PA	HSTD	39 44 175 09	45
ATHENE, MOUNT	MTN	44 23 168 36	88
ATHENE, MOUNT	MTN	44 23 168 36	90
ATHENREE	LOC	37 27 175 58	17
ATHOL	LOC	45 31 168 35	99
ATIA POINT	PNT	42 26 173 42	73
ATIAMURI	LOC	38 24 176 02	28
ATIAMURI	LOC	38 24 176 02	29
ATIAMURI, LAKE	LAKE	38 23 176 02	28
ATIAMURI, LAKE	LAKE	38 23 176 02	29
ATIHAU ISLAND	ISLD	35 55 175 06	9
ATIU ISLAND	ISLD	36 38 175 53	16
ATIWHAKATU STREAM	STRM	40 54 175 32	48
ATKINSON STREAM	STRM	41 52 172 30	65
ATOA (TRIG)	HILL	35 49 174 04	7
ATTEMPT HILL (TRIG)	HILL	40 51 173 52	54
ATTEMPT HILL (TRIG)	HILL	40 51 173 52	61
ATTICA, MOUNT	MTN	44 07 169 01	78
ATTILA, MOUNT (TRIG)	HILL	40 35 176 18	50
ATUANUI (TRIG)	HILL	36 27 174 27	10
ATUANUI (TRIG)	HILL	36 27 174 27	11
AUAHINE (TRIG)	HILL	36 39 174 20	10
AUAHITOTARA (TRIG)	PEAK	39 28 175 46	37
AUBREY PEAK	PEAK	45 37 167 06	105
AUCKLAND	METR	36 51 174 46	11
AUCKLAND	METR	36 51 174 46	12
AUCKLAND CENTENNIAL PARK	PARK	37 00 174 31	12
AUGARDE, MOUNT	MTN	42 07 173 04	66
AUGUSTUS, MOUNT (TRIG)	MTN	41 41 171 51	63
AUGUSTUS, MOUNT (TRIG)	MTN	41 41 171 51	64
AUKOPAE	LOC	38 56 175 06	26
AUKOPAE	LOC	38 56 175 06	27
AURERE	LOC	35 00 173 26	3
AURERE STREAM	STRM	34 59 173 26	3
AURIPO	LOC	45 03 169 47	100
AURIPO	LOC	45 03 169 47	101
AUROA	LOC	39 29 174 03	34
AUROA POINT	PNT	39 05 177 58	33
AURUM, MOUNT	MTN	44 46 168 38	90
AURUM, MOUNT	MTN	44 46 168 38	95
AUSTRIA (TRIG)	HILL	34 34 172 50	2
AUTAWA (TRIG)	HILL	39 11 174 27	35
AVALANCHE GLACIER	GLCR	44 26 168 45	90
AVALANCHE, MOUNT	MTN	44 26 168 45	88
AVALANCHE, MOUNT	MTN	44 26 168 45	90
AVALANCHE STREAM	STRM	44 11 170 40	86
AVALON	SBRB	41 12 174 55	52
AVALON	SBRB	41 12 174 55	55
AVALON PEAK	PEAK	43 14 170 37	74
AVERNUS, LAKE	LAKE	42 35 172 05	70
AVERY (TRIG)	HILL	41 07 172 07	56
AVERY (TRIG)	HILL	41 07 172 07	62
AVIEMORE	HSTD	44 37 170 13	92
AVIEMORE	LOC	44 40 170 21	92
AVIEMORE, LAKE	LAKE	44 37 170 18	92
AVOCA	LOC	35 49 173 53	6
AVOCA	LOC	35 49 173 53	7
AVOCA	LOC	43 10 171 52	80
AVOCA	LOC	43 10 171 52	81
AVOCA COL	SAD	43 01 171 26	75
AVOCA COL	SAD	43 01 171 26	80
AVOCA, MOUNT	MTN	43 02 171 24	75
AVOCA, MOUNT	MTN	43 02 171 24	80
AVOCA RIVER	STRM	39 56 176 18	47
AVOCA RIVER	STRM	43 11 171 32	80
AVON BURN	STRM	44 27 169 42	91
AVON RIVER	STRM	41 39 173 39	66
AVON RIVER	STRM	43 31 172 44	82
AVON RIVER	STRM	43 31 172 44	83
AVON SADDLE	SAD	41 49 173 31	66
AVONDALE	SBRB	36 54 174 41	11
AVONDALE	SBRB	36 54 174 41	12
AVONDALE	SBRB	36 54 174 41	14
AVONDALE	HSTD	41 41 173 38	67
AWAAWAKINO	LOC	37 58 177 27	24
AWAAWAROA BAY	BAY	36 50 175 06	13
AWAHOA BAY	BAY	35 45 174 33	8
AWAHOU	LOC	38 03 176 13	20
AWAHOU	LOC	38 03 176 13	21
AWAHOU NORTH	LOC	40 11 175 49	46
AWAHOU SOUTH	LOC	40 13 175 47	46
AWAHOU STREAM	STRM	38 03 176 13	20
AWAHOU STREAM	STRM	38 03 176 13	21
AWAHURI	LOC	40 17 175 31	45
AWAHURI	LOC	40 17 175 31	46
AWAI STREAM	STRM	39 04 174 11	34
AWAITI	LOC	37 23 175 37	15
AWAITI CANAL	CANL	37 18 175 32	15
AWAKANAE STREAM	STRM	36 48 175 30	13
AWAKANAE STREAM	STRM	36 48 175 30	16
AWAKAPONGA	LOC	37 56 176 45	22
AWAKARI RIVER	STRM	41 55 171 28	63
AWAKAU	LOC	38 42 174 43	26
AWAKERI	LOC	38 00 176 53	22
AWAKERI	LOC	38 00 176 53	23
AWAKERI SPRINGS	LOC	38 01 176 52	22
AWAKERI SPRINGS	LOC	38 01 176 52	23
AWAKIA STREAM	STRM	46 13 169 25	111
AWAKIA STREAM	STRM	46 13 169 25	113
AWAKINO	LOC	38 39 174 38	26
AWAKINO POINT	LOC	35 55 173 55	7
AWAKINO RIVER	STRM	35 56 173 54	6
AWAKINO RIVER	STRM	35 56 173 54	7
AWAKINO RIVER	STRM	38 40 174 37	26
AWAKINO RIVER	STRM	44 42 170 26	92
AWAKINO RIVER (EAST BRANCH)	STRM	44 46 170 24	92
AWAKINO RIVER (WEST BRANCH)	STRM	44 46 170 24	92
AWAKINO STREAM	STRM	35 48 173 51	6
AWAMANGU	LOC	46 06 169 39	111
AWAMANGU	LOC	46 06 169 39	113
AWAMARINO	LOC	38 16 174 48	18
AWAMARINO	LOC	38 16 174 48	26
AWAMOKO	LOC	44 56 170 52	93
AWAMOKO STREAM	STRM	44 54 170 53	93
AWANA BAY	BAY	36 13 175 29	9
AWANA STREAM	STRM	36 12 175 29	9
AWANUI	LOC	35 03 173 16	3
AWANUI	LOC	37 47 177 39	24
AWANUI RIVER	STRM	35 01 173 16	3
AWANUI STREAM	STRM	39 41 176 50	42
AWANUI STREAM	STRM	39 41 176 50	43
AWAPATU STREAM	STRM	39 23 175 47	37
AWAPIKOPIKO STREAM	STRM	40 21 176 00	49
AWAPIRI	HSTD	41 50 173 44	67

AWAPOKO RIVER	STRM	34 59 173 26	3
AWAPOTO RIVER	STRM	40 52 173 00	57
AWAPUNI	SBRB	40 23 175 34	48
AWAPUNI	SBRB	40 23 175 34	49
AWARAU RIVER	STRM	42 00 171 53	64
AWAROA	LOC	35 16 173 18	3
AWAROA BAY	BAY	40 51 173 02	57
AWAROA CREEK	LOC	35 44 174 22	5
AWAROA CREEK	LOC	35 44 174 22	7
AWAROA CREEK	LOC	35 44 174 22	8
AWAROA HEAD	HEAD	40 51 173 03	57
AWAROA RIVER	STRM	35 20 173 14	3
AWAROA RIVER	STRM	36 10 174 03	7
AWAROA RIVER	STRM	37 19 174 46	14
AWAROA RIVER	STRM	38 06 174 55	18
AWAROA RIVER	STRM	40 52 173 00	57
AWAROA STREAM	STRM	37 28 175 02	14
AWAROA STREAM	STRM	37 35 175 05	18
AWARUA	LOC	35 35 173 50	4
AWARUA	LOC	35 35 173 50	6
AWARUA	LOC	35 35 173 50	7
AWARUA	LOC	46 30 168 23	109
AWARUA BAY	BAY	46 34 168 28	109
AWARUA PLAINS	PLNS	46 31 168 30	109
AWARUA POINT	PNT	44 16 168 03	89
AWARUA RIVER	STRM	35 38 173 51	6
AWARUA RIVER	STRM	35 38 173 51	7
AWARUA ROCK	ROCK	35 47 174 33	5
AWARUA ROCK	ROCK	35 47 174 33	8
AWATAIKATO POINT	PNT	43 38 169 23	78
AWATANE	LOC	38 10 175 19	18
AWATANE	LOC	38 10 175 19	19
AWATEA	LOC	46 22 169 32	113
AWATERE	HSTD	37 41 178 21	25
AWATERE RIVER	STRM	37 38 178 22	25
AWATERE RIVER	STRM	41 37 174 10	60
AWATERE (TRIG)	HILL	41 37 174 05	60
AWATERE-ITI STREAM	STRM	42 04 173 20	66
AWATOITOI	LOC	40 56 175 56	49
AWATOITOI	LOC	40 56 175 56	51
AWATOTO	LOC	39 32 176 55	40
AWATOTO	LOC	39 32 176 55	41
AWATOTO	LOC	39 32 176 55	42
AWATOTO STATION	RSTN	39 33 176 55	40
AWATOTO STATION	RSTN	39 33 176 55	41
AWATOTO STATION	RSTN	39 33 176 55	42
AWATOTO STATION	RSTN	39 33 176 55	43
AWATUNA	LOC	39 26 174 03	34
AWATUNA	LOC	42 38 171 04	68
AWATUNA	LOC	42 38 171 04	69
AWE BURN	STRM	45 27 167 21	96
AWFUL, MOUNT	MTN	44 09 169 04	78
AWHEA RIVER	STRM	41 30 175 31	53
AWHEAITI STREAM	STRM	41 31 175 30	53
AWHITU	LOC	37 05 174 38	12
AWHITU	LOC	37 05 174 38	14
AWHITU CENTRAL	LOC	37 06 174 35	12
AWHITU CENTRAL	LOC	37 06 174 35	14
AWKWARD, MOUNT	MTN	44 00 169 32	79
AXIS, MOUNT	MTN	42 55 171 20	69
AYESHA STREAM	STRM	41 52 171 48	63
AYESHA STREAM	STRM	41 52 171 48	64
AYLESBURY	LOC	43 32 172 14	81
AYLESBURY	LOC	43 32 172 14	85
AZIM, MOUNT	PEAK	39 22 175 52	37

B

BAAL	MTN	44 10 168 40	88
BACK CREEK	STRM	45 29 170 34	102
BACK CREEK	STRM	45 50 168 05	106
BACK CREEK	STRM	45 50 168 05	107
BACK CREEK	STRM	46 31 169 23	113
BACK RANGE STREAM	STRM	41 41 173 31	66
BACK RIVER	LOC	35 02 173 32	3
BACK RIVER	LOC	35 02 173 32	4
BACK STREAM	STRM	46 02 169 23	111
BACK STREAM	STRM	46 02 169 23	113
BAD PASSAGE	STRA	46 02 166 32	104
BAIGENT, MOUNT	MTN	41 34 172 26	62
BAIN HILL (TRIG)	HILL	43 55 169 00	78
BAIN, MOUNT	MTN	45 36 167 08	105
BAINESSE	LOC	40 25 175 23	48
BAINHAM	LOC	40 46 172 33	56
BAINHAM	LOC	40 46 172 33	57
BAIRD, MOUNT	MTN	45 18 167 20	96
BAIRD RANGE	MTNS	43 27 170 13	74
BAIRD RANGE	MTNS	43 27 170 13	77
BAKER CREEK	STRM	41 15 172 06	56
BAKER CREEK	STRM	41 15 172 06	62
BAKER CREEK	STRM	43 49 169 50	76
BAKER CREEK	STRM	43 49 169 50	79
BAKER, MOUNT (TRIG)	HILL	39 43 175 50	46
BAKER, MOUNT (TRIG)	HILL	40 42 175 46	49
BAKER, MOUNT (TRIG)	HILL	40 42 175 46	51
BAKER PEAK	PEAK	43 52 169 49	76
BAKER PEAK	PEAK	43 52 169 49	79
BAKER SADDLE	SAD	43 37 170 06	76
BAKER SADDLE	SAD	43 37 170 06	77
BALACLAVA, MOUNT (TRIG)	MTN	42 11 172 51	65
BALCAIRN	LOC	43 13 172 42	82
BALCLUTHA	TOWN	46 14 169 44	111
BALCLUTHA	TOWN	46 14 169 44	113
BALD CONE (TRIG)	HILL	47 13 167 36	114
BALD HILL	PEAK	41 44 172 07	64
BALD HILL (TRIG)	MTN	43 47 169 13	78
BALD HILL (TRIG)	HILL	46 58 167 58	114
BALD HILL (TRIG)	HILL	46 58 167 58	115
BALD HILL (TRIG)	HILL	37 14 174 48	12
BALD HILL (TRIG)	HILL	37 14 174 48	14
BALD HILL (TRIG)	PEAK	42 18 171 55	63
BALD HILL (TRIG)	PEAK	42 18 171 55	64
BALD HILL (TRIG)	HILL	45 32 170 14	101
BALD KNOB	PEAK	41 10 172 16	56
BALD KNOB	PEAK	41 10 172 16	62
BALD MOUNTAIN	MTNS	44 15 168 30	88
BALD PEAK (TRIG)	PEAK	45 23 168 10	98
BALD RANGE	MTN	42 45 171 28	69
BALD ROCK (TRIG)	HILL	36 07 174 27	7
BALD ROCK (TRIG)	HILL	36 07 174 27	8
BALD (TRIG)	HILL	40 56 175 51	49
BALD (TRIG)	HILL	40 56 175 51	51
BALDY HILL (TRIG)	MTN	43 05 171 44	80
BALDY, MOUNT (TRIG)	PEAK	41 26 173 37	59
BALDY, MOUNT (TRIG)	PEAK	41 26 173 37	60
BALDY (TRIG)	HILL	40 42 172 27	56
BALDY (TRIG)	HILL	40 42 172 27	57
BALDY (TRIG)	PEAK	42 17 172 15	64
BALDY (TRIG)	MTN	42 01 172 26	65
BALFOUR	LOC	45 51 168 35	107

BALFOUR GLACIER	GLCR	43 33 170 04	76
BALFOUR GLACIER	GLCR	43 33 170 04	77
BALFOUR, MOUNT (TRIG)	MTN	42 27 173 00	72
BALFOUR RANGE	MTNS	43 34 170 03	76
BALFOUR RANGE	MTNS	43 34 170 03	77
BALFOUR RIVER	STRM	43 32 169 59	76
BALFOUR RIVER	STRM	43 32 169 59	77
BALL GLACIER	GLCR	43 37 170 10	74
BALL GLACIER	GLCR	43 37 170 10	77
BALLANCE	LOC	40 24 175 48	49
BALLENY REEF	REEF	46 06 166 33	104
BALLOON CREEK	STRM	41 10 172 41	56
BALLOON CREEK	STRM	41 10 172 41	58
BALLOON HILL (TRIG)	HILL	41 10 172 37	56
BALLOON HILL (TRIG)	HILL	41 10 172 37	58
BALLOON, MOUNT	MTN	44 48 167 47	94
BALLOON STREAM	STRM	44 23 170 24	92
BALMACAAN SADDLE	SAD	43 39 171 01	75
BALMACAAN SADDLE	SAD	43 39 171 01	87
BALMACAAN STREAM	STRM	43 37 171 05	75
BALMORAL	LOC	42 50 172 44	71
BALMORAL STREAM	STRM	46 11 169 40	111
BALMORAL STREAM	STRM	46 11 169 40	113
BALMORAL (TRIG)	HILL	44 40 170 37	92
BALMORAL (TRIG)	HILL	44 40 170 37	93
BAMFORD KNOB	PEAK	43 24 170 29	74
BAMFORD KNOB	PEAK	43 24 170 29	77
BANDIT PEAK	PEAK	43 22 170 50	75
BANDOLERO COL	SAD	43 21 170 52	75
BANKS CREEK	STRM	41 24 173 35	59
BANKS PENINSULA	PEN	43 44 172 52	83
BANKSIDE	LOC	43 42 172 06	85
BANNATYNE, MOUNT	MTN	43 01 171 11	75
BANNISTER	PEAK	40 45 175 27	48
BANNOCK BRAE RANGE	MTNS	43 43 169 44	76
BANNOCK BRAE RANGE	MTNS	43 43 169 44	79
BANNOCK BRAE (TRIG)	MTN	43 39 169 39	76
BANNOCK BRAE (TRIG)	MTN	43 39 169 39	79
BANNOCK BURN	STRM	45 05 169 10	99
BANNOCKBURN	LOC	45 06 169 10	99
BAR POINT	PNT	40 34 172 33	57
BARBER, MOUNT (TRIG)	MTN	45 30 167 13	96
BARBER STREAM	STRM	41 52 173 10	66
BARCLAYS CREEK	STRM	44 21 170 03	92
BARE CONE	MTN	44 50 167 29	94
BARE HILL (TRIG)	HILL	46 00 168 35	107
BARE HILL (TRIG)	HILL	40 49 172 21	56
BARE ISLAND	ISLD	39 50 177 02	42
BARE ISLAND	ISLD	39 50 177 02	43
BARE KNOB (TRIG)	PEAK	40 56 173 02	57
BARE PEAK (TRIG)	PEAK	45 22 168 03	97
BARE PEAK (TRIG)	PEAK	45 22 168 03	98
BARE ROCKY RANGE	MTNS	43 43 169 50	76
BARE ROCKY RANGE	MTNS	43 43 169 50	79
BAREACRE (TRIG)	PEAK	39 25 176 00	37
BAREFELL (TRIG)	MTN	42 10 173 08	66
BARFF, MOUNT	MTN	44 25 168 39	88
BARFF, MOUNT	MTN	44 25 168 39	90
BARING HEAD	HEAD	41 25 174 52	52
BARING HEAD	HEAD	41 25 174 52	55
BARING, MOUNT (TRIG)	MTN	41 49 172 31	65
BARK BAY	BAY	40 55 173 03	57
BARKER, MOUNT	MTN	44 44 169 11	90
BARKER, MOUNT (TRIG)	HILL	43 21 171 37	80
BARKES CORNER	LOC	37 44 176 07	20
BARKES CORNER	LOC	37 44 176 07	21
BARLOW, MOUNT	MTN	43 19 170 37	74
BARLOW RIVER	STRM	43 21 170 31	74
BARN ISLANDS	ISLS	44 05 168 18	88
BARN RIVER	STRM	44 03 168 23	88
BARNEGO	LOC	46 14 169 44	111
BARNEGO	LOC	46 14 169 44	113
BARNHILL CREEK	STRM	45 46 168 13	107
BARNICOAT, MOUNT	MTN	43 33 170 12	74
BARNICOAT, MOUNT	MTN	43 33 170 12	77
BARNICOAT RANGE	MTNS	41 21 173 15	59
BARR, MOUNT	HILL	41 01 172 11	56
BARR, MOUNT	HILL	41 01 172 11	62
BARRACK CREEK	STRM	42 51 171 34	69
BARRACOUTA POINT	PNT	46 33 168 14	109
BARRHILL	LOC	43 40 171 51	80
BARRHILL	LOC	43 40 171 51	84
BARRIER, CAPE	CAPE	36 21 175 32	9
BARRIER PEAK	PEAK	44 51 167 43	94
BARRIER RANGE	MTNS	44 13 169 42	79
BARRIER RIVER	STRM	44 25 168 13	88
BARRIER RIVER	STRM	44 25 168 13	89
BARRINGTON PEAK	PEAK	44 33 168 11	88
BARRINGTON PEAK	PEAK	44 33 168 11	89
BARRON, MOUNT (TRIG)	MTN	42 50 171 32	69
BARRON, MOUNT (TRIG)	MTN	42 30 172 12	70
BARRON PEAK	PEAK	43 54 169 46	76
BARRON PEAK	PEAK	43 54 169 46	79
BARRON RANGE	MTNS	42 51 171 31	69
BARRON STREAM	STRM	41 05 172 46	57
BARRON STREAM	STRM	41 05 172 46	58
BARROSA, MOUNT	MTN	43 37 171 14	75
BARRY, MOUNT	MTN	43 11 170 49	75
BARRY, MOUNT	MTN	44 17 168 41	88
BARRY, MOUNT	MTN	44 17 168 41	90
BARRYTOWN	LOC	42 15 171 20	63
BARRYVILLE	LOC	38 30 175 34	27
BARRYVILLE	LOC	38 30 175 34	28
BARTH, MOUNT	MTN	44 10 169 36	79
BARTLETTS	LOC	38 51 177 54	32
BARTLETTS	LOC	38 51 177 54	33
BARTLETTS CREEK	STRM	41 31 173 36	59
BARTLETTS CREEK	STRM	41 31 173 36	60
BARTON, MOUNT	HILL	44 30 167 54	89
BARTON, MOUNT	HILL	44 30 167 54	94
BARTON, MOUNT (TRIG)	PEAK	41 02 175 06	52
BARTON, MOUNT (TRIG)	PEAK	41 33 175 20	53
BARTON, MOUNT (TRIG)	PEAK	41 02 175 06	53
BARTON, MOUNT (TRIG)	PEAK	41 02 175 06	55
BARTRUM CREEK	STRM	43 08 170 45	74
BASIN CREEK	STRM	42 25 172 24	71
BASIN CREEK	STRM	43 06 171 29	75
BASIN CREEK	STRM	43 06 171 29	80
BASIN CREEK	STRM	46 03 167 32	105
BASIN CREEK	STRM	46 03 167 32	106
BASIN CREEK	STRM	47 10 167 39	114
BASIN STREAM	STRM	44 25 170 27	92
BASTION PEAK	PEAK	43 18 171 01	75
BASTION, THE (TRIG)	HILL	45 58 168 25	107
BATEMAN CREEK	STRM	42 03 172 00	64
BATES, MOUNT (TRIG)	MTN	46 12 166 59	105
BATLEY	LOC	36 14 174 19	7
BATLEY	LOC	36 14 174 19	8
BATON RIVER	STRM	41 17 172 48	58
BATON SADDLE	SAD	41 15 172 35	56

BATON SADDLE	SAD	41 15 172 35	58
BATON SADDLE	SAD	41 20 172 44	58
BATTERSEA	LOC	41 08 175 25	53
BATTERY STREAM	STRM	41 21 175 08	52
BATTERY STREAM	STRM	41 21 175 08	53
BATTERY STREAM	STRM	41 21 175 08	55
BATTLEMENT PEAK	PEAK	44 22 168 17	88
BATTLEMENT PEAK	PEAK	44 22 168 17	89
BATTY CREEK	STRM	42 25 171 17	68
BATTY CREEK	STRM	42 25 171 17	69
BAUZA ISLAND	ISLD	45 18 166 55	96
BAWBAW (TRIG)	PEAK	41 13 175 08	52
BAWBAW (TRIG)	PEAK	41 13 175 08	53
BAWBAW (TRIG)	PEAK	41 13 175 08	55
BAY OF ISLANDS	BAY	35 13 174 12	5
BAY OF MANY COVES	BAY	41 11 174 10	54
BAY OF MANY COVES	BAY	41 11 174 10	60
BAY OF MANY COVES	BAY	41 11 174 10	61
BAY OF PLENTY	BAY	37 48 177 12	23
BAY PEAKS	PEAK	45 14 168 38	95
BAY PEAKS	PEAK	45 14 168 38	99
BAY VIEW	LOC	39 25 176 52	40
BAY VIEW	LOC	39 25 176 52	41
BAY VIEW	LOC	39 25 176 52	42
BAY VIEW	LOC	41 15 173 19	59
BAYLYS BEACH	LOC	35 57 173 44	6
BAYONET PEAKS	PEAK	45 10 168 41	95
BAYONET PEAKS	PEAK	45 10 168 41	99
BAYOU CREEK	STRM	43 50 169 06	78
BAYOU HILL (TRIG)	HILL	43 50 169 06	78
BAYSWATER	LOC	46 06 168 05	106
BAYSWATER	LOC	46 06 168 05	107
BEACHLANDS	LOC	36 53 175 00	12
BEACHLANDS	LOC	36 53 175 00	13
BEACHLANDS	LOC	36 53 175 00	14
BEACON	MTN	44 21 168 17	88
BEACON	MTN	44 21 168 17	89
BEACON HILL	MTN	44 26 170 19	92
BEACON HILL (TRIG)	LOC	46 08 169 19	110
BEACON HILL (TRIG)	LOC	46 08 169 19	112
BEACON HILL (TRIG)	LOC	46 08 169 19	113
BEACON POINT	PNT	44 40 169 08	90
BEACON, THE	MTN	42 19 173 17	66
BEACONSFIELD	LOC	40 05 175 39	46
BEALE, MOUNT (TRIG)	HILL	40 33 172 41	57
BEALEY	LOC	43 02 171 38	80
BEALEY, MOUNT	MTN	42 58 171 33	69
BEALEY RANGE	MTNS	44 01 169 30	79
BEALEY RIVER	STRM	43 00 171 36	69
BEANS BURN	STRM	44 39 168 18	89
BEATRIX BAY	BAY	41 02 174 01	54
BEATRIX BAY	BAY	41 02 174 01	60
BEATRIX BAY	BAY	41 02 174 01	61
BEATTIE, LAKE	LAKE	45 30 166 47	96
BEATTIE (TRIG)	MTN	42 12 173 20	66
BEAU SADDLE	SAD	42 48 172 27	71
BEAUMONT	LOC	45 49 169 32	111
BEAUMONT CREEK	STRM	45 54 167 59	106
BEAUMONT CREEK	STRM	45 54 167 59	107
BEAUMONT, MOUNT	MTN	43 06 170 56	75
BEAUMONT RIVER	STRM	45 49 169 31	111
BEAUMONT STATION	HSTD	45 44 169 32	111
BEAUMONT (TRIG)	HILL	45 52 168 01	106
BEAUMONT (TRIG)	HILL	45 52 168 01	107
BEAUTIFUL, MOUNT (TRIG)	HILL	42 48 173 21	72
BEAUTIFUL, MOUNT (TRIG)	HILL	42 48 173 21	73
BEAUTIFUL RIVER	STRM	41 12 172 26	56
BEAUTIFUL RIVER	STRM	41 12 172 26	62
BEAUTIFUL VALLEY	LOC	44 07 171 02	87
BECK, MOUNT (TRIG)	HILL	44 15 168 15	88
BECK, MOUNT (TRIG)	HILL	44 15 168 15	89
BECKENHAM HILLS	HSTD	42 53 173 03	72
BECKETT STREAM	STRM	42 54 171 58	70
BECKMAN, MOUNT	MTN	42 20 172 00	70
BECKS	LOC	45 00 169 45	91
BECKS	LOC	45 00 169 45	100
BECKS	LOC	45 00 169 45	101
BEDDOES, LAKE	LAKE	44 55 167 33	94
BEDDOES, LAKE	LAKE	44 55 167 33	97
BEEBYS KNOB	PEAK	41 44 172 56	65
BEECHE, MOUNT	MTN	42 05 171 39	63
BEECHE, MOUNT	MTN	42 05 171 39	64
BEEHIVE	HILL	45 30 167 30	97
BEEHIVE CREEK	STRM	40 10 175 49	46
BEEHIVE ISLAND	ISLD	36 27 174 49	11
BEEHIVE (TRIG)	HILL	40 32 176 14	50
BEEHIVES (TRIG)	HILL	39 20 174 03	34
BEGGS CREEK	STRM	44 58 169 32	91
BEGLEY CREEK	STRM	42 05 172 48	65
BEGLEY SADDLE	SAD	42 05 172 48	65
BEHIND PEAKS	MTNS	45 20 167 06	96
BEL, MOUNT	MTN	44 14 168 42	88
BELFAST	POPL	43 27 172 38	82
BELFAST	POPL	43 27 172 38	83
BELFAST	POPL	43 27 172 38	85
BELFIELD	LOC	44 06 171 19	84
BELFIELD	LOC	44 06 171 19	87
BELFRY PEAK	PEAK	44 06 169 46	79
BELGROVE	LOC	41 27 172 58	58
BELGROVE	LOC	41 27 172 58	59
BELL BLOCK	USAT	39 02 174 09	34
BELL CREEK	STRM	42 06 171 46	63
BELL CREEK	STRM	42 06 171 46	64
BELL HILL	LOC	42 33 171 33	69
BELL HILL (TRIG)	HILL	42 34 171 37	69
BELL HILL (TRIG)	HILL	42 34 171 37	70
BELL MOUNT	HILL	45 51 167 41	106
BELL POINT	PNT	44 41 167 34	94
BELLE BURN	STRM	45 49 169 31	111
BELLE, MOUNT	MTN	44 47 167 59	89
BELLE, MOUNT	MTN	44 47 167 59	94
BELLS CREEK	STRM	44 28 169 07	90
BELLS ISLAND	ISLD	41 18 173 10	59
BELLS JUNCTION	LOC	39 33 175 31	36
BELLS JUNCTION	LOC	39 33 175 31	37
BELLS SADDLE	SAD	45 17 170 37	102
BELVEDERE PEAK (TRIG)	PEAK	42 06 172 43	65
BEN AVON	MTN	44 25 169 37	91
BEN BOLT (TRIG)	HILL	46 00 168 29	107
BEN BOLT (TRIG)	HILL	37 02 175 44	16
BEN BOLT (TRIG)	HILL	37 02 175 44	17
BEN CALLUM (TRIG)	HILL	45 57 168 31	107
BEN CLIBERICK	MTN	42 48 172 24	71
BEN CRUACHAN	MTN	45 03 168 52	95
BEN CRUACHAN	MTN	45 03 168 52	99
BEN DHU (TRIG)	MTN	44 04 170 06	86
BEN HOPE (TRIG)	MTN	43 58 171 08	87
BEN LOMOND	HILL	39 41 176 32	42
BEN LOMOND	HILL	39 41 176 32	43
BEN LOMOND	HILL	39 41 176 32	47

BEN LOMOND (TRIG)	MTN	45 01 168 37	95
BEN LOMOND (TRIG)	MTN	45 01 168 37	99
BEN LOMOND (TRIG)	HILL	40 07 176 34	43
BEN LOMOND (TRIG)	HILL	39 59 175 20	45
BEN LOMOND (TRIG)	HILL	40 07 176 34	47
BEN LOMOND (TRIG)	MTN	42 52 172 55	71
BEN LOMOND (TRIG)	MTN	42 46 173 03	72
BEN LOMOND (TRIG)	MTN	42 52 172 55	72
BEN LOMOND (TRIG)	MTN	44 56 170 30	92
BEN MCLEOD	MTN	43 44 170 57	87
BEN MCLEOD RANGE	MTNS	43 45 170 52	87
BEN MORE	MTN	43 21 171 43	80
BEN MORE	MTN	44 57 168 23	90
BEN MORE	MTN	44 57 168 32	95
BEN MORE	MTN	44 57 168 32	99
BEN MORE STREAM	STRM	41 59 174 00	67
BEN MORE STREAM	STRM	43 22 171 38	80
BEN MORE (TRIG)	HILL	45 55 168 27	107
BEN MORE (TRIG)	HILL	41 55 174 00	67
BEN MORE (TRIG)	HILL	42 42 172 43	71
BEN MURRAY (TRIG)	MTN	41 37 172 25	62
BEN NEVIS	MTN	45 10 168 50	95
BEN NEVIS	MTN	45 10 168 50	99
BEN NEVIS (TRIG)	HILL	40 09 176 40	43
BEN NEVIS (TRIG)	HILL	40 09 176 40	47
BEN OHAU RANGE	MTNS	44 00 170 01	77
BEN OHAU RANGE	MTNS	44 00 170 01	79
BEN OHAU (TRIG)	MTN	44 16 169 54	79
BENBOWN (TRIG)	HILL	41 20 173 35	59
BENCH ISLAND	ISLD	46 55 168 14	109
BENCH ISLAND	ISLD	46 55 168 14	115
BENCRUACHAN	HSTD	42 39 173 16	72
BENCRUACHAN	HSTD	42 39 173 16	73
BENDIGO	LOC	44 56 169 20	91
BENDIGO CREEK	STRM	44 56 169 19	91
BENDROSE STREAM	STRM	44 18 170 09	86
BENGER BURN	STRM	45 38 169 16	110
BENGER BURN (SOUTH BRANCH)	STRM	45 39 169 21	110
BENHAR	LOC	46 13 169 48	111
BENHAR	LOC	46 13 169 48	113
BENIO	LOC	46 03 169 05	110
BENIO	LOC	46 03 169 05	112
BENMORE	LOC	46 00 168 21	107
BENMORE, LAKE	LAKE	44 25 170 13	92
BENMORE PEAK	MTN	44 25 170 06	92
BENMORE RANGE	MTNS	44 24 170 07	92
BENMORE (TRIG)	HILL	44 27 170 00	92
BENNETS	LOC	43 19 172 18	81
BENNETS	LOC	43 19 172 18	85
BENNETT STREAM	STRM	42 39 173 16	72
BENNETT STREAM	STRM	42 39 173 16	73
BENNETTS SIDING	RSDG	39 39 175 46	46
BENNEYDALE	LOC	38 31 175 22	27
BENVORLICH (TRIG)	HILL	40 38 176 15	50
BERESFORD PASS	PASS	44 20 168 16	88
BERESFORD PASS	PASS	44 20 168 16	89
BERESFORD RANGE	MTNS	46 27 169 25	113
BERGHAN POINT	PNT	34 55 173 34	3
BERLINS	LOC	41 52 171 50	63
BERLINS	LOC	41 52 171 50	64
BERLINS BLUFF (TRIG)	HILL	41 54 171 50	63
BERLINS BLUFF (TRIG)	HILL	41 54 171 50	64
BERNARD BURN	STRM	44 53 167 35	94
BERNARD LAKE	LAKE	44 53 167 38	94
BERNARD STREAM	STRM	43 51 171 03	87
BERNERS, MOUNT (TRIG)	HILL	41 42 172 00	64
BERRY CREEK	STRM	43 05 170 33	74
BERTHA, MOUNT	MTN	44 07 169 13	78
BERWICK	LOC	45 56 170 06	103
BESSONS DAM	LAKE	42 04 171 23	63
BESTS ISLAND	ISLD	41 18 173 09	59
BETA CREEK	STRM	41 56 171 41	63
BETA CREEK	STRM	41 56 171 41	64
BETA, MOUNT	MTN	44 05 168 35	88
BETHLEHEM	LOC	37 42 176 06	20
BETHLEHEM	LOC	37 42 176 06	21
BETSY ISLAND	ISLD	47 08 167 32	114
BETTISON STREAM	STRM	43 23 170 34	74
BETTISON STREAM	STRM	43 23 170 34	77
BETTY HILL (TRIG)	MTN	44 01 170 06	77
BETTY HILL (TRIG)	MTN	44 01 170 06	86
BEVAN, MOUNT	MTN	44 24 168 41	88
BEVAN, MOUNT	MTN	44 24 168 41	90
BEVEN COL	SAD	44 24 168 41	88
BEVEN COL	SAD	44 24 168 41	90
BEXLEY	LOC	43 21 172 05	81
BEXLEY	LOC	43 21 172 05	85
BICKERSTAFFE	LOC	36 08 174 20	7
BICKERSTAFFE	LOC	36 08 174 20	8
BIDEFORD	LOC	40 52 175 52	49
BIDEFORD	LOC	40 52 175 52	51
BIG BAY	BAY	36 30 174 45	11
BIG BAY	LOC	37 03 174 39	12
BIG BAY	BAY	37 03 174 38	12
BIG BAY	LOC	37 03 174 39	14
BIG BAY	BAY	37 03 174 38	14
BIG BAY	BAY	41 07 174 09	54
BIG BAY	BAY	40 52 172 08	56
BIG BAY	BAY	41 07 174 09	60
BIG BAY	BAY	41 07 174 09	61
BIG BAY	BAY	43 37 172 53	82
BIG BAY	BAY	43 37 172 53	83
BIG BAY	BAY	44 18 168 03	89
BIG BEN RANGE	MTNS	43 24 171 43	80
BIG BEN SADDLE	SAD	43 15 172 07	81
BIG BEN (TRIG)	MTN	43 24 171 41	80
BIG BEN (TRIG)	PEAK	39 05 176 23	39
BIG BEN (TRIG)	PEAK	39 05 176 23	40
BIG BEN (TRIG)	MTN	44 50 170 24	92
BIG BOLTON	MTN	41 49 173 41	67
BIG BUSH GULLY	STRM	42 40 173 26	73
BIG BUSH STREAM	STRM	42 22 172 51	71
BIG BUSH STREAM	STRM	42 22 172 51	72
BIG CASTLE	MTN	41 53 173 29	66
BIG CREEK	STRM	43 19 170 25	74
BIG CREEK	STRM	46 10 170 09	103
BIG DEEP CREEK	STRM	41 47 172 10	64
BIG FACE (TRIG)	HILL	41 23 175 16	53
BIG GEORDIE	MTN	44 58 168 28	95
BIG GEORDIE	MTN	44 58 168 28	98
BIG GLORY BAY	BAY	46 59 168 07	115
BIG GOAT HILL	MTN	43 13 171 21	75
BIG GOAT HILL	MTN	43 13 171 21	80
BIG GULLY	STRM	41 50 173 49	67
BIG GULLY	STRM	45 16 170 28	102
BIG HILL RANGE	MTNS	43 26 170 59	75
BIG HILL STREAM	STRM	39 37 176 24	47
BIG HILL (TRIG)	HILL	45 57 168 15	107
BIG HILL (TRIG)	HILL	41 51 173 51	67
BIG HILL (TRIG)	HILL	44 59 170 56	93
BIG HOPWOOD BURN	STRM	44 24 169 20	91
BIG ISLAND	ISLD	47 08 167 31	114
BIG JAR	MTN	43 04 171 08	75
BIG KURI BAY	BAY	47 07 168 03	115
BIG LAGOON	LAGN	41 33 174 06	60
BIG LAGOON	LAKE	46 21 168 10	109
BIG MOGGY ISLAND	ISLD	47 09 167 24	114
BIG OMAHA	LOC	36 20 174 44	11
BIG RIVER	STRM	40 46 172 15	56
BIG RIVER	LOC	42 15 171 55	63
BIG RIVER	STRM	42 14 171 45	63
BIG RIVER	STRM	42 20 171 32	63
BIG RIVER	STRM	42 14 171 45	64
BIG RIVER	LOC	42 15 171 55	64
BIG RIVER	STRM	46 13 166 56	104
BIG RIVER	STRM	46 13 166 56	105
BIG ROCK STREAM	STRM	45 49 170 01	111
BIG SAND PASS	PASS	46 55 167 47	114
BIG SANDHILL (TRIG)	HILL	46 56 167 48	114
BIG SOUTH CAPE ISLAND	ISLD	47 15 167 24	114
BIG STREAM	STRM	45 45 170 21	103
BIG WAINIHINIHI RIVER	STRM	42 45 171 20	69
BIGNELL REEF	REEF	43 51 168 54	78
BILLHOOK PEAK (TRIG)	PEAK	42 28 172 36	71
BILLY BURN	STRM	45 02 167 52	94
BILLY BURN	STRM	45 02 167 52	97
BILLY BURN	STRM	45 02 167 52	98
BILLY CREEK	STRM	45 14 168 33	95
BILLY CREEK	STRM	45 14 168 33	99
BILLY GOAT POINT	PNT	36 44 174 55	11
BILLY GOAT POINT	PNT	36 44 174 55	12
BILLY SADDLE	SAD	45 19 168 29	95
BILLY SADDLE	SAD	45 19 168 29	99
BINSER SADDLE	SAD	43 00 171 51	70
BINSER SADDLE	SAD	43 00 171 51	80
BINSER, MOUNT (TRIG)	MTN	43 02 171 51	80
BINSER, MOUNT (TRIG)	MTN	43 02 171 51	81
BIRCH CREEK	STRM	43 57 169 29	78
BIRCH CREEK	STRM	43 57 169 29	79
BIRCH CREEK	STRM	44 22 169 39	91
BIRCH HILL	HSTD	41 39 173 17	66
BIRCH HILL	MTN	44 23 169 33	91
BIRCH KNOB	MTN	43 57 169 27	78
BIRCH KNOB	MTN	43 57 169 27	79
BIRCH NOOK (TRIG)	HILL	43 00 171 34	80
BIRCH TOPPING (TRIG)	PEAK	42 35 172 54	71
BIRCH TOPPING (TRIG)	PEAK	42 35 172 54	72
BIRCHFIELD	LOC	41 41 171 48	63
BIRCHFIELD	LOC	41 41 171 48	64
BIRCHVILLE	LOC	41 06 175 05	52
BIRCHVILLE	LOC	41 06 175 05	55
BIRCHWOOD	LOC	45 57 167 47	106
BIRD CREEK	STRM	42 01 171 42	63
BIRD CREEK	STRM	42 01 171 42	64
BIRD ISLAND	ISLD	40 16 176 41	50
BIRD ISLAND	ISLD	40 59 174 02	54
BIRD ISLAND	ISLD	40 59 174 02	60
BIRD ISLAND	ISLD	40 59 174 02	61
BIRD ISLAND	ISLD	45 55 170 33	103
BIRD ISLAND	ISLD	46 46 168 25	109
BIRD ISLAND	ISLD	46 46 168 25	115
BIRD, MOUNT (TRIG)	MTN	43 14 170 20	74
BIRD ROCK	ROCK	34 57 173 41	4
BIRD ROCK	ROCK	35 10 174 18	5
BIRD ROCKS	ROCK	36 07 175 21	9
BIRDLINGS BROOK	STRM	43 48 172 21	85
BIRDLINGS FLAT	LOC	43 50 172 42	83
BIRDLINGS FLAT	LOC	43 50 172 42	85
BIRDS EYE STREAM	STRM	43 03 172 28	81
BIRDS EYE STREAM	STRM	43 03 172 28	82
BIRDWOOD RANGE	MTNS	43 05 171 25	75
BIRDWOOD RANGE	MTNS	43 05 171 25	80
BIRETTA, MOUNT	MTN	43 41 170 15	77
BIRETTA, MOUNT	MTN	43 41 170 15	86
BIRKENHEAD	SBRB	36 49 174 43	11
BIRKENHEAD	SBRB	36 49 174 43	12
BIRLEY PASS	PASS	44 57 167 59	94
BIRLEY PASS	PASS	44 57 167 59	97
BIRLEY PASS	PASS	44 57 167 59	98
BIRNAM, MOUNT	MTN	44 10 169 14	78
BIRTHDAY CREEK	STRM	42 32 173 22	72
BIRTHDAY CREEK	STRM	42 32 173 22	73
BISCUIT STREAM	STRM	40 58 175 54	51
BISHOP BURN	STRM	45 42 167 02	105
BISHOPDALE	SBRB	41 18 173 15	59
BISHOPS AND CLERKS ISLANDS	ISLS	46 40 167 48	108
BISHOPS AND CLERKS ISLANDS	ISLS	46 40 167 48	114
BISHOPS BAY	BAY	44 39 169 03	90
BISHOPS CAP (TRIG)	PEAK	41 31 173 10	59
BITTERNESS, MOUNT (TRIG)	MTN	44 45 170 18	92
BLACK BIRCH CREEK	STRM	42 59 173 08	72
BLACK BIRCH CREEK	STRM	43 35 170 53	75
BLACK BIRCH STREAM	STRM	41 43 173 53	67
BLACK CONE	PEAK	45 18 167 37	97
BLACK CREEK	STRM	42 54 173 06	72
BLACK FOREST	LOC	44 25 170 16	92
BLACK FOREST STREAM	STRM	44 25 170 15	92
BLACK GIANTS	MTN	45 31 167 08	96
BLACK GULLY	STRM	45 53 169 14	110
BLACK GULLY	LOC	45 54 169 21	110
BLACK GULLY	LOC	45 54 169 21	111
BLACK HEAD	HEAD	41 02 174 14	54
BLACK HEAD	HEAD	41 02 174 14	60
BLACK HEAD	HEAD	41 02 174 14	61
BLACK HEAD	HEAD	45 56 170 26	103
BLACK HILL	HILL	45 45 168 56	110
BLACK HILL (TRIG)	MTN	43 23 171 25	75
BLACK HILL (TRIG)	MTN	43 23 171 25	80
BLACK HILL (TRIG)	MTN	43 11 172 00	81
BLACK HILL (TRIG)	MTN	45 40 168 35	107
BLACK HILL RANGE	MTNS	43 25 171 25	75
BLACK HILL RANGE	MTNS	43 25 171 25	80
BLACK HORN (TRIG)	HILL	46 33 169 13	112
BLACK JACK (TRIG)	HILL	36 43 175 44	16
BLACK LAKES	LAKE	41 22 172 18	62
BLACK, MOUNT	HILL	45 45 167 40	106
BLACK, MOUNT (TRIG)	PEAK	45 13 169 04	99
BLACK MOUNTAIN	MTN	43 34 170 49	75
BLACK PEAK	PEAK	44 38 168 25	89
BLACK PEAK	PEAK	44 49 168 29	89
BLACK PEAK	PEAK	44 35 168 50	90
BLACK PEAK	PEAK	44 49 168 29	95
BLACK POINT	LOC	44 54 170 47	93
BLACK RANGE	MTNS	43 04 171 36	80
BLACK REEF	REEF	39 38 177 05	42
BLACK REEF	REEF	39 38 177 05	43
BLACK REEF	REEF	41 44 171 28	63
BLACK ROCK	LOC	45 48 170 00	111
BLACK ROCK	ROCK	45 45 169 55	111
BLACK ROCK	ROCK	47 10 167 58	115
BLACK ROCK POINT	PNT	46 47 167 51	108
BLACK ROCK POINT	PNT	46 47 167 51	109
BLACK ROCK POINT	PNT	46 47 167 51	114
BLACK ROCK STREAM	STRM	45 32 170 19	101
BLACK ROCK STREAM	STRM	45 47 170 02	111
BLACK ROCK (TRIG)	PEAK	42 56 172 15	70
BLACK ROCK (TRIG)	HILL	45 30 170 21	101
BLACK ROCKS	ROCK	35 12 174 07	4
BLACK ROCKS	ROCK	35 07 174 01	4
BLACK ROCKS	ROCK	35 07 174 01	5
BLACK ROCKS	ROCK	35 12 174 07	5
BLACK ROCKS	ROCK	36 42 175 52	16
BLACK ROCKS	ROCK	41 37 175 14	53
BLACK ROCKS, THE	ROCK	36 07 173 52	7
BLACK SERPENT (TRIG)	MTN	42 16 172 49	65
BLACK SPUR CREEK	STRM	45 16 168 19	95
BLACK SPUR CREEK	STRM	45 16 168 19	98
BLACK STREAM	STRM	46 01 169 34	111
BLACK STREAM	STRM	46 01 169 34	113
BLACK UMBRELLA RANGE	MTNS	45 42 169 00	110
BLACK UMBRELLA (TRIG)	HILL	45 45 169 00	110
BLACK VALLEY STREAM	STRM	41 32 173 40	60
BLACKBALL	LOC	42 22 171 25	69
BLACKBALL CREEK	STRM	42 23 171 25	69
BLACKBALL PEAK (TRIG)	PEAK	42 20 171 20	69
BLACKBURN	LOC	39 52 176 17	47
BLACKBURN, MOUNT (ROTTEN TOMMY)	MTN	43 45 170 12	77
BLACKBURN, MOUNT (ROTTEN TOMMY)	MTN	43 45 170 12	86
BLACKBURN STREAM	STRM	41 40 171 59	64
BLACKBURN STREAM	STRM	42 32 173 22	72
BLACKBURN STREAM	STRM	42 32 173 22	73
BLACKDEUGH BURN	STRM	45 58 169 28	111
BLACKHEAD	HSTD	40 10 176 50	43
BLACKHEAD POINT	PNT	40 13 176 47	43
BLACKLOCK STREAM	STRM	46 02 166 46	104
BLACKMANS	LOC	45 15 169 18	100
BLACKMOUNT	LOC	45 49 167 40	106
BLACKPOOL	LOC	36 47 175 00	12
BLACKPOOL	LOC	36 47 175 00	13
BLACKS POINT	LOC	42 08 171 53	63
BLACKS POINT	LOC	42 08 171 53	64
BLACKS STREAM	STRM	43 30 172 02	81
BLACKS STREAM	STRM	43 30 172 02	85
BLACKSTONE HILL (TRIG)	MTN	45 00 169 49	100
BLACKSTONE HILL (TRIG)	MTN	45 00 169 49	101
BLACKWATER	LOC	42 15 171 46	63
BLACKWATER	LOC	42 15 171 46	64
BLACKWATER CREEK	STRM	41 17 172 06	62
BLACKWATER CREEK	STRM	42 14 171 45	63
BLACKWATER CREEK	STRM	42 14 171 45	64
BLACKWATER CREEK	STRM	42 27 171 29	69
BLACKWATER CREEK	STRM	43 41 169 32	76
BLACKWATER CREEK	STRM	43 41 169 32	79
BLACKWATER LAKE	LAKE	43 07 171 55	80
BLACKWATER LAKE	LAKE	43 07 171 55	81
BLACKWATER RIVER	STRM	42 15 171 41	63
BLACKWATER RIVER	STRM	41 51 171 48	63
BLACKWATER RIVER	STRM	41 51 171 48	64
BLACKWATER RIVER	STRM	42 15 171 41	64
BLACKWATER RIVER	STRM	41 47 172 22	65
BLACKWATER STREAM	STRM	40 39 175 21	48
BLACKWOOD BAY	BAY	41 13 174 06	54
BLACKWOOD BAY	BAY	41 13 174 06	60
BLACKWOOD BAY	BAY	41 13 174 06	61
BLAIKIES CREEK	STRM	47 06 167 52	114
BLAIKIES HILL	HILL	47 03 167 50	114
BLAIR PEAK	PEAK	43 17 170 52	75
BLAIRICH	HSTD	41 42 173 55	67
BLAIRICH PASS	PASS	41 40 173 48	67
BLAIRICH RIVER	STRM	41 42 173 55	67
BLAIRICH (TRIG)	MTN	41 43 173 48	67
BLAIRLOGIE	HSTD	40 58 175 59	51
BLAKE	PEAK	40 51 175 29	48
BLAKE	PEAK	40 51 175 29	49
BLAKETOWN	SBRB	42 27 171 12	68
BLAKETOWN	SBRB	42 27 171 12	69
BLANCHARDS BLUFF	CLIF	43 16 170 06	76
BLANCHARDS CREEK	STRM	43 17 170 08	74
BLAND BAY	BAY	35 21 174 21	5
BLANDSWOOD	LOC	43 54 171 14	87
BLEAK HILL (TRIG)	HILL	46 26 169 12	112
BLENHEIM	TOWN	41 31 173 57	60
BLIGH SOUND	SND	44 46 167 29	94
BLIND BAY	BAY	36 16 175 26	9
BLIND RIVER	LOC	41 41 174 08	67
BLIND RIVER	STRM	41 40 174 09	67
BLIND SADDLE	SAD	42 20 173 26	66
BLIND SADDLE	SAD	42 20 173 26	72
BLIND SADDLE	SAD	42 20 173 26	73
BLIND SPUR STREAM	STRM	43 43 170 45	86
BLIND STREAM	STRM	42 38 172 57	71
BLIND STREAM	STRM	42 38 172 57	72
BLINKERS STREAM	STRM	42 24 173 02	72
BLIZZARD PEAK	PEAK	43 41 169 58	76
BLIZZARD PEAK	PEAK	43 41 169 58	77
BLIZZARD PEAK	PEAK	43 41 169 58	79
BLOCK HILL (TRIG)	MTN	42 58 172 19	71
BLOCKHOUSE BAY	SBRB	36 56 174 42	12
BLOCKHOUSE BAY	SBRB	36 56 174 42	14
BLONDIN STREAM	STRM	43 40 171 18	75
BLONDIN STREAM	STRM	43 40 171 18	87
BLOOMFIELD, MOUNT	MTN	43 09 170 52	75
BLOOMFIELD RANGE	MTNS	43 09 170 54	75
BLOWHARD STREAM	STRM	43 10 172 17	81
BLOWHARD (TRIG)	MTN	41 44 173 07	66
BLOXHAM, LAKE	LAKE	45 09 167 25	94
BLOXHAM, LAKE	LAKE	45 09 167 25	97
BLUE BOTTLE CREEK	STRM	42 46 171 04	68
BLUE BOTTLE CREEK	STRM	42 46 171 04	69
BLUE CLIFFS	LOC	44 30 170 58	93
BLUE CLIFFS RIDGE	RDGE	41 44 172 22	65
BLUE CREEK	STRM	41 28 172 34	58
BLUE CREEK	STRM	44 41 168 47	90
BLUE CREEK	STRM	45 28 169 05	99
BLUE DUCK CREEK	STRM	41 23 172 06	62
BLUE DUCK CREEK	STRM	41 47 171 54	63
BLUE DUCK CREEK	STRM	41 47 171 54	64
BLUE DUCK CREEK	STRM	44 52 170 13	92
BLUE GLEN CREEK	STRM	41 39 172 54	65
BLUE GREY RIVER	STRM	42 25 172 06	70
BLUE HILL (TRIG)	HILL	41 12 173 27	59
BLUE LAKE	LAKE	39 08 175 40	37
BLUE LAKE	LAKE	39 08 175 40	38
BLUE LAKE	LAKE	42 04 172 40	65
BLUE LAKE	LAKE	44 52 169 49	91
BLUE LAKE	LAKE	45 29 168 56	99
BLUE LAKES	LAKE	43 42 170 10	77
BLUE LAKES	LAKE	43 42 170 10	86
BLUE MOUNTAIN STREAM	STRM	41 53 174 00	67
BLUE MOUNTAIN (TRIG)	HILL	43 01 172 26	81
BLUE MOUNTAIN (TRIG)	MTN	41 55 173 20	66
BLUE MOUNTAIN (TRIG)	MTN	41 51 173 57	67
BLUE MOUNTAINS	LOC	41 11 175 02	52
BLUE MOUNTAINS	LOC	41 11 175 02	55
BLUE MOUNTAINS	MTNS	45 55 169 22	111
BLUE RIVER	STRM	44 10 169 16	78
BLUE RIVER (MOERAKI RIVER)	STRM	43 44 169 18	78
BLUE RIVER NORTH BRANCH	STRM	44 08 169 16	78
BLUE RIVER SOUTH BRANCH	STRM	44 09 169 16	78
BLUE ROCK STREAM	STRM	42 44 172 33	71
BLUE ROCK (TRIG)	HILL	41 50 172 23	65
BLUE SPUR	LOC	42 43 171 01	68
BLUE SPUR	LOC	42 43 171 01	69
BLUE SPUR	LOC	45 54 169 40	111
BLUE STREAM	STRM	42 43 171 56	70
BLUESKIN BAY	BAY	45 44 170 35	103
BLUESTONE CREEK	STRM	44 38 170 38	93
BLUFF	POPL	46 36 168 20	109
BLUFF HARBOUR	HARB	46 34 168 20	109
BLUFF HILL	SBRB	39 29 176 55	40
BLUFF HILL	SBRB	39 29 176 55	41
BLUFF HILL	SBRB	39 29 176 55	42
BLUFF RIVER	STRM	42 10 173 32	66
BLUFF STREAM	STRM	42 08 173 36	66
BLUFF, THE	CLIF	34 41 172 54	2
BLUFF, THE	PNT	36 16 174 14	10
BLUFF, THE	PNT	42 52 173 19	72
BLUFF, THE	PNT	42 52 173 19	73
BLUFF, THE (TRIG)	HILL	45 17 170 51	102
BLUFF, THE (TRIG)	HILL	46 37 168 20	109
BLUFFY CREEK	STRM	40 55 172 13	56
BLUMINE ISLAND	ISLD	41 10 174 14	54
BLUMINE ISLAND	ISLD	41 10 174 14	60
BLUMINE ISLAND	ISLD	41 10 174 14	61
BLYTH, MOUNT (TRIG)	MTN	44 34 170 52	93
BLYTHE DOWNS	HSTD	42 56 173 10	72
BLYTHE DOWNS	HSTD	42 56 173 10	73
BLYTHE RIVER	STRM	42 56 173 16	72
BLYTHE RIVER	STRM	42 56 173 16	73
BOANERGES	MTN	43 59 169 46	79
BOAR HILL (TRIG)	HILL	39 24 176 25	39
BOAR HILL (TRIG)	HILL	39 24 176 25	40
BOAT GROUP	ISLS	47 08 167 32	114
BOAT HARBOUR	HARB	45 12 167 49	97
BOAT HARBOUR	HARB	45 12 167 49	98
BOATMANS CREEK	STRM	42 00 171 53	63
BOATMANS CREEK	STRM	42 00 171 53	64
BOB STREAM	STRM	42 03 173 45	67
BOBBYS HEAD	HEAD	45 32 170 46	102
BOBS KNOB	PEAK	41 09 173 59	54
BOBS KNOB	PEAK	41 09 173 59	60
BOBS KNOB	PEAK	41 09 173 59	61
BOBS PEAK	PEAK	45 02 168 35	95
BOBS PEAK	PEAK	45 02 168 35	99
BOBS PEAK (TRIG)	HILL	41 01 173 45	60
BOBS PEAK (TRIG)	HILL	41 01 173 45	61
BOBS POINT	PNT	46 51 168 08	109
BOBS POINT	PNT	46 51 168 08	115
BOBY STREAM	STRM	43 04 172 37	82
BODDINGTON RANGE	MTNS	42 16 172 59	66
BODDYTOWN	LOC	42 29 171 13	68
BODDYTOWN	LOC	42 29 171 13	69
BOG BURN	STRM	46 09 168 16	107
BOG LAKE	LAKE	45 11 167 50	94
BOG LAKE	LAKE	45 11 167 50	97
BOG LAKE	LAKE	45 11 167 50	98
BOGGYBURN	LOC	46 03 168 23	107
BOLD HILL (TRIG)	MTN	43 13 171 54	80
BOLD HILL (TRIG)	MTN	43 13 171 54	81
BOLD PEAK	PEAK	44 51 168 18	89
BOLD PEAK	PEAK	44 51 168 18	95
BOLTONS GULLY	STRM	44 02 170 12	77
BOLTONS GULLY	STRM	44 02 170 12	86
BOMBAY	LOC	37 12 174 59	12
BOMBAY	LOC	37 12 174 59	13
BOMBAY	LOC	37 12 174 59	14
BOMBAY ROCK	ROCK	46 31 168 16	109
BON ACCORD HARBOUR	HARB	36 26 174 50	11
BONAR GLACIER	GLCR	44 24 168 43	88
BONAR GLACIER	GLCR	44 24 168 43	90
BONAR KNOB	PEAK	44 09 168 13	88
BONAR, MOUNT (TRIG)	MTN	43 05 170 39	74
BONAR RANGE	MTNS	43 06 170 42	74
BONAR RIVER	STRM	44 16 168 48	78
BONDS CREEK	STRM	45 31 169 45	100
BONDS CREEK	STRM	45 31 169 45	101
BONDS PEAK	PEAK	43 10 171 02	75
BONNY DOON CREEK	STRM	40 43 172 35	56
BONNY DOON CREEK	STRM	40 43 172 35	57
BONNY GLEN	LOC	40 03 175 18	45
BONPLAND, MOUNT	MTN	44 50 168 17	89
BONPLAND, MOUNT	MTN	44 50 168 17	95
BOO BOO STREAM	STRM	41 47 174 14	67
BOOM STREAM	STRM	37 04 175 48	16
BOOM STREAM	STRM	37 04 175 48	17
BORLAND BURN	STRM	45 46 167 36	105
BORLAND BURN	STRM	45 46 167 36	106
BORLAND BURN (MIDDLE BRANCH)	STRM	45 44 167 30	105
BORLAND BURN (NORTH BRANCH)	STRM	45 44 167 30	105
BORLAND BURN (NORTH BRANCH)	STRM	45 44 167 30	106
BORLAND BURN (SOUTH BRANCH)	STRM	45 45 167 31	105
BORLAND LODGE	HSTD	45 47 167 32	105
BORLAND LODGE	HSTD	45 47 167 32	106
BORLAND (TRIG)	MTN	45 43 167 28	105
BORLAND (TRIG)	MTN	45 43 167 28	106
BORTONS	LOC	44 53 170 46	93
BOSCAWEN, MOUNT	MTN	42 29 172 14	70
BOSTAQUET BAY	BAY	36 27 174 52	11
BOTTLE POINT	PNT	40 45 173 50	61
BOULDER BANK	BNK	41 14 173 18	59
BOULDER BANK	BNK	41 31 174 05	60
BOULDER HILL (TRIG)	HILL	45 48 170 22	103
BOULDER LAKE	LAKE	40 54 172 35	56
BOULDER LAKE	LAKE	40 54 172 35	57
BOULDER RIVER	STRM	40 48 172 33	56
BOULDER RIVER	STRM	40 48 172 33	57
BOULDER STREAM	STRM	41 39 173 07	58
BOULDER STREAM	STRM	41 39 173 07	59
BOULDER STREAM	STRM	41 50 172 37	65
BOULDER STREAM	STRM	41 46 173 12	66
BOULDERSTONE STREAM	STRM	43 12 171 24	75
BOULDERSTONE STREAM	STRM	43 12 171 24	80
BOUNDARY CREEK	STRM	41 34 173 31	59
BOUNDARY CREEK	STRM	43 00 173 06	72
BOUNDARY CREEK	STRM	43 32 171 05	75
BOUNDARY CREEK	STRM	43 29 171 24	75
BOUNDARY CREEK	STRM	43 58 169 28	79
BOUNDARY CREEK	STRM	43 29 171 24	80
BOUNDARY CREEK	STRM	44 21 169 10	90
BOUNDARY CREEK	STRM	44 51 169 02	90

BOUNDARY CREEK	STRM	44 44 169 51	91
BOUNDARY CREEK	STRM	44 50 170 15	92
BOUNDARY CREEK	STRM	45 18 167 47	97
BOUNDARY CREEK	STRM	45 18 167 47	98
BOUNDARY CREEK	STRM	45 34 169 36	100
BOUNDARY CREEK	STRM	45 08 170 15	101
BOUNDARY CREEK	STRM	45 22 170 14	101
BOUNDARY CREEK	STRM	46 08 167 41	106
BOUNDARY CREEK	STRM	46 08 167 41	108
BOUNDARY CREEK	STRM	45 49 168 47	110
BOUNDARY CREEK	STRM	46 25 169 03	112
BOUNDARY PEAK (TRIG)	PEAK	41 51 172 03	64
BOUNDARY SPUR	SPR	44 08 169 22	78
BOUNDARY STREAM	STRM	41 36 174 10	60
BOUNDARY STREAM	STRM	42 01 173 55	67
BOUNDARY STREAM	STRM	41 48 173 52	67
BOUNDARY STREAM	STRM	42 33 172 56	71
BOUNDARY STREAM	STRM	42 33 172 56	72
BOUNDARY STREAM	STRM	43 10 171 24	75
BOUNDARY STREAM	STRM	43 55 170 33	77
BOUNDARY STREAM	STRM	43 10 171 24	80
BOUNDARY STREAM	STRM	43 32 171 40	80
BOUNDARY STREAM	STRM	43 03 171 54	80
BOUNDARY STREAM	STRM	43 31 171 47	80
BOUNDARY STREAM	STRM	43 03 171 54	81
BOUNDARY STREAM	STRM	43 55 170 33	86
BOUNDARY STREAM	STRM	44 03 170 08	86
BOUNDARY STREAM	STRM	43 46 171 13	87
BOUNDARY (TRIG)	HILL	41 04 173 46	60
BOUNDARY (TRIG)	HILL	41 04 173 46	61
BOUNTY HAVEN	BAY	44 51 167 30	94
BOURKES ROCK (TRIG)	PEAK	42 01 172 01	64
BOURNE STREAM	STRM	42 40 173 07	72
BOVIS, MOUNT (TRIG)	HILL	40 29 176 20	50
BOVIS, MOUNT (TRIG)	MTN	42 07 171 29	63
BOWEN CHANNEL	CHAN	45 45 166 40	104
BOWEN COL	SAD	44 35 167 56	89
BOWEN COL	SAD	44 35 167 56	94
BOWEN FALLS	FALL	44 40 167 56	89
BOWEN FALLS	FALL	44 40 167 56	94
BOWEN, MOUNT (TRIG)	HILL	40 40 175 44	49
BOWEN RIVER	STRM	44 40 167 56	89
BOWEN RIVER	STRM	44 40 167 56	94
BOWENS PEAK	PEAK	45 00 168 38	95
BOWENS PEAK	PEAK	45 00 168 38	99
BOWENTOWN	LOC	37 28 175 59	17
BOWENTOWN HEADS	HEAD	37 28 175 59	17
BOWLERS CREEK	STRM	45 55 169 39	111
BOWLERS CREEK	LOC	45 53 169 39	111
BOWSCALE TARN	LAKE	42 08 172 57	66
BOWYANG, MOUNT	MTN	44 42 168 36	90
BOWYERS STREAM	STRM	43 44 171 32	84
BOYD STREAM	STRM	41 30 172 28	62
BOYDS CREEK	STRM	43 27 169 46	76
BOYLE RIVER	STRM	42 36 172 24	71
BOYS COL	SAD	44 29 168 30	88
BOYS COL	SAD	44 29 168 30	89
BRABAZON, MOUNT (TRIG)	MTN	43 36 170 49	75
BRADLEY, MOUNT	MTN	43 42 172 43	83
BRADLEY, MOUNT (TRIG)	HILL	41 21 173 36	59
BRADLEYS LANDING	LOC	36 00 173 55	7
BRADSHAW, MOUNT	MTN	45 51 166 34	104
BRADSHAW SOUND	SND	45 18 167 02	96
BRAEBURN	LOC	41 11 173 00	58
BRAEBURN	LOC	41 11 173 00	59
BRAEBURN RANGE	MTNS	41 48 172 33	65
BRAEMORE	HSTD	39 52 175 30	45
BRAEMORE	HSTD	39 52 175 30	46
BRAG CREEK	STRM	43 56 169 17	78
BRAGG CREEK	STRM	41 22 173 57	54
BRAGG CREEK	STRM	41 22 173 57	60
BRAIGH	LOC	36 00 174 25	7
BRAIGH	LOC	36 00 174 25	8
BRAMPTON SHOAL	SHL	35 15 174 04	4
BRAMPTON SHOAL	SHL	35 15 174 04	5
BRANCH BURN	STRM	44 50 169 03	90
BRANCH CREEK	STRM	42 09 172 22	65
BRANCH CREEK	STRM	44 02 169 13	78
BRANCH RIVER	STRM	41 36 173 57	60
BRANCH RIVER	STRM	41 40 173 10	66
BRANCH STREAM	STRM	42 03 173 45	67
BRANXHOLME	LOC	46 18 168 20	107
BRANXHOLME	LOC	46 18 168 20	109
BRASS PEAK	PEAK	43 45 170 13	77
BRASS PEAK	PEAK	43 45 170 13	86
BRASSKNOCKER CREEK	STRM	45 07 169 25	100
BRAVO ISLAND	ISLD	46 57 168 08	115
BRAXTON BURN	STRM	45 44 168 13	106
BRAXTON BURN	STRM	45 44 168 13	107
BRAY CREEK	STRM	42 24 171 24	69
BREAK CREEK	STRM	41 10 172 06	56
BREAK CREEK	STRM	41 10 172 06	62
BREAKSEA ISLAND	ISLD	45 35 166 38	104
BREAKSEA ISLANDS	ISLS	47 07 168 12	115
BREAKSEA ISLANDS	ISLS	46 47 168 33	115
BREAKSEA SOUND	SND	45 35 166 44	104
BREAM BAY	BAY	35 56 174 33	8
BREAM HEAD	HEAD	35 51 174 35	8
BREAM HEAD (TRIG)	HILL	35 51 174 35	8
BREAM ISLANDS	ISLS	35 50 174 35	8
BREAM TAIL	HEAD	36 03 174 35	8
BREAST CREEK	STRM	44 36 169 32	91
BREAST HILL	MTN	44 34 169 21	91
BRECHIN BURN	STRM	43 04 172 00	81
BREEZER STREAM	STRM	41 42 173 19	66
BRENDA PEAK	PEAK	44 31 168 17	88
BRENDA PEAK	PEAK	44 31 168 17	89
BRETT, CAPE	CAPE	35 10 174 20	5
BREWERY CREEK	STRM	41 37 172 31	58
BREWSTER GLACIER	GLCR	44 05 169 26	78
BREWSTER GLACIER	GLCR	44 05 169 26	79
BREWSTER, MOUNT	MTN	44 04 169 27	78
BREWSTER, MOUNT	MTN	44 04 169 27	79
BRIAN BORU	HILL	41 54 173 56	67
BRIDE BURN	STRM	44 35 168 21	88
BRIDE BURN	STRM	44 35 168 21	89
BRIDE PEAKS	PEAK	44 31 168 19	88
BRIDE PEAKS	PEAK	44 31 168 19	89
BRIDGE CREEK	STRM	42 26 171 14	68
BRIDGE CREEK	STRM	42 26 171 14	69
BRIDGE CREEK	STRM	42 55 172 24	71
BRIDGE HILL	LOC	45 16 169 23	100
BRIDGE PA	LOC	39 39 176 45	42
BRIDGE PA	LOC	39 39 176 45	43
BRIDGE PEAK	PEAK	40 56 175 16	48
BRIDGE STREAM	STRM	42 50 172 16	70
BRIDGES CREEK	STRM	44 41 168 28	89
BRIDGES SADDLE	SAD	44 40 168 33	90
BRIENS (TRIG)	HILL	39 40 176 21	47
BRIG ROCK	ROCK	44 32 167 47	94
BRIGHT, LAKE	LAKE	45 42 167 08	105
BRIGHTON	POPL	45 57 170 20	103
BRIGHTWATER	POPL	41 23 173 06	58
BRIGHTWATER	POPL	41 23 173 06	59
BRINNS HEAD	HEAD	45 40 170 39	102
BRISTED STREAM	STRM	43 05 171 20	75
BRISTED STREAM	STRM	43 05 171 20	80
BRIXTON	LOC	39 01 174 13	34
BROAD BAY	SBRB	45 51 170 37	103
BROAD BAY	BAY	47 16 167 36	114
BROAD GULLY	LOC	44 50 171 03	93
BROAD HEAD	HEAD	47 16 167 38	114
BROAD STREAM	STRM	45 47 170 05	111
BROADFIELD	LOC	43 36 172 28	81
BROADFIELD	LOC	43 36 172 28	82
BROADFIELD	LOC	43 36 172 28	85
BROADLANDS	LOC	38 31 176 20	29
BROADLEAF STREAM	STRM	43 09 171 57	80
BROADLEAF STREAM	STRM	43 09 171 57	81
BROADWOOD	LOC	35 16 173 23	3
BROD BAY	BAY	45 24 167 41	97
BRODIES CREEK	STRM	34 52 173 26	3
BRODRICK PASS	PASS	43 58 169 43	79
BRODRICK PEAK	PEAK	43 30 170 24	74
BRODRICK PEAK	PEAK	43 30 170 24	77
BROKE-ADRIFT PASSAGE	STRA	46 06 166 34	104
BROKEN HILL (TRIG)	MTN	43 10 171 46	80
BROKEN HILLS	LOC	37 07 175 44	17
BROKEN ISLANDS	ISLS	36 14 175 18	9
BROKEN LEG KNOB	PEAK	42 29 173 06	72
BROKEN RIVER	STRM	43 13 171 56	80
BRONTE	LOC	41 16 173 05	58
BRONTE	LOC	41 16 173 05	59
BROOKBY	LOC	36 59 174 59	12
BROOKBY	LOC	36 59 174 59	14
BROOKBY (TRIG)	HILL	41 35 173 49	60
BROOKDALE	HSTD	42 42 173 19	72
BROOKDALE	HSTD	42 42 173 19	73
BROOKES, MOUNT	MTN	38 37 174 40	26
BROOKLANDS	LOC	43 24 172 42	82
BROOKLANDS	LOC	43 24 172 42	83
BROOKLANDS	LOC	46 08 169 59	111
BROOKLYN	SBRB	41 18 174 46	52
BROOKLYN	SBRB	41 18 174 46	55
BROOKLYN	LOC	41 06 172 57	57
BROOKLYN	LOC	41 06 172 57	58
BROOKLYN STREAM	STRM	41 06 173 00	57
BROOKLYN STREAM	STRM	41 06 173 00	58
BROOKSIDE	LOC	43 42 172 03	85
BROOM STREAM	STRM	42 38 172 46	71
BROOM STREAM	STRM	42 38 172 46	72
BROOM STREAM	STRM	43 10 172 11	81
BROOME, MOUNT	MTN	44 14 169 07	78
BROTHER PEAKS (TRIG)	HILL	45 23 170 20	101
BROTHERS POINT, THE	PNT	46 40 169 12	112
BROTHERS STREAM	STRM	41 32 173 35	59
BROTHERS STREAM	STRM	44 40 170 36	92
BROTHERS, THE	ISLD	41 07 174 26	54
BROTHERS, THE	ISLS	47 10 167 30	114
BROTHERS, THE (TRIG)	HILL	43 43 171 22	84
BROTHERS, THE (TRIG)	HILL	43 43 171 22	87
BROTHERS, THE (TRIG)	HILL	45 56 166 34	104
BROTHERS, THE (TRIG)	MTN	42 59 172 23	71
BROUGH CREEK	STRM	41 39 172 52	65
BROUGHTON ARM	BAY	45 34 166 56	104
BROW PEAK (TRIG)	MTN	44 55 168 48	90
BROW PEAK (TRIG)	MTN	44 55 168 48	95
BROWN COW	HILL	40 45 172 34	56
BROWN COW	HILL	40 45 172 34	60
BROWN CREEK	STRM	41 52 171 56	64
BROWN CREEK	STRM	42 20 171 46	70
BROWN DOME (TRIG)	HILL	46 19 169 24	111
BROWN DOME (TRIG)	HILL	46 19 169 24	113
BROWN GREY RIVER	STRM	42 24 172 06	70
BROWN HILL	PEAK	42 56 171 51	70
BROWN, LAKE	LAKE	44 44 167 50	89
BROWN, LAKE	LAKE	44 44 167 50	94
BROWN, MOUNT	MTN	44 39 169 11	90
BROWN, MOUNT	MTN	43 51 170 03	76
BROWN, MOUNT	MTN	43 51 170 03	77
BROWN, MOUNT	MTN	43 51 170 03	79
BROWN, MOUNT (TRIG)	HILL	43 55 169 01	78
BROWN, MOUNT (TRIG)	HILL	43 05 172 37	82
BROWN, MOUNT (TRIG)	HILL	41 51 172 11	64
BROWN, MOUNT (TRIG)	MTN	42 51 171 13	68
BROWN, MOUNT (TRIG)	MTN	42 51 171 13	69
BROWN OWL	SBRB	41 06 175 05	52
BROWN OWL	SBRB	41 06 175 05	55
BROWN PEAK	PEAK	45 37 167 54	106
BROWN RIVER	STRM	40 51 172 27	56
BROWN RIVER	STRM	42 40 171 32	69
BROWN SADDLE	SAD	43 43 171 12	87
BROWNE ISLAND	ISLD	44 09 168 15	88
BROWNE, LAKE	LAKE	45 24 167 04	96
BROWNE, MOUNT	MTN	43 02 171 01	75
BROWNING CREEK	STRM	43 49 169 48	78
BROWNING CREEK	STRM	43 49 169 48	79
BROWNING, LAKE	LAKE	42 57 171 21	69
BROWNING, MOUNT	MTN	43 51 169 51	76
BROWNING, MOUNT	MTN	43 51 169 51	79
BROWNING RANGE	MTNS	42 55 171 15	68
BROWNING RANGE	MTNS	42 55 171 15	69
BROWNING RANGE	MTNS	44 05 169 03	78
BROWNING RANGE	MTNS	44 00 169 02	78
BROWNINGS PASS	PASS	42 57 171 21	69
BROWNLEE, LAKE	LAKE	44 54 167 43	94
BROWNS	LOC	46 09 168 25	107
BROWNS BAY	SBRB	36 43 174 45	11
BROWNS BAY	SBRB	36 43 174 45	12
BROWNS BEACH	BCH	44 15 171 24	87
BROWNS ISLAND	ISLD	36 50 174 54	11
BROWNS ISLAND	ISLD	36 50 174 54	12
BROWNS STREAM	STRM	42 40 172 46	71
BRUCE BAY	BAY	43 35 169 35	76
BRUCE BAY	LOC	43 36 169 35	76
BRUCE, MOUNT	MTN	43 43 170 16	77
BRUCE, MOUNT	MTN	43 43 170 16	86
BRUCE, MOUNT (TRIG)	MTN	43 03 171 37	80
BRUCE ROCKS	ROCK	45 58 170 17	103
BRUCE SADDLE	SAD	43 06 171 32	80
BRUCE STREAM	STRM	43 01 171 38	80
BRUCES HILL (TRIG)	PEAK	40 45 175 38	48
BRUCES HILL (TRIG)	PEAK	40 45 175 38	49
BRUCES HILL (TRIG)	PEAK	40 45 175 38	51
BRUNNER	LOC	42 26 171 20	69
BRUNNER, LAKE (MOANA)	LAKE	42 37 171 27	69
BRUNNER, MOUNT	MTN	43 42 170 03	76
BRUNNER, MOUNT	MTN	43 42 170 03	77
BRUNNER, MOUNT	MTN	43 42 170 03	79
BRUNNER RANGE	MTNS	41 56 172 04	64
BRUNSWICK	LOC	39 51 175 02	45
BRUNTON, LAKE	LAKE	46 39 168 53	112
BRUNTWOOD	LOC	37 51 175 26	19
BRYAN O'LYNN (TRIG)	PEAK	42 38 171 43	70
BRYANS HILL (TRIG)	HILL	43 31 171 40	80
BRYANT HILL (TRIG)	HILL	40 25 175 41	49
BRYANT RANGE	MTNS	41 19 173 25	59
BRYANTS STREAM	STRM	41 18 173 33	59
BRYCE BURN	STRM	45 59 167 36	105
BRYCE BURN	STRM	45 59 167 36	106
BRYCE, MOUNT	MTN	43 05 171 12	75
BRYDONE	LOC	46 16 168 48	110
BRYDONE	LOC	46 16 168 48	112
BRYNAVON	LOC	35 41 174 27	5
BRYNAVON	LOC	35 41 174 27	8
BRYNDERWYN	LOC	36 06 174 25	7
BRYNDERWYN	LOC	36 06 174 25	8
BRYNDWR	SBRB	43 30 172 35	82
BRYNDWR	SBRB	43 30 172 35	83
BRYNDWR	SBRB	43 30 172 35	85
BRYNEIRA RANGE	MTNS	44 33 168 11	88
BRYNEIRA RANGE	MTNS	44 33 168 11	89
BUCCLEUCH	LOC	43 41 171 25	84
BUCCLEUCH	LOC	43 41 171 25	87
BUCHANAN CREEK	STRM	45 45 168 14	107
BUCHANAN PEAKS	PEAK	44 33 168 59	90
BUCK, MOUNT	MTN	44 49 168 32	90
BUCK, MOUNT	MTN	44 49 168 32	95
BUCKLAND	LOC	37 14 174 56	12
BUCKLAND	LOC	37 14 174 56	14
BUCKLAND	LOC	37 53 175 38	19
BUCKLAND CREEK	STRM	41 52 171 42	63
BUCKLAND CREEK	STRM	41 52 171 42	64
BUCKLANDS BEACH	SBRB	36 52 174 54	11
BUCKLANDS BEACH	SBRB	36 52 174 54	12
BUCKLANDS CROSSING	LOC	45 37 170 36	102
BUCKLER BURN	STRM	44 52 168 23	89
BUCKLER BURN	STRM	44 52 168 23	95
BULL AND COW	ROCK	47 09 167 32	114
BULL CREEK	STRM	41 56 172 38	65
BULL CREEK	STRM	42 54 171 58	70
BULL CREEK	LOC	46 11 170 08	103
BULL CREEK	STRM	46 11 170 08	103
BULL CREEK	STRM	46 15 167 46	106
BULL CREEK	STRM	46 15 167 46	108
BULL HILL (TRIG)	PEAK	41 21 175 20	53
BULL, MOUNT	MTN	44 00 169 30	79
BULL PADDOCK STREAM	STRM	41 48 172 57	66
BULL POINT	PNT	46 57 168 05	115
BULL RANGE	MTNS	41 11 173 40	60
BULL STREAM	STRM	42 10 173 02	66
BULLER BAY	BAY	41 44 171 32	63
BULLER RIVER	STRM	41 44 171 35	63
BULLERS CREEK	STRM	47 07 167 54	114
BULLERS CREEK	STRM	47 07 167 54	115
BULLOCK BOW SADDLE	SAD	43 43 170 48	87
BULLOCK CREEK	STRM	42 06 171 20	63
BULLOCK CREEK	STRM	43 29 169 53	76
BULLOCK CREEK	STRM	43 13 172 25	81
BULLOCK CREEK	STRM	45 33 169 13	100
BULLOCK GULLY	STRM	42 20 173 06	66
BULLOCK STREAM	STRM	42 25 172 44	71
BULLOCKY CREEK	STRM	45 34 169 44	100
BULLOCKY CREEK	STRM	45 34 169 44	101
BULLS	POPL	40 11 175 23	45
BULRUSH LAKE	LAKE	34 43 173 00	2
BULWER	LOC	40 56 173 57	54
BULWER	LOC	40 56 173 57	61
BUNCOMBE	MTN	44 20 168 39	88
BUNCOMBE	MTN	44 20 168 39	90
BUNGTOWN	LOC	45 54 169 47	111
BUNGTOWN STREAM	STRM	45 58 169 49	111
BUNKER HILL	HILL	36 03 174 22	7
BUNKER HILL	HILL	36 03 174 22	8
BUNKER ISLETS	ISLS	46 52 168 16	109
BUNKER ISLETS	ISLS	46 52 168 16	115
BUNKERS STREAM	STRM	42 24 172 56	71
BUNKERS STREAM	STRM	42 24 172 56	72
BUNNYTHORPE	POPL	40 17 175 38	48
BUNNYTHORPE	POPL	40 17 175 38	49
BURGAN STREAM	STRM	45 35 169 56	101
BURGESS ISLAND	ISLD	36 10 174 04	7
BURGESS ISLAND	ISLD	35 54 175 07	9
BURGESS, MOUNT	MTN	44 03 170 38	86
BURGOO STREAM	STRM	40 58 172 28	56
BURGOO STREAM	STRM	40 58 172 28	57
BURKE, MOUNT	MTN	44 05 169 18	78
BURKE, MOUNT	MTN	44 34 169 11	90
BURKE PASS	PASS	44 05 170 36	86
BURKE PASS	LOC	44 05 170 39	86
BURKE RIVER	STRM	44 02 169 22	78
BURLEY, MOUNT (TRIG)	HILL	41 53 171 49	63
BURLEY, MOUNT (TRIG)	HILL	41 53 171 49	64
BURMEISTER TOPS	MTNS	44 01 168 40	88
BURMEISTER MORASS	SWMP	44 00 168 43	88
BURN CREEK	STRM	42 09 172 31	65
BURN, MOUNT	MTN	42 12 172 29	66
BURN STREAM	STRM	46 01 169 53	111
BURN STREAM	STRM	46 01 169 53	113
BURNBRAE	LOC	42 03 172 16	64
BURNET STREAM	STRM	43 04 171 20	75
BURNET STREAM	STRM	43 04 171 20	80
BURNETT, MOUNT	MTN	45 47 166 48	104
BURNETT, MOUNT	MTN	43 48 170 12	77
BURNETT, MOUNT	MTN	43 48 170 12	86
BURNETT, MOUNT (TRIG)	HILL	40 38 172 38	56
BURNETT, MOUNT (TRIG)	HILL	40 38 172 38	57
BURNETT MOUNTAINS	MTNS	43 45 170 13	77
BURNETT MOUNTAINS	MTNS	43 45 170 13	86
BURNETT STREAM	STRM	44 20 170 53	92
BURNETTS FACE	LOC	41 45 171 49	63
BURNETTS FACE	LOC	41 45 171 49	64
BURNHAM	LOC	43 37 172 18	81
BURNHAM	LOC	43 37 172 18	85
BURNS, MOUNT	MTN	45 45 167 24	105
BURNS, MOUNT	MTN	43 45 169 59	76
BURNS, MOUNT	MTN	43 45 169 59	78
BURNS, MOUNT	MTN	43 45 169 59	79
BURNT COUNTRY CREEK	STRM	41 51 173 32	66
BURNT HILL	HSTD	43 22 172 09	81
BURNT HILL	HSTD	43 22 172 09	85
BURNT HILL (TRIG)	HILL	43 23 172 08	81
BURNT HILL (TRIG)	HILL	43 23 172 08	85
BURNT HUT HILL (TRIG)	HILL	43 01 173 03	82
BURNT SADDLE	SAD	41 57 173 55	67
BURNT TOP	MTN	44 04 169 20	78
BURR STREAM	STRM	41 52 173 40	67
BURROUGH HEAD (TRIG)	HEAD	43 11 170 12	74
BURSTER RANGE	MTNS	43 25 170 16	74
BURSTER RANGE	MTNS	43 25 170 16	77
BURTON CREEK	STRM	42 13 171 42	63
BURTON CREEK	STRM	42 13 171 42	64
BURTON GLACIER	GLCR	43 27 170 19	74
BURTON GLACIER	GLCR	43 27 170 19	77
BURWOOD	SBRB	43 30 172 40	82
BURWOOD	SBRB	43 30 172 40	83
BURWOOD	SBRB	43 30 172 40	85
BUSBY HEAD	HEAD	35 52 174 32	8
BUSCOT, THE	MTN	44 24 170 02	92
BUSH CONE (TRIG)	HILL	46 34 169 11	112
BUSH CREEK	STRM	43 21 171 09	75
BUSH CREEK	STRM	44 56 168 50	90
BUSH CREEK	STRM	44 56 168 50	95
BUSH GULLY	STRM	42 24 172 55	71
BUSH GULLY	STRM	42 24 172 55	72
BUSH SIDING	LOC	46 28 168 40	112
BUSH STREAM	STRM	43 37 170 55	75
BUSH STREAM	STRM	43 52 170 07	76
BUSH STREAM	STRM	43 52 170 07	77
BUSH STREAM	STRM	43 52 170 07	79
BUSH STREAM	STRM	43 27 171 45	80
BUSH STREAM	STRM	43 52 170 07	86
BUSH (TRIG)	HILL	40 07 176 42	43
BUSH (TRIG)	HILL	40 07 176 42	47
BUSHEY	LOC	45 28 170 45	102
BUSHGROVE	HSTD	40 55 175 57	49
BUSHGROVE	HSTD	40 55 175 57	51
BUSHSIDE	LOC	43 38 171 29	75
BUSHSIDE	LOC	43 38 171 29	80
BUSHSIDE	LOC	43 38 171 29	84
BUSHY CREEK	STRM	43 11 172 37	82
BUSHY CREEK	STRM	46 10 168 55	110
BUSHY CREEK	STRM	46 10 168 55	112
BUSHY KNOLL (TRIG)	HILL	38 42 177 27	31
BUSHY KNOLL (TRIG)	HILL	38 42 177 27	33
BUSHY POINT	PNT	41 16 174 16	54
BUSHY POINT	PNT	41 16 174 16	61
BUSHY POINT	PNT	46 27 168 20	109
BUSHY SADDLE	SAD	42 21 173 26	72
BUSHY SADDLE	SAD	42 21 173 26	73
BUSTER CREEK	STRM	45 04 169 31	100
BUSTER, MOUNT (TRIG)	MTN	44 56 170 13	92
BUTCHER SADDLE	SAD	40 44 175 23	48
BUTCHERS CREEK	STRM	41 47 174 00	67
BUTCHERS CREEK	STRM	42 46 171 05	68
BUTCHERS CREEK	STRM	42 46 171 05	69
BUTCHERS CREEK	STRM	45 18 169 20	100
BUTCHERS DAM	DAM	45 17 169 21	100
BUTCHERS GULLY	LOC	45 18 169 20	100
BUTE ISLAND	ISLD	45 11 167 40	97
BUTEMENT, MOUNT	MTN	44 51 168 31	90
BUTEMENT, MOUNT	MTN	44 51 168 31	95
BUTLER, MOUNT	MTN	43 15 170 56	75
BUTLER RANGE	MTNS	43 24 170 31	74
BUTLER RANGE	MTNS	43 14 170 56	75
BUTLER RANGE	MTNS	43 24 170 31	77
BUTLER RIVER	STRM	43 25 170 25	74
BUTLER RIVER	STRM	43 25 170 25	77
BUTLER SADDLE	SAD	43 19 170 56	75
BUTLER SADDLE	SAD	43 47 170 51	87
BUTTERS, MOUNT (TRIG)	PEAK	40 34 176 02	49
BUTTRESS POINT	PNT	43 38 169 30	76
BUTTRESS POINT	PNT	43 38 169 30	79
BUTZBACH, MOUNT	MTN	43 44 169 45	76
BUTZBACH, MOUNT	MTN	43 44 169 45	79
BUX, LAKE	LAKE	44 10 168 40	88
BUXTON CREEK	STRM	42 51 173 19	72
BUXTON CREEK	STRM	42 51 173 19	73
BYRNE, MOUNT (TRIG)	MTN	42 45 171 52	70
BYRON STREAM	STRM	41 44 173 26	66
BYWASH CREEK	STRM	42 25 171 42	70

C

CABERFEIDH	LOC	46 30 169 29	113
CABIN STREAM	STRM	42 57 172 29	71
CABLE BAY	LOC	35 00 173 29	3
CABLE BAY	BAY	41 09 173 24	59
CADMAN, LAKE	LAKE	45 52 166 44	104
CADMUS, MOUNT (TRIG)	HILL	40 34 176 21	50
CAIRN	MTN	42 19 173 29	66
CAIRN HILL	MTN	43 40 171 05	75
CAIRN HILL	MTN	43 40 171 05	87
CAIRN HILL (TRIG)	HILL	43 21 171 57	80
CAIRN HILL (TRIG)	HILL	43 21 171 57	81
CAIRN PEAK	PEAK	42 55 171 15	68
CAIRN PEAK	PEAK	42 55 171 15	69
CAIRN, THE	MTN	44 22 170 08	92
CAIRN, THE (TRIG)	HILL	46 18 169 11	110
CAIRN, THE (TRIG)	HILL	46 18 169 11	112
CAIRNBRAE	LOC	43 40 171 41	80
CAIRNBRAE	LOC	43 40 171 41	84
CAIRNHILL (TRIG)	HILL	45 19 169 23	100
CAIRNMUIR GULLY	STRM	45 05 169 14	100
CAIRNMUIR HILL (TRIG)	MTN	45 08 169 16	100
CAIRNMUIR MOUNTAINS	MTNS	45 09 169 16	100
CALDERVALE	LOC	41 09 172 07	56
CALDERVALE	LOC	41 09 172 07	62
CALF CREEK	STRM	42 35 172 35	71
CALF SADDLE	SAD	42 04 173 48	67
CALLAGHANS	LOC	42 40 171 09	68
CALLAGHANS	LOC	42 40 171 09	69
CALLAGHANS CREEK	STRM	42 22 171 28	69
CALLERY CREEK	STRM	44 08 168 16	88
CALLERY RIVER	STRM	43 24 170 11	74
CALLERY RIVER	STRM	43 24 170 11	77
CALLERY SADDLE	SAD	43 26 170 21	74
CALLERY SADDLE	SAD	43 26 170 21	77
CALLIOPE, MOUNT (TRIG)	MTN	44 07 168 55	78
CALLIOPE SADDLE	SAD	46 25 169 23	113
CALM PEAK (TRIG)	PEAK	45 28 166 45	96
CAM RIVER	STRM	41 52 173 41	67
CAM RIVER	STRM	43 23 172 39	82
CAM RIVER	STRM	43 23 172 39	83
CAM RIVER	STRM	43 23 172 39	85
CAMBERLEY	SBRB	39 38 176 49	42
CAMBERLEY	SBRB	39 38 176 49	43
CAMBRIANS	LOC	44 55 169 45	91
CAMBRIDGE	POPL	37 53 175 28	19
CAMDEN	HSTD	41 51 173 41	67
CAMEL BACKS	HILL	45 29 167 28	97
CAMEL, MOUNT	MTN	34 49 173 10	2
CAMEL, MOUNT	MTN	34 49 173 10	3
CAMEL, THE	MTN	41 57 172 49	65
CAMELBACK, MOUNT (TRIG)	MTN	42 53 170 59	68
CAMELBACK, MOUNT (TRIG)	MTN	42 53 170 59	69
CAMELHEAD	PEAK	40 39 175 27	48
CAMELOT RIVER	STRM	45 19 167 12	96
CAMERON COL	SAD	43 21 170 59	75
CAMERON, MOUNT	MTN	44 06 169 17	78

CAMERON, MOUNT (TRIG)	HILL	39 27 176 39	39
CAMERON, MOUNT (TRIG)	HILL	39 27 176 39	40
CAMERON, MOUNT (TRIG)	HILL	39 27 176 39	42
CAMERON, MOUNT (TRIG)	HILL	40 50 176 01	49
CAMERON, MOUNT (TRIG)	HILL	40 50 176 01	51
CAMERON, MOUNT (TRIG)	HILL	41 20 174 52	52
CAMERON, MOUNT (TRIG)	HILL	41 20 174 52	55
CAMERON, MOUNT (TRIG)	MTN	45 30 168 52	99
CAMERON MOUNTAINS	MTNS	45 58 167 00	105
CAMERON RIVER	STRM	43 26 171 10	75
CAMERON STREAM	STRM	42 42 171 59	70
CAMERONS	LOC	42 33 171 09	68
CAMERONS	LOC	42 33 171 09	69
CAMERONS CREEK	STRM	44 09 169 18	78
CAMERONS CREEK	STRM	45 31 169 02	99
CAMERONS LOOKOUT (TRIG)	HILL	40 59 175 56	51
CAMP CREEK	STRM	42 50 170 52	68
CAMP CREEK	STRM	43 31 170 45	74
CAMP CREEK	STRM	44 24 169 11	90
CAMP CREEK	STRM	44 42 169 29	91
CAMP CREEK	STRM	44 42 169 53	91
CAMP CREEK	STRM	45 05 170 15	101
CAMP CREEK	STRM	46 10 167 43	106
CAMP CREEK	STRM	46 10 167 43	108
CAMP HILL	MTN	44 35 169 34	91
CAMP HILL (TRIG)	MTN	45 02 167 19	94
CAMP HILL (TRIG)	HILL	45 02 168 55	95
CAMP HILL (TRIG)	MTN	45 02 167 19	96
CAMP HILL (TRIG)	HILL	45 02 168 55	99
CAMP HILL (TRIG)	HILL	45 09 170 11	101
CAMP, LAKE	LAKE	43 37 171 03	75
CAMP OVEN DOME	MTN	44 25 168 27	88
CAMP OVEN DOME	MTN	44 25 168 27	89
CAMP PEAKS	PEAK	44 23 169 13	90
CAMP SADDLE	SAD	43 14 170 50	75
CAMP STREAM	STRM	39 17 176 39	39
CAMP STREAM	STRM	39 17 176 39	40
CAMP STREAM	STRM	42 58 172 02	70
CAMP STREAM	STRM	42 42 171 58	70
CAMP STREAM	STRM	42 35 172 44	71
CAMP STREAM	STRM	43 59 170 12	77
CAMP STREAM	STRM	43 59 169 57	77
CAMP STREAM	STRM	43 59 169 57	79
CAMP STREAM	STRM	43 13 171 47	80
CAMP STREAM	STRM	43 48 170 39	86
CAMP STREAM	STRM	43 59 170 12	86
CAMP VALLEY	LOC	44 13 170 49	87
CAMPBELL, CAPE	CAPE	41 44 174 16	67
CAMPBELL CREEK	STRM	45 26 169 10	99
CAMPBELL, MOUNT	MTN	44 00 169 15	78
CAMPBELL, MOUNT	MTN	44 42 168 39	90
CAMPBELL, MOUNT	MTN	42 56 171 26	69
CAMPBELL, MOUNT (TRIG)	PEAK	45 16 168 12	95
CAMPBELL, MOUNT (TRIG)	PEAK	45 16 168 12	98
CAMPBELL, MOUNT (TRIG)	PEAK	41 07 172 51	57
CAMPBELL, MOUNT (TRIG)	PEAK	41 07 172 51	58
CAMPBELL PARK	LOC	44 51 170 32	92
CAMPBELL PASS	PASS	42 55 171 27	69
CAMPBELL POINT	PNT	46 25 169 48	113
CAMPBELL RANGE	MTNS	42 53 171 24	69
CAMPBELL STREAM	STRM	42 29 173 17	72
CAMPBELL STREAM	STRM	42 29 173 17	73
CAMPBELLS BAY	SBRB	36 45 174 46	11
CAMPBELLS BAY	SBRB	36 45 174 46	12
CAMPBELLS CREEK	STRM	40 10 176 26	47
CAMPBELLS CREEK	STRM	45 03 169 13	100
CAMPING CREEK	STRM	45 40 169 05	110
CAMPING STREAM	STRM	42 23 172 37	71
CAMSELL, MOUNT	MTN	42 59 171 17	68
CAMSELL, MOUNT	MTN	42 59 171 17	69
CANADIAN STREAM	STRM	45 46 169 31	111
CANDLELIGHT CREEK	STRM	42 27 171 23	69
CANDLESTICK STREAM	STRM	42 51 172 02	70
CANDLESTICKS,THE	MTNS	42 52 172 01	70
CANN, MOUNT (TRIG)	MTN	42 09 172 20	65
CANNIBAL BAY	BAY	46 28 169 46	113
CANNIBAL COVE	BAY	41 05 174 15	54
CANNIBAL COVE	BAY	41 05 174 15	61
CANNINGTON	LOC	44 20 170 53	87
CANNINGTON	LOC	44 20 170 53	93
CANNINGTON CREEK	STRM	40 51 172 08	56
CANNISTER CREEK	STRM	41 44 173 27	66
CANOE CREEK	STRM	42 12 171 19	63
CANON PEAK	PEAK	44 15 168 50	78
CANTERBURY PLAINS	PLN	43 45 171 56	84
CANTON STREAM	STRM	45 45 169 58	111
CANVASTOWN	LOC	41 18 173 40	60
CANYON CREEK	STRM	44 15 169 37	79
CANYON CREEK	STRM	45 03 167 34	94
CANYON CREEK	STRM	45 03 167 34	97
CAP BURN	STRM	45 16 170 14	101
CAP CREEK	STRM	46 01 167 50	106
CAP (TRIG)	HILL	40 49 175 49	49
CAP (TRIG)	HILL	40 49 175 49	51
CAPE FOULWIND	LOC	41 45 171 29	63
CAPE REINGA	LOC	34 26 172 41	2
CAPE RIVER	STRM	41 26 175 27	53
CAPLES RIVER	STRM	44 56 168 22	89
CAPLES RIVER	STRM	44 56 168 22	95
CAPLESTON	LOC	42 04 171 55	63
CAPLESTON	LOC	42 04 171 55	64
CAPTAIN CREEK	STRM	41 22 173 26	59
CAPTAIN CREEK	STRM	41 22 172 07	62
CAPTAIN, MOUNT (TRIG)	MTN	42 29 172 43	71
CAPTAINS PEAK	PEAK	43 39 170 43	74
CAPTAINS PEAK	PEAK	43 39 170 43	86
CARD CREEK	STRM	42 34 171 13	68
CARD CREEK	STRM	42 34 171 13	69
CARDIFF	LOC	39 22 174 14	34
CARDIFF	LOC	39 22 174 14	44
CARDRONA	LOC	44 53 169 01	90
CARDRONA, MOUNT	MTN	44 51 168 56	90
CARDRONA, MOUNT	MTN	44 51 168 56	95
CARDRONA RIVER	STRM	44 41 169 12	90
CAREW	LOC	43 58 171 21	84
CAREW	LOC	43 58 171 21	87
CAREW BAY	BAY	42 38 171 25	69
CAREWS PEAK (TRIG)	PEAK	43 50 172 52	83
CAREYS CREEK	STRM	45 43 170 34	103
CARGILL, MOUNT (TRIG)	HILL	45 49 170 33	103
CARL CREEK	STRM	44 05 168 39	88
CARLETON	LOC	43 18 172 17	81
CARLETON	LOC	43 18 172 17	85
CARLUKE	LOC	41 13 173 36	59
CARLUKE	LOC	41 13 173 36	60
CARLYLE STREAM	STRM	42 35 172 28	71
CARLYON, MOUNT (TRIG)	HILL	40 05 176 37	43
CARLYON, MOUNT (TRIG)	HILL	40 05 176 37	47
CARNARVON	LOC	40 17 175 22	48
CARNEYS CREEK	STRM	43 29 170 49	74
CAROLINE	LOC	45 50 168 22	107
CAROLINE BAY	BAY	44 23 171 15	93
CAROLINE BAY	BAY	46 45 168 30	109
CAROLINE BAY	BAY	46 45 168 30	115
CAROLINE BURN	STRM	46 02 167 18	105
CAROLINE CREEK	STRM	42 09 172 40	65
CAROLINE PEAK	PEAK	45 57 167 12	105
CAROLINE STREAM	STRM	42 45 173 20	72
CAROLINE STREAM	STRM	42 45 173 20	73
CARRIAGE DRIVE	MTN	43 16 171 32	80
CARRICK, LAKE	LAKE	45 50 166 46	104
CARRICK RANGE	MTNS	45 05 169 04	99
CARRICK RIVER	STRM	45 57 166 46	104
CARRICKTOWN	LOC	45 08 169 08	99
CARRINGTON	LOC	40 58 175 31	51
CARRINGTON	LOC	40 58 175 31	53
CARRINGTON, MOUNT	MTN	42 30 172 15	70
CARSONS STREAM	STRM	45 51 169 29	111
CARSWELL	LOC	40 56 175 54	49
CARSWELL	LOC	40 56 175 54	51
CARTER PASSAGE	PASS	46 55 168 13	115
CARTERS BEACH	BCH	37 43 174 49	18
CARTERS BEACH	LOC	41 45 171 34	63
CARTERS MILL	LOC	43 57 168 51	78
CARTERS SADDLE	SAD	42 13 173 14	66
CARTERTON	POPL	41 01 175 32	51
CARTERTON	POPL	41 01 175 32	53
CASCADE BAY	BAY	44 06 168 17	88
CASCADE COVE	BAY	45 48 166 36	104
CASCADE CREEK	STRM	41 50 171 43	63
CASCADE CREEK	STRM	41 50 171 43	64
CASCADE CREEK	STRM	42 06 172 20	65
CASCADE CREEK	STRM	44 15 169 28	78
CASCADE CREEK	STRM	44 15 169 28	79
CASCADE CREEK	STRM	44 29 168 40	88
CASCADE CREEK	STRM	44 54 168 05	89
CASCADE CREEK	LOC	44 54 168 05	89
CASCADE CREEK	STRM	44 29 168 40	90
CASCADE CREEK	STRM	45 15 168 28	95
CASCADE CREEK	STRM	45 15 168 28	98
CASCADE PEAK	PEAK	44 39 167 56	89
CASCADE PEAK	PEAK	44 39 167 56	94
CASCADE POINT	PNT	44 00 168 22	88
CASCADE RANGE	MTNS	43 07 171 17	75
CASCADE RIVER	STRM	44 02 168 22	88
CASCADE SADDLE	SAD	44 29 168 38	88
CASCADE SADDLE	SAD	44 29 168 38	90
CASCADE STREAM	STRM	46 15 167 56	106
CASCADE STREAM	STRM	46 15 167 56	107
CASCADE STREAM	STRM	46 15 167 56	108
CASCADE STREAM	STRM	46 15 167 56	109
CASEY CREEK	STRM	44 05 168 51	78
CASEY SADDLE	SAD	42 56 171 49	70
CASEY STREAM	STRM	42 54 171 52	70
CASHMERE	SBRB	43 35 172 38	82
CASHMERE	SBRB	43 35 172 38	83
CASHMERE	SBRB	43 35 172 38	85
CASIANI, LAKE	LAKE	41 54 172 16	64
CASS	LOC	43 02 171 45	80
CASS, MOUNT (TRIG)	HILL	43 05 172 49	82
CASS RIVER	STRM	43 53 170 30	77
CASS RIVER	STRM	43 00 171 45	80
CASS RIVER	STRM	43 53 170 30	86
CASS RIVER (EAST BRANCH)	STRM	43 39 170 24	74
CASS RIVER (EAST BRANCH)	STRM	43 39 170 24	77
CASS RIVER (EAST BRANCH)	STRM	43 39 170 24	86
CASS RIVER (WEST BRANCH)	STRM	43 39 170 24	74
CASS RIVER (WEST BRANCH)	STRM	43 39 170 24	77
CASS RIVER (WEST BRANCH)	STRM	43 39 170 24	86
CASS SADDLE	SAD	43 06 171 41	80
CASSIN, MOUNT (TRIG)	HILL	41 50 171 46	63
CASSIN, MOUNT (TRIG)	HILL	41 50 171 46	64
CASSINO PEAK	PEAK	43 27 170 28	74
CASSINO PEAK	PEAK	43 27 170 28	77
CASTALIA, LAKE	LAKE	44 13 168 55	78
CASTALY RIVER	STRM	42 39 173 16	72
CASTALY RIVER	STRM	42 39 173 16	73
CASTLE DENT HUT	BLDG	45 47 169 41	111
CASTLE DOWNS (TRIG)	HILL	45 51 168 18	107
CASTLE DOWNS SWAMP	SWMP	45 48 168 13	107
CASTLE HILL	LOC	40 43 175 57	49
CASTLE HILL	LOC	40 43 175 57	51
CASTLE HILL	MTN	44 07 169 18	78
CASTLE HILL	HSTD	43 14 171 43	80
CASTLE HILL (TRIG)	HILL	43 12 171 26	75
CASTLE HILL (TRIG)	HILL	43 12 171 26	80
CASTLE HILL (TRIG)	HILL	45 29 168 38	99
CASTLE HILL (TRIG)	HILL	45 26 168 40	99
CASTLE HILL PEAK	PEAK	43 16 171 46	80
CASTLE ISLAND	ISLD	36 52 175 54	16
CASTLE ISLAND	ISLD	36 52 175 54	17
CASTLE, MOUNT	MTN	44 51 167 47	94
CASTLE POINT	PNT	40 54 176 14	50
CASTLE RIVER	STRM	41 31 175 25	53
CASTLE RIVER	STRM	41 59 173 27	66
CASTLE RIVER	STRM	44 51 167 47	94
CASTLE ROCK (TRIG)	HILL	36 48 175 34	13
CASTLE ROCK (TRIG)	HILL	36 48 175 34	16
CASTLE STREAM	STRM	42 30 172 34	71
CASTLE (TRIG)	HILL	40 43 175 56	49
CASTLE (TRIG)	HILL	40 43 175 56	51
CASTLECLIFF	SBRB	39 57 174 59	45
CASTLEPOINT	LOC	40 54 176 13	50
CASTLEPOINT STREAM	STRM	40 54 176 13	50
CASTLEROCK	LOC	45 43 168 24	107
CASTOR	MTN	44 13 168 53	78
CASTOR BAY	SBRB	36 45 174 46	11
CASTOR BAY	SBRB	36 45 174 46	12
CASWELL SOUND	SND	45 00 167 08	96
CAT CREEK	STRM	41 33 172 42	58
CAT CREEK	STRM	41 33 173 30	59
CAT CREEK	STRM	42 11 172 57	65
CAT HILL	HILL	42 50 172 59	72
CATARACT CREEK	STRM	43 07 171 00	75
CATHEDRAL PEAKS	MTNS	45 23 167 27	97
CATHERINE COVE	BAY	40 53 173 53	54
CATHERINE COVE	BAY	40 53 173 53	61
CATHERINE, LAKE	LAKE	43 13 171 34	80
CATHERINE, MOUNT	MTN	43 26 171 16	75
CATHERINE, MOUNT (TRIG)	MTN	43 54 171 01	87
CATHERINE STREAM	STRM	42 47 173 12	72
CATHERINE STREAM	STRM	42 47 173 12	73
CATLEY, MOUNT	MTN	42 20 172 43	65
CATLEY, MOUNT	MTN	42 20 172 43	71
CATLINS CONE (TRIG)	PEAK	46 23 169 17	112
CATLINS CONE (TRIG)	PEAK	46 23 169 17	113
CATLINS, LAKE	LAKE	46 29 169 38	113
CATLINS RIVER	STRM	46 29 169 37	113
CATLINS STATE FOREST PARK	PARK	46 20 169 00	110
CATLINS STATE FOREST PARK	PARK	46 19 169 08	110
CATLINS STATE FOREST PARK	PARK	46 20 169 00	112
CATLINS STATE FOREST PARK	PARK	46 27 169 14	112
CATLINS STATE FOREST PARK	PARK	46 19 169 08	112
CATLINS STATE FOREST PARK	PARK	46 35 169 04	112
CATLINS STATE FOREST PARK	PARK	46 27 169 14	113
CATLINS STATE FOREST PARK	PARK	46 31 169 39	113
CATON PEAK	PEAK	46 03 166 53	104
CATON PEAK	PEAK	46 03 166 53	105
CATSEARS SADDLE	SAD	41 39 173 47	60
CATSEYE BAY	BAY	44 49 167 23	94
CATSEYE SADDLE	SAD	44 53 167 27	94
CATSEYE SADDLE	SAD	44 53 167 27	97
CATTLE CREEK	STRM	41 44 174 08	67
CATTLE CREEK	STRM	44 31 169 56	92
CATTLE CREEK	STRM	44 31 170 41	93
CATTLE CREEK	LOC	44 31 170 41	93
CATTLE FLAT	LOC	45 40 168 38	107
CATTLE STREAM	STRM	43 16 171 02	75
CATTLE VALLEY	LOC	44 04 170 57	87
CATTLEMOUNT (TRIG)	HILL	36 06 174 27	8
CAVALLI ISLANDS	ISLS	35 00 173 56	4
CAVE	LOC	44 19 170 57	87
CAVE BAY	BAY	35 27 174 44	5
CAVE CREEK	STRM	45 28 169 20	100
CAVE CREEK NORTH	STRM	42 02 171 26	63
CAVE HILL	HILL	44 23 171 00	93
CAVE POINT	PNT	46 41 167 47	108
CAVE POINT	PNT	46 41 167 47	114
CAVE STREAM	STRM	41 34 172 41	58
CAVE STREAM	STRM	41 48 173 12	66
CAVE STREAM	STRM	43 12 171 45	80
CAVENDISH	LOC	43 44 171 23	84
CAVENDISH	LOC	43 44 171 23	87
CAVENDISH RIVER	STRM	46 13 166 52	104
CAVENDISH RIVER	STRM	46 13 166 52	105
CAVERHILL	LOC	42 47 173 19	72
CAVERHILL	LOC	42 47 173 19	73
CAVERN CREEK	STRM	41 07 172 29	56
CAVERN CREEK	STRM	41 07 172 29	57
CAVERN CREEK	STRM	41 07 172 29	62
CAVERSHAM	SBRB	45 54 170 29	103
CAVES STREAM	STRM	43 40 171 26	75
CAVES STREAM	STRM	43 40 171 26	80
CAVES STREAM	STRM	43 40 171 26	84
CAWTE, MOUNT (TRIG)	HILL	41 16 173 50	54
CAWTE, MOUNT (TRIG)	HILL	41 16 173 50	60
CAWTE, MOUNT (TRIG)	HILL	41 16 173 50	61
CECIL, MOUNT	MTN	44 35 170 55	93
CECIL PEAK	PEAK	45 07 168 38	95
CECIL PEAK	HSTD	45 08 168 41	95
CECIL PEAK	PEAK	45 07 168 38	99
CECIL PEAK	HSTD	45 08 168 41	99
CEDER HILL (TRIG)	HILL	46 24 169 28	113
CEMETERY CREEK	STRM	45 06 169 36	100
CENTAUR PEAKS	PEAK	44 38 168 34	90
CENTRE BURN	STRM	45 43 168 09	106
CENTRE BURN	STRM	45 43 168 09	107
CENTRE BUSH	LOC	46 04 168 20	107
CENTRE CREEK	STRM	43 09 171 32	80
CENTRE HILL (TRIG)	HILL	45 35 168 06	98
CENTRE HILL (TRIG)	HILL	43 00 172 57	71
CENTRE HILL (TRIG)	HILL	43 00 172 57	72
CENTRE ISLAND	ISLD	45 14 167 46	97
CENTRE ISLAND	ISLD	46 27 167 51	108
CENTRE ISLAND	ISLD	46 27 167 51	109
CENTRE PASS	PASS	45 36 167 09	105
CENTRE PEAK (TRIG)	HILL	40 47 172 20	56
CENTRE SPUR	RDGE	45 15 168 30	95
CENTRE SPUR	RDGE	45 15 168 30	99
CERBERUS, MOUNT	MTN	45 17 168 12	98
CHAIN GULLY	STRM	45 07 170 10	101
CHAIN HILLS	MTNS	44 42 169 40	91
CHALICE, LAKE	LAKE	41 34 173 19	59
CHALKY INLET	BAY	46 04 166 30	104
CHALKY ISLAND	ISLD	46 03 166 31	104
CHALKY POINT	PNT	46 04 166 32	104
CHAMBERLAIN	LOC	44 15 170 49	87
CHAMBERLAIN, LAKE	LAKE	45 23 167 03	96
CHANCELLOR DOME	MTN	43 31 170 08	74
CHANCELLOR DOME	MTN	43 31 170 08	77
CHANCELLOR ROCKS	ROCK	41 50 174 12	67
CHANEYS	LOC	43 26 172 39	82
CHANEYS	LOC	43 26 172 39	83
CHANEYS	LOC	43 26 172 39	85
CHANNEL ISLAND	ISLD	36 25 175 20	9
CHANNEL ISLAND	ISLD	36 25 175 20	16
CHAOS, MOUNT	MTN	44 37 168 16	89
CHAPMANS CREEK	STRM	43 49 171 16	87
CHARING CROSS	LOC	43 33 172 09	81
CHARING CROSS	LOC	43 33 172 09	85
CHARLES, MOUNT (TRIG)	HILL	45 52 170 42	103
CHARLES, PORT	BAY	36 31 175 28	16
CHARLES SOUND	SND	45 03 167 05	96
CHARLESTON	LOC	41 54 171 26	63
CHARLIES KNOB (TRIG)	MTN	43 36 170 31	74
CHARLIES KNOB (TRIG)	MTN	43 36 170 31	77
CHARLTON	LOC	46 09 168 53	110
CHARLTON	LOC	46 09 168 53	112
CHARLTON, MOUNT	MTN	44 50 168 00	89
CHARLTON, MOUNT	MTN	44 50 168 00	94
CHARMING CREEK	STRM	41 36 171 55	62
CHARON, MOUNT (TRIG)	MTN	42 29 172 45	71
CHARON, MOUNT (TRIG)	MTN	42 29 172 45	72
CHARTERIS BAY	LOC	43 39 172 43	82
CHARTERIS BAY	BAY	43 39 172 42	82
CHARTERIS BAY	BAY	43 39 172 42	83
CHARTERIS BAY	LOC	43 39 172 43	83
CHARTERIS BAY	BAY	43 39 172 42	85
CHARWELL RIVER	STRM	42 30 173 18	72
CHARWELL RIVER	STRM	42 30 173 18	73
CHARWELL RIVER, RIGHT BRANCH	STRM	42 25 173 22	72
CHARWELL RIVER, RIGHT BRANCH	STRM	42 25 173 22	73
CHASLANDS	LOC	46 35 169 19	113
CHASLANDS MISTAKE	HEAD	46 38 169 22	113
CHASM CREEK	STRM	44 39 168 07	89
CHASM CREEK	STRM	45 25 169 18	100
CHASM ISLAND	ISLD	46 34 169 36	113
CHASM STREAM	STRM	41 33 171 59	62
CHASTLETON (TRIG)	HILL	44 07 170 55	87
CHATTERTON RIVER	STRM	42 33 172 48	71
CHATTERTON RIVER	STRM	42 33 172 48	72
CHATTO CREEK	STRM	45 10 169 30	100
CHATTO CREEK	LOC	45 08 169 31	100
CHATTON	LOC	45 59 168 55	110
CHATTON NORTH	LOC	45 56 168 58	110
CHEDDAR VALLEY	LOC	38 02 177 06	23
CHEDDAR VALLEY	HSTD	42 39 173 08	72
CHEDDAR VALLEY	HSTD	42 39 173 08	73
CHEESEMAN, MOUNT	MTN	43 10 171 39	80
CHELTENHAM	POPL	40 08 175 40	46
CHERTSEY	LOC	43 48 171 56	84
CHEST PEAK (TRIG)	MTN	43 06 172 01	81
CHESTER BURN	STRM	45 18 167 29	97
CHESTERFIELD	LOC	42 37 171 05	68
CHESTERFIELD	LOC	42 37 171 05	69
CHETWODE ISLANDS	ISLD	40 54 174 05	54
CHETWODE ISLANDS	ISLS	40 54 174 05	61
CHEVALIER, MOUNT	MTN	43 34 170 39	74
CHEVALIER, POINT	PNT	36 51 174 42	11
CHEVALIER, POINT	PNT	36 51 174 42	12
CHEVIOT	POPL	42 49 173 16	72
CHEVIOT	POPL	42 49 173 16	73
CHEVIOT HILLS	HILL	45 38 167 45	106
CHEW TOBACCO BAY	BAY	47 00 168 12	115
CHEW TOBACCO POINT	PNT	46 59 168 13	115
CHIMERA STREAM	STRM	43 16 171 16	75
CHIMNEY	HILL	45 48 168 04	106
CHIMNEY	HILL	45 48 168 04	107
CHIMNEY CREEK	STRM	44 44 170 13	92
CHIMNEY PEAKS	PEAK	45 44 167 47	106
CHIMNEYS ISLAND	ISLD	47 08 167 31	114
CHINAMAN STREAM	STRM	41 50 172 56	65
CHINAMAN, THE (TRIG)	HILL	45 48 169 31	111
CHISHOLM, MOUNT (TRIG)	MTN	45 41 167 01	104
CHISHOLM, MOUNT (TRIG)	MTN	45 41 167 01	105
CHORLTON	LOC	43 41 173 01	82
CHORLTON	LOC	43 41 173 01	83
CHOWBOK COL	SAD	43 19 170 57	75
CHRISTABEL, LAKE	LAKE	42 25 172 15	70
CHRISTCHURCH	METR	43 32 172 38	82
CHRISTCHURCH	METR	43 32 172 38	83
CHRISTCHURCH	METR	43 32 172 38	85
CHRISTINA, MOUNT	MTN	44 48 168 03	89
CHRISTMAS CREEK	STRM	45 43 170 21	103
CHRISTMAS CREEK	LOC	45 43 170 21	103
CHRISTMAS VILLAGE BAY	BAY	46 45 167 59	109
CHRISTMAS VILLAGE BAY	BAY	46 45 167 59	115
CHRISTOPHER RIVER	STRM	42 17 172 33	65
CHROME STREAM	STRM	41 41 173 09	66
CHRYSTALLS BEACH	LOC	46 11 170 06	103
CHUDLEIGH, MOUNT	MTN	43 35 170 17	74
CHUDLEIGH, MOUNT	MTN	43 35 170 17	77
CHUMMIE CREEK	STRM	41 26 172 36	58
CHURCH HILL (TRIG)	MTN	44 43 168 46	90
CHURCH HILL (TRIG)	MTN	44 43 168 46	95
CHURCHILL	LOC	37 25 175 04	14
CILICIA PEAK	PEAK	44 23 168 31	88
CILICIA PEAK	PEAK	44 23 168 31	89
CIRCLE HILL	LOC	46 03 169 58	111
CIRCLE HILL	LOC	46 03 169 58	113
CITHERON	MTN	44 04 169 14	78
CLANDEBOYE	LOC	44 13 171 23	84
CLANDEBOYE	LOC	44 13 171 23	87
CLAPCOTT CREEK	STRM	43 59 169 27	78
CLAPCOTT CREEK	STRM	43 59 169 27	79
CLARA, MOUNT (TRIG)	MTN	42 20 172 42	65
CLARA, MOUNT (TRIG)	MTN	42 20 172 42	71
CLARE PEAK	PEAK	45 38 167 55	106
CLAREMONT	LOC	44 23 171 09	93
CLARENCE	LOC	42 09 173 56	67
CLARENCE RESERVE	HSTD	42 23 173 27	72
CLARENCE RESERVE	HSTD	42 23 173 27	73
CLARENCE RIVER	STRM	42 10 173 56	67
CLARENDON	LOC	46 03 170 02	103
CLARENDON	LOC	46 03 170 02	111
CLAREVILLE	LOC	41 01 175 31	51
CLAREVILLE	LOC	41 01 175 31	53
CLARIS	LOC	36 15 175 28	9
CLARK, LAKE	LAKE	44 08 168 40	88
CLARK, LAKE	LAKE	45 04 167 32	94
CLARK, LAKE	LAKE	45 04 167 32	97
CLARK POINT	PNT	41 08 174 17	54
CLARK POINT	PNT	41 08 174 17	61
CLARK RIVER	STRM	40 51 172 28	56
CLARK RIVER	STRM	40 51 172 28	57
CLARK RIVER	STRM	41 33 172 47	58
CLARK RIVER	STRM	41 19 172 43	58
CLARKE GLACIER	GLCR	43 15 170 54	75
CLARKE HILL (TRIG)	HILL	44 01 168 40	88
CLARKE, MOUNT	MTN	43 49 169 20	78
CLARKE, MOUNT	MTN	44 33 168 29	88
CLARKE, MOUNT	MTN	44 33 168 29	89
CLARKE, MOUNT	MTN	43 51 169 50	76
CLARKE, MOUNT	MTN	43 51 169 50	79
CLARKE PASS	PASS	43 51 169 35	76
CLARKE PASS	PASS	43 51 169 35	79
CLARKE RIVER	STRM	42 22 171 50	70
CLARKE RIVER	STRM	43 59 169 31	79
CLARKE SADDLE	SAD	43 35 170 09	74
CLARKE SADDLE	SAD	43 35 170 09	77
CLARKES JUNCTION	LOC	45 44 170 03	111
CLARKES MOUND	MTN	43 55 169 33	76
CLARKES MOUND	MTN	43 55 169 33	79
CLARKES PASS	PASS	43 00 171 15	75
CLARKES STREAM	STRM	45 43 169 52	111
CLARKS BEACH	LOC	37 08 174 42	12
CLARKS BEACH	LOC	37 08 174 42	14
CLARKS CREEK	STRM	37 06 174 48	12
CLARKS CREEK	STRM	37 06 174 48	14
CLARKSVILLE	LOC	46 08 169 55	111
CLARKSVILLE	LOC	46 08 169 55	113
CLARKVILLE	LOC	43 25 172 37	82
CLARKVILLE	LOC	43 25 172 37	83
CLARKVILLE	LOC	43 25 172 37	85
CLASSEN GLACIER	GLCR	43 29 170 27	77
CLAVERLEY	LOC	42 36 173 28	73
CLAY KNOB	PEAK	42 43 172 31	71
CLAY POINT	PNT	40 53 173 59	54
CLAY POINT	PNT	40 53 173 59	61
CLAYTON	LOC	43 55 170 53	87
CLEAR, MOUNT (TRIG)	MTN	42 20 173 22	72
CLEAR, MOUNT (TRIG)	MTN	42 20 173 22	73
CLEAR STREAM	STRM	44 40 170 10	92
CLEAR WATER RIVER	STRM	43 27 169 51	76
CLEARBURN	LOC	44 21 170 00	92
CLEARWATER, LAKE	LAKE	43 36 171 03	75
CLEDDAU RIVER	STRM	44 41 167 58	89
CLEDDAU RIVER	STRM	44 41 167 58	94
CLEFT CREEK	STRM	44 39 168 07	89
CLENT HILLS	MTNS	43 36 171 13	75
CLENT HILLS SADDLE	SAD	43 27 171 17	75
CLENT HILLS SADDLE	SAD	43 27 171 17	80
CLENT HILLS STREAM	STRM	43 34 171 11	75
CLERKE, MOUNT	MTN	45 41 166 41	104
CLEUGHEARN PEAK (TRIG)	MTN	45 50 167 24	105
CLEVEDON	LOC	36 59 175 03	12
CLEVEDON	LOC	36 59 175 03	13
CLEVEDON	LOC	36 59 175 03	14
CLIFDEN	LOC	46 03 167 43	106
CLIFF COVE	BAY	45 58 166 45	104

CLIFF ROAD STATION	RSTN	40 04 175 25	45
CLIFF ROAD STATION	RSTN	40 04 175 25	46
CLIFF (TRIG)	HILL	40 47 173 49	54
CLIFF (TRIG)	HILL	40 47 173 49	61
CLIFFORD BAY	BAY	41 41 174 11	67
CLIFTON	LOC	39 38 177 01	42
CLIFTON	LOC	39 38 177 01	43
CLIFTON	LOC	40 51 172 52	57
CLIFTON	LOC	46 28 168 22	109
CLIFTON	LOC	46 12 169 24	111
CLIFTON	LOC	46 12 169 24	113
CLIMAX COL	SAD	44 23 168 21	88
CLIMAX COL	SAD	44 23 168 21	89
CLIMAX PEAK	PEAK	44 28 168 22	88
CLIMAX PEAK	PEAK	44 28 168 22	89
CLIMIE (TRIG)	PEAK	41 09 175 09	52
CLIMIE (TRIG)	PEAK	41 09 175 09	53
CLIMIE (TRIG)	PEAK	41 09 175 09	55
CLINTON	POPL	46 12 169 22	111
CLINTON	POPL	46 12 169 22	113
CLINTON RIVER	STRM	42 16 173 44	67
CLINTON RIVER	STRM	44 56 167 56	89
CLINTON RIVER	STRM	44 56 167 56	94
CLINTON RIVER (NORTH BRANCH)	STRM	44 53 167 53	89
CLINTON RIVER (NORTH BRANCH)	STRM	44 53 167 53	94
CLINTON RIVER (WEST BRANCH)	STRM	44 53 167 53	89
CLINTON RIVER (WEST BRANCH)	STRM	44 53 167 53	94
CLIO, MOUNT	MTN	44 09 168 51	78
CLIVE	USAT	39 35 176 55	42
CLIVE	USAT	39 35 176 55	43
CLIVE, MOUNT (TRIG)	HILL	40 37 175 49	49
CLOCK POINT HILL (TRIG)	HILL	41 05 173 38	60
CLOHER, MOUNT	MTN	43 22 170 21	74
CLOHER, MOUNT	MTN	43 22 170 21	77
CLOUD HILL (TRIG)	HILL	44 27 169 53	91
CLOUDESLEY, MOUNT	MTN	43 12 171 39	80
CLOUDMAKER, LAKE	LAKE	44 18 168 43	88
CLOUDMAKER, LAKE	LAKE	44 18 168 43	90
CLOUDY BAY	BAY	41 27 174 04	54
CLOUDY BAY	BAY	41 27 174 04	60
CLOUDY PASS	PASS	44 48 167 33	94
CLOUDY PEAK	PEAK	43 28 170 47	74
CLOUDY PEAK	PEAK	43 28 170 47	75
CLOUDY PEAK RANGE	MTNS	43 24 170 44	74
CLOUDY PEAK (TRIG)	PEAK	44 55 169 32	91
CLOUDY RANGE	HSTD	42 26 173 16	72
CLOUDY RANGE	HSTD	42 26 173 16	73
CLOUDY RANGE (TRIG)	MTN	42 23 173 13	72
CLOUDY RANGE (TRIG)	MTN	42 23 173 13	73
CLOUDY STREAM	STRM	43 31 170 48	74
CLOUSTONVILLE	LOC	41 01 175 07	52
CLOUSTONVILLE	LOC	41 01 175 07	53
CLOUSTONVILLE	LOC	41 01 175 07	55
CLOVA BAY	BAY	41 06 174 02	54
CLOVA BAY	BAY	41 06 174 02	60
CLOVA BAY	BAY	41 06 174 02	61
CLUB ROCKS	ROCK	37 32 177 11	23
CLUDEN PASS	PASS	44 49 169 43	91
CLUDEN STREAM	STRM	44 48 169 31	91
CLUNES STREAM	STRM	46 05 167 48	106
CLUNES STREAM	STRM	46 05 167 48	108
CLUTHA RIVER	STRM	45 39 169 24	111
CLUTHA RIVER (KOAU BRANCH)	STRM	46 21 169 49	111
CLUTHA RIVER (KOAU BRANCH)	STRM	46 21 169 49	113
CLUTHA RIVER (MATAU BRANCH)	STRM	46 20 169 50	111
CLUTHA RIVER (MATAU BRANCH)	STRM	46 20 169 50	113
CLYDE	POPL	45 11 169 19	100
CLYDE RIVER	STRM	43 40 170 58	75
CLYDE (TRIG)	HILL	40 55 175 55	49
CLYDE (TRIG)	HILL	40 55 175 55	51
CLYDESDALE	LOC	40 17 175 19	45
CLYDESDALE	LOC	40 17 175 19	48
CLYDEVALE	LOC	46 06 169 31	111
CLYDEVALE	LOC	46 06 169 31	113
COAL CREEK	STRM	40 01 175 55	46
COAL CREEK	STRM	41 22 172 44	58
COAL CREEK	STRM	41 48 171 37	63
COAL CREEK	STRM	41 48 171 37	64
COAL CREEK	STRM	41 55 171 55	64
COAL CREEK	STRM	41 41 172 26	65
COAL CREEK	STRM	42 12 172 16	65
COAL CREEK	STRM	42 27 171 14	68
COAL CREEK	STRM	42 27 171 14	69
COAL CREEK	STRM	43 15 171 58	81
COAL CREEK	STRM	44 18 170 52	87
COAL CREEK	STRM	44 46 169 31	91
COAL CREEK	STRM	45 12 168 59	99
COAL CREEK	STRM	45 29 169 19	100
COAL CREEK	STRM	45 22 169 18	100
COAL CREEK	STRM	45 04 169 31	100
COAL CREEK	STRM	45 19 170 16	101
COAL CREEK	STRM	45 40 168 00	106
COAL CREEK	STRM	45 56 167 58	106
COAL CREEK	STRM	45 40 167 45	106
COAL CREEK	STRM	45 40 168 00	107
COAL CREEK	STRM	46 03 168 27	107
COAL CREEK	STRM	45 56 167 58	107
COAL CREEK FLAT	LOC	45 30 169 18	100
COAL HILL	HILL	45 31 168 09	98
COAL HILL (TRIG)	MTN	43 47 171 08	87
COAL ISLAND	ISLD	46 08 166 38	104
COAL PIT SADDLE	SAD	45 04 168 57	99
COAL POINT	PNT	46 19 169 55	111
COAL POINT	PNT	46 19 169 55	113
COAL RIVER	STRM	43 47 170 33	77
COAL RIVER	STRM	43 47 170 33	86
COAL RIVER	STRM	45 30 166 43	96
COAL STREAM	STRM	38 28 177 40	31
COAL STREAM	STRM	44 08 170 53	87
COALGATE	LOC	43 29 171 58	81
COAST HILL	HILL	41 09 174 22	54
COAST HILL	HILL	41 09 174 22	61
COAST (TRIG)	HILL	41 07 174 23	54
COAST (TRIG)	HILL	41 07 174 23	61
COATES BAY	BAY	36 14 174 17	7
COATES BAY	BAY	36 14 174 17	8
COATES, MOUNT	MTN	43 29 170 35	74
COATES, MOUNT	MTN	43 29 170 35	77
COATESVILLE	LOC	36 43 174 38	11
COATESVILLE	LOC	36 43 174 38	12
COBB, LAKE	LAKE	41 03 172 31	56
COBB, LAKE	LAKE	41 03 172 31	57
COBB, LAKE	LAKE	41 03 172 31	58
COBB RESERVOIR	LAKE	41 07 172 40	56
COBB RESERVOIR	LAKE	41 07 172 40	57
COBB RESERVOIR	LAKE	41 07 172 40	58
COBB RIVER	STRM	41 08 172 36	56
COBB RIVER	STRM	41 08 172 36	57
COBB RIVER	STRM	41 08 172 36	58
COBDEN	SBRB	42 26 171 12	68
COBDEN	SBRB	42 26 171 12	69
COCHRAN STREAM	STRM	42 52 171 57	70
COCKABULLA CREEK	STRM	43 15 170 08	74
COCKAYNE GLACIER	GLCR	43 17 170 52	75
COCKAYNE, MOUNT	MTN	43 09 171 40	80
COCKEYE CREEK	STRM	42 34 171 13	68
COCKEYE CREEK	STRM	42 34 171 13	69
CODFISH ISLAND	ISLD	46 46 167 43	108
CODFISH ISLAND	ISLD	46 46 167 43	114
COFFEE CREEK	STRM	41 59 172 12	64
COLAC BAY	LOC	46 22 167 53	108
COLAC BAY	BAY	46 22 167 55	108
COLAC BAY	BAY	46 22 167 55	109
COLAC BAY	LOC	46 22 167 53	109
COLD PEAK	PEAK	45 10 168 11	98
COLD STREAM	STRM	39 25 173 58	34
COLD STREAM	STRM	42 17 173 26	66
COLDSTREAM	LOC	43 18 172 37	82
COLDSTREAM	LOC	43 18 172 37	83
COLDSTREAM	LOC	44 09 171 31	84
COLDWATER CREEK	STRM	42 04 172 56	65
COLE CREEK	STRM	43 45 169 11	78
COLENSO (TRIG)	PEAK	39 44 176 03	47
COLERIDGE, LAKE	LAKE	43 18 171 30	80
COLERIDGE PASS	PASS	43 18 171 38	80
COLERIDGE STREAM	STRM	43 20 171 35	80
COLL CREEK	STRM	41 59 171 51	63
COLL CREEK	STRM	41 59 171 51	64
COLLIE CREEK	STRM	43 43 169 22	78
COLLIERS JUNCTION	LOC	39 37 175 35	46
COLLINGWOOD	POPL	40 41 172 41	56
COLLINGWOOD	POPL	40 41 172 41	57
COLLINS BAY	BAY	45 07 168 41	95
COLLINS BAY	BAY	45 07 168 41	99
COLLINS CREEK	STRM	45 08 168 41	95
COLLINS CREEK	STRM	45 08 168 41	99
COLLINS RIVER	STRM	41 09 173 32	59
COLLYER	MTN	44 10 168 36	88
COLONEL GULLY STREAM	STRM	41 47 173 53	67
COLONIAL HEAD	HEAD	45 09 166 58	96
COLONIAL KNOB (TRIG)	HILL	41 09 174 48	52
COLONIAL KNOB (TRIG)	HILL	41 09 174 48	55
COLUMN ROCKS (TRIG)	MTN	44 54 169 10	90
COLVILLE	LOC	36 38 175 28	13
COLVILLE	LOC	36 38 175 28	16
COLVILLE BAY	BAY	36 37 175 27	13
COLVILLE BAY	BAY	36 37 175 27	16
COLVILLE, CAPE	CAPE	36 28 175 21	9
COLVILLE, CAPE	CAPE	36 28 175 21	16
COLVILLE CHANNEL	CHAN	36 25 175 27	9
COLWELL, LAKE	LAKE	45 32 167 10	96
COLYERS ISLAND	ISLD	46 33 168 18	109
COLYTON	LOC	40 14 175 39	46
COMET, THE (TRIG)	PEAK	39 29 176 18	39
COMMAND PEAK	PEAK	45 08 167 06	96
COMMANDER PEAK	MTN	45 26 167 05	96
COMMANDER, THE	MTN	43 27 170 36	74
COMMANDER, THE	MTN	43 27 170 36	77
COMPANY CREEK	STRM	43 16 170 07	74
COMPANY CREEK	STRM	43 16 170 07	76
CONDIES HEAD (TRIG)	HILL	45 11 169 12	100
CONE BURN	STRM	46 02 168 46	110
CONE BURN	STRM	46 02 168 46	112
CONE CREEK	STRM	39 59 175 59	46
CONE ISLAND	ISLD	34 57 173 46	4
CONE PEAK	PEAK	45 33 167 27	97
CONE PEAK	PEAK	45 52 167 02	105
CONE PEAK (TRIG)	HILL	40 59 173 53	54
CONE PEAK (TRIG)	HILL	40 59 173 53	60
CONE PEAK (TRIG)	HILL	40 59 173 53	61
CONE ROCK	ROCK	34 57 173 42	4
CONE SADDLE	SAD	40 59 175 21	48
CONE, THE (TRIG)	HILL	46 00 168 25	107
CONE, THE (TRIG)	MTN	38 00 175 04	18
CONE, THE (TRIG)	HILL	46 04 169 13	110
CONE, THE (TRIG)	HILL	46 04 169 13	112
CONE (TRIG)	PEAK	40 58 175 21	48
CONE (TRIG)	PEAK	40 58 175 21	53
CONE (TRIG)	MTN	44 55 170 22	92
CONE (TRIG)	MTN	44 56 170 22	92
CONICAL HILL	PEAK	42 04 171 59	64
CONICAL HILL	MTN	43 40 169 51	76
CONICAL HILL	MTN	43 40 169 51	79
CONICAL HILL	LOC	46 04 169 14	110
CONICAL HILL	LOC	46 04 169 14	112
CONICAL HILL (TRIG)	PEAK	41 34 172 38	58
CONICAL HILL (TRIG)	PEAK	42 22 172 00	70
CONICAL HILL (TRIG)	HILL	46 14 169 26	111
CONICAL HILL (TRIG)	HILL	46 14 169 26	113
CONICAL KNOB	PEAK	41 24 173 24	59
CONICAL PEAK (TRIG)	HILL	36 19 174 40	11
CONICAL PEAK (TRIG)	PEAK	45 16 170 35	102
CONNEMARA	HSTD	42 43 173 17	72
CONNEMARA	HSTD	42 43 173 17	73
CONNORS CREEK	STRM	42 00 172 55	65
CONNS CREEK	LOC	41 44 171 47	63
CONNS CREEK	LOC	41 44 171 47	64
CONRAD, MOUNT	MTN	43 34 170 25	74
CONRAD, MOUNT	MTN	43 34 170 25	77
CONROYS DAM	DAM	45 17 169 19	100
CONROYS GULLY	LOC	45 16 169 20	100
CONSOLATION PEAK	PEAK	44 51 168 05	89
CONSPICUOUS (TRIG)	HILL	39 56 175 58	46
CONSTANCE, LAKE	LAKE	42 05 172 40	65
CONSTITUTION HILL (TRIG)	HILL	42 45 173 06	72
CONSTITUTION, MOUNT	MTN	44 18 169 15	78
CONTOUR CHAN	STRM	45 58 170 07	103
CONWAY FLAT	LOC	42 37 173 28	72
CONWAY HILLS	HSTD	42 25 173 19	72
CONWAY HILLS	HSTD	42 25 173 19	73
CONWAY PEAK	PEAK	43 32 170 12	74
CONWAY PEAK	PEAK	43 32 170 12	77
CONWAY RIVER	STRM	42 37 173 28	72
CONWAY RIVER	STRM	42 37 173 28	73
CONWAY SPUR (TRIG)	PEAK	42 25 173 14	72
CONWAY SPUR (TRIG)	PEAK	42 25 173 14	73
COOK BLUFF	CLIF	43 27 169 46	76
COOK CHANNEL	CHAN	45 47 166 37	104
COOK CREEK	STRM	36 08 174 30	8
COOK, MOUNT	MTN	43 36 170 09	74
COOK, MOUNT	MTN	43 36 170 09	77
COOK RANGE, MOUNT	MTN	43 39 170 09	77
COOK RANGE, MOUNT	MTN	43 39 170 09	86
COOK RIVER	STRM	43 26 169 48	76
COOK SADDLE	SAD	43 27 170 04	76
COOK SADDLE	SAD	43 27 170 04	77
COOK STRAIT	STRA	41 24 174 36	55
COOKS ARM	BAY	47 12 167 38	114
COOKS BAY	BAY	36 50 175 45	16
COOKS BEACH	LOC	36 50 175 43	16
COOKSON, MOUNT	PEAK	42 33 173 09	72
COOKSON, MOUNT	PEAK	42 33 173 09	73
COOLEYS STREAM	STRM	41 07 175 06	52
COOLEYS STREAM	STRM	41 07 175 06	53
COOLEYS STREAM	STRM	41 07 175 06	55
COOMBE ROCKS	ROCK	41 21 174 09	54
COOMBE ROCKS	ROCK	41 21 174 09	60
COONOOR	LOC	40 26 176 06	49
COONOOR	LOC	40 26 176 06	50
COOPER CREEK	STRM	37 54 175 02	18
COOPER ISLAND	ISLD	45 44 166 50	104
COOPER LAGOON	LAGN	43 52 172 18	85
COOPERS BEACH	LOC	34 59 173 31	3
COOPERS CASTLE	HILL	36 10 175 24	9
COOPERS CREEK	STRM	43 18 172 10	81
COOPERS CREEK	LOC	43 17 172 07	81
COOPERS CREEK	STRM	44 13 171 23	84
COOPERS CREEK	STRM	44 13 171 23	87
COOPERS CREEK	LOC	44 01 171 15	87
COOPERS KNOB (TRIG)	HILL	43 40 172 37	82
COOPERS KNOB (TRIG)	HILL	43 40 172 37	83
COOPERS KNOB (TRIG)	HILL	43 40 172 37	85
COOPTOWN	LOC	43 45 172 49	83
COOTE HILL (TRIG)	MTN	45 02 167 31	94
COOTE HILL (TRIG)	MTN	45 02 167 31	97
COPERNICUS, MOUNT	MTN	42 00 171 45	63
COPERNICUS, MOUNT	MTN	42 00 171 45	64
COPLAND GLACIER	GLCR	43 38 170 05	76
COPLAND GLACIER	GLCR	43 38 170 05	77
COPLAND GLACIER	GLCR	43 38 170 05	79
COPLAND, MOUNT	MTN	43 36 170 02	76
COPLAND, MOUNT	MTN	43 36 170 02	77
COPLAND PASS	PASS	43 39 170 06	76
COPLAND PASS	PASS	43 39 170 06	77
COPLAND PASS	PASS	43 39 170 06	79
COPLAND RANGE	MTNS	43 34 169 55	76
COPLAND RIVER	STRM	43 37 169 50	76
COPPERMINE CREEK	STRM	43 49 169 09	78
COPPERMINE ISLAND	ISLD	35 53 174 46	8
COPPERMINE SADDLE	SAD	41 21 173 21	59
CORA LYNN	LOC	43 01 171 40	80
CORALIE BAY	BAY	36 36 175 47	16
CORBIES CREEK	STRM	44 38 170 04	92
CORBYVALE	LOC	41 29 172 03	62
CORDING ISLANDS	ISLS	46 04 166 41	104
CORMACKS	LOC	45 05 170 54	102
CORNER CREEK	STRM	43 10 171 33	80
CORNER KNOB (TRIG)	HILL	43 01 171 43	80
CORNER PEAK	PEAK	44 29 169 20	91
CORNER POST	MTN	44 18 168 45	88
CORNER POST	MTN	44 18 168 45	90
CORNISH HEAD	HEAD	45 37 170 42	102
CORNWALLIS	LOC	37 01 174 36	11
CORNWALLIS	LOC	37 01 174 36	14
COROGLEN	LOC	36 55 175 41	15
COROGLEN	LOC	36 55 175 41	16
COROGLEN	LOC	36 55 175 41	17
COROMANDEL	POPL	36 45 175 30	13
COROMANDEL	POPL	36 45 175 30	16
COROMANDEL HARBOUR	HARB	36 48 175 27	13
COROMANDEL HARBOUR	HARB	36 48 175 27	16
COROMANDEL PENINSULA	PEN	37 02 175 42	16
COROMANDEL RANGE	MTNS	37 17 175 46	17
COROMANDEL STATE FOREST PARK	PARK	36 32 175 24	9
COROMANDEL STATE FOREST PARK	PARK	36 38 175 33	13
COROMANDEL STATE FOREST PARK	PARK	37 02 175 50	16
COROMANDEL STATE FOREST PARK	PARK	36 38 175 33	16
COROMANDEL STATE FOREST PARK	PARK	36 32 175 24	16
COROMANDEL STATE FOREST PARK	PARK	37 02 175 50	17
COROMANDEL STATE FOREST PARK	PARK	37 18 175 50	17
CORONATION PEAK	PEAK	45 14 167 16	96
CORONET CREEK	STRM	44 53 168 50	90
CORONET CREEK	STRM	44 53 168 50	95
CORONET PEAK	LOC	44 55 168 44	90
CORONET PEAK	LOC	44 55 168 44	95
CORONET PEAK SKI FIELD	LOC	44 55 168 44	90
CORONET PEAK SKI FIELD	LOC	44 55 168 44	95
CORONET PEAK (TRIG)	MTN	44 55 168 44	90
CORONET PEAK (TRIG)	MTN	44 55 168 44	95
CORRIEDALE	LOC	44 59 170 48	93
CORRY (TRIG)	HILL	39 49 175 02	45
COSGROVE ISLAND	ISLD	46 34 169 37	113
COSMOS PEAKS	PEAK	44 34 168 18	88
COSMOS PEAKS	PEAK	44 34 168 18	89
COSSEYS RESERVOIR	LAKE	37 04 175 06	13
COSSEYS RESERVOIR	LAKE	37 04 175 06	14
COSSEYS RESERVOIR	LAKE	37 04 175 06	15
COSTELLO, MOUNT (TRIG)	MTN	42 18 173 04	66
COTTERELL PEAK	PEAK	42 00 172 48	65
COTTERS CREEK	STRM	44 12 169 30	79
COTTON, MOUNT (TRIG)	MTN	43 15 171 30	80
COTTON (TRIG)	HILL	41 45 172 21	65
COULAIR PEAK	PEAK	43 21 170 59	75
COULOIR PEAK	PEAK	44 49 167 43	94
COULTER HILL	HILL	36 58 175 47	16
COULTER HILL	HILL	36 58 175 47	17
COUNTESS PEAK	PEAK	45 06 168 02	97
COUNTESS PEAK	PEAK	45 06 168 02	98
COUNTESS STREAM	STRM	42 40 172 54	71
COUNTESS STREAM	STRM	42 40 172 54	72
COUNTING STREAM	STRM	42 38 173 02	72
COUNTRY STREAM	STRM	43 08 170 47	75
COURTENAY	LOC	43 28 172 14	81
COURTENAY	LOC	43 28 172 14	85
COURTNEY, MOUNT (TRIG)	HILL	41 50 171 55	63
COURTNEY, MOUNT (TRIG)	HILL	41 50 171 55	64
COUTTS CREEK	STRM	39 57 175 24	45
COUTTS CREEK	STRM	39 57 175 24	46
COUTTS ISLAND	LOC	43 26 172 38	82
COUTTS ISLAND	LOC	43 26 172 38	83
COUTTS ISLAND	LOC	43 26 172 38	85
COW CREEK	STRM	41 40 172 38	65
COW CREEK	STRM	41 49 173 46	67
COW ISLAND	ISLD	46 57 168 11	115
COW SADDLE	SAD	40 46 175 30	48
COW SADDLE	SAD	40 46 175 30	49
COW SADDLE	SAD	40 46 175 30	51
COW SADDLE	SAD	40 53 172 35	56
COW SADDLE	SAD	40 53 172 35	57
COW STREAM	STRM	41 51 173 34	66
COW STREAM	STRM	42 25 172 40	71
COWAN CREEK	STRM	44 02 169 15	78
COWES	LOC	36 49 175 09	13
COWHIDE CREEK	STRM	43 07 170 37	74
COX RIVER	STRM	42 52 171 57	70
COX SADDLE	SAD	42 47 171 55	70
COZENS CREEK	STRM	41 17 172 55	58
COZETTE BURN	STRM	45 19 167 16	96
CRADDOCK STREAM	STRM	43 33 171 02	75
CRAIG FLAT	LOC	45 44 169 29	111
CRAIG PEAK	PEAK	43 32 170 03	76
CRAIG PEAK	PEAK	43 32 170 03	77
CRAIGELLACHIE	LOC	45 50 169 34	111
CRAIGELLACHIE (TRIG)	MTN	44 56 168 35	90
CRAIGELLACHIE (TRIG)	MTN	44 56 168 35	95
CRAIGIE BURN	STRM	44 19 169 10	90
CRAIGIE HILL (TRIG)	HILL	45 40 168 43	110
CRAIGIEBURN	LOC	42 17 171 36	63
CRAIGIEBURN	LOC	43 06 171 52	80
CRAIGIEBURN	LOC	43 06 171 52	81
CRAIGIEBURN CREEK	STRM	40 58 172 49	57
CRAIGIEBURN CREEK	STRM	42 18 171 36	63
CRAIGIEBURN RANGE	MTNS	43 07 171 33	80
CRAIGIEBURN STATE FOREST PARK	PARK	43 06 171 34	80
CRAIGLOCHART	HSTD	41 38 173 40	60
CRAIGROYSTON PEAK	PEAK	44 32 168 45	90
CRAIGS PEAK (TRIG)	HILL	41 45 174 02	67
CRAIL BAY	HSTD	41 09 173 58	54
CRAIL BAY	BAY	41 07 173 58	54
CRAIL BAY	BAY	41 07 173 58	60
CRAIL BAY	HSTD	41 09 173 58	60
CRAIL BAY	HSTD	41 09 173 58	61
CRAIL BAY	BAY	41 07 173 58	61
CRATE CREEK	STRM	42 17 172 00	64
CRATER CREEK	STRM	45 26 170 12	101
CRATER HEAD	HEAD	34 09 172 07	2
CRAWFORD CREEK	STRM	42 58 171 14	68
CRAWFORD CREEK	STRM	42 58 171 14	69
CRAWFORD, MOUNT (TRIG)	PEAK	40 49 175 21	48
CRAWFORD RANGE	MTNS	42 43 172 05	70
CRAYFISH HEIGHTS	MTN	45 13 167 00	96
CRAYFISH ISLAND	ISLD	45 48 166 34	104
CREIGHTON PEAK (TRIG)	PEAK	42 07 172 09	64
CRESCENT ISLAND	ISLD	44 37 169 04	90
CRESCENT MOUNT	MTN	45 39 167 24	105
CRIBB CREEK	STRM	42 24 173 31	73
CRICHTON	LOC	46 09 169 52	111
CRICHTON	LOC	46 09 169 52	113
CRICHTON, MOUNT	MTN	45 02 168 29	95
CRICHTON, MOUNT	MTN	45 02 168 29	98
CRICHTONS HILL (TRIG)	HILL	40 54 173 58	54
CRICHTONS HILL (TRIG)	HILL	40 54 173 58	61
CRICKLEWOOD	HSTD	38 58 177 13	41
CRICKLEWOOD	LOC	44 10 170 51	87
CRIFFEL PEAK (TRIG)	MTN	44 47 169 10	90
CRIFFEL RANGE	MTNS	44 53 169 05	90
CRIMEA CREEK	STRM	42 14 172 56	65
CRIMEA RANGE	MTNS	42 16 172 50	65
CRIPPLETOWN	LOC	44 56 169 18	91
CROESUS KNOB	PEAK	42 18 171 23	63
CROFTON	LOC	40 06 175 23	45
CROFTON DOWNS	SBRB	41 15 174 46	52
CROFTON DOWNS	SBRB	41 15 174 46	55
CROISILLES HARBOUR	HARB	41 06 173 40	60
CROISILLES HILL (TRIG)	HILL	41 06 173 35	59
CROMBIE STREAM	STRM	46 16 167 10	105
CROMEL STREAM	STRM	45 38 168 23	107
CROMWELL	POPL	45 03 169 12	100
CROMWELL GORGE	GORG	45 09 169 19	100
CRONADUN	LOC	42 02 171 52	63
CRONADUN	LOC	42 02 171 52	64
CROOK BURN	STRM	46 04 169 31	111
CROOK BURN	STRM	46 04 169 31	113
CROOKED ARM	BAY	45 21 167 02	96
CROOKED MARY CREEK	STRM	42 24 172 08	70
CROOKED RIVER	STRM	42 36 171 29	69
CROOKSTON	LOC	45 51 169 20	110
CROOKSTON	LOC	45 51 169 20	111
CROP KNOB	MTN	43 06 170 59	75
CROPP RIVER	STRM	43 04 171 02	75
CROPP, MOUNT (TRIG)	HILL	42 40 172 43	71
CROSBIE STREAM	STRM	37 01 175 37	13
CROSBIE STREAM	STRM	37 01 175 37	15
CROSBIE STREAM	STRM	37 01 175 37	16
CROSS CREEK	LOC	41 10 175 12	52
CROSS CREEK	STRM	41 10 175 16	53
CROSS CREEK	LOC	41 10 175 12	53
CROSS CREEK	LOC	41 10 175 12	55
CROSS EDEN CREEK	STRM	45 08 170 00	101
CROSSANS CORNER	LOC	45 55 169 09	110
CROSSBOW SADDLE	SAD	43 21 170 51	75
CROSSCUT, MOUNT	MTN	44 46 168 02	89
CROSSCUT, MOUNT	MTN	42 06 172 08	64
CROSSLEY, MOUNT	MTN	42 50 172 04	70
CROSSLEY STREAM	STRM	42 49 172 07	70
CROW CREEK	STRM	43 57 169 15	78
CROW RIVER	STRM	41 18 172 28	58
CROW RIVER	STRM	43 00 171 31	69
CROWFOOT, MOUNT	MTN	45 33 167 03	96
CROWFOOT, MOUNT	MTN	45 33 167 03	105
CROWLES BAY	BAY	35 11 174 01	4
CROWLES BAY	BAY	35 11 174 01	5
CROWN RANGE	MTNS	44 57 168 55	90
CROWN RANGE	MTNS	44 57 168 55	95
CROWN ROCK (TRIG)	ROCK	45 39 169 03	110
CROWN TERRACE	LOC	44 59 168 53	95
CROWN TERRACE	LOC	44 59 168 53	99
CROWS NEST	MTN	41 59 173 40	67
CROYDON	LOC	46 03 168 54	110
CROYDON	LOC	46 03 168 54	112
CROZIER STREAM	STRM	41 36 173 11	59
CRUSHINGTON	LOC	42 09 171 54	63
CRUSHINGTON	LOC	42 09 171 54	64
CRYSTAL BROOK	STRM	42 49 173 15	72
CRYSTAL BROOK	HSTD	42 48 173 13	72
CRYSTAL BROOK	HSTD	42 48 173 13	73
CRYSTAL BROOK	STRM	42 49 173 15	73
CRYSTAL PEAK	PEAK	42 10 172 44	65
CUB STREAM	STRM	41 10 172 28	56
CUB STREAM	STRM	41 10 172 28	57
CUB STREAM	STRM	41 10 172 28	58
CUCKOO RIVER	STRM	41 16 172 17	56
CUCKOO RIVER	STRM	41 16 172 17	62
CUCKOO SADDLE	SAD	42 04 173 46	67
CULDAFF POINT	PNT	40 56 174 05	54
CULDAFF POINT	PNT	40 56 174 05	61
CULLEN CREEK	STRM	41 17 173 51	54
CULLEN CREEK	STRM	41 17 173 51	60
CULLEN CREEK	STRM	41 17 173 51	61
CULLEN, MOUNT (TRIG)	MTN	41 20 173 50	54
CULLEN, MOUNT (TRIG)	MTN	41 20 173 50	60
CULLEN, MOUNT (TRIG)	MTN	41 20 173 50	61
CULLENS (TRIG)	HILL	39 48 176 13	47
CULLIFORD HILL (TRIG)	HILL	41 30 172 33	58
CULVERDEN	LOC	42 47 172 51	71
CULVERDEN	LOC	42 47 172 51	72
CULVERDON, MOUNT (TRIG)	HILL	42 43 172 49	71
CULVERDON, MOUNT (TRIG)	HILL	42 43 172 49	72
CUMINE PEAK	PEAK	43 25 170 32	74
CUMINE PEAK	PEAK	43 25 170 32	77

CUNARIS SOUND	SND	45 58 166 40	**104**
CUNNINGHAM, MOUNT	MTN	44 32 168 32	**88**
CUNNINGHAM, MOUNT	MTN	44 32 168 32	**89**
CUNNINGHAM, MOUNT	MTN	44 32 168 32	**90**
CUPOLA, MOUNT	MTN	41 59 172 43	**65**
CUPOLA (TRIG)	PEAK	45 37 168 31	**99**
CUPOLA (TRIG)	PEAK	45 37 168 31	**107**
CURIE, MOUNT	MTN	42 02 171 30	**63**
CURIOUS COVE	LOC	41 15 174 07	**54**
CURIOUS COVE	LOC	41 15 174 07	**60**
CURIOUS COVE	LOC	41 15 174 07	**61**
CURLEW ISLAND	ISLD	45 47 166 37	**104**
CURRANS CREEK	STRM	46 33 168 39	**112**
CURRENT BASIN	CHAN	40 57 173 47	**61**
CURTIS, MOUNT	PEAK	41 54 172 04	**64**
CUSACK, MOUNT	MTN	45 36 167 03	**105**
CUST	LOC	43 19 172 22	**81**
CUST	LOC	43 19 172 22	**85**
CUST RIVER	STRM	43 23 172 41	**82**
CUST RIVER	STRM	43 23 172 41	**85**
CUTHBERT, MOUNT	MTN	45 48 167 25	**105**
CUTHILL	LOC	36 46 174 42	**11**
CUTHILL	LOC	36 46 174 42	**12**
CUTTANCE CREEK	STRM	43 57 169 21	**78**
CUTTANCE, MOUNT	MTN	43 56 169 20	**78**
CUTTER ROCKS	ROCK	44 10 168 14	**88**
CUVIER ISLAND	ISLD	36 26 175 46	**16**
D			
DACRE	LOC	46 19 168 36	**112**
DAGG SOUND	SND	45 23 166 46	**96**
DAGG (TRIG)	PEAK	40 51 175 31	**48**
DAGG (TRIG)	PEAK	40 51 175 31	**49**
DAGG (TRIG)	PEAK	40 51 175 31	**51**
DAGON	MTN	44 12 168 37	**88**
DAIRY FLAT	LOC	36 40 174 38	**11**
DAIRY FLAT	LOC	36 40 174 38	**12**
DAIRY STREAM	STRM	36 40 174 39	**11**
DAIRY STREAM	STRM	36 40 174 39	**12**
DALE CREEK	STRM	43 20 170 26	**74**
DALE CREEK	STRM	45 30 167 59	**97**
DALE CREEK	STRM	45 30 167 59	**98**
DALE HILL (TRIG)	HILL	45 20 167 58	**97**
DALE HILL (TRIG)	HILL	45 20 167 58	**98**
DALEFIELD	LOC	41 02 175 29	**53**
DALGETY, MOUNT	MTN	44 18 170 36	**86**
DALGETY RANGE	MTNS	44 16 170 36	**86**
DAMFOOL, MOUNT	MTN	43 01 171 27	**75**
DAMFOOL, MOUNT	MTN	43 01 171 27	**80**
DAMONS BAY	BAY	43 53 172 59	**83**
DAMPER, MOUNT (TRIG)	MNT	38 55 174 50	**26**
DAMPIER, MOUNT	MTN	43 35 170 08	**74**
DAMPIER, MOUNT	MTN	43 35 170 08	**77**
DAMPIER RANGE	MTNS	42 46 171 57	**70**
DAN, LAKE	LAKE	44 09 168 40	**88**
DAN PEAK	PEAK	43 14 170 50	**75**
DANA	MTN	44 06 169 13	**78**
DANA PEAKS	PEAK	45 13 167 36	**97**
DANAE, MOUNT	MTN	45 30 167 02	**96**
DANBY HILL	HILL	45 27 167 55	**97**
DANBY HILL	HILL	45 27 167 55	**98**
DANDYS SADDLE	SAD	44 47 168 38	**90**
DANDYS SADDLE	SAD	44 47 168 38	**95**
DANE RIVER	STRM	42 04 173 20	**66**
DANGER ROCK	ROCK	35 21 174 23	**5**
DANGEROUS CREEK	STRM	41 23 173 46	**60**
DANIEL, MOUNT	MTN	44 46 167 43	**94**
DANIELLS, LAKE	LAKE	42 18 172 18	**65**
DANNEVIRKE	TOWN	40 12 176 06	**47**
DANSEYS PASS	LOC	44 59 170 30	**92**
DARBY, LAKE	LAKE	43 10 170 25	**74**
DARBY, MOUNT (TRIG)	HILL	46 36 169 02	**112**
D'ARCHIAC, MOUNT	MTN	43 28 170 35	**74**
D'ARCHIAC, MOUNT	MTN	43 28 170 35	**77**
DARFIELD	POPL	43 29 172 07	**81**
DARFIELD	POPL	43 29 172 07	**85**
DARGAVILLE	TOWN	35 56 173 52	**6**
DARGAVILLE	TOWN	35 56 173 52	**7**
DARK CLOUD RANGE	MTNS	45 55 166 51	**104**
DARK, MOUNT	MTN	43 53 170 03	**76**
DARK, MOUNT	MTN	43 53 170 03	**77**
DARK, MOUNT	MTN	43 53 170 03	**79**
DARK RIVER	STRM	44 50 167 37	**94**
DARK SUMMIT (TRIG)	HILL	36 27 174 37	**11**
DARKNESS PEAK	PEAK	44 24 168 22	**88**
DARKNESS PEAK	PEAK	44 24 168 22	**89**
DARNLEY CREEK	STRM	43 19 170 18	**74**
DARRAN MOUNTAINS	MTNS	44 43 168 03	**89**
DARRAN PASS	PASS	44 42 168 01	**89**
DART RIVER	STRM	41 25 172 39	**58**
DART RIVER	STRM	44 51 168 22	**89**
DART RIVER	STRM	44 51 168 22	**95**
DART STREAM	STRM	42 04 173 42	**67**
DARTMOOR	HSTD	39 29 176 42	**39**
DARTMOOR	HSTD	39 29 176 42	**40**
DARTMOOR	HSTD	39 29 176 42	**42**
DARTS BUSH STREAM	STRM	44 12 170 02	**79**
DARWIN GLACIER	GLCR	43 32 170 19	**74**
DARWIN GLACIER	GLCR	43 32 170 19	**77**
DASHER, MOUNT	MTN	45 09 170 29	**102**
DASHWOOD	LOC	41 39 174 04	**60**
DASHWOOD	LOC	41 39 174 04	**67**
DASHWOOD PASS	PASS	41 37 174 03	**60**
DATAMOS	MTN	44 12 168 44	**88**
DAVAAR	HSTD	42 57 173 04	**72**
DAVID MOUNT	MTN	44 54 170 25	**92**
DAVID PEAKS	PEAK	44 58 168 09	**98**
DAVID ROCKS	ROCK	36 42 175 00	**12**
DAVID ROCKS	ROCK	36 42 175 00	**13**
DAVIDSONS TOP (TRIG)	MTN	45 36 169 42	**100**
DAVIDSONS TOP (TRIG)	MTN	45 36 169 42	**101**
DAVIE, MOUNT	MTN	42 58 171 24	**69**
DAVY CREEK	STRM	41 31 172 39	**58**
DAVY, MOUNT (TRIG)	MTN	42 23 171 21	**69**
DAWN RIVULET	STRM	43 59 168 47	**88**
DAWSON BURN	STRM	46 03 166 46	**104**
DAWSON FALLS	LOC	39 20 174 06	**34**
DAWSON, MOUNT (TRIG)	HILL	39 09 175 07	**36**
DAYS BAY	SBRB	41 16 174 54	**52**
DAYS BAY	SBRB	41 16 174 54	**55**
DE FILIPPI CREEK	STRM	41 50 172 00	**64**
DE LA BECHE	MTN	43 31 170 16	**74**
DE LA BECHE	MTN	43 31 170 16	**77**
DEAD HORSE CREEK	STRM	44 45 169 16	**91**
DEAD MANS CREEK	STRM	44 07 170 31	**86**
DEAD MANS HILL	HILL	42 43 173 21	**72**
DEADMAN STREAM	STRM	42 03 173 58	**67**
DEADMANS POINT	PNT	36 51 175 24	**13**
DEADMANS POINT	PNT	36 51 175 24	**16**
DEADWOOD CREEK	STRM	45 41 167 04	**105**
DEADWOOD (TRIG)	HILL	41 00 175 05	**52**
DEADWOOD (TRIG)	HILL	41 00 175 05	**55**
DEAN BURN	STRM	45 57 167 40	**106**
DEAN HILL	HILL	45 49 167 34	**105**
DEAN HILL	HILL	45 49 167 34	**106**
DEBORAH	LOC	45 06 170 55	**102**
DECANTER BAY	BAY	43 39 173 00	**82**
DECANTER BAY	BAY	43 39 173 00	**83**
DECEIT PEAKS	MTNS	47 05 167 41	**114**
DECEPTION RIVER	STRM	42 48 171 36	**69**
DECEPTION RIVER	STRM	42 48 171 36	**70**
DECHEN, MOUNT	MTN	43 48 169 45	**76**
DECHEN, MOUNT	MTN	43 48 169 45	**79**
DEE CREEK	STRM	41 51 171 58	**64**
DEE CREEK	STRM	44 03 168 23	**88**
DEE HILL (TRIG)	HILL	44 06 168 25	**88**
DEE STREAM	STRM	42 01 173 47	**67**
DEELAW	MTN	43 54 169 09	**78**
DEEP COVE	BAY	45 27 167 08	**96**
DEEP CREEK	STRM	38 32 177 44	**31**
DEEP CREEK	STRM	41 09 172 41	**56**
DEEP CREEK	STRM	41 09 172 41	**57**
DEEP CREEK	STRM	41 09 172 41	**58**
DEEP CREEK	STRM	41 21 173 38	**60**
DEEP CREEK	STRM	42 12 171 56	**63**
DEEP CREEK	STRM	42 12 171 56	**64**
DEEP CREEK	STRM	42 33 171 28	**69**
DEEP CREEK	STRM	43 14 170 11	**74**
DEEP CREEK	STRM	43 59 170 53	**87**
DEEP CREEK	STRM	44 54 168 41	**90**
DEEP CREEK	LOC	44 42 171 03	**93**
DEEP CREEK	STRM	44 54 168 41	**95**
DEEP CREEK	STRM	45 27 169 46	**100**
DEEP CREEK	STRM	45 03 170 30	**102**
DEEP CREEK	STRM	45 31 170 33	**102**
DEEP CREEK	STRM	45 40 169 51	**111**
DEEP CREEK	STRM	45 48 169 43	**111**
DEEP STREAM	STRM	39 17 176 48	**40**
DEEP STREAM	STRM	44 39 170 21	**92**
DEEP STREAM	STRM	45 00 170 13	**92**
DEEP STREAM	LOC	45 42 170 18	**103**
DEEP STREAM	STRM	45 42 170 18	**103**
DEEP STREAM	STRM	46 15 167 46	**106**
DEEP STREAM	STRM	46 15 167 46	**108**
DEEP WATER COVE	BAY	35 12 174 18	**5**
DEEPDALE RIDGE	RDGE	41 50 172 09	**64**
DEEPDALE RIVER	STRM	41 47 172 09	**64**
DEEPDELL CREEK	STRM	45 19 170 31	**102**
DEER SPUR CREEK	STRM	44 32 169 22	**91**
DEER VALLEY	STRM	42 24 172 24	**71**
DEIFFENBACH POINT	PNT	41 14 174 09	**54**
DEIFFENBACH POINT	PNT	41 14 174 09	**60**
DEIFFENBACH POINT	PNT	41 14 174 09	**61**
DEIGHTON CREEK	STRM	45 27 170 21	**101**
DEIGHTON CREEK	STRM	45 27 170 21	**102**
DELAWARE BAY	BAY	41 08 173 28	**59**
DELTA BURN	STRM	45 19 167 27	**97**
DELTA CREEK	STRM	41 58 171 40	**63**
DELTA CREEK	STRM	41 58 171 40	**64**
DELTA, MOUNT (TRIG)	MTN	44 09 168 29	**88**
DELTA STREAM	STRM	42 20 172 36	**65**
DELTA STREAM	STRM	42 20 172 36	**71**
DELTA TARN	LAKE	44 08 168 28	**88**
DENIS CREEK	STRM	41 57 171 40	**63**
DENIS CREEK	STRM	41 57 171 40	**64**
DENIS CREEK	STRM	43 54 168 57	**78**
DENNISTON	LOC	41 44 171 48	**63**
DENNISTON	LOC	41 44 171 48	**64**
DENNISTOUN PASS	PASS	43 25 170 37	**74**
DENNISTOUN PASS	PASS	43 25 170 37	**77**
DENNY, LAKE	LAKE	43 40 171 07	**75**
DENNY, LAKE	LAKE	43 40 171 07	**87**
DENNY STREAM	STRM	43 40 171 07	**75**
DENNY STREAM	STRM	43 40 171 07	**87**
DEPTH PEAK	MTN	45 28 166 50	**96**
DERAA (TRIG)	PEAK	41 09 175 12	**52**
DERAA (TRIG)	PEAK	41 09 175 12	**53**
DERAA (TRIG)	PEAK	41 09 175 12	**55**
DERDAN HILL (TRIG)	HILL	45 35 170 38	**102**
DERWENT CRAGS	ROCK	43 06 171 03	**75**
DESOLATION (TRIG)	HILL	39 32 176 21	**39**
DEUCE, THE	MTN	44 01 169 20	**78**
DEVIL RANGE	MTNS	40 59 172 39	**56**
DEVIL RANGE	MTNS	40 59 172 39	**57**
DEVIL RANGE	MTNS	40 59 172 39	**58**
DEVIL RIVER	STRM	40 59 172 44	**56**
DEVIL RIVER	STRM	40 59 172 44	**57**
DEVIL RIVER	STRM	40 59 172 44	**58**
DEVIL RIVER PEAK (TRIG)	HILL	40 58 172 38	**56**
DEVIL RIVER PEAK (TRIG)	HILL	40 58 172 38	**57**
DEVIL RIVER PEAK (TRIG)	HILL	40 58 172 38	**58**
DEVILS ARMCHAIR	MTN	44 41 167 52	**89**
DEVILS ARMCHAIR	MTN	44 41 167 52	**94**
DEVILS BACKBONE (TRIG)	HILL	41 40 173 27	**66**
DEVILS CREEK	STRM	41 25 173 35	**59**
DEVILS CREEK	STRM	42 47 172 27	**71**
DEVILS CREEK	STRM	44 59 169 18	**100**
DEVILS DIP SADDLE, THE	SAD	40 54 172 40	**56**
DEVILS DIP SADDLE, THE	SAD	40 54 172 40	**57**
DEVILS GAP (TRIG)	HILL	43 50 172 49	**83**
DEVILS HILL (TRIG)	MTN	42 47 173 02	**72**
DEVILS PEAK	PEAK	43 59 171 00	**87**
DEVILS STAIRCASE	HILL	41 05 173 50	**54**
DEVILS STAIRCASE	HILL	41 05 173 50	**60**
DEVILS STAIRCASE	HILL	41 05 173 50	**61**
DEVILS STAIRCASE	MTN	45 15 168 45	**95**
DEVILS STAIRCASE	MTN	45 15 168 45	**99**
DEVILS STREAM	STRM	44 01 170 57	**87**
DEVILS STREAM	STRM	45 44 169 50	**111**
DEVILS THUMB (TRIG)	PEAK	41 27 172 37	**58**
DEVILSKIN SADDLE	SAD	42 29 172 18	**71**
DEVILSKIN STREAM	STRM	42 32 172 17	**71**
DEVINE (TRIG)	HILL	41 13 175 02	**52**
DEVINE (TRIG)	HILL	41 13 175 02	**55**
DEVONPORT	SBRB	36 49 174 48	**11**
DEVONPORT	SBRB	36 49 174 48	**12**
DEWAR, MOUNT	MTN	42 05 171 33	**63**
DIADEM RANGE	MTNS	44 24 169 46	**91**
DIAMOND CREEK	STRM	42 06 172 18	**65**
DIAMOND CREEK	STRM	44 45 167 47	**94**
DIAMOND HARBOUR	HARB	43 38 172 44	**82**
DIAMOND HARBOUR	HARB	43 38 172 44	**83**
DIAMOND LAKE	LAKE	41 05 172 37	**56**
DIAMOND LAKE	LAKE	41 05 172 37	**57**
DIAMOND LAKE	LAKE	41 05 172 37	**58**
DIAMOND, LAKE	LAKE	44 45 168 22	**89**
DIAMOND, LAKE	LAKE	44 45 168 22	**95**
DIAMOND LAKES	LAKE	41 06 172 37	**56**
DIAMOND LAKES	LAKE	41 06 172 37	**57**
DIAMOND LAKES	LAKE	41 06 172 37	**58**
DIANA, LAKE	LAKE	44 15 168 54	**78**
DICK, MOUNT	MTN	45 16 168 41	**95**
DICK, MOUNT	MTN	45 16 168 41	**99**
DICKSON PASS	PASS	43 04 170 57	**75**
DICKSON RIVER	STRM	43 02 170 54	**75**
DIEDRICH, MOUNT (TRIG)	MTN	42 57 171 05	**68**
DIEDRICH, MOUNT (TRIG)	MTN	42 57 171 05	**69**
DIEDRICH RANGE	MTNS	42 59 171 07	**68**
DIEDRICH RANGE	MTNS	42 59 171 07	**69**
DIFFICULTY, MOUNT (TRIG)	PEAK	45 03 169 05	**99**
DIFFICULTY, MOUNT (TRIG)	HILL	45 09 170 37	**102**
DIGGERS CREEK	STRM	42 13 172 17	**65**
DIGGERS HILL (TRIG)	HILL	45 51 167 38	**106**
DIGGERS VALLEY	LOC	35 11 173 20	**3**
DIGGINGS PEAK (TRIG)	PEAK	44 58 170 17	**92**
DILEMMA CREEK	STRM	42 03 171 26	**63**
DILEMMA PEAK	PEAK	43 38 170 05	**76**
DILEMMA PEAK	PEAK	43 38 170 05	**77**
DILEMMA PEAK	PEAK	43 38 170 05	**79**
DILLMANSTOWN	LOC	42 39 171 12	**68**
DILLMANSTOWN	LOC	42 39 171 12	**69**
DILLON CONE (TRIG)	MTN	42 16 173 13	**66**
DILLON CREEK	STRM	41 40 173 45	**67**
DILLON RIVER	STRM	42 24 173 05	**72**
DIME, LAKE	LAKE	43 50 169 17	**78**
DINGLE BURN	STRM	44 25 169 24	**91**
DINGLE PEAK	PEAK	44 29 169 22	**91**
DINGO CREEK	STRM	45 15 169 59	**101**
DIOMEDE, MOUNT	MTN	44 01 169 14	**78**
DIORITE STREAM	STRM	44 26 168 13	**88**
DIORITE STREAM	STRM	44 26 168 13	**89**
DIP CREEK	STRM	44 37 169 32	**91**
DIP CREEK	STRM	45 13 169 26	**100**
DIPTON	LOC	45 54 168 23	**107**
DIPTON STREAM	STRM	46 01 168 19	**107**
DIPTON WEST	LOC	45 53 168 21	**107**
DISCOVERY CREEK	STRM	41 05 172 28	**56**
DISCOVERY CREEK	STRM	41 05 172 28	**57**
DISCOVERY CREEK	STRM	41 05 172 28	**62**
DISMAL SADDLE	SAD	44 48 168 33	**90**
DISMAL SADDLE	SAD	44 48 168 33	**95**
DISPUTE, LAKE	LAKE	45 03 168 33	**95**
DISPUTE, LAKE	LAKE	45 03 168 33	**99**
DISPUTE, MOUNT	MTN	44 08 168 57	**78**
DIVIDE HEAD	HEAD	45 57 166 39	**104**
DIVIDE, THE	SAD	44 50 168 07	**89**
DIXON, MOUNT (TRIG)	MTN	42 43 171 49	**70**
DOBSON	LOC	42 28 171 18	**68**
DOBSON	LOC	42 28 171 18	**69**
DOBSON, MOUNT	MTN	43 56 169 45	**76**
DOBSON, MOUNT	MTN	43 56 169 45	**79**
DOBSON RIVER	STRM	44 11 169 52	**79**
DOCHERTY CREEK	STRM	43 25 170 07	**74**
DOCHERTY CREEK	STRM	43 25 170 07	**77**
DOCHERTY, MOUNT	HILL	43 47 169 19	**78**
DOCHERTY STREAM	STRM	43 18 170 03	**76**
DOCTOR CREEK	STRM	42 56 171 00	**68**
DOCTOR CREEK	STRM	42 56 171 00	**69**
DOCTOR HILL	HILL	42 56 170 57	**68**
DOCTORS CREEK	STRM	41 46 172 14	**64**
DODSONS VALLEY	SBRB	41 15 173 20	**59**
DOG BROOK	STRM	42 39 173 02	**72**
DOG HILL (TRIG)	HILL	41 48 174 05	**67**
DOG HILL (TRIG)	HILL	42 33 173 02	**72**
DOG HILL (TRIG)	PEAK	42 24 173 17	**72**
DOG HILL (TRIG)	PEAK	42 24 173 17	**73**
DOG ISLAND	ISLD	46 39 168 24	**109**
DOG KENNEL	LOC	44 52 171 03	**93**
DOG STREAM	STRM	42 06 173 01	**66**
DOGS HILL (TRIG)	MTN	43 34 171 07	**75**
DOLOMITE POINT	PNT	42 07 171 20	**63**
DOME	PEAK	42 59 171 40	**70**
DOME BURN	STRM	45 45 168 50	**110**
DOME CREEK	STRM	45 38 168 36	**99**
DOME VALLEY	LOC	36 22 174 38	**11**
DOMET, MOUNT	MTN	44 52 170 23	**92**
DOMETT	LOC	42 52 173 13	**72**
DOMETT	LOC	42 52 173 13	**73**
DOMETT, MOUNT	PEAK	41 04 172 19	**56**
DOMETT, MOUNT	PEAK	41 04 172 19	**62**
DOMETT RANGE	MTNS	41 02 172 18	**56**
DOMETT RANGE	MTNS	41 02 172 18	**62**
DON CREEK	STRM	46 23 168 54	**112**
DON JUAN (TRIG)	HILL	39 20 176 28	**39**
DON JUAN (TRIG)	HILL	39 20 176 28	**40**
DONALD CREEK	STRM	41 32 172 44	**58**
DONALD CREEK	STRM	44 00 168 23	**88**
DONALD GLACIER	GLCR	44 14 168 51	**78**
DONALD HILL	MTN	43 21 171 24	**75**
DONALD HILL	MTN	43 21 171 24	**80**
DONALD, MOUNT	MTN	45 04 167 25	**94**
DONALD, MOUNT	MTN	45 04 167 25	**96**
DONALD, MOUNT	MTN	45 04 167 25	**97**
DONALD, MOUNT (TRIG)	MTN	42 59 172 45	**71**
DONALD RIVER	STRM	39 22 176 26	**39**
DONALD RIVER	STRM	39 22 176 26	**40**
DONALD RIVER	STRM	44 14 168 47	**78**
DONALD STUARTS CREEK	STRM	44 55 169 45	**91**
DONALDS CREEK	STRM	41 41 173 58	**67**
DONNE GLACIER	GLCR	44 36 168 02	**89**
DONNE RIVER	STRM	44 42 167 58	**89**
DONNE RIVER	STRM	44 42 167 58	**94**
DONNELLY CREEK	STRM	42 53 170 50	**68**
DONNELLYS CROSSING	LOC	35 42 173 36	**6**
DONOGHUES	LOC	42 54 170 47	**68**
DONOVAN (TRIG)	HILL	40 50 175 41	**49**
DONOVAN (TRIG)	HILL	40 50 175 41	**51**
DOOLAN CREEK	STRM	42 17 171 36	**63**
DOOLAN CREEK	STRM	42 17 171 36	**64**
DOOLANS CREEK	STRM	45 04 169 01	**99**
DOOLANS CREEK (LEFT BRANCH)	STRM	45 05 168 59	**99**
DOOLANS CREEK (RIGHT BRANCH)	STRM	45 05 168 59	**99**
DOOM CREEK	STRM	41 24 173 36	**60**
DOON RIVER	STRM	45 09 167 29	**94**
DOON RIVER	STRM	45 09 167 29	**97**
DORA, LAKE	LAKE	45 13 167 03	**96**
DORA, MOUNT	MTN	42 08 172 44	**65**
DORE PASS	PASS	44 56 167 58	**94**
DORE PASS	PASS	44 56 167 58	**97**
DORE PASS	PASS	44 56 167 58	**98**
DORES STREAM	STRM	40 14 176 10	**47**
DOREY STREAM	STRM	44 12 169 53	**79**
DORIE	LOC	43 53 172 05	**85**
DORIS MOUNT	MTN	44 07 169 02	**78**
DORSET CREEK	STRM	40 49 175 24	**48**
DORSET, POINT	PNT	41 20 174 50	**52**
DORSET, POINT	PNT	41 20 174 50	**55**
DOT, MOUNT	MTN	44 34 168 03	**88**
DOT, MOUNT	MTN	44 34 168 03	**89**
DOTTREL, MOUNT (TRIG)	MTN	44 56 169 08	**90**
DOUBLE BAY	BAY	41 11 173 56	**54**
DOUBLE BAY	BAY	41 11 173 56	**60**
DOUBLE BAY	BAY	41 11 173 56	**61**
DOUBLE CONE	PEAK	45 04 168 49	**95**
DOUBLE CONE	PEAK	45 04 168 49	**99**
DOUBLE HILL STREAM	STRM	43 19 171 22	**75**
DOUBLE HILL STREAM	STRM	43 19 171 22	**80**
DOUBLE HILL (TRIG)	HILL	43 18 171 19	**75**
DOUBLE HILL (TRIG)	HILL	43 18 171 19	**80**
DOUBLE HILL (TRIG)	HILL	45 45 170 32	**103**
DOUBLE ISLAND	ISLD	36 38 175 54	**16**
DOUBLE PEAK	PEAK	45 12 167 16	**96**
DOUBTFUL CREEK	STRM	43 05 171 37	**80**
DOUBTFUL ISLAND	ISLD	45 12 167 42	**97**
DOUBTFUL RANGE	MTNS	42 35 172 17	**70**
DOUBTFUL RANGE	MTNS	42 35 172 17	**71**
DOUBTFUL RIVER	STRM	42 33 172 21	**71**
DOUBTFUL SOUND	SND	45 16 166 51	**96**
DOUBTLESS BAY	BAY	34 55 173 28	**3**
DOUGAL CREEK	STRM	44 01 168 22	**88**
DOUGHBOY BAY	BAY	47 02 167 41	**114**
DOUGHBOY CREEK	STRM	43 41 169 32	**76**
DOUGHBOY CREEK	STRM	43 41 169 32	**79**
DOUGHBOY CREEK	STRM	47 02 167 42	**114**
DOUGHBOY HILL (TRIG)	HILL	47 02 167 44	**114**
DOUGLAS	LOC	39 18 174 28	**35**
DOUGLAS	LOC	39 18 174 28	**44**
DOUGLAS	LOC	44 47 170 52	**93**
DOUGLAS CREEK	STRM	43 07 170 44	**74**
DOUGLAS GLACIER	GLCR	43 42 169 58	**76**
DOUGLAS GLACIER	GLCR	43 42 169 58	**77**
DOUGLAS GLACIER	GLCR	43 42 169 58	**79**
DOUGLAS, LAKE	LAKE	43 58 169 06	**78**
DOUGLAS MOUNT (TRIG)	MTN	43 42 169 34	**76**
DOUGLAS MOUNT (TRIG)	MTN	43 42 169 34	**79**
DOUGLAS NEVE	GLCR	43 41 170 00	**76**
DOUGLAS NEVE	GLCR	43 41 170 00	**77**
DOUGLAS NEVE	GLCR	43 41 170 00	**79**
DOUGLAS PEAK	PEAK	43 32 170 12	**74**
DOUGLAS PEAK	PEAK	43 32 170 12	**77**
DOUGLAS RANGE	MTNS	40 58 172 33	**56**
DOUGLAS RANGE	MTNS	40 58 172 33	**57**
DOUGLAS RANGE	MTNS	40 58 172 33	**58**
DOUGLAS RIVER	STRM	43 40 169 50	**76**
DOUGLAS RIVER	STRM	43 40 169 50	**79**
DOUGLAS SADDLE	SAD	43 00 170 56	**75**
DOUGLAS SADDLE	SAD	44 06 169 13	**78**
DOUGLAS STREAM	STRM	44 32 170 20	**92**
DOVE RIVER	STRM	41 16 172 50	**58**
DOVE RIVER	STRM	42 48 172 33	**71**
DOVEDALE	LOC	41 17 172 54	**58**
DOVEDALE CREEK	STRM	45 11 169 43	**100**
DOVEDALE CREEK	STRM	45 11 169 43	**101**
DOVEDALE (TRIG)	HILL	41 20 172 59	**58**
DOVEDALE (TRIG)	HILL	41 20 172 59	**59**
DOWNE, MOUNT	MTN	43 24 170 18	**74**
DOWNE, MOUNT	MTN	43 24 170 18	**77**
DOWNEY CREEK	STRM	41 06 172 28	**56**
DOWNEY CREEK	STRM	41 06 172 28	**57**
DOWNEY CREEK	STRM	41 06 172 28	**62**
DOWNIE CREEK	STRM	42 08 172 31	**65**
DOYLESTON	LOC	43 45 172 19	**85**
DOZY STREAM	STRM	42 50 172 22	**71**
DRAGONFLY PEAK	PEAK	44 25 168 53	**90**
DRAKE RANGE	MTNS	44 10 168 54	**78**
DRAKE RIVER	STRM	44 11 168 47	**78**
DREYERS ROCK	LOC	40 47 175 47	**49**
DREYERS ROCK	LOC	40 47 175 47	**51**
DRIFT BAY	BAY	45 07 168 45	**95**
DRIFT BAY	BAY	45 07 168 45	**99**
DROMEDARY HILL	MTN	44 30 169 39	**91**
DROMORE	LOC	43 51 171 51	**84**
DROWNING CREEK	STRM	45 59 169 02	**110**
DRUMDUAN (TRIG)	HILL	41 11 173 24	**59**
DRUMMOND	LOC	46 09 168 09	**107**
DRUMMOND CREEK	STRM	45 20 168 53	**95**
DRUMMOND CREEK	STRM	45 20 168 53	**99**
DRUMMOND PEAK	PEAK	43 28 170 15	**74**
DRUMMOND PEAK	PEAK	43 28 170 15	**77**
DRURY	POPL	37 06 174 57	**12**
DRURY	POPL	37 06 174 57	**14**
DRY ACHERON STREAM	STRM	43 24 171 34	**80**
DRY CREEK	STRM	42 52 171 27	**69**
DRY CREEK	STRM	43 12 170 30	**74**
DRY CREEK	STRM	43 52 171 02	**87**
DRY CREEK	STRM	44 53 169 24	**91**
DRY CREEK (LITTLE MAN RIVER)	STRM	43 13 170 25	**74**
DRY RIVER	STRM	41 15 175 23	**53**
DRY RIVER	STRM	40 51 172 50	**57**
DRY RIVER (TRIG)	HILL	41 18 175 22	**53**
DRY STREAM	STRM	42 50 172 52	**71**
DRY STREAM	STRM	42 50 172 52	**72**
DRY STREAM	STRM	44 14 170 05	**79**
DRYBREAD	LOC	44 59 169 40	**91**
DRYBREAD	LOC	44 59 169 40	**100**
DRYBURGH, MOUNT	HILL	44 40 170 26	**92**
DRYDEN BAY	BAY	41 10 174 10	**54**
DRYDEN BAY	BAY	41 10 174 10	**60**
DRYDEN BAY	BAY	41 10 174 10	**61**
DRYSDALE CREEK	STRM	42 03 172 00	**64**
DU FAUR PEAK	PEAK	43 40 170 05	**76**
DU FAUR PEAK	PEAK	43 40 170 05	**77**
DU FAUR PEAK	PEAK	43 40 170 05	**79**
DU FRESNE, MOUNT	MTN	43 33 170 06	**74**
DU FRESNE, MOUNT	MTN	43 33 170 06	**77**
DUBIOUS STREAM	STRM	42 09 173 33	**66**
DUBLIN BAY	BAY	44 39 169 09	**90**
DUCHESS STREAM	STRM	42 28 172 19	**71**
DUCK COVE	BAY	45 45 166 39	**104**
DUCK CREEK	STRM	42 50 171 01	**68**
DUCK CREEK	STRM	42 50 171 01	**69**
DUCK CREEK	STRM	43 07 172 13	**81**
DUCK CREEK	STRM	46 33 168 22	**109**
DUCK CREEK	STRM	46 55 167 46	**114**
DUCK POINT	LOC	45 47 170 18	**103**
DUCK STREAM	STRM	44 11 170 42	**86**
DUESSA PEAK	PEAK	42 13 172 35	**65**
DUFFERS CREEK	STRM	42 19 171 34	**63**
DUFFERS CREEK	STRM	42 19 171 34	**69**
DUFFERS CREEK	STRM	42 59 170 38	**74**
DUFFERS SADDLE	SAD	45 11 169 05	**99**
DUKESHEAD (TRIG)	HILL	41 21 173 52	**54**
DUKESHEAD (TRIG)	HILL	41 21 173 52	**60**
DULL BURN	STRM	46 07 169 36	**111**
DULL BURN	STRM	46 07 169 36	**113**
DUMBARTON	LOC	45 36 169 19	**100**
DUMB-BELL LAKE	LAKE	44 15 169 46	**79**
DUMGREE (TRIG)	HILL	41 37 174 00	**60**
DUMPLING HILL	HILL	44 46 167 45	**94**

DUN FIUNARY	MTN	43 57 170 01	77
DUN FIUNARY	MTN	43 57 170 01	79
DUN SADDLE	SAD	41 21 173 22	59
DUNBACK	LOC	45 23 170 38	102
DUNBACK HILL (TRIG)	HILL	45 25 170 33	102
DUNBAR STREAM	STRM	43 28 171 09	75
DUNCAN CREEK	STRM	44 00 168 23	88
DUNCAN, LAKE	LAKE	45 14 167 23	96
DUNCAN, LAKE	LAKE	45 14 167 23	97
DUNCAN, MOUNT (TRIG)	HILL	41 19 173 53	54
DUNCAN, MOUNT (TRIG)	HILL	41 19 173 53	60
DUNCAN, MOUNT (TRIG)	HILL	41 19 173 53	61
DUNCAN RIVER	STRM	44 12 168 23	88
DUNCAN STREAM	STRM	44 05 170 04	79
DUNCAN STREAM	STRM	43 40 172 59	83
DUNCANS KNOB	MTN	44 26 168 48	90
DUNDAS CREEK	STRM	40 10 175 50	46
DUNDAS, MOUNT (TRIG)	PEAK	40 44 175 27	48
DUNEARN	LOC	46 00 168 10	107
DUNEDIN	METR	45 53 170 30	103
DUNGANVILLE	LOC	42 33 171 19	69
DUNLOP STREAM	STRM	45 54 166 56	104
DUNLOP STREAM	STRM	45 54 166 56	105
DUNMORE	LOC	37 39 174 58	18
DUNMORE (TRIG)	HILL	39 18 176 34	39
DUNMORE (TRIG)	HILL	39 18 176 34	40
DUNN SADDLE	SAD	42 50 171 24	69
DUNNS CREEK	STRM	42 51 171 28	69
DUNNS STREAM	STRM	39 31 174 07	34
DUNOLLIE	SBRB	42 24 171 16	68
DUNOLLIE	SBRB	42 24 171 16	69
DUNOLLY	LOC	40 04 175 36	46
DUNPHY CREEK	STRM	41 59 171 56	64
DUNROBIN	LOC	45 48 169 20	110
DUNSANDEL	LOC	43 40 172 11	81
DUNSANDEL	LOC	43 40 172 11	85
DUNSANDEL CREEK	STRM	41 53 174 03	67
DUNSDALE	LOC	46 11 168 35	107
DUNSDALE	HILL	46 08 168 40	110
DUNSDALE	HILL	46 08 168 40	112
DUNSDALE STREAM	STRM	46 08 168 36	110
DUNSDALE STREAM	STRM	46 08 168 36	112
DUNSTAN CREEK	STRM	45 00 169 46	91
DUNSTAN MOUNTAINS	MTNS	44 56 169 31	91
DUNSTAN PASS	PASS	44 46 169 42	91
DUNSTAN PEAK	PEAK	44 51 169 43	91
DUNSTAN RANGE	MTNS	44 35 169 43	91
DUNSTAN STREAM	STRM	44 25 170 39	92
DUNSTAN (TRIG)	MTN	45 03 169 22	100
DUNSTERVILLE PEAKS	PEAK	45 11 167 02	96
DUNTON CREEK	STRM	45 10 167 53	94
DUNTON CREEK	STRM	45 10 167 53	97
DUNTON CREEK	STRM	45 10 167 53	98
DUNTON PEAK	PEAK	45 14 168 00	97
DUNTON PEAK	PEAK	45 14 168 00	98
DUNTON RANGE	MTNS	45 13 168 01	97
DUNTON RANGE	MTNS	45 13 168 01	98
DUNTROON	LOC	44 52 170 41	93
DUPPA, MOUNT (TRIG)	PEAK	41 13 173 30	59
DURIES PEAK	PEAK	44 40 168 45	90
D'URVILLE ISLAND	ISLD	40 50 173 51	54
D'URVILLE ISLAND	ISLD	40 50 173 51	61
D'URVILLE PENINSULA	PEN	40 52 173 54	61
D'URVILLE PENINSULA (TRIG)	HILL	40 52 173 54	54
D'URVILLE RIVER	STRM	41 55 172 39	65
D'URVILLE ROCKS	ROCK	36 43 175 04	13
DURWARDS CREEK	STRM	44 18 168 15	88
DURWARDS CREEK	STRM	44 18 168 15	89
DUSKY HILL (TRIG)	HILL	45 50 169 09	110
DUSKY SOUND	SND	45 47 166 26	104
DUTHIE, MOUNT (TRIG)	MTN	38 34 174 40	26
DUVAUCHELLE	LOC	43 45 172 56	83
DYERS PASS	PASS	43 37 172 39	82
DYERS PASS	PASS	43 37 172 39	83
DYERS PASS	PASS	43 37 172 39	85
DYERVILLE	LOC	41 15 175 24	53
DYKE HEAD	HEAD	43 53 173 01	83
DYNAMITE GULLY	STRM	42 43 172 41	71
DYNAMITE POINT	PNT	46 55 168 01	109
DYNAMITE POINT	PNT	46 55 168 01	115

E

EALING	LOC	44 03 171 25	84
EALING	LOC	44 03 171 25	87
EARL MOUNTAINS	MTNS	44 57 167 59	94
EARLE, MOUNT	MTN	43 29 170 36	74
EARLE, MOUNT	MTN	43 29 170 36	77
EARNSCLEUGH	LOC	45 13 169 19	100
EARNSLAW BURN	STRM	44 44 168 23	89
EARNSLAW, MOUNT	MTN	44 38 168 24	89
EARS, MOUNT (TRIG)	HILL	40 48 173 55	54
EARS, MOUNT (TRIG)	HILL	40 48 173 55	61
EARSHELL COVE	BAY	45 44 166 35	104
EARTHQUAKE FLAT	LOC	38 16 176 20	21
EARTHQUAKE FLAT	LOC	38 16 176 20	29
EAST ARM (PORT HARDY)	BAY	40 47 173 54	61
EAST BAY	BAY	35 00 173 50	4
EAST BAY	BAY	41 09 174 19	54
EAST BAY	BAY	41 09 174 19	61
EAST BEACH	BCH	34 52 173 11	3
EAST BRANCH (LITTLE VALLEY CREEK)	STRM	45 19 169 29	100
EAST BRANCH HUNTER RIVER	STRM	44 02 169 37	79
EAST CAPE	CAPE	36 14 175 05	9
EAST CAPE	CAPE	37 41 178 33	25
EAST CAPE	LOC	37 41 178 33	25
EAST CAPE	CAPE	47 01 168 14	115
EAST CHATTON	LOC	45 59 169 00	110
EAST DIADEM CREEK	STRM	44 23 169 51	91
EAST DOME (TRIG)	PEAK	45 32 168 41	99
EAST GORE	SBRB	46 06 168 57	110
EAST GORE	SBRB	46 06 168 57	112
EAST HEAD	HEAD	41 13 174 19	54
EAST HEAD	HEAD	41 13 174 19	61
EAST HEAD	HEAD	42 26 173 42	73
EAST HEAD	HEAD	43 41 173 05	82
EAST HEAD	HEAD	43 41 173 05	83
EAST ISLAND (WHANGAOKENO ISLAND)	ISLD	37 41 178 35	25
EAST PEAK	PEAK	44 44 168 05	89
EAST SENTINEL	MTN	43 30 170 38	74
EAST TAIERI	POPL	45 54 170 20	103
EAST TAKAKA	LOC	40 55 172 50	57
EAST TAMAKI	SBRB	36 57 174 53	12
EAST TAMAKI	SBRB	36 57 174 53	14
EAST TAMAKI HEIGHTS	SBRB	36 55 174 56	12
EAST TAMAKI HEIGHTS	SBRB	36 55 174 56	14
EASTBOURNE	USAT	41 18 174 54	52
EASTBOURNE	USAT	41 18 174 54	55
EASTERN BUSH	LOC	45 59 167 46	106
EASTERN HOHONU RIVER	STRM	42 37 171 25	69
EASTERN HUTT RIVER	STRM	41 02 175 13	53
EASTERN PASSAGE	STRA	46 04 166 33	104
EASTERN WAIOTAURU	STRM	40 55 175 12	48
EASY HARBOUR	HARB	47 10 167 34	114
EBENEZER PEAK	PEAK	43 26 170 09	74
EBENEZER PEAK	PEAK	43 26 170 09	77
ECHO STREAM	STRM	43 57 169 50	79
ECHOLANDS	LOC	38 52 175 20	27
ECOLOGY STREAM	STRM	39 12 176 01	38
EDELWEISS, MOUNT (TRIG)	PEAK	41 34 173 13	59
EDEN CREEK	STRM	45 12 170 03	101
EDENDALE	POPL	46 19 168 47	110
EDENDALE	POPL	46 19 168 47	112
EDGAR, MOUNT	MTN	44 44 167 45	94
EDGE PEAK	PEAK	45 52 167 30	105
EDGE PEAK	PEAK	45 52 167 30	106
EDGECUMBE	POPL	37 59 176 49	22
EDGECUMBE	POPL	37 59 176 49	23
EDGECUMBE, MOUNT	MTN	45 46 166 54	104
EDGECUMBE, MOUNT	MTN	45 46 166 54	105
EDGECUMBE, MOUNT (TRIG)	MTN	38 07 176 44	22
EDIEVALE	LOC	45 48 169 21	110
EDIEVALE	LOC	45 48 169 21	111
EDISON, MOUNT	MTN	43 22 170 39	74
EDISON, MOUNT	MTN	43 22 170 39	77
EDISON, MOUNT	MTN	42 40 172 20	71
EDITH, MOUNT (TRIG)	MTN	43 54 171 05	87
EDITH RIVER	STRM	44 58 167 29	94
EDITH RIVER	STRM	44 58 167 29	97
EDITH SADDLE	SAD	44 58 167 35	94
EDITH SADDLE	SAD	44 58 167 35	97
EDITOR HILL (TRIG)	HILL	41 08 173 41	60
EDWARD, MOUNT	MTN	44 00 170 36	77
EDWARD, MOUNT	MTN	44 00 170 36	78
EDWARD, MOUNT	MTN	44 28 168 35	88
EDWARD, MOUNT	MTN	44 28 168 35	90
EDWARD, MOUNT (TRIG)	MTN	45 04 168 56	95
EDWARD, MOUNT (TRIG)	MTN	45 04 168 56	99
EDWARD STREAM	STRM	44 14 170 26	86
EDWARDS ISLAND	ISLD	46 50 168 13	109
EDWARDS ISLAND	ISLD	46 50 168 13	115
EDWARDS PASS	PASS	42 24 172 46	71
EDWARDS RIVER	STRM	42 59 171 36	70
EDWARDS RIVER	STRM	42 27 172 36	71
EDWARDS RIVER, EAST BRANCH	STRM	42 58 171 38	70
EDWARDSON SOUND	SND	45 57 166 38	104
EDWIN BURN	STRM	46 15 167 18	105
EEL CREEK	STRM	42 38 171 24	69
EEL CREEK	STRM	45 53 167 21	105
EGAR THOMPSON, MOUNT	MTN	43 47 170 04	76
EGAR THOMPSON, MOUNT	MTN	43 47 170 04	77
EGAR THOMPSON, MOUNT	MTN	43 47 170 04	79
EGG ISLAND	ISLD	37 33 175 59	17
EGGELING, LAKE	LAKE	43 59 169 09	78
EGGELING, MOUNT	MTN	44 00 169 02	78
EGGELLING, MOUNT (TRIG)	MTN	44 07 168 28	88
EGLINTON, MOUNT	MTN	45 01 167 58	94
EGLINTON, MOUNT	MTN	45 01 167 58	97
EGLINTON, MOUNT	MTN	45 01 167 58	98
EGLINTON RIVER	STRM	45 10 167 49	94
EGLINTON RIVER	STRM	45 10 167 49	97
EGLINTON RIVER	STRM	45 10 167 49	98
EGLINTON RIVER (EAST BRANCH)	STRM	45 03 167 59	97
EGLINTON RIVER (EAST BRANCH)	STRM	45 03 167 59	98
EGLINTON RIVER (WEST BRANCH)	STRM	45 04 167 59	97
EGLINTON RIVER (WEST BRANCH)	STRM	45 04 167 59	98
EGMONT, CAPE	CAPE	39 17 173 45	34
EGMONT, MOUNT (TARANAKI, MOUNT)	MTN	39 18 174 04	34
EGMONT NATIONAL PARK	PARK	39 17 174 04	34
EGMONT PEAK (TRIG)	HILL	39 44 175 47	46
EGMONT VILLAGE	LOC	39 09 174 10	34
EGREMONT (TRIG)	HILL	46 23 169 02	112
EIFFELTON	LOC	44 02 171 41	84
EIGHT MILE CREEK	STRM	42 33 171 17	69
EIGHT MILE JUNCTION	LOC	38 25 175 07	27
EIGHTY-EIGHT VALLEY STREAM	STRM	41 24 173 02	58
EIGHTY-EIGHT VALLEY STREAM	STRM	41 24 173 02	59
EINSTEIN, MOUNT	MTN	42 00 171 36	63
EKETAHUNA	POPL	40 39 175 42	49
ELAINE BAY	HSTD	41 03 173 46	60
ELAINE BAY	HSTD	41 03 173 46	61
ELAINE STREAM	STRM	45 19 167 16	96
ELBOW CREEK	STRM	45 48 167 57	106
ELBOW CREEK	STRM	45 48 167 57	107
ELDER, MOUNT (TRIG)	MTN	44 54 167 20	94
ELDER, MOUNT (TRIG)	MTN	44 54 167 20	96
ELDER STREAM	STRM	44 28 170 59	93
ELDER (TRIG)	MTN	42 13 172 59	66
ELDERSLIE	LOC	45 02 170 51	102
ELDON, MOUNT	MTN	45 16 168 08	98
ELDRIG PEAK	PEAK	45 45 167 26	105
ELEANOR, MOUNT (TRIG)	HILL	43 59 168 36	88
ELEANOR, MOUNT (TRIG)	HILL	42 46 173 20	72
ELEANOR, MOUNT (TRIG)	HILL	42 46 173 20	73
ELECTRIC RIVER	STRM	45 52 167 21	105
ELEPHANT HILL	LOC	44 49 170 51	93
ELEPHANT HILL STREAM	STRM	44 52 170 52	93
ELEPHANT HILL (TRIG)	HILL	44 48 170 48	93
ELEPHANT, THE	MTN	44 35 167 51	89
ELEPHANT, THE	MTN	44 35 167 51	94
ELESPIE	MTN	44 23 168 20	88
ELESPIE	MTN	44 23 168 20	89
ELFIN BAY	BAY	44 57 168 22	95
ELFIN BAY	LOC	44 58 168 23	95
ELFIN BAY	BAY	44 57 168 22	98
ELFIN BAY	LOC	44 58 168 23	98
ELIE DE BEAUMONT	MTN	43 29 170 20	74
ELIE DE BEAUMONT	MTN	43 29 170 20	77
ELIOT, MOUNT	MTN	43 02 171 14	75
ELISE PEAK	PEAK	41 59 172 55	65
ELIZABETH ISLAND	ISLD	45 25 167 07	96
ELIZABETH, MOUNT	MTN	42 41 171 49	70
ELIZABETH, POINT	PNT	42 23 171 13	68
ELIZABETH, POINT	PNT	42 23 171 13	69
ELIZABETH REEF	REEF	35 31 174 29	5
ELIZABETH RIVER	STRM	45 25 167 08	96
ELLA, MOUNT	MTN	42 05 172 35	65
ELLA RANGE	MTNS	42 04 172 34	65
ELLA (TRIG)	HILL	43 07 172 51	82
ELLANGOWAN STREAM	STRM	43 47 173 06	83
ELLEN, MOUNT (TRIG)	HILL	42 48 173 08	72
ELLEN, MOUNT (TRIG)	HILL	42 48 173 08	73
ELLERSLIE	SBRB	36 54 174 50	11
ELLERSLIE	SBRB	36 54 174 50	12
ELLERSLIE	SBRB	36 54 174 50	14
ELLERY, LAKE	LAKE	44 03 168 39	88
ELLERY, MOUNT (TRIG)	HILL	44 03 168 41	88
ELLESMERE	LOC	43 40 172 06	81
ELLESMERE	LOC	43 40 172 06	85
ELLESMERE, LAKE (WAIHORA)	LAKE	43 47 172 31	83
ELLESMERE, LAKE (WAIHORA)	LAKE	43 47 172 31	85
ELLETTS BEACH	LOC	37 05 174 49	12
ELLETTS BEACH	LOC	37 05 174 49	14
ELLIOT, MOUNT	MTN	44 47 167 47	94
ELLIOT, MOUNT	MTN	43 47 169 47	76
ELLIOT, MOUNT	MTN	43 47 169 47	79
ELLIOT, MOUNT (TRIG)	MTN	42 30 171 50	70
ELLIOTT, MOUNT (TRIG)	MTN	41 53 173 31	66
ELLIOTT STREAM	STRM	42 14 173 21	66
ELLIS CREEK	STRM	42 27 172 03	70
ELLIS CREEK	STRM	42 59 170 41	74
ELLIS, MOUNT	MTN	44 05 169 09	78
ELLIS RIVER	STRM	41 18 172 42	58
ELM TREE CREEK	STRM	45 36 167 52	97
ELM TREE CREEK	STRM	45 36 167 52	98
ELMER, LAKE	LAKE	41 04 172 17	56
ELMER, LAKE	LAKE	41 04 172 17	62
ELSDON	SBRB	41 08 174 50	52
ELSDON	SBRB	41 08 174 50	55
ELSTHORPE	LOC	39 55 176 49	42
ELSTHORPE	LOC	39 55 176 49	43
ELSTOW	LOC	37 31 175 38	15
ELSTOW CANAL	CANL	37 20 175 31	15
ELTERWATER, LAKE	LAKE	41 48 174 09	67
ELTHAM	POPL	39 26 174 18	34
ELTHAM	POPL	39 26 174 18	35
ELTHAM	POPL	39 26 174 18	45
ELTHAM	POPL	39 26 174 18	47
ELWOOD, MOUNT	MTN	45 00 167 31	94
ELWOOD, MOUNT	MTN	45 00 167 31	97
EMELIUS ARM	BAY	45 06 167 09	96
EMERALD STREAM	STRM	45 39 167 20	105
EMILY CREEK	STRM	44 03 169 09	78
EMILY HILL (TRIG)	MTN	43 32 171 15	75
EMILY, LAKE	LAKE	43 33 171 14	75
EMILY PASS	PASS	44 01 169 10	78
EMILY PEAK	PEAK	44 45 168 12	89
EMILY PEAKS	MTN	42 09 172 26	65
EMMA, LAKE	LAKE	43 38 171 06	75
EMU PLAIN	PLN	42 39 172 54	71
EMU PLAIN	PLN	42 39 172 54	72
EMU PLAINS	HSTD	42 39 172 52	71
EMU PLAINS	HSTD	42 39 172 52	72
EMU POINT	PNT	36 48 174 55	11
EMU POINT	PNT	36 48 174 55	12
EMU STREAM	STRM	43 12 171 48	80
ENCHANTED STREAM	STRM	41 45 173 12	66
ENCHANTED STREAM	STRM	41 56 173 27	66
END PEAK	PEAK	44 41 168 55	90
END PEAK	PEAK	45 03 167 54	94
END PEAK	PEAK	45 03 167 54	97
END PEAK	PEAK	45 03 167 54	98
END PEAK	PEAK	45 52 167 06	105
ENDEAVOUR INLET	LOC	41 07 174 10	54
ENDEAVOUR INLET	BAY	41 07 174 10	54
ENDEAVOUR INLET	BAY	41 07 174 10	60
ENDEAVOUR INLET	LOC	41 07 174 10	60
ENDEAVOUR INLET	LOC	41 07 174 10	61
ENDEAVOUR INLET	BAY	41 07 174 10	61
ENDERBY, MOUNT	MTN	44 02 169 34	79
ENFIELD	LOC	45 03 170 52	102
ENID PEAK	PEAK	42 12 172 37	65
ENNER GLYNN	SBRB	41 18 173 15	59
ENSOR STREAM	STRM	43 18 171 22	75
ENSOR STREAM	STRM	43 18 171 22	80
ENTRANCE ISLAND	ISLD	45 07 167 48	94
ENTRANCE ISLAND	ISLD	45 07 167 48	97
ENTRANCE ISLAND	ISLD	45 07 167 48	98
ENVS, MOUNT	MTN	43 14 171 38	80
EOSTRE, MOUNT	MTN	44 27 168 52	90
EPPING, MOUNT	MTN	42 05 171 40	63
EPPING, MOUNT	MTN	42 05 171 40	64
EPUNI	SBRB	41 13 174 56	52
EPUNI	SBRB	41 13 174 56	55
EPWORTH	LOC	44 15 171 15	87
EREBUS, MOUNT	MTN	44 42 168 11	89
EREBUS, MOUNT	MTN	43 38 170 32	74
EREBUS, MOUNT	MTN	43 38 170 32	77
EREWHON	HSTD	39 31 175 58	37
EREWHON	HSTD	43 31 170 51	75
EREWHON COL	COL	43 12 170 56	75
EREWHON PARK	HSTD	43 34 170 56	75
ERIC TWINS	MTNS	43 24 170 38	74
ERIN ISLAND	ISLD	45 13 167 41	97
ERINGA (TRIG)	HILL	41 10 175 39	51
ERINGA (TRIG)	HILL	41 10 175 39	53
ERMEDALE	LOC	46 15 168 00	106
ERMEDALE	LOC	46 15 168 00	107
ERMEDALE	LOC	46 15 168 00	108
ERMEDALE	LOC	46 15 168 00	109
ERNEST ISLAND	ISLD	47 14 167 39	114
ERNEST ISLANDS	ISLS	46 57 167 40	114
ERNEST, MOUNT	MTN	44 16 169 15	78
EROS CREEK	STRM	44 20 168 34	88
EROS CREEK	STRM	44 20 168 34	90
ERSKINE, LAKE	LAKE	44 50 168 00	89
ERSKINE, LAKE	LAKE	44 50 168 00	94
ERUA	LOC	39 14 175 24	36
ERUA	LOC	39 14 175 24	37
ESCAPE REEFS	REEF	46 29 167 57	108
ESCAPE REEFS	REEF	46 29 167 57	109
ESK BURN	STRM	45 17 167 25	96
ESK BURN	STRM	45 17 167 25	97
ESK HEAD	HSTD	42 50 172 18	71
ESK HEAD (TRIG)	PEAK	42 52 172 14	70
ESK RIVER	STRM	39 24 176 53	40
ESK RIVER	STRM	39 24 176 53	41
ESK RIVER	STRM	39 24 176 53	42
ESK RIVER	STRM	43 06 171 57	81
ESK SADDLE	SAD	45 12 167 24	96
ESK SADDLE	SAD	45 12 167 24	97
ESK VALLEY	LOC	44 32 171 04	93
ESKDALE	LOC	39 24 176 50	40
ESKDALE	LOC	39 24 176 50	41
ESKDALE	LOC	39 24 176 50	42
ESTUARY BURN	STRM	44 27 169 07	90
ETA CREEK	STRM	41 59 171 38	63
ETA CREEK	STRM	41 59 171 38	64
ETAL STREAM	STRM	45 52 168 08	106
ETAL STREAM	STRM	45 52 168 08	107
ETAL (TRIG)	MTN	45 48 168 02	106
ETAL (TRIG)	MTN	45 48 168 02	107
ETHELTON	LOC	42 53 173 04	72
ETHNE SADDLE	SAD	45 01 167 24	94
ETHNE SADDLE	SAD	45 01 167 24	96
ETHNE SADDLE	SAD	45 01 167 24	97
ETNA, MOUNT (TRIG)	HILL	43 22 171 48	80
ETTRICK	LOC	45 38 169 21	100
ETTRICK BURN	STRM	45 15 167 43	97
EUCLID, MOUNT	MTN	41 58 171 36	63
EULALIE MOUND (TRIG)	MTN	42 19 172 47	65
EULALIE MOUND (TRIG)	MTN	42 19 172 47	71
EULALIE MOUND (TRIG)	MTN	42 19 172 47	72
EUREKA	MTN	43 50 169 29	76
EUREKA	MTN	43 50 169 29	79
EVANS BAY	BAY	41 18 174 49	52
EVANS BAY	BAY	41 18 174 49	55
EVANS CREEK	STRM	43 07 170 37	74
EVANS FLAT	LOC	45 54 169 38	111
EVANS, MOUNT	MTN	43 11 170 56	75
EVANS, MOUNT	MTN	45 48 166 40	104
EVANS, MOUNT	HILL	40 57 172 55	57
EVANS, MOUNT (TRIG)	HILL	43 39 172 47	82
EVANS, MOUNT (TRIG)	HILL	43 39 172 47	83
EVANS PASS	PASS	43 36 172 45	82
EVANS PASS	PASS	43 36 172 45	83
EVANS PEAK	PEAK	45 16 167 04	96
EVANS RIVER	STRM	42 39 171 38	70
EVANSDALE	LOC	45 43 170 34	103
EVELYN, LAKE	LAKE	43 15 171 32	80
EVELYN, MOUNT	MTN	45 06 170 28	102
EVERSLEY	LOC	44 05 170 49	87
EVES STREAM	STRM	41 43 173 05	66
EVES VALLEY STREAM	STRM	41 17 173 07	58
EVES VALLEY STREAM	STRM	41 17 173 07	59
EWE BURN	STRM	45 20 167 45	97
EWE BURN	STRM	45 20 167 45	98
EWE RANGE	MTNS	44 35 169 54	91
EWELME STREAM	STRM	42 25 173 38	73
EXCELLENT SADDLE	SAD	43 09 171 14	75
EXCELSIOR CREEK	STRM	45 38 167 41	106
EXCELSIOR PEAK	PEAK	45 38 167 49	106
EXE STREAM	STRM	44 12 170 43	86
EXETER PEAK	PEAK	43 33 170 42	74
EXHIBITION GULLY	STRM	44 20 170 03	92
EXPEDITION PEAK	PEAK	45 00 167 21	94
EXPEDITION PEAK	PEAK	45 00 167 21	96
EYLES, LAKE	LAKE	45 15 167 28	97
EYRE CREEK	LOC	45 35 168 28	98
EYRE CREEK	STRM	45 32 168 34	99
EYRE CREEK	LOC	45 35 168 28	99
EYRE MOUNTAINS	MTNS	45 26 168 23	98
EYRE PEAK (TRIG)	PEAK	45 20 168 28	95
EYRE PEAK (TRIG)	PEAK	45 20 168 28	98
EYRE RIVER	STRM	43 26 172 33	81
EYRE RIVER	STRM	43 26 172 33	85
EYRETON	LOC	43 25 172 33	82
EYRETON	LOC	43 25 172 33	83
EYRETON	LOC	43 25 172 33	85

F

FABIANS CREEK	STRM	41 31 173 35	59
FAERIE QUEENE (TRIG)	MTN	42 16 172 31	65
FAGAN CREEK	STRM	42 16 171 18	63
FAIRBURN	LOC	35 07 173 25	3
FAIRDOWN	LOC	41 44 171 42	63
FAIRDOWN	LOC	41 44 171 42	64
FAIRFAX	LOC	46 13 168 03	106
FAIRFAX	LOC	46 13 168 03	107
FAIRFAX	LOC	46 13 168 03	108
FAIRFIELD	LOC	43 52 171 48	84
FAIRFIELD	POPL	45 54 170 22	103
FAIRHALL	LOC	41 32 173 54	60
FAIRHALL RIVER	STRM	41 30 173 54	60
FAIRLIE	POPL	44 06 170 50	87
FAIRLIGHT	LOC	45 25 168 40	99
FAIRTON	LOC	43 52 171 49	84
FAIRVIEW	LOC	44 25 171 11	93
FAIRY BAY	BAY	41 07 173 52	54
FAIRY BAY	BAY	41 07 173 52	60
FAIRY BAY	BAY	41 07 173 52	61
FAIRY HILL	HILL	36 13 174 34	8
FALL BURN	STRM	44 45 169 16	91
FALLS CREEK	STRM	41 25 172 02	62
FALLS CREEK	STRM	42 53 170 57	68
FALLS CREEK	STRM	44 14 168 25	88
FALLS CREEK	STRM	44 49 168 05	89
FALLS DAM	DAM	44 52 169 55	92
FALLS RIVER	STRM	40 56 173 03	57
FALSE CREEK	STRM	41 12 172 22	56
FALSE CREEK	STRM	41 12 172 22	62
FALSE INLET	PEN	46 29 169 45	113
FALSE LAKE	LAKE	45 49 166 54	104
FALSE LAKE	LAKE	45 49 166 54	105
FALSTONE CREEK	STRM	44 24 170 12	92
FAMILY PEAKS	PEAK	45 42 167 47	106
FAN STREAM	STRM	43 25 170 41	74
FANAL ISLAND	ISLD	35 56 175 09	9
FANGHILL STREAM	STRM	43 08 171 21	75
FANGHILL STREAM	STRM	43 08 171 21	80
FANNIN BAY	BAY	45 49 166 32	104
FANNIN, MOUNT	MTN	45 20 167 18	96
FANTHAMS PEAK	PEAK	39 19 174 04	34
FARADAY, MOUNT (TRIG)	MTN	42 11 171 30	63
FARDOWNER PEAK	PEAK	43 20 170 23	74
FAREWELL, CAPE	CAPE	40 30 172 41	57
FAREWELL SPIT	SPIT	40 30 172 50	57
FARMER CREEK	STRM	42 02 172 01	64
FARMER POINT	PNT	34 48 173 11	3
FARMER ROCKS	ROCK	34 09 172 10	2
FARQUHARSON CREEK	STRM	42 57 171 15	68
FARQUHARSON CREEK	STRM	42 57 171 15	69
FARQUHARSON SADDLE	SAD	42 58 171 18	69
FARRAR, MOUNT	MTN	43 19 170 39	74
FARRAR PEAK	PEAK	44 15 168 51	78
FAST BURN	STRM	44 23 169 23	91
FASTNESS PEAK	PEAK	44 22 168 48	90
FAUST (TRIG)	MTN	42 29 172 26	71
FEATHERSTON	POPL	41 07 175 19	53
FEBRERO POINT	PNT	45 17 166 50	96
FEILDING	POPL	40 14 175 34	45
FEILDING	POPL	40 14 175 34	46
FELDWICK	LOC	46 00 167 50	106
FELL, MOUNT	PEAK	41 27 173 25	59
FELL, THE	STRM	42 14 173 22	66
FENCOURT	LOC	37 52 175 29	19
FENDALTON	SBRB	43 31 172 36	82
FENDALTON	SBRB	43 31 172 36	83
FENDALTON	SBRB	43 31 172 36	85
FENHAM CREEK	STRM	46 05 167 47	106
FENIAN CREEK	STRM	41 12 172 11	56
FENIAN CREEK	STRM	41 12 172 11	62
FENIAN RANGE	MTNS	41 11 172 16	56
FENIAN RANGE	MTNS	41 11 172 16	62
FENIAN (TRIG)	PEAK	41 14 172 15	56
FENIAN (TRIG)	PEAK	41 14 172 15	62
FEREDAY ISLAND	ISLD	43 48 172 09	85
FERGUS, LAKE	LAKE	44 51 168 07	89
FERGUSON CREEK	STRM	43 10 170 30	74
FERGUSON CREEK	STRM	44 07 169 34	79

FERGUSON, MOUNT	MTN	44 04 169 34	79
FERGUSON, MOUNT	MTN	44 40 168 33	90
FERGUSON, MOUNT	MTN	43 29 170 07	74
FERGUSON, MOUNT	MTN	43 14 170 34	74
FERGUSON, MOUNT	MTN	43 29 170 07	77
FERGUSONS	LOC	42 58 170 44	68
FERGUSONS	LOC	42 58 170 44	74
FERGUSSON ISLAND	ISLD	45 24 167 06	96
FERN BURN	STRM	40 45 169 00	90
FERN FLAT	LOC	35 07 173 33	3
FERN FLAT	LOC	35 07 173 33	4
FERN FLAT	LOC	40 02 175 21	45
FERN GULLY CREEK	STRM	44 40 170 21	92
FERNDALE	LOC	46 11 169 00	110
FERNDALE	LOC	46 11 169 00	112
FERNHILL	LOC	39 35 176 45	42
FERNHILL	LOC	39 35 176 45	43
FERNHILL	LOC	45 03 168 38	99
FERNIEHURST	LOC	42 38 173 20	72
FERNIEHURST	HSTD	42 36 173 20	72
FERNIEHURST	LOC	42 38 173 20	73
FERNIEHURST	HSTD	42 36 173 20	73
FERNSIDE	RSTN	41 05 175 21	53
FERNSIDE	LOC	43 19 172 32	81
FERNSIDE	LOC	43 19 172 32	82
FERNSIDE	LOC	43 19 172 32	83
FERNSIDE	LOC	43 19 172 32	85
FERNTOWN	LOC	40 40 172 39	56
FERNTOWN	LOC	40 40 172 39	57
FERNY GAIR (TRIG)	MTN	41 47 173 39	67
FERRY HILL (TRIG)	HILL	46 00 170 09	103
FETT STREAM	STRM	44 14 170 33	86
FETTERCAIRN (TRIG)	HILL	44 44 170 30	92
FETTES PEAK	PEAK	43 45 169 52	76
FETTES PEAK	PEAK	43 45 169 52	79
FEZ CREEK	STRM	44 20 168 32	88
FEZ CREEK	STRM	44 20 168 32	89
FIDGET STREAM	STRM	42 08 173 36	66
FIDGET STREAM	STRM	42 08 173 36	67
FIELD (TRIG)	HILL	40 51 175 07	48
FIELD (TRIG)	HILL	40 51 175 07	52
FIELD (TRIG)	HILL	40 51 175 07	55
FIERY COL	SAD	44 33 168 14	88
FIERY COL	SAD	44 33 168 14	89
FIFE ROCK	ROCK	46 48 168 23	109
FIFE ROCK	ROCK	46 48 168 23	115
FIGHTING BAY	BAY	41 20 174 12	54
FIGHTING BAY	BAY	41 20 174 12	60
FIGHTING BAY	BAY	41 20 174 12	61
FINDLAY, MOUNT	MTN	43 04 171 18	75
FINDLAY, MOUNT	MTN	43 04 171 18	80
FINEGAND	LOC	46 16 169 44	111
FINEGAND	LOC	46 16 169 44	113
FINGALS HEAD	MTN	44 14 168 44	88
FINLAY HILL	MTN	43 29 170 41	74
FINLAYSONS BROOK	STRM	36 00 174 25	7
FINLAYSONS BROOK	STRM	36 00 174 25	8
FINNIS STREAM	STRM	38 18 175 16	27
FIORDLAND NATIONAL PARK	PARK	44 45 167 45	94
FIORDLAND NATIONAL PARK	PARK	45 09 167 18	96
FIORDLAND NATIONAL PARK	PARK	45 53 166 57	104
FIORDLAND NATIONAL PARK	PARK	45 53 166 57	105
FIRE WOOD STREAM	STRM	44 02 170 42	86
FIREWOOD CREEK	STRM	37 41 175 08	18
FIRST ARM	BAY	45 19 166 57	96
FIRST CREEK	STRM	43 51 170 12	77
FIRST CREEK	STRM	43 51 170 12	86
FIRST WATERFALL STREAM	STRM	43 41 170 37	86
FIRTH OF THAMES	BAY	37 05 175 25	13
FIRTH OF THAMES	BAY	37 05 175 25	15
FIRTH, MOUNT (TRIG)	HILL	41 05 175 18	53
FISH CREEK	STRM	45 11 169 14	100
FISH LAKE	LAKE	42 07 172 55	65
FISH RIVER	STRM	44 07 169 21	78
FISHERMAN ISLAND	ISLD	41 00 173 03	57
FISHERMAN ISLAND	ISLD	41 00 173 03	58
FISHERMAN ISLAND	ISLD	41 00 173 03	59
FISHERMANS HILL (TRIG)	HILL	46 25 169 46	113
FISHERMANS POINT	PNT	43 51 172 23	85
FISHERMANS ROCK	ROCK	41 25 174 58	52
FISHERMANS ROCK	ROCK	41 25 174 58	55
FISHERS STREAM	STRM	46 01 169 57	111
FISHERS STREAM	STRM	46 01 169 57	113
FISHTAIL, MOUNT (TRIG)	PEAK	41 27 173 30	59
FISHTAIL STREAM	STRM	41 23 173 25	59
FITCHETT, MOUNT	MTN	45 38 167 03	105
FITZGERALD, MOUNT (TRIG)	MTN	43 42 172 50	83
FITZGERALD STREAM	STRM	43 29 170 30	74
FITZGERALD STREAM	STRM	43 29 170 30	77
FITZROY	SBRB	39 03 174 06	34
FITZROY BAY	BAY	41 23 174 52	52
FITZROY BAY	BAY	41 01 173 48	54
FITZROY BAY	BAY	41 23 174 52	55
FITZROY BAY	BAY	41 01 173 48	60
FITZROY BAY	BAY	41 01 173 48	61
FITZWILLIAM, MOUNT	MTN	43 10 171 31	80
FIVE FINGERS PENINSULA	PEN	45 42 166 30	104
FIVE FINGERS POINT	PNT	45 45 166 27	104
FIVE FORKS	LOC	45 03 170 46	102
FIVE GULLY STREAM	STRM	43 11 172 09	81
FIVE MILE CREEK	STRM	43 16 170 06	74
FIVE MILE CREEK	STRM	45 11 169 15	100
FIVE MILE LAGOON	LAKE	43 17 170 05	74
FIVE MILE LAGOON	LAKE	43 17 170 05	76
FIVE MILE STREAM	STRM	36 57 175 39	13
FIVE MILE STREAM	STRM	36 57 175 39	15
FIVE MILE STREAM	STRM	36 57 175 39	16
FIVE MILE STREAM	STRM	42 20 172 58	65
FIVE MILE STREAM	STRM	42 20 172 58	71
FIVE MILE STREAM	STRM	42 20 172 58	72
FIVE RIVERS	LOC	45 38 168 28	107
FLAG CREEK	STRM	40 51 176 04	49
FLAG CREEK	STRM	40 51 176 04	51
FLAG PEAK (TRIG)	HILL	43 50 172 59	83
FLAG SWAMP	LOC	45 33 170 41	102
FLAG (TRIG)	PEAK	45 17 169 03	99
FLAGPOLE STREAM	STRM	43 21 171 54	80
FLAGPOLE (TRIG)	HILL	43 21 171 51	80
FLAGPOLE (TRIG)	HILL	43 21 171 51	81
FLAGSTAFF CREEK	STRM	42 28 171 46	70
FLAGSTAFF CREEK	STRM	43 39 169 36	76
FLAGSTAFF CREEK	STRM	43 39 169 36	79
FLAGSTAFF FLAT	FLAT	42 29 171 47	70
FLAGSTAFF (TRIG)	HILL	45 36 168 55	99
FLAGSTAFF (TRIG)	HILL	40 12 176 36	43
FLAGSTAFF (TRIG)	HILL	40 12 176 36	47
FLAGSTAFF (TRIG)	HILL	41 16 175 38	51
FLAGSTAFF (TRIG)	HILL	41 16 175 38	53
FLAMBOROUGH HEAD (TRIG)	HILL	46 24 168 56	112
FLANAGAN CREEK	STRM	40 54 172 27	56
FLANAGANS SUMMIT	PEAK	44 13 168 49	78
FLAT CREEK	STRM	41 04 172 53	57
FLAT CREEK	STRM	41 04 172 53	58
FLAT CREEK	STRM	41 15 173 35	59
FLAT CREEK	STRM	41 56 172 12	64
FLAT HILL (TRIG)	HILL	46 35 168 17	109
FLAT HILL (TRIG)	HILL	45 14 170 21	101
FLAT HILL (TRIG)	HILL	45 38 168 49	110
FLAT ISLAND	ISLD	34 59 173 52	4
FLAT ISLAND	ISLD	36 43 175 52	16
FLAT, MOUNT	MTN	45 36 167 25	105
FLAT, MOUNT	MTN	45 36 167 25	106
FLAT POINT	PNT	41 15 175 58	51
FLAT POINT	PNT	44 47 167 26	94
FLAT ROCK	ROCK	36 27 174 55	9
FLAT ROCK	ROCK	36 27 174 55	11
FLAT TOP	MTN	44 01 169 18	78
FLAT TOP PEAK	PEAK	44 51 168 00	89
FLATSPUR	HSTD	40 57 175 59	49
FLATSPUR	HSTD	40 57 175 59	51
FLAX HILL (TRIG)	HILL	42 30 173 20	72
FLAX HILL (TRIG)	HILL	42 30 173 20	73
FLAX ISLANDS	ISLS	35 55 175 06	9
FLAXBOURNE	HSTD	41 45 174 11	67
FLAXBOURNE RIVER	STRM	41 51 174 11	67
FLAXMERE	LOC	39 38 176 47	42
FLAXMERE	LOC	39 38 176 47	43
FLAXTON	LOC	43 21 172 38	82
FLAXTON	LOC	43 21 172 38	83
FLAXTON	LOC	43 21 172 38	85
FLAXY CREEK	STRM	38 39 176 34	30
FLAXY CREEK	STRM	45 50 168 08	106
FLAXY CREEK	STRM	45 50 168 08	107
FLEA BAY	BAY	43 53 173 01	83
FLECKED PEAK	PEAK	45 07 167 41	94
FLECKED PEAK	PEAK	45 07 167 41	97
FLEETWOOD PEAK	PEAK	45 04 167 16	94
FLEETWOOD PEAK	PEAK	45 04 167 16	96
FLEMING RIVER	STRM	46 35 169 25	113
FLEMINGTON	LOC	40 09 176 27	47
FLEMINGTON	LOC	44 01 171 44	84
FLETCHER CREEK	STRM	41 59 171 53	63
FLETCHER CREEK	STRM	41 59 171 53	64
FLETCHER, MOUNT	MTN	43 27 170 30	74
FLETCHER, MOUNT	MTN	43 27 170 30	77
FLINTS BUSH	LOC	46 16 168 09	107
FLINTS BUSH	LOC	46 16 168 09	109
FLOCK HILL	HSTD	43 08 171 46	80
FLOCK HILL (TRIG)	MTN	43 11 171 45	80
FLOCK HOUSE	HSTD	40 16 175 17	45
FLODDEN CREEK	STRM	45 56 169 14	110
FLOOD BURN	STRM	44 44 168 43	90
FLOOD BURN	STRM	44 44 168 43	95
FLORA SADDLE	SAD	41 11 172 44	58
FLORA STREAM	STRM	41 10 172 41	56
FLORA STREAM	STRM	41 10 172 41	58
FLORENCE HILL (TRIG)	HILL	46 34 169 28	113
FLORENCE, LAKE	LAKE	42 53 171 30	69
FLORENCE, MOUNT (TRIG)	HILL	46 38 168 59	112
FLORENCE STREAM	STRM	45 41 167 20	105
FLORENCE STREAM (NORTH BRANCH)	STRM	45 42 167 14	105
FLORENCE (TRIG)	HILL	44 35 170 43	93
FLOUR CASK BAY	BAY	47 17 167 29	114
FOG HILL	HILL	36 54 175 37	13
FOG HILL	HILL	36 54 175 37	15
FOG HILL	HILL	36 54 175 37	16
FOG PEAK	PEAK	44 31 168 48	90
FOGGY PEAK	MTN	43 17 171 45	80
FOGGY TOP	MTN	44 08 169 10	78
FOHN SADDLE	SAD	44 32 168 16	88
FOHN SADDLE	SAD	44 32 168 16	89
FOIBLE STREAM	STRM	42 36 172 11	70
FOLEYS CREEK	STRM	42 37 171 16	68
FOLEYS CREEK	STRM	42 37 171 16	69
FOLIAGE HILL	HILL	44 57 167 54	94
FOLIAGE HILL	HILL	44 57 167 54	97
FOLIAGE HILL	HILL	44 57 167 54	98
FOOKS STREAM	STRM	42 54 172 05	70
FOOT ARM	BAY	45 11 167 06	96
FOOTSTOOL, THE	MTN	43 41 170 04	76
FOOTSTOOL, THE	MTN	43 41 170 04	77
FOOTSTOOL, THE	MTN	43 41 170 04	79
FORBES, MOUNT	MTN	43 30 170 35	74
FORBES, MOUNT	MTN	43 30 170 35	77
FORBES, MOUNT	MTN	45 48 166 41	104
FORBES, MOUNT (TRIG)	PEAK	45 20 166 52	96
FORBES MOUNTAINS	MTNS	44 33 168 26	88
FORBES MOUNTAINS	MTNS	44 33 168 26	89
FORBES RIVER	STRM	43 28 170 42	74
FORD STREAM	STRM	43 26 171 42	80
FORDELL	LOC	39 58 175 12	45
FORDEN PEAK	PEAK	45 17 167 11	96
FOREST BURN	STRM	45 30 167 39	97
FOREST CREEK	STRM	43 40 170 58	87
FOREST RANGE	MTNS	46 28 169 04	112
FOREST RANGE (TRIG)	HILL	46 29 169 06	112
FORGOTTEN PEAK	PEAK	46 02 166 59	104
FORGOTTEN PEAK	PEAK	46 02 166 59	105
FORGOTTEN RIVER	STRM	44 29 168 16	88
FORGOTTEN RIVER	STRM	44 29 168 16	89
FORGOTTEN RIVER COL	SAD	44 27 168 21	88
FORGOTTEN RIVER COL	SAD	44 27 168 21	89
FORK STREAM	STRM	44 02 170 27	77
FORK STREAM	STRM	44 02 170 27	86
FORKS, THE	LOC	43 16 170 14	74
FORSTER, MOUNT	MTN	45 41 166 46	104
FORSYTH	LOC	45 57 169 44	111
FORSYTH BAY	BAY	41 00 174 02	54
FORSYTH BAY	BAY	41 00 174 02	60
FORSYTH BAY	BAY	41 00 174 02	61
FORSYTH CREEK	STRM	41 21 172 50	58
FORSYTH ISLAND	ISLD	40 58 174 04	54
FORSYTH ISLAND	ISLD	40 58 174 04	60
FORSYTH ISLAND	ISLD	40 58 174 04	61
FORSYTH, LAKE	LAKE	43 48 172 45	83
FORT HILL (TRIG)	HILL	46 03 170 00	111
FORTIFICATION	LOC	46 31 169 00	112
FORTIFICATION CREEK	STRM	45 34 169 40	100
FORTIFICATION CREEK	STRM	45 34 169 40	101
FORTIFICATION HILL (TRIG)	HILL	46 30 168 57	112
FORTIFICATION STREAM	STRM	45 48 170 14	103
FORTROSE	LOC	46 34 168 48	112
FORTROSE (TRIG)	HILL	46 37 168 51	112
FORTUNE, MOUNT (TRIG)	HILL	45 19 170 40	102
FOSSIL CREEK	STRM	42 04 171 27	63
FOSSIL STREAM	STRM	42 54 172 09	70
FOSTER CREEK	STRM	41 23 173 36	59
FOSTER CREEK	STRM	41 23 173 36	60
FOSTER STREAM	STRM	43 14 171 58	81
FOSTERS HILL (TRIG)	MTN	43 13 171 59	81
FOSTERS HILL (TRIG)	HILL	41 00 175 42	51
FOSTERS HILL (TRIG)	HILL	41 00 175 42	53
FOULWIND, CAPE	CAPE	41 45 171 28	63
FOUR BROTHERS PASS	PASS	44 27 168 16	88
FOUR BROTHERS PASS	PASS	44 27 168 16	89
FOUR MILE RIVER	STRM	41 57 171 25	63
FOUR PEAKS	LOC	44 02 171 08	87
FOUR PEAKS RANGE	MTNS	43 57 171 02	87
FOUR RIVERS	LOC	41 47 172 18	65
FOURTEEN MILE BLUFF	CLIF	42 18 171 17	68
FOURTEEN MILE BLUFF	CLIF	42 18 171 17	69
FOVEAUX STRAIT	STRA	46 42 168 08	109
FOWLER CREEK	STRM	41 20 172 42	58
FOWLER PASS	PASS	45 19 167 20	96
FOWLERS PASS	PASS	42 19 172 43	65
FOX CREEK	STRM	40 56 172 09	56
FOX CREEK	STRM	42 42 171 03	68
FOX CREEK	STRM	42 42 171 03	69
FOX CREEK	STRM	43 09 172 23	81
FOX GLACIER	GLCR	43 31 170 07	74
FOX GLACIER	LOC	43 28 170 01	76
FOX GLACIER	GLCR	43 31 170 07	77
FOX GLACIER	LOC	43 28 170 01	77
FOX PEAK	PEAK	43 50 170 47	87
FOX RANGE	MTNS	43 31 170 02	76
FOX RANGE	MTNS	43 31 170 02	77
FOX RIVER	STRM	42 02 171 23	63
FOX RIVER	STRM	43 28 169 59	76
FOX RIVER	STRM	43 28 169 59	77
FOXHILL	LOC	41 26 172 59	58
FOXHILL	LOC	41 26 172 59	59
FOXS CREEK	STRM	43 13 172 40	82
FOXTON	POPL	40 28 175 17	48
FOXTON BEACH	POPL	40 28 175 15	48
FOY PASS	PASS	42 45 171 51	70
FRANCES, MOUNT (TRIG)	MTN	43 55 171 09	87
FRANCES RIVER	STRM	43 25 170 48	74
FRANCIS BURN	STRM	46 15 167 16	105
FRANCIS STREAM	STRM	44 22 170 50	93
FRANKLIN, MOUNT	MTN	44 04 169 03	78
FRANKLIN, MOUNT	MTN	42 03 172 41	65
FRANKLIN, MOUNT	MTN	42 52 171 40	70
FRANKLIN, MOUNT (TRIG)	HILL	45 54 167 54	106
FRANKLIN MOUNTAINS	MTNS	44 58 167 45	94
FRANKLIN MOUNTAINS	MTNS	44 58 167 45	97
FRANKTON	POPL	45 02 168 44	95
FRANKTON	POPL	45 02 168 44	99
FRANKTON ARM	BAY	45 03 168 40	95
FRANKTON ARM	BAY	45 03 168 40	99
FRANZ JOSEF	LOC	43 24 170 11	74
FRANZ JOSEF	LOC	43 24 170 11	77
FRANZ JOSEF GLACIER	GLCR	43 28 170 12	74
FRANZ JOSEF GLACIER	GLCR	43 28 170 12	77
FRASER CREEK	STRM	43 54 169 42	76
FRASER CREEK	STRM	43 54 169 42	79
FRASER CREEK	STRM	44 50 168 13	89
FRASER DAM	DAM	45 13 169 13	100
FRASER GULLY	STRM	41 42 172 43	65
FRASER, LAKE	LAKE	45 53 166 31	104
FRASER, MOUNT	MTN	42 38 171 50	70
FRASER PEAK (TRIG)	PEAK	43 00 170 54	75
FRASER RIVER	STRM	45 15 169 22	100
FRASER STREAM	STRM	43 49 170 21	77
FRASER STREAM	STRM	44 15 170 06	79
FRASER STREAM	STRM	43 49 170 21	86
FRASERS STREAM	STRM	44 01 171 03	87
FRASERTOWN	POPL	38 58 177 24	41
FRAZER STREAM	STRM	40 43 172 22	56
FREAR BAY	BAY	34 58 173 42	4
FRED BURN	STRM	45 23 167 55	97
FRED BURN	STRM	45 23 167 55	98
FRED BURN	STRM	46 13 166 51	104
FRED BURN	STRM	46 13 166 51	105
FREDERICK, MOUNT (TRIG)	MTN	41 42 171 51	63
FREDERICK, MOUNT (TRIG)	MTN	41 42 171 51	64
FREDS HILL	HILL	45 36 169 24	100
FREDS STREAM	STRM	43 50 170 07	76
FREDS STREAM	STRM	43 50 170 07	77
FREDS STREAM	STRM	43 50 170 07	79
FREEHOLD CREEK	STRM	44 16 169 50	79
FREEMAN BURN	STRM	45 27 167 23	96
FREEMAN BURN	STRM	45 27 167 23	97
FRENCH BAY	BAY	43 48 172 57	83
FRENCH FARM	LOC	43 47 172 54	83
FRENCH HILL (TRIG)	HILL	43 46 172 52	83
FRENCH, MOUNT	MTN	44 25 168 43	88
FRENCH, MOUNT	MTN	44 25 168 43	90
FRENCH, MOUNT (TRIG)	MTN	42 41 171 21	69
FRENCH PASS	LOC	37 53 175 32	19
FRENCH PASS	PASS	40 55 173 50	54
FRENCH PASS	LOC	40 56 173 50	54
FRENCH PASS	PASS	40 55 173 50	61
FRENCH PASS	LOC	40 56 173 50	61
FRENCHMAN ISLAND	ISLD	35 52 174 32	8
FRENCHMAN PEAK	PEAK	44 34 168 11	88
FRENCHMAN PEAK	PEAK	44 34 168 11	89
FRENCHMANS SWAMP	LOC	35 18 174 10	5
FRESHWATER RIVER	STRM	46 54 167 58	109
FRESHWATER RIVER	STRM	46 54 167 58	114
FREW CREEK	STRM	43 03 171 03	75
FREW SADDLE	SAD	43 05 171 06	75
FREYBERG, MOUNT	MTN	42 20 172 23	71
FREYBERG RANGE	MTNS	42 20 172 22	71
FRIEDA CREEK	STRM	44 06 168 21	88
FRIEDA, MOUNT	MTN	43 06 171 06	75
FRITZ GLACIER	GLCR	43 29 170 10	74
FRITZ GLACIER	GLCR	43 29 170 10	77
FRITZ RANGE	MTNS	43 29 170 10	74
FRITZ RANGE	MTNS	43 29 170 10	77
FROSTY CREEK	STRM	42 48 170 56	68
FROSTY CREEK	STRM	42 48 170 56	69
FROTH CREEK	STRM	43 13 170 46	74
FRUID BURN	STRM	45 42 169 33	111
FRUITLANDS	LOC	45 21 169 18	100
FUCHSIA CREEK	STRM	42 34 171 12	68
FUCHSIA CREEK	STRM	42 34 171 12	69
FUCHSIA CREEK	STRM	45 03 170 45	102
FUCHSIA CREEK	LOC	45 04 170 42	102
FUGEL, MOUNT	PEAK	41 24 172 14	62
FULL MOON SADDLE	SAD	43 12 170 56	75
FULLARTON STREAM	STRM	45 20 170 16	101
FULTON MOUNT (TRIG)	MTN	45 02 169 21	100
FURKERT PASS	PASS	45 42 167 09	105
FURMISTER CREEK	STRM	42 14 171 48	63
FURMISTER CREEK	STRM	42 14 171 48	64
FURNEAUX, MOUNT (TRIG)	HILL	41 05 174 13	54
FURNEAUX, MOUNT (TRIG)	HILL	41 05 174 13	60
FURNEAUX, MOUNT (TRIG)	HILL	41 05 174 13	61
FUTURITY ROCK	ROCK	44 25 168 23	88
FUTURITY ROCK	ROCK	44 25 168 23	89
FYFE PASS	PASS	43 45 169 59	76
FYFE PASS	PASS	43 45 169 59	77
FYFE PASS	PASS	43 45 169 59	79
FYFE RIVER	STRM	41 37 172 31	58
FYFFE, MOUNT (TRIG)	MTN	42 19 173 37	66

G

GABLE END FORELAND	CAPE	38 32 178 17	32
GABLE ISLET	ISLD	38 32 178 18	32
GABRIEL STREAM	STRM	42 44 172 17	71
GABRIELS GULLY	LOC	45 53 169 40	111
GAER ARM	BAY	45 17 167 09	96
GALA WATER	STRM	39 41 176 34	42
GALA WATER	STRM	39 41 176 34	43
GALA WATER	STRM	39 41 176 34	47
GALATEA	LOC	38 25 176 45	30
GALE, MOUNT (TRIG)	MTN	41 27 173 16	59
GALILEO, MOUNT	MTN	41 56 171 43	63
GALILEO, MOUNT	MTN	41 56 171 43	64
GALLOWAY	LOC	45 13 169 28	100
GALPIN (TRIG)	HILL	40 00 175 26	45
GALPIN (TRIG)	HILL	40 00 175 26	46
GALWAY POINT (TRIG)	PNT	43 24 169 54	76
GAMMA CREEK	STRM	41 58 171 40	63
GAMMA CREEK	STRM	41 58 171 40	64
GAMMACK RANGE	MTNS	43 43 170 19	77
GAMMACK RANGE	MTNS	43 43 170 19	86
GAMMONS CREEK	LOC	43 17 172 09	81
GANNET ISLAND	ISLD	37 58 174 33	18
GANNET POINT	PNT	41 03 174 13	54
GANNET POINT	PNT	41 03 174 13	60
GANNET POINT	PNT	41 03 174 13	61
GAP ROAD	LOC	46 10 168 19	107
GAPES VALLEY	LOC	44 07 171 09	87
GARDEN OF ALLAH	GLCR	43 18 170 43	74
GARDEN OF EDEN	GLCR	43 20 170 41	74
GARDEN POINT	PNT	45 20 167 44	97
GARDEN POINT	PNT	46 47 168 00	109
GARDEN POINT	PNT	46 47 168 00	115
GARDINERS CREEK	STRM	47 08 167 47	114
GARDNER BURN	STRM	45 50 167 09	105
GARGARUS	MTN	43 11 171 29	80
GARGARUS SADDLE	SAD	43 10 171 29	75
GARGARUS SADDLE	SAD	43 10 171 29	80
GARIBALDI, MOUNT	MTN	41 14 172 20	56
GARIBALDI, MOUNT	MTN	41 14 172 20	62
GARIBALDI RIDGE	RDGE	41 14 172 24	56
GARIBALDI RIDGE	RDGE	41 14 172 24	62
GARNET PEAK (TRIG)	PEAK	42 33 172 25	71
GARNOCK BURN	STRM	45 36 167 35	105
GARNOCK BURN	STRM	45 36 167 35	106
GARRY RIVER	STRM	43 15 172 23	81
GARRY STREAM	STRM	46 24 169 32	113
GARSTON	LOC	45 28 168 41	99
GARVIE MOUNTAINS	MTNS	45 26 168 55	99
GASPIPE (TRIG)	HILL	39 14 174 28	35
GASPIPE (TRIG)	HILL	39 14 174 28	44
GATE PA	SBRB	37 43 176 08	20
GATE PA	SBRB	37 43 176 08	21
GATES	MTN	44 28 168 20	88
GATES	MTN	44 28 168 20	89
GATES CREEK	STRM	43 38 169 24	78
GATES, MOUNT	HILL	43 39 169 25	76
GATES, MOUNT	HILL	43 39 169 25	78
GATES, MOUNT (TRIG)	HILL	43 39 169 25	79
GAULT, LAKE	LAKE	43 26 169 59	76
GAULT, LAKE	LAKE	43 26 169 59	77
GAUNT CREEK	STRM	43 19 170 18	74
GAWLER DOWNS (TRIG)	HILL	43 45 171 22	84
GAWLER DOWNS (TRIG)	HILL	43 45 171 22	87
GAWLER STREAM	STRM	43 45 171 19	84
GAWLER STREAM	STRM	43 45 171 19	87
GELT RIVER	STRM	42 31 173 18	72
GELT RIVER	STRM	42 31 173 18	73
GENDARME, MOUNT	MTN	44 47 167 56	94
GENDARME, MOUNT	MTN	44 47 167 56	89
GENOA PEAK	PEAK	42 57 171 10	68
GENOA PEAK	PEAK	42 57 171 10	69
GENTLE ANNIE GORGE	GORG	42 21 171 57	70
GENTLE ANNIE POINT	PNT	41 30 171 57	62
GENTLE ANNIE SADDLE	SAD	40 55 175 27	48
GENTLE ANNIE (TRIG)	HILL	41 10 173 30	59
GEORGE, LAKE	LAKE	46 21 167 46	108
GEORGE, MOUNT	MTN	45 28 167 14	96
GEORGE RIVER	STRM	42 03 173 27	66
GEORGE RIVER	STRM	44 56 167 25	94
GEORGE RIVER	STRM	44 56 167 25	96
GEORGE RIVER	STRM	44 56 167 25	97
GEORGE SADDLE	SAD	42 06 173 45	67
GEORGE SOUND	SND	44 50 167 21	94
GEORGE SOUND (SOUTH WEST ARM)	BAY	44 59 167 24	94
GEORGE SPUR (TRIG)	MTN	42 09 173 44	67
GEORGE STREAM	STRM	42 07 173 50	67
GEORGES HILL (TRIG)	HILL	44 42 169 32	91
GEORGETOWN	LOC	44 55 170 51	93
GEORGINA, LAKE	LAKE	43 19 171 34	80
GEORGINA, MOUNT (TRIG)	MTN	43 19 171 36	80
GERALD, MOUNT	MTN	43 45 170 38	77
GERALD, MOUNT	MTN	43 45 170 38	86
GERALDINE	POPL	44 06 171 14	87
GERALDINE DOWNS	LOC	44 05 171 14	87
GERALDINE FLAT	LOC	44 09 171 14	87
GERMAN CREEK	STRM	44 16 171 14	87
GERMAN, MOUNT	MTN	43 47 170 12	77
GERMAN, MOUNT	MTN	43 47 170 12	86
GERMAN STREAM	STRM	45 58 169 48	111
GERTRUDE SADDLE	SAD	44 45 168 01	89
GIBBS CREEK	STRM	41 26 172 34	58
GIBBS CREEK	STRM	43 20 170 03	76
GIBBS HILL (TRIG)	HILL	40 49 172 59	57
GIBBS, LAKE	LAKE	43 25 170 01	76
GIBBS, LAKE	LAKE	43 25 170 01	77
GIBBSTON	LOC	45 02 168 58	99
GIBRALTAR BURN	STRM	45 51 167 50	106
GIBRALTAR HILL (TRIG)	HILL	45 50 167 51	106
GIBSON BEACH	BCH	37 41 174 48	18
GIBSON SPUR (TRIG)	MTN	42 03 173 48	67
GIBSON STREAM	STRM	42 01 173 49	67
GIBSON STREAM	STRM	44 36 170 18	92
GIBSONS CREEK	STRM	41 30 173 52	60
GIBSONS CREEK	STRM	45 45 169 31	111
GIDEON, MOUNT	MTN	43 12 171 20	75
GIDEON, MOUNT	MTN	43 12 171 20	80
GILBERT ISLANDS	ISLS	45 36 166 40	104
GILBERT, MOUNT (TRIG)	MTN	44 53 168 35	90
GILBERT, MOUNT (TRIG)	MTN	44 53 168 35	95
GILBERTS GULLY	LOC	45 16 169 23	100
GILES CREEK	STRM	42 03 171 50	63
GILES CREEK	STRM	42 03 171 50	64

GILES, MOUNT (TRIG)	MTN	42 21 173 07	72
GILL HILL (TRIG)	HILL	43 59 168 50	78
GILLESPIE PASS	PASS	44 10 169 04	78
GILLESPIES BEACH	BCH	43 25 169 49	76
GILLESPIES POINT (TRIG)	PNT	43 24 169 51	76
GILLIES (TRIG)	HILL	41 19 175 20	53
GILLOWS DAM	DAM	41 47 171 34	63
GILRAY, MOUNT (TRIG)	PEAK	45 01 169 03	99
GIMMERBURN	LOC	45 10 170 00	101
GIRDLESTONE	PEAK	39 18 175 34	37
GIRDLESTONE	PEAK	39 18 175 34	38
GIRDLESTONE SADDLE	SAD	40 43 175 25	48
GIRDLESTONE (TRIG)	PEAK	40 48 175 26	48
GISBORNE	TOWN	38 40 178 01	32
GISBORNE	TOWN	38 40 178 01	33
GISBORNE, MOUNT	HILL	37 31 177 11	23
GISBORNE POINT	LOC	38 03 176 27	21
GISBORNE POINT	LOC	38 03 176 27	22
GIZEH, MOUNT	MTN	43 02 171 26	75
GIZEH, MOUNT	MTN	43 02 171 26	80
GLACIER DOME	MTN	44 20 168 48	90
GLACIER GULLY	STRM	42 14 172 38	65
GLADE HOUSE	HSTD	44 55 167 56	89
GLADE HOUSE	HSTD	44 55 167 56	94
GLADE HOUSE	HSTD	44 55 167 56	97
GLADE HOUSE	HSTD	44 55 167 56	98
GLADE PASS	PASS	44 54 167 59	89
GLADE PASS	PASS	44 54 167 59	94
GLADFIELD	LOC	46 08 168 07	106
GLADFIELD	LOC	46 08 168 07	107
GLADIATOR	MTN	43 43 169 58	76
GLADIATOR	MTN	43 43 169 58	77
GLADIATOR	MTN	43 43 169 58	79
GLADSTONE	LOC	40 40 175 19	48
GLADSTONE	LOC	41 05 175 38	51
GLADSTONE	LOC	41 05 175 38	53
GLADSTONE	HSTD	41 54 173 35	66
GLADSTONE	LOC	42 32 171 09	68
GLADSTONE	LOC	42 32 171 09	69
GLADSTONE	LOC	44 36 169 19	91
GLADSTONE	SBRB	46 21 168 24	109
GLADSTONE, MOUNT	MTN	45 34 167 09	105
GLADSTONE, MOUNT (TRIG)	MTN	41 59 173 36	66
GLADSTONE PEAK	PEAK	45 39 167 55	106
GLADSTONE STREAM	STRM	44 09 170 04	79
GLADWISH, MOUNT (TRIG)	MTN	44 19 169 34	91
GLAISNOCK RIVER	STRM	45 00 167 42	94
GLAISNOCK RIVER	STRM	45 00 167 42	97
GLAISNOCK WILDERNESS AREA	PARK	44 55 167 34	94
GLAISNOCK WILDERNESS AREA	PARK	44 55 167 34	97
GLASGOW BAY	BAY	41 18 174 14	54
GLASGOW BAY	BAY	41 18 174 14	60
GLASGOW BAY	BAY	41 18 174 14	61
GLASGOW RANGE	MTNS	41 36 172 04	62
GLASNEVIN	LOC	43 06 172 44	82
GLASSEYE CREEK	STRM	41 24 172 04	62
GLAZEBROOK STREAM	STRM	41 51 173 21	66
GLEDKNOWE (TRIG)	HILL	45 57 170 14	103
GLEN AFTON	LOC	37 37 175 02	18
GLEN ALPIN PASS	PASS	45 47 166 46	104
GLEN BOUIE STREAM	STRM	44 39 170 03	92
GLEN COLWYN	HSTD	42 37 173 23	72
GLEN COLWYN	HSTD	42 37 173 23	73
GLEN CREEK	STRM	44 31 170 03	92
GLEN EDEN	SBRB	36 55 174 39	11
GLEN EDEN	SBRB	36 55 174 39	12
GLEN EDEN	SBRB	36 55 174 39	14
GLEN INNES	SBRB	36 53 174 51	11
GLEN INNES	SBRB	36 53 174 51	12
GLEN JON STREAM	STRM	42 52 173 05	72
GLEN MASSEY	LOC	37 40 175 04	18
GLEN MURRAY	LOC	37 27 174 58	14
GLEN OROUA	LOC	40 20 175 25	48
GLEN PARK	LOC	45 26 170 40	102
GLENALLAN STREAM	STRM	42 37 172 46	71
GLENARIFFE STREAM	STRM	43 19 171 23	75
GLENARIFFE STREAM	STRM	43 19 171 23	80
GLENAVY	LOC	44 55 171 06	93
GLENBERVIE	LOC	35 40 174 21	5
GLENBERVIE	LOC	35 40 174 21	7
GLENBERVIE	LOC	35 40 174 21	8
GLENBROOK	LOC	37 12 174 45	12
GLENBROOK	LOC	37 12 174 45	14
GLENBROOK BEACH	LOC	37 10 174 43	12
GLENBROOK BEACH	LOC	37 10 174 43	14
GLENBURN	HSTD	43 04 172 17	81
GLENCAIRN CREEK	STRM	44 38 168 39	90
GLENCAIRN, MOUNT	MTN	43 58 169 53	79
GLENCOE RIVER	STRM	42 46 172 33	71
GLENDHU BAY	LOC	44 40 169 00	90
GLENDHU (TRIG)	HILL	42 58 173 02	72
GLENDU	HSTD	41 22 175 44	51
GLENDU	HSTD	41 22 175 44	53
GLENDU ROCKS	ROCK	41 23 175 45	51
GLENDU ROCKS	ROCK	41 23 175 45	53
GLENDUAN	LOC	41 11 173 22	59
GLENFIELD	LOC	36 47 174 43	11
GLENFIELD	LOC	36 47 174 43	12
GLENGARRY	LOC	41 50 172 15	64
GLENGARRY	SBRB	46 24 168 23	109
GLENGARRY PEAK	PEAK	45 14 167 08	96
GLENGARRY STREAM	STRM	41 50 172 15	64
GLENGARRY (TRIG)	HILL	43 07 172 46	82
GLENGYLE	MTN	44 28 168 42	88
GLENGYLE	MTN	44 28 168 42	90
GLENHAM	LOC	46 25 168 51	112
GLENHOPE	LOC	41 39 172 39	58
GLENHOPE	LOC	41 39 172 39	65
GLENHOPE	HSTD	42 35 172 33	71
GLENISLA, MOUNT	MTN	43 56 169 53	79
GLENITI	LOC	44 23 171 11	93
GLENKENICH	LOC	45 58 169 14	110
GLENLEDI	LOC	46 11 170 05	103
GLENLEDI STREAM	STRM	46 12 170 06	103
GLENLEE	HSTD	41 53 173 36	66
GLENLEE NORTH	MTN	41 49 173 38	67
GLENLEITH	SBRB	45 51 170 29	103
GLENMARK	HSTD	43 01 172 47	82
GLENMARY, MOUNT	MTN	43 59 169 53	79
GLENNIE, MOUNT (TRIG)	PEAK	41 34 173 01	58
GLENNIE, MOUNT (TRIG)	PEAK	41 34 173 01	59
GLENOMARU	LOC	46 23 169 40	113
GLENOMARU STREAM	STRM	46 20 169 44	113
GLENOMARU (TRIG)	HILL	46 21 169 40	111
GLENOMARU (TRIG)	HILL	46 21 169 40	113
GLENORCHY	LOC	44 51 168 23	89
GLENORCHY	LOC	44 51 168 23	95
GLENORE	LOC	46 06 169 52	111
GLENORE	LOC	46 06 169 52	113
GLENRAE RIVER	STRM	42 49 172 30	71
GLENRAE SADDLE	SAD	42 19 172 38	65
GLENRAE SADDLE	SAD	42 19 172 38	71
GLENROCK STREAM	STRM	43 19 171 24	75
GLENROCK STREAM	STRM	43 19 171 24	80
GLENROSS	HSTD	39 27 176 27	39
GLENROSS	HSTD	39 27 176 27	40
GLENROY RIVER	STRM	42 00 172 20	65
GLENROY RIVER, EAST BRANCH	STRM	42 01 172 20	65
GLENSIDE	SBRB	41 12 174 49	52
GLENSIDE	SBRB	41 12 174 49	55
GLENTHORNE STREAM	STRM	43 13 171 27	75
GLENTHORNE STREAM	STRM	43 13 171 27	80
GLENTUI	LOC	43 14 172 17	81
GLENTUI RIVER	STRM	43 14 172 18	81
GLENTUNNEL	LOC	43 29 171 56	80
GLENTUNNEL	LOC	43 29 171 56	81
GLENURE	LOC	45 53 168 31	107
GLENURE HILL	HSTD	45 53 168 29	107
GLENVAR	LOC	36 42 174 43	11
GLENVAR	LOC	36 42 174 43	12
GLINKES GULLY	LOC	36 05 173 51	7
GLOIN PEAK, MOUNT	MTN	43 41 169 48	76
GLOIN PEAK, MOUNT	MTN	43 41 169 48	79
GLORIANA PEAK	PEAK	42 16 172 29	65
GLORIOUS, MOUNT	MTN	43 40 169 56	76
GLORIOUS, MOUNT	MTN	43 40 169 56	77
GLORIOUS, MOUNT	MTN	43 40 169 56	79
GLORIT	LOC	36 28 174 27	10
GLORIT	LOC	36 28 174 27	11
GLOSTER RIVER	STRM	42 16 173 18	66
GLYNN WYE	HSTD	42 36 172 31	71
GLYNN WYE RANGE	MTNS	42 40 172 25	71
GOAL PASSAGE	STRA	45 18 166 53	96
GOAT CREEK	STRM	41 36 172 12	62
GOAT HILL	PEAK	42 50 171 36	69
GOAT HILL	PEAK	42 50 171 36	70
GOAT HILL (TRIG)	HILL	41 25 173 11	59
GOAT HILL (TRIG)	HILL	41 06 173 38	60
GOAT HILLS STREAM	STRM	42 30 173 19	72
GOAT HILLS STREAM	STRM	42 30 173 19	73
GOAT ISLAND	ISLD	36 16 174 48	11
GOAT PASS	PASS	42 54 171 37	69
GOAT PASS	PASS	42 54 171 37	70
GOAT POINT	PNT	43 50 173 06	83
GODLEY GLACIER	GLCR	43 27 170 32	74
GODLEY GLACIER	GLCR	43 27 170 32	77
GODLEY HEAD	HEAD	43 35 172 48	82
GODLEY HEAD	HEAD	43 35 172 48	83
GODLEY PEAK	PEAK	43 22 171 17	75
GODLEY PEAK	PEAK	43 22 171 17	80
GODLEY RIVER	STRM	43 47 170 32	77
GODLEY STREAM	STRM	43 24 171 16	75
GODLEY STREAM	STRM	43 24 171 16	80
GOETHE, MOUNT	MTN	43 19 170 51	75
GOG (TRIG)	HILL	47 12 167 33	114
GOLA PEAK (TRIG)	MTN	42 57 172 21	71
GOLD ARM	BAY	45 06 167 08	96
GOLD BURN	STRM	44 52 168 49	90
GOLD BURN	STRM	44 52 168 49	95
GOLD BURN	STRM	46 12 166 43	104
GOLD BURN (EAST BRANCH)	STRM	46 12 166 43	104
GOLD BURN (WEST BRANCH)	STRM	46 12 166 43	104
GOLD CREEK	STRM	39 23 176 25	39
GOLD CREEK	STRM	39 23 176 25	40
GOLD CREEK	STRM	39 45 176 14	47
GOLD, MOUNT	MTN	44 35 169 10	90
GOLDEN BAY	BAY	40 40 172 49	57
GOLDEN CROSS	LOC	37 20 175 47	17
GOLDEN CROWN (TRIG)	HILL	39 38 176 19	47
GOLDEN DOWNS	LOC	41 33 172 53	58
GOLDEN SPRINGS	SPR	38 28 176 18	29
GOLDEN VALLEY	LOC	37 22 175 54	17
GOLDIE HILL (TRIG)	HILL	46 02 167 28	106
GOLDIE HILL (TRIG)	HILL	46 02 167 28	105
GOLDNEY RIVER	STRM	43 15 171 34	80
GOLDSBOROUGH	LOC	42 41 171 07	68
GOLDSBOROUGH	LOC	42 41 171 07	69
GOLGOTHA	HILL	43 28 171 50	80
GOLLANS STREAM	STRM	41 22 174 52	52
GOLLANS STREAM	STRM	41 22 174 52	55
GOMORRAH, MOUNT (TRIG)	PEAK	41 23 172 35	58
GONVILLE	SBRB	39 56 175 01	45
GOODWOOD	LOC	45 32 170 43	102
GOOSE BAY	BAY	42 29 173 32	72
GOOSE BAY	BAY	42 29 173 32	73
GOOSE COVE	BAY	45 41 166 33	104
GOOSE ISLAND	ISLD	47 11 167 32	114
GOOSEBERRY STREAM	STRM	44 00 170 54	87
GOOSEY, MOUNT (TRIG)	MTN	42 26 173 07	72
GORDON	LOC	37 41 175 49	19
GORDON	LOC	37 41 175 49	20
GORDON CREEK	STRM	41 34 172 53	58
GORDON CREEK	STRM	42 08 171 35	63
GORDON CREEK	STRM	43 30 169 44	76
GORDON GULLY	STRM	43 28 171 04	75
GORDON, MOUNT (TRIG)	MTN	42 21 173 01	72
GORDON PEAK	MTN	45 25 169 27	100
GORDON RANGE	MTNS	41 33 173 00	58
GORDON RANGE	MTNS	41 33 173 00	59
GORDON STREAM	STRM	41 56 173 08	66
GORDON STREAM	STRM	46 02 168 44	110
GORDON STREAM	STRM	46 02 168 44	112
GORDONS PYRAMID (TRIG)	HILL	41 11 172 41	56
GORDONS PYRAMID (TRIG)	HILL	41 11 172 41	57
GORDONS STREAM	STRM	44 29 171 01	93
GORDONS VALLEY	LOC	44 27 171 02	93
GORDONTON	LOC	37 40 175 18	19
GORE	TOWN	46 06 168 56	110
GORE	TOWN	46 06 168 56	112
GORE BASIN (TRIG)	MTN	42 20 173 19	66
GORE BASIN (TRIG)	MTN	42 20 173 19	72
GORE BASIN (TRIG)	MTN	42 20 173 19	73
GORE BAY	LOC	42 52 173 18	72
GORE BAY	LOC	42 52 173 18	73
GORE, MOUNT (TRIG)	MTN	42 19 171 59	64
GORE, MOUNT (TRIG)	MTN	42 19 171 59	70
GORE, PORT	HARB	41 01 174 14	54
GORE, PORT	HARB	41 01 174 14	60
GORE, PORT	HARB	41 01 174 14	61
GORE STREAM	STRM	42 15 173 21	66
GORGE BURN	STRM	45 18 168 15	95
GORGE BURN	STRM	45 18 167 26	97
GORGE BURN	STRM	45 18 168 15	98
GORGE CREEK	STRM	42 11 171 24	63
GORGE CREEK	STRM	44 12 168 17	88
GORGE CREEK	STRM	45 00 169 55	92
GORGE CREEK	STRM	45 32 167 56	97
GORGE CREEK	STRM	45 32 167 56	98
GORGE CREEK	LOC	45 23 169 16	100
GORGE CREEK	STRM	45 23 169 18	100
GORGE CREEK	STRM	45 00 169 55	101
GORGE CREEK	STRM	45 41 169 06	110
GORGE CREEK	STRM	47 09 167 59	115
GORGE CREEK, THE	STRM	40 57 172 49	57
GORGE HILL (TRIG)	HILL	44 43 170 33	92
GORGE HILL (TRIG)	HILL	46 05 170 03	103
GORGE ISLANDS	ISLS	44 11 168 11	88
GORGE PLATEAU (TRIG)	MTN	44 16 168 21	88
GORGE RIVER	STRM	44 11 168 12	88
GORGE ROAD	LOC	46 28 168 42	112
GORGE STREAM	STRM	39 23 176 31	39
GORGE STREAM	STRM	39 23 176 31	40
GORGE STREAM	STRM	39 23 176 31	42
GORGE STREAM	STRM	39 38 176 30	47
GORGE STREAM	STRM	42 36 172 34	71
GORGE STREAM	STRM	46 15 167 56	106
GORGE STREAM	STRM	46 15 167 56	107
GORGE STREAM	STRM	46 15 167 56	108
GORGE STREAM	STRM	46 15 167 56	109
GORGE STREAM	STRM	46 28 169 15	112
GORGE STREAM	STRM	46 28 169 15	113
GORILLA STREAM	STRM	43 46 170 08	77
GORILLA STREAM	STRM	43 46 170 08	80
GORMAN STREAM	STRM	44 29 170 41	93
GOSLING STREAM	STRM	41 46 173 24	66
GOUGHS BAY	BAY	43 49 173 06	83
GOULAND CREEK	STRM	40 57 172 15	56
GOULAND DOWNS	PLAT	40 54 172 19	56
GOULAND, MOUNT (TRIG)	HILL	40 57 172 23	56
GOULAND RANGE	MTNS	40 57 172 23	56
GOULDS ROAD	LOC	43 39 172 08	81
GOULDS ROAD	LOC	43 39 172 08	85
GOULTER HILL (TRIG)	HILL	41 33 173 48	60
GOULTER RIVER	STRM	41 39 173 13	59
GOVERNORS BAY	LOC	43 38 172 39	82
GOVERNORS BAY	BAY	43 38 172 40	82
GOVERNORS BAY	LOC	43 38 172 39	83
GOVERNORS BAY	BAY	43 38 172 40	83
GOVERNORS BAY	LOC	43 38 172 39	85
GOVERNORS BAY	BAY	43 38 172 40	85
GOW, MOUNT	MTN	43 50 169 43	76
GOW, MOUNT	MTN	43 50 169 43	79
GOWAN HILL (TRIG)	HILL	45 55 168 04	106
GOWAN HILL (TRIG)	HILL	45 55 168 04	107
GOWAN RIVER	STRM	41 48 172 36	65
GOWANBRIDGE	LOC	41 43 172 33	65
GOWS CREEK	STRM	42 24 171 31	69
GRACE BURN	STRM	46 13 166 47	104
GRACE CREEK	STRM	41 10 172 28	56
GRACE CREEK	STRM	41 10 172 28	57
GRACE CREEK	STRM	41 10 172 28	62
GRACE, LAKE	LAKE	42 56 171 59	70
GRACE, MOUNT (TRIG)	HILL	41 20 174 56	52
GRACE, MOUNT (TRIG)	HILL	41 20 174 56	55
GRACEFIELD	SBRB	41 14 174 55	52
GRACEFIELD	SBRB	41 14 174 55	55
GRAEME (TRIG)	HILL	43 40 172 58	82
GRAEME (TRIG)	HILL	43 40 172 58	83
GRAF SPEE	MTN	43 33 170 40	74
GRAHAM CREEK	STRM	41 39 172 50	65
GRAHAM, MOUNT (TRIG)	MTN	42 50 171 06	68
GRAHAM, MOUNT (TRIG)	MTN	42 50 171 06	69
GRAHAM RIVER	STRM	41 16 174 04	54
GRAHAM RIVER	STRM	41 13 172 50	58
GRAHAM RIVER	STRM	41 16 174 04	60
GRAHAM RIVER	STRM	41 16 174 04	61
GRAHAM RIVER, NORTH BRANCH	STRM	41 12 172 49	58
GRAHAM RIVER, SOUTH BRANCH	STRM	41 12 172 49	58
GRAHAM SADDLE	SAD	43 30 170 16	74
GRAHAM SADDLE	SAD	43 30 170 16	77
GRAHAMS BEACH	LOC	37 03 174 40	12
GRAHAMS BEACH	LOC	37 03 174 40	14
GRAHAMS POINT	PNT	41 04 173 34	59
GRAHAMS STREAM	STRM	37 00 175 51	16
GRAHAMS STREAM	STRM	37 00 175 51	17
GRAMPIAN MOUNTAINS	MTNS	44 17 170 31	86
GRAMPIAN STREAM	STRM	44 28 170 40	92
GRAND DUCHESS, THE	MTN	42 27 172 18	71
GRAND PLATEAU	PLAT	43 35 170 10	74
GRAND PLATEAU	PLAT	43 35 170 10	77
GRANDVIEW CREEK	STRM	44 36 169 18	91
GRANDVIEW MOUNTAIN	MTN	44 39 169 21	91
GRANGE RIDGE	RDGE	41 10 172 23	56
GRANGE RIDGE	RDGE	41 10 172 23	62
GRANITE CREEK	STRM	41 17 172 06	62
GRANITE CREEK	STRM	41 41 172 07	64
GRANITE CREEK	STRM	42 57 171 00	68
GRANITE CREEK	STRM	42 56 170 43	68
GRANITE CREEK	STRM	42 57 171 00	69
GRANITE CREEK	STRM	42 27 171 47	70
GRANITE CREEK	STRM	42 34 171 41	70
GRANITE HILL (TRIG)	PEAK	42 37 171 38	70
GRANITE KNOB	HILL	47 06 167 47	114
GRANITE PINNACLE	PEAK	42 08 172 17	65
GRANITY	LOC	41 38 171 51	62
GRANITY CREEK	STRM	41 28 172 34	58
GRANITY CREEK	STRM	41 42 172 32	65
GRANITY CREEK	STRM	42 06 172 20	65
GRANITY STREAM	STRM	46 12 167 55	106
GRANITY STREAM	STRM	46 12 167 55	107
GRANITY STREAM	STRM	46 12 167 55	108
GRANT (TRIG)	HILL	40 41 175 55	49
GRANT BURN	STRM	46 14 167 01	105
GRANT STREAM	STRM	42 56 172 09	70
GRANTHAM RIVER	STRM	42 34 172 42	71
GRANTS LOOKOUT (TRIG)	HILL	41 05 174 09	54
GRANTS LOOKOUT (TRIG)	HILL	41 05 174 09	60
GRANTS LOOKOUT (TRIG)	HILL	41 05 174 09	61
GRANTS TOP (TRIG)	MTN	43 52 171 04	84
GRANVILLE	LOC	42 19 171 39	63
GRANVILLE	LOC	42 19 171 39	69
GRANVILLE	LOC	42 19 171 39	70
GRASMERE	HSTD	43 04 171 44	80
GRASMERE	SBRB	46 23 168 20	109
GRASMERE, LAKE	LAKE	43 04 171 46	80
GRASS BURN	STRM	46 01 167 51	106
GRASSMERE, LAKE	LAKE	41 44 174 10	67
GRASSY CREEK	STRM	45 56 167 42	106
GRAVE TALBOT PASS	PASS	44 44 167 59	89
GRAVE TALBOT PASS	PASS	44 44 167 59	94
GRAVE, LAKE	LAKE	44 49 167 37	94
GRAVE, MOUNT	MTN	44 36 167 57	89
GRAVE, MOUNT	MTN	44 36 167 57	94
GRAY HILL	PEAK	42 57 171 58	70
GRAY RIVER	STRM	46 06 166 44	104
GRAYS CORNER	LOC	44 52 171 04	93
GRAYS HILLS	HILL	44 16 170 24	86
GRAYS HILLS	LOC	44 20 170 22	92
GRAYS RIVER	STRM	44 15 170 21	86
GRAYSON PEAK	PEAK	44 53 170 21	92
GREANEY, LAKE	LAKE	44 06 168 47	78
GREAT BARRIER ISLAND	ISLD	36 13 175 24	9
GREAT EXHIBITION BAY	BAY	34 36 173 04	2
GREAT ISLAND	ISLD	34 10 172 08	2
GREAT ISLAND	ISLD	43 51 172 10	85
GREAT ISLAND	ISLD	45 60 166 33	104
GREAT MERCURY ISLAND	ISLD	36 37 175 48	16
GREAT MOSS SWAMP	SWMP	45 34 169 53	101
GREAT ROCK	MTN	44 40 169 23	91
GREAT UNKNOWN	MTN	43 20 170 35	74
GREATFORD	LOC	40 08 175 25	45
GREATFORD	LOC	40 08 175 25	46
GREBE RIVER	STRM	45 35 167 22	105
GRECIAN STREAM	STRM	41 08 172 42	57
GRECIAN STREAM	STRM	41 08 172 42	58
GREEN BURN	STRM	42 24 173 27	72
GREEN BURN	STRM	42 24 173 27	73
GREEN BURN	STRM	45 44 168 13	107
GREEN BUSH, THE (TRIG)	HILL	45 47 169 34	111
GREEN GULLY	STRM	44 51 170 15	92
GREEN HEAD	HEAD	45 40 170 39	102
GREEN HILL	PEAK	42 52 171 49	70
GREEN HILL (TRIG)	HILL	42 47 172 40	71
GREEN HILLS	HSTD	42 25 173 22	72
GREEN HILLS	HSTD	42 25 173 22	73
GREEN HILLS	LOC	44 49 171 03	93
GREEN ISLAND	ISLD	36 39 175 51	16
GREEN ISLAND	ISLD	45 57 170 23	103
GREEN ISLAND	USAT	45 54 170 25	103
GREEN ISLAND	ISLD	46 46 168 34	115
GREEN LAKE	LAKE	45 48 167 24	105
GREEN, MOUNT	MTN	43 30 170 19	74
GREEN, MOUNT	MTN	43 30 170 19	77
GREEN POINT	PNT	41 07 174 48	52
GREEN POINT	PNT	41 07 174 48	55
GREEN SADDLE	SAD	40 55 172 33	56
GREEN SADDLE	SAD	40 55 172 33	57
GREEN VALLEY	VLY	44 46 167 46	94
GREEN VALLEY	LOC	45 17 170 31	102
GREENDALE	LOC	43 35 172 05	81
GREENDALE	LOC	43 35 172 05	85
GREENFIELD	LOC	46 06 169 35	111
GREENFIELD	LOC	46 06 169 35	113
GREENHILLS	LOC	46 33 168 18	109
GREENHITHE	LOC	36 46 174 40	11
GREENHITHE	LOC	36 46 174 40	12
GREENLAND, MOUNT	MTN	44 39 168 41	90
GREENLAND, MOUNT (TRIG)	MTN	42 57 170 50	68
GREENLAND RESERVOIR	LAKE	45 26 169 38	100
GREENLAW COL	SAD	43 01 171 25	75
GREENLAW COL	SAD	43 01 171 25	80
GREENLAW, MOUNT	MTN	43 01 171 25	75
GREENLAW, MOUNT	MTN	43 01 171 25	80
GREENPARK	LOC	43 41 172 30	81
GREENPARK	STRM	43 10 172 29	82
GREENPARK	LOC	43 10 172 29	83
GREENPARK	LOC	43 10 172 29	85
GREENPARK HUTS	BLDG	43 46 172 33	83
GREENPARK HUTS	BLDG	43 46 172 33	85
GREENPOINT	LOC	46 35 168 18	109
GREENSTONE	LOC	42 38 171 17	68
GREENSTONE	LOC	42 38 171 17	69
GREENSTONE RIVER	STRM	42 38 171 12	68
GREENSTONE RIVER	STRM	42 38 171 12	69
GREENSTONE RIVER	STRM	44 56 168 20	95
GREENSTONE RIVER	STRM	44 56 168 20	98
GREENSTREET	LOC	43 49 171 40	84
GREENVALE	LOC	45 53 169 03	110
GREER CREEK	STRM	43 39 169 43	76
GREER CREEK	STRM	43 39 169 43	79
GREERTON	SBRB	37 43 176 08	20
GREERTON	SBRB	37 43 176 08	21
GREIG STREAM	STRM	41 50 173 06	66
GREIGS	LOC	42 19 171 17	63
GREIGS	LOC	42 19 171 17	68
GREIGS	LOC	42 19 171 17	69
GRENVILLE POINT	PNT	34 46 173 09	3
GRETA	LOC	42 54 173 01	72
GRETA RIVER	STRM	42 54 173 07	72
GRETA STREAM	STRM	44 15 169 53	79
GREVILLE HARBOUR	HARB	40 50 173 48	61
GREY GLACIER	GLCR	43 27 170 29	74
GREY GLACIER	GLCR	43 27 170 29	77
GREY HEIGHTS (TRIG)	HILL	36 26 174 52	11
GREY HILL (TRIG)	HILL	42 32 172 39	71
GREY LYNN	SBRB	36 52 174 44	11
GREY LYNN	SBRB	36 52 174 44	12
GREY, MOUNT	MTN	45 33 167 15	96
GREY, MOUNT (TRIG)	MTN	43 07 172 33	81
GREY, MOUNT (TRIG)	MTN	43 07 172 33	82
GREY PASS	PASS	43 26 170 30	74
GREY PASS	PASS	43 26 170 30	77
GREY RANGE	MTNS	43 07 171 34	80
GREY RIVER	STRM	41 54 173 35	66
GREY RIVER	STRM	42 27 171 12	68
GREY RIVER	STRM	42 27 171 12	69
GREY RIVER	STRM	43 10 172 29	81
GREY RIVER	STRM	43 10 172 29	82
GREYMOUTH	TOWN	42 27 171 12	68
GREYMOUTH	TOWN	42 27 171 12	69
GREYTOWN	POPL	41 05 175 27	53
GRIDIRON (TRIG)	MTN	42 14 173 26	66
GRIDLAND (TRIG)	HILL	40 02 175 54	46
GRIFFIN CREEK	STRM	42 46 171 21	69
GRIFFIN, MOUNT (TRIG)	MTN	42 48 171 21	69
GRIFFITHS, MOUNT	MTN	42 59 171 17	68
GRIFFITHS, MOUNT	MTN	42 59 171 17	69
GRIFFITHS SADDLE	SAD	42 59 171 17	68
GRIFFITHS SADDLE	SAD	42 59 171 17	69
GRIFFITHS SADDLE	SAD	42 59 171 17	75
GRIFFITHS STREAM	STRM	43 03 171 18	75
GRIFFITHS STREAM	STRM	44 02 171 03	87
GRINDLEY RIDGE	RDGE	41 06 172 19	56
GRINDLEY RIDGE	RDGE	41 06 172 19	62
GRONO, MOUNT (TRIG)	PEAK	45 16 166 57	96
GROPER ISLAND	ISLD	35 54 175 03	9
GROPERS BUSH	LOC	46 14 168 02	106
GROPERS BUSH	LOC	46 14 168 02	107
GROPERS BUSH	LOC	46 14 168 02	108
GROPERS BUSH	LOC	46 14 168 02	109
GROVE BURN	STRM	46 10 167 32	105
GROVE BURN	STRM	46 10 167 32	106
GROVE BURN	STRM	46 10 167 32	108
GROVE BUSH	LOC	46 18 168 29	107
GROVE BUSH	LOC	46 18 168 29	109
GROVES SWAMP	SWMP	42 50 170 57	68
GROVETOWN	LOC	41 29 173 58	60
GROW BURN	STRM	45 34 168 54	99
GROWLER, THE	STRM	43 31 170 45	74
GUARDIAN, MOUNT (TRIG)	MTN	42 35 173 26	73

GUARDIAN PEAK	PEAK	43 19 170 41	74
GUARDS BAY	BAY	40 59 174 06	54
GUARDS BAY	BAY	40 59 174 06	60
GUARDS BAY	BAY	40 59 174 06	61
GUFFIES CREEK	STRM	44 50 170 15	92
GUIDE RIVER	STRM	42 16 173 04	66
GUINEVERE, MOUNT	MTN	42 57 171 29	69
GUINEVERE, MOUNT (TRIG)	MTN	42 09 172 43	65
GULCH GLACIER	GLCR	43 36 170 04	76
GULCH GLACIER	GLCR	43 36 170 04	77
GULCHES HEAD	HEAD	46 05 166 35	104
GULL ROCK POINT	PNT	46 48 168 02	109
GULL ROCK POINT	PNT	46 48 168 02	115
GUM TREE FLAT	LOC	44 48 171 01	93
GUMMIES BUSH	LOC	46 17 168 02	108
GUMMIES BUSH	LOC	46 17 168 02	109
GUMTOWN	LOC	35 42 174 13	5
GUMTOWN	LOC	35 42 174 13	7
GUMTOWN	LOC	35 42 174 13	8
GUNN, LAKE	LAKE	44 53 168 05	89
GUNN, MOUNT	MTN	44 45 168 05	89
GUNN PEAK	PEAK	43 21 170 22	74
GUNN RIVER	STRM	43 23 170 25	74
GUNN RIVER	STRM	43 23 170 25	77
GUNNER DOWNS	PLAT	41 02 172 11	56
GUNNER DOWNS	PLAT	41 02 172 11	62
GUNNER RIVER	STRM	40 57 172 08	56
GUNNER RIVER	STRM	40 57 172 08	62
GUNNS BUSH	HSTD	44 39 170 58	93
GUT, THE	STRA	45 18 166 57	96
GUTHRIE	LOC	38 17 176 09	21
GUTHRIE	LOC	38 17 176 09	29
GUY, MOUNT (TRIG)	MTN	43 36 171 05	75
GUYON, LAKE	LAKE	42 17 172 39	65
GWAVAS	LOC	39 47 176 29	47
GYZEH (TRIG)	PEAK	45 35 168 19	98

H

HAAST	LOC	43 53 169 03	78
HAAST, MOUNT	MTN	43 34 170 11	74
HAAST, MOUNT	MTN	43 34 170 11	77
HAAST, MOUNT (TRIG)	MTN	42 19 172 05	64
HAAST, MOUNT (TRIG)	MTN	42 19 172 05	70
HAAST PASS	PASS	44 06 169 21	78
HAAST RANGE	MTNS	44 10 168 45	88
HAAST RIVER	STRM	43 50 169 02	78
HAAST SPIT (TRIG)	HILL	43 50 169 03	78
HABUKININI CREEK	STRM	46 27 168 48	112
HACKET RIVER	STRM	44 15 168 07	88
HACKETT CREEK	STRM	41 23 173 13	59
HACKTHORNE	LOC	43 48 171 35	84
HADFIELD	LOC	43 45 171 59	84
HADLOW	LOC	44 22 171 10	93
HAE HAE TE MOANA RIVER	STRM	44 12 171 14	87
HAE HAE TE MOANA RIVER (NTH BRANCH)	STRM	44 04 171 10	87
HAE HAE TE MOANA RIVER (STH BRANCH)	STRM	44 04 171 10	87
HAECKEL PEAK	PEAK	43 32 170 21	74
HAECKEL PEAK	PEAK	43 32 170 21	77
HAEHANGA (TRIG)	HILL	38 58 174 32	35
HAGGARD CREEK	STRM	41 56 171 47	63
HAGGARD CREEK	STRM	41 56 171 47	64
HAHA STREAM	STRM	35 41 173 49	6
HAHEI	LOC	36 51 175 48	16
HAIDINGER, MOUNT	MTN	43 33 170 12	74
HAIDINGER, MOUNT	MTN	43 33 170 12	77
HAIDINGER, MOUNT (TRIG)	HILL	40 42 172 34	56
HAIDINGER, MOUNT (TRIG)	HILL	40 42 172 34	57
HAILES KNOB (TRIG)	PEAK	41 06 172 49	57
HAILES KNOB (TRIG)	PEAK	41 06 172 49	58
HAIRINI	LOC	38 01 175 22	19
HAIRINI	SBRB	37 44 176 10	20
HAIRINI	SBRB	37 44 176 10	21
HAITAI STREAM	STRM	41 23 175 27	53
HAKAKINO	HSTD	41 05 175 47	51
HAKANOA, LAKE	LAKE	37 33 175 10	15
HAKAONGA (TRIG)	HILL	37 33 178 15	25
HAKAPOUA, LAKE	LAKE	46 10 166 57	104
HAKAPOUA, LAKE	LAKE	46 10 166 57	105
HAKARIMATA RANGE	MTNS	37 38 175 08	18
HAKARIMATA (TRIG)	HILL	37 40 175 07	18
HAKARU	LOC	36 09 174 31	8
HAKARU RIVER	STRM	36 13 174 28	8
HAKATARAMEA	HSTD	44 36 170 34	92
HAKATARAMEA	LOC	44 44 170 30	92
HAKATARAMEA DOWNS	LOC	44 26 170 40	93
HAKATARAMEA PASS	PASS	44 19 170 35	86
HAKATARAMEA RIVER	STRM	44 20 170 38	86
HAKATARAMEA RIVER	STRM	44 20 170 38	93
HAKATERE	LOC	43 37 171 10	75
HAKATERE	LOC	44 03 171 49	84
HAKERETEKE STREAM	STRM	38 20 176 23	21
HAKERETEKE STREAM	STRM	38 20 176 23	29
HAKU	LOC	38 25 174 52	26
HAKURANGI (TRIG)	HILL	38 00 178 17	25
HALCOMBE	POPL	40 09 175 30	45
HALCOMBE	POPL	40 09 175 30	46
HALCOMBE, MOUNT	MTN	43 31 170 11	74
HALCOMBE, MOUNT	MTN	43 31 170 11	77
HALDANE	LOC	46 38 169 01	112
HALDANE BAY	BAY	46 40 169 02	112
HALDON	HSTD	44 22 170 15	92
HALDON (TRIG)	HILL	40 52 176 10	50
HALDON (TRIG)	HILL	40 52 176 10	51
HALDONS, THE	HSTD	41 44 173 59	67
HALF, LAKE	LAKE	34 44 173 00	2
HALF MOON BAY	BAY	42 15 173 49	67
HALF MOON STREAM	STRM	42 17 173 09	66
HALF MOON (TRIG)	HILL	40 51 175 55	49
HALF MOON (TRIG)	HILL	40 51 175 55	51
HALF PASSAGE ROCK	ROCK	46 49 168 24	109
HALF PASSAGE ROCK	ROCK	46 49 168 24	115
HALFMOON BAY	BAY	46 54 168 09	109
HALFMOON BAY	LOC	46 54 168 08	109
HALFMOON BAY	BAY	46 54 168 09	115
HALFMOON BAY	LOC	46 54 168 08	115
HALFMOON SADDLE	SAD	43 05 171 24	75
HALFMOON SADDLE	SAD	43 05 171 24	80
HALFWAY BAY	LOC	45 12 168 42	95
HALFWAY BAY	LOC	45 12 168 42	99
HALFWAY BLUFF	CLIF	44 03 168 20	88
HALFWAY PEAK	PEAK	44 34 168 00	89
HALFWAY PEAK	PEAK	45 04 167 42	94
HALFWAY PEAK	PEAK	44 34 168 00	94
HALFWAY PEAK	PEAK	45 04 167 42	97
HALFWAY POINT	PNT	40 50 173 56	54
HALFWAY POINT	PNT	40 50 173 56	61
HALFWAY ROCKS	ROCK	46 28 168 10	109
HALFWAY SADDLE	SAD	44 20 168 27	88
HALFWAY SADDLE	SAD	44 20 168 27	89
HALKETT	LOC	43 30 172 19	81
HALKETT	LOC	43 30 172 19	85
HALL ARM	BAY	45 27 167 07	96
HALL, LAKE	LAKE	45 18 167 23	96
HALL, MOUNT	MTN	41 49 173 36	66
HALL RANGE	MTNS	43 42 170 27	77
HALL RANGE	MTNS	43 42 170 27	86
HALL RIVER	STRM	43 40 169 26	76
HALL RIVER	STRM	43 40 169 26	78
HALL RIVER	STRM	43 40 169 26	79
HALL STREAM	STRM	43 29 171 56	80
HALLAM COVE	BAY	41 00 173 49	54
HALLAM COVE	BAY	41 00 173 49	60
HALLAM COVE	BAY	41 00 173 49	61
HALLS HILL (TRIG)	HILL	36 34 174 40	11
HALSWELL	LOC	43 35 172 34	82
HALSWELL	LOC	43 35 172 34	83
HALSWELL	LOC	43 35 172 34	85
HALSWELL, POINT	PNT	41 17 174 50	52
HALSWELL, POINT	PNT	41 17 174 50	55
HALSWELL RIVER	STRM	43 46 172 36	83
HALSWELL RIVER	STRM	43 46 172 36	85
HAMAMA	LOC	40 55 172 47	57
HAMBONE CREEK	STRM	43 43 169 22	78
HAMENGA STREAM	STRM	35 42 173 59	5
HAMENGA STREAM	STRM	35 42 173 59	7
HAMER, LAKE	LAKE	44 08 168 31	88
HAMILTON	TOWN	37 47 175 17	18
HAMILTON	TOWN	37 47 175 17	19
HAMILTON	LOC	45 15 170 09	101
HAMILTON BAY	BAY	40 59 173 51	54
HAMILTON BAY	BAY	40 59 173 51	60
HAMILTON BAY	BAY	40 59 173 51	61
HAMILTON BURN	STRM	45 42 168 08	106
HAMILTON BURN	STRM	45 42 168 08	107
HAMILTON CREEK	STRM	43 08 171 37	80
HAMILTON, MOUNT	MTN	43 33 170 20	74
HAMILTON, MOUNT	MTN	43 33 170 20	77
HAMILTON, MOUNT (TRIG)	MTN	45 37 168 01	106
HAMILTON, MOUNT (TRIG)	MTN	45 37 168 01	107
HAMILTON PEAK	PEAK	43 07 171 41	80
HAMILTON RIVER	STRM	41 57 172 54	65
HAMLEY PEAK	PEAK	45 14 167 02	96
HAMPDEN	LOC	45 20 170 49	102
HAMPSTEAD	SBRB	43 55 171 46	84
HAMUA	LOC	40 34 175 44	49
HAMURANA	LOC	38 02 176 16	20
HAMURANA	LOC	38 02 176 16	21
HAMUTINUI (TRIG)	MTN	38 10 177 37	24
HAMUTINUI (TRIG)	MTN	38 10 177 37	31
HANATA ISLAND	ISLD	43 37 169 27	76
HANATA ISLAND	ISLD	43 37 169 27	78
HANATA ISLAND	ISLD	43 37 169 27	79
HANDYSIDE (TRIG)	PEAK	42 34 172 34	71
HANGAROA	LOC	38 41 177 36	31
HANGAROA	LOC	38 41 177 36	33
HANGAROA RIVER	STRM	38 50 177 31	31
HANGAROA RIVER	STRM	38 50 177 31	33
HANGATIKI	LOC	38 15 175 11	18
HANGATIKI	LOC	38 15 175 11	27
HANGAWERA (TRIG)	HILL	37 33 175 28	15
HANGORE BANK	BNK	37 04 174 43	12
HANGORE BANK	BNK	37 04 174 43	14
HANKINSON, LAKE	LAKE	45 04 167 34	94
HANKINSON, LAKE	LAKE	45 04 167 34	97
HANLAN, LAKE	LAKE	41 25 172 06	62
HANLEY, MOUNT	MTN	45 01 168 31	95
HANLEY, MOUNT	MTN	45 01 168 31	99
HANMER PLAIN	PLN	42 33 172 45	71
HANMER RANGE	MTNS	42 30 172 50	71
HANMER RIVER	STRM	42 35 172 47	71
HANMER RIVER	STRM	42 35 172 47	72
HANMER SPRINGS	POPL	42 31 172 50	71
HANMER SPRINGS	POPL	42 31 172 50	72
HANS ISLAND	ISLD	42 48 171 09	68
HANS ISLAND	ISLD	42 48 171 09	69
HANSARD POINT	PNT	45 01 167 09	96
HANSENS HILL (TRIG)	HILL	35 29 174 24	5
HAOWHENUA POINT	PNT	36 12 175 03	9
HAPAPAWERA (TRIG)	HILL	36 42 175 34	13
HAPAPAWERA (TRIG)	HILL	36 42 175 34	16
HAPARANGI (TRIG)	HILL	38 14 176 12	20
HAPARANGI (TRIG)	HILL	38 14 176 12	21
HAPARANGI (TRIG)	HILL	38 14 176 12	29
HAPARAPARA RIVER	STRM	37 48 177 39	24
HAPOKAPOKA STREAM	STRM	39 39 175 20	45
HAPONGA (TRIG)	HILL	35 24 173 33	3
HAPONGA (TRIG)	HILL	35 24 173 33	4
HAPONGA (TRIG)	HILL	35 24 173 33	6
HAPPY CREEK	STRM	40 40 175 56	49
HAPPY VALLEY	LOC	37 10 175 07	13
HAPPY VALLEY	LOC	37 10 175 07	14
HAPPY VALLEY	LOC	37 10 175 07	15
HAPPY VALLEY	HSTD	43 00 173 06	82
HAPPY VALLEY	LOC	46 08 167 47	106
HAPPY VALLEY	LOC	46 08 167 47	108
HAPPY VALLEY SADDLE	SAD	41 27 172 06	62
HAPPY VALLEY STREAM	STRM	42 11 173 48	67
HAPUAKOHE RANGE	MTNS	37 21 175 22	15
HAPUKA RIVER	STRM	43 55 168 54	78
HAPUKA ROCK	ROCK	46 28 167 49	108
HAPUKU	LOC	42 19 173 45	67
HAPUKU	LOC	42 19 173 45	73
HAPUKU RIVER	STRM	42 20 173 44	67
HAPUKU RIVER	STRM	42 20 173 44	73
HAPUKU ROCKS	ROCK	40 43 173 58	61
HAPURUA STREAM	STRM	38 47 175 00	26
HAPURUA STREAM	STRM	38 47 175 00	27
HARAKEHE HEAD	HEAD	45 54 170 40	103
HARAKEKE	LOC	41 13 173 01	58
HARAKEKE	LOC	41 13 173 01	59
HARAKEKE ISLAND	ISLD	35 09 174 08	4
HARAKEKE ISLAND	ISLD	35 09 174 08	5
HARAKEKE TAUTORO ISLAND	ISLD	44 16 171 22	87
HARAPEPE	LOC	37 56 175 07	18
HARATA, MOUNT (TRIG)	MTN	42 22 171 55	70
HARATAHI CREEK	STRM	36 30 174 17	10
HARATAUNGA STREAM	STRM	36 41 175 33	13
HARATAUNGA STREAM	STRM	36 41 175 33	16
HARAWEKA ISLAND	ISLD	34 59 173 57	4
HARAWERA (TRIG)	HILL	39 39 175 17	45
HARBOUR ISLANDS	ISLS	45 35 166 46	104
HARD CREEK	STRM	41 52 171 55	63
HARD CREEK	STRM	41 52 171 55	64
HARDING CREEK, MOUNT	STRM	43 48 171 40	84
HARDY, MOUNT (TRIG)	HILL	40 53 172 37	56
HARDY, MOUNT (TRIG)	HILL	40 53 172 37	57
HARDY, PORT	HARB	40 45 173 53	61
HARES EARS	ISLD	45 16 166 50	96
HAREWOOD	LOC	43 29 172 33	82
HAREWOOD	LOC	43 29 172 33	83
HAREWOOD	LOC	43 29 172 33	85
HARGREAVES RUN (TRIG)	HILL	36 16 174 18	10
HARIHARI	LOC	43 09 170 34	74
HARIHARI, LAKE	LAKE	38 13 174 44	18
HARIKI BEACH	LOC	37 46 177 41	24
HARINGTON POINT	LOC	45 47 170 44	103
HARLEY CREEK	STRM	41 42 172 39	65
HARMAN, MOUNT	MTN	42 56 171 22	69
HARMAN PASS	PASS	42 56 171 25	69
HARMAN RIVER	STRM	42 55 171 20	69
HARMAN STREAM	STRM	43 11 172 06	81
HARNETTS CREEK	STRM	42 21 173 42	73
HARO CREEK	STRM	43 07 170 39	74
HAROHARO (TRIG)	HILL	38 06 176 30	21
HAROHARO (TRIG)	HILL	38 06 176 30	22
HAROTO BAY	LOC	37 48 174 57	18
HAROTO BAY	BAY	37 48 174 57	18
HARPER, MOUNT	MTN	43 00 171 25	69
HARPER, MOUNT	MTN	43 00 171 25	75
HARPER, MOUNT	MTN	43 00 171 25	80
HARPER, MOUNT (TRIG)	MTN	43 40 171 03	75
HARPER, MOUNT (TRIG)	MTN	43 40 171 03	87
HARPER PASS	PASS	42 44 171 53	70
HARPER RANGE	MTNS	43 40 171 04	87
HARPER RIVER	STRM	43 14 171 25	80
HARPER SADDLE	SAD	43 35 170 07	74
HARPER SADDLE	SAD	43 35 170 07	76
HARPER SADDLE	SAD	43 35 170 07	77
HARRIET, MOUNT (TRIG)	HILL	36 24 174 29	10
HARRIET, MOUNT (TRIG)	HILL	36 24 174 29	11
HARRIS, LAKE	LAKE	44 44 168 11	89
HARRIS, MOUNT	HILL	44 03 169 02	78
HARRIS MOUNT (TRIG)	HILL	44 50 170 58	93
HARRIS MOUNTAINS	MTNS	44 40 168 49	90
HARRIS STREAM	STRM	44 10 169 51	79
HARRIS (TRIG)	HILL	40 46 175 33	48
HARRIS (TRIG)	HILL	40 46 175 33	49
HARRIS (TRIG)	HILL	40 46 175 33	51
HARRISON RIVER	STRM	44 38 167 54	89
HARRISON RIVER	STRM	44 38 167 54	94
HARRISON SADDLE	SAD	44 54 167 27	94
HARRISON SADDLE	SAD	44 53 167 27	96
HARRISON SADDLE	SAD	44 54 167 27	97
HARRISVILLE	LOC	37 15 174 57	12
HARRISVILLE	LOC	37 15 174 57	14
HARRY, MOUNT	MTN	42 54 171 07	68
HARRY, MOUNT	MTN	42 54 171 07	69
HARTE, MOUNT (TRIG)	MTN	41 48 172 26	65
HARTLEY TARN	LAKE	43 53 170 26	77
HARTLEY TARN	LAKE	43 53 170 26	86
HARTS HILL	HILL	45 28 167 39	97
HARURU	LOC	35 17 174 03	4
HARURU	LOC	35 17 174 03	5
HARVEY CREEK	STRM	41 23 172 05	62
HARVEYS FLAT	LOC	45 50 170 11	103
HARWICH ISLAND	ISLD	44 33 169 05	90
HARWOOD	LOC	45 49 170 40	103
HARWOODS HOLE	CAVE	40 57 172 52	57
HASSING PEAK	PEAK	43 59 169 35	79
HASTINGS	TOWN	39 39 176 51	42
HASTINGS	TOWN	39 39 176 51	43
HASTWELLS	LOC	40 43 175 42	49
HASTWELLS	LOC	40 43 175 42	51
HASZARD, MOUNT	MTN	43 46 170 26	77
HASZARD, MOUNT	MTN	43 46 170 26	86
HASZARD RIDGE	RDGE	43 44 170 26	77
HASZARD RIDGE	RDGE	43 44 170 26	86
HATAITAI	SBRB	41 18 174 48	52
HATAITAI	SBRB	41 18 174 48	55
HATEA RIVER	STRM	35 45 174 21	5
HATEA RIVER	STRM	35 45 174 21	7
HATEA RIVER	STRM	35 45 174 21	8
HATEPE	LOC	38 51 176 01	28
HATEPE	LOC	38 51 176 01	29
HATEPE	LOC	38 51 176 01	38
HATFIELDS BEACH	LOC	36 34 174 42	11
HATPIN CREEK	STRM	42 19 171 33	63
HATTERS BAY	BAY	42 04 171 22	63
HATUMA	LOC	40 02 176 30	47
HATUMA, LAKE	LAKE	40 01 176 31	43
HATUMA, LAKE	LAKE	40 01 176 31	47
HAUARAHI STREAM	STRM	37 07 175 18	13
HAUARAHI STREAM	STRM	37 07 175 18	15
HAUHA STREAM	STRM	39 28 174 29	35
HAUHA STREAM	STRM	39 28 174 29	44
HAUHAUPONAMU STREAM	STRM	37 48 177 52	24
HAUHUNGAROA RANGE	MTNS	38 44 175 33	27
HAUHUNGAROA RANGE	MTNS	38 44 175 33	28
HAUHUNGAROA RANGE	MTNS	38 44 175 33	38
HAUHUNGAROA (TRIG)	HILL	38 50 175 34	27
HAUHUNGAROA (TRIG)	HILL	38 50 175 34	28
HAUHUNGAROA (TRIG)	HILL	38 50 175 34	38
HAUHUNGATAHI WILDERNESS AREA	WILD	39 15 175 28	36
HAUHUNGATAHI WILDERNESS AREA	WILD	39 15 175 28	37
HAUHUNGATAHI (TRIG)	PEAK	39 14 175 27	36
HAUHUNGATAHI (TRIG)	PEAK	39 14 175 27	37
HAUITI	LOC	38 23 178 18	32
HAULASHORE ISLAND	ISLD	41 16 173 15	59
HAUMAKARIRI STREAM	STRM	39 51 175 30	45
HAUMAKARIRI STREAM	STRM	39 51 175 30	46
HAUMOANA	USAT	39 36 176 57	42
HAUMOANA	USAT	39 36 176 57	43
HAUMURI BLUFFS	PNT	42 34 173 30	73
HAUNGA	HILL	35 09 173 45	4
HAUNUI	LOC	40 37 176 03	49
HAUONE	LOC	37 51 176 39	21
HAUONE	LOC	37 51 176 39	22
HAUONE STREAM	STRM	37 51 176 38	21
HAUONE STREAM	STRM	37 51 176 38	22
HAUPARA POINT	PNT	37 35 178 19	25
HAUPARU BAY	LOC	38 03 176 25	20
HAUPARU BAY	LOC	38 03 176 25	21
HAUPATUA STREAM	STRM	38 12 178 02	24
HAUPATUA STREAM	STRM	38 12 178 02	32
HAUPEEHI (TRIG)	HILL	38 29 175 12	27
HAUPIRI	LOC	42 34 171 49	70
HAUPIRI, LAKE	LAKE	42 34 171 41	70
HAUPIRI RANGE	MTNS	40 54 172 39	56
HAUPIRI RANGE	MTNS	40 54 172 39	57
HAUPIRI RIVER	STRM	42 31 171 48	70
HAURAKI CREEK	STRM	43 22 169 58	76
HAURAKI CREEK	STRM	43 22 169 58	77
HAURAKI GULF	GULF	36 38 175 04	13
HAURAKI PLAINS	PLN	37 19 175 32	15
HAURAKI STREAM	STRM	38 02 176 14	20
HAURAKI STREAM	STRM	38 02 176 14	21
HAURANGI STATE FOREST PARK	PARK	41 31 175 19	53
HAURERE POINT	PNT	37 58 177 27	23
HAURERE POINT	PNT	37 58 177 27	24
HAUROKO BURN	STRM	45 48 167 08	105
HAUROKO, LAKE	LAKE	46 00 167 19	105
HAURUIA, MOUNT	HILL	36 13 175 05	9
HAUTANOA	LOC	38 07 178 20	25
HAUTAPU	LOC	37 52 175 27	19
HAUTAPU CHANNEL	CHAN	36 44 175 25	13
HAUTAPU CHANNEL	CHAN	36 44 175 25	16
HAUTAPU POINT	PNT	36 07 175 30	9
HAUTAPU RIVER	STRM	38 59 176 48	40
HAUTAPU RIVER	STRM	39 45 175 50	46
HAUTAWA STREAM	STRM	39 51 175 30	46
HAUTU PA	LOC	38 59 175 50	37
HAUTU PA	LOC	38 59 175 50	38
HAUTU PRISON FARM	LOC	39 00 175 51	37
HAUTU PRISON FARM	LOC	39 00 175 51	38
HAUTURU	LOC	38 06 174 56	18
HAUTURU ISLAND	ISLD	37 13 175 54	17
HAUTURU, MOUNT (TRIG)	HILL	36 12 175 05	9
HAUTURU STREAM	STRM	35 24 173 14	3
HAUTURU (TRIG)	HILL	36 54 175 28	13
HAUTURU (TRIG)	HILL	36 54 175 28	15
HAUTURU (TRIG)	HILL	36 54 175 28	16
HAUTURU (TRIG)	HILL	38 12 175 02	18
HAUWAI	LOC	41 45 174 09	67
HAUWAI STREAM	STRM	38 52 175 27	27
HAUWAI STREAM	STRM	38 25 176 05	28
HAUWAI STREAM	STRM	38 25 176 05	29
HAVELOCK	POPL	41 17 173 46	60
HAVELOCK	POPL	41 17 173 46	61
HAVELOCK CREEK	STRM	43 31 169 52	76
HAVELOCK NORTH	USAT	39 40 176 53	42
HAVELOCK NORTH	USAT	39 40 176 53	43
HAVELOCK RIVER	STRM	43 31 170 48	74
HAWAI	LOC	37 55 177 32	24
HAWAI RIVER	STRM	37 55 177 32	24
HAWARDEN	POPL	42 56 172 39	71
HAWDON, LAKE	LAKE	43 06 171 51	80
HAWDON RIVER	STRM	43 00 171 45	70
HAWDON RIVER, EAST BRANCH	STRM	42 56 171 45	70
HAWEA FLAT	LOC	44 39 169 17	91
HAWEA, LAKE	LAKE	44 28 169 17	91
HAWEA RIVER	STRM	44 37 169 15	91
HAWEA STREAM	STRM	39 48 176 48	42
HAWEA STREAM	STRM	39 48 176 48	43
HAWERA	TOWN	39 35 174 17	34
HAWERA	TOWN	39 35 174 17	35
HAWERA	TOWN	39 35 174 17	44
HAWERA STREAM	STRM	35 26 173 59	4
HAWERA (TRIG)	PEAK	42 12 171 28	63
HAWES HEAD	HEAD	45 03 167 04	96
HAWK CREEK	STRM	42 55 171 10	68
HAWK CREEK	STRM	42 55 171 10	69
HAWK HILLS	HSTD	42 24 173 22	72
HAWK HILLS	HSTD	42 24 173 22	73
HAWK RANGE (TRIG)	PEAK	42 23 173 22	72
HAWK RANGE (TRIG)	PEAK	42 23 173 22	73
HAWKDUN RANGE	MTNS	44 49 169 59	92
HAWKE BAY	BAY	39 23 177 12	41
HAWKENS JUNCTION	LOC	37 57 176 45	22
HAWKER CREEK	STRM	42 26 172 04	70
HAWKES KNOB (TRIG)	PEAK	40 52 172 21	56
HAWKEY STREAM	STRM	44 16 170 33	86
HAWKINS	LOC	43 29 172 03	81
HAWKINS	LOC	43 29 172 03	85
HAWKINS HILL (TRIG)	HILL	41 19 174 44	52
HAWKINS HILL (TRIG)	HILL	41 19 174 44	55
HAWKINS, MOUNT	MTN	43 46 169 42	76
HAWKINS, MOUNT	MTN	43 46 169 42	79
HAWKINS RIVER	STRM	43 37 172 09	81
HAWKINS RIVER	STRM	43 37 172 09	85
HAWKS BURN	STRM	45 12 169 11	99
HAWKS CRAG	CRAG	41 52 171 47	63
HAWKS CRAG	CRAG	41 52 171 47	64
HAWKSBURY BUSH	LOC	45 34 170 41	102
HAWKSWOOD	LOC	42 39 173 20	72
HAWKSWOOD	LOC	42 39 173 20	73
HAWTREY (TRIG)	HILL	41 17 174 55	52
HAWTREY (TRIG)	HILL	41 17 174 55	55
HAY, LAKE	LAKE	45 49 167 03	105
HAY, MOUNT (TRIG)	MTN	43 57 170 34	77
HAY, MOUNT (TRIG)	MTN	43 57 170 34	86
HAY RIVER	STRM	45 46 167 08	105
HAYCOCK SADDLE	SAD	42 07 173 41	67
HAYCOCK (TRIG)	HILL	41 42 173 24	66
HAYDON DOWNS	HSTD	42 55 172 25	71
HAYES, LAKE	LAKE	44 59 168 49	99
HAYES, LAKE	LAKE	44 59 168 49	95
HAYS GAP	LOC	46 26 169 47	113
HAYS STREAM	STRM	37 06 174 57	12
HAYS STREAM	STRM	37 06 174 57	14
HAYSTACK CREEK	STRM	41 31 172 16	62
HAYSTACK, THE	ROCK	40 54 174 05	54
HAYSTACK, THE	HILL	41 17 172 18	56
HAYSTACK, THE	ROCK	40 54 174 05	61
HAYSTACK, THE	HILL	41 17 172 18	62
HAYSTACK, THE	PEAK	41 34 172 20	62
HAYTER STREAM	STRM	44 11 170 42	86
HAYTOR (TRIG)	HILL	43 40 172 55	82
HAYTOR (TRIG)	HILL	43 40 172 55	83
HAYWARD POINT	PNT	46 30 169 43	113
HAYWARDS	LOC	41 09 174 59	52
HAYWARDS	LOC	41 09 174 59	55
HAZELBURGH GROUP	ISLS	46 49 168 28	109
HAZELBURGH GROUP	ISLS	46 49 168 28	115
HAZELBURN	LOC	44 12 170 59	87
HAZLETTS	LOC	46 16 168 06	106
HAZLETTS	LOC	46 16 168 06	107
HAZLETTS	LOC	46 16 168 06	109
HEAD OF THE BAY	BAY	43 39 172 40	82
HEAD OF THE BAY	BAY	43 39 172 40	83
HEAD OF THE BAY	BAY	43 39 172 40	85
HEAD, MOUNT	MTN	44 34 168 26	88
HEAD, MOUNT	MTN	44 34 168 26	89
HEADACHE STREAM	STRM	41 53 173 59	67
HEADLONG PEAK	PEAK	44 33 168 36	88
HEADLONG PEAK	PEAK	44 33 168 36	90
HEALE, MOUNT (TRIG)	HILL	40 34 175 47	49
HEALEY'S CREEK	STRM	47 10 167 45	114
HEAO STATION	RSTN	38 59 174 59	36
HEAO STREAM	STRM	39 11 174 52	35
HEAPHY BLUFF	CLIF	40 59 172 06	56
HEAPHY BLUFF	CLIF	40 59 172 06	62
HEAPHY RIVER	STRM	40 59 172 06	56
HEAPHY RIVER	STRM	40 59 172 06	62
HEAPHY TRACK	TRCK	41 02 172 07	56
HEAPHY TRACK	TRCK	41 02 172 07	62
HEATH MOUNTAINS	MTNS	45 44 167 04	105
HEATHCOTE	SBRB	43 35 172 43	82
HEATHCOTE	SBRB	43 35 172 43	83
HEATHCOTE	SBRB	43 35 172 43	85

HEATHCOTE RIVER	STRM	43 34 172 42	82
HEATHCOTE RIVER	STRM	43 34 172 42	83
HEATHCOTE RIVER	STRM	43 34 172 42	85
HEATHERLEA	LOC	40 36 175 18	48
HEATON, LAKE	LAKE	40 07 175 17	45
HEAVE UP	MTN	44 00 169 16	78
HECLA, MOUNT (TRIG)	MTN	43 29 171 28	75
HECLA, MOUNT (TRIG)	MTN	43 29 171 28	80
HECTOR	LOC	41 36 171 53	62
HECTOR COL	SAD	44 24 168 41	88
HECTOR COL	SAD	44 24 168 41	90
HECTOR, LAKE	LAKE	45 59 166 31	104
HECTOR, MOUNT (TRIG)	PEAK	40 57 175 17	48
HECTOR, MOUNT (TRIG)	PEAK	40 57 175 17	53
HECTOR MOUNTAINS	MTNS	45 16 168 50	95
HECTOR MOUNTAINS	MTNS	45 16 168 50	99
HECTOR RIVER	STRM	40 55 175 23	48
HECTORS STREAM	STRM	45 08 170 40	102
HEDDON BUSH	LOC	46 05 168 09	107
HEDGEHOPE	LOC	46 12 168 32	107
HEDGEHOPE STREAM	STRM	46 18 168 26	107
HEDIN PEAK	PEAK	44 30 168 21	88
HEDIN PEAK	PEAK	44 30 168 21	89
HEENEY CREEK	STRM	45 23 170 13	101
HEIDELBERG	SBRB	46 26 168 23	109
HEIMAMA STREAM	STRM	39 27 173 50	34
HEIPIPI	LOC	38 38 176 54	30
HEKERANGI POINT	PNT	39 14 177 51	33
HELEN PEAKS	PEAK	45 25 168 20	98
HELENA BAY	BAY	35 26 174 22	5
HELENA BAY	LOC	35 26 174 21	5
HELENA PEAKS	PEAK	46 02 167 12	105
HELENSBROOK	LOC	46 07 169 58	111
HELENSVILLE	POPL	36 41 174 27	10
HELENSVILLE	POPL	36 41 174 27	11
HELENSVILLE	POPL	36 41 174 27	12
HELLENE CREEK	STRM	45 21 170 35	102
HELLFIRE STREAM	STRM	41 56 172 55	65
HELLS GATE	PASS	40 59 175 18	53
HELMET HILL (TRIG)	HILL	46 05 167 25	105
HELMET HILL (TRIG)	HILL	46 05 167 25	108
HELMET PEAK	PEAK	43 22 170 42	74
HELVETIA	LOC	37 11 174 52	12
HELVETIA	LOC	37 11 174 52	14
HEMATITE STREAM	STRM	42 43 173 12	72
HEMATITE STREAM	STRM	42 43 173 12	73
HEMPHILL CREEK	STRM	41 32 172 11	62
HEN & CHICKENS GROUP	ISLS	35 56 174 44	8
HENDERSON	SBRB	36 53 174 38	11
HENDERSON	SBRB	36 53 174 38	12
HENDERSON BAY	BAY	34 45 173 08	2
HENDERSON BURN	STRM	44 59 167 41	94
HENDERSON BURN	STRM	44 59 167 41	97
HENDERSON, LAKE	LAKE	41 05 172 31	56
HENDERSON, LAKE	LAKE	41 05 172 31	57
HENDERSON, LAKE	LAKE	41 05 172 31	58
HENDERSON POINT	PNT	34 44 173 07	2
HENDES CREEK	STRM	43 12 170 41	74
HENLEY	LOC	45 59 170 10	103
HENNAH, MOUNT	MTN	43 16 171 33	80
HENNESSY CREEK	STRM	41 36 172 12	62
HENRIETTA BAY	BAY	46 47 168 30	109
HENRIETTA BAY	BAY	46 47 168 30	115
HENRIETTA, LAKE	LAKE	43 14 171 30	80
HENRY BURN	STRM	45 37 166 58	104
HENRY BURN	STRM	45 37 166 58	105
HENRY CREEK	STRM	45 14 167 48	97
HENRY CREEK	STRM	45 14 167 48	98
HENRY, MOUNT (TRIG)	MTN	45 00 167 30	94
HENRY, MOUNT (TRIG)	MTN	45 00 167 30	97
HENRY PASS	PASS	45 01 167 30	94
HENRY PASS	PASS	45 01 167 30	97
HENRY RIVER	STRM	42 21 172 16	71
HENRY SADDLE	SAD	42 22 172 27	71
HEPBURN CREEK	LOC	36 26 174 40	11
HERANGI HILL	HILL	34 28 172 40	2
HERANGI RANGE	MTNS	38 25 174 45	26
HERANGI (TRIG)	HILL	38 33 174 47	26
HERBERT	LOC	45 14 170 47	102
HERBERT, MOUNT	MTN	44 49 167 34	94
HERBERT, MOUNT (TRIG)	HILL	46 24 169 06	112
HERBERT RANGE	MTNS	41 19 172 20	62
HERBERTVILLE	LOC	40 30 176 33	50
HERCULES, MOUNT (TRIG)	MTN	43 10 170 28	74
HEREHERE STREAM	STRM	39 40 176 52	42
HEREHERE STREAM	STRM	39 40 176 52	43
HEREHERETAUNGA (TRIG)	HILL	37 44 177 49	24
HEREKAREAO (TRIG)	HILL	35 15 173 17	3
HEREKINO	LOC	35 16 173 13	3
HEREKINO HARBOUR	HARB	35 18 173 10	3
HEREKOPARE ISLAND	ISLD	46 52 168 13	109
HEREKOPARE ISLAND	ISLD	46 52 168 13	115
HERENGAWE, LAKE	LAKE	39 48 174 38	44
HEREPO	LOC	43 07 170 34	74
HEREPURU STREAM	STRM	37 52 176 41	21
HEREPURU STREAM	STRM	37 52 176 41	22
HERETANIWHA (TRIG)	HILL	43 35 169 33	76
HERETANIWHA POINT	PNT	43 35 169 33	76
HERETAUNGA	SBRB	41 09 175 01	52
HERETAUNGA	SBRB	41 09 175 01	55
HERIOT	POPL	45 50 169 16	110
HERIOT BURN	STRM	45 50 169 17	110
HERMAN CREEK	STRM	43 35 169 41	76
HERMANN, MOUNT	MTN	43 41 169 43	76
HERMANN, MOUNT	MTN	43 41 169 43	79
HERMIT STREAM	STRM	46 22 169 22	113
HERON, LAKE	LAKE	43 28 171 11	75
HERON RIVER	STRM	47 03 168 09	115
HERRICK CREEK	STRM	45 38 166 55	104
HERRICK CREEK	STRM	45 38 166 55	105
HERRIES, LAKE	LAKE	45 22 167 24	96
HERRIES, LAKE	LAKE	45 22 167 24	97
HERRING STREAM	STRM	41 10 172 54	58
HESLINGTON, MOUNT (TRIG)	HILL	41 24 173 07	58
HESLINGTON, MOUNT (TRIG)	HILL	41 24 173 07	59
HEVELDT, MOUNT	MTN	44 06 168 47	78
HEVELDT, MOUNT	MTN	44 06 168 47	88
HEWLETT POINT	PNT	35 48 174 20	7
HEWLETT POINT	PNT	35 48 174 20	8
HEWSON RANGE	MTNS	43 47 171 00	87
HEWSON RIVER	STRM	43 51 171 04	87
HEXTON	LOC	38 37 177 58	32
HEXTON	LOC	38 37 177 58	33
HEYWOOD PEAK	PEAK	45 35 167 08	105
HEYWOOD POINT	LOC	45 46 170 41	103
HEYWOOD POINT	PNT	45 45 170 42	103
HICKS BAY	BAY	37 35 178 18	25
HICKS BAY	LOC	37 35 178 17	25
HICKSON, MOUNT	MTN	43 53 169 48	76
HICKSON, MOUNT	MTN	43 53 169 48	79
HICTORY BAY	BAY	43 47 173 07	83
HIDDEN BURN	STRM	45 18 168 14	95
HIDDEN BURN	STRM	45 18 168 14	98
HIDDEN CREEK	STRM	43 10 171 36	80
HIDDEN FALLS CREEK	STRM	44 38 168 07	89
HIDDEN ISLAND	ISLD	45 04 168 39	95
HIDDEN ISLAND	ISLD	45 04 168 39	99
HIDDEN LAKE	LAKE	45 15 167 18	96
HIGGINS BROOK	STRM	40 44 172 29	56
HIGGINS BROOK	STRM	40 44 172 29	57
HIGGINS, MOUNT (TRIG)	HILL	40 45 172 31	56
HIGGINS, MOUNT (TRIG)	HILL	40 45 172 31	57
HIGH BARE PEAK (TRIG)	HILL	43 46 172 45	83
HIGH BURN	STRM	44 18 169 23	78
HIGH CLAYTONS	MTNS	43 50 170 57	87
HIGH MAUNGANUI (TRIG)	HILL	41 17 175 07	52
HIGH MAUNGANUI (TRIG)	HILL	41 17 175 07	53
HIGH MAUNGANUI (TRIG)	HILL	41 17 175 07	55
HIGH MISTY (TRIG)	PEAK	41 12 175 05	52
HIGH MISTY (TRIG)	PEAK	41 12 175 05	55
HIGH PEAK	PEAK	43 28 171 44	80
HIGH PEAK ROCKS	ROCK	35 33 174 43	8
HIGH PEAK SADDLE	SAD	43 27 171 47	80
HIGHBANK	LOC	43 37 171 45	80
HIGHBANK	LOC	43 37 171 45	84
HIGHCLIFF	LOC	45 53 170 34	103
HIGHFIELD, MOUNT (TRIG)	MTN	42 38 173 06	72
HIGHLAND SADDLE	SAD	44 47 168 58	90
HIGHLAND SADDLE	SAD	44 47 168 58	95
HIGHLAY HILL (TRIG)	HILL	45 19 170 26	102
HIHI	LOC	34 59 173 34	3
HIHI	LOC	34 59 173 34	4
HIHI STREAM	STRM	37 07 175 38	15
HIHI STREAM	STRM	37 07 175 38	17
HIHI (TRIG)	HILL	37 05 175 42	15
HIHI (TRIG)	HILL	37 05 175 42	16
HIHI (TRIG)	HILL	37 05 175 42	17
HIHIROROA STREAM	STRM	38 28 177 46	31
HIHIROROA STREAM	STRM	38 28 177 46	32
HIHITAHI	LOC	39 34 175 42	37
HIHITAHI (TRIG)	PEAK	39 33 175 44	37
HIKAPU REACH	STRA	41 12 173 52	54
HIKAPU REACH	STRA	41 12 173 52	60
HIKAPU REACH	STRA	41 12 173 52	61
HIKAWERA	LOC	41 16 175 37	51
HIKAWERA	LOC	41 16 175 37	53
HIKIHIKI BANK	BNK	37 03 174 49	12
HIKIHIKI BANK	BNK	37 03 174 49	14
HIKIPARI PASS	PASS	44 39 168 01	89
HIKUAI	LOC	37 04 175 46	16
HIKUAI	LOC	37 04 175 46	17
HIKUAI STREAM	STRM	37 04 175 48	16
HIKUAI STREAM	STRM	37 04 175 48	17
HIKUMUTU	LOC	38 58 175 17	36
HIKUMUTU STREAM	STRM	38 57 175 14	27
HIKUMUTU STREAM	STRM	38 57 175 14	36
HIKURANGI	POPL	35 36 174 17	5
HIKURANGI	POPL	35 36 174 17	7
HIKURANGI	POPL	35 36 174 17	8
HIKURANGI RIVER	STRM	35 42 174 02	5
HIKURANGI RIVER	STRM	35 42 174 02	7
HIKURANGI STREAM	STRM	39 48 175 59	46
HIKURANGI (TRIG)	HILL	35 03 173 28	3
HIKURANGI (TRIG)	HILL	35 32 173 55	4
HIKURANGI (TRIG)	HILL	35 46 174 06	5
HIKURANGI (TRIG)	HILL	35 46 174 06	7
HIKURANGI (TRIG)	HILL	37 17 175 47	17
HIKURANGI (TRIG)	HILL	38 12 175 19	18
HIKURANGI (TRIG)	HILL	38 12 175 19	19
HIKURANGI (TRIG)	MTN	37 55 178 04	25
HIKURANGI (TRIG)	HILL	38 48 175 18	27
HIKURANGI (TRIG)	MTN	38 21 176 51	30
HIKURANGI (TRIG)	PEAK	39 48 176 05	47
HIKURUA STREAM	STRM	35 06 173 55	4
HIKUTAIA	LOC	37 17 175 39	15
HIKUTAIA	LOC	37 17 175 39	17
HIKUTAIA RIVER	STRM	37 18 175 39	15
HIKUTAIA RIVER	STRM	37 18 175 39	17
HIKUTAWATAWA (TRIG)	HILL	36 44 175 33	13
HIKUTAWATAWA (TRIG)	HILL	36 44 175 33	16
HIKUWAI	LOC	38 10 178 16	25
HIKUWAI	LOC	38 10 178 16	32
HIKUWAI BEACH	LOC	37 59 177 18	23
HIKUWAI RIVER	STRM	38 18 178 16	32
HILDA BURN	STRM	45 42 166 57	104
HILDA BURN	STRM	45 42 166 57	105
HILDA, LAKE	LAKE	45 17 167 24	96
HILDA, LAKE	LAKE	45 17 167 24	97
HILDERTHORPE	LOC	45 00 171 03	93
HILDERTHORPE	LOC	45 00 171 03	102
HILL END (TRIG)	HILL	40 48 176 05	49
HILL END (TRIG)	HILL	40 48 176 05	51
HILL SADDLE	SAD	43 21 171 50	80
HILL TOP	LOC	43 45 172 52	83
HILLEND	LOC	46 08 169 44	111
HILLEND	LOC	46 08 169 44	113
HILLERSDEN	LOC	41 36 173 26	59
HILLERSDEN STREAM	STRM	41 32 173 36	59
HILLGROVE	LOC	45 22 170 49	102
HILLPOINT STREAM	STRM	45 59 168 07	107
HILLS CREEK	STRM	45 00 169 55	91
HILLS CREEK	LOC	44 57 169 55	92
HILLS CREEK	STRM	45 00 169 55	92
HILLS PEAK	PEAK	42 53 171 35	69
HILLSBOROUGH	LOC	39 05 174 09	34
HILTON	LOC	44 09 171 10	87
HILTON, MOUNT (TRIG)	MTN	42 57 172 30	71
HIMATANGI	LOC	40 24 175 19	48
HIMATANGI BEACH	LOC	40 23 175 14	48
HINAHINA	LOC	46 29 169 40	113
HINAHINA COVE	BAY	46 32 169 40	113
HINAHINA HILL (TRIG)	HILL	46 31 169 38	113
HINAHINA STREAM	STRM	46 32 169 40	113
HINAKURA	LOC	41 18 175 39	51
HINAKURA	LOC	41 18 175 39	53
HINATAU RIVER	STRM	43 03 170 23	74
HINAU	LOC	39 54 175 50	46
HINAU	LOC	42 11 171 44	63
HINAU	LOC	42 11 171 44	64
HINAU (TRIG)	HILL	39 53 175 52	46
HINDLEY BURN	STRM	46 00 167 32	105
HINDLEY BURN	STRM	46 00 167 32	106
HINDLEY CREEK	STRM	43 59 168 47	78
HINDLEY PEAK	PEAK	45 53 167 29	105
HINDLEY PEAK	PEAK	45 53 167 29	106
HINDON	HSTD	45 44 170 12	103
HINDON	LOC	45 44 170 18	103
HINDON CROSSING	LOC	45 46 170 19	103
HINDON STATION	RSTN	45 43 170 20	103
HINDS	LOC	44 00 171 34	84
HINDS RIVER	STRM	44 07 171 39	84
HINDS RIVER (NORTH BRANCH)	STRM	43 49 171 26	87
HINDS RIVER (SOUTH BRANCH)	STRM	43 49 171 26	87
HINEHOPU	LOC	38 02 176 29	21
HINEHOPU	LOC	38 02 176 29	22
HINEMAIAIA STREAM	STRM	38 54 176 06	38
HINEMAIAIA STREAM	STRM	38 54 176 06	39
HINEMOA	LOC	40 36 175 53	49
HINEMOA POINT	PNT	38 07 176 18	20
HINEMOA POINT	PNT	38 07 176 18	21
HINERUA	HSTD	39 51 176 14	47
HINGAIA POINT	PNT	36 11 175 07	9
HINGE PEAK	PEAK	43 12 171 04	75
HINUERA	LOC	37 53 175 46	19
HIRA	LOC	41 13 173 24	59
HIRAKIMATA (TRIG)	HILL	36 11 175 25	9
HIRERE FALLS	FALL	44 52 167 51	89
HIRERE FALLS	FALL	44 52 167 51	94
HIRIKI (TRIG)	HILL	34 27 172 41	2
HIRUHARAMA	LOC	37 56 178 16	25
HITCHIN, MOUNT	MTN	43 07 170 49	74
HITCHIN, MOUNT	MTN	43 07 170 49	75
HITOKI STREAM	STRM	39 10 174 34	35
HIWERA	HSTD	39 40 175 55	46
HIWI SADDLE	SAD	38 38 175 12	27
HIWI (TRIG)	HILL	39 39 174 40	44
HIWINUI	LOC	40 16 175 42	46
HIWINUI	LOC	40 16 175 42	49
HIWIPANGO	LOC	41 31 172 56	58
HOANGA	LOC	35 53 173 54	7
HOARY HEAD (TRIG)	HILL	41 08 172 48	57
HOARY HEAD (TRIG)	HILL	41 08 172 48	58
HOBSONVILLE	LOC	36 48 174 39	11
HOBSONVILLE	LOC	36 48 174 39	12
HOCHSTETTER, LAKE	LAKE	42 27 171 40	69
HOCHSTETTER, LAKE	LAKE	42 27 171 40	70
HOCHSTETTER, MOUNT	MTN	42 31 172 01	70
HODDER RIVER	STRM	41 53 173 38	67
HODDERVILLE	LOC	38 08 175 44	19
HODGE CREEK	STRM	41 14 172 32	56
HODGE CREEK	STRM	41 14 172 32	58
HODGE CREEK	STRM	41 21 172 08	62
HODGEN VALLEY STREAM	STRM	41 20 172 56	58
HODGES, MOUNT	MTN	45 42 166 46	104
HODGKINSON CREEK	STRM	44 15 169 36	79
HODGKINSON, MOUNT (TRIG)	MTN	43 48 170 05	76
HODGKINSON, MOUNT (TRIG)	MTN	43 48 170 05	77
HODGKINSON, MOUNT (TRIG)	MTN	43 48 170 05	79
HODGSON STREAM	STRM	41 49 172 42	65
HODGSON (TRIG)	HILL	41 48 172 38	65
HOE-O-TAINUI	LOC	37 31 175 25	15
HOG BURN	STRM	45 10 170 11	101
HOG SWAMP CREEK	STRM	41 40 174 07	67
HOGGET (TRIG)	PEAK	39 22 176 13	39
HOGS BACK (TRIG)	MTN	43 11 171 41	80
HOHONU	LOC	42 42 171 16	68
HOHONU	LOC	42 42 171 16	69
HOHONU RANGE	MTN	42 41 171 23	69
HOIATAIKAHU (TRIG)	HILL	38 02 177 29	24
HOKIANGA HARBOUR	HARB	35 26 173 25	6
HOKIO BEACH	LOC	40 36 175 11	48
HOKITIKA	TOWN	42 43 170 58	68
HOKITIKA	TOWN	42 43 170 58	69
HOKITIKA RIVER	STRM	42 43 170 57	68
HOKITIKA RIVER	STRM	43 01 171 01	75
HOKITIKA SADDLE	SAD	43 01 171 14	75
HOKONUI	LOC	46 08 168 29	107
HOKONUI HILLS	HILL	45 58 168 33	107
HOKONUI HILLS	HILL	46 04 168 44	110
HOKONUI HILLS	HILL	46 04 168 44	112
HOKORAKO CREEK	STRM	36 13 174 18	7
HOKORAKO CREEK	STRM	36 13 174 18	8
HOKOROA	HSTD	38 20 178 04	32
HOKOWHITU	SBRB	40 22 175 38	48
HOKOWHITU	SBRB	40 22 175 38	49
HOKURI CREEK	STRM	44 25 168 03	88
HOKURI CREEK	STRM	44 25 168 03	89
HOLDSWORTH, MOUNT	MTN	44 01 169 35	79
HOLDSWORTH, MOUNT (TRIG)	PEAK	40 52 175 25	48
HOLLOW TOP (TRIG)	HILL	41 52 174 09	67
HOLLY BURN	STRM	46 12 167 38	106
HOLLY BURN	STRM	46 12 167 38	108
HOLLYFORD	LOC	44 46 168 08	89
HOLLYFORD RIVER	STRM	44 20 168 00	89
HOLME STATION	HSTD	44 26 171 04	93
HOLMWOOD ISLAND	ISLD	45 31 167 31	97
HOLYOAKE STREAM	STRM	41 01 173 00	57
HOLYOAKE STREAM	STRM	41 01 173 00	58
HOME BAY	BAY	36 46 174 56	11
HOME BAY	BAY	36 46 174 56	12
HOME BAY	BAY	42 42 172 10	70
HOME CREEK	STRM	43 27 171 12	75
HOME CREEK	STRM	45 35 167 37	97
HOME CREEK	STRM	45 50 168 08	106
HOME CREEK	STRM	45 50 168 08	107
HOME HILL	MTN	44 55 168 17	89
HOME HILL	MTN	44 55 168 17	95
HOME HILL	MTN	45 21 168 33	95
HOME HILL	MTN	44 55 168 17	98
HOME HILL	MTN	45 21 168 33	99
HOME POINT	PNT	35 19 174 23	5
HOME STREAM	STRM	42 38 173 00	72
HOMEBROOK	HSTD	38 24 177 28	31
HOMEBUSH	HSTD	40 21 176 23	50
HOMEBUSH	LOC	40 59 175 40	51
HOMEBUSH	LOC	40 59 175 40	53
HOMEBUSH	LOC	43 29 172 01	81
HOMEBUSH	LOC	43 29 172 01	85
HOMER SADDLE	SAD	44 46 167 59	89
HOMER SADDLE	SAD	44 46 167 59	94
HOMER TUNNEL	TUNL	44 46 167 59	89
HOMER TUNNEL	TUNL	44 46 167 59	94
HOMESTEAD CREEK	STRM	41 45 172 44	65
HOMESTEAD PEAK	PEAK	44 28 168 46	90
HOMESTEAD SPUR (TRIG)	MTN	42 18 173 32	66
HOMESTEAD STREAM	STRM	42 48 172 12	70
HOMEWOOD	HSTD	41 10 175 59	51
HOMEWOOD	HSTD	41 05 173 57	54
HOMEWOOD	HSTD	41 05 173 57	60
HOMEWOOD	HSTD	41 05 173 57	61
HOMMINY COVE	BAY	43 58 168 34	88
HOMUNGA BAY	BAY	37 22 175 56	17
HOMUNGA STREAM	STRM	37 23 175 52	17
HONEYCOMB LIGHT	LTH	41 21 175 50	51
HONEYCOMB ROCK	ROCK	41 21 175 49	51
HONEYMOON VALLEY	LOC	35 08 173 29	3
HONGIORA	ISLD	36 57 176 04	17
HONIKIWI	LOC	38 09 175 07	18
HOODOO SADDLE	SAD	39 23 176 16	39
HOOK	LOC	44 41 171 09	93
HOOK BUSH	HSTD	44 39 170 58	93
HOOK RIVER	STRM	44 41 171 09	93
HOOKER GLACIER	GLCR	43 50 169 39	76
HOOKER GLACIER	GLCR	43 40 170 07	77
HOOKER GLACIER	GLCR	43 50 169 39	79
HOOKER GLACIER	GLCR	43 40 170 07	86
HOOKER, MOUNT	MTN	43 50 169 40	76
HOOKER, MOUNT	MTN	43 50 169 40	79
HOOKER RANGE	MTNS	43 44 169 56	76
HOOKER RANGE	MTNS	43 44 169 56	79
HOOKER RIVER	STRM	43 46 170 09	77
HOOKER RIVER	STRM	43 46 170 09	86
HOOKS BAY	BAY	36 45 175 11	13
HOON HAY	SBRB	43 34 172 36	82
HOON HAY	SBRB	43 34 172 36	83
HOON HAY	SBRB	43 34 172 36	85
HOOPER POINT	PNT	34 25 172 51	2
HOOPERS INLET	LOC	45 51 170 40	103
HOOPERS INLET	BAY	45 53 170 40	103
HOPE	POPL	41 21 173 09	58
HOPE	POPL	41 21 173 09	59
HOPE ARM	BAY	45 33 167 31	97
HOPE, LAKE	LAKE	45 08 168 50	95
HOPE, LAKE	LAKE	45 08 168 50	99
HOPE MOUNT	MTN	43 44 170 41	86
HOPE, MOUNT (TRIG)	MTN	41 40 172 35	65
HOPE PASS	PASS	42 37 172 06	70
HOPE POINT	PNT	35 27 174 44	5
HOPE RANGE	MTNS	41 34 172 38	58
HOPE RIVER	STRM	41 39 172 39	58
HOPE RIVER	STRM	41 42 172 37	65
HOPE RIVER	STRM	42 36 172 34	71
HOPE RIVER	STRM	44 05 168 19	88
HOPE SADDLE	SAD	41 38 172 43	58
HOPE STREAM	STRM	36 34 175 23	16
HOPELANDS	LOC	40 21 175 57	49
HOPELESS CREEK	STRM	41 57 172 48	65
HOPELESS, MOUNT	MTN	41 57 172 44	65
HOPEONE	LOC	38 21 177 07	31
HOPES CREEK	STRM	45 20 169 33	100
HOPKINS, MOUNT	MTN	43 48 169 58	76
HOPKINS, MOUNT	MTN	43 48 169 58	77
HOPKINS, MOUNT	MTN	43 48 169 58	79
HOPKINS RIVER	STRM	44 06 169 52	79
HOPKIRK (TRIG)	HILL	40 15 175 50	46
HOPUHOPU	LOC	37 38 175 10	18
HOPURUAHINE STREAM	STRM	38 43 177 03	30
HORACE WALKER GLACIER	GLCR	43 40 169 57	76
HORACE WALKER GLACIER	GLCR	43 40 169 57	79
HORAHORA	LOC	35 41 174 30	5
HORAHORA	LOC	35 41 174 30	8
HORAHORA	LOC	37 59 175 38	19
HORAHORA RIVER	STRM	35 40 174 30	5
HORAHORA RIVER	STRM	35 40 174 30	8
HOREA (TRIG)	HILL	37 47 174 51	18
HOREKE	LOC	35 22 173 36	3
HOREKE	LOC	35 22 173 36	4
HOREKE	LOC	35 22 173 36	6
HORIZON, LAKE	LAKE	45 42 167 07	105
HORN, CAPE	CAPE	36 56 174 44	12
HORN, CAPE	CAPE	36 56 174 44	14
HORN, MOUNT	MTN	45 04 169 17	100
HORN RANGE, THE	MTNS	45 07 168 59	99
HORNBY	SBRB	43 33 172 32	81
HORNBY	SBRB	43 33 172 32	82
HORNBY	SBRB	43 33 172 32	83
HORNBY	SBRB	43 33 172 32	85
HOROEKA	LOC	40 27 176 13	50
HOROERA POINT	PNT	37 38 178 29	25
HOROHORO	LOC	38 14 176 10	20
HOROHORO	LOC	38 14 176 10	21
HOROHORO	LOC	38 14 176 10	29
HOROHORO (TRIG)	HILL	38 16 176 08	21
HOROHORO (TRIG)	HILL	38 16 176 08	28
HOROHORO (TRIG)	HILL	38 16 176 08	29
HOROHORO (TRIG)	HILL	39 05 175 52	37
HOROHORO (TRIG)	HILL	39 05 175 52	38
HOROKINO	LOC	38 28 175 28	27
HOROKIWI STREAM	STRM	41 06 174 54	52
HOROKIWI STREAM	STRM	41 06 174 54	55
HOROMANGA	LOC	38 22 176 45	30
HOROMANGA RIVER	STRM	38 22 176 45	30
HOROMIA STREAM	STRM	39 32 175 07	36
HOROPITO	LOC	39 21 175 23	36
HOROPITO	LOC	39 21 175 23	37
HOROPITO STREAM	STRM	39 59 175 57	46
HORORATA	LOC	43 32 171 57	80
HORORATA	LOC	43 32 171 57	81
HOROROA POINT	PNT	35 00 173 51	4
HOROTEA, LAKE	LAKE	39 18 176 09	38
HOROTEA, LAKE	LAKE	39 18 176 09	39
HOROTIU	LOC	37 42 175 12	18
HOROWEKA STREAM	STRM	38 34 178 02	32
HOROWHENUA, LAKE	LAKE	40 37 175 15	48
HORRELLVILLE	LOC	43 20 172 20	81
HORRELLVILLE	LOC	43 20 172 20	85
HORRIBLE, MOUNT	MTN	41 45 173 44	67
HORRIBLE, MOUNT (TRIG)	MTN	42 21 173 18	72
HORRIBLE, MOUNT (TRIG)	MTN	42 21 173 18	73
HORRIBLE, MOUNT (TRIG)	MTN	44 35 170 02	92
HORRIBLE STREAM	STRM	42 25 172 48	71
HORRIBLE STREAM	STRM	42 25 172 48	72
HORSE BURN	STRM	45 15 170 16	101
HORSE GULLY	STRM	42 07 172 55	65
HORSE GULLY	STRM	44 28 169 53	91
HORSE RANGE	MTNS	45 18 170 34	102
HORSESHOE BAY	BAY	46 53 168 08	109
HORSESHOE BAY	BAY	46 53 168 08	115
HORSESHOE HILL (TRIG)	PEAK	42 34 172 31	71
HORSESHOE LAKE	LAKE	39 55 176 46	42
HORSESHOE LAKE	LAKE	39 55 176 46	43
HORSHAM DOWN	LOC	37 42 175 15	19
HORSHAM DOWNS	LOC	37 42 175 15	18
HORSLEY DOWNS	LOC	42 53 172 38	71
HORUHORU ROCK	ROCK	36 44 175 10	13
HOSPITAL HILL	LOC	38 01 177 15	23
HOSPITAL HILL	SBRB	39 29 176 54	40
HOSPITAL HILL	SBRB	39 29 176 54	41
HOSPITAL HILL	SBRB	39 29 176 54	42
HOSSACK RIVER	STRM	42 24 173 04	72
HOSSACK SADDLE	SAD	42 27 173 02	72
HOT LAKE	LAKE	38 05 176 44	22
HOT SPRING CREEK	STRM	43 12 170 39	74
HOT WATER BEACH	LOC	36 53 175 49	16
HOT WATER BEACH	LOC	36 53 175 49	17
HOTEO	LOC	36 23 174 32	10
HOTEO	LOC	36 23 174 32	11
HOTEO NORTH	LOC	36 19 174 30	10
HOTEO NORTH	LOC	36 19 174 30	11
HOTEO RIVER	STRM	36 26 174 26	10

HOTEO RIVER	STRM	36 26 174 26	11
HOTOANANGA LAKE	LAKE	37 40 175 11	18
HOUCHENS (TRIG)	HILL	37 53 174 54	18
HOUGH SADDLE	SAD	41 20 172 35	58
HOUHORA	LOC	34 48 173 06	2
HOUHORA	LOC	34 48 173 06	3
HOUHORA BAY	BAY	34 49 173 10	3
HOUHORA HARBOUR	HARB	34 48 173 07	2
HOUHORA HARBOUR	HARB	34 48 173 07	3
HOUHORA HEADS	HEAD	34 50 173 10	2
HOUHORA HEADS	HEAD	34 50 173 10	3
HOUHOU	LOC	42 42 171 00	68
HOUHOU	LOC	42 42 171 00	69
HOUIPAPA	LOC	46 29 169 33	113
HOUND BURN	STRM	45 13 170 16	101
HOUPOTO	LOC	37 52 177 35	24
HOUSE CREEK	STRM	41 53 173 35	66
HOUSE HILL (TRIG)	HILL	44 12 170 19	86
HOUSEROOF HILL	MTN	45 55 166 58	104
HOUSEROOF HILL	MTN	45 55 166 58	105
HOUTO	LOC	35 45 174 00	5
HOUTO	LOC	35 45 174 00	7
HOUTO (TRIG)	HILL	35 46 173 59	5
HOUTO (TRIG)	HILL	35 46 173 59	7
HOVELLS WATCHING DOG (TRIG)	HILL	37 37 178 17	25
HOWARD	LOC	41 46 172 40	65
HOWARD JUNCTION	LOC	41 42 172 38	65
HOWARD RIVER	STRM	41 43 172 41	65
HOWDEN, LAKE	LAKE	44 49 168 08	89
HOWE CREEK	STRM	44 02 169 16	78
HOWE KNOB	PEAK	44 03 169 06	78
HOWE, MOUNT (TRIG)	MTN	42 44 171 39	70
HOWE POINT	PNT	35 10 174 07	4
HOWE POINT	PNT	35 10 174 07	5
HOWE (TRIG)	HILL	40 17 176 24	50
HOWELLS POINT	PNT	46 23 168 02	109
HOWICK	SBRB	36 54 174 56	11
HOWICK	SBRB	36 54 174 56	12
HOWICK	SBRB	36 54 174 56	14
HOWITT, MOUNT	MTN	43 43 169 57	76
HOWITT, MOUNT	MTN	43 43 169 57	79
HOWITT PEAKS	PEAK	45 06 167 38	94
HOWITT PEAKS	PEAK	45 06 167 38	97
HOWITT POINT	PNT	42 36 171 28	69
HUAERO STREAM	STRM	37 54 177 43	24
HUANGARUA RIVER	STRM	41 12 175 28	53
HUANUI	HSTD	38 18 178 01	32
HUANUI (TRIG)	HILL	38 56 174 39	26
HUAPAI	LOC	36 46 174 32	10
HUAPAI	LOC	36 46 174 32	11
HUAPAI	LOC	36 46 174 32	12
HUAPE STREAM	STRM	38 13 177 06	23
HUAPE STREAM	STRM	38 13 177 06	31
HUARAHI (TRIG)	HILL	38 27 174 53	26
HUARAU	LOC	36 07 174 19	7
HUARAU	LOC	36 07 174 19	8
HUAROA POINT	PNT	36 36 174 50	11
HUAROA POINT	PNT	36 36 174 50	12
HUARUA (TRIG)	HILL	35 52 174 11	7
HUATOKE STREAM	STRM	39 03 174 05	34
HUATOKITOKI STREAM	STRM	40 12 176 35	43
HUATOKITOKI STREAM	STRM	40 12 176 35	47
HUB CREEK	STRM	45 15 166 58	96
HUEHUE STREAM	STRM	35 29 173 47	4
HUEHUE STREAM	STRM	35 29 173 47	6
HUFFAN STREAM	STRM	40 55 173 03	57
HUGHES CREEK	STRM	43 21 170 29	74
HUGHES CREEK	STRM	43 21 170 29	77
HUHATAHI STREAM	STRM	38 50 174 59	26
HUIA	LOC	37 00 174 34	12
HUIA	LOC	37 00 174 34	14
HUIA BANK	BNK	37 02 174 35	12
HUIA BANK	BNK	37 02 174 35	14
HUIA RESERVOIR	LAKE	36 58 174 32	12
HUIA RESERVOIR	LAKE	36 58 174 32	14
HUIA RIVER	STRM	41 17 172 16	62
HUIA (TRIG)	HILL	35 05 173 48	4
HUIAKAMA	LOC	39 16 174 34	35
HUIAKAMA	LOC	39 16 174 34	44
HUIARAU RANGE	MTNS	38 39 177 01	30
HUIARAU (TRIG)	HILL	38 28 175 43	28
HUIARUA	HSTD	38 06 178 03	25
HUIHUITAHA STREAM	STRM	38 04 175 40	19
HUIKOMAKO (TRIG)	HILL	38 31 174 39	26
HUIKUMU STREAM	STRM	39 24 175 04	36
HUINGA	LOC	39 22 174 26	35
HUINGA	LOC	39 22 174 26	44
HUIRANGI	LOC	39 03 174 15	34
HUIROA	LOC	39 15 174 29	35
HUIROA	LOC	39 15 174 29	44
HUIRU (TRIG)	HILL	40 32 176 20	50
HUITATARIKI STREAM	STRM	37 52 178 02	25
HUKANUI	LOC	40 34 175 41	49
HUKANUI STREAM	STRM	38 52 177 07	30
HUKANUI (TRIG)	HILL	39 15 176 33	39
HUKANUI (TRIG)	HILL	39 15 176 33	40
HUKAPAPA	LOC	39 04 175 23	36
HUKAPAPA	LOC	39 04 175 23	37
HUKARAHI (TRIG)	HILL	36 46 175 42	16
HUKARERE	LOC	42 15 171 42	63
HUKARERE	LOC	42 15 171 42	64
HUKAROA (TRIG)	HILL	39 28 175 15	36
HUKATERE	LOC	34 54 173 06	2
HUKATERE	LOC	34 54 173 06	3
HUKATERE	LOC	36 11 174 10	7
HUKATERE STREAM	STRM	35 14 173 06	3
HUKAWAI	LOC	42 18 171 47	63
HUKAWAI	LOC	42 18 171 47	64
HUKERE STREAM	STRM	41 54 172 48	65
HUKERENUI	LOC	35 31 174 12	5
HUKIHIKI CREEK	STRM	46 37 169 22	113
HUKITAWA STREAM	STRM	38 44 176 52	30
HULKA, MOUNT	MTN	43 18 170 38	74
HUMBOLDT CREEK	STRM	44 42 168 08	89
HUMBOLDT, MOUNT	MTN	42 11 172 37	65
HUMBOLDT MOUNTAINS	MTNS	44 44 168 15	89
HUMBOLDT TOWER	MTN	44 29 168 33	88
HUMBOLDT TOWER	MTN	44 29 168 33	90
HUMMOCK PEAK (TRIG)	PEAK	45 18 168 18	95
HUMMOCK PEAK (TRIG)	PEAK	45 18 168 18	98
HUMMOCK (TRIG)	HILL	45 33 170 23	101
HUMMOCK (TRIG)	HILL	45 33 170 23	102
HUMP BURN	STRM	46 09 167 24	105
HUMP BURN	STRM	46 09 167 24	108
HUMP RIDGE	RDGE	46 07 167 20	105
HUMP RIDGE	RDGE	46 07 167 20	108
HUMP, THE (TRIG)	MTN	46 07 167 20	105
HUMPHREYS	LOC	42 44 171 06	68
HUMPHREYS	LOC	42 44 171 06	69
HUMPHRIES, MOUNT	MTN	43 49 169 54	76

HUMPHRIES, MOUNT	MTN	43 49 169 54	79
HUMPHRIES, MOUNT (TRIG)	HILL	39 19 174 49	35
HUMPHRIES, MOUNT (TRIG)	HILL	39 19 174 49	44
HUMUHUMU, LAKE	LAKE	36 20 174 07	10
HUNAHUNA STREAM	STRM	35 15 173 07	3
HUNDALEE	LOC	42 36 173 25	72
HUNDALEE	LOC	42 36 173 25	73
HUNGAHUNGA	LOC	37 41 175 44	19
HUNGRY HILL (TRIG)	HILL	41 52 174 06	67
HUNT HILL	HILL	43 41 169 30	76
HUNT HILL	HILL	43 41 169 30	79
HUNT, MOUNT	MTN	42 53 171 45	70
HUNT SADDLE	SAD	42 49 171 30	69
HUNTER	LOC	44 37 171 02	93
HUNTER HILLS, THE	MTNS	44 31 170 50	93
HUNTER, MOUNT	MTN	42 20 172 03	64
HUNTER, MOUNT	MTN	42 20 172 03	70
HUNTER MOUNTAINS	MTNS	45 38 167 24	105
HUNTER PASS	PASS	44 52 167 42	94
HUNTER RIVER	STRM	44 17 169 27	79
HUNTER STREAM	STRM	44 37 168 28	88
HUNTER STREAM	STRM	44 37 168 28	89
HUNTERS CREEK	STRM	37 38 176 08	20
HUNTERS GULLY	STRM	41 39 172 52	65
HUNTERS STREAM	STRM	43 19 172 28	81
HUNTERS STREAM	STRM	43 19 172 28	85
HUNTERVILLE	POPL	39 56 175 34	45
HUNTERVILLE	POPL	39 56 175 34	46
HUNTINGDON	LOC	43 59 171 44	84
HUNTLY	POPL	37 34 175 10	14
HUNTLY	POPL	37 34 175 10	15
HUNTS CREEK	STRM	42 49 171 28	69
HUNUA	LOC	37 05 175 04	13
HUNUA	LOC	37 05 175 04	14
HUNUA	LOC	37 05 175 04	15
HUNUA RANGES	MTNS	37 01 175 13	13
HUNUA RANGES	MTNS	37 01 175 13	15
HUNUA STREAM	STRM	37 03 175 05	12
HUNUA STREAM	STRM	37 03 175 05	13
HUNUA STREAM	STRM	37 03 175 05	14
HUPARA	LOC	35 07 174 00	5
HURA CREEK	STRM	42 51 171 27	69
HURA SADDLE	SAD	42 52 171 24	69
HURIPARI STREAM	STRM	39 49 175 11	45
HURIWAI RIVER	STRM	37 27 174 43	14
HURLEYVILLE	LOC	39 39 174 30	44
HURRICANE COL	SAD	44 22 168 23	88
HURRICANE COL	SAD	44 22 168 23	89
HURUHAKARIKI (TRIG)	HILL	40 33 175 30	48
HURUHAKARIKI (TRIG)	HILL	40 33 175 30	49
HURUHI HARBOUR	HARB	36 36 175 46	16
HURUHURUMAKU CLIFFS	CLIF	38 07 174 41	18
HURUHURUMAKU STREAM	STRM	38 29 175 45	28
HURUHURUNUI STREAM	STRM	39 11 177 50	33
HURUIKI (TRIG)	HILL	35 26 174 19	5
HURUNUI	LOC	42 53 172 46	71
HURUNUI	LOC	42 53 172 46	72
HURUNUI MOUTH	LOC	42 54 173 16	72
HURUNUI MOUTH	LOC	42 54 173 16	73
HURUNUI PEAK (TRIG)	MTN	42 47 172 35	71
HURUNUI RIVER	STRM	42 55 173 17	72
HURUNUI RIVER	STRM	42 55 173 17	73
HURUNUI RIVER, SOUTH BRANCH	STRM	42 50 172 21	71
HURUNUI STREAM	STRM	37 49 175 59	20
HURURU STREAM	STRM	37 57 176 20	20
HURURU STREAM	STRM	37 57 176 20	21
HUSBAND CREEK	STRM	41 45 172 17	65
HUSS MOUNT	MTN	43 28 170 26	74
HUSS MOUNT	MTN	43 28 170 26	77
HUT BRANCH	STRM	42 53 172 19	71
HUT BURN	STRM	45 06 168 23	95
HUT BURN	STRM	45 06 168 23	98
HUT CREEK	STRM	42 45 171 34	69
HUT CREEK	STRM	44 56 168 02	89
HUT CREEK	STRM	44 51 169 55	92
HUT CREEK	STRM	44 50 170 15	92
HUT PEAK	PEAK	43 56 169 48	76
HUT PEAK	PEAK	43 56 169 48	79
HUT STREAM	STRM	41 56 173 08	66
HUT STREAM	STRM	43 13 171 09	75
HUT STREAM	STRM	43 05 172 27	81
HUTEWAI STREAM	STRM	40 02 175 54	46
HUTIA (TRIG)	HILL	39 15 174 55	35
HUTIA (TRIG)	HILL	39 15 174 55	36
HUTIWAI STREAM	STRM	38 49 174 36	26
HUTIWAI STREAM	STRM	38 29 174 44	26
HUTIWAI (TRIG)	HILL	38 51 174 40	26
HUTOIA STREAM	STRM	35 19 173 38	4
HUTT RIVER	STRM	41 14 174 54	52
HUTT RIVER	STRM	41 14 174 54	55
HUTT STREAM	STRM	43 25 171 35	80
HUTT, MOUNT (TRIG)	MTN	43 28 171 32	80
HUTTON, MOUNT	MTN	43 36 170 23	74
HUTTON, MOUNT	MTN	43 36 170 23	77
HUTTON, MOUNT (TRIG)	MTN	41 54 172 37	65
HUXLEY RIVER	STRM	44 00 169 49	79
HUXLEY, MOUNT	MTN	44 04 169 41	79
HYDE	LOC	45 18 170 15	101
HYDE, MOUNT (TRIG)	MTN	44 45 168 48	90
HYDE, MOUNT (TRIG)	MTN	44 45 168 48	95
HYDE, MOUNT (TRIG)	HILL	45 47 170 17	103
HYDE ROCK (TRIG)	MTN	45 23 169 12	100
HYDE (TRIG)	PEAK	39 16 175 42	37
HYDE (TRIG)	PEAK	39 16 175 42	38
HYPERIA	MTN	44 15 168 45	88

I

IAN, MOUNT	MTN	44 29 168 29	88
IAN, MOUNT	MTN	44 29 168 29	89
IANTHE LAKE	LAKE	43 04 170 37	74
ICEBURG, LAKE	LAKE	44 49 167 52	89
ICEBURG, LAKE	LAKE	44 49 167 52	94
IDA BURN	STRM	45 04 169 45	100
IDA BURN	STRM	45 04 169 45	101
IDA BURN (NORTH BRANCH)	STRM	44 52 169 55	92
IDA, LAKE	LAKE	42 43 171 23	69
IDA, LAKE	LAKE	43 14 171 32	80
IDA, MOUNT (TRIG)	MTN	43 13 171 32	80
IDA, MOUNT (TRIG)	MTN	44 56 170 05	92
IDA RANGE	MTNS	44 57 170 08	92
IDA VALLEY	LOC	45 02 169 49	100
IDA VALLEY	LOC	45 02 169 49	101
IDABURN	LOC	44 59 169 59	92
IDABURN	LOC	44 59 169 59	101
IDABURN DAM	DAM	45 02 169 54	100
IDABURN DAM	DAM	45 02 169 54	101
IGNIMBRITE SADDLE	SAD	39 07 176 00	37
IGNIMBRITE SADDLE	SAD	39 07 176 00	38
IHAKARA	LOC	40 36 175 20	48

IHUMEKA STREAM	STRM	38 39 177 27	31
IHUMEKA STREAM	STRM	38 39 177 27	33
IHUNGIA	LOC	38 03 178 10	25
IHUNGIA RIVER	STRM	37 59 178 10	25
IHUNUI (TRIG)	HILL	37 42 174 58	18
IHURAUA	LOC	40 44 175 49	49
IHURAUA	LOC	40 44 175 49	51
IHURAUA RIVER	STRM	40 38 175 52	49
IHUTOTO	HILL	38 35 177 01	30
IKAMATUA	LOC	42 16 171 41	63
IKAMATUA	LOC	42 16 171 41	64
IKAMATUA PLAIN	PLN	42 18 171 43	63
IKAMATUA PLAIN	PLN	42 18 171 43	64
IKANUI STREAM	STRM	40 06 176 52	43
IKAWETEA STREAM	STRM	39 31 176 15	39
IKAWHENUA RANGE	MTNS	38 29 176 53	30
IMPEY, MOUNT (TRIG)	MTN	41 45 173 16	66
INACCESSIBLE, MOUNT	MTN	45 53 166 38	104
INAHA	LOC	39 34 174 10	34
INAHA STREAM	STRM	39 35 174 10	34
INANGAHUA	LOC	41 52 171 57	64
INANGAHUA JUNCTION	LOC	41 52 171 56	63
INANGAHUA JUNCTION	LOC	41 52 171 56	64
INANGAHUA LANDING	LOC	41 55 171 54	63
INANGAHUA LANDING	LOC	41 55 171 54	64
INANGAHUA RIVER	STRM	41 51 171 57	63
INANGAHUA RIVER	STRM	41 51 171 57	64
INANGATAHI STREAM	STRM	39 12 176 37	39
INANGATAHI STREAM	STRM	39 12 176 37	40
INCH CLUTHA	ISLD	46 17 169 47	111
INCH CLUTHA	ISLD	46 17 169 47	113
INCH VALLEY	LOC	45 25 170 39	102
INCHBONNIE	LOC	42 44 171 29	69
INCHOLME	LOC	45 07 170 47	102
INDIAN ISLAND	ISLD	45 47 166 35	104
INFRAMENTA, MOUNT	MTN	43 02 171 04	75
INGAHAPE STREAM	STRM	39 38 174 23	35
INGAHAPE STREAM	STRM	39 38 174 23	44
INGLEWOOD	POPL	39 10 174 11	34
INKERMAN SADDLE	SAD	43 34 170 47	75
INLAND KAIKOURA RANGE	MTNS	42 03 173 34	66
INNES BURN	STRM	44 26 170 21	92
INNES, LAKE	LAKE	46 11 166 58	105
INTERVENTION SADDLE	SAD	44 26 168 19	88
INTERVENTION SADDLE	SAD	44 26 168 19	89
INUMIA STREAM	STRM	35 09 173 47	4
INVERCARGILL	TOWN	46 25 168 22	109
INVERNESS	HSTD	42 41 173 18	72
INVERNESS	HSTD	42 41 173 18	73
INVINCIBLE CREEK	STRM	44 44 168 28	89
INVINCIBLE CREEK	STRM	44 44 168 28	95
INVITATION COL	SAD	44 23 168 24	88
INVITATION COL	SAD	44 23 168 24	89
IONA	HSTD	42 39 173 16	72
IONA	HSTD	42 39 173 16	73
IONIA, MOUNT	MTN	44 23 168 35	88
IONIA, MOUNT	MTN	44 23 168 35	90
IOTA BLUFF (TRIG)	HILL	44 02 168 21	88
IOTA CREEK	STRM	42 01 171 37	63
IOTA, MOUNT	MTN	44 03 168 22	88
IRENE, MOUNT	MTN	45 11 167 21	96
IRENE PASS	PASS	45 13 167 16	96
IRENE RIVER	STRM	45 07 167 14	94
IRENE RIVER	STRM	45 07 167 14	96
IRIRANGI	LOC	39 33 175 41	37
IRIS BURN	STRM	45 29 167 35	97
IRIS, MOUNT	MTN	42 06 172 48	65
IRIS (TRIG)	HILL	40 24 176 24	50
IRISHMAN CREEK	STRM	44 13 170 20	86
IRISHMAN STREAM	STRM	44 03 169 55	79
IRON BAR POINT (TRIG)	HILL	44 06 168 17	88
IRON CREEK	STRM	43 12 171 51	80
IRON HILL	HILL	41 06 172 37	56
IRON HILL	HILL	41 06 172 37	57
IRON HILL	HILL	41 06 172 37	58
IRONSTONE CREEK	STRM	40 59 172 50	57
IRONSTONE CREEK	STRM	40 59 172 50	58
IRTHING STREAM	STRM	45 40 168 25	107
IRWELL	LOC	43 42 172 07	85
IRWELL RIVER	STRM	43 45 172 23	85
ISAACS, MOUNT	MNT	36 20 175 31	9
ISABEL, MOUNT	MTN	43 44 170 01	76
ISABEL, MOUNT	MTN	43 44 170 01	77
ISABEL, MOUNT	MTN	43 44 170 01	79
ISIS STREAM	STRM	41 51 173 42	67
ISLA BANK	LOC	46 13 168 08	106
ISLA BANK	LOC	46 13 168 08	107
ISLAND BAY	SBRB	41 20 174 46	52
ISLAND BAY	BAY	41 21 174 46	52
ISLAND BAY	SBRB	41 20 174 46	55
ISLAND BAY	BAY	41 21 174 46	55
ISLAND BAY	BAY	43 53 172 52	83
ISLAND BLOCK	LOC	37 19 175 08	14
ISLAND BLOCK	LOC	37 19 175 08	15
ISLAND BLOCK	LOC	45 45 168 30	111
ISLAND CREEK	STRM	41 49 171 38	63
ISLAND CREEK	STRM	41 49 171 38	64
ISLAND CREEK	STRM	45 32 169 09	99
ISLAND HILL	HILL	46 55 167 49	114
ISLAND HILL (TRIG)	HILL	43 06 172 12	81
ISLAND HILL (TRIG)	PEAK	42 47 171 14	68
ISLAND HILL (TRIG)	PEAK	42 47 171 14	69
ISLAND LAKE	LAKE	41 02 172 29	56
ISLAND LAKE	LAKE	41 02 172 29	57
ISLAND LAKE	LAKE	41 02 172 29	58
ISLAND LAKE	LAKE	42 09 172 56	65
ISLAND LAKE	LAKE	45 47 167 22	105
ISLAND SADDLE	SAD	42 11 172 48	65
ISLAND STREAM	LOC	45 10 170 48	102
ISLAND STREAM	STRM	45 10 170 46	102
ISLAND STREAM NORTH BRANCH	STRM	45 11 170 44	102
ISLAND STREAM SOUTH BRANCH	STRM	45 11 170 44	102
ISLAND VIEW	LOC	37 26 175 58	17
ISLET COVE	BAY	45 57 166 45	104
ISLET POINT	PNT	45 02 167 05	96
ISLINGTON	SBRB	43 33 172 31	81
ISLINGTON	SBRB	43 33 172 31	82
ISLINGTON	SBRB	43 33 172 31	83
ISLINGTON	SBRB	43 33 172 31	85
ISOBEL, MOUNT (TRIG)	MTN	42 29 172 51	71
ISOBEL, MOUNT (TRIG)	MTN	42 29 172 51	72
ISOLATED HILL	HILL	41 54 173 58	67
ISOLATED HILL (TRIG)	HILL	42 41 173 01	72
ISOLATED SADDLE	SAD	42 08 173 05	66
ISOLATION, MOUNT	MTN	44 44 167 57	89
ISOLATION, MOUNT	MTN	44 44 167 57	94
ISTHMUS PEAK	PEAK	44 28 169 12	90
ISTHMUS SOUND	SND	46 03 166 42	104
ITALIAN GULLY	STRM	42 55 170 47	68
IVEAGH BAY	BAY	42 38 171 29	69

IVYDALE	LOC	35 22 173 34	3
IVYDALE	LOC	35 22 173 34	4
IVYDALE	LOC	35 22 173 34	6
IWIKAU VILLAGE	LOC	39 14 175 33	36
IWIKAU VILLAGE	LOC	39 14 175 33	37
IWIKAU VILLAGE	LOC	39 14 175 33	38
IWITAHI	LOC	38 50 176 16	29
IWITUAROA RANGE	MTNS	40 55 172 08	56
IZARD, MOUNT	MTN	43 11 171 38	80

J

JACK CREEK	STRM	42 52 171 17	68
JACK CREEK	STRM	42 52 171 17	69
JACK, MOUNT	MTN	43 49 169 39	76
JACK, MOUNT	MTN	43 49 169 39	79
JACK (TRIG)	MTN	41 45 173 33	66
JACKETTS ISLAND	ISLD	41 09 173 02	57
JACKETTS ISLAND	ISLD	41 09 173 02	58
JACKETTS ISLAND	ISLD	41 09 173 02	59
JACKS BROTHER	MTN	41 47 173 30	66
JACKS HILL	MTN	43 12 171 15	75
JACKS PASS	PASS	42 29 172 50	72
JACKS SADDLE	SAD	42 51 172 27	71
JACKS STREAM	STRM	42 52 172 30	71
JACKS STREAM	STRM	43 59 170 08	77
JACKSON BAY	BAY	43 58 168 42	88
JACKSON BAY	LOC	43 58 168 37	88
JACKSON, CAPE	CAPE	41 00 174 19	54
JACKSON, CAPE	CAPE	41 00 174 19	61
JACKSON CREEK	STRM	42 22 172 16	70
JACKSON HEAD	HEAD	43 58 168 37	88
JACKSON PEAKS	MTNS	45 25 167 35	97
JACKSON, MOUNT	MTN	43 54 169 47	76
JACKSON, MOUNT	MTN	43 54 169 47	79
JACKSON, MOUNT	MTN	44 07 168 41	88
JACKSON, MOUNT (TRIG)	MTN	42 14 173 16	66
JACKSON RIVER	STRM	44 03 168 44	88
JACKSON STREAM	STRM	43 27 171 45	80
JACKSON (TRIG)	HILL	39 22 174 30	35
JACKSON (TRIG)	HILL	39 22 174 30	44
JACKSONS	LOC	42 45 171 32	69
JACKY LEE ISLAND	ISLD	46 51 168 13	109
JACKY LEE ISLAND	ISLD	46 51 168 13	115
JACOB, MOUNT	MTN	43 38 169 43	76
JACOB, MOUNT	MTN	43 38 169 43	79
JACOBS BLUFF (TRIG)	HILL	43 33 169 39	76
JACOBS CREEK	STRM	45 26 166 55	96
JACOBS HILL (TRIG)	HILL	46 28 169 42	113
JACOBS LADDER (TRIG)	HILL	42 14 173 50	67
JACOBS RIVER	LOC	43 34 169 41	76
JACOBS RIVER (MAKAWHIO RIVER)	STRM	43 34 169 38	76
JACOBS RIVER ESTUARY	ESTY	46 21 168 00	108
JACOBS RIVER ESTUARY	ESTY	46 21 168 00	109
JACOBS STREAM	STRM	43 33 171 12	75
JAG ROCKS	ROCK	40 47 174 03	54
JAG ROCKS	ROCK	40 47 174 03	61
JAGGED COL	SAD	43 20 171 01	75
JAGGED PEAK	PEAK	43 20 171 01	75
JAGGED SPUR	RDGE	43 43 169 50	76
JAGGED SPUR	RDGE	43 43 169 50	79
JAGGED STREAM	STRM	43 18 171 04	75
JAM STREAM	STRM	42 04 173 43	67
JAMES PEAK (TRIG)	PEAK	45 15 168 51	95
JAMES PEAK (TRIG)	PEAK	45 15 168 51	99
JAMESTOWN	LOC	44 24 168 03	88
JAMESTOWN	LOC	44 24 168 03	89
JAMESTOWN SADDLE	SAD	44 23 168 06	88
JAMESTOWN SADDLE	SAD	44 23 168 06	89
JAMIES KNOB (TRIG)	HILL	41 35 174 07	60
JANE, LAKE	LAKE	45 43 167 07	105
JANE PEAK	PEAK	45 20 168 19	95
JANE PEAK	PEAK	45 20 168 19	98
JAQUIERY, LAKE	LAKE	45 50 167 15	105
JAQUIERY, PASS	PASS	45 29 167 02	96
JAQUIERY STREAM	STRM	45 46 167 18	105
JASPER, LAKE	LAKE	41 40 173 58	67
JEAN BATTEN PEAK	PEAK	44 52 168 10	89
JEANETTE, LAKE	LAKE	41 31 172 23	62
JEANIE BURN	STRM	45 58 166 52	104
JEANIE BURN	STRM	45 58 166 52	105
JED RIVER	STRM	42 51 173 19	72
JED RIVER	STRM	42 51 173 19	73
JENKINS HILL (TRIG)	HILL	41 20 173 17	59
JERRY RIVER	STRM	44 12 168 15	88
JERUSALEM	LOC	39 33 175 05	36
JERUSALEM CREEK	STRM	44 22 168 00	89
JERVOIS, MOUNT	MTN	42 22 172 33	71
JERVOIS STREAM	STRM	42 25 172 35	71
JESS CREEK	STRM	41 54 171 48	63
JESS CREEK	STRM	41 54 171 48	64
JESSIE PEAK	PEAK	45 04 168 29	95
JESSIE PEAK	PEAK	45 04 168 29	98
JEWELL, LAKE	LAKE	41 09 172 23	56
JEWELL, LAKE	LAKE	41 09 172 23	62
JOAN, LAKE	LAKE	43 10 170 24	74
JOE CREEK	STRM	44 16 168 37	88
JOE GLACIER	GLCR	44 29 168 22	88
JOE GLACIER	GLCR	44 29 168 22	89
JOE PEAK	PEAK	44 17 168 30	88
JOE PEAK	PEAK	44 17 168 30	89
JOE RIVER	STRM	44 25 168 30	88
JOE RIVER	STRM	44 25 168 30	89
JOES RIVER	STRM	44 44 167 51	89
JOES RIVER	STRM	44 44 167 51	94
JOES SADDLE	SAD	46 30 169 25	113
JOEYS ISLAND	ISLD	46 34 168 23	109
JOHN INGLIS GLACIER	GLCR	44 26 168 24	88
JOHN INGLIS GLACIER	GLCR	44 26 168 24	89
JOHN ISLANDS	ISLS	45 34 166 48	104
JOHN O'GROATES RIVER	STRM	44 31 167 50	89
JOHN O'GROATES RIVER	STRM	44 31 167 50	94
JOHN O'GROATS HILL	HILL	45 56 169 25	111
JOHN POINT	PNT	47 07 168 09	115
JOHN, MOUNT OBSERVATORY (TRIG)	MTN	43 59 170 28	77
JOHN, MOUNT OBSERVATORY (TRIG)	MTN	43 59 170 28	86
JOHNS CREEK	STRM	44 36 169 19	91
JOHNSON CREEK	STRM	41 22 173 36	59
JOHNSON, LAKE	LAKE	45 00 168 44	95
JOHNSON, LAKE	LAKE	45 00 168 44	99
JOHNSON, MOUNT	MTN	43 36 170 16	74
JOHNSON, MOUNT	MTN	43 36 170 16	77
JOHNSON RIVER	STRM	41 29 172 17	62
JOHNSONVILLE	SBRB	41 13 174 48	52
JOHNSONVILLE	SBRB	41 13 174 48	55
JOHNSTON, MOUNT	MTN	42 10 171 33	63
JOHNSTONE	LOC	46 01 169 46	111
JOHNSTONE	LOC	46 01 169 46	113
JOHNSTONE STREAM	STRM	43 34 171 11	75
JOHNSTONE (TRIG)	MTN	38 23 177 26	31

JOLLIE BROOK	STRM	42 48 172 20	71
JOLLIE BROOK (TRIG)	MTN	42 43 172 23	71
JOLLIE, MOUNT	MTN	43 25 170 51	75
JOLLIE RANGE	MTNS	43 21 170 52	75
JOLLIE RIVER	STRM	43 52 170 10	77
JOLLIE RIVER	STRM	43 52 170 10	86
JOLLIES PASS	PASS	42 30 172 53	71
JOLLIES PASS	PASS	42 30 172 53	72
JON, MOUNT	HILL	42 51 173 02	72
JONATHAN, MOUNT (TRIG)	MTN	42 44 172 36	71
JONES CREEK	STRM	41 41 171 47	63
JONES CREEK	STRM	41 41 171 47	64
JONES, MOUNT	MTN	44 23 169 27	91
JONES, MOUNT (TRIG)	PEAK	41 24 172 40	58
JONES SADDLE	SAD	44 55 168 37	90
JONES SADDLE	SAD	44 55 168 37	95
JONES STREAM	STRM	42 25 172 37	71
JORDAN	HSTD	41 49 173 46	67
JORDAN RIVER	STRM	41 50 173 44	67
JORDAN SADDLE	SAD	43 03 171 30	80
JORDAN STREAM	STRM	42 15 173 45	67
JORDAN STREAM	STRM	43 00 171 32	80
JOSEPH, MOUNT	MTN	43 52 170 22	77
JOSEPH, MOUNT	MTN	43 52 170 22	86
JOSEPH STREAM	STRM	43 52 170 26	77
JOSEPH STREAM	STRM	43 52 170 26	86
JOSEPHVILLE	LOC	45 48 168 25	107
JOURDAIN CONE	PEAK	43 11 170 58	75
JUDEA	SBRB	37 42 176 08	20
JUDEA	SBRB	37 42 176 08	21
JUDGE CREEK	STRM	45 40 169 25	111
JUDGEFORD	LOC	41 07 174 57	52
JUDGEFORD	LOC	41 07 174 57	55
JUDGES CREEK	STRM	42 04 172 56	66
JULIA CREEK	STRM	42 54 171 26	69
JULIA, LAKE	LAKE	42 43 171 22	69
JUMBO	PEAK	40 51 175 26	48
JUMBO CREEK	STRM	43 40 169 44	76
JUMBO CREEK	STRM	43 40 169 44	79
JUMBO, MOUNT	MTN	44 17 168 59	78
JUMBUCK, LAKE	LAKE	44 02 168 24	88
JUMPED UP STREAM	STRM	39 40 176 19	47
JUNCTION BURN	STRM	45 09 167 30	94
JUNCTION BURN	STRM	45 09 167 30	97
JUNCTION CREEK	STRM	42 06 172 31	65
JUNCTION CREEK	STRM	41 45 173 37	67
JUNCTION HILL (TRIG)	MTN	44 14 168 20	88
JUNCTION ISLANDS	ISLS	36 14 175 19	9
JUNCTION PEAK	PEAK	43 25 170 21	74
JUNCTION PEAK	PEAK	43 25 170 21	77
JUNCTION (TRIG)	HILL	34 32 172 50	2
JUNCTION (TRIG)	MTN	42 06 172 29	65
JUNE BAY	BAY	45 53 167 21	105
JUNO, MOUNT	MTN	44 14 168 56	78
JUNO RIVER	STRM	45 02 167 06	96
JUPITER CREEK	STRM	41 18 172 26	62
JURA GLACIER	GLCR	44 34 168 26	88
JURA GLACIER	GLCR	44 34 168 26	89

■ K

KAAWA	LOC	37 31 174 53	14
KAAWA STREAM	STRM	37 30 174 44	14
KAEO	LOC	35 06 173 47	4
KAEO RIVER	STRM	35 05 173 46	4
KAHAHAKURI STREAM	STRM	39 59 176 30	47
KAHAKAHA STREAM	STRM	39 47 175 12	45
KAHAO STREAM	STRM	41 05 174 54	52
KAHAO STREAM	STRM	41 05 174 54	55
KAHAROA	LOC	38 00 176 14	20
KAHAROA	LOC	38 00 176 14	21
KAHAROA STREAM	STRM	38 19 177 10	31
KAHAROA (TRIG)	MTN	38 21 177 13	31
KAHAWAI POINT	PNT	35 29 174 43	5
KAHEKE STREAM	STRM	40 00 175 55	46
KAHEREKOAU MOUNTAINS	MTNS	45 54 167 19	105
KAHIKA	LOC	39 11 176 56	40
KAHIKA	LOC	39 11 176 56	41
KAHIKA STREAM	STRM	39 11 176 58	40
KAHIKA STREAM	STRM	39 11 176 58	41
KAHIKATEA	HILL	41 16 174 07	54
KAHIKATEA	HILL	41 16 174 07	60
KAHIKATEA	HILL	41 16 174 07	61
KAHIKATEA RANGE	MTNS	38 23 177 12	31
KAHIKATOA	LOC	35 18 173 34	3
KAHIKATOA	LOC	35 18 173 34	4
KAHIWIROA	PEAK	40 52 175 21	48
KAHOE	LOC	35 03 173 41	4
KAHOKA STREAM	STRM	37 58 177 48	24
KAHOKAWA BEACH	BCH	34 32 172 44	2
KAHUA POINT	BAY	38 02 174 47	18
KAHUHURU STREAM	STRM	37 42 175 00	18
KAHUI (TRIG)	HILL	39 19 173 56	34
KAHUIKA	LOC	46 31 169 27	113
KAHUITARA (TRIG)	HILL	39 01 177 26	33
KAHUNUI STREAM	STRM	38 24 177 17	31
KAHUNUI (TRIG)	MTN	38 37 177 23	31
KAHUPARERE, LAKE	LAKE	36 22 174 09	10
KAHUPUTOI (TRIG)	HILL	35 25 173 41	4
KAHUPUTOI (TRIG)	HILL	35 25 173 41	6
KAHURA STREAM	STRM	39 23 175 01	36
KAHURANAKI	HSTD	39 47 176 51	42
KAHURANAKI	HSTD	39 47 176 51	43
KAHURANAKI (TRIG)	HILL	39 48 176 52	42
KAHURANAKI (TRIG)	HILL	39 48 176 52	43
KAHURANGI POINT	PNT	40 46 172 13	56
KAHURANGI RIVER	STRM	40 47 172 13	56
KAHURAUPONGA CREEK	STRM	40 03 175 12	45
KAHUTAEWAO CREEK	STRM	36 23 174 23	10
KAHUTAEWAO CREEK	STRM	36 23 174 23	11
KAHUTARA	LOC	41 14 175 20	53
KAHUTARA RIVER	STRM	42 26 173 35	73
KAHUTARA (TRIG)	HILL	36 40 175 34	13
KAHUTARA (TRIG)	HILL	36 40 175 34	16
KAHUTEA COL	SAD	43 00 171 23	75
KAHUTEA COL	SAD	43 00 171 23	80
KAHUTERAWA STREAM	STRM	40 24 175 35	48
KAHUTERAWA STREAM	STRM	40 24 175 35	49
KAHUTUTAEATUA STREAM	STRM	40 08 176 16	47
KAHUWERA STREAM	STRM	35 35 174 00	4
KAHUWERA STREAM	STRM	35 35 174 00	5
KAHUWERA STREAM	STRM	35 35 174 00	7
KAHUWERA (TRIG)	HILL	38 28 175 04	26
KAHUWERA (TRIG)	HILL	38 28 175 04	27
KAI IWI	POPL	39 51 174 56	45
KAI IWI STREAM	STRM	39 53 174 54	44
KAI IWI STREAM	STRM	39 53 174 54	45
KAIAKA	LOC	35 07 173 26	3
KAIAPOI	USAT	43 23 172 39	82
KAIAPOI	USAT	43 23 172 39	83
KAIAPOI	USAT	43 23 172 39	85
KAIARANGI (TRIG)	HILL	38 39 177 23	31
KAIARANGI (TRIG)	HILL	38 39 177 23	33
KAIATA	LOC	42 28 171 15	68
KAIATA	LOC	42 28 171 15	69
KAIATA CREEK	STRM	42 28 171 14	68
KAIATA CREEK	STRM	42 28 171 14	69
KAIATA RANGE	MTNS	42 29 171 19	68
KAIATA RANGE	MTNS	42 29 171 19	69
KAIATE FALLS	LOC	37 46 176 14	20
KAIATE FALLS	LOC	37 46 176 14	21
KAIAUA	LOC	37 07 175 18	13
KAIAUA	LOC	37 07 175 18	15
KAIAUA	HSTD	38 18 178 20	32
KAIAUA BAY	BAY	38 19 178 20	32
KAIAUAI STREAM	STRM	39 09 174 08	34
KAIEWE JUNCTION	LOC	39 39 175 49	46
KAIHERE	LOC	37 22 175 25	15
KAIHIHI STREAM	STRM	39 09 173 51	34
KAIHIKU	LOC	46 14 169 34	111
KAIHIKU	LOC	46 14 169 34	113
KAIHIKU RANGE	MTNS	46 17 169 30	111
KAIHIKU RANGE	MTNS	46 17 169 30	113
KAIHIKU STREAM	STRM	46 11 169 40	111
KAIHIKU STREAM	STRM	46 11 169 40	113
KAIHIKU (TRIG)	HILL	46 16 169 27	111
KAIHIKU (TRIG)	HILL	46 16 169 27	113
KAIHINU	LOC	42 41 171 00	68
KAIHINU	LOC	42 41 171 00	69
KAIHINU (TRIG)	HILL	40 30 175 33	48
KAIHINU (TRIG)	HILL	40 30 175 33	49
KAIHOKA LAKES	LAKE	40 33 172 36	57
KAIHU	LOC	35 46 173 42	6
KAIHU RIVER	STRM	35 57 173 52	6
KAIITI POINT	PNT	36 29 175 20	9
KAIIWI, LAKE	LAKE	35 49 173 39	6
KAIIWI (TRIG)	HILL	35 50 173 39	6
KAIK	LOC	45 22 170 51	102
KAIKAI BEACH	BCH	35 36 173 24	6
KAIKAIKARORO (TRIG)	HILL	37 47 176 00	20
KAIKAIKURI STREAM	STRM	41 18 175 39	51
KAIKAIKURI STREAM	STRM	41 18 175 39	53
KAIKARANGI	LOC	39 55 175 36	46
KAIKINO STREAM	STRM	34 58 173 13	3
KAIKOHE	POPL	35 25 173 48	4
KAIKOHE	POPL	35 25 173 48	6
KAIKOKOPU CANAL	CANL	37 47 176 29	21
KAIKOKOPU CANAL	CANL	37 47 176 29	22
KAIKOKOPU, LAKE	LAKE	40 23 175 16	48
KAIKOKOPU STREAM	STRM	46 07 167 15	105
KAIKOPU STREAM	STRM	39 51 176 58	42
KAIKOPU STREAM	STRM	39 51 176 58	43
KAIKORAI STREAM	STRM	45 56 170 24	103
KAIKOU	LOC	35 35 173 58	4
KAIKOU	LOC	35 35 173 58	5
KAIKOU	LOC	35 35 173 58	7
KAIKOU RIVER	STRM	35 39 174 02	5
KAIKOU RIVER	STRM	35 39 174 02	7
KAIKOURA	TOWN	42 24 173 41	73
KAIKOURA ISLAND	ISLD	36 11 175 19	9
KAIKOURA PENINSULA	PEN	42 25 173 42	73
KAIKOURA STREAM	STRM	38 44 177 35	31
KAIKOURA STREAM	STRM	38 44 177 35	33
KAIKOURA (TRIG)	HILL	37 45 177 54	24
KAIKOURA (TRIG)	HILL	42 24 173 39	73
KAIMAI MAMAKU STATE FOREST PARK	PARK	37 31 175 48	17
KAIMAI MAMAKU STATE FOREST PARK	PARK	37 48 175 57	20
KAIMAI RANGE	MTNS	37 45 175 54	20
KAIMAMAKU	LOC	35 30 174 18	5
KAIMAMAKU STREAM	STRM	35 34 174 14	5
KAIMANAWA (TRIG)	PEAK	39 25 175 54	37
KAIMANAWA MOUNTAINS	MTNS	39 13 175 54	37
KAIMANAWA MOUNTAINS	MTNS	39 13 175 54	38
KAIMANAWA STATE FOREST PARK	PARK	39 09 175 53	37
KAIMANAWA STATE FOREST PARK	PARK	39 09 175 53	38
KAIMANAWA STATE FOREST PARK	PARK	39 01 176 08	39
KAIMANAWA (TRIG)	HILL	38 35 176 14	29
KAIMANGO STREAM	STRM	38 08 174 57	18
KAIMARAMA	LOC	36 52 175 39	16
KAIMARAMA RIVER	STRM	36 51 175 40	16
KAIMARO STREAM	STRM	35 41 173 49	6
KAIMATA	LOC	39 10 174 17	34
KAIMATA	LOC	39 10 174 17	35
KAIMATA	LOC	42 32 171 24	69
KAIMATA RANGE	MTNS	42 44 171 40	70
KAIMATANGI (TRIG)	PEAK	39 01 176 30	39
KAIMATANGI (TRIG)	PEAK	39 01 176 30	40
KAIMATATAI	LOC	46 27 169 48	113
KAIMAUMAU	LOC	34 55 173 16	3
KAIMIKO (TRIG)	HILL	39 09 174 29	35
KAIMIRO	LOC	39 12 174 09	34
KAIMOHO POINT	PNT	37 56 178 24	25
KAIMOHU ISLAND	ISLD	47 12 167 27	114
KAINGA	LOC	43 25 172 40	82
KAINGA	LOC	43 25 172 40	83
KAINGA	LOC	43 25 172 40	85
KAINGAPOUPOU (TRIG)	HILL	38 08 177 41	24
KAINGAROA	LOC	35 02 173 20	3
KAINGAROA FOREST	LOC	38 24 176 34	30
KAINGAROA (TRIG)	HILL	38 33 176 27	29
KAINGAROA (TRIG)	HILL	38 33 176 27	30
KAIPAITANGATA STREAM	STRM	41 02 175 30	53
KAIPAKATI POINT	PNT	42 02 171 22	63
KAIPAKI	LOC	37 53 175 23	19
KAIPARA ENTRANCE	CHAN	36 25 174 10	10
KAIPARA FLATS	FLAT	36 30 174 24	10
KAIPARA FLATS	LOC	36 25 174 33	11
KAIPARA FLATS	FLAT	36 30 174 24	11
KAIPARA HARBOUR	HARB	36 12 174 06	7
KAIPARA HARBOUR	HARB	36 18 174 18	10
KAIPARA HEAD	HEAD	36 24 174 08	10
KAIPARA RIVER	STRM	36 42 174 27	10
KAIPARA RIVER	STRM	36 42 174 27	11
KAIPARA RIVER	STRM	36 42 174 27	12
KAIPARA STREAM	STRM	38 08 176 34	21
KAIPARA STREAM	STRM	38 08 176 34	22
KAIPARAHOURA STREAM	STRM	40 15 176 34	47
KAIPARAHOURA STREAM	STRM	40 15 176 34	50
KAIPARORO	LOC	40 42 175 39	48
KAIPARORO	LOC	40 42 175 39	49
KAIPARORO	LOC	40 42 175 39	51
KAIPARORO (TRIG)	PEAK	40 42 175 35	48
KAIPARORO (TRIG)	PEAK	40 42 175 35	49
KAIPARORO (TRIG)	PEAK	40 42 175 35	51
KAIPATIKI CREEK	STRM	35 18 174 03	4
KAIPATIKI CREEK	STRM	35 18 174 03	5
KAIPAUA (TRIG)	HILL	35 13 173 21	3
KAIPAWA (TRIG)	HILL	36 44 175 31	13
KAIPAWA (TRIG)	HILL	36 44 175 31	16
KAIPIKARI	LOC	39 02 174 24	35
KAIPO BAY	BAY	44 24 167 55	89
KAIPO RIVER	STRM	39 05 176 18	39
KAIPO RIVER	STRM	44 25 167 55	89
KAIPO SADDLE	SAD	39 03 176 08	38
KAIPO SADDLE	SAD	39 03 176 08	39
KAIPONO (TRIG)	MTN	38 18 177 35	31
KAIRA CREEK	STRM	36 15 174 24	10
KAIRA CREEK	STRM	36 15 174 24	11
KAIRAE (TRIG)	HILL	39 47 175 06	45
KAIRAKAU BEACH	LOC	39 57 176 56	42
KAIRAKAU BEACH	LOC	39 57 176 56	43
KAIRAKI	LOC	43 23 172 42	82
KAIRAKI	LOC	43 23 172 42	83
KAIRANGA	LOC	40 21 175 32	48
KAIRANGA	LOC	40 21 175 32	49
KAIRANGI	LOC	38 00 175 30	19
KAIRARA	LOC	35 48 173 49	6
KAIRARA STREAM	STRM	35 48 173 51	6
KAIRARA STREAM	STRM	35 48 173 51	7
KAIRIMU STREAM	STRM	38 18 174 47	26
KAIRUA	LOC	37 42 176 16	20
KAIRUA	LOC	37 42 176 16	21
KAIRURU (TRIG)	HILL	38 27 176 18	29
KAITAIA	POPL	35 07 173 16	3
KAITAKE RANGE	MTNS	39 10 173 58	34
KAITANE STREAM	STRM	39 25 174 59	36
KAITANGATA	POPL	46 17 169 51	111
KAITANGATA	POPL	46 17 169 51	113
KAITAPEHA (TRIG)	HILL	41 14 174 11	54
KAITAPEHA (TRIG)	HILL	41 14 174 11	60
KAITAPEHA (TRIG)	HILL	41 14 174 11	61
KAITAPU STREAM	STRM	39 34 175 43	37
KAITARAKIHI	HILL	37 08 175 41	15
KAITARAKIHI	HILL	37 08 175 41	17
KAITARATAHI	LOC	38 32 177 54	32
KAITARINGA STREAM	STRM	38 31 175 03	26
KAITARINGA STREAM	STRM	38 31 175 03	27
KAITATARA STREAM	STRM	39 50 175 31	46
KAITAWA	LOC	38 48 177 08	31
KAITAWA	LOC	40 30 175 53	49
KAITAWA CREEK	STRM	40 30 175 55	49
KAITEMAKO	LOC	37 45 176 12	20
KAITEMAKO	LOC	37 45 176 12	21
KAITERITERI	LOC	41 02 173 01	57
KAITERITERI	LOC	41 02 173 01	58
KAITERITERI	LOC	41 02 173 01	59
KAITIEKE	LOC	39 06 175 16	36
KAITIEKE STREAM	STRM	39 25 174 57	35
KAITIEKE STREAM	STRM	39 25 174 57	36
KAITIEKE STREAM	STRM	39 05 175 15	36
KAITIEKE (TRIG)	HILL	39 21 174 38	35
KAITIEKE (TRIG)	HILL	39 21 174 38	44
KAITIRAEA	PNT	40 58 174 01	54
KAITIRAEA	PNT	40 58 174 01	60
KAITIRAEA	PNT	40 58 174 01	61
KAITOA (TRIG)	HILL	42 17 173 43	67
KAITOKE	LOC	36 53 175 44	16
KAITOKE	LOC	36 53 175 44	17
KAITOKE	LOC	41 05 175 11	52
KAITOKE	LOC	41 05 175 11	53
KAITOKE	LOC	41 05 175 11	55
KAITOKE CREEK	STRM	36 14 175 29	9
KAITOKE, LAKE	LAKE	39 58 175 04	45
KAITORETE SPIT	SPIT	43 50 172 32	83
KAITORETE SPIT	SPIT	43 50 172 32	85
KAITUNA	LOC	40 54 175 33	48
KAITUNA	LOC	40 54 175 33	49
KAITUNA	LOC	40 31 176 17	50
KAITUNA	LOC	40 54 175 33	51
KAITUNA LAGOON	LAKE	43 47 172 38	83
KAITUNA LAGOON	LAKE	43 47 172 38	85
KAITUNA PASS	PASS	43 42 172 41	83
KAITUNA PASS	PASS	43 42 172 41	85
KAITUNA RIVER	STRM	37 45 176 25	20
KAITUNA RIVER	STRM	37 45 176 25	21
KAITUNA RIVER	STRM	40 42 172 37	56
KAITUNA RIVER	STRM	40 42 172 37	57
KAITUNA RIVER	STRM	41 17 173 47	60
KAITUNA RIVER	STRM	43 47 172 39	83
KAITUNA RIVER	STRM	43 47 172 39	85
KAITUNA STREAM	STRM	37 08 175 45	17
KAITUNA STREAM	STRM	46 11 167 15	105
KAIUMA SADDLE	SAD	41 12 173 47	60
KAIUMA SADDLE	SAD	41 12 173 47	61
KAIUMA STREAM	STRM	41 12 173 41	60
KAIWAI (TRIG)	HILL	40 02 176 27	47
KAIWAIWAI	LOC	41 10 175 25	53
KAIWAKA	LOC	36 10 174 26	8
KAIWAKA RIVER	STRM	36 09 174 23	7
KAIWAKA RIVER	STRM	36 09 174 23	8
KAIWAKA STATION	RSTN	36 10 174 26	7
KAIWAKA STATION	RSTN	36 10 174 26	8
KAIWAKA STREAM	STRM	39 18 176 47	40
KAIWARA RIVER	STRM	42 53 173 04	72
KAIWERA	LOC	46 10 169 06	110
KAIWERA	LOC	46 10 169 06	112
KAIWERA STREAM	STRM	46 09 169 10	110
KAIWERA STREAM	STRM	46 09 169 10	112
KAIWERA STREAM (EAST BRANCH)	STRM	46 14 169 08	110
KAIWERA STREAM (EAST BRANCH)	STRM	46 14 169 08	112
KAIWERA STREAM (WEST BRANCH)	STRM	46 14 169 08	110
KAIWERA STREAM (WEST BRANCH)	STRM	46 14 169 08	112
KAIWHA	HILL	37 45 176 13	20
KAIWHA	HILL	37 45 176 13	21
KAIWHAIKI	LOC	39 50 175 05	45
KAIWHAKA (TRIG)	HILL	38 30 177 31	31
KAIWHAKAUKA STREAM	STRM	39 07 175 04	36
KAIWHARAWHARA	SBRB	41 15 174 48	52
KAIWHARAWHARA	SBRB	41 15 174 48	55
KAIWHATA RIVER	STRM	41 12 175 59	51
KAIWHETU (TRIG)	HILL	34 57 173 32	3
KAIWHIRI (TRIG)	PEAK	41 30 175 20	53
KAIWHITU ISLAND	ISLD	36 15 174 11	7
KAIWHITU ISLAND	ISLD	36 15 174 11	10
KAIWINIKA (TRIG)	HILL	38 29 178 00	32
KAKA	HILL	38 49 174 49	26
KAKA	LOC	41 33 172 42	58
KAKA HILL	HILL	42 20 171 36	69
KAKA HILL	HILL	42 20 171 36	70
KAKA HILL (TRIG)	MTN	43 20 171 34	80
KAKA HILL (TRIG)	HILL	41 16 173 20	59
KAKA POINT	LOC	46 23 169 47	113
KAKA SADDLE	SAD	40 55 172 23	56
KAKAHI	LOC	38 56 175 23	36
KAKAHI	LOC	38 56 175 23	37
KAKAHI STREAM	STRM	38 53 175 03	26
KAKAHI STREAM	STRM	38 53 175 03	27
KAKAHO CREEK	STRM	45 18 170 50	102
KAKAHO STREAM	STRM	38 35 175 45	28
KAKAHU	LOC	44 10 171 03	87
KAKAHU BUSH	LOC	44 10 171 06	87
KAKAHU HILL (TRIG)	HILL	44 08 171 03	87
KAKAHU RIVER	STRM	44 14 171 12	87
KAKAHU STREAM	STRM	37 55 175 51	20
KAKANUI	LOC	36 32 174 27	10
KAKANUI	LOC	36 32 174 27	11
KAKANUI	LOC	45 11 170 54	102
KAKANUI MOUNTAINS	MTNS	45 07 170 24	101
KAKANUI MOUNTAINS	MTNS	45 07 170 24	102
KAKANUI PEAK (TRIG)	PEAK	45 08 170 26	102
KAKANUI POINT	PNT	36 32 174 25	10
KAKANUI POINT	PNT	36 32 174 25	11
KAKANUI POINT	PNT	45 12 170 54	102
KAKANUI RIVER	STRM	45 12 170 54	102
KAKANUI RIVER (NORTH BRANCH)	STRM	45 03 170 36	102
KAKANUI RIVER (SOUTH BRANCH)	STRM	45 03 170 36	102
KAKANUI (TRIG)	HILL	37 39 178 24	25
KAKANUI (TRIG)	PEAK	40 58 175 08	52
KAKANUI (TRIG)	PEAK	40 58 175 08	53
KAKANUI (TRIG)	PEAK	40 58 175 08	55
KAKAPO BROOK	STRM	42 35 172 31	71
KAKAPO CREEK	STRM	44 58 167 41	94
KAKAPO CREEK	STRM	44 58 167 41	97
KAKAPO HILL (TRIG)	HILL	46 11 166 51	104
KAKAPO HILL (TRIG)	HILL	46 11 166 51	105
KAKAPO, LAKE	LAKE	45 55 167 02	105
KAKAPO, MOUNT (TRIG)	HILL	42 37 172 29	71
KAKAPO PEAK (TRIG)	HILL	41 01 172 33	56
KAKAPO PEAK (TRIG)	HILL	41 01 172 33	57
KAKAPO PEAK (TRIG)	HILL	41 01 172 33	58
KAKAPO RANGE	MTNS	45 50 166 38	104
KAKAPO RIVER	STRM	41 16 172 16	62
KAKAPO SADDLE	SAD	41 23 172 20	62
KAKAPO SPUR	RDGE	41 09 172 32	56
KAKAPO SPUR	RDGE	41 09 172 32	57
KAKAPO SPUR	RDGE	41 09 172 32	58
KAKAPO STREAM	STRM	39 05 176 05	38
KAKAPO STREAM	STRM	39 05 176 05	39
KAKAPOTAHI	LOC	42 58 170 41	68
KAKAPOTAHI	LOC	42 59 170 41	74
KAKAPOTAHI RIVER	STRM	42 59 170 41	74
KAKAPUAKA	LOC	46 15 169 43	111
KAKAPUAKA	LOC	46 15 169 43	113
KAKARAHONUI (TRIG)	HILL	38 31 176 43	30
KAKARAIA FLATS	FLAT	36 27 174 24	10
KAKARAIA FLATS	FLAT	36 27 174 24	11
KAKARAMEA	LOC	39 43 174 27	44
KAKARAMEA (TRIG)	PEAK	38 59 175 42	37
KAKARAMEA (TRIG)	PEAK	38 59 175 42	38
KAKARIKI	HSTD	37 50 178 23	25
KAKARIKI	LOC	40 08 175 27	45
KAKARIKI	LOC	40 08 175 27	46
KAKARIKI	LOC	40 34 175 38	48
KAKARIKI	LOC	40 34 175 38	49
KAKARIKI STREAM	STRM	39 02 177 04	41
KAKATAHI	LOC	39 39 175 20	45
KAKATAHI STREAM	STRM	39 40 175 20	45
KAKATARAHAE	HILL	36 54 175 34	13
KAKATARAHAE	HILL	36 54 175 34	15
KAKATARAHAE	HILL	36 54 175 34	16
KAKATARAHAE STREAM	STRM	36 52 175 30	13
KAKATARAHAE STREAM	STRM	36 52 175 30	16
KAKAWAU (TRIG)	HILL	42 31 171 15	68
KAKAWAU (TRIG)	HILL	42 31 171 15	69
KAKEPUKU (TRIG)	HILL	38 04 175 15	18
KAKEPUKU (TRIG)	HILL	38 04 175 15	19
KAMAHI	LOC	46 20 168 43	112
KAMAKA	LOC	42 26 171 24	69
KAMO	SBRB	35 41 174 17	5
KAMO	SBRB	35 41 174 17	7
KAMO	SBRB	35 41 174 17	8
KAMORE STREAM	STRM	35 18 173 52	4
KANAE BAY	BAY	41 19 174 09	54
KANAE BAY	BAY	41 19 174 09	60
KANAE BAY	BAY	41 19 174 09	61
KANAKANAIA	LOC	38 25 177 59	32
KANE, MOUNT	MTN	44 57 167 44	94
KANE, MOUNT	MTN	44 57 167 44	97
KANETETOE ISLAND	ISLD	46 53 168 17	109
KANETETOE ISLAND	ISLD	46 53 168 17	115
KANGAROO CREEK	STRM	42 25 171 28	69
KANGAROO LAKE	LAKE	42 37 171 33	69
KANGEROO CREEK	STRM	45 45 168 02	106
KANGEROO CREEK	STRM	45 45 168 02	107
KANIERE	LOC	42 45 171 00	68
KANIERE	LOC	42 45 171 00	69
KANIERE, LAKE	LAKE	42 51 171 09	68
KANIERE, LAKE	LAKE	42 51 171 09	69
KANIERE RIVER	STRM	42 45 171 00	68
KANIERE RIVER	STRM	42 45 171 00	69
KANINIHI POINT	PNT	47 17 167 34	114
KANIWHANIWHA	LOC	37 55 175 05	18
KANIWHANIWHA STREAM	STRM	37 53 175 08	18
KANOHI	LOC	36 36 174 30	10
KANOHI	LOC	36 36 174 30	11
KANOHI	LOC	36 36 174 30	12
KANOHINUI (TRIG)	HILL	38 28 176 53	30
KANONO, LAKE	LAKE	36 22 174 09	10
KAOKAOROA RANGE	MTNS	39 47 176 45	42
KAOKAOROA RANGE	MTNS	39 47 176 45	43
KAPAENUI STREAM	STRM	38 24 175 14	27
KAPAKAPANUI (TRIG)	HILL	40 56 175 10	48
KAPAKAPANUI (TRIG)	HILL	40 56 175 10	52
KAPAKAPANUI (TRIG)	HILL	40 56 175 10	55
KAPARA (TRIG)	HILL	39 31 174 42	35
KAPARA (TRIG)	HILL	39 31 174 42	44
KAPIAPIA ROCK	ROCK	37 32 174 43	14
KAPIRO	LOC	35 11 173 55	4
KAPITEA CREEK	STRM	42 36 171 06	68
KAPITEA CREEK	STRM	42 36 171 06	69
KAPITEA RESERVOIR	LAKE	42 41 171 12	68
KAPITEA RESERVOIR	LAKE	42 41 171 12	69
KAPITI	LOC	46 04 170 01	111
KAPITI ISLAND	ISLD	40 52 174 55	52
KAPITI ISLAND	ISLD	40 52 174 55	55
KAPOAIAIA STREAM	STRM	39 16 173 45	34
KAPONGA	POPL	39 26 174 09	34
KAPOWAI RIVER	STRM	36 54 175 42	16
KAPOWAI RIVER	STRM	36 54 175 42	17
KAPOWAIRUA	LOC	34 26 172 52	2
KAPUA	LOC	44 47 170 58	93
KAPUARANGI (TRIG)	HILL	38 03 177 36	24
KAPUAWHIO STREAM	STRM	39 06 175 52	37
KAPUAWHIO STREAM	STRM	39 06 175 52	38
KAPUKA	LOC	46 28 168 36	112
KAPUKA SOUTH	LOC	46 30 168 39	112
KAPUNATIKI CREEK	STRM	44 13 171 27	84
KAPUNATIKI CREEK	STRM	44 13 171 27	87
KAPUNI	LOC	39 29 174 08	34
KAPUNI STREAM	STRM	39 32 174 11	34

KARA	LOC	35 43 174 12	5
KARA	LOC	35 43 174 12	7
KARA	LOC	35 43 174 12	8
KARAHAKI STREAM	STRM	39 44 174 34	44
KARAITIANA (TRIG)	HILL	39 32 175 58	37
KARAKA	LOC	37 06 174 52	12
KARAKA	LOC	37 06 174 52	14
KARAKA BAY	BAY	36 09 175 21	9
KARAKA BAY	BAY	38 21 178 20	32
KARAKA BAY	BAY	41 21 174 10	54
KARAKA BAY	BAY	41 21 174 10	60
KARAKA, LAKE	LAKE	36 19 174 02	10
KARAKA, LAKE	LAKE	36 37 174 18	10
KARAKA POINT	PNT	36 24 174 23	10
KARAKA POINT	PNT	36 24 174 23	11
KARAKA (TRIG)	HILL	37 08 175 33	13
KARAKA (TRIG)	HILL	37 08 175 33	15
KARAKARIKI	LOC	37 46 175 07	18
KARAKATUWHERO RIVER	STRM	37 37 178 20	25
KARAMEA	POPL	41 15 172 07	56
KARAMEA	HILL	41 17 172 07	56
KARAMEA	POPL	41 15 172 07	62
KARAMEA	HILL	41 17 172 07	62
KARAMEA BIGHT	BAY	41 42 171 34	63
KARAMEA ISLAND	ISLD	39 52 176 59	42
KARAMEA ISLAND	ISLD	39 52 176 59	43
KARAMEA RIVER	STRM	41 15 172 06	56
KARAMEA RIVER	STRM	41 15 172 06	62
KARAMU	LOC	37 53 175 09	18
KARAMURAMU ISLAND	ISLD	36 56 175 09	13
KARAMURAMU ISLAND	ISLD	36 56 175 09	15
KARANGAHAKE	LOC	37 25 175 43	17
KARANGAHAKE (TRIG)	HILL	37 26 175 43	17
KARANGAHAPE CLIFFS	CLIF	38 48 175 49	28
KARANGAHAPE CLIFFS	CLIF	38 48 175 49	29
KARANGAHAPE CLIFFS	CLIF	38 48 175 49	38
KARANGAITI (TRIG)	HILL	38 50 175 15	27
KARANGARUA	LOC	43 32 169 50	76
KARANGARUA RANGE	MTNS	43 39 169 55	76
KARANGARUA RANGE	MTNS	43 39 169 55	79
KARANGARUA RIVER	STRM	43 30 169 44	76
KARANGARUA SADDLE	SAD	43 44 169 56	76
KARANGARUA SADDLE	SAD	43 44 169 56	79
KARANGARUA (TRIG)	MTN	43 36 169 46	76
KARANGI (TRIG)	HILL	34 59 173 42	4
KARAPIRO	LOC	37 55 175 32	19
KARAPIRO, LAKE	LAKE	37 57 175 37	19
KARAPIRO STREAM	STRM	37 54 175 29	19
KARAPITI STREAM	STRM	38 18 176 15	21
KARAPITI STREAM	STRM	38 18 176 15	29
KARATIA	LOC	34 33 172 51	2
KARAUI POINT	PNT	34 57 173 42	4
KAREHANA BAY	SBRB	41 05 174 52	52
KAREHANA BAY	SBRB	41 05 174 52	55
KAREKARE	LOC	36 59 174 29	12
KAREMU STREAM	STRM	39 50 174 58	45
KARENGORENGO STREAM	STRM	37 42 175 49	19
KARENGORENGO STREAM	STRM	37 42 175 49	20
KAREPONIA	LOC	35 03 173 17	3
KARERARERA BAY	BAY	35 13 174 17	5
KARERE	LOC	40 24 175 31	48
KARERE	LOC	40 24 175 31	49
KARETU	LOC	35 22 174 09	4
KARETU	LOC	35 22 174 09	5
KARETU, MOUNT (TRIG)	MTN	43 12 172 29	81
KARETU, MOUNT (TRIG)	MTN	43 12 172 29	82
KARETU RIVER	STRM	43 12 172 27	81
KARETU RIVER	STRM	43 12 172 27	82
KARETU STREAM	STRM	35 22 174 09	5
KARETU STREAM	STRM	38 26 174 55	26
KAREWA ISLAND	ISLD	37 32 176 08	17
KAREWA (TRIG)	HILL	37 56 178 11	25
KAREWAREWA	LOC	39 52 175 55	46
KARIKARI BAY	BAY	34 51 173 21	3
KARIKARI, CAPE	CAPE	34 47 173 24	3
KARIKARI PENINSULA	PEN	34 53 173 21	3
KARIKARINGA (TRIG)	PEAK	39 12 175 53	37
KARIKARINGA (TRIG)	PEAK	39 12 175 53	38
KARIKARIRUA (TRIG)	HILL	39 28 174 42	35
KARIKARIRUA (TRIG)	HILL	39 28 174 42	44
KARIOI	LOC	39 27 175 31	36
KARIOI	LOC	39 27 175 31	37
KARIOI, MOUNT (TRIG)	HILL	37 52 174 48	18
KARIOITAHI	LOC	37 16 174 41	12
KARIOITAHI	LOC	37 16 174 41	14
KARIPARIPA POINT	PNT	35 11 174 18	5
KARITANE	LOC	45 39 170 39	102
KAROKIO STREAM	STRM	39 35 175 24	36
KARORE BANK	BNK	37 01 174 44	12
KARORE BANK	BNK	37 01 174 44	14
KARORI	SBRB	41 17 174 44	52
KARORI	SBRB	41 17 174 44	55
KARORI ROCK	ROCK	41 20 174 39	52
KARORI ROCK	ROCK	41 20 174 39	55
KARORI STREAM	STRM	41 20 174 41	52
KARORI STREAM	STRM	41 20 174 41	55
KARORO	SBRB	42 28 171 11	68
KARORO	SBRB	42 28 171 11	69
KARORO CREEK	STRM	46 24 169 47	113
KARUHIRUHI	LOC	35 27 173 28	6
KATAKI	LOC	45 24 170 50	102
KATAKI BEACH	BCH	45 25 170 50	102
KATAWA HEAD	HEAD	43 44 173 07	83
KATHERINE BAY	BAY	36 07 175 22	9
KATHERINE, LAKE	LAKE	45 00 167 27	94
KATHERINE, LAKE	LAKE	45 00 167 27	97
KATHRYN PEAK	PEAK	45 46 167 03	105
KATIKARA STREAM	STRM	39 08 173 53	34
KATIKATI	POPL	37 33 175 55	17
KATIKATI ENTRANCE	CHAN	37 28 175 59	17
KATIKI POINT	PNT	45 24 170 52	102
KATIPO CREEK	STRM	41 02 172 06	56
KATIPO CREEK	STRM	41 02 172 06	62
KATTOTHYRST	MTN	45 10 170 30	102
KATUI	LOC	35 42 173 34	6
KAUAEKEKE STREAM	STRM	39 35 175 50	37
KAUAEKEKE (TRIG)	PEAK	39 33 175 48	37
KAUAEKEKE (TRIG)	HILL	39 39 175 35	46
KAUAEPARAOA STREAM	STRM	34 33 172 46	2
KAUAERANGA	LOC	37 09 175 36	13
KAUAERANGA	LOC	37 09 175 36	15
KAUAERANGA RIVER	STRM	37 09 175 33	15
KAUAERANGA (TRIG)	HILL	35 37 174 04	5
KAUAERANGA (TRIG)	HILL	35 37 174 04	7
KAUANA	LOC	46 01 168 22	107
KAUANGAROA	LOC	39 56 175 17	45
KAUARAPAOA STREAM	STRM	39 48 175 05	45
KAUAUROA BAY	BAY	41 03 173 58	54
KAUAUROA BAY	BAY	41 03 173 58	60
KAUAUROA BAY	BAY	41 03 173 58	61
KAUAUROA (TRIG)	HILL	41 02 173 58	54
KAUAUROA (TRIG)	HILL	41 02 173 58	60
KAUAUROA (TRIG)	HILL	41 02 173 58	61
KAUHANGAROA STREAM	STRM	39 06 175 16	36
KAUHAUROA STREAM	STRM	38 58 177 25	33
KAUKAPAKAPA	LOC	36 37 174 30	10
KAUKAPAKAPA	LOC	36 37 174 30	11
KAUKAPAKAPA	LOC	36 37 174 30	12
KAUKAPAKAPA RIVER	STRM	36 38 174 27	10
KAUKAPAKAPA RIVER	STRM	36 38 174 27	11
KAUKAPAKAPA RIVER	STRM	36 38 174 27	12
KAUKATEA STREAM	STRM	39 56 175 18	45
KAUKAU (TRIG)	HILL	41 14 174 46	52
KAUKAU (TRIG)	HILL	41 14 174 46	55
KAUKORE STREAM	STRM	39 29 175 03	36
KAUKUMOUTITI STREAM	STRM	37 49 176 00	20
KAUMATUA STREAM	STRM	39 41 176 18	47
KAUMINGI STREAM	STRM	40 58 175 54	51
KAUPOKONUI	LOC	39 33 174 05	34
KAUPOKONUI STREAM	STRM	39 34 174 03	34
KAURAPATAKA, LAKE	LAKE	42 47 171 42	70
KAURI	LOC	35 39 174 18	5
KAURI	LOC	35 39 174 18	7
KAURI	LOC	35 39 174 18	8
KAURI FLAT	LOC	37 46 174 52	18
KAURI HILL (TRIG)	HILL	36 01 174 06	7
KAURI MOUNT	MTN	35 46 174 33	5
KAURI MOUNT	MTN	35 46 174 33	8
KAURI POINT	PNT	35 10 174 02	4
KAURI POINT	PNT	35 10 174 02	5
KAURI POINT	PNT	36 52 175 09	13
KAURI POINT	PNT	37 31 175 59	17
KAURI STREAM	STRM	37 51 174 55	18
KAURITUTAHI CREEK	STRM	37 05 174 38	12
KAURITUTAHI CREEK	STRM	37 05 174 38	14
KAURIWHATI STREAM	STRM	35 17 173 39	4
KAUROA	LOC	37 51 174 55	18
KAURU HILL	LOC	45 06 170 45	102
KAURU HILL (TRIG)	HILL	45 06 170 42	102
KAURU RIVER	STRM	45 05 170 49	102
KAUWAEWAKA STREAM	STRM	38 47 177 47	31
KAUWAEWAKA STREAM	STRM	38 47 177 47	32
KAUWAEWAKA STREAM	STRM	38 47 177 47	33
KAUWHATA	LOC	40 17 175 32	48
KAUWHATA	LOC	40 17 175 32	49
KAWAHA POINT	PNT	38 06 176 15	20
KAWAHA POINT	PNT	38 06 176 15	21
KAWAKAPUTA BAY	BAY	46 23 167 50	108
KAWAKAWA	LOC	34 55 173 19	3
KAWAKAWA	LOC	35 08 174 04	4
KAWAKAWA	LOC	35 08 174 04	5
KAWAKAWA BAY	BAY	36 57 175 09	13
KAWAKAWA BAY	LOC	36 57 175 10	13
KAWAKAWA BAY	LOC	36 57 175 10	14
KAWAKAWA BAY	BAY	36 57 175 09	15
KAWAKAWA BAY	LOC	36 57 175 10	15
KAWAKAWA BAY	BAY	38 41 175 51	28
KAWAKAWA BAY	BAY	38 41 175 51	29
KAWAKAWA BAY	BAY	38 41 175 51	38
KAWAKAWA (TRIG)	HILL	35 21 174 03	4
KAWAKAWA (TRIG)	HILL	35 21 174 03	5
KAWAKAWA (TRIG)	HILL	41 33 175 17	53
KAWARAU FALLS	LOC	45 02 168 45	95
KAWARAU FALLS	LOC	45 02 168 45	99
KAWARAU GORGE	LOC	45 03 169 09	99
KAWARAU RIVER	STRM	45 02 168 45	95
KAWARAU RIVER	STRM	45 02 168 45	99
KAWAROA STREAM	STRM	38 03 174 53	18
KAWATI POINT	PNT	36 24 174 50	11
KAWATIRI	LOC	41 42 172 37	65
KAWAU BAY	BAY	36 25 174 45	11
KAWAU ISLAND	ISLD	36 25 174 51	11
KAWAU POINT	PNT	36 27 174 53	11
KAWAUNUI STREAM	STRM	38 23 176 21	29
KAWAUTAHI	LOC	39 02 175 16	36
KAWAUTAHI STREAM	STRM	39 04 175 13	36
KAWEKA RANGE	MTNS	39 14 176 20	39
KAWEKA STATE FOREST PARK	PARK	39 20 176 22	39
KAWEKA (TRIG)	PEAK	39 17 176 23	39
KAWEKA (TRIG)	PEAK	39 17 176 23	40
KAWEKU	LOC	45 56 168 42	110
KAWERAU	POPL	38 05 176 42	21
KAWERAU	POPL	38 05 176 42	22
KAWERUA	LOC	35 38 173 27	6
KAWHAKA CREEK	STRM	42 43 171 05	68
KAWHAKA CREEK	STRM	42 43 171 05	69
KAWHAKA PASS	PASS	42 48 171 17	68
KAWHAKA PASS	PASS	42 48 171 17	69
KAWHATAU RIVER	STRM	39 47 175 48	46
KAWHIA	LOC	38 04 174 49	18
KAWHIA HARBOUR	HARB	38 05 174 50	18
KAWITI	LOC	35 25 173 58	4
KAWITI	LOC	35 25 173 58	5
KAY CREEK	STRM	44 51 168 14	89
KAY CREEK	STRM	44 51 168 14	95
KAYE, MOUNT	MTN	44 06 169 24	78
KAYE, MOUNT	MTN	44 06 169 24	79
KEA PASS	PASS	43 07 171 05	75
KEAN, POINT	PNT	42 25 173 43	73
KEDRON RIVER	STRM	42 32 172 15	70
KEENAN CREEK	STRM	46 10 167 43	106
KEENAN CREEK	STRM	46 10 167 43	108
KEHU PEAK	PEAK	42 02 172 45	65
KEIKEINUI (TRIG)	HILL	39 35 175 03	36
KEINTON COMBE	HSTD	42 36 173 07	72
KEKERENGU	LOC	42 00 174 01	67
KEKERENGU RIVER	STRM	42 00 174 01	67
KELCEYS BUSH	HSTD	44 42 170 58	93
KELCHERS	LOC	44 47 170 51	93
KELLARD, MOUNT	MTN	45 32 166 50	96
KELLARD, MOUNT	MTN	45 32 166 50	104
KELLY RANGE	MTNS	42 48 171 32	69
KELLY SADDLE	SAD	42 47 171 33	69
KELLYS BAY	LOC	36 15 174 05	7
KELLYS BAY	LOC	36 15 174 05	10
KELLYS CREEK	STRM	42 48 171 35	69
KELLYS CREEK	STRM	42 26 171 36	69
KELLYS CREEK	STRM	42 26 171 36	70
KELLYS HILL (TRIG)	PEAK	42 47 171 34	69
KELLYS STREAM	STRM	41 14 175 24	53
KELLYVILLE	LOC	37 16 175 03	12
KELLYVILLE	LOC	37 16 175 03	13
KELLYVILLE	LOC	37 16 175 03	14
KELP POINT	PNT	47 13 167 37	114
KELSO	POPL	45 54 169 14	110
KELSTON	SBRB	36 54 174 40	11
KELSTON	SBRB	36 54 174 40	12
KELSTON	SBRB	36 54 174 40	14
KELVIN GROVE	SBRB	40 20 175 38	48
KELVIN GROVE	SBRB	40 20 175 38	49
KELVIN HEIGHTS	LOC	45 03 168 41	95
KELVIN HEIGHTS	LOC	45 03 168 41	99
KELVIN, MOUNT (TRIG)	MTN	41 56 171 37	63
KELVIN, MOUNT (TRIG)	MTN	41 56 171 37	64
KELVIN PEAK (TRIG)	HILL	46 04 168 46	110
KELVIN PEAK (TRIG)	HILL	46 04 168 46	112
KEMP, MOUNT	MTN	42 20 172 05	70
KEMPE POINT	PNT	41 02 174 18	54
KEMPE POINT	PNT	41 02 174 18	61
KENANA	LOC	35 03 173 34	3
KENANA	LOC	35 03 173 34	4
KENANA RIVER	STRM	35 03 173 34	3
KENANA RIVER	STRM	35 03 173 34	4
KENDALL CREEK	STRM	41 24 172 24	62
KENDALL, MOUNT	PEAK	41 22 172 24	62
KENEPURU HEAD	LOC	41 10 174 07	54
KENEPURU HEAD	LOC	41 10 174 07	60
KENEPURU HEAD	LOC	41 10 174 07	61
KENEPURU SADDLE	SAD	41 08 174 08	54
KENEPURU SADDLE	SAD	41 08 174 08	60
KENEPURU SADDLE	SAD	41 08 174 08	61
KENEPURU SOUND	SND	41 12 173 58	54
KENEPURU SOUND	SND	41 12 173 58	60
KENEPURU SOUND	SND	41 12 173 58	61
KENNAWAY HILL	HILL	43 02 170 51	75
KENNEDY BAY	BAY	36 41 175 34	13
KENNEDY BAY	LOC	36 40 175 32	13
KENNEDY BAY	LOC	36 40 175 32	16
KENNEDY BAY	BAY	36 41 175 34	16
KENNEDY CREEK	STRM	42 46 171 04	68
KENNEDY CREEK	STRM	42 46 171 04	69
KENNEDY FALLS	FALL	42 55 171 38	70
KENNEDY STREAM	STRM	42 49 172 07	70
KENNEDYS POINT	PNT	36 49 175 01	12
KENNEDYS POINT	PNT	36 49 175 01	13
KENNET	HILL	42 03 173 21	66
KENNET RIVER	STRM	42 02 173 23	66
KENNETH BURN	STRM	45 38 167 05	105
KENNETHS PEAK (TRIG)	HILL	46 29 169 18	112
KENNETHS PEAK (TRIG)	HILL	46 29 169 18	113
KENNINGTON	LOC	46 24 168 27	109
KENNY CREEK	STRM	45 58 168 07	106
KENNY CREEK	STRM	45 58 168 07	107
KENSINGTON, MOUNT	MTN	43 18 170 38	74
KENT PASSAGE	STRA	35 13 174 04	4
KENT PASSAGE	STRA	35 13 174 04	5
KEPKA, MOUNT	MTN	44 46 167 48	94
KEPLER MOUNTAINS	MTNS	45 22 167 25	97
KEREKERE STREAM	STRM	41 02 175 11	52
KEREKERE STREAM	STRM	41 02 175 11	53
KEREKERE STREAM	STRM	41 02 175 11	55
KEREONE	LOC	37 42 175 37	19
KEREPEHI	LOC	37 18 175 33	15
KERERU	LOC	39 38 176 25	47
KERERU STREAM	STRM	40 21 176 17	50
KERERU STREAM	STRM	41 47 171 54	63
KERERU STREAM	STRM	41 47 171 54	64
KERERU (TRIG)	HILL	40 36 176 24	50
KERERUHUAHUA (TRIG)	MTN	38 10 177 54	24
KERERUHUAHUA (TRIG)	MTN	38 10 177 54	32
KERERUTAHI	LOC	38 03 177 07	23
KERETA	LOC	36 55 175 26	13
KERETA	LOC	36 55 175 26	15
KERETA	LOC	36 55 175 26	16
KERETA, LAKE	LAKE	36 36 174 17	10
KEREU RIVER	STRM	37 43 177 43	24
KERIKERI	LOC	35 14 173 57	4
KERIKERI	LOC	35 14 173 57	5
KERIKERI INLET	LOC	35 13 174 01	4
KERIKERI INLET	BAY	35 12 174 01	4
KERIKERI INLET	LOC	35 13 174 01	5
KERIKERI INLET	BAY	35 12 174 01	5
KERIKERI RIVER	STRM	35 13 173 58	4
KERIKERI RIVER	STRM	37 44 174 57	18
KERR, MOUNT	MTN	42 49 171 19	69
KERR POINT	PNT	34 24 172 59	2
KERRYTOWN	LOC	44 17 171 12	87
KETEMARINGI (TRIG)	HILL	38 39 175 33	27
KETEMARINGI (TRIG)	HILL	38 39 175 33	28
KETETAHI SPRINGS	SPR	39 06 175 39	37
KETETAHI SPRINGS	SPR	39 06 175 39	38
KETU BAY	BAY	40 59 173 59	54
KETU BAY	BAY	40 59 173 59	60
KETU BAY	BAY	40 59 173 59	61
KEY PEAK	PEAK	45 13 167 10	96
KEY SUMMIT (TRIG)	HILL	44 49 168 08	89
KEYSTONE, THE	MTN	44 04 169 17	78
KHANDALLAH	SBRB	41 14 174 48	52
KHANDALLAH	SBRB	41 14 174 48	55
KIA ORA	LOC	45 05 170 50	102
KIDNAPPERS, CAPE	CAPE	39 39 177 06	42
KIDNAPPERS, CAPE	CAPE	39 39 177 06	43
KIEKIE (TRIG)	HILL	39 26 175 06	36
KIHIKIHI	POPL	38 03 175 21	19
KIHIKIHI STREAM	STRM	38 27 174 55	26
KIHONA,LAKE	LAKE	34 38 172 54	2
KIKITANGEO (TRIG)	HILL	36 21 174 30	10
KIKITANGEO (TRIG)	HILL	36 21 174 30	11
KIKIWA	LOC	41 41 172 53	65
KIKOWHERO STREAM	STRM	39 39 176 38	42
KIKOWHERO STREAM	STRM	39 39 176 38	43
KIKOWHERO STREAM	STRM	39 39 176 38	47
KILBIRNIE	SBRB	41 19 174 47	52
KILBIRNIE	SBRB	41 19 174 47	55
KILGRAM	HSTD	41 53 174 03	67
KILLIECRANKIE CREEK	STRM	45 14 168 31	95
KILLIECRANKIE CREEK	STRM	45 14 168 31	99
KILLINCHY	LOC	43 44 172 15	85
KILMARNOCK (TRIG)	PEAK	41 31 172 02	62
KIMBELL	LOC	44 03 170 45	86
KIMBELL SPUR	RDGE	41 07 172 31	56
KIMBELL SPUR	RDGE	41 07 172 31	57
KIMBELL SPUR	RDGE	41 07 172 31	58
KIMBERLEY	LOC	43 26 172 07	81
KIMBERLEY	LOC	43 26 172 07	85
KIMBOLTON	POPL	40 04 175 47	46
KIMIHIA	LOC	37 33 175 11	15
KIMIHIA, LAKE	LAKE	37 32 175 11	15
KINA	LOC	41 11 173 04	58
KINA	LOC	41 11 173 04	59
KINAKI, MOUNT (TRIG)	MTN	45 00 169 20	100
KINAKINA	ISLD	46 37 169 22	113
KINBRACE	LOC	44 34 170 46	93
KINGSDOWN	HSTD	43 07 172 09	81
KINGSDOWN	LOC	44 28 171 13	93
KINGSEAT	LOC	37 08 174 48	12
KINGSEAT	LOC	37 08 174 48	14
KINGSTON	POPL	45 20 168 43	95
KINGSTON	POPL	45 20 168 43	99
KINI CREEK	STRM	43 37 169 42	76
KINI CREEK	STRM	43 37 169 42	79
KINI, LAKE	LAKE	43 36 169 37	76
KINIHI, MOUNT	MTN	43 42 169 41	79
KINKEL, MOUNT	MTN	43 17 170 53	75
KINLEITH	LOC	38 17 175 53	28
KINLEITH	LOC	38 17 175 53	29
KINLOCH	LOC	38 40 175 40	28
KINLOCH	LOC	38 40 175 40	38
KINLOCH	LOC	44 51 168 21	89
KINLOCH	LOC	44 51 168 21	95
KINNAIRD MOUNT (TRIG)	MTN	43 45 169 27	76
KINNAIRD MOUNT (TRIG)	MTN	43 45 169 27	78
KINNAIRD MOUNT (TRIG)	MTN	43 45 169 27	79
KINOHAKU	LOC	38 10 174 49	18
KINSEY, MOUNT	MTN	43 41 170 08	77
KINSEY, MOUNT	MTN	43 41 170 08	86
KINZETT CREEK	STRM	41 27 172 44	58
KINZETT STREAM	STRM	41 21 172 31	58
KIOKIO	LOC	38 10 175 17	18
KIOKIO	LOC	38 10 175 17	19
KIORENUI VILLAGE	LOC	38 28 176 42	30
KIRI STREAM	STRM	39 09 174 00	34
KIRIKAU	LOC	39 01 175 07	36
KIRIKIRI STREAM	STRM	37 12 175 34	13
KIRIKIRI STREAM	STRM	37 12 175 34	15
KIRIKIRI STREAM	STRM	37 46 176 09	20
KIRIKIRI STREAM	STRM	37 48 176 18	20
KIRIKIRI STREAM	STRM	37 48 176 18	21
KIRIKIRI STREAM	STRM	37 46 176 09	21
KIRIKIRITOKI STREAM	STRM	35 34 174 19	5
KIRIKIRITOKI STREAM	STRM	35 34 174 19	7
KIRIKIRITOKI STREAM	STRM	35 34 174 19	8
KIRIKOPUNI	LOC	35 51 174 01	7
KIRIKOPUNI STATION	RSTN	35 52 174 01	7
KIRIOKE	LOC	35 29 173 47	4
KIRIOKE	LOC	35 29 173 47	6
KIRIOPUKAE, LAKE	LAKE	38 48 177 07	30
KIRIOPUKAE, LAKE	LAKE	38 48 177 07	31
KIRIPAKA	LOC	35 39 174 25	5
KIRIPAKA	LOC	35 39 174 25	7
KIRIPAKA	LOC	35 39 174 25	8
KIRIRAUKAWA, MOUNT	HILL	36 12 175 05	9
KIRITA BAY	LOC	36 52 175 25	13
KIRITA BAY	BAY	36 52 175 25	16
KIRITAE STREAM	STRM	39 32 174 24	35
KIRITAE STREAM	STRM	39 32 174 24	44
KIRITAKI	LOC	40 14 175 59	46
KIRITEHERE	LOC	38 20 174 43	26
KIRITEHERE STREAM	STRM	38 20 174 42	26
KIRIWHAKAPAPA	LOC	40 49 175 34	48
KIRIWHAKAPAPA	LOC	40 49 175 34	49
KIRIWHAKAPAPA	LOC	40 49 175 34	51
KIRIWHAKAPAPA STREAM	STRM	40 49 175 37	48
KIRIWHAKAPAPA STREAM	STRM	40 49 175 37	49
KIRIWHAKAPAPA STREAM	STRM	40 49 175 37	51
KIRK STREAM	STRM	43 18 170 53	75
KIRKLANDS HILL	HILL	47 04 167 55	114
KIRKLANDS HILL	HILL	47 04 167 55	115
KIRKLISTON RANGE	MTNS	44 30 170 32	92
KIRWEE	LOC	43 30 172 13	81
KIRWEE	LOC	43 30 172 13	85
KISBEE BAY	BAY	46 07 166 42	104
KITCHENER RIVER	STRM	44 25 168 50	90
KITTO CREEK	STRM	41 54 171 36	63
KIWI BURN	STRM	46 13 166 44	104
KIWI CREEK	STRM	39 20 176 17	39
KIWI CREEK	STRM	41 34 172 41	58
KIWI, LAKE	LAKE	46 10 166 48	104
KIWI, MOUNT (TRIG)	HILL	41 04 174 04	54
KIWI, MOUNT (TRIG)	HILL	41 04 174 04	60
KIWI, MOUNT (TRIG)	HILL	41 04 174 04	61
KIWI RIVER	STRM	42 38 172 15	70
KIWI SADDLE	SAD	39 20 176 19	39
KIWI SADDLE	SAD	41 24 172 30	58
KIWI SADDLE	SAD	41 23 172 16	62
KIWI SADDLE	SAD	42 40 172 14	70
KIWI STREAM	STRM	39 20 174 47	35
KIWI STREAM	STRM	39 20 174 47	44
KIWI STREAM	STRM	41 27 172 29	58
KIWI STREAM	STRM	41 27 172 29	62
KIWI STREAM	STRM	43 09 171 21	75
KIWITAHI	LOC	37 44 175 35	19
KIWITAHI STATION	LOC	37 42 175 36	19
KIWITEA	LOC	40 07 175 43	46
KIWITEA STREAM	STRM	40 13 175 36	46
KNAPDALE	LOC	46 01 168 55	110
KNIFE AND STEEL HARBOUR	HARB	46 14 167 01	105
KNIGHTS POINTS	PNT	43 43 169 14	78
KNIGHTS STREAM	STRM	43 43 173 06	83
KNOB (TRIG)	HILL	40 44 176 06	49
KNOB (TRIG)	HILL	40 44 176 06	51
KNOB, THE (TRIG)	HILL	45 48 167 45	106
KNOB, THE (TRIG)	MTN	46 09 166 42	104
KNOBBIES, THE	ISLS	46 45 167 35	108
KNOBBIES, THE	ISLS	46 45 167 35	114
KNOBBY CREEK	STRM	45 38 168 57	99
KNOBBY RANGE	MTNS	45 26 169 24	100
KNOBS FLAT	LOC	44 59 168 01	97
KNOBS FLAT	LOC	44 59 168 01	98
KNOLL PEAK (TRIG)	PEAK	45 54 167 28	105
KNOLL PEAK (TRIG)	PEAK	45 54 167 28	106
KNOLL POINT	PNT	42 38 171 25	69
KNOLL, THE	HILL	44 19 168 12	88
KNOLL, THE	HILL	44 19 168 12	89
KNOWLES TOP (TRIG)	HILL	43 13 172 15	81
KNUCKLE HILL (TRIG)	HILL	40 38 172 34	56
KNUCKLE HILL (TRIG)	HILL	40 38 172 34	57
KNUCKLE PEAK	PEAK	44 48 168 55	90
KNUCKLE PEAK	PEAK	44 48 168 55	95
KNUCKLE POINT	PNT	34 51 173 28	3
KNUCKLES (TRIG)	MTN	43 14 171 35	80
KOAMARU, CAPE	CAPE	41 05 174 23	54
KOARO STREAM	STRM	39 12 176 28	39
KOARO STREAM	STRM	39 12 176 28	40
KOAU STREAM	STRM	39 31 176 21	39
KOEKE	HSTD	39 43 175 35	46
KOEKE JUNCTION	LOC	39 42 175 36	46
KOETI, MOUNT (TRIG)	MTN	42 48 171 47	70
KOETI PASS	PASS	42 47 171 50	70
KOHAIHAI BLUFF	CLIF	41 06 172 06	56
KOHAIHAI BLUFF	CLIF	41 06 172 06	62
KOHAIHAI RIVER	STRM	41 07 172 06	56
KOHAIHAI RIVER	STRM	41 07 172 06	62
KOHATU	LOC	41 27 172 50	58
KOHATU (TRIG)	HILL	41 27 172 48	58
KOHAU (TRIG)	HILL	34 31 173 00	2
KOHE	LOC	35 19 173 17	3
KOHE CREEK	STRM	46 02 166 36	104
KOHEKOHE	LOC	37 12 174 39	12
KOHEKOHE	LOC	37 12 174 39	14

KOHEKOHE	HSTD	40 59 176 02	51
KOHEKOHE (TRIG)	HILL	35 35 173 29	6
KOHEROA (TRIG)	HILL	35 28 174 11	5
KOHERURAHI POINT	PNT	36 56 175 08	13
KOHERURAHI POINT	PNT	36 56 175 08	14
KOHERURAHI POINT	PNT	36 56 175 08	15
KOHI	LOC	39 43 174 36	44
KOHI POINT	PNT	37 56 177 01	22
KOHI POINT	PNT	37 56 177 01	23
KOHI STREAM	STRM	39 45 174 34	44
KOHIKA	LOC	44 33 171 03	93
KOHIKA STREAM	STRM	44 35 171 09	93
KOHIKU	LOC	40 35 176 10	50
KOHINGA (TRIG)	PEAK	39 25 176 21	39
KOHINUI	LOC	40 25 175 57	49
KOHIOAWA BEACH	BCH	37 53 176 44	22
KOHIRIKIRIKI (TRIG)	HILL	38 41 177 31	31
KOHIRIKIRIKI (TRIG)	HILL	38 41 177 31	33
KOHITANE (TRIG)	HILL	39 00 177 29	33
KOHIWAI STREAM	STRM	41 00 176 04	51
KOHUAMARUA BLUFF	CLIF	43 15 170 07	74
KOHUKOHU	LOC	35 22 173 32	3
KOHUKOHU	LOC	35 22 173 32	6
KOHUKOHUNUI (TRIG)	HILL	37 02 175 13	13
KOHUKOHUNUI (TRIG)	HILL	37 02 175 13	15
KOHUMARU	LOC	35 05 173 33	3
KOHUMARU	LOC	35 05 173 33	4
KOHUMARU STREAM	STRM	35 02 173 34	3
KOHUMARU STREAM	STRM	35 02 173 34	4
KOHUNGAHUNGA	HILL	36 57 175 50	16
KOHUNGAHUNGA	HILL	36 57 175 50	17
KOHURATAHI	LOC	39 06 174 46	35
KOHURAU	HILL	44 48 170 19	92
KOHURONAKI (TRIG)	HILL	34 29 172 50	2
KOHURU STREAM	STRM	38 20 177 04	30
KOIRA	LOC	38 59 175 06	36
KOITIATA	LOC	40 04 175 08	45
KOITIATA, LAKE	LAKE	40 07 175 12	45
KOITIATA STREAM	STRM	40 07 175 10	45
KOKAKO	LOC	38 49 177 09	31
KOKAKO (TRIG)	HILL	37 46 175 02	18
KOKAKONUI STREAM	STRM	39 01 175 07	36
KOKATAHI	LOC	42 50 171 02	68
KOKATAHI	LOC	42 50 171 02	69
KOKATAHI RIVER	STRM	42 50 171 01	68
KOKATAHI RIVER	STRM	42 50 171 01	69
KOKIRI	LOC	42 30 171 23	69
KOKOAMO	LOC	44 53 170 43	93
KOKOHITOA (TRIG)	HILL	39 02 176 54	40
KOKOHITOA (TRIG)	HILL	39 02 176 54	41
KOKOMIKO STREAM	STRM	38 39 175 19	27
KOKOMOKA (TRIG)	HILL	38 50 176 31	30
KOKOMUKATARANGA (TRIG)	HILL	37 41 178 31	25
KOKONGA	LOC	45 13 170 15	101
KOKOPUMATARA STREAM	STRM	38 07 177 47	24
KOKOTA	BNK	34 33 172 58	2
KOMAKO	LOC	40 06 175 54	46
KOMAKORAU	LOC	37 39 175 16	18
KOMAKORAU	LOC	37 39 175 16	19
KOMAKORAU STREAM	STRM	37 37 175 12	18
KOMAKORAU STREAM	STRM	37 37 175 12	19
KOMAPARA (TRIG)	MTN	37 48 178 07	25
KOMATA	LOC	37 21 175 40	15
KOMATA	LOC	37 21 175 40	17
KOMATA NORTH	LOC	37 20 175 40	15
KOMATA NORTH	LOC	37 20 175 40	17
KOMATA REEFS	LOC	37 21 175 44	17
KOMATA RIVER	STRM	37 21 175 39	17
KOMOKORIKI	LOC	36 30 174 32	10
KOMOKORIKI	LOC	36 30 174 32	11
KOMUTUMUTU STREAM	STRM	38 04 176 11	20
KOMUTUMUTU STREAM	STRM	38 04 176 11	21
KONEWA STREAM	STRM	40 05 175 54	46
KONGAHU	LOC	41 18 172 06	62
KONGAHU POINT	PNT	41 27 171 59	62
KONIHI STREAM	STRM	38 19 177 01	30
KONINI	LOC	40 30 175 47	49
KONINI STREAM	STRM	37 04 175 12	13
KONINI STREAM	STRM	37 04 175 12	15
KONINI STREAM	STRM	39 05 175 18	36
KONONI	LOC	45 58 169 31	111
KOPAATUAKI (TRIG)	HILL	38 32 178 00	32
KOPAKI	LOC	38 29 175 17	27
KOPAKORAHI STREAM	STRM	38 20 175 48	28
KOPAKORAHI STREAM	STRM	38 20 175 48	29
KOPANE	LOC	40 19 175 28	48
KOPANE	LOC	40 19 175 28	49
KOPARA	LOC	42 34 171 44	70
KOPAURIURI STREAM	STRM	38 29 175 19	27
KOPEKA RIVER	STRM	47 08 167 56	114
KOPEKA RIVER	STRM	47 08 167 56	115
KOPEOPEO	LOC	37 57 176 57	22
KOPEOPEO	LOC	37 57 176 57	23
KOPEOPEO CANAL	CANL	37 55 176 52	22
KOPEOPEO CANAL	CANL	37 55 176 52	23
KOPIKOPIKO	LOC	40 32 175 38	48
KOPIKOPIKO	LOC	40 32 175 38	49
KOPOAI, LAKE	LAKE	36 03 173 50	7
KOPONGATAHI POINT	PNT	37 34 177 59	24
KOPONGATAHI POINT	PNT	37 34 177 59	25
KOPONUI (TRIG)	HILL	37 58 175 00	18
KOPU	LOC	37 11 175 35	13
KOPU	LOC	37 11 175 35	15
KOPUA	LOC	40 05 176 17	47
KOPUA (TRIG)	PEAK	39 10 176 42	40
KOPUAPOUNAMU RIVER	STRM	37 42 178 19	25
KOPUAPOUNAMU STREAM	STRM	38 38 177 13	31
KOPUARAHI	LOC	37 13 175 30	13
KOPUARAHI	LOC	37 13 175 30	15
KOPUARANGA	LOC	40 50 175 40	48
KOPUARANGA	LOC	40 30 175 40	49
KOPUARANGA	LOC	40 50 175 40	51
KOPUARANGA RIVER	STRM	40 54 175 41	49
KOPUARANGA RIVER	STRM	40 54 175 41	51
KOPUAWHARA STATION	RSTN	39 02 177 51	33
KOPUAWHARA STREAM	STRM	39 05 177 55	33
KOPUERA, LAKE	LAKE	37 26 175 08	14
KOPUERA, LAKE	LAKE	37 26 175 08	15
KOPUERA STREAM	STRM	37 17 175 06	14
KOPUERA STREAM	STRM	37 17 175 06	15
KOPUKU	LOC	37 16 175 11	13
KOPUKU	LOC	37 16 175 11	15
KOPUKU STREAM	STRM	37 17 175 08	15
KOPUNI STREAM	STRM	39 11 177 50	33
KOPUOKAI (TRIG)	HILL	35 05 173 25	3
KOPUOKAI (TRIG)	HILL	36 46 174 25	10
KOPUOKAI (TRIG)	HILL	36 46 174 25	11
KOPUPARAPARA (TRIG)	MTN	38 33 176 56	30
KOPURERERUA STREAM	STRM	37 42 176 09	20
KOPURERERUA STREAM	STRM	37 42 176 09	21

KOPURIKI	LOC	38 21 176 48	30
KOPURIKI STREAM	STRM	38 19 176 49	30
KOPUROA CANAL	CANL	37 45 176 21	20
KOPUROA CANAL	CANL	37 45 176 21	21
KOPURU BEACH	BCH	36 04 173 51	7
KOPURU (TRIG)	HILL	36 03 173 51	6
KOPURU (TRIG)	HILL	36 03 173 51	7
KOPUTARA, LAKE	LAKE	40 24 175 16	48
KOPUTAROA	LOC	40 35 175 20	48
KOPUTAUAKI BAY	BAY	36 44 175 27	13
KOPUTAUAKI BAY	BAY	36 44 175 27	16
KORAKONUI	LOC	38 09 175 25	19
KORAKORIKI STREAM	STRM	39 01 175 06	36
KORANGA	LOC	38 28 177 25	31
KORANGA	HSTD	38 25 177 20	31
KORANGA RIVER	STRM	38 24 177 17	31
KORAPUKI ISLAND	ISLD	36 40 175 51	16
KOREMOA	LOC	36 07 173 56	7
KORERE	LOC	41 32 172 48	58
KORERE (TRIG)	HILL	41 32 172 49	58
KORINITI	LOC	39 40 175 09	45
KOROHE PA	LOC	38 58 175 52	37
KOROHE PA	LOC	38 58 175 52	38
KOROKORO	SBRB	41 13 174 52	52
KOROKORO	SBRB	41 13 174 52	55
KOROKORO STREAM	STRM	41 13 174 52	52
KOROKORO STREAM	STRM	41 13 174 52	55
KOROMATUA	LOC	37 50 175 12	18
KOROMATUA	LOC	37 50 175 12	19
KOROMATUA STREAM	STRM	37 49 175 09	18
KOROMIKO	LOC	41 20 173 58	54
KOROMIKO	LOC	41 20 173 58	60
KOROMIKO	LOC	41 20 173 58	61
KOROPEKE (TRIG)	HILL	40 32 175 51	49
KOROPONUI (TRIG)	HILL	40 18 176 14	50
KOROPUKU STREAM	STRM	42 50 171 43	70
KORORA	LOC	40 30 176 11	50
KOROTETI STREAM	STRM	39 22 175 49	37
KOTAKOTAIA STREAM	STRM	38 35 175 31	27
KOTAKOTAIA STREAM	STRM	38 35 175 31	28
KOTARA	HSTD	38 54 177 31	33
KOTARE	LOC	38 53 174 44	26
KOTEKARAKA (TRIG)	HILL	37 26 174 47	14
KOTEKIEKIE STREAM	STRM	39 23 174 49	35
KOTEKIEKIE STREAM	STRM	39 23 174 49	44
KOTEMAORI	LOC	39 04 177 02	41
KOTEPATO STREAM	STRM	38 20 177 19	31
KOTERUATO STREAM	STRM	37 13 175 12	13
KOTERUATO STREAM	STRM	37 13 175 12	15
KOTINGA	LOC	40 53 172 47	57
KOTIPU (TRIG)	HILL	35 11 173 24	3
KOTITI STREAM	STRM	39 50 174 57	45
KOTOKO (TRIG)	HILL	39 06 176 59	40
KOTOKO (TRIG)	HILL	39 06 176 59	41
KOTORE RANGE	MTNS	38 50 176 57	30
KOTOREPUPUAI STREAM	STRM	37 13 175 39	15
KOTOREPUPUAI STREAM	STRM	37 13 175 39	17
KOTUKU	LOC	42 33 171 28	69
KOTUKU (TRIG)	HILL	37 44 174 55	18
KOTUKUTUKU STREAM	STRM	38 41 175 46	28
KOTUKUTUKU STREAM	STRM	38 41 175 46	38
KOTUKUTUKU (TRIG)	HILL	38 36 175 16	27
KOUKOUPO STREAM	STRM	39 39 175 26	45
KOUKOUPO STREAM	STRM	39 39 175 26	46
KOURARAU	HSTD	41 06 175 42	51
KOURARAU	HSTD	41 06 175 42	53
KOURARAU DAM	HSTD	41 05 175 42	51
KOURARAU DAM	HSTD	41 05 175 42	53
KOURARAU STREAM	STRM	41 05 175 42	51
KOURARAU STREAM	STRM	41 05 175 42	53
KOURATAHI STREAM	STRM	37 33 174 59	14
KOURAWHERO	LOC	36 25 174 36	11
KOURAWHERO STREAM	STRM	36 24 174 33	11
KOUTU	LOC	35 29 173 25	6
KOUTU	SBRB	38 08 176 14	20
KOUTU	SBRB	38 08 176 14	21
KOUTUAMOA POINT	PNT	37 54 178 24	25
KOUTUNUI HEAD	HEAD	38 03 178 22	25
KOUTUNUI POINT	PNT	38 07 178 21	25
KOWAI BUSH	LOC	43 18 171 55	80
KOWAI BUSH	LOC	43 18 171 55	81
KOWAI RIVER	STRM	43 19 171 59	80
KOWAI RIVER	STRM	43 12 172 46	82
KOWAI RIVER (NORTH BRANCH)	STRM	43 12 172 45	82
KOWAI RIVER (SOUTH BRANCH)	STRM	43 12 172 45	82
KOWAI RIVER (WEST BRANCH)	STRM	43 20 171 47	80
KOWARE (TRIG)	HILL	34 51 173 27	3
KOWHAI	LOC	42 25 173 37	73
KOWHAI BEACH	BCH	34 47 173 09	3
KOWHAI CREEK	STRM	45 45 168 03	106
KOWHAI CREEK	STRM	45 45 168 03	107
KOWHAI RIVER	STRM	42 25 173 38	73
KOWHAI SADDLE	SAD	42 17 173 37	66
KOWHAI SADDLE	SAD	42 17 173 37	67
KOWHAI STREAM	STRM	43 10 172 25	81
KOWHAI STREAM	STRM	43 58 171 16	87
KOWHAIROA (TRIG)	HILL	35 00 173 44	4
KOWHATU	LOC	44 33 170 40	93
KOWHATUHURI POINT	PNT	35 08 174 05	4
KOWHATUHURI POINT	PNT	35 08 174 05	5
KOWHATUPIKO (TRIG)	HILL	39 18 174 32	35
KOWHATUPIKO (TRIG)	HILL	39 18 174 32	44
KOWHITIRANGI	LOC	42 53 171 01	68
KOWHITIRANGI	LOC	42 53 171 01	69
KRUSE, MOUNT (TRIG)	MTN	42 16 172 44	65
KUAKA POINT	PNT	34 55 173 16	3
KUAMAHANGA STREAM	STRM	41 06 175 47	51
KUAOTUNU	LOC	36 43 175 44	16
KUATAIKA (TRIG)	HILL	36 55 174 28	10
KUATAIKA (TRIG)	HILL	36 55 174 28	11
KUATAIKA (TRIG)	HILL	36 55 174 28	12
KUHARUA (TRIG)	HILL	38 56 175 42	37
KUHARUA (TRIG)	HILL	38 56 175 42	38
KUHATAHI STREAM	STRM	38 01 175 52	20
KUHUNUI (TRIG)	HILL	39 40 175 10	45
KUKU	LOC	40 41 175 14	48
KUKUMOA	LOC	38 00 177 16	23
KUKUNUI (TRIG)	HILL	35 54 174 23	7
KUKUNUI (TRIG)	HILL	35 54 174 23	8
KUKUPA	LOC	43 43 172 54	83
KUMARA	POPL	42 38 171 11	68
KUMARA	POPL	42 38 171 11	69
KUMARA JUNCTION	LOC	42 35 171 08	68
KUMARA JUNCTION	LOC	42 35 171 08	69
KUMARA RESERVOIR	LAKE	42 42 171 11	68
KUMARA RESERVOIR	LAKE	42 42 171 11	69
KUMEROA	LOC	40 20 175 59	49
KUMETEWHIWHIA (TRIG)	HILL	35 13 173 27	3
KUMEU	POPL	36 47 174 34	11
KUMEU	POPL	36 47 174 34	12

KUMEU RIVER	STRM	36 46 174 30	10
KUMEU RIVER	STRM	36 46 174 30	11
KUMEU RIVER	STRM	36 46 174 30	12
KUMI POINT	PNT	35 39 174 31	5
KUMI POINT	PNT	35 39 174 31	8
KUMUTOTO BAY	BAY	41 13 174 04	54
KUMUTOTO BAY	BAY	41 13 174 04	60
KUMUTOTO BAY	BAY	41 13 174 04	61
KUNDY ISLAND	ISLD	47 07 167 33	114
KUPE	LOC	39 15 174 23	35
KUPE	LOC	39 15 174 23	44
KUPE BEACH	BCH	35 26 174 26	5
KURANUI	LOC	37 40 175 30	19
KURANUI (TRIG)	HILL	39 47 174 50	44
KURATAHI (TRIG)	HILL	39 38 175 41	46
KURATAU	LOC	38 54 175 47	28
KURATAU	LOC	38 54 175 47	38
KURATAU JUNCTION	LOC	38 53 175 41	28
KURATAU JUNCTION	LOC	38 53 175 41	38
KURATAU, LAKE	LAKE	38 52 175 43	28
KURATAU, LAKE	LAKE	38 52 175 43	38
KURATAU RIVER	STRM	38 53 175 47	28
KURATAU RIVER	STRM	38 53 175 47	38
KURI BUSH	LOC	46 02 170 13	103
KURI, MOUNT	MTN	44 12 169 00	78
KURI POINT	PNT	47 08 168 03	115
KURI STREAM	STRM	39 14 174 48	35
KURI (TRIG)	HILL	40 54 172 58	57
KURIPAPANGO	LOC	39 24 176 20	39
KURITUNU STREAM	STRM	38 12 174 56	18
KURIWAI CREEK	STRM	46 22 168 50	112
KURIWAO	LOC	46 13 169 26	111
KURIWAO	LOC	46 13 169 26	113
KURIWAO HILL (TRIG)	HILL	46 24 168 49	112
KURIWAO PEAK	HILL	46 14 169 22	111
KURIWAO PEAK	HILL	46 14 169 22	113
KURIWAO STREAM	STRM	46 12 169 27	111
KURIWAO STREAM	STRM	46 12 169 27	113
KURIWAO (TRIG)	HILL	46 15 169 16	110
KURIWAO (TRIG)	HILL	46 15 169 16	112
KURIWAO (TRIG)	HILL	46 15 169 16	113
KUROW	LOC	44 44 170 28	92
KUROW HILL (TRIG)	HILL	44 44 170 27	92
KUROW RIVER	STRM	44 45 170 29	92
KURUNUI STREAM	STRM	38 28 177 46	32
KUTARERE	LOC	38 03 177 09	23
KUWAKATAI, LAKE	LAKE	36 32 174 14	10
KYE BURN	STRM	45 12 170 14	101
KYEBURN	LOC	45 09 170 15	101
KYEBURN DIGGINGS	LOC	44 59 170 17	92
KYEBURN DIGGINGS	LOC	44 59 170 17	101
KYEBURN, MOUNT (TRIG)	MTN	44 56 170 18	92
KYLE	LOC	43 56 172 03	85

L

LA FONTAINE STREAM	STRM	43 04 170 31	74
LA GRIPPE (TRIG)	MTN	42 42 172 29	71
LA PEROUSE	MTN	43 36 170 05	76
LA PEROUSE	MTN	43 36 170 05	77
LA PEROUSE GLACIER	GLCR	43 35 170 04	76
LA PEROUSE GLACIER	GLCR	43 35 170 04	77
LACEBARK STREAM	STRM	42 12 173 34	66
LACHLAN (TRIG)	HILL	39 16 177 00	40
LACHLAN (TRIG)	HILL	39 16 177 00	41
LADBROOKS	LOC	43 37 172 37	81
LADBROOKS	LOC	43 37 172 37	82
LADBROOKS	LOC	43 37 172 37	83
LADY ALICE ISLAND	ISLD	35 54 174 44	8
LADY BARKLY	LOC	46 06 168 21	107
LADY FRANKLIN BANK	BNK	36 21 174 12	10
LADY LAKE	LAKE	42 36 171 35	69
LADY OF THE SNOWS	MTN	44 43 167 44	94
LAGMHOR	LOC	43 53 171 38	84
LAGOON BAY	BAY	46 46 168 29	109
LAGOON BAY	BAY	46 46 168 29	115
LAGOON CREEK	STRM	45 32 167 50	97
LAGOON CREEK	STRM	45 32 167 50	98
LAGOON PEAK (TRIG)	MTN	43 23 171 14	75
LAGOON SADDLE	SAD	43 03 171 36	80
LAGOON VALLEY	LOC	44 41 169 19	91
LAGOON (TRIG)	HILL	43 16 171 01	75
LAHEYS CREEK	STRM	45 04 169 28	100
LAINGHOLM	LOC	36 59 174 38	12
LAINGHOLM	LOC	36 59 174 38	14
LAINGHOLM POINT	PNT	36 58 174 39	12
LAINGHOLM POINT	PNT	36 58 174 39	14
LAINGS HILL	MTN	43 17 171 35	80
LAIRDVALE	LOC	38 52 175 16	27
LAKE ALICE	LOC	40 08 175 20	45
LAKE COLERIDGE	LOC	43 22 171 32	80
LAKE CREEK	STRM	44 13 169 29	79
LAKE FERRY	LOC	41 24 175 09	52
LAKE FERRY	LOC	41 24 175 09	53
LAKE FERRY	LOC	41 24 175 09	55
LAKE GRASSMERE	LOC	41 43 174 08	67
LAKE HAWEA	LOC	44 37 169 15	91
LAKE HILL (TRIG)	HILL	43 29 171 11	75
LAKE HILL (TRIG)	HILL	43 21 171 35	80
LAKE HILL (TRIG)	HILL	42 19 172 39	65
LAKE MOERAKI	LOC	43 43 169 16	78
LAKE OHAU LODGE	BLDG	44 14 169 49	79
LAKE OHIA	LOC	34 59 173 23	3
LAKE OMAPERE	LOC	35 20 173 48	4
LAKE PARINGA	LOC	43 43 169 25	76
LAKE PARINGA	LOC	43 43 169 25	78
LAKE PARINGA	LOC	43 43 169 25	79
LAKE PUKAKI	LOC	44 11 170 09	86
LAKE RAUPO STATION	HSTD	42 59 172 48	71
LAKE RAUPO STATION	HSTD	42 59 172 48	72
LAKE ROTOMA	LOC	38 03 176 34	21
LAKE ROTOMA	LOC	38 03 176 34	22
LAKE STREAM	STRM	42 18 172 06	64
LAKE STREAM	STRM	43 27 171 11	75
LAKE SUMNER STATE FOREST PARK	PARK	42 40 172 03	70
LAKE TAYLOR	HSTD	42 47 172 16	71
LAKE TEKAPO	LOC	44 01 170 29	77
LAKE TEKAPO	LOC	44 01 170 29	86
LAKEMAN, MOUNT (TRIG)	MTN	42 33 172 12	70
LAKES, THE	LAKE	39 22 176 22	39
LAKESIDE	LOC	43 49 172 21	85
LAKESIDE	LOC	46 14 169 50	111
LAKESIDE	LOC	46 14 169 50	113
LAMB VALLEY	STRM	41 39 172 39	58
LAMBERT, CAPE	CAPE	40 59 174 14	54
LAMBERT, CAPE	CAPE	40 59 174 14	60
LAMBERT, CAPE	CAPE	40 59 174 14	61
LAMBERT COL	SAD	43 18 170 47	75
LAMBERT GLACIER	GLCR	43 18 170 46	74
LAMBERT MOUNT	MTN	43 18 170 45	74

LAMBERT RIVER	STRM	43 14 170 45	74
LAMBING SADDLE	SAD	45 16 168 38	95
LAMBING SADDLE	SAD	45 16 168 38	99
LAMMERLAW RANGE	MTNS	45 43 169 43	111
LAMMERLAW STREAM	STRM	45 49 169 52	111
LAMMERLAW TOP (TRIG)	HILL	45 40 169 38	111
LAMMERMOOR RANGE	MTNS	45 42 169 45	111
LAMMERMOOR (TRIG)	HILL	45 43 169 44	111
LANCE, MOUNT (TRIG)	MTN	42 58 172 27	71
LANCELOT, MOUNT	MTN	42 56 171 30	69
LANDING BAY	BAY	46 00 166 29	104
LANDING CREEK	STRM	40 56 172 14	56
LANDING CREEK	STRM	41 57 171 54	64
LANDS END	HSTD	41 13 175 51	51
LANDSBOROUGH RIVER	STRM	43 57 169 29	79
LANDSLIP CREEK	STRM	43 56 170 11	77
LANDSLIP CREEK	STRM	43 56 170 11	86
LANERCOST	HSTD	42 39 173 16	72
LANERCOST	HSTD	42 39 173 16	73
LANGDALE	HSTD	40 56 176 03	49
LANGDALE	HSTD	40 56 176 03	51
LANGDON (TRIG)	PEAK	39 02 175 27	36
LANGDON (TRIG)	PEAK	39 02 175 27	37
LANGRIDGE	HSTD	42 00 173 25	66
LANGS BEACH	BCH	36 03 174 32	8
LANSDOWN	LOC	44 41 171 01	93
LANSDOWNE	LOC	43 37 172 35	82
LANSDOWNE	LOC	43 37 172 35	83
LANSDOWNE	LOC	43 37 172 35	85
LANSDOWNE (TRIG)	HILL	41 35 173 32	59
LAPITH PEAK	PEAK	44 39 168 33	90
LARGE BURN	STRM	45 05 167 21	94
LARGE BURN	STRM	45 05 167 21	96
LARGS PEAK	PEAK	44 58 167 59	97
LARGS PEAK	PEAK	44 58 167 59	98
LARKINS, MOUNT	MTN	44 53 168 30	89
LARKINS, MOUNT	MTN	44 53 168 30	95
LARNACH STREAM	STRM	45 50 168 36	107
LARRIKIN CREEK	STRM	41 36 172 13	62
LARRY SADDLE	SAD	42 04 172 07	64
LARRYS CREEK	LOC	42 00 171 54	63
LARRYS CREEK	LOC	42 00 171 54	64
LASCHELLES CREEK	STRM	44 05 168 31	88
LATHROP, MOUNT	MTN	42 55 171 17	68
LATHROP, MOUNT	MTN	42 55 171 17	69
LAUDER	LOC	45 03 169 40	100
LAUDER CREEK	STRM	45 00 169 42	91
LAUDER CREEK	STRM	45 00 169 42	100
LAURAS LEG	PNT	46 59 168 12	115
LAURISTON	LOC	43 43 171 47	84
LAVERICKS (TRIG)	HILL	43 45 173 01	83
LAVERICKS BAY	BAY	43 43 173 06	83
LAW CREEK	STRM	43 19 170 25	74
LAW HILL (TRIG)	HILL	43 48 169 16	78
LAW, LAKE	LAKE	43 49 169 16	78
LAW PEAK	MTN	43 52 169 22	78
LAWRENCE	POPL	45 55 169 41	111
LAWRENCE RIVER	STRM	43 28 170 51	75
LAWRENCE SADDLE	SAD	41 20 172 15	62
LAWSON CREEK	STRM	42 10 171 19	63
LE BONS BAY	BAY	43 44 173 06	83
LE BONS BAY	LOC	43 46 173 04	83
LEAD HILLS (TRIG)	HILL	40 54 172 33	56
LEAD HILLS (TRIG)	HILL	40 54 172 33	57
LEADER DALE	STRM	42 24 172 49	71
LEADER DALE	STRM	42 24 172 49	72
LEADER FALLS	FALL	44 37 168 00	89
LEADER RIVER	STRM	42 44 173 19	72
LEADER RIVER	STRM	42 44 173 19	73
LEADERVALE	HSTD	42 38 173 16	72
LEADERVALE	HSTD	42 38 173 16	73
LEAMINGTON	SBRB	37 55 175 29	19
LEAMINGTON	HSTD	42 44 173 14	72
LEAMINGTON	LOC	42 47 173 11	72
LEAMINGTON	LOC	42 47 173 11	73
LEAMINGTON	HSTD	42 44 173 14	73
LEAMINGTON STREAM	STRM	42 43 173 17	72
LEAMINGTON STREAM	STRM	42 43 173 17	73
LEAN PEAK	PEAK	43 39 170 06	76
LEAN PEAK	PEAK	43 39 170 06	77
LEAN PEAK	PEAK	43 39 170 06	79
LEANING MOUNT	MTN	44 16 169 31	79
LEANING PEAK (TRIG)	PEAK	45 30 167 16	96
LEANING ROCK (TRIG)	MTN	45 04 169 21	100
LEAPING BURN	STRM	44 33 168 54	90
LEARMONT, MOUNT	MTN	42 58 171 18	68
LEARMONT, MOUNT	MTN	42 58 171 18	69
LEATHAM	HSTD	41 45 173 12	66
LEATHAM RIVER	STRM	41 43 173 10	66
LEATHERWOOD SADDLE	SAD	45 13 166 56	96
LEE BROOK	STRM	41 58 173 29	66
LEE CREEK	STRM	45 59 170 08	103
LEE FLAT	LOC	45 48 170 02	111
LEE ISLAND	ISLD	45 02 167 52	94
LEE ISLAND	ISLD	45 02 167 52	97
LEE ISLAND	ISLD	45 02 167 52	98
LEE RIVER	STRM	41 24 173 09	59
LEE RIVER	STRM	43 53 172 17	85
LEE STREAM	LOC	45 48 170 08	103
LEE STREAM	STRM	45 50 170 16	103
LEE STREAM	STRM	45 50 170 16	111
LEEB GLACIER	GLCR	43 13 170 54	75
LEEB, LAKE	LAKE	44 08 168 40	88
LEES CREEK	STRM	41 57 172 54	65
LEES KNOB	HILL	47 06 167 48	114
LEES PASS	PASS	43 02 172 22	81
LEES VALLEY	LOC	43 09 172 12	81
LEESTON	LOC	43 46 172 18	85
LEIGH	LOC	36 18 174 48	11
LEITCH, MOUNT	MTN	42 20 171 21	69
LEITH HILL (TRIG)	MTN	43 13 171 41	80
LEITHEN BURN	STRM	45 51 169 07	110
LEITHFIELD	LOC	43 12 172 44	82
LEITHFIELD BEACH	LOC	43 13 172 45	82
LENDENFELD PEAK	MTN	43 34 170 10	74
LENDENFELD PEAK	MTN	43 34 170 10	77
LENNOX PASS	PASS	44 39 168 26	89
LEPPERTON	LOC	39 04 174 12	34
LESLIE HILLS	HSTD	42 40 172 51	71
LESLIE HILLS	HSTD	42 40 172 51	72
LESLIE, MOUNT (TRIG)	PEAK	42 36 172 52	71
LESLIE, MOUNT (TRIG)	PEAK	42 36 172 52	72
LESLIE PASS	PASS	42 36 172 50	71
LESLIE PASS	PASS	42 36 172 50	72
LESLIE RIVER	STRM	41 13 172 35	56
LESLIE RIVER	STRM	41 13 172 35	58
LESLIE STREAM	STRM	42 40 172 47	71
LESLIE STREAM	STRM	42 40 172 47	72
LESSONG MONUMENT (TRIG)	PEAK	39 33 176 18	39
LETHAM BURN	STRM	45 48 167 57	106

LETHAM BURN	STRM	45 48 167 57	107
LETHAM (TRIG)	MTN	45 47 167 59	106
LETHAM (TRIG)	MTN	45 47 167 59	107
LETITIA, LAKE	LAKE	43 03 171 57	80
LETITIA, LAKE	LAKE	43 03 171 57	81
LEVELS	LOC	44 19 171 12	87
LEVELS VALLEY	LOC	44 19 171 06	87
LEVEN STREAM	STRM	44 12 169 15	78
LEVIN	TOWN	40 37 175 17	48
LEVY, PORT	HARB	43 39 172 50	82
LEVY, PORT	HARB	43 39 172 50	83
LEWIS PASS	PASS	42 23 172 24	71
LEWIS RIVER	STRM	40 56 172 08	56
LEWIS RIVER	STRM	42 31 172 23	71
LIBRETTO RANGE	MTNS	42 26 172 26	71
LICHFIELD	LOC	38 07 175 49	19
LICHFIELD	LOC	38 07 175 49	20
LIEBIG RANGE	MTNS	43 37 170 21	74
LIEBIG RANGE	MTNS	43 37 170 21	77
LIEBIG RANGE	MTNS	43 37 170 21	86
LIGAR BAY	BAY	40 49 172 54	57
LIGAR CREEK	STRM	45 48 167 39	106
LIGAR, PORT	HARB	40 56 173 59	54
LIGAR, PORT	HARB	40 56 173 59	61
LIGHT RIVER	STRM	44 47 167 38	94
LILIAN, LAKE	LAKE	43 11 171 31	80
LILL BURN	STRM	46 01 167 38	105
LILL BURN	STRM	46 01 167 38	106
LILLBURN HILL (TRIG)	MTN	43 02 172 10	81
LILLBURN RIVER	STRM	43 05 172 10	81
LILYBANK	LOC	43 42 170 34	77
LILYBANK	LOC	43 42 170 34	86
LIMA, MOUNT	MTN	44 38 168 36	90
LIMBURN STREAM	STRM	42 00 173 48	67
LIMEHILLS	LOC	46 04 168 20	107
LIMESTONE CREEK	STRM	39 58 175 58	46
LIMESTONE CREEK	STRM	43 48 171 21	87
LIMESTONE CREEK	STRM	44 04 168 23	88
LIMESTONE DOWNS	LOC	37 29 174 46	14
LIMESTONE GLENS	HSTD	42 50 173 03	72
LIMESTONE HILL (TRIG)	HILL	42 12 173 31	66
LIMESTONE HILL (TRIG)	HILL	42 36 173 21	72
LIMESTONE HILL (TRIG)	HILL	42 36 173 21	73
LIMESTONE ISLAND	ISLD	35 47 174 21	5
LIMESTONE ISLAND	ISLD	35 47 174 21	7
LIMESTONE ISLAND	ISLD	35 47 174 21	8
LIMESTONE STREAM	STRM	42 11 173 28	66
LIMESTONE STREAM	STRM	41 54 173 36	66
LIMESTONE STREAM	STRM	42 37 173 28	72
LIMESTONE STREAM	STRM	42 37 173 28	73
LIMESTONE VALLEY	LOC	44 12 170 48	87
LINCOLN	LOC	43 39 172 29	81
LINCOLN	LOC	43 39 172 29	82
LINCOLN	LOC	43 39 172 29	83
LINCOLN	LOC	43 39 172 29	85
LINDEN	SBRB	41 10 174 50	52
LINDEN	SBRB	41 10 174 50	55
LINDIS PASS	PASS	44 35 169 39	91
LINDIS PEAK (TRIG)	MTN	44 44 169 28	91
LINDIS RIVER	STRM	44 30 169 34	91
LINDIS RIVER	STRM	44 53 169 20	91
LINDIS VALLEY	LOC	44 45 169 30	91
LINDS BRIDGE	LOC	46 20 168 20	109
LINDSAY CREEK	STRM	41 03 172 41	56
LINDSAY CREEK	STRM	41 03 172 41	57
LINDSAY CREEK	STRM	41 03 172 41	58
LINDSAY, LAKE	LAKE	40 59 172 38	56
LINDSAY, LAKE	LAKE	40 59 172 38	57
LINDSAY, LAKE	LAKE	40 59 172 38	58
LINDSAY, MOUNT (TRIG)	HILL	44 08 168 38	88
LINDSAY PEAK	PEAK	44 04 169 19	78
LINKWATER	LOC	41 18 173 49	54
LINKWATER	LOC	41 18 173 49	60
LINKWATER	LOC	41 18 173 49	61
LINN BURN	STRM	45 20 169 57	101
LINTLEY	LOC	45 47 168 28	107
LINTLEY RANGE	MTNS	45 42 168 30	107
LINTON	LOC	40 26 175 33	48
LINTON	LOC	40 26 175 33	49
LINTON CREEK	STRM	42 24 173 30	73
LINTON CREEK	STRM	45 57 167 52	106
LINTON CREEK	STRM	45 57 167 52	107
LINTON MILITARY CAMP	LOC	40 25 175 35	48
LINTON MILITARY CAMP	LOC	40 25 175 35	49
LINTON, MOUNT (TRIG)	HILL	45 54 167 46	106
LINWOOD	SBRB	43 32 172 40	82
LINWOOD	SBRB	43 32 172 40	83
LINWOOD	SBRB	43 32 172 40	85
LION ROCK	ROCK	35 07 174 03	4
LION ROCK	ROCK	35 07 174 03	5
LION ROCK	ROCK	36 12 175 03	9
LION ROCK	ROCK	36 57 174 28	12
LION, THE (TRIG)	MTN	44 37 167 48	89
LION, THE (TRIG)	MTN	44 37 167 48	94
LISMORE	LOC	43 54 171 29	84
LITTLE AKALOA BAY	BAY	43 40 173 00	82
LITTLE AKALOA BAY	BAY	43 40 173 00	83
LITTLE BARRIER ISLAND	ISLD	36 12 175 05	9
LITTLE BEN (TRIG)	HILL	41 28 173 06	58
LITTLE BEN (TRIG)	HILL	41 28 173 06	59
LITTLE BREAST HILL	MTN	44 33 169 29	91
LITTLE CAIRN PEAK	PEAK	45 52 168 15	107
LITTLE CREEK	STRM	45 40 167 38	106
LITTLE CRIFFEL (TRIG)	MTN	44 48 169 08	90
LITTLE CROW RIVER	STRM	41 19 172 32	58
LITTLE DEEPDALE CREEK	STRM	41 44 172 06	64
LITTLE DEVIL CREEK	STRM	44 38 168 29	89
LITTLE HOHONU RIVER	STRM	42 38 171 18	69
LITTLE HOPE RIVER	STRM	41 39 172 39	58
LITTLE HOPWOOD BURN	STRM	44 24 169 21	91
LITTLE HUIA	LOC	37 01 174 33	12
LITTLE HUIA	LOC	37 01 174 33	14
LITTLE HUMMOCK (TRIG)	HILL	45 30 170 26	102
LITTLE ISLAND	ISLD	45 44 166 34	104
LITTLE ISLAND	ISLD	45 59 166 35	104
LITTLE KOWAI RIVER	STRM	43 19 171 57	80
LITTLE KYE BURN	STRM	44 59 170 13	92
LITTLE LAKE	LAKE	42 20 172 37	71
LITTLE LOTTERY RIVER	STRM	42 32 172 59	72
LITTLE MAN RIVER (DRY CREEK)	STRM	43 13 170 25	74
LITTLE MOGGY ISLAND	ISLD	47 08 167 25	114
LITTLE, MOUNT	MTN	43 43 170 14	77
LITTLE, MOUNT	MTN	43 43 170 14	86
LITTLE MOUNT ALLAN	LOC	45 44 170 21	103
LITTLE MOUNT ANGLEM (TRIG)	MTN	46 46 167 57	108
LITTLE MOUNT ANGLEM (TRIG)	MTN	46 46 167 57	109
LITTLE MOUNT ANGLEM (TRIG)	MTN	46 46 167 57	114
LITTLE MOUNT ANGLEM (TRIG)	MTN	46 46 167 57	115
LITTLE MOUNT PEEL (TRIG)	MTN	43 53 171 13	87
LITTLE OMARAMA STREAM	STRM	44 35 169 52	91
LITTLE ONAHAU RIVER	STRM	40 48 172 46	57
LITTLE OPAWA RIVER	STRM	44 14 170 53	87
LITTLE PEAK (TRIG)	HILL	45 39 170 18	101
LITTLE PEAK (TRIG)	HILL	45 47 169 48	111
LITTLE PEVERLL	HILL	43 02 171 55	80
LITTLE PEVERLL	HILL	43 02 171 55	81
LITTLE POMAHAKA RIVER	STRM	45 31 169 11	100
LITTLE RAKAIA	LOC	43 51 172 13	85
LITTLE RIVER	STRM	43 27 171 36	80
LITTLE RIVER	LOC	43 46 172 47	83
LITTLE SHIEL HILL	MTN	44 40 168 43	90
LITTLE SOLANDER ISLAND	ISLD	46 34 166 51	108
LITTLE TOTARA RIVER	STRM	41 52 171 28	63
LITTLE TWIN	PEAK	41 20 173 24	59
LITTLE VALLEY	LOC	45 19 169 28	100
LITTLE VALLEY CREEK	STRM	45 16 169 29	100
LITTLE WAIHI	LOC	37 46 176 29	21
LITTLE WAIHI	LOC	37 46 176 29	22
LITTLE WANGANUI	LOC	41 22 172 05	62
LITTLE WANGANUI HEAD	HEAD	41 24 172 03	62
LITTLE WANGANUI RIVER	STRM	41 24 172 04	62
LITTLE WANGANUI SADDLE	SAD	41 24 172 18	62
LIVERPOOL, MOUNT	MTN	44 26 168 38	88
LIVERPOOL, MOUNT	MTN	44 26 168 38	90
LIVINGSTONE	LOC	39 56 175 39	46
LIVINGSTONE	LOC	44 58 170 35	92
LIVINGSTONE MOUNTAINS	MTNS	45 03 168 06	97
LIVINGSTONE MOUNTAINS	MTNS	45 03 168 06	98
LIZARD ISLE	ISLD	35 55 175 07	9
LIZARD STREAM	STRM	42 13 173 25	66
LLAWRENNY PEAKS	PEAK	44 40 167 49	94
LLOYD, MOUNT	MTN	43 49 170 04	76
LLOYD, MOUNT	MTN	43 49 170 04	77
LLOYD, MOUNT	MTN	43 49 170 04	79
LLOYD PEAK	PEAK	44 47 167 55	89
LLOYD PEAK	PEAK	44 47 167 55	94
LLOYDS HILL (TRIG)	HILL	36 37 174 38	11
LLOYDS HILL (TRIG)	HILL	36 37 174 38	12
LO CREEK	STRM	44 03 169 00	78
LOBURN	LOC	43 15 172 33	82
LOBURN	LOC	43 15 172 33	83
LOBURN NORTH	LOC	43 13 172 29	81
LOBURN NORTH	LOC	43 13 172 29	82
LOCH BURN	STRM	45 09 167 38	94
LOCH BURN	STRM	45 09 167 38	97
LOCH KATRINE	LAKE	42 43 172 12	70
LOCH NORRIE	LOC	36 39 174 30	10
LOCH NORRIE	LOC	36 39 174 30	11
LOCH NORRIE	LOC	36 39 174 30	12
LOCHAR BURN	STRM	44 63 169 16	91
LOCHIEL	HSTD	42 35 172 47	71
LOCHIEL	HSTD	42 35 172 47	72
LOCHIEL	LOC	46 12 168 20	107
LOCHINDORB	LOC	46 20 169 31	111
LOCHINDORB	LOC	46 20 169 31	113
LOCHMARA BAY	BAY	41 14 174 00	54
LOCHMARA BAY	BAY	41 14 174 00	60
LOCHMARA BAY	BAY	41 14 174 00	61
LOCHNAGAR	MTN	44 36 168 34	88
LOCHNAGAR	LAKE	44 35 168 36	88
LOCHNAGAR	MTN	44 36 168 34	90
LOCHNAGAR	LAKE	44 35 168 36	90
LOCHY RIVER	STRM	45 12 168 42	95
LOCHY RIVER	STRM	45 12 168 42	99
LOCK CREEK	STRM	42 19 172 08	70
LOCKETT, LAKE	LAKE	41 05 172 38	56
LOCKETT, LAKE	LAKE	41 05 172 38	57
LOCKETT, LAKE	LAKE	41 05 172 38	58
LOCKETT RANGE	MTNS	41 04 172 34	56
LOCKETT RANGE	MTNS	41 04 172 34	57
LOCKETT RANGE	MTNS	41 04 172 34	58
LOCKHARTS STREAM	STRM	44 11 170 40	86
LODESTONE (TRIG)	HILL	41 10 172 45	58
LODGE, MOUNT	MTN	42 06 171 32	63
LOGAN BURN	STRM	45 29 169 56	101
LOGANBRAE	LOC	45 27 169 54	101
LOIS, LAKE	LAKE	45 31 167 21	96
LOIS, LAKE	LAKE	45 31 167 21	97
LONG BAY	LOC	36 41 174 45	11
LONG BAY	LOC	36 41 174 45	12
LONG BAY	BAY	43 53 172 51	83
LONG BURN	STRM	45 11 168 39	95
LONG BURN	STRM	45 11 168 39	99
LONG BURN	STRM	45 55 166 55	104
LONG BURN	STRM	45 55 166 55	105
LONG CREEK	STRM	40 39 172 27	56
LONG CREEK	STRM	40 39 172 27	57
LONG CREEK	STRM	42 18 173 42	67
LONG CREEK	STRM	43 05 171 36	80
LONG FLAT CREEK	STRM	44 07 169 33	79
LONG GULLY	STRM	41 35 172 54	58
LONG GULLY	STRM	41 42 172 41	65
LONG GULLY	STRM	44 49 169 23	91
LONG GULLY	STRM	44 58 169 47	91
LONG GULLY	GLLY	45 04 169 08	99
LONG GULLY STREAM	STRM	41 28 172 49	58
LONG ISLAND	ISLD	41 07 174 17	54
LONG ISLAND	ISLD	41 07 174 17	61
LONG ISLAND	ISLD	45 46 166 42	104
LONG LOOKOUT POINT	PNT	43 39 173 03	82
LONG LOOKOUT POINT	PNT	43 39 173 03	83
LONG POINT	PNT	39 10 177 49	33
LONG POINT	PNT	41 49 174 13	67
LONG POINT	PNT	46 16 167 06	105
LONG POINT	POIN	46 35 169 35	113
LONG RANGE LAKE	LAKE	40 08 176 46	43
LONG REEF	REEF	46 13 166 41	104
LONG SOUND	SND	46 08 166 44	104
LONG SPUR CREEK	STRM	44 41 169 33	91
LONG VALLEY CREEK	STRM	45 25 169 39	100
LONGBEACH	LOC	44 06 171 41	84
LONGBEACH CREEK	STRM	46 37 169 16	112
LONGBEACH CREEK	STRM	46 37 169 16	113
LONGBURN	POPL	40 23 175 32	48
LONGBURN	POPL	40 23 175 32	49
LONGBUSH	LOC	41 09 175 37	51
LONGBUSH	LOC	41 09 175 37	53
LONGBUSH	LOC	46 23 168 29	109
LONGFELLOW, MOUNT (TRIG)	MTN	42 42 172 18	71
LONGFELLOW (TRIG)	HILL	39 30 176 22	39
LONGFORD	LOC	41 47 172 22	65
LONGLANDS	LOC	39 40 176 49	42
LONGLANDS	LOC	39 40 176 49	43
LONGRIDGE	LOC	45 52 168 39	107
LONGRIDGE	LOC	45 52 168 39	110
LONGRIDGE NORTH	LOC	45 47 168 33	107
LONGRIDGE POINT	PNT	44 12 168 09	88
LONGRIDGE STREAM	STRM	45 55 168 35	107
LONGRIDGE (TRIG)	HILL	45 46 168 31	107
LONGSIGHT, MOUNT	MTN	44 46 167 33	94
LONGSLIP CREEK	STRM	44 30 169 46	91
LONGSLIP, MOUNT (TRIG)	MTN	44 32 169 40	91
LONGWOOD	LOC	46 21 167 59	108
LONGWOOD	LOC	46 21 167 59	109
LONGWOOD RANGE	MTNS	46 16 167 50	106
LONGWOOD RANGE	MTNS	46 16 167 50	108
LOOKING GLASS BAY	BAY	44 55 167 13	96
LOOKOUT BLUFF	CLIF	45 16 170 52	102
LOOKOUT HILL	HILL	39 39 176 30	43
LOOKOUT HILL	HILL	39 39 176 30	47
LOOKOUT HILL	HILL	45 22 167 46	97
LOOKOUT HILL (TRIG)	MTN	44 36 169 00	90
LOOKOUT HILL (TRIG)	HILL	45 22 167 46	98
LOOKOUT PEAK	PEAK	41 09 173 45	60
LOOKOUT PEAK	PEAK	41 09 173 45	61
LOOKOUT PEAK	PEAK	42 46 171 57	70
LOOKOUT POINT	PNT	46 37 168 19	109
LOOKOUT RANGE	MTNS	41 31 172 36	58
LOOKOUT (TRIG)	HILL	39 55 175 14	45
LOOKOUT (TRIG)	HILL	41 11 173 34	59
LOOKOUT (TRIG)	MTN	42 01 173 29	66
LOOKOUT (TRIG)	MTN	42 54 172 56	71
LOOKOUT (TRIG)	MTN	42 54 172 56	72
LOOKUP CREEK	STRM	43 47 170 56	87
LOOKUP, MOUNT (TRIG)	MTN	45 12 168 15	95
LOOKUP, MOUNT (TRIG)	MTN	45 12 168 15	98
LORA GORGE	LOC	46 04 168 30	107
LORA STREAM	STRM	46 04 168 29	107
LORD ASHLEY BAY	BAY	40 57 174 05	54
LORD ASHLEY BAY	BAY	40 57 174 05	61
LORD RANGE	MTNS	43 15 170 49	75
LORD RIVER	STRM	43 16 170 47	75
LORD, MOUNT (TRIG)	MTN	43 15 170 52	75
LORDS RIVER	STRM	47 06 168 04	115
LORN PEAK	PEAK	45 21 168 47	95
LORN PEAK	PEAK	45 21 168 47	99
LORNEVILLE	LOC	46 21 168 21	109
LORT, MOUNT	MTN	45 40 166 38	104
LOST STREAM	STRM	41 53 173 04	66
LOTS WIFE (TRIG)	HILL	45 28 170 28	102
LOTTERY RIVER	STRM	42 39 173 02	72
LOTTIN POINT	PNT	37 32 178 10	25
LOUDON HILL (TRIG)	HILL	45 52 167 46	106
LOUGHNAN, MOUNT	MTN	43 26 170 28	74
LOUGHNAN, MOUNT	MTN	43 26 170 28	77
LOUISA STREAM	STRM	39 41 176 52	42
LOUISA STREAM	STRM	39 41 176 52	43
LOUPER PEAK	PEAK	43 14 170 57	75
LOUPER STREAM	STRM	43 16 170 59	75
LOVELLS FLAT	LOC	46 11 169 50	111
LOVELLS FLAT	LOC	46 11 169 50	113
LOVELLS STREAM	STRM	46 10 169 50	111
LOVELLS STREAM	STRM	46 10 169 50	113
LOW BURN	STRM	45 00 169 13	90
LOW BURN	STRM	45 00 169 13	100
LOW BURN	STRM	45 50 169 31	111
LOW CREEK	STRM	43 55 169 31	76
LOW CREEK	STRM	43 55 169 31	79
LOW CREEK	STRM	44 15 168 17	88
LOW SPUR	MTN	43 55 169 27	76
LOW SPUR	MTN	43 55 169 27	78
LOW SPUR	MTN	43 55 169 27	79
LOWBURN	LOC	45 00 169 13	100
LOWCLIFFE	LOC	44 07 171 35	84
LOWER BEN LOMOND (TRIG)	MTN	44 55 170 31	92
LOWER BULLER GORGE	GORG	41 51 171 43	63
LOWER BULLER GORGE	GORG	41 51 171 43	64
LOWER HUIA RESERVOIR	LAKE	36 59 174 34	12
LOWER HUIA RESERVOIR	LAKE	36 59 174 34	14
LOWER HUTT	USAT	41 13 174 55	52
LOWER HUTT	USAT	41 13 174 55	55
LOWER KAIMAI	LOC	37 48 176 02	20
LOWER KAWHATAU	LOC	39 47 175 49	46
LOWER MANORBURN DAM	DAM	45 14 169 26	100
LOWER MOUTERE	LOC	41 08 173 00	57
LOWER MOUTERE	LOC	41 08 173 00	58
LOWER MOUTERE	LOC	41 08 173 00	59
LOWER NEVIS	LOC	45 14 168 58	99
LOWER NIHOTUPU RESERVOIR	LAKE	36 58 174 37	12
LOWER NIHOTUPU RESERVOIR	LAKE	36 58 174 37	14
LOWER OTOKO PASS	PASS	43 51 169 42	76
LOWER OTOKO PASS	PASS	43 51 169 42	79
LOWER SELWYN HUTS	BLDG	43 44 172 27	85
LOWER SHOTOVER	LOC	45 00 168 46	95
LOWER SHOTOVER	LOC	45 00 168 46	99
LOWER WAIAUA	LOC	37 59 177 22	23
LOWER WAIHOU	LOC	35 25 173 23	3
LOWER WAIHOU	LOC	35 25 173 23	6
LOWGARTH	LOC	39 23 174 13	34
LOWRIE PEAK (TRIG)	HILL	39 56 175 19	45
LOWRY BAY	SBRB	41 15 174 55	52
LOWRY BAY	SBRB	41 15 174 55	55
LOWRY HILLS	HSTD	42 48 173 06	72
LOWRY PEAKS RANGE	MTNS	42 47 173 02	72
LOWRY (TRIG)	HILL	41 16 174 55	52
LOWRY (TRIG)	HILL	41 16 174 55	55
LOWTHER	LOC	45 40 168 26	107
LOWTHER PEAK (TRIG)	PEAK	45 40 168 29	107
LOWTHER SADDLE	SAD	41 27 173 16	59
LUCAS CREEK	STRM	36 46 174 40	11
LUCAS CREEK	STRM	36 46 174 40	12
LUCAS PEAK (TRIG)	HILL	43 53 172 55	83
LUCIA, MOUNT	MTN	43 39 170 21	74
LUCIA, MOUNT	MTN	43 39 170 21	77
LUCIA, MOUNT	MTN	43 39 170 21	86
LUCIA, MOUNT (TRIG)	MTN	42 26 172 26	71
LUCIFER	MTN	44 14 168 43	88
LUCKY POINT	PNT	41 16 174 17	54
LUCKY POINT	PNT	41 16 174 17	61
LUCKY POINT	PNT	46 43 167 57	108
LUCKY POINT	PNT	46 43 167 57	109
LUCKY POINT	PNT	46 43 167 57	114
LUCKY POINT	PNT	46 43 167 57	115
LUCRETIA STREAM	STRM	42 28 172 21	71
LUCY STREAM	STRM	42 50 172 10	70
LUDS RIVER	STRM	41 13 173 24	59
LUG CREEK	STRM	45 27 170 10	101
LUGGATE	LOC	44 45 169 16	91
LUGGATE CREEK	STRM	44 45 169 14	90
LUKE CREEK	STRM	42 22 173 40	73
LUMALUMA CREEK	STRM	45 51 166 42	104
LUMP, THE	HILL	45 56 166 42	104
LUMSDEN	POPL	45 44 168 27	107
LUNA CREEK	STRM	45 00 168 26	95
LUNA, LAKE	LAKE	44 57 168 30	89
LUNA, LAKE	LAKE	44 57 168 30	95
LUNA, LAKE	LAKE	44 57 168 30	98
LUNA, LAKE	LAKE	44 57 168 30	99
LUNA, MOUNT (TRIG)	PEAK	41 24 172 28	62
LUNA RIDGE	RDGE	41 22 172 28	58
LUNA RIDGE	RDGE	41 22 172 28	62
LUNAR, MOUNT	MTN	41 33 172 16	62
LUPIN	TRIG	40 41 175 10	48
LUXMORE, MOUNT	MTN	45 23 167 35	97
LYALL BAY	SBRB	41 20 174 48	52
LYALL BAY	SBRB	41 20 174 48	55
LYALL, MOUNT	MTN	45 48 166 41	104
LYALL, MOUNT	MTN	45 17 167 32	97
LYALLDALE	LOC	44 30 171 06	93
LYCIA, MOUNT	MTN	44 07 169 00	78
LYDIA, MOUNT	MTN	44 28 168 30	88
LYDIA, MOUNT	MTN	44 28 168 30	89
LYDIA (TRIG)	HILL	40 52 175 37	48
LYDIA (TRIG)	HILL	40 52 175 37	49
LYDIA (TRIG)	HILL	40 52 175 37	51
LYELL	LOC	41 48 172 03	64
LYELL CREEK	STRM	41 48 172 03	64
LYELL GLACIER	GLCR	43 18 170 51	75
LYELL, MOUNT (TRIG)	PEAK	41 46 172 04	64
LYELL RANGE	MTNS	41 43 172 08	64
LYNCH STREAM	STRM	36 57 175 51	16
LYNCH STREAM	STRM	36 57 175 51	17
LYNCH (TRIG)	HILL	38 25 177 29	31
LYNDHURST	LOC	43 42 171 43	84
LYNDON, LAKE	LAKE	43 18 171 42	80
LYNDON, MOUNT	MTN	43 18 171 41	80
LYNDON PASS	PASS	42 34 172 56	71
LYNDON PASS	PASS	42 34 172 56	72
LYNDON STREAM	STRM	42 38 173 00	72
LYNMORE	SBRB	38 09 176 17	20
LYNMORE	SBRB	38 09 176 17	21
LYNN CREEK	STRM	43 52 171 15	87
LYNTON DOWNS	HSTD	42 23 173 28	73
LYSTER (TRIG)	HILL	39 52 175 11	45
LYTTELTON	USAT	43 36 172 42	82
LYTTELTON	USAT	43 36 172 42	83
LYTTELTON	USAT	43 36 172 42	85
LYTTELTON HARBOUR	HARB	43 37 172 45	82
LYTTELTON HARBOUR	HARB	43 37 172 45	83
LYTTLE PEAK	PEAK	43 36 169 59	76
LYTTLE PEAK	PEAK	43 36 169 59	77
LYTTLE, LAKE	LAKE	43 25 169 57	76
LYTTLE, MOUNT	MTN	44 47 168 05	89
LYVIA RIVER	STRM	45 28 167 10	96
L11 RIVER	STRM	43 43 172 27	85

M

MABEL BUSH	LOC	46 17 168 32	107
MABEL BUSH	LOC	46 17 168 32	109
MABEL, MOUNT (TRIG)	PEAK	41 23 175 24	53
MACANDREW BAY	SBRB	45 52 170 35	103
MACARTHUR, LAKE	LAKE	45 55 166 36	104
MACAULEY RIVER	STRM	43 45 170 32	77
MACAULEY RIVER	STRM	43 45 170 32	86
MACCOINNICH, MOUNT	HILL	42 50 173 17	72
MACCOINNICH, MOUNT	HILL	42 50 173 17	73
MACDONALDS CREEK	STRM	43 18 170 13	74
MACDONALDS PEAK	PEAK	44 50 168 57	90
MACDONALDS PEAK	PEAK	44 50 168 57	95
MACETOWN	LOC	44 52 168 49	90
MACETOWN	LOC	44 52 168 49	95
MACFARLANE MOUND	HILL	44 02 168 44	88
MACFARLANE, MOUNT	MTN	43 55 169 23	78
MACFARLANE RIVER	STRM	43 58 169 27	78
MACFARLANE RIVER	STRM	43 58 169 27	79
MACGREGOR CREEK	STRM	43 06 170 44	74
MACGREGOR MOUNT	MTN	44 22 170 37	92
MACKAY CREEK	STRM	44 44 167 48	94
MACKAY DOWNS	DOWN	40 51 172 14	56
MACKAY ROCKS	MTN	43 30 170 14	74
MACKAY ROCKS	MTN	43 30 170 14	77
MACKAYS BURN	STRM	45 37 169 44	100
MACKAYTOWN	LOC	37 25 175 42	17
MACKENZIE PASS	PASS	44 12 170 36	86
MACKENZIE PASS	PASS	45 35 167 08	105
MACKENZIE RIVER	STRM	44 11 170 30	86
MACKENZIE STREAM	STRM	42 42 172 04	70
MACKENZIES PEAK	PEAK	44 02 170 02	79
MACKFORD	LOC	38 42 174 42	26
MACKINNON, LAKE	LAKE	45 07 167 23	94
MACKINNON, LAKE	LAKE	45 07 167 23	96
MACKINNON, LAKE	LAKE	45 07 167 23	97
MACKINNON PASS	PASS	44 48 167 46	94
MACKINTOSH KNOB	MTN	42 06 173 45	67
MACKLEY RIVER	STRM	41 50 171 54	63
MACKLEY RIVER	STRM	41 50 171 54	64
MACLENNAN	LOC	46 32 169 28	113
MACLENNAN RANGE	MTNS	46 31 169 18	112
MACLENNAN RANGE	MTNS	46 31 169 18	113
MACLENNAN RIVER	STRM	46 33 169 28	113
MACNAMARA CREEK	STRM	46 11 166 38	104
MACPHERSON CREEK	STRM	43 57 169 19	78
MACPHERSON KNOB	HILL	40 43 172 26	56
MACPHERSON KNOB	HILL	40 43 172 26	57
MACPHERSON KNOB	PEAK	43 58 169 17	78
MACPHERSON, MOUNT	MTN	44 45 167 59	89
MACPHERSON, MOUNT	MTN	44 45 167 59	94
MACPHERSON PASS	PASS	45 18 167 20	96
MACRAES FLAT	LOC	45 23 170 26	102
MACS KNOB (TRIG)	PEAK	42 40 172 08	70
MADELINE, MOUNT	MTN	44 37 168 03	89
MADMANS CREEK	STRM	41 53 171 29	63
MAEREWHENUA	LOC	44 55 170 37	92
MAEREWHENUA RIVER	STRM	44 51 170 42	93
MAEREWHENUA RIVER (NORTH BRANCH)	STRM	44 57 170 34	92
MAEREWHENUA RIVER (SOUTH BRANCH)	STRM	44 57 170 34	92
MAEWA	LOC	40 12 175 33	45
MAEWA	LOC	40 12 175 33	46
MAEWA (TRIG)	HILL	39 42 175 17	45
MAGGIE CREEK	STRM	41 39 172 30	65
MAGGIE CREEK	STRM	41 44 172 42	65
MAGOG	MTN	43 05 171 50	80
MAGOG	HILL	47 11 167 34	114
MAHAKIPAWA ARM	BAY	41 17 173 49	54
MAHAKIPAWA ARM	BAY	41 17 173 49	60
MAHAKIPAWA ARM	BAY	41 17 173 49	61
MAHAKIRAU	LOC	36 51 175 37	16
MAHAKIRAU RIVER	STRM	36 51 175 40	16
MAHAKIRUA STREAM	STRM	38 33 176 59	30
MAHANA	LOC	41 16 173 03	58
MAHANA	LOC	41 16 173 03	59
MAHANGA	HSTD	39 00 177 53	33
MAHANGA, MOUNT	MTN	42 06 172 38	65
MAHANGA RANGE	MTNS	42 00 172 39	65
MAHANGA (TRIG)	HILL	39 00 177 50	33
MAHARA ISLAND	ISLD	45 32 167 32	97
MAHARAHARA	LOC	40 15 175 58	46
MAHARAHARA	LOC	40 15 175 58	49
MAHARAHARA STATION	RSTN	40 17 176 00	49

MAHARAHARA WEST	LOC	40 15 175 55	46
MAHARAHARA WEST	LOC	40 15 175 55	49
MAHARAHARA (TRIG)	PEAK	40 11 175 55	46
MAHARAKEKE STREAM	STRM	40 01 176 27	47
MAHAU SOUND	SND	41 14 173 53	54
MAHAU SOUND	SND	41 14 173 53	60
MAHAU SOUND	SND	41 14 173 53	61
MAHAUKURA (TRIG)	HILL	38 00 175 07	18
MAHENO	LOC	45 10 170 50	102
MAHENO STREAM	STRM	38 00 177 34	24
MAHENO (TRIG)	HILL	36 04 174 04	7
MAHIA	LOC	39 05 177 55	33
MAHIA BEACH	LOC	39 05 177 52	33
MAHIA PENINSULA	PEN	39 10 177 53	33
MAHINA BAY	LOC	41 16 174 54	52
MAHINA BAY	LOC	41 16 174 54	55
MAHINAPUA, LAKE	LAKE	42 48 170 55	68
MAHINEPUA	LOC	35 00 173 50	4
MAHINEPUA BAY	BAY	35 00 173 51	4
MAHINERANGI, LAKE	LAKE	45 50 169 56	111
MAHITAHI	LOC	43 39 169 36	76
MAHITAHI	LOC	43 39 169 36	79
MAHITAHI RIVER	STRM	43 36 169 35	76
MAHITAHI RIVER	STRM	43 36 169 35	79
MAHOE	LOC	39 23 174 10	34
MAHOE STREAM	STRM	38 10 174 52	18
MAHOE (TRIG)	HILL	40 25 176 18	50
MAHOENUI	LOC	38 35 174 50	26
MAHORA	SBRB	39 38 176 51	42
MAHORA	SBRB	39 38 176 51	43
MAHORA (TRIG)	HILL	35 58 173 46	6
MAHUNGARAPE ISLAND	ISLD	36 48 175 45	16
MAHURANGI	LOC	36 29 174 44	11
MAHURANGI HARBOUR	HARB	36 29 174 43	11
MAHURANGI ISLAND	ISLD	36 50 175 49	16
MAHURANGI RIVER	STRM	36 25 174 42	11
MAHURANGI WEST	LOC	36 30 174 41	11
MAHURAUITI STREAM	STRM	40 03 176 14	47
MAHURAUNUI STREAM	STRM	40 03 176 13	47
MAHUTA	LOC	36 00 173 48	6
MAHUTA	RSTN	37 35 175 06	14
MAHUTA	RSTN	37 35 175 06	15
MAHUTA GAP	PASS	36 00 173 47	6
MAIHIIHI	LOC	38 13 175 23	19
MAIKAIKATOA STREAM	STRM	39 03 174 44	35
MAIKI HILL	HILL	35 15 174 07	4
MAIKI HILL	HILL	35 15 174 07	5
MAIMAI	LOC	42 09 171 45	63
MAIMAI	LOC	42 09 171 45	64
MAIMAI CREEK	STRM	42 08 171 46	63
MAIMAI CREEK	STRM	42 08 171 46	64
MAIMAI PLAINS	PLN	42 09 171 43	63
MAIMAI PLAINS	PLN	42 09 171 43	64
MAIN DIVIDE	MTNS	42 26 172 18	71
MAINUI (TRIG)	HILL	39 41 175 01	45
MAINWARING, MOUNT	MTN	45 29 167 13	96
MAIORO	LOC	37 19 174 41	14
MAIORO GAP	PASS	37 20 174 41	14
MAIORO SANDS	LOC	37 21 174 44	14
MAIRAKI DOWNS (TRIG)	HILL	43 16 172 23	81
MAIRANGI BAY	SBRB	36 44 174 45	11
MAIRANGI BAY	SBRB	36 44 174 45	12
MAIRE STREAM	STRM	35 17 173 17	3
MAIRE STREAM	STRM	37 30 174 58	14
MAIRETAHI CREEK	STRM	36 33 174 21	10
MAIRETAHI CREEK	STRM	36 33 174 21	11
MAIROA	LOC	38 23 174 59	26
MAIROA	LOC	38 23 174 59	27
MAIROA STREAM	STRM	38 28 174 56	26
MAIRS SADDLE	SAD	43 02 170 50	75
MAITAHI	LOC	35 52 173 45	6
MAITLAND	LOC	46 00 169 01	110
MAITLAND, MOUNT	MTN	44 10 169 43	79
MAITLAND, MOUNT	MTN	43 58 169 37	79
MAITLAND STREAM	STRM	44 09 169 51	79
MAJOR, MOUNT	MTN	42 07 173 29	66
MAJOR PEAK	PEAK	44 55 168 29	89
MAJOR PEAK	PEAK	44 55 168 29	95
MAJOR SADDLE	SAD	39 09 176 02	38
MAJOR SADDLE	SAD	39 09 176 02	39
MAKAHI STREAM	STRM	41 20 173 46	60
MAKAHI STREAM	STRM	41 20 173 46	61
MAKAHIKA STREAM	STRM	40 40 175 21	48
MAKAHIKA STREAM	STRM	41 15 175 45	51
MAKAHIKA STREAM	STRM	41 13 175 45	53
MAKAHIKATOA STREAM	STRM	39 24 175 40	37
MAKAHIKATOA STREAM	STRM	39 28 176 03	39
MAKAHIWI (TRIG)	HILL	39 00 175 12	36
MAKAHU	LOC	39 18 174 35	35
MAKAHU	LOC	39 18 174 35	44
MAKAHU RIVER	STRM	39 12 176 30	39
MAKAHU RIVER	STRM	39 12 176 30	40
MAKAHU STREAM	STRM	39 20 174 37	35
MAKAHU STREAM	STRM	39 20 174 37	44
MAKAHU (TRIG)	HILL	39 17 174 39	35
MAKAHU (TRIG)	HILL	39 17 174 39	44
MAKAIRO STREAM	STRM	40 25 175 57	49
MAKAKA	LOC	37 57 174 49	18
MAKAKA STREAM	STRM	38 55 177 16	41
MAKAKAHI RIVER	STRM	40 28 175 48	49
MAKAKAHI (TRIG)	HILL	40 41 175 36	48
MAKAKAHI (TRIG)	HILL	40 41 175 36	49
MAKAKAHO	LOC	39 33 174 54	35
MAKAKAHO	LOC	39 33 174 54	36
MAKAKAHO JUNCTION	LOC	39 35 174 50	35
MAKAKAHO JUNCTION	LOC	39 35 174 50	44
MAKAKAHO STREAM	STRM	39 35 174 51	35
MAKAKAHO STREAM	STRM	39 35 174 51	44
MAKAKOERE STREAM	STRM	38 26 177 16	31
MAKAPUA STREAM	STRM	38 54 177 17	41
MAKARA	LOC	41 16 174 42	52
MAKARA	LOC	41 16 174 42	55
MAKARA BEACH	LOC	41 13 174 43	52
MAKARA BEACH	LOC	41 13 174 43	55
MAKARA RIVER	STRM	41 18 175 28	53
MAKARA STREAM	STRM	39 07 174 21	36
MAKARA STREAM	STRM	39 51 176 44	42
MAKARA STREAM	STRM	39 51 176 44	43
MAKARA STREAM	STRM	41 13 174 43	52
MAKARA STREAM	STRM	41 13 174 43	55
MAKARA (TRIG)	HILL	41 26 175 23	53
MAKARAKA	LOC	38 39 177 58	32
MAKARAKA	LOC	38 39 177 58	33
MAKARAKA STREAM	STRM	39 59 175 36	46
MAKARAKAI STREAM	STRM	38 58 174 41	35
MAKARAKAI (TRIG)	PEAK	38 57 174 42	35
MAKARANUI	LOC	39 25 175 21	36
MAKARAU	LOC	36 33 174 29	10
MAKARAU	LOC	36 33 174 29	11
MAKARAU RIVER	STRM	36 33 174 28	10
MAKARAU RIVER	STRM	36 33 174 28	11
MAKAREAO	LOC	45 23 170 39	102
MAKAREAO STREAM	STRM	38 54 177 28	33
MAKARETU	LOC	39 55 176 16	47
MAKARETU RIVER	STRM	39 59 176 29	47
MAKARETU STREAM	STRM	40 40 175 21	48
MAKARETURETU STREAM	STRM	39 27 176 24	39
MAKAREWA	LOC	46 20 168 21	109
MAKAREWA JUNCTION	LOC	46 17 168 20	109
MAKAREWA RIVER	STRM	46 10 168 31	107
MAKAREWA RIVER	STRM	46 22 168 15	109
MAKAREWA STREAM	STRM	45 49 167 39	106
MAKARI STREAM	STRM	38 58 177 39	33
MAKARIKA	HSTD	37 57 178 13	25
MAKARIKA STREAM	STRM	37 56 178 14	25
MAKARORA	LOC	44 14 169 14	78
MAKARORA RIVER	STRM	44 08 169 20	78
MAKARORO RIVER	STRM	39 50 176 19	47
MAKATOTE RIVER	STRM	39 16 175 21	36
MAKATOTE RIVER	STRM	39 16 175 21	37
MAKATOTE STREAM	STRM	37 54 178 16	25
MAKATOTE STREAM	STRM	39 33 175 53	37
MAKAURI	LOC	38 38 177 57	32
MAKAURI	LOC	38 38 177 57	33
MAKAWAKAWA STREAM	STRM	40 05 175 54	46
MAKAWHIO POINT	PNT	43 33 169 39	76
MAKAWHIO RIVER (JACOBS RIVER)	STRM	43 34 169 38	76
MAKERETU STREAM	STRM	38 54 177 33	33
MAKERIKERI RIVER	STRM	43 17 172 33	81
MAKERIKERI RIVER	STRM	43 17 172 33	82
MAKERUA	LOC	40 31 175 27	48
MAKETAWA STREAM	STRM	39 09 174 16	34
MAKETU	LOC	37 46 176 27	21
MAKETU	LOC	37 46 176 27	22
MAKETU PA	PA	38 05 174 49	18
MAKETU STREAM	STRM	39 35 175 27	36
MAKETU STREAM	STRM	39 35 175 27	37
MAKIEKIE CREEK	STRM	40 07 175 51	46
MAKIKIHI	LOC	44 38 171 09	93
MAKIKIHI RIVER	STRM	44 38 171 10	93
MAKINO	LOC	40 10 175 36	46
MAKINO RIVER	STRM	39 11 176 24	39
MAKINO RIVER	STRM	39 11 176 24	40
MAKINO STREAM	STRM	39 01 174 38	35
MAKINO STREAM	STRM	39 12 174 26	35
MAKINO STREAM	STRM	39 32 174 23	35
MAKINO STREAM	STRM	39 19 175 13	36
MAKINO STREAM	STRM	39 23 175 06	36
MAKINO STREAM	STRM	39 32 174 23	44
MAKINO STREAM	STRM	39 42 175 49	46
MAKINO STREAM	STRM	40 16 175 31	46
MAKINO (TRIG)	HILL	39 29 174 25	35
MAKINO (TRIG)	HILL	39 29 174 25	44
MAKINO (TRIG)	HILL	39 43 175 59	46
MAKIRIKI STREAM	STRM	40 49 176 03	49
MAKIRIKI STREAM	STRM	40 49 176 03	51
MAKIRIKIRI SOUTH	LOC	40 05 175 19	45
MAKIRIKIRI STREAM	STRM	39 32 176 13	39
MAKIRIKIRI STREAM	STRM	40 04 175 10	45
MAKIRIKIRI STREAM	STRM	39 52 175 07	45
MAKIRIKIRI (TRIG)	PEAK	39 37 176 11	47
MAKO POINT	PNT	37 02 174 38	12
MAKO POINT	PNT	37 02 174 38	14
MAKOHINE STREAM	STRM	39 53 175 41	46
MAKOHINE VALLEY	LOC	39 45 175 45	46
MAKOKAKO STREAM	STRM	39 45 174 49	44
MAKOKOMIKO STREAM	STRM	39 04 175 12	36
MAKOKOMIKO STREAM	STRM	39 13 175 23	36
MAKOKOMIKO STREAM	STRM	39 13 175 23	37
MAKOKOMIKO (TRIG)	PEAK	39 11 176 08	38
MAKOKOMIKO (TRIG)	PEAK	39 11 176 08	39
MAKOKOMUKA STREAM	STRM	38 02 178 00	24
MAKOKOMUKA STREAM	STRM	38 02 178 00	25
MAKOMAKO	LOC	37 58 174 54	18
MAKOMAKO	LOC	40 27 175 44	49
MAKOMETE STREAM	STRM	38 01 178 16	25
MAKOMIKO STREAM	STRM	38 56 175 14	36
MAKOMIKO STREAM	STRM	39 16 175 57	37
MAKOMIKO STREAM	STRM	39 16 175 57	38
MAKOPUA STREAM	STRM	39 45 175 54	46
MAKORAKO (TRIG)	PEAK	39 09 176 03	38
MAKORAKO (TRIG)	PEAK	39 09 176 03	39
MAKORO STREAM	STRM	39 37 174 28	44
MAKOROKIO STREAM	STRM	40 41 175 16	48
MAKORORI	LOC	38 39 178 08	32
MAKORORI POINT	PNT	38 40 178 06	32
MAKOTUKU	LOC	40 07 176 14	47
MAKOTUKU RIVER	STRM	39 28 175 18	36
MAKOTUKU STREAM	STRM	39 47 175 16	45
MAKOTUKUTUKU STREAM	STRM	41 30 175 12	53
MAKOURA STREAM	STRM	39 00 175 07	36
MAKOURA STREAM	STRM	40 42 176 09	49
MAKOWHAI STREAM	STRM	40 15 175 19	45
MAKUHOU STREAM	STRM	39 58 175 18	45
MAKUKUPARA STREAM	STRM	40 28 176 17	50
MAKURI	LOC	40 32 176 01	49
MAKURI ITI STREAM	STRM	40 30 176 03	49
MAKURI RIVER	STRM	40 29 175 55	49
MAKURI STREAM	STRM	39 22 174 26	35
MAKURI STREAM	STRM	39 22 174 26	44
MAKURI STREAM	STRM	40 33 175 58	49
MAKURI (TRIG)	HILL	39 20 174 27	35
MAKURI (TRIG)	HILL	39 20 174 27	44
MAKURI (TRIG)	HILL	40 31 175 59	49
MALASPINA REACH	STRA	45 21 167 02	96
MALCOLM, MOUNT (TRIG)	HILL	44 13 168 11	88
MALCOLM, MOUNT (TRIG)	PEAK	45 01 169 00	99
MALCOLM PEAK	PEAK	43 18 170 49	75
MALCOLM RANGE	MTNS	44 14 168 13	88
MALCOLMS KNOB (TRIG)	KNOB	43 27 169 46	76
MALING, MOUNT	MTN	42 14 172 26	65
MALING, MOUNT (TRIG)	MTN	42 11 172 45	65
MALING PASS	PASS	42 13 172 42	65
MALINGS PEAK	PEAK	44 52 168 47	90
MALINGS PEAK	PEAK	44 52 168 47	95
MALINGSON, MOUNT (TRIG)	PEAK	42 27 173 04	72
MALITA, MOUNT (TRIG)	PEAK	41 23 173 16	59
MALLOCKVALE	HSTD	42 57 172 32	71
MALONES DAM	DAM	45 54 169 43	111
MALTE BRUN	MTN	43 34 170 18	74
MALTE BRUN	MTN	43 34 170 18	77
MALTE BRUN PASS	PASS	43 34 170 18	74
MALTE BRUN PASS	PASS	43 34 170 18	77
MALTE BRUN RANGE	MTNS	43 34 170 17	74
MALTE BRUN RANGE	MTNS	43 34 170 17	77
MALVERN HILLS	HSTD	41 46 173 34	66
MALVERN, MOUNT (TRIG)	MTN	41 53 173 50	67
MAMAKU	LOC	38 06 176 05	20
MAMAKU	LOC	38 06 176 05	21
MAMAKU PLATEAU	PLAT	38 03 176 04	20
MAMAKU POINT	PNT	46 52 168 09	109
MAMAKU POINT	PNT	46 52 168 09	115
MAMARANUI	LOC	35 50 173 45	6
MAMMOTH (TRIG)	MTN	41 59 172 25	65
MAMONA	LOC	45 55 170 13	103
MAN OF WAR PASSAGE	STRA	36 11 175 20	9
MAN, LAKE	LAKE	42 33 172 13	70
MANA	SBRB	41 05 174 52	52
MANA	SBRB	41 05 174 52	55
MANA ISLAND	ISLD	41 05 174 47	52
MANA ISLAND	ISLD	41 05 174 47	55
MANAIA	LOC	36 51 175 29	13
MANAIA	LOC	36 51 175 29	16
MANAIA	POPL	39 33 174 07	34
MANAIA HARBOUR	HARB	36 51 175 27	13
MANAIA HARBOUR	HARB	36 51 175 27	16
MANAIA RIVER	STRM	36 51 175 28	13
MANAIA RIVER	STRM	36 51 175 28	16
MANAIA STREAM	STRM	35 19 173 58	4
MANAIA STREAM	STRM	35 19 173 58	5
MANAIA (TRIG)	HILL	35 49 174 31	8
MANAKAIAUA RIVER	STRM	43 34 169 38	76
MANAKAU	POPL	40 43 175 13	48
MANAKAU (TRIG)	MTN	42 14 173 37	66
MANANGAATIUHI STREAM	STRM	38 32 176 59	30
MANANUI	LOC	42 46 170 55	68
MANAOHOU STREAM	STRM	38 26 176 56	30
MANAPOURI	LOC	45 34 167 36	97
MANAPOURI, LAKE	LAKE	45 31 167 29	97
MANAROA	LOC	41 07 174 02	54
MANAROA	LOC	41 07 174 02	60
MANAROA	LOC	41 07 174 02	61
MANAROA ROA BEACH	LOC	40 17 175 14	45
MANAWA (TRIG)	HILL	40 48 176 01	49
MANAWA (TRIG)	HILL	40 48 176 01	51
MANAWAANGIANGI STREAM	STRM	40 19 176 30	50
MANAWAORA	LOC	35 17 174 13	5
MANAWAORA BAY	BAY	35 17 174 12	5
MANAWAPOU RIVER	STRM	39 39 174 21	44
MANAWARU	LOC	37 38 175 46	19
MANAWATA (TRIG)	HILL	37 45 176 01	20
MANAWATU GORGE	GORG	40 18 175 46	49
MANAWATU RIVER	STRM	40 28 175 13	48
MANDAMUS RIVER	STRM	42 45 172 33	71
MANDEVILLE	LOC	45 59 168 48	110
MANDEVILLE NORTH	LOC	43 23 172 33	82
MANDEVILLE NORTH	LOC	43 23 172 33	83
MANDEVILLE NORTH	LOC	43 23 172 33	85
MANEAROA (TRIG)	HILL	39 17 175 04	36
MANGA	HSTD	38 24 178 10	32
MANGAARUHE RIVER	STRM	38 54 177 26	33
MANGAARUHE RIVER	STRM	38 54 177 26	41
MANGAAWAKINO STREAM	STRM	38 41 174 44	26
MANGAEHU STREAM	STRM	39 23 174 28	35
MANGAEHU STREAM	STRM	39 23 174 28	44
MANGAEHUEHU STREAM	STRM	39 30 175 28	36
MANGAEHUEHU STREAM	STRM	39 30 175 28	37
MANGAETOROA STREAM	STRM	39 34 175 15	36
MANGAETUROA	LOC	39 27 175 14	36
MANGAHAHURU STREAM	STRM	35 39 174 18	5
MANGAHAHURU STREAM	STRM	35 39 174 18	7
MANGAHAHURU STREAM	STRM	35 39 174 18	8
MANGAHANENE STREAM	STRM	37 57 175 35	19
MANGAHAO	LOC	40 26 175 47	49
MANGAHAO HYDRO ELECTRIC POWER STN	BLDG	40 35 175 27	48
MANGAHAO RIVER	STRM	40 20 175 49	49
MANGAHARAKEKE STREAM	STRM	38 10 175 31	19
MANGAHARAKEKE STREAM	STRM	37 49 175 20	19
MANGAHARAKEKE STREAM	STRM	38 25 176 22	29
MANGAHARAKEKE STREAM	STRM	38 19 176 44	30
MANGAHAUHAU STREAM	STRM	38 41 177 40	31
MANGAHAUHAU STREAM	STRM	38 41 177 40	33
MANGAHAUINI	LOC	38 07 178 18	25
MANGAHAUINI RIVER	STRM	38 08 178 19	25
MANGAHAUPAPA STREAM	STRM	37 44 177 59	24
MANGAHAUPAPA STREAM	STRM	37 44 177 59	25
MANGAHEI STREAM	STRM	40 13 176 14	47
MANGAHEIA	HSTD	38 21 178 15	32
MANGAHEIA RIVER	STRM	38 22 178 17	32
MANGAHEWA STREAM	STRM	39 02 174 21	34
MANGAHEWA STREAM	STRM	39 02 174 21	35
MANGAHIA STREAM	STRM	37 53 175 00	18
MANGAHIA STREAM	STRM	38 56 174 32	26
MANGAHINA STREAM	STRM	39 23 176 43	40
MANGAHINA STREAM	STRM	39 23 176 43	42
MANGAHINATORE STREAM	STRM	37 43 178 00	24
MANGAHINATORE STREAM	STRM	37 43 178 00	25
MANGAHOANGA STREAM	STRM	38 10 176 54	22
MANGAHOANGA STREAM	STRM	38 10 176 54	23
MANGAHOANGA STREAM	STRM	38 26 176 20	29
MANGAHOTU STREAM	STRM	38 34 175 01	26
MANGAHOTU STREAM	STRM	38 34 175 01	27
MANGAHOUANGA STREAM	STRM	38 55 176 49	40
MANGAHOUANGA STREAM	STRM	38 55 176 49	41
MANGAHOUHOU	LOC	38 58 175 39	37
MANGAHOUHOU	LOC	38 58 175 39	38
MANGAHOUHOUITI STREAM	STRM	39 05 175 50	37
MANGAHOUHOUITI STREAM	STRM	39 05 175 50	38
MANGAHOUHOUNUI STREAM	STRM	39 02 175 49	37
MANGAHOUHOUNUI STREAM	STRM	39 02 175 49	38
MANGAHOUI STREAM	STRM	38 36 177 47	31
MANGAHOWHI STREAM	STRM	39 47 175 19	45
MANGAHOWHI STREAM	STRM	39 54 175 22	45
MANGAHUIA STREAM	STRM	39 55 175 55	46
MANGAHUIA STREAM	STRM	40 31 176 21	50
MANGAHUIA (TRIG)	PEAK	39 54 176 03	46
MANGAHUIA (TRIG)	PEAK	39 54 176 03	47
MANGAHUME STREAM	STRM	39 28 173 52	34
MANGAHUTIWAI STREAM	STRM	38 49 174 37	26
MANGAIO STREAM	STRM	39 26 175 01	36
MANGAIO STREAM	STRM	39 23 175 44	37
MANGAIO (TRIG)	PEAK	39 21 175 46	37
MANGAIO (TRIG)	PEAK	39 21 175 46	38
MANGAITI	LOC	37 30 175 41	15
MANGAITI	LOC	37 30 175 41	17
MANGAITI STREAM	STRM	37 30 175 41	17
MANGAITI STREAM	STRM	38 31 175 10	27
MANGAITI STREAM	STRM	39 48 175 05	45
MANGAKAHIA RIVER	STRM	35 38 173 51	6
MANGAKAHIA RIVER	STRM	35 42 174 02	7
MANGAKAHU STREAM	STRM	38 43 175 17	27
MANGAKAHU VALLEY	LOC	38 45 175 25	27
MANGAKAKAHO STREAM	STRM	38 37 176 54	30
MANGAKAPUA STREAM	STRM	38 52 177 23	41
MANGAKARA STREAM	STRM	38 02 175 40	19
MANGAKARA STREAM	STRM	38 50 174 54	26
MANGAKARA STREAM	STRM	38 44 175 47	28
MANGAKARA STREAM	STRM	38 44 175 47	38
MANGAKARA STREAM	STRM	39 05 176 42	40
MANGAKARETU STREAM	STRM	35 16 173 46	4
MANGAKINO	POPL	38 22 175 46	28
MANGAKINO STREAM	STRM	35 43 174 20	5
MANGAKINO STREAM	STRM	35 43 174 20	7
MANGAKINO STREAM	STRM	35 43 174 20	8
MANGAKINO STREAM	STRM	37 28 175 45	17
MANGAKINO STREAM	STRM	37 49 174 58	18
MANGAKINO STREAM	STRM	38 24 175 46	28
MANGAKIRI STREAM	STRM	37 25 175 50	17
MANGAKIRIKIRI STREAM	STRM	37 08 175 36	13
MANGAKIRIKIRI STREAM	STRM	37 08 175 36	15
MANGAKIRIKIRI STREAM	STRM	38 01 177 41	24
MANGAKOKAKO STREAM	STRM	40 15 176 05	50
MANGAKOMUA STREAM	STRM	38 10 175 31	19
MANGAKOPIKOPIKO STREAM	STRM	39 22 176 49	40
MANGAKOPIKOPIKO STREAM	STRM	39 22 176 49	42
MANGAKOTAHA STREAM	STRM	38 07 175 54	20
MANGAKOTUKUTUKU STREAM	STRM	37 35 175 05	18
MANGAKOTUKUTUKU STREAM	STRM	38 09 176 33	21
MANGAKOTUKUTUKU STREAM	STRM	38 09 176 33	22
MANGAKOWHIA STREAM	STRM	38 27 175 02	26
MANGAKOWHIA STREAM	STRM	38 27 175 02	27
MANGAKOWHIRIWHIRI STREAM	STRM	38 26 175 48	28
MANGAKOWHITIWHITI STREAM	STRM	38 57 175 56	37
MANGAKOWHITIWHITI STREAM	STRM	38 57 175 56	38
MANGAKURA	LOC	36 25 174 27	10
MANGAKURA	LOC	36 25 174 27	11
MANGAKURI RIVER	STRM	39 57 176 55	43
MANGAMAHA STREAM	STRM	37 42 178 03	25
MANGAMAHAKI STREAM	STRM	38 28 177 49	32
MANGAMAHOE, LAKE	LAKE	39 07 174 08	34
MANGAMAHOE STREAM	STRM	39 47 175 30	46
MANGAMAHU	LOC	39 49 175 22	45
MANGAMAHU STREAM	STRM	39 49 175 22	45
MANGAMAHU (TRIG)	HILL	39 45 175 29	45
MANGAMAHU (TRIG)	HILL	39 45 175 29	46
MANGAMAHUE	PEAK	39 53 176 04	47
MANGAMAIA STREAM	STRM	38 21 177 47	31
MANGAMAIA STREAM	STRM	38 21 177 47	32
MANGAMAIO STREAM	STRM	38 58 174 28	35
MANGAMAIO (TRIG)	HILL	39 00 174 30	35
MANGAMAIRE	LOC	40 31 175 45	49
MANGAMAIRE RIVER	STRM	39 15 176 01	38
MANGAMAIRE RIVER	STRM	39 15 176 01	39
MANGAMAIRE STREAM	STRM	39 10 174 34	35
MANGAMAIRE STREAM	STRM	39 07 175 19	36
MANGAMAIRE STREAM	STRM	40 29 175 47	49
MANGAMAIRE STREAM	STRM	40 16 176 13	50
MANGAMAIRE STREAM	STRM	40 19 176 38	50
MANGAMAKO STREAM	STRM	38 15 176 49	30
MANGAMANGI STREAM	STRM	39 35 174 20	44
MANGAMARAHIA STREAM	STRM	39 28 176 03	39
MANGAMATE STREAM	STRM	39 47 176 29	47
MANGAMATUKUTUKU STREAM	STRM	38 09 178 00	24
MANGAMATUKUTUKU STREAM	STRM	38 09 178 00	32
MANGAMAUKU STREAM	STRM	39 48 176 30	47
MANGAMAUNU	LOC	42 18 173 45	67
MANGAMAUNU STREAM	STRM	38 09 178 02	25
MANGAMAUNU STREAM	STRM	38 09 178 02	32
MANGAMAUNU (TRIG)	HILL	38 10 178 00	24
MANGAMAUNU (TRIG)	HILL	38 10 178 00	25
MANGAMAUNU (TRIG)	HILL	38 10 178 00	32
MANGAMAWHETE STREAM	STRM	39 11 174 17	34
MANGAMINGI	LOC	39 25 174 27	35
MANGAMINGI	LOC	39 25 174 27	44
MANGAMINGI SADDLE	SAD	39 09 176 05	38
MANGAMINGI SADDLE	SAD	39 09 176 05	39
MANGAMINGI STREAM	STRM	39 18 175 17	36
MANGAMINGI STREAM	STRM	39 08 176 09	38
MANGAMINGI STREAM	STRM	39 08 176 09	39
MANGAMOEAHU STREAM	STRM	39 10 174 24	35
MANGAMOKO STREAM	STRM	39 54 175 41	46
MANGAMOKU STREAM	STRM	39 54 175 05	45
MANGAMOTEO STREAM	STRM	38 44 177 33	31
MANGAMOTEO STREAM	STRM	38 44 177 33	33
MANGAMUKA	LOC	35 13 173 33	3
MANGAMUKA	LOC	35 13 173 33	4
MANGAMUKA BRIDGE	LOC	35 15 173 33	3
MANGAMUKA BRIDGE	LOC	35 15 173 33	4
MANGAMUKA RIVER	STRM	35 19 173 32	3
MANGAMUTU	LOC	40 27 175 48	49
MANGAMUTU STREAM	STRM	35 21 173 55	4
MANGAMUTU STREAM	STRM	35 21 173 55	6
MANGAMUTU STREAM	STRM	38 47 176 05	28
MANGAMUTU STREAM	STRM	38 47 176 05	29
MANGAMUTU STREAM	STRM	38 47 176 05	38
MANGANESE POINT	PNT	35 48 174 27	8
MANGANGARARA STREAM	STRM	39 07 176 59	40
MANGANGARARA STREAM	STRM	39 07 176 59	41
MANGANUI RIVER	STRM	35 57 174 00	7
MANGANUI RIVER	STRM	36 00 174 11	8
MANGANUI RIVER	STRM	38 40 174 40	26
MANGANUI RIVER	STRM	39 04 174 17	34
MANGANUI RIVER	STRM	39 04 174 17	35
MANGANUI STREAM	STRM	37 45 175 51	20
MANGANUI STREAM	STRM	41 21 175 08	52
MANGANUI STREAM	STRM	41 21 175 08	53
MANGANUI STREAM	STRM	41 21 175 08	55
MANGANUI (TRIG)	HILL	38 39 174 40	26
MANGANUIATEAO RIVER	STRM	39 24 175 03	36
MANGANUIOHOU RIVER	STRM	38 51 176 54	30
MANGANUIOTAHU STREAM	STRM	39 39 174 53	45
MANGANUKU STREAM	STRM	38 17 177 23	31
MANGAOAI STREAM	STRM	38 28 177 54	32
MANGAOHAE	LOC	38 21 174 53	26
MANGAOHAE STREAM	STRM	38 22 174 53	26
MANGAOHAERE (TRIG)	HILL	38 58 175 13	36
MANGAOHANE STREAM	STRM	39 32 176 02	39
MANGAOHANE (TRIG)	PEAK	39 33 176 11	39
MANGAOHARA STREAM	STRM	40 02 176 31	43
MANGAOHARA STREAM	STRM	40 02 176 31	47
MANGAOHAU STREAM	STRM	40 27 176 32	50
MANGAOHO STREAM	STRM	39 51 176 31	47
MANGAOHOI STREAM	STRM	38 00 175 19	19
MANGAOHUTU	LOC	39 03 175 07	36
MANGAOHUTU STREAM	STRM	39 04 175 03	36
MANGAOKAHU STREAM	STRM	37 50 175 01	18
MANGAOKEWA	LOC	38 27 175 19	27
MANGAOKEWA STREAM	STRM	38 15 175 12	27
MANGAOKURA STREAM	STRM	38 01 177 48	24
MANGAOMATUA STREAM	STRM	37 36 178 03	25
MANGAONE	LOC	40 32 175 52	49
MANGAONE RIVER	STRM	39 29 176 42	40
MANGAONE RIVER	STRM	39 29 176 42	42
MANGAONE RIVER	STRM	40 31 175 53	49
MANGAONE SIDING	RSDG	38 14 176 47	22
MANGAONE SIDING	RSDG	38 14 176 47	30
MANGAONE STREAM	STRM	35 29 173 49	4
MANGAONE STREAM	STRM	35 29 173 49	6
MANGAONE STREAM	STRM	37 49 175 20	19

MANGAONE STREAM	STRM	38 00 176 44	21
MANGAONE STREAM	STRM	38 00 176 44	22
MANGAONE STREAM	STRM	38 47 174 44	26
MANGAONE STREAM	STRM	38 54 177 30	33
MANGAONE STREAM	STRM	38 58 177 40	33
MANGAONE STREAM	STRM	39 07 174 20	34
MANGAONE STREAM	STRM	39 03 174 53	35
MANGAONE STREAM	STRM	39 25 174 57	35
MANGAONE STREAM	STRM	39 07 174 19	35
MANGAONE STREAM	STRM	39 05 174 40	35
MANGAONE STREAM	STRM	39 25 174 57	36
MANGAONE STREAM	STRM	38 57 177 07	41
MANGAONE STREAM	STRM	39 50 174 53	44
MANGAONE STREAM	STRM	39 50 174 59	45
MANGAONE STREAM	STRM	40 17 175 37	46
MANGAONE STREAM	STRM	39 45 175 38	46
MANGAONE STREAM	STRM	40 48 175 05	48
MANGAONE STREAM	STRM	40 31 176 20	50
MANGAONE STREAM	STRM	40 48 175 05	52
MANGAONE STREAM	STRM	40 48 175 05	55
MANGAONGA STREAM	STRM	39 00 174 26	35
MANGAONGA STREAM	STRM	39 10 177 00	40
MANGAONGA STREAM	STRM	39 10 177 00	41
MANGAONGOKI STREAM	STRM	38 52 175 41	28
MANGAONGOKI STREAM	STRM	38 52 175 41	38
MANGAONOHO	LOC	39 54 175 39	46
MANGAONUA STREAM	STRM	37 47 175 24	19
MANGAONUKU STREAM	STRM	39 55 176 32	42
MANGAONUKU STREAM	STRM	39 55 176 32	43
MANGAONUKU STREAM	STRM	39 55 176 32	47
MANGAOPARO RIVER	STRM	37 51 178 20	25
MANGAOPOU STREAM	STRM	38 52 177 38	33
MANGAORA STREAM	STRM	38 03 174 51	18
MANGAORAKA STREAM	STRM	39 00 174 11	34
MANGAORAKEI STREAM	STRM	39 05 175 10	36
MANGAORANGA	LOC	40 41 175 45	49
MANGAORANGA STREAM	STRM	40 39 175 42	49
MANGAORAPA	LOC	40 20 176 30	50
MANGAORAPA STREAM	STRM	40 17 176 34	50
MANGAORE	LOC	40 35 175 27	48
MANGAORE STREAM	STRM	40 32 175 23	48
MANGAORONGA STREAM	STRM	38 09 175 13	19
MANGAORONGA STREAM	STRM	38 17 177 51	32
MANGAORONGO	LOC	38 12 175 20	19
MANGAORONGO STREAM	STRM	38 09 175 13	18
MANGAORONGO STREAM	STRM	38 34 174 52	26
MANGAORONGO STREAM	STRM	38 36 176 57	30
MANGAORUA STREAM	STRM	38 09 175 42	19
MANGAOTAKI	LOC	38 25 174 53	26
MANGAOTAKI RIVER	STRM	38 33 174 55	26
MANGAOTAMA STREAM	STRM	37 57 175 17	18
MANGAOTAMA STREAM	STRM	37 57 175 17	19
MANGAOTANE STREAM	STRM	38 07 177 42	24
MANGAOTARA STREAM	STRM	38 48 177 32	31
MANGAOTARA STREAM	STRM	38 48 177 32	33
MANGAOTUKU STREAM	STRM	39 19 174 32	35
MANGAOTUKU STREAM	STRM	39 19 174 32	44
MANGAOWATA STREAM	STRM	39 04 174 44	35
MANGAOWATA (TRIG)	HILL	39 04 174 44	35
MANGAOWIRA STREAM	STRM	37 39 178 22	25
MANGAPA	LOC	35 11 173 38	4
MANGAPA RIVER	STRM	35 14 173 41	4
MANGAPA RIVER	STRM	37 49 176 02	20
MANGAPAE STREAM	STRM	39 47 175 49	46
MANGAPAHI STREAM	STRM	38 58 177 40	33
MANGAPAI	LOC	35 52 174 18	7
MANGAPAI	LOC	35 52 174 18	8
MANGAPAI RIVER	STRM	35 49 174 21	7
MANGAPAI RIVER	STRM	35 49 174 21	8
MANGAPAI STREAM	STRM	37 26 174 45	14
MANGAPAKA STREAM	STRM	39 04 174 39	35
MANGAPAKEHA STREAM	STRM	40 55 176 04	49
MANGAPAKEHA STREAM	STRM	40 55 176 04	51
MANGAPAKEHA (TRIG)	HILL	40 57 175 57	49
MANGAPAKEHA (TRIG)	HILL	40 57 175 57	51
MANGAPAPA RIVER	STRM	39 48 175 30	46
MANGAPAPA SADDLE	SAD	39 09 176 14	39
MANGAPAPA STREAM	STRM	37 24 174 57	14
MANGAPAPA STREAM	STRM	38 04 174 57	18
MANGAPAPA STREAM	STRM	38 29 174 43	26
MANGAPAPA STREAM	STRM	38 44 175 04	27
MANGAPAPA STREAM	STRM	38 22 177 47	31
MANGAPAPA STREAM	STRM	38 22 177 47	32
MANGAPAPA STREAM	STRM	39 09 176 35	39
MANGAPAPA STREAM	STRM	39 09 176 35	40
MANGAPAPA STREAM	STRM	39 40 174 52	44
MANGAPAPA (TRIG)	HILL	38 58 174 48	35
MANGAPARO	LOC	38 53 174 59	26
MANGAPARO	LOC	38 53 174 59	27
MANGAPEHI	LOC	38 31 175 18	27
MANGAPEHI STREAM	STRM	38 26 175 05	27
MANGAPIKO	LOC	37 59 175 16	18
MANGAPIKO	LOC	37 59 175 16	19
MANGAPIKO STREAM	STRM	37 32 174 58	14
MANGAPIKO STREAM	STRM	37 28 175 18	15
MANGAPIKO STREAM	STRM	37 59 175 12	18
MANGAPIKO STREAM	STRM	37 59 175 12	19
MANGAPIKO VALLEY	LOC	37 28 175 19	15
MANGAPIOPIO STREAM	STRM	38 44 177 32	31
MANGAPIOPIO STREAM	STRM	38 44 177 32	33
MANGAPIPI STREAM	STRM	39 58 175 38	46
MANGAPIU STREAM	STRM	35 42 174 10	5
MANGAPIU STREAM	STRM	35 42 174 10	7
MANGAPOHIO STREAM	STRM	39 59 176 24	47
MANGAPOHUE STREAM	STRM	38 14 175 18	27
MANGAPOIKE RIVER	STRM	38 52 177 39	31
MANGAPOIKE RIVER	STRM	38 54 177 29	33
MANGAPOUA STREAM	STRM	39 02 174 22	35
MANGAPOURI STREAM	STRM	37 58 176 14	20
MANGAPOURI STREAM	STRM	37 58 176 14	21
MANGAPOURI STREAM	STRM	37 36 178 02	25
MANGAPU RIVER	STRM	38 15 175 12	27
MANGAPUAKA STREAM	STRM	40 13 176 13	47
MANGAPUKA STREAM	STRM	40 21 176 17	50
MANGAPUNIPUNI STREAM	STRM	39 44 174 49	44
MANGAPURU STREAM	STRM	39 00 176 57	40
MANGAPURU STREAM	STRM	39 00 176 57	41
MANGAPURUA STREAM	STRM	39 16 174 58	36
MANGAPURUA (TRIG)	HILL	39 13 175 05	36
MANGARA STREAM	STRM	39 56 175 20	45
MANGARAKAI STREAM	STRM	38 08 178 15	25
MANGARAKAU	LOC	40 38 172 29	56
MANGARAKAU	LOC	40 38 172 29	57
MANGARAMA STREAM	STRM	38 20 175 07	27
MANGARANGIORA STREAM	STRM	38 52 177 38	31
MANGARANGIORA STREAM	STRM	38 52 177 38	33
MANGARANGIORA STREAM	STRM	39 19 176 40	39
MANGARANGIORA STREAM	STRM	39 19 176 40	40
MANGARANGIORA STREAM	STRM	39 19 176 40	42
MANGARAPA STREAM	STRM	38 15 175 12	27
MANGARARA STREAM	STRM	39 55 176 44	42
MANGARARA STREAM	STRM	39 55 176 44	43
MANGARATA STREAM	STRM	38 13 175 33	19
MANGARAUKOKORE STREAM	STRM	37 51 178 04	25
MANGARAWA	LOC	40 18 175 54	49
MANGARE STREAM	STRM	38 08 175 36	19
MANGARE STREAM	STRM	39 09 174 44	35
MANGAREHU STREAM	STRM	37 08 175 37	13
MANGAREHU STREAM	STRM	37 08 175 37	15
MANGAREIA STREAM	STRM	40 52 175 52	49
MANGAREIA STREAM	STRM	40 52 175 52	51
MANGARERE STREAM	STRM	39 50 175 48	46
MANGAREWA STREAM	STRM	38 13 175 41	28
MANGAREWA STREAM	STRM	39 04 174 12	34
MANGAREWA STREAM	STRM	39 17 174 41	35
MANGAREWA STREAM	STRM	39 17 174 41	44
MANGAREWA WEST (TRIG)	HILL	39 14 174 43	35
MANGAREWA WEST (TRIG)	HILL	39 14 174 43	44
MANGAREWAREWA STREAM	STRM	38 45 177 21	31
MANGARIMU	LOC	39 57 175 52	46
MANGAROA	LOC	39 40 176 49	42
MANGAROA	LOC	39 40 176 49	43
MANGAROA	LOC	41 07 175 07	52
MANGAROA	LOC	41 07 175 07	53
MANGAROA	LOC	41 07 175 07	55
MANGAROA RIVER	STRM	41 06 175 08	52
MANGAROA RIVER	STRM	41 06 175 08	55
MANGAROA STREAM	STRM	37 53 175 48	19
MANGAROA STREAM	STRM	37 53 175 48	20
MANGAROA STREAM	STRM	38 12 178 15	25
MANGAROA STREAM	STRM	38 54 175 02	26
MANGAROA STREAM	STRM	38 54 175 02	27
MANGAROA STREAM	STRM	38 12 178 15	32
MANGAROA STREAM	STRM	39 10 176 48	40
MANGAROA STREAM	STRM	39 40 176 52	42
MANGAROA STREAM	STRM	39 40 176 52	43
MANGAROA STREAM	STRM	40 37 175 38	48
MANGAROA STREAM	STRM	40 37 175 38	49
MANGAROUHI STREAM	STRM	40 04 176 40	43
MANGAROUHI STREAM	STRM	40 04 176 40	47
MANGARUAKI STREAM	STRM	38 27 177 55	32
MANGATAHAE STREAM	STRM	38 25 175 43	28
MANGATAHAE STREAM	STRM	38 40 177 20	31
MANGATAHI STREAM	STRM	39 37 176 34	42
MANGATAHI STREAM	STRM	39 52 176 32	42
MANGATAHI STREAM	STRM	39 37 176 34	43
MANGATAHI STREAM	STRM	39 52 176 32	43
MANGATAHI STREAM	STRM	39 37 176 34	47
MANGATAHI STREAM	STRM	39 52 176 32	47
MANGATAHU STREAM	STRM	38 17 177 47	32
MANGATAINOKA	POPL	40 25 175 52	49
MANGATAINOKA RIVER	STRM	39 10 176 24	39
MANGATAINOKA RIVER	STRM	40 24 175 54	49
MANGATAINOKA SADDLE	SAD	39 08 176 16	39
MANGATAIORE	LOC	35 10 173 26	3
MANGATAIPA	LOC	35 14 173 31	3
MANGATANA STREAM	STRM	39 04 174 28	35
MANGATANGI	LOC	37 12 175 12	13
MANGATANGI	LOC	37 12 175 12	15
MANGATANGI RESERVOIR	LAKE	37 06 175 13	13
MANGATANGI RESERVOIR	LAKE	37 06 175 13	15
MANGATANGI STREAM	STRM	37 15 175 11	13
MANGATANGI STREAM	STRM	37 15 175 11	15
MANGATANGI STREAM	STRM	38 10 174 45	18
MANGATANGI (TRIG)	HILL	37 08 175 11	13
MANGATANGI (TRIG)	HILL	37 08 175 11	15
MANGATAPU STREAM	STRM	38 04 175 49	20
MANGATARA	LOC	35 57 173 49	6
MANGATARA STREAM	STRM	39 33 176 42	39
MANGATARA STREAM	STRM	39 33 176 42	40
MANGATARA STREAM	STRM	39 33 176 42	42
MANGATARA STREAM	STRM	39 33 176 42	43
MANGATARAIRE	LOC	35 22 173 41	4
MANGATARAIRE	LOC	35 22 173 41	6
MANGATARAMEA STREAM	STRM	39 12 176 09	38
MANGATARAMEA STREAM	STRM	39 12 176 09	39
MANGATARAMEA STREAM	STRM	39 26 176 14	39
MANGATARATA	LOC	37 17 175 22	15
MANGATARATA	HSTD	38 06 178 08	25
MANGATARATA STREAM	STRM	37 14 175 24	15
MANGATARATA STREAM	STRM	39 59 176 40	43
MANGATARATA STREAM	STRM	39 59 176 40	47
MANGATARERE (TRIG)	HILL	40 57 175 30	48
MANGATARERE (TRIG)	HILL	40 57 175 30	49
MANGATARERE (TRIG)	HILL	40 57 175 30	53
MANGATARU STREAM	STRM	37 32 174 54	14
MANGATAUNOKA STREAM	STRM	39 30 175 03	36
MANGATAURA STREAM	STRM	39 50 176 18	47
MANGATAWA STREAM	STRM	35 28 173 41	4
MANGATAWA STREAM	STRM	35 28 173 41	6
MANGATAWA STREAM	STRM	38 53 174 43	26
MANGATAWAI STREAM	STRM	39 08 175 49	37
MANGATAWAI STREAM	STRM	39 08 175 49	38
MANGATAWAI (TRIG)	HILL	39 11 175 05	36
MANGATAWHIRI	LOC	37 13 175 07	13
MANGATAWHIRI	LOC	37 13 175 07	14
MANGATAWHIRI	LOC	37 13 175 07	15
MANGATAWHIRI RIVER	STRM	37 04 175 10	13
MANGATAWHIRI RIVER	STRM	37 17 175 03	14
MANGATAWHIRI RIVER	STRM	37 04 175 10	15
MANGATE STREAM	STRM	38 08 176 40	21
MANGATE STREAM	STRM	38 08 176 40	22
MANGATEA	LOC	38 21 175 08	27
MANGATEA STREAM	STRM	37 29 175 19	15
MANGATEITEI STREAM	STRM	39 25 175 24	36
MANGATEITEI STREAM	STRM	39 25 175 24	37
MANGATEPARU	LOC	37 35 175 30	19
MANGATEPOPO STREAM	STRM	39 01 175 32	36
MANGATEPOPO STREAM	STRM	39 01 175 32	37
MANGATEPOPO STREAM	STRM	39 01 175 32	38
MANGATERA	LOC	40 11 176 07	47
MANGATERA RIVER	STRM	39 40 176 05	47
MANGATERA STREAM	STRM	40 15 176 06	47
MANGATETE STREAM	STRM	35 01 173 18	3
MANGATETE STREAM	STRM	38 22 176 10	29
MANGATETE STREAM	STRM	38 38 177 34	31
MANGATETE STREAM	STRM	39 05 174 57	36
MANGATEWAI	HSTD	39 59 176 18	47
MANGATEWAI RIVER	STRM	39 59 176 21	47
MANGATEWAIITI STREAM	STRM	40 08 176 12	47
MANGATEWAINUI RIVER	STRM	40 11 176 12	47
MANGATI	LOC	38 03 175 08	18
MANGATI STREAM	STRM	37 39 174 50	18
MANGATIA STREAM	STRM	37 25 174 57	14
MANGATINI STREAM	STRM	41 36 171 55	62
MANGATIPONA STREAM	STRM	39 54 175 18	45
MANGATIPUA STREAM	STRM	39 03 175 41	37
MANGATIPUA STREAM	STRM	39 03 175 41	38
MANGATITI	LOC	40 33 176 07	50
MANGATITI STREAM	STRM	38 41 176 27	29
MANGATITI STREAM	STRM	38 41 176 27	30
MANGATITI STREAM	STRM	39 19 175 01	36
MANGATITI STREAM	STRM	40 35 176 09	49
MANGATITI STREAM	STRM	40 35 176 09	50
MANGATITI (TRIG)	HILL	40 34 176 08	50
MANGATOA STREAM	STRM	35 27 173 44	4
MANGATOA STREAM	STRM	35 27 173 44	6
MANGATOETOE	LOC	35 08 173 27	3
MANGATOETOE STREAM	STRM	38 36 177 48	32
MANGATOETOE STREAM	STRM	41 36 175 15	53
MANGATOETOE (TRIG)	HILL	39 11 175 46	37
MANGATOETOE (TRIG)	HILL	39 11 175 46	38
MANGATOETOE (TRIG)	PEAK	41 35 175 18	53
MANGATOETOENUI STREAM	STRM	39 13 175 46	37
MANGATOETOENUI STREAM	STRM	39 13 175 46	38
MANGATOI	LOC	37 54 176 14	20
MANGATOI	LOC	37 54 176 14	21
MANGATOI CREEK	STRM	41 16 175 41	51
MANGATOI CREEK	STRM	41 16 175 41	53
MANGATOKERAU	HSTD	38 16 178 12	32
MANGATOKERAU RIVER	STRM	38 18 178 15	32
MANGATOKETOKE STREAM	STRM	37 37 175 12	18
MANGATOKETOKE STREAM	STRM	37 37 175 12	19
MANGATOKI	LOC	39 26 174 13	34
MANGATOKI STREAM	STRM	39 30 174 15	34
MANGATORO	LOC	40 16 176 13	50
MANGATORO STREAM	STRM	38 52 174 39	26
MANGATORO STREAM	STRM	40 16 176 13	50
MANGATOROMIRO STREAM	STRM	39 26 174 29	35
MANGATOROMIRO STREAM	STRM	39 26 174 29	44
MANGATOTO STREAM	STRM	38 55 177 00	40
MANGATOTO STREAM	STRM	38 55 177 00	41
MANGATU	LOC	35 42 173 39	6
MANGATU RIVER	STRM	38 23 177 49	32
MANGATU STREAM	STRM	35 44 173 40	6
MANGATU STREAM	STRM	36 26 174 28	10
MANGATU STREAM	STRM	36 26 174 28	11
MANGATU STREAM	STRM	38 35 175 23	27
MANGATU STREAM	STRM	38 43 175 39	28
MANGATU STREAM	STRM	38 43 175 39	38
MANGATUAHAUA STREAM	STRM	38 15 174 52	26
MANGATUKITUKI STREAM	STRM	39 33 174 54	35
MANGATUKITUKI STREAM	STRM	39 33 174 54	36
MANGATUKUTUKU STREAM	STRM	38 40 175 19	27
MANGATUMARU STREAM	STRM	38 41 177 37	31
MANGATUMARU STREAM	STRM	38 41 177 37	33
MANGATUNA	LOC	38 18 178 16	32
MANGATUNA	LOC	40 18 176 20	50
MANGATUPO STREAM	STRM	38 46 177 24	31
MANGATUPO STREAM	STRM	38 46 177 24	33
MANGATUPOTO	LOC	38 42 175 14	27
MANGATURANGA STREAM	STRM	39 05 177 09	41
MANGATURUTU STREAM	STRM	39 13 176 22	39
MANGATURUTURU RIVER	STRM	39 19 175 16	36
MANGATUTAEKURI (TRIG)	HILL	37 47 178 24	25
MANGATUTARA STREAM	STRM	37 57 177 45	24
MANGATUTU	LOC	38 14 175 27	19
MANGATUTU STREAM	STRM	38 06 175 24	19
MANGATUTU STREAM	STRM	37 35 178 15	25
MANGATUTU STREAM	STRM	38 24 176 01	28
MANGATUTU STREAM	STRM	38 24 176 01	29
MANGATUTU STREAM	STRM	39 26 176 33	39
MANGATUTU STREAM	STRM	39 26 176 33	40
MANGATUTU STREAM	STRM	39 26 176 33	42
MANGATUTU STREAM	STRM	39 59 175 37	46
MANGATUTU (TRIG)	HILL	40 00 175 38	46
MANGATUTUNUI STREAM	STRM	39 12 176 29	39
MANGATUTUNUI STREAM	STRM	39 12 176 29	40
MANGAUIKA STREAM	STRM	38 00 175 12	18
MANGAURUROA STREAM	STRM	39 30 176 02	39
MANGAWAIITI STREAM	STRM	39 17 174 54	35
MANGAWAIITI STREAM	STRM	39 17 174 54	44
MANGAWAIITI STREAM, EAST BRANCH	STRM	39 18 174 53	35
MANGAWAIITI STREAM, EAST BRANCH	STRM	39 18 174 53	44
MANGAWARA	LOC	37 31 175 15	15
MANGAWARA STREAM	STRM	37 35 175 13	15
MANGAWEHI STREAM	STRM	38 42 177 37	31
MANGAWEHI STREAM	STRM	38 42 177 37	33
MANGAWEKA	POPL	39 48 175 48	46
MANGAWEKA STATION	RSTN	39 49 175 47	46
MANGAWEKA (TRIG)	PEAK	39 49 176 05	47
MANGAWHAI	LOC	36 08 174 34	8
MANGAWHAI HARBOUR	HARB	36 05 174 36	8
MANGAWHAI HEADS	LOC	36 05 174 35	8
MANGAWHARARIKI RIVER	STRM	39 48 175 49	46
MANGAWHARE	LOC	35 57 173 52	6
MANGAWHARE	LOC	35 57 173 52	7
MANGAWHATA	LOC	40 24 175 26	48
MANGAWHATA STREAM	STRM	38 34 175 07	27
MANGAWHATI POINT	PNT	35 49 174 23	7
MANGAWHATI POINT	PNT	35 49 174 23	8
MANGAWHATU STREAM	STRM	37 40 178 06	25
MANGAWHERO	LOC	35 29 173 32	6
MANGAWHERO	LOC	38 15 175 16	18
MANGAWHERO	LOC	38 15 175 16	19
MANGAWHERO	LOC	38 15 175 16	27
MANGAWHERO RIVER	STRM	39 52 175 18	45
MANGAWHERO STREAM	STRM	35 16 173 22	3
MANGAWHERO STREAM	STRM	38 12 175 13	18
MANGAWHERO STREAM	STRM	37 48 175 50	19
MANGAWHERO STREAM	STRM	37 53 175 25	19
MANGAWHERO STREAM	STRM	38 12 175 13	19
MANGAWHERO STREAM	STRM	39 33 174 04	34
MANGAWHERO STREAM	STRM	38 57 177 19	41
MANGAWHERO STREAM	STRM	40 15 176 34	47
MANGAWHEROITI STREAM	STRM	39 30 174 05	34
MANGAWHIO	LOC	39 42 174 45	44
MANGAWHIO, LAKE	LAKE	39 39 174 48	44
MANGAWHIO STREAM	STRM	38 09 176 38	21
MANGAWHIO STREAM	STRM	38 09 176 38	22
MANGAWHIO STREAM	STRM	38 17 175 41	28
MANGAWIRI STREAM	STRM	38 29 176 45	30
MANGERE	SBRB	36 58 174 48	12
MANGERE	SBRB	36 58 174 48	14
MANGERE RIVER	STRM	35 42 174 07	5
MANGERE RIVER	STRM	35 42 174 07	7
MANGERE STREAM	STRM	35 42 174 11	5
MANGERE STREAM	STRM	35 42 174 11	7
MANGERE STREAM	STRM	35 42 174 11	8
MANGERTON RIDGE	RDGE	42 00 172 56	65
MANGIMANGI STREAM	STRM	39 35 174 20	34
MANGIMANGI STREAM	STRM	39 35 174 20	35
MANGIMANGI STREAM	STRM	39 35 174 20	44
MANGLES RIVER	STRM	41 48 172 22	65
MANGLES VALLEY	LOC	41 49 172 23	65
MANGOIHE STREAM	STRM	39 33 175 05	36
MANGOIRA STREAM	STRM	39 55 175 55	46
MANGOIWA STREAM	STRM	39 38 175 43	46
MANGONUI	LOC	34 59 173 32	3
MANGONUI HARBOUR	HARB	34 59 173 32	3
MANGONUIOWAE STREAM	STRM	35 18 173 20	3
MANGORAWA STREAM	STRM	37 58 176 15	20
MANGOREI STREAM	STRM	39 06 174 07	34
MANGOREWA RIVER	STRM	37 50 176 24	20
MANGOREWA RIVER	STRM	37 50 176 24	21
MANGOREWA STREAM	STRM	37 58 176 10	21
MANGOTAI STREAM	STRM	39 49 175 10	45
MANGUNGU	LOC	35 21 173 34	3
MANGUNGU	LOC	35 21 173 34	4
MANGUNGU	LOC	35 21 173 34	6
MANIA STREAM	STRM	37 35 175 55	20
MANIATUTU SIDING	RSDG	37 49 176 27	21
MANIATUTU SIDING	RSDG	37 49 176 27	22
MANILLA STREAM	STRM	43 00 172 29	71
MANLY	LOC	36 38 174 46	11
MANLY	LOC	36 38 174 46	12
MANNERING, MOUNT	MTN	43 29 170 25	74
MANNERING, MOUNT	MTN	43 29 170 25	77
MANNING STREAM	STRM	43 39 170 29	77
MANNING STREAM	STRM	43 39 170 29	86
MANOEKA	LOC	37 47 176 17	20
MANOEKA	LOC	37 47 176 17	21
MANOR BURN	STRM	45 15 169 25	100
MANOR PARK	SBRB	41 09 174 59	52
MANOR PARK	SBRB	41 09 174 59	55
MANORBURN RESERVOIR	LAKE	45 23 169 37	100
MANSON CREEK	STRM	39 20 176 17	39
MANSON, MOUNT (TRIG)	MTN	43 06 171 44	80
MANSON (TRIG)	PEAK	39 17 176 15	39
MANSONS SIDING	RSDG	39 05 175 23	36
MANSONS SIDING	RSDG	39 05 175 23	37
MANTELL, MOUNT (TRIG)	MTN	41 59 172 17	65
MANUAITI (TRIG)	HILL	37 58 174 48	18
MANUHERIKIA RIVER	STRM	44 51 169 55	91
MANUHERIKIA RIVER	STRM	45 16 169 24	100
MANUHERIKIA RIVER (EAST BRANCH)	STRM	44 45 169 54	91
MANUHERIKIA RIVER (WEST BRANCH)	STRM	44 45 169 54	91
MANUI	LOC	39 46 175 48	46
MANUKA BAY	BAY	42 54 173 18	72
MANUKA BAY	BAY	42 54 173 18	73
MANUKA CREEK	STRM	42 09 172 13	64
MANUKA CREEK	STRM	44 32 169 52	91
MANUKA CREEK	LOC	46 03 169 48	111
MANUKA CREEK	LOC	46 03 169 48	113
MANUKA ISLAND	HSTD	41 41 173 10	66
MANUKA ISLAND	ISLD	46 12 169 42	111
MANUKA ISLAND	ISLD	46 12 169 42	113
MANUKA LAKE	LAKE	43 32 171 15	75
MANUKA PEAK (TRIG)	PEAK	43 16 171 11	75
MANUKA POINT (TRIG)	HILL	43 17 171 14	75
MANUKA STREAM	STRM	41 49 173 27	66
MANUKA STREAM	STRM	45 34 170 20	101
MANUKA STREAM	STRM	46 05 169 51	111
MANUKA STREAM	STRM	46 05 169 51	113
MANUKA (TRIG)	HILL	39 50 175 49	46
MANUKAIAPU (TRIG)	PEAK	39 19 175 49	37
MANUKAIAPU (TRIG)	PEAK	39 19 175 49	38
MANUKAU	LOC	35 14 173 12	3
MANUKAU CITY CENTRE	SBRB	37 00 174 52	12
MANUKAU CITY CENTRE	SBRB	37 00 174 52	14
MANUKAU ENTRANCE	CHAN	37 03 174 31	12
MANUKAU HARBOUR	HARB	37 02 174 43	12
MANUKAU HARBOUR	HARB	37 02 174 43	14
MANUNUI	SBRB	38 54 175 20	27
MANUOHA (TRIG)	MTN	38 39 177 07	31
MANUREWA	USAT	37 01 174 54	12
MANUREWA	USAT	37 01 174 54	14
MANUREWA POINT	PNT	41 31 175 32	53
MANURIKI STREAM	STRM	37 53 177 40	24
MANURUHI	HILL	38 33 176 54	30
MANUTAHI	HSTD	37 54 178 21	25
MANUTAHI	LOC	39 40 174 34	44
MANUTUKE	LOC	38 41 177 55	32
MANUTUKE	LOC	38 41 177 55	33
MANUWHAKAPAKAPA BAY	BAY	40 55 173 46	61
MANY ISLANDS	ISLS	45 46 166 31	104
MAORI BAY	BAY	41 10 173 51	54
MAORI BAY	BAY	41 10 173 51	60
MAORI BAY	BAY	41 10 173 51	61
MAORI CREEK	STRM	41 32 172 07	62
MAORI CREEK	STRM	42 33 171 19	69
MAORI CREEK	STRM	45 12 169 43	100
MAORI CREEK	STRM	45 12 169 43	101
MAORI GULLY	STRM	41 31 172 11	62
MAORI HEAD	HEAD	45 54 170 34	103
MAORI LAKES	LAKE	43 35 171 10	75
MAORI, MOUNT	MTN	44 26 168 37	88
MAORI, MOUNT	MTN	44 26 168 37	90
MAORI RIVER	STRM	43 47 169 07	78
MAORI SADDLE	SAD	44 05 169 09	78
MAORI STREAM	STRM	39 06 176 53	40
MAORI STREAM	STRM	39 06 176 53	41
MAORIBANK	SBRB	41 07 175 06	52
MAORIBANK	SBRB	41 07 175 06	55
MAPARA STREAM	STRM	38 30 175 05	27
MAPARA STREAM	STRM	38 42 175 58	28
MAPARA STREAM	STRM	38 42 175 58	29
MAPARA STREAM	STRM	38 42 175 58	38
MAPAU	LOC	36 09 174 03	7
MAPIU	LOC	38 35 175 13	27
MAPIU STREAM	STRM	38 30 175 03	27
MAPOURIKA, LAKE	LAKE	43 19 170 12	74
MAPOURIKI (TRIG)	MTN	38 42 176 49	30
MAPUA	LOC	41 15 173 06	58
MAPUA	LOC	41 15 173 06	59
MARA	LOC	40 40 176 15	50
MARAEHAKO STREAM	STRM	37 40 177 48	24
MARAEHARA	HSTD	37 45 178 25	25
MARAEHARA RIVER	STRM	37 47 178 28	25
MARAEKAKAHO	LOC	39 39 176 38	42
MARAEKAKAHO	LOC	39 39 176 38	43
MARAEKAKAHO	LOC	39 39 176 38	47
MARAEKAKAHO RIVER	STRM	39 39 176 38	42
MARAEKAKAHO RIVER	STRM	39 39 176 38	43
MARAEKAKAHO RIVER	STRM	39 39 176 38	47
MARAEMANUKA STREAM	STRM	38 29 175 40	28
MARAENUI	SBRB	39 31 176 54	40
MARAENUI	SBRB	39 31 176 54	41
MARAENUI	SBRB	39 31 176 54	42
MARAEROA	LOC	35 21 173 38	4
MARAETAHA	LOC	38 50 177 53	32
MARAETAHA	LOC	38 50 177 53	33
MARAETAHA RIVER	STRM	38 47 177 56	32
MARAETAHA RIVER	STRM	38 47 177 56	33
MARAETAI	LOC	36 53 175 02	12
MARAETAI	LOC	36 53 175 02	13
MARAETAI	LOC	36 53 175 02	14
MARAETAI	LOC	38 22 175 45	28
MARAETAI BAY	BAY	41 15 174 09	54
MARAETAI BAY	BAY	41 15 174 09	60

MARAETAI BAY	BAY	41 15 174 09	61
MARAETAI STREAM	STRM	37 24 174 44	14
MARAETAUA (TRIG)	HILL	38 24 175 07	27
MARAETOI, LAKE	LAKE	38 22 175 47	28
MARAETOTARA RIVER	STRM	39 38 176 59	42
MARAETOTARA RIVER	STRM	39 38 176 59	43
MARAEWHITI POINT	PNT	34 49 173 23	3
MARAHAU	LOC	41 00 173 00	57
MARAHAU	LOC	41 00 173 00	58
MARAHAU	LOC	41 00 173 00	59
MARAHAU, LAKE	LAKE	39 51 174 49	44
MARAHAU RIVER	STRM	41 00 173 00	57
MARAHAU RIVER	STRM	41 00 173 00	58
MARAHAU RIVER	STRM	41 00 173 00	59
MARAKEKE	LOC	40 01 176 27	47
MARAKERAKE	LOC	45 04 170 44	102
MARAMARUA	LOC	37 15 175 14	13
MARAMARUA	LOC	37 15 175 14	15
MARAMARUA MILL	LOC	37 15 175 12	13
MARAMARUA MILL	LOC	37 15 175 12	15
MARAMARUA RIVER	STRM	37 18 175 05	14
MARAMARUA RIVER	STRM	37 18 175 05	15
MARAMATAHA RIVER	STRM	38 39 175 19	27
MARANGAE STREAM	STRM	39 10 174 52	35
MARANGAE (TRIG)	HILL	39 10 174 54	35
MARANGAI	HSTD	39 58 175 18	45
MARAREWA	LOC	41 26 172 51	58
MARAROA RIVER	STRM	45 35 167 43	97
MARAROA RIVER	STRM	45 11 168 09	98
MARATEA POINT	PNT	35 27 174 43	5
MARATHON FLAT	HSTD	41 43 174 00	67
MARATOTO	LOC	37 19 175 46	17
MARATOTO, LAKE	LAKE	37 53 175 18	18
MARATOTO, LAKE	LAKE	37 53 175 18	19
MARAU POINT	PNT	38 17 178 21	32
MARAU (TRIG)	HILL	38 17 178 20	32
MARAWITI	LOC	43 39 171 46	80
MARAWITI	LOC	43 39 171 46	84
MARBLE POINT	HSTD	42 40 172 46	71
MARCHANT, LAKE	LAKE	45 04 167 20	94
MARCHANT, LAKE	LAKE	45 04 167 20	96
MARCHANT, MOUNT (TRIG)	HILL	40 35 175 56	49
MARCHANT (TRIG)	PEAK	41 02 175 16	53
MARCHBURN RIVER	STRM	41 32 173 39	60
MARCOS HILL (TRIG)	HILL	39 06 174 44	35
MARE BURN	STRM	45 17 170 17	101
MAREAROA	LOC	38 33 175 32	27
MAREAROA	LOC	38 33 175 32	28
MAREE, LOCH	LAKE	45 41 167 03	105
MAREIKURA STREAM	STRM	35 51 174 01	7
MARERETU	LOC	36 03 174 18	7
MARERETU	LOC	36 03 174 18	8
MARETU STREAM	STRM	38 32 177 37	31
MAREWA	SBRB	39 30 176 55	40
MAREWA	SBRB	39 30 176 55	41
MAREWA	SBRB	39 30 176 55	42
MARGARET STREAM	STRM	45 57 166 53	104
MARGARET STREAM	STRM	45 57 166 53	105
MARGUERITE PEAKS (TRIG)	PEAK	45 01 167 29	94
MARGUERITE PEAKS (TRIG)	PEAK	45 01 167 29	97
MARIA ISLAND	ISLD	36 43 175 00	12
MARIA ISLAND	ISLD	36 43 175 00	13
MARIA, MOUNT (TRIG)	MTN	42 22 172 38	71
MARIA VAN DIEMEN, CAPE	CAPE	34 29 172 39	2
MARIAN, LAKE	LAKE	44 47 168 05	89
MARIMA	LOC	40 30 175 42	49
MARIMA (TRIG)	HILL	40 28 175 41	49
MARINA, LAKE	LAKE	41 28 172 14	62
MARINO MOUNTAINS	MTNS	41 32 172 27	61
MARINO MOUNTAINS	MTNS	41 32 172 27	62
MARINUI STREAM	STRM	46 31 169 04	112
MARION BAY	BAY	42 41 172 14	70
MARION, LAKE	LAKE	42 41 172 14	70
MARION, MOUNT	MTN	43 07 171 06	75
MARION TOWER	MTN	44 29 168 34	88
MARION TOWER	MTN	44 29 168 34	90
MARIRI	LOC	41 09 173 01	57
MARIRI	LOC	41 09 173 01	58
MARIRI	LOC	41 09 173 01	59
MARITANA STREAM	STRM	42 30 172 28	71
MARIWERA STREAM	STRM	46 03 167 33	105
MARIWERA STREAM	STRM	46 03 167 33	106
MARK, MOUNT	MTN	43 57 169 04	78
MARK RANGE	MTNS	43 57 169 07	78
MARKET CROSS	LOC	41 15 172 08	56
MARKET CROSS	LOC	41 15 172 08	62
MARLEYS HILL	HILL	43 37 172 37	82
MARLEYS HILL	HILL	43 37 172 37	83
MARLEYS HILL	HILL	43 37 172 37	85
MARLOW	LOC	35 32 174 07	4
MARLOW	LOC	35 32 174 07	5
MARO (TRIG)	HILL	38 52 175 12	27
MAROA STREAM	STRM	40 25 176 01	49
MAROANUI (TRIG)	HILL	38 31 176 01	28
MAROANUI (TRIG)	HILL	38 31 176 01	29
MAROHEMO	LOC	36 09 174 19	7
MAROHEMO	LOC	36 09 174 19	8
MAROKOPA	LOC	38 18 174 43	26
MAROKOPA RIVER	STRM	38 19 174 43	26
MAROMAKU	LOC	35 29 174 06	4
MAROMAKU	LOC	35 29 174 06	5
MAROMAUKU STREAM	STRM	38 57 177 29	33
MARONAN	LOC	43 55 171 33	84
MAROPEA RIVER	STRM	39 40 176 05	47
MAROPEA (TRIG)	PEAK	39 45 176 11	47
MAROPIU	LOC	35 49 173 44	6
MAROTERE ISLANDS	ISLS	35 54 174 44	8
MARQUEE, THE	MTN	43 21 171 03	75
MARR CREEK	STRM	41 45 172 35	65
MARRINGTON PEAKS	MTNS	45 18 167 07	96
MARSDEN	LOC	42 34 171 13	68
MARSDEN	LOC	42 34 171 13	69
MARSDEN BAY	LOC	35 50 174 28	8
MARSDEN, MOUNT (TRIG)	MTN	44 52 168 43	90
MARSDEN, MOUNT (TRIG)	MTN	44 52 168 43	95
MARSDEN POINT	LOC	35 51 174 29	8
MARSH BURN	STRM	46 01 167 50	106
MARSH, MOUNT (TRIG)	HILL	40 42 175 53	49
MARSH, MOUNT (TRIG)	HILL	40 42 175 53	51
MARSHALL, LAKE	LAKE	46 10 166 58	105
MARSHALL, MOUNT	MTN	42 10 171 34	63
MARSHALL PASS	PASS	44 49 167 52	89
MARSHALL PASS	PASS	44 49 167 52	94
MARSHALL RANGE	MTNS	41 08 172 25	56
MARSHALL RANGE	MTNS	41 08 172 25	62
MARSHALL ROCKS	ROCK	46 11 166 37	104
MARSHALL (TRIG)	HILL	39 55 175 48	46
MARSHLAND	LOC	43 29 172 39	82
MARSHLAND	LOC	43 29 172 39	83
MARSHLAND	LOC	43 29 172 39	85
MARSHLANDS	LOC	41 27 174 00	54
MARSHLANDS	LOC	41 27 174 00	60
MARTHA, MOUNT	MTN	44 25 169 33	91
MARTIN, MOUNT	MTN	45 19 167 24	96
MARTIN, MOUNT	MTN	45 19 167 24	97
MARTINBOROUGH	POPL	41 13 175 27	53
MARTINS BAY	BAY	35 32 173 23	6
MARTINS BAY	BAY	36 27 174 46	11
MARTINS BAY	BAY	44 22 167 58	89
MARTINS BAY	LOC	44 22 168 00	89
MARTON	POPL	40 05 175 23	45
MARTON	POPL	40 05 175 23	46
MARTON BLOCK	LOC	39 56 175 55	46
MARTON CREEK	STRM	39 55 175 26	45
MARTON CREEK	STRM	39 55 175 26	46
MARTYR HILL (TRIG)	MTN	44 11 168 32	88
MARTYR RIVER	STRM	44 05 168 29	88
MARTYR SADDLE	SAD	44 07 168 34	88
MARUA	LOC	35 34 174 22	5
MARUA	LOC	35 34 174 22	7
MARUA	LOC	35 34 174 22	8
MARUAKOA	LOC	45 02 170 47	102
MARUARUA STREAM	STRM	35 37 174 14	5
MARUARUA STREAM	STRM	35 37 174 14	7
MARUARUA STREAM	STRM	35 37 174 14	8
MARUIA	LOC	42 11 172 13	64
MARUIA RIVER	STRM	41 47 172 13	64
MARUIA RIVER, LEFT HAND BRANCH	STRM	42 22 172 22	71
MARUIA RIVER, RIGHT HAND BRANCH	STRM	42 22 172 22	71
MARUIA SADDLE	SAD	42 02 172 18	65
MARUIA SPRINGS	LOC	42 23 172 20	71
MARUIA STREAM	STRM	39 44 175 38	46
MARUMARU	HSTD	38 55 177 27	33
MARY BURN	STRM	44 15 170 19	86
MARY ISLAND	ISLD	45 59 167 19	105
MARY, LAKE	LAKE	44 03 168 43	88
MARY MARUIA SADDLE	SAD	42 23 172 09	70
MARY, MOUNT (TRIG)	HILL	39 39 176 21	47
MARY, MOUNT (TRIG)	HILL	44 08 170 17	86
MARY RANGE	MTNS	44 10 170 17	86
MARY RIVER	STRM	42 54 171 25	69
MARYBANK	SBRB	39 57 175 04	45
MARYBANK	SBRB	41 14 173 19	59
MARYMERE, LAKE	LAKE	43 07 171 51	80
MARYS RANGE	MTNS	44 46 170 19	92
MASON BAY	BAY	46 55 167 45	114
MASON HEAD	HEAD	46 53 167 45	114
MASON HILLS	HSTD	42 31 173 08	72
MASON HILLS	HSTD	42 31 173 08	73
MASON, LAKE	LAKE	42 44 172 10	70
MASON, MOUNT	MTN	42 37 171 47	70
MASON, MOUNT (TRIG)	PEAK	45 03 169 00	99
MASON, MOUNT (TRIG)	MTN	42 54 172 30	71
MASON RIVER	STRM	42 29 173 11	72
MASON RIVER	STRM	42 29 173 11	73
MASONS FLAT	LOC	42 54 172 35	71
MASONS HILL (TRIG)	HILL	46 08 167 35	106
MASONS HILL (TRIG)	HILL	46 08 167 35	108
MASSEY	SBRB	36 50 174 37	11
MASSEY	SBRB	36 50 174 37	12
MASSEY UNIVERSITY	UNIV	40 23 175 37	48
MASSEY UNIVERSITY	UNIV	40 23 175 37	49
MASSON CREEK	STRM	46 04 167 33	105
MASSON CREEK	STRM	46 04 167 33	106
MASTERTON	TOWN	40 57 175 39	49
MASTERTON	TOWN	40 57 175 39	51
MASTERTON	TOWN	40 57 175 39	53
MATA	LOC	35 19 173 30	3
MATA	LOC	35 51 174 23	7
MATA	LOC	35 51 174 23	8
MATA CREEK	STRM	44 55 169 51	91
MATA RIVER	STRM	37 53 178 17	25
MATAHANA STREAM	STRM	38 17 176 07	21
MATAHANA STREAM	STRM	38 17 176 07	28
MATAHANA STREAM	STRM	38 17 176 07	29
MATAHANEA	LOC	38 08 177 16	23
MATAHAPA	LOC	38 07 177 09	23
MATAHI	LOC	38 15 177 07	31
MATAHINA	LOC	38 10 176 47	22
MATAHINA, LAKE	LAKE	38 08 176 49	22
MATAHINA SIDING	RSDG	38 11 176 48	22
MATAHIWI	LOC	39 36 175 09	36
MATAHIWI	LOC	39 36 175 09	45
MATAHIWI	LOC	40 53 175 35	48
MATAHIWI	LOC	40 53 175 35	49
MATAHIWI	LOC	40 53 175 35	51
MATAHORUA STREAM	STRM	39 09 177 02	40
MATAHORUA STREAM	STRM	39 09 177 02	41
MATAHUI POINT	PNT	37 34 175 58	20
MATAHURU	LOC	37 26 175 18	15
MATAHURU STREAM	STRM	37 28 175 13	15
MATAI	LOC	37 50 175 44	19
MATAI	LOC	42 22 171 30	69
MATAI BAY	BAY	34 50 173 25	3
MATAI RIVER	STRM	41 16 173 17	59
MATAI (TRIG)	HILL	39 31 174 35	35
MATAI (TRIG)	HILL	39 31 174 35	44
MATAIAPONGA (TRIG)	HILL	39 46 175 35	46
MATAIKOKAKO (TRIG)	HILL	36 58 175 12	13
MATAIKOKAKO (TRIG)	HILL	36 58 175 12	15
MATAIKONA	HSTD	40 47 176 16	50
MATAIKONA RIVER	STRM	40 47 176 16	50
MATAIMOANA (TRIG)	HILL	39 32 175 00	36
MATAIPUKU (TRIG)	HILL	37 41 178 17	25
MATAKA	HILL	35 10 174 07	4
MATAKA	HILL	35 10 174 07	5
MATAKANA	LOC	36 21 174 43	11
MATAKANA ISLAND	ISLD	37 33 176 03	17
MATAKANA ISLAND	ISLD	37 33 176 03	20
MATAKANA POINT	PNT	37 36 176 02	20
MATAKANA RIVER, LEFT BRANCH	STRM	36 23 174 42	11
MATAKANA RIVER, MIDDLE BRANCH	STRM	36 22 174 43	11
MATAKANUI	LOC	45 01 169 34	100
MATAKAOA POINT	PNT	37 34 178 19	25
MATAKAWAU	LOC	37 07 174 37	12
MATAKAWAU	LOC	37 07 174 37	14
MATAKAWAU CREEK	STRM	37 07 174 40	12
MATAKAWAU CREEK	STRM	37 07 174 40	14
MATAKAWAU POINT	LOC	37 07 174 40	12
MATAKAWAU POINT	LOC	37 07 174 40	14
MATAKETAKE RANGE	MTNS	43 50 169 15	78
MATAKI LODGE	HSTD	41 58 172 31	65
MATAKI (TRIG)	HILL	35 23 173 39	4
MATAKI (TRIG)	HILL	35 23 173 39	6
MATAKITAKI	LOC	41 59 172 20	65
MATAKITAKI RIVER	STRM	41 48 172 19	65
MATAKITAKI RIVER, EAST BRANCH	STRM	42 13 172 31	65
MATAKITAKI RIVER, WEST BRANCH	STRM	42 13 172 31	65
MATAKITAKI STATION	HSTD	41 59 172 29	65
MATAKITAKI (TRIG)	HILL	37 27 174 55	14
MATAKOHE	LOC	36 08 174 11	7
MATAKOHE RIVER	STRM	36 07 174 12	7
MATAKOHE RIVER	STRM	36 07 174 12	8
MATAKOTEA STREAM	STRM	37 49 174 58	18
MATAKUHIA RANGE	MTNS	38 43 177 16	31
MATAKUHIA STREAM	STRM	39 01 176 38	39
MATAKUHIA STREAM	STRM	39 01 176 38	40
MATAMATA	POPL	37 49 175 46	19
MATAMAU	LOC	40 09 176 10	47
MATANEHUNEHU STREAM	STRM	39 11 173 48	34
MATANGI	LOC	37 48 175 24	19
MATANGIRAU	LOC	35 03 173 48	4
MATAORA BAY	BAY	37 18 175 55	17
MATAPAUA BAY	BAY	36 45 175 48	16
MATAPIHI	LOC	37 42 176 12	20
MATAPIHI	LOC	37 42 176 12	21
MATAPIRO	LOC	39 36 176 37	42
MATAPIRO	LOC	39 36 176 37	43
MATAPIRO	LOC	39 36 176 37	47
MATAPOURI	LOC	35 34 174 30	5
MATAPOURI	LOC	35 34 174 30	8
MATAPOURI BAY	BAY	35 34 174 31	5
MATAPOURI BAY	BAY	35 34 174 31	8
MATAPU	LOC	39 29 174 13	34
MATARAE	LOC	45 37 170 09	101
MATARANGI	LOC	36 44 175 40	16
MATARAU	LOC	35 39 174 13	5
MATARAU	LOC	35 39 174 13	7
MATARAU	LOC	35 39 174 13	8
MATARAUA	LOC	35 32 173 45	4
MATARAUA	LOC	35 32 173 45	6
MATARAWA	LOC	41 03 175 27	53
MATARAWA STREAM	STRM	38 12 175 51	28
MATARAWA STREAM	STRM	39 56 175 03	45
MATARIKI	LOC	41 25 172 44	58
MATAROA	LOC	39 39 175 43	46
MATARU STREAM	STRM	38 59 174 51	35
MATARUA CREEK	STRM	40 28 175 46	49
MATATA	LOC	37 53 176 45	22
MATATAPU ROCKS	ROCK	37 39 176 25	21
MATATAPU ROCKS	ROCK	37 39 176 25	22
MATATARA STREAM	STRM	39 51 175 09	45
MATATOKI	LOC	37 12 175 36	13
MATATOKI	LOC	37 12 175 36	15
MATATOKI STREAM	STRM	37 13 175 36	13
MATATOKI STREAM	STRM	37 13 175 36	15
MATAU	LOC	39 10 174 35	35
MATAU	LOC	46 19 169 49	111
MATAU	LOC	46 19 169 49	113
MATAU STREAM	STRM	39 06 174 33	35
MATAURA	POPL	46 12 168 52	110
MATAURA	POPL	46 12 168 52	112
MATAURA ISLAND	LOC	46 26 168 47	112
MATAURA RANGE	MTNS	45 39 168 37	107
MATAURA RIVER	STRM	46 35 168 48	112
MATAURA SADDLE	SAD	45 19 168 25	95
MATAURA SADDLE	SAD	45 19 168 25	98
MATAURA STREAM	STRM	37 22 175 52	17
MATAURA (TRIG)	HILL	46 14 168 53	110
MATAURA (TRIG)	HILL	46 14 168 53	112
MATAURAURA (TRIG)	HILL	38 56 177 08	41
MATAURI BAY	BAY	35 02 173 55	4
MATAURI BAY	LOC	35 03 173 54	4
MATAWAI	LOC	38 21 177 32	31
MATAWAI (TRIG)	MTN	38 21 177 34	31
MATAWAIA	LOC	35 31 173 57	4
MATAWHANA	HILL	38 13 175 42	19
MATAWHAURA (TRIG)	HILL	38 02 176 29	21
MATAWHAURA (TRIG)	HILL	38 02 176 29	22
MATAWHERA	LOC	35 24 173 29	3
MATAWHERA	LOC	35 24 173 29	6
MATAWHERO	HILL	36 12 175 25	9
MATAWHERO	LOC	38 39 177 56	32
MATAWHERO	LOC	38 39 177 56	33
MATAWHERO STATION	RSTN	38 40 177 58	32
MATAWHERO STATION	RSTN	38 40 177 58	33
MATAWHERO STREAM	STRM	36 36 174 27	10
MATAWHERO STREAM	STRM	36 36 174 27	11
MATAWHERO STREAM	STRM	36 36 174 27	12
MATAWHEROHIA	LOC	35 08 173 46	4
MATAWHEROHIA POINT	PNT	34 49 173 25	3
MATEA	LOC	38 44 176 31	30
MATEMATEAONGA RANGE	MTNS	39 21 174 42	35
MATEMATEAONGA RANGE	MTNS	39 21 174 42	44
MATEMATEAONGA (TRIG)	HILL	39 23 174 41	35
MATEMATEAONGA (TRIG)	HILL	39 23 174 41	44
MATES CREEK	STRM	41 25 173 21	59
MATHER CREEK	STRM	44 01 169 23	78
MATHERS PEAK	PEAK	43 47 169 43	76
MATHERS PEAK	PEAK	43 47 169 43	79
MATHESON, LAKE	LAKE	43 26 169 58	76
MATHESONS CORNER	LOC	45 50 169 20	110
MATHESONS CORNER	LOC	45 50 169 20	111
MATHEWS STREAM	STRM	39 37 176 23	47
MATHIAS CREEK	STRM	43 44 169 15	78
MATHIAS PASS	PASS	43 06 171 07	75
MATHIAS RIVER	STRM	43 17 171 19	75
MATIERE	LOC	38 46 175 06	27
MATIHE POINT	PNT	36 16 174 08	10
MATIHETIHE	LOC	35 26 173 17	3
MATILDA, LAKE	LAKE	45 28 167 12	96
MATINGARAHI	LOC	37 00 175 17	13
MATINGARAHI	LOC	37 00 175 17	15
MATINGARAHI POINT	PNT	37 01 175 17	13
MATINGARAHI POINT	PNT	37 01 175 17	15
MATIRA	LOC	37 35 174 51	14
MATIRANGI STREAM	STRM	39 06 174 34	35
MATIRANGI (TRIG)	HILL	39 07 174 40	35
MATIRI HILL (TRIG)	HILL	41 46 172 19	65
MATIRI RANGE	MTNS	41 33 172 21	62
MATIRI RIVER	STRM	41 47 172 18	65
MATIRI RIVER, EAST BRANCH	STRM	41 41 172 20	65
MATIRI RIVER, WEST BRANCH	STRM	41 41 172 19	65
MATIRI, LAKE	LAKE	41 39 172 20	62
MATIRI, LAKE	LAKE	41 39 172 20	65
MATTERHORN	MTN	45 33 167 10	96
MATTHEWS, MOUNT (TRIG)	PEAK	41 21 175 01	52
MATTHEWS, MOUNT (TRIG)	PEAK	41 21 175 01	55
MATUKITUKI RIVER	STRM	44 38 169 01	90
MATUKITUKI RIVER (EAST BRANCH)	STRM	44 29 168 49	90
MATUKITUKI RIVER (WEST BRANCH)	STRM	44 29 168 49	90
MATUKITUKI SADDLE	SAD	44 24 168 40	88
MATUKITUKI SADDLE	SAD	44 24 168 40	90
MATUKU (TRIG)	HILL	39 39 175 57	46
MAUD CREEK	STRM	41 43 172 41	65
MAUD GLACIER	GLCR	43 27 170 31	74
MAUD GLACIER	GLCR	43 27 170 31	77
MAUD ISLAND	ISLD	41 01 173 53	54
MAUD ISLAND	ISLD	41 01 173 53	60
MAUD ISLAND	ISLD	41 01 173 53	61
MAUD (TRIG)	HILL	41 48 172 42	65
MAUDE, MOUNT	MTN	43 59 170 38	86
MAUITAHI ISLAND	ISLD	35 54 174 42	8
MAUIUI	HILL	38 33 175 46	28
MAUKORO CANAL	CANL	37 14 175 24	15
MAUKORO (TRIG)	HILL	37 28 175 30	15
MAUKU	LOC	37 12 174 49	12
MAUKU	LOC	37 12 174 49	14
MAUKU STREAM	STRM	37 11 174 48	12
MAUKU STREAM	STRM	37 11 174 48	14
MAUKU STREAM	STRM	39 07 174 51	35
MAUKUKU (TRIG)	HILL	39 37 175 23	37
MAUKUKU (TRIG)	HILL	39 37 175 23	45
MAUKUKU (TRIG)	HILL	39 37 175 23	46
MAUKURATAWHAI (TRIG)	MTN	42 26 172 51	71
MAUKURATAWHAI (TRIG)	MTN	42 26 172 51	72
MAUMAUPAKI (TRIG)	HILL	36 58 175 34	13
MAUMAUPAKI (TRIG)	HILL	36 58 175 34	15
MAUMAUPAKI (TRIG)	HILL	36 58 175 34	16
MAUNGAHARURU RANGE	MTNS	39 08 176 45	40
MAUNGAHATOA (TRIG)	HILL	35 05 173 37	4
MAUNGAHAUMI (TRIG)	MTN	38 18 177 40	31
MAUNGAHAUMIA STREAM	STRM	37 35 175 32	19
MAUNGAHEREMONA (TRIG)	HILL	35 10 173 15	3
MAUNGAHUKA	PEAK	40 55 175 20	48
MAUNGAITI (TRIG)	HILL	38 21 175 56	28
MAUNGAITI (TRIG)	HILL	38 21 175 56	29
MAUNGAKAKA (TRIG)	HILL	37 39 178 28	25
MAUNGAKARAMEA	LOC	35 51 174 12	7
MAUNGAKARAMEA	LOC	35 51 174 12	8
MAUNGAKATOTE (TRIG)	HILL	39 00 175 35	37
MAUNGAKATOTE (TRIG)	HILL	39 00 175 35	38
MAUNGAKAWA (TRIG)	HILL	37 25 175 24	15
MAUNGAKAWA (TRIG)	HILL	37 48 175 37	19
MAUNGAKAWA (TRIG)	HILL	40 56 175 02	48
MAUNGAKAWA (TRIG)	HILL	40 56 175 02	52
MAUNGAKAWA (TRIG)	HILL	40 56 175 02	55
MAUNGAKAWAKAWA (TRIG)	HILL	35 30 173 49	4
MAUNGAKAWAKAWA (TRIG)	HILL	35 30 173 49	6
MAUNGAKOTUKUTUKU STREAM	STRM	40 54 175 04	52
MAUNGAKOTUKUTUKU STREAM	STRM	40 54 175 04	55
MAUNGAKU (TRIG)	PEAK	38 59 175 32	36
MAUNGAKU (TRIG)	PEAK	38 59 175 32	37
MAUNGAKU (TRIG)	PEAK	38 59 175 32	38
MAUNGAMANGERO (TRIG)	HILL	38 23 174 47	26
MAUNGANAMU (TRIG)	HILL	38 44 176 08	28
MAUNGANAMU (TRIG)	HILL	38 44 176 08	29
MAUNGANUI	HILL	41 09 173 31	59
MAUNGANUI BLUFF	CLIF	35 46 173 33	6
MAUNGANUI, MOUNT (TRIG)	MTN	37 38 176 10	20
MAUNGANUI POINT	PNT	36 07 175 19	9
MAUNGANUI (TRIG)	HILL	35 45 173 34	6
MAUNGANUI (TRIG)	HILL	36 49 175 07	13
MAUNGANUI (TRIG)	HILL	38 21 177 39	31
MAUNGANUI (TRIG)	PEAK	40 58 175 03	52
MAUNGANUI (TRIG)	PEAK	40 58 175 03	55
MAUNGAONGAONGA (TRIG)	HILL	38 20 176 21	21
MAUNGAONGAONGA (TRIG)	HILL	38 20 176 21	29
MAUNGAORANGI (TRIG)	PEAK	39 05 176 10	39
MAUNGAPAKEHA (TRIG)	HILL	40 53 175 55	49
MAUNGAPAKEHA (TRIG)	HILL	40 53 175 55	51
MAUNGAPARERUA STREAM	STRM	35 13 173 55	4
MAUNGAPOHATU	LOC	38 34 177 06	30
MAUNGAPOHATU (TRIG)	MTN	38 34 177 08	31
MAUNGAPURUPURU (TRIG)	HILL	40 52 175 58	49
MAUNGAPURUPURU (TRIG)	HILL	40 52 175 58	51
MAUNGARAHIRI (TRIG)	HILL	38 34 175 18	27
MAUNGARAHO (TRIG)	HILL	36 02 173 58	7
MAUNGARAKI	SBRB	41 13 174 53	52
MAUNGARAKI	SBRB	41 13 174 53	55
MAUNGARAKI (TRIG)	HILL	41 05 175 44	51
MAUNGARAKI (TRIG)	HILL	41 05 175 44	53
MAUNGARAMARAMA CREEK	STRM	40 24 175 54	49
MAUNGARATAITI, LAKE	LAKE	39 55 175 31	45
MAUNGARATAITI, LAKE	LAKE	39 55 175 31	46
MAUNGARATANUI, LAKE	LAKE	39 55 175 31	45
MAUNGARATANUI, LAKE	LAKE	39 55 175 31	46
MAUNGARAU (TRIG)	HILL	39 26 174 53	35
MAUNGARAU (TRIG)	HILL	40 44 175 55	49
MAUNGARAU (TRIG)	HILL	40 44 175 55	51
MAUNGAROA	LOC	39 07 175 06	36
MAUNGAROA STREAM	STRM	39 12 175 11	36
MAUNGAROA (TRIG)	HILL	38 06 178 16	25
MAUNGAROA (TRIG)	HILL	39 11 175 10	36
MAUNGARU RANGE	MTNS	35 48 173 56	7
MAUNGARU (TRIG)	HILL	35 50 173 58	7
MAUNGATANIWHA	HSTD	38 55 176 56	40
MAUNGATANIWHA	HSTD	38 55 176 56	41
MAUNGATANIWHA RANGE	MTNS	35 10 173 28	3
MAUNGATANIWHA (TRIG)	HILL	35 10 173 31	3
MAUNGATANIWHA (TRIG)	MTN	38 49 176 48	30
MAUNGATAPERE	POPL	35 45 174 13	5
MAUNGATAPERE	POPL	35 45 174 13	7
MAUNGATAPERE	POPL	35 45 174 13	8
MAUNGATAPERE (TRIG)	HILL	35 47 174 11	5
MAUNGATAPERE (TRIG)	HILL	35 47 174 11	7
MAUNGATAPERE (TRIG)	HILL	35 47 174 11	8
MAUNGATAPU	SBRB	37 43 176 11	20
MAUNGATAPU	SBRB	37 43 176 11	21
MAUNGATAPU (TRIG)	PEAK	41 19 173 25	59
MAUNGATAUTARI	LOC	37 58 175 34	19
MAUNGATAUTARI (TRIG)	HILL	38 01 175 34	19
MAUNGATERA (TRIG)	HILL	38 54 176 07	28
MAUNGATERA (TRIG)	HILL	38 54 176 07	29
MAUNGATERA (TRIG)	HILL	38 54 176 07	38
MAUNGATI	LOC	44 28 170 57	93
MAUNGATIKA	MTN	44 29 169 27	91
MAUNGATIRO	LOC	44 38 170 37	92
MAUNGATOATOU STREAM	STRM	38 30 177 08	31
MAUNGATUA	LOC	45 53 170 19	103
MAUNGATUA (TRIG)	HILL	45 53 170 07	103
MAUNGATUROTO	POPL	36 06 174 21	7
MAUNGATUROTO	POPL	36 06 174 21	8
MAUNGATUROTO (TRIG)	HILL	35 22 173 53	4
MAUNGATUROTO (TRIG)	HILL	35 19 173 43	4
MAUNGATUROTO (TRIG)	HILL	35 22 173 53	6
MAUNGAWARU (TRIG)	MTN	38 02 177 44	24
MAUNGAWERA	LOC	44 39 169 13	91
MAUNGAWHAKAMANA (TRIG)	HILL	38 08 176 35	21
MAUNGAWHAKAMANA (TRIG)	HILL	38 08 176 35	22
MAUNGAWHIO LAGOON	LAGN	39 04 177 53	33
MAUNGAWHIORANGI (TRIG)	HILL	38 11 177 15	23
MAUNSELL (TRIG)	HILL	40 52 176 05	49
MAUNSELL (TRIG)	HILL	40 52 176 05	51
MAUNU	LOC	35 44 174 17	5
MAUNU	LOC	35 44 174 17	7
MAUNU	LOC	35 44 174 17	8
MAUNUKIORA STREAM	STRM	38 21 175 38	28
MAURI (TRIG)	HILL	39 26 174 59	36
MAURICEVILLE	LOC	40 47 175 42	49

MAURICEVILLE	LOC	40 47 175 42	51
MAURICEVILLE WEST	LOC	40 46 175 41	48
MAURICEVILLE WEST	LOC	40 46 175 41	49
MAURICEVILLE WEST	LOC	40 46 175 41	51
MAURIKURA STREAM	STRM	39 23 175 05	36
MAURY, MOUNT	MTN	45 20 167 30	97
MAVIS, LAKE	LAKE	42 54 171 39	70
MAVORA, MOUNT	MTN	45 05 168 11	98
MAWARO	LOC	44 17 170 54	87
MAWHAI POINT	PNT	38 11 178 22	25
MAWHERAITI	LOC	42 11 171 43	63
MAWHERAITI	LOC	42 11 171 43	64
MAWHERAITI RIVER	STRM	42 17 171 39	63
MAWHERAITI RIVER	STRM	42 17 171 39	64
MAX, MOUNT	MTN	45 13 167 31	97
MAXIMILIAN RANGE	MTNS	43 27 170 18	74
MAXIMILIAN RANGE	MTNS	43 27 170 18	77
MAXWELL	LOC	39 49 174 52	44
MAXWELL PASS	PASS	41 36 174 00	60
MAY CREEK	STRM	42 45 171 24	69
MAY CREEK	STRM	42 24 172 06	70
MAY HILLS	HILL	44 24 167 58	89
MAY STREAM	STRM	41 46 173 07	66
MAYFAIR	SBRB	39 38 176 52	42
MAYFAIR	SBRB	39 38 176 52	43
MAYFIELD	LOC	43 49 171 25	84
MAYFIELD	LOC	43 49 171 25	87
MAYMORN	LOC	41 07 175 08	52
MAYMORN	LOC	41 07 175 08	53
MAYMORN	LOC	41 07 175 08	55
MAYMORN (TRIG)	PEAK	41 01 175 12	52
MAYMORN (TRIG)	PEAK	41 01 175 12	53
MAYMORN (TRIG)	PEAK	41 01 175 12	55
MAYNE ISLANDS	ISLS	36 25 174 47	11
MAYOR ISLAND	ISLD	37 17 176 15	17
MAYTOWN	LOC	44 43 171 03	93
MCARTHNY HILL (TRIG)	HILL	45 50 170 41	103
MCARTHUR CREEK	STRM	44 16 168 36	88
MCARTHUR TOPS	MTNS	44 04 168 34	88
MCARTHURS HILL (TRIG)	HILL	46 33 169 30	113
MCBAIN CREEK	STRM	43 33 169 58	77
MCCARDELL GLACIER	GLCR	43 48 169 44	76
MCCARDELL GLACIER	GLCR	43 48 169 44	79
MCCARTIE, MOUNT (TRIG)	HILL	40 26 176 25	50
MCCLURE PEAK	PEAK	43 26 170 37	74
MCCLURE PEAK	PEAK	43 26 170 37	77
MCCONNOCHIE CREEK	STRM	42 11 171 56	64
MCCORMICK, MOUNT	MTN	41 18 174 04	54
MCCORMICK, MOUNT	MTN	41 18 174 04	60
MCCORMICK, MOUNT	MTN	41 18 174 04	61
MCCORMICKS CREEK	STRM	45 24 170 38	102
MCCOY STREAM	STRM	43 22 170 47	75
MCCULLAUGH CREEK	STRM	43 52 169 37	76
MCCULLAUGH CREEK	STRM	43 52 169 37	79
MCCULLAUGH, MOUNT	MTN	43 50 169 37	76
MCCULLAUGH, MOUNT	MTN	43 50 169 37	79
MCCULLOUCHS CREEK	STRM	43 10 170 30	74
MCCULLOUGHS CREEK	STRM	43 16 170 25	74
MCDONALD CREEK	STRM	44 52 167 30	94
MCDONALD MOUNT	MTN	43 39 169 47	76
MCDONALD MOUNT	MTN	43 39 169 47	79
MCDONALD, MOUNT	HILL	44 04 170 16	86
MCDONALD, MOUNT (TRIG)	HILL	43 02 172 31	81
MCDONALD, MOUNT (TRIG)	HILL	43 02 172 31	82
MCDONNELL PEAK	PEAK	45 38 167 08	105
MCDOUGALL, MOUNT	MTN	45 01 167 41	94
MCDOUGALL, MOUNT	MTN	45 01 167 41	97
MCFETRICK PEAK	PEAK	43 24 170 19	74
MCFETRICK PEAK	PEAK	43 24 170 19	77
MCGAVOCK, MOUNT (TRIG)	MTN	46 08 166 55	105
MCGAVOCK, MOUNT (TRIG)	MTN	46 08 166 55	104
MCGREGOR, LAKE	LAKE	43 56 170 28	77
MCGREGOR, LAKE	LAKE	43 56 170 28	86
MCGREGOR ROCK	ROCK	36 03 174 37	8
MCGULSH, MOUNT	MTN	44 27 167 55	89
MCHARDIES CREEK	STRM	45 32 169 57	101
MCINTOSH CREEK	STRM	44 15 168 37	88
MCINTOSH, MOUNT	MTN	44 50 168 28	89
MCINTOSH, MOUNT	MTN	44 50 168 28	95
MCISAACS STREAM	STRM	36 52 175 35	13
MCISAACS STREAM	STRM	36 52 175 35	16
MCIVOR CREEK	STRM	45 50 167 38	106
MCIVOR, LAKE	LAKE	45 06 167 31	94
MCIVOR, LAKE	LAKE	45 06 167 31	97
MCIVORS HILL (TRIG)	HILL	45 50 167 40	106
MCKAY BLUFF	CLIF	41 10 173 22	59
MCKAY CREEK	STRM	42 56 170 53	68
MCKAY CREEK	STRM	44 13 168 26	88
MCKAY CREEK	STRM	45 37 169 11	100
MCKAY, LAKE	LAKE	44 51 169 13	91
MCKAY, MOUNT	MTN	42 05 172 44	65
MCKAYS CROSSING	LOC	40 58 174 59	52
MCKAYS CROSSING	LOC	40 58 174 59	55
MCKAYS STREAM	STRM	44 34 170 39	92
MCKELLAR, LAKE	LAKE	44 51 168 09	89
MCKELLAR STREAM	STRM	42 06 172 31	65
MCKELLAR STREAM	STRM	45 59 168 49	110
MCKENZIE BURN	STRM	45 18 167 26	97
MCKENZIE COL	SAD	43 11 170 55	75
MCKENZIE COVE	BAY	36 03 174 32	8
MCKENZIE CREEK	STRM	44 20 168 05	88
MCKENZIE CREEK	STRM	44 20 168 05	89
MCKENZIE FALLS	FALL	44 37 167 45	94
MCKENZIE, MOUNT	MTN	43 57 169 43	79
MCKENZIE, MOUNT (TRIG)	HILL	44 17 168 10	88
MCKENZIE, MOUNT (TRIG)	HILL	44 17 168 10	89
MCKENZIE STREAM	STRM	44 06 170 04	79
MCKENZIES CREEK	STRM	44 40 169 29	91
MCKERROW CREEK	STRM	43 50 169 46	76
MCKERROW CREEK	STRM	43 50 169 46	79
MCKERROW, LAKE	LAKE	44 27 168 03	88
MCKERROW, LAKE	LAKE	44 27 168 03	89
MCKERROW, MOUNT	MTN	43 47 169 57	76
MCKERROW, MOUNT	MTN	43 47 169 57	77
MCKERROW, MOUNT	MTN	43 47 169 57	79
MCKERROW RANGE	MTNS	44 15 169 17	78
MCKERROW (TRIG)	HILL	41 19 174 58	52
MCKERROW (TRIG)	HILL	41 19 174 58	55
MCKINLAYS CREEK	STRM	45 06 168 35	95
MCKINLAYS CREEK	STRM	45 06 168 35	99
MCKINNEY STREAM	STRM	37 32 175 55	17
MCKINNON STREAM	STRM	43 35 170 32	74
MCKINNON STREAM	STRM	43 35 170 32	77
MCLAREN FALLS	LOC	37 48 176 03	20
MCLAREN, MOUNT (TRIG)	HILL	41 05 173 44	60
MCLAREN, MOUNT (TRIG)	HILL	41 05 173 44	61
MCLEAN, MOUNT	HILL	44 01 168 45	88
MCLEANS	LOC	44 48 170 59	93
MCLEANS ISLAND	LOC	43 28 172 28	81
MCLEANS ISLAND	LOC	43 28 172 28	82
MCLEANS ISLAND	LOC	43 28 172 28	85
MCLENNAN CREEK	STRM	43 30 171 26	75
MCLENNAN CREEK	STRM	43 30 171 26	80
MCLENNON CREEK	STRM	43 57 169 31	79
MCLEOD BAY	LOC	35 48 174 30	8
MCLEOD (TRIG)	HILL	40 49 175 38	48
MCLEOD (TRIG)	HILL	40 49 175 38	49
MCLEOD (TRIG)	HILL	40 49 175 38	51
MCMAHON, MOUNT	HILL	41 07 174 06	54
MCMAHON, MOUNT	HILL	41 07 174 06	60
MCMAHON, MOUNT	HILL	41 07 174 06	61
MCMILLAN, MOUNT	MTN	43 26 170 41	74
MCMILLAN STREAM	STRM	42 42 172 06	70
MCMILLAN STREAM	STRM	44 08 170 03	79
MCMURRAY CREEK	STRM	41 57 171 53	63
MCMURRAY CREEK	STRM	41 57 171 53	64
MCNAB	LOC	46 05 169 00	112
MCNABB CREEK	STRM	41 10 172 18	56
MCNABB CREEK	STRM	41 10 172 18	62
MCNEILL (TRIG)	HILL	39 27 176 42	40
MCNEILL (TRIG)	HILL	39 27 176 42	42
MCPHEES ROCK (TRIG)	MTN	45 28 170 00	101
MCRAE, LAKE	LAKE	42 11 173 20	66
MCRAE, MOUNT	MTN	43 26 170 51	75
MCRAE RIVER	STRM	41 51 173 43	67
MCTAGGART CREEK	STRM	43 38 169 49	76
MCTAVISH CREEK	STRM	44 18 168 35	88
MCWHIRTER, MOUNT	MTN	43 08 171 03	75
MEAD	LOC	43 43 172 01	85
MEAD STREAM	STRM	42 01 173 48	67
MEADOW BURN	STRM	45 57 168 49	110
MEADOWBANK	LOC	45 28 170 41	102
MEANY, MOUNT (TRIG)	PEAK	39 18 176 13	39
MEDBURY	LOC	42 52 172 41	71
MEDHURST, MOUNT	MTN	43 18 171 01	75
MEDINA	HSTD	42 41 173 25	72
MEDINA RIVER	STRM	42 41 173 26	72
MEDINA RIVER	STRM	42 41 173 26	73
MEDLEY PEAK	PEAK	45 15 167 03	96
MEDWAY RIVER	STRM	41 46 173 52	67
MEDWAY SADDLE	SAD	41 55 173 46	67
MEEANEE	LOC	39 33 176 53	40
MEEANEE	LOC	39 33 176 53	41
MEEANEE	LOC	39 33 176 53	42
MEEANEE	LOC	39 33 176 53	43
MEGGAT BURN	STRM	45 58 170 07	103
MEIKLEBURN SADDLE	SAD	43 53 170 55	87
MEIKLEJOHNS BAY	BAY	45 01 168 26	95
MEIKLEJOHNS BAY	BAY	45 01 168 26	98
MELINA, MOUNT	MTN	44 27 169 32	91
MELLING	SBRB	41 12 174 54	52
MELLING	SBRB	41 12 174 54	55
MELLISH STREAM	STRM	43 28 171 13	75
MELVILLE COVE	BAY	41 03 174 11	54
MELVILLE COVE	BAY	41 03 174 11	60
MELVILLE COVE	BAY	41 03 174 11	61
MEMPHIS, MOUNT (TRIG)	MTN	45 36 167 10	105
MENDIP HILLS	HSTD	42 38 173 17	72
MENDIP HILLS	HSTD	42 38 173 17	73
MENTEATH, MOUNT	MTN	45 35 167 05	105
MENZIES FERRY	LOC	46 21 168 49	112
MENZIES STREAM	STRM	43 39 172 58	82
MENZIES STREAM	STRM	43 39 172 58	83
MERCER	LOC	37 17 175 03	14
MERCER GLACIER	GLCR	44 23 168 35	88
MERCER GLACIER	GLCR	44 23 168 35	90
MERCURY BAY	BAY	36 49 175 44	16
MERCURY CREEK	STRM	41 20 172 27	62
MERCURY ISLANDS	ISLS	36 38 175 52	16
MERCURY PEAK	PEAK	44 13 168 55	78
MEREDITH, MOUNT (TRIG)	HILL	41 03 176 00	51
MEREMERE	POPL	37 19 175 04	14
MEREMERE	POPL	37 19 175 04	15
MEREMERE	LOC	39 34 174 26	35
MEREMERE	LOC	39 34 174 26	44
MERINO DOWNS	LOC	45 58 169 06	110
MERITA	LOC	34 51 173 26	3
MERRIE RANGE	MTNS	45 42 167 10	105
MERRIJIGS	LOC	42 12 171 54	63
MERRIJIGS	LOC	42 12 171 54	64
MERRIVALE	LOC	46 05 167 52	106
MERTON	LOC	45 38 170 36	102
MERTON CREEK	STRM	46 02 167 43	106
MESOPOTAMIA	HSTD	43 39 170 54	75
MESOPOTAMIA	HSTD	43 39 170 54	87
MESSENGER, MOUNT	MNT	38 54 174 56	26
META, MOUNT	MTN	43 04 171 06	75
META RANGE	MTNS	43 03 171 05	75
META SADDLE	SAD	43 03 171 05	75
METHVEN	POPL	43 38 171 39	80
METHVEN	POPL	43 38 171 39	84
METHVEN	POPL	43 38 171 39	85
MEYBILLE BAY	BAY	42 05 171 21	63
MEYER (TRIG)	HILL	44 47 170 37	92
MEYER (TRIG)	HILL	44 47 170 37	93
MIC MAC CREEK	STRM	43 38 169 30	79
MICAWBER, MOUNT	MTN	42 02 171 38	63
MICAWBER, MOUNT	MTN	42 02 171 38	64
MICHAEL CREEK	STRM	42 46 171 46	70
MICHAEL, MOUNT (TRIG)	HILL	44 03 170 52	87
MICHAEL, MOUNT (TRIG)	PEAK	45 00 169 08	99
MICMAC CREEK	STRM	43 38 169 30	76
MID BURN	STRM	45 10 167 46	94
MID BURN	STRM	45 10 167 46	97
MID DOME (TRIG)	PEAK	45 35 168 32	99
MID HILL	MTN	43 04 171 34	80
MID POINT	PNT	41 02 172 06	56
MID POINT	PNT	41 02 172 06	62
MIDDLE CREEK	STRM	40 34 176 25	50
MIDDLE CREEK	STRM	42 22 173 41	73
MIDDLE CREEK	STRM	43 29 171 27	75
MIDDLE CREEK	STRM	43 29 171 27	80
MIDDLE CREEK	STRM	46 17 168 10	107
MIDDLE FIORD	FIOR	45 12 167 43	97
MIDDLE FIORD (NORTH WEST ARM)	BAY	45 08 167 36	94
MIDDLE FIORD (NORTH WEST ARM)	BAY	45 08 167 36	97
MIDDLE FIORD (SOUTH WEST ARM)	BAY	45 08 167 36	94
MIDDLE FIORD (SOUTH WEST ARM)	BAY	45 08 167 36	97
MIDDLE GABLE	PNT	35 36 174 32	5
MIDDLE GABLE	PNT	35 36 174 32	8
MIDDLE GULLY STREAM	STRM	42 02 173 12	66
MIDDLE HILL	MTN	43 24 171 07	75
MIDDLE HILL (TRIG)	HILL	40 47 176 07	49
MIDDLE HILL (TRIG)	HILL	40 47 176 07	51
MIDDLE HILL (TRIG)	HILL	42 09 173 49	67
MIDDLE HILL (TRIG)	HILL	41 50 174 04	67
MIDDLE ISLAND	ISLD	36 38 175 52	16
MIDDLE ISLAND	ISLD	36 57 176 05	17
MIDDLE PEAK	PEAK	44 46 168 59	90
MIDDLE VALLEY	LOC	44 06 170 55	87
MIDDLEHURST	HSTD	42 00 173 27	66
MIDDLEMARCH	LOC	45 31 170 07	101
MIDDLETON, LAKE	LAKE	44 17 169 51	79
MIDDLETON (TRIG)	HILL	44 16 169 51	79
MIDHIRST	POPL	39 18 174 16	34
MIDHIRST	POPL	39 18 174 16	44
MIDWAY POINT	PNT	37 32 178 13	25
MIHI	LOC	38 29 176 16	29
MIHIANGA STREAM	STRM	38 26 175 43	28
MIHIWAKA	LOC	45 47 170 36	103
MIHIWAKA (TRIG)	HILL	45 47 170 36	103
MIKE, LAKE	LAKE	45 50 166 54	104
MIKE, LAKE	LAKE	45 50 166 54	105
MIKE RIVER	STRM	45 47 166 51	104
MIKE RIVER	STRM	45 47 166 51	105
MIKIMIKI	LOC	40 51 175 37	48
MIKIMIKI	LOC	40 51 175 37	49
MIKIMIKI	LOC	40 51 175 37	51
MIKIMIKI STREAM	STRM	40 51 175 37	48
MIKIMIKI STREAM	STRM	40 51 175 37	49
MIKIMIKI STREAM	STRM	40 51 175 37	51
MIKO	LOC	41 33 171 55	62
MIKONUI RIVER	STRM	42 54 170 46	68
MILBURN	LOC	46 05 170 01	111
MILFORD	SBRB	36 46 174 46	11
MILFORD	SBRB	36 46 174 46	12
MILFORD	LOC	44 15 171 23	84
MILFORD	LOC	44 15 171 23	87
MILFORD SOUND	LOC	44 41 167 56	89
MILFORD SOUND	SND	44 36 167 49	89
MILFORD SOUND	SND	44 36 167 49	94
MILFORD SOUND	LOC	44 41 167 56	94
MILFORD TRACK	TRCK	44 41 167 49	89
MILFORD TRACK	TRCK	44 41 167 49	94
MILL BROOK	STRM	35 59 174 25	7
MILL BROOK	STRM	35 59 174 25	8
MILL CREEK	LOC	36 53 175 40	15
MILL CREEK	LOC	36 53 175 40	16
MILL CREEK	LOC	36 53 175 40	17
MILL CREEK	STRM	41 13 174 45	52
MILL CREEK	STRM	41 13 174 45	55
MILL CREEK	STRM	42 29 171 11	68
MILL CREEK	STRM	42 29 171 11	69
MILL CREEK	STRM	44 29 168 51	90
MILL CREEK	STRM	46 29 169 41	113
MILL STREAM	STRM	41 31 173 52	60
MILLARS FLAT	LOC	45 40 169 25	111
MILLER PEAK (TRIG)	PEAK	45 10 167 35	97
MILLER STREAM	STRM	42 08 173 52	67
MILLER (TRIG)	HILL	40 50 175 57	49
MILLER (TRIG)	HILL	40 50 175 57	51
MILLERS CREEK	STRM	45 01 169 43	100
MILLERTON	LOC	41 38 171 53	62
MILLERTON	LOC	41 38 171 53	63
MILLINGTON, MOUNT	MTN	43 48 169 36	76
MILLINGTON, MOUNT	MTN	43 48 169 36	79
MILLON BAY	BAY	36 24 174 46	11
MILLS CREEK	STRM	42 05 171 37	63
MILLS PEAK	PEAK	44 37 167 56	89
MILLS PEAK	PEAK	44 37 167 56	94
MILLTON STREAM	STRM	43 10 172 04	81
MILLTOWN	LOC	42 48 171 12	68
MILLTOWN	LOC	42 48 171 12	69
MILLTOWN	LOC	43 50 172 16	85
MILNTHORPE	LOC	40 43 172 41	56
MILNTHORPE	LOC	40 43 172 41	57
MILSON	SBRB	40 20 175 37	48
MILSON	SBRB	40 20 175 37	49
MILTON	POPL	46 07 169 58	111
MILTON	POPL	46 07 169 58	113
MIMI RIVER	STRM	38 58 174 26	35
MIMIHA STREAM	STRM	35 26 174 22	5
MIMIHA STREAM	STRM	38 39 176 55	30
MIMIHA STREAM	STRM	39 09 176 39	40
MIMIHAU	LOC	46 19 168 54	110
MIMIHAU	LOC	46 19 168 54	112
MIMIHAU STREAM	STRM	46 19 168 51	110
MIMIHAU STREAM	STRM	46 19 168 51	112
MIMIHAU STREAM (NORTH BRANCH)	STRM	46 18 169 01	110
MIMIHAU STREAM (NORTH BRANCH)	STRM	46 18 169 01	112
MIMIHAU STREAM (SOUTH BRANCH)	STRM	46 18 169 01	110
MIMIHAU STREAM (SOUTH BRANCH)	STRM	46 18 169 01	112
MIMIWHANGATA BAY	BAY	35 26 174 24	5
MINA	LOC	42 49 173 15	72
MINA	LOC	42 49 173 15	73
MINARET BAY	LOC	44 25 169 07	90
MINARET BURN	STRM	44 32 169 05	90
MINARET PEAKS	PEAK	44 26 169 00	90
MINARETS	MTN	43 31 170 16	74
MINARETS	MTN	43 31 170 16	77
MINCHIN, LAKE	LAKE	42 50 171 49	70
MINCHIN PASS	PASS	42 47 171 49	70
MINCHIN STREAM	STRM	42 51 171 49	70
MINDEN	LOC	37 43 176 03	20
MINE POINT	PNT	38 44 175 59	28
MINE POINT	PNT	38 44 175 59	29
MINE POINT	PNT	38 44 175 59	38
MINEHAHA	LOC	41 55 172 12	64
MINER RIVER	STRM	41 24 173 14	59
MINERAL BELT (TRIG)	HILL	40 54 173 49	60
MINERAL BELT (TRIG)	HILL	40 54 173 49	61
MINERS HEAD	HEAD	36 04 175 21	9
MINERVA, LAKE	LAKE	45 20 167 21	96
MINGAIROA (TRIG)	HILL	37 41 177 59	24
MINGAIROA (TRIG)	HILL	37 41 177 59	25
MINGHA RIVER	STRM	42 59 171 36	69
MINGHA RIVER	STRM	42 59 171 36	70
MINGINUI	LOC	38 38 176 44	30
MINGINUI STREAM	STRM	38 39 176 43	30
MINIHA STREAM	STRM	37 52 176 42	21
MINIHA STREAM	STRM	37 52 176 42	22
MINIM MERE	LAKE	44 05 168 47	78
MINOR PEAK	PEAK	44 56 168 28	89
MINOR PEAK	PEAK	44 56 168 28	95
MINOR PEAK	PEAK	44 56 168 28	98
MINOS	MTN	44 37 168 15	89
MINZION BURN	STRM	45 41 169 27	111
MIRAMAR	SBRB	41 19 174 49	52
MIRAMAR	SBRB	41 19 174 49	55
MIRANDA	LOC	37 11 175 19	13
MIRANDA	LOC	37 11 175 19	15
MIRANDA STREAM	STRM	37 11 175 19	13
MIRANDA STREAM	STRM	37 11 175 19	15
MIRFIN CREEK	STRM	42 11 171 36	63
MIROMIRO (TRIG)	MTN	42 29 172 40	71
MIROROA	HILL	39 26 176 23	39
MIROROA	HILL	39 26 176 23	40
MIRZA	LOC	41 52 174 07	67
MIRZA CREEK	STRM	41 53 174 08	67
MISERY, MOUNT	HILL	41 53 173 52	67
MISERY, MOUNT	MTN	42 58 170 59	68
MISERY, MOUNT	MTN	42 58 170 59	69
MISERY, MOUNT	HILL	43 29 171 51	80
MISERY, MOUNT	HILL	43 29 171 51	81
MISERY, MOUNT	MTN	43 51 170 43	86
MISERY, MOUNT (TRIG)	MTN	43 03 171 42	80
MISERY, MOUNT (TRIG)	HILL	38 30 174 41	26
MISERY, MOUNT (TRIG)	HILL	37 48 176 11	20
MISERY, MOUNT (TRIG)	HILL	37 48 176 11	21
MISERY, MOUNT (TRIG)	HILL	40 50 176 07	49
MISERY, MOUNT (TRIG)	HILL	40 50 176 07	50
MISERY, MOUNT (TRIG)	HILL	40 50 176 07	51
MISERY, MOUNT (TRIG)	HILL	41 18 174 40	52
MISERY, MOUNT (TRIG)	HILL	41 18 174 40	55
MISERY, MOUNT (TRIG)	HILL	40 32 172 37	57
MISERY, MOUNT (TRIG)	MTN	44 45 169 41	91
MISERY, MOUNT (TRIG)	HILL	46 11 169 55	111
MISERY, MOUNT (TRIG)	HILL	46 11 169 55	113
MISERY STREAM	STRM	41 55 173 03	66
MISSION BAY	SBRB	36 51 174 50	11
MISSION BAY	SBRB	36 51 174 50	12
MISSION BAY	BAY	38 54 175 56	28
MISSION BAY	BAY	38 54 175 56	29
MISSION BAY	BAY	38 54 175 56	38
MISSION BUSH	LOC	37 13 174 44	12
MISSION BUSH	LOC	37 13 174 44	14
MISTAKE CREEK	STRM	43 15 171 14	75
MISTAKE CREEK	STRM	44 55 168 02	89
MISTAKE HILL	MTN	43 12 171 12	75
MISTAKE PEAK (TRIG)	PEAK	43 47 170 30	77
MISTAKE PEAK (TRIG)	PEAK	43 47 170 30	86
MISTAKE RIVER	STRM	43 50 170 30	77
MISTAKE RIVER	STRM	43 50 170 30	86
MISTY PEAK	PEAK	43 38 169 52	76
MISTY PEAK	PEAK	44 06 169 06	78
MISTY PEAK	PEAK	43 38 169 52	79
MISTY RIVER	STRM	45 14 167 12	96
MITCHAM	LOC	43 45 171 52	84
MITCHEL CREEK	STRM	42 07 172 13	64
MITCHELL, MOUNT	MTN	43 29 170 04	76
MITCHELL, MOUNT	MTN	43 29 170 04	77
MITCHELL, MOUNT (TRIG)	HILL	39 52 175 16	45
MITCHELLS	LOC	42 38 171 25	69
MITCHELSON, MOUNT	MTN	44 48 167 53	89
MITCHELSON, MOUNT	MTN	44 48 167 53	94
MITIHAU (TRIG)	HILL	39 33 175 20	36
MITIMITI	LOC	35 26 173 16	3
MITIMITI STREAM	STRM	37 22 174 54	14
MITITAI	LOC	36 01 173 56	7
MITRE CREEK	STRM	44 56 169 03	90
MITRE PEAK	PEAK	42 00 173 36	66
MITRE PEAK	PEAK	44 38 167 51	89
MITRE PEAK	PEAK	44 38 167 51	94
MITRE PEAK (TRIG)	PEAK	42 12 172 55	65
MITRE ROCKS	ROCK	38 23 178 20	32
MITRE (TRIG)	PEAK	40 48 175 27	48
MIZAR, MOUNT (TRIG)	MTN	42 49 172 24	71
MIZZEN PEAK	PEAK	42 37 172 49	71
MIZZEN PEAK	PEAK	42 37 172 49	72
MOA CREEK	STRM	45 10 169 40	100
MOA CREEK	LOC	45 12 169 39	100
MOA CREEK	STRM	46 18 167 56	108
MOA CREEK	STRM	46 18 167 56	109
MOA HILL	MTN	43 06 171 18	75
MOA HILL	MTN	43 06 171 18	80
MOA STREAM	STRM	43 07 171 20	75
MOA STREAM	STRM	43 07 171 20	80
MOAKAUTEURE STREAM	STRM	38 25 175 57	28
MOAKAUTEURE STREAM	STRM	38 25 175 57	29
MOAKURARUA STREAM	STRM	38 03 175 12	18
MOANA	LOC	42 35 171 29	69
MOANA (LAKE BRUNNER)	LAKE	42 37 171 27	69
MOANA (TRIG)	HILL	39 35 174 42	35
MOANA (TRIG)	HILL	39 35 174 42	44
MOANARUA ISLAND	ISLD	35 21 174 23	5
MOANATUATUA SWAMP	SWMP	37 57 175 23	19
MOANUI STREAM	STRM	38 25 177 21	31
MOANUI (TRIG)	MTN	38 22 177 24	31
MOAWHANGO	LOC	39 35 175 52	37
MOAWHANGO	LOC	39 35 175 52	46
MOAWHANGO, LAKE	LAKE	39 24 175 45	37
MOAWHANGO RIVER	STRM	39 42 175 56	46
MOAWHANGO RIVER, WEST BRANCH	STRM	39 20 175 53	37
MODIC CREEK	STRM	43 55 169 25	78
MOEANGIANGI RIVER	STRM	39 15 177 01	40
MOEANGIANGI RIVER	STRM	39 15 177 01	41
MOEATOA	LOC	38 23 174 44	26
MOEAWATEA	LOC	39 32 174 39	35
MOEAWATEA	LOC	39 32 174 39	44
MOEAWATEA STREAM	STRM	39 33 174 38	35
MOEAWATEA STREAM	STRM	39 33 174 38	44
MOEHAU	LOC	35 27 173 37	4
MOEHAU	LOC	35 27 173 37	6
MOEHAU RANGE	MTNS	36 32 175 24	9
MOEHAU RANGE	MTNS	36 32 175 24	16
MOEMOE (TRIG)	PEAK	39 33 176 06	39
MOENGAWAHINE	LOC	35 39 174 03	5
MOENGAWAHINE	LOC	35 39 174 03	7
MOENGAWAHINE STREAM	STRM	35 38 174 05	5
MOENGAWAHINE STREAM	STRM	35 38 174 05	7
MOENUI	LOC	41 17 173 48	60
MOENUI	LOC	41 17 173 48	61
MOERAKI	LOC	45 21 170 49	102
MOERAKI HILL (TRIG)	HILL	43 44 169 20	78
MOERAKI, LAKE	LAKE	43 44 169 17	78
MOERAKI RIVER (BLUE RIVER)	STRM	43 44 169 18	78
MOERAKI (TRIG)	HILL	45 23 170 51	102
MOERANGI	LOC	38 00 174 56	18
MOERANGI	LOC	38 54 175 36	27
MOERANGI	LOC	38 54 175 36	28
MOERANGI	LOC	38 54 175 36	38
MOERANGI STREAM	STRM	38 45 176 51	30
MOERANGI (TRIG)	MTN	38 44 176 43	30
MOEREWA	LOC	35 08 174 01	4
MOEREWA	LOC	35 08 174 01	5
MOEROA	LOC	39 27 174 38	35
MOEROA	LOC	39 27 174 38	44
MOETAHANGA (TRIG)	HILL	38 19 175 38	28
MOETANGI STREAM	STRM	35 26 173 17	3
MOETANGI STREAM	STRM	35 26 173 17	6
MOEWAKA STREAM	STRM	37 23 174 49	14
MOEWHARE	LOC	35 52 174 15	7
MOEWHARE	LOC	35 52 174 15	8
MOFFAT, MOUNT	MTN	43 28 170 27	74
MOFFAT, MOUNT	MTN	43 28 170 27	77
MOFFAT PEAK	PEAK	45 01 168 08	98
MOFFAT STREAM	STRM	44 23 170 24	92
MOHAKA	LOC	39 07 177 12	41
MOHAKA RIVER	STRM	39 08 177 12	41
MOHAKATINO	HSTD	38 45 174 42	26
MOHAKATINO RIVER	STRM	38 44 174 36	26

MOHAU STREAM	STRM	37 36 178 02	25
MOHEI BAY	BAY	35 25 174 22	5
MOHI MOUNTAIN (TRIG)	HILL	36 37 175 49	16
MOHINUI (TRIG)	HILL	36 14 174 23	7
MOHINUI (TRIG)	HILL	36 14 174 23	8
MOHINUI (TRIG)	HILL	36 14 174 23	10
MOHINUI (TRIG)	HILL	36 14 174 23	11
MOHUITI	LOC	35 16 173 29	3
MOHUNGA (TRIG)	HILL	36 08 175 20	9
MOIKAU (TRIG)	HILL	41 25 175 15	53
MOIRS HILL (TRIG)	HILL	36 28 174 36	11
MOKAI	LOC	38 32 175 54	28
MOKAI	LOC	38 32 175 54	29
MOKAI PATEA RANGE	MTNS	39 45 176 06	47
MOKAIHAHA STREAM	STRM	38 09 175 58	20
MOKARA	LOC	39 08 176 54	40
MOKARA	LOC	39 08 176 54	41
MOKAU	LOC	35 25 174 20	5
MOKAU	LOC	38 42 174 37	26
MOKAU RIVER	STRM	38 34 174 54	26
MOKAU STREAM	STRM	35 19 174 21	5
MOKAU STREAM	STRM	38 44 177 06	30
MOKAU STREAM	STRM	38 44 177 06	31
MOKAUITI	LOC	38 35 175 10	27
MOKAUITI STREAM	STRM	38 33 174 53	26
MOKE CREEK	STRM	44 58 168 38	95
MOKE CREEK	STRM	44 58 168 38	99
MOKE CREEK (WEST BRANCH)	STRM	45 00 168 34	95
MOKE CREEK (WEST BRANCH)	STRM	45 00 168 34	99
MOKE, LAKE	LAKE	45 00 168 34	95
MOKE, LAKE	LAKE	45 00 168 34	99
MOKENO, LAKE	LAKE	36 21 174 04	10
MOKI STREAM	STRM	38 59 174 37	35
MOKIHINUI	LOC	41 32 171 58	62
MOKIHINUI RIVER	STRM	41 31 171 56	62
MOKIHINUI RIVER, NORTH BRANCH	STRM	41 33 172 11	62
MOKIHINUI RIVER, SOUTH BRANCH	STRM	41 33 172 11	62
MOKIHINUI RIVER, SOUTH BRANCH	STRM	41 40 172 09	64
MOKOHINAU ISLANDS	ISLS	35 55 175 06	9
MOKOIA	LOC	39 38 174 23	35
MOKOIA	LOC	39 38 174 23	44
MOKOIA ISLAND	ISLD	38 05 176 17	20
MOKOIA ISLAND	ISLD	38 05 176 17	21
MOKOIWI STREAM	STRM	37 51 178 08	25
MOKOMOKO INLET	BAY	46 31 168 17	109
MOKOMOKOMA STREAM	STRM	38 59 176 40	40
MOKOMOKONUI RIVER	STRM	39 03 176 35	39
MOKOMOKONUI RIVER	STRM	39 03 176 35	40
MOKONUIARANGI (TRIG)	HILL	38 33 177 32	31
MOKOOTIPI (TRIG)	HILL	38 07 175 09	19
MOKORETA	LOC	46 25 169 04	112
MOKORETA RIVER	STRM	46 22 168 49	112
MOKORETA (TRIG)	HILL	46 20 169 08	112
MOKORO STREAM	STRM	39 03 176 24	39
MOKORO STREAM	STRM	39 03 176 24	40
MOKOROA STREAM	STRM	36 53 174 27	10
MOKOROA STREAM	STRM	36 53 174 27	11
MOKOROA STREAM	STRM	36 53 174 27	12
MOKOTUA	LOC	46 28 168 33	109
MOKOTUA STREAM	STRM	46 29 168 23	109
MOKOTUNA STREAM	STRM	35 27 174 13	5
MOKUKU STREAM	STRM	37 44 177 45	24
MOLE HILL CREEK	STRM	45 03 170 38	102
MOLE HILL (TRIG)	HILL	42 02 173 56	67
MOLE HILL (TRIG)	HILL	45 03 170 37	102
MOLE HILL (TRIG)	HILL	45 46 169 13	110
MOLE SADDLE	SAD	41 57 172 35	65
MOLE STREAM	STRM	42 00 172 30	65
MOLE, THE (TRIG)	HILL	45 53 168 07	106
MOLE, THE (TRIG)	HILL	45 53 168 07	107
MOLESWORTH	LOC	36 06 174 33	8
MOLESWORTH	HSTD	42 05 173 15	66
MOLESWORTH STREAM	STRM	42 05 173 16	66
MOLLOY BAY	BAY	42 35 171 29	69
MOLLOYS LOOKOUT (TRIG)	HILL	42 31 171 27	69
MOLLY CREEK	STRM	43 21 170 00	76
MOLLY CREEK	STRM	43 21 170 00	77
MOLYNEUX BAY	BAY	46 22 169 50	113
MOLYNEUX, PORT	LOC	46 22 169 47	113
MOMO (TRIG)	HILL	39 35 175 21	36
MOMONANUI STREAM	STRM	39 04 176 35	39
MOMONANUI STREAM	STRM	39 04 176 35	40
MONA BAY	BAY	36 09 175 27	9
MONA (TRIG)	HILL	38 54 175 04	26
MONA (TRIG)	HILL	38 54 175 04	27
MONASTARY PEAK	PEAK	43 41 170 15	77
MONASTARY PEAK	PEAK	43 41 170 15	86
MONAVALE	LOC	37 56 175 26	19
MONAVALE	LOC	44 18 170 52	87
MONCRIEFF COL	SAD	44 24 168 46	90
MONEYMORE	LOC	46 10 169 55	111
MONEYMORE	LOC	46 10 169 55	113
MONK, LAKE	LAKE	46 01 166 58	104
MONK, LAKE	LAKE	46 01 166 58	105
MONKEY FACE	HILL	42 26 173 25	72
MONKEY FACE	HILL	42 26 173 25	73
MONKEY ISLAND	ISLD	46 18 167 43	108
MONOA	HILL	35 23 174 17	5
MONOTIS, MOUNT	MTN	42 41 171 52	70
MONOWAI	LOC	45 47 167 37	106
MONOWAI, LAKE	LAKE	45 54 167 25	105
MONOWAI RIVER	STRM	45 49 167 31	105
MONOWAI RIVER	STRM	45 49 167 31	106
MONRO, MOUNT	MTN	41 55 173 45	67
MONRO PEAK	PEAK	43 51 169 27	76
MONS BOREAS (TRIG)	MTN	42 46 172 24	71
MONS SEX MILLIA (TRIG)	PEAK	42 32 172 27	71
MONTALTO	LOC	43 48 171 21	84
MONTALTO	LOC	43 48 171 21	87
MONTGOMERIE RIVER	STRM	42 09 172 00	64
MONTGOMERY, MOUNT	MTN	43 46 169 59	76
MONTGOMERY, MOUNT	MTN	43 46 169 59	77
MONTGOMERY, MOUNT	MTN	43 46 169 59	79
MONTROSE	HSTD	42 42 172 47	71
MONTROSE	HSTD	42 42 172 47	72
MONTSERRAT (TRIG)	HILL	43 04 172 56	82
MONUMENT	HILL	42 31 173 25	72
MONUMENT	HILL	42 31 173 25	73
MONUMENT SADDLE	SAD	44 51 168 31	90
MONUMENT SADDLE	SAD	44 51 168 31	95
MOONLIGHT	LOC	45 25 170 20	101
MOONLIGHT CREEK	STRM	44 58 168 38	90
MOONLIGHT CREEK	STRM	44 58 168 38	95
MOONLIGHT SADDLE	SAD	44 52 168 31	89
MOONLIGHT SADDLE	SAD	44 52 168 31	90
MOONLIGHT SADDLE	SAD	44 52 168 31	95
MOONLIGHT SADDLE	SAD	45 50 167 50	106
MOONLIGHT STREAM	STRM	43 44 170 51	87
MOONRAKER	MTN	44 19 168 45	88
MOONRAKER	MTN	44 19 168 45	90
MOORCOCK SADDLE	SAD	39 58 176 09	47
MOORES TAIPO (TRIG)	HILL	41 01 175 57	51
MOORHOUSE RANGE	MTNS	43 42 171 11	87
MORAINE CREEK	STRM	43 11 171 09	75
MORAINE CREEK	STRM	44 41 168 07	89
MORAN CREEK	STRM	41 19 172 40	58
MORATTI (TRIG)	HILL	39 11 174 19	34
MORATTI (TRIG)	HILL	39 11 174 19	35
MOREHUREHU, LAKE	LAKE	34 39 173 00	2
MOREMONUI GULLY	GLLY	35 55 173 42	6
MORERE	LOC	38 59 177 47	33
MORETON, LAKE	LAKE	44 41 167 44	94
MORETON, MOUNT	MTN	43 21 170 36	74
MORGAN, LAKE	LAKE	42 40 171 43	70
MORGAN RANGE	MTNS	41 09 172 20	56
MORGAN RANGE	MTNS	41 09 172 20	62
MORGAN RIVER	STRM	42 41 171 38	70
MORGAN TARN	LAKE	41 57 171 36	63
MORINUI STREAM	STRM	39 07 175 08	36
MORINUI (TRIG)	HILL	39 14 175 08	36
MORLAND	HSTD	41 03 175 49	51
MORLEY STREAM	STRM	45 56 167 57	106
MORLEY STREAM	STRM	45 56 167 57	107
MORLEY (TRIG)	HILL	45 50 167 58	106
MORLEY (TRIG)	HILL	45 50 167 58	107
MORNA	HSTD	42 41 172 49	71
MORNA	HSTD	42 41 172 49	72
MORNINGTON	SBRB	45 53 170 28	103
MORRINSVILLE	POPL	37 39 175 32	19
MORRIS, MOUNT	MTN	41 52 173 07	66
MORRIS TARN	LAKE	42 37 172 15	70
MORRISON CREEK	STRM	42 05 171 38	63
MORRISON CREEK	STRM	42 05 171 38	64
MORRISON, MOUNT	MTN	42 49 171 51	70
MORRISON (TRIG)	HILL	41 09 175 30	53
MORRISONS	LOC	45 16 170 29	102
MORRISONS BUSH	LOC	41 07 175 26	53
MORSE RIVER	STRM	43 44 169 39	76
MORSE RIVER	STRM	43 44 169 39	79
MORTON JONES, CAPE	CAPE	34 08 172 10	2
MORTON MAINS	LOC	46 21 168 39	112
MORTON STREAM	STRM	44 26 170 37	92
MORVEN	LOC	44 49 171 07	93
MOSGIEL	USAT	45 53 170 21	103
MOSQUITO CREEK	STRM	42 33 171 16	68
MOSQUITO CREEK	STRM	42 33 171 16	69
MOSQUITO HILL (TRIG)	HILL	43 53 169 05	78
MOSS BURN	STRM	45 42 168 14	107
MOSS PASS	PASS	42 04 172 38	65
MOSSBURN	LOC	45 40 168 14	107
MOSSES DIP	SAD	41 42 173 22	66
MOSSY CREEK	STRM	42 15 171 43	63
MOSSY CREEK	STRM	42 15 171 43	64
MOSSY STREAM	STRM	41 44 171 55	64
MOTAIREHE	LOC	36 07 175 23	9
MOTAIREHE STREAM	STRM	36 07 175 23	9
MOTAKOTAKO	LOC	37 56 174 50	18
MOTATAPU, MOUNT	MTN	44 44 168 50	90
MOTATAPU, MOUNT	MTN	44 44 168 50	95
MOTATAPU RIVER	STRM	44 36 168 57	90
MOTATAPU RIVER (NORTH BRANCH)	STRM	44 45 168 55	90
MOTATAPU RIVER (NORTH BRANCH)	STRM	44 45 168 55	95
MOTATAPU RIVER (SOUTH BRANCH)	STRM	44 45 168 55	90
MOTATAPU RIVER (SOUTH BRANCH)	STRM	44 45 168 55	95
MOTATAU	LOC	35 29 174 02	4
MOTATAU	LOC	35 29 174 02	5
MOTATAU (TRIG)	HILL	35 36 174 02	4
MOTATAU (TRIG)	HILL	35 36 174 02	5
MOTATAU (TRIG)	HILL	35 36 174 02	7
MOTEA	LOC	40 19 176 15	50
MOTEO	LOC	39 31 176 46	40
MOTEO	LOC	39 31 176 46	42
MOTERE (TRIG)	HILL	38 46 175 30	27
MOTERE (TRIG)	HILL	38 46 175 30	38
MOTITI ISLAND	ISLD	37 38 176 25	21
MOTITI ISLAND	ISLD	37 38 176 25	22
MOTITI (TRIG)	HILL	39 02 175 55	37
MOTITI (TRIG)	HILL	39 02 175 55	38
MOTOA STREAM	STRM	39 35 175 06	36
MOTU	LOC	38 15 177 33	31
MOTU KAPITI ISLAND	ISLD	35 28 174 44	5
MOTU RIMU	LOC	46 28 168 26	109
MOTU RIVER	STRM	37 52 177 36	24
MOTUAIURI ISLAND	ISLD	38 04 178 22	25
MOTUANAURU ISLAND	ISLD	41 02 173 39	60
MOTUARA ISLAND	ISLD	41 05 174 16	54
MOTUARA ISLAND	ISLD	41 05 174 16	61
MOTUARIKI ISLAND	ISLD	43 56 170 31	77
MOTUARIKI ISLAND	ISLD	43 56 170 31	86
MOTUAROHIA ISLAND	ISLD	35 14 174 10	4
MOTUAROHIA ISLAND	ISLD	35 14 174 10	5
MOTUARUHE STREAM	STRM	39 36 175 09	36
MOTUEKA	TOWN	41 07 173 01	57
MOTUEKA	TOWN	41 07 173 01	58
MOTUEKA	TOWN	41 07 173 01	59
MOTUEKA ISLAND	ISLD	36 49 175 48	16
MOTUEKA RIVER	STRM	41 05 173 01	57
MOTUEKA RIVER	STRM	41 05 173 01	58
MOTUEKA RIVER	STRM	41 05 173 01	59
MOTUEKAITI ISLAND	ISLD	34 59 173 52	4
MOTUHAKU ISLAND	ISLD	36 10 175 17	9
MOTUHARAKEKE ISLAND	ISLD	35 00 173 58	4
MOTUHOA ISLAND	ISLD	37 39 176 04	20
MOTUHOA ISLAND	ISLD	37 39 176 04	21
MOTUHORA ISLAND	ISLD	37 51 176 58	22
MOTUHORA ISLAND	ISLD	37 51 176 58	23
MOTUHUA POINT	PNT	36 43 175 45	16
MOTUIHE ISLAND	ISLD	36 49 174 57	11
MOTUIHE ISLAND	ISLD	36 49 174 57	12
MOTUIWI ISLAND	ISLD	35 03 173 56	4
MOTUKAHA ISLAND	ISLD	37 38 176 26	22
MOTUKAHAKAHA BAY	BAY	34 57 173 39	4
MOTUKAHAUA	ISLD	36 39 175 22	13
MOTUKAHAUA	ISLD	36 39 175 22	16
MOTUKAIKA	LOC	44 24 170 59	93
MOTUKAIKA RIVER	STRM	44 24 171 00	93
MOTUKARAKA	LOC	35 22 173 30	3
MOTUKARAKA	LOC	35 22 173 30	6
MOTUKARAKA ISLAND	ISLD	36 53 174 59	12
MOTUKARAMARAMA	ISLD	36 41 175 24	13
MOTUKARAMARAMA	ISLD	36 41 175 24	16
MOTUKARARA	LOC	43 44 172 35	83
MOTUKARARA	LOC	43 44 172 35	85
MOTUKAUERE ISLAND	ISLD	37 28 175 04	14
MOTUKAURI	LOC	35 24 173 27	3
MOTUKAURI	LOC	35 24 173 27	6
MOTUKAURI ISLAND	ISLD	35 20 174 23	5
MOTUKAWAITI ISLAND	ISLD	35 02 173 57	4
MOTUKAWANUI ISLAND	ISLD	35 00 173 56	4
MOTUKAWAO GROUP	ISLS	36 41 175 23	13
MOTUKAWAO GROUP	ISLS	36 41 175 23	16
MOTUKEHUA ISLAND	ISLD	35 24 174 22	5
MOTUKEO (TRIG)	HILL	38 36 178 04	32
MOTUKETEKETE ISLAND	ISLD	36 28 174 48	11
MOTUKIEKIE ISLAND	ISLD	35 13 174 12	5
MOTUKIEKIE ROCKS	ROCK	42 20 171 16	68
MOTUKIEKIE ROCKS	ROCK	42 20 171 16	69
MOTUKIORE	LOC	35 24 173 34	3
MOTUKIORE	LOC	35 24 173 34	4
MOTUKIORE	LOC	35 24 173 34	6
MOTUKOPAKE ISLAND	ISLD	36 45 175 25	13
MOTUKOPAKE ISLAND	ISLD	36 45 175 25	16
MOTUKORANGA ISLAND	ISLD	36 45 175 49	16
MOTUKORARI ISLAND	ISLD	35 13 174 19	5
MOTUKORUENGA ISLAND	ISLD	36 44 175 50	16
MOTUKORURE ISLAND	ISLD	36 48 175 46	16
MOTUKOTARE ISLAND	ISLD	37 41 177 43	24
MOTUKUMARA ROCK	ROCK	35 14 174 19	5
MOTUMAIRE ISLAND	ISLD	35 16 174 06	4
MOTUMAIRE ISLAND	ISLD	35 16 174 06	5
MOTUMAOHO	LOC	37 41 175 28	19
MOTUMATAI (TRIG)	PEAK	39 19 175 59	37
MOTUMATAI (TRIG)	PEAK	39 19 175 59	38
MOTUMATAI (TRIG)	HILL	41 05 175 49	51
MOTUMATE STREAM	STRM	38 25 177 58	32
MOTUNAU	LOC	42 58 172 59	72
MOTUNAU BEACH	LOC	43 07 173 04	82
MOTUNAU ISLAND	ISLD	43 04 173 04	82
MOTUNAU ROCKS	ROCK	38 14 174 43	18
MOTUNUI	LOC	39 00 174 18	34
MOTUNUI	LOC	39 00 174 18	35
MOTUNUI ISLAND	ISLD	37 47 177 39	24
MOTUNUIA ISLAND	ISLD	37 27 175 11	15
MOTUOAPA	LOC	38 56 175 53	37
MOTUOAPA	LOC	38 56 175 53	38
MOTUOAPA PENINSULA	PEN	38 56 175 52	37
MOTUOAPA PENINSULA	PEN	38 56 175 52	38
MOTUOPAO ISLAND	ISLD	34 28 172 38	2
MOTUORA ISLAND	ISLD	36 30 174 47	11
MOTUOROI ISLAND	ISLD	38 15 178 20	32
MOTUORUHI	ISLD	36 45 175 24	13
MOTUORUHI	ISLD	36 45 175 24	16
MOTUOTAU ISLAND	ISLD	37 38 176 12	20
MOTUPIA ISLAND	ISLD	34 37 172 48	2
MOTUPIKO	LOC	41 27 172 49	58
MOTUPIKO RIVER	STRM	41 27 172 50	58
MOTUPIKO RIVER	STRM	41 39 172 50	65
MOTUPIPI	LOC	40 51 172 51	57
MOTUPOTAKA	ISLD	36 38 175 22	13
MOTUPOTAKA	ISLD	36 38 175 22	16
MOTUPUHA (TRIG)	HILL	39 29 175 59	37
MOTUPUTA ISLAND	ISLD	37 37 176 27	22
MOTUREKAREKA ISLAND	ISLD	36 29 174 47	11
MOTUREMU ISLAND	ISLD	36 26 174 23	10
MOTUREMU ISLAND	ISLD	36 26 174 23	11
MOTUREWA	ISLD	35 43 174 34	5
MOTUREWA	ISLD	35 43 174 34	8
MOTURIKI ISLAND	ISLD	37 38 176 11	20
MOTUROA ISLAND	ISLD	34 46 173 21	3
MOTUROA ISLAND	ISLD	35 13 174 05	4
MOTUROA ISLAND	ISLD	35 13 174 05	5
MOTUROA ISLAND	ISLD	36 17 174 16	10
MOTUROA ISLANDS	ISLS	34 47 173 22	3
MOTUROA (TRIG)	HILL	39 52 176 39	42
MOTUROA (TRIG)	HILL	39 52 176 39	43
MOTUROA (TRIG)	HILL	39 52 176 39	47
MOTURUA	ISLD	36 42 175 24	13
MOTURUA	ISLD	36 42 175 24	16
MOTURUA ISLAND	ISLD	35 14 174 11	5
MOTURUNA CREEK	STRM	35 20 173 32	3
MOTUTAIKO ISLAND	ISLD	36 13 175 17	9
MOTUTAIKO ISLAND	ISL	38 51 175 57	28
MOTUTAIKO ISLAND	ISL	38 51 175 57	29
MOTUTAIKO ISLAND	ISL	38 51 175 57	38
MOTUTAKAPOU (TRIG)	HILL	38 08 175 30	19
MOTUTAKAPUPU ISLAND	ISLD	34 59 173 58	4
MOTUTANGI	LOC	34 53 173 09	2
MOTUTANGI	LOC	34 53 173 09	3
MOTUTANGI SWAMP	SWMP	34 54 173 11	3
MOTUTAPERE	HILL	37 07 175 41	15
MOTUTAPERE	HILL	37 07 175 41	17
MOTUTAPERE	HILL	37 38 175 50	20
MOTUTAPERE ISLAND	ISLD	34 58 173 56	4
MOTUTAPERE ISLAND	ISLD	36 47 175 26	13
MOTUTAPERE ISLAND	ISLD	36 47 175 26	16
MOTUTAPU ISLAND	ISLD	36 46 174 55	11
MOTUTAPU ISLAND	ISLD	36 46 174 55	12
MOTUTARA BAY	BAY	34 52 173 17	3
MOTUTARA ISLAND	ISLD	35 23 174 23	5
MOTUTARA POINT	PNT	35 39 174 32	5
MOTUTARA POINT	PNT	35 31 174 29	5
MOTUTARA POINT	PNT	35 39 174 32	8
MOTUTARA ROCK	ROCK	35 11 174 18	5
MOTUTERE POINT	PNT	38 53 175 57	28
MOTUTERE POINT	PNT	38 53 175 57	29
MOTUTERE POINT	PNT	38 53 175 57	38
MOTUTERE (TRIG)	HILL	36 50 175 34	13
MOTUTERE (TRIG)	HILL	36 50 175 34	16
MOTUTI	LOC	35 23 173 26	3
MOTUTI	LOC	35 23 173 26	6
MOTUTOA	LOC	35 30 173 26	6
MOTUTOHE ISLAND	ISLD	35 29 174 28	5
MOTUWAIREKA STREAM	STRM	41 05 176 05	51
MOTUWI	ISLD	36 41 175 24	13
MOTUWI	ISLD	36 41 175 24	16
MOUAT LAKE	LAKE	46 02 167 01	105
MOUATS SADDLE	SAD	46 31 169 27	113
MOUKAHU (TRIG)	HILL	39 39 175 01	45
MOUMAHAKI, LAKE	LAKE	39 41 174 40	44
MOUMAHAKI STREAM	STRM	39 47 174 44	44
MOUMOUKAI	LOC	37 06 175 09	13
MOUMOUKAI	LOC	37 06 175 09	15
MOUMOUKAI (TRIG)	HILL	38 58 177 46	33
MOUNT ALBERT	SBRB	36 53 174 43	11
MOUNT ALBERT	SBRB	36 53 174 43	12
MOUNT ALGIDUS	HSTD	43 15 171 22	75
MOUNT ALGIDUS	HSTD	43 15 171 22	80
MOUNT ALLAN	RSTN	45 45 170 21	103
MOUNT ASPIRING NATIONAL PARK	PARK	44 08 169 08	78
MOUNT ASPIRING NATIONAL PARK	PARK	44 31 168 30	88
MOUNT ASPIRING NATIONAL PARK	PARK	44 31 168 30	89
MOUNT BENGER	HSTD	42 51 172 52	71
MOUNT BENGER	HSTD	42 51 172 52	72
MOUNT BIGGS	LOC	40 12 175 29	45
MOUNT BIGGS	LOC	40 12 175 29	46
MOUNT BROWN CREEK	STRM	42 57 171 54	70
MOUNT BRUCE	LOC	40 45 175 36	48
MOUNT BRUCE	LOC	40 45 175 36	49
MOUNT BRUCE	LOC	40 45 175 36	51
MOUNT CAMPBELL CREEK	STRM	45 20 169 28	100
MOUNT CARGILL	LOC	45 48 170 34	103
MOUNT COOK	POPL	43 44 170 06	76
MOUNT COOK	LOC	43 51 170 10	77
MOUNT COOK	POPL	43 44 170 06	77
MOUNT COOK	POPL	43 44 170 06	79
MOUNT COOK	LOC	43 51 170 10	86
MOUNT COOK	POPL	43 44 170 06	86
MOUNT COOK NATIONAL PARK	PARK	43 36 170 17	74
MOUNT COOK NATIONAL PARK	PARK	43 36 170 17	77
MOUNT CREIGHTON	LOC	45 00 168 26	95
MOUNT CREIGHTON	LOC	45 00 168 26	98
MOUNT CURL	HSTD	39 57 175 30	45
MOUNT CURL	HSTD	39 57 175 30	46
MOUNT EDEN	SBRB	36 53 174 46	11
MOUNT EDEN	SBRB	36 53 174 46	12
MOUNT FURNEAUX	HSTD	42 23 173 31	73
MOUNT FYFFE	HSTD	42 21 173 36	73
MOUNT GERALD CREEK	STRM	43 47 170 33	77
MOUNT GERALD CREEK	STRM	43 47 170 33	86
MOUNT HILTON	HSTD	42 58 172 32	71
MOUNT HOLDSWORTH LODGE	BLDG	40 54 175 28	48
MOUNT HUTT	LOC	43 31 171 37	80
MOUNT HUTT RANGE	MTNS	43 29 171 31	80
MOUNT MAUNGANUI	USAT	37 39 176 12	20
MOUNT MAUNGANUI	USAT	37 39 176 12	21
MOUNT PALM	HSTD	42 43 173 03	72
MOUNT PEEL	HSTD	43 50 171 15	87
MOUNT PISA	LOC	44 56 169 16	91
MOUNT PLEASANT	LOC	41 20 173 58	54
MOUNT PLEASANT	LOC	41 20 173 58	60
MOUNT PLEASANT	LOC	41 20 173 58	61
MOUNT PLEASANT	SBRB	43 34 172 43	82
MOUNT PLEASANT	SBRB	43 34 172 43	83
MOUNT POSSESSION	HSTD	43 39 171 14	75
MOUNT POSSESSION	HSTD	43 39 171 14	87
MOUNT RICHARDS	LOC	40 07 175 51	46
MOUNT RICHMOND STATE FOREST PARK	PARK	41 30 173 13	59
MOUNT RICHMOND STATE FOREST PARK	PARK	41 43 172 56	66
MOUNT ROSKILL	SBRB	36 55 174 45	11
MOUNT ROSKILL	SBRB	36 55 174 45	12
MOUNT ROSKILL	SBRB	36 55 174 45	14
MOUNT SOMERS RANGE	MTNS	43 34 171 18	75
MOUNT SOMERS RANGE	MTNS	43 34 171 18	80
MOUNT STEWART	HSTD	42 37 173 10	72
MOUNT STEWART	HSTD	42 37 173 10	73
MOUNT STOKER	LOC	45 36 170 16	101
MOUNT STUART	LOC	46 05 169 56	111
MOUNT STUART	LOC	46 05 169 56	113
MOUNT WELLINGTON	SBRB	36 55 174 49	11
MOUNT WELLINGTON	SBRB	36 55 174 49	12
MOUNT WELLINGTON	SBRB	36 55 174 49	14
MOUNT WESLEY	LOC	35 58 173 52	6
MOUNT WESLEY	LOC	35 58 173 52	7
MOUNT WILLIAM RANGE	MTNS	41 48 171 48	63
MOUNT WILLIAM RANGE	MTNS	41 48 171 48	64
MOUNTAIN CAMP CREEK	STRM	41 20 173 39	60
MOUNTAIN CREEK	STRM	41 39 172 09	62
MOUNTAIN CREEK	STRM	41 50 171 33	63
MOUREA	LOC	38 03 176 20	20
MOUREA	LOC	38 03 176 20	21
MOUREESES BAY	BAY	35 29 174 27	5
MOUTAHIAURU ISLAND	ISLD	38 04 178 23	25
MOUTERE BLUFF	CLIF	41 13 173 05	58
MOUTERE BLUFF	CLIF	41 13 173 05	59
MOUTERE INLET	BAY	41 09 173 02	58
MOUTERE INLET	BAY	41 09 173 02	59
MOUTERE RIVER	STRM	40 50 172 09	56
MOUTERE RIVER	STRM	41 09 173 00	58
MOUTERE RIVER	STRM	41 09 173 00	59
MOUTOA	LOC	40 31 175 24	48
MOUTOA FLOODWAY	CANL	40 30 175 16	48
MOUTOHORA	LOC	38 17 177 32	31
MOUTOHORA (TRIG)	MTN	38 16 177 29	31
MOUTOKI ISLAND	ISLD	37 50 176 53	22
MOUTOKI ISLAND	ISLD	37 50 176 53	23
MOWBRAY RIVER	STRM	43 53 170 59	87
MOWHANAU BEACH	LOC	39 53 174 54	44
MOWHANAU STREAM	STRM	39 53 174 54	45
MOWLEM (TRIG)	HILL	41 15 174 58	52
MOWLEM (TRIG)	HILL	41 15 174 58	55
MUARANGI (TRIG)	HILL	36 17 174 04	10
MUDDY CREEK	STRM	40 36 172 37	56
MUDDY CREEK	STRM	40 36 172 37	57
MUDDY CREEK	STRM	45 04 169 40	100
MUDDY CREEK	STRM	46 34 168 30	109
MUDDY STREAM	STRM	42 22 172 39	71
MUDGIE, LAKE	LAKE	42 44 171 11	68
MUDGIE, LAKE	LAKE	42 44 171 11	69
MUELLER GLACIER	GLCR	43 44 170 02	76
MUELLER GLACIER	GLCR	43 44 170 02	77
MUELLER GLACIER	GLCR	43 44 170 02	79
MUELLER, LAKE	LAKE	43 25 170 02	76
MUELLER, LAKE	LAKE	43 25 170 02	77
MUELLER, MOUNT (TRIG)	MTN	42 22 172 18	71
MUELLER PASS	PASS	43 46 169 49	76
MUELLER PASS	PASS	44 03 169 13	78
MUELLER PASS	PASS	43 46 169 49	79
MUELLER PEAK (TRIG)	PEAK	43 14 170 50	75
MUELLER RIVER	STRM	44 02 168 58	78
MUHUNOA	LOC	40 39 175 12	48
MUHUNOA EAST	LOC	40 41 175 18	48
MUIR CREEK	STRM	44 01 169 23	78
MUKAHANGA	HSTD	40 46 173 56	61
MULLER	HSTD	42 03 173 23	66
MULLET POINT	PNT	36 27 174 47	11
MUNGO PASS	PASS	43 03 171 13	75
MUNGO RIVER	STRM	43 03 171 07	75
MUNRO BAY	BAY	35 48 174 29	8
MUNRO PEAK	PEAK	44 13 168 50	78
MUNRO PEAK	PEAK	43 51 169 27	78
MUNRO PEAK	PEAK	43 51 169 27	79
MUNRO STREAM	STRM	39 22 176 48	40
MUNRO STREAM	STRM	39 22 176 48	42
MUNTZ, MOUNT (TRIG)	MTN	42 22 172 49	71
MUNTZ, MOUNT (TRIG)	MTN	42 22 172 49	72
MURCHISON	POPL	41 48 172 20	65
MURCHISON GLACIER	GLCR	43 34 170 23	74
MURCHISON GLACIER	GLCR	43 34 170 23	77
MURCHISON, MOUNT	MTN	43 00 171 23	75
MURCHISON, MOUNT	MTN	43 00 171 23	80
MURCHISON, MOUNT (TRIG)	MTN	41 44 172 30	65
MURCHISON MOUNTAINS	MTNS	45 15 167 32	97
MURCHISON RIVER	STRM	43 39 170 13	74
MURCHISON RIVER	STRM	43 39 170 13	77
MURCHISON RIVER	STRM	43 39 170 13	86
MURDERERS COVE	BAY	47 14 167 25	114
MURDOCK CREEK	STRM	43 52 169 38	76
MURDOCK CREEK	STRM	43 52 169 38	79
MURIEL CREEK	STRM	42 57 171 01	68
MURIEL CREEK	STRM	42 57 171 01	69

Mu-No

MURIHIKU, LAKE	LAKE	46 24 168 16	109
MURIMOTU	LOC	39 33 175 42	37
MURIMOTU ISLAND	ISLD	34 25 173 03	2
MURIWAI	LOC	38 45 177 55	32
MURIWAI	LOC	38 45 177 55	33
MURIWAI BEACH	LOC	36 50 174 26	10
MURIWAI BEACH	BCH	36 46 174 23	10
MURIWAI BEACH	LOC	36 50 174 26	11
MURIWAI BEACH	BCH	36 46 174 23	11
MURIWAI STREAM	STRM	35 42 173 32	6
MURPHY ISLAND	ISLD	47 17 167 30	114
MURPHY STREAM	STRM	43 28 170 42	74
MURPHY (TRIG)	STRM	42 03 173 13	66
MURPHYS CREEK	STRM	45 27 170 30	102
MURPHYS SADDLE	SAD	44 54 168 37	90
MURPHYS SADDLE	SAD	44 54 168 37	95
MURRAY CREEK	STRM	41 40 172 27	65
MURRAY CREEK	STRM	42 50 171 01	68
MURRAY CREEK	STRM	42 50 171 01	69
MURRAY CREEK	STRM	45 48 168 23	107
MURRAY, LAKE	LAKE	43 54 170 28	77
MURRAY, LAKE	LAKE	43 54 170 28	86
MURRAY, MOUNT (TRIG)	MTN	42 33 172 16	71
MURRAY, MOUNT (TRIG)	HILL	45 13 169 57	101
MURRAY RIVER	STRM	46 47 168 00	109
MURRAY RIVER	STRM	46 47 168 00	114
MURRAY RIVER	STRM	46 47 168 00	115
MURRAY SADDLE	SAD	42 59 170 58	68
MURRAY SADDLE	SAD	42 59 170 58	69
MURRAY SADDLE	SAD	42 59 170 58	75
MURRYS CREEK	STRM	45 13 169 49	100
MURRYS CREEK	STRM	45 13 169 49	101
MURTY CREEK	STRM	42 01 172 23	65
MURUMURU (TRIG)	HILL	39 20 175 07	36
MURUPARA	POPL	38 27 176 42	30
MUSEUM RANGE	MTNS	45 15 167 15	96
MUSGRAVE BROOK	STRM	41 40 173 36	66
MUSGRAVE, MOUNT	MTN	43 48 170 43	86
MUSIC CREEK	STRM	44 06 168 44	88
MUSICK POINT	PNT	36 51 174 54	11
MUSICK POINT	PNT	36 51 174 54	12
MUSKET BAY	BAY	44 30 167 50	94
MUSTERERS COL	SAD	43 22 170 52	75
MUTTON COVE	BAY	40 47 173 00	57
MUTTONBIRD ISLANDS	ISLS	46 51 168 15	109
MUTTONBIRD ISLANDS	ISLS	47 11 167 26	114
MUTTONBIRD ISLANDS	ISLS	46 51 168 15	115
MUTTONTOWN	LOC	45 12 169 21	100
MUTU MUTU POINT	PNT	44 26 171 16	93
MUTUERA STREAM	STRM	38 36 177 24	31
MUTURANGI STREAM	STRM	38 06 174 57	18
MUZZLE STREAM	STRM	42 07 173 38	66
MUZZLE STREAM	STRM	42 07 173 38	67
MYERS, MOUNT	MTN	43 35 169 54	76
MYRMIDON	MTN	43 34 170 43	74
MYROSS BUSH	LOC	46 23 168 25	109
MYSTERY BURN	STRM	45 20 167 36	97
MYSTERY COL	SAD	44 26 168 34	88
MYSTERY COL	SAD	44 26 168 34	90
MYSTERY LAKE	LAKE	43 33 171 02	75
MYTH TARN	LAKE	45 08 167 22	94
MYTH TARN	LAKE	45 08 167 22	96

N

NABHRA (TRIG)	HILL	41 07 175 00	52
NABHRA (TRIG)	HILL	41 07 175 00	55
NAENAE	SBRB	41 12 174 57	52
NAENAE	SBRB	41 12 174 57	55
NAIKE	LOC	37 31 174 57	14
NAIKE STREAM	STRM	37 30 174 55	14
NAMU, MOUNT	MTN	45 12 167 04	96
NAMU RIVER	STRM	45 10 167 00	96
NAMUNAMU, LAKE	LAKE	39 53 175 28	45
NAMUNAMU, LAKE	LAKE	39 53 175 28	46
NANCY RIVER	STRM	42 32 171 51	70
NANCY SOUND	SND	45 06 167 01	96
NANCY-TASS SADDLE	SAD	42 30 171 57	70
NANI ISLAND	ISLD	36 46 175 03	12
NANI ISLAND	ISLD	36 46 175 03	13
NANSEN PEAK	MTN	44 30 168 24	88
NANSEN PEAK	PEAK	44 30 168 24	89
NANTES, MOUNT	MTN	45 35 167 03	105
NAPENAPE	LOC	42 57 173 15	72
NAPENAPE	LOC	42 57 173 15	73
NAPIER	TOWN	39 30 176 54	40
NAPIER	TOWN	39 30 176 54	41
NAPIER	TOWN	39 30 176 54	42
NAPIER, MOUNT (TRIG)	MTN	45 09 167 02	96
NAPOLEON	HILL	41 56 174 01	67
NARBEY STREAM	STRM	43 50 173 03	83
NARDOO CREEK	STRM	42 01 172 31	65
NARDOO STREAM	STRM	45 49 169 52	111
NARDOO (TRIG)	MTN	42 03 172 28	65
NARROW BEND	CHAN	46 09 166 44	104
NARROW NECK	LOC	45 26 166 55	96
NARROWS CREEK	STRM	45 02 167 43	94
NARROWS CREEK	STRM	45 02 167 43	97
NASEBY	LOC	45 02 170 09	101
NATHAN POINT	PNT	38 07 174 48	18
NATHAN STREAM	STRM	42 36 172 27	71
NATIONAL PARK	POPL	39 10 175 24	36
NATIONAL PARK	POPL	39 10 175 24	37
NATIVE ISLAND	ISLD	46 55 168 09	109
NATIVE ISLAND	ISLD	46 55 168 09	115
NATS CREEK	STRM	43 55 168 58	78
NAUMAI	LOC	36 06 173 59	7
NAVIGATOR RANGE	MTNS	43 36 170 01	76
NAVIGATOR RANGE	MTNS	43 36 170 01	77
NAVIRE ROCK	ROCK	35 58 175 08	9
NAZOMI	MTN	43 37 170 08	74
NAZOMI	MTN	43 37 170 08	77
NEALE BURN	STRM	44 55 167 55	89
NEALE BURN	STRM	44 55 167 55	94
NEAVE, MOUNT	MTN	43 11 171 01	75
NEAVESVILLE	LOC	37 10 175 42	17
NECK, THE	PNT	46 56 168 12	115
NED, THE (TRIG)	HILL	41 39 173 55	60
NEDS CREEK	STRM	45 03 169 30	100
NEDS HILL (TRIG)	HILL	40 42 176 01	49
NEDS HILL (TRIG)	HILL	40 42 176 01	51
NEE ISLAND	ISLD	45 15 166 52	96
NEEDLE	PEAK	41 54 171 48	63
NEEDLE	PEAK	41 54 171 48	64
NEEDLE PEAK	PEAK	45 54 166 50	104
NEEDLE POINT	PNT	41 57 171 25	63
NEEDLE ROCK	ROCK	36 44 175 51	16
NEEDLES	ROCK	35 07 174 05	4
NEEDLES CREEK	STRM	41 50 174 10	67
NEEDLES POINT	PNT	36 02 175 25	9
NEEDLES POINT	PNT	41 52 174 10	67
NEILL SADDLE	SAD	40 57 175 20	48
NEILL SADDLE	SAD	40 57 175 20	53
NEILS BEACH	LOC	44 00 168 39	88
NEILSON CREEK	STRM	43 56 169 17	78
NELL STREAM	STRM	43 24 171 10	75
NELSON	TOWN	41 16 173 17	59
NELSON CREEK	STRM	42 23 171 26	69
NELSON CREEK	LOC	42 24 171 31	69
NELSON CREEK, LEFT BRANCH	STRM	42 25 171 33	69
NELSON CREEK, RIGHT BRANCH	STRM	42 29 171 35	69
NELSON CREEK, RIGHT BRANCH	STRM	42 29 171 35	70
NELSON HAVEN	HARB	41 15 173 18	59
NELSON ISLAND	ISLD	36 10 175 18	9
NELSON LAKES NATIONAL PARK	PARK	41 56 172 41	65
NELSON STREAM	STRM	44 18 170 56	87
NELSON TOPS, THE	MTNS	42 37 172 09	70
NELSONS MONUMENT	ISLD	40 44 173 54	61
NENTHORN	LOC	45 29 170 22	101
NENTHORN STREAM	STRM	45 38 170 14	101
NEREUS	MTN	44 39 168 12	89
NERGER, MOUNT	MTN	44 00 169 07	78
NERINE, LAKE	LAKE	44 38 168 12	89
NESBITS CREEK	STRM	41 45 173 08	66
NESCHACKER HILL (TRIG)	MTN	42 38 172 19	71
NESSING, MOUNT	LOC	44 16 170 47	87
NESSING, MOUNT	MTN	44 21 170 42	93
NEST (TRIG)	HILL	38 48 175 05	26
NEST (TRIG)	HILL	38 48 175 05	27
NESTOR GULLY	STRM	41 41 172 48	65
NESTOR (TRIG)	HILL	41 42 172 46	65
NET ROCK	ROCK	35 13 174 19	5
NETHERBY	LOC	37 35 175 17	18
NETHERBY	LOC	37 35 175 17	19
NETHERBY	SBRB	43 54 171 47	84
NETHERTON	LOC	37 21 175 37	15
NETHERWOOD	HSTD	41 43 173 29	66
NEUDORF SADDLE	SAD	41 17 172 56	58
NEUMAN RANGE	MTNS	43 55 169 55	79
NEUTRAL HILL	MTN	43 46 170 47	87
NEVER NEVER, LAKE	LAKE	44 34 167 57	89
NEVER NEVER, LAKE	LAKE	44 34 167 57	94
NEVILLE (TRIG)	HILL	40 51 173 47	61
NEVIS BURN	STRM	45 10 169 00	99
NEVIS CROSSING	LOC	45 11 169 00	99
NEVIS RIVER	STRM	45 04 169 02	99
NEW BRIGHTON	SBRB	43 30 172 44	82
NEW BRIGHTON	SBRB	43 30 172 44	83
NEW CREEK	STRM	41 47 172 01	64
NEW CREEK	LOC	41 47 172 01	64
NEW CREEK	STRM	41 45 172 35	65
NEW LYNN	SBRB	36 55 174 40	11
NEW LYNN	SBRB	36 55 174 40	12
NEW LYNN	SBRB	36 55 174 40	14
NEW PLYMOUTH	TOWN	39 04 174 04	34
NEW RIVER	STRM	42 33 171 08	68
NEW RIVER	STRM	42 33 171 08	69
NEW RIVER ESTUARY	ESTY	46 29 168 20	109
NEWBURY	LOC	40 19 175 34	48
NEWBURY	LOC	40 19 175 34	49
NEWCOMBE, MOUNT (TRIG)	MTN	42 36 171 50	70
NEWHAVEN	LOC	46 29 169 43	113
NEWLAND	LOC	43 53 171 51	84
NEWLAND STREAM	STRM	44 15 169 01	78
NEWLANDS	SBRB	41 14 174 49	52
NEWLANDS	SBRB	41 14 174 49	55
NEWMAN	LOC	40 37 175 43	49
NEWMARKET	SBRB	36 52 174 46	11
NEWMARKET	SBRB	36 52 174 46	12
NEWNES CREEK	STRM	41 44 171 46	63
NEWNES CREEK	STRM	41 44 171 46	64
NEWSTEAD	LOC	37 47 175 21	19
NEWTON CREEK	STRM	42 51 171 22	69
NEWTON CREEK	STRM	45 00 167 42	94
NEWTON CREEK	STRM	45 00 167 42	97
NEWTON CREEK	STRM	47 08 167 55	114
NEWTON CREEK	STRM	47 08 167 55	115
NEWTON FLAT	LOC	41 47 172 10	64
NEWTON, MOUNT	MTN	42 52 171 20	69
NEWTON PEAK	PEAK	43 19 170 43	74
NEWTON RANGE	MTNS	42 53 171 16	68
NEWTON RANGE	MTNS	42 53 171 16	69
NEWTON RIVER	STRM	41 47 172 11	64
NEWTON RIVER	STRM	45 55 166 26	104
NEWTON ROCK	ROCK	46 48 168 04	109
NEWTON ROCK	ROCK	46 48 168 04	115
NEWTON SADDLE	SAD	42 50 171 24	69
NEWTOWN STREAM	STRM	43 04 172 00	81
NGA HORO ISLAND	ISLD	36 58 176 05	17
NGAAWAPURUA STREAM	STRM	38 37 177 14	31
NGAAWAPURUA STREAM	STRM	39 14 176 15	39
NGAERE	LOC	39 23 174 18	34
NGAERE	LOC	39 23 174 18	35
NGAERE	LOC	39 23 174 18	44
NGAHAPE	LOC	38 09 175 21	19
NGAHAPE	LOC	41 07 175 55	51
NGAHAPE STREAM	STRM	40 02 176 31	47
NGAHERE	LOC	42 24 171 26	69
NGAHINAPOURI	LOC	37 54 175 12	18
NGAHORE (TRIG)	HILL	37 47 177 48	24
NGAIO	SBRB	41 15 174 46	52
NGAIO	SBRB	41 15 174 46	55
NGAIO DOWNS	HSTD	42 04 173 57	67
NGAIOTONGA	LOC	35 19 174 17	5
NGAKAPUA, LAKE	LAKE	35 01 173 12	3
NGAKAROA STREAM	STRM	38 30 177 54	32
NGAKARU, LAKE	LAKE	36 39 174 20	10
NGAKAUAU STREAM	STRM	40 56 176 11	50
NGAKAUTUAKINA POINT	PNT	37 38 176 01	20
NGAKAWAU	LOC	41 37 171 53	62
NGAKAWAU RIVER	STRM	41 36 171 53	62
NGAKAWAU RIVER	STRM	41 40 172 00	64
NGAKEKETA, LAKE	LAKE	34 31 172 46	2
NGAKIRIPARAURI STREAM	STRM	35 46 173 37	6
NGAKOAOHIA STREAM	STRM	38 03 175 12	18
NGAKONUI	LOC	38 50 175 19	27
NGAKONUI	HSTD	41 16 175 41	51
NGAKONUI	HSTD	41 16 175 41	53
NGAKONUI STREAM	STRM	38 50 175 20	27
NGAKURU	LOC	38 20 176 11	21
NGAKURU	LOC	38 20 176 11	29
NGAMAHANGA STREAM	STRM	39 02 177 13	41
NGAMAIA (TRIG)	PEAK	40 39 175 32	48
NGAMAIA (TRIG)	PEAK	40 39 175 32	49
NGAMANAURARU BAY	BAY	36 12 175 03	9
NGAMATAPOURI	LOC	39 35 174 49	35
NGAMATAPOURI	LOC	39 35 174 49	44
NGAMATEA	HSTD	39 24 176 08	39
NGAMOKO	HILL	38 41 176 56	30
NGAMOKO RANGE	MTNS	38 45 177 11	31
NGAMOKO (TRIG)	MTN	38 46 177 10	31
NGAMOTU LAGOON	LAGN	39 04 177 26	33
NGAMOTU LAGOON	LAGN	39 04 177 26	41
NGAMUTU (TRIG)	HILL	39 08 175 23	36
NGAMUTU (TRIG)	HILL	39 08 175 23	37
NGAMUWAHINE RIVER	STRM	37 49 176 01	20
NGANGIHO (TRIG)	HILL	38 35 176 03	28
NGANGIHO (TRIG)	HILL	38 35 176 03	29
NGAPAENGA	LOC	38 21 174 55	26
NGAPAERURU	LOC	40 15 176 14	50
NGAPAKIRI (TRIG)	MTN	38 42 177 19	31
NGAPAKORO (TRIG)	HILL	38 25 174 58	26
NGAPAKORO (TRIG)	HILL	38 25 174 58	27
NGAPARA	LOC	44 57 170 45	93
NGAPEKE	LOC	37 43 176 13	20
NGAPEKE	LOC	37 43 176 13	21
NGAPIPITO	LOC	35 26 173 55	4
NGAPOIPOIATORE (TRIG)	HILL	38 22 176 07	28
NGAPOIPOIATORE (TRIG)	HILL	38 22 176 07	29
NGAPOUATU (TRIG)	PEAK	38 59 176 27	39
NGAPOUATU (TRIG)	PEAK	38 59 176 27	40
NGAPUHI	LOC	35 27 173 47	4
NGAPUHI	LOC	35 27 173 47	6
NGAPUKE	LOC	38 53 175 25	27
NGAPUKETURUA	HILL	38 14 174 45	18
NGAPUKETURUA STREAM	STRM	40 35 175 34	48
NGAPUKETURUA STREAM	STRM	40 35 175 34	49
NGAPUKETURUA (TRIG)	HILL	38 44 176 32	30
NGAPUKETURUA (TRIG)	MTN	38 29 177 13	31
NGAPUKETURUA (TRIG)	PEAK	39 05 176 02	38
NGAPUKETURUA (TRIG)	PEAK	39 05 176 02	39
NGAPUKETURUA (TRIG)	PEAK	40 40 175 30	48
NGAPUKETURUA (TRIG)	PEAK	40 40 175 30	49
NGAPUNA	SBRB	38 09 176 16	20
NGAPUNA	SBRB	38 09 176 16	21
NGAPUNA	LOC	45 28 170 09	101
NGAPUNARUA STREAM	STRM	38 13 178 07	32
NGAPUTAHI	LOC	38 36 176 50	30
NGARAHU (TRIG)	HILL	35 07 173 47	4
NGARAKAUWHAKARARA (TRIG)	HILL	39 32 175 11	36
NGARARA STREAM	STRM	41 14 175 33	51
NGARARA STREAM	STRM	41 14 175 33	53
NGARARAHAE BAY	BAY	38 25 174 38	26
NGARARATUNUA	LOC	35 41 174 15	5
NGARARATUNUA	LOC	35 41 174 15	7
NGARARATUNUA	LOC	35 41 174 15	8
NGARIMU BAY	LOC	37 04 175 31	13
NGARIMU BAY	LOC	37 04 175 31	15
NGARIMU BAY	LOC	37 04 175 31	16
NGAROMA	LOC	38 18 175 35	27
NGAROMA	LOC	38 18 175 35	28
NGAROTO	LOC	37 59 175 19	18
NGAROTO	LOC	37 59 175 19	19
NGAROTO, LAKE	LAKE	37 58 175 18	18
NGAROTO, LAKE	LAKE	37 58 175 18	19
NGARUA	LOC	37 40 175 40	19
NGARUA STREAM	STRM	37 20 175 30	15
NGARUAWAHIA	POPL	37 40 175 09	18
NGARUPUPU POINT	PNT	38 29 174 38	26
NGARURORO RIVER	STRM	39 34 176 55	42
NGARURORO RIVER	STRM	39 34 176 55	43
NGARURU	HSTD	41 40 173 14	66
NGARURU, LAKE	LAKE	39 53 175 27	45
NGARURU, LAKE	LAKE	39 53 175 27	46
NGARURU (TRIG)	HILL	39 54 175 27	45
NGARURU (TRIG)	HILL	39 54 175 27	46
NGATAKI	LOC	34 44 173 03	2
NGATAMAHINE POINT	PNT	36 10 175 05	9
NGATAMAHINERUA (TRIG)	HILL	37 40 175 51	20
NGATAMAWAHINE STREAM	STRM	38 21 176 46	30
NGATAPA	LOC	38 35 177 47	32
NGATARAWA	LOC	39 38 176 44	42
NGATARAWA	LOC	39 38 176 44	43
NGATAU RIVER	STRM	44 03 169 09	78
NGATAUHAO (TRIG)	HILL	39 23 175 08	36
NGATAUS KNOB	PEAK	43 36 169 51	76
NGATEA	LOC	37 17 175 30	15
NGATERETERE (TRIG)	MTN	38 09 177 33	24
NGATIAWA RIVER	STRM	40 54 175 06	48
NGATIAWA RIVER	STRM	40 54 175 06	52
NGATIAWA RIVER	STRM	40 54 175 06	55
NGATIMOTI	LOC	41 12 172 53	58
NGATIRA	LOC	38 06 175 52	20
NGATIWHETU	LOC	34 39 172 56	2
NGATOHUAHIRA (TRIG)	HILL	37 43 178 22	25
NGATOKA (TRIG)	HILL	35 54 174 18	7
NGATOKA (TRIG)	HILL	35 54 174 18	8
NGATORO STREAM	STRM	39 08 174 17	34
NGATORONUI STREAM	STRM	39 10 174 14	34
NGATU, LAKE	LAKE	35 02 173 12	3
NGATUHOA STREAM	STRM	37 50 176 02	20
NGATUMOROKI (TRIG)	HILL	34 41 172 59	2
NGATURI	LOC	40 28 175 55	49
NGATURI CREEK	STRM	40 28 175 55	49
NGATUTURA POINT	PNT	37 31 174 45	14
NGATUTURU (TRIG)	HILL	35 29 174 03	4
NGATUTURU (TRIG)	HILL	35 29 174 03	5
NGAUOTEKAKA (TRIG)	HILL	38 27 178 02	32
NGAUPIKO POINT	PNT	36 14 174 19	7
NGAUPIKO POINT	PNT	36 14 174 19	8
NGAUPOKO (TRIG)	HILL	39 37 175 00	36
NGAUPOKO (TRIG)	HILL	39 37 175 00	45
NGAURANGA	LOC	41 15 174 49	52
NGAURANGA	LOC	41 15 174 49	55
NGAURUHOE, MOUNT	MTN	39 10 175 38	37
NGAURUHOE, MOUNT	MTN	39 10 175 38	38
NGAURUKEHU	RSDG	39 36 175 42	46
NGAUTUKU (TRIG)	HILL	38 22 176 01	28
NGAUTUKU (TRIG)	HILL	38 22 176 01	29
NGAWAIAWHITU STREAM	STRM	39 20 176 09	38
NGAWAIAWHITU STREAM	STRM	39 20 176 09	39
NGAWAKA	LOC	39 37 175 47	46
NGAWAPURUA	LOC	40 23 175 54	49
NGAWERO	LOC	37 57 176 10	20
NGAWERO	LOC	37 57 176 10	21
NGAWHA	LOC	35 23 173 52	4
NGAWHA	LOC	35 23 173 52	6
NGAWHA SPRINGS	LOC	35 25 173 52	4
NGAWHA SPRINGS	LOC	35 25 173 52	6
NGAWHAKARARA (TRIG)	PEAK	40 33 175 35	48
NGAWHAKARARA (TRIG)	PEAK	40 33 175 35	49
NGAWHAKATATARA (TRIG)	HILL	38 06 177 37	24
NGAWHAKATATARA (TRIG)	HILL	37 40 178 03	25
NGAWIRO	HSTD	42 41 173 05	72
NGONGOTAHA	UGAT	38 05 176 13	20
NGONGOTAHA	LOC	38 05 176 13	21
NGONGOTAHA STREAM	STRM	38 05 176 13	20
NGONGOTAHA STREAM	STRM	38 05 176 13	21
NGONGOTAHA VALLEY	LOC	38 07 176 09	20
NGONGOTAHA VALLEY	LOC	38 07 176 09	21
NGUNGURU	LOC	35 38 174 30	5
NGUNGURU	LOC	35 38 174 30	8
NGUNGURU BAY	BAY	35 41 174 32	5
NGUNGURU BAY	BAY	35 41 174 32	8
NGUNGURU RIVER	STRM	35 38 174 31	5
NGUNGURU RIVER	STRM	35 38 174 26	7
NGUNGURU RIVER	STRM	35 38 174 31	8
NGUROA BAY	BAY	40 31 172 37	57
NGUTUKOKO (TRIG)	HILL	41 02 175 47	51
NGUTUNUI	LOC	38 05 175 07	18
NGUTUNUI STREAM	STRM	38 06 175 08	18
NGUTUWERA STREAM	STRM	38 06 175 46	19
NGUTUWERA STREAM	STRM	38 06 175 46	20
NIAGARA	LOC	46 36 169 07	112
NICHOLAS, MOUNT	LOC	45 06 168 26	95
NICHOLAS, MOUNT	LOC	45 06 168 26	98
NICHOLAS, MOUNT (TRIG)	MTN	45 08 168 24	95
NICHOLAS, MOUNT (TRIG)	MTN	45 08 168 24	98
NICHOLAS SADDLE	SAD	45 10 168 24	95
NICHOLAS SADDLE	SAD	45 10 168 24	98
NICHOLSON CREEK	STRM	43 30 169 45	76
NICHOLSON, MOUNT	MTN	43 19 170 48	75
NIDD STREAM	STRM	41 57 173 52	67
NIGEL, LAKE	LAKE	45 18 168 26	95
NIGEL, LAKE	LAKE	45 18 168 26	98
NIGER PEAK (TRIG)	MTN	44 31 168 51	90
NIGGER STREAM	STRM	43 00 172 03	70
NIGGERHEAD (TRIG)	PEAK	42 40 172 12	70
NIGHTCAPS	POPL	45 58 168 02	106
NIGHTCAPS	POPL	45 58 168 02	107
NIGHTFALL STREAM	STRM	44 10 168 42	88
NIGHTINGALE STREAM	STRM	42 16 172 46	65
NIHONIHO	LOC	38 47 175 03	26
NIHONIHO	LOC	38 47 175 03	27
NIHONUI (TRIG)	HILL	37 26 174 42	14
NIKAU	LOC	40 29 175 43	49
NIKAU	LOC	41 33 171 56	62
NILE HEAD	HEAD	40 44 173 52	61
NIMROD, MOUNT	MTN	44 26 170 48	93
NINA BROOK	STRM	41 40 174 00	67
NINA RIVER	STRM	42 29 172 23	71
NINE MILE BEACH	BCH	41 50 171 27	63
NINE MILE BLUFF	CLIF	42 20 171 16	68
NINE MILE BLUFF	CLIF	42 20 171 16	69
NINE MILE CREEK	STRM	44 47 169 30	91
NINEPIN ROCK	ROCK	40 55 174 03	54
NINEPIN ROCK	ROCK	40 55 174 03	61
NINETY MILE BEACH	BCH	34 45 172 58	2
NIOBE PEAK	PEAK	44 34 168 14	88
NIOBE PEAK	PEAK	44 34 168 14	89
NIREAHA	LOC	40 37 175 38	48
NIREAHA	LOC	40 37 175 38	49
NISSON HILL (TRIG)	HILL	44 01 168 48	78
NISSON, LAKE	LAKE	44 01 168 48	78
NITA PEAKS (TRIG)	PEAK	44 59 167 28	94
NITA PEAKS (TRIG)	PEAK	44 59 167 28	97
NITZ CREEK	STRM	44 58 167 41	94
NITZ CREEK	STRM	44 58 167 41	97
NIVALUS, LAKE	LAKE	42 21 171 57	70
NOB, MOUNT	MTN	44 15 168 42	88
NOBBLER, MOUNT (TRIG)	MTN	45 01 170 21	101
NOBLE ISLAND	ISLD	47 13 167 39	114
NOBLE, MOUNT	MTN	45 34 167 03	105
NOBLE, MOUNT (TRIG)	MTN	42 52 172 24	71
NOBLES	LOC	42 20 171 43	63
NOBLES	LOC	42 20 171 43	64
NOBLES	LOC	42 20 171 43	70
NOBLES STREAM	STRM	46 10 170 05	103
NOELS PEAK (TRIG)	MTN	41 45 172 28	65
NOISES, THE	ISLS	36 42 174 58	11
NOISES, THE	ISLS	36 42 174 58	12
NOKOMAI	LOC	45 30 168 41	99
NOKOMAI RIVER	STRM	45 34 168 39	99
NONOTI	LOC	42 50 173 14	72
NONOTI	LOC	42 50 173 14	73
NOPERA	HSTD	41 11 173 57	54
NOPERA	HSTD	41 11 173 57	60
NOPERA	HSTD	41 11 173 57	61
NORMA, LAKE	LAKE	45 20 167 16	96
NORMA (TRIG)	MTN	42 26 172 22	71
NORMANBY	POPL	39 32 174 16	34
NORMANBY	POPL	39 32 174 16	44
NORMANBY	LOC	44 27 171 15	93
NORMANDALE	SBRB	41 12 174 53	52
NORMANDALE	SBRB	41 12 174 53	55
NORMANS ISLAND	ISLD	45 47 166 32	104
NORRIS GULLY STREAM	STRM	41 28 172 50	58
NORRIS, MOUNT (TRIG)	HILL	41 30 172 52	58
NORSEWOOD	POPL	40 05 176 13	47
NORTH ARM	BAY	45 29 167 22	96
NORTH ARM	BAY	45 29 167 22	97
NORTH ARM	BAY	46 53 168 00	109
NORTH ARM	BAY	47 11 167 40	114
NORTH ARM	BAY	46 53 168 00	115
NORTH BAXTON BURN	STRM	45 42 168 06	106
NORTH BAXTON BURN	STRM	45 42 168 06	107
NORTH BRANCH	STRM	43 36 170 30	74
NORTH BRANCH	STRM	43 36 170 30	77
NORTH BRANCH HUXLEY RIVER	STRM	44 01 169 45	79
NORTH BRANCH NERGER CREEK	STRM	43 55 168 58	78
NORTH BRANCH TEMPLE STREAM	STRM	44 07 169 49	79
NORTH BRANCH WILKIN RIVER	STRM	44 17 168 54	78
NORTH BRANCH YOUNG RIVER	STRM	44 11 169 09	78
NORTH BRAXTON (TRIG)	MTN	45 40 168 01	106
NORTH BRAXTON (TRIG)	MTN	45 40 168 01	107
NORTH CAPE	CAPE	34 25 173 03	2
NORTH CHANNEL	CHAN	36 23 174 50	11
NORTH CLYDE	SBRB	39 02 177 26	33
NORTH COL	SAD	44 39 168 11	89
NORTH COVE	BAY	36 25 174 50	11
NORTH CREEK	STRM	41 39 172 56	65
NORTH DEAN (TRIG)	HILL	43 02 172 39	82
NORTH DUNEDIN	SBRB	45 52 170 31	103
NORTH EAST GORGE STREAM	STRM	43 40 170 38	74
NORTH EAST ISLAND	ISLD	34 08 172 10	2
NORTH EAST VALLEY	SBRB	45 51 170 32	103
NORTH EGMONT CHALET	LOC	39 16 174 06	34
NORTH ESK RIVER	STRM	42 49 172 14	70
NORTH ETAL CREEK	STRM	45 46 168 01	106
NORTH ETAL CREEK	STRM	45 46 168 01	107
NORTH FIORD	FIOR	45 07 167 48	94
NORTH FIORD	FIOR	45 07 167 48	97
NORTH GABLE	PNT	35 36 174 32	5
NORTH GABLE	PNT	35 36 174 32	8
NORTH HEAD	HEAD	35 23 174 23	5
NORTH HEAD	HEAD	35 31 173 22	6
NORTH HEAD	HEAD	36 24 174 03	10
NORTH HEAD	HEAD	36 50 174 49	11
NORTH HEAD	HEAD	36 50 174 49	12
NORTH HEAD	HEAD	40 56 173 04	57

NORTH HEAD	HEAD	43 48 173 07	83
NORTH HEAD	HEAD	46 44 168 32	109
NORTH HEAD	HEAD	46 39 169 07	112
NORTH HEAD	HEAD	46 44 168 32	115
NORTH HEAD STREAM	STRM	46 05 167 57	106
NORTH HEAD STREAM	STRM	46 05 167 57	107
NORTH ISLAND	ISLD	46 49 168 14	109
NORTH ISLAND	ISLD	46 49 168 14	115
NORTH KAWEKA (TRIG)	PEAK	39 16 176 23	39
NORTH KAWEKA (TRIG)	PEAK	39 16 176 23	40
NORTH MATHIAS RIVER	STRM	43 11 171 08	75
NORTH MAVORA, LAKE	LAKE	45 14 168 10	98
NORTH OPUHA RIVER	STRM	44 00 170 53	87
NORTH PEAK	PEAK	43 19 171 00	75
NORTH PEAK	PEAK	45 58 168 35	107
NORTH PEAK STREAM	STRM	45 56 168 38	107
NORTH PORT	HARB	45 59 166 34	104
NORTH RANGE	MTNS	45 43 168 18	107
NORTH RED HEAD	HEAD	46 45 167 42	108
NORTH RED HEAD	HEAD	46 45 167 42	114
NORTH RIVER	STRM	35 57 174 24	7
NORTH RIVER	LOC	35 57 174 25	7
NORTH RIVER	STRM	35 57 174 24	8
NORTH RIVER	LOC	35 57 174 25	8
NORTH ROUGH RIDGE	RDGE	45 07 169 51	100
NORTH ROUGH RIDGE	RDGE	45 07 169 51	101
NORTH STREAM	STRM	43 08 171 15	75
NORTH TAIERI	LOC	45 50 170 21	103
NORTH TRAP	ROCK	47 22 168 54	115
NORTH WEST BAY	BAY	41 05 173 53	54
NORTH WEST BAY	BAY	41 05 173 53	60
NORTH WEST BAY	BAY	41 05 173 53	61
NORTH WEST BAY	BAY	46 45 167 37	108
NORTH WEST BAY	BAY	46 45 167 37	114
NORTH WEST NELSON STATE FOREST PARK	PARK	41 05 172 15	56
NORTH WEST NELSON STATE FOREST PARK	PARK	41 05 172 15	62
NORTHAMPTON, MOUNT (TRIG)	MTN	42 18 172 57	65
NORTHCOTE	SBRB	36 49 174 44	11
NORTHCOTE	SBRB	36 49 174 44	12
NORTHCOTE	SBRB	43 29 172 38	82
NORTHCOTE	SBRB	43 29 172 38	83
NORTHCOTE	SBRB	43 29 172 38	85
NORTHOPE	LOC	46 13 168 16	107
NORTHUMBERLAND, MOUNT (TRIG)	MTN	42 19 172 51	65
NORTON	TRIG	40 27 175 15	48
NORTON RESERVE	LOC	44 43 171 03	93
NORWEST LAKE	LAKE	45 28 167 20	96
NORWOOD	LOC	43 39 172 15	81
NORWOOD	LOC	43 39 172 15	85
NOTOWN	LOC	42 27 171 27	69
NOVARA PEAK (THE TWINS)	PEAK	43 37 170 15	74
NOVARA PEAK (THE TWINS)	PEAK	43 37 170 15	77
NOVARO, MOUNT (TRIG)	MTN	42 31 172 07	70
NOX, MOUNT	MTN	44 39 168 16	89
NUGGET HILL (TRIG)	HILL	45 49 167 55	106
NUGGET HILL (TRIG)	HILL	45 49 167 55	107
NUGGET KNOB (TRIG)	PEAK	41 26 172 26	62
NUGGET POINT	PNT	45 01 167 06	96
NUGGET POINT	PNT	46 27 169 49	113
NUGGET STREAM	STRM	46 25 169 48	113
NUGGETY CREEK	STRM	41 28 172 34	58
NUGGETY CREEK	STRM	41 45 172 24	65
NUGGETY (TRIG)	HILL	41 46 172 30	65
NUHAKA	POPL	39 03 177 44	33
NUHAKA RIVER	STRM	39 04 177 45	33
NUINUIKAI (TRIG)	HILL	38 30 178 17	32
NUKIWAI	HSTD	42 45 172 59	72
NUKUHAKARI BAY	BAY	38 23 174 39	26
NUKUHAU	SBRB	38 41 176 04	28
NUKUHAU	SBRB	38 41 176 04	29
NUKUHAU	SBRB	38 41 176 04	38
NUKUHAU LODGE	HSTD	39 36 174 40	35
NUKUHAU LODGE	HSTD	39 36 174 40	44
NUKUHOU NORTH	LOC	38 08 177 08	23
NUKUHOU RIVER	STRM	38 01 177 06	23
NUKUMARU	LOC	39 49 174 48	44
NUKUROA	LOC	44 45 171 08	93
NUKUTAUNGA ISLAND	ISLD	34 59 173 58	4
NUKUTAWHITI	LOC	35 39 173 52	6
NUKUTAWHITI	LOC	35 39 173 52	7
NUKUWAIATA ISLAND	ISLD	40 54 174 04	54
NUKUWAIATA ISLAND	ISLD	40 54 174 04	61
NUNS VEIL, THE	HILL	43 42 170 15	77
NUNS VEIL, THE	HILL	43 42 170 15	86
NURSE CREEK	STRM	44 59 167 55	94
NURSE CREEK	STRM	44 59 167 55	97
NURSE CREEK	STRM	44 59 167 55	98
NYDIA BAY	BAY	41 10 173 47	54
NYDIA BAY	BAY	41 10 173 47	60
NYDIA BAY	BAY	41 10 173 47	61
NYDIA SADDLE	SAD	41 08 173 47	60
NYDIA SADDLE	SAD	41 08 173 47	61

O

OAIA ISLAND	ISLD	36 51 174 25	10
OAIA ISLAND	ISLD	36 51 174 25	11
OAKEN, MOUNT	MTN	43 15 171 25	75
OAKEN, MOUNT	MTN	43 15 171 25	80
OAKLANDS	SBRB	43 35 172 34	82
OAKLANDS	SBRB	43 35 172 34	83
OAKLANDS	SBRB	43 35 172 34	85
OAKLEIGH	LOC	35 50 174 19	7
OAKLEIGH	LOC	35 50 174 19	8
OAKURA	LOC	35 23 174 27	5
OAKURA	POPL	39 07 173 57	34
OAKURA RIVER	STRM	39 07 173 57	34
OAMARU	TOWN	45 06 170 58	102
OAMARU RIVER	STRM	39 05 176 16	39
OAMARU STREAM	STRM	38 09 175 03	18
OAOITI STREAM	STRM	39 23 173 47	34
OAONUI	LOC	39 23 173 49	34
OAONUI STREAM	STRM	39 24 173 47	34
OAPUI (TRIG)	HILL	39 09 174 24	35
OARO	LOC	42 31 173 30	73
OARO RIVER	STRM	42 31 173 30	73
OATES, MOUNT	MTN	42 55 171 39	70
OBELISK	HILL	45 10 170 41	102
OBELISK CREEK	STRM	45 23 169 18	100
OBELISK (TRIG)	MTN	45 19 169 12	100
OBLONG HILL (TRIG)	MTN	45 58 167 21	105
OBLONG PEAK	PEAK	44 14 168 58	78
OBSERVATION HILL	MTN	43 40 170 35	77
OBSERVATION HILL	MTN	43 40 170 35	86
OCEAN BEACH	LOC	35 51 174 33	8
OCEAN BEACH	BCH	35 49 174 34	8
OCEAN BEACH	LOC	39 45 177 00	42
OCEAN BEACH	LOC	39 45 177 00	43
OCEAN BEACH	LOC	46 35 168 18	109
OCEAN BEACH	BCH	46 58 168 11	115
OCEAN GROVE	LOC	45 54 170 33	103
OCEAN PEAK (TRIG)	MTN	44 45 168 11	89
OCEAN VIEW	LOC	45 56 170 20	103
O'CONNOR, MOUNT	MTN	43 00 171 06	75
O'CONNOR, MOUNT (TRIG)	MTN	43 20 171 15	75
O'CONNOR, MOUNT (TRIG)	PEAK	41 28 172 09	62
ODYSSEY PEAK	PEAK	44 43 167 54	89
ODYSSEY PEAK	PEAK	44 43 167 54	94
OEO	LOC	39 32 173 59	34
OEO STREAM	STRM	39 32 173 57	34
OGILVIE LAGOON	LAKE	42 51 170 55	68
OHAAKI	LOC	38 31 176 19	29
OHAE STREAM	STRM	35 38 173 26	6
OHAEAWAI	LOC	35 21 173 53	4
OHAEAWAI	LOC	35 21 173 53	6
OHAI	LOC	45 56 167 57	106
OHAI	LOC	45 56 167 57	107
OHAKANA ISLAND	ISLD	37 59 177 04	23
OHAKARI (TRIG)	HILL	39 07 174 54	35
OHAKARI (TRIG)	HILL	39 07 174 54	36
OHAKEA	LOC	40 12 175 23	45
OHAKUNE	POPL	39 25 175 25	36
OHAKUNE	POPL	39 25 175 25	37
OHAKURI	LOC	38 25 176 05	28
OHAKURI	LOC	38 25 176 05	29
OHAKURI, LAKE	LAKE	38 25 176 07	29
OHANE STREAM	STRM	38 23 177 01	30
OHANE STREAM	STRM	39 03 176 34	39
OHANE STREAM	STRM	39 03 176 34	40
OHANGAI	LOC	39 35 174 23	35
OHANGAI	LOC	39 35 174 23	44
OHANGAIA STREAM	STRM	39 22 175 07	36
OHAO POINT	PNT	34 31 173 00	2
OHAOKO SADDLE	SAD	39 02 176 14	39
OHAPI	LOC	44 10 171 18	84
OHAPI	LOC	44 10 171 18	87
OHAPI CREEK	STRM	44 14 171 23	84
OHAPI CREEK	STRM	44 14 171 23	87
OHAPUKU	LOC	43 23 172 37	82
OHAPUKU	LOC	43 23 172 37	83
OHAPUKU	LOC	43 23 172 37	85
OHARA STREAM	STRM	39 36 176 26	47
OHARAE STREAM	STRM	35 08 173 20	3
OHARIU BAY	BAY	41 13 174 43	52
OHARIU BAY	BAY	41 13 174 43	55
OHARIU STREAM	STRM	41 14 174 43	52
OHARIU STREAM	STRM	41 14 174 43	55
OHAU	LOC	40 40 175 15	48
OHAU HILL (TRIG)	HILL	41 15 174 38	52
OHAU HILL (TRIG)	HILL	41 15 174 38	55
OHAU HYDRO ELECTRICITY CANAL	CANL	44 15 170 02	79
OHAU, LAKE	LAKE	44 14 169 51	79
OHAU PEAK	PEAK	44 19 169 46	91
OHAU POINT	PNT	41 14 174 39	52
OHAU POINT	PNT	41 14 174 39	55
OHAU POINT	PNT	42 15 173 50	67
OHAU RIVER	STRM	40 41 175 09	48
OHAU RIVER	STRM	44 19 170 10	79
OHAUA	LOC	38 32 176 59	30
OHAUA STREAM	STRM	38 10 176 57	22
OHAUA STREAM	STRM	38 10 176 57	23
OHAUITI	LOC	37 46 176 11	20
OHAUITI	LOC	37 46 176 11	21
OHAUPARA STREAM	STRM	37 58 176 10	20
OHAUPARA STREAM	STRM	37 58 176 10	21
OHAUPO	LOC	37 55 175 18	18
OHAUPO	LOC	37 55 175 18	19
OHAUTIRA	LOC	37 46 174 59	18
OHAUTIRA STREAM	STRM	37 46 174 58	18
OHAWE BEACH	LOC	39 35 174 12	34
OHETA STREAM	STRM	37 36 178 02	24
OHETA STREAM	STRM	37 36 178 02	25
OHIA STREAM	STRM	35 08 173 42	4
OHIA, LAKE	LAKE	34 58 173 22	3
OHIAPOPOKO (TRIG)	TRIG	37 50 174 54	18
OHIE STREAM	STRM	39 48 174 44	44
OHIKAITI RIVER	STRM	41 51 171 44	63
OHIKAITI RIVER	STRM	41 51 171 44	64
OHIKANUI RIVER	STRM	41 51 171 43	63
OHIKANUI RIVER	STRM	41 51 171 43	64
OHINAU ISLAND	ISLD	36 44 175 53	16
OHINAUITI ISLAND	ISLD	36 43 175 53	16
OHINE STREAM	STRM	37 31 175 35	15
OHINEAKAI	LOC	38 00 178 20	25
OHINEMAEMAE (TRIG)	HILL	38 59 177 27	33
OHINEMAKA RIVER	STRM	43 38 169 30	76
OHINEMAKA RIVER	STRM	43 38 169 30	79
OHINEMURI RIVER	STRM	37 26 175 43	17
OHINEMUTU	SBRB	38 08 176 15	20
OHINEMUTU	SBRB	38 08 176 15	21
OHINENUI STREAM	STRM	38 07 176 07	20
OHINENUI STREAM	STRM	38 07 176 07	21
OHINEPAKA	LOC	39 01 177 20	41
OHINEPANEA	LOC	37 50 176 34	21
OHINEPANEA	LOC	37 50 176 34	22
OHINEPANEA STATION	RSTN	37 49 176 34	21
OHINEPANEA STATION	RSTN	37 49 176 34	22
OHINEPOUTEA	HSTD	37 51 178 06	25
OHINETAHI	LOC	43 38 172 39	82
OHINETAHI	LOC	43 38 172 39	83
OHINETAHI	LOC	43 38 172 39	85
OHINETAMATEA RIVER	STRM	43 27 169 46	76
OHINETAPU STREAM	STRM	40 09 175 50	46
OHINETEWAI (TRIG)	HILL	38 00 176 43	21
OHINETEWAI (TRIG)	HILL	38 00 176 43	22
OHINETUHUA POINT	PNT	38 45 175 45	28
OHINETUHUA POINT	PNT	38 45 175 45	38
OHINEWAI	LOC	37 29 175 10	14
OHINEWAI	LOC	37 29 175 10	15
OHINEWAI, LAKE	LAKE	37 10 175 10	15
OHINEWAI STREAM	STRM	36 33 175 21	9
OHINEWAI STREAM	STRM	36 33 175 21	16
OHINEWAIRUA	HSTD	39 32 175 56	37
OHINEWHIRO (TRIG)	HILL	38 41 174 50	26
OHINGAITI	POPL	39 52 175 42	46
OHINIPAKA (TRIG)	HILL	39 32 174 46	35
OHINIPAKA (TRIG)	HILL	39 32 174 46	44
OHIWA	LOC	37 59 177 10	23
OHIWA HARBOUR	HARB	37 59 177 09	23
OHIWAI (TRIG)	HILL	37 04 175 49	16
OHIWAI (TRIG)	HILL	37 04 175 49	17
OHO CREEK	STRM	45 49 166 48	104
OHO, MOUNT (TRIG)	HILL	44 59 169 16	100
OHO SADDLE	SAD	45 50 166 52	104
OHOKA	LOC	43 22 172 35	82
OHOKA	LOC	43 22 172 35	83
OHOKA	LOC	43 22 172 35	85
OHOPE	LOC	37 58 177 03	23
OHORA STREAM	STRM	38 19 177 01	30
OHOTE STREAM	STRM	37 47 175 09	18
OHOTU	LOC	39 43 175 50	46
OHOURERE STREAM	STRM	37 44 176 05	20
OHUHA STREAM	STRM	39 02 175 15	36
OHUI	LOC	37 04 175 53	16
OHUI	LOC	37 04 175 53	17
OHUI SIDING	RSDG	38 09 176 48	22
OHUIA LAGOON	LAGN	39 04 177 28	33
OHUINGA (TRIG)	PEAK	39 52 176 08	47
OHURA	POPL	38 51 174 59	26
OHURA	POPL	38 51 174 59	27
OHURA RIVER	STRM	39 02 175 04	36
OHURAKURA	LOC	39 14 176 43	40
OHURI	LOC	35 26 173 32	3
OHURI	LOC	35 26 173 32	6
OHURI RIVER	STRM	35 27 173 32	6
OHUTU STREAM	STRM	38 23 176 48	30
OHUTU STREAM	STRM	39 39 176 03	47
OHUTU (TRIG)	PEAK	39 36 176 08	47
OHUTUTEA BAY	BAY	35 11 174 19	5
OILSKIN PASS	PASS	44 56 167 35	94
OILSKIN PASS	PASS	44 56 167 35	97
OINGO LAKE	LAKE	39 34 176 45	40
OINGO LAKE	LAKE	39 34 176 45	42
OINGO LAKE	LAKE	39 34 176 45	43
OIO	LOC	39 03 175 23	36
OIO	LOC	39 03 175 23	37
OIO STREAM	STRM	39 05 175 15	36
OIO STREAM, EAST BRANCH	STRM	39 05 175 17	36
OIO STREAM, WEST BRANCH	STRM	39 05 175 17	36
OIRA CREEK	STRM	37 06 174 55	12
OIRA CREEK	STRM	37 06 174 55	14
OIRATITI STREAM	STRM	38 03 177 27	24
OKAERIA	LOC	37 20 175 17	15
OKAHAU POINT	PNT	45 23 170 52	102
OKAHAUTAUMANGA (TRIG)	HILL	35 08 173 32	3
OKAHU	LOC	35 09 173 16	3
OKAHU	LOC	36 00 174 03	7
OKAHU ISLAND	ISLD	35 12 174 13	5
OKAHU STREAM	STRM	35 19 173 30	3
OKAHU STREAM	STRM	35 57 174 03	7
OKAHU STREAM	STRM	38 37 176 44	30
OKAHU STREAM	STRM	38 34 176 46	30
OKAHU STREAM	STRM	39 21 173 46	34
OKAHU STREAM	STRM	39 36 175 18	36
OKAHU STREAM	STRM	39 36 175 18	45
OKAHU (TRIG)	HILL	37 22 174 45	14
OKAHU (TRIG)	HILL	38 14 176 38	21
OKAHU (TRIG)	HILL	38 14 176 38	22
OKAHU (TRIG)	HILL	38 14 176 38	30
OKAHU (TRIG)	HILL	39 37 175 35	36
OKAHU (TRIG)	HILL	39 37 175 35	46
OKAHUATA (TRIG)	MTN	38 19 177 22	31
OKAHUKURA	LOC	38 48 175 14	27
OKAHUKURA PENINSULA	PEN	36 22 174 20	10
OKAHUKURA STREAM	STRM	38 25 175 24	27
OKAIA STREAM	STRM	38 40 175 55	28
OKAIA STREAM	STRM	38 40 175 55	29
OKAIAWA	POPL	39 32 174 12	34
OKAIHAE (TRIG)	HILL	38 51 175 12	27
OKAIHAU	LOC	35 19 173 46	4
OKAINS BAY	BAY	43 41 173 04	83
OKAINS BAY	LOC	43 43 173 02	83
OKAITERUA STREAM	STRM	45 51 168 22	107
OKAKA	LOC	35 20 173 40	4
OKAKI (TRIG)	HILL	36 00 173 50	6
OKAKI (TRIG)	HILL	36 00 173 50	7
OKAMA STREAM	STRM	38 26 175 54	28
OKAMA STREAM	STRM	38 26 175 54	29
OKAOKO ROCK	ROCK	35 22 174 23	5
OKAPA (TRIG)	HILL	35 32 174 05	4
OKAPA (TRIG)	HILL	35 32 174 05	5
OKAPEKA (TRIG)	HILL	38 25 177 18	31
OKAPU	LOC	38 02 174 51	18
OKAPUA CREEK	STRM	46 01 168 54	110
OKARAHIA STREAM	STRM	42 34 173 30	73
OKARAMIO	LOC	41 25 173 46	60
OKARAMIO RIVER	STRM	41 24 173 46	60
OKARARI STREAM	STRM	35 19 174 00	4
OKARARI STREAM	STRM	35 19 174 00	5
OKAREKA, LAKE	LAKE	38 10 176 22	20
OKAREKA, LAKE	LAKE	38 10 176 22	21
OKARI LAGOON	LAGN	41 50 171 28	63
OKARI RIVER	STRM	41 49 171 28	63
OKARITO	LOC	43 13 170 10	74
OKARITO LAGOON	LAGN	43 12 170 13	74
OKARITO RIVER	STRM	43 14 170 12	74
OKARO CREEK	STRM	36 18 174 09	10
OKARO, LAKE	LAKE	38 18 176 24	21
OKARO, LAKE	LAKE	38 18 176 24	29
OKARORO (TRIG)	HILL	36 12 174 10	7
OKATAINA, LAKE	LAKE	38 08 176 25	20
OKATAINA, LAKE	LAKE	38 08 176 25	21
OKATAKATA ISLANDS	ISLD	35 00 173 17	3
OKATO	POPL	39 12 173 53	34
OKAU	LOC	38 52 174 40	26
OKAU	LOC	40 51 176 14	50
OKAU STREAM	STRM	40 51 176 15	50
OKAUAI STREAM	STRM	39 32 175 04	36
OKAUAKA STREAM	STRM	38 36 175 24	27
OKAUAMO (TRIG)	HILL	39 20 175 13	36
OKAUAWA STREAM	STRM	39 38 176 30	43
OKAUAWA STREAM	STRM	39 38 176 30	47
OKAUIA	LOC	37 47 175 50	19
OKAUIA	LOC	37 47 175 50	20
OKAUIA PA	LOC	37 49 175 52	20
OKAURA STREAM	STRM	38 34 177 13	31
OKAWA STREAM	STRM	39 33 176 42	39
OKAWA STREAM	STRM	39 33 176 42	40
OKAWA STREAM	STRM	39 33 176 42	42
OKAWAWA STREAM	STRM	35 39 173 34	6
OKE ISLAND	ISLD	45 38 166 51	104
O'KEEFE CREEK	STRM	41 53 171 31	63
OKEHU STREAM	STRM	39 53 174 53	44
OKEHU STREAM	STRM	39 53 174 53	45
OKERE FALLS	LOC	38 01 176 21	20
OKERE FALLS	LOC	38 01 176 21	21
OKETE	LOC	37 49 174 56	18
OKETE STREAM	STRM	37 49 174 55	18
OKIATO	LOC	35 18 174 08	4
OKIATO	LOC	35 18 174 08	5
OKIORE	LOC	38 11 177 17	23
OKIRAU STREAM	STRM	39 36 174 33	35
OKIRAU STREAM	STRM	39 36 174 33	44
OKITU	LOC	38 40 178 05	32
OKIWA BAY	BAY	41 16 173 56	54
OKIWA BAY	BAY	41 16 173 56	60
OKIWA BAY	BAY	41 16 173 56	61
OKIWA (TRIG)	HILL	39 45 174 53	44
OKIWI	LOC	36 09 175 24	9
OKIWI BAY	BAY	41 06 173 40	60
OKIWI BAY	BAY	42 13 173 52	67
OKIWIRIKI (TRIG)	HILL	38 32 175 09	27
OKOA (TRIG)	HILL	39 47 175 17	45
OKOEKE STREAM	STRM	38 59 176 32	39
OKOEKE STREAM	STRM	38 59 176 32	40
OKOHA	HSTD	41 03 174 06	54
OKOHA	HSTD	41 03 174 06	60
OKOHA	HSTD	41 03 174 06	61
OKOIA	LOC	39 56 175 18	45
OKOKEWA ISLAND	ISLD	36 09 175 19	9
OKOKI	LOC	39 01 174 29	35
OKOROA (TRIG)	HILL	39 29 174 59	36
OKOROIRE	LOC	37 57 175 48	19
OKOROIRE	LOC	37 57 175 48	20
OKOROMAI BAY	BAY	36 37 174 49	11
OKOROMAI BAY	BAY	36 37 174 49	12
OKOROMAI POINT	PNT	35 20 174 21	5
OKOROPUNGA STREAM	STRM	41 26 175 39	53
OKOTINGA (TRIG)	HILL	39 30 175 33	36
OKOTINGA (TRIG)	HILL	39 30 175 33	37
OKOWHAO, LAKE	LAKE	37 32 175 08	14
OKOWHAO, LAKE	LAKE	37 32 175 08	15
OKUKU	LOC	43 13 172 25	81
OKUKU HILL (TRIG)	MTN	43 05 172 19	81
OKUKU PASS	PASS	43 06 172 27	81
OKUKU PASS	PASS	43 06 172 27	82
OKUKU RANGE	MTNS	43 05 172 23	81
OKUKU RESERVOIR	RESR	42 44 171 14	68
OKUKU RESERVOIR	RESR	42 44 171 14	69
OKUKU RIVER	STRM	43 17 172 28	81
OKUKU RIVER (SOUTH BRANCH)	STRM	43 07 172 22	81
OKUKU RIVER (WEST BRANCH)	STRM	43 12 172 28	81
OKUKU RIVER (WEST BRANCH)	STRM	43 12 172 28	82
OKUKU SADDLE	SAD	43 04 172 19	81
OKUPATA STREAM	STRM	38 04 174 55	18
OKUPATA STREAM	STRM	39 01 175 32	36
OKUPATA STREAM	STRM	39 01 175 32	37
OKUPATA STREAM	STRM	39 01 175 32	38
OKUPU	LOC	36 15 175 26	9
OKURA	LOC	36 41 174 43	11
OKURA	LOC	36 41 174 43	12
OKURA RIVER	STRM	35 14 173 59	4
OKURA RIVER	STRM	36 40 174 44	11
OKURA RIVER	STRM	36 40 174 44	12
OKURAKURA STREAM	STRM	39 15 176 47	40
OKUREI POINT	PNT	37 45 176 28	21
OKUREI POINT	PNT	37 45 176 28	22
OKURI BAY	BAY	40 59 173 47	60
OKURI BAY	BAY	40 59 173 47	61
OKURI (TRIG)	HILL	40 59 173 46	60
OKURI (TRIG)	HILL	40 59 173 46	61
OKURU	LOC	43 55 168 56	78
OKURU RIVER	STRM	43 54 168 55	78
OKUTI RIVER	STRM	43 47 172 47	83
OKUTI VALLEY	LOC	43 47 172 49	83
OKUTUA CREEK	STRM	43 11 170 15	74
OLAF, MOUNT	MTN	43 35 170 24	74
OLAF, MOUNT	MTN	43 35 170 24	77
OLD HUT CREEK	STRM	45 32 169 26	100
OLD HUTT CREEK	STRM	45 04 170 15	101
OLD MAN CREEK	STRM	44 30 169 57	92
OLD MAN PEAK	PEAK	43 31 171 22	75
OLD MAN PEAK	PEAK	43 31 171 22	80
OLD MAN PEAK	PEAK	44 36 169 41	91
OLD MAN RANGE	MTNS	43 32 171 22	75
OLD MAN RANGE	MTNS	43 32 171 22	80
OLD MAN RANGE	MTNS	45 22 169 12	100
OLD MAN ROCK	ROCK	36 43 175 51	16
OLD MAN ROCK	ROCK	46 22 167 44	108
OLD MAN, THE	STRM	44 02 168 23	88
OLD MAN (TRIG)	MTN	43 59 170 23	77
OLD MAN (TRIG)	MTN	43 59 170 23	86
OLD MANS HEAD	PNT	40 48 173 57	54
OLD MANS POINT	PNT	40 48 173 57	61
OLD MOTUPUHA (TRIG)	PEAK	39 28 176 00	37
OLD SOW (TRIG)	PEAK	41 26 172 41	58
OLD WOMAN RANGE	MTNS	45 16 169 04	99
OLDEROG CREEK	STRM	42 51 171 19	69
OLDNAM (TRIG)	HILL	43 04 172 53	82
O'LEARY PASS	PASS	44 29 168 26	88
O'LEARY PASS	PASS	44 29 168 26	89
O'LEARY PASS	PASS	44 31 168 01	89
OLIVE, MOUNT	PEAK	41 17 172 32	56
OLIVE, MOUNT	PEAK	41 17 172 32	58
OLIVER POINT	PNT	45 35 166 40	104
OLIVER, MOUNT (TRIG)	HILL	41 16 173 53	54
OLIVER, MOUNT (TRIG)	HILL	41 16 173 53	60
OLIVER, MOUNT (TRIG)	HILL	41 16 173 53	61
OLIVINE ICE PLATEAU	PLAT	44 27 168 22	88
OLIVINE ICE PLATEAU	PLAT	44 27 168 22	89
OLIVINE RANGE	MTNS	44 18 168 29	88
OLIVINE RANGE	MTNS	44 18 168 29	89
OLIVINE RIVER	STRM	44 27 168 13	88
OLIVINE RIVER	STRM	44 27 168 13	89
OLLIVER, MOUNT (TRIG)	MTN	43 43 170 04	76
OLLIVER, MOUNT (TRIG)	MTN	43 43 170 04	77
OLLIVER, MOUNT (TRIG)	MTN	43 43 170 04	79
OLLIVER STREAM	STRM	43 30 171 09	75
OLYMPUS, MOUNT	MTN	43 11 171 37	80
OLYMPUS, MOUNT (TRIG)	MTN	41 38 173 30	59
OMAHA	LOC	36 20 174 47	11
OMAHA BAY	BAY	36 20 174 49	11
OMAHA FLATS	LOC	36 21 174 45	11
OMAHAKI	HSTD	39 29 176 23	39
OMAHAKI STREAM	STRM	39 32 176 22	39
OMAHAKI STREAM	STRM	39 32 176 22	40
OMAHINE STREAM	STRM	37 51 175 52	20
OMAHINE STREAM	STRM	39 44 174 41	44
OMAHU	LOC	37 16 175 40	15
OMAHU	LOC	37 16 175 40	17
OMAHU STREAM	STRM	35 39 173 52	6
OMAHU STREAM	STRM	35 39 173 52	7
OMAHU STREAM	STRM	37 31 175 41	15
OMAHU STREAM	STRM	37 31 175 41	17
OMAHUTA	LOC	35 14 173 35	3
OMAHUTA	LOC	35 14 173 35	4
OMAIA ISLAND	ISLD	35 00 173 16	3
OMAIO	LOC	37 49 177 38	24
OMAIO BAY	BAY	37 48 177 38	24
OMAKA RIVER	STRM	41 30 173 52	60
OMAKAU	LOC	45 06 169 36	100
OMAKERE	LOC	40 03 176 45	43
OMAKERE STREAM	STRM	40 01 176 42	43
OMAKERE (TRIG)	HILL	40 06 176 47	43
OMAKURA STREAM	STRM	35 16 173 32	3
O'MALLEY STREAM	STRM	42 30 173 06	72
OMAMARI	LOC	35 52 173 40	6
OMANA	LOC	35 54 174 06	7

OMANAIA	LOC	35 27 173 33	6
OMANAIA RIVER	STRM	35 25 173 30	3
OMANAIA RIVER	STRM	35 25 173 30	6
OMANAWA	LOC	37 48 176 05	20
OMANAWA	LOC	37 48 176 05	21
OMANAWA FALLS	LOC	37 51 176 06	20
OMANAWA FALLS	LOC	37 51 176 06	21
OMANAWA RIVER	STRM	37 46 176 04	20
OMANAWA RIVER	STRM	37 46 176 04	21
OMANU	SBRB	37 39 176 13	20
OMANU	SBRB	37 39 176 13	21
OMANU BEACH	SBRB	37 40 176 14	20
OMANU BEACH	SBRB	37 40 176 14	21
OMANU CREEK	STRM	41 49 171 36	63
OMANU CREEK	STRM	41 49 171 36	64
OMANUKA LAGOON	LAKE	40 20 175 19	48
OMAO STREAM	STRM	35 26 173 38	4
OMAO STREAM	STRM	35 26 173 38	6
OMAPERE	LOC	35 32 173 23	6
OMAPERE, LAKE	LAKE	35 21 173 48	4
OMAPERE, LAKE	LAKE	35 21 173 48	6
OMARAE STREAM	STRM	39 29 175 29	36
OMARAE STREAM	STRM	39 29 175 29	37
OMARAMA	LOC	44 29 169 58	92
OMARAMA SADDLE	SAD	44 40 169 49	91
OMARAMA STREAM	STRM	44 36 169 52	91
OMAROWA STREAM	STRM	39 08 176 34	39
OMAROWA STREAM	STRM	39 08 176 34	40
OMARU RIVER	STRM	36 01 174 09	7
OMARU STREAM	STRM	39 29 174 44	35
OMARU STREAM	STRM	39 29 174 44	44
OMARUAPAKIHAU (TRIG)	HILL	40 45 176 17	50
OMARUKOKERE STREAM	STRM	39 15 176 18	39
OMARUMUTU	LOC	37 59 177 24	23
OMARUMUTU	LOC	37 59 177 24	24
OMATA	LOC	39 05 174 01	34
OMATA STREAM	STRM	39 42 174 43	44
OMATAI (TRIG)	HILL	35 04 173 31	3
OMATANE	LOC	39 44 175 55	46
OMAUI	LOC	46 31 168 15	109
OMAUI ISLAND	ISLD	46 31 168 13	109
OMAUKORA STREAM	STRM	38 16 177 20	31
OMAUMAU RIVER	STRM	36 27 174 25	10
OMAUMAU RIVER	STRM	36 27 174 25	11
OMAUNU	LOC	35 08 173 44	4
OMAUNU STREAM	STRM	35 08 173 42	4
OMEGA (TRIG)	PEAK	41 00 175 18	53
OMEO CREEK	STRM	45 16 169 17	100
OMERUITI (TRIG)	HILL	38 54 176 24	29
OMERUITI (TRIG)	HILL	38 54 176 24	39
OMERUITI (TRIG)	HILL	38 54 176 24	40
OMIHA	LOC	36 49 175 03	12
OMIHA	LOC	36 49 175 03	13
OMIHI	LOC	43 02 172 51	82
OMIHI STREAM	STRM	43 05 172 47	82
OMIMI	LOC	45 41 170 36	103
OMOANA	LOC	39 25 174 34	35
OMOANA	LOC	39 25 174 34	44
OMOANA SADDLE	SAD	39 25 174 32	35
OMOANA SADDLE	SAD	39 25 174 32	44
OMOEROA BLUFF	CLIF	43 18 170 02	76
OMOEROA HILL (TRIG)	HILL	43 22 170 05	76
OMOEROA HILL (TRIG)	HILL	43 22 170 05	77
OMOEROA RIVER	STRM	43 19 170 02	76
OMOEROA SADDLE	SAD	43 25 170 07	74
OMOEROA SADDLE	SAD	43 25 170 07	77
OMOHO STREAM	STRM	36 41 175 33	13
OMOHO STREAM	STRM	36 41 175 33	16
OMOHO STREAM	STRM	38 40 175 51	28
OMOHO STREAM	STRM	38 40 175 51	29
OMOKOITI FLATS	FLAT	36 32 174 20	10
OMOKOROA	LOC	37 40 176 02	20
OMOKOROA BEACH	LOC	37 38 176 03	20
OMORI	LOC	38 54 175 46	28
OMORI	LOC	38 54 175 46	38
OMOTO	LOC	42 28 171 15	68
OMOTO	LOC	42 28 171 15	69
ONAERO RIVER	STRM	39 00 174 22	35
ONAHAU BAY	BAY	41 14 173 58	54
ONAHAU BAY	BAY	41 14 173 58	60
ONAHAU BAY	BAY	41 14 173 58	61
ONAHAU RIVER	STRM	40 48 172 46	57
ONAHAU (TRIG)	HILL	41 14 173 57	54
ONAHAU (TRIG)	HILL	41 14 173 57	60
ONAHAU (TRIG)	HILL	41 14 173 57	61
ONAMALUTU RIVER	STRM	41 29 173 49	60
ONAUKU BAY	BAY	41 08 174 22	54
ONAUKU BAY	BAY	41 08 174 22	61
ONAWE PENINSULA	PEN	43 46 172 56	83
ONE TREE HILL	SBRB	36 54 174 48	11
ONE TREE HILL	SBRB	36 54 174 48	12
ONE TREE HILL	SBRB	36 54 174 48	14
ONE TREE HILL	HSTD	42 39 173 16	72
ONE TREE HILL	HSTD	42 39 173 16	73
ONE TREE HILL (TRIG)	HILL	37 10 175 06	13
ONE TREE HILL (TRIG)	HILL	37 10 175 06	14
ONE TREE HILL (TRIG)	HILL	37 10 175 06	15
ONE TREE POINT	LOC	35 49 174 27	7
ONE TREE POINT	LOC	35 49 174 27	8
ONE TREE SADDLE	SAD	42 55 171 07	68
ONE TREE SADDLE	SAD	42 55 171 07	69
ONE TREE SADDLE	SAD	42 34 172 58	72
ONEHUNGA	SBRB	36 55 174 47	12
ONEHUNGA	SBRB	36 55 174 47	14
ONEHUNGA BAY	BAY	41 07 174 20	54
ONEHUNGA BAY	BAY	41 07 174 20	61
ONEKAINGA (TRIG)	HILL	35 29 174 26	5
ONEKAKA	LOC	40 46 172 42	56
ONEKAKA	LOC	40 46 172 42	57
ONEKAWA	SBRB	39 30 176 53	40
ONEKAWA	SBRB	39 30 176 53	41
ONEKAWA	SBRB	39 30 176 53	42
ONEMANA	LOC	37 09 175 53	17
ONEONE, MOUNT (TRIG)	HILL	43 02 170 25	74
ONEONE RIVER	STRM	43 02 170 26	74
ONEPOTO (TRIG)	HILL	37 17 174 53	14
ONERAHI	SBRB	35 46 174 22	5
ONERAHI	SBRB	35 46 174 22	7
ONERAHI	SBRB	35 46 174 22	8
ONERIRI	LOC	36 17 174 22	10
ONERIRI	LOC	36 17 174 22	11
ONEROA	LOC	36 47 175 01	12
ONEROA	LOC	36 47 175 01	13
ONEROA BAY	BAY	35 15 174 08	4
ONEROA BAY	BAY	35 15 174 08	5
ONETAI STREAM	STRM	35 44 173 51	6
ONETAI STREAM	STRM	37 16 175 39	15
ONETAI STREAM	STRM	37 16 175 39	17
ONETANGI	LOC	36 47 175 05	13
ONETANGI BAY	BAY	36 47 175 05	13
ONEWHERO	LOC	37 20 174 55	14
ONEWHERO BAY	BAY	35 14 174 04	4
ONEWHERO BAY	BAY	35 14 174 04	5
ONGAHORO (TRIG)	HILL	38 16 176 14	21
ONGAHORO (TRIG)	HILL	38 16 176 14	29
ONGANGANA STREAM	STRM	39 28 175 02	36
ONGAONGA	POPL	39 55 176 25	47
ONGAONGA STREAM	STRM	39 57 176 28	47
ONGARAHU STREAM	STRM	38 25 175 58	28
ONGARAHU STREAM	STRM	38 25 175 58	29
ONGARUANUKU	MTN	44 33 167 58	89
ONGARUANUKU	MTN	44 33 167 58	94
ONGARUE	LOC	38 43 175 17	27
ONGARUE ELECTRIC SUBSTATION	BLDG	38 45 175 11	27
ONGARUE RIVER	STRM	38 53 175 15	27
ONGARURU	LOC	38 08 178 19	25
ONGARURU	LOC	38 08 178 19	32
ONGOHI STREAM	STRM	36 34 175 22	9
ONGOHI STREAM	STRM	36 34 175 22	16
ONLY ISLAND	ISLD	45 58 166 52	104
ONLY ISLAND	ISLD	45 58 166 52	105
ONOKE	LOC	35 25 173 25	3
ONOKE	LOC	35 25 173 25	6
ONOKE, LAKE	LAKE	41 23 175 08	52
ONOKE, LAKE	LAKE	41 23 175 08	53
ONOKE, LAKE	LAKE	41 23 175 08	55
ONSLOW, LAKE	LAKE	45 33 169 38	100
ONSLOW, MOUNT	MTN	43 27 170 46	74
ONUKUTAUIRA STREAM	STRM	38 08 175 57	20
OONAH BURN	STRM	45 31 167 18	96
OPAEA	LOC	39 37 175 48	46
OPAHEKE	LOC	37 06 174 57	12
OPAHEKE	LOC	37 06 174 57	14
OPAHEKEHEKE ISLAND	ISLD	36 37 174 23	10
OPAHEKEHEKE ISLAND	ISLD	36 37 174 23	11
OPAHERU SADDLE	SAD	38 33 176 51	30
OPAHI	LOC	35 29 174 01	4
OPAHI	LOC	35 29 174 01	5
OPAKAU ISLAND	ISLD	36 12 175 18	9
OPAKAU STREAM	STRM	38 14 175 57	20
OPAKAU STREAM	STRM	38 14 175 57	28
OPAKAU STREAM	STRM	38 14 175 57	29
OPAKI	LOC	40 53 175 40	48
OPAKI	LOC	40 53 175 40	51
OPAKU	LOC	39 41 174 33	44
OPANGA (TRIG)	HILL	39 45 175 18	45
OPANGO (TRIG)	HILL	35 20 173 20	3
OPANI-APUTA POINT	PNT	41 05 173 58	54
OPANI-APUTA POINT	PNT	41 05 173 58	60
OPANI-APUTA POINT	PNT	41 05 173 58	61
OPAOPAO STREAM	STRM	35 17 173 41	4
OPAPA	LOC	37 59 177 26	23
OPAPA	LOC	39 48 176 41	42
OPAPA	LOC	39 48 176 41	43
OPAPA	LOC	39 48 176 41	47
OPAPE	LOC	37 59 177 26	24
OPARA	LOC	35 26 173 27	3
OPARA	LOC	35 26 173 27	6
OPARA STREAM	STRM	43 42 173 03	83
OPARARA	LOC	41 13 172 08	56
OPARARA	LOC	41 13 172 08	62
OPARARA RIVER	STRM	41 12 172 07	56
OPARARA RIVER	STRM	41 12 172 07	62
OPARAU	LOC	38 03 174 56	18
OPARAU RIVER	STRM	38 03 174 55	18
OPARURE	LOC	38 19 175 07	27
OPATO STREAM	STRM	38 17 177 21	31
OPAU STREAM	STRM	39 18 176 37	39
OPAU STREAM	STRM	39 18 176 37	40
OPAWA	SBRB	43 33 172 40	82
OPAWA	SBRB	43 33 172 40	83
OPAWA	SBRB	43 33 172 40	85
OPAWA RIVER	STRM	41 30 174 03	60
OPAWE STREAM	STRM	40 08 175 52	46
OPEN BAY	BAY	41 07 174 48	52
OPEN BAY	BAY	41 07 174 48	55
OPEN BAY ISLANDS	ISLD	43 52 168 53	78
OPEN CREEK	STRM	42 36 173 24	72
OPEN CREEK	STRM	42 36 173 24	73
OPERA RANGE	MTNS	42 24 172 30	71
OPERIKI PA	LOC	39 39 175 10	45
OPHIR	LOC	45 07 169 36	100
OPIHI	LOC	44 13 171 04	87
OPIHI BAY	BAY	41 18 174 08	54
OPIHI BAY	BAY	41 18 174 08	60
OPIHI BAY	BAY	41 18 174 08	61
OPIHI RIVER	STRM	44 02 170 45	86
OPIHI RIVER	STRM	44 02 170 45	87
OPIHI RIVER	STRM	44 17 171 21	87
OPIKI	LOC	40 27 175 28	48
OPIKI	LOC	40 27 175 28	49
OPIO	LOC	45 57 168 05	106
OPIO	LOC	45 57 168 05	107
OPIO STREAM	STRM	46 07 167 58	106
OPIO STREAM	STRM	46 07 167 58	107
OPITO	LOC	36 43 175 48	16
OPITO BAY	BAY	36 43 175 48	16
OPITONUI RIVER	STRM	36 46 175 36	13
OPITONUI RIVER	STRM	36 46 175 36	16
OPONAE	LOC	38 16 177 18	31
OPONAE STREAM	STRM	38 16 177 18	31
OPONONI	LOC	35 30 173 24	6
OPORAE	HSTD	40 25 176 14	50
OPORAE STREAM	STRM	40 25 176 14	50
OPORAE (TRIG)	HILL	40 22 176 13	50
OPORO	LOC	46 18 168 17	107
OPORO	LOC	46 18 168 17	109
OPOTIKI	POPL	38 01 177 17	23
OPOTIKI STREAM	STRM	38 49 175 14	27
OPOTIKI (TRIG)	HILL	38 48 175 11	27
OPOTORU RIVER	STRM	37 50 174 52	18
OPOUAHI, LAKE	LAKE	39 09 176 50	40
OPOUAHI, LAKE	LAKE	39 09 176 50	41
OPOUAWE RIVER	STRM	41 34 175 25	53
OPOUNUI POINT	PNT	35 01 173 54	4
OPOURI PEAK	PEAK	41 11 173 45	60
OPOURI PEAK	PEAK	41 11 173 45	61
OPOURI RIVER	STRM	41 13 173 36	60
OPOURI SADDLE	SAD	41 08 173 44	60
OPOURIAO	LOC	38 07 177 00	22
OPOURIAO	LOC	38 07 177 00	23
OPOURIKI STREAM	STRM	46 19 167 57	108
OPOURIKI STREAM	STRM	46 19 167 57	109
OPOUTAMA	LOC	39 04 177 50	33
OPOUTAMA STREAM	STRM	39 04 177 50	33
OPOUTEKE	LOC	35 42 173 50	6
OPOUTEKE RIVER	STRM	35 40 173 53	6
OPOUTEKE RIVER	STRM	35 40 173 53	7
OPOUTEKE STREAM	STRM	35 41 173 50	6
OPOUTERE	LOC	37 06 175 53	17
OPU CREEK	STRM	36 11 174 17	7
OPU CREEK	STRM	36 11 174 17	8
OPUA	LOC	35 19 174 07	4
OPUA	LOC	35 19 174 07	5
OPUAHAU (TRIG)	HILL	37 17 176 14	17
OPUATIA	LOC	37 25 175 00	14
OPUATIA STREAM	STRM	37 23 174 55	14
OPUAWHANGA	LOC	35 31 174 21	5
OPUHA	LOC	44 10 171 00	87
OPUHA RIVER	STRM	44 14 170 53	87
OPUHA RIVER	STRM	44 11 171 00	87
OPUIAKI RIVER	STRM	37 49 176 02	20
OPUNAKE	POPL	39 27 173 51	34
OPURAKAU (TRIG)	HILL	38 25 176 57	30
OPUREHU RIVER	STRM	35 15 173 32	3
OPUREHU RIVER	STRM	35 15 173 32	4
OPUREKE (TRIG)	PEAK	38 55 176 33	39
OPUREKE (TRIG)	PEAK	38 55 176 33	40
OPURUA (TRIG)	HILL	39 02 177 34	33
ORAHIRI STREAM	STRM	38 12 175 12	18
ORAKA BEACH	LOC	39 05 177 54	33
ORAKA POINT	PNT	46 24 167 53	108
ORAKA POINT	PNT	46 24 167 53	109
ORAKA STREAM	STRM	37 54 175 48	19
ORAKA STREAM	STRM	37 54 175 48	20
ORAKA STREAM	STRM	38 07 175 54	20
ORAKA (TRIG)	HILL	46 23 167 52	108
ORAKA (TRIG)	HILL	46 23 167 52	109
ORAKAU	LOC	38 04 175 24	19
ORAKEI	SBRB	36 52 174 49	11
ORAKEI	SBRB	36 52 174 49	12
ORAKEI STREAM	STRM	37 31 175 24	15
ORAKEIKORAKO	LOC	38 29 176 09	28
ORAKEIKORAKO	LOC	38 29 176 09	29
ORAKIPAOA	LOC	44 16 171 19	87
ORAKONUI STREAM	STRM	38 31 176 11	29
ORANGAPAI	LOC	45 14 170 08	101
ORANGI (TRIG)	HILL	37 49 175 06	18
ORANGIKAHU (TRIG)	HILL	35 25 174 18	5
ORANGIKINO (TRIG)	PEAK	38 57 176 28	39
ORANGIKINO (TRIG)	PEAK	38 57 176 28	40
ORANGIMEA	LOC	39 41 174 51	44
ORANGIPONGO	LOC	39 54 175 41	46
ORANGIPUKU RIVER	STRM	42 39 171 26	69
ORANGITUTAETUTU (TRIG)	HILL	38 26 177 03	30
ORANGIWHAO (TRIG)	HILL	38 08 174 44	18
ORAORA	LOC	35 32 173 30	6
ORAORA STREAM	STRM	35 36 173 24	6
ORARI	LOC	44 09 171 17	84
ORARI	LOC	44 09 171 17	87
ORARI BRIDGE	LOC	44 03 171 16	87
ORARI RIVER	STRM	44 15 171 25	84
ORARI RIVER	STRM	44 15 171 25	87
ORATIA	LOC	36 55 174 37	11
ORATIA	LOC	36 55 174 37	12
ORATIA	LOC	36 55 174 37	14
ORAUEA RIVER	STRM	46 08 167 43	106
ORAUEA RIVER	STRM	46 08 167 43	108
ORAUEA STREAM	STRM	45 57 167 52	106
ORAUEA STREAM	STRM	45 57 167 52	107
ORAUKURANGI	PEAK	38 18 177 14	31
ORAUTA	LOC	35 25 173 58	4
ORAUTA	LOC	35 25 173 58	5
ORAUTA STREAM	STRM	35 24 173 58	4
ORAUTA STREAM	STRM	35 24 173 58	5
ORAUTOHA	LOC	39 20 175 14	36
ORAUTOHA STREAM	STRM	39 19 175 14	36
ORAWAU	LOC	35 16 173 28	3
ORAWIA	LOC	46 03 167 47	106
ORBELL, LAKE	LAKE	45 18 167 40	97
ORCHARD BAY	BAY	40 58 174 03	54
ORCHARD BAY	BAY	40 58 174 03	60
ORCHARD BAY	BAY	40 58 174 03	61
ORCHARD CREEK	STRM	41 24 172 44	58
ORCHARD SPUR (TRIG)	RDGE	41 38 173 52	60
ORE STREAM	STRM	44 12 169 15	78
OREKOPA STREAM	STRM	38 20 174 57	26
OREORE	LOC	39 33 175 18	36
OREPUKI	LOC	46 17 167 45	108
ORERE	LOC	36 59 175 13	13
ORERE	LOC	36 59 175 13	15
ORERE POINT	LOC	36 58 175 14	13
ORERE POINT	PNT	36 58 175 15	13
ORERE POINT	PNT	36 58 175 15	15
ORERE POINT	LOC	36 58 175 14	15
ORERE POINT	PNT	45 13 170 54	102
ORERE RIVER	STRM	36 58 175 15	13
ORERE RIVER	STRM	36 58 175 15	15
ORETE POINT	PNT	37 36 177 54	24
ORETI BEACH	LOC	46 26 168 14	109
ORETI PLAINS	LOC	46 08 168 14	107
ORETI RIVER	STRM	46 28 168 16	109
OREWA	POPL	36 35 174 42	11
OREWA	POPL	36 35 174 42	12
OREWA RIVER	STRM	36 36 174 42	11
OREWA RIVER	STRM	36 36 174 42	12
OREWHA (TRIG)	HILL	38 26 177 39	31
ORGAN RANGE	MTNS	42 39 172 33	71
ORGAN STREAM	STRM	42 41 172 34	71
ORGANS ISLAND	ISLD	41 48 171 37	63
ORGANS ISLAND	ISLD	41 48 171 37	64
ORIATOU POINT	PNT	34 33 172 57	2
ORINGI	LOC	40 15 176 01	46
ORINGI	LOC	40 16 176 01	49
ORINI	LOC	37 34 175 19	15
ORINOCO	LOC	41 14 172 53	58
ORIRA	LOC	35 19 173 35	3
ORIRA	LOC	35 19 173 35	4
ORIRA RIVER	STRM	35 20 173 34	3
ORIRA RIVER	STRM	35 20 173 34	4
ORMOND	LOC	38 33 177 55	32
ORMONDVILLE	LOC	40 07 176 16	47
OROI (TRIG)	HILL	37 59 177 28	23
OROI (TRIG)	HILL	37 59 177 28	24
OROKAWA BAY	BAY	37 23 175 56	17
OROKO CREEK	STRM	43 12 170 14	74
OROMAHOE	LOC	35 19 173 59	4
OROMAHOE	LOC	35 19 173 59	5
ORONGO	LOC	37 12 175 33	13
ORONGO	LOC	37 12 175 33	15
ORONGO BAY	LOC	35 18 174 09	4
ORONGO BAY	LOC	35 18 174 09	5
ORONGO POINT	PNT	36 25 174 21	10
ORONGO STREAM	STRM	37 53 175 02	18
ORONGO (TRIG)	HILL	36 25 174 21	10
ORONGO (TRIG)	HILL	36 25 174 21	11
ORONGORONGO RIVER	STRM	41 25 174 54	52
ORONGORONGO RIVER	STRM	41 25 174 54	55
ORONGORONGO STATION	HSTD	41 25 174 54	52
ORONGORONGO STATION	HSTD	41 25 174 54	55
ORONGORONGO (TRIG)	PEAK	41 13 175 05	52
ORONGORONGO (TRIG)	PEAK	41 13 175 05	55
ORONUI STREAM	STRM	37 53 178 01	24
ORONUI STREAM	STRM	37 53 178 01	25
OROPI	LOC	37 50 176 10	20
OROPI	LOC	37 50 176 10	21
OROTERE	LOC	35 07 173 50	4
OROTERE (TRIG)	HILL	35 08 173 50	4
OROUA DOWNS	LOC	40 22 175 19	48
OROUA RIVER	STRM	40 17 175 31	46
OROUA RIVER	STRM	40 26 175 26	48
O'ROURKE (TRIG)	HILL	41 57 172 21	65
OROWAITI RIVER	STRM	41 45 171 39	63
OROWAITI RIVER	STRM	41 45 171 39	64
OROWHANA (TRIG)	HILL	35 36 173 45	4
OROWHANA (TRIG)	HILL	35 36 173 45	6
OROWHANO (TRIG)	HILL	35 14 173 14	3
ORPHANS ROCK	ROCK	47 11 167 44	114
ORR HILL (TRIG)	HILL	41 00 173 48	60
ORR HILL (TRIG)	HILL	41 00 173 48	61
ORR, MOUNT (TRIG)	MTN	44 45 170 38	93
ORR STREAM	STRM	41 58 173 18	66
ORTON	LOC	37 23 175 02	14
ORTON	LOC	44 09 171 25	84
ORTON	LOC	44 09 171 25	87
ORUA BAY	BAY	37 03 174 36	12
ORUA BAY	LOC	37 03 174 36	12
ORUA BAY	LOC	37 03 174 36	14
ORUA BAY	BAY	37 03 174 36	14
ORUAEA BAY	BAY	35 32 174 28	5
ORUAHINEAWE (TRIG)	HILL	38 36 176 12	29
ORUAITI	LOC	35 00 173 36	3
ORUAITI	LOC	35 00 173 36	4
ORUAITI RIVER	STRM	35 01 173 35	3
ORUAITI RIVER	STRM	35 01 173 35	4
ORUAIWI	LOC	38 50 175 27	27
ORUAKERETAKI STREAM	STRM	40 16 176 03	46
ORUANUI	LOC	38 35 176 02	28
ORUANUI	LOC	38 35 176 02	29
ORUARONGO	TRIG	40 30 175 15	48
ORUATAIAKA (TRIG)	HILL	37 43 178 13	25
ORUATEMANU ISLAND	ISLD	35 00 173 48	4
ORUATIPOKI STREAM	STRM	38 49 177 17	31
ORUAWHARO	LOC	36 16 174 25	10
ORUAWHARO	LOC	36 16 174 25	11
ORUAWHARO RIVER	STRM	36 18 174 17	10
ORUKUTIA STREAM	STRM	38 07 177 26	23
ORUKUTIA STREAM	STRM	38 07 177 26	24
ORUPE STREAM	STRM	39 06 175 09	36
ORURU	LOC	35 03 173 30	3
ORURU RIVER	STRM	35 01 173 29	3
ORURU (TRIG)	HILL	35 03 173 31	3
ORUTUA RIVER	STRM	37 38 178 27	25
ORWELL CREEK	STRM	42 21 171 32	69
OSBORNE	LOC	45 46 170 35	103
O'SHANESSY, MOUNT	MTN	42 39 171 43	70
OSPREY HEAD	HEAD	34 59 173 32	3
OSSA, MOUNT	MTN	42 02 172 04	64
OSTEND	LOC	36 48 175 02	12
OSTEND	LOC	36 48 175 02	13
OSTLER, MOUNT	HILL	44 15 170 03	79
OSWALD STREAM	STRM	45 38 168 21	107
OTA CREEK	LOC	46 17 168 48	110
OTA CREEK	STRM	46 18 168 50	110
OTA CREEK	LOC	46 17 168 48	112
OTA CREEK	STRM	46 18 168 50	112
OTAENGA STREAM	STRM	35 35 173 50	4
OTAENGA STREAM	STRM	35 35 173 50	6
OTAGO HARBOUR	HARB	45 50 170 37	103
OTAGO PENINSULA	PEN	45 51 170 38	103
OTAGO RETREAT	PASS	46 09 166 37	104
OTAHA	LOC	35 08 173 56	4
OTAHI STREAM	STRM	39 27 173 50	34
OTAHOME	HSTD	40 57 176 09	49
OTAHOME	HSTD	40 57 176 09	50
OTAHOME	HSTD	40 57 176 09	51
OTAHOUA	HILL	40 59 175 45	51
OTAHU FLAT	LOC	45 59 167 43	106
OTAHU RIVER	STRM	37 14 175 53	17
OTAHUHU	SBRB	36 57 174 51	12
OTAHUHU	SBRB	36 57 174 51	14
OTAHUTI	LOC	46 14 168 12	107
OTAIHANGA	LOC	40 53 175 01	48
OTAIHANGA	LOC	40 53 175 01	52
OTAIHANGA	LOC	40 53 175 01	55
OTAIHANGA (TRIG)	HILL	39 12 174 58	36
OTAIKA	LOC	35 47 174 18	5
OTAIKA	LOC	35 47 174 18	7
OTAIKA	LOC	35 47 174 18	8
OTAIKA STREAM	STRM	35 47 174 19	5
OTAIKA STREAM	STRM	35 47 174 19	7
OTAIKA STREAM	STRM	35 47 174 19	8
OTAIKA VALLEY	LOC	35 47 174 14	5
OTAIKA VALLEY	LOC	35 47 174 14	7
OTAIKA VALLEY	LOC	35 47 174 14	8
OTAINGA (TRIG)	HILL	35 15 173 31	3
OTAIO	LOC	44 35 171 09	93
OTAIO GORGE	LOC	44 32 170 56	93
OTAIO RIVER	STRM	44 33 171 11	93
OTAIRI	LOC	39 50 175 30	45
OTAIRI	LOC	39 50 175 30	46
OTAITAI BUSH	LOC	46 20 168 03	109
OTAITAPU (TRIG)	HILL	37 56 177 37	24
OTAKAHA STREAM	STRM	41 33 175 13	53
OTAKAIANGI	LOC	35 37 174 11	5
OTAKAIANGI	LOC	35 37 174 11	7
OTAKARAMU STREAM (SOUTH BRANCH)	STRM	46 09 168 56	110
OTAKARAMU STREAM (SOUTH BRANCH)	STRM	46 09 168 56	112
OTAKARARA STREAM	STRM	39 26 176 33	39
OTAKARARA STREAM	STRM	39 26 176 33	40
OTAKARARA STREAM	STRM	39 26 176 33	42
OTAKEAO STREAM	STRM	36 55 175 26	13
OTAKEAO STREAM	STRM	36 55 175 26	15
OTAKEAO STREAM	STRM	36 55 175 26	16
OTAKEHO	LOC	39 33 174 02	34
OTAKEHO STREAM	STRM	39 34 174 03	34
OTAKETAKE STREAM	STRM	38 40 175 54	28
OTAKETAKE STREAM	STRM	38 40 175 54	29
OTAKI	POPL	40 46 175 09	48
OTAKI	POPL	40 46 175 09	55
OTAKI BEACH	LOC	40 44 175 07	48
OTAKI FORKS	LOC	40 52 175 14	48
OTAKI RIVER	STRM	40 46 175 06	48
OTAKIRI	LOC	37 59 176 45	22
OTAKIRI STATION	RSTN	37 57 176 47	22
OTAKOU	LOC	45 49 170 42	103
OTAKOWAI STREAM	STRM	39 18 176 48	40
OTAKOWAI STREAM	STRM	39 18 176 48	42
OTAMA	LOC	36 42 175 46	16
OTAMA	LOC	45 58 168 52	110

OTAMA CREEK	STRM	45 58 168 50	110
OTAMA RIVER	STRM	36 43 175 46	16
OTAMAARIKI STREAM	STRM	38 39 176 43	30
OTAMAKAPUA	LOC	39 53 175 47	46
OTAMAKOKORE STREAM	STRM	38 18 176 15	29
OTAMAMUA (TRIG)	HILL	35 23 174 12	5
OTAMANGAKAU, LAKE	LAKE	39 00 175 38	37
OTAMANGAKAU, LAKE	LAKE	39 00 175 38	38
OTAMARAHO STREAM	STRM	40 16 176 04	46
OTAMARAKAU	LOC	37 50 176 36	21
OTAMARAKAU	LOC	37 50 176 36	22
OTAMAROA	LOC	37 36 177 59	24
OTAMAROA	LOC	37 36 177 59	25
OTAMAROA STREAM	STRM	38 27 175 26	27
OTAMATAPAIO RIVER	STRM	44 33 170 06	92
OTAMATEA RIVER	STRM	36 14 174 19	7
OTAMATEA RIVER	STRM	36 14 174 19	8
OTAMATEA RIVER	STRM	38 45 176 23	29
OTAMATEANUI STREAM	STRM	39 17 176 00	37
OTAMATEANUI STREAM	STRM	39 17 176 00	38
OTAMATEAROA, LAKE	LAKE	37 18 174 41	14
OTAMAURI	HSTD	39 30 176 30	39
OTAMAURI	HSTD	39 30 176 30	40
OTAMAURI	HSTD	39 30 176 30	42
OTAMAURI STREAM	STRM	39 33 176 28	39
OTAMAURI STREAM	STRM	39 33 176 28	40
OTAMAWAIRUA STREAM	STRM	39 05 175 25	36
OTAMAWAIRUA STREAM	STRM	39 05 175 25	37
OTAMITA	LOC	46 01 168 51	110
OTAMITA STREAM	STRM	46 01 168 51	110
OTAMITA STREAM	STRM	46 01 168 51	112
OTAMORE (TRIG)	HILL	39 27 175 04	36
OTANE	LOC	38 26 177 07	31
OTANE	POPL	39 54 176 38	42
OTANE	POPL	39 54 176 38	43
OTANE	POPL	39 54 176 38	47
OTANE STREAM	STRM	38 25 177 07	31
OTANERAU BAY	BAY	41 10 174 20	54
OTANERAU BAY	BAY	41 10 174 20	61
OTANERITO BAY	BAY	43 51 173 04	83
OTANEROA POINT	PNT	35 16 174 18	5
OTANEURI STREAM	STRM	38 18 177 01	30
OTANEWAINUKU (TRIG)	HILL	37 54 176 12	20
OTANEWAINUKU (TRIG)	HILL	37 54 176 12	21
OTANGANE STREAM	STRM	40 32 175 41	48
OTANGANE STREAM	STRM	40 32 175 41	49
OTANGAROA	LOC	35 07 173 38	4
OTANGAROA STREAM	STRM	37 29 174 43	14
OTANGIHIA (TRIG)	HILL	39 06 176 36	39
OTANGIHIA (TRIG)	HILL	39 06 176 36	40
OTANGIMOANA STREAM	STRM	38 44 176 25	29
OTANGIWAI	LOC	38 43 175 07	27
OTANGURU STREAM	STRM	36 45 175 40	16
OTANOMOMO	LOC	46 18 169 45	111
OTANOMOMO	LOC	46 18 169 45	113
OTAO	LOC	35 19 174 02	4
OTAO	LOC	35 19 174 02	5
OTAPIRI	LOC	46 03 168 26	107
OTAPIRI GORGE	LOC	46 03 168 27	107
OTAPIRI STREAM	STRM	46 16 168 27	107
OTAPOKURA (TRIG)	HILL	37 53 178 15	25
OTAPUKAWA STREAM	STRM	38 23 177 07	31
OTARA	SBRB	36 58 174 52	12
OTARA	SBRB	36 58 174 52	14
OTARA	LOC	38 03 177 20	23
OTARA	LOC	46 38 168 53	112
OTARA POINT	PNT	35 25 174 23	5
OTARA RIVER	STRM	38 00 177 17	23
OTARAIA	LOC	46 12 169 05	110
OTARAIA	LOC	46 12 169 05	112
OTARAIA HILL (TRIG)	HILL	46 13 169 06	110
OTARAIA HILL (TRIG)	HILL	46 13 169 06	112
OTARAMA	LOC	43 17 171 56	80
OTARAMA	LOC	43 17 171 56	81
OTARAMA PEAK	PEAK	43 14 171 50	80
OTARAMARAE	LOC	38 01 176 22	20
OTARAMARAE	LOC	38 01 176 22	21
OTARAO STREAM	STRM	35 42 174 01	5
OTARAO STREAM	STRM	35 42 174 01	7
OTARAPAOA (TRIG)	HILL	37 40 177 58	24
OTARAPAOA (TRIG)	HILL	37 40 177 58	25
OTARAWAIRERE BAY	BAY	37 57 177 01	22
OTARAWAIRERE BAY	BAY	37 57 177 01	23
OTARAWHATA ISLAND	ISLD	37 32 177 59	25
OTATARA	HSTD	39 33 176 49	40
OTATARA	HSTD	39 33 176 49	41
OTATARA	HSTD	39 33 176 49	42
OTATARA	HSTD	39 33 176 49	43
OTATARA	USAT	46 26 168 18	109
OTATOKI CREEK	STRM	43 10 170 15	74
OTAUA	LOC	35 30 173 43	4
OTAUA	LOC	35 30 173 43	6
OTAUA	LOC	37 18 174 44	14
OTAUA STREAM	STRM	35 28 173 41	4
OTAUA STREAM	STRM	35 28 173 41	6
OTAUNGA STREAM	STRM	38 44 175 45	28
OTAUNGA STREAM	STRM	38 44 175 45	38
OTAUNOA RANGE	MTNS	38 48 176 58	30
OTAUPARI STREAM	STRM	39 34 175 05	36
OTAUTAU	POPL	46 09 168 00	106
OTAUTAU	POPL	46 09 168 00	107
OTAUTAU	POPL	46 09 168 00	108
OTAUTAU STREAM	STRM	46 09 168 00	106
OTAUTAU STREAM	STRM	46 09 168 00	107
OTAUTAU STREAM	STRM	46 09 168 00	108
OTAUTAU (TRIG)	HILL	46 09 167 58	106
OTAUTAU (TRIG)	HILL	46 09 167 58	107
OTAUTAU (TRIG)	HILL	46 09 167 58	108
OTAUTORA STREAM	STRM	38 04 175 38	19
OTAUTU (TRIG)	HILL	39 17 175 15	36
OTAWA (TRIG)	HILL	37 48 176 15	20
OTAWA (TRIG)	HILL	37 48 176 15	21
OTAWAKI (TRIG)	HILL	39 45 175 08	45
OTAWHAO STREAM	STRM	40 19 176 00	49
OTAWHIRI STREAM	STRM	39 02 176 35	39
OTAWHIRI STREAM	STRM	39 02 176 35	40
OTAWHITI STREAM	STRM	39 25 174 49	35
OTAWHITI STREAM	STRM	39 25 174 49	44
OTE MAKURA STREAM	STRM	42 29 173 32	73
OTEAO (TRIG)	HILL	36 59 175 42	16
OTEAO (TRIG)	HILL	36 59 175 42	17
OTEHA STREAM	STRM	36 44 174 41	11
OTEHA STREAM	STRM	36 44 174 41	12
OTEHAKE RIVER	STRM	42 46 171 43	70
OTEHAKE RIVER, EAST BRANCH	STRM	42 51 171 43	70
OTEHAKE RIVER, WEST BRANCH	STRM	42 51 171 43	70
OTEHAKE WILDERNESS AREA	WILD	42 47 171 42	70
OTEHE	PNT	37 36 174 46	18
OTEHEI BAY	BAY	35 13 174 14	5
OTEHIRINAKI	LOC	37 50 177 37	24

OTEKAIEKE	LOC	44 50 170 34	92
OTEKAIEKE HILL (TRIG)	MTN	44 53 170 28	92
OTEKAIEKE RIVER	STRM	44 49 170 35	92
OTEKAWA CREEK	STRM	36 19 174 16	10
OTEKE STREAM	STRM	38 10 174 49	18
OTEKURA	LOC	46 26 169 45	113
OTEMATATA	POPL	44 37 170 11	92
OTEMATATA RIVER	STRM	44 36 170 12	92
OTEMATEA CHANNEL	CHAN	36 20 174 14	10
OTEPO (TRIG)	HILL	35 08 173 20	3
OTEPO (TRIG)	HILL	39 09 175 10	36
OTEPO (TRIG)	HILL	40 53 172 13	56
OTEPOPO	LOC	45 14 170 47	102
OTERAMIKA	LOC	46 26 168 37	112
OTERANGA BAY	BAY	41 18 174 38	52
OTERANGA BAY	BAY	41 18 174 38	55
OTERANGA HEAD	HEAD	41 19 174 38	52
OTERANGA HEAD	HEAD	41 19 174 38	55
OTERANGA STREAM	STRM	41 18 174 38	52
OTERANGA STREAM	STRM	41 18 174 38	55
OTERAWHANGA (TRIG)	HILL	41 04 174 15	54
OTERAWHANGA (TRIG)	HILL	41 04 174 15	60
OTERAWHANGA (TRIG)	HILL	41 04 174 15	61
OTEREI RIVER	STRM	41 29 175 35	53
OTEWA	LOC	38 14 175 18	18
OTEWA	LOC	38 14 175 18	19
OTIAKE	LOC	44 48 170 30	92
OTIAKE RIVER	STRM	44 48 170 32	92
OTIKERAMA	LOC	46 05 169 02	110
OTIKERAMA	LOC	46 05 169 02	112
OTIPI (TRIG)	MTN	38 08 177 37	24
OTIPUA	LOC	44 27 171 10	93
OTIRA	LOC	42 50 171 34	69
OTIRA RIVER	STRM	42 45 171 38	69
OTIRANGI	LOC	38 55 177 55	33
OTIRANUI (TRIG)	HILL	39 28 175 19	36
OTIRIA	LOC	35 09 174 00	4
OTIRIA	LOC	35 09 174 00	5
OTIRIA STREAM	STRM	35 08 174 04	4
OTIRIA STREAM	STRM	35 08 174 04	5
OTITIA ROCK	ROCK	43 37 169 27	76
OTITIA ROCK	ROCK	43 37 169 27	78
OTITIA ROCK	ROCK	43 37 169 27	79
OTIWHITI	HSTD	39 51 175 30	45
OTIWHITI	HSTD	39 51 175 30	46
OTOHI (TRIG)	HILL	38 37 176 47	30
OTOHUAO POINT	HEAD	43 38 172 59	82
OTOHUAO POINT	HEAD	43 38 172 59	83
OTOI	HSTD	38 57 177 04	41
OTOI ROCK	ROCK	35 23 173 13	3
OTOKI STREAM	STRM	39 38 174 23	35
OTOKI STREAM	STRM	39 38 174 23	44
OTOKIA	LOC	45 57 170 11	103
OTOKIA CREEK	STRM	45 57 170 20	103
OTOKIA HILL (TRIG)	HILL	45 54 170 12	103
OTOKO	LOC	38 27 177 37	31
OTOKO	HSTD	39 44 175 20	45
OTOKO LAKE	LAKE	43 49 169 43	76
OTOKO LAKE	LAKE	43 49 169 43	79
OTOKO RIVER	STRM	43 46 169 31	76
OTOKO RIVER	STRM	43 46 169 31	79
OTOKORO STREAM	STRM	39 22 175 49	37
OTOMAROTO STREAM	STRM	39 16 174 52	35
OTOMAROTO STREAM	STRM	39 16 174 52	44
OTONGA	LOC	35 34 174 17	5
OTONGA	LOC	35 34 174 17	7
OTONGA	LOC	35 34 174 17	8
OTONGA	HILL	37 48 175 01	18
OTONGA POINT	PNT	34 56 173 36	3
OTONGA POINT	PNT	34 56 173 36	4
OTONGA POINT	PNT	37 18 175 55	17
OTOPE STREAM	STRM	40 17 176 04	49
OTORANOHO (TRIG)	HILL	39 30 175 05	36
OTOREHINAITI SADDLE	SAD	39 09 176 13	39
OTORO STREAM	STRM	40 15 176 20	50
OTOROA	LOC	35 05 173 51	4
OTOROHANGA	POPL	38 11 175 13	18
OTOROHANGA	POPL	38 11 175 13	19
OTOROKUA POINT (TRIG)	PNT	43 25 169 48	76
OTOTOA, LAKE	LAKE	36 31 174 14	10
OTOTOKA STREAM	STRM	39 52 174 50	44
OTTERSON STREAM	STRM	41 55 173 35	66
OTU BAY	BAY	40 45 173 50	61
OTUAREIAWA STREAM	STRM	39 41 175 55	46
OTUATAKAHI STREAM	STRM	38 12 174 56	18
OTUAURI (TRIG)	HILL	37 57 178 21	25
OTUHAEREROA ISLAND	ISLD	41 02 173 40	60
OTUHANGITOI STREAM	STRM	39 42 175 20	45
OTUHI	LOC	35 48 174 10	7
OTUHIANGA (TRIG)	HILL	36 08 174 07	7
OTUHIE, LAKE	LAKE	40 41 172 25	56
OTUHOE (TRIG)	HILL	38 58 175 52	37
OTUHOE (TRIG)	HILL	38 58 175 52	38
OTUITI STREAM	STRM	39 00 175 06	36
OTUKEHU (TRIG)	HILL	39 02 175 06	36
OTUKERE STREAM	STRM	35 14 173 33	3
OTUKERE STREAM	STRM	35 14 173 33	4
OTUKOROITI POINT	PNT	40 49 172 10	56
OTUKOTARA (TRIG)	HILL	38 49 176 25	29
OTUKOU	LOC	39 02 175 39	37
OTUKOU	LOC	39 02 175 39	38
OTUMAHI, LAKE	LAKE	38 03 176 51	22
OTUMAHI, LAKE	LAKE	38 03 176 51	23
OTUMAIKA (TRIG)	HILL	37 17 175 23	15
OTUMAKIORE (TRIG)	PEAK	38 58 176 30	39
OTUMAKIORE (TRIG)	PEAK	38 58 176 30	40
OTUMOETAI	SBRB	37 40 176 08	20
OTUMOETAI	SBRB	37 40 176 08	21
OTUMOTU POINTS	PNT	43 42 169 16	78
OTUNUA STREAM	STRM	39 12 177 51	33
OTUNUI	LOC	38 54 175 09	27
OTUNUI STREAM	STRM	38 56 175 09	27
OTUPAE (TRIG)	PEAK	39 30 176 11	39
OTUPORIKI STREAM	STRM	39 40 175 09	45
OTUPOTO STREAM	STRM	38 42 175 46	28
OTUPOTO STREAM	STRM	38 42 175 46	38
OTUPUA STREAM	STRM	39 06 176 20	39
OTUREHUA	LOC	45 01 169 55	101
OTURERE STREAM	STRM	39 11 175 47	37
OTURERE STREAM	STRM	39 11 175 47	38
OTURIA (TRIG)	HILL	35 16 173 33	3
OTURIA (TRIG)	HILL	35 16 173 33	4
OTUROA	LOC	38 03 176 11	20
OTUROA	LOC	38 03 176 11	21
OTURU	LOC	35 06 173 17	3
OTURU STREAM	STRM	37 02 175 50	16
OTURU STREAM	STRM	37 02 175 50	17
OTURUA STREAM	STRM	39 21 176 02	38
OTURUA STREAM	STRM	39 21 176 02	39
OTUTOKONUI (TRIG)	HILL	39 41 175 58	46

OTUWHARE	LOC	37 49 177 39	24
OTUWHERO INLET	BAY	41 01 173 00	57
OTUWHERO INLET	BAY	41 01 173 00	58
OTUWHERO INLET	BAY	41 01 173 00	59
OTUWHERO RIVER	STRM	41 01 173 00	57
OTUWHERO RIVER	STRM	41 01 173 00	58
OTUWHETI STREAM	STRM	37 10 175 51	17
OTWAY	LOC	37 30 175 36	15
OUAHA (TRIG)	HILL	38 50 176 03	28
OUAHA (TRIG)	HILL	38 50 176 03	29
OUAHA (TRIG)	HILL	38 50 176 03	38
OUE	LOC	35 28 173 30	6
OUE (TRIG)	HILL	38 03 174 53	18
OUEARI	HILL	38 23 177 05	30
OUEARI	HILL	38 23 177 05	31
OUETEHEUHEU STREAM	STRM	37 51 176 25	21
OUETEHEUHEU STREAM	STRM	37 51 176 25	22
OUNUORA RIVER	STRM	36 53 175 40	15
OUNUORA RIVER	STRM	36 53 175 40	16
OUNUORA RIVER	STRM	36 53 175 40	17
OURAWERA STREAM	STRM	46 22 167 50	108
OURI STREAM	STRM	39 31 173 56	34
OURUHIA	LOC	43 27 172 39	82
OURUHIA	LOC	43 27 172 39	83
OURUHIA	LOC	43 27 172 39	85
OUSE STREAM	STRM	41 59 173 51	67
OUTER ISLAND	ISLD	41 04 173 01	57
OUTER ISLAND	ISLD	41 04 173 01	58
OUTER ISLAND	ISLD	41 04 173 01	59
OUTLOOK HILL (TRIG)	HILL	41 19 174 39	52
OUTLOOK HILL (TRIG)	HILL	41 19 174 39	55
OUTPOST, THE	MTN	43 52 169 35	76
OUTPOST, THE	MTN	43 52 169 35	79
OUTRAM	POPL	45 52 170 14	103
OUTRAM PEAK	PEAK	43 21 170 42	74
OVEN HILL CREEK	STRM	45 39 169 25	100
OVERDALE	LOC	43 47 172 00	84
OVERHEAD CONE	MTN	44 54 167 31	94
OVERHEAD CONE	MTN	44 54 167 31	97
OVERSEEN PEAK	MTN	46 08 166 52	104
OVERSEEN PEAK	MTN	46 08 166 52	106
OVERTON	LOC	40 03 175 29	45
OVERTON	LOC	40 03 175 29	46
OWAE STREAM	STRM	35 22 174 08	5
OWAHANGA	LOC	40 41 176 20	50
OWAHANGA HILL (TRIG)	HILL	40 34 176 27	50
OWAHANGA RIVER	STRM	40 41 176 21	50
OWAI STREAM	STRM	35 26 174 22	5
OWAIRAKA STREAM	STRM	38 06 175 26	19
OWAIRAKA VALLEY	LOC	38 06 175 27	19
OWAIRUA (TRIG)	HILL	39 06 175 12	36
OWAKA	POPL	46 27 169 39	113
OWAKA RIVER	STRM	46 28 169 41	113
OWAKA STREAM	STRM	38 12 177 00	22
OWAKA STREAM	STRM	38 12 177 00	30
OWAKA VALLEY	LOC	46 26 169 35	113
OWARE	LOC	46 19 168 55	110
OWARE	LOC	46 19 168 55	112
OWARE STREAM	STRM	46 22 168 53	112
OWEKA	LOC	41 53 171 54	63
OWEKA	LOC	41 53 171 54	64
OWEKA STREAM	STRM	37 34 178 09	25
OWEN CREEK	STRM	41 38 172 10	62
OWEN HEAD	HEAD	47 07 168 08	115
OWEN ISLAND	ISLD	47 08 168 09	115
OWEN JUNCTION	LOC	41 42 172 30	65
OWEN, MOUNT	MTN	45 18 167 34	97
OWEN, MOUNT (TRIG)	MTN	41 33 172 33	58
OWEN RIVER	STRM	41 41 172 27	65
OWEN RIVER	LOC	41 42 172 30	65
OWHAKATORO STREAM	STRM	38 03 176 59	22
OWHAKATORO STREAM	STRM	38 03 176 59	23
OWHAKURA	LOC	39 33 175 34	36
OWHAKURA	LOC	39 33 175 34	37
OWHANGO	POPL	39 00 175 22	36
OWHANGO	POPL	39 00 175 22	37
OWHAREITI, LAKE	LAKE	35 24 173 56	4
OWHAREITI, LAKE	LAKE	35 24 173 56	5
OWHATA	LOC	35 18 173 11	3
OWHATA	LOC	38 08 176 18	20
OWHATA	LOC	38 08 176 18	21
OWHIO STREAM	STRM	38 58 177 13	41
OWHIRO	LOC	38 10 174 52	18
OWHIRO	RSTN	45 54 170 19	103
OWHIRO BAY	BAY	41 21 174 45	52
OWHIRO BAY	BAY	41 21 174 45	55
OWHIRO STREAM	STRM	45 54 170 16	103
OWHITI BAY	BAY	36 46 175 09	13
OWHIWA	LOC	35 45 174 26	5
OWHIWA	LOC	35 45 174 26	7
OWHIWA	LOC	35 45 174 26	8
OX BURN	STRM	44 46 168 25	89
OX BURN	STRM	44 46 168 25	96
OXFORD	POPL	43 18 172 12	81
OXFORD	POPL	43 18 172 12	85
OXFORD, MOUNT	MTN	43 13 172 05	81
OYSTER POINT	PNT	36 35 174 25	10
OYSTER POINT	PNT	36 35 174 25	11
OYSTER STREAM	STRM	42 00 173 11	66

■ P

PA CREEK	STRM	40 36 175 50	49
PA HILL	HILL	35 59 173 56	7
PA ISLAND	ISLD	34 58 173 43	4
PADDLE HILL CREEK	STRM	43 37 171 11	75
PADDOCK HILL	HILL	45 38 167 38	106
PADDOCK HILL (TRIG)	PEAK	42 40 171 29	69
PADDOCK ROCKS	ROCK	40 55 173 46	61
PADDY RIDGE	RDGE	41 16 172 40	56
PADDY RIDGE	RDGE	41 16 172 40	58
PADDYS CREEK	STRM	42 24 171 58	70
PADDYS CREEK	STRM	46 15 167 47	106
PADDYS CREEK	STRM	46 15 167 47	108
PAEHOKA (TRIG)	HILL	36 42 174 28	10
PAEHOKA (TRIG)	HILL	36 42 174 28	11
PAEHOKA (TRIG)	HILL	36 42 174 28	12
PAEKAKARIKI	POPL	40 59 174 57	52
PAEKAKARIKI	POPL	40 59 174 57	55
PAEMAKO	LOC	38 30 174 58	26
PAEMAKO	LOC	38 30 174 58	27
PAENGA	LOC	41 56 172 12	64
PAENGAROA	LOC	37 49 176 25	20
PAENGAROA	LOC	37 49 176 25	21
PAEPAERAHI	LOC	38 04 175 30	19
PAERATA	LOC	37 10 174 54	12
PAERATA	LOC	37 10 174 54	14
PAERATA RIDGE	LOC	38 02 177 14	23
PAERATA STREAM	STRM	35 49 174 02	7
PAERAU	LOC	45 25 169 57	101

PAERAU POINT	PNT	38 20 178 20	32
PAEROA	POPL	37 23 175 40	15
PAEROA	POPL	37 23 175 40	17
PAEROA	HILL	38 23 176 15	29
PAEROA RANGE	MTNS	38 23 176 16	29
PAEROA (TRIG)	HILL	40 10 176 16	47
PAEWAI STREAM	STRM	39 00 176 39	39
PAEWAI STREAM	STRM	39 00 176 39	40
PAEWHENUA	LOC	38 16 175 24	27
PAGES SADDLE	SAD	40 56 172 54	57
PAH POINT (TRIG)	HILL	42 37 171 28	69
PAHAOA RIVER	STRM	41 24 175 43	53
PAHARA (TRIG)	HILL	34 51 173 06	2
PAHARA (TRIG)	HILL	34 51 173 06	3
PAHARAKEKE STREAM	STRM	41 19 175 12	53
PAHAU	LOC	42 48 172 48	71
PAHAU	LOC	42 48 172 48	72
PAHAU DOWNS	HSTD	42 45 172 43	71
PAHAU PASS	PASS	42 36 172 42	71
PAHAU RIVER	STRM	42 50 172 54	71
PAHAU RIVER	STRM	42 50 172 54	72
PAHAUTANE	LOC	42 03 171 22	63
PAHAUTEA	LOC	41 14 175 23	53
PAHAUTEA (TRIG)	HILL	38 53 176 19	29
PAHEKEHEKE STREAM	STRM	38 18 176 47	30
PAHI	LOC	36 10 174 14	7
PAHI	LOC	36 10 174 14	8
PAHI RIVER	STRM	36 10 174 14	7
PAHI RIVER	STRM	36 10 174 14	8
PAHI STREAM	STRM	36 29 175 21	9
PAHI STREAM	STRM	36 29 175 21	16
PAHIA	LOC	46 20 167 45	108
PAHIA HILL	HILL	46 19 167 43	108
PAHIA POINT	PNT	46 19 167 46	108
PAHIATUA	POPL	40 27 175 50	49
PAHIATUA STATION	RSTN	40 27 175 49	49
PAHIKO (TRIG)	HILL	37 33 175 47	17
PAHIRI PEAK (TRIG)	PEAK	45 31 167 13	96
PAHOIA	LOC	37 39 176 00	20
PAHOU	LOC	37 59 176 58	22
PAHOU	LOC	37 59 176 58	23
PAHUREHURE INLET	BAY	37 03 174 51	12
PAHUREHURE INLET	BAY	37 03 174 51	14
PAIAKA (TRIG)	HILL	39 10 174 36	35
PAIAKARAHI STREAM	STRM	37 18 175 42	17
PAIHIA	LOC	35 17 174 05	4
PAIHIA	LOC	35 17 174 05	5
PAIHIKOKURI STREAM	STRM	35 16 173 25	3
PAIHIKOKURI (TRIG)	HILL	35 15 173 27	3
PAIKAURI (TRIG)	HILL	34 58 173 37	4
PAINGA STREAM	STRM	38 49 177 17	31
PAIOKATUTU STREAM	STRM	35 13 173 36	4
PAIRERE STREAM	STRM	37 57 175 40	19
PAIWAI (TRIG)	HILL	40 30 175 44	49
PAIWATA STREAM	STRM	46 14 169 34	111
PAIWATA STREAM	STRM	46 14 169 34	113
PAKANAE	LOC	35 30 173 25	6
PAKARAE	LOC	38 31 178 15	32
PAKARAE RIVER	STRM	38 33 178 15	32
PAKARAKA	LOC	35 22 173 57	4
PAKARAKA RANGE	MTNS	37 44 175 29	19
PAKATOA ISLAND	ISLD	36 48 175 12	13
PAKAUMANU (TRIG)	HILL	38 26 175 15	27
PAKAUTUTU	HSTD	39 11 176 30	39
PAKAUTUTU	HSTD	39 11 176 30	40
PAKAWAU	LOC	40 36 172 41	57
PAKAWAU CREEK	STRM	40 35 172 41	57
PAKAWAU INLET	BAY	40 35 172 41	57
PAKEHAUA STREAM	STRM	35 19 174 18	5
PAKEHO	LOC	38 22 175 03	26
PAKEHO	LOC	38 22 175 03	27
PAKIHAUKEA PASS	PASS	44 39 168 01	89
PAKIHI ISLAND	ISLD	36 55 175 10	13
PAKIHI ISLAND	ISLD	36 55 175 10	15
PAKIHI STREAM	STRM	37 56 174 55	18
PAKIHI STREAM	STRM	38 06 177 24	23
PAKIHI STREAM	STRM	38 06 177 24	24
PAKIHI (TRIG)	HILL	38 44 175 32	27
PAKIHI (TRIG)	HILL	38 44 175 32	28
PAKIHI (TRIG)	HILL	38 44 175 32	38
PAKIHIKURA	LOC	39 56 175 43	46
PAKIHIKURA STREAM	STRM	39 57 175 38	46
PAKIHIKURA (TRIG)	HILL	39 57 175 42	46
PAKIHIROA	HSTD	37 51 178 05	25
PAKIPAKI	LOC	39 42 176 47	42
PAKIPAKI	LOC	39 42 176 47	43
PAKIRA (TRIG)	HILL	39 42 174 56	45
PAKIRARAHI (TRIG)	HILL	37 11 175 41	15
PAKIRARAHI (TRIG)	HILL	37 11 175 41	17
PAKIRI	LOC	36 16 174 44	11
PAKIRI RIVER	STRM	36 15 174 43	11
PAKIRI STREAM	STRM	36 15 174 43	11
PAKOKA RIVER	STRM	37 56 174 51	18
PAKOTAI	LOC	35 41 173 54	7
PAKOWHAI	HSTD	38 45 177 54	32
PAKOWHAI	HSTD	38 45 177 54	33
PAKOWHAI	LOC	39 35 176 52	42
PAKOWHAI	LOC	39 35 176 52	43
PAKOWHAI RIVER	STRM	40 42 176 13	50
PAKURANGA	SBRB	36 55 174 53	12
PAKURANGA	SBRB	36 55 174 53	14
PAKURATAHI	LOC	41 05 175 12	52
PAKURATAHI	LOC	41 05 175 12	53
PAKURATAHI FORKS	LOC	41 03 175 12	52
PAKURATAHI FORKS	LOC	41 03 175 12	53
PAKURATAHI FORKS	LOC	41 03 175 12	55
PAKURATAHI RIVER	STRM	41 03 175 12	52
PAKURATAHI RIVER	STRM	41 03 175 12	53
PAKURATAHI RIVER	STRM	41 03 175 12	55
PAKURI STREAM	STRM	38 30 176 09	28
PAKURI STREAM	STRM	38 30 176 09	29
PALLISER BAY	BAY	41 26 175 04	52
PALLISER BAY	BAY	41 26 175 04	55
PALLISER, CAPE	CAPE	41 37 175 15	53
PALM BEACH	LOC	36 47 175 03	12
PALM BEACH	LOC	36 47 175 03	13
PALMER CREEK	STRM	44 02 168 53	78
PALMER HEAD	HEAD	41 20 174 49	52
PALMER HEAD	HEAD	41 20 174 49	55
PALMER RANGE	MTNS	43 20 171 15	75
PALMER ROAD STATION	RSTN	39 29 174 10	34
PALMER SADDLE	SAD	42 21 173 14	72
PALMER SADDLE	SAD	42 21 173 14	73
PALMER STREAM	STRM	42 18 173 15	72
PALMER STREAM	STRM	42 18 173 15	73
PALMERSTON	POPL	45 29 170 43	102
PALMERSTON NORTH	TOWN	40 22 175 37	48
PALMERSTON NORTH	TOWN	40 22 175 37	49
PALMSIDE	HSTD	42 46 172 59	72
PAMAPURIA	LOC	35 08 173 21	3

PAMOTUMOTU (TRIG)	HILL	38 15 175 28	19
PAMOTUMOTU (TRIG)	HILL	38 15 175 28	27
PAN, LAKE	LAKE	45 12 167 03	96
PAN, MOUNT (TRIG)	MTN	42 41 172 22	71
PANAKI ISLAND	ISLD	34 59 173 57	4
PANANEHE ISLAND	ISLD	34 25 172 51	2
PANATEWAEWAE, TRIG	PEAK	40 43 175 19	48
PANCAKE RANGE	MTNS	43 02 172 12	81
PANCAKE STREAM	STRM	43 05 172 16	81
PANDORA	LOC	34 27 172 47	2
PANDORA RIVER	STRM	45 10 166 59	96
PANEKIRI RANGE	MTNS	38 49 177 03	30
PANEL CREEK	STRM	43 45 169 23	78
PANEMANGA (TRIG)	PEAK	39 04 176 25	39
PANEMANGA (TRIG)	PEAK	39 04 176 25	40
PANETAPU	LOC	38 10 175 29	19
PANGAKI STREAM	STRM	38 30 174 56	26
PANGARARA (TRIG)	HILL	38 39 175 21	27
PANGATOTARA	LOC	41 10 172 55	58
PANGURU	LOC	35 23 173 23	3
PANGURU	LOC	35 23 173 23	6
PANIRAU STREAM	STRM	38 43 174 51	26
PANITUTAE (TRIG)	HILL	38 07 175 40	19
PANMURE	SBRB	36 54 174 51	11
PANMURE	SBRB	36 54 174 51	12
PANMURE	SBRB	36 54 174 51	14
PANOKO STREAM	STRM	39 12 176 11	39
PANUI (TRIG)	HILL	40 32 176 28	50
PAOANUI POINT	PNT	40 05 176 54	43
PAOKUHUKURA (TRIG)	HILL	39 02 177 44	33
PAONEONE (TRIG)	HILL	37 39 178 21	25
PAOPAOHAONUI STREAM	STRM	39 07 174 00	34
PAORAAMEKA (TRIG)	HILL	39 35 175 14	36
PAORAE STREAM	STRM	38 57 174 56	26
PAOTAMARIKI (TRIG)	HILL	39 40 175 13	45
PAPAAROHA	LOC	36 42 175 26	13
PAPAAROHA	LOC	36 42 175 26	16
PAPAHAUA (TRIG)	HILL	39 31 175 15	36
PAPAHUA STREAM	STRM	40 17 176 06	49
PAPAHUA STREAM	STRM	40 17 176 06	50
PAPAITONGA, LAKE	LAKE	40 39 175 13	48
PAPAKA STREAM	STRM	44 21 171 13	87
PAPAKAI	LOC	39 03 175 37	37
PAPAKAI	LOC	39 03 175 37	38
PAPAKAI (TRIG)	HILL	36 56 175 35	13
PAPAKAI (TRIG)	HILL	36 56 175 35	15
PAPAKAI (TRIG)	HILL	36 56 175 35	16
PAPAKAI (TRIG)	PEAK	39 03 175 36	37
PAPAKAI (TRIG)	PEAK	39 03 175 36	38
PAPAKAIO	LOC	44 59 170 59	93
PAPAKANUI SPIT	SPIT	36 26 174 13	10
PAPAKAURI STREAM	STRM	35 22 174 14	5
PAPAKAURI (TRIG)	HILL	38 38 174 51	26
PAPAKERI CREEK	STRM	43 35 169 38	76
PAPAKIRI STREAM	STRM	39 13 176 53	40
PAPAKIRI STREAM	STRM	39 13 176 53	41
PAPAKURA	USAT	37 04 174 57	12
PAPAKURA	USAT	37 04 174 57	14
PAPAKURA CHANNEL	CHAN	37 02 174 41	12
PAPAKURA CHANNEL	CHAN	37 02 174 41	14
PAPAKURA (TRIG)	HILL	35 02 173 44	4
PAPAMOA	LOC	37 44 176 18	20
PAPAMOA	LOC	37 44 176 18	21
PAPAMOA BEACH	BCH	37 43 176 20	20
PAPAMOA BEACH	BCH	37 43 176 20	21
PAPAMOA (TRIG)	HILL	37 44 176 17	20
PAPAMOA (TRIG)	HILL	37 44 176 17	21
PAPAMOA (TRIG)	HILL	38 08 177 29	24
PAPANUI	SBRB	43 30 172 37	82
PAPANUI	SBRB	43 30 172 37	83
PAPANUI	SBRB	43 30 172 37	85
PAPANUI BEACH	BCH	45 52 170 45	103
PAPANUI INLET	BAY	45 51 170 42	103
PAPANUI JUNCTION	LOC	39 41 175 33	46
PAPANUI POINT	PNT	37 53 174 46	18
PAPAPOHATU (TRIG)	HILL	39 03 175 53	37
PAPAPOHATU (TRIG)	HILL	39 03 175 53	38
PAPARAHIA STREAM	STRM	38 32 174 38	26
PAPARANGI	LOC	39 42 174 59	45
PAPARANGI	SBRB	41 13 174 49	52
PAPARANGI	SBRB	41 13 174 49	55
PAPARATA	LOC	37 10 175 03	12
PAPARATA	LOC	37 10 175 03	13
PAPARATA	LOC	37 10 175 03	14
PAPARAUPONGA STREAM	STRM	39 29 176 23	39
PAPARIMU	LOC	37 09 175 07	13
PAPARIMU	LOC	37 09 175 07	14
PAPARIMU	LOC	37 09 175 07	15
PAPARITU (TRIG)	HILL	38 48 177 42	31
PAPARITU (TRIG)	HILL	38 48 177 42	33
PAPAROA	LOC	36 06 174 14	7
PAPAROA	LOC	36 06 174 14	8
PAPAROA CREEK	STRM	36 08 174 13	7
PAPAROA CREEK	STRM	36 08 174 13	8
PAPAROA CREEK	STRM	42 23 171 25	69
PAPAROA POINT	PNT	38 08 174 42	18
PAPAROA POINT	PNT	42 14 173 51	67
PAPAROA RANGE	MTNS	42 05 171 33	63
PAPAROA STREAM	STRM	35 32 173 50	4
PAPAROA STREAM	STRM	35 32 173 50	6
PAPAROA STREAM	STRM	36 07 174 14	7
PAPAROA STREAM	STRM	36 07 174 14	8
PAPAROA STREAM	STRM	38 58 175 08	36
PAPARORE	LOC	35 00 173 12	3
PAPATAHI (TRIG)	PEAK	41 19 175 03	52
PAPATAHI (TRIG)	PEAK	41 19 175 03	55
PAPATAHORA STREAM	STRM	35 38 174 04	5
PAPATAHORA STREAM	STRM	35 38 174 04	7
PAPATANGI (TRIG)	HILL	38 09 175 42	19
PAPATAWA	LOC	40 19 175 55	49
PAPATEA BAY	BAY	37 39 177 51	24
PAPATIKI STREAM	STRM	38 56 174 29	26
PAPATOETOE	USAT	36 59 174 51	12
PAPATOETOE	USAT	36 59 174 51	14
PAPATOTARA	LOC	46 10 167 38	106
PAPATOTARA	LOC	46 10 167 38	108
PAPATOWAI	LOC	46 34 169 28	113
PAPATU (TRIG)	HILL	38 42 177 50	32
PAPATU (TRIG)	HILL	38 42 177 50	33
PAPAUMA (TRIG)	HILL	39 03 175 03	36
PAPAWAI	LOC	41 07 175 29	53
PAPAWAI BAY	BAY	41 00 173 45	60
PAPAWAI BAY	BAY	41 00 173 45	61
PAPOKEKA STREAM	STRM	38 37 177 31	31
PAPONGA	LOC	35 18 173 27	3
PAPS, THE	HILL	46 48 167 59	109
PAPS, THE	HILL	46 48 167 59	114
PAPS, THE	HILL	46 48 167 59	115
PAPUA	LOC	35 24 173 33	3
PAPUA	LOC	35 24 173 33	4
PAPUA	LOC	35 24 173 33	6
PAPUERU	LOC	38 39 176 53	30
PAPUNI	LOC	38 41 177 20	31
PARA	LOC	41 22 173 56	54
PARA	LOC	41 22 173 56	60
PARADISE	LOC	44 44 168 22	89
PARADISE	LOC	44 44 168 22	95
PARADISE, LAKE	LAKE	45 27 166 50	96
PARAHAKA	LOC	35 54 174 15	7
PARAHAKA	LOC	35 54 174 15	8
PARAHAKI STREAM	STRM	38 45 176 51	30
PARAHAKI (TRIG)	HILL	35 43 174 20	5
PARAHAKI (TRIG)	HILL	35 43 174 20	7
PARAHAKI (TRIG)	HILL	35 43 174 20	8
PARAHEKA (TRIG)	HILL	38 18 178 05	32
PARAHI	LOC	36 03 174 07	7
PARAHIRAHI (TRIG)	HILL	35 25 173 50	4
PARAHIRAHI (TRIG)	HILL	35 25 173 50	6
PARAKAI	LOC	36 40 174 26	10
PARAKAI	LOC	36 40 174 26	11
PARAKAO	LOC	35 43 173 57	5
PARAKAO	LOC	35 43 173 57	7
PARAKAU STREAM	STRM	36 54 175 45	16
PARAKAU STREAM	STRM	36 54 175 45	17
PARAKAUMANGA STREAM	STRM	38 56 175 39	28
PARAKAUMANGA STREAM	STRM	38 56 175 39	37
PARAKAUMANGA STREAM	STRM	38 56 175 39	38
PARAKETU STREAM	STRM	38 39 175 18	27
PARAKIORE (TRIG)	HILL	35 40 174 17	5
PARAKIORE (TRIG)	HILL	35 40 174 17	7
PARAKIORE (TRIG)	HILL	35 40 174 17	8
PARAKIWAI	LOC	37 14 175 51	17
PARAMENA REEF	REEF	35 14 174 13	5
PARANGI, LAKE	LAKE	38 02 174 49	18
PARANUI	LOC	35 03 173 28	3
PARANUI DRAIN	DRN	37 31 175 22	15
PARANUI PEAK	PEAK	44 35 167 59	89
PARANUI PEAK	PEAK	44 35 167 59	94
PARANUI STREAM	STRM	35 01 173 28	3
PARANUI STREAM	STRM	40 02 175 50	46
PARAOANUI PA	LOC	38 18 177 07	31
PARAOANUI POINT	PNT	36 12 174 08	7
PARAPARA	LOC	35 01 173 26	3
PARAPARA	LOC	40 43 172 41	56
PARAPARA	LOC	40 43 172 41	57
PARAPARA INLET	BAY	40 43 172 41	56
PARAPARA INLET	BAY	40 43 172 41	57
PARAPARA PEAK (TRIG)	HILL	40 50 172 40	56
PARAPARA PEAK (TRIG)	HILL	40 50 172 40	57
PARAPARA RIVER	STRM	40 44 172 41	56
PARAPARA RIVER	STRM	40 44 172 41	57
PARAPARA STREAM	STRM	34 59 173 29	3
PARAPARA STREAM	STRM	38 12 175 15	18
PARAPARA STREAM	STRM	38 12 175 15	19
PARAPARA STREAM	STRM	42 16 173 45	67
PARAPARA (TRIG)	HILL	38 50 175 07	27
PARAPARA (TRIG)	HILL	40 43 172 40	56
PARAPARA (TRIG)	HILL	40 43 172 40	57
PARAPARAUMU	POPL	40 55 175 00	48
PARAPARAUMU	POPL	40 55 175 00	52
PARAPARAUMU	POPL	40 55 175 00	55
PARAPARAUMU BEACH	POPL	40 53 174 59	52
PARAPARAUMU BEACH	POPL	40 53 174 59	55
PARARAKE (TRIG)	HILL	35 00 173 25	3
PARARAKI STREAM	STRM	41 32 175 11	53
PARARATA SADDLE	SAD	38 58 174 56	36
PARARIKI, MOUNT	MTN	44 34 168 00	89
PARARIKI, MOUNT	MTN	44 34 168 00	94
PARARIKI STREAM	STRM	38 20 177 57	32
PARASITE CREEK	STRM	43 59 169 25	79
PARASOL CREEK	STRM	45 45 169 07	110
PARATAHI ISLAND	ISLD	37 00 174 28	12
PARATAIKO RANGE	MTNS	35 36 173 34	6
PARATAWA STREAM	STRM	37 50 175 08	18
PARATUA STREAM	STRM	39 40 176 41	42
PARATUA STREAM	STRM	39 40 176 41	43
PARAU	LOC	36 58 174 37	12
PARAU	LOC	36 58 174 37	14
PARAWA	LOC	45 33 168 32	99
PARAWAI	LOC	37 09 175 34	13
PARAWAI	LOC	37 09 175 34	15
PARAWANUI, LAKE	LAKE	36 04 173 51	7
PARAWERA	LOC	38 05 175 26	19
PARAWHENUAMEA STREAM	STRM	37 48 176 22	20
PARAWHENUAMEA STREAM	STRM	37 48 176 22	21
PAREKARANGI	LOC	38 26 176 19	29
PAREKURA BAY	BAY	35 16 174 16	5
PAREKURA BAY	LOC	35 16 174 14	5
PAREMATA	LOC	38 23 178 16	32
PAREMATA	SBRB	41 07 174 52	52
PAREMATA	SBRB	41 07 174 52	55
PAREMOREMO	LOC	36 45 174 39	11
PAREMOREMO	LOC	36 45 174 39	12
PARENGARENGA HARBOUR	HARB	34 32 172 59	2
PAREOKAWA (TRIG)	STRM	35 17 173 19	3
PAREORA	LOC	44 29 171 13	93
PAREORA RIVER	STRM	44 30 171 13	93
PAREORA RIVER (SOUTH BRANCH)	STRM	44 24 171 03	93
PAREORA WEST	LOC	44 26 171 08	93
PARERA	LOC	45 47 170 19	103
PARERANUI STREAM	STRM	38 59 176 30	39
PARERANUI STREAM	STRM	38 59 176 30	40
PARETAI	LOC	46 20 169 47	111
PARETAI	LOC	46 20 169 47	113
PARETETAITONGA	PEAK	39 17 175 33	36
PARETETAITONGA	PEAK	39 17 175 33	37
PARETETAITONGA	PEAK	39 17 175 33	38
PAREWANUI	LOC	40 14 175 19	45
PARI STREAM	STRM	39 50 176 00	46
PARIHAKA STREAM	STRM	37 11 175 47	17
PARIKAKA STREAM	STRM	39 58 176 19	47
PARIKANAPA (TRIG)	HILL	38 45 177 42	31
PARIKANAPA (TRIG)	HILL	38 45 177 42	33
PARIKAWA	LOC	42 05 173 57	67
PARIKINO	LOC	39 48 175 09	45
PARINGA HILL	HILL	43 40 169 28	76
PARINGA HILL	HILL	43 40 169 28	78
PARINGA HILL	HILL	43 40 169 28	79
PARINGA LAKE	LAKE	43 43 169 24	78
PARINGA RIVER	STRM	43 38 169 26	78
PARINGA RIVER	STRM	43 38 169 26	79
PARINGATATA (TRIG)	HILL	46 29 169 27	113
PARINUI	LOC	39 20 174 59	36
PARIOKARA	LOC	37 47 177 40	24
PARIOKARIWA POINT	PNT	38 53 174 31	26
PARIOKONOHI POINT	PNT	38 36 178 12	32
PARIPOKAI (TRIG)	HILL	39 20 175 01	36
PARIS	MTN	43 37 170 42	74
PARITATA PENINSULA	PEN	37 47 174 55	18
PARITEA (TRIG)	HILL	39 19 174 55	35
PARITEA (TRIG)	HILL	39 19 174 55	36
PARITU STREAM	STRM	37 08 175 52	17
PARIWHAKAOHA RIVER	STRM	40 47 172 44	56
PARIWHAKAOHA RIVER	STRM	40 47 172 44	57
PARK BURN	STRM	44 58 169 16	91
PARK DOME	MTN	43 10 170 56	75
PARK HILL	LOC	45 49 169 14	110
PARK, MOUNT	MTN	43 03 171 13	75
PARK, MOUNT	MTN	44 49 167 59	89
PARK, MOUNT	MTN	44 49 167 59	94
PARK PASS	PASS	44 36 168 13	88
PARK PASS	PASS	44 36 168 13	89
PARK POINT	PNT	36 49 174 59	12
PARK RIVER	STRM	40 49 175 23	48
PARKER CREEK	STRM	43 16 170 25	74
PARKER, MOUNT (TRIG)	HILL	44 48 170 41	93
PARKHILL	HSTD	42 56 172 32	71
PARKHURST	LOC	36 39 174 24	10
PARKHURST	LOC	36 39 174 24	11
PARKVALE	SBRB	39 39 176 52	42
PARKVALE	SBRB	39 39 176 52	43
PARKVILLE	LOC	40 40 175 41	49
PARNASSUS	LOC	42 43 173 17	72
PARNASSUS	LOC	42 43 173 17	73
PARNASSUS, MOUNT (TRIG)	MTN	42 41 173 11	72
PARNASSUS, MOUNT (TRIG)	MTN	42 41 173 11	73
PARNELL	SBRB	36 51 174 47	11
PARNELL	SBRB	36 51 174 47	12
PAROA	LOC	37 57 176 56	22
PAROA	LOC	37 57 176 56	23
PAROA	LOC	42 31 171 10	68
PAROA	LOC	42 31 171 10	69
PAROA BAY	LOC	35 17 174 11	5
PAROA BAY	BAY	35 16 174 10	5
PAROANUI	LOC	35 03 173 37	4
PARONUI	LOC	35 03 173 37	3
PARORE	LOC	35 55 173 51	6
PARORE	LOC	35 55 173 51	7
PARROT ISLAND	ISLD	45 43 166 32	104
PARRY CHANNEL	CHAN	35 53 174 38	8
PARSONS CREEK	STRM	44 15 169 49	79
PARSONS ROCK STREAM	STRM	44 42 170 15	92
PARUA BAY	BAY	35 01 173 54	4
PARUA BAY	LOC	35 46 174 27	5
PARUA BAY	BAY	35 47 174 27	5
PARUA BAY	BAY	35 47 174 27	7
PARUA BAY	LOC	35 46 174 27	7
PARUA BAY	BAY	35 47 174 27	8
PARUA BAY	LOC	35 46 174 27	8
PARYPHANTA SADDLE	SAD	41 15 172 17	56
PARYPHANTA SADDLE	SAD	41 15 172 17	62
PASCOE (TRIG)	HILL	40 45 173 57	61
PASKE CREEK	STRM	42 05 172 48	65
PASKE, MOUNT	MTN	42 06 172 45	65
PASKE SADDLE	SAD	42 07 172 43	65
PASS BURN	STRM	44 37 169 32	91
PASS BURN	STRM	44 59 168 14	95
PASS BURN	STRM	44 59 168 14	98
PASS PEAK (TRIG)	HILL	44 35 170 09	92
PASS STREAM	STRM	42 39 172 55	71
PASS STREAM	STRM	42 39 172 55	72
PASSAGE ISLANDS	ISLS	45 46 166 34	104
PASSAGE ISLANDS	ISLS	46 01 166 32	104
PASSAGE POINT	PNT	45 44 166 44	104
PASSCHENDAELE	MTN	44 27 168 23	88
PASSCHENDAELE	MTN	44 27 168 23	89
PASTURE HILL (TRIG)	MTN	45 10 168 22	95
PASTURE HILL (TRIG)	MTN	45 10 168 22	98
PATAKA (TRIG)	HILL	39 02 174 40	35
PATAKANUI STREAM	STRM	41 17 175 17	53
PATAKOROKORO (TRIG)	HILL	35 30 173 58	4
PATAKOROKORO (TRIG)	HILL	35 30 173 58	5
PATANGA, MOUNT	PEAK	45 17 167 15	96
PATANGATA	LOC	39 55 176 43	42
PATANGATA	LOC	39 55 176 43	43
PATANUI STREAM	STRM	41 09 176 01	51
PATAUA	LOC	35 43 174 30	5
PATAUA	LOC	35 43 174 30	8
PATAUA ISLAND	ISLD	35 43 174 32	5
PATAUA ISLAND	ISLD	35 43 174 32	8
PATAUA RIVER	STRM	35 43 174 31	5
PATAUA RIVER	STRM	35 43 174 31	8
PATE, THE	MTN	45 48 167 52	106
PATEA	POPL	39 45 174 28	44
PATEA RIVER	STRM	39 46 174 29	44
PATEAROA	LOC	45 17 170 03	101
PATERANGI	LOC	37 57 175 15	18
PATERANGI	LOC	37 57 175 15	19
PATERSON INLET	BAY	46 56 168 03	115
PATERSON, MOUNT	MTN	43 47 169 40	76
PATERSON, MOUNT	MTN	43 47 169 40	79
PATERSONS PASS	PASS	44 55 168 38	90
PATERSONS PASS	PASS	44 55 168 38	95
PATETE (TRIG)	HILL	39 32 174 30	35
PATETE (TRIG)	HILL	39 32 174 30	44
PATETONGA	LOC	37 24 175 28	15
PATH BURN	STRM	45 13 168 19	95
PATH BURN	STRM	45 13 168 19	98
PATIENCE BAY	BAY	45 23 167 45	97
PATIKAIKAI (TRIG)	HILL	39 09 176 47	40
PATITI POINT	PNT	44 25 171 16	93
PATOKA	LOC	39 21 176 36	39
PATOKA	HSTD	39 21 176 36	40
PATOKA	HSTD	39 21 176 36	42
PATOKA STREAM	STRM	39 20 176 41	39
PATOKA STREAM	STRM	39 20 176 41	40
PATOKA STREAM	STRM	39 20 176 41	42
PATONS ROCK	LOC	40 47 172 46	57
PATRIARCH	HSTD	41 37 173 17	59
PATRIARCH MOUNT	MTN	44 16 169 22	78
PATRIARCH, MOUNT (TRIG)	PEAK	41 25 172 30	58
PATRIARCH, MOUNT (TRIG)	MTN	41 37 173 13	59
PATTEN, MOUNT	HILL	45 39 166 45	104
PATTEN PASSAGE	STRA	41 11 174 15	54
PATTEN PASSAGE	STRA	41 11 174 15	60
PATTEN PASSAGE	STRA	41 11 174 15	61
PATTERSON HILL (TRIG)	MTN	43 14 171 55	80
PATTERSON HILL (TRIG)	MTN	43 14 171 55	81
PATUHA (TRIG)	HILL	39 10 173 58	34
PATUHAMO POINT	PNT	37 12 175 54	17
PATUKI	HSTD	40 44 173 57	61
PATUKI, MOUNT	MTN	44 40 168 01	89
PATUKURI (TRIG)	HILL	36 39 174 27	10
PATUKURI (TRIG)	HILL	36 39 174 27	11
PATUKURI (TRIG)	HILL	36 39 174 27	12
PATUMAHOE	LOC	37 11 174 50	12
PATUMAHOE	LOC	37 11 174 50	14
PATURAU RIVER	LOC	40 39 172 26	56
PATURAU RIVER	STRM	40 39 172 26	56
PATURAU RIVER	STRM	40 39 172 26	57
PATURAU (TRIG)	HILL	40 42 172 29	56
PATURAU (TRIG)	HILL	40 42 172 29	57
PATUTAHI	LOC	38 38 177 53	32
PATUTAHI	LOC	38 38 177 53	33
PATUTAHI RIVER	STRM	35 36 174 00	4
PATUTAHI RIVER	STRM	35 36 174 00	5
PATUTAHI RIVER	STRM	35 36 174 00	7
PATUWAHINE (TRIG)	PEAK	39 04 176 51	40
PATUWAHINE (TRIG)	PEAK	39 04 176 51	41
PAUA	LOC	34 33 172 55	2
PAUANUI	LOC	37 01 175 52	16
PAUANUI	LOC	37 01 175 52	17
PAUANUI (TRIG)	HILL	35 19 173 14	3
PAUANUI (TRIG)	HILL	37 02 175 52	16
PAUANUI (TRIG)	HILL	37 02 175 52	17
PAUARIKI STREAM	STRM	38 08 178 15	25
PAUATAHANUI	LOC	41 06 174 55	52
PAUATAHANUI	LOC	41 06 174 55	55
PAUL, MOUNT (TRIG)	MTN	42 33 172 58	72
PAUL, MOUNT (TRIG)	HILL	45 37 170 29	102
PAULINA, MOUNT (TRIG)	MTN	45 02 167 09	96
PAUTOUTO (TRIG)	HILL	35 14 173 32	3
PAVILION PEAK	PEAK	44 28 169 37	91
PAWAIROTO	HILL	38 29 177 06	30
PAWARENGA	LOC	35 21 173 15	3
PAXTON POINT	PNT	34 42 173 04	2
PAYNE CREEK	STRM	41 51 171 49	63
PAYNE CREEK	STRM	41 51 171 49	64
PEA SOUP CREEK	STRM	41 54 172 15	64
PEACH COVE	BAY	35 52 174 34	8
PEACHE SADDLE	SAD	43 34 171 20	75
PEACHE SADDLE	SAD	43 34 171 20	80
PEACHE SADDLE	SAD	43 34 171 20	84
PEACHGROVE BAY	BAY	36 37 175 49	16
PEAK HILL (TRIG)	MTN	43 19 171 30	80
PEAK, THE	PEAK	39 01 174 43	35
PEAK, THE (TRIG)	HILL	40 05 176 27	47
PEAK, THE (TRIG)	PEAK	41 23 174 57	52
PEAK, THE (TRIG)	PEAK	41 23 174 57	55
PEAK (TRIG)	HILL	39 14 175 05	36
PEAK (TRIG)	HILL	40 55 176 08	49
PEAK (TRIG)	HILL	40 55 176 08	50
PEAK (TRIG)	HILL	40 55 176 08	51
PEAKED HILL (TRIG)	HILL	42 33 173 24	72
PEAKED HILL (TRIG)	HILL	42 33 173 24	73
PEAKS, THE	LOC	42 50 172 35	71
PEANTER PEAK	PEAK	41 55 172 50	65
PEARCE (TRIG)	HILL	43 43 172 56	83
PEARL ISLAND	ISLD	47 11 167 42	114
PEARSE RIVER	STRM	41 14 172 49	58
PEARSON CREEK	STRM	43 40 169 21	78
PEARSON, LAKE	LAKE	43 06 171 47	80
PEARSON, MOUNT	MTN	43 58 169 35	79
PEARSON SADDLE	SAD	44 19 168 51	90
PEBBLY HILL (TRIG)	HILL	46 13 168 37	110
PEBBLY HILL (TRIG)	HILL	46 13 168 37	112
PEBBLY HILLS	LOC	46 12 168 35	107
PECK VALLEY CREEK	STRM	44 31 170 10	92
PECKSNIFF, MOUNT	MTN	42 10 171 30	63
PECULIAR, MOUNT	MTN	43 41 169 53	76
PECULIAR, MOUNT	MTN	43 41 169 53	79
PEEBLES	LOC	44 58 170 56	93
PEEL CREEK, MOUNT	STRM	43 52 171 07	87
PEEL FOREST	LOC	43 55 171 16	87
PEEL, MOUNT (TRIG)	MTN	43 51 171 10	87
PEEL, MOUNT (TRIG)	HILL	41 08 172 36	56
PEEL, MOUNT (TRIG)	HILL	41 08 172 36	57
PEEL, MOUNT (TRIG)	HILL	41 08 172 36	58
PEEL, MOUNT (TRIG)	HILL	46 03 168 40	110
PEEL, MOUNT (TRIG)	HILL	46 03 168 40	112
PEEL RANGE	MTNS	41 07 172 34	56
PEEL RANGE	MTNS	41 07 172 34	57
PEEL RANGE	MTNS	41 07 172 34	58
PEEL STREAM	STRM	41 13 172 35	56
PEEL STREAM	STRM	41 13 172 35	58
PEEP-O-DAY	LOC	39 57 175 49	46
PEEP-O-DAY (TRIG)	HILL	40 40 175 50	49
PEG COL	SAD	43 20 171 02	75
PEGASUS BAY	BAY	43 22 172 55	82
PEGASUS BAY	BAY	43 22 172 55	83
PEGASUS CREEK	STRM	47 09 167 42	114
PEGASUS PEAK	PEAK	44 12 168 52	78
PEGGIOH	HSTD	41 51 174 01	67
PEGGIOH	MTN	41 50 173 56	67
PEGMATITE CREEK	STRM	43 49 169 27	76
PEGMATITE CREEK	STRM	43 49 169 27	78
PEGMATITE CREEK	STRM	43 49 169 27	79
PEHIMATEA (TRIG)	HILL	38 22 174 41	26
PEHIRI	LOC	38 39 177 37	31
PEHIRI	LOC	38 39 177 37	33
PEHU (TRIG)	HILL	39 18 175 07	36
PEKAPEKA BAY	BAY	35 01 173 44	4
PEKAPEKA STREAM	STRM	39 26 176 43	40
PEKAPEKA STREAM	STRM	39 26 176 43	42
PEKAPEKARAU	LOC	35 46 173 55	7
PEKATAHI	RSTN	38 03 176 59	22
PEKATAHI	RSTN	38 03 176 59	23
PEKEPEKE (TRIG)	HILL	38 29 176 38	30
PEKERAU	LOC	35 00 173 21	3
PELION, MOUNT (TRIG)	MTN	42 00 172 05	64
PELL CREEK	STRM	41 54 171 54	63
PELL CREEK	STRM	41 54 171 54	64
PELL STREAM	STRM	42 20 172 16	65
PELL STREAM	STRM	42 20 172 16	71
PELORUS BRIDGE	LOC	41 18 173 34	59
PELORUS RIVER	STRM	41 16 173 46	60
PELORUS SOUND	SND	41 08 173 52	54
PELORUS SOUND	SND	41 08 173 52	60
PELORUS SOUND	SND	41 08 173 52	61
PEMBER, MOUNT	MTN	43 03 172 05	81
PEMBER, MOUNT	MTN	45 37 167 02	105
PEMBERTON	LOC	39 55 175 53	46
PEMBROKE	LOC	39 19 174 14	34
PEMBROKE, MOUNT	MTN	44 34 167 53	89
PEMBROKE, MOUNT	MTN	44 34 167 53	94
PEMBROKE WILDERNESS AREA	PARK	44 34 167 53	89
PEMBROKE WILDERNESS AREA	PARK	44 34 167 53	94
PENCARROW HEAD	HEAD	41 22 174 51	52
PENCARROW HEAD	HEAD	41 22 174 51	55
PENDARVES	LOC	43 53 171 59	84
PENDER, MOUNT	MTN	45 42 166 52	104
PENDLE HILL (TRIG)	HILL	42 55 173 07	72
PENDULO REACH	STRA	45 18 167 00	96
PENGUIN BAY	BAY	41 08 173 50	54
PENGUIN BAY	BAY	41 08 173 50	60
PENGUIN BAY	BAY	41 08 173 50	61
PENGUIN BAY	BAY	46 31 169 42	113
PENGUIN ISLAND	ISLD	37 04 175 56	16
PENGUIN ISLAND	ISLD	37 04 175 56	17
PENGUIN ISLAND	ISLD	40 51 173 55	54

PENGUIN ISLAND	ISLD	40 51 173 55	61
PENINSULA, THE	PEN	44 37 169 07	90
PENINSULA (TRIG)	MTN	42 02 173 51	67
PENK RIVER	STRM	41 50 173 44	67
PENNY PASS	PASS	42 47 171 50	70
PENNY STREAM	STRM	42 47 171 53	70
PENNYWEIGHT HILL (TRIG)	HILL	44 56 169 54	91
PENTLAND HILL (TRIG)	HILL	44 40 170 50	93
PENTLAND HILLS	LOC	44 41 170 48	93
PEPE STREAM	STRM	37 00 175 51	16
PEPE STREAM	STRM	37 00 175 51	17
PEPENUI STREAM	STRM	38 57 175 25	36
PEPENUI STREAM	STRM	38 57 175 25	37
PEPEPE	LOC	37 36 174 56	18
PEPIN ISLAND	ISLD	41 09 173 25	59
PERAKI BAY	BAY	43 52 172 49	83
PERAKI CREEK	STRM	43 52 172 49	83
PERANO HEAD	HEAD	41 12 174 22	54
PERCIVAL, MOUNT (TRIG)	MTN	42 28 172 56	71
PERCIVAL, MOUNT (TRIG)	MTN	42 28 172 56	72
PERCIVAL RIVER	STRM	42 35 172 47	71
PERCIVAL RIVER	STRM	42 35 172 47	72
PERCY, MOUNT (TRIG)	HILL	40 49 176 15	50
PERCY PEAK (TRIG)	HILL	40 51 172 22	56
PERCY SADDLE	SAD	45 34 167 19	96
PERCY SADDLE	SAD	45 34 167 19	105
PERCY SMITH, MOUNT	MTN	43 50 169 53	76
PERCY SMITH, MOUNT	MTN	43 50 169 53	79
PERCY STREAM	STRM	45 36 167 22	105
PERFORATED POINT	PNT	34 48 173 10	3
PERIA	LOC	35 06 173 29	3
PERIA	LOC	37 48 175 43	19
PERIA STREAM	STRM	35 06 173 30	3
PERINGA RIVER	STRM	43 38 169 26	76
PERPENDICULAR PEAK	PEAK	45 49 166 52	104
PERPENDICULAR POINT	PNT	34 50 173 10	3
PERPENDICULAR POINT	PNT	42 05 171 21	63
PERRY, MOUNT (TRIG)	HILL	40 53 172 24	56
PERRY SADDLE	SAD	40 54 172 24	56
PERSEUS, MOUNT	MTN	44 16 168 55	78
PERTH COL	SAD	43 20 170 43	74
PERTH RIVER	STRM	43 17 170 24	74
PETE STREAM	STRM	43 00 171 53	70
PETE STREAM	STRM	43 00 171 53	80
PETER CREEK	STRM	43 13 170 43	74
PETER, MOUNT (TRIG)	PEAK	42 31 173 14	72
PETER, MOUNT (TRIG)	PEAK	42 31 173 14	73
PETER STREAM	STRM	44 29 170 41	93
PETERMANN, MOUNT	MTN	43 25 170 34	74
PETERMANN, MOUNT	MTN	43 25 170 34	77
PETERS PASS	PASS	42 25 172 45	71
PETERS POINT	PNT	46 51 168 06	109
PETERS POINT	PNT	46 51 168 06	115
PETERSON, MOUNT	MTN	44 13 169 41	79
PETONE	SBRB	41 14 174 53	52
PETONE	SBRB	41 14 174 53	55
PETREL ISLANDS	ISLS	45 44 166 31	104
PETTICOAT LANE	STRM	43 24 171 20	75
PETTICOAT LANE	STRM	43 24 171 20	80
PEVERIL PEAK (TRIG)	PEAK	43 00 171 55	70
PEVERIL PEAK (TRIG)	PEAK	43 00 171 55	80
PEVERIL PEAK (TRIG)	PEAK	43 00 171 55	81
PFEIFER, MOUNT (TRIG)	MTN	42 49 171 40	70
PHANTOM RIVER	STRM	43 51 171 04	87
PHILLIPS, MOUNT	MTN	44 40 167 53	89
PHILLIPS, MOUNT	MTN	44 40 167 53	94
PHILLIPS, MOUNT	HILL	45 43 166 37	104
PHILLIPS, MOUNT (TRIG)	MTN	41 44 173 22	66
PHILLIPS SADDLE	SAD	43 29 171 48	80
PHILOSOPHERS KNOB (TRIG)	MTN	42 20 172 30	65
PHILOSOPHERS KNOB (TRIG)	MTN	42 20 172 30	71
PHIPPS PEAK	PEAK	42 54 171 36	69
PHOEBE	LOC	42 45 173 14	72
PHOEBE	LOC	42 45 173 14	73
PHOEBE CREEK	STRM	44 34 168 54	90
PHOENIX DAM	DAM	45 53 169 43	111
PHYLLIS, LAKE	LAKE	41 28 172 14	62
PIAERE	LOC	37 56 175 41	19
PIAKA	LOC	35 32 174 09	4
PIAKA	LOC	35 32 174 09	5
PIAKATU POINT	PNT	43 39 169 22	78
PIAKATU (TRIG)	HILL	43 39 169 23	78
PIAKAU STREAM	STRM	39 10 174 15	34
PIAKO RIVER	STRM	37 12 175 30	13
PIAKO RIVER	STRM	37 12 175 30	15
PIAKONUI STREAM	STRM	37 43 175 37	19
PIANO FLAT	LOC	45 34 169 01	99
PIAPIA BAY	BAY	35 01 173 52	4
PIBRAC	MTN	43 38 170 10	74
PIBRAC	MTN	43 38 170 10	77
PIBRAC	MTN	43 38 170 10	86
PIC D'ARGENT COL	SAD	44 25 168 21	88
PIC D'ARGENT COL	SAD	44 25 168 21	89
PICKELHAUBE	MTN	44 19 168 50	90
PICKELHAUBE GLACIER	GLCR	44 14 168 52	78
PICKERSGILL ISLAND	ISLD	41 10 174 17	54
PICKERSGILL ISLAND	ISLD	41 10 174 17	61
PICTON	TOWN	41 18 174 00	54
PICTON	TOWN	41 18 174 00	60
PICTON	TOWN	41 18 174 00	61
PICTON HARBOUR	HARB	41 16 174 01	54
PICTON HARBOUR	HARB	41 16 174 01	60
PICTON HARBOUR	HARB	41 16 174 01	61
PIERCY ISLAND	ISLD	35 10 174 20	5
PIG BAY	BAY	41 01 174 12	54
PIG BAY	BAY	41 01 174 12	60
PIG BAY	BAY	41 01 174 12	61
PIG BURN	STRM	45 12 170 06	101
PIG CREEK	STRM	45 24 168 35	99
PIG CREEK	STRM	45 47 167 32	105
PIG CREEK	STRM	45 47 167 32	106
PIG HUNTING CREEK	STRM	44 28 171 14	93
PIG ISLAND	ISLD	44 57 168 25	89
PIG ISLAND	ISLD	44 57 168 25	95
PIG ISLAND	ISLD	44 57 168 25	98
PIG ISLAND	ISLD	46 24 167 59	108
PIG ISLAND	ISLD	46 24 167 59	109
PIG SPUR STREAM	STRM	42 57 172 08	70
PIG WHARE SADDLE	SAD	41 43 173 42	67
PIGEON BAY	BAY	43 39 172 54	82
PIGEON BAY	LOC	43 41 172 54	83
PIGEON BAY	BAY	43 39 172 54	83
PIGEON BUSH	LOC	41 09 175 17	53
PIGEON CREEK	STRM	41 24 173 03	58
PIGEON CREEK	STRM	41 24 173 03	59
PIGEON FLAT	LOC	45 48 170 33	103
PIGEON ISLAND	ISLD	44 55 168 24	89
PIGEON ISLAND	ISLD	44 55 168 24	95
PIGEON ISLAND	ISLD	45 43 166 33	104
PIGEON SADDLE	SAD	40 50 172 58	57
PIGSKIN, LAKE	LAKE	34 42 173 01	2
PIHA	LOC	36 57 174 28	12
PIHAKOA POINT	PNT	34 50 173 27	3
PIHAMA	LOC	39 30 173 56	34
PIHANGA (TRIG)	PEAK	39 03 175 46	37
PIHANGA (TRIG)	PEAK	39 03 175 46	38
PIHANUI	HSTD	38 59 177 07	41
PIKARORO BAY	BAY	47 02 168 13	115
PIKARORO POINT	PNT	47 02 168 13	115
PIKE PEAK	PEAK	41 27 172 21	62
PIKE STREAM	STRM	42 14 171 32	63
PIKES PEAK	PEAK	43 43 170 29	77
PIKES PEAK	PEAK	43 43 170 29	86
PIKES, THE (TRIG)	MTN	41 58 173 54	67
PIKIARIKI (TRIG)	HILL	39 18 175 11	36
PIKIAWATEA (TRIG)	PEAK	39 06 176 07	38
PIKIAWATEA (TRIG)	PEAK	39 06 176 07	39
PIKIKIRUNA (TRIG)	HILL	41 00 172 52	57
PIKIKIRUNA (TRIG)	HILL	41 00 172 52	58
PIKIWAHINE	LOC	35 55 174 08	7
PIKOPIKO	LOC	46 07 167 44	106
PIKOPIKO	LOC	46 07 167 44	108
PIKOPIKO STREAM	STRM	38 42 175 41	28
PIKOPIKO STREAM	STRM	38 42 175 41	38
PIKOWAI	LOC	37 52 176 40	21
PIKOWAI	LOC	37 52 176 40	22
PIKOWAI STREAM	STRM	37 51 176 40	21
PIKOWAI STREAM	STRM	37 51 176 40	22
PILBROW HILL	HILL	36 04 174 25	7
PILBROW HILL	HILL	36 04 174 25	8
PILCH POINT	PNT	40 30 172 39	57
PILLANS HEAD	HEAD	46 34 169 32	113
PILLANS PASS	PASS	45 36 167 10	105
PILLAR POINT	PNT	40 30 172 43	57
PILLAR ROCK	ROCK	35 15 174 19	5
PINAKI (TRIG)	HILL	36 10 173 57	7
PINCHBACK RANGE	MTNS	41 30 172 46	58
PINCHBACK (TRIG)	HILL	41 33 172 46	58
PINCHGUT STREAM	STRM	43 07 172 20	81
PINDERS POND	LAKE	45 35 169 19	100
PINE BUSH	LOC	46 28 168 48	112
PINE STREAM	STRM	39 29 174 34	35
PINE STREAM	STRM	39 29 174 34	44
PINE TREE SADDLE	SAD	42 35 173 22	72
PINE TREE SADDLE	SAD	42 35 173 22	73
PINE VALLEY STREAM	STRM	41 32 173 33	59
PINEDALE	LOC	38 04 175 49	19
PINEDALE	LOC	38 04 175 49	20
PINEHAVEN	SBRB	41 10 175 01	52
PINEHAVEN	SBRB	41 10 175 01	55
PINELHEUGH CREEK	STRM	45 31 169 28	100
PINELHEUGH (TRIG)	MTN	45 28 169 30	100
PINNACLE	MTN	41 49 173 17	66
PINNACLE	PEAK	42 24 172 03	70
PINNACLE STREAM	STRM	41 50 173 22	66
PINNACLE (TRIG)	MTN	44 15 169 46	79
PINNACLE (TRIG)	PEAK	45 26 168 36	99
PINNACLE (TRIG)	PEAK	40 53 175 29	48
PINNACLES, THE	HILL	37 03 175 43	16
PINNACLES, THE	HILL	37 03 175 43	17
PINNACLES, THE	MTN	41 53 173 27	66
PINOHIA	HSTD	41 13 173 51	54
PINOHIA	HSTD	41 13 173 51	60
PINOHIA	HSTD	41 13 173 51	61
PIONEER PASS	PASS	43 34 170 14	74
PIONEER PASS	PASS	43 34 170 14	77
PIOPIO	POPL	38 28 175 01	26
PIOPIO	POPL	38 28 175 01	27
PIOPIO (TRIG)	PEAK	39 39 176 13	47
PIOPIOTEA STREAM	STRM	39 04 175 24	36
PIOPIOTEA STREAM	STRM	39 04 175 24	37
PIOS BEACH	LOC	37 28 175 59	17
PIPECLAY GULLY	GLLY	45 05 169 09	99
PIPIKARETU POINT	PNT	45 48 170 45	103
PIPINUI POINT	PNT	41 10 174 44	52
PIPINUI POINT	PNT	41 10 174 44	55
PIPIPI (TRIG)	HILL	39 23 174 55	35
PIPIPI (TRIG)	HILL	39 23 175 14	36
PIPIPI (TRIG)	HILL	39 23 174 55	36
PIPIPI (TRIG)	HILL	39 49 175 19	45
PIPIRIKI	LOC	39 29 175 03	36
PIPIROA	LOC	37 13 175 29	13
PIPIROA	LOC	37 13 175 29	15
PIPIWAI	LOC	35 37 174 01	5
PIPIWAI	LOC	35 37 174 01	7
PIPIWAI STREAM	STRM	35 40 174 02	5
PIPIWAI STREAM	STRM	35 40 174 02	7
PIRARUHE STREAM	STRM	39 19 175 01	36
PIRAU	HILL	37 59 174 53	18
PIRAUAU (TRIG)	HILL	38 06 178 06	25
PIRAUNUI STREAM	STRM	37 34 175 39	19
PIRIAKA	LOC	38 56 175 21	27
PIRIAKA	LOC	38 56 175 21	36
PIRIMAI	SBRB	39 31 176 52	40
PIRIMAI	SBRB	39 31 176 52	41
PIRIMAI	SBRB	39 31 176 52	42
PIRINOA	LOC	41 21 175 12	52
PIRINOA	LOC	41 21 175 12	53
PIRINOA	LOC	41 21 175 12	55
PIRIPAI	LOC	37 56 176 58	22
PIRIPAI	LOC	37 56 176 58	23
PIRIPAUA	LOC	38 50 177 10	31
PIRIPIRI	LOC	38 16 174 53	18
PIRIPIRI	LOC	38 16 174 53	26
PIRIPIRI POINT	PNT	36 40 174 45	11
PIRIPIRI POINT	PNT	36 40 174 45	12
PIRIPIRI STREAM	STRM	39 13 175 46	37
PIRIPIRI STREAM	STRM	39 13 175 46	38
PIRIPIRI STREAM	STRM	40 03 175 59	46
PIRIPIRI (TRIG)	HILL	41 19 174 03	54
PIRIPIRI (TRIG)	HILL	41 19 174 03	60
PIRIPIRI (TRIG)	HILL	41 19 174 03	61
PIRONGIA	LOC	38 00 175 11	18
PIRONGIA STATE FOREST PARK	PARK	37 57 175 02	18
PIRONGIA (TRIG)	MTN	38 00 175 06	18
PIROPIRO	LOC	38 37 175 24	27
PIROPIRO STREAM	STRM	38 40 175 29	27
PIRORUA STREAM	STRM	38 10 174 57	18
PISA, MOUNT (TRIG)	MTN	44 52 169 11	90
PISA RANGE	MTNS	44 53 169 11	90
PISGAH HILL	HILL	40 55 172 54	57
PISGAH, MOUNT	MTN	45 07 167 30	94
PISGAH, MOUNT	MTN	45 07 167 30	97
PISGAH, MOUNT (TRIG)	MTN	45 05 170 23	101
PISGAH, MOUNT (TRIG)	MTN	45 05 170 23	102
PITANGI STREAM	STRM	39 46 175 10	45
PITO PEAKS	PEAK	43 24 170 57	75
PITOKUKU ISLAND	ISLD	36 15 175 30	9
PITOTE STREAM	STRM	37 48 174 58	18
PITT HEAD	HEAD	40 57 173 04	57
PIVOT PEAK	PEAK	44 27 168 34	88
PIVOT PEAK	PEAK	44 27 168 34	90
PIVOT, THE (TRIG)	MTN	43 59 169 21	78
PLATEAU CREEK	STRM	44 12 168 17	88
PLEASANT BAY	BAY	45 14 167 48	97
PLEASANT BAY	BAY	45 14 167 48	98
PLEASANT CREEK	STRM	45 45 168 01	106
PLEASANT CREEK	STRM	45 45 168 01	107
PLEASANT, MOUNT (TRIG)	HILL	43 35 172 44	82
PLEASANT, MOUNT (TRIG)	HILL	43 35 172 44	83
PLEASANT, MOUNT (TRIG)	HILL	40 22 176 37	50
PLEASANT, MOUNT (TRIG)	HILL	40 56 173 51	54
PLEASANT, MOUNT (TRIG)	HILL	40 56 173 51	61
PLEASANT, MOUNT (TRIG)	HILL	45 31 170 38	102
PLEASANT POINT	POPL	44 16 171 08	87
PLEASANT RANGE	MTNS	45 41 167 07	105
PLEASANT RIVER	STRM	45 34 170 44	102
PLEASANT VALLEY	LOC	44 05 171 11	87
PLEASANT VALLEY	LOC	45 31 170 42	102
PLECKVILLE	LOC	40 40 175 46	49
PLENTY, MOUNT	MTN	43 15 171 44	80
PLIMMERTON	SBRB	41 05 174 52	52
PLIMMERTON	SBRB	41 05 174 52	55
PLOVER CRAG	MTN	43 50 169 26	76
PLOVER CRAG	MTN	43 50 169 26	78
PLOVER CRAG	MTN	43 50 169 26	79
PLUNKETT STREAM	STRM	41 20 173 46	60
PLUNKETT STREAM	STRM	41 20 173 46	61
PLUTO PEAK	PEAK	44 37 168 23	89
PLUVIUS, MOUNT	MTN	45 07 167 22	94
PLUVIUS, MOUNT	MTN	45 07 167 22	96
POACHERS PASS	PASS	43 15 171 08	75
POARANGITAUTAHI (TRIG)	HILL	39 10 174 48	35
POERUA	LOC	42 42 171 31	69
POERUA RIVER	STRM	42 38 171 31	69
POERUA RIVER	STRM	43 03 170 24	74
POERUA, LAKE	LAKE	42 42 171 30	69
POHA (TRIG)	HILL	38 39 177 40	31
POHAKA (TRIG)	HILL	39 36 175 53	46
POHANGINA	LOC	40 11 175 48	46
POHANGINA RIVER	STRM	40 16 175 46	46
POHANGINA RIVER	STRM	40 02 176 03	47
POHANGINA SADDLE	SAD	39 57 176 07	47
POHARA	LOC	40 50 172 53	57
POHARA BEACH	BCH	40 50 172 52	57
POHARA MARAE	LOC	38 04 175 38	19
POHATU (TRIG)	HILL	46 01 167 57	106
POHATU (TRIG)	HILL	46 01 167 57	107
POHATUHAHA (TRIG)	PEAK	39 40 176 16	47
POHEHE (TRIG)	PEAK	40 36 175 35	48
POHEHE (TRIG)	PEAK	40 36 175 35	49
POHOKURA	LOC	39 10 174 40	35
POHOKURA	LOC	38 58 176 32	39
POHOKURA	LOC	38 58 176 32	40
POHOKURA KNOB (TRIG)	HILL	39 13 174 42	35
POHOKURA SADDLE	SAD	39 11 174 38	35
POHOKURA (TRIG)	PEAK	38 57 176 43	40
POHONUI	LOC	39 46 175 34	46
POHOWAITAI ISLAND	ISLD	47 13 167 19	114
POHUEHUE	LOC	36 28 174 39	11
POHUENUI	HSTD	41 01 173 59	54
POHUENUI	HSTD	41 01 173 59	60
POHUENUI	HSTD	41 01 173 59	61
POHUENUI RIVER	STRM	35 58 174 27	7
POHUENUI RIVER	STRM	35 58 174 27	8
POHUERORO STREAM	STRM	37 42 177 53	24
POINT BURN	STRM	45 20 167 44	97
POINT HOWARD	SBRB	41 13 174 54	52
POINT HOWARD	SBRB	41 13 174 54	55
POINT WELLS	LOC	36 20 174 45	11
POISON BAY	BAY	44 39 167 37	94
POISON CREEK	STRM	44 48 169 20	91
POKAEWHENUA STREAM	STRM	37 21 175 17	15
POKAIATUA (TRIG)	HILL	39 36 175 04	36
POKAIATUA (TRIG)	HILL	39 36 175 04	45
POKAIKIRI (TRIG)	MTN	38 20 177 28	31
POKAINGAKAKAHU	HILL	38 29 176 49	30
POKAIROA STREAM	STRM	38 18 176 47	30
POKAITU STREAM	STRM	38 17 176 08	21
POKAITU STREAM	STRM	38 17 176 08	29
POKAIWHENUA STREAM	STRM	37 59 175 40	19
POKAKA	LOC	39 18 175 23	36
POKAKA	LOC	39 18 175 23	37
POKAKA (TRIG)	HILL	35 17 173 56	4
POKAPU	LOC	35 26 173 59	4
POKAPU	LOC	35 26 173 59	5
POKARE (TRIG)	HILL	37 49 176 34	21
POKARE (TRIG)	HILL	37 49 176 34	22
POKEKA STREAM	STRM	39 32 174 47	35
POKEKA STREAM	STRM	39 32 174 47	44
POKENO	POPL	37 15 175 01	12
POKENO	POPL	37 15 175 01	13
POKENO	POPL	37 15 175 01	14
POKERE	LOC	35 29 174 00	4
POKERE	LOC	35 29 174 00	5
POKOHINU POINT	PNT	37 48 177 37	24
POKOKINI	HSTD	41 06 173 56	54
POKOKINI	HSTD	41 06 173 56	60
POKOKINI	HSTD	41 06 173 56	61
POKOKO STREAM	STRM	39 37 175 29	45
POKOKO STREAM	STRM	39 37 175 29	46
POKOPOKO STREAM	STRM	37 50 176 25	20
POKOPOKO STREAM	STRM	37 50 176 25	21
POKOPOKO STREAM	STRM	39 35 176 03	39
POKOPOKO STREAM	STRM	39 18 176 40	40
POKOPOKO STREAM	STRM	39 35 176 03	47
POKOPOKO (TRIG)	HILL	39 35 176 05	39
POKOPOKO (TRIG)	HILL	39 35 176 05	47
POKORORO	LOC	41 13 172 50	58
POKORORO RIVER	STRM	41 12 172 52	58
POKORUA, LAKE	LAKE	37 12 174 38	12
POKORUA, LAKE	LAKE	37 12 174 38	14
POKURU	LOC	38 04 175 14	18
POKURU	LOC	38 04 175 14	19
POLAR RANGE	MTNS	42 56 171 41	70
POLEY CREEK	STRM	45 32 170 29	102
POLEY STREAM	STRM	41 32 175 25	53
POLLEN ISLAND	ISLD	36 52 174 40	11
POLLEN ISLAND	ISLD	36 52 174 40	12
POLLOCK STREAM	STRM	43 42 170 30	77
POLLOCK STREAM	STRM	43 42 170 30	86
POLLOCKS HILL (TRIG)	HILL	46 24 169 40	113
POLLOK	LOC	37 08 174 37	12
POLLOK	LOC	37 08 174 37	14
POLLUX	MTN	44 14 168 52	78
POLNOON BURN	STRM	44 44 168 43	90
POMAHAKA	LOC	46 01 169 14	110
POMAHAKA RIVER	STRM	45 34 169 12	100
POMAHAKA RIVER	STRM	46 09 169 34	113
POMARANGAI	LOC	38 22 174 48	26
POMARE	SBRB	41 10 174 58	52
POMARE	SBRB	41 10 174 58	55
POMARE BAY	BAY	35 17 174 08	4
POMARE BAY	BAY	35 17 174 08	5
POMMEL, THE	MTN	44 17 168 40	88
POMMEL, THE	MTN	44 17 168 40	90
POMONA ISLAND	ISLD	45 31 167 28	97
POMPEYS PILLAR	ROCK	43 51 173 05	83
POND BURN	STRM	45 02 168 14	95
POND BURN	STRM	45 02 168 14	98
PONGA	LOC	37 07 175 01	12
PONGA	LOC	37 07 175 01	13
PONGA	LOC	37 07 175 01	14
PONGAKAWA	LOC	37 50 176 28	21
PONGAKAWA	LOC	37 50 176 28	22
PONGAKAWA STATION	RSTN	37 49 176 29	21
PONGAKAWA STATION	RSTN	37 49 176 29	22
PONGAKAWA STREAM	STRM	37 49 176 31	21
PONGAKAWA STREAM	STRM	37 49 176 31	22
PONGAKAWA VALLEY	LOC	37 54 176 31	21
PONGAKAWA VALLEY	LOC	37 54 176 31	22
PONGARARA STREAM	STRM	39 37 175 25	45
PONGARARA STREAM	STRM	39 37 175 25	46
PONGAROA	LOC	40 33 176 11	50
PONGAROA RIVER	STRM	40 35 176 14	50
PONGAWHAKATIKI (TRIG)	HILL	37 41 175 02	18
PONSONBY	SBRB	36 51 174 44	11
PONSONBY	SBRB	36 51 174 44	12
PONUI ISLAND	ISLD	36 52 175 11	13
PONUI, LAKE	LAKE	41 21 175 07	52
PONUI, LAKE	LAKE	41 21 175 07	55
PONUI STREAM	STRM	39 09 177 08	41
PONUI STREAM	STRM	39 57 176 55	42
PONUI STREAM	STRM	39 57 176 55	43
PONUI STREAM	STRM	40 42 175 51	49
PONUI STREAM	STRM	40 42 175 51	51
PONUI (TRIG)	HILL	36 52 175 11	13
POOL BURN	STRM	45 10 169 40	100
POOL BURN	STRM	45 10 169 40	101
POOLBURN	LOC	45 08 169 41	100
POOLBURN	LOC	45 08 169 41	101
POOLBURN RESERVOIR	LAKE	45 19 169 44	100
POOLBURN RESERVOIR	LAKE	45 19 169 44	101
POOR KNIGHTS ISLANDS	ISLS	35 28 174 44	5
POPES HILL (TRIG)	HILL	40 55 175 30	48
POPES HILL (TRIG)	HILL	40 55 175 30	49
POPES HILL (TRIG)	HILL	40 55 175 30	51
POPES NOSE	MTN	44 24 168 45	90
POPES PASS	PASS	42 56 171 22	69
POPLAR STREAM	STRM	44 36 170 39	92
POPLARS RANGE	MTNS	42 33 172 27	71
POPLARS, THE	HSTD	42 36 172 26	71
POPOITI (TRIG)	HILL	41 09 175 34	51
POPOITI (TRIG)	HILL	41 09 175 34	53
POPORANGI STREAM	STRM	39 34 176 27	47
POPORO STREAM	STRM	37 22 174 53	14
POPOTAI ISLAND	ISLD	43 52 168 53	78
POPOTUNOA	LOC	46 06 169 23	111
POPOTUNOA	LOC	46 06 169 23	113
POPOTUNOA HILL (TRIG)	HILL	46 11 169 22	111
POPOTUNOA HILL (TRIG)	HILL	46 11 169 22	113
POPUANUI (TRIG)	HILL	39 18 174 35	35
POPUANUI (TRIG)	HILL	39 18 174 35	44
PORAENUI POINT	PNT	35 12 174 04	4
PORAENUI POINT	PNT	35 12 174 04	5
PORAITI	HSTD	39 29 176 50	40
PORAITI	HSTD	39 29 176 50	41
PORAITI	HSTD	39 29 176 50	42
PORANGAHAU	POPL	40 18 176 37	50
PORANGAHAU RIVER	STRM	40 17 176 40	50
PORANGAHAU STREAM	STRM	40 01 176 27	47
PORARARI	LOC	42 05 171 21	63
PORERE (TRIG)	HILL	39 03 175 16	36
POREWA	LOC	40 02 175 28	45
POREWA	LOC	40 02 175 28	46
POREWA STREAM	STRM	40 05 175 27	45
POREWA STREAM	STRM	40 07 175 53	46
POREWA STREAM	STRM	40 05 175 27	46
PORI	LOC	40 36 175 56	49
PORI (TRIG)	HILL	40 37 175 57	49
PORIRUA	USAT	41 08 174 50	52
PORIRUA	USAT	41 08 174 50	55
PORIRUA EAST	SBRB	41 09 174 52	52
PORIRUA EAST	SBRB	41 09 174 52	55
PORIRUA HARBOUR	HARB	41 06 174 52	52
PORIRUA HARBOUR	HARB	41 06 174 52	55
PORIRUA (TRIG)	HILL	41 03 174 51	52
PORIRUA (TRIG)	HILL	41 03 174 51	55
PORM, LAKE	LAKE	44 10 168 40	88
PORONUI	HSTD	39 01 176 17	39
POROOTARARO	LOC	38 33 175 19	27
POROPORO	LOC	37 59 176 56	22
POROPORO	LOC	37 59 176 56	23
POROPORO RIVER	STRM	37 47 178 26	25
PORORARI RIVER	STRM	42 06 171 20	63
PORORUA (TRIG)	HILL	37 28 175 19	15
POROTI	LOC	35 44 174 07	5
POROTI	LOC	35 44 174 07	7
POROUTAWHAO	LOC	40 34 175 16	48
PORPOISE BAY	BAY	46 39 169 07	112
PORPOISE POINT	PNT	45 45 166 40	104
PORT ADVENTURE	BAY	47 04 168 11	115
PORT ALBERT	LOC	36 17 174 26	10
PORT ALBERT	LOC	36 17 174 26	11
PORT ARTHUR (TRIG)	HILL	38 54 175 08	27
PORT AWANUI	LOC	37 49 178 27	25
PORT CHALMERS	USAT	45 49 170 37	103
PORT CHARLES	BAY	36 31 175 28	9
PORT CHARLES	LOC	36 31 175 28	9
PORT CHARLES	LOC	36 31 175 28	16
PORT COOPER SADDLE	SAD	41 56 173 16	66
PORT CRAIG	LOC	46 13 167 22	105
PORT CRAIG	LOC	46 13 167 22	108
PORT FITZROY	BAY	36 11 175 21	9
PORT FITZROY	LOC	36 10 175 22	9
PORT JACKSON	BAY	36 29 175 21	9
PORT JACKSON	BAY	36 29 175 21	16
PORT LEVY	LOC	43 39 172 49	82
PORT LEVY	LOC	43 39 172 49	83
PORT MOTUEKA	LOC	41 08 173 01	57
PORT MOTUEKA	LOC	41 08 173 01	58
PORT MOTUEKA	LOC	41 08 173 01	59
PORT NELSON	SBRB	41 15 173 17	59
PORT OHOPE	LOC	37 59 177 06	23
PORT PEGASUS	BAY	47 13 167 40	114
PORT ROBINSON	LOC	42 53 173 19	72
PORT ROBINSON	LOC	42 53 173 19	73
PORT WAIKATO	LOC	37 24 174 44	14
PORT WHANGAREI	SBRB	35 45 174 19	5
PORT WHANGAREI	SBRB	35 45 174 19	7

PORT WHANGAREI	SBRB	35 45 174 19	8
PORTAGE	LOC	41 12 174 02	54
PORTAGE	LOC	41 12 174 02	60
PORTAGE	LOC	41 12 174 02	61
PORTER CREEK	STRM	41 39 172 57	66
PORTER RIVER	STRM	43 15 171 44	80
PORTERS KNOB	PEAK	41 40 173 01	66
PORTERS PASS	PASS	43 18 171 45	80
PORTLAND	LOC	35 48 174 20	7
PORTLAND	LOC	35 48 174 20	8
PORTLAND ISLAND	ISLD	39 17 177 52	33
PORTOBELLO	SBRB	45 51 170 39	103
PORTUGUESE HILL (TRIG)	HILL	45 40 169 27	111
POSEIDON CREEK	STRM	44 44 167 50	94
POSEIDON PEAK	PEAK	44 35 168 14	88
POSEIDON PEAK	PEAK	44 35 168 14	89
POSSESSION, MOUNT (TRIG)	MTN	43 40 171 09	75
POSSESSION, MOUNT (TRIG)	MTN	43 40 171 09	87
POSSIBILITY COL	SAD	44 29 168 20	88
POSSIBILITY COL	SAD	44 29 168 20	89
POSTAL RIVER	STRM	41 12 172 11	56
POSTAL RIVER	STRM	41 12 172 11	62
POTAE (TRIG)	PEAK	39 39 176 10	47
POTAHI POINT	PNT	38 01 174 48	18
POTAKA	LOC	37 34 178 08	25
POTANGOTANGO (TRIG)	HILL	39 30 174 37	35
POTANGOTANGO (TRIG)	HILL	39 30 174 37	44
POTATO CREEK	STRM	44 40 170 36	92
POTATO POINT	PNT	45 45 170 38	103
POTERITERI LAKE	LAKE	46 07 167 08	105
POTERITERI PEAK	PEAK	46 02 167 05	105
POTIKI BAY	BAY	36 33 175 32	9
POTIKI BAY	BAY	36 33 175 32	16
POTTERS	LOC	45 26 169 08	99
POTTERS CREEK	STRM	43 20 170 12	74
POTTERS CREEK	STRM	43 20 170 12	77
POTTERS CREEK	STRM	45 09 169 00	99
POTTS, MOUNT	MTN	43 30 170 56	75
POTTS PEAK (TRIG)	PEAK	37 51 177 58	24
POTTS RANGE	MTNS	43 29 170 54	75
POTTS RIVER	STRM	43 35 170 55	75
POTUA STREAM	STRM	39 05 177 21	41
POU (TRIG)	HILL	41 12 175 43	51
POU (TRIG)	HILL	41 12 175 43	53
POUAHIRI CREEK	STRM	46 22 167 49	108
POUAKAI (TRIG)	PEAK	39 14 174 01	34
POUARUA CANAL	CANL	37 15 175 24	15
POUARUA, LAKE	LAKE	38 58 176 24	39
POUARUA, LAKE	LAKE	38 58 176 24	40
POUATU (TRIG)	HILL	39 02 174 50	35
POUAWA	LOC	38 37 178 11	32
POUAWA RIVER	STRM	38 37 178 11	32
POUERUA (TRIG)	HILL	35 23 173 56	4
POUIATOA (TRIG)	HILL	39 05 174 31	35
POUKAWA	LOC	39 46 176 44	42
POUKAWA	LOC	39 46 176 44	43
POUKAWA, LAKE	LAKE	39 47 176 42	42
POUKAWA, LAKE	LAKE	39 47 176 42	43
POUKIORE	LOC	39 52 175 38	46
POUKOURA INLET	BAY	35 09 174 02	4
POUKOURA INLET	BAY	35 09 174 02	5
POULTER HILL	PEAK	42 54 172 00	70
POULTER RANGE	MTNS	42 50 171 55	70
POULTER RIVER	STRM	43 05 171 54	80
POULTER RIVER	STRM	43 05 171 54	81
POULTER RIVER, EAST BRANCH	STRM	42 57 171 54	70
POUNAWEA	LOC	46 29 169 41	113
POUPOU STREAM	STRM	37 38 175 55	20
POUPOUATUA (TRIG)	HILL	40 07 176 05	47
POURAKINO RIVER	STRM	46 21 167 59	107
POURAKINO RIVER	STRM	46 21 167 59	108
POURAKINO RIVER	STRM	46 21 167 59	109
POURAKINO VALLEY	LOC	46 13 167 56	106
POURAKINO VALLEY	LOC	46 13 167 56	107
POURAKINO VALLEY	LOC	46 13 167 56	108
POURAKINO VALLEY	LOC	46 13 167 56	109
POURANGA (TRIG)	HILL	39 02 175 48	37
POURANGA (TRIG)	HILL	39 02 175 48	38
POURANGAKI RIVER	STRM	39 49 175 58	46
POURAUREROA STREAM	STRM	37 13 175 06	13
POURAUREROA STREAM	STRM	37 13 175 06	14
POURAUREROA STREAM	STRM	37 13 175 06	15
POURERERE	HSTD	40 06 176 52	43
POURERERE STREAM	STRM	40 06 176 52	43
POUREWA ISLAND	ISLD	38 23 178 21	32
POURI STREAM	STRM	39 22 174 49	35
POURI STREAM	STRM	39 22 174 49	44
POUTAHI (TRIG)	HILL	39 25 175 10	36
POUTAKATAKA (TRIG)	HILL	38 19 176 10	21
POUTAKATAKA (TRIG)	HILL	38 19 176 10	29
POUTAKI STREAM	STRM	39 40 176 24	47
POUTAMA ISLAND	ISLD	47 16 167 24	114
POUTAWA BANK	BNK	37 06 174 44	12
POUTAWA BANK	BNK	37 06 174 44	14
POUTI (TRIG)	HILL	39 35 175 34	36
POUTI (TRIG)	HILL	39 35 175 34	37
POUTO	LOC	36 22 174 11	10
POUTO STREAM	STRM	37 36 174 54	18
POUTOA, LAKE	LAKE	36 38 174 19	10
POUWHAKAURA	LOC	39 50 175 45	46
POVERTY BAY	BAY	38 43 177 59	32
POVERTY BAY	BAY	38 43 177 59	33
POVERTY HILL (TRIG)	HILL	46 13 169 54	111
POVERTY HILL (TRIG)	HILL	46 13 169 54	113
POWER CREEK	STRM	43 38 169 30	76
POWER CREEK	STRM	43 38 169 30	79
POWER HILL (TRIG)	HILL	45 48 170 24	103
POWER HOUSE STREAM	STRM	43 34 170 55	75
POWER KNOB	MTN	43 49 169 28	76
POWER KNOB	MTN	43 49 169 28	79
POWER STREAM	STRM	43 02 171 36	80
PRATT, LAKE	LAKE	43 21 170 10	74
PRATT, LAKE	LAKE	43 21 170 10	77
PRATT STREAM	STRM	44 24 171 00	93
PREBBLE HILL (TRIG)	HILL	43 13 171 46	80
PREBBLETON	LOC	43 35 172 31	81
PREBBLETON	LOC	43 35 172 31	82
PREBBLETON	LOC	43 35 172 31	83
PREBBLETON	LOC	43 35 172 31	85
PRECIPICE CREEK	STRM	44 48 168 23	95
PRECIPICE HILL	MTN	44 49 168 27	89
PRECIPICE HILL	MTN	44 49 168 27	95
PRECIPICE PEAK	PEAK	45 32 167 23	96
PRECIPICE PEAK	PEAK	45 32 167 23	97
PREECE POINT	PNT	36 47 175 29	13
PREECE POINT	PNT	36 47 175 29	16
PRELUDE PEAK	PEAK	43 19 170 52	75
PRESERVATION INLET	BAY	46 08 166 35	104
PRETTY BRIDGE STREAM	STRM	41 27 172 58	58
PRICE, MOUNT	MTN	43 19 170 21	74
PRICE PEAK	PEAK	43 37 170 01	76
PRICE PEAK	PEAK	43 37 170 01	77
PRICE RANGE	MTNS	43 22 170 21	74
PRICE RANGE	MTNS	43 22 170 21	77
PRICE RIVER	STRM	43 07 171 00	75
PRICES INLET	BAY	46 55 168 03	109
PRICES INLET	BAY	46 55 168 03	115
PRICES POINT	PNT	35 00 173 15	3
PRICES POINT	PNT	46 55 168 04	109
PRICES POINT	PNT	46 55 168 04	115
PRICES STREAM	STRM	43 48 172 41	83
PRIESTLY, MOUNT	MTN	42 04 171 33	63
PRINCE OF WALES (TRIG)	MTN	44 46 168 39	90
PRINCE OF WALES (TRIG)	MTN	44 46 168 39	95
PRINCES ISLAND	ISLD	34 11 172 03	2
PRINCESS BATH	LAKE	42 11 172 41	65
PRINCESS BURN	STRM	45 56 167 06	105
PRINCESS, MOUNT (TRIG)	MTN	42 11 172 41	65
PRINCESS MOUNTAINS	MTNS	45 59 167 09	105
PRINCESS STREAM	STRM	42 13 172 45	65
PRINCHESTER CREEK	STRM	45 36 167 59	97
PRINCHESTER CREEK	STRM	45 36 167 59	98
PRINGLE STREAM	STRM	44 25 170 29	92
PROGRESS JUNCTION	LOC	42 09 171 52	63
PROGRESS JUNCTION	LOC	42 09 171 52	64
PROMINENT CONE (TRIG)	PEAK	39 16 176 02	38
PROMINENT CONE (TRIG)	PEAK	39 16 176 02	39
PROSPECT CREEK	STRM	44 54 167 43	94
PROSPECT HILL (TRIG)	HILL	43 18 171 07	75
PROSPECT HILL (TRIG)	MTN	45 14 169 13	100
PROSPECT MOUNT	MTN	44 30 169 31	91
PROSPECT, MOUNT	LOC	45 24 167 54	97
PROSPECT, MOUNT	LOC	45 24 167 54	98
PROSPECT, MOUNT (TRIG)	PEAK	45 25 167 57	97
PROSPECT, MOUNT (TRIG)	PEAK	45 25 167 57	98
PROSPECTOR CREEK	STRM	41 43 172 49	65
PROSPECTOR PEAK	PEAK	44 36 168 10	89
PROVE ISLAND	ISLD	45 46 166 33	104
PROVIDENCE, CAPE	CAPE	46 01 166 28	104
PROVIDENCE ROCKS	ROCK	46 02 166 28	104
PRUDENCE PEAK	PEAK	43 49 169 58	76
PRUDENCE PEAK	PEAK	43 49 169 58	77
PRUDENCE PEAK	PEAK	43 49 169 58	79
PRYSE PEAK (TRIG)	PEAK	46 56 168 00	115
PUAHA	LOC	43 45 172 50	83
PUAHUE	LOC	38 03 175 26	19
PUAKATO (TRIG)	HILL	38 14 178 10	32
PUANENE STREAM	STRM	37 49 176 29	21
PUANENE STREAM	STRM	37 49 176 29	22
PUANGIANGI ISLAND	ISLD	40 46 173 59	61
PUAO	LOC	39 44 174 49	44
PUAROA STREAM	STRM	38 17 174 47	26
PUDDING HILL	HILL	41 50 173 29	66
PUDDING HILL STREAM	STRM	43 37 171 32	80
PUDDING VALLEY CREEK	STRM	43 40 171 07	87
PUERUA	LOC	46 19 169 41	111
PUERUA	LOC	46 19 169 41	113
PUERUA RIVER	STRM	46 21 169 48	111
PUERUA RIVER	STRM	46 21 169 48	113
PUETO STREAM	STRM	38 37 176 15	29
PUG CREEK	STRM	43 22 170 04	76
PUG CREEK	STRM	43 22 170 04	77
PUHA	LOC	38 27 177 50	32
PUHANGATOHORAKA (TRIG)	HILL	35 07 173 32	3
PUHARAKEKE CREEK	STRM	36 37 174 21	10
PUHARAKEKE CREEK	STRM	36 37 174 21	11
PUHATA	LOC	35 18 173 13	3
PUHATA STREAM	STRM	35 18 173 12	3
PUHEKE (TRIG)	HILL	34 52 173 20	3
PUHEKI (TRIG)	HILL	38 59 175 04	36
PUHERUA (TRIG)	HILL	39 42 175 53	46
PUHI PUHI RIVER	STRM	42 19 173 43	67
PUHIKERERU (TRIG)	MTN	37 59 177 43	24
PUHINUI CREEK	STRM	35 16 174 15	5
PUHIPUHI	LOC	35 29 174 16	5
PUHIPUHI	HILL	38 11 176 36	21
PUHIPUHI	HILL	38 11 176 36	22
PUHITAHI CREEK	STRM	37 08 174 48	12
PUHITAHI CREEK	STRM	37 08 174 48	14
PUHOI	LOC	36 31 174 39	11
PUHOI RIVER	STRM	36 32 174 43	11
PUHOKIO STREAM	STRM	39 49 176 59	42
PUHOKIO STREAM	STRM	39 49 176 59	43
PUHUKA	LOC	44 22 171 14	93
PUIARAU (TRIG)	HILL	38 47 177 21	31
PUKAHU	LOC	39 41 176 50	42
PUKAHU	LOC	39 41 176 50	43
PUKAHU STREAM	STRM	37 22 174 57	14
PUKAHUNUI STREAM	STRM	38 55 176 43	40
PUKAKA STREAM	STRM	41 26 174 00	54
PUKAKA STREAM	STRM	41 26 174 00	60
PUKAKI HYDRO ELECTRICITY CANAL	CANL	44 16 170 02	79
PUKAKI, LAKE	LAKE	44 03 170 10	86
PUKAKI RIVER	STRM	44 20 170 13	86
PUKANUI, MOUNT (TRIG)	MTN	43 45 171 13	87
PUKAPAKA CREEK	STRM	41 33 174 03	60
PUKAPUKA	LOC	36 29 174 40	11
PUKAPUKA (TRIG)	HILL	37 06 175 12	13
PUKAPUKA (TRIG)	HILL	37 06 175 12	15
PUKAREAO STREAM	STRM	38 30 176 58	30
PUKARORO ROCK	ROCK	42 32 173 30	73
PUKARORONUI (TRIG)	HILL	38 52 177 43	33
PUKATEA BAY	BAY	40 57 173 53	54
PUKATEA BAY	BAY	40 57 173 53	61
PUKATEA STREAM	STRM	40 44 172 19	56
PUKAWA	LOC	38 55 175 45	28
PUKAWA	LOC	38 55 175 45	37
PUKAWA	LOC	38 55 175 45	38
PUKE MAKARIRI	MTN	44 21 169 35	91
PUKEAKURA (TRIG)	HILL	38 33 178 06	32
PUKEAMARU	HSTD	37 41 178 16	25
PUKEAMARU (TRIG)	MTN	37 39 178 15	25
PUKEAMUKU (TRIG)	HILL	40 44 176 13	50
PUKEARUHE	LOC	38 54 174 31	26
PUKEARUHE	LOC	46 02 168 22	107
PUKEATUA	LOC	38 04 175 33	19
PUKEATUA (TRIG)	HILL	35 07 174 02	4
PUKEATUA (TRIG)	HILL	35 07 174 02	5
PUKEATUA (TRIG)	HILL	37 58 175 44	19
PUKEATUA (TRIG)	HILL	38 02 175 34	19
PUKEATUA (TRIG)	HILL	37 52 178 22	25
PUKEATUA (TRIG)	PEAK	40 54 175 11	48
PUKEATUA (TRIG)	PEAK	40 54 175 11	52
PUKEATUA (TRIG)	PEAK	40 54 175 11	55
PUKEAWA	LOC	46 09 169 37	111
PUKEAWA	LOC	46 09 169 37	113
PUKEHAMOAMOA	HSTD	39 33 176 42	39
PUKEHAMOAMOA	LOC	39 33 176 42	40
PUKEHAMOAMOA	LOC	39 33 176 42	42
PUKEHAMOAMOA	LOC	39 33 176 42	43
PUKEHAMOAMOA	LOC	39 33 176 42	47
PUKEHANGI	HILL	37 17 175 48	17
PUKEHIKI	LOC	45 52 170 37	103
PUKEHINA	LOC	37 49 176 31	21
PUKEHINA	LOC	37 49 176 31	22
PUKEHINA BEACH	BCH	37 47 176 30	21
PUKEHINA BEACH	BCH	37 47 176 30	22
PUKEHINAU (TRIG)	HILL	35 06 173 37	4
PUKEHINAU (TRIG)	HILL	40 55 175 44	49
PUKEHINAU (TRIG)	HILL	40 55 175 44	51
PUKEHIWITAHI (TRIG)	HILL	45 28 170 47	102
PUKEHOE (TRIG)	HILL	38 52 177 45	31
PUKEHOE (TRIG)	HILL	38 52 177 45	33
PUKEHOIHO (TRIG)	HILL	38 36 174 56	26
PUKEHOU	LOC	39 50 176 38	42
PUKEHOU	LOC	39 50 176 38	43
PUKEHOU	LOC	39 50 176 38	47
PUKEHOU (TRIG)	MTN	37 57 177 39	24
PUKEHOU (TRIG)	HILL	40 45 175 11	48
PUKEHOUA (TRIG)	HILL	38 01 175 10	18
PUKEHUIA	LOC	35 53 174 02	7
PUKEHUIA (TRIG)	HILL	35 14 174 17	5
PUKEHUIA (TRIG)	HILL	39 38 175 37	46
PUKEHURUHURU (TRIG)	MTN	38 39 177 15	31
PUKEIAHONOA (TRIG)	HILL	37 59 177 36	24
PUKEINOI	LOC	38 08 174 53	18
PUKEITI (TRIG)	HILL	39 12 173 59	34
PUKEKAMAKA (TRIG)	HILL	37 19 175 20	15
PUKEKAPIA	LOC	37 32 175 07	14
PUKEKAPIA	LOC	37 32 175 07	15
PUKEKAREA (TRIG)	HILL	34 31 172 43	2
PUKEKARORO	LOC	36 08 174 25	7
PUKEKARORO	LOC	36 08 174 25	8
PUKEKARORO (TRIG)	HILL	36 08 174 27	7
PUKEKARORO (TRIG)	HILL	36 08 174 27	8
PUKEKAWA	LOC	37 20 174 59	14
PUKEKAWA (TRIG)	LOC	37 34 174 49	14
PUKEKAWA (TRIG)	HILL	37 20 174 59	14
PUKEKIEKIE (TRIG)	HILL	38 36 174 59	26
PUKEKIEKIE (TRIG)	HILL	38 36 174 59	27
PUKEKIWI (TRIG)	HILL	39 41 175 23	45
PUKEKO STREAM	STRM	39 02 174 35	35
PUKEKOHE	POPL	37 12 174 54	12
PUKEKOHE	POPL	37 12 174 54	14
PUKEKOHE EAST	LOC	37 12 174 57	12
PUKEKOHE EAST	LOC	37 12 174 57	14
PUKEKOHE (TRIG)	HILL	36 02 174 13	7
PUKEKOHE (TRIG)	HILL	36 02 174 13	8
PUKEKOIKOI	HSTD	41 09 174 10	54
PUKEKOIKOI	HSTD	41 09 174 10	60
PUKEKOIKOI	HSTD	41 09 174 10	61
PUKEKOMA	LOC	46 06 169 44	111
PUKEKOMA	LOC	46 06 169 44	113
PUKEKOTARE (TRIG)	HILL	36 56 175 45	16
PUKEKOTARE (TRIG)	HILL	36 56 175 45	17
PUKEKUMERA (TRIG)	HILL	41 02 176 01	51
PUKEKURA	LOC	37 56 175 30	19
PUKEKURA	LOC	43 01 170 40	74
PUKEKURA STREAM	STRM	34 39 172 52	2
PUKEKURA (TRIG)	HILL	37 57 175 31	19
PUKEMAIRE	HILL	46 05 168 39	110
PUKEMAIRE	HILL	46 05 168 39	112
PUKEMAKO CAMP	LOC	38 31 175 31	27
PUKEMANUKA (TRIG)	HILL	38 02 178 16	25
PUKEMAORI	LOC	46 04 167 49	106
PUKEMAORI	LOC	46 04 167 49	108
PUKEMATEKEO (TRIG)	HILL	36 20 174 43	11
PUKEMIRO	LOC	35 16 173 22	3
PUKEMIRO	LOC	37 37 175 02	18
PUKEMIRO (TRIG)	HILL	35 35 173 54	4
PUKEMIRO (TRIG)	HILL	35 35 173 54	6
PUKEMIRO (TRIG)	HILL	35 35 173 54	7
PUKEMIRO (TRIG)	HILL	38 59 174 52	35
PUKEMOKEMOKE (TRIG)	HILL	37 35 175 22	19
PUKEMORE (TRIG)	HILL	37 32 175 13	15
PUKEMOREMORE	HILL	35 24 174 16	5
PUKEMOREMORE	LOC	37 49 175 28	19
PUKEMOREMORE (TRIG)	HILL	37 49 175 29	19
PUKEMOREMORE (TRIG)	HILL	38 04 177 03	22
PUKEMOREMORE (TRIG)	HILL	38 04 177 03	23
PUKEMOREMORE (TRIG)	PEAK	40 43 175 28	48
PUKEMUTU	LOC	46 01 168 14	107
PUKENUI	LOC	34 49 173 07	2
PUKENUI	LOC	34 49 173 07	3
PUKENUI	HILL	38 07 174 58	18
PUKENUI BEACH	BCH	39 02 177 53	33
PUKENUI (TRIG)	HILL	36 41 175 36	13
PUKENUI (TRIG)	HILL	36 41 175 36	16
PUKENUI (TRIG)	MTN	38 48 177 05	30
PUKENUI (TRIG)	HILL	39 23 175 00	36
PUKENUI (TRIG)	HILL	41 23 175 25	53
PUKENUIORAHO (TRIG)	HILL	38 09 177 13	23
PUKEOHEKE (TRIG)	HILL	40 05 176 53	43
PUKEOKAHU	LOC	39 37 176 00	46
PUKEONAKE (TRIG)	PEAK	39 09 175 34	37
PUKEONAKE (TRIG)	PEAK	39 09 175 34	38
PUKEOPU (TRIG)	HILL	38 36 177 29	31
PUKEORARA (TRIG)	HILL	38 57 177 42	33
PUKEOTAHINGA (TRIG)	HILL	37 20 174 51	14
PUKEOTARUMAI (TRIG)	HILL	37 42 178 31	25
PUKEOWARE	LOC	37 15 174 46	12
PUKEOWARE	LOC	37 15 174 46	14
PUKEPAHI (TRIG)	HILL	46 26 169 30	113
PUKEPITO	LOC	46 09 169 40	111
PUKEPITO	LOC	46 09 169 40	113
PUKEPOTO	LOC	35 10 173 13	3
PUKEPOTO MAIN OUTFALL	DRN	35 07 173 14	3
PUKEPOTO (TRIG)	HILL	38 46 175 13	27
PUKEPOTO (TRIG)	HILL	40 26 176 12	50
PUKEPUKE LAGOON	LAKE	40 20 175 16	48
PUKEPUKE (TRIG)	MTN	38 40 177 10	31
PUKERAKI (TRIG)	HILL	38 07 178 03	25
PUKERANGI	LOC	45 38 170 15	101
PUKERATA (TRIG)	HILL	39 03 175 09	36
PUKERAU	LOC	46 06 169 06	110
PUKERAU	LOC	46 06 169 06	112
PUKERAU POINT	PNT	41 04 173 34	59
PUKERAU STREAM	STRM	46 05 169 00	110
PUKERAU STREAM	STRM	46 05 169 00	112
PUKERIMU	LOC	37 55 175 24	19
PUKERIMU	LOC	38 30 175 15	27
PUKERIMU STREAM	STRM	38 13 175 56	20
PUKERIMU (TRIG)	MTN	37 48 177 51	24
PUKEROA	HSTD	39 47 175 30	45
PUKEROA	HSTD	39 47 175 30	46
PUKEROA (TRIG)	HILL	37 51 176 25	21
PUKEROA (TRIG)	HILL	37 51 176 25	22
PUKEROA (TRIG)	HILL	38 29 175 33	27
PUKEROA (TRIG)	HILL	38 29 175 33	28
PUKEROA (TRIG)	MTN	38 48 176 38	30
PUKEROA (TRIG)	HILL	39 49 175 31	45
PUKEROA (TRIG)	HILL	39 49 175 31	46
PUKERONUI (TRIG)	HILL	38 53 177 42	33
PUKERORO	LOC	37 53 175 26	19
PUKERORO (TRIG)	HILL	41 13 175 53	51
PUKERUA BAY	BAY	41 02 174 54	52
PUKERUA BAY	SBRB	41 02 174 53	52
PUKERUA BAY	BAY	41 02 174 54	55
PUKERUA BAY	SBRB	41 02 174 53	55
PUKERUA (TRIG)	HILL	37 23 175 10	14
PUKERUA (TRIG)	HILL	37 23 175 10	15
PUKERURU (TRIG)	HILL	38 44 177 23	31
PUKERURU (TRIG)	HILL	38 44 177 23	33
PUKERURU (TRIG)	PEAK	41 01 175 10	52
PUKERURU (TRIG)	PEAK	41 01 175 10	53
PUKERURU (TRIG)	PEAK	41 01 175 10	55
PUKETA	LOC	42 26 173 35	73
PUKETAHA	LOC	37 43 175 20	19
PUKETAHA (TRIG)	PEAK	41 17 175 02	52
PUKETAHA (TRIG)	PEAK	41 17 175 02	55
PUKETAKAHIA POINT	PNT	34 56 173 33	3
PUKETAPU	LOC	39 31 176 47	40
PUKETAPU	LOC	39 31 176 47	42
PUKETAPU (TRIG)	MTN	38 31 177 02	30
PUKETAPU (TRIG)	HILL	38 58 177 37	33
PUKETAPU (TRIG)	HILL	39 25 176 46	40
PUKETAPU (TRIG)	HILL	39 25 176 46	42
PUKETAPU (TRIG)	HILL	45 30 170 44	102
PUKETARATA (TRIG)	HILL	38 08 175 18	18
PUKETARATA (TRIG)	HILL	38 08 175 18	19
PUKETARATARA (TRIG)	HILL	36 20 174 27	10
PUKETARATARA (TRIG)	HILL	36 20 174 27	11
PUKETARUWHENUA (TRIG)	HILL	38 19 174 45	26
PUKETAUTAHI (TRIG)	HILL	39 30 176 40	39
PUKETAUTAHI (TRIG)	HILL	39 30 176 40	40
PUKETAUTAHI (TRIG)	HILL	39 30 176 40	42
PUKETAWA (TRIG)	HILL	37 23 175 44	17
PUKETAWA (TRIG)	HILL	38 40 174 51	26
PUKETAWAI (TRIG)	HILL	38 41 175 00	26
PUKETAWAI (TRIG)	HILL	38 41 175 00	27
PUKETAWAI (TRIG)	HILL	38 13 175 14	27
PUKETEITEI (TRIG)	HILL	41 07 175 52	51
PUKETERAKI	LOC	45 39 170 39	102
PUKETERAKI RANGE	MTNS	42 46 172 14	70
PUKETERAKI RANGE	MTNS	43 05 172 01	81
PUKETERAKI (TRIG)	MTN	43 02 172 06	81
PUKETI	LOC	35 10 173 46	4
PUKETI	LOC	46 02 169 36	111
PUKETI	LOC	46 02 169 36	113
PUKETI, LAKE	LAKE	37 17 174 40	14
PUKETI POINT	PNT	41 08 173 26	59
PUKETI (TRIG)	HILL	35 48 173 42	6
PUKETIHI	LOC	38 55 174 55	26
PUKETIKA	MTN	44 32 169 32	91
PUKETIKITIKI (TRIG)	HILL	39 00 177 06	41
PUKETIRO	LOC	46 30 169 29	113
PUKETITIRI	LOC	39 17 176 32	39
PUKETITIRI	LOC	39 17 176 32	40
PUKETITOI (TRIG)	HILL	35 43 174 05	5
PUKETITOI (TRIG)	HILL	35 43 174 05	7
PUKETOI	LOC	40 31 176 08	49
PUKETOI	LOC	40 31 176 08	50
PUKETOI RANGE	MTNS	40 35 176 00	49
PUKETOI (TRIG)	PEAK	40 35 176 00	49
PUKETOKA (TRIG)	HILL	37 18 175 16	15
PUKETOKI	HILL	38 08 175 25	19
PUKETOKI (TRIG)	HILL	37 27 175 55	17
PUKETONA	LOC	35 18 173 57	4
PUKETOTARA	HILL	36 52 174 28	10
PUKETOTARA	HILL	36 52 174 28	11
PUKETOTARA	HILL	36 52 174 28	12
PUKETOTARA	LOC	38 02 175 10	18
PUKETOTARA PENINSULA	PEN	36 17 174 19	10
PUKETOTARA STREAM	STRM	35 14 173 55	4
PUKETOWAI (TRIG)	HILL	35 16 173 40	4
PUKETUI	LOC	37 05 175 45	16
PUKETUI	LOC	37 05 175 45	17
PUKETUI (TRIG)	HILL	37 08 175 43	17
PUKETUI (TRIG)	HILL	38 45 175 18	27
PUKETUROTO	MTN	44 33 168 02	88
PUKETUROTO	MTN	44 33 168 02	89
PUKETURUA	LOC	38 04 175 42	19
PUKETUTU	LOC	38 26 175 14	27
PUKETUTU ISLAND	ISLD	34 59 173 26	3
PUKETUTU ISLAND	ISLD	36 58 174 44	12
PUKETUTU ISLAND	ISLD	36 58 174 44	14
PUKETUTU (TRIG)	HILL	34 57 173 35	3
PUKETUTU (TRIG)	HILL	35 10 173 18	3
PUKETUTU (TRIG)	HILL	34 57 173 35	4
PUKETUTU (TRIG)	HILL	36 42 174 29	10
PUKETUTU (TRIG)	HILL	36 42 174 29	11
PUKETUTU (TRIG)	HILL	37 12 175 01	12
PUKETUTU (TRIG)	HILL	37 12 175 01	13
PUKETUTU (TRIG)	HILL	37 12 175 01	14
PUKETUTU (TRIG)	HILL	38 18 175 51	28
PUKETUTU (TRIG)	HILL	38 18 175 51	29
PUKEURI	LOC	45 02 171 02	102
PUKEWAO (TRIG)	HILL	46 33 168 53	112
PUKEWHAKAAHU (TRIG)	HILL	38 06 175 31	19
PUKEWHAKATARATARA (TRIG)	HILL	36 52 175 27	13
PUKEWHAKATARATARA (TRIG)	HILL	36 52 175 27	16
PUKEWHAO (TRIG)	HILL	35 22 173 36	3
PUKEWHAO (TRIG)	HILL	35 22 173 36	4
PUKEWHAO (TRIG)	HILL	35 22 173 36	6
PUKEWHARAREKE (TRIG)	HILL	36 51 175 32	13
PUKEWHARAREKE (TRIG)	HILL	36 51 175 32	16
PUKEWHARARIKI (TRIG)	HILL	35 23 173 42	4
PUKEWHARARIKI (TRIG)	HILL	35 50 173 49	6
PUKEWHARARIKI (TRIG)	HILL	35 23 173 42	6
PUKEWHARARIKI (TRIG)	PEAK	39 23 176 10	39
PUKEWHARARIKI (TRIG)	HILL	39 45 175 13	45
PUKEWHAU	HILL	37 13 175 49	17
PUKEWHERO PEAK	PEAK	43 31 170 31	74
PUKEWHERO PEAK	PEAK	43 31 170 31	77
PUKEWHERO (TRIG)	HILL	38 41 174 41	26
PUKEWHINAU (TRIG)	HILL	40 28 176 15	50
PUKIO	LOC	41 15 175 21	53
PUKURANUI STREAM	STRM	37 57 177 37	24
PUKURAU STREAM	STRM	36 57 175 07	13
PUKURAU STREAM	STRM	36 57 175 07	14
PUKURAU STREAM	STRM	36 57 175 07	15
PUKUTUARO CLIFF	CLIF	43 01 170 33	74
PULHAM STREAM	STRM	37 13 175 44	17
PUNAATAWAKE BAY	BAY	40 46 173 49	61
PUNAKAIKI	LOC	42 07 171 20	63
PUNAKAIKI RIVER	STRM	42 07 171 20	63
PUNAKITERE	LOC	35 29 173 42	4
PUNAKITERE	LOC	35 29 173 42	6
PUNAKITERE RIVER	STRM	35 28 173 39	4
PUNAKITERE RIVER	STRM	35 28 173 39	6

PUNAKITERE VALLEY	LOC	35 28 173 52	4
PUNAKITERE VALLEY	LOC	35 28 173 52	6
PUNANUI STREAM	STRM	43 01 172 20	81
PUNAROMIA	LOC	38 12 176 21	20
PUNAROMIA	LOC	38 12 176 21	21
PUNARUKU	LOC	35 22 174 19	5
PUNARUKU STREAM	STRM	35 22 174 19	5
PUNAWAI	LOC	43 47 171 32	84
PUNEHU	LOC	35 26 173 23	3
PUNEHU	LOC	35 26 173 23	6
PUNEHU STREAM	STRM	39 30 173 54	34
PUNEKETORO STREAM	STRM	39 12 176 34	39
PUNEKETORO STREAM	STRM	39 12 176 34	40
PUNGAERE	LOC	35 11 173 51	4
PUNGAEREERE STREAM	STRM	39 21 173 46	34
PUNGAPUNGA	LOC	38 54 175 23	27
PUNGAPUNGA RIVER	STRM	38 54 175 20	27
PUNGAREHU	LOC	39 17 173 48	34
PUNGAREHU	LOC	39 49 175 09	45
PUNGAREHU (TRIG)	MTN	38 13 177 38	24
PUNGAREHU (TRIG)	MTN	38 13 177 38	31
PUNGAREHUNUI (TRIG)	MTN	37 49 178 08	25
PUNGATAUA	LOC	39 37 175 54	46
PUNGATIKI STREAM	STRM	37 29 174 50	14
PUNI	LOC	37 14 174 51	12
PUNI	LOC	37 14 174 51	14
PUNIHO	LOC	39 12 173 50	34
PUNINGA	HSTD	38 53 177 52	33
PUNIU RIVER	STRM	38 01 175 13	18
PUNIU RIVER	STRM	38 01 175 13	19
PUNIU RIVER	STRM	38 12 175 35	27
PUNIWHAKAU	LOC	39 20 174 37	35
PUNIWHAKAU	LOC	39 20 174 37	44
PUNIWHAKAU STREAM	STRM	39 20 174 37	35
PUNIWHAKAU STREAM	STRM	39 20 174 37	44
PUNIWHAKAU (TRIG)	HILL	39 19 174 38	35
PUNIWHAKAU (TRIG)	HILL	39 19 174 38	44
PUPONGA	LOC	40 31 172 43	57
PUPONGA POINT	PNT	37 01 174 37	12
PUPONGA POINT	PNT	37 01 174 37	14
PUPONGA POINT	PNT	40 32 172 44	57
PUPONGA, PORT	HARB	40 32 172 44	57
PUPUIA ISLAND	ISLD	36 13 174 10	7
PUPUKE	LOC	35 07 173 43	4
PUPUKE, LAKE	LAKE	36 47 174 46	11
PUPUKE, LAKE	LAKE	36 47 174 46	12
PUPUKE RIVER	STRM	35 06 173 43	4
PUPUTAHA STREAM	STRM	38 30 175 14	27
PUPUWHARAU, LAKE	LAKE	38 05 176 43	22
PURAHAUA STREAM	STRM	46 17 169 40	111
PURAHAUA STREAM	STRM	46 17 169 40	113
PURAHOTAKAHA (TRIG)	MTN	37 54 177 46	24
PURAKANUI	LOC	45 45 170 38	103
PURAKANUI BAY	BAY	45 44 170 37	103
PURAKAUITI	LOC	46 32 169 31	113
PURAKAUNUI	LOC	46 31 169 33	113
PURAKAUNUI RIVER	STRM	46 33 169 37	113
PURAMAHOI	LOC	40 48 172 45	57
PURANGI	LOC	36 52 175 44	16
PURANGI	LOC	39 10 174 32	35
PURAROTO STREAM	STRM	39 26 175 01	36
PURAROTO (TRIG)	HILL	39 27 174 56	36
PURAU	LOC	43 39 172 45	82
PURAU	LOC	43 39 172 45	83
PURAU BAY	BAY	43 38 172 45	82
PURAU BAY	BAY	43 38 172 45	83
PURAU STREAM	STRM	43 38 172 45	82
PURAU STREAM	STRM	43 38 172 45	83
PUREKIREKI	LOC	46 21 169 28	113
PUREMUTAHURI STREAM	STRM	37 45 177 41	24
PUREORA STATE FOREST PARK	PARK	38 32 175 37	27
PUREORA STATE FOREST PARK	PARK	38 32 175 37	28
PUREORA (TRIG)	HILL	36 41 174 22	10
PUREORA (TRIG)	HILL	36 41 174 22	11
PUREORA (TRIG)	MTN	38 33 175 38	28
PURERE STREAM	STRM	38 00 175 48	19
PURERE STREAM	STRM	38 00 175 48	20
PURERUA	LOC	35 09 174 02	4
PURERUA	LOC	35 09 174 02	5
PURERUA PENINSULA	PEN	35 08 174 03	4
PURERUA PENINSULA	PEN	35 08 174 03	5
PURIMU STREAM	STRM	40 09 176 29	47
PURIRI	LOC	37 14 175 38	15
PURIRI	LOC	37 14 175 38	17
PURIRI POINT	PNT	36 12 174 15	7
PURIRI POINT	PNT	36 12 174 15	8
PURIRI RIVER	STRM	37 14 175 37	13
PURIRI RIVER	STRM	37 14 175 37	15
PUROA	HILL	36 33 175 30	9
PUROA	HILL	36 33 175 30	16
PURPLE HILL (TRIG)	MTN	43 07 171 49	80
PURSER, LAKE	LAKE	45 49 166 47	104
PURUA	LOC	35 38 174 07	5
PURUA	LOC	35 38 174 07	7
PURUA (TRIG)	HILL	35 38 174 08	5
PURUA (TRIG)	HILL	35 38 174 08	7
PURUKOHUKOHU STREAM	STRM	38 27 176 20	29
PURURIRI (TRIG)	HILL	40 32 175 31	48
PURURIRI (TRIG)	HILL	40 32 175 31	49
PURURU	LOC	38 20 175 18	27
PURURU STREAM	STRM	38 18 175 16	27
PUSSY RIVER	STRM	42 35 172 13	70
PUTAKOLO HEAD	HEAD	43 47 173 08	83
PUTANGIRUA PINNACLES	LOC	41 27 175 15	53
PUTAPUTA STREAM	STRM	41 03 175 10	52
PUTAPUTA STREAM	STRM	41 03 175 10	53
PUTAPUTA STREAM	STRM	41 03 175 10	55
PUTARA	LOC	40 40 175 34	48
PUTARA	LOC	40 40 175 34	49
PUTARURU	POPL	38 04 175 47	19
PUTATAKA (TRIG)	HILL	37 24 174 46	14
PUTAUHINA ISLAND	ISLD	47 13 167 23	114
PUTEKETEKE, MOUNT	MTN	45 44 167 16	105
PUTEORE (TRIG)	HILL	39 22 174 48	35
PUTEORE (TRIG)	HILL	39 22 174 48	44
PUTIKI	SBRB	39 57 175 03	45
PUTORINO	LOC	39 08 177 00	41
PUTORINO	LOC	39 59 175 34	46
PUTTICK, MOUNT	MTN	42 21 172 02	70
PUWAI BAY	BAY	47 15 167 23	114
PUWERA	LOC	35 48 174 19	7
PUWERA	LOC	35 48 174 19	8
PUWERA STREAM	STRM	35 47 174 19	7
PUWERA STREAM	STRM	35 47 174 19	8
PUWHENUA (TRIG)	HILL	37 56 176 07	20
PUWHENUA (TRIG)	HILL	37 56 176 07	21
PUYSEGUR POINT	PNT	46 09 166 36	104
PUZZLE PEAK (TRIG)	PEAK	41 01 174 10	54
PUZZLE PEAK (TRIG)	PEAK	41 01 174 10	60
PUZZLE PEAK (TRIG)	PEAK	41 01 174 10	61
PYE CREEK	STRM	43 04 170 26	74
PYE, MOUNT (TRIG)	HILL	46 25 169 17	112
PYE, MOUNT (TRIG)	HILL	46 25 169 17	113
PYES PA	LOC	37 49 176 08	20
PYES PA	LOC	37 49 176 08	21
PYKE CREEK	STRM	44 05 169 23	78
PYKE CREEK	STRM	44 05 169 23	79
PYKE, MOUNT (TRIG)	MTN	44 22 168 09	89
PYKE, MOUNT (TRIG)	MTN	44 22 168 09	88
PYKE RIVER	STRM	44 30 168 11	88
PYKE RIVER	STRM	44 30 168 11	89
PYKE SADDLE	SAD	44 15 168 17	88
PYKE SADDLE	SAD	44 15 168 17	89
PYKES HILL	HILL	44 27 169 03	90
PYRAMID	PEAK	41 15 172 23	56
PYRAMID	PEAK	41 15 172 23	62
PYRAMID	LOC	45 55 168 49	110
PYRAMID CREEK	STRM	45 54 168 49	110
PYRAMID, THE	PEAK	42 38 171 57	70
PYRAMID, THE (TRIG)	HILL	44 12 170 01	79
PYRAMID (TRIG)	MTN	43 27 171 06	75
PYRAMID (TRIG)	HILL	41 39 173 40	60
PYRAMID (TRIG)	HILL	45 54 168 49	110
PYRAMID VALLEY	LOC	42 58 172 36	71

Q

QUAIL BURN	STRM	44 27 169 56	91
QUAIL ISLAND	ISLD	43 38 172 41	82
QUAIL ISLAND	ISLD	43 38 172 41	83
QUAIL ISLAND	ISLD	43 38 172 41	85
QUAIL, MOUNT (TRIG)	MTN	42 31 172 16	70
QUAIL VALLEY STREAM	STRM	41 27 172 58	58
QUAIL VALLEY STREAM	STRM	41 27 172 58	59
QUAKER SADDLE	SAD	43 33 171 18	75
QUAKER SADDLE	SAD	43 33 171 18	80
QUARANTINE ISLAND	ISLD	45 50 170 38	103
QUARRY CREEK	STRM	43 57 169 29	79
QUARRY HILLS	LOC	46 32 169 02	112
QUARTZ CREEK	STRM	41 29 173 36	59
QUARTZ CREEK	STRM	43 47 171 03	87
QUARTZ CREEK	STRM	44 38 169 08	90
QUARTZ HILL	HILL	43 22 171 46	80
QUARTZ HILL (TRIG)	PEAK	41 15 174 41	52
QUARTZ HILL (TRIG)	PEAK	41 15 174 41	55
QUARTZ REEF CREEK	STRM	45 00 169 14	100
QUEEN CHARLOTTE SOUND	SND	41 14 174 05	54
QUEEN CHARLOTTE SOUND	SND	41 14 174 05	60
QUEEN CHARLOTTE SOUND	SND	41 14 174 05	61
QUEENS FLAT	LOC	44 58 170 47	93
QUEENS HILL (TRIG)	HILL	46 07 169 36	111
QUEENS HILL (TRIG)	HILL	46 07 169 36	113
QUEENSBERRY	LOC	44 50 169 19	91
QUEENSBERRY HILL (TRIG)	MTN	44 56 169 01	90
QUEENSTOWN	POPL	45 02 168 40	95
QUEENSTOWN	POPL	45 02 168 40	99
QUERY PEAK	PEAK	43 44 169 47	76
QUERY PEAK	PEAK	43 44 169 47-	79
QUILL, LAKE	LAKE	44 49 167 44	94
QUOICH CREEK	STRM	45 32 168 34	99
QUOIN POINT	PNT	46 09 170 10	103
QUOIN (TRIG)	PEAK	41 00 175 14	53

R

RABBIT HILL (TRIG)	MTN	43 20 171 42	80
RABBIT ISLAND	ISLD	36 43 175 49	16
RABBIT ISLAND	ISLD	37 04 175 56	16
RABBIT ISLAND	ISLD	37 04 175 56	17
RABBIT ISLAND	ISLD	41 16 173 09	59
RABBIT PASS	PASS	44 19 168 51	90
RABBITERS PEAK	PEAK	44 03 169 47	79
RACECOURSE HILL	LOC	43 27 172 04	81
RACECOURSE HILL	LOC	43 27 172 04	85
RACECOURSE STATION	RSTN	39 46 174 36	44
RACHEL RANGE	MTNS	42 10 173 08	66
RADDLE, MOUNT	MTN	44 14 168 28	88
RADIANT RANGE	MTNS	41 28 172 08	62
RADOVE, MOUNT	MTN	43 42 170 26	77
RADOVE, MOUNT	MTN	43 42 170 26	86
RAEOTUTEMAHUTA	LOC	41 35 175 21	53
RAEPAHU (TRIG)	HILL	38 29 175 23	27
RAEPERE CREEK	STRM	36 11 174 22	7
RAEPERE CREEK	STRM	36 12 174 14	7
RAEPERE CREEK	STRM	36 12 174 14	8
RAEPERE CREEK	STRM	36 11 174 22	8
RAES JUNCTION	LOC	45 47 169 28	111
RAETAHINGA POINT	PNT	36 53 174 26	10
RAETAHINGA POINT	PNT	36 53 174 26	11
RAETEA (TRIG)	HILL	35 13 173 25	3
RAETIHI	POPL	39 26 175 17	36
RAETIHI (TRIG)	HILL	39 23 175 25	36
RAETIHI (TRIG)	HILL	39 23 175 25	37
RAGAN, MOUNT	MTN	44 16 168 51	78
RAGGED PEAK	PEAK	43 07 170 52	75
RAGGED POINT	PNT	40 50 173 47	61
RAGGED RANGE	MTNS	43 14 171 05	75
RAGGEDY RANGE	MTNS	45 08 169 39	100
RAGGEDY (TRIG)	HILL	45 04 170 02	101
RAGLAN	POPL	37 48 174 53	18
RAGLAN HARBOUR	HARB	37 46 174 56	18
RAGLAN RANGE	MTNS	41 52 172 58	66
RAHANUI	LOC	37 57 174 48	18
RAHIRI	LOC	35 17 173 39	4
RAHOPAKAPAKA STREAM	STRM	38 17 176 08	28
RAHOPAKAPAKA STREAM	STRM	38 17 176 08	29
RAHOTIA (TRIG)	HILL	41 16 174 10	54
RAHOTIA (TRIG)	HILL	41 16 174 10	60
RAHOTIA (TRIG)	HILL	41 16 174 10	61
RAHOTU	LOC	39 20 173 48	34
RAHU RIVER	STRM	42 18 172 11	64
RAHU RIVER	STRM	42 18 172 11	70
RAHU RIVER, LEFT BRANCH	STRM	42 19 172 07	64
RAHU RIVER, LEFT BRANCH	STRM	42 19 172 07	70
RAHU RIVER, RIGHT BRANCH	STRM	42 19 172 07	64
RAHU SADDLE	SAD	42 19 172 07	64
RAHU SADDLE	SAD	42 19 172 07	70
RAHUI	LOC	41 50 171 52	63
RAHUI	LOC	41 50 171 52	64
RAHUI, LAKE	LAKE	41 44 171 52	63
RAHUI, LAKE	LAKE	41 44 171 52	64
RAHUI (TRIG)	HILL	39 24 174 25	35
RAHUI (TRIG)	HILL	39 24 174 25	44
RAHUIMOKAIROA (TRIG)	HILL	39 11 177 53	33
RAI RIVER	STRM	41 18 173 34	59
RAI SADDLE	SAD	41 11 173 33	59
RAI VALLEY	LOC	41 14 173 35	59
RAIKAIA	POPL	43 45 172 02	85
RAIKAIA (TRIG)	HILL	43 47 172 02	85
RAIN PEAK	PEAK	41 40 172 18	65
RAINBOW	LOC	38 43 176 05	28
RAINBOW	LOC	38 43 176 05	29
RAINBOW	LOC	38 43 176 05	38
RAINBOW COL	SAD	44 23 168 47	90
RAINBOW ISLES	ISLD	46 35 169 28	113
RAINBOW RIVER	STRM	42 02 172 54	65
RAINCLIFF STREAM	STRM	44 11 170 59	87
RAINEY RIVER	STRM	41 20 173 31	59
RAINY POINT (TRIG)	HILL	39 17 174 24	35
RAINY POINT (TRIG)	HILL	39 17 174 24	44
RAINY RIVER	STRM	41 37 172 47	58
RAINYTOP	MTN	43 50 169 24	76
RAINYTOP	MTN	43 50 169 24	78
RAINYTOP	MTN	43 50 169 24	79
RAIO	LOC	34 50 173 08	2
RAIO	LOC	34 50 173 08	3
RAKAHOUKA	LOC	46 20 168 29	109
RAKAIA HUTS	BLDG	43 53 172 14	85
RAKAIA RIVER	STRM	43 54 172 13	85
RAKATU, LAKE	LAKE	45 36 167 38	105
RAKATU, LAKE	LAKE	45 36 167 38	106
RAKAU	LOC	41 24 172 48	58
RAKAUANANGA POINT	PNT	36 38 174 48	11
RAKAUANANGA POINT	PNT	36 38 174 48	12
RAKAUHAU (TRIG)	HILL	40 39 176 19	50
RAKAUMAHI (TRIG)	HILL	39 32 174 51	35
RAKAUMAHI (TRIG)	HILL	39 32 174 51	44
RAKAUMANGA	LOC	37 32 175 08	14
RAKAUMANGA	LOC	37 32 175 08	15
RAKAUNUI	LOC	38 07 174 53	18
RAKAUNUI	LOC	40 36 176 08	50
RAKAUNUI STREAM	STRM	42 26 173 35	73
RAKAUNUI (TRIG)	HILL	40 36 176 05	49
RAKAUNUI (TRIG)	HILL	40 36 176 05	50
RAKAUPUHIPUHI STREAM	STRM	40 28 176 19	50
RAKAUROA	LOC	38 25 177 34	31
RAKAUTAHI (TRIG)	HILL	40 05 175 50	46
RAKAUTANGI (TRIG)	HILL	39 22 175 06	36
RAKAUTAO	LOC	35 26 173 52	4
RAKAUTAPU (TRIG)	HILL	38 22 176 56	30
RAKAUTARA	LOC	42 16 173 48	67
RAKAUTARA STREAM	STRM	42 17 173 47	67
RAKAUWHAKAHUE STREAM	STRM	38 17 175 21	27
RAKAWHIA (TRIG)	HILL	38 39 177 19	31
RAKEAHUA, MOUNT (TRIG)	HILL	46 57 167 53	114
RAKEAHUA RIVER	STRM	46 59 167 53	114
RAKETAPAUMA PA	LOC	39 33 175 39	37
RAKINO CHANNEL	CHAN	36 44 174 56	11
RAKINO CHANNEL	CHAN	36 44 174 56	12
RAKINO ISLAND	ISLD	36 43 174 57	11
RAKINO ISLAND	ISLD	36 43 174 57	12
RAKIS TABLE (TRIG)	HILL	45 00 170 44	93
RAKIS TABLE (TRIG)	HILL	45 00 170 44	102
RAKITU ISLAND	ISLD	36 08 175 30	9
RALFES KNOB	PEAK	43 17 170 20	74
RALPH, MOUNT	MTN	42 04 172 07	64
RAM CREEK	STRM	41 52 171 59	64
RAM HILL	MTN	44 06 169 49	79
RAM HILL STREAM	STRM	45 48 168 24	107
RAM HILL (TRIG)	HILL	45 48 168 24	107
RAMANUI	LOC	39 20 174 59	36
RAMARAMA	LOC	37 09 174 57	12
RAMARAMA	LOC	37 09 174 57	14
RAMARAMA STREAM	STRM	37 17 175 54	17
RAMATAMA STREAM	STRM	42 45 172 43	71
RAMEKA CREEK	STRM	40 52 172 49	57
RAMESES, MOUNT	MTN	42 26 171 57	70
RAMIHA (TRIG)	HILL	40 25 175 44	49
RAMPART, THE	MTN	44 01 169 12	78
RAMSAY GLACIER	GLCR	43 16 170 55	75
RAMSAY, MOUNT	MTN	44 01 169 27	78
RAMSAY, MOUNT	MTN	44 01 169 27	79
RAMSAY, MOUNT	MTN	42 06 171 33	63
RAMSAY, MOUNT	MTN	43 16 170 53	75
RAMSHEAD SADDLE	SAD	41 42 173 45	67
RANANA	LOC	39 35 175 07	36
RANFURLY	LOC	45 08 170 06	101
RANGAKAUIKA (TRIG)	HILL	39 28 175 25	36
RANGAKAUIKA (TRIG)	HILL	39 28 175 25	37
RANGAMAHOE (TRIG)	HILL	42 50 173 34	73
RANGANUI (TRIG)	HILL	39 23 175 03	36
RANGATAUA	LOC	39 26 175 27	36
RANGATAUA	LOC	39 26 175 27	37
RANGATAUA BAY	BAY	37 42 176 13	20
RANGATAUA BAY	BAY	37 42 176 13	21
RANGATIRA CREEK	STRM	44 14 171 16	87
RANGATIRA MOUNT	MTN	43 24 170 31	74
RANGATIRA MOUNT	MTN	43 24 170 31	77
RANGATIRA VALLEY	LOC	44 12 171 12	87
RANGAUNU BAY	BAY	34 49 173 16	3
RANGAUNU HARBOUR	HARB	34 58 173 17	3
RANGER STREAM	STRM	42 52 171 52	70
RANGI POINT	LOC	35 28 173 23	6
RANGI SADDLE	SAD	39 50 176 08	47
RANGI TAIPO (TRIG)	PEAK	42 46 171 30	69
RANGIAETA (TRIG)	HILL	42 15 173 48	67
RANGIAHAU ISLAND	ISLD	36 13 175 18	9
RANGIAHUA	LOC	35 19 173 38	4
RANGIAHUA	LOC	38 57 177 19	41
RANGIAOHIA	LOC	38 01 175 23	19
RANGIATEA	LOC	38 13 175 21	19
RANGIHAEATA	LOC	40 48 172 47	57
RANGIHAEATA HEAD	HEAD	40 48 172 48	57
RANGIHAU STREAM	STRM	36 57 175 39	15
RANGIHAU STREAM	STRM	36 57 175 39	16
RANGIHAU STREAM	STRM	36 57 175 39	17
RANGIHOUA BAY	BAY	35 10 174 05	4
RANGIHOUA BAY	BAY	35 10 174 05	5
RANGIKAHU (TRIG)	HILL	37 39 174 48	18
RANGIKOHUA STREAM	STRM	38 32 175 01	26
RANGIKOHUA STREAM	STRM	38 32 175 01	27
RANGIKOHUA (TRIG)	HILL	38 01 178 08	25
RANGIKURA	LOC	39 46 174 33	44
RANGINUI (TRIG)	HILL	38 22 175 28	27
RANGIORA	LOC	35 23 173 31	3
RANGIORA	LOC	35 23 173 31	6
RANGIORA	POPL	43 19 172 36	82
RANGIORA	POPL	43 19 172 36	83
RANGIORA	POPL	43 19 172 36	85
RANGIORA BAY	BAY	34 29 173 00	2
RANGIOTEATUA (TRIG)	PEAK	39 50 176 08	47
RANGIOTU	LOC	40 25 175 26	48
RANGIPO	LOC	39 05 175 49	37
RANGIPO	LOC	39 05 175 49	38
RANGIPO DESERT	PLN	39 19 175 40	37
RANGIPO DESERT	PLN	39 19 175 40	38
RANGIPO (TRIG)	HILL	37 08 175 17	13
RANGIPO (TRIG)	HILL	37 08 175 17	15
RANGIPO (TRIG)	HILL	37 09 175 51	17
RANGIPOUA (TRIG)	MTN	37 49 177 46	24
RANGIPU	LOC	37 49 174 51	18
RANGIPUANOANO (TRIG)	HILL	38 38 175 07	27
RANGIPUKEA ISLAND	ISLD	36 50 175 25	13
RANGIPUKEA ISLAND	ISLD	36 50 175 25	16
RANGIPUTA	LOC	34 53 173 18	3
RANGIRIRI	LOC	37 26 175 08	14
RANGIRIRI	LOC	37 26 175 08	15
RANGIRIRI CREEK	STRM	37 09 174 40	12
RANGIRIRI CREEK	STRM	37 09 174 40	14
RANGIRIRI STREAM	STRM	38 24 177 38	31
RANGIRIRI WEST	LOC	37 26 175 07	14
RANGIRIRI WEST	LOC	37 26 175 07	15
RANGIRIRI (TRIG)	HILL	38 55 175 11	27
RANGITAIKI	LOC	38 53 176 22	29
RANGITAIKI RIVER	STRM	37 55 176 53	22
RANGITAIKI RIVER	STRM	37 55 176 53	23
RANGITANE RIVER	STRM	35 12 173 59	4
RANGITANE RIVER	STRM	35 12 173 59	5
RANGITANE (TRIG)	HILL	39 47 175 59	46
RANGITAPU (TRIG)	HILL	40 03 176 49	43
RANGITATA	LOC	44 04 171 22	84
RANGITATA	LOC	44 04 171 22	87
RANGITATA COL	SAD	43 19 170 48	75
RANGITATA DIVERSION RACE	STRM	43 35 171 44	80
RANGITATA DIVERSION RACE	STRM	43 35 171 44	84
RANGITATA ISLAND	LOC	44 06 171 27	84
RANGITATA ISLAND	LOC	44 06 171 27	87
RANGITATA RIVER	STRM	44 11 171 31	84
RANGITATA RIVER (MIDDLE CHANNEL)	STRM	44 11 171 29	84
RANGITATA RIVER (SOUTH CHANNEL)	STRM	44 11 171 30	84
RANGITATAU	LOC	39 46 174 48	44
RANGITIHI	LOC	35 08 173 20	3
RANGITIKEI RIVER	STRM	40 16 175 14	45
RANGITIKEI RIVER	STRM	39 40 176 02	46
RANGITIKEI RIVER	STRM	40 17 175 13	48
RANGITIRA BEACH	BCH	36 34 174 14	10
RANGITOPUNI STREAM	STRM	36 45 174 36	11
RANGITOPUNI STREAM	STRM	36 45 174 36	12
RANGITOTO	LOC	38 21 175 16	27
RANGITOTO CHANNEL	CHAN	36 48 174 49	11
RANGITOTO CHANNEL	CHAN	36 48 174 49	12
RANGITOTO ISLAND	ISLD	36 47 174 52	11
RANGITOTO ISLAND	ISLD	36 47 174 52	12
RANGITOTO ISLANDS	ISLS	40 46 173 59	61
RANGITOTO, MOUNT (TRIG)	MTN	43 00 170 48	75
RANGITOTO POINT	PNT	37 48 174 50	18
RANGITOTO (TRIG)	HILL	36 47 174 51	11
RANGITOTO (TRIG)	HILL	36 47 174 51	12
RANGITOTO (TRIG)	HILL	36 54 175 44	16
RANGITOTO (TRIG)	HILL	36 54 175 44	17
RANGITOTO (TRIG)	HILL	38 22 175 25	27
RANGITOTO (TRIG)	HILL	39 56 176 42	42
RANGITOTO (TRIG)	HILL	39 56 176 42	43
RANGITOTO (TRIG)	HILL	40 06 176 20	47
RANGITOTO (TRIG)	HILL	40 57 176 05	49
RANGITOTO (TRIG)	HILL	40 57 176 05	51
RANGITUKIA	LOC	37 46 178 27	25
RANGITUKIA STREAM	STRM	37 51 175 08	18
RANGITUMAU	LOC	40 51 175 42	49
RANGITUMAU	LOC	40 51 175 42	51
RANGIURU	LOC	37 47 176 22	20
RANGIURU	LOC	37 47 176 22	21
RANGIURU (TRIG)	HILL	37 52 176 20	20
RANGIURU (TRIG)	HILL	37 52 176 20	21
RANGIWAEA ISLAND	ISLD	37 38 176 07	20
RANGIWAEA ISLAND	ISLD	37 38 176 07	21
RANGIWAEA JUNCTION	LOC	39 33 175 35	37
RANGIWAHIA	LOC	39 54 175 54	46
RANGIWHAIA STREAM	STRM	39 32 175 27	36
RANGIWHAIA STREAM	STRM	39 32 175 27	37
RANGIWHAKAEA BAY	BAY	36 05 175 25	9
RANGIWHAKAOMA (TRIG)	HILL	39 34 174 36	35
RANGIWHAKAOMA (TRIG)	HILL	39 34 174 36	44
RANKIN PEAK	PEAK	43 23 170 39	74
RANKIN STREAM	STRM	43 38 170 29	74
RANKIN STREAM	STRM	43 38 170 29	77
RANKLE BURN	STRM	46 02 169 21	110
RANKLE BURN	STRM	46 02 169 21	111
RANKLE BURN	STRM	46 02 169 21	113
RANKLEBURN	LOC	46 02 169 21	111
RANKLEBURN	LOC	46 02 169 21	113
RANOLF, MOUNT (TRIG)	HILL	41 06 172 31	56
RANOLF, MOUNT (TRIG)	HILL	41 06 172 31	57
RANOLF, MOUNT (TRIG)	HILL	41 06 172 31	58
RANUI	LOC	36 52 174 36	11
RANUI	LOC	36 52 174 36	12
RANUI	LOC	37 47 174 59	18
RANUNCULUS, MOUNT (TRIG)	MTN	42 35 171 57	70
RAORAOROA STREAM	STRM	39 21 176 16	39
RAORIAKA	LOC	39 47 175 06	45
RAOULIA, MOUNT (TRIG)	MTN	42 05 171 42	63
RAOULIA, MOUNT (TRIG)	MTN	42 05 171 42	64
RAPAHOE	LOC	42 23 171 15	68
RAPAHOE	LOC	42 23 171 15	69
RAPAKI	LOC	43 36 172 41	82
RAPAKI	LOC	43 36 172 41	83
RAPAKI	LOC	43 36 172 41	85
RAPANUI	LOC	39 53 174 57	45
RAPANUI STREAM	STRM	38 48 174 35	26
RAPARAHI STREAM	STRM	38 09 175 42	19
RAPARAPAHOE CANAL	CANL	37 45 176 21	20
RAPARAPAHOE CANAL	CANL	37 45 176 21	21
RAPARAPAHOE STREAM	STRM	37 46 176 19	20
RAPARAPAHOE STREAM	STRM	37 46 176 19	21
RAPARAPARIRIKI STREAM	STRM	37 51 178 05	25
RAPARAPAWAI STREAM	STRM	40 16 175 59	46
RAPAURA	LOC	41 28 173 54	60
RAPID CREEK	STRM	43 01 171 01	75
RAPID STREAM	STRM	41 42 171 45	63
RAPID STREAM	STRM	41 42 171 45	64
RAPPAHANNOCK	STRM	42 05 172 14	64
RAPPAHANNOCK SADDLE	SAD	42 06 172 19	65
RAPURAPU STREAM	STRM	37 52 175 52	20
RAPUWAI	LOC	44 09 171 02	87
RARA (TRIG)	HILL	40 41 176 13	50
RARANGI	LOC	41 24 174 03	54
RARANGI	LOC	41 24 174 03	60
RARATOKA ISLAND	ISLD	46 20 167 50	108
RARAWA BEACH	BCH	34 43 173 05	2
RARAWA (TRIG)	HILL	34 45 173 05	2
RAREWAREWA (TRIG)	HILL	35 37 174 09	5
RAREWAREWA (TRIG)	HILL	35 37 174 09	7
RAROA PA	LOC	38 11 177 03	22
RAROA PA	LOC	38 11 177 03	23
RAROA STREAM	STRM	38 09 177 03	22
RAROA STREAM	STRM	38 09 177 03	23
RASSELAS, LAKE	LAKE	43 42 169 21	78
RASTUS BURN	STRM	45 00 168 49	95
RASTUS BURN	STRM	45 00 168 49	99
RAT ISLAND	ISLD	47 08 167 34	114

Ra-Ro

RATA	LOC	40 00 175 31	45
RATA	LOC	40 00 175 31	46
RATA BURN	STRM	46 05 167 16	105
RATA CREEK	STRM	43 13 170 30	74
RATA HILL (TRIG)	HILL	40 58 173 00	57
RATA HILL (TRIG)	HILL	40 58 173 00	58
RATA HILL (TRIG)	HILL	40 58 173 00	59
RATA RANGE	MTNS	46 26 169 30	113
RATA (TRIG)	HILL	39 13 174 04	34
RATA (TRIG)	HILL	39 05 174 42	35
RATA (TRIG)	HILL	39 00 174 36	35
RATA (TRIG)	HILL	39 14 174 30	35
RATA (TRIG)	HILL	39 06 175 00	36
RATA (TRIG)	HILL	40 39 175 59	49
RATAHAU (TRIG)	PEAK	39 00 175 20	36
RATAITI	LOC	39 54 175 31	45
RATAITI	LOC	39 54 175 31	46
RATAMAROKE (TRIG)	HILL	37 25 175 21	15
RATANA	LOC	40 03 175 10	45
RATANUI	LOC	46 30 169 37	113
RATANUI (TRIG)	HILL	38 23 174 53	26
RATANUI (TRIG)	HILL	39 33 174 32	35
RATANUI (TRIG)	HILL	39 08 175 02	36
RATANUI (TRIG)	HILL	39 33 174 32	44
RATANUI (TRIG)	HILL	39 39 175 06	45
RATAPIKO, LAKE	LAKE	39 12 174 20	34
RATAPIKO, LAKE	LAKE	39 12 174 20	35
RATAPU (TRIG)	PEAK	40 37 175 35	48
RATAPU (TRIG)	PEAK	40 37 175 35	49
RATAROA STREAM	STRM	37 49 176 01	20
RATAROA (TRIG)	HILL	37 14 175 18	13
RATAROA (TRIG)	HILL	37 14 175 18	15
RATATOMOKIA (TRIG)	HILL	38 45 175 02	26
RATATOMOKIA (TRIG	HILL	38 45 175 02	27
RATAWERA (TRIG)	HILL	37 24 175 23	15
RATORUTORU (TRIG)	HILL	35 08 173 39	4
RATTRAY STREAM	STRM	44 36 170 24	92
RAU (TRIG)	HILL	38 43 174 56	26
RAUHOMAUMAU ISLAND	ISLD	35 38 174 33	8
RAUHORI STREAM	STRM	36 32 174 30	10
RAUHORI STREAM	STRM	36 32 174 30	11
RAUIRI HEAD	HEAD	37 59 174 50	18
RAUIRI (TRIG)	HILL	37 59 174 50	18
RAUKATAU	HILL	38 40 177 01	30
RAUKAWA BAY	BAY	34 32 172 43	2
RAUKAWA RANGE	MTNS	39 47 176 38	42
RAUKAWA RANGE	MTNS	39 47 176 38	43
RAUKAWA RANGE	MTNS	39 47 176 38	47
RAUKAWA ROCK	ROCK	41 12 174 22	54
RAUKOKORE	LOC	37 38 177 53	24
RAUKOKORE RIVER	STRM	37 39 177 52	24
RAUKUMARA RANGE	MTNS	38 00 177 55	24
RAUKUMARA (TRIG)	MTN	37 46 178 07	25
RAUKURA POINT	PNT	36 56 175 11	13
RAUKURA POINT	PNT	36 56 175 11	15
RAUMAI	LOC	40 13 175 46	46
RAUMATI BEACH	POPL	40 55 174 59	52
RAUMATI BEACH	POPL	40 55 174 59	55
RAUMATI SOUTH	POPL	40 56 174 59	52
RAUMATI SOUTH	POPL	40 56 174 59	55
RAUNGAEHE RANGE	MTNS	38 05 176 53	22
RAUNGAEHE RANGE	MTNS	38 05 176 53	23
RAUPIU STREAM	STRM	39 42 175 20	45
RAUPO	LOC	36 07 173 59	7
RAUPO	LOC	42 19 171 35	63
RAUPO	LOC	42 19 171 35	69
RAUPO BAY	BAY	34 52 173 17	3
RAUPO BAY	BAY	43 40 173 02	82
RAUPO BAY	BAY	43 40 173 02	83
RAUPO LAGOON	LAKE	44 19 169 52	79
RAUPOROA BAY	BAY	36 32 175 31	9
RAUPOROA BAY	BAY	36 32 175 31	16
RAUPUNGA	LOC	39 05 177 09	41
RAUREKA	SBRB	39 39 176 49	42
RAUREKA	SBRB	39 39 176 49	43
RAURIMU	LOC	39 07 175 24	36
RAURIMU	LOC	39 07 175 24	37
RAUTAWIRI STREAM	STRM	38 29 176 18	29
RAVENSBOURNE	SBRB	45 52 170 33	103
RAWA STREAM	STRM	39 33 173 59	34
RAWEA STREAM	STRM	38 04 177 35	24
RAWENE	LOC	35 24 173 30	3
RAWENE	LOC	35 24 173 30	6
RAWHIA	LOC	35 19 173 36	3
RAWHIA	LOC	35 19 173 36	4
RAWHITI	LOC	35 14 174 16	5
RAWHITIROA	LOC	39 26 174 22	34
RAWHITIROA	LOC	39 26 174 22	35
RAWHITIROA	LOC	39 26 174 22	44
RAWHITIROA (TRIG)	HILL	39 49 175 42	46
RAWTOR (TRIG)	HILL	43 43 171 00	87
RAYMONDS GAP	LOC	46 05 167 53	106
RAYMONDS GAP	LOC	46 05 167 53	107
RAYMONDS GAP	LOC	46 05 167 53	108
RAZORBACK POINT	PNT	42 08 171 20	63
RAZORBACK (TRIG)	HILL	40 40 176 11	50
REA RIVER	STRM	45 15 167 10	96
RECTORY PEAK	PEAK	45 17 167 12	96
RED BEACH	LOC	36 36 174 42	11
RED BEACH	LOC	36 36 174 42	12
RED BLUFF	CLIF	36 12 175 29	9
RED HEAD PEAK	PEAK	46 45 167 43	108
RED HEAD PEAK	PEAK	46 45 167 43	114
RED HILL	SBRB	37 04 174 59	12
RED HILL	SBRB	37 04 174 59	14
RED HILL RANGE	MTNS	44 18 168 21	88
RED HILL RANGE	MTNS	44 18 168 21	89
RED HILL STREAM	STRM	42 11 173 29	66
RED HILL (TRIG)	MTN	43 19 171 38	80
RED HILL (TRIG)	HILL	36 51 175 43	16
RED HILL (TRIG)	MTN	41 38 173 03	58
RED HILL (TRIG)	MTN	41 38 173 03	59
RED HILLS RIDGE	RDGE	41 42 173 02	66
RED HILLS (TRIG)	MTN	44 18 168 21	88
RED HILLS (TRIG)	MTN	44 18 168 21	89
RED JACKS	LOC	42 24 171 27	69
RED JACKS CREEK	STRM	42 24 171 26	69
RED LION, THE	MTN	43 11 170 55	75
RED MERCURY ISLAND	ISLD	36 37 175 56	16
RED MOUNTAIN	MTN	43 30 171 03	75
RED MOUNTAIN	MTN	44 19 168 21	88
RED MOUNTAIN	MTN	44 19 168 21	89
RED PEAK	MTN	43 19 170 59	75
RED RIVER	STRM	40 22 176 21	50
RED SADDLE	SAD	43 07 172 01	81
REDAN	LOC	46 22 168 58	112
REDAN STREAM	STRM	46 21 168 54	112
REDCLIFF CREEK	STRM	45 40 167 38	106
REDCLIFFE POINT	PNT	43 52 173 02	83
REDCLIFFE SADDLE	SAD	43 26 171 27	80
REDCLIFFE STREAM	STRM	43 22 171 30	80
REDCLIFFS	CLIF	43 34 172 44	82
REDCLIFFS	CLIF	43 34 172 44	83
REDHILL	LOC	36 04 173 53	7
REDRUTH	LOC	44 25 171 14	93
REDVALE	LOC	36 41 174 42	11
REDVALE	LOC	36 41 174 42	12
REDWOOD	SBRB	41 11 174 49	52
REDWOOD	SBRB	41 11 174 49	55
REDWOOD PASS	PASS	41 35 174 04	60
REDWOODS VALLEY	LOC	41 18 173 05	58
REDWOODS VALLEY	LOC	41 18 173 05	59
REEF POINT	PNT	40 59 173 56	54
REEF POINT	PNT	40 59 173 56	60
REEF POINT	PNT	40 59 173 56	61
REEF SADDLE	SAD	44 41 168 34	90
REEF SPUR (TRIG)	MTN	43 50 169 16	78
REEFTON	TOWN	42 07 171 52	63
REEFTON	TOWN	42 07 171 52	64
REEFTON SADDLE	SAD	42 08 171 49	63
REEFTON SADDLE	SAD	42 08 171 49	64
REENA	LOC	35 26 173 20	3
REENA	LOC	35 26 173 20	6
REES RIVER	STRM	44 51 168 22	89
REES RIVER	STRM	44 51 168 22	95
REES SADDLE	SAD	44 33 168 34	88
REES SADDLE	SAD	44 33 168 34	90
REEVES, MOUNT	MTN	45 39 167 07	105
REEVES, MOUNT	MTN	42 58 171 11	68
REEVES, MOUNT	MTN	42 58 171 11	69
REEVES (TRIG)	PEAK	41 01 175 21	53
REFUGE ISLAND	ISLD	42 37 171 28	69
REGINA CREEK	STRM	43 40 169 50	76
REGINA CREEK	STRM	43 40 169 50	79
REHI STREAM	STRM	38 20 176 12	21
REHI STREAM	STRM	38 20 176 12	29
REHIA	LOC	36 03 174 02	7
REHIA (TRIG)	HILL	36 06 174 06	7
REHUOTANE (TRIG)	HILL	35 38 174 32	5
REHUOTANE (TRIG)	HILL	35 38 174 32	8
REHUTAI	LOC	35 58 173 47	6
REIDS STREAM	STRM	46 00 170 15	103
REIDSTON	LOC	45 09 170 51	102
REIKORANGI	LOC	40 54 175 05	48
REIKORANGI	LOC	40 54 175 05	52
REIKORANGI	LOC	40 54 175 05	55
REIKORANGI STREAM	STRM	40 54 175 05	48
REIKORANGI STREAM	STRM	40 54 175 05	52
REIKORANGI STREAM	STRM	40 54 175 05	55
REINGA, CAPE	CAPE	34 25 172 41	2
REMARKABLE PEAK	PEAK	43 04 170 56	75
REMARKABLES, THE	MTNS	45 05 168 48	95
REMARKABLES, THE	MTNS	45 05 168 48	99
REMOTE PEAKS	PEAK	44 19 168 27	88
REMOTE PEAKS	PEAK	44 19 168 27	89
REMUERA	SBRB	36 53 174 48	11
REMUERA	SBRB	36 53 174 48	12
RENALL STATION	RSTN	40 57 175 38	48
RENALL STATION	RSTN	40 57 175 38	49
RENALL STATION	RSTN	40 57 175 38	51
RENALL STATION	RSTN	40 57 175 38	53
RENATA STREAM	STRM	41 01 175 12	52
RENATA STREAM	STRM	41 01 175 12	53
RENATA STREAM	STRM	41 01 175 12	55
RENATA (TRIG)	PEAK	40 59 175 12	52
RENATA (TRIG)	PEAK	40 59 175 12	53
RENATA (TRIG)	PEAK	40 59 175 12	55
RENEGADE, MOUNT	MTN	43 21 170 52	75
RENOWN	LOC	37 34 175 03	14
RENWICK	USAT	41 31 173 50	60
REOTAHI BAY	LOC	35 50 174 30	8
REPIA	LOC	36 05 173 57	7
REPONGAERE, LAKE	LAKE	38 36 177 52	32
REPOROA	LOC	38 26 176 21	29
REPOROA STREAM	STRM	39 35 176 03	47
REPORUA	LOC	37 52 178 24	25
REPULSE, MOUNT	MTN	44 35 168 43	88
REPULSE, MOUNT	MTN	44 35 168 43	90
RERE	LOC	38 32 177 37	31
REREKINO (TRIG)	PEAK	39 00 174 40	35
REREPI (TRIG)	HILL	38 47 177 51	32
REREPI (TRIG)	HILL	38 47 177 51	33
REREWHAKAAITU	LOC	38 19 176 30	21
REREWHAKAAITU	LOC	38 19 176 30	30
REREWHAKAAITU, LAKE	LAKE	38 18 176 30	21
REREWHAKAAITU, LAKE	LAKE	38 18 176 30	30
REREWHAKAAITU RIVER	STRM	41 25 175 40	53
RESERVOIR, THE	LAKE	46 39 169 04	112
RESOLUTION BAY	BAY	41 08 174 14	54
RESOLUTION BAY	BAY	41 08 174 14	60
RESOLUTION BAY	BAY	41 08 174 14	61
RESOLUTION ISLAND	ISLD	45 40 166 38	104
RETARUKE	LOC	39 07 175 08	36
RETARUKE RIVER	STRM	39 07 175 04	36
RETFORD STREAM	STRM	45 10 167 53	97
RETFORD STREAM	STRM	45 10 167 53	98
RETREAT CREEK	STRM	44 20 168 23	88
RETREAT CREEK	STRM	44 20 168 23	89
RETREAT HILL (TRIG)	MTN	43 06 172 17	81
RETREAT PINNACLES	MTN	44 21 168 26	88
RETREAT PINNACLES	MTN	44 21 168 26	89
RETURN CHANNEL	CHAN	46 01 166 32	104
REWA	LOC	39 59 175 38	46
REWANUI	LOC	42 23 171 19	69
REWAREWA	LOC	38 18 175 19	27
REWITI	LOC	36 45 174 27	10
REWITI	LOC	36 45 174 27	11
REWITI	LOC	36 45 174 27	12
REYNOLDS CREEK	STRM	43 21 170 27	74
REYNOLDS CREEK	STRM	43 46 169 33	76
REYNOLDS CREEK	STRM	43 21 170 27	77
REYNOLDS CREEK	STRM	43 46 169 33	79
REYNOLDS MOUNT	MTN	43 43 169 35	76
REYNOLDS MOUNT	MTN	43 43 169 35	79
RIAMAKI	LOC	39 12 175 12	36
RIARIAKI (TRIG)	HILL	39 13 175 13	36
RIBBLE STREAM	STRM	41 53 173 37	66
RIBBLE STREAM	STRM	41 53 173 37	67
RIBBLE, THE	STRM	42 24 172 58	71
RIBBLE, THE	STRM	42 24 172 58	72
RIBBON WOOD STREAM	STRM	43 43 170 35	86
RIBBONWOOD CREEK	STRM	44 27 169 42	91
RIBBONWOOD STREAM	STRM	43 24 171 10	75
RICCARTON	SBRB	43 32 172 35	82
RICCARTON	SBRB	43 32 172 35	83
RICCARTON	SBRB	43 32 172 35	85
RICHARD BURN	STRM	45 56 166 55	104
RICHARD BURN	STRM	45 56 166 55	105
RICHARDS, MOUNT	MTN	45 34 166 43	104
RICHARDS, MOUNT	MTN	44 13 168 30	88
RICHARDS POINT	PNT	46 50 167 43	114
RICHARDSON GLACIER	GLCR	43 49 169 57	76
RICHARDSON GLACIER	GLCR	43 49 169 57	77
RICHARDSON GLACIER	GLCR	43 49 169 57	79
RICHARDSON, MOUNT (TRIG)	MTN	43 11 172 13	81
RICHARDSON MOUNTAINS	MTNS	44 52 168 33	90
RICHARDSON MOUNTAINS	MTNS	44 52 168 33	95
RICHIE, MOUNT	MTN	43 38 169 47	76
RICHIE, MOUNT	MTN	43 38 169 47	79
RICHMOND	USAT	41 21 173 12	59
RICHMOND	SBRB	43 31 172 39	82
RICHMOND	SBRB	43 31 172 39	83
RICHMOND	SBRB	43 31 172 39	85
RICHMOND	LOC	45 01 171 03	93
RICHMOND	LOC	45 01 171 03	102
RICHMOND BAY	BAY	41 01 173 58	54
RICHMOND BAY	BAY	41 01 173 58	60
RICHMOND BAY	BAY	41 01 173 58	61
RICHMOND BROOK	STRM	41 40 174 00	67
RICHMOND BROOK	HSTD	41 43 173 57	67
RICHMOND DOWNS	LOC	37 47 175 40	19
RICHMOND, MOUNT	MTN	43 32 170 26	74
RICHMOND, MOUNT	MTN	43 32 170 26	77
RICHMOND, MOUNT	MTN	45 14 168 07	98
RICHMOND, MOUNT (TRIG)	PEAK	41 28 173 24	59
RICHMOND RANGE	MTNS	41 27 173 30	59
RICHMOND STREAM	STRM	41 25 173 21	59
RICHTER, LAKE	LAKE	45 29 167 30	97
RIDGE CREEK	STRM	44 23 168 29	88
RIDGE CREEK	STRM	44 23 168 29	89
RIDGE PEAK	PEAK	45 12 168 24	95
RIDGE PEAK	PEAK	45 12 168 24	98
RIDGE (TRIG)	HILL	40 50 175 44	49
RIDGE (TRIG)	HILL	40 50 175 44	51
RIDGELANDS	HSTD	40 09 175 35	46
RIDLAND SADDLE	SAD	43 07 170 49	75
RIGEL, MOUNT	MTN	44 11 169 34	79
RIGHT BOWER, THE	MTN	43 59 169 19	78
RIGNEY	LOC	45 43 169 28	111
RILEY, MOUNT (TRIG)	PEAK	41 25 173 42	60
RILEY, MOUNT (TRIG)	MTN	42 32 171 20	69
RILEY (TRIG)	HILL	40 55 175 49	49
RILEY (TRIG)	HILL	40 55 175 49	51
RIMARIKI ISLAND	ISLD	35 26 174 26	5
RIMMER, LAKE	LAKE	45 56 166 35	104
RIMU	LOC	42 46 171 00	68
RIMU	LOC	42 46 171 00	69
RIMU	LOC	46 24 168 32	109
RIMU, MOUNT (TRIG)	HILL	41 14 173 37	59
RIMU, MOUNT (TRIG)	HILL	41 14 173 37	60
RIMUHAU (TRIG)	HILL	38 42 177 46	31
RIMUHAU (TRIG)	HILL	38 42 177 46	33
RIMUROA (TRIG)	HILL	38 38 178 02	32
RIMUTAKA RANGE	MTNS	41 17 175 05	52
RIMUTAKA RANGE	MTNS	41 17 175 05	55
RIMUTAKA STATE FOREST PARK	PARK	41 15 175 05	52
RIMUTAKA STATE FOREST PARK	PARK	41 15 175 05	55
RIMUTAKA (TRIG)	PEAK	41 07 175 14	53
RING CREEK	STRM	41 49 173 46	67
RINGAWHATI (TRIG)	HILL	40 47 175 12	48
RINGAWHATI (TRIG)	HILL	40 47 175 12	52
RINGWAY	LOC	46 10 168 00	106
RINGWAY	LOC	46 10 168 00	107
RINGWAY	LOC	46 10 168 00	108
RINTOUL, MOUNT (TRIG)	PEAK	41 31 173 14	59
RIPIA RIVER	STRM	39 13 176 31	39
RIPIA RIVER	STRM	39 13 176 31	40
RIPONUI	LOC	35 34 174 09	4
RIPONUI	LOC	35 34 174 09	5
RIPONUI	LOC	35 34 174 09	7
RIPPONVALE	LOC	45 02 169 09	99
RIRIPO STREAM	STRM	39 35 175 07	36
RIRIPO STREAM	STRM	39 35 175 07	45
RIRIWHA (TRIG)	HILL	34 58 173 47	4
RISSINGTON	LOC	39 25 176 43	40
RISSINGTON	LOC	39 25 176 43	42
RITEAKAWARAU (TRIG)	HILL	36 36 174 33	10
RITEAKAWARAU (TRIG)	HILL	36 36 174 33	11
RITEAKAWARAU (TRIG)	HILL	36 36 174 33	12
RIVERDALE	POPL	45 54 168 44	110
RIVERHEAD	LOC	36 46 174 36	11
RIVERHEAD	LOC	36 46 174 36	12
RIVERLANDS	LOC	41 31 173 59	60
RIVERLEA	LOC	39 26 174 05	34
RIVERSDALE	HSTD	42 39 173 13	72
RIVERSDALE	HSTD	42 39 173 13	73
RIVERSDALE BEACH	BCH	41 05 176 04	51
RIVERSIDE	LOC	44 01 171 50	84
RIVERSIDE	LOC	45 53 170 16	103
RIVERTON	POPL	46 22 168 01	108
RIVERTON	POPL	46 22 168 01	109
RIVERTON (TRIG)	HILL	46 23 168 01	108
RIVERTON (TRIG)	HILL	46 23 168 01	109
RIWAKA	LOC	41 05 173 00	57
RIWAKA	LOC	41 05 173 00	58
RIWAKA	LOC	41 05 173 00	59
RIWAKA RIVER	STRM	41 04 173 00	57
RIWAKA RIVER	STRM	41 04 173 00	58
RIWAKA RIVER, NORTH BRANCH	STRM	41 03 172 55	57
RIWAKA RIVER, NORTH BRANCH	STRM	41 03 172 55	58
RIWAKA RIVER, SOUTH BRANCH	STRM	41 03 172 55	57
RIWAKA RIVER, SOUTH BRANCH	STRM	41 03 172 55	58
ROA	LOC	42 21 171 23	69
ROA, MOUNT (TRIG)	MNT	38 50 174 44	26
ROAD HILL (TRIG)	HILL	40 58 175 51	51
ROARING BILLY, THE	STRM	43 56 169 18	78
ROARING LION CREEK	STRM	45 22 168 51	95
ROARING LION CREEK	STRM	45 22 168 51	99
ROARING LION RIVER	STRM	41 12 172 26	56
ROARING LION RIVER	STRM	41 12 172 26	62
ROARING MEG	STRM	40 52 175 14	48
ROARING MEG	STRM	40 52 175 14	52
ROARING MEG	STRM	40 52 175 14	55
ROARING MEG	STRM	45 00 169 04	99
ROARING MEG	STRM	45 05 170 31	102
ROARING MEG CREEK	STRM	42 20 171 28	69
ROARING MEG POWER STATION	PHSE	45 00 169 05	99
ROARING SWINE CREEK	STRM	43 58 169 13	78
ROB ROY CREEK	STRM	45 47 168 47	110
ROB ROY CREEK (WEST BRANCH)	STRM	45 44 168 46	110
ROB ROY GLACIER	GLCR	44 28 168 45	90
ROB ROY PEAK	PEAK	44 27 168 43	88
ROB ROY PEAK	PEAK	44 27 168 43	90
ROB ROY STREAM	STRM	44 29 168 40	88
ROB ROY STREAM	STRM	44 29 168 40	90
ROBB SADDLE	SAD	44 52 167 38	94
ROBERT CREEK	STRM	45 23 168 34	95
ROBERT CREEK	STRM	45 23 168 34	99
ROBERTS, MOUNT (TRIG)	MTN	43 15 170 53	75
ROBERTSON CREEK	STRM	44 40 168 39	90
ROBERTSON, MOUNT (TRIG)	MTN	41 21 174 01	54
ROBERTSON, MOUNT (TRIG)	MTN	41 21 174 01	60
ROBERTSON POINT	PNT	41 21 174 07	54
ROBERTSON POINT	PNT	41 21 174 07	60
ROBERTSON RIVER	STRM	47 11 167 48	114
ROBIN HOOD BAY	BAY	41 22 174 05	54
ROBIN HOOD BAY	BAY	41 22 174 05	60
ROBIN HOOD BAY	BAY	43 52 172 48	83
ROBIN SADDLE	SAD	45 12 167 22	96
ROBINSON CREEK	STRM	42 07 173 14	66
ROBINSON CREEK	STRM	43 49 169 12	78
ROBINSON CREEK	STRM	44 04 168 23	88
ROBINSON RIVER	STRM	42 27 172 00	70
ROBINSON SADDLE	SAD	42 12 173 15	66
ROBSON STREAM	STRM	41 29 172 28	62
ROBSON STREAM	STRM	42 27 173 15	72
ROBSON STREAM	STRM	42 27 173 15	73
ROBYNES CREEK	STRM	42 47 172 28	71
ROCHE PASS	PASS	42 47 171 58	70
ROCHFORT, LAKE	LAKE	41 46 171 44	63
ROCHFORT, LAKE	LAKE	41 46 171 44	64
ROCHFORT, MOUNT (TRIG)	PEAK	41 46 171 45	63
ROCHFORT, MOUNT (TRIG)	PEAK	41 46 171 45	64
ROCK AND PILLAR	LOC	45 24 170 11	101
ROCK AND PILLAR CREEK	STRM	45 22 170 00	101
ROCK AND PILLAR RANGE	MTNS	45 22 170 08	101
ROCK BURN	STRM	44 40 168 19	89
ROCK PEAK	PEAK	38 11 175 00	18
ROCK POINT	PNT	41 08 174 47	52
ROCK POINT	PNT	41 08 174 47	55
ROCK, THE	HILL	41 50 173 59	67
ROCK (TRIG)	MTN	41 54 172 27	65
ROCKFORD	LOC	43 20 172 02	81
ROCKLANDS	HSTD	41 51 171 53	63
ROCKLANDS	HSTD	41 51 171 53	64
ROCKS AHEAD STREAM	STRM	39 17 176 18	39
ROCKS CREEK	STRM	44 49 169 55	91
ROCKS POINT	PNT	40 51 172 08	56
ROCKS, THE (TRIG)	PEAK	41 22 173 21	59
ROCKVILLE	LOC	40 44 172 38	56
ROCKVILLE	LOC	40 44 172 38	57
ROCKY BAY	BAY	35 36 174 32	5
ROCKY BAY	BAY	35 36 174 32	8
ROCKY BAY	BAY	36 36 175 47	16
ROCKY CREEK	STRM	39 17 176 09	39
ROCKY CREEK	STRM	41 22 173 46	60
ROCKY CREEK	STRM	41 42 172 53	65
ROCKY CREEK	STRM	42 50 170 52	68
ROCKY CREEK	STRM	42 46 171 25	69
ROCKY CREEK	STRM	43 27 170 00	76
ROCKY CREEK	STRM	43 27 170 00	77
ROCKY DOME (TRIG)	HILL	46 19 169 31	111
ROCKY DOME (TRIG)	HILL	46 19 169 31	113
ROCKY GULLY	STRM	41 43 172 33	65
ROCKY GULLY	STRM	44 15 170 54	87
ROCKY GULLY	STRM	44 20 170 46	93
ROCKY HILL (TRIG)	HILL	45 34 169 24	100
ROCKY, MOUNT	HILL	46 52 167 57	109
ROCKY, MOUNT	HILL	46 52 167 57	115
ROCKY, MOUNT	HILL	46 52 167 57	114
ROCKY MOUNT (TRIG)	PEAK	45 24 168 59	99
ROCKY PEAK	PEAK	44 47 168 47	90
ROCKY PEAK	PEAK	44 55 169 38	91
ROCKY PEAK	PEAK	44 47 168 47	95
ROCKY PEAK (TRIG)	HILL	45 25 169 53	100
ROCKY PEAK (TRIG)	HILL	45 25 169 53	101
ROCKY POINT	PNT	35 07 174 05	4
ROCKY POINT	PNT	35 07 174 05	5
ROCKY POINT	PNT	36 13 174 17	7
ROCKY POINT	PNT	36 13 174 17	8
ROCKY POINT	PNT	36 12 175 07	9
ROCKY POINT	PNT	41 37 175 17	53
ROCKY POINT	PNT	44 28 169 19	91
ROCKY POINT	PNT	45 11 167 45	97
ROCKY POINT (TRIG)	PEAK	39 20 176 15	39
ROCKY RIVER	STRM	40 49 172 37	56
ROCKY RIVER	STRM	41 09 172 55	57
ROCKY RIVER	STRM	40 49 172 37	57
ROCKY RIVER	STRM	41 09 172 55	58
ROCKY STREAM	STRM	43 04 172 26	81
ROCKY TOP	MTN	44 47 170 18	92
ROCKY TOP	MTN	45 49 167 24	105
ROCKY TOR	PEAK	41 43 172 08	64
ROCKY VALLEY CREEK	STRM	46 14 170 03	111
RODERICK, MOUNT (TRIG)	MTN	42 47 172 30	71
RODGER INLET	BAY	45 52 167 27	105
RODGER INLET	BAY	45 52 167 27	106
RODING RIVER	STRM	41 24 173 08	59
RODNEY, CAPE	CAPE	36 17 174 49	11
RODNEY (TRIG)	HILL	42 32 172 42	71
ROE BURN	STRM	45 48 168 23	107
ROE, LAKE	LAKE	45 42 167 09	105
ROEBUCK CREEK	STRM	41 25 173 21	59
ROGER HEAD	HEAD	46 45 167 38	108
ROGER HEAD	HEAD	46 45 167 38	114
ROGERSON RIVER	STRM	42 31 172 49	71
ROIMATA POINT	PNT	35 28 174 27	5
ROIMATA (TRIG)	HILL	39 29 174 28	35
ROIMATA (TRIG)	HILL	39 29 174 28	44
ROKAIWHANA STREAM	STRM	40 11 176 03	46
ROKEBY	LOC	43 44 171 55	84
ROKEBY STREAM	STRM	42 26 172 28	71
ROKEBY (TRIG)	MTN	42 25 172 30	71
ROKOAWEKE POINT	PNT	35 34 174 31	5
ROKOAWEKE POINT	PNT	35 34 174 31	8
ROLLESBY RANGE	MTNS	44 09 170 37	86
ROLLESTON	LOC	43 36 172 23	81
ROLLESTON	LOC	43 36 172 23	85
ROLLESTON, MOUNT	MTN	42 55 171 31	69
ROLLESTON RANGE	MTNS	43 10 171 14	75
ROLLESTON RIVER	STRM	42 51 171 34	69
ROLLING PIN	MTN	44 22 168 43	88
ROLLING PIN	MTN	44 22 168 43	90
ROLLING RIVER	STRM	41 27 172 35	58
ROMAHAPA	LOC	46 21 169 43	113
RONA ISLAND	ISLD	45 30 167 32	97
RONALD ADAIR, MOUNT	MTN	43 36 170 27	74
RONALD ADAIR, MOUNT	MTN	43 36 170 27	77
RONALD, LAKE	LAKE	44 38 167 43	94
RONGA, MOUNT (TRIG)	HILL	41 09 173 38	60
RONGA RIVER	STRM	41 13 173 36	59
RONGA SADDLE	SAD	41 08 173 36	59
RONGAHERE	LOC	45 59 169 29	111
RONGAHERE	LOC	45 59 169 29	113
RONGOITI JUNCTION	LOC	39 41 175 42	46
RONGOKOKAKO	LOC	40 39 175 39	48
RONGOKOKAKO	LOC	40 39 175 39	49
RONGOMAI	LOC	40 36 175 48	49
RONGOTEA	POPL	40 17 175 25	48
RONGOTEA (TRIG)	PEAK	39 46 176 07	47

ROO STREAM	STRM	45 42 167 02	**105**
ROON, MOUNT	MTN	43 29 170 10	**74**
ROON, MOUNT	MTN	43 29 170 10	**77**
ROONEY RIVER	STRM	45 55 167 17	**105**
ROROKOKO STREAM	STRM	40 58 175 50	**49**
ROROKOKO STREAM	STRM	40 58 175 50	**51**
ROSA, MOUNT	MTN	43 39 170 09	**74**
ROSA, MOUNT	MTN	43 39 170 09	**77**
ROSA, MOUNT	MTN	43 39 170 09	**86**
ROSA, MOUNT (TRIG)	MTN	43 08 171 56	**80**
ROSA, MOUNT (TRIG)	MTN	43 08 171 56	**81**
ROSAMOND, MOUNT	MTN	42 56 171 24	**69**
ROSEBANK	SBRB	46 15 169 43	**111**
ROSEBANK	SBRB	46 15 169 43	**113**
ROSEBERY	LOC	45 02 170 57	**102**
ROSEBERY, MOUNT (TRIG)	HILL	46 20 169 21	**111**
ROSEBERY, MOUNT (TRIG)	HILL	46 20 169 21	**113**
ROSES SADDLE	SAD	44 49 168 51	**90**
ROSES SADDLE	SAD	44 49 168 51	**95**
ROSEWILL	LOC	44 20 171 09	**87**
ROSEWILL STREAM	STRM	44 21 171 12	**87**
ROSLYN	SBRB	40 20 175 37	**48**
ROSLYN	SBRB	40 20 175 37	**49**
ROSLYN BUSH	LOC	46 21 168 27	**109**
ROSS	POPL	42 54 170 49	**68**
ROSS, LAKE	LAKE	44 54 167 57	**89**
ROSS, LAKE	LAKE	44 54 167 57	**94**
ROSS, MOUNT	MTN	43 01 171 08	**75**
ROSS, MOUNT	MTN	43 36 170 39	**74**
ROSS, MOUNT (TRIG)	PEAK	41 27 175 21	**53**
ROSS, MOUNT (TRIG)	MTN	42 15 172 00	**64**
ROSS, MOUNT (TRIG)	MTN	42 21 173 14	**72**
ROSS, MOUNT (TRIG)	MTN	42 21 173 14	**73**
ROSS MOUNT (TRIG)	HILL	45 36 170 12	**101**
ROSS STREAM	STRM	44 23 170 21	**92**
ROSS STREAM	STRM	45 37 170 16	**101**
ROSS (TRIG)	PEAK	40 13 175 53	**46**
ROSSMORE	HSTD	41 40 173 58	**67**
ROSY PEAK	PEAK	44 10 168 50	**78**
ROTHERHAM	LOC	42 42 172 57	**71**
ROTHERHAM	LOC	42 42 172 57	**72**
ROTHESAY BAY	SBRB	36 44 174 45	**11**
ROTHESAY BAY	SBRB	36 44 174 45	**12**
ROTO	LOC	38 54 175 00	**26**
ROTO	LOC	38 54 175 00	**27**
ROTOAIRA, LAKE	LAKE	39 04 175 43	**37**
ROTOAIRA, LAKE	LAKE	39 04 175 43	**38**
ROTOATUA, LAKE	LAKE	38 05 176 26	**21**
ROTOATUA, LAKE	LAKE	38 05 176 26	**22**
ROTOEHU	LOC	38 02 176 32	**21**
ROTOEHU	LOC	38 02 176 32	**22**
ROTOEHU, LAKE	LAKE	38 01 176 32	**21**
ROTOEHU, LAKE	LAKE	38 01 176 32	**22**
ROTOHOUHOU STREAM	STRM	38 18 176 14	**21**
ROTOHOUHOU STREAM	STRM	38 18 176 14	**29**
ROTOITI	LOC	38 03 176 29	**21**
ROTOITI	LOC	38 03 176 29	**22**
ROTO-ITI	HSTD	42 57 172 50	**71**
ROTO-ITI	HSTD	42 57 172 50	**72**
ROTOITI, LAKE	LAKE	38 03 176 26	**20**
ROTOITI, LAKE	LAKE	38 03 176 26	**21**
ROTOITI, LAKE	LAKE	38 03 176 26	**22**
ROTOITI, LAKE	LAKE	41 50 172 50	**65**
ROTOITI, LAKE	LAKE	42 24 173 36	**73**
ROTOITIPAKU, LAKE	LAKE	38 04 176 43	**21**
ROTOITIPAKU, LAKE	LAKE	38 04 176 43	**22**
ROTOKAKAHI	LOC	35 20 173 17	**3**
ROTOKAKAHI, LAKE	LAKE	38 13 176 19	**20**
ROTOKAKAHI, LAKE	LAKE	38 13 176 19	**21**
ROTOKAKAHI, LAKE	LAKE	38 13 176 19	**29**
ROTOKAKAHI RIVER	STRM	35 20 173 17	**3**
ROTOKARE, LAKE	LAKE	39 27 174 25	**35**
ROTOKARE, LAKE	LAKE	39 27 174 25	**44**
ROTOKAURI	LOC	37 46 175 12	**18**
ROTOKAURI, LAKE	LAKE	37 46 175 12	**18**
ROTOKAUTUTU	LOC	37 53 178 18	**25**
ROTOKAWA	LOC	38 38 176 13	**29**
ROTOKAWA, LAKE	LAKE	38 38 176 11	**29**
ROTOKAWAU, LAKE	LAKE	34 52 173 19	**3**
ROTOKAWAU, LAKE	LAKE	36 21 174 09	**10**
ROTOKAWAU, LAKE	LAKE	37 29 175 11	**15**
ROTOKAWAU, LAKE	LAKE	38 04 176 23	**20**
ROTOKAWAU, LAKE	LAKE	38 04 176 23	**21**
ROTOKINO	LOC	43 12 170 22	**74**
ROTOKINO, LAKE	LAKE	43 10 170 26	**74**
ROTOKOHU	LOC	41 58 171 54	**63**
ROTOKOHU	LOC	41 58 171 54	**64**
ROTOKOHU, LAKE	LAKE	38 05 176 31	**21**
ROTOKOHU, LAKE	LAKE	38 05 176 31	**22**
ROTOKOHU STREAM	STRM	37 23 175 39	**15**
ROTOKOHU STREAM	STRM	37 23 175 39	**17**
ROTOMA, LAKE	LAKE	38 03 176 35	**21**
ROTOMA, LAKE	LAKE	38 03 176 35	**22**
ROTOMAHANA	LOC	38 19 176 24	**21**
ROTOMAHANA	LOC	38 19 176 24	**29**
ROTOMAHANA, LAKE	LAKE	38 16 176 26	**21**
ROTOMAHANA, LAKE	LAKE	38 16 176 26	**22**
ROTOMAHANA, LAKE	LAKE	38 16 176 26	**30**
ROTOMANU	LOC	42 39 171 34	**69**
ROTOMANU STATION	RSTN	42 39 171 32	**69**
ROTONGAIO BAY	BAY	38 48 176 04	**28**
ROTONGAIO BAY	BAY	38 48 176 04	**29**
ROTONGAIO BAY	BAY	38 48 176 04	**38**
ROTONGAIO, LAKE	LAKE	38 57 177 01	**41**
ROTONGARO	LOC	37 32 175 05	**14**
ROTONGARO	LOC	37 32 175 05	**15**
ROTONGARO, LAKE	LAKE	37 29 175 07	**14**
ROTONGARO, LAKE	LAKE	37 29 175 07	**15**
ROTONGAROITI, LAKE	LAKE	37 29 175 07	**14**
ROTONGAROITI, LAKE	LAKE	37 29 175 07	**15**
ROTONGATA	LOC	38 08 175 35	**19**
ROTONUIAHA, LAKE	LAKE	38 57 177 02	**41**
ROTOORANGI	LOC	37 59 175 28	**19**
ROTOPAUNGA (TRIG)	PEAK	39 07 175 40	**37**
ROTOPAUNGA (TRIG)	PEAK	39 07 175 40	**38**
ROTOPOUNAMU, LAKE	LAKE	39 01 177 53	**33**
ROTOPOUNAMU, LAKE	LAKE	39 02 175 44	**37**
ROTOPOUNAMU, LAKE	LAKE	39 02 175 44	**38**
ROTOPOUUA, LAKE	LAKE	36 19 174 06	**10**
ROTOROA	LOC	41 48 172 35	**65**
ROTOROA ISLAND	ISLD	36 49 175 12	**13**
ROTOROA, LAKE	LAKE	35 04 173 12	**3**
ROTOROA, LAKE	LAKE	37 48 175 16	**18**
ROTOROA, LAKE	LAKE	37 48 175 16	**19**
ROTOROA, LAKE	LAKE	38 03 176 43	**22**
ROTOROA, LAKE	LAKE	38 57 177 02	**41**
ROTOROA, LAKE	LAKE	41 51 172 38	**65**
ROTORUA	TOWN	38 08 176 14	**20**
ROTORUA	TOWN	38 08 176 14	**21**
ROTORUA, LAKE	LAKE	38 05 176 16	**20**
ROTORUA, LAKE	LAKE	38 05 176 16	**21**
ROTORUA, LAKE	LAKE	42 24 173 35	**73**
ROTOTAHI	HSTD	38 26 178 16	**32**
ROTOTAWAI	HSTD	41 13 175 21	**53**
ROTOTEKOITI, LAKE	LAKE	43 39 169 46	**76**
ROTOTEKOITI, LAKE	LAKE	43 39 169 46	**79**
ROTOTUNA	LOC	36 15 174 02	**10**
ROTOTUNA	LOC	37 44 175 16	**18**
ROTOTUNA	LOC	37 44 175 16	**19**
ROTOTUNA, LAKE	LAKE	36 15 174 02	**10**
ROTOTUNA, LAKE	LAKE	39 34 174 47	**35**
ROTOTUNA, LAKE	LAKE	39 34 174 47	**44**
ROTOWARO	LOC	37 35 175 04	**18**
ROUGH AND TUMBLE CREEK	STRM	41 32 172 04	**62**
ROUGH BURN	STRM	44 24 169 07	**90**
ROUGH CREEK	STRM	41 53 171 56	**64**
ROUGH CREEK	STRM	41 51 172 56	**65**
ROUGH CREEK	STRM	42 20 173 11	**66**
ROUGH CREEK	STRM	42 57 171 34	**69**
ROUGH CREEK	STRM	43 54 169 33	**76**
ROUGH CREEK	STRM	43 35 169 49	**76**
ROUGH CREEK	STRM	43 54 169 33	**79**
ROUGH HILL	HSTD	41 26 175 25	**53**
ROUGH HILL (TRIG)	HILL	41 26 175 25	**53**
ROUGH RIDGE	MTN	43 51 169 32	**76**
ROUGH RIDGE	RDGE	43 57 169 07	**78**
ROUGH RIDGE	MTN	43 51 169 32	**79**
ROUGH RIDGE	RDGE	45 18 169 50	**100**
ROUGH RIDGE	RDGE	45 18 169 50	**101**
ROUGH RIVER	STRM	42 17 171 39	**63**
ROUGH STREAM	STRM	41 29 175 25	**53**
ROUGH STREAM	STRM	42 11 171 56	**64**
ROUGH STREAM	STRM	42 49 172 21	**71**
ROUGH'NS CREEK	STRM	41 34 172 53	**58**
ROUND DOWN (TRIG)	HILL	45 46 168 51	**110**
ROUND HEAD	HEAD	44 55 167 14	**96**
ROUND HILL	MTN	43 25 171 20	**75**
ROUND HILL	MTN	43 25 171 20	**80**
ROUND HILL	MTN	44 47 168 31	**89**
ROUND HILL	MTN	44 47 168 31	**90**
ROUND HILL	MTN	44 47 168 31	**95**
ROUND HILL	MTN	45 10 168 38	**95**
ROUND HILL	MTN	45 10 168 38	**99**
ROUND HILL	HILL	45 02 170 52	**102**
ROUND HILL	LOC	46 20 167 50	**108**
ROUND HILL	LOC	46 02 169 48	**111**
ROUND HILL	LOC	46 02 169 48	**113**
ROUND HILL CREEK	STRM	43 25 171 21	**75**
ROUND HILL CREEK	STRM	43 25 171 21	**80**
ROUND HILL (TRIG)	MTN	43 51 170 06	**76**
ROUND HILL (TRIG)	MTN	43 51 170 06	**77**
ROUND HILL (TRIG)	MTN	43 51 170 06	**79**
ROUND HILL (TRIG)	MTN	43 51 170 06	**86**
ROUND HILL (TRIG)	HILL	44 05 171 02	**87**
ROUND HILL (TRIG)	HILL	44 49 169 01	**90**
ROUND HILL (TRIG)	PEAK	45 20 168 35	**95**
ROUND HILL (TRIG)	PEAK	45 20 168 35	**99**
ROUND HILL (TRIG)	HILL	45 10 169 09	**99**
ROUND HILL (TRIG)	HILL	45 30 168 36	**99**
ROUND HILL (TRIG)	HILL	46 18 167 47	**108**
ROUND HILL (TRIG)	MTN	43 49 170 40	**86**
ROUND HILL (TRIG)	HILL	44 28 170 37	**92**
ROUND HILL (TRIG)	HILL	44 46 170 53	**93**
ROUND HILL (TRIG)	HILL	44 28 170 37	**93**
ROUND HILL (TRIG)	HILL	45 02 170 18	**101**
ROUND HILL (TRIG)	MTN	45 30 169 57	**101**
ROUND HILL (TRIG)	HILL	45 13 170 26	**102**
ROUND HILL (TRIG)	HILL	45 42 168 42	**110**
ROUND HILL (TRIG)	HILL	46 01 169 48	**111**
ROUND HILL (TRIG)	HILL	46 01 169 48	**113**
ROUND PEAKS	PEAK	45 02 168 21	**95**
ROUND PEAKS	PEAK	45 02 168 21	**98**
ROUND RIDGE HILL (TRIG)	HILL	45 48 170 10	**103**
ROUND TOP	PEAK	42 55 171 06	**68**
ROUND TOP	PEAK	42 55 171 06	**69**
ROUND TOP (TRIG)	HILL	43 29 171 43	**80**
ROUNDABOUT, LAKE	LAKE	43 38 171 06	**75**
ROUTE BURN	STRM	44 45 168 20	**89**
ROUTE BURN (NORTH BRANCH)	STRM	44 44 168 13	**89**
ROUTEBURN FALLS	FALL	44 44 168 12	**89**
ROVER SADDLE	SAD	42 48 171 47	**70**
ROW, MOUNT	MTN	42 48 171 55	**70**
ROW STREAM	STRM	42 52 171 57	**70**
ROWALLAN BURN	STRM	46 10 167 31	**105**
ROWALLAN BURN	STRM	46 10 167 31	**106**
ROWALLAN BURN	STRM	46 10 167 31	**108**
ROWALLAN BURN (EAST BRANCH)	STRM	46 09 167 31	**105**
ROWALLAN BURN (EAST BRANCH)	STRM	46 09 167 31	**106**
ROWALLAN BURN (EAST BRANCH)	STRM	46 09 167 31	**108**
ROWALLAN BURN (WEST BRANCH)	STRM	46 09 167 31	**105**
ROWALLAN BURN (WEST BRANCH)	STRM	46 09 167 31	**106**
ROWALLAN BURN (WEST BRANCH)	STRM	46 09 167 31	**108**
ROWAN	LOC	39 24 174 07	**34**
ROWE, MOUNT (TRIG)	HILL	37 02 175 40	**15**
ROWE, MOUNT (TRIG)	HILL	37 02 175 40	**16**
ROWE, MOUNT (TRIG)	HILL	37 02 175 40	**17**
ROXBURGH	POPL	45 33 169 19	**100**
ROXBURGH EAST	LOC	45 33 169 19	**100**
ROXBURGH HYDRO	LOC	45 29 169 19	**100**
ROXBURGH, LAKE	LAKE	45 01 167 41	**94**
ROXBURGH, LAKE	LAKE	45 01 167 41	**97**
ROXBURGH, LAKE	LAKE	45 25 169 19	**100**
ROYAL CREEK	STRM	44 00 169 39	**79**
ROYAL MOUNT (TRIG)	HILL	45 31 170 43	**102**
ROYAL, MOUNT (TRIG)	HILL	45 32 170 27	**102**
ROYAL STREAM	STRM	42 39 173 16	**72**
ROYAL STREAM	STRM	42 39 173 16	**73**
ROYS BAY	BAY	44 42 169 07	**90**
ROYS HILL	HSTD	39 38 176 43	**42**
ROYS HILL	HSTD	39 38 176 43	**43**
ROYS PEAK (TRIG)	MTN	44 42 169 03	**90**
ROYS PENINSULA	PEN	44 38 169 02	**90**
RUAHAKOAKOA	TRIG	37 33 178 05	**25**
RUAHEMA STREAM	STRM	38 07 177 16	**23**
RUAHINE	HILL	38 09 175 21	**19**
RUAHINE	LOC	39 51 175 54	**46**
RUAHINE	LOC	46 21 167 47	**108**
RUAHINE RANGE	MTNS	40 11 175 56	**46**
RUAHINE STATE FOREST PARK	PARK	40 10 175 57	**46**
RUAHINE STATE FOREST PARK	PARK	39 51 176 07	**47**
RUAHINE (TRIG)	HILL	38 47 175 39	**28**
RUAHINE (TRIG)	HILL	38 47 175 39	**38**
RUAHOREHORE STREAM	STRM	37 24 175 52	**17**
RUAKAKA	LOC	35 54 174 27	**7**
RUAKAKA	LOC	35 54 174 27	**8**
RUAKAKA RIVER	STRM	35 54 174 28	**8**
RUAKAKA (TRIG)	HILL	37 24 175 06	**14**
RUAKAKA (TRIG)	HILL	37 24 175 06	**15**
RUAKAWA	HSTD	39 44 176 39	**42**
RUAKAWA	HSTD	39 44 176 39	**43**
RUAKAWA	HSTD	39 44 176 39	**47**
RUAKITURI	LOC	38 46 177 24	**31**
RUAKITURI	LOC	38 46 177 24	**33**
RUAKITURI RIVER	STRM	38 50 177 31	**31**
RUAKITURI RIVER	STRM	38 50 177 31	**33**
RUAKITURI STREAM	STRM	39 07 177 11	**41**
RUAKIWI	LOC	37 42 174 55	**18**
RUAKOKOPUTUNA	LOC	41 19 175 25	**53**
RUAKOKOPUTUNA RIVER	STRM	41 19 175 28	**53**
RUAKORORA STREAM	STRM	39 47 175 01	**45**
RUAMAHANGA	LOC	37 01 175 31	**13**
RUAMAHANGA	LOC	37 01 175 31	**15**
RUAMAHANGA	LOC	37 01 175 31	**16**
RUAMAHANGA RIVER	STRM	41 22 175 08	**52**
RUAMAHANGA RIVER	STRM	41 22 175 08	**53**
RUAMAHANGA STREAM	STRM	40 05 175 28	**45**
RUAMAHANGA STREAM	STRM	40 05 175 28	**46**
RUAMAHUAITI ISLAND	ISLD	36 58 176 05	**17**
RUAMAHUANUI ISLAND	ISLD	36 57 176 06	**17**
RUANUI	LOC	39 37 175 39	**46**
RUAOTEHUIA STREAM	STRM	37 15 175 10	**13**
RUAOTEHUIA STREAM	STRM	37 15 175 10	**15**
RUAPANI, LAKE	LAKE	38 44 177 08	**31**
RUAPAPA	HSTD	38 57 177 10	**41**
RUAPEHU, MOUNT	MTN	39 18 175 34	**37**
RUAPEHU, MOUNT	MTN	39 18 175 34	**38**
RUAPEKA STREAM	STRM	37 56 175 32	**19**
RUAPEKAPEKA	LOC	35 27 174 09	**4**
RUAPEKAPEKA	LOC	35 27 174 09	**5**
RUAPUKE	LOC	37 55 174 47	**18**
RUAPUKE ISLAND	ISLD	46 46 168 31	**109**
RUAPUKE ISLAND	ISLD	46 46 168 31	**115**
RUAPUNA	LOC	43 52 171 20	**84**
RUAPUNA	LOC	43 52 171 20	**87**
RUARANGI	LOC	35 56 174 17	**7**
RUARANGI	LOC	35 56 174 17	**8**
RUAROA	LOC	35 08 173 20	**3**
RUAROA	LOC	40 11 176 03	**46**
RUATAHUNA	LOC	38 37 176 58	**30**
RUATAHUNA STREAM	STRM	38 37 176 56	**30**
RUATAHUNGA STREAM	STRM	38 04 177 58	**24**
RUATAIKO (TRIG)	HILL	38 19 177 08	**31**
RUATANGATA WEST	LOC	35 40 174 10	**5**
RUATANGATA WEST	LOC	35 40 174 10	**7**
RUATANIWHA	LOC	39 56 176 31	**42**
RUATANIWHA	LOC	39 56 176 31	**43**
RUATANIWHA	LOC	39 56 176 31	**47**
RUATANIWHA INLET	BAY	40 40 172 41	**56**
RUATANIWHA INLET	BAY	40 40 172 41	**57**
RUATAPU	LOC	42 48 170 53	**68**
RUATEA STREAM	STRM	39 06 176 14	**39**
RUATITI	LOC	39 17 175 11	**36**
RUATITI STREAM	STRM	39 19 175 12	**36**
RUATO	LOC	38 04 176 26	**21**
RUATO	LOC	38 04 176 26	**22**
RUATO STREAM	STRM	35 23 173 38	**4**
RUATO STREAM	STRM	35 23 173 38	**6**
RUATO STREAM	STRM	37 56 176 18	**21**
RUATOKI NORTH	LOC	38 08 177 00	**22**
RUATOKI NORTH	LOC	38 08 177 00	**23**
RUATORIA	LOC	37 53 178 19	**25**
RUATUNA, LAKE	LAKE	37 56 175 17	**18**
RUATUNA, LAKE	LAKE	37 56 175 17	**19**
RUATUPAPAKU (TRIG)	HILL	38 15 177 03	**22**
RUATUPAPAKU (TRIG)	HILL	38 15 177 03	**30**
RUAWAHIA (TRIG)	MTN	38 14 176 30	**21**
RUAWAHIA (TRIG)	MTN	38 14 176 30	**22**
RUAWAHIA (TRIG)	MTN	38 14 176 30	**30**
RUAWAI	POPL	36 08 174 04	**7**
RUAWAIHIA (TRIG)	HILL	39 44 175 02	**45**
RUAWARO	LOC	37 32 175 02	**14**
RUAWHATA	LOC	40 23 175 50	**49**
RUBERSLAW (TRIG)	PEAK	42 42 171 24	**69**
RUBICON, LAKE	LAKE	43 18 171 50	**80**
RUBICON RIVER	STRM	43 19 171 54	**80**
RUBIESLAW CREEK	STRM	42 44 171 25	**69**
RUBY BAY	BAY	41 14 173 06	**58**
RUBY BAY	BAY	41 14 173 06	**59**
RUBY CREEK	STRM	45 37 169 22	**100**
RUBY ISLAND	ISLD	44 41 169 06	**90**
RUBY, LAKE	LAKE	42 42 171 22	**69**
RUERA CREEK	STRM	43 35 169 39	**76**
RUERA, MOUNT	MTN	44 06 168 59	**78**
RUERA RIVER	STRM	43 38 169 58	**76**
RUERA RIVER	STRM	43 38 169 58	**77**
RUERA RIVER	STRM	43 38 169 58	**79**
RUFFE CREEK	STRM	41 59 172 12	**64**
RUGGED ISLANDS	ISLS	46 42 167 43	**108**
RUGGED ISLANDS	ISLS	46 42 167 43	**114**
RUGGED MOUNTAIN (TRIG)	MTN	44 43 167 38	**94**
RUGGED PEAK	PEAK	44 47 167 32	**94**
RUGGEDY FLAT	FLAT	46 49 167 49	**114**
RUGGEDY MOUNTAINS	MTNS	46 47 167 44	**114**
RUHTRA STREAM	STRM	46 01 168 40	**110**
RUHTRA STREAM	STRM	46 01 168 40	**112**
RUKUHIA STATION	RSTN	37 52 175 17	**18**
RUKUHIA STATION	RSTN	37 52 175 17	**19**
RUKUWAI	LOC	35 45 174 28	**5**
RUKUWAI	LOC	35 45 174 28	**8**
RUM RIVER	STRM	45 16 167 07	**96**
RUMBLING BURN	STRM	44 33 169 03	**90**
RUNANGA	USAT	42 24 171 15	**68**
RUNANGA	USAT	42 24 171 15	**69**
RUNANGA, LAKE	LAKE	39 35 176 42	**42**
RUNANGA, LAKE	LAKE	39 35 176 42	**43**
RUNARUNA	LOC	35 19 173 21	**3**
RUNAWAY, CAPE	CAPE	37 32 177 59	**24**
RUNAWAY, CAPE	CAPE	37 32 177 59	**25**
RUNCIMAN	LOC	37 07 174 57	**12**
RUNCIMAN	LOC	37 07 174 57	**14**
RUNUNDER POINT	PNT	41 19 174 14	**54**
RUNUNDER POINT	PNT	41 19 174 14	**61**
RURIMA ISLAND	ISLD	37 50 176 52	**22**
RURIMA ISLAND	ISLD	37 50 176 52	**23**
RURU	LOC	42 35 171 30	**69**
RURU (TRIG)	HILL	37 48 175 34	**19**
RURUANGA STREAM	STRM	38 04 176 43	**21**
RURUANGA STREAM	STRM	38 04 176 43	**22**
RURUNUI (TRIG)	HILL	39 36 174 52	**35**
RURUNUI (TRIG)	HILL	39 36 174 52	**44**
RUSSEL, MOUNT	MTN	42 51 171 39	**70**
RUSSELL	POPL	35 16 174 07	**4**
RUSSELL	POPL	35 16 174 07	**5**
RUSSELL PEAK (TRIG)	PEAK	43 21 171 50	**80**
RUSSELL RANGE	MTNS	43 21 171 50	**80**
RUSSELLS FLAT	LOC	43 23 171 56	**80**
RUSSELLS FLAT	LOC	43 23 171 56	**81**
RUSSET BURN	STRM	45 52 167 10	**105**
RUTHERFORD PASS	PASS	43 38 170 21	**74**
RUTHERFORD PASS	PASS	43 38 170 21	**77**
RUTHERGLEN	LOC	42 32 171 11	**68**
RUTHERGLEN	LOC	42 32 171 11	**69**
RUTLAND, MOUNT	MTN	42 03 172 13	**64**
RUTLAND, MOUNT (TRIG)	PEAK	41 14 173 42	**60**
RYAL BUSH	LOC	46 16 168 20	**107**
RYAL BUSH	LOC	46 16 168 20	**109**
RYALL, MOUNT (TRIG)	MTN	42 16 171 22	**63**
RYAN PEAK	PEAK	43 34 169 55	**76**
RYANS CREEK	STRM	44 13 168 08	**88**
RYTON RIVER	STRM	43 17 171 32	**80**

S

SABINE RIVER	STRM	41 54 172 41	**65**
SABINE RIVER, EAST BRANCH	STRM	42 00 172 41	**65**
SABINE RIVER, WEST BRANCH	STRM	42 00 172 41	**65**
SADD, MOUNT (TRIG)	MTN	42 22 172 43	**71**
SADDLE BACK PEAK	PEAK	45 11 167 10	**96**
SADDLE CREEK	STRM	43 52 169 38	**76**
SADDLE CREEK	STRM	43 52 169 38	**79**
SADDLE CREEK	STRM	47 08 167 47	**114**
SADDLE HILL	HILL	41 52 173 54	**67**
SADDLE HILL	MTN	45 53 166 44	**104**
SADDLE HILL	HILL	45 46 168 05	**106**
SADDLE HILL	HILL	45 46 168 05	**107**
SADDLE HILL (TRIG)	HILL	43 48 172 52	**83**
SADDLE HILL (TRIG)	MTN	45 00 167 25	**94**
SADDLE HILL (TRIG)	MTN	45 00 167 25	**97**
SADDLE HILL (TRIG)	HILL	40 59 173 49	**54**
SADDLE HILL (TRIG)	PEAK	41 17 173 26	**59**
SADDLE HILL (TRIG)	HILL	40 59 173 49	**60**
SADDLE HILL (TRIG)	HILL	40 59 173 49	**61**
SADDLE HILL (TRIG)	MTN	45 00 167 25	**96**
SADDLE POINT	PNT	46 43 167 59	**108**
SADDLE POINT	PNT	46 43 167 59	**109**
SADDLE POINT	PNT	46 43 167 59	**115**
SADDLE ROCKS	ROCK	40 41 173 58	**61**
SADDLE STREAM	STRM	41 45 171 54	**63**
SADDLE STREAM	STRM	41 45 171 54	**64**
SADDLE STREAM	STRM	43 33 171 22	**75**
SADDLE STREAM	STRM	43 33 171 22	**80**
SADDLE STREAM	STRM	43 50 171 07	**87**
SADDLE (TRIG)	HILL	40 26 176 06	**49**
SADDS STREAM	STRM	42 25 172 41	**71**
SAFE COVE	BAY	45 01 167 52	**94**
SAFE COVE	BAY	45 01 167 52	**97**
SAFE COVE	BAY	45 01 167 52	**98**
SAIES	LOC	35 03 173 42	**4**
SAIL POINT	PNT	36 12 174 03	**7**
SAIL ROCK	ROCK	36 00 174 42	**8**
SAIL ROCK (TRIG)	HILL	42 57 173 13	**72**
SAIL ROCK (TRIG)	HILL	42 57 173 13	**73**
SAILORS CUTTING	LOC	44 33 170 05	**92**
SAINT ALBANS	SBRB	43 31 172 38	**82**
SAINT ALBANS	SBRB	43 31 172 38	**83**
SAINT ALBANS	SBRB	43 31 172 38	**85**
SAINT ANDREW, MOUNT (TRIG)	MTN	42 31 172 32	**71**
SAINT ANDREW STREAM	STRM	41 38 171 58	**62**
SAINT ANDREWS	LOC	44 32 171 11	**93**
SAINT ANNE POINT	PNT	44 34 167 47	**94**
SAINT ARNAUD	LOC	41 48 172 51	**65**
SAINT ARNAUD RANGE	MTNS	41 56 172 49	**65**
SAINT ARNAUD (TRIG)	MTN	41 49 172 54	**65**
SAINT BATHANS	LOC	44 52 169 48	**91**
SAINT BATHANS, MOUNT (TRIG)	MTN	44 44 169 46	**91**
SAINT BATHANS RANGE	MTNS	44 43 169 45	**91**
SAINT BERNARD (TRIG)	PEAK	42 08 173 26	**66**
SAINT CLAIR	SBRB	45 55 170 29	**103**
SAINT CUTHBERT, MOUNT (TRIG)	MTN	44 33 170 00	**92**
SAINT CUTHBERT RANGE	MTNS	44 35 170 01	**92**
SAINT GEORGE STREAM	STRM	41 38 171 59	**62**
SAINT HELIERS	SBRB	36 51 174 52	**11**
SAINT HELIERS	SBRB	36 51 174 52	**12**
SAINT JAMES	HSTD	42 27 172 48	**71**
SAINT JAMES	HSTD	42 27 172 48	**72**
SAINT JAMES RANGE	MTNS	42 20 172 43	**71**
SAINT JOHNS HILL	SBRB	39 55 175 02	**45**
SAINT JUST, MOUNT (TRIG)	MTN	44 49 168 47	**90**
SAINT JUST, MOUNT (TRIG)	MTN	44 49 168 47	**95**
SAINT KILDA	SBRB	45 54 170 30	**103**
SAINT LEONARDS	SBRB	39 38 176 50	**42**
SAINT LEONARDS	SBRB	39 38 176 50	**43**
SAINT LEONARDS	SBRB	45 51 170 34	**103**
SAINT MARY MOUNT	MTN	44 16 169 39	**79**
SAINT MARY (TRIG)	MTN	42 26 172 35	**71**
SAINT OMER	HSTD	41 11 173 58	**54**
SAINT OMER	LOC	41 11 173 57	**60**
SAINT OMER	HSTD	41 11 173 58	**61**
SAINT PATRICK, LAKE	LAKE	45 37 167 13	**105**
SAINT PATRICK, MOUNT (TRIG)	MTN	42 18 171 20	**63**
SAINT PATRICK, MOUNT (TRIG)	MTN	42 18 171 20	**69**
SAINT PATRICK, MOUNT (TRIG)	MTN	42 27 172 44	**71**
SAINT PATRICK STREAM	STRM	41 40 171 58	**64**
SAINT PATRICKS	LOC	45 48 168 31	**107**
SAINT PAUL (TRIG)	HILL	36 17 175 28	**9**
SAINT PAULS DOME	MTN	45 21 167 21	**96**
SAINT PAULS DOME	MTN	45 21 167 21	**97**
SAINT QUINTIN FALLS	FALL	44 50 167 48	**94**
SAINT RONANS STREAM	STRM	41 57 172 54	**65**
SAINT WINIFRED STREAM	STRM	43 25 170 41	**74**
SAINTS CREEK	STRM	44 57 167 50	**94**
SAINTS CREEK	STRM	44 57 167 50	**97**
SALAMIS	MTN	44 05 169 08	**78**
SALE, MOUNT (TRIG)	MTN	44 55 168 55	**90**
SALE, MOUNT (TRIG)	MTN	44 55 168 55	**95**
SALISBURY	LOC	44 26 171 13	**93**
SALISBURY	LOC	45 49 170 21	**103**
SALLY, LAKE	LAKE	42 52 171 40	**70**
SALMON CREEK	STRM	43 11 171 57	**81**
SALMOND, MOUNT (TRIG)	MTN	45 04 168 53	**95**
SALMOND, MOUNT (TRIG)	MTN	45 04 168 53	**99**
SALT LAKE	LAKE	45 35 170 05	**101**
SALTWATER CREEK	STRM	43 16 172 42	**82**
SALTWATER CREEK	LOC	43 16 172 42	**82**
SALTWATER CREEK	LOC	43 16 172 42	**83**
SALTWATER CREEK	STRM	43 16 172 42	**83**
SALTWATER LAGOON	LAGN	43 06 170 21	**74**
SALTWATER STREAM	STRM	41 40 173 14	**66**
SAM CREEK	STRM	41 00 172 49	**57**
SAM CREEK	STRM	41 00 172 49	**58**
SAM PEAK	PEAK	43 31 170 04	**76**
SAM PEAK	PEAK	43 31 170 04	**77**
SAMS CREEK	STRM	41 04 172 46	**57**
SAMS CREEK	STRM	41 04 172 46	**58**
SANATORIUM HILL	LOC	37 52 175 33	**19**
SAND HILL POINT	PNT	46 15 167 19	**105**
SAND HILL POINT	PNT	46 15 167 19	**108**
SANDFLY STREAM	STRM	41 50 172 56	**66**
SANDHILLS CREEK	STRM	40 40 172 24	**56**
SANDHILLS (TRIG)	HILL	34 37 172 54	**2**

SANDROCK BLUFF	CLIF	44 07 168 16	88
SANDSPIT	LOC	36 24 174 43	11
SANDSTONE CREEK	STRM	41 39 172 30	58
SANDSTONE CREEK	STRM	42 47 170 55	68
SANDSTONE STREAM	STRM	45 59 168 49	110
SANDSTONE (TRIG)	HILL	45 55 168 41	110
SANDY BAY	BAY	34 26 172 42	2
SANDY BAY	BAY	35 32 174 29	5
SANDY BAY	BAY	41 00 173 01	57
SANDY BAY	BAY	41 00 173 01	58
SANDY BAY	BAY	41 00 173 01	59
SANDY BAY	BAY	46 27 169 47	113
SANDY CREEK	STRM	45 41 169 08	110
SANDY KNOLLS	LOC	43 34 172 19	81
SANDY KNOLLS	LOC	43 34 172 19	85
SANDY KNOLLS (TRIG)	HILL	43 31 172 20	81
SANDY KNOLLS (TRIG)	HILL	43 31 172 20	85
SANDY PEAK (TRIG)	PEAK	41 14 172 27	56
SANDY PEAK (TRIG)	PEAK	41 14 172 27	62
SANDY POINT	PNT	46 30 168 18	109
SANDY SADDLE	SAD	42 20 173 34	66
SANDY SADDLE	SAD	42 20 173 34	73
SANDY STREAM	STRM	42 13 172 45	65
SANDYMOUNT	LOC	45 52 170 40	103
SANDYMOUNT (TRIG)	HILL	45 53 170 40	103
SANSON	POPL	40 13 175 25	45
SANSON	POPL	40 13 175 25	46
SANTOFT	LOC	40 09 175 14	45
SARA HILL (TRIG)	MTN	44 22 168 04	88
SARA HILL (TRIG)	MTN	44 22 168 04	89
SARAH, LAKE	LAKE	43 03 171 47	80
SARJEANT (TRIG)	HILL	39 54 175 16	45
SATURN CREEK	STRM	41 18 172 27	56
SATURN CREEK	STRM	41 18 172 27	62
SAUL (TRIG)	HILL	41 37 173 50	60
SAUL, MOUNT (TRIG)	PEAK	42 36 172 43	71
SAUNDERS, CAPE	CAPE	45 53 170 44	103
SAUNDERS, MOUNT (TRIG)	MTN	42 15 173 35	66
SAUVAGE POINT	PNT	40 57 173 46	61
SAVAGE BURN	STRM	44 44 168 37	90
SAVAGE BURN	STRM	44 44 168 37	95
SAVANNAH RANGE	MTNS	42 56 171 47	70
SAWDON STREAM	STRM	44 11 170 30	86
SAWYER BURN	STRM	44 27 169 16	91
SAWYERS BAY	SBRB	45 49 170 36	103
SAWYERS CREEK	STRM	42 12 171 48	63
SAWYERS CREEK	STRM	42 12 171 48	64
SAWYERS CREEK	STRM	42 28 171 12	68
SAWYERS CREEK	STRM	42 28 171 12	69
SAWYERS CREEK	STRM	42 23 173 27	72
SAWYERS CREEK	STRM	42 23 173 27	73
SAWYERS CREEK	STRM	44 16 169 50	79
SAXON RIVER	STRM	40 50 172 16	56
SAXTON PASS	PASS	42 04 173 13	66
SAXTON RIVER	STRM	42 06 173 09	66
SAXTON SADDLE	SAD	41 57 173 13	66
SAXTON (TRIG)	MTN	41 58 173 09	66
SCAMANDER STREAM	STRM	43 19 171 33	80
SCARBOROUGH	LOC	44 26 171 15	93
SCARCLIFFE	MTN	43 10 171 20	75
SCARCLIFFE	MTN	43 10 171 20	80
SCARFACE, MOUNT	MTN	42 50 171 48	70
SCARGILL	LOC	42 56 172 57	72
SCARGILL CREEK	STRM	42 56 172 57	71
SCARGILL CREEK	STRM	42 56 172 57	72
SCARLETT RANGE	MTNS	41 20 172 15	62
SCAW FELL	MTN	42 40 172 25	71
SCEPTRE PEAK	PEAK	43 21 170 40	74
SCHEHALLIEN, MOUNT	MTN	42 32 172 29	71
SCHOOL CREEK	STRM	42 48 172 53	71
SCHOOL CREEK	STRM	42 48 172 53	72
SCHOOLHOUSE CREEK	STRM	45 12 169 00	99
SCHOOLHOUSE FLAT	LOC	45 13 168 59	99
SCONE CREEK	STRM	43 23 170 34	74
SCONE CREEK	STRM	43 23 170 34	77
SCOTSBURN STREAM	STRM	43 58 171 16	87
SCOTSMAN VALLEY	LOC	37 47 175 29	19
SCOTT BURN	STRM	46 55 167 51	114
SCOTT CREEK	STRM	44 45 168 20	89
SCOTT CREEK	STRM	44 45 168 20	95
SCOTT, MOUNT	HILL	45 35 170 29	102
SCOTT, MOUNT (TRIG)	MTN	44 59 168 56	95
SCOTT, MOUNT (TRIG)	MTN	44 59 168 56	99
SCOTT, MOUNT (TRIG)	MTN	42 23 172 35	71
SCOTT PEAK	PEAK	43 41 170 00	76
SCOTT PEAK	PEAK	43 41 170 00	77
SCOTT PEAK	PEAK	43 41 170 00	79
SCOTT POINT	PNT	34 32 172 47	2
SCOTT POINT	PNT	41 08 174 13	54
SCOTT POINT	PNT	41 08 174 13	60
SCOTT POINT	PNT	41 08 174 13	61
SCOTT (TRIG)	HILL	39 14 174 58	36
SCOTTS GAP	LOC	46 03 167 55	106
SCOTTS GAP	LOC	46 03 167 55	107
SCOTTS KNOB	MTN	41 51 173 03	66
SCOTTY CREEK	STRM	42 01 172 11	64
SCOTTYS CREEK	STRM	42 48 171 29	69
SCOTTYS SADDLE	SAD	42 48 171 23	69
SCOUR STREAM	STRM	43 39 170 54	75
SCOUR STREAM	STRM	43 39 170 54	87
SCOUR STREAM	STRM	44 26 170 40	93
SCROGGS HILL	LOC	45 55 170 18	103
SCROGGS HILL (TRIG)	HILL	45 55 170 19	103
SCRUB BURN	STRM	45 20 170 15	101
SCRUB ROUGH CREEK	STRM	41 47 173 50	67
SCRUB (TRIG)	HILL	40 32 175 35	48
SCRUB (TRIG)	HILL	40 32 175 35	49
SCRUB (TRIG)	HILL	40 42 176 15	50
SCRUBBY FLAT CREEK	STRM	44 11 169 31	79
SCRUBBY GULLY	STRM	45 06 169 47	100
SCRUBBY GULLY	STRM	45 06 169 47	101
SCRUBBY HILL (TRIG)	HILL	46 32 169 10	112
SCRUBBY KNOWE	HILL	46 02 169 25	111
SCRUBBY KNOWE	HILL	46 02 169 25	113
SCUFFLE ISLAND	ISLD	40 47 173 49	54
SCUFFLE ISLAND	ISLD	40 47 173 49	61
SCULLY REEF	REEF	36 51 175 13	13
SEA VIEW PEAK	PEAK	45 47 167 02	105
SEA VIEW (TRIG)	HILL	40 57 176 00	49
SEA VIEW (TRIG)	HILL	40 57 176 00	51
SEABREEZE POINT	PNT	44 39 167 38	94
SEACLIFF	LOC	45 41 170 37	102
SEADOWN	LOC	44 18 171 17	87
SEADOWN (TRIG)	HILL	43 09 172 40	82
SEAFIELD	LOC	43 55 171 54	84
SEAFORD	LOC	40 35 172 41	57
SEAFORTH	LOC	44 20 171 16	87
SEAFORTH RIVER	STRM	45 37 166 58	105
SEAGROVE	LOC	37 06 174 47	12
SEAGROVE	LOC	37 06 174 47	14
SEAGULL HILL (TRIG)	HILL	44 59 170 00	92
SEAGULL HILL (TRIG)	HILL	44 59 170 00	101
SEAGULL LAKE	LAKE	43 31 171 15	75
SEAL COL	SAD	44 30 168 23	88
SEAL COL	SAD	44 30 168 23	89
SEAL CREEK	STRM	47 10 167 52	114
SEAL ISLAND	ISLD	42 02 171 22	63
SEAL ISLANDS	ISLS	45 47 166 29	104
SEAL POINT	PNT	47 11 167 50	114
SEAL ROCKS	ROCK	44 00 168 31	88
SEAL ROCKS	ROCK	46 45 168 36	115
SEALERS BAY	BAY	46 46 167 39	108
SEALERS BAY	BAY	46 46 167 39	114
SEALY, MOUNT	MTN	43 46 170 03	76
SEALY, MOUNT	MTN	43 46 170 03	77
SEALY, MOUNT	MTN	43 46 170 03	79
SEALY PASS	PASS	43 25 170 33	74
SEALY PASS	PASS	43 25 170 33	77
SEALY STREAM	STRM	44 22 168 20	88
SEALY STREAM	STRM	44 22 168 20	89
SEATOUN	SBRB	41 19 174 50	52
SEATOUN	SBRB	41 19 174 50	55
SEAVIEW	LOC	42 42 170 59	68
SEAWARD DOWNS	LOC	46 23 168 45	112
SEAWARD KAIKOURA RANGE	MTNS	42 15 173 34	66
SEAWARD RIVER	STRM	42 51 172 23	71
SEBASTOPOL, MOUNT (TRIG)	MTN	42 15 172 53	65
SEBASTOPOL (TRIG)	MTN	43 45 170 06	76
SEBASTOPOL (TRIG)	MTN	43 45 170 06	77
SEBASTOPOL (TRIG)	MTN	43 45 170 06	79
SEBASTOPOL (TRIG)	MTN	43 45 170 06	86
SECOND CREEK	STRM	43 50 170 13	77
SECOND CREEK	STRM	43 50 170 13	86
SECOND WATERFALL STREAM	STRM	43 40 170 38	86
SECRETARY ISLAND	ISLD	45 14 166 56	96
SEDDON	POPL	41 40 174 04	67
SEDDON COL	SAD	43 09 170 56	75
SEDDONVILLE	LOC	41 33 171 59	62
SEDGEMERE	LOC	43 50 172 19	85
SEDGEMERE, LAKE	LAKE	42 08 172 55	65
SEFTON	LOC	43 15 172 40	82
SEFTON	LOC	43 15 172 40	83
SEFTON, MOUNT	MTN	43 41 170 02	76
SEFTON, MOUNT	MTN	43 41 170 02	77
SEFTON, MOUNT	MTN	43 41 170 02	79
SEIGE GLACIER	GLCR	43 16 170 32	74
SELBOURNE, MOUNT	MTN	44 01 168 56	78
SELBOURNE RANGE	MTNS	44 06 168 55	78
SELBOURNE SPUR (TRIG)	HILL	44 01 168 51	78
SELFE, LAKE	LAKE	43 14 171 31	80
SELFE, MOUNT (TRIG)	MTN	42 50 172 30	71
SELWYN	LOC	37 55 175 51	19
SELWYN	LOC	37 55 175 51	20
SELWYN	LOC	43 39 172 15	81
SELWYN	LOC	43 39 172 15	85
SELWYN HUTS	BLDG	43 43 172 27	85
SELWYN, MOUNT (TRIG)	MTN	44 52 168 39	90
SELWYN, MOUNT (TRIG)	MTN	44 52 168 39	95
SELWYN RIVER	STRM	43 45 172 27	85
SELWYN RIVER (NORTH BRANCH)	STRM	43 20 171 49	80
SENTINEL PEAK	PEAK	44 24 169 14	91
SENTINEL ROCK	ROCK	36 05 174 36	8
SENTINEL ROCK	ROCK	40 53 174 08	54
SENTINEL ROCK	ROCK	40 53 174 08	61
SENTINEL ROCK	ROCK	40 53 174 08	61
SENTINEL, THE	MTN	44 12 168 57	78
SENTRY HILL	LOC	39 03 174 12	34
SEPARATION POINT	PNT	40 47 173 00	57
SEPARATION STREAM	STRM	43 30 170 30	74
SEPARATION STREAM	STRM	43 30 170 30	77
SERGEANTS HILL	LOC	41 46 171 39	63
SERGEANTS HILL	LOC	41 46 171 39	64
SERPENTINE CREEK	STRM	42 14 172 46	65
SERPENTINE CREEK	STRM	44 25 169 54	91
SERPENTINE CREEK	STRM	45 27 169 52	100
SERPENTINE CREEK	STRM	45 27 169 52	101
SERPENTINE RIVER	STRM	41 24 173 12	59
SERPENTINE SADDLE	SAD	44 39 168 10	89
SERPENTINE STREAM	STRM	45 10 170 50	102
SERPENTINE (TRIG)	HILL	41 20 173 12	59
SETON PEAK	PEAK	44 37 168 46	90
SETTLERS STREAM	STRM	37 00 175 37	13
SETTLERS STREAM	STRM	37 00 175 37	15
SETTLERS STREAM	STRM	37 00 175 37	16
SEVEN MILE CREEK	STRM	42 23 171 15	68
SEVEN MILE CREEK	STRM	42 23 171 15	69
SEVENTEEN MILE BLUFF	CLIF	42 17 171 18	63
SEVERN RIVER	STRM	42 08 173 03	66
SEVERN SADDLE	SAD	41 49 173 03	66
SEVERN (TRIG)	MTN	42 05 173 04	66
SEWELL PEAK (TRIG)	PEAK	42 24 171 21	69
SEXTON CREEK	STRM	38 37 176 15	29
SEYMOUR, MOUNT (TRIG)	MTN	42 18 172 45	65
SEYMOUR PEAK	PEAK	43 26 170 30	74
SEYMOUR PEAK	PEAK	43 26 170 30	77
SEYMOUR STREAM	STRM	42 13 173 24	66
SHAFTESBURY	LOC	37 37 175 47	19
SHAFTESBURY	LOC	37 37 175 47	20
SHAG HARBOUR	HARB	40 52 173 04	57
SHAG ISLANDS	ISLS	45 44 166 46	104
SHAG LAKE	LAKE	35 47 173 36	6
SHAG POINT	PNT	36 19 175 26	9
SHAG POINT	LOC	45 28 170 49	102
SHAG POINT	PNT	45 29 170 50	102
SHAG POINT	PNT	45 52 167 27	105
SHAG POINT	PNT	45 52 167 27	106
SHAG RIVER	STRM	45 29 170 49	102
SHAG RIVER	STRM	45 41 166 33	104
SHAG ROCK	CLIF	42 49 173 21	72
SHAG ROCK	CLIF	42 49 173 21	73
SHAG ROCK	ROCK	46 35 168 16	109
SHAG VALLEY	LOC	45 19 170 33	102
SHAGGY HILL (TRIG)	MTN	43 22 171 09	75
SHAGREE CREEK	STRM	46 14 170 00	111
SHAGREE CREEK	STRM	46 14 170 00	113
SHALE PEAK (TRIG)	PEAK	42 37 172 38	71
SHALLOW BEACH	BCH	45 29 167 36	97
SHALLOW CREEK	STRM	45 59 166 32	104
SHALLOW LAKE	LAKE	45 43 167 20	105
SHANNON	POPL	40 33 175 25	48
SHANNON	LOC	45 40 170 05	101
SHANTY CREEK	STRM	45 20 169 21	100
SHANTY TOWN	LOC	42 32 171 11	68
SHANTY TOWN	LOC	42 32 171 11	69
SHARK COVE	BAY	45 44 166 58	104
SHARK COVE	BAY	45 44 166 58	105
SHARK ISLAND	ISLD	46 50 167 43	114
SHARKS BAY CREEK	STRM	45 31 168 44	99
SHARKS HEAD	HEAD	40 36 172 29	56
SHARKS HEAD	HEAD	40 36 172 29	57
SHARPRIDGE CREEK	STRM	45 57 167 52	106
SHATTERED PEAK	PEAK	43 54 169 27	76
SHATTERED PEAK	PEAK	43 54 169 27	78
SHATTERED PEAK	PEAK	43 54 169 27	79
SHAW STREAM	STRM	42 10 172 02	64
SHEARER CREEK	STRM	42 57 170 47	68
SHEARER SWAMP	SWMP	42 55 170 45	68
SHEEPSKIN CREEK	STRM	44 45 169 18	91
SHEEPWASH CREEK	STRM	45 32 170 09	101
SHEEPWASH CREEK	STRM	45 53 168 07	106
SHEEPWASH CREEK	STRM	45 53 168 07	107
SHEEPWASH CREEK	STRM	45 39 168 39	107
SHEERDOWN PEAK	PEAK	44 42 167 56	89
SHEERDOWN PEAK	PEAK	44 42 167 56	94
SHEFFIELD	LOC	43 23 172 01	81
SHEFFIELD	LOC	43 23 172 01	85
SHELIA, LAKE	LAKE	46 50 167 50	109
SHELIA, LAKE	LAKE	46 50 167 50	114
SHELL BAY	BAY	43 50 173 05	83
SHELLY BEACH	LOC	36 34 174 23	10
SHELLY BEACH	LOC	36 34 174 23	11
SHELTER ISLAND	ISLD	45 16 166 53	96
SHELTER POINT	PNT	47 06 168 13	115
SHENANDOAH	LOC	41 52 172 15	64
SHENANDOAH RIVER	STRM	41 59 172 12	64
SHENANDOAH SADDLE	SAD	42 01 172 15	64
SHEPHERD SADDLE	SAD	45 26 168 24	98
SHEPHERDS CREEK	STRM	44 55 169 46	91
SHEPHERDS CREEK	STRM	44 53 169 24	91
SHEPHERDS CREEK	STRM	44 27 170 12	92
SHEPHERDS CREEK	STRM	45 05 169 10	99
SHEPHERDS CREEK	STRM	45 09 169 44	100
SHEPHERDS CREEK	STRM	45 09 169 44	101
SHEPHERDS HUT CREEK	STRM	45 33 169 55	100
SHEPHERDS HUT CREEK	STRM	45 33 169 55	101
SHEPHERDS HUT CREEK	STRM	45 12 170 09	101
SHEPHERDS PASS	PASS	44 36 168 25	88
SHEPHERDS PASS	PASS	44 36 168 25	89
SHEPPARD, LAKE	LAKE	42 46 172 15	70
SHEPPARD (TRIG)	HILL	43 43 172 36	83
SHEPPARD (TRIG)	HILL	43 43 172 36	85
SHERENDEN	LOC	39 30 176 35	39
SHERENDEN	LOC	39 30 176 35	40
SHERENDEN	LOC	39 30 176 35	42
SHERIDAN CREEK	STRM	40 53 175 13	48
SHERRY RIVER	STRM	41 22 172 44	58
SHERWOOD	HSTD	42 32 173 04	72
SHERWOOD	LOC	43 45 171 49	84
SHERWOOD DOWNS	LOC	43 58 170 52	87
SHERWOOD RISE	LOC	35 45 174 22	5
SHERWOOD RISE	LOC	35 45 174 22	7
SHERWOOD RISE	LOC	35 45 174 22	8
SHEWELL, MOUNT	HILL	41 01 173 51	54
SHEWELL, MOUNT	HILL	41 01 173 51	60
SHEWELL, MOUNT	HILL	41 01 173 51	61
SHIEL BURN	STRM	44 42 168 43	90
SHIELS PEAK	PEAK	43 37 169 57	76
SHIELS PEAK	PEAK	43 37 169 57	77
SHIFTON STREAM	STRM	43 12 172 05	81
SHIN RIVER	STRM	41 54 173 40	67
SHINGLE CREEK	STRM	42 09 172 13	64
SHINGLE CREEK	LOC	45 25 169 17	100
SHINGLE CREEK	STRM	45 25 169 19	100
SHINGLE HILL (TRIG)	MTN	43 25 171 26	75
SHINGLE HILL (TRIG)	MTN	44 09 169 47	79
SHINGLE HILL (TRIG)	MTN	43 25 171 26	80
SHINGLE PEAK (TRIG)	PEAK	41 57 173 21	60
SHINGLE TOP	MTN	43 59 169 33	79
SHINGLEY STREAM	STRM	41 47 173 23	66
SHIP COVE	BAY	41 06 174 15	54
SHIP COVE	BAY	41 06 174 15	60
SHIP COVE	BAY	41 06 174 15	61
SHIP CREEK	STRM	43 45 169 09	78
SHIPWREAK BAY	BAY	35 11 173 07	3
SHIRLEY	SBRB	43 30 172 39	82
SHIRLEY	SBRB	43 30 172 39	83
SHIRLEY	SBRB	43 30 172 39	85
SHIRLEY, LAKE	LAKE	45 04 167 15	94
SHIRLEY, LAKE	LAKE	45 04 167 15	96
SHOAL BAY	BAY	36 49 174 46	11
SHOAL BAY	BAY	36 49 174 46	12
SHOE ISLAND	ISLD	37 00 175 55	16
SHOE ISLAND	ISLD	37 00 175 55	17
SHOE (TRIG)	HILL	37 00 175 55	16
SHOE (TRIG	HILL	37 00 175 55	17
SHORT BURN	STRM	45 12 168 42	95
SHORT BURN	STRM	45 12 168 42	99
SHORT SPUR CREEK	STRM	44 42 169 30	91
SHOTOVER RIVER	STRM	45 01 168 46	90
SHOTOVER RIVER	STRM	45 01 168 46	95
SHOTOVER RIVER	STRM	45 01 168 46	99
SHOTOVER SADDLE	SAD	44 31 168 41	88
SHOTOVER SADDLE	SAD	44 31 168 41	90
SHRIMPTON MOUNT	MTN	44 15 169 17	78
SHRIVES, MOUNT	MTN	44 41 170 55	93
SHY LAKE	LAKE	45 36 166 53	104
SIBBALD, MOUNT	MTN	43 33 170 33	74
SIBBALD, MOUNT	MTN	43 33 170 33	77
SIBBALD RANGE	MTNS	43 35 170 34	74
SIBBALD RANGE	MTNS	43 35 170 34	77
SIBERIA SADDLE	SAD	44 07 169 02	78
SIBERIA STREAM	STRM	41 53 173 04	66
SIBERIA STREAM	STRM	44 14 169 02	78
SIDEY STREAM	STRM	45 38 170 15	101
SIERRA RANGE, THE	MTNS	43 40 169 59	76
SIERRA RANGE, THE	MTNS	43 40 169 59	77
SIERRA RANGE, THE	MTNS	43 40 169 59	79
SILCOCK CREEK	STRM	42 02 172 02	64
SILVER BROOK	STRM	42 44 172 33	71
SILVER BURN	STRM	44 27 169 22	91
SILVER CREEK	STRM	44 28 170 02	92
SILVER ISLAND	ISLD	44 27 169 21	91
SILVER PEAK (TRIG)	PEAK	43 00 170 47	74
SILVER PEAK (TRIG)	HILL	45 45 170 27	103
SILVER RANGE	MTNS	39 52 176 49	42
SILVER RANGE	MTNS	39 52 176 49	43
SILVER STREAM	STRM	42 57 172 41	71
SILVER STREAM	STRM	45 51 170 24	103
SILVERDALE	LOC	36 37 174 41	11
SILVERDALE	LOC	36 37 174 41	12
SILVERHOPE	LOC	39 58 175 32	45
SILVERHOPE	LOC	39 58 175 32	46
SILVERHORN (TRIG)	MTN	44 50 168 37	95
SILVERHORN (TRIG)	MTN	44 50 168 37	90
SILVERMINE CREEK	STRM	41 16 172 28	56
SILVERMINE CREEK	STRM	41 16 172 28	62
SILVERSTREAM	SBRB	41 09 175 01	52
SILVERSTREAM	SBRB	41 09 175 01	55
SILVERSTREAM	STRM	41 48 173 07	66
SIMCOX	TRIG	40 43 175 10	48
SIMLA (TRIG)	HILL	36 55 174 31	10
SIMLA (TRIG)	HILL	36 55 174 31	11
SIMLA (TRIG)	HILL	36 55 174 31	12
SIMMOND'S ISLAND	ISLD	34 45 173 09	3
SIMONIN PASS	PASS	44 21 168 22	88
SIMONIN PASS	PASS	44 21 168 22	89
SIMPSON ROCK	ROCK	36 00 175 07	9
SINBAD GULLY	STRM	44 40 167 54	89
SINBAD GULLY	STRM	44 40 167 54	94
SINBADS MISTAKE	BAY	47 03 168 12	115
SINCLAIR CREEK	STRM	41 32 172 12	62
SINCLAIR HEAD	HEAD	41 22 174 43	52
SINCLAIR HEAD	HEAD	41 22 174 43	55
SINCLAIR, MOUNT	MTN	43 39 170 49	75
SINCLAIR, MOUNT	MTN	43 48 169 56	76
SINCLAIR, MOUNT	MTN	43 48 169 56	79
SINCLAIR, MOUNT (TRIG)	HILL	43 43 172 52	83
SINCLAIR RANGE	MTNS	43 41 170 49	87
SINCLAIR RIVER	STRM	43 25 170 49	75
SINCLAIRS CASTLE	CLIF	41 51 171 43	63
SINCLAIRS CASTLE	CLIF	41 51 171 43	64
SIR WILLIAMS PEAK	PEAK	44 36 168 24	88
SIR WILLIAMS PEAK	PEAK	44 36 168 24	89
SIRDAR CREEK	STRM	41 59 171 30	63
SISTER PEAKS (TRIG)	HILL	45 20 170 22	101
SISTER PEAKS (TRIG)	HILL	45 20 170 22	102
SISTERS STREAM	STRM	42 47 172 19	71
SISTERS, THE	ISLD	46 38 169 15	112
SISTERS, THE	ISLD	46 38 169 15	113
SISTERS, THE	ISLS	47 11 167 47	114
SISTERS, THE (TRIG)	HILL	45 29 170 14	101
SISYPHUS PEAK	PEAK	44 23 168 50	90
SIX MILE	LOC	41 53 172 20	65
SIX MILE CREEK	STRM	41 27 171 59	62
SIX MILE CREEK	STRM	41 53 172 19	65
SIX MILE CREEK	STRM	41 55 172 55	65
SIX MILE CREEK	STRM	45 21 170 15	101
SIX MILE CREEK	STRM	45 28 170 10	101
SIX MILE STREAM	STRM	41 44 173 02	66
SIXTEEN MILE CREEK	STRM	44 40 168 39	90
SKEDADDLE, MOUNT	MTN	42 41 172 31	71
SKEET RIVER	STRM	41 19 172 42	58
SKEET SADDLE	SAD	41 21 172 35	58
SKELMORLIE PEAK	PEAK	44 57 167 58	94
SKELMORLIE PEAK	PEAK	44 57 167 58	97
SKELMORLIE PEAK	PEAK	44 57 167 58	98
SKIDDAW, MOUNT (TRIG)	MTN	42 40 172 27	71
SKIDDAW STREAM	STRM	42 37 172 30	71
SKIFFINGTON SWAMP	SWMP	43 26 170 00	76
SKIFFINGTON SWAMP	SWMP	43 26 170 00	77
SKINNERS HILL (TRIG)	HILL	39 00 174 45	35
SKIPPERS	LOC	44 51 168 41	90
SKIPPERS	LOC	44 51 168 41	95
SKIPPERS CREEK	STRM	44 51 168 42	90
SKIPPERS CREEK	STRM	44 51 168 42	95
SKIPPERS RANGE	MTNS	44 27 168 08	88
SKIPPERS RANGE	MTNS	44 27 168 08	89
SKIPPERS SADDLE	SAD	44 57 168 42	90
SKIPPERS SADDLE	SAD	44 57 168 42	95
SKULL CREEK	STRM	35 49 174 23	7
SKULL CREEK	STRM	35 49 174 23	8
SLAB HUT CREEK	STRM	42 10 171 45	63
SLAB HUT CREEK	STRM	42 10 171 45	64
SLAPJACK SADDLE	SAD	45 05 169 04	99
SLATE CREEK	STRM	44 19 168 34	88
SLATE CREEK	STRM	44 19 168 34	90
SLATE RANGE	MTNS	40 52 172 18	56
SLATE RANGE	MTNS	45 32 168 38	99
SLATE RIVER	STRM	40 46 172 37	56
SLATE RIVER	STRM	40 46 172 37	57
SLATE RIVER PEAK	HILL	40 54 172 37	56
SLATE RIVER PEAK	HILL	40 54 172 37	57
SLATY CREEK	STRM	40 41 172 26	56
SLATY CREEK	STRM	40 41 172 26	57
SLATY CREEK	STRM	42 16 171 32	63
SLATY CREEK	STRM	42 38 171 33	69
SLATY CREEK	LOC	42 19 171 31	69
SLATY PEAK	PEAK	41 29 173 16	59
SLIP BAY	BAY	42 52 171 09	68
SLIP BAY	BAY	42 52 171 09	69
SLIP (TRIG)	HILL	39 46 176 03	47
SLIPPER ISLAND	ISLD	37 03 175 57	16
SLIPPER ISLAND	ISLD	37 03 175 57	17
SLIPPER LAKE	LAKE	36 11 174 38	8
SLIPPERY CREEK	STRM	41 15 172 30	56
SLIPPERY CREEK	STRM	41 15 172 30	58
SLIPPERY CREEK	STRM	41 28 172 43	58
SLIPS (TRIG)	HILL	41 45 172 47	65
SLOPE POINT	PNT	46 41 169 00	112
SLOPE POINT	LOC	46 40 169 00	112
SLOVENS STREAM	STRM	43 12 171 53	80
SLY BURN	STRM	44 59 168 16	95
SLY BURN	STRM	44 59 168 16	98
SMALL CRAFT HARBOUR ISLAND	ISLS	45 58 166 39	104
SMART CREEK	STRM	42 44 171 18	69
SMART, MOUNT	MTN	42 42 171 19	69
SMEDLEY	HSTD	39 47 176 20	47
SMITE PEAK	MTN	43 21 171 14	75
SMITE RIVER	STRM	43 26 171 11	75
SMITH, MOUNT (TRIG)	MTN	43 51 169 14	78
SMITH PEAK	PEAK	43 16 170 38	74
SMITH STREAM	STRM	39 50 176 14	47
SMITH (TRIG)	HILL	41 16 173 32	59
SMITHFIELD	LOC	44 22 171 15	93
SMITHS CREEK	STRM	44 34 169 33	91
SMITHS LOOKOUT	HILL	47 14 167 32	114
SMITHS PONDS	LAKE	44 08 168 31	88
SMITHS RIDGE (TRIG)	HILL	40 41 175 40	48
SMITHS RIDGE (TRIG)	HILL	40 41 175 40	49
SMITHY CREEK	STRM	44 58 168 01	97
SMITHY CREEK	STRM	44 58 168 01	98
SMOKY CREEK	STRM	46 42 167 50	108
SMOKY CREEK	STRM	46 42 167 50	109
SMOKY CREEK	STRM	46 42 167 50	114
SMOOTH PEAK (TRIG)	PEAK	45 20 168 16	95
SMOOTH PEAK (TRIG)	PEAK	45 20 168 16	98
SMOOTH POINT	PNT	47 12 167 43	114
SMOOTHWATER BAY	BAY	43 58 168 35	88
SMOOTHWATER POINT	PNT	43 58 168 35	88
SMOOTHWATER RIVER	STRM	43 58 168 35	88
SMUGGLERS BAY	BAY	35 52 174 32	8
SMYTH RANGE	MTNS	43 11 170 45	74
SNAG BAY	BAY	44 24 169 08	90
SNAG BURN	STRM	45 11 167 39	97
SNAKE POINT	PNT	41 12 174 10	54
SNAKE POINT	PNT	41 12 174 10	60
SNAKE POINT	PNT	41 12 174 10	61
SNAPPER KNOLL	HILL	36 04 174 21	7
SNAPPER KNOLL	HILL	36 04 174 21	8
SNELLS BEACH	LOC	36 25 174 44	11
SNOW CREEK	STRM	42 21 171 57	70

SNOW RIVER	STRM	40 50 172 37	56
SNOW RIVER	STRM	40 50 172 37	57
SNOW RIVER	STRM	44 13 170 27	86
SNOW WHITE CREEK	STRM	45 38 167 30	105
SNOW WHITE CREEK	STRM	45 38 167 30	106
SNOW WHITE GLACIER	GLCR	44 26 168 35	88
SNOW WHITE GLACIER	GLCR	44 26 168 35	90
SNOWBALL SADDLE	SAD	44 27 168 33	88
SNOWBALL SADDLE	SAD	44 27 168 33	89
SNOWBALL SADDLE	SAD	44 27 168 33	90
SNOWDEN PEAK	PEAK	45 17 168 03	97
SNOWDEN PEAK	PEAK	45 17 168 03	98
SNOWDEN RANGE	MTNS	41 02 172 36	56
SNOWDEN RANGE	MTNS	41 02 172 36	57
SNOWDEN RANGE	MTNS	41 02 172 36	58
SNOWDEN (TRIG)	HILL	40 48 175 43	49
SNOWDEN (TRIG)	HILL	40 48 175 43	51
SNOWDRIFT SADDLE	SAD	44 28 168 31	88
SNOWDRIFT SADDLE	SAD	44 28 168 31	89
SNOWFLAKE	MTN	42 17 173 32	66
SNOWFLAKE STREAM	STRM	42 19 173 34	66
SNOWY CREEK	STRM	44 31 168 33	88
SNOWY CREEK	STRM	44 31 168 33	90
SNOWY GORGE CREEK	STRM	44 19 169 40	79
SNOWY PEAK	PEAK	44 39 168 45	90
SNOWY RIVER	STRM	42 15 171 41	63
SNOWY RIVER	STRM	42 15 171 41	64
SNOWY STREAM	STRM	42 09 173 37	67
SNOWY STREAM	STRM	43 27 171 29	80
SNOWY TOP	PEAK	44 24 169 46	91
SNUFFLE NOSE	PNT	43 53 172 50	83
SOAKER, MOUNT	MTN	45 23 167 15	96
SOCKBURN	SBRB	43 33 172 33	82
SOCKBURN	SBRB	43 33 172 33	83
SOCKBURN	SBRB	43 33 172 33	85
SOHO CREEK	STRM	44 49 168 53	90
SOHO CREEK	STRM	44 49 168 53	95
SOHO, MOUNT	MTN	44 52 168 52	90
SOHO, MOUNT	MTN	44 52 168 52	95
SOLANDER ISLAND	ISLD	46 35 166 54	108
SOLITARY CONE	PEAK	45 24 167 08	96
SOLITARY, MOUNT	MTN	45 44 167 00	104
SOLITARY, MOUNT	MTN	45 44 167 00	105
SOLOMON ISLAND	ISLD	47 13 167 26	114
SOLOMONS THRONE (TRIG)	HILL	42 38 173 13	72
SOLOMONS THRONE (TRIG)	HILL	42 38 173 13	73
SOLUTION COL	SAD	44 27 168 22	88
SOLUTION COL	SAD	44 27 168 22	89
SOLUTION, MOUNT	MTN	43 54 169 39	76
SOLUTION, MOUNT	MTN	43 54 169 39	79
SOLUTION RANGE	MTNS	43 54 169 39	76
SOLUTION RANGE	MTNS	43 54 169 39	79
SOLWAY STATION	RSTN	40 57 175 37	48
SOLWAY STATION	RSTN	40 57 175 37	49
SOLWAY STATION	RSTN	40 57 175 37	51
SOLWAY STATION	RSTN	40 57 175 37	53
SOMERS, MOUNT	LOC	43 42 171 24	84
SOMERS, MOUNT	LOC	43 42 171 24	87
SOMERS, MOUNT (TRIG)	MTN	43 37 171 23	75
SOMERS, MOUNT (TRIG)	MTN	43 37 171 23	80
SOMERS, MOUNT (TRIG)	MTN	43 37 171 23	84
SOMERTON	LOC	43 46 171 55	84
SOMES ISLAND	ISLD	41 15 174 53	52
SOMES ISLAND	ISLD	41 15 174 53	55
SOMNUS	MTN	44 40 168 13	89
SONORA CREEK	STRM	45 06 169 17	100
SOUCIS, CAPE	CAPE	41 03 173 36	59
SOUTER PEAK	PEAK	44 04 168 58	78
SOUTERS CREEK	STRM	42 29 171 35	69
SOUTH ARM	BAY	45 31 167 26	97
SOUTH ARM	BAY	47 13 167 38	114
SOUTH ARM (PORT HARDY)	BAY	40 48 173 52	54
SOUTH ARM (PORT HARDY)	BAY	40 48 173 52	61
SOUTH BAXTON BURN	STRM	45 42 168 07	106
SOUTH BAXTON BURN	STRM	45 42 168 07	107
SOUTH BAY	BAY	42 26 173 41	73
SOUTH BAY	LOC	42 25 173 41	73
SOUTH BEACH	LOC	42 29 171 11	68
SOUTH BEACH	LOC	42 29 171 11	69
SOUTH BRANCH HUXLEY RIVER	STRM	44 01 169 45	79
SOUTH BRANCH NERGER CREEK	STRM	43 55 168 58	78
SOUTH BRANCH TEMPLE STREAM	STRM	44 07 169 49	79
SOUTH BRANCH YOUNG RIVER	STRM	44 11 169 09	78
SOUTH BRAXTON	MTN	45 42 168 01	106
SOUTH BRAXTON	MTN	45 42 168 01	107
SOUTH CAPE	CAPE	47 17 167 32	114
SOUTH CASTOR PEAK (TRIG)	HILL	41 08 173 35	59
SOUTH COVE	BAY	36 27 174 50	11
SOUTH DEAN	HILL	43 03 172 38	82
SOUTH FIORD	FIOR	45 21 167 41	97
SOUTH HEAD	HEAD	35 32 173 22	6
SOUTH HEAD	LOC	36 28 174 15	10
SOUTH HEAD	HEAD	36 26 174 14	10
SOUTH HEAD	HEAD	37 03 174 31	12
SOUTH HEAD	HEAD	40 55 173 03	57
SOUTH HEAD	HEAD	43 49 173 06	83
SOUTH HEAD CONE	PEAK	40 35 172 32	57
SOUTH HILLEND	LOC	46 03 168 14	107
SOUTH ISLET	ISLD	46 48 168 30	109
SOUTH ISLET	ISLD	46 48 168 30	115
SOUTH JURY (TRIG)	HILL	41 08 175 31	53
SOUTH MALVERN	LOC	43 28 171 54	80
SOUTH MALVERN	LOC	43 28 171 54	81
SOUTH MATHIAS RIVER	STRM	43 10 171 05	75
SOUTH MAVORA LAKE	LAKE	45 18 168 10	98
SOUTH OPUHA RIVER	STRM	43 58 170 45	86
SOUTH OPUHA RIVER	STRM	44 00 170 53	87
SOUTH PEAK	PEAK	43 23 170 57	75
SOUTH POINT	PNT	45 49 166 32	104
SOUTH POINT	PNT	46 48 168 30	109
SOUTH POINT	PNT	46 48 168 30	115
SOUTH PORT	HARB	46 02 166 36	104
SOUTH RED HEAD POINT	PNT	47 05 167 33	114
SOUTH ROUGH RIDGE HILL (TRIG)	MTN	45 24 169 46	100
SOUTH ROUGH RIDGE HILL (TRIG)	MTN	45 24 169 46	101
SOUTH TRAP	ROCK	47 33 168 52	115
SOUTH WEST ARM	BAY	44 59 167 24	96
SOUTH WEST ARM	BAY	46 56 167 58	114
SOUTH WEST ARM	BAY	46 56 167 58	115
SOUTH WEST CAPE	CAPE	47 17 167 27	114
SOUTH WEST ISLAND	ISLD	34 11 172 04	2
SOUTH WEST POINT	PNT	45 14 166 52	96
SOUTHBRIDGE	LOC	43 49 172 15	85
SOUTHBROOK	LOC	43 20 172 36	82
SOUTHBROOK	LOC	43 20 172 36	83
SOUTHBROOK	LOC	43 20 172 36	85
SOUTHBURN	LOC	44 27 171 06	93
SOUTHBURN CREEK	STRM	44 30 171 11	93
SOUTHERN ALPS	MTNS	42 43 171 54	70
SOUTHERN ALPS	MTNS	43 07 171 13	75
SOUTHERN WAIOTAURU	STRM	40 55 175 12	48
SOUTHERN WAIOTAURU	STRM	40 55 175 12	52
SOUTHERN WAIOTAURU	STRM	40 55 175 12	55
SOUTHEY, MOUNT	MTN	42 12 172 45	65
SOUTHSHORE	LOC	43 33 172 45	82
SOUTHSHORE	LOC	43 33 172 45	83
SOUTRA HILL (TRIG)	MTN	45 32 169 50	100
SOUTRA HILL (TRIG)	MTN	45 32 169 50	101
SOW BURN	STRM	45 22 170 03	101
SPAIN CREEK	STRM	45 04 169 45	100
SPAIN CREEK	STRM	45 04 169 45	101
SPAR BUSH	LOC	46 15 168 15	107
SPAR BUSH	LOC	46 15 168 15	109
SPARRMAN, MOUNT	MTN	45 48 166 38	104
SPEARGRASS CREEK	STRM	41 46 172 46	65
SPEARGRASS FLAT	LOC	44 58 168 46	95
SPEARGRASS FLAT	LOC	44 58 168 46	99
SPEARGRASS HOMESTEAD	HSTD	41 48 172 47	65
SPECIMEN CREEK	STRM	41 33 172 09	62
SPECTACLE LAKE	LAKE	36 11 174 38	8
SPECULATION HILL	MTN	43 14 170 41	74
SPENCE BURN	STRM	45 42 167 57	106
SPENCE, MOUNT	MTN	43 46 169 58	76
SPENCE, MOUNT	MTN	43 46 169 58	77
SPENCE, MOUNT	MTN	43 46 169 58	79
SPENCE PEAK	PEAK	45 43 167 51	106
SPENCER GLACIER	GLCR	43 28 170 17	74
SPENCER GLACIER	GLCR	43 28 170 17	77
SPENCER MOUNT	MTN	43 25 170 14	74
SPENCER MOUNT	MTN	43 25 170 14	77
SPENCERVILLE	LOC	43 26 172 42	82
SPENCERVILLE	LOC	43 26 172 42	83
SPENCERVILLE	LOC	43 26 172 42	85
SPENSER MOUNTAINS	MTNS	42 13 172 34	65
SPEY RIVER	STRM	40 59 172 27	56
SPEY RIVER	STRM	40 59 172 27	62
SPEY RIVER	STRM	45 32 167 17	96
SPEY STREAM	STRM	42 33 173 20	72
SPEY STREAM	STRM	42 33 173 20	73
SPHINX, LAKE	LAKE	45 50 167 05	105
SPHINX SADDLE	SAD	43 02 171 28	75
SPHINX SADDLE	SAD	43 02 171 28	80
SPHINX (TRIG)	HILL	41 48 172 16	64
SPIDER LAKES	LAKE	43 37 171 07	75
SPIDER WEB	MTN	42 41 172 30	71
SPIKE	MTN	44 19 168 44	88
SPIKE	MTN	44 19 168 44	90
SPILLERS HILL (TRIG)	MTN	45 33 169 46	100
SPILLERS HILL (TRIG)	MTN	45 33 169 46	101
SPIRE PEAK	PEAK	45 24 167 27	97
SPIRIT BURN	STRM	45 54 168 22	107
SPIRITS BAY	BAY	34 26 172 48	2
SPLIT HILL (TRIG)	HILL	45 31 170 14	101
SPLIT PEAKS	PEAK	43 36 170 44	74
SPONGE SWAMP	SWMP	44 02 168 45	88
SPOON RIVER	STRM	44 09 168 15	88
SPOT HILL	MTN	45 00 167 19	96
SPOT (TRIG)	HILL	40 49 175 44	49
SPOT (TRIG)	HILL	40 49 175 44	51
SPOTSWOOD	SBRB	39 04 174 02	34
SPOTSWOOD	LOC	42 44 173 16	72
SPOTSWOOD	LOC	42 44 173 16	73
SPOTTS CREEK	STRM	44 47 169 05	90
SPRAY RIVER	STRM	41 44 173 28	66
SPRAY STREAM	STRM	42 11 173 28	66
SPREYDON	SBRB	43 33 172 37	82
SPREYDON	SBRB	43 33 172 37	83
SPREYDON	SBRB	43 33 172 37	85
SPRING CREEK	POPL	41 27 173 58	54
SPRING CREEK	POPL	41 27 173 58	60
SPRING GROVE	LOC	41 23 173 05	58
SPRING GROVE	LOC	41 23 173 05	59
SPRING GROVE	HSTD	42 56 172 53	71
SPRING GROVE	HSTD	42 56 172 53	72
SPRING GULLY	STRM	45 04 171 01	102
SPRING HILL (TRIG)	MTN	43 02 172 14	81
SPRING HILL (TRIG)	HILL	40 40 176 01	49
SPRINGBANK	LOC	43 19 172 26	81
SPRINGBANK	LOC	43 19 172 26	85
SPRINGBROOK	LOC	44 30 171 11	93
SPRINGBURN	LOC	43 40 171 28	75
SPRINGBURN	LOC	43 40 171 28	80
SPRINGBURN	LOC	43 40 171 28	84
SPRINGBURN	LOC	43 40 171 28	87
SPRINGDALE	LOC	37 32 175 34	15
SPRINGFIELD	LOC	35 53 174 20	7
SPRINGFIELD	LOC	35 53 174 20	8
SPRINGFIELD	LOC	43 20 171 56	80
SPRINGFIELD	LOC	43 20 171 56	81
SPRINGHILL	LOC	39 52 176 23	47
SPRINGHILLS	LOC	46 11 168 29	107
SPRINGS FLAT	LOC	35 40 174 19	5
SPRINGS FLAT	LOC	35 40 174 19	7
SPRINGS FLAT	LOC	35 40 174 19	8
SPRINGS JUNCTION	LOC	42 20 172 11	64
SPRINGS JUNCTION	LOC	42 20 172 11	70
SPRINGSTON	LOC	43 38 172 25	81
SPRINGSTON	LOC	43 39 172 26	85
SPRINGSTON SOUTH	LOC	43 41 172 26	81
SPRINGSTON SOUTH	LOC	43 41 172 26	85
SPRINGVALE	LOC	45 12 169 26	100
SPRINGVALE	HSTD	46 21 169 39	113
SPURS, THE	MTN	43 09 171 28	75
SPURS, THE	MTN	43 09 171 28	80
SPURTELTON CREEK	STRM	43 00 172 50	71
SPURTELTON CREEK	STRM	43 00 172 50	72
SPY GLASS POINT	PNT	42 33 173 31	73
SPYE	LOC	43 00 172 54	71
SPYE	LOC	43 00 172 54	72
SPYE	LOC	43 00 172 54	82
SPYLAW BURN	STRM	45 46 169 09	110
SPYLAW HILL (TRIG)	HILL	45 45 169 26	111
SQUALLY COVE	BAY	41 03 173 44	60
SQUARE TOP	MTN	45 53 166 45	104
SQUARE TOP ISLAND	ISLD	36 28 175 24	9
SQUARE TOP ISLAND	ISLD	36 28 175 24	16
STACE CREEK	STRM	41 21 174 04	54
STACE CREEK	STRM	41 21 174 04	60
STACK, THE	MTN	44 44 169 02	90
STAFFA ROCK	ROCK	34 48 173 19	3
STAFFORD	LOC	42 40 171 05	68
STAFFORD	LOC	42 40 171 05	69
STAFFORD BAY	BAY	43 59 168 33	88
STAFFORD CREEK	STRM	41 38 174 07	60
STAFFORD, MOUNT	MTN	44 14 169 41	79
STAFFORD RANGE	MTNS	44 03 168 36	88
STAFFORD RIVER	STRM	43 59 168 33	88
STAG HILL	MTN	43 07 171 38	80
STAG HILL	HILL	45 24 170 22	101
STAG HILL	HILL	45 24 170 22	102
STAG PASS	PASS	44 23 168 18	88
STAG PASS	PASS	44 23 168 18	89
STAG STREAM	STRM	42 31 173 21	72
STAG STREAM	STRM	42 31 173 21	73
STAG STREAM	STRM	45 51 168 22	107
STAIR CASE CREEK	STRM	43 58 169 06	78
STAIR PEAK	PEAK	44 45 168 31	89
STAIR PEAK	PEAK	44 45 168 31	90
STAIR PEAK	PEAK	44 45 168 31	95
STAIRCASE	LOC	43 14 171 58	80
STAIRCASE	LOC	43 14 171 58	81
STAIRCASE	MTN	44 13 168 34	88
STAIRCASE CREEK	STRM	45 15 168 45	95
STAIRCASE CREEK	STRM	45 15 168 45	99
STAIRCASE GULLY	STRM	43 13 171 56	80
STAIRCASE GULLY	STRM	43 13 171 56	81
STAIRCASE SADDLE	SAD	44 26 170 19	92
STAIRCASE SADDLE	SAD	45 50 166 55	104
STAIRCASE SADDLE	SAD	45 50 166 55	105
STANLEY BROOK	STRM	41 18 172 49	58
STANLEY BROOK	LOC	41 19 172 49	58
STANLEY, LAKE	LAKE	41 01 172 37	56
STANLEY, LAKE	LAKE	41 01 172 37	57
STANLEY, LAKE	LAKE	41 01 172 37	58
STANLEY, MOUNT (TRIG)	HILL	41 07 173 49	54
STANLEY, MOUNT (TRIG)	HILL	41 07 173 49	60
STANLEY, MOUNT (TRIG)	HILL	41 07 173 49	61
STANLEY, MOUNT (TRIG)	MTN	42 16 172 41	65
STANLEY POINT	PNT	34 49 173 10	3
STANLEY RIVER	STRM	41 03 172 40	56
STANLEY RIVER	STRM	41 03 172 40	57
STANLEY RIVER	STRM	41 03 172 40	58
STANLEY RIVER	STRM	42 24 172 37	71
STANMORE BAY	LOC	36 37 174 44	11
STANMORE BAY	LOC	36 37 174 44	12
STANTON RIVER	STRM	42 40 173 08	72
STANTON RIVER	STRM	42 40 173 08	73
STANWAY	LOC	40 06 175 33	46
STAPP, MOUNT	MTN	42 40 171 51	70
STAR HILL	HILL	41 52 173 33	66
STAR HILL (TRIG)	MTN	41 38 173 08	58
STAR HILL (TRIG)	MTN	41 38 173 08	59
STARBOROUGH CREEK	STRM	41 40 174 05	67
STARGAZER	MTN	44 21 168 43	88
STARGAZER	MTN	44 21 168 43	90
STARLIGHT CREEK	STRM	45 25 168 41	99
STARLING HEAD	HEAD	47 04 168 13	115
START (TRIG)	HILL	41 25 175 15	53
STARVATION BLUFF (TRIG)	HILL	46 26 169 25	113
STARVATION HILL (TRIG)	HILL	43 17 172 15	81
STATION BAY	BAY	36 45 174 56	11
STATION BAY	BAY	36 45 174 56	12
STATION BURN	STRM	45 08 168 22	95
STATION BURN	STRM	45 08 168 22	98
STATION BURN	STRM	45 40 168 54	110
STATION CREEK	STRM	42 08 171 57	64
STATION CREEK	STRM	42 11 172 13	64
STATION CREEK	STRM	42 00 172 29	65
STATION CREEK	STRM	41 42 172 40	65
STATION CREEK	STRM	42 14 172 17	65
STATION CREEK	STRM	41 45 173 12	66
STATION CREEK	STRM	41 39 174 09	67
STATION CREEK	STRM	44 00 170 53	87
STATION CREEK	STRM	44 38 169 30	91
STATION CREEK	STRM	44 37 170 14	92
STATION PEAK (TRIG)	PEAK	44 45 170 34	92
STATION STREAM	STRM	41 54 173 35	66
STATION STREAM	STRM	43 42 170 32	77
STATION STREAM	STRM	43 42 170 32	86
STATION STREAM	STRM	44 38 170 37	92
STAVELEY	LOC	43 39 171 26	75
STAVELEY	LOC	43 39 171 26	80
STAVELEY	LOC	43 39 171 26	84
STAVELEY	LOC	43 39 171 26	87
STEADMAN SADDLE	SAD	43 04 171 08	75
STEELE, MOUNT	MTN	42 03 171 44	63
STEELE, MOUNT	MTN	42 03 171 44	64
STEEP HEAD	HEAD	46 31 168 13	109
STEEP HEAD	HEAD	46 58 168 11	115
STEEP HEAD SPUR (TRIG)	HILL	44 08 168 20	88
STEEP HILL	MTN	44 43 167 48	94
STEEP PEAK	PEAK	45 30 167 19	96
STEEP POINT	PNT	40 53 172 07	56
STEEPFACE HILL (TRIG)	MTN	43 25 171 32	80
STEEPLE BURN	STRM	45 38 168 47	99
STEEPLE BURN	STRM	45 40 168 53	110
STEEPLE (TRIG)	PEAK	45 33 168 45	99
STEEP-TO ISLAND	ISLD	46 06 166 40	104
STEPHENS BAY	BAY	41 02 173 01	57
STEPHENS BAY	BAY	41 02 173 01	58
STEPHENS BAY	BAY	41 02 173 01	59
STEPHENS, CAPE	CAPE	40 42 173 57	61
STEPHENS ISLAND	ISLD	40 40 174 00	61
STEPHENS PEAK	PEAK	45 26 166 48	96
STEPHENSON ISLAND	ISLD	34 58 173 47	4
STEPHENSON, MOUNT	MTN	43 51 169 24	78
STERNDALE STREAM	STRM	44 14 171 01	87
STERNS SADDLE	SAD	39 17 176 21	39
STEVEN BURN	STRM	45 38 168 56	99
STEVENS, MOUNT (TRIG)	HILL	40 48 172 27	56
STEVENS, MOUNT (TRIG)	HILL	40 48 172 27	57
STEVENSON, MOUNT	MTN	42 03 171 41	63
STEVENSON, MOUNT	MTN	42 03 171 41	64
STEVENSON, MOUNT	MTN	43 50 170 18	77
STEVENSON, MOUNT	MTN	43 50 170 18	86
STEVENSON STREAM	STRM	43 40 171 26	75
STEVENSON STREAM	STRM	43 40 171 26	80
STEVENSON STREAM	STRM	43 40 171 26	84
STEVENSON STREAM	STRM	43 40 171 26	87
STEVENSONS ARM	BAY	44 39 169 08	90
STEVENSONS ISLAND	ISLD	44 36 169 08	90
STEW CREEK	STRM	43 46 169 31	76
STEW CREEK	STRM	43 46 169 31	79
STEWARDS GULLY	LOC	43 25 172 40	85
STEWART CREEK	STRM	42 09 173 53	67
STEWART CREEK	STRM	42 53 171 22	69
STEWART ISLAND	ISLD	40 53 173 54	54
STEWART ISLAND	ISLD	40 53 173 54	61
STEWART KNOB	PEAK	44 02 169 24	78
STEWART KNOB	PEAK	44 02 169 24	79
STEWART, MOUNT	MTN	41 25 173 18	59
STEWART, MOUNT	MTN	42 58 171 30	69
STEWART PASS	PASS	44 09 168 59	78
STEWART STREAM	STRM	43 57 169 57	77
STEWART STREAM	STRM	43 57 169 57	79
STEWARTS CREEK	STRM	44 08 169 20	78
STEWARTS GULLY	LOC	43 25 172 40	82
STEWARTS GULLY	LOC	43 25 172 40	83
STEYNING STREAM	STRM	42 28 172 35	71
STILLWATER	LOC	36 39 174 43	11
STILLWATER	LOC	36 39 174 43	12
STILLWATER	LOC	42 26 171 21	69
STILLWATER CREEK	STRM	42 26 171 21	69
STILLWATER RIVER	STRM	45 04 167 19	94
STILLWATER RIVER	STRM	45 04 167 19	96
STINA BURN	STRM	44 51 167 30	94
STINKING CREEK	STRM	45 35 167 33	105
STINKING CREEK	STRM	45 35 167 33	106
STINKING STREAM	STRM	42 40 172 47	71
STIRLING	LOC	46 15 169 47	111
STIRLING	LOC	46 15 169 47	113
STIRLING FALLS	FALL	44 36 167 51	89
STIRLING FALLS	FALL	44 36 167 51	94
STIRLING POINT	PNT	46 37 168 21	109
STITTS BLUFF	CLIF	41 51 171 48	63
STITTS BLUFF	CLIF	41 51 171 48	64
STOAT CREEK	STRM	42 24 173 06	72
STOCKTON	HSTD	41 38 171 54	62
STOCKTON, MOUNT (TRIG)	PEAK	41 39 171 55	63
STOCKTON, MOUNT (TRIG)	PEAK	41 39 171 55	64
STOCKYARD CREEK	STRM	44 46 168 44	90
STOCKYARD CREEK	STRM	44 46 168 44	95
STODDART, MOUNT	MTN	43 17 170 47	75
STOKE	SBRB	41 19 173 14	59
STOKER, MOUNT (TRIG)	HILL	45 36 170 15	101
STOKES, MOUNT (TRIG)	HILL	41 05 174 06	54
STOKES, MOUNT (TRIG)	HILL	41 05 174 06	60
STOKES, MOUNT (TRIG)	HILL	41 05 174 06	61
STOKES VALLEY	SBRB	41 11 174 59	52
STOKES VALLEY	SBRB	41 11 174 59	55
STONE BLACK (TRIG)	HILL	44 12 170 53	87
STONE HUT STREAM	STRM	43 42 170 36	86
STONEBURN	LOC	45 26 170 34	102
STONEHENGE (TRIG)	MTN	45 28 170 03	101
STONEMAN, THE (TRIG)	HILL	45 44 169 36	111
STONEY CREEK	STRM	41 35 172 12	62
STONEY HILL (TRIG)	HILL	40 53 173 02	57
STONEY POINT	PNT	45 32 167 34	97
STONY BATTER (TRIG)	HILL	36 46 175 10	13
STONY BAY	BAY	36 31 175 25	9
STONY BAY	BAY	36 31 175 25	16
STONY BAY	BAY	43 51 173 03	83
STONY CREEK	STRM	40 58 175 52	51
STONY CREEK	STRM	41 25 175 30	53
STONY CREEK	STRM	42 11 171 43	63
STONY CREEK	STRM	42 11 171 43	64
STONY CREEK	STRM	43 22 170 12	74
STONY CREEK	STRM	43 29 169 57	76
STONY CREEK	STRM	43 29 169 57	77
STONY CREEK	STRM	43 22 170 12	77
STONY CREEK	STRM	43 16 172 39	82
STONY CREEK	STRM	43 16 172 39	83
STONY CREEK	STRM	44 52 168 41	90
STONY CREEK	STRM	44 37 170 38	93
STONY CREEK	STRM	44 52 168 41	95
STONY CREEK	STRM	45 26 167 50	97
STONY CREEK	STRM	45 26 167 50	98
STONY CREEK	STRM	45 36 169 56	101
STONY CREEK	STRM	45 17 169 58	101
STONY CREEK	STRM	45 03 170 45	102
STONY CREEK	STRM	45 31 170 47	102
STONY CREEK	STRM	46 15 167 58	106
STONY CREEK	STRM	46 15 167 58	107
STONY CREEK	STRM	46 15 167 58	108
STONY CREEK	STRM	46 11 169 49	111
STONY CREEK	LOC	46 11 169 46	111
STONY CREEK	STRM	46 11 169 49	113
STONY CREEK	LOC	46 11 169 46	113
STONY PEAK	PEAK	44 21 169 43	91
STONY PEAK (TRIG)	LOC	46 11 169 15	110
STONY PEAK (TRIG)	LOC	46 11 169 15	112
STONY RIDGE (TRIG)	HILL	44 58 170 52	93
STONY RIVER	STRM	39 10 173 49	34
STONY RIVER	STRM	44 22 170 15	92
STONY SADDLE	SAD	44 47 168 33	90
STONY SADDLE	SAD	44 47 168 33	95
STONY STREAM	STRM	44 00 171 09	87
STONY STREAM	STRM	37 23 175 47	17
STONY STREAM	STRM	41 41 171 46	63
STONY STREAM	STRM	41 41 171 46	64
STONY STREAM	STRM	42 45 172 07	70
STONY STREAM	STRM	42 27 172 37	71
STONY STREAM	STRM	43 40 170 37	74
STONY STREAM	STRM	44 00 169 56	77
STONY STREAM	STRM	43 40 170 37	77
STONY STREAM	STRM	44 00 169 56	79
STONY STREAM	STRM	44 38 170 20	92
STONY STREAM	STRM	45 49 169 47	111
STONY TARN	LAKE	43 52 170 27	77
STONY TARN	LAKE	43 52 170 27	86
STONY (TRIG)	HILL	40 49 175 42	49
STONY (TRIG)	HILL	40 49 175 42	51
STONYHURST	HSTD	42 58 173 10	72
STONYHURST	HSTD	42 58 173 10	73
STOP ISLAND	ISLD	45 46 166 32	104
STOPPER, THE	MTN	45 53 166 38	104
STORM, MOUNT (TRIG)	MTN	43 08 172 06	81
STORMY (TRIG)	PEAK	41 17 172 14	56
STORMY (TRIG)	PEAK	41 17 172 14	62
STORY, LAKE	LAKE	45 45 167 10	105
STOUR RIVER	STRM	43 34 171 16	75
STOUR RIVER	STRM	43 34 171 16	80
STOUR RIVER (EAST BRANCH)	STRM	43 36 171 18	75
STOUR RIVER (EAST BRANCH)	STRM	43 36 171 18	80
STOUR RIVER (WEST BRANCH)	STRM	43 39 171 15	75
STOUT, MOUNT	MTN	43 05 171 10	75
STRACHAN CREEK	STRM	44 02 169 20	78
STRACHAN, MOUNT	MTN	43 47 169 47	76
STRACHAN, MOUNT	MTN	43 47 169 47	79
STRACHAN PASS	PASS	43 15 170 52	75
STRACHAN PEAK (TRIG)	PEAK	41 23 173 58	54
STRACHAN PEAK (TRIG)	PEAK	41 23 173 58	60
STRACHAN RANGE	MTNS	43 45 169 37	76
STRACHAN RANGE	MTNS	43 45 169 37	79
STRACHANS	LOC	44 47 170 31	92
STRANRAER HILL (TRIG)	HILL	45 01 170 12	101
STRATFORD	TOWN	39 21 174 17	34
STRATFORD	TOWN	39 21 174 17	35
STRATFORD	TOWN	39 21 174 17	44
STRATFORD CREEK	STRM	44 59 169 11	90
STRATFORD MOUNTAIN HOUSE	BLDG	39 19 174 07	34
STRATHMORE	LOC	39 17 174 34	35
STRATHMORE	LOC	39 17 174 34	44
STRAUCHON GLACIER	GLCR	43 37 170 04	76
STRAUCHON GLACIER	GLCR	43 37 170 04	77
STRAUCHON RIVER	STRM	43 39 170 01	76
STRAUCHON RIVER	STRM	43 39 170 01	77
STRAUCHON RIVER	STRM	43 39 170 01	79
STREAK HILL (TRIG)	HILL	34 36 172 57	2
STREAMLANDS	LOC	36 24 174 37	11

STRIPE HEAD	HEAD	46 01 166 36	104
STRIPE POINT	PNT	44 33 167 49	94
STRONACH HILL	HILL	45 38 169 04	99
STRONVAR	LOC	41 04 175 55	51
STRONVAR (TRIG)	MTN	41 46 173 26	66
STRUAN	LOC	44 35 170 39	93
STRUCHON, MOUNT	MTN	43 58 169 42	79
STUART, MOUNT	MTN	44 07 169 15	78
STUART MOUNTAINS	MTNS	45 04 167 39	94
STUART MOUNTAINS	MTNS	45 04 167 39	97
STUART STREAM	STRM	46 03 169 40	111
STUART STREAM	STRM	46 03 169 40	113
STUARTS	LOC	46 32 169 27	113
STUCKS HILL (TRIG)	HILL	46 15 167 44	106
STUCKS HILL (TRIG)	HILL	46 15 167 44	108
STUDENTS PEAK	PEAK	44 48 168 00	89
STUDENTS PEAK	PEAK	44 48 168 00	94
STUDHOLME	LOC	44 44 171 08	93
STUDHOLME, MOUNT (TRIG)	MTN	44 39 170 54	93
STUDHOLME SADDLE	SAD	39 18 176 22	39
STUDHOLME SADDLE	SAD	39 18 176 22	40
STUDLEIGH RANGE	MTNS	42 47 172 06	70
STUMP BAY	BAY	38 57 175 49	37
STUMP BAY	BAY	38 57 175 49	38
STYLES GULLEY	STRM	45 47 170 19	103
STYX	SBRB	43 28 172 38	82
STYX	SBRB	43 28 172 38	83
STYX	SBRB	43 28 172 38	85
STYX CREEK	STRM	45 26 169 57	101
STYX RIVER	STRM	42 53 171 06	68
STYX RIVER	STRM	42 53 171 06	69
STYX RIVER	STRM	42 27 172 48	71
STYX RIVER	STRM	43 24 172 42	82
STYX RIVER	STRM	43 24 172 42	83
STYX RIVER	STRM	43 24 172 42	85
STYX SADDLE	SAD	42 54 171 19	69
SUDDEN VALLEY STREAM	STRM	42 59 171 45	70
SUGAR LOAF	MTN	43 54 170 43	86
SUGAR LOAF	HILL	43 57 170 55	87
SUGAR LOAF	MTN	45 04 168 16	95
SUGAR LOAF	MTN	45 04 168 16	98
SUGAR LOAF	HILL	45 14 169 17	100
SUGAR LOAF (TRIG)	MTN	43 02 171 47	80
SUGAR LOAF (TRIG)	MTN	44 42 168 18	89
SUGAR LOAF (TRIG)	MTN	44 42 168 18	95
SUGAR LOAF (TRIG)	HILL	41 12 173 43	60
SUGARLOAF	HILL	43 37 172 39	82
SUGARLOAF	HILL	43 37 172 39	83
SUGARLOAF	HILL	43 37 172 39	85
SUGARLOAF ISLAND	ISLD	34 47 173 22	3
SUGARLOAF, MOUNT (TRIG)	MTN	43 28 171 12	75
SUGARLOAF PASS	PASS	44 41 168 16	89
SUGARLOAF PASS	PASS	44 41 168 16	95
SUGARLOAF ROCK	ROCK	35 34 174 42	8
SUGARLOAF (TRIG)	HILL	41 20 174 54	52
SUGARLOAF (TRIG)	HILL	41 20 174 54	55
SUGARLOAF (TRIG)	PEAK	41 13 172 47	58
SULPHUR SPRINGS	HSTD	42 57 172 53	71
SULPHUR SPRINGS	HSTD	42 57 172 53	72
SUMMER HILL	LOC	46 19 169 51	111
SUMMER HILL	LOC	46 19 169 51	113
SUMMERHILL	LOC	43 16 172 20	81
SUMMERLEA	LOC	41 32 171 56	62
SUMMIT ROCK (TRIG)	MTN	45 26 170 04	101
SUMMIT (TRIG)	PEAK	40 28 176 07	49
SUMMIT (TRIG)	PEAK	40 28 176 07	50
SUMNER	SBRB	43 35 172 44	82
SUMNER	SBRB	43 35 172 44	83
SUMNER HEAD	HEAD	43 34 172 47	82
SUMNER HEAD	HEAD	43 34 172 47	83
SUMNER, LAKE	LAKE	42 42 172 13	70
SUNDAY CREEK	STRM	42 38 171 04	68
SUNDAY CREEK	STRM	42 38 171 04	69
SUNDAY CREEK	STRM	42 25 171 29	69
SUNDAY TARN	LAKE	43 54 170 25	77
SUNDAY TARN	LAKE	43 54 170 25	86
SUNNY KNOB (TRIG)	MTN	42 45 172 29	71
SUNNY NOOK	LOC	35 57 173 52	6
SUNNY NOOK	LOC	35 57 173 52	7
SUNNYSIDE (TRIG)	HILL	45 48 167 37	106
SUNSET VALLEY	STRM	42 14 172 29	65
SUNSHINE BAY	BAY	45 03 168 38	95
SUNSHINE BAY	BAY	45 03 168 38	99
SUPPER COVE	BAY	45 42 166 57	104
SUPPER COVE	BAY	45 42 166 57	105
SUPPLY BAY	BAY	45 32 167 36	97
SURF (TRIG)	PEAK	41 28 175 17	53
SURFDALE	LOC	36 48 175 01	12
SURFDALE	LOC	36 48 175 01	13
SURLY CREEK	STRM	44 00 169 25	78
SURLY CREEK	STRM	44 00 169 25	79
SURPRISE CREEK	STRM	44 47 167 53	89
SURPRISE CREEK	STRM	44 47 167 53	94
SURVILLE CLIFFS	CLIF	34 24 173 01	2
SUTER, MOUNT	MTN	44 49 168 00	89
SUTHERLAND FALLS	FALL	44 48 167 44	94
SUTHERLAND, LAKE	LAKE	45 00 167 34	94
SUTHERLAND, LAKE	LAKE	45 00 167 34	97
SUTHERLAND SOUND	SND	44 43 167 33	94
SUTHERLANDS	LOC	44 17 171 03	87
SUTHERLANDS PEAK	PEAK	44 24 170 06	92
SUTTON	LOC	45 34 170 07	101
SUTTON MOUNT	MTN	44 14 169 46	79
SUTTON, MOUNT	MTN	44 29 170 24	92
SUTTON STREAM	STRM	44 36 170 18	92
SUTTON STREAM	STRM	45 36 170 08	101
SUTTON (TRIG)	MTN	41 53 172 30	65
SWAG SADDLE	SAD	41 23 172 15	62
SWALE STREAM	STRM	41 57 173 52	67
SWAMP CREEK	STRM	44 39 168 08	89
SWAMP STREAM	STRM	42 49 173 15	72
SWAMP STREAM	STRM	42 49 173 15	73
SWAMPY GULLY	STRM	41 41 172 48	65
SWAMPY HILL (TRIG)	HILL	45 31 170 25	102
SWAMPY SPUR (TRIG)	HILL	45 48 170 30	103
SWAMPY SUMMIT (TRIG)	HILL	45 48 170 28	103
SWAN BURN	STRM	41 04 172 06	56
SWAN BURN	STRM	41 04 172 06	62
SWAN LAGOON	LAKE	44 19 169 56	79
SWAN LAKE	LAKE	34 45 173 00	2
SWAN, LAKE	LAKE	45 29 166 48	96
SWANNANOA	LOC	43 23 172 29	81
SWANNANOA	LOC	43 23 172 29	82
SWANNANOA	LOC	43 23 172 29	83
SWANNANOA	LOC	43 23 172 29	85
SWANSON	LOC	36 52 174 34	11
SWANSON	LOC	36 52 174 34	12
SWEENEY LAKE	LAKE	43 47 169 25	76
SWEENEY LAKE	LAKE	43 47 169 25	78
SWEENEY LAKE	LAKE	43 47 169 25	79
SWEEP (TRIG)	HILL	40 44 175 47	49
SWEEP (TRIG)	HILL	40 44 175 47	51
SWEEPS STREAM	STRM	43 40 170 47	74
SWEEPS STREAM	STRM	43 40 170 47	86
SWEETS SADDLE	SAD	41 38 173 31	59
SWEETS STREAM	STRM	41 40 173 32	66
SWEETWATER	LOC	35 03 173 13	3
SWELL STREAM	STRM	38 34 178 01	32
SWIFT RIVER	STRM	43 31 171 26	75
SWIFT RIVER	STRM	43 31 171 26	80
SWIN BURN	STRM	45 12 170 15	101
SWIN RIVER	STRM	43 29 171 11	75
SWIN RIVER (NORTH BRANCH)	STRM	43 30 171 15	75
SWIN RIVER (SOUTH BRANCH)	STRM	43 30 171 15	75
SWINBURN PEAK (TRIG)	HILL	45 10 170 21	101
SWINDLE, MOUNT	MTN	43 53 169 18	78
SWISS CREEK	STRM	42 58 170 49	68
SWORD PEAK	PEAK	43 23 170 39	74
SWYNCOMBE	HSTD	42 21 173 32	73
SWYNCOMBE (TRIG)	HILL	42 20 173 32	73
SYDNEY KING, MOUNT	MTN	43 31 170 26	74
SYDNEY KING, MOUNT	MTN	43 31 170 26	77
SYDNEY, MOUNT (TRIG)	HILL	44 36 170 41	93
SYLVAN, LAKE	LAKE	44 42 168 19	89
SYLVAN, LAKE	LAKE	44 42 168 19	95
SYLVESTER, LAKE	LAKE	41 06 172 38	56
SYLVESTER, LAKE	LAKE	41 06 172 38	57
SYLVESTER, LAKE	LAKE	41 06 172 38	58
SYLVIA STREAM	STRM	42 30 172 23	71
SYME, MOUNT	MTN	44 38 168 02	89
SYMMETRY PEAKS (TRIG)	PEAK	45 17 168 34	95
SYMMETRY PEAKS (TRIG)	PEAK	45 17 168 34	99
SYMONDS HILL (TRIG)	HILL	41 05 173 40	60

T

TABLE CAPE	CAPE	39 06 178 00	33
TABLE FLAT (TRIG)	HILL	39 58 175 57	46
TABLE HILL	HILL	44 19 170 00	79
TABLE HILL	LOC	46 04 169 55	111
TABLE HILL	LOC	46 04 169 55	113
TABLE HILL (TRIG)	HILL	47 02 167 51	114
TABLE HILL (TRIG)	HILL	40 43 172 34	56
TABLE HILL (TRIG)	HILL	40 43 172 34	57
TABLE HILL (TRIG)	HILL	45 16 170 41	102
TABLE HILL (TRIG)	HILL	46 05 169 52	111
TABLE HILL (TRIG)	HILL	46 05 169 52	113
TABLE RIDGE	RDGE	46 27 169 10	112
TABLE (TRIG)	HILL	40 39 176 06	49
TABLELANDS	LOC	38 00 177 19	23
TABLELANDS	LOC	41 14 175 32	51
TABLELANDS	LOC	41 14 175 32	53
TACHALLS CREEK	STRM	41 50 174 08	67
TADMOR	LOC	41 26 172 45	58
TADMOR RIVER	STRM	41 22 172 48	58
TADMOR SADDLE (TRIG)	HILL	41 36 172 40	58
TAEMARO	LOC	34 57 173 34	3
TAEMARO	LOC	34 57 173 34	4
TAEMARO BAY	BAY	34 56 173 35	3
TAEMARO BAY	BAY	34 56 173 35	4
TAEORE, LAKE	LAKE	34 41 173 01	2
TAFF TOR	PEAK	42 41 171 24	69
TAHAENUI RIVER	STRM	39 03 177 40	33
TAHAIA	LOC	38 16 175 17	27
TAHAIA (TRIG)	HILL	38 15 175 15	18
TAHAIA (TRIG)	HILL	38 15 175 15	19
TAHAIA (TRIG)	HILL	38 15 175 15	27
TAHAKOPA	LOC	46 31 169 23	113
TAHAKOPA BAY	BAY	46 34 169 30	113
TAHAKOPA RIVER	STRM	46 33 169 28	113
TAHANGA (TRIG)	HILL	36 44 175 48	16
TAHAROA	LOC	38 09 174 44	18
TAHAROA, LAKE	LAKE	35 48 173 39	6
TAHAROA, LAKE	LAKE	38 10 174 45	18
TAHARUA RIVER	STRM	38 55 176 16	39
TAHATEKAPUA (TRIG)	HILL	39 27 175 32	36
TAHATEKAPUA (TRIG)	HILL	39 27 175 32	37
TAHATIKA	LOC	46 24 169 32	113
TAHAWAI	LOC	37 31 175 56	17
TAHEKE	LOC	35 27 173 39	4
TAHEKE	LOC	35 27 173 39	6
TAHEKE RIVER	STRM	35 40 174 27	5
TAHEKE RIVER	STRM	35 40 174 27	7
TAHEKE RIVER	STRM	35 40 174 27	8
TAHEKENUI STREAM	STRM	39 04 177 15	41
TAHEKEROA	LOC	36 32 174 34	11
TAHEKEROA RIVER	STRM	36 34 174 31	10
TAHEKEROA RIVER	STRM	36 34 174 31	11
TAHERE	LOC	35 41 174 26	5
TAHERE	LOC	35 41 174 26	7
TAHERE	LOC	35 41 174 26	8
TAHORA	LOC	38 17 177 07	31
TAHORA	LOC	39 02 174 48	35
TAHORA SADDLE	SAD	39 04 174 48	35
TAHORAITI	LOC	40 14 176 04	47
TAHORAKURI	LOC	38 34 176 14	29
TAHORANUI RIVER	STRM	35 08 173 57	4
TAHUAHUA (TRIG)	HILL	41 13 174 07	54
TAHUAHUA (TRIG)	HILL	41 13 174 07	60
TAHUAHUA (TRIG)	HILL	41 13 174 07	61
TAHUNA	LOC	37 30 175 30	15
TAHUNA SIDING	RSDG	38 05 176 47	22
TAHUNAMAERE STREAM	STRM	39 25 174 36	35
TAHUNAMAERE STREAM	STRM	39 25 174 36	44
TAHUNANUI	SBRB	41 17 173 15	59
TAHUNATARA POINT	PNT	38 43 175 57	28
TAHUNATARA POINT	PNT	38 43 175 57	29
TAHUNATARA POINT	PNT	38 43 175 57	38
TAHUNGA	LOC	38 38 177 31	31
TAHUNGA	LOC	38 38 177 31	33
TAHUOKARETU STREAM	STRM	40 25 176 19	50
TAHUPO (TRIG)	HILL	39 25 174 47	35
TAHUPO (TRIG)	HILL	39 25 174 47	44
TAHURANGI STREAM	STRM	39 05 175 44	37
TAHURANGI STREAM	STRM	39 05 175 44	38
TAHUROA	LOC	37 43 175 31	19
TAHURUA POINT	PNT	37 32 178 02	25
TAIAROA HEAD	HEAD	45 47 170 44	103
TAIEPA (TRIG)	HILL	40 30 175 50	49
TAIEPAKOWHAI (TRIG)	HILL	37 39 174 56	18
TAIERI BEACH	LOC	46 05 170 11	103
TAIERI ISLAND	ISLD	46 03 170 14	103
TAIERI MOUTH	LOC	46 04 170 11	103
TAIERI RIDGE	RDGE	45 26 170 16	101
TAIERI RIVER	STRM	46 03 170 12	103
TAIERI STREAM	STRM	37 25 175 46	17
TAIHAPE	TOWN	39 41 175 48	46
TAIHARURU	LOC	35 44 174 32	5
TAIHARURU	LOC	35 44 174 32	8
TAIHARURU BAY	BAY	35 44 174 33	8
TAIHARURU HEAD	HEAD	35 43 174 34	8
TAIHARURU RIVER	STRM	35 43 174 33	8
TAIHIKI RIVER	STRM	37 09 174 42	12
TAIHIKI RIVER	STRM	37 09 174 42	14
TAIHOA	LOC	37 50 175 48	19
TAIHOA	LOC	37 50 175 48	20
TAIKARAWA STREAM	STRM	35 26 173 16	3
TAIKIRAU	LOC	35 29 174 04	4
TAIKIRAU	LOC	35 29 174 04	5
TAIKIRAU STREAM	STRM	35 26 173 59	4
TAIKIRAU STREAM	STRM	35 26 173 59	5
TAIKO	LOC	44 21 171 04	93
TAIKO STREAM	STRM	44 24 171 03	93
TAIKO (TRIG)	HILL	40 35 175 38	48
TAIKO (TRIG)	HILL	40 35 175 38	49
TAIKOREA	LOC	40 22 175 24	48
TAIKOREA	TRIG	40 21 175 21	48
TAILINGS CREEK	STRM	41 52 171 30	63
TAIMATE	HSTD	41 47 174 09	67
TAINGAEHE	LOC	36 11 174 02	7
TAIOMA	LOC	45 48 170 20	103
TAIPA	LOC	35 00 173 28	3
TAIPA RIVER	STRM	35 00 173 28	3
TAIPARE BAY	BAY	41 00 173 43	60
TAIPO RIVER	STRM	41 22 172 22	62
TAIPO RIVER	STRM	42 45 171 23	69
TAIPOITI	LOC	42 08 171 50	63
TAIPOITI	LOC	42 08 171 50	64
TAIPOURI STREAM	STRM	38 06 177 24	23
TAIPOURI STREAM	STRM	38 06 177 24	24
TAIPUHA	LOC	36 00 174 18	7
TAIPUHA	LOC	36 00 174 18	8
TAIPUHA STREAM	STRM	36 00 174 18	7
TAIPUHA STREAM	STRM	36 00 174 18	8
TAIRUA	LOC	37 01 175 51	16
TAIRUA	LOC	37 01 175 51	17
TAIRUA HARBOUR	HARB	37 01 175 51	16
TAIRUA HARBOUR	HARB	37 01 175 51	17
TAIRUA RIVER	STRM	37 04 175 49	17
TAIRUA RIVER, FIRST BRANCH	STRM	37 04 175 46	17
TAIRUA RIVER, FORTH BRANCH	STRM	37 08 175 44	17
TAIRUA RIVER, SECOND BRANCH	STRM	37 05 175 44	17
TAIRUA RIVER, THIRD BRANCH	STRM	37 07 175 44	17
TAITA	SBRB	41 11 174 58	52
TAITA	SBRB	41 11 174 58	55
TAITA STREAM	STRM	35 09 173 47	4
TAITA (TRIG)	HILL	35 05 173 45	4
TAITAI (TRIG)	HILL	37 53 178 11	25
TAITAPU	LOC	43 40 172 33	82
TAITAPU	LOC	43 40 172 33	83
TAITAPU	LOC	43 40 172 33	85
TAKAHE STREAM	STRM	43 09 171 21	75
TAKAHE STREAM	STRM	43 09 171 21	80
TAKAHIWAI	LOC	35 50 174 24	7
TAKAHIWAI	LOC	35 50 174 24	8
TAKAHUE	LOC	35 12 173 21	3
TAKAHUE RIVER	STRM	35 02 173 20	3
TAKAKA	POPL	40 51 172 48	57
TAKAKA RIVER	STRM	40 49 172 48	57
TAKAKURI STREAM	STRM	35 05 173 39	4
TAKAKURI (TRIG)	HILL	35 06 173 40	4
TAKAMATUA	LOC	43 47 172 58	83
TAKAMORE	LOC	37 52 178 16	25
TAKANINI	SBRB	37 03 174 55	12
TAKANINI	SBRB	37 03 174 55	14
TAKAPARU (TRIG)	HILL	37 57 175 54	20
TAKAPAU	LOC	38 21 178 12	32
TAKAPAU	POPL	40 02 176 21	47
TAKAPAU (TRIG)	HILL	40 02 176 22	47
TAKAPUNA	USAT	36 48 174 46	11
TAKAPUNA	USAT	36 48 174 46	12
TAKAPURAU (TRIG)	HILL	39 55 175 46	46
TAKAPUTAHI	LOC	38 05 177 35	24
TAKAPUTAHI RIVER	STRM	38 04 177 41	24
TAKARANGI (TRIG)	HILL	38 46 177 54	32
TAKARANGI (TRIG)	HILL	38 46 177 54	33
TAKARO	SBRB	40 21 175 36	48
TAKARO	SBRB	40 21 175 36	49
TAKARO LODGE	BLDG	45 17 167 58	97
TAKARO LODGE	BLDG	45 17 167 58	98
TAKATU	LOC	36 22 174 46	11
TAKAURUNGA (TRIG)	HILL	37 53 175 56	20
TAKERAU BAY	BAY	34 56 173 33	3
TAKIROA	LOC	44 51 170 39	93
TAKITIMU MOUNTAINS	MTNS	45 43 167 51	106
TAKITU STREAM	STRM	35 41 173 49	6
TAKOU	LOC	39 25 174 38	35
TAKOU	LOC	39 25 174 38	44
TAKOU BAY	LOC	35 07 173 55	4
TAKOU BAY	BAY	35 06 173 57	4
TAKOU RIVER	STRM	35 06 173 55	4
TAKOU STREAM	STRM	35 06 173 54	4
TAKUTAI	LOC	42 44 170 56	68
TALBOT, MOUNT	MTN	44 45 168 00	89
TALBOT RIVER	STRM	44 46 167 53	89
TALBOT RIVER	STRM	44 46 167 53	94
TALLA BURN	STRM	45 44 169 33	111
TAMA LAKES	LAKE	39 12 175 37	37
TAMA LAKES	LAKE	39 12 175 37	38
TAMA (TRIG)	HILL	39 11 175 38	37
TAMA (TRIG)	HILL	39 11 175 38	38
TAMAHERE	LOC	37 50 175 22	19
TAMAITEMIOKA ISLAND	ISLD	47 13 167 20	114
TAMAKI	SBRB	36 54 174 51	11
TAMAKI	SBRB	36 54 174 51	12
TAMAKI, MOUNT	MTN	43 38 170 21	74
TAMAKI, MOUNT	MTN	43 38 170 21	77
TAMAKI, MOUNT	MTN	43 38 170 21	86
TAMAKI RIVER	STRM	36 51 174 53	11
TAMAKI RIVER	STRM	36 51 174 53	12
TAMAKI RIVER	STRM	40 16 176 04	46
TAMAKI RIVER	STRM	40 16 176 04	47
TAMAKI RIVER, WEST BRANCH	STRM	40 08 176 03	46
TAMAKI STRAIT	STRA	36 51 175 02	12
TAMAKI STRAIT	STRA	36 51 175 02	13
TAMAKOMAKO STREAM	STRM	39 40 175 39	46
TAMARERE (TRIG)	MTN	38 05 177 52	24
TAMATEA	SBRB	39 31 176 52	40
TAMATEA	SBRB	39 31 176 52	41
TAMATEA	SBRB	39 31 176 52	42
TAMATEA PEAK	PEAK	45 42 167 10	105
TAMATERAU	LOC	35 46 174 25	5
TAMATERAU	LOC	35 46 174 25	7
TAMATERAU	LOC	35 46 174 25	8
TAMIHANA	LOC	37 44 175 44	19
TAMUMU	HSTD	39 58 176 42	42
TAMUMU	HSTD	39 58 176 42	43
TAMURENUI, LAKE	LAKE	38 02 176 44	22
TANATANA	LOC	38 11 177 07	23
TANAWA (TRIG)	HILL	40 45 176 09	50
TANAWA (TRIG)	HILL	40 45 176 09	51
TANCRED, MOUNT	MTN	43 05 171 07	75
TANE	LOC	40 35 175 51	49
TANEATUA	LOC	38 04 177 01	22
TANEATUA	LOC	38 04 177 01	23
TANEHOPUWAI	LOC	38 23 175 08	27
TANEHUA (TRIG)	HILL	37 00 175 45	16
TANEHUA (TRIG)	HILL	37 00 175 45	17
TANEKAHA	LOC	35 36 174 13	5
TANEKAHA	LOC	35 36 174 13	7
TANEKAHA	LOC	35 36 174 13	8
TANEKAHA CREEK	STRM	42 05 172 49	65
TANGAHOE RIVER	STRM	39 39 174 21	44
TANGAHOE STREAM	STRM	39 19 174 59	36
TANGARAKAU	LOC	39 01 174 51	35
TANGARAKAU RIVER	STRM	39 14 174 53	35
TANGAREWAI STREAM	STRM	39 58 176 19	47
TANGARUHE STREAM	STRM	40 18 176 32	50
TANGATUPURA STREAM	STRM	40 01 176 36	43
TANGATUPURA STREAM	STRM	40 01 176 36	47
TANGIHANGA	HSTD	38 33 177 53	32
TANGIHANGA (TRIG)	HILL	38 56 177 39	33
TANGIHUA	LOC	35 51 174 09	7
TANGIHUA RANGE	MTNS	35 53 174 07	7
TANGIHUA (TRIG)	HILL	35 52 174 05	7
TANGIMOANA	LOC	40 18 175 16	48
TANGINGATAHI POINT	PNT	38 47 175 47	28
TANGINGATAHI POINT	PNT	38 47 175 47	38
TANGITERORIA	LOC	35 50 174 03	7
TANGITIKI BAY	BAY	36 14 174 05	7
TANGITU	LOC	38 37 175 13	27
TANGITU STREAM	STRM	39 04 174 33	35
TANGITU (TRIG)	HILL	35 10 173 41	4
TANGITU (TRIG)	HILL	39 04 174 34	35
TANGIWAI	LOC	39 28 175 35	37
TANGOAKE	LOC	34 38 172 58	2
TANGOIO	LOC	39 20 176 55	40
TANGOIO	LOC	39 20 176 55	41
TANGOIO	LOC	39 20 176 55	42
TANGOIO BLUFF	CLIF	39 20 176 56	40
TANGOIO BLUFF	CLIF	39 20 176 56	41
TANGOIO BLUFF	CLIF	39 20 176 56	42
TANGOWAHINE	LOC	35 52 173 56	7
TANGOWAHINE STREAM	STRM	35 52 173 56	7
TANGOWAHINE (TRIG)	HILL	35 52 173 53	6
TANGOWAHINE (TRIG)	HILL	35 52 173 53	7
TANILBA, MOUNT (TRIG)	MTN	44 59 167 12	96
TANIWHA	LOC	37 25 175 18	15
TANIWHA STREAM	STRM	37 24 175 17	15
TANNERS POINT	PNT	37 29 175 57	17
TANOA	LOC	36 12 174 21	8
TANUTANU STREAM	STRM	35 13 173 06	3
TAOKERE STREAM	STRM	39 40 175 25	45
TAOKERE STREAM	STRM	39 40 175 25	46
TAONUI	LOC	40 15 175 36	46
TAONUI STREAM	STRM	39 25 175 21	36
TAONUI STREAM	STRM	39 25 175 21	37
TAONUI STREAM	STRM	40 26 175 27	48
TAOROA JUNCTION	LOC	39 42 175 57	46
TAOTAOROA	LOC	37 55 175 38	19
TAPA STREAM	STRM	36 51 175 28	13
TAPA STREAM	STRM	36 51 175 28	16
TAPANUI	POPL	45 57 169 16	110
TAPAPA	LOC	37 59 175 51	20
TAPAPA STREAM	STRM	35 11 173 29	3
TAPAPAKANGA STREAM	STRM	36 59 175 16	13
TAPAPAKANGA STREAM	STRM	36 59 175 16	15
TAPARAHAIA STREAM	STRM	35 29 174 18	5
TAPARAMAPUA STREAM	STRM	37 58 174 53	18
TAPATU	HSTD	37 42 178 13	25
TAPAWERA	LOC	41 23 172 49	58
TAPEKA POINT	PNT	35 15 174 07	4
TAPEKA POINT	PNT	35 15 174 07	5
TAPIRIMOKO POINT	PNT	38 22 174 40	26
TAPLEY STREAM	STRM	43 07 172 22	81
TAPOKOPOKO (TRIG)	PEAK	41 22 174 58	52
TAPOKOPOKO (TRIG)	PEAK	41 22 174 58	55
TAPORA	LOC	36 21 174 18	10
TAPORA BANK	BNK	36 24 174 16	10
TAPOTUPOTU BAY	BAY	34 26 172 43	2
TAPU	LOC	36 59 175 30	13
TAPU	LOC	36 59 175 30	15
TAPU	LOC	36 59 175 30	16
TAPU RIVER	STRM	36 59 175 30	13
TAPU RIVER	STRM	36 59 175 30	15
TAPU RIVER	STRM	36 59 175 30	16
TAPUAE STREAM	STRM	39 06 173 59	34
TAPUAE STREAM	STRM	39 07 175 07	36
TAPUAE (TRIG)	HILL	38 18 175 05	26
TAPUAE (TRIG)	HILL	39 35 175 39	37
TAPUAE (TRIG)	HILL	39 35 175 39	46
TAPUAEHARURU BAY	BAY	38 43 176 03	28
TAPUAEHARURU BAY	BAY	38 43 176 03	29
TAPUAEHARURU BAY	BAY	38 43 176 03	38
TAPUAEHARURU (TRIG)	HILL	37 36 177 59	24
TAPUAEHARURU (TRIG)	HILL	37 36 177 59	25
TAPUAENGOTO STREAM	STRM	39 25 176 09	39
TAPUAENUKU (TRIG)	MTN	42 00 173 40	67
TAPUAEROA RIVER	STRM	37 53 178 17	25
TAPUAETAHI STREAM	STRM	35 08 173 59	4
TAPUAETAHI STREAM	STRM	35 08 173 59	5
TAPUAETAHI (TRIG)	HILL	36 55 175 50	16
TAPUAETAHI (TRIG)	HILL	36 55 175 50	17
TAPUATA	LOC	40 13 176 05	47
TAPUHI	LOC	35 28 174 12	5
TAPUI	LOC	45 01 170 41	102
TAPUI STREAM	STRM	40 28 176 33	50
TAPUIOMARUAHINE (TRIG)	PEAK	39 09 176 10	39
TAPUKETARU (TRIG)	HILL	35 39 173 46	6
TAPUWAE	LOC	35 22 173 26	3
TAPUWAE	LOC	35 22 173 26	6
TAPUWAE	LOC	38 34 175 22	27
TAPUWAI POINT	PNT	36 07 175 26	9
TARA	LOC	36 07 174 31	8
TARA CREEK	STRM	36 06 174 34	8
TARA TAMA	PEAK	42 49 171 25	69
TARA (TRIG)	MTN	44 45 170 42	93
TARADALE	SBRB	39 32 176 51	40
TARADALE	SBRB	39 32 176 51	41
TARADALE	SBRB	39 32 176 51	42
TARAERE BAY	BAY	34 35 172 58	2
TARAHIKI ISLAND	ISLD	36 47 175 13	13
TARAIRE STREAM	STRM	35 06 173 51	4
TARAKAHU (TRIG)	HILL	35 27 173 54	4
TARAKAHU (TRIG)	HILL	35 32 173 46	4
TARAKAHU (TRIG)	HILL	35 32 173 46	6
TARAKAMUKU (TRIG)	HILL	40 23 175 45	49
TARAKENGARARA (TRIG)	HILL	37 42 178 26	25
TARAKIHINUI STREAM	STRM	38 51 177 54	33
TARAKOHE	LOC	40 50 172 54	57

TARAMAKAU	LOC	42 41 171 15	68
TARAMAKAU	LOC	42 41 171 15	69
TARAMAKAU RIVER	STRM	42 34 171 08	68
TARAMAKAU RIVER	STRM	42 34 171 08	69
TARAMEA STREAM	STRM	40 35 175 34	48
TARAMEA STREAM	STRM	40 35 175 34	49
TARAMOA	LOC	46 16 168 14	109
TARAMOUKOU STREAM	STRM	39 08 174 22	35
TARAMOUKOU (TRIG)	HILL	39 08 174 22	35
TARANAKI, MOUNT (EGMONT, MOUNT)	MTN	39 18 174 04	34
TARANAKI PEAK	PEAK	43 39 170 26	74
TARANAKI PEAK	PEAK	43 39 170 26	77
TARANAKI PEAK	PEAK	43 39 170 26	86
TARANAKI POINT	PNT	37 58 174 47	18
TARANAKI (TRIG)	HILL	36 29 174 28	10
TARANAKI (TRIG)	HILL	36 29 174 28	11
TARANGA ISLAND	ISLD	35 58 174 43	8
TARANOHO STREAM	STRM	36 57 175 39	15
TARANOHO STREAM	STRM	36 57 175 39	16
TARANUI	LOC	45 12 170 54	102
TARAOHINERE (TRIG)	HILL	38 46 177 44	31
TARAOHINERE (TRIG)	HILL	38 46 177 44	33
TARAPATIKI	LOC	38 51 177 12	31
TARAPEKE STREAM	STRM	39 39 176 20	47
TARAPONUI (TRIG)	PEAK	39 08 176 44	40
TARARA	LOC	46 31 169 35	113
TARARERE STREAM	STRM	39 16 176 53	40
TARARERE STREAM	STRM	39 16 176 53	41
TARAROA STREAM	STRM	37 22 175 01	14
TARARU	LOC	37 07 175 31	13
TARARU	LOC	37 07 175 31	15
TARARU	LOC	37 07 175 31	16
TARARU STREAM	STRM	37 07 175 31	13
TARARU STREAM	STRM	37 07 175 31	15
TARARU STREAM	STRM	37 07 175 31	16
TARARU (TRIG)	HILL	37 05 175 33	13
TARARUA	MTN	44 14 168 32	88
TARARUA PEAKS	PEAK	40 55 175 19	48
TARARUA RANGE	MTNS	40 44 175 25	48
TARARUA STATE FOREST PARK	PARK	40 51 175 23	48
TARATA	LOC	39 09 174 22	34
TARATA	LOC	39 09 174 22	35
TARATA STREAM	STRM	39 07 175 10	36
TARATA (TRIG)	HILL	39 42 176 00	46
TARATAHI	HSTD	40 59 175 35	51
TARATAHI	HSTD	40 59 175 35	53
TARATARA (TRIG)	HILL	35 04 174 00	4
TARATARA (TRIG)	HILL	35 05 173 40	4
TARATUIA POINT	PNT	37 37 177 53	24
TARAUKAWA (TRIG)	HILL	41 16 174 14	54
TARAUKAWA (TRIG)	HILL	41 16 174 14	60
TARAUKAWA (TRIG)	HILL	41 16 174 14	61
TARAUNUI	LOC	35 44 174 28	5
TARAUNUI	LOC	35 44 174 28	8
TARAWAMAOMAO POINT	PNT	34 26 172 41	2
TARAWERA	LOC	39 02 176 34	39
TARAWERA	LOC	39 02 176 34	40
TARAWERA, LAKE	LAKE	38 12 176 25	20
TARAWERA, LAKE	LAKE	38 12 176 27	21
TARAWERA, LAKE	LAKE	38 12 176 27	22
TARAWERA, MOUNT	MTN	38 13 176 31	21
TARAWERA, MOUNT	MTN	38 13 176 31	22
TARAWERA, MOUNT	MTN	38 13 176 31	30
TARAWERA RIDGE (TRIG)	RDGE	38 14 176 32	21
TARAWERA RIDGE (TRIG)	RDGE	38 14 176 32	22
TARAWERA RIDGE (TRIG)	RDGE	38 14 176 32	30
TARAWERA RIVER	STRM	37 54 176 47	22
TAREHA	LOC	39 16 176 51	40
TAREHA	LOC	39 16 176 51	41
TAREHA POINT	PNT	35 12 174 03	4
TAREHA POINT	PNT	35 12 174 03	5
TARERE (TRIG)	HILL	39 35 174 29	35
TARERE (TRIG)	HILL	39 35 174 29	44
TAREREPO (TRIG)	HILL	39 16 174 29	35
TAREREPO (TRIG)	HILL	39 16 174 29	44
TAREWA (TRIG)	HILL	38 52 177 51	33
TAREWAREWA STREAM	STRM	38 35 178 11	32
TARIKI	LOC	39 14 174 15	34
TARIKI	LOC	39 14 174 15	44
TARINGAMOTU	LOC	38 51 175 15	27
TARINGAMOTU RIVER	STRM	38 51 175 15	27
TARINGAMOTU VALLEY	LOC	38 50 175 22	27
TARINGAPEKA STREAM	STRM	37 30 174 55	14
TARINGATURA CREEK	STRM	45 52 168 08	106
TARINGATURA CREEK	STRM	45 52 168 08	107
TARINGATURA HILL (TRIG)	HILL	45 51 168 13	107
TARINGATURA HILLS	HILL	45 54 168 14	107
TARLETON, LAKE	LAKE	42 46 170 56	68
TARLETON, MOUNT	MTN	43 07 171 03	75
TARNDALE	HSTD	38 13 177 47	24
TARNDALE	HSTD	38 13 177 47	32
TARNDALE	HSTD	42 11 172 56	65
TARNDALE, MOUNT (TRIG)	MTN	42 10 172 53	65
TARONUI BAY	LOC	35 08 173 59	4
TARONUI BAY	BAY	35 07 173 58	4
TARONUI BAY	LOC	35 08 173 59	5
TARONUI BAY	BAY	35 07 173 58	5
TARRAS	LOC	44 50 169 25	91
TARRAS CREEK	STRM	44 49 169 27	91
TARUAHUNA PASS	PASS	42 54 171 41	70
TARUARAU RIVER	STRM	39 30 176 20	39
TARUKENGA	LOC	38 05 176 09	20
TARUKENGA	LOC	38 05 176 09	21
TARUNA	HSTD	42 52 172 32	71
TARURUTANGI	LOC	39 05 174 10	34
TASMAN	LOC	41 11 173 03	58
TASMAN	LOC	41 11 173 03	59
TASMAN BAY	BAY	41 00 173 14	59
TASMAN GLACIER	GLCR	43 35 170 13	74
TASMAN GLACIER	GLCR	43 35 170 13	77
TASMAN, MOUNT	MTN	43 34 170 09	74
TASMAN MOUNTAINS	MTNS	41 01 172 22	56
TASMAN MOUNTAINS	MTNS	41 01 172 22	62
TASMAN RIVER	STRM	43 53 170 10	77
TASMAN RIVER	STRM	43 53 170 10	86
TASMAN SADDLE	SAD	43 31 170 21	74
TASMAN SADDLE	SAD	43 31 170 21	77
TASS RIVER	STRM	42 27 171 59	70
TATA ISLANDS	ISLS	40 48 172 55	57
TATAIAHAPI PA	LOC	38 10 177 07	23
TATAPOURI POINT	PNT	38 39 178 09	32
TATAPOURI (TRIG)	HILL	38 39 178 08	32
TATARA (TRIG)	HILL	38 40 174 57	26
TATARA (TRIG)	HILL	38 40 174 57	27
TATARAAKINA (TRIG)	PEAK	39 03 176 38	39
TATARAAKINA (TRIG)	PEAK	39 03 176 38	40
TATARAIMAKA	LOC	39 10 173 55	34
TATARANIA (TRIG)	HILL	39 27 174 45	35
TATARANIA (TRIG)	HILL	39 27 174 45	44
TATARARIKI	LOC	36 04 173 56	7
TATARE	LOC	43 22 170 12	77
TATARE RANGE	MTNS	43 25 170 20	74
TATARE RANGE	MTNS	43 25 170 20	77
TATARE STREAM	STRM	43 21 170 10	74
TATARE STREAM	STRM	43 21 170 10	77
TATAWEKA STREAM	STRM	38 26 177 15	31
TATAWEKA (TRIG)	HILL	36 04 175 23	9
TATU	LOC	38 56 174 57	26
TATU	LOC	38 56 174 57	36
TATU (TRIG)	HILL	38 55 174 55	26
TATU (TRIG)	HILL	38 55 174 55	36
TATUANUI	LOC	37 37 175 36	19
TATUAOTEMAUMU (TRIG)	HILL	38 26 178 11	32
TAUAKIRA	HSTD	39 42 175 14	45
TAUAKIRA (TRIG)	HILL	39 42 175 13	45
TAUANUI, LAKE	LAKE	35 30 173 52	4
TAUANUI, LAKE	LAKE	35 30 173 52	6
TAUANUI RIVER	STRM	41 19 175 12	53
TAUANUI (TRIG)	HILL	35 30 173 52	4
TAUANUI (TRIG)	HILL	35 30 173 52	6
TAUHARA (TRIG)	HILL	38 42 176 10	28
TAUHARA (TRIG)	HILL	38 42 176 10	29
TAUHEI	LOC	37 36 175 26	19
TAUHEI STREAM	STRM	37 35 175 21	19
TAUHERENIKAU	LOC	41 07 175 23	53
TAUHERENIKAU RIVER	STRM	41 10 175 19	53
TAUHERENIKAU (TRIG)	PEAK	41 02 175 20	53
TAUHOA	LOC	36 23 174 27	10
TAUHOA	LOC	36 23 174 27	11
TAUHOA CHANNEL	CHAN	36 25 174 17	10
TAUHOA RIVER	STRM	36 24 174 23	10
TAUHOA RIVER	STRM	36 24 174 23	11
TAUKAWAU POINT	PNT	35 26 174 26	5
TAUKOPU (TRIG)	HILL	39 47 175 42	46
TAUKORO STREAM	STRM	39 46 175 19	45
TAUMAHARUA (TRIG)	HILL	37 22 175 43	15
TAUMAHARUA (TRIG)	HILL	37 22 175 43	17
TAUMAIHI ISLAND	ISLD	37 39 176 25	21
TAUMAIHI ISLAND	ISLD	37 39 176 25	22
TAUMAIHI (TRIG)	HILL	38 08 177 21	23
TAUMAITI	HILL	36 53 174 26	10
TAUMAITI	HILL	36 53 174 26	11
TAUMAITI	HILL	36 53 174 26	12
TAUMAKA ISLAND	ISLD	43 52 168 53	78
TAUMAOTEAWHENGAIAO (TRIG)	MTN	37 44 178 07	25
TAUMARERE	LOC	35 07 174 05	4
TAUMARERE	LOC	35 07 174 05	5
TAUMARUITI	LOC	38 54 175 16	27
TAUMARUNUI	TOWN	38 53 175 16	27
TAUMATA	LOC	46 09 169 28	111
TAUMATA	LOC	46 09 169 28	113
TAUMATA CREEK	STRM	36 32 174 18	10
TAUMATA KARAMU (TRIG)	HILL	38 46 177 28	31
TAUMATA KARAMU (TRIG)	HILL	38 46 177 28	33
TAUMATA STREAM	STRM	39 15 174 48	35
TAUMATA STREAM	STRM	39 15 174 48	44
TAUMATA (TRIG)	HILL	35 04 173 24	3
TAUMATAMAHOE (TRIG)	HILL	35 11 173 16	3
TAUMATAMIERE (TRIG)	HILL	38 10 176 52	22
TAUMATAMIERE (TRIG)	HILL	38 10 176 52	23
TAUMATAOKARETU (TRIG)	HILL	38 14 177 33	24
TAUMATAOKARETU (TRIG)	HILL	38 14 177 33	31
TAUMATAOMIRO (TRIG)	HILL	37 44 178 29	25
TAUMATAOREI (TRIG)	HILL	37 41 178 23	25
TAUMATAORIAKI (TRIG)	HILL	39 00 177 49	33
TAUMATAOTEATUA (TRIG)	HILL	40 29 176 27	50
TAUMATAPOUPOU STREAM	STRM	38 32 177 43	31
TAUMATARA POINT	PNT	34 48 173 23	3
TAUMATATAHI	LOC	39 33 174 47	35
TAUMATATAHI	LOC	39 33 174 47	44
TAUMATATOTARA	HILL	38 15 174 54	18
TAUMATAWHAKATANGIHANGAKAUAUO-TAMATEAPOKAIWHENUAKITANATAHU (TRIG)	HILL	40 21 176 32	50
TAUMATAWHAUWHAU (TRIG)	HILL	35 33 173 43	4
TAUMATAWHAUWHAU (TRIG)	HILL	35 33 173 43	6
TAUMATINI (TRIG)	HILL	39 40 174 54	44
TAUMATINI (TRIG)	HILL	39 40 174 54	45
TAUMUTU	LOC	43 51 172 21	85
TAUNAKI (TRIG)	HILL	35 04 173 26	3
TAUNAMAU CREEK	STRM	46 21 168 08	107
TAUNAMAU CREEK	STRM	46 21 168 08	109
TAUNGARUAWAHINE (TRIG)	HILL	38 56 177 35	33
TAUNGATA (TRIG)	PEAK	40 49 175 15	48
TAUNGATARA STREAM	STRM	39 29 173 53	34
TAUNGATERA (TRIG)	HILL	38 47 176 14	29
TAUNGAURUROA POINT	PNT	38 25 174 38	26
TAUNGAWHA (TRIG)	HILL	39 04 175 05	36
TAUNOA STREAM	STRM	46 17 167 44	106
TAUNOA STREAM	STRM	46 17 167 44	108
TAUNOKO	LOC	39 30 174 58	36
TAUPAKI	LOC	36 50 174 34	11
TAUPAKI	LOC	36 50 174 34	12
TAUPERIKAKA POINT	HILL	43 45 169 09	78
TAUPEUPE SADDLE	SAD	38 38 177 02	30
TAUPIRI	LOC	37 37 175 12	18
TAUPIRI BAY	BAY	35 17 174 18	5
TAUPIRI ISLAND	ISLD	34 29 172 39	2
TAUPIRI RANGE	MTNS	37 33 175 12	15
TAUPIRI (TRIG)	HILL	37 36 175 11	18
TAUPO	TOWN	38 42 176 05	28
TAUPO	TOWN	38 42 176 05	29
TAUPO	TOWN	38 42 176 05	38
TAUPO BAY	LOC	35 00 173 43	4
TAUPO BAY	BAY	35 00 173 43	4
TAUPO, LAKE	LAKE	38 55 175 49	28
TAUPO, LAKE	LAKE	38 55 175 49	29
TAUPO, LAKE	LAKE	38 55 175 49	38
TAUPO POINT	PNT	40 47 172 57	57
TAUPORAE (TRIG)	HILL	39 48 175 40	46
TAURAKAWA (TRIG)	HILL	39 21 174 42	35
TAURAKAWA (TRIG)	HILL	39 21 174 42	44
TAURANGA	TOWN	37 41 176 10	20
TAURANGA	TOWN	37 41 176 10	21
TAURANGA	HILL	38 29 177 11	31
TAURANGA BAY	LOC	35 00 173 47	4
TAURANGA BAY	BAY	35 00 173 47	4
TAURANGA BAY	BAY	41 46 171 27	63
TAURANGA ENTRANCE	CHAN	37 38 176 10	20
TAURANGA HARBOUR	HARB	37 34 176 00	17
TAURANGA HARBOUR	HARB	37 34 176 00	20
TAURANGA RIVER	STRM	38 17 177 07	31
TAURANGA STREAM	STRM	38 12 177 18	31
TAURANGA VALLEY	LOC	35 02 173 47	4
TAURANGA-TAUPO RIVER	STRM	38 55 175 54	29
TAURANGA-TAUPO RIVER	STRM	38 55 175 54	37
TAURANGA-TAUPO RIVER	STRM	38 55 175 54	38
TAURANGAKAUTUKU RIVER	STRM	37 42 178 19	25
TAURANGAKOAU (TRIG)	HILL	37 51 177 40	24
TAURANGAKOHU (TRIG)	HILL	38 10 175 27	19
TAURANGANUI	LOC	37 20 174 49	14
TAURANGARURU	LOC	37 15 174 40	12
TAURANGARURU	LOC	37 15 174 40	14
TAURANGI (TRIG)	HILL	38 40 175 00	26
TAURANGI (TRIG)	HILL	38 40 175 00	27
TAURAROA	LOC	35 53 174 14	7
TAURAROA	LOC	35 53 174 14	8
TAURAROA	LOC	38 18 175 24	27
TAURAROA RIVER	STRM	35 55 174 08	7
TAURAROA STREAM	STRM	39 51 175 05	45
TAUREKAITAI STREAM	STRM	40 10 176 33	47
TAUREWA	LOC	39 05 175 33	36
TAUREWA	LOC	39 05 175 33	37
TAUREWA	LOC	39 05 175 33	38
TAUREWA (TRIG)	PEAK	39 04 175 27	36
TAUREWA (TRIG)	PEAK	39 04 175 27	37
TAURIKO	LOC	37 44 176 06	20
TAURIKO	LOC	37 44 176 06	21
TAURIKURA	LOC	35 50 174 33	8
TAURIMU STREAM	STRM	39 07 175 08	36
TAUROA PEAK	PEAK	43 22 170 43	74
TAUROA PENINSULA	PEN	35 12 173 05	3
TAUROA POINT	PNT	35 10 173 04	3
TAUROA STREAM	STRM	35 53 174 26	7
TAUROA STREAM	STRM	35 53 174 26	8
TAUROA (TRIG)	HILL	35 11 173 05	3
TAURUS, MOUNT	MTN	44 18 168 51	90
TAUTANE STREAM	STRM	40 30 176 35	50
TAUTAPAWA STREAM	STRM	39 36 175 51	37
TAUTAPAWA STREAM	STRM	39 36 175 51	46
TAUTARAKAPUA STREAM	STRM	39 10 174 59	36
TAUTARUA (TRIG)	HILL	40 26 175 59	49
TAUTAU STREAM	STRM	37 47 176 06	20
TAUTAU STREAM	STRM	37 47 176 06	21
TAUTEREI STREAM	STRM	37 43 174 49	18
TAUTORO	LOC	35 29 173 51	4
TAUTORO	LOC	35 29 173 51	6
TAUTORO (TRIG)	HILL	35 30 173 52	4
TAUTORO (TRIG)	HILL	35 30 173 52	6
TAUTUKU	LOC	46 35 169 25	113
TAUTUKU BAY	BAY	46 35 169 27	113
TAUTUKU, MOUNT (TRIG)	HILL	46 25 169 22	113
TAUTUKU PENINSULA	PEN	46 36 169 27	113
TAUTUKU RIVER	STRM	46 36 169 25	113
TAUWERU	LOC	40 58 175 48	51
TAUWERU RIVER	STRM	41 04 175 38	51
TAUWERU RIVER	STRM	41 04 175 38	53
TAUWHARE	LOC	37 46 175 27	19
TAUWHARE	LOC	38 18 177 07	31
TAUWHARE (TRIG)	HILL	35 25 173 20	3
TAUWHARE (TRIG)	HILL	35 25 173 20	6
TAUWHARE (TRIG)	HILL	39 37 175 11	36
TAUWHARE (TRIG)	HILL	39 37 175 11	45
TAUWHAREPARE	LOC	38 16 178 06	32
TAUWHAREWERA STREAM	STRM	40 27 176 12	50
TAVERNERS	STRM	42 46 171 43	70
TAWA	USAT	41 10 174 49	52
TAWA	USAT	41 10 174 49	55
TAWAHA	HSTD	41 10 175 26	53
TAWAI	LOC	44 53 171 00	93
TAWAI (TRIG)	HILL	38 21 177 10	31
TAWAKE TOHUNGA (TRIG)	PEAK	39 17 176 05	38
TAWAKE TOHUNGA (TRIG)	PEAK	39 17 176 05	39
TAWANUI	LOC	46 28 169 32	113
TAWAPATA	LOC	39 13 177 55	33
TAWAPIKO (TRIG)	HILL	39 38 175 08	45
TAWAPUKU RIVER	STRM	35 34 173 50	4
TAWAPUKU RIVER	STRM	35 34 173 50	6
TAWAPUKU RIVER	STRM	35 34 173 50	7
TAWARAU RIVER	STRM	38 16 174 50	26
TAWARE (TRIG)	HILL	35 06 173 21	3
TAWARIKI (TRIG)	HILL	38 44 174 41	26
TAWATAIA	LOC	40 37 175 48	49
TAWATAIA CREEK	STRM	40 36 175 48	49
TAWERA (TRIG)	HILL	40 45 175 36	48
TAWERA (TRIG)	HILL	40 45 175 36	49
TAWERA (TRIG)	HILL	40 45 175 36	51
TAWERO POINT	PNT	41 04 173 57	54
TAWERO POINT	PNT	41 04 173 57	60
TAWERO POINT	PNT	41 04 173 57	61
TAWHAI	LOC	42 09 171 47	63
TAWHAI	LOC	42 09 171 47	64
TAWHANA	LOC	38 01 178 14	25
TAWHANA	LOC	38 26 177 07	31
TAWHARANUI	LOC	36 23 174 47	11
TAWHARANUI PENINSULA	PEN	36 22 174 48	11
TAWHAREKIRI LAKES	LAKE	43 50 169 05	78
TAWHATA	LOC	39 04 175 03	36
TAWHERO (TRIG)	PEAK	40 44 175 34	48
TAWHERO (TRIG)	PEAK	40 44 175 34	49
TAWHERO (TRIG)	PEAK	40 44 175 34	51
TAWHIROKO POINT	PNT	45 22 170 52	102
TAWHITI	LOC	45 23 169 17	100
TAWHITI RAHI ISLAND	ISLD	35 27 174 43	5
TAWHITI STREAM	STRM	39 37 174 21	34
TAWHITI STREAM	STRM	39 37 174 21	35
TAWHITI STREAM	STRM	39 34 174 39	35
TAWHITI STREAM	STRM	39 37 174 21	44
TAWHITI STREAM	STRM	39 34 174 39	44
TAWHITI (TRIG)	HILL	38 04 178 21	25
TAWHITIAPAKA (TRIG)	HILL	38 13 177 50	24
TAWHITIAPAKA (TRIG)	HILL	38 13 177 50	32
TAWHITINUI ISLAND	ISLD	41 03 173 48	54
TAWHITINUI ISLAND	ISLD	41 03 173 48	60
TAWHITINUI ISLAND	ISLD	41 03 173 48	61
TAWHITINUI REACH	STRA	41 02 173 50	54
TAWHITINUI REACH	STRA	41 02 173 50	60
TAWHITINUI REACH	STRA	41 02 173 50	61
TAWHITIRAHI (TRIG)	HILL	36 50 175 32	13
TAWHITIRAHI (TRIG)	HILL	36 50 175 32	16
TAWHITIRAUPEKA (TRIG)	HILL	38 47 174 52	26
TAWHIUAU (TRIG)	MTN	38 28 176 48	30
TAWHIWHI	LOC	39 37 174 49	44
TAWHIWHI (TRIG)	HILL	39 39 174 49	44
TAWIRIKOHUKOHU (TRIG)	PEAK	40 41 175 25	48
TAY STREAM	STRM	44 16 170 08	86
TAYLOR, LAKE	LAKE	42 46 172 14	70
TAYLOR, MOUNT (TRIG)	HILL	36 25 174 50	11
TAYLOR, MOUNT (TRIG)	MTN	43 31 171 19	75
TAYLOR, MOUNT (TRIG)	MTN	43 31 171 19	80
TAYLOR PASS	PASS	41 38 173 58	60
TAYLOR RANGE	MTNS	43 29 171 18	75
TAYLOR RANGE	MTNS	43 29 171 18	80
TAYLOR RIVER	STRM	41 31 173 58	60
TAYLOR STREAM	STRM	41 22 172 31	58
TAYLOR STREAM	STRM	41 53 172 19	65
TAYLORS CREEK	STRM	46 19 167 56	108
TAYLORS CREEK	STRM	46 19 167 56	109
TAYLORS MISTAKE	SBRB	43 35 172 46	82
TAYLORS MISTAKE	BAY	43 35 172 47	82
TAYLORS MISTAKE	BAY	43 35 172 47	83
TAYLORS MISTAKE	SBRB	43 35 172 46	83
TAYLORS STREAM	STRM	43 33 171 22	75
TAYLORS STREAM	STRM	43 44 171 32	84
TAYLORS STREAM	STRM	43 33 171 22	80
TAYLORS STREAM	STRM	45 59 168 28	107
TAYLORVILLE	LOC	42 26 171 19	68
TAYLORVILLE	LOC	42 26 171 19	69
TE AHIOTEATUA (TRIG)	HILL	38 51 177 18	31
TE AHITAHUTAHU (TRIG)	HILL	38 09 177 18	23
TE AHITAITAI STREAM	STRM	41 14 175 34	51
TE AHITAITAI STREAM	STRM	41 14 175 34	53
TE AHOPONGA (TRIG)	HILL	35 02 173 25	3
TE AHUAHU	LOC	35 20 173 51	4
TE AHUMATU (TRIG)	HILL	36 15 175 26	9
TE AITANGAAMAHAKI (TRIG)	HILL	38 42 177 24	31
TE AITANGAAMAHAKI (TRIG)	HILL	38 42 177 24	33
TE AKAROA	PNT	40 57 174 00	54
TE AKAROA	PNT	40 57 174 00	61
TE AKATARAWA (TRIG)	HILL	44 36 170 14	92
TE AKATARERE (TRIG)	HILL	38 03 175 35	19
TE AKATEA	LOC	37 39 175 03	18
TE AKAU	LOC	37 41 174 51	18
TE AKAU POINT	PNT	36 08 175 29	9
TE AKAU SOUTH	LOC	37 43 174 51	18
TE AKEOHIKOPIRO (TRIG)	HILL	38 01 175 06	18
TE ANAAU GLOW-WORM CAVES	CAVE	45 18 167 44	97
TE ANANUIARAU BAY	BAY	36 11 175 05	9
TE ANAOHITI (TRIG)	HILL	39 08 174 58	36
TE ANAPUTA POINT	PNT	36 32 175 32	16
TE ANAU	POPL	45 25 167 43	97
TE ANAU DOWNS	LOC	45 11 167 50	97
TE ANAU DOWNS	LOC	45 11 167 50	98
TE ANAU HILL (TRIG)	HILL	45 20 167 43	97
TE ANAU, LAKE	LAKE	45 13 167 45	97
TE ANAU, LAKE	LAKE	45 13 167 45	98
TE ANGA	LOC	38 16 174 50	18
TE ANGA	LOC	38 16 174 50	26
TE AO WHEKERE (TRIG)	MTN	42 11 173 42	67
TE APITI STREAM	STRM	39 55 176 56	42
TE APITI STREAM	STRM	39 55 176 56	43
TE APITI (TRIG)	HILL	38 46 177 37	31
TE APITI (TRIG)	HILL	38 46 177 37	33
TE APUTA	LOC	38 48 175 40	28
TE APUTA	LOC	38 48 175 40	38
TE ARAI	LOC	36 12 174 36	8
TE ARAI POINT	LOC	36 11 174 37	8
TE ARAI POINT	PNT	36 10 174 39	8
TE ARAI RIVER	STRM	38 41 177 56	32
TE ARAI RIVER	STRM	38 41 177 56	33
TE ARAI (TRIG)	HILL	35 08 173 34	3
TE ARAI (TRIG)	HILL	35 08 173 34	4
TE ARAKURA	LOC	40 17 175 33	48
TE ARAKURA	LOC	40 17 175 33	49
TE ARAOHAKERE (TRIG)	HILL	38 52 174 54	26
TE ARAROA	LOC	37 38 178 22	25
TE ARERO STREAM	STRM	38 51 176 07	28
TE ARERO STREAM	STRM	38 51 176 07	29
TE ARERO STREAM	STRM	38 51 176 07	38
TE AROHA	POPL	37 32 175 42	15
TE AROHA	POPL	37 32 175 42	17
TE AROHA, LAKE	LAKE	45 20 167 48	97
TE AROHA, LAKE	LAKE	45 20 167 48	98
TE AROHA STREAM	STRM	38 38 177 51	32
TE AROHA STREAM	STRM	38 38 177 51	33
TE AROHA WEST	LOC	37 35 175 44	19
TE AROHA (TRIG)	HILL	37 32 175 44	17
TE AROWHENUA	HSTD	41 45 173 24	66
TE ATATU NORTH	SBRB	36 50 174 39	11
TE ATATU NORTH	SBRB	36 50 174 39	12
TE ATATU SOUTH	SBRB	36 52 174 39	11
TE ATATU SOUTH	SBRB	36 52 174 39	12
TE ATUA (TRIG)	HILL	40 00 176 48	42
TE ATUA (TRIG)	HILL	40 00 176 48	43
TE ATUAHAUTAPU (TRIG)	HILL	38 05 177 33	24
TE ATUAOPARAPARA	HILL	39 48 176 09	47
TE AU, LAKE	LAKE	45 16 167 23	96
TE AU SADDLE	SAD	45 14 167 20	96
TE AU (TRIG)	HILL	40 52 175 05	48
TE AU (TRIG)	HILL	40 52 175 05	52
TE AU (TRIG)	HILL	40 52 175 05	55
TE AUPAPA (TRIG)	HILL	40 30 175 54	49
TE AUTE COLLEGE	SCH	39 50 176 38	42
TE AUTE COLLEGE	SCH	39 50 176 38	43
TE AUTE COLLEGE	SCH	39 50 176 38	47
TE AWA	LOC	44 12 171 15	87
TE AWAMUTU	POPL	38 01 175 20	18
TE AWAMUTU	POPL	38 01 175 20	19
TE AWANGA	LOC	39 38 176 59	42
TE AWANGA	LOC	39 38 176 59	43
TE AWAOTEAOUHI STREAM	STRM	36 04 174 09	7
TE AWAPUTAHI (TRIG)	HILL	40 23 176 27	50
TE EKAOU CREEK	STRM	40 07 175 54	46
TE HAKAOTUMAKOKIRI (TRIG)	HILL	38 48 177 36	31
TE HANA	LOC	36 15 174 31	10
TE HANA	LOC	36 15 174 31	11
TE HAPUA	LOC	34 31 172 55	2
TE HARA POINT	PNT	37 44 174 49	18
TE HARANGA (TRIG)	HILL	38 43 177 54	32
TE HARANGA (TRIG)	HILL	38 43 177 54	33
TE HAROTO	LOC	39 08 176 36	39
TE HAROTO	LOC	39 08 176 36	40
TE HAU	MTN	44 33 167 55	89
TE HAU	MTN	44 33 167 55	94
TE HAU STREAM	STRM	38 36 176 17	29
TE HAUKE	LOC	39 47 176 41	42
TE HAUKE	LOC	39 47 176 41	43
TE HAUKE	LOC	39 47 176 41	47
TE HAUPA ISLAND	ISLD	36 31 174 45	11
TE HEKA STREAM	STRM	39 50 176 31	42
TE HEKA STREAM	STRM	39 50 176 31	43
TE HEKA STREAM	STRM	39 50 176 31	47
TE HEKENGA (TRIG)	PEAK	39 53 176 06	47
TE HENGA	LOC	36 54 174 27	10
TE HENGA	LOC	36 54 174 27	11
TE HENUI STREAM	STRM	39 03 174 05	34
TE HERUHERU (TRIG)	HILL	36 09 175 22	9
TE HERUNGA (TRIG)	HILL	37 35 175 00	18
TE HERUOTARAIA POINT	PNT	39 09 177 50	33
TE HERUOTUREIA (TRIG)	PEAK	39 03 176 52	40
TE HERUOTUREIA (TRIG)	PEAK	39 03 176 52	41
TE HEUHEU	PEAK	39 16 175 35	37
TE HEUHEU	PEAK	39 16 175 35	38
TE HIAPO (TRIG)	HILL	38 47 175 35	27
TE HIAPO (TRIG)	HILL	38 47 175 35	28
TE HIAPO (TRIG)	HILL	38 47 175 35	38
TE HIHI	LOC	37 07 174 50	12
TE HIHI	LOC	37 07 174 50	14
TE HIHI CREEK	STRM	37 06 174 48	12
TE HIHI CREEK	STRM	37 06 174 48	14

TE HIWERA (TRIG)	HILL	38 56 177 28	33
TE HOANGA STREAM	STRM	35 35 173 56	4
TE HOANGA STREAM	STRM	35 35 173 56	7
TE HOE	LOC	37 31 175 19	15
TE HOE	HSTD	39 02 176 50	40
TE HOE	HSTD	39 02 176 50	41
TE HOE RIVER	STRM	39 01 176 49	40
TE HOE RIVER	STRM	39 01 176 49	41
TE HOE STREAM	STRM	40 41 175 52	49
TE HOE (TRIG)	HILL	37 29 175 22	15
TE HORO	HSTD	37 48 178 27	25
TE HORO	LOC	40 48 175 07	48
TE HORO	LOC	40 48 175 07	52
TE HORO	LOC	40 48 175 07	55
TE HORO BEACH	LOC	40 48 175 05	48
TE HORO BEACH	LOC	40 48 175 05	52
TE HORO BEACH	LOC	40 48 175 05	55
TE HOROA	LOC	39 34 175 39	37
TE HOUKA	LOC	46 14 169 40	111
TE HOUKA	LOC	46 14 169 40	113
TE HUAHUA	LOC	35 21 173 29	3
TE HUE	HSTD	37 44 178 19	25
TE HUE	HSTD	39 40 175 21	45
TE HUE POINT	PNT	36 11 175 03	9
TE HUE STREAM	STRM	37 17 175 43	17
TE HUIA	LOC	35 06 173 50	4
TE HUKA ISLAND	ISLD	37 41 177 45	24
TE HUMENGA POINT	PNT	41 32 175 11	53
TE HURUHURU (TRIG)	MTN	44 24 170 44	93
TE HUTEWAI	LOC	37 52 174 51	18
TE IHUORURUMAIOTERANGI (TRIG)	HILL	38 58 176 58	40
TE IHUORURUMAIOTERANGI (TRIG)	HILL	38 58 176 58	41
TE IKAARONGAMAI BAY	BAY	38 33 178 16	32
TE IRINGA	LOC	35 27 173 47	4
TE IRINGA	LOC	35 27 173 47	6
TE IRINGA (TRIG)	HILL	38 16 174 45	18
TE IRINGA (TRIG)	HILL	38 16 174 45	26
TE IRINGA (TRIG)	PEAK	39 00 176 13	39
TE IRINGA (TRIG)	PEAK	39 23 176 17	39
TE KAHA	LOC	37 45 177 41	24
TE KAHA POINT	PNT	37 47 174 50	18
TE KAHA POINT	PNT	37 44 177 40	24
TE KAHA (TRIG)	HILL	38 59 175 27	36
TE KAHA (TRIG)	HILL	38 59 175 27	37
TE KAHIKA, LAKE	LAKE	34 37 173 00	2
TE KAHIKA STREAM	STRM	37 58 177 45	24
TE KAHIKATOA (TRIG)	HILL	35 01 173 46	4
TE KAHO (TRIG)	HILL	38 17 178 11	32
TE KAHUKURI STREAM	STRM	35 40 173 54	7
TE KAIHEKIAPANUI (TRIG)	HILL	38 54 177 40	33
TE KAKA (TRIG)	HILL	37 00 175 32	13
TE KAKA (TRIG)	HILL	37 00 175 32	15
TE KAKA (TRIG)	HILL	37 00 175 32	16
TE KAKA (TRIG)	HILL	38 59 175 56	37
TE KAKA (TRIG)	HILL	38 59 175 56	38
TE KAKAHO ISLAND	ISLD	40 53 174 06	54
TE KAKAHO ISLAND	ISLD	40 53 174 06	61
TE KAO	LOC	34 40 172 58	2
TE KAO BAY	BAY	34 36 172 58	2
TE KAO STREAM	STRM	34 38 172 58	2
TE KAPU (TRIG)	HILL	39 09 177 53	33
TE KAPUA (TRIG)	HILL	37 43 178 09	25
TE KAPUA (TRIG)	HILL	38 29 177 52	32
TE KAPUAARANGI (TRIG)	HILL	38 03 177 25	23
TE KAPUAARANGI (TRIG)	HILL	38 03 177 25	24
TE KARAE	LOC	35 17 173 30	3
TE KARAE STREAM	STRM	35 18 173 31	3
TE KARAKA	LOC	35 26 173 24	3
TE KARAKA	LOC	35 26 173 24	6
TE KARAKA	LOC	38 28 177 52	32
TE KARAKA ISLAND	ISLD	36 50 175 49	16
TE KARAKA POINT	PNT	37 12 175 53	17
TE KAUAE (TRIG)	HILL	38 17 176 28	21
TE KAUAE (TRIG)	HILL	38 17 176 28	22
TE KAUAE (TRIG)	HILL	38 17 176 28	30
TE KAUKAU POINT	PNT	41 34 175 26	53
TE KAURI	LOC	37 33 175 08	14
TE KAURI	LOC	37 33 175 08	15
TE KAURI LODGE	HSTD	38 05 174 59	18
TE KAURI STREAM	STRM	38 05 174 55	18
TE KAUWAE POINT	PNT	38 41 175 52	28
TE KAUWAE POINT	PNT	38 41 175 52	29
TE KAUWAE POINT	PNT	38 41 175 52	38
TE KAUWHATA	LOC	37 24 175 09	14
TE KAUWHATA	LOC	37 24 175 09	15
TE KAWA	HILL	38 05 175 18	18
TE KAWA	LOC	38 06 175 17	18
TE KAWA	HILL	38 05 175 18	19
TE KAWA	LOC	38 06 175 17	19
TE KAWA STREAM	STRM	43 40 172 49	83
TE KAWA WEST	LOC	38 06 175 14	18
TE KAWA WEST	LOC	38 06 175 14	19
TE KAWAU POINT	PNT	36 27 174 16	10
TE KAWAU (TRIG)	HILL	38 34 174 53	26
TE KEHO (TRIG)	HILL	37 18 175 54	17
TE KEI STREAM	STRM	38 39 177 13	31
TE KIE (TRIG)	HILL	35 40 173 51	6
TE KIE (TRIG)	HILL	35 40 173 51	7
TE KIKOOTERANGI (TRIG)	HILL	38 21 174 57	26
TE KINGA	LOC	42 36 171 30	69
TE KINGA (TRIG)	PEAK	42 39 171 29	69
TE KIRI	LOC	39 26 173 59	34
TE KITEROA	LOC	45 56 169 05	110
TE KIWI STREAM	STRM	39 05 177 17	41
TE KOHAIAKAHU POINT	PNT	38 48 176 03	28
TE KOHAIAKAHU POINT	PNT	38 48 176 03	29
TE KOHAIAKAHU POINT	PNT	38 48 176 03	38
TE KOHANGA	LOC	37 19 174 51	14
TE KOHATU (TRIG)	HILL	38 36 175 41	28
TE KOHU STREAM	STRM	38 46 176 39	30
TE KOKOMUKA (TRIG)	HILL	37 41 178 10	25
TE KONI (TRIG)	HILL	39 37 175 14	36
TE KONI (TRIG)	HILL	39 37 175 14	45
TE KOOTI (TRIG)	MTN	42 41 172 38	71
TE KOOTI'S LOOKOUT (TRIG)	HILL	39 01 176 48	40
TE KOOTI'S LOOKOUT (TRIG)	HILL	39 01 176 48	41
TE KOPAHOU (TRIG)	HILL	41 20 174 43	52
TE KOPAHOU (TRIG)	HILL	41 20 174 43	55
TE KOPARETANGIHANGA (TRIG)	HILL	38 51 177 26	31
TE KOPARETANGIHANGA (TRIG)	HILL	38 51 177 26	33
TE KOPUA	LOC	38 04 175 14	18
TE KOPUA	LOC	38 04 175 14	19
TE KOPUA ISLAND	ISLD	35 19 174 19	5
TE KOPURU	POPL	36 02 173 55	6
TE KOPURU	POPL	36 02 173 55	7
TE KOPURU (TRIG)	HILL	39 40 175 04	45
TE KORAHA	LOC	38 13 174 56	18
TE KORIHI (TRIG)	HILL	35 06 173 30	3
TE KOUMA	LOC	36 49 175 29	13
TE KOUMA	LOC	36 49 175 29	16
TE KOUMA HARBOUR	HARB	36 50 175 27	13
TE KOUMA HARBOUR	HARB	36 50 175 27	16
TE KOURA	LOC	38 46 175 15	27
TE KOWHAI	LOC	36 10 174 06	7
TE KOWHAI	LOC	37 44 175 09	18
TE KUHA	LOC	41 50 171 40	63
TE KUHA	LOC	41 50 171 40	64
TE KUITI	POPL	38 20 175 10	27
TE KUME (TRIG)	HILL	35 14 174 02	4
TE KUME (TRIG)	HILL	35 14 174 02	5
TE KUMI	HSTD	37 43 178 01	25
TE KUMI	LOC	38 19 175 19	27
TE KURI POINT	PNT	36 13 174 04	7
TE KURI (TRIG)	HILL	36 11 173 58	7
TE MAARI STREAM	STRM	37 58 174 53	18
TE MAHIA	HSTD	41 13 173 58	54
TE MAHIA	HSTD	41 13 173 58	60
TE MAHIA	HSTD	41 13 173 58	61
TE MAHIMAHI STREAM	STRM	35 05 173 54	4
TE MAHOE	LOC	38 07 176 49	22
TE MAIKA	LOC	38 06 174 46	18
TE MAIPI (TRIG)	HILL	41 06 175 54	51
TE MAIRE	LOC	36 06 173 55	7
TE MAIRE	LOC	38 57 175 12	36
TE MAIRE STREAM	STRM	38 57 175 11	36
TE MAIRE STREAM	STRM	41 17 175 17	53
TE MANIHI (TRIG)	PEAK	39 23 176 19	39
TE MANUKA (TRIG)	MTN	38 17 177 37	31
TE MAPARA	LOC	38 29 175 05	26
TE MAPARA	LOC	38 29 175 05	27
TE MAPOU (TRIG)	HILL	39 22 174 52	35
TE MAPOU (TRIG)	HILL	39 22 174 52	44
TE MARA STREAM	STRM	40 49 175 36	48
TE MARA STREAM	STRM	40 49 175 36	49
TE MARA STREAM	STRM	40 49 175 36	51
TE MARAMA STREAM	STRM	38 29 174 40	26
TE MARUA	LOC	41 06 175 07	52
TE MARUA	LOC	41 06 175 07	53
TE MARUA	LOC	41 06 175 07	55
TE MARUA	HSTD	40 46 173 57	61
TE MATA	LOC	36 58 175 30	13
TE MATA	LOC	36 58 175 30	15
TE MATA	LOC	36 58 175 30	16
TE MATA	LOC	37 53 174 52	18
TE MATA RIVER	STRM	36 58 175 30	13
TE MATA RIVER	STRM	36 58 175 30	15
TE MATA RIVER	STRM	36 58 175 30	16
TE MATA (TRIG)	HILL	39 11 175 01	36
TE MATA (TRIG)	HILL	39 42 176 55	42
TE MATA (TRIG)	HILL	39 42 176 55	43
TE MATAI	LOC	37 47 176 21	20
TE MATAI	LOC	37 47 176 21	21
TE MATAI (TRIG)	PEAK	39 07 176 25	39
TE MATAI (TRIG)	PEAK	39 07 176 25	40
TE MATAU STREAM	STRM	40 02 176 22	47
TE MAUKU POINT	PNT	38 27 174 38	26
TE MAUNGA	SBRB	37 41 176 14	20
TE MAUNGA	SBRB	37 41 176 14	21
TE MAUNGA (TRIG)	PEAK	41 24 175 20	53
TE MAWHAI	LOC	38 03 175 19	18
TE MAWHAI	LOC	38 03 175 19	19
TE MIKO	LOC	42 05 171 22	63
TE MIRO	LOC	37 49 175 33	19
TE MIRO (TRIG)	HILL	37 50 175 32	19
TE MOANA	LOC	44 03 171 07	87
TE MOANANUI	LOC	37 25 175 41	15
TE MOANANUI	LOC	37 25 175 41	17
TE MOEHAU JUNCTION	LOC	39 36 175 48	46
TE MOTO MOTO STREAM	STRM	42 31 173 29	73
TE MOTU ISLAND	ISLD	38 06 174 48	18
TE NAIHI RIVER	STRM	44 07 168 49	78
TE NAMU (TRIG)	HILL	39 48 175 35	46
TE NGAE	LOC	38 05 176 20	20
TE NGAE	LOC	38 05 176 20	21
TE NGAIO POINT	PNT	36 23 174 17	10
TE NGAIRE	LOC	35 02 173 51	4
TE NGARU	LOC	45 47 170 40	103
TE NGARU STREAM	STRM	39 21 176 55	40
TE NGARU STREAM	STRM	39 21 176 55	41
TE NGARU STREAM	STRM	39 21 176 55	42
TE NGAU (TRIG)	HILL	35 33 174 10	4
TE NGAU (TRIG)	HILL	35 33 174 10	5
TE NGAU (TRIG)	HILL	35 33 174 10	7
TE NIU (TRIG)	HILL	37 39 174 53	18
TE NUNUHE ROCK	ROCK	35 11 174 12	5
TE OHAKI PA	LOC	37 48 175 51	19
TE OHAKI PA	LOC	37 48 175 51	20
TE OINEOHU POINT	PNT	38 49 175 50	28
TE OINEOHU POINT	PNT	38 49 175 50	29
TE OINEOHU POINT	PNT	38 49 175 50	38
TE OKA BAY	BAY	43 51 172 47	83
TE OKA STREAM	STRM	43 51 172 47	83
TE OKA (TRIG)	HILL	43 49 172 47	83
TE ONEPU STREAM	STRM	38 17 176 54	30
TE OPAI LAGOON	LAKE	41 17 175 15	52
TE OPAI LAGOON	LAKE	41 17 175 15	53
TE OPAU STREAM	STRM	35 29 173 49	4
TE OPAU STREAM	STRM	35 29 173 49	6
TE ORE ORE	LOC	40 57 175 42	49
TE ORE ORE	LOC	40 57 175 42	51
TE ORE ORE	LOC	40 57 175 42	53
TE ORIWA STREAM	STRM	35 31 174 27	5
TE ORORORA POINT	PNT	36 57 175 52	16
TE OROROA POINT	PNT	36 57 175 52	17
TE PAE (TRIG)	HILL	40 12 176 28	47
TE PAEROA LAGOON	LAGN	39 03 177 31	33
TE PAHI ISLAND	ISLD	35 11 174 05	4
TE PAHI ISLAND	ISLD	35 11 174 05	5
TE PAHU	LOC	37 55 175 08	18
TE PAHU STREAM	STRM	37 54 175 08	18
TE PAKI	LOC	34 30 172 48	2
TE PAKI POINT	PNT	35 26 174 44	5
TE PAKI STREAM	STRM	37 43 175 07	18
TE PAKI (TRIG)	HILL	34 28 172 46	2
TE PAKI (TRIG)	HILL	40 36 175 28	48
TE PAPATAPU	LOC	37 57 174 52	18
TE PARAUA (TRIG)	HILL	37 40 177 49	24
TE PEITA CREEK	STRM	41 47 172 30	65
TE PEKA	LOC	46 31 168 51	112
TE PEKAOTERANGIHEKEIHO (TRIG)	HILL	37 35 178 06	25
TE PENE	LOC	35 04 173 54	4
TE PIRITA	LOC	43 38 171 53	80
TE PIRITA	LOC	43 38 171 53	81
TE PIRITA	LOC	43 38 171 53	84
TE PITO	HILL	38 11 177 40	24
TE PITO	HILL	38 11 177 40	31
TE POHUE	LOC	39 15 176 41	40
TE POHUE (TRIG)	HILL	37 49 178 24	25
TE POI	LOC	37 53 175 50	19
TE POI	LOC	37 53 175 50	20
TE POKAPOKA (TRIG)	HILL	38 40 176 39	30
TE POPO	LOC	39 16 174 22	35
TE POPO	LOC	39 16 174 22	44
TE POPO STREAM	STRM	39 16 174 16	34
TE POROPORO POINT	PNT	38 42 175 46	28
TE POROPORO POINT	PNT	38 42 175 46	38
TE POUWHAKATUTU	LOC	38 33 176 03	28
TE POUWHAKATUTU	LOC	38 33 176 03	29
TE PUA	LOC	36 41 174 26	10
TE PUA	LOC	36 41 174 26	11
TE PUA POINT	PNT	34 32 172 57	2
TE PUAEHARURI STREAM	STRM	37 08 175 18	13
TE PUAEHARURI STREAM	STRM	37 08 175 18	15
TE PUHI	LOC	35 08 173 26	3
TE PUHI STREAM	STRM	35 07 173 20	3
TE PUHI (TRIG)	HILL	38 12 175 09	18
TE PUIA SPRINGS	LOC	38 03 178 18	25
TE PUIA STREAM	STRM	35 18 173 20	3
TE PUKE	POPL	37 47 176 20	20
TE PUKE	POPL	37 47 176 20	21
TE PUKE (TRIG)	HILL	35 15 174 02	4
TE PUKE (TRIG)	HILL	35 15 174 02	5
TE PUKE (TRIG)	HILL	37 09 175 38	15
TE PUKE (TRIG)	HILL	37 09 175 38	17
TE PUKE (TRIG)	PEAK	38 58 175 22	36
TE PUKE (TRIG)	PEAK	38 58 175 22	37
TE PUKEOHIKARUA	PEAK	39 11 176 17	39
TE PUNA	LOC	37 42 176 04	20
TE PUNA INLET	BAY	35 10 174 01	4
TE PUNA INLET	BAY	35 10 174 01	5
TE PUNA STREAM	STRM	37 41 176 02	20
TE PUNINGA	LOC	37 34 175 33	15
TE PUROA (TRIG)	HILL	37 42 175 06	18
TE PURU	LOC	37 03 175 31	13
TE PURU	LOC	37 03 175 31	15
TE PURU	LOC	37 03 175 31	16
TE PURU STREAM	STRM	37 03 175 31	13
TE PURU STREAM	STRM	37 03 175 31	15
TE PURU STREAM	STRM	37 03 175 31	16
TE RAE	LOC	40 34 172 42	57
TE RAHAU CANAL	CANL	37 58 176 57	22
TE RAHAU CANAL	CANL	37 58 176 57	23
TE RAHU	LOC	37 59 175 20	19
TE RAINA	LOC	38 50 175 40	28
TE RAINA	LOC	38 50 175 40	38
TE RAITE	HILL	34 48 173 05	2
TE RAITE	HILL	34 48 173 05	3
TE RAKE POINT	PNT	34 25 172 54	2
TE RAMANUIAPAKURA (TRIG)	HILL	38 37 177 37	31
TE RAMANUKA (TRIG)	HILL	34 44 173 01	2
TE RANGA	LOC	37 54 176 16	20
TE RANGA	LOC	37 45 176 07	20
TE RANGA	LOC	37 54 176 16	21
TE RANGA	LOC	37 45 176 07	21
TE RANGA (TRIG)	HILL	35 09 173 39	4
TE RANGA (TRIG)	HILL	35 20 174 16	5
TE RANGA (TRIG)	HILL	38 24 174 39	26
TE RANGAARUANUKU (TRIG)	HILL	38 28 176 59	30
TE RANGANUIATOI	MTN	37 49 177 59	24
TE RANGANUIATOI	MTN	37 49 177 59	25
TE RANGAWHAKARUA (TRIG)	PEAK	39 08 176 11	39
TE RANGI (TRIG)	HILL	35 24 174 14	5
TE RANGIITA	LOC	38 55 175 54	28
TE RANGIITA	LOC	38 55 175 54	29
TE RANGIITA	LOC	38 55 175 54	37
TE RANGIITA	LOC	38 55 175 54	38
TE RANGINUI (TRIG)	HILL	37 39 177 57	24
TE RAPA	LOC	37 45 175 14	18
TE RAPA	LOC	37 45 175 14	19
TE RAPA	HSTD	41 54 174 05	67
TE RAUAMOA	LOC	38 06 175 03	18
TE RAUKAUWHAKAMATAKU POINT	PNT	41 35 175 21	53
TE RAUMAUKU	LOC	38 10 175 10	18
TE RAUONE BEACH	LOC	45 48 170 44	103
TE RAUPO	LOC	34 47 173 06	2
TE RAUPO	LOC	34 47 173 06	3
TE RAUPUA	HILL	35 31 173 31	6
TE RAWA	HSTD	41 04 173 54	54
TE RAWA	HSTD	41 04 173 54	60
TE RAWA	HSTD	41 04 173 54	61
TE RAWHITI INLET	BAY	35 14 174 12	5
TE REI (TRIG)	PEAK	39 30 175 52	37
TE REINGA	LOC	38 50 177 31	31
TE REINGA	LOC	38 50 177 31	33
TE REINGA BAY	BAY	34 56 173 32	3
TE REINGA (TRIG)	HILL	38 05 177 40	24
TE REINGA (TRIG)	HILL	38 48 177 30	31
TE REINGA (TRIG)	HILL	38 48 177 30	33
TE REINGAOTEMOKO	HILL	38 31 176 51	30
TE RERE PA	LOC	38 01 177 19	23
TE REREATUKAHIA STREAM	STRM	37 35 175 55	20
TE REREKOTURUTUKU (TRIG)	HILL	39 00 175 04	36
TE RERENGA	LOC	36 46 175 36	16
TE RERENGA STREAM	STRM	37 54 176 15	20
TE RERENGA STREAM	STRM	37 54 176 15	21
TE REWA POINT	PNT	35 27 173 23	6
TE REWAREWA POINT	PNT	41 04 174 50	52
TE REWAREWA POINT	PNT	41 04 174 50	55
TE REWHATAU STREAM	STRM	37 40 178 06	25
TE ROA BAY	BAY	35 14 174 18	5
TE ROHOTAIEPA RIVER	STRM	42 58 170 39	74
TE ROKOTAI (TRIG)	HILL	36 29 174 15	10
TE RORE	LOC	35 11 173 23	3
TE RORE	LOC	37 56 175 12	18
TE RORE STREAM	STRM	35 09 173 21	3
TE ROTETE (TRIG)	PEAK	39 24 175 47	37
TE ROTI	LOC	39 30 174 17	34
TE ROTI	LOC	39 30 174 17	35
TE ROTI	LOC	39 30 174 17	44
TE ROTO KARE	LAKE	39 34 176 48	40
TE ROTO KARE	LAKE	39 34 176 48	42
TE ROTO KARE	LAKE	39 34 176 48	43
TE ROTO O KIWA	LAKE	39 49 176 40	42
TE ROTO O KIWA	LAKE	39 49 176 40	43
TE ROTO O KIWA	LAKE	39 49 176 40	47
TE ROTOMANOAO (TRIG)	HILL	35 12 173 40	4
TE ROUITI PA	LOC	39 05 176 16	39
TE RUATAKAIKARE (TRIG)	PEAK	39 13 176 13	39
TE RUAUHI (TRIG)	HILL	38 04 177 07	23
TE RURUKU BAY	BAY	36 12 174 08	7
TE TAHEKE (TRIG)	HILL	38 01 176 22	20
TE TAHEKE (TRIG)	HILL	38 01 176 22	21
TE TAHI	LOC	38 02 175 08	18
TE TAHI (TRIG)	HILL	38 49 177 25	31
TE TAHI (TRIG)	HILL	38 49 177 25	33
TE TAHO	LOC	43 13 170 27	74
TE TAHUA (TRIG)	HILL	38 31 175 17	27
TE TAPUAE	HILL	38 31 176 58	30
TE TAPUI	HILL	37 50 175 39	19
TE TARAHIORAHIRI (TRIG)	HILL	35 40 173 56	7
TE TATAU POUNAMU WILDERNESS AREA	WILD	39 08 175 43	37
TE TATAU POUNAMU WILDERNESS AREA	WILD	39 08 175 43	38
TE TAU BANK	BNK	36 59 174 40	12
TE TAU BANK	BNK	36 59 174 40	14
TE TAWAI POINT	PNT	38 47 175 44	28
TE TAWAI POINT	PNT	38 47 175 44	38
TE TEHI STREAM	STRM	38 44 176 40	30
TE TEKO	LOC	38 02 176 48	22
TE TEKO (TRIG)	HILL	38 13 175 49	19
TE TEKO (TRIG)	HILL	38 13 175 49	20
TE TII	LOC	35 09 174 00	4
TE TII	LOC	35 09 174 00	5
TE TIPUA	LOC	46 11 168 46	110
TE TIPUA	LOC	46 11 168 46	112
TE TIRINGA STREAM	STRM	38 59 176 00	38
TE TIRINGA STREAM	STRM	38 59 176 00	39
TE TIROA POINT	PNT	38 46 175 45	28
TE TIROA POINT	PNT	38 46 175 45	38
TE TITOKI POINT	PNT	36 13 175 03	9
TE TOHE STREAM	STRM	40 19 176 31	50
TE TOI STREAM	STRM	38 07 174 54	18
TE TORO	LOC	37 10 174 40	12
TE TORO	LOC	37 10 174 40	14
TE TOTARA STREAM	STRM	38 44 176 52	30
TE TOTARA (TRIG)	HILL	37 59 175 53	20
TE TOTIPO HEAD	HEAD	34 28 173 00	2
TE (TRIG)	MTN	38 45 177 03	30
TE TUA	LOC	46 10 167 41	106
TE TUA	LOC	46 10 167 41	108
TE TUHI	LOC	39 43 175 09	45
TE TUHI JUNCTION	LOC	39 38 174 58	45
TE TUHI POINT	PNT	38 42 175 54	28
TE TUHI POINT	PNT	38 42 175 54	29
TE TUHI POINT	PNT	38 42 175 54	38
TE TUHI (TRIG)	HILL	39 43 175 06	45
TE TUMU	LOC	37 47 176 24	21
TE TUTU (TRIG)	HILL	36 44 175 42	16
TE UKE	LOC	37 50 174 58	18
TE UKU LANDING	LOC	37 49 174 59	18
TE UKU (TRIG)	HILL	37 52 174 58	18
TE UMAKURI POINT	PNT	35 21 173 11	3
TE UMUOTAMAIHU (TRIG)	MTN	37 59 178 02	25
TE UNUUNUAKAPUATEARIKI STREAM	STRM	39 27 175 33	36
TE UNUUNUAKAPUATEARIKI STREAM	STRM	39 27 175 33	37
TE UPOKOOHINEPAKI POINT	PNT	37 50 178 27	25
TE UPOKOOKOHU (TRIG)	HILL	37 58 177 33	24
TE URA (TRIG)	HILL	35 58 174 03	7
TE URI	LOC	40 15 176 23	47
TE URI	LOC	40 15 176 23	50
TE URI STREAM	STRM	40 18 176 32	50
TE WAEWAE	LOC	46 12 167 40	106
TE WAEWAE	LOC	46 12 167 40	108
TE WAEWAE BAY	BAY	46 13 167 30	105
TE WAEWAE BAY	BAY	46 13 167 30	106
TE WAEWAE BAY	BAY	46 13 167 30	108
TE WAI O TUPURITIA STREAM	STRM	39 08 176 09	39
TE WAIITI	LOC	37 56 177 31	24
TE WAIITI	LOC	38 37 176 59	30
TE WAIOTUKAPITI STREAM	STRM	38 49 176 51	30
TE WAIPOKA STREAM	STRM	35 22 173 26	3
TE WAIROA	LOC	38 13 176 22	20
TE WAIROA	LOC	38 13 176 22	21
TE WAIROA	LOC	38 13 176 22	29
TE WAITERE	LOC	38 08 174 48	18
TE WAITI HILL (TRIG)	HILL	38 14 177 25	24
TE WAITI HILL (TRIG)	HILL	38 14 177 25	31
TE WAITI STREAM	STRM	38 07 177 23	23
TE WAITI STREAM	STRM	37 40 177 50	24
TE WAKA (TRIG)	PEAK	39 14 176 39	39
TE WAKA (TRIG)	PEAK	39 14 176 39	40
TE WAKATEHAUA ISLAND	ISLD	34 41 172 54	2
TE WANA (TRIG)	MTN	38 30 177 15	31
TE WARO (TRIG)	HILL	38 27 176 13	29
TE WARO (TRIG)	HILL	39 12 175 19	36
TE WERA	HSTD	38 28 177 26	31
TE WERA	LOC	39 14 174 35	35
TE WERA	LOC	39 14 174 35	44
TE WERA, MOUNT	MTN	44 40 168 03	89
TE WERAAKAUANGA (TRIG)	HILL	38 05 177 29	24
TE WERAHI BEACH	BCH	34 27 172 40	2
TE WERAHI STREAM	STRM	34 28 172 40	2
TE WERAITI (TRIG)	HILL	37 50 175 55	20
TE WETA (TRIG)	HILL	38 22 176 13	29
TE WHA STREAM	STRM	37 35 175 05	18
TE WHAIAU, LAKE	LAKE	39 01 175 37	37
TE WHAIAU, LAKE	LAKE	39 01 175 37	38
TE WHAITI	LOC	38 35 176 47	30
TE WHAKARAE	LOC	38 56 175 12	27
TE WHAKARAE	LOC	38 56 175 12	36
TE WHAKAUMU (TRIG)	HILL	38 15 176 56	22
TE WHAKAUMU (TRIG)	HILL	38 15 176 56	30
TE WHAKAUMUATANGIHIA (TRIG)	HILL	37 48 178 16	25
TE WHANGA	HSTD	41 02 175 42	51
TE WHANGA	HSTD	41 02 175 42	53
TE WHARANGI (TRIG)	HILL	35 18 173 23	3
TE WHARAU	LOC	35 55 173 53	6
TE WHARAU	LOC	35 55 173 53	7
TE WHARAU	LOC	41 10 175 50	51
TE WHARAU RIVER	STRM	42 00 171 53	63
TE WHARAU RIVER	STRM	42 00 171 53	64
TE WHATA (TRIG)	HILL	39 25 176 16	39
TE WHAU	LOC	35 09 173 53	4
TE WHAU POINT	PNT	36 38 175 26	13
TE WHAU POINT	PNT	36 38 175 26	16
TE WHAU (TRIG)	HILL	35 09 173 53	4
TE WHETU	LOC	38 10 175 57	20
TE WHIORAU (TRIG)	HILL	37 57 177 31	24
TE WI BAY	BAY	35 12 174 19	5
TE WIRIKI STREAM	STRM	41 48 172 30	65
TEACHIMATE BAY	BAY	46 39 169 14	112
TEACHIMATE BAY	BAY	46 39 169 14	113
TEAL CREEK	STRM	44 15 169 13	78
TEAL RIVER	STRM	41 14 173 24	59
TEAM STREAM	STRM	42 02 173 10	66
TEARDROP, LAKE	LAKE	45 14 167 11	96
TECHNICAL, MOUNT	MTN	42 25 172 21	71
TEDDINGTON	LOC	43 40 172 39	82
TEDDINGTON	LOC	43 40 172 39	83
TEDDINGTON	LOC	43 40 172 39	85
TEDDY, MOUNT (TRIG)	HILL	40 52 172 17	56
TEDDYS HILL	MTN	43 22 171 06	75
TEER CREEK	STRM	44 00 168 29	88
TEER HILL (TRIG)	HILL	44 01 168 30	88
TEHEKEOTEWHARE (TRIG)	HILL	38 18 176 59	30
TEHEOIRI (TRIG)	HILL	35 02 173 50	4
TEHEPOUTU POINT	PNT	34 31 172 42	2
TEKAPO HYDRO ELECTRICITY CANAL	CANL	44 01 170 27	86
TEKAPO, LAKE	LAKE	43 53 170 32	77
TEKAPO, LAKE	LAKE	43 53 170 32	86
TEKAPO MILITARY CAMP	BLDG	44 00 170 24	77

TEKAPO MILITARY CAMP	BLDG	44 00 170 24	86
TEKAPO RIVER	STRM	44 00 170 29	77
TEKAPO RIVER	STRM	44 00 170 29	86
TEKOA, MOUNT (TRIG)	MTN	42 40 172 38	71
TEKOA RANGE	MTNS	42 41 172 37	71
TEKOE	MTN	43 46 169 51	76
TEKOE	MTN	43 46 169 51	79
TEKURA ROCKS	ROCK	34 55 173 35	3
TEKURA ROCKS	ROCK	34 55 173 35	4
TELFORD BURN	STRM	45 50 167 53	106
TELFORD PEAK	PEAK	45 46 167 50	106
TEME RIVER	STRM	41 42 173 36	66
TEMPLE PEAK	PEAK	44 48 168 29	89
TEMPLE PEAK	PEAK	44 48 168 29	95
TEMPLE STREAM	STRM	44 09 169 50	79
TEMPLE VIEW	LOC	37 49 175 13	18
TEMPLE VIEW	LOC	37 49 175 13	19
TEMPLETON	LOC	43 33 172 28	81
TEMPLETON	LOC	43 33 172 28	82
TEMPLETON	LOC	43 33 172 28	85
TEMUKA	POPL	44 15 171 17	84
TEMUKA	POPL	44 15 171 17	87
TEN CHAIN CREEK	STRM	44 50 169 55	92
TEN HOUR GORGE CREEK	STRM	44 21 168 31	88
TEN HOUR GORGE CREEK	STRM	44 21 168 31	89
TEN MILE CREEK	STRM	42 20 171 16	63
TEN MILE CREEK	STRM	42 20 171 16	69
TENGAWAI RIVER	STRM	44 10 170 47	86
TENGAWAI RIVER	STRM	44 15 171 08	87
TENNANTS PEAK (TRIG)	PEAK	45 24 168 46	99
TENNYSON INLET	BAY	41 05 173 47	60
TENNYSON INLET	HSTD	41 08 173 45	60
TENNYSON INLET	HSTD	41 08 173 45	61
TENNYSON INLET	BAY	41 05 173 47	61
TENNYSON, LAKE	LAKE	42 12 172 44	65
TENNYSON MOUNT (TRIG)	PEAK	45 27 168 50	99
TENT PEAK	PEAK	43 21 171 01	75
TENT PEAK	PEAK	44 10 169 28	79
TENT (TRIG)	HILL	40 52 175 11	48
TENT (TRIG)	HILL	40 52 175 11	52
TENT (TRIG)	HILL	40 52 175 11	55
TERAKO, MOUNT (TRIG)	MTN	42 27 173 09	72
TERAKO, MOUNT (TRIG)	MTN	42 27 173 09	73
TERAWHITI, CAPE	CAPE	41 18 174 37	52
TERAWHITI, CAPE	CAPE	41 18 174 37	55
TERAWHITI HILL (TRIG)	HILL	41 17 174 38	52
TERAWHITI HILL (TRIG)	HILL	41 17 174 38	55
TERMINUS CREEK	STRM	44 55 167 45	94
TERRA NOVA PASS	PASS	43 26 170 37	74
TERRA NOVA PASS	PASS	43 26 170 37	77
TERRACE CREEK	STRM	44 20 169 26	91
TERRACE CREEK	STRM	46 11 168 15	107
TERRACE CREEK (SOUTH BRANCH)	STRM	44 20 169 25	91
TERRACE EDGE (TRIG)	HILL	44 02 168 29	88
TERRACE END	SBRB	40 21 175 38	48
TERRACE END	SBRB	40 21 175 38	49
TERRACE PEAK	PEAK	44 20 169 21	91
TERRES, MOUNT	MTN	44 28 167 55	89
TERRIBLE KNOB (TRIG)	PEAK	42 43 172 05	70
TERROR PEAK	PEAK	44 40 167 49	94
TESCHEMAKERS	LOC	45 09 170 51	102
TETEHE (TRIG)	HILL	37 25 174 44	14
TEVIOT	LOC	45 36 169 22	100
TEVIOT, MOUNT (TRIG)	MTN	45 36 169 32	100
TEVIOT RIVER	STRM	45 32 169 19	100
TEVIOT RIVER (NORTH BRANCH)	STRM	45 32 169 38	100
TEVIOT RIVER (SOUTH BRANCH)	STRM	45 33 169 39	100
THAMES	TOWN	37 09 175 33	13
THAMES	TOWN	37 09 175 33	15
THE BRANCH	HSTD	41 41 173 11	66
THE FIVE BRIDGES	LOC	38 20 178 10	32
THE GATES	HSTD	42 35 173 06	72
THE GRAMPIANS	HSTD	42 45 172 41	71
THE GROVE	LOC	41 17 173 55	54
THE GROVE	LOC	41 17 173 55	60
THE GROVE	LOC	41 17 173 55	61
THE HERMITAGE	HSTD	42 44 173 03	72
THE HOOK	LOC	38 57 175 46	37
THE HOOK	LOC	38 57 175 46	38
THE HOSSACK	HSTD	42 32 172 58	71
THE HOSSACK	HSTD	42 32 172 58	72
THE KAIK	LOC	43 50 172 57	83
THE KEY	LOC	45 33 167 54	97
THE KEY	LOC	45 33 167 54	98
THE LAKES	HSTD	42 24 173 36	73
THE PINES BEACH	LOC	43 23 172 42	82
THE PINES BEACH	LOC	43 23 172 42	83
THE PLATEAU	LOC	41 05 175 09	52
THE PLATEAU	LOC	41 05 175 09	53
THE PLATEAU	LOC	41 05 175 09	55
THE POINT	LOC	43 30 171 41	80
THE ROCKS	LOC	46 23 168 02	109
THE SPIRAL	LOC	39 07 175 24	36
THE SPIRAL	LOC	39 07 175 24	37
THE THREE BRIDGES	LOC	38 15 178 15	32
THE WARREN	LOC	43 20 172 12	81
THE WARREN	LOC	43 20 172 12	85
THELMA PEAK	PEAK	43 27 170 13	74
THELMA PEAK	PEAK	43 27 170 13	77
THERMA GLACIER	GLCR	44 22 168 44	88
THERMA GLACIER	GLCR	44 22 168 44	90
THESIS PEAK	PEAK	43 06 171 31	80
THETA, MOUNT (TRIG)	MTN	44 10 168 25	88
THETA TARN	LAKE	44 12 168 27	88
THICKET BURN	STRM	46 00 167 30	105
THIRD COVE	BAY	45 31 166 52	96
THIRD WATERFALL STREAM	STRM	43 40 170 38	74
THIRD WATERFALL STREAM	STRM	43 40 170 38	77
THIRTEEN MILE BUSH STREAM	STRM	43 20 171 51	80
THISBE STREAM	STRM	46 24 169 26	113
THOMAS BURN	STRM	45 32 167 56	97
THOMAS BURN	STRM	45 32 167 56	98
THOMAS, LAKE	LAKE	45 59 166 30	104
THOMAS, LAKE	LAKE	45 28 167 57	97
THOMAS, LAKE	LAKE	45 28 167 57	98
THOMAS, MOUNT (TRIG)	MTN	43 56 169 13	78
THOMAS, MOUNT (TRIG)	MTN	43 10 172 21	81
THOMAS RANGE	MTNS	43 53 169 18	78
THOMAS RIVER	STRM	43 56 169 09	78
THOMAS STREAM	STRM	42 05 173 26	66
THOMPSON, LAKE	LAKE	44 48 167 59	89
THOMPSON, LAKE	LAKE	42 08 172 38	65
THOMPSON, MOUNT	MTN	45 39 167 03	105
THOMPSON, MOUNT	MTN	43 43 170 01	76
THOMPSON, MOUNT	MTN	43 43 170 01	77
THOMPSON, MOUNT	MTN	43 43 170 01	79
THOMPSON SOUND	SND	45 09 166 58	96
THOMPSON STREAM	STRM	42 51 171 51	70
THOMPSON STREAM	STRM	43 53 169 53	76
THOMPSON (TRIG)	PEAK	40 46 175 15	48
THOMPSONS POINT	PNT	36 46 175 03	13
THOMS ROCK	ROCK	41 21 174 40	52
THOMS ROCK	ROCK	41 21 174 40	55
THOMSON CREEK	STRM	44 12 168 41	88
THOMSON HILL(TRIG)	HILL	41 21 172 43	58
THOMSON, LAKE	LAKE	45 02 167 32	94
THOMSON, LAKE	LAKE	45 02 167 32	97
THOMSON MOUNTAINS	MTNS	45 07 168 15	95
THOMSON MOUNTAINS	MTNS	45 07 168 15	98
THOMSON RIDGE	RDGE	46 51 167 56	109
THOMSON RIDGE	RDGE	46 51 167 56	114
THOMSON STREAM	STRM	43 53 169 53	79
THOMSONS CREEK	STRM	45 06 169 40	100
THOMSONS CREEK	STRM	45 46 169 09	110
THOMSONS CROSSING	LOC	46 11 168 20	107
THOMSONS SADDLE	SAD	44 58 169 28	91
THOMSONS SADDLE	SAD	44 58 169 28	100
THORNBURY	LOC	46 17 168 06	109
THORNDIKE, MOUNT	MTN	43 09 170 57	75
THORNTON	LOC	37 55 176 52	22
THORNTON	LOC	37 55 176 52	23
THORNTON BAY	LOC	37 04 175 31	13
THORNTON BAY	LOC	37 04 175 31	15
THORNTON BAY	LOC	37 04 175 31	16
THORPE	LOC	41 17 172 53	58
THREE DUCKS LAKE	LAKE	45 00 167 17	94
THREE DUCKS LAKE	LAKE	45 00 167 17	96
THREE KINGS ISLANDS	ISLS	34 10 172 07	2
THREE KINGS RANGE	MTNS	39 23 175 54	37
THREE KINGS, THE	PEAK	40 50 175 26	48
THREE MILE BUSH	LOC	35 42 174 17	5
THREE MILE BUSH	LOC	35 42 174 17	7
THREE MILE BUSH	LOC	35 42 174 17	8
THREE MILE LAGOON	LAGN	43 15 170 07	76
THREE MILE STREAM	STRM	42 42 172 12	70
THREE O'CLOCK STREAM	STRM	45 41 170 21	102
THREE PEAKS	PEAK	41 55 172 31	65
THREE SISTERS	PEAK	41 59 171 36	63
THREE SISTERS (TRIG)	HILL	46 32 168 15	109
THREE STEEPLES	ROCK	41 43 171 28	63
THREE STREAMS	LOC	37 49 174 54	18
THUMB POINT	PNT	36 45 175 10	13
THUMBS, THE	MTN	43 36 170 43	74
THUNDERBOLT CREEK	STRM	39 10 175 54	37
THUNDERBOLT CREEK	STRM	39 10 175 54	38
THURSO STREAM	STRM	42 21 172 33	65
THURSO STREAM	STRM	42 21 172 33	71
TI POINT	LOC	36 19 174 47	11
TI TREE POINT	PNT	40 27 176 24	50
TIA ISLAND	ISLD	47 04 168 13	115
TIAKAKA (TRIG)	HILL	39 31 175 24	36
TIAKAKA (TRIG)	HILL	39 31 175 24	37
TIAKITAHUNA	LOC	40 24 175 30	48
TIAKITAHUNA	LOC	40 24 175 30	49
TIDAL CREEK	STRM	41 23 172 05	62
TIGER STREAM	STRM	41 44 171 55	63
TIGER STREAM	STRM	41 44 171 55	64
TIHIA (TRIG)	PEAK	39 00 175 44	37
TIHIA (TRIG)	PEAK	39 00 175 44	38
TIHIROA	LOC	38 06 175 11	18
TIHOI	LOC	38 37 175 37	28
TIHOREA (TRIG)	PEAK	38 59 176 20	39
TIKAO	LOC	43 48 172 54	83
TIKIKARU (TRIG)	HILL	38 26 175 06	27
TIKINUI	LOC	36 08 173 58	7
TIKIPUNGA	SBRB	35 41 174 20	5
TIKIPUNGA	SBRB	35 41 174 20	7
TIKIPUNGA	SBRB	35 41 174 20	8
TIKIRAU (TRIG)	HILL	37 33 178 00	24
TIKIRAU (TRIG)	HILL	37 33 178 00	25
TIKIRERE STREAM	STRM	39 36 175 52	37
TIKITAPU, LAKE	LAKE	38 12 176 20	20
TIKITAPU, LAKE	LAKE	38 12 176 20	21
TIKITERE	LOC	38 04 176 22	20
TIKITERE	LOC	38 04 176 22	21
TIKITIKI	LOC	37 48 178 25	25
TIKITIKI ISLAND	ISLD	35 09 174 08	4
TIKITIKI ISLAND	ISLD	35 09 174 08	5
TIKITIKI (TRIG)	HILL	37 33 174 55	14
TIKITIKI (TRIG)	HILL	38 30 175 04	26
TIKITIKI (TRIG)	HILL	38 30 175 04	27
TIKOKINO	POPL	39 49 176 27	47
TIKOKOPU STREAM	STRM	36 44 174 31	10
TIKOKOPU STREAM	STRM	36 44 174 31	11
TIKOKOPU STREAM	STRM	36 44 174 31	12
TIKOPUTA STREAM	STRM	38 44 174 51	26
TIKORAKI POINT	PNT	45 22 170 52	102
TIKORANGI	LOC	39 02 174 17	34
TIKORANGI (TRIG)	HILL	34 32 172 52	2
TIKORANGI (TRIG)	HILL	35 48 174 19	7
TIKORANGI (TRIG)	HILL	35 48 174 19	8
TIKORANGI (TRIG)	HILL	38 35 176 44	30
TIKORE ISLAND	ISLD	46 34 168 19	109
TIKOTATAHI BAY	BAY	47 06 168 10	115
TIKOTIKO	LOC	37 29 175 00	14
TIKOTIKO STREAM	STRM	37 28 175 01	14
TILBY POINT	PNT	37 40 176 07	20
TILBY POINT	PNT	37 40 176 07	21
TIM BURN	STRM	44 45 169 31	91
TIMA BURN	STRM	45 39 169 24	100
TIMAHANGA STREAM	STRM	39 30 176 15	39
TIMARU	TOWN	44 24 171 15	93
TIMARU RIVER	STRM	44 32 169 19	91
TIMARU STREAM	STRM	39 07 173 55	34
TIMBER BAY	LOC	40 15 176 06	47
TIMBER CREEK	STRM	45 39 169 11	100
TIMMS STREAM	STRM	41 33 173 31	59
TIMMS STREAM	STRM	42 22 172 48	71
TIMPANYS	LOC	46 27 168 31	109
TIMPENDEAN	HSTD	42 59 172 42	71
TIMUTIMU HEAD	HEAD	43 54 172 57	83
TIN HUT STREAM	STRM	43 46 170 24	86
TIN HUT STREAM	STRM	41 51 173 35	66
TIN HUT STREAM	STRM	43 46 170 24	77
TIN RANGE	MTNS	47 07 167 46	114
TINAKORI	HSTD	40 56 175 52	49
TINAKORI	HSTD	40 56 175 52	51
TINDALE CREEK	STRM	42 09 171 26	63
TINIROTO	LOC	38 46 177 34	31
TINIROTO	LOC	38 46 177 34	33
TINIROTO LAKES	LAKE	38 46 177 33	31
TINIROTO LAKES	LAKE	38 46 177 33	33
TINKERS SADDLE	SAD	42 11 173 27	66
TINKERTOWN	LOC	45 58 168 02	106
TINKERTOWN	LOC	45 58 168 02	107
TINLINE CREEK	STRM	42 24 173 09	72
TINLINE CREEK	STRM	42 24 173 09	73
TINLINE DOWNS	HSTD	42 33 173 05	72
TINLINE, MOUNT (TRIG)	MTN	42 27 173 07	72
TINLINE RIVER	STRM	41 19 173 30	59
TINOPAI	LOC	36 15 174 15	10
TINTOCK (TRIG)	HILL	40 47 175 53	49
TINTOCK (TRIG)	HILL	40 47 175 53	51
TINUI	LOC	40 53 176 04	49
TINUI	LOC	40 53 176 04	51
TINUI HILL (TRIG)	HILL	40 49 176 09	49
TINUI HILL (TRIG)	HILL	40 49 176 09	50
TINUI HILL (TRIG)	HILL	40 49 176 09	51
TINUI ISLAND	ISLD	40 47 173 58	54
TINUI ISLAND	ISLD	40 47 173 58	61
TINUI RIVER	STRM	40 53 176 05	49
TINUI RIVER	STRM	40 53 176 05	50
TINUI RIVER	STRM	40 53 176 05	51
TINWALD	USAT	43 55 171 44	84
TINWALD BURN	STRM	44 56 169 18	91
TIPAPA	HSTD	42 58 172 59	72
TIRAKI STREAM	STRM	38 56 176 06	38
TIRAKI STREAM	STRM	38 56 176 06	39
TIRAU	POPL	37 59 175 46	19
TIRAU (TRIG)	HILL	38 01 175 44	19
TIRAUMEA	LOC	40 38 176 03	49
TIRAUMEA RIVER	STRM	40 24 175 54	49
TIRAUMEA RIVER	STRM	41 47 172 22	65
TIRAUMEA SADDLE	SAD	41 55 172 38	65
TIRIKAHU STREAM	STRM	38 57 176 24	39
TIRIKAHU STREAM	STRM	38 57 176 24	40
TIRIKAWA (TRIG)	HILL	34 27 172 44	2
TIRIRAUKAU (TRIG)	HILL	39 52 175 31	45
TIRIRAUKAU (TRIG)	HILL	39 52 175 31	46
TIRIRAUKAWA	LOC	39 45 175 40	46
TIRITEA	LOC	40 25 175 40	48
TIRITEA	LOC	40 25 175 40	49
TIRITEA STREAM	STRM	40 23 175 36	48
TIRITIRI MATANGI ISLAND	ISLD	36 36 174 53	11
TIRITIRI MATANGI ISLAND	ISLD	36 36 174 53	12
TIROA	LOC	38 31 175 29	27
TIROHANGA	LOC	38 01 177 24	23
TIROHANGA	LOC	46 26 169 47	113
TIROHANGA POINT	PNT	37 34 176 02	20
TIROHANGA STREAM	STRM	35 24 174 06	4
TIROHANGA STREAM	STRM	35 24 174 06	5
TIROHANGA STREAM	STRM	39 15 174 48	35
TIROHANGA STREAM	STRM	39 15 174 48	44
TIROHANGA (TRIG)	HILL	38 16 178 09	32
TIROHANGA (TRIG)	HILL	39 07 177 03	41
TIROHIA	LOC	37 26 175 39	15
TIROHIA	LOC	37 26 175 39	17
TIROITI	LOC	45 16 170 16	101
TIROMOANA	LOC	42 02 171 23	63
TIROROA	LOC	41 52 171 47	63
TIROROA	LOC	41 52 171 47	64
TIROTIROWHETU (TRIG)	HILL	39 01 177 09	41
TIRUA POINT	PNT	38 23 174 38	26
TISBURY	LOC	46 27 168 25	109
TITAHA (TRIG)	HILL	35 15 173 22	3
TITAHI BAY	SBRB	41 06 174 50	52
TITAHI BAY	SBRB	41 06 174 50	55
TITAN BLUFF (TRIG)	HILL	46 28 169 25	113
TITAN ROCKS (TRIG)	PEAK	45 32 168 59	99
TITAN STREAM	STRM	43 16 171 19	75
TITAN STREAM	STRM	43 16 171 19	80
TITAPU (TRIG)	PEAK	39 39 176 06	47
TITAU STREAM	STRM	39 23 176 07	39
TITI ISLAND	ISLD	40 57 174 08	54
TITI ISLAND	ISLD	40 57 174 08	61
TITIHUATAHU (TRIG)	HILL	35 26 173 53	4
TITIHUATAHU (TRIG)	HILL	35 26 173 53	6
TITINUI STREAM	STRM	37 56 177 35	24
TITIOKURA	HSTD	39 13 176 42	40
TITIPU ISLAND	ISLD	36 14 174 10	7
TITIPUA STREAM	STRM	46 15 168 31	107
TITIPUA STREAM	STRM	46 15 168 31	109
TITIRANGI	SBRB	36 56 174 39	12
TITIRANGI	SBRB	36 56 174 39	14
TITIRANGI BAY	BAY	41 00 174 08	54
TITIRANGI BAY	BAY	41 00 174 08	60
TITIRANGI BAY	BAY	41 00 174 08	61
TITIRANGI (TRIG)	HILL	38 24 178 19	32
TITIRAUPENGA (TRIG)	MTN	38 31 175 42	28
TITIROA	LOC	46 29 168 46	112
TITIROA, MOUNT	MTN	45 40 167 31	105
TITIROA, MOUNT	MTN	45 40 167 31	106
TITIROA STREAM	STRM	46 34 168 46	112
TITITIRA HEAD	HEAD	43 38 169 25	78
TITOKI	LOC	35 44 174 04	5
TITOKI	LOC	35 44 174 04	7
TITOKI STREAM	STRM	37 43 175 32	19
TIWAI POINT	PNT	46 36 168 22	109
TOA BRIDGE	LOC	38 17 175 21	27
TOAROHA RANGE	MTNS	42 58 171 11	68
TOAROHA RANGE	MTNS	42 58 171 11	69
TOAROHA RIVER	STRM	42 53 171 07	68
TOAROHA RIVER	STRM	42 53 171 07	69
TOAROHA SADDLE	SAD	43 02 171 10	75
TOATOA	LOC	35 03 173 26	3
TOATOA	LOC	38 07 177 30	24
TOATOA (TRIG)	HILL	38 08 177 31	24
TOBY, MOUNT	MTN	43 40 170 43	86
TODEA STREAM	STRM	40 02 175 54	46
TOE RAG CREEK	STRM	40 43 172 29	56
TOE RAG CREEK	STRM	40 43 172 29	57
TOENEPI STREAM	STRM	37 42 175 33	19
TOENGA (TRIG)	HILL	41 10 174 10	54
TOENGA (TRIG)	HILL	41 10 174 10	60
TOENGA (TRIG)	HILL	41 10 174 10	61
TOETOE	LOC	35 46 174 19	5
TOETOE	LOC	35 46 174 19	7
TOETOE	LOC	35 46 174 19	8
TOETOE POINT	PNT	36 17 174 09	10
TOETOE STREAM	STRM	38 50 175 01	26
TOETOE STREAM	STRM	38 50 175 01	27
TOETOE (TRIG)	HILL	34 36 172 52	2
TOETOEHATIKO (TRIG)	HILL	35 39 173 36	6
TOETOES BAY	BAY	46 36 168 40	112
TOETOES (TRIG)	HILL	46 32 168 47	112
TOI FLAT	LOC	40 21 176 17	50
TOIRO	LOC	46 16 169 39	111
TOIRO	LOC	46 16 169 39	113
TOIRO (TRIG)	HILL	38 37 175 06	27
TOIROA (TRIG)	HILL	38 10 178 19	25
TOIROA (TRIG)	HILL	38 10 178 19	32
TOITOI FLAT	FLAT	47 05 168 00	114
TOITOI FLAT	FLAT	47 05 168 00	115
TOITOI RIVER	STRM	47 07 168 00	114
TOITOI RIVER	STRM	47 07 168 00	115
TOKAANU	POPL	38 58 175 46	37
TOKAANU	POPL	38 58 175 46	38
TOKAKAHAKAHA ISLAND	ISLD	37 10 175 53	17
TOKAKORIRI CREEK	STRM	43 42 169 17	78
TOKANUI	LOC	38 04 175 20	18
TOKANUI	LOC	38 04 175 20	19
TOKANUI	POPL	46 34 168 57	112
TOKANUI RIVER	STRM	46 37 168 50	112
TOKAORA	LOC	39 35 174 13	34
TOKAPIKO (TRIG)	HILL	38 25 175 12	27
TOKARAHI	LOC	44 58 170 39	93
TOKARAHU POINT	PNT	36 42 175 47	16
TOKAROA POINT	PNT	37 00 175 52	16
TOKAROA POINT	PNT	37 00 175 52	17
TOKATA ISLAND	ISLD	37 50 176 52	22
TOKATA ISLAND	ISLD	37 50 176 52	23
TOKATA POINT	PNT	37 51 177 35	24
TOKATEA ROCKS	ROCK	38 18 178 21	32
TOKATOKA	LOC	36 04 173 59	7
TOKATOKA POINT	PNT	34 25 173 01	2
TOKATU POINT	PNT	36 22 174 52	11
TOKAWHERO POINT	PNT	36 07 175 31	9
TOKEAWA STREAM	STRM	40 12 175 47	46
TOKENUI STREAM	STRM	38 10 177 24	24
TOKENUI STREAM	STRM	38 10 177 24	31
TOKERAU	LOC	38 00 176 22	20
TOKERAU BEACH	LOC	34 54 173 22	3
TOKERAU BEACH	BCH	34 56 173 23	3
TOKIAHURU STREAM	STRM	39 29 175 28	36
TOKIAHURU STREAM	STRM	39 29 175 28	37
TOKIAMEHA (TRIG)	HILL	37 59 178 14	25
TOKIAMINGA STREAM	STRM	38 25 176 21	29
TOKIMATAA POINT	PNT	37 19 176 15	17
TOKIRIMA	LOC	38 57 175 01	36
TOKITOKIRAU STREAM	STRM	39 22 175 07	36
TOKO	LOC	39 20 174 24	35
TOKO	LOC	39 20 174 24	44
TOKO MOUTH	LOC	46 13 170 03	103
TOKO MOUTH	LOC	46 13 170 03	111
TOKO NGAWA POINT	PNT	41 01 173 01	57
TOKO NGAWA POINT	PNT	41 01 173 01	58
TOKO NGAWA POINT	PNT	41 01 173 01	59
TOKO STREAM	STRM	39 21 174 25	35
TOKO STREAM	STRM	39 21 174 25	44
TOKOITI	LOC	46 08 169 59	111
TOKOMAIRIRO	STRM	46 13 170 03	103
TOKOMAIRIRO	STRM	46 13 170 03	111
TOKOMAIRIRO RIVER (EAST BRANCH)	STRM	46 07 169 57	111
TOKOMAIRIRO RIVER (EAST BRANCH)	STRM	46 07 169 57	113
TOKOMAIRIRO RIVER (WEST BRANCH)	STRM	46 07 169 57	111
TOKOMAIRIRO RIVER (WEST BRANCH)	STRM	46 07 169 57	113
TOKOMARU	POPL	40 28 175 30	48
TOKOMARU	POPL	40 28 175 30	49
TOKOMARU BAY	LOC	38 08 178 19	25
TOKOMARU BAY	BAY	38 08 178 21	25
TOKOMARU BAY	BAY	38 08 178 21	32
TOKOMARU RIVER	STRM	40 32 175 24	48
TOKOMATA (TRIG)	HILL	34 57 173 37	3
TOKOMATA (TRIG)	HILL	34 57 173 37	4
TOKORANGI	LOC	40 05 175 29	45
TOKORANGI	LOC	40 05 175 29	46
TOKOROA	POPL	38 14 175 52	19
TOKOROA	POPL	38 14 175 52	20
TOKOROA	POPL	38 14 175 52	28
TOKOROA	POPL	38 14 175 52	29
TOKOROA BAY	BAY	43 50 172 44	83
TOLAGA BAY	BAY	38 22 178 19	32
TOLAGA BAY	LOC	38 22 178 18	32
TOLE, MOUNT	MTN	44 03 169 31	79
TOLEDO COL	SAD	43 21 170 50	75
TOLSON RIVER	STRM	46 54 167 58	109
TOLSON RIVER	STRM	46 54 167 58	114
TOLSON RIVER	STRM	46 54 167 58	115
TOM BOWLING BAY	BAY	34 25 172 57	2
TOM CREEK	STRM	43 10 170 33	74
TOMARATA	LOC	36 14 174 39	8
TOMARATA	LOC	36 14 174 39	11
TOMARATA LAKE	LAKE	36 12 174 39	8
TOMATEA POINT	PNT	40 36 172 41	57
TOMLINSONS SADDLE	SAD	41 53 173 47	67
TOMMY FLAT CREEK	STRM	45 36 170 34	102
TOMMY POINT	PNT	44 45 167 30	94
TOMMY STREAM	STRM	41 49 173 21	66
TOMMYS STREAM	STRM	43 00 172 32	71
TOMOANA	LOC	39 38 176 52	42
TOMOANA	LOC	39 38 176 52	43
TOMOGALAK STREAM	STRM	45 46 168 39	107
TOMS CREEK	STRM	42 46 171 38	70
TOMS STREAM	STRM	43 34 170 37	74
TONE RIVER	STRM	42 02 173 25	66
TONE SADDLE	SAD	42 09 173 23	66
TONGA ISLAND	ISLD	40 53 173 04	57
TONGA ROADSTEAD	ANCH	40 53 173 03	57
TONGAPORUTU	LOC	38 49 174 36	26
TONGAPORUTU RIVER	STRM	38 49 174 35	26
TONGARIRO	LOC	39 02 175 39	37
TONGARIRO	LOC	39 02 175 39	38
TONGARIRO, MOUNT	MTN	39 08 175 38	37
TONGARIRO, MOUNT	MTN	39 08 175 38	38
TONGARIRO NATIONAL PARK	PARK	39 13 175 36	37
TONGARIRO NATIONAL PARK	PARK	39 13 175 36	38
TONGARIRO RIVER	STRM	38 57 175 47	37
TONGARIRO RIVER	STRM	38 57 175 47	38
TONOA	LOC	36 12 174 21	7
TONY CREEK	STRM	41 18 172 06	62
TOOMEY STREAM	STRM	37 21 175 43	17
TOOTH PEAK	PEAK	44 59 168 19	95
TOOTH PEAK	PEAK	44 59 168 19	98
TOP MCMILLAN STREAM	STRM	44 07 170 03	79
TOP VALLEY STREAM	STRM	41 34 173 30	59
TOPEHAEHAE STREAM	STRM	37 43 175 32	19
TOPHEAVY	MTN	44 04 169 25	78
TOPHEAVY	MTN	44 04 169 25	79
TOPHOUSE	LOC	41 46 172 54	65
TOPSY, LAKE	LAKE	43 46 169 18	78
TOPUNI	LOC	36 13 174 28	7
TOPUNI	LOC	36 13 174 28	8
TOPUNI RIVER	STRM	36 15 174 28	8
TOPUNI RIVER	STRM	36 15 174 28	10
TOPUNI RIVER	STRM	36 15 174 28	11
TOR HILL	HILL	45 01 167 22	94
TOR HILL	HILL	45 01 167 22	96
TORA	HSTD	41 31 175 30	53
TORBAY	SBRB	36 42 174 45	11
TORBAY	SBRB	36 42 174 45	12
TOREA BAY	BAY	41 14 174 02	54
TOREA BAY	BAY	41 14 174 02	60
TOREA BAY	BAY	41 14 174 02	61
TOREADOR PEAK	PEAK	44 22 168 25	88
TOREADOR PEAK	PEAK	44 22 168 25	89
TOREHAPA STREAM	STRM	37 56 176 13	20
TOREHAPA STREAM	STRM	37 56 176 13	21
TOREHAPE	LOC	37 21 175 25	15
TOREPARU STREAM	STRM	37 57 174 47	18
TORERE	LOC	37 57 177 30	24

TORERE RIVER	STRM	37 57 177 29	24
TORLESSE, MOUNT (TRIG)	MTN	43 15 171 49	80
TORLESSE RANGE	MTNS	43 14 171 49	80
TORMORE	HILL	42 49 173 09	72
TORMORE	LOC	42 53 173 08	72
TORMORE	HILL	42 49 173 09	73
TORMORE	LOC	42 53 173 08	73
TORNADO GLACIER	GLCR	44 22 168 26	88
TORNADO GLACIER	GLCR	44 22 168 26	89
TOROA POINT	PNT	36 42 174 46	11
TOROA POINT	PNT	36 42 174 46	12
TOROPAPA STREAM	STRM	39 09 176 34	39
TOROPAPA STREAM	STRM	39 09 176 34	40
TORRENT BAY	BAY	40 57 173 04	57
TORRENT RIVER	STRM	40 57 173 03	57
TORRENT RIVER	STRM	40 57 173 03	58
TORRENT RIVER	STRM	40 57 173 03	59
TORUMANO (TRIG)	HILL	44 57 169 20	91
TORUMANO (TRIG)	HILL	44 57 169 20	100
TORY CHANNEL	CHAN	41 14 174 15	54
TORY CHANNEL	CHAN	41 14 174 15	60
TORY CHANNEL	CHAN	41 14 174 15	61
TOTANGI STREAM	STRM	38 32 177 45	32
TOTARA	HILL	35 26 173 57	4
TOTARA	LOC	37 10 175 33	13
TOTARA	LOC	37 10 175 33	15
TOTARA	LOC	45 08 170 52	102
TOTARA CREEK	STRM	40 56 175 24	48
TOTARA CREEK	STRM	44 15 171 06	87
TOTARA CREEK	STRM	44 30 170 04	92
TOTARA CREEK	STRM	45 19 169 57	101
TOTARA FLAT	LOC	42 18 171 37	63
TOTARA FLAT	LOC	42 18 171 37	64
TOTARA NORTH	LOC	35 02 173 43	4
TOTARA PARK	SBRB	41 07 175 05	52
TOTARA PARK	SBRB	41 07 175 05	55
TOTARA PEAK	PEAK	44 29 170 08	92
TOTARA PEAK (TRIG)	MTN	43 15 171 06	87
TOTARA POINT	PNT	38 07 174 47	18
TOTARA RIVER	STRM	41 52 171 28	63
TOTARA RIVER	STRM	42 52 170 49	68
TOTARA SADDLE	SAD	41 25 173 17	59
TOTARA SADDLE	SAD	42 04 173 49	67
TOTARA SADDLE	SAD	42 59 170 51	75
TOTARA STREAM	STRM	38 42 174 43	26
TOTARA STREAM	STRM	38 22 176 10	29
TOTARA STREAM	STRM	39 25 174 44	35
TOTARA STREAM	STRM	39 25 174 44	44
TOTARA STREAM	STRM	40 20 176 00	49
TOTARA STREAM	STRM	43 17 171 04	75
TOTARA (TRIG)	HILL	43 04 172 52	82
TOTARA (TRIG)	HILL	39 13 174 23	35
TOTARA (TRIG)	PEAK	42 30 173 25	72
TOTARA (TRIG)	PEAK	42 30 173 25	73
TOTARA VALLEY	LOC	44 14 171 00	87
TOTARANUI	LOC	40 49 173 00	57
TOUCAN STREAM	STRM	40 47 172 20	56
TOUWAI BAY	BAY	35 02 173 47	4
TOUWAI STREAM	STRM	35 02 173 47	4
TOWAI	LOC	35 30 174 09	4
TOWAI	LOC	35 30 174 09	5
TOWAI (TRIG)	HILL	40 25 176 09	50
TOWER HILL (TRIG)	HILL	45 46 168 34	107
TOWER HILLS	MTN	45 54 166 45	104
TOWER PEAK	PEAK	46 01 167 03	105
TOWER PEAK	PEAK	45 39 167 48	106
TOWER ROCKS	ROCK	40 42 173 57	61
TOWER (TRIG)	HILL	40 45 173 51	61
TOWING HEAD	HEAD	45 24 166 45	96
TOWNLEY MOUNTAINS	MTNS	45 38 167 12	105
TOWNSEND CREEK	STRM	42 45 171 47	70
TOWNSEND, MOUNT	MTN	43 44 169 56	76
TOWNSEND, MOUNT	MTN	43 44 169 56	79
TOWNSHEND RIVER	STRM	43 12 172 08	81
TOWY RIVER	STRM	42 27 173 16	72
TOWY RIVER	STRM	42 27 173 16	73
TRACK BURN	STRM	46 10 167 24	105
TRACK BURN	STRM	46 10 167 24	108
TRAIL STREAM	STRM	41 56 173 39	66
TRAIL STREAM	STRM	41 56 173 39	67
TRAILLS HILL	HILL	46 59 167 48	114
TRANSIT BEACH	BCH	44 36 167 44	94
TRANSIT RIVER	STRM	44 36 167 45	94
TRASS VALLEY STREAM	STRM	41 25 173 00	58
TRAVERS, MOUNT (TRIG)	MTN	42 01 172 44	65
TRAVERS RANGE	MTNS	41 57 172 44	65
TRAVERS RIVER	STRM	41 52 172 49	65
TRAVERS SADDLE	SAD	42 02 172 44	65
TREACEY, MOUNT	MTN	42 43 171 21	69
TREADWELL, MOUNT	MTN	43 04 171 13	75
TREBLE CONE	MTN	44 38 168 53	90
TREBLE CONE SKI FIELD	LOC	44 38 168 54	90
TREBLE MOUNTAIN	MTN	46 00 166 42	104
TREGEAR, MOUNT	MTN	43 05 171 09	75
TRENT, MOUNT	MTN	43 56 169 45	79
TRENT RIVER	STRM	42 36 171 58	70
TRENT SADDLE	SAD	42 42 171 48	70
TRENTHAM	SBRB	41 08 175 03	52
TRENTHAM	SBRB	41 08 175 03	55
TRENTHAM	LOC	44 02 170 53	87
TRIANGLE CREEK	STRM	43 08 171 29	75
TRIANGLE CREEK	STRM	43 08 171 29	80
TRIANGLE PEAK	PEAK	44 53 168 01	89
TRIBUTE CREEK	STRM	43 11 170 38	74
TRIDENT PEAK	PEAK	44 09 168 58	78
TRIG HILL (TRIG)	MTN	44 43 169 22	91
TRIG ISLAND (TRIG)	HILL	45 10 170 34	102
TRINITY	MTN	44 23 168 23	88
TRINITY	MTN	44 23 168 23	89
TRINITY LAKES	LAKE	45 32 167 23	96
TRINITY LAKES	LAKE	45 32 167 23	97
TRIO ISLANDS	ISLS	40 50 174 00	54
TRIO ISLANDS	ISLS	40 50 174 00	61
TRIPLE PEAK	PEAK	44 29 168 56	90
TRIPLEX CREEK	STRM	39 47 176 16	47
TRIPOD HILL	HILL	45 38 167 06	105
TRIPP, MOUNT (TRIG)	MTN	43 42 171 11	87
TRIPP SET	LOC	44 00 171 13	87
TRIPPS PEAK	MTN	43 57 171 03	87
TRIREME PEAK	PEAK	43 22 170 43	74
TROOPER (TRIG)	HILL	40 58 176 05	51
TROTTER, MOUNT	HILL	45 31 170 34	102
TROTTERS CREEK	STRM	45 31 170 42	102
TROTTERS GORGE	LOC	45 24 170 48	102
TROUP, LAKE	LAKE	45 29 167 08	96
TROUP, MOUNT	MTN	45 29 167 07	96
TROVATORE (TRIG)	MTN	42 23 172 26	71
TROYTE RIVER	STRM	43 43 169 53	76
TROYTE RIVER	STRM	43 43 169 53	79
TRUDGE COL	SAD	42 53 171 45	70
TRUDGE STREAM	STRM	42 51 171 47	70
TRUMPER STREAM	STRM	42 51 172 23	71
TRUMPETER POINT	PNT	46 57 168 04	115
TRURAN PASS	PASS	43 03 170 51	75
TRYPHENA	LOC	36 18 175 29	9
TRYPHENA HARBOUR	HARB	36 19 175 29	9
TUAHENI POINT	PNT	38 43 178 04	32
TUAHIWI	LOC	43 20 172 39	82
TUAHIWI	LOC	43 20 172 39	83
TUAHIWI	LOC	43 20 172 39	85
TUAHU (TRIG)	HILL	39 04 174 26	35
TUAHUKUKU (TRIG)	HILL	39 34 174 45	35
TUAHUKUKU (TRIG)	HILL	39 34 174 45	44
TUAI	LOC	38 49 177 09	31
TUAKAU	LOC	37 16 174 56	12
TUAKAU	LOC	37 16 174 56	14
TUAKITOTO, LAKE	LAKE	46 13 169 49	111
TUAKITOTO, LAKE	LAKE	46 13 169 49	113
TUAMARINA	POPL	41 26 173 58	54
TUAMARINA	POPL	41 26 173 58	60
TUAMARINA RIVER	STRM	41 26 173 58	54
TUAMARINA RIVER	STRM	41 26 173 58	60
TUAMARINA (TRIG)	HILL	41 25 173 59	54
TUAMARINA (TRIG)	HILL	41 25 173 59	60
TUAMOTU ISLAND	ISLD	38 42 178 03	32
TUANUIOTAKOU (TRIG)	HILL	39 29 174 56	36
TUANUIOTEKAHAKAHA (TRIG)	MTN	38 11 177 44	24
TUANUIOTEKAHAKAHA (TRIG)	MTN	38 11 177 44	32
TUAPA ISLAND	ISLD	38 07 174 52	18
TUAPAKA (TRIG)	HILL	40 50 175 10	48
TUAPEKA FLAT	LOC	45 57 169 38	111
TUAPEKA MOUTH	LOC	46 01 169 31	111
TUAPEKA MOUTH	LOC	46 01 169 31	113
TUAPEKA RIVER	STRM	46 01 169 31	111
TUAPEKA WEST	LOC	45 56 169 33	111
TUAPIRO CREEK	STRM	37 30 175 56	17
TUATAPERE	POPL	46 08 167 41	106
TUATAPERE	POPL	46 08 167 41	108
TUATEAWA	LOC	36 39 175 34	13
TUATEAWA	LOC	36 39 175 34	16
TUATEAWA STREAM	STRM	36 39 175 34	13
TUATEAWA STREAM	STRM	36 39 175 34	16
TUATINI	LOC	38 07 178 19	25
TUATINI	LOC	38 07 178 19	32
TUBMAN HILL	HILL	40 55 172 18	56
TUBMAN RANGE	MTNS	40 55 172 18	56
TUCK STREAM	STRM	46 26 169 33	113
TUFA (TRIG)	PEAK	39 20 175 38	37
TUFA (TRIG)	PEAK	39 20 175 38	38
TUFT (TRIG)	HILL	39 45 175 58	46
TUHA STREAM	STRM	39 51 175 45	46
TUHA (TRIG)	HILL	39 52 175 48	46
TUHARA	LOC	39 02 177 30	33
TUHAWAIKI ISLAND	ISLD	46 30 169 43	113
TUHAWAIKI POINT	PNT	44 27 171 15	93
TUHAWAIKI, MOUNT	MTN	44 41 168 05	89
TUHINGAMATA (TRIG)	HILL	38 42 175 34	27
TUHINGAMATA (TRIG)	HILL	38 42 175 34	28
TUHINGAMATA (TRIG)	HILL	38 43 176 00	28
TUHINGAMATA (TRIG)	HILL	38 43 176 00	29
TUHINGAMATA (TRIG)	HILL	38 42 175 34	38
TUHINGAMATA (TRIG)	HILL	38 43 176 00	38
TUHIPA	LOC	35 25 173 57	4
TUHIRANGI (TRIG)	HILL	36 32 174 29	10
TUHIRANGI (TRIG)	HILL	36 32 174 29	11
TUHIRANGI (TRIG)	HILL	39 31 175 38	37
TUHITARATA	LOC	41 18 175 16	53
TUHUA	LOC	38 46 175 10	27
TUHUA (TRIG)	HILL	38 47 175 27	27
TUHUA (TRIG)	PEAK	42 49 171 11	68
TUHUA (TRIG)	PEAK	42 49 171 11	69
TUI	LOC	41 33 172 44	58
TUI GLEN	SBRB	41 15 173 19	59
TUI STREAM	STRM	37 32 175 41	17
TUI TARN	LAKE	43 52 170 27	77
TUI TARN	LAKE	43 52 170 27	86
TUIPAKE (TRIG)	HILL	39 07 174 30	35
TUKE, MOUNT	MTN	42 40 171 58	70
TUKE RIVER	STRM	43 01 170 52	75
TUKEMOKIHI	LOC	38 54 177 36	33
TUKEMOKIHI STREAM	STRM	38 54 177 46	33
TUKIKARAMEA	LOC	37 52 175 12	18
TUKINO SKI FIELD	SKI	39 17 175 37	37
TUKINO SKI FIELD	SKI	39 17 175 37	38
TUKIPO RIVER	STRM	39 59 176 30	47
TUKITUKI RIVER	STRM	39 36 176 57	42
TUKITUKI RIVER	STRM	39 36 176 57	43
TUKITUKIPAPA STREAM	STRM	39 00 177 01	41
TUKUTAHORA (TRIG)	PEAK	39 04 175 00	36
TUKUTAPA (TRIG)	HILL	38 56 177 11	41
TUKUTUPERE STREAM	STRM	37 55 175 51	20
TUMAI	LOC	45 34 170 42	102
TUMAI (TRIG)	HILL	39 06 174 36	35
TUMBLEDOWN BAY	BAY	43 51 172 46	83
TUMMIL RIVER	STRM	41 40 173 39	67
TUMMIL, THE	HSTD	41 40 173 39	67
TUMU BAY	BAY	37 37 176 26	22
TUMUNUI	LOC	38 16 176 19	21
TUMUNUI	LOC	38 16 176 19	29
TUMUNUI HILL	HILL	38 17 176 18	21
TUMUNUI HILL	HILL	38 17 176 18	29
TUNA	LOC	39 16 174 18	34
TUNA	LOC	39 16 174 18	35
TUNA	LOC	39 16 174 18	44
TUNAEKE STREAM	STRM	37 47 175 08	18
TUNAKINO RIVER	STRM	41 13 173 37	60
TUNAKORE STREAM	STRM	40 17 176 18	50
TUNAKOTEKOTE	LOC	38 55 175 17	27
TUNAMARO STREAM	STRM	39 03 176 24	39
TUNAMARO STREAM	STRM	39 03 176 24	40
TUNANUI STREAM	STRM	39 01 177 46	33
TUNAPARA	LOC	39 30 175 13	36
TUNAPOTO STREAM	STRM	39 30 174 48	35
TUNAPOTO STREAM	STRM	39 30 174 48	44
TUNATAU STREAM	STRM	39 45 175 54	46
TUNAWAEA STREAM	STRM	38 25 175 23	27
TUNING FORK CREEK	STRM	44 03 168 44	88
TUNNEL CREEK	STRM	43 49 169 32	76
TUNNEL CREEK	STRM	43 49 169 32	79
TUNNEL HILL (TRIG)	HILL	44 49 169 53	91
TUNNEL (TRIG)	HILL	41 06 175 10	52
TUNNEL (TRIG)	HILL	41 06 175 10	53
TUNNEL (TRIG)	HILL	41 06 175 10	55
TUNUPO (TRIG)	PEAK	39 58 176 04	47
TUPAPAKURUA STREAM	STRM	39 11 175 18	36
TUPARI (TRIG)	PEAK	39 41 176 11	47
TUPAROA	LOC	37 55 178 23	25
TURAKINA	POPL	40 03 175 13	45
TURAKINA RIVER	STRM	40 04 175 08	45
TURAKIRAE HEAD	HEAD	41 27 174 55	52
TURAKIRAE HEAD	HEAD	41 27 174 55	55
TURAKIRAI (TRIG)	HILL	39 16 174 36	35
TURAKIRAI (TRIG)	HILL	39 16 174 36	44
TURANGAAPO STREAM	STRM	38 41 174 52	26
TURANGANUI RIVER	STRM	38 40 178 01	32
TURANGANUI RIVER	STRM	38 40 178 01	33
TURANGANUI RIVER	STRM	41 21 175 09	53
TURANGAOMOANA	LOC	37 45 175 50	19
TURANGAOMOANA	LOC	37 45 175 50	20
TURANGARERE	LOC	39 35 175 44	37
TURANGARERE	LOC	39 35 175 44	46
TURANGATAIROA (TRIG)	HILL	39 35 175 43	37
TURANGATAIROA (TRIG)	HILL	39 35 175 43	46
TURANGI	TOWN	39 00 175 48	37
TURANGI	TOWN	39 00 175 48	38
TUREPOREPO STREAM	STRM	38 11 176 15	20
TUREPOREPO STREAM	STRM	38 11 176 15	21
TURIHAUA	HSTD	38 38 178 10	32
TURIHAUA POINT	PNT	38 38 178 10	32
TURIHAUA STREAM	STRM	38 38 178 09	32
TURIMAWIWI RIVER	STRM	40 44 172 19	56
TURIOHINETERANGI (TRIG)	HILL	39 34 175 59	37
TURIPOTO STREAM	STRM	38 38 174 41	26
TURIRI RANGE	MTNS	40 05 176 27	47
TURITEA STREAM	STRM	38 05 175 10	18
TURIWHATE	LOC	42 44 171 18	68
TURIWHATE	LOC	42 44 171 18	69
TURIWHATE, MOUNT (TRIG)	MTN	42 46 171 17	68
TURIWHATE, MOUNT (TRIG)	MTN	42 46 171 17	69
TURIWIRI	LOC	35 57 173 55	6
TURIWIRI	LOC	35 57 173 55	7
TURIWIRI (TRIG)	HILL	35 57 173 54	6
TURIWIRI (TRIG)	HILL	35 57 173 54	7
TURK RIDGE	RDGE	42 08 172 47	65
TURKS HEAD	HEAD	44 23 168 33	88
TURKS HEAD	HEAD	44 23 168 33	89
TURKS HEAD	HEAD	44 23 168 33	90
TURKS HEAD (TRIG)	MTN	42 10 173 17	66
TURN PEAK	PEAK	45 05 167 04	96
TURN ROUND HILL	HILL	44 48 167 31	94
TURNAGAIN, CAPE	CAPE	40 30 176 37	50
TURNBULL, MOUNT	MTN	42 51 172 03	70
TURNBULL, MOUNT (TRIG)	MTN	45 08 168 19	95
TURNBULL, MOUNT (TRIG)	MTN	45 08 168 19	98
TURNBULL RIVER	STRM	43 55 168 54	78
TURNBULL STREAM	STRM	42 58 171 54	70
TURNBULL (TRIG)	HILL	39 23 175 28	36
TURNBULL (TRIG)	HILL	39 23 175 28	37
TURNER CREEK	STRM	44 49 168 22	89
TURNER CREEK	STRM	44 49 168 22	95
TURNER, MOUNT	MTN	44 13 169 05	78
TURNER PASS	PASS	44 37 168 02	89
TURNER PEAK	PEAK	43 39 170 09	74
TURNER PEAK	PEAK	43 39 170 09	77
TURNER PEAK (TRIG)	HILL	40 56 173 56	54
TURNER PEAK (TRIG)	HILL	40 56 173 56	61
TURNLEY CREEK	STRM	44 06 168 37	88
TUROA SKI FIELD	LOC	39 18 175 32	36
TUROA SKI FIELD	LOC	39 18 175 32	37
TUROA SKI FIELD	LOC	39 18 175 32	38
TURPENTINE	PEAK	42 26 172 08	70
TURRET HEAD	MTN	44 40 168 23	89
TURRET PEAK	PEAK	43 11 171 18	75
TURRET PEAK	PEAK	43 11 171 18	80
TURRET PEAKS	PEAK	44 17 169 05	78
TURRET PEAKS	PEAK	45 07 167 45	94
TURRET PEAKS	PEAK	45 07 167 45	97
TURRET RANGE	MTNS	45 33 167 20	96
TURTONS SADDLE	SAD	43 22 171 22	75
TURTONS SADDLE	SAD	43 22 171 22	80
TURTONS STREAM	STRM	43 26 171 22	75
TURTONS STREAM	STRM	43 26 171 22	80
TURUA	LOC	37 14 175 34	13
TURUA	LOC	37 14 175 34	15
TUSK, THE	MTN	43 06 170 53	75
TUSSOCK CREEK	LOC	46 15 168 25	107
TUSSOCK CREEK	STRM	46 16 168 26	107
TUSSOCK CREEK	LOC	46 15 168 25	109
TUSSOCK PEAK	PEAK	45 37 167 00	104
TUSSOCK PEAK	PEAK	45 37 167 00	105
TUTAEKURI RIVER	STRM	39 34 176 55	40
TUTAEKURI RIVER	STRM	38 58 177 22	41
TUTAEKURI RIVER	STRM	39 34 176 55	42
TUTAEKURI RIVER	STRM	42 33 171 59	70
TUTAEMARO (TRIG)	HILL	38 50 177 07	30
TUTAEMARO (TRIG)	HILL	38 50 177 07	31
TUTAEMATAI	LOC	35 20 174 18	5
TUTAENUI	LOC	40 01 175 24	45
TUTAENUI	LOC	40 01 175 24	46
TUTAENUI STREAM	STRM	39 09 177 04	41
TUTAENUI STREAM	STRM	40 12 175 21	45
TUTAEPAWHATI BAY	BAY	47 07 168 04	115
TUTAETI STREAM	STRM	38 50 175 25	27
TUTAETOKO STREAM	STRM	38 05 177 21	23
TUTAETOKO (TRIG)	HILL	38 13 177 21	31
TUTAEUAUA STREAM	STRM	38 41 175 49	28
TUTAEWAEROA STREAM	STRM	38 41 175 46	28
TUTAEWAEROA STREAM	STRM	38 41 175 46	38
TUTAEWHAKAPIKI (TRIG)	HILL	37 38 177 59	24
TUTAEWHAKAPIKI (TRIG)	HILL	37 38 177 59	25
TUTAKI	LOC	41 50 172 28	65
TUTAKI RIVER	STRM	41 50 172 28	65
TUTAKI RIVER, EAST BRANCH	STRM	41 54 172 28	65
TUTAKI RIVER, WEST BRANCH	STRM	41 54 172 28	65
TUTAMOE	HILL	35 46 173 48	6
TUTAMOE	LOC	35 39 173 39	6
TUTAMOE RANGE	MTNS	35 43 173 43	6
TUTAMOE (TRIG)	HILL	38 14 177 58	32
TUTARA (TRIG)	HILL	37 48 178 21	25
TUTEKEHUA	LOC	35 16 173 31	3
TUTEREMOANA (TRIG)	HILL	40 51 174 55	52
TUTEREMOANA (TRIG)	HILL	40 51 174 55	55
TUTIRA	LOC	39 12 176 53	40
TUTIRA	LOC	39 12 176 53	41
TUTIRA, LAKE	LAKE	39 14 176 53	40
TUTIRA, LAKE	LAKE	39 14 176 53	41
TUTOKO, MOUNT	MTN	44 36 168 01	89
TUTOKO, MOUNT	MTN	44 36 168 01	94
TUTOKO RIVER	STRM	44 41 167 58	89
TUTOKO RIVER	STRM	44 41 167 58	94
TUTU BURN	STRM	45 21 167 32	97
TUTU STREAM	STRM	42 35 172 35	71
TUTU (TRIG)	HILL	39 49 175 15	45
TUTUKAKA	LOC	35 37 174 31	5
TUTUKAKA	LOC	35 37 174 31	8
TUTUKAKA HARBOUR	HARB	35 37 174 32	8
TUTUKAKA HEAD	HEAD	35 37 174 33	5
TUTUKAKA HEAD	HEAD	35 37 174 33	8
TUTUKAKA HEAD	HEAD	35 37 174 33	11
TUTUMAI (TRIG)	HILL	38 57 175 19	36
TUTUMATAI (TRIG)	HILL	37 51 178 16	25
TUTURAU	LOC	46 15 168 51	110
TUTURAU	LOC	46 15 168 51	112
TUTURUMURI	LOC	41 25 175 29	53
TUTURUWAHINE (TRIG)	HILL	37 39 175 00	18
TUTUTAWA	LOC	39 19 174 32	35
TUTUTAWA	LOC	39 19 174 32	44
TUTUTAWA (TRIG)	HILL	39 19 174 34	35
TUTUTAWA (TRIG)	HILL	39 19 174 34	44
TUTUWHINAU (TRIG)	HILL	37 58 178 18	25
TUWATAWATA (TRIG)	MTN	38 42 176 45	30
TWAIN COL	SAD	43 44 170 01	76
TWAIN COL	SAD	43 44 170 01	77
TWAIN COL	SAD	43 44 170 01	79
TWEED RIVER	STRM	42 15 173 18	66
TWELVE MILE CREEK	STRM	42 26 171 23	69
TWENTY FIVE MILE CREEK	STRM	44 39 168 28	89
TWENTY FIVE MILE-SADDLE	SAD	44 34 168 32	88
TWENTY FIVE MILE-SADDLE	SAD	44 34 168 32	89
TWENTY FIVE MILE-SADDLE	SAD	44 34 168 32	90
TWILIGHT BEACH	BCH	34 30 172 47	2
TWILIGHT COL	SAD	43 29 170 36	74
TWILIGHT COL	SAD	43 29 170 36	77
TWILIGHT, MOUNT	MTN	44 18 168 54	90
TWIN PEAKS	PEAK	44 30 169 04	90
TWIN SISTERS	MTN	44 47 167 42	94
TWIN STREAM	STRM	43 55 170 08	76
TWIN STREAM	STRM	43 55 170 08	77
TWINLAW (TRIG)	HILL	45 59 167 53	106
TWINS, THE	ISLD	36 46 175 48	16
TWINS, THE	MTN	44 43 168 01	89
TWINS, THE	PEAK	41 14 172 39	56
TWINS, THE	PEAK	41 14 172 39	58
TWINS, THE (NOVARA PEAK)	PEAK	43 37 170 15	74
TWINS, THE (NOVARA PEAK)	PEAK	43 37 170 15	77
TWINS (TRIG)	HILL	41 48 172 34	65
TWIZEL	POPL	44 16 170 06	79
TWIZEL	POPL	44 16 170 06	86
TWIZEL RIVER	STRM	44 19 170 11	86
TWO LEGGED STREAM	STRM	44 24 170 40	93
TWO MILE STREAM	STRM	42 11 173 23	66
TWO MILE STREAM	STRM	44 28 170 40	93
TWO PEAKS (TRIG)	HILL	40 02 176 39	43
TWO PEAKS (TRIG)	HILL	40 02 176 39	47
TWO PETERS	MTN	44 19 168 39	88
TWO PETERS	MTN	44 19 168 39	90
TWO THUMB BAY	BAY	44 57 167 11	96
TWO THUMB RANGE	MTNS	43 33 170 40	74
TWO THUMB RANGE	MTNS	43 52 170 40	86
TWO THUMB STREAM	STRM	43 38 170 40	74
TWYFORD	LOC	39 36 176 48	42
TWYFORD	LOC	39 36 176 48	43
TYLER	MTN	44 21 168 37	88
TYLER	MTN	44 21 168 37	90
TYNDALL CREEK	STRM	42 54 171 15	68
TYNDALL CREEK	STRM	42 54 171 15	69
TYNDALL, MOUNT	MTN	44 32 168 38	88
TYNDALL, MOUNT	MTN	44 32 168 38	90
TYNDAR, MOUNT	MTN	44 10 168 54	78
TYTLER ROCKS (TRIG)	MTN	42 16 173 29	66
TYTLER STREAM	STRM	42 13 173 26	66

■ U

U PASS	PASS	44 52 168 00	89
UAWA RIVER	STRM	38 23 178 18	32
UEPANGO STREAM	STRM	38 46 175 15	27
UEROA (TRIG)	HILL	39 36 174 57	36
UEROA (TRIG)	HILL	39 36 174 57	45
UGLY RIVER	STRM	41 12 172 19	56
UGLY RIVER	STRM	41 12 172 19	62
ULIC (TRIG)	HILL	40 47 175 48	49
ULIC (TRIG)	HILL	40 47 175 48	51
ULVA ISLAND	ISLD	46 56 168 08	115
UMAREAREA STREAM	STRM	38 04 175 11	18
UMAUMAKARORO (TRIG)	HILL	35 13 173 29	3
UMAWERA	LOC	35 17 173 34	3
UMAWERA	LOC	35 17 173 34	4
UMBRELLA MOUNTAINS	MTN	45 35 169 06	99
UMERE	LOC	41 16 172 11	56
UMERE	LOC	41 16 172 11	62
UMUKARIKARI (TRIG)	PEAK	39 08 175 54	37
UMUKARIKARI (TRIG)	PEAK	39 08 175 54	38
UMUPUIA BEACH	BCH	36 54 175 04	13
UMUPUIA BEACH	BCH	36 54 175 04	14
UMUPUIA BEACH	BCH	36 54 175 04	15
UMURUA STREAM	STRM	38 06 176 10	20
UMURUA STREAM	STRM	38 06 176 10	21
UMUTAOROA	LOC	40 08 176 05	47
UMUTOI	LOC	40 00 175 58	46
UNA, MOUNT	MTN	42 13 172 35	65
UNAHI	LOC	35 00 173 15	3
UNCLE BAY	BAY	42 39 171 28	69
UNDERWOOD	LOC	46 20 168 20	109
UNDERWOOD, PORT	HARB	41 20 174 07	54
UNDERWOOD, PORT	HARB	41 20 174 07	60
UNION, MOUNT (TRIG)	MTN	42 04 173 33	66
UNITED CREEK	STRM	41 22 173 17	59
UNKNOWN COL	SAD	43 05 171 12	75
UNKNOWN, LAKE	LAKE	44 38 168 16	89
UNKNOWN STREAM	STRM	43 03 171 19	75
UNUHIA STREAM	STRM	35 03 173 39	4
UNUWHAO (TRIG)	HILL	34 26 172 53	2
UPCOT	HSTD	41 54 173 35	66
UPCOT SADDLE	SAD	41 56 173 31	66
UPCOT STREAM	STRM	41 55 173 32	66
UPOKOKAHARA (TRIG)	HILL	38 56 176 57	40
UPOKOKAHARA (TRIG)	HILL	38 56 176 57	41
UPOKOKOTIO STREAM	STRM	37 54 176 05	20
UPOKOKOTIO STREAM	STRM	37 54 176 05	21
UPOKOMATU STREAM	STRM	38 49 175 19	27
UPOKONGARO	LOC	39 52 175 07	45
UPOKONGARO STREAM	STRM	39 52 175 07	45
UPOKONGARURU STREAM	STRM	41 05 175 48	51
UPOKONUI STREAM	STRM	39 34 174 53	35
UPOKOONGAURU STREAM	STRM	37 55 176 18	20
UPOKOONGAURU STREAM	STRM	37 55 176 18	21
UPOKORAU	LOC	35 09 173 50	4
UPOKORAU STREAM	STRM	39 37 174 32	35
UPOKORAU STREAM	STRM	39 37 174 32	44
UPOKORORO STREAM	STRM	39 48 176 25	47
UPPER ATIAMURI	LOC	38 21 176 01	28
UPPER ATIAMURI	LOC	38 21 176 01	29
UPPER BULLER GORGE	GORG	41 47 172 07	64
UPPER CHARLTON	LOC	46 06 168 51	110
UPPER CHARLTON	LOC	46 06 168 51	112
UPPER GREY RIVER	STRM	42 27 172 00	70
UPPER HUTT	USAT	41 07 175 04	52
UPPER HUTT	USAT	41 07 175 04	55
UPPER HUTT STATION	RSTN	41 08 175 04	52

UPPER HUTT STATION	RSTN	41 08 175 04	55
UPPER KAWHATAU	LOC	39 49 175 58	46
UPPER MANGATAWHIRI RESERVOIR	LAKE	37 05 175 09	13
UPPER MANGATAWHIRI RESERVOIR	LAKE	37 05 175 09	15
UPPER MATAKITAKI	LOC	42 01 172 22	65
UPPER MOUTERE	LOC	41 16 173 00	58
UPPER MOUTERE	LOC	41 16 173 00	59
UPPER NIHOTUPU RESERVOIR	LAKE	36 57 174 34	12
UPPER NIHOTUPU RESERVOIR	LAKE	36 57 174 34	14
UPPER PEAK	PEAK	44 45 168 16	89
UPPER PEAK	PEAK	44 45 168 16	95
UPPER RETARUKE	LOC	39 08 175 15	36
UPPER STUDHOLME PASS	PASS	43 58 169 35	79
UPPER TAKAKA	LOC	41 02 172 49	57
UPPER TAKAKA	LOC	41 02 172 49	58
UPPER WAIAUA	LOC	38 03 177 27	23
UPPER WAIAUA	LOC	38 03 177 27	24
UPPER WAITATI	LOC	45 46 170 32	103
UPPER WAITOHI	LOC	44 13 171 07	87
UPTON BROOK	STRM	41 47 173 34	66
UPTON DOWNS	HSTD	41 44 173 53	67
UPUKERORA RIVER	STRM	45 24 167 45	97
UPUKERORA RIVER	STRM	45 24 167 45	98
URAWHITIKI POINT	PNT	38 05 174 46	18
UREKAWA STREAM	STRM	39 44 174 29	44
URENUI	POPL	39 00 174 23	35
URENUI RIVER	STRM	38 59 174 23	35
URENUI (TRIG)	HILL	39 02 174 27	35
URETANE	LOC	44 46 171 03	93
URETARA ISLAND	ISLD	38 00 177 07	23
URETARA STREAM	STRM	37 34 175 54	20
UREWERA NATIONAL PARK	PARK	38 30 177 00	30
URGUHART CREEK	STRM	42 59 170 38	74
URIAH, MOUNT	MTN	42 01 171 39	63
URIAH, MOUNT	MTN	42 01 171 39	64
URQUHART KNOB	PEAK	43 07 170 46	74
URQUHART PEAK	PEAK	43 08 171 07	75
URQUHARTS BAY	LOC	35 51 174 32	8
URRALL	LOC	43 43 171 45	84
URUKOKOMUKA STREAM	STRM	38 23 177 47	31
URUKOKOMUKA STREAM	STRM	38 23 177 47	32
URUMATUI STREAM	STRM	39 07 177 54	33
URUNGAIO	LOC	35 19 173 31	3
URUPA POINT	PNT	35 28 174 44	5
URUPUKAPUKA ISLAND	ISLD	35 13 174 14	5
URUROARAHI POINT	PNT	36 35 175 45	16
URUTARANGA STREAM	STRM	38 28 177 54	32
URUTAWA (TRIG)	HILL	38 13 177 28	24
URUTAWA (TRIG)	HILL	38 13 177 28	31
URUTI	LOC	38 57 174 32	26
URUTI	LOC	38 57 174 32	35
URUTI POINT	PNT	41 08 176 04	51
URUTI STREAM	STRM	38 57 174 32	35
URUWHENUA	LOC	41 00 172 50	57
URUWHENUA	LOC	41 00 172 50	58
USELESS BAY	BAY	46 09 166 44	104
USELESS LAKE	LAKE	45 44 166 35	104
UTAKURA	LOC	35 21 173 40	4
UTAKURA RIVER	STRM	35 22 173 46	4
UTAKURA RIVER	STRM	35 22 173 46	6
UTIKU	LOC	39 44 175 50	46
UTIKU (TRIG)	HILL	40 25 175 46	49
UTUHINA STREAM	STRM	38 07 176 15	20

V

UTUHINA STREAM	STRM	38 07 176 15	21
UTUWAI	LOC	40 01 175 56	46
UWHIROA STREAM	STRM	35 15 173 12	3
UWIRU STREAM	STRM	35 13 173 35	4
VALETTA	LOC	43 46 171 29	84
VALHALLA STREAM	STRM	42 01 174 00	67
VALIANT, MOUNT	MTN	42 53 171 47	70
VALLEY CREEK	STRM	41 43 172 20	65
VALLEY CREEK	STRM	45 41 169 09	110
VALLEY CREEK	STRM	46 00 169 09	110
VALLEY OF DARKNESS, THE	STRM	43 47 169 31	76
VALLEY OF DARKNESS, THE	STRM	43 47 169 31	79
VALLEY PEAK	PEAK	46 03 166 37	104
VALLEY STREAM	STRM	42 49 172 15	70
VALPYS PASS	PASS	44 38 168 21	89
VAN (TRIG)	HILL	40 42 176 07	49
VAN (TRIG)	HILL	40 42 176 07	50
VAN (TRIG)	HILL	40 42 176 07	51
VANCOUVER ARM	BAY	45 31 166 56	96
VANGUARD PEAK (TRIG)	PEAK	44 51 168 45	90
VANGUARD PEAK (TRIG)	PEAK	44 51 168 45	95
VAUGHAN, MOUNT (TRIG)	MTN	41 41 172 03	64
VEIL STREAM	STRM	43 23 170 41	74
VENUS CREEK	STRM	41 19 172 26	62
VERNON, MOUNT (TRIG)	HILL	39 58 176 33	42
VERNON, MOUNT (TRIG)	HILL	39 58 176 33	43
VERNON, MOUNT (TRIG)	HILL	39 58 176 33	47
VERNON (TRIG)	HILL	41 34 173 59	60
VERONA STREAM	STRM	39 16 175 07	36
VERONICA CHANNEL	CHAN	35 18 174 07	4
VERONICA CHANNEL	CHAN	35 18 174 07	5
VERTER BURN	STRM	45 51 170 01	111
VESTA, MOUNT	MTN	44 15 168 56	78
VICTOIRE, MOUNT	MTN	43 25 170 31	74
VICTOIRE, MOUNT	MTN	43 25 170 31	77
VICTOR LAKE	LAKE	45 55 166 48	104
VICTOR, MOUNT	MTN	44 02 169 11	78
VICTORIA GLACIER	GLCR	43 30 170 09	74
VICTORIA GLACIER	GLCR	43 30 170 09	77
VICTORIA, LAKE	LAKE	45 20 167 27	97
VICTORIA, MOUNT	MTN	44 29 168 28	88
VICTORIA, MOUNT	MTN	44 29 168 28	89
VICTORIA, MOUNT	MTN	42 02 172 07	64
VICTORIA, MOUNT (TRIG)	HILL	41 51 174 03	67
VICTORIA RANGE	MTNS	42 08 172 07	64
VICTORIA RANGE	MTNS	43 29 170 07	76
VICTORIA RANGE	MTNS	43 29 170 07	77
VICTORIA RIVER	STRM	35 02 173 20	3
VICTORIA (TRIG)	HILL	44 43 170 36	92
VICTORIA VALLEY	LOC	35 10 173 25	3
VICTORY ISLAND	ISLD	40 44 173 55	61
VIEW HILL	LOC	43 18 172 03	81
VIEW HILL SADDLE	SAD	41 31 172 01	62
VIEW HILL (TRIG)	HILL	43 19 172 03	81
VIEW HILL (TRIG)	HILL	43 42 172 59	83
VIEW HILL (TRIG)	HILL	43 19 172 03	85
VIEW POINT (TRIG)	HILL	41 03 176 05	51
VINCENT CREEK	STRM	43 04 171 02	75
VINCENT, LAKE	LAKE	46 36 168 49	112
VINCENT PEAK	PEAK	45 39 167 08	105
VINE CREEK	STRM	42 56 171 00	68
VINE CREEK	STRM	42 56 171 00	69
VINE CREEK	STRM	43 15 170 26	74
VINEGAR HILL	LOC	39 56 175 38	46
VINING (TRIG)	HILL	37 08 175 13	13
VINING (TRIG)	HILL	37 08 175 13	15
VIRGIN FLAT	FLAT	41 51 171 31	63
VIRGINIA	LOC	42 55 172 21	71
VIRGINIA PEAK (TRIG)	MTN	42 54 172 20	71
VOGELTOWN	SBRB	39 05 174 04	34
VOLTA GLACIER	GLCR	44 22 168 47	90
VON RIVER	STRM	45 05 168 26	95
VON RIVER	STRM	45 05 168 26	98
VON RIVER (NORTH BRANCH)	STRM	45 11 168 19	95
VON RIVER (NORTH BRANCH)	STRM	45 11 168 19	98
VON RIVER (SOUTH BRANCH)	STRM	45 11 168 19	95
VON RIVER (SOUTH BRANCH)	STRM	45 11 168 19	98
VULCAN GLACIER	GLCR	44 22 168 47	90
VULCAN (TRIG)	HILL	43 03 173 00	82

W

WAAHI, LAKE	LAKE	37 34 175 08	14
WAAHI, LAKE	LAKE	37 34 175 08	15
WADDINGTON	LOC	43 24 172 02	81
WADDINGTON	LOC	43 24 172 02	85
WADE, LAKE	LAKE	45 03 167 31	94
WADE, LAKE	LAKE	45 03 167 31	97
WADESTOWN	SBRB	41 16 174 46	52
WADESTOWN	SBRB	41 16 174 46	55
WAENGA	LOC	45 05 169 16	100
WAERENGA	LOC	37 22 175 13	15
WAERENGA STREAM	STRM	37 23 175 17	15
WAERENGAAHIKA	LOC	38 36 177 55	32
WAERENGAOKURI	LOC	38 41 177 47	32
WAERENGAOKURI	LOC	38 41 177 47	33
WAETITI STREAM	STRM	38 20 175 40	28
WAEWAEPA RANGE	MTNS	40 28 176 03	49
WAEWAETOREA ISLAND	ISLD	35 12 174 13	5
WAGGON CREEK	STRM	41 49 171 28	63
WAHAATUA STREAM	STRM	38 10 177 24	23
WAHAATUA STREAM	STRM	38 10 177 24	24
WAHAKARI, LAKE	LAKE	34 39 172 55	2
WAHANUI	HSTD	38 59 177 08	41
WAHAPO, LAKE	LAKE	43 15 170 16	74
WAHAROA	LOC	37 46 175 45	19
WAHATUARA (TRIG)	HILL	40 24 176 11	50
WAHIANOA RIVER	STRM	39 27 175 38	37
WAHIEROA (TRIG)	HILL	37 54 176 50	22
WAHIEROA (TRIG)	HILL	37 54 176 50	23
WAHINGAMUKU (TRIG)	HILL	38 03 178 13	25
WAIAMARU (TRIG)	HILL	39 11 174 55	35
WAIAMARU (TRIG)	HILL	39 11 174 55	36
WAIANAKARUA	LOC	45 16 170 48	102
WAIANAKARUA RIVER MIDDLE BRANCH	STRM	45 16 170 43	102
WAIANAKARUA RIVER NORTH BRANCH	STRM	45 16 170 49	102
WAIANAKARUA RIVER SOUTH BRANCH	STRM	45 17 170 45	102
WAIANIWA	LOC	46 18 168 15	107
WAIANIWA	LOC	46 18 168 15	109
WAIANIWA CREEK	STRM	46 21 168 15	109
WAIANUANU (TRIG)	HILL	37 46 175 56	20
WAIAPI	LOC	44 15 171 13	87
WAIAPU RIVER	STRM	37 47 178 27	25
WAIARE	LOC	35 09 173 48	4
WAIAREKA JUNCTION	LOC	45 06 170 55	102
WAIARIARI	LOC	44 40 171 04	93
WAIARIKI RIVER	STRM	35 32 174 14	5
WAIARIKI STREAM	STRM	41 20 174 39	52
WAIARIKI STREAM	STRM	41 20 174 39	55
WAIARIKIKI	LOC	46 16 168 68	108
WAIARIKIKI	LOC	46 16 168 68	112
WAIARIKIKI STREAM	STRM	46 17 168 59	110
WAIARIKIKI STREAM	STRM	46 17 168 59	112
WAIARO	LOC	36 36 175 25	13
WAIARO	LOC	36 36 175 25	16
WAIARUA STREAM	STRM	38 57 176 31	39
WAIARUA STREAM	STRM	38 57 176 31	40
WAIARUHE	LOC	40 17 176 00	49
WAIARUHE RIVER	STRM	35 18 173 58	4
WAIARUMU STREAM	STRM	37 55 175 33	19
WAIATAPAUA BAY	BAY	35 20 174 22	5
WAIATARUA	LOC	36 56 174 35	12
WAIATARUA	LOC	36 56 174 35	14
WAIATIU STREAM	STRM	38 40 176 43	30
WAIATOTO	LOC	43 59 168 48	78
WAIATOTO RIVER	STRM	43 59 168 47	78
WAIATUA STREAM	STRM	35 17 173 09	3
WAIATUPURITIA SADDLE	SAD	39 05 176 09	38
WAIATUPURITIA SADDLE	SAD	39 05 176 09	39
WAIAU	LOC	36 49 175 32	16
WAIAU	POPL	42 39 173 03	72
WAIAU BAY	BAY	36 37 174 46	11
WAIAU BAY	BAY	36 37 174 46	12
WAIAU BEACH	LOC	37 09 174 43	12
WAIAU BEACH	LOC	37 09 174 43	14
WAIAU CAVES	CAVE	46 01 167 45	106
WAIAU, LAKE	LAKE	39 48 174 41	44
WAIAU PA	LOC	37 08 174 45	12
WAIAU PA	LOC	37 08 174 45	14
WAIAU PASS	PASS	42 06 172 39	65
WAIAU RIVER	STRM	36 47 175 31	13
WAIAU RIVER	STRM	36 47 175 31	16
WAIAU RIVER	STRM	38 10 178 15	25
WAIAU RIVER	STRM	38 10 178 15	32
WAIAU RIVER	STRM	38 58 177 24	33
WAIAU RIVER	STRM	38 58 177 24	41
WAIAU RIVER	STRM	42 47 173 22	72
WAIAU RIVER	STRM	42 47 173 22	73
WAIAU RIVER	STRM	45 30 167 36	97
WAIAU RIVER	STRM	46 12 167 37	106
WAIAU RIVER	STRM	46 12 167 37	108
WAIAU STREAM	STRM	39 00 174 20	34
WAIAU STREAM	STRM	39 00 174 20	35
WAIAU STREAM	STRM	39 51 174 41	44
WAIAUA	LOC	38 01 177 25	23
WAIAUA	LOC	38 01 177 25	24
WAIAUA BAY	BAY	35 04 173 56	4
WAIAUA RIVER	STRM	37 59 177 23	23
WAIAUA RIVER	STRM	37 59 177 23	24
WAIAUA RIVER	STRM	39 28 173 52	34
WAIAUTE STREAM	STRM	38 09 176 36	21
WAIAUTE STREAM	STRM	38 09 176 36	22
WAICOE STREAM	STRM	45 48 167 38	106
WAICOLO STREAM	STRM	46 07 167 58	106
WAICOLO STREAM	STRM	46 07 167 58	107
WAIHAHA	LOC	35 20 174 14	5
WAIHAHA	LOC	38 44 175 45	28
WAIHAHA	LOC	38 44 175 45	38
WAIHAHA RIVER	STRM	38 44 175 45	28
WAIHAHA RIVER	STRM	38 44 175 45	38
WAIHAO DOWNS	LOC	44 48 170 55	93
WAIHAO FORKS	LOC	44 48 170 56	93
WAIHAO RIVER	STRM	44 46 171 10	93
WAIHAO RIVER (NORTH BRANCH)	STRM	44 48 170 56	93
WAIHAO RIVER (SOUTH BRANCH)	STRM	44 48 170 56	93
WAIHAORUNGA	LOC	44 44 170 50	93
WAIHAPA	LOC	35 05 173 41	4
WAIHAPI CREEK	STRM	43 24 169 55	76
WAIHARAKEKE	LOC	37 16 175 52	17
WAIHARAKEKE	LOC	38 08 174 52	18
WAIHARAKEKE STREAM	STRM	35 08 174 04	4
WAIHARAKEKE STREAM	STRM	35 22 173 44	4
WAIHARAKEKE STREAM	STRM	35 08 174 04	5
WAIHARAKEKE STREAM	STRM	37 15 175 52	17
WAIHARAKEKE STREAM	STRM	38 09 174 51	18
WAIHARAKEKE WEST STREAM	STM	37 35 175 31	19
WAIHARARA	LOC	34 57 173 11	3
WAIHAREHARE BAY	BAY	38 31 178 17	32
WAIHARURU STREAM	STRM	39 29 175 27	36
WAIHARURU STREAM	STRM	39 29 175 27	37
WAIHARURU STREAM	STRM	38 55 176 06	38
WAIHARURU STREAM	STRM	38 55 176 06	39
WAIHAU BAY	BAY	37 37 177 56	24
WAIHAU BAY	LOC	37 37 177 55	24
WAIHAU BAY	BAY	38 27 178 19	32
WAIHAU STREAM	STRM	39 26 176 40	39
WAIHAU STREAM	STRM	39 26 176 40	40
WAIHAU STREAM	STRM	39 26 176 40	42
WAIHAUPAI STREAM	STRM	35 47 173 35	6
WAIHEKAU STREAM	STRM	37 35 175 38	19
WAIHEKE CHANNEL	CHAN	36 50 175 10	13
WAIHEKE ISLAND	ISLD	36 48 175 07	13
WAIHEKE RIVER	STRM	42 33 171 59	70
WAIHI	POPL	37 24 175 50	17
WAIHI	LOC	38 57 175 44	37
WAIHI	LOC	38 57 175 44	38
WAIHI BEACH	POPL	37 25 175 57	17
WAIHI ESTUARY	ESTY	37 46 176 29	21
WAIHI ESTUARY	ESTY	37 46 176 29	22
WAIHI GORGE	LOC	44 00 171 10	87
WAIHI POINT	PNT	41 01 174 19	54
WAIHI POINT	PNT	41 01 174 19	61
WAIHI RIVER	STRM	44 16 171 19	87
WAIHI STREAM	STRM	38 57 175 45	37
WAIHI STREAM	STRM	38 57 175 45	38
WAIHI STREAM	STRM	38 56 177 09	41
WAIHI STREAM	STRM	40 26 176 18	50
WAIHIHI BAY	BAY	35 15 174 07	4
WAIHIHI BAY	BAY	35 15 174 07	5
WAIHINAU BAY	BAY	40 57 173 58	54
WAIHINAU BAY	BAY	40 57 173 58	61
WAIHINGAIA STREAM	STRM	41 22 175 48	51
WAIHIRERE	LOC	38 35 177 57	32
WAIHO RIVER	STRM	43 17 170 03	76
WAIHOA STREAM	STRM	35 50 174 10	7
WAIHOAKA	LOC	46 14 167 42	106
WAIHOAKA	LOC	46 14 167 42	108
WAIHOANGA STREAM	STRM	35 17 173 43	4
WAIHOANGA STREAM	STRM	35 22 173 44	4
WAIHOANGA STREAM	STRM	35 22 173 44	6
WAIHOHONU STREAM	STRM	39 12 175 47	37
WAIHOHONU STREAM	STRM	39 12 175 47	38
WAIHOHONU (TRIG)	HILL	39 12 175 45	37
WAIHOHONU (TRIG)	HILL	39 12 175 45	38
WAIHOKI	LOC	40 37 176 10	50
WAIHOKI STREAM	STRM	40 37 176 10	50
WAIHOKI VALLEY	LOC	40 38 176 10	50
WAIHOLA	LOC	46 01 170 06	103
WAIHOLA HILL (TRIG)	HILL	46 00 170 03	103
WAIHOLA, LAKE	LAKE	46 01 170 05	103
WAIHOPAI RIVER	STRM	35 29 173 19	6
WAIHOPAI RIVER	STRM	41 31 173 44	60
WAIHOPAI RIVER	STRM	41 39 173 37	67
WAIHOPAI SADDLE	SAD	41 55 173 13	66
WAIHOPAI (TRIG)	HILL	41 33 173 40	60
WAIHOPO	LOC	34 47 173 05	2
WAIHOPO	LOC	34 47 173 05	3
WAIHOPO LAKE	LAKE	34 45 173 03	2
WAIHOPO LAKE	LAKE	34 45 173 03	3
WAIHOPUHOPU STREAM	STRM	37 03 175 18	13
WAIHOPUHOPU STREAM	STRM	37 03 175 18	15
WAIHORA (ELLESMERE, LAKE)	LAKE	43 47 172 31	83
WAIHORA (ELLESMERE, LAKE)	LAKE	43 47 172 31	85
WAIHORA BAY	BAY	38 42 175 47	28
WAIHORA BAY	BAY	38 42 175 47	38
WAIHORA RIVER	STRM	38 27 177 52	32
WAIHORA STREAM	STRM	38 41 175 48	28
WAIHORA STREAM	STRM	38 25 177 58	32
WAIHORA STREAM	STRM	39 29 174 53	35
WAIHORA STREAM	STRM	39 29 174 53	44
WAIHORA STREAM	STRM	40 58 176 03	51
WAIHORA STREAM	STRM	41 17 175 17	53
WAIHOROIHIKA STREAM	STRM	38 43 177 03	30
WAIHOU	LOC	37 34 175 40	19
WAIHOU RIVER	STRM	35 25 173 23	3
WAIHOU RIVER	STRM	35 20 173 41	4
WAIHOU RIVER	STRM	35 25 173 23	6
WAIHOU RIVER	STRM	37 10 175 32	13
WAIHOU RIVER	STRM	37 10 175 32	15
WAIHOU STREAM	STRM	38 37 176 56	30
WAIHOU VALLEY	LOC	35 18 173 43	4
WAIHUA	LOC	39 06 177 17	41
WAIHUA RIVER	STRM	39 06 177 17	41
WAIHUA STREAM	STRM	38 15 176 50	22
WAIHUA STREAM	STRM	38 15 176 50	30
WAIHUAHUA SWAMP	SWMP	34 54 173 13	3
WAIHUE	LOC	35 50 173 51	6
WAIHUE	LOC	35 50 173 51	7
WAIHUKA	LOC	35 09 173 46	4
WAIHUKA RIVER	STRM	38 29 177 50	31
WAIHUKA RIVER	STRM	38 29 177 50	32
WAIHUKA STREAM	STRM	38 41 175 19	27
WAI-ITI	LOC	41 26 173 00	58
WAI-ITI	LOC	41 26 173 00	59
WAIITI CREEK	STRM	42 22 171 44	70
WAI-ITI RIVER	STRM	41 21 173 07	58
WAI-ITI RIVER	STRM	41 21 173 07	59
WAIITI STREAM	STRM	37 57 177 29	24
WAIITI STREAM	STRM	37 40 178 27	25
WAIITI STREAM	STRM	38 17 177 07	31
WAIITI STREAM	STRM	39 28 176 42	39
WAIITI STREAM	STRM	39 28 176 42	40
WAIITI STREAM	STRM	39 28 176 42	42
WAIITI (TRIG)	HILL	38 57 174 43	35
WAIKAHAWAI POINT	PNT	37 58 178 23	25
WAIKAHIKATEA STREAM	STRM	36 37 174 30	10
WAIKAHIKATEA STREAM	STRM	36 37 174 30	11
WAIKAHIKATEA STREAM	STRM	36 37 174 30	12
WAIKAIA	POPL	45 44 168 51	108
WAIKAIA HILL (TRIG)	HILL	45 54 168 54	110
WAIKAIA RIVER	STRM	45 53 168 48	110
WAIKAIA RIVER (EAST BRANCH)	STRM	45 27 169 07	99
WAIKAIA RIVER (WEST BRANCH)	STRM	45 28 169 05	99
WAIKAINGA STREAM	STRM	35 06 173 31	3
WAIKAKA	LOC	45 55 169 01	110
WAIKAKA STREAM	STRM	38 45 175 04	26
WAIKAKA STREAM	STRM	38 45 175 04	27
WAIKAKA STREAM	STRM	46 07 168 57	110
WAIKAKA STREAM (EAST BRANCH)	STRM	45 59 169 02	110
WAIKAKA VALLEY	LOC	46 02 169 04	110
WAIKAKA VALLEY	LOC	46 02 169 04	112
WAIKAKA (TRIG)	HILL	38 41 175 07	27
WAIKAKA (TRIG)	HILL	46 08 169 02	110
WAIKAKA (TRIG)	HILL	46 08 169 02	112
WAIKAKAHI	LOC	44 51 171 01	93
WAIKAKAHO RIVER	STRM	41 27 173 54	54
WAIKAKAHO RIVER	STRM	41 27 173 54	60
WAIKAKAPO STREAM	STRM	46 08 167 16	105
WAIKAKARIKI RIVER	STRM	37 48 177 42	24
WAIKAKARIKI STREAM	STRM	38 37 177 55	32
WAIKAMAKA RIVER	STRM	39 42 176 05	47
WAIKAMIHI STREAM	STRM	37 58 176 45	22
WAIKANA	LOC	46 14 168 57	110
WAIKANA	LOC	46 14 168 57	112
WAIKANAE	POPL	40 53 175 04	48
WAIKANAE	POPL	40 53 175 04	52
WAIKANAE	POPL	40 53 175 04	55
WAIKANAE BEACH	POPL	40 52 175 01	48
WAIKANAE BEACH	POPL	40 52 175 01	52
WAIKANAE BEACH	POPL	40 52 175 01	55
WAIKANAE, LAKE	LAKE	34 36 172 53	2
WAIKANAE RIVER	STRM	40 52 175 00	48
WAIKANAE RIVER	STRM	40 52 175 00	52
WAIKANAE RIVER	STRM	40 52 175 00	55
WAIKANAE STREAM	STRM	34 38 172 51	2
WAIKANAE STREAM	STRM	36 36 175 31	13
WAIKANAE STREAM	STRM	36 36 175 31	16
WAIKANAPANAPA	LOC	37 36 177 58	24
WAIKANAPANAPA	LOC	37 36 177 58	25
WAIKANAPITI STREAM	STRM	38 05 176 37	21
WAIKANAPITI STREAM	STRM	38 05 176 37	22
WAIKAPIRO, LAKE	LAKE	39 14 176 53	40
WAIKAPIRO, LAKE	LAKE	39 14 176 53	41
WAIKARAKA	LOC	35 46 174 23	5
WAIKARAKA	LOC	35 46 174 23	7
WAIKARAKA	LOC	35 46 174 23	8
WAIKARAKA STREAM	STRM	35 18 173 44	4
WAIKARAKA STREAM	STRM	41 09 176 01	51
WAIKARAMU, LAKE	LAKE	34 55 173 14	3
WAIKARE	LOC	35 21 174 14	5
WAIKARE CREEK	STRM	35 44 174 29	5
WAIKARE CREEK	STRM	35 44 174 29	8
WAIKARE INLET	BAY	35 19 174 10	5
WAIKARE, LAKE	LAKE	37 26 175 12	15
WAIKARE, LAKE	LAKE	39 40 174 48	44
WAIKARE RIVER	STRM	35 21 174 13	5
WAIKARE RIVER	STRM	38 19 177 00	30
WAIKARE STREAM	STRM	39 11 175 28	36
WAIKARE STREAM	STRM	39 11 175 28	37
WAIKAREHU STREAM	STRM	35 17 173 39	4
WAIKAREITI, LAKE	LAKE	38 43 177 10	31
WAIKAREMOANA, LAKE	LAKE	38 46 177 06	30
WAIKARETAHEKE RIVER	STRM	38 56 177 16	41
WAIKARETU	LOC	37 33 174 50	14
WAIKARI	POPL	42 58 172 41	71
WAIKARI	SBRB	45 57 170 29	103
WAIKARI NORTH (TRIG)	HILL	42 53 173 00	72
WAIKARI RIVER	STRM	39 10 177 05	41
WAIKARI RIVER	STRM	42 53 173 03	72
WAIKARIKARI	LOC	39 27 176 25	39
WAIKARIKARI	LOC	39 27 176 25	40
WAIKARO POINT	PNT	36 07 175 26	9
WAIKAROKARO STREAM	STRM	39 23 176 20	39
WAIKATO	LOC	40 37 172 41	56
WAIKATO	LOC	40 37 172 41	57
WAIKATO RIVER	STRM	37 22 174 42	14
WAIKATO RIVER	STRM	39 14 175 47	37
WAIKATO RIVER	STRM	39 14 175 47	38
WAIKAURA	LOC	44 51 170 37	92
WAIKAUWIA (TRIG)	HILL	39 04 174 51	35
WAIKAWA	LOC	41 16 174 03	54
WAIKAWA	LOC	41 16 174 03	60
WAIKAWA	LOC	41 16 174 03	61
WAIKAWA	LOC	46 37 169 08	112
WAIKAWA BAY	BAY	41 16 174 03	54
WAIKAWA BAY	BAY	41 16 174 03	60
WAIKAWA BAY	BAY	41 16 174 03	61
WAIKAWA BEACH	LOC	40 41 175 09	48
WAIKAWA HARBOUR	HARB	46 38 169 09	112
WAIKAWA POINT	PNT	37 41 177 44	24
WAIKAWA RIVER	STRM	46 36 169 08	112
WAIKAWA RIVER (EAST BRANCH)	STRM	46 31 169 08	112
WAIKAWA RIVER (WEST BRANCH)	STRM	46 31 169 08	112
WAIKAWA STREAM	STRM	35 10 173 21	3
WAIKAWA STREAM	STRM	40 41 175 09	48
WAIKAWA VALLEY	LOC	46 31 169 07	112
WAIKAWA (TRIG)	HILL	46 39 169 10	112
WAIKAWAU	LOC	36 36 175 30	13
WAIKAWAU	LOC	36 57 175 28	13
WAIKAWAU	LOC	36 57 175 28	15
WAIKAWAU	LOC	36 36 175 30	16
WAIKAWAU	LOC	36 57 175 28	16
WAIKAWAU	LOC	38 28 174 41	26
WAIKAWAU BAY	BAY	36 36 175 32	13
WAIKAWAU BAY	BAY	36 36 175 32	16
WAIKAWAU RIVER	STRM	36 57 175 28	13
WAIKAWAU RIVER	STRM	36 36 175 31	13
WAIKAWAU RIVER	STRM	36 57 175 28	15
WAIKAWAU RIVER	STRM	36 57 175 28	16
WAIKAWAU RIVER	STRM	36 36 175 31	16
WAIKAWAU RIVER	STRM	38 29 174 38	26
WAIKAWAU STREAM	STRM	37 28 174 43	14
WAIKEENE STREAM	STRM	42 24 173 28	72
WAIKEENE STREAM	STRM	42 24 173 28	73
WAIKEKE STREAM	STRM	37 23 175 12	15
WAIKERE, LAKE	LAKE	35 48 173 38	6
WAIKERIA	LOC	38 08 175 24	19
WAIKERIKERI	LOC	45 09 169 22	100
WAIKERIKERI CREEK	STRM	45 11 169 24	100
WAIKEWAI CREEK	STRM	43 52 172 21	85
WAIKIEKIE	LOC	35 57 174 14	7
WAIKIEKIE	LOC	35 57 174 14	8
WAIKIEKIE (TRIG)	HILL	35 56 174 14	7
WAIKIEKIE (TRIG)	HILL	35 56 174 14	8
WAIKINO	LOC	37 24 175 47	17
WAIKINO CREEK	STRM	35 20 174 11	5
WAIKINO STREAM	STRM	38 45 175 43	28
WAIKINO STREAM	STRM	38 45 175 43	38
WAIKIRI (TRIG)	HILL	38 46 174 38	26
WAIKIRIKIRI	LOC	38 11 177 00	22
WAIKIRIKIRI	LOC	38 11 177 00	23
WAIKITE	LOC	38 20 176 18	21
WAIKITE	LOC	38 20 176 18	29
WAIKITE VALLEY	LOC	38 20 176 17	29

WAIKITI RIVER	STRM	42 34 171 53	70
WAIKIWI	SBRB	46 23 168 21	109
WAIKIWI STREAM	STRM	46 24 168 15	109
WAIKOAU	LOC	39 14 176 49	40
WAIKOAU	LOC	39 14 176 49	41
WAIKOAU RIVER	STRM	39 16 176 53	40
WAIKOAU RIVER	STRM	39 16 176 53	41
WAIKOAU RIVER	STRM	46 09 167 27	105
WAIKOAU RIVER	STRM	46 09 167 27	108
WAIKOAU RIVER (NORTH BRANCH)	STRM	46 08 167 27	105
WAIKOAU RIVER (NORTH BRANCH)	STRM	46 08 167 27	108
WAIKOHU	HSTD	38 28 177 47	32
WAIKOHU RIVER	STRM	38 27 177 46	31
WAIKOHU RIVER	STRM	38 27 177 46	32
WAIKOHU STREAM	STRM	37 56 178 16	25
WAIKOHU (TRIG)	HILL	38 23 177 43	31
WAIKOIKOI	LOC	46 00 169 09	110
WAIKOIKOI STREAM	STRM	46 02 169 14	110
WAIKOKO STREAM	STRM	38 39 177 44	31
WAIKOKO STREAM	STRM	38 39 177 44	33
WAIKOKO STREAM	STRM	39 08 175 49	37
WAIKOKO STREAM	STRM	39 08 175 49	38
WAIKOKO STREAM	STRM	43 48 172 40	83
WAIKOKOMIKO STREAM	STRM	39 22 176 47	40
WAIKOKOMIKO STREAM	STRM	39 22 176 47	42
WAIKOKOPU	LOC	39 05 177 50	33
WAIKOKOPU STREAM	STRM	38 14 176 50	22
WAIKOKOPU STREAM	STRM	38 14 176 50	30
WAIKOKOWAI	LOC	37 34 175 03	14
WAIKONINI STREAM	STRM	39 27 176 37	39
WAIKONINI STREAM	STRM	39 27 176 37	40
WAIKONINI STREAM	STRM	39 27 176 37	42
WAIKOPIKOPIKO STREAM	STRM	46 38 169 01	112
WAIKOPUA CREEK	STRM	36 54 174 58	12
WAIKOPUA CREEK	STRM	36 54 174 58	14
WAIKORE (TRIG)	HILL	38 42 176 20	29
WAIKOREA	LOC	37 34 174 53	14
WAIKOREA STREAM	STRM	37 37 174 47	18
WAIKOROPUPU RIVER	STRM	40 49 172 48	57
WAIKOUAITI	LOC	45 36 170 41	102
WAIKOUAITI RIVER	STRM	45 38 170 40	102
WAIKOUAITI RIVER (NORTH BRANCH)	STRM	45 37 170 35	102
WAIKOUAITI RIVER (SOUTH BRANCH)	STRM	45 37 170 35	102
WAIKOUKOU STREAM	STRM	36 44 174 31	10
WAIKOUKOU STREAM	STRM	36 44 174 31	11
WAIKOUKOU STREAM	STRM	36 44 174 31	12
WAIKOUKOU VALLEY	LOC	36 45 174 30	10
WAIKOUKOU VALLEY	LOC	36 45 174 30	11
WAIKOUKOU VALLEY	LOC	36 45 174 30	12
WAIKOURA CREEK	LOC	44 57 170 53	93
WAIKOURA STREAM	STRM	38 42 175 23	27
WAIKOURO	LOC	46 06 167 59	106
WAIKOURO	LOC	46 06 167 59	107
WAIKOURO	LOC	46 06 167 59	108
WAIKOWHAI STREAM	STRM	43 25 169 50	76
WAIKOWHEWHE STREAM	STRM	38 14 176 49	22
WAIKOWHEWHE STREAM	STRM	38 14 176 49	30
WAIKOWHEWHE (TRIG)	HILL	38 14 176 42	21
WAIKOWHEWHE (TRIG)	HILL	38 14 176 42	22
WAIKOWHEWHE (TRIG)	HILL	38 14 176 42	30
WAIKUKU	LOC	43 18 172 41	82
WAIKUKU	LOC	43 18 172 41	83
WAIKUKU BEACH	BCH	34 26 173 00	2
WAIKUKU BEACH	LOC	43 17 172 43	82
WAIKUKU BEACH	LOC	43 17 172 43	83
WAIKUKU STREAM	STRM	38 04 174 59	18
WAIKUKU (TRIG)	HILL	40 29 175 52	49
WAIKUKUPA RIVER	STRM	43 20 170 01	76
WAIKUKUPA RIVER	STRM	43 20 170 01	77
WAIKUMETE STREAM	STRM	37 18 175 26	15
WAIKUNE	LOC	39 13 175 24	36
WAIKUNE	LOC	39 13 175 24	37
WAIKURA	HSTD	37 39 178 03	25
WAIKURA RIVER	STRM	37 44 177 59	24
WAIKURA RIVER	STRM	37 44 177 59	25
WAIKURA RIVER	STRM	38 39 177 37	31
WAIKURA RIVER	STRM	38 39 177 37	33
WAIMA	LOC	35 29 173 35	4
WAIMA	LOC	35 29 173 35	6
WAIMA RIVER	STRM	35 25 173 33	3
WAIMA RIVER	STRM	35 25 173 33	4
WAIMA RIVER	STRM	35 25 173 33	6
WAIMA RIVER	STRM	35 43 173 37	6
WAIMA RIVER	STRM	41 54 174 07	67
WAIMA VALLEY	LOC	35 29 173 36	4
WAIMA VALLEY	LOC	35 29 173 36	6
WAIMAHAKA	LOC	46 31 168 49	112
WAIMAHAKA STREAM	STRM	46 32 168 46	112
WAIMAHANA BAY	BAY	34 57 173 37	4
WAIMAHE STREAM	STRM	35 20 173 31	3
WAIMAHORA	LOC	38 18 175 22	27
WAIMAHORA STREAM	STRM	38 18 175 22	27
WAIMAHORA STREAM	STRM	40 09 175 11	45
WAIMAI STREAM	STRM	37 38 174 47	18
WAIMAIRE	LOC	41 32 171 56	62
WAIMAIRI BEACH	SBRB	43 29 172 44	82
WAIMAIRI BEACH	SBRB	43 29 172 44	83
WAIMAKARIRI COL	SAD	42 54 171 30	69
WAIMAKARIRI RIVER	STRM	43 23 172 43	82
WAIMAKARIRI RIVER	STRM	43 23 172 43	83
WAIMAKARIRI RIVER	STRM	43 23 172 43	85
WAIMAKARIRI STREAM	STRM	37 54 175 48	20
WAIMAMAKU	LOC	35 33 173 29	6
WAIMAMAKU CREEK	STRM	36 13 174 04	7
WAIMAMAKU RIVER	STRM	35 35 173 25	6
WAIMANA	LOC	38 09 177 05	22
WAIMANA	LOC	38 09 177 05	23
WAIMANA RIVER	STRM	38 04 177 00	22
WAIMANA RIVER	STRM	38 04 177 00	23
WAIMANGARARA RIVER	STRM	42 22 173 41	73
WAIMANGAROA	LOC	41 43 171 46	63
WAIMANGAROA	LOC	41 43 171 46	64
WAIMANGAROA RIVER	STRM	41 42 171 45	63
WAIMANGAROA RIVER	STRM	41 42 171 45	64
WAIMANGO STREAM	STRM	34 50 173 23	3
WAIMANGU	LOC	38 17 176 23	21
WAIMANGU	LOC	38 17 176 23	29
WAIMANGU POINT	PNT	36 59 175 17	13
WAIMANGU POINT	PNT	36 59 175 17	15
WAIMANGU STREAM	STRM	36 59 175 17	13
WAIMANGU STREAM	STRM	36 59 175 17	15
WAIMANONI	LOC	35 02 173 15	3
WAIMAOMAO BAY	BAY	36 10 175 06	9
WAIMAPU	LOC	37 45 176 10	20
WAIMAPU	LOC	37 45 176 10	21
WAIMAPU STREAM	STRM	37 44 176 09	20
WAIMAPU STREAM	STRM	37 44 176 09	21
WAIMARAMA	LOC	39 49 176 59	42
WAIMARAMA	LOC	39 49 176 59	43
WAIMARARA (TRIG)	HILL	41 25 174 56	52
WAIMARARA (TRIG)	HILL	41 25 174 56	55
WAIMARINO RIVER	STRM	38 57 175 51	37
WAIMARINO RIVER	STRM	38 57 175 51	38
WAIMARINO STREAM	STRM	39 16 175 21	36
WAIMATA	LOC	37 26 175 53	17
WAIMATA	LOC	38 30 178 02	32
WAIMATA RIVER	STRM	38 40 178 02	32
WAIMATA RIVER	STRM	40 32 176 30	50
WAIMATA STREAM	STRM	37 26 175 51	17
WAIMATA STREAM	STRM	38 44 177 49	32
WAIMATA STREAM	STRM	38 44 177 49	33
WAIMATAO STREAM	STRM	39 49 175 11	45
WAIMATAU STREAM	STRM	38 12 177 53	24
WAIMATAU STREAM	STRM	38 12 177 53	32
WAIMATE	POPL	44 44 171 03	93
WAIMATE CHANNEL	CHAN	36 46 175 25	13
WAIMATE CHANNEL	CHAN	36 46 175 25	16
WAIMATE CREEK	STRM	44 45 171 10	93
WAIMATE ISLAND	ISLD	36 46 175 25	13
WAIMATE ISLAND	ISLD	36 46 175 25	16
WAIMATE NORTH	LOC	35 19 173 53	4
WAIMATENUI	LOC	35 37 173 43	6
WAIMATUA	LOC	46 27 168 28	109
WAIMATUA CREEK	STRM	46 28 168 23	109
WAIMATUKU	LOC	46 18 168 10	109
WAIMATUKU STREAM	STRM	46 22 168 10	109
WAIMAUKU	LOC	36 46 174 30	10
WAIMAUKU	LOC	36 46 174 30	11
WAIMAUKU	LOC	36 46 174 30	12
WAIMAUNGA	LOC	42 14 171 42	63
WAIMAUNGA	LOC	42 14 171 42	64
WAIMAUNU STREAM	STRM	39 03 177 45	33
WAIMEA CREEK	STRM	41 49 171 35	63
WAIMEA CREEK	STRM	42 38 171 04	68
WAIMEA CREEK	STRM	42 38 171 04	69
WAIMEA HILL (TRIG)	HILL	45 59 168 42	110
WAIMEA INLET	BAY	41 19 173 10	59
WAIMEA PLAINS	PLNS	45 51 168 31	107
WAIMEA RIVER	STRM	41 17 173 08	59
WAIMEA STREAM	STRM	35 26 173 36	4
WAIMEA STREAM	STRM	35 26 173 36	6
WAIMEA STREAM	STRM	42 07 173 02	66
WAIMEA STREAM	STRM	45 58 168 45	110
WAIMEAMEA RIVER	STRM	46 16 167 43	106
WAIMEAMEA RIVER	STRM	46 16 167 43	108
WAIMEHA STREAM	STRM	38 05 176 56	22
WAIMEHA STREAM	STRM	38 05 176 56	23
WAIMIHA	LOC	38 37 175 19	27
WAIMIHA STREAM	STRM	38 37 175 20	27
WAIMIHIA	LOC	38 49 176 17	29
WAIMIMI	HSTD	40 59 176 05	51
WAIMIMIHA, LAKE	LAKE	35 09 173 10	3
WAIMIRO	LOC	40 27 176 13	50
WAIMONGA CREEK	STRM	45 27 169 46	100
WAIMONGA CREEK	STRM	45 27 169 46	101
WAIMONOA STREAM	STRM	38 34 175 45	28
WAIMOTU	LOC	45 12 170 50	102
WAIMOTU CREEK	STRM	46 11 167 37	106
WAIMOTU CREEK	STRM	46 11 167 37	108
WAIMUMU	LOC	46 08 168 49	110
WAIMUMU	LOC	46 08 168 49	112
WAIMUMU STREAM	STRM	46 12 168 52	110
WAIMUMU STREAM	STRM	46 12 168 52	112
WAIMUTU STREAM	STRM	40 01 175 16	45
WAINGAKE STREAM	STRM	38 47 177 48	32
WAINGAKE STREAM	STRM	38 47 177 48	33
WAINGAKIA	PEAK	39 08 176 05	38
WAINGAKIA	PEAK	39 08 176 05	39
WAINGAKIA STREAM	STRM	37 59 178 08	25
WAINGAKIA STREAM	STRM	39 19 176 02	38
WAINGAKIA STREAM	STRM	39 19 176 02	39
WAINGARARA	LOC	38 03 177 04	22
WAINGARARA	LOC	38 03 177 04	23
WAINGARARA STREAM	STRM	35 46 173 41	6
WAINGARARA STREAM	STRM	38 03 177 07	23
WAINGARARA (TRIG)	HILL	39 00 174 49	35
WAINGARO	LOC	37 41 175 00	18
WAINGARO LANDING	LOC	37 45 174 57	18
WAINGARO RIVER	STRM	37 45 174 57	18
WAINGARO RIVER	STRM	40 53 172 49	57
WAINGARO STREAM	STRM	36 46 175 36	13
WAINGARO STREAM	STRM	36 46 175 36	16
WAINGARO STREAM	STRM	42 37 173 19	72
WAINGARO STREAM	STRM	42 37 173 19	73
WAINGAROMIA RIVER	STRM	38 24 177 51	32
WAINGATA, LAKE	LAKE	36 21 174 09	10
WAINGATA STREAM	STRM	38 03 178 01	24
WAINGATA STREAM	STRM	38 03 178 01	25
WAINGAWA	LOC	40 58 175 35	51
WAINGAWA	LOC	40 58 175 35	53
WAINGAWA RIVER	STRM	41 00 175 40	51
WAINGAWA RIVER	STRM	41 00 175 40	53
WAINGONGORO RIVER	STRM	39 35 174 12	34
WAINGONGORO STREAM	STRM	39 49 176 59	42
WAINGONGORO STREAM	STRM	39 49 176 59	43
WAINGONGORO STREAM	STRM	41 03 175 40	51
WAINGONGORO STREAM	STRM	41 03 175 40	53
WAINIHINIHI	LOC	42 46 171 20	69
WAINIHINIHI CREEK	STRM	42 49 171 14	68
WAINIHINIHI CREEK	STRM	42 49 171 14	69
WAINONO LAGOON	LAGN	44 42 171 09	93
WAINUI	LOC	35 01 173 51	4
WAINUI	LOC	36 36 174 35	11
WAINUI	LOC	36 36 174 35	12
WAINUI	LOC	38 01 177 05	23
WAINUI	LOC	38 41 178 04	32
WAINUI	LOC	43 49 172 54	83
WAINUI BAY	BAY	35 01 173 51	4
WAINUI BEACH	BCH	39 52 174 45	44
WAINUI CREEK	STRM	44 53 169 26	91
WAINUI INLET	BAY	40 48 172 56	57
WAINUI JUNCTION	LOC	35 10 173 11	3
WAINUI JUNCTION	LOC	39 39 175 50	46
WAINUI, LAKE	LAKE	36 06 173 53	7
WAINUI RIVER	STRM	35 06 173 38	4
WAINUI RIVER	STRM	37 38 175 58	20
WAINUI RIVER	STRM	40 30 176 34	50
WAINUI RIVER	STRM	40 50 172 56	57
WAINUI SADDLE	SAD	40 56 172 55	57
WAINUI STREAM	STRM	36 33 174 39	11
WAINUI STREAM	STRM	37 49 174 51	18
WAINUI STREAM	STRM	38 21 175 47	28
WAINUI STREAM	STRM	41 05 175 02	52
WAINUI STREAM	STRM	41 05 175 02	55
WAINUI (TRIG)	PEAK	41 01 174 59	52
WAINUI (TRIG)	PEAK	41 01 174 59	55
WAINUIOMAPU STREAM	STRM	40 51 175 53	49
WAINUIOMAPU STREAM	STRM	40 51 175 53	51
WAINUIOMATA	USAT	41 15 174 57	52
WAINUIOMATA	USAT	41 15 174 57	55
WAINUIOMATA RIVER	STRM	41 25 174 53	52
WAINUIOMATA RIVER	STRM	41 25 174 53	55
WAINUIORU RIVER	STRM	41 16 175 44	51
WAINUIORU RIVER	STRM	41 16 175 44	53
WAINUIOTOTO BAY	BAY	36 42 175 36	16
WAIOAKURA STREAM	STRM	40 36 176 15	50
WAIOEKA PA	LOC	38 05 177 18	23
WAIOEKA RIVER	STRM	38 00 177 16	23
WAIOHAU	LOC	38 14 176 51	22
WAIOHAU	LOC	38 14 176 51	30
WAIOHIKA	LOC	38 36 177 57	32
WAIOHIKI	LOC	39 33 176 50	40
WAIOHIKI	LOC	39 33 176 50	41
WAIOHIKI	LOC	39 33 176 50	42
WAIOHIKI	LOC	39 33 176 50	43
WAIOHINE RIVER	STRM	41 06 175 30	53
WAIOHINE (TRIG)	HILL	40 58 175 25	48
WAIOHIPA STREAM	STRM	38 12 174 43	18
WAIOHO STREAM	STRM	37 59 176 58	22
WAIOHO STREAM	STRM	37 59 176 58	23
WAIOHOTU STREAM	STRM	37 58 175 51	20
WAIOKOTORE STREAM	STRM	39 40 176 07	47
WAIOKUMURAU STREAM	STRM	35 36 173 44	6
WAIOKURA STREAM	STRM	39 35 174 08	34
WAIOMIO	LOC	35 10 174 06	4
WAIOMIO	LOC	35 10 174 06	5
WAIOMIO STREAM	STRM	35 07 174 05	4
WAIOMIO STREAM	STRM	35 07 174 05	5
WAIOMOKO RIVER	STRM	38 35 178 13	32
WAIOMOU	LOC	37 56 175 50	19
WAIOMOU	LOC	37 56 175 50	20
WAIOMOU STREAM	STRM	37 50 175 50	20
WAIOMU	LOC	37 02 175 31	13
WAIOMU	LOC	37 02 175 31	15
WAIOMU	LOC	37 02 175 31	16
WAIONE	LOC	40 28 176 17	50
WAIONE STREAM	STRM	37 24 175 52	17
WAIONE STREAM	STRM	37 57 175 35	19
WAIONE STREAM	STRM	38 07 175 56	20
WAIONE STREAM	STRM	38 40 175 21	27
WAIONE STREAM	STRM	38 40 176 35	30
WAIONE STREAM	STRM	39 00 175 31	36
WAIONE STREAM	STRM	39 00 175 31	37
WAIONEHU STREAM	STRM	35 59 174 27	8
WAIONEKE	LOC	36 33 174 17	10
WAIONEPU CREEK	STRM	46 38 169 01	112
WAIONEPU RIVER	STRM	35 50 174 10	7
WAIONGANA STREAM	STRM	39 00 174 11	34
WAIONUI INLET	BAY	36 26 174 13	10
WAIOPEHU (TRIG)	PEAK	40 44 175 21	48
WAIOPOAHU STREAM	STRM	37 52 177 35	24
WAIOPU STREAM	STRM	38 06 177 32	24
WAIORAHI STREAM	STRM	37 45 176 08	20
WAIORAHI STREAM	STRM	37 45 176 08	21
WAIORAKA STREAM	STRM	38 06 175 45	19
WAIORATENE STREAM	STRM	38 47 176 06	29
WAIOROKO STREAM	STRM	38 33 174 38	26
WAIORONGOMAI	LOC	37 34 175 46	17
WAIORONGOMAI	LOC	37 52 178 12	25
WAIORONGOMAI	HSTD	41 16 175 09	52
WAIORONGOMAI	HSTD	41 16 175 09	53
WAIORONGOMAI	HSTD	41 16 175 09	55
WAIORONGOMAI RIVER	STRM	37 52 178 12	25
WAIORONGOMAI RIVER	STRM	41 16 175 10	52
WAIORONGOMAI RIVER	STRM	41 16 175 10	53
WAIORONGOMAI RIVER	STRM	41 16 175 10	55
WAIORONGOMAI SADDLE	SAD	41 16 175 05	52
WAIORONGOMAI SADDLE	SAD	41 16 175 05	55
WAIORORE	LOC	37 46 177 41	24
WAIOTAHI	LOC	38 02 177 12	23
WAIOTAHI BEACH	LOC	38 00 177 14	23
WAIOTAHI PA	LOC	38 02 177 11	23
WAIOTAHI RIVER	STRM	38 00 177 12	23
WAIOTAHI RIVER, OHIAO BRANCH	STRM	38 12 177 11	31
WAIOTAHI VALLEY	LOC	38 05 177 11	23
WAIOTAKA STREAM	STRM	38 57 175 50	37
WAIOTAMA	LOC	35 49 174 06	7
WAIOTAMA RIVER	STRM	35 49 174 06	7
WAIOTANE STREAM	STRM	35 39 173 27	6
WAIOTAOU	LOC	38 21 176 22	29
WAIOTAPU STREAM	STRM	38 29 176 18	29
WAIOTAPU VILLAGE	LOC	38 19 176 25	21
WAIOTAPU VILLAGE	LOC	38 19 176 25	29
WAIOTAURU RIVER	STRM	40 52 175 14	48
WAIOTAURU RIVER	STRM	40 52 175 14	52
WAIOTAURU RIVER	STRM	40 52 175 14	55
WAIOTEATUA STREAM	STRM	37 36 175 09	18
WAIOTEHUE	LOC	35 14 173 19	3
WAIOTEMARAMA	LOC	35 33 173 26	6
WAIOTIRA	LOC	35 56 174 12	7
WAIOTIRA	LOC	35 56 174 12	8
WAIOTIRA STREAM	STRM	35 59 174 10	7
WAIOTU	LOC	35 32 174 14	5
WAIOTU RIVER	STRM	35 31 174 13	5
WAIOTUKAPUNA STREAM	STRM	38 43 177 03	30
WAIOURU	POPL	39 28 175 41	37
WAIOURU STREAM	STRM	39 31 175 42	37
WAIOWAKA STREAM	STRM	40 38 176 12	50
WAIOWHATA STREAM	STRM	35 38 173 43	6
WAIPA RIVER	STRM	37 40 175 09	18
WAIPA STREAM	STRM	38 02 175 40	19
WAIPA STREAM	STRM	39 05 175 50	37
WAIPA STREAM	STRM	39 05 175 50	38
WAIPA VALLEY	LOC	38 26 175 23	27
WAIPAHEKE STREAM	STRM	37 18 175 44	17
WAIPAHI	LOC	46 06 169 14	110
WAIPAHI	LOC	46 06 169 14	112
WAIPAHI RIVER	STRM	46 05 169 15	110
WAIPAHI RIVER	STRM	46 05 169 15	112
WAIPAHIHI	SBRB	38 43 176 06	28
WAIPAHIHI	SBRB	38 43 176 06	29
WAIPAHIHI	SBRB	38 43 176 06	38
WAIPAHIHI STREAM	STRM	37 53 175 43	19
WAIPAHIHI STREAM	STRM	39 06 175 04	36
WAIPAHIHI STREAM	STRM	39 16 175 46	37
WAIPAHIHI STREAM	STRM	39 16 175 46	38
WAIPAHIHI (TRIG)	PEAK	39 16 175 49	37
WAIPAHIHI (TRIG)	PEAK	39 16 175 49	38
WAIPAIPAI	LOC	35 35 174 27	5
WAIPAIPAI	LOC	35 35 174 27	8
WAIPAKIHI RIVER	STRM	39 14 175 47	37
WAIPAKIHI RIVER	STRM	39 14 175 47	38
WAIPANGO	LOC	46 18 167 59	108
WAIPANGO	LOC	46 18 167 59	109
WAIPAO STREAM	STRM	35 44 174 06	5
WAIPAO STREAM	STRM	35 44 174 06	7
WAIPAOA	HSTD	38 17 177 51	32
WAIPAOA	LOC	38 31 177 54	32
WAIPAOA RIVER	STRM	38 43 177 56	32
WAIPAOA RIVER	STRM	38 43 177 56	33
WAIPAOA STREAM	STRM	38 41 177 19	31
WAIPAPA	LOC	35 12 173 55	4
WAIPAPA	LOC	38 18 175 41	28
WAIPAPA BAY	BAY	42 13 173 52	67
WAIPAPA, LAKE	LAKE	38 19 175 42	28
WAIPAPA POINT	PNT	46 40 168 51	112
WAIPAPA RIVER	STRM	35 18 173 40	4
WAIPAPA RIVER	STRM	37 40 176 00	20
WAIPAPA RIVER	STRM	38 18 175 41	28
WAIPAPA STREAM	STRM	35 12 173 58	4
WAIPAPA STREAM	STRM	35 53 174 25	7
WAIPAPA STREAM	STRM	35 53 174 25	8
WAIPAPA STREAM	STRM	37 56 176 00	20
WAIPAPA STREAM	STRM	37 56 176 39	21
WAIPAPA STREAM	STRM	37 56 176 39	22
WAIPAPA STREAM	STRM	37 39 178 30	25
WAIPAPA STREAM	STRM	38 46 174 44	26
WAIPAPA STREAM	STRM	39 20 174 38	35
WAIPAPA STREAM	STRM	39 16 175 03	36
WAIPAPA STREAM	STRM	39 16 177 01	40
WAIPAPA STREAM	STRM	39 16 177 01	41
WAIPAPA STREAM	STRM	39 52 176 45	42
WAIPAPA STREAM	STRM	39 52 176 45	43
WAIPAPA STREAM	STRM	39 20 174 38	44
WAIPAPA STREAM	STRM	46 40 168 57	112
WAIPAPAKAURI	LOC	35 02 173 13	3
WAIPAPAKAURI BEACH	LOC	35 03 173 10	2
WAIPAPAKAURI BEACH	LOC	35 03 173 10	3
WAIPAPAKAURI OUTFALL	DRN	35 01 173 15	3
WAIPARA	POPL	43 04 172 45	82
WAIPARA RIVER	STRM	43 09 172 48	82
WAIPARA RIVER	STRM	44 15 168 39	88
WAIPARA RIVER, MIDDLE BRANCH	STRM	43 00 172 29	71
WAIPARA RIVER, NORTH BRANCH	STRM	43 00 172 33	71
WAIPARA RIVER, SOUTH BRANCH	STRM	43 03 172 33	81
WAIPARA SADDLE	SAD	44 24 168 39	88
WAIPARA SADDLE	SAD	44 24 168 39	90
WAIPARA (TRIG)	HILL	34 35 172 51	2
WAIPARATI (TRIG)	HILL	39 06 176 38	39
WAIPARATI (TRIG)	HILL	39 06 176 38	40
WAIPARE STREAM	STRM	38 01 175 52	20
WAIPARERA	LOC	35 43 174 28	5
WAIPARERA	LOC	35 43 174 28	8
WAIPARERA CREEK	STRM	34 56 173 13	3
WAIPARERA, LAKE	LAKE	34 57 173 11	2
WAIPARERA, LAKE	LAKE	34 57 173 11	3
WAIPARI RIVER	STRM	38 10 175 32	19
WAIPARI STREAM	STRM	38 58 175 30	36
WAIPARI STREAM	STRM	38 58 175 30	37
WAIPARI STREAM	STRM	38 58 175 30	38
WAIPARU	LOC	45 48 168 46	110
WAIPARU (TRIG)	PEAK	46 48 168 49	110
WAIPATI RIVER	STRM	46 37 169 21	113
WAIPATIKI	LOC	40 22 176 17	50
WAIPATIKI BEACH	LOC	39 18 176 58	40
WAIPATIKI BEACH	LOC	39 18 176 58	41
WAIPATIKI BEACH	LOC	39 18 176 58	42
WAIPATIKI STREAM	STRM	39 18 176 58	40
WAIPATIKI STREAM	STRM	39 18 176 58	41
WAIPATIKI STREAM	STRM	40 22 176 18	50
WAIPAUA STREAM	STRM	40 44 176 16	50
WAIPAWA	POPL	39 57 176 35	42
WAIPAWA	POPL	39 57 176 35	43
WAIPAWA	POPL	39 57 176 35	47
WAIPAWA RIVER	STRM	39 59 176 39	42
WAIPAWA RIVER	STRM	39 59 176 39	43
WAIPAWA RIVER	STRM	39 59 176 39	47
WAIPAWA SADDLE	SAD	39 49 176 09	47
WAIPAWA STREAM	STRM	40 58 175 48	51
WAIPAWA (TRIG)	HILL	41 25 175 31	53
WAIPEHI STREAM	STRM	38 53 175 58	28
WAIPEHI STREAM	STRM	38 53 175 58	29
WAIPEHI STREAM	STRM	38 53 175 58	38
WAIPIATA	LOC	45 11 170 10	101
WAIPINGAU STREAM	STRM	38 53 174 32	26
WAIPIPI	LOC	37 13 174 41	12
WAIPIPI	LOC	37 13 174 41	14
WAIPIRO	LOC	38 01 178 20	25
WAIPIRO BAY	BAY	38 01 178 21	25
WAIPIROPIRO STREAM	STRM	39 41 176 44	42
WAIPIROPIRO STREAM	STRM	39 41 176 44	43
WAIPIROPIRO STREAM	STRM	39 41 176 44	47
WAIPOAKA STREAM	STRM	36 02 174 19	7
WAIPOAKA STREAM	STRM	36 02 174 19	8
WAIPOHATU STREAM	STRM	46 37 169 01	112
WAIPOPO	LOC	44 17 171 19	87
WAIPORI	LOC	45 49 169 53	111
WAIPORI FALLS	LOC	45 55 169 59	111
WAIPORI, LAKE	LAKE	45 58 170 07	103
WAIPORI RIVER	STRM	45 50 169 48	111
WAIPORI STREAM	STRM	40 39 175 55	49
WAIPOUA FOREST	LOC	35 39 173 33	6
WAIPOUA RIVER	STRM	35 38 173 30	6
WAIPOUA RIVER	STRM	40 58 175 40	48
WAIPOUA RIVER	STRM	40 58 175 40	49
WAIPOUA RIVER	STRM	40 58 175 40	51
WAIPOUA SETTLEMENT	LOC	35 39 173 30	6
WAIPOUNAMU	LOC	45 52 168 46	110
WAIPOUWERAWERA STREAM	STRM	38 40 176 05	28
WAIPOUWERAWERA STREAM	STRM	38 40 176 05	29
WAIPU	LOC	35 59 174 27	7
WAIPU	LOC	35 59 174 27	8
WAIPU CAVES	LOC	35 56 174 21	7
WAIPU CAVES	LOC	35 56 174 21	8
WAIPU COVE	BAY	36 02 174 30	8
WAIPU GORGE	GORG	36 04 174 24	7
WAIPU GORGE	GORG	36 04 174 24	8
WAIPU, LAKE	LAKE	40 03 175 09	45
WAIPU RIVER	STRM	36 00 174 29	8
WAIPUKA STREAM	STRM	39 45 177 00	42
WAIPUKA STREAM	STRM	39 45 177 00	43
WAIPUKU STREAM	STRM	39 14 174 16	34
WAIPUKURAU	TOWN	40 00 176 33	42
WAIPUKURAU	TOWN	40 00 176 33	43
WAIPUKURAU	TOWN	40 00 176 33	47
WAIPUNA	LOC	39 30 175 11	36
WAIPUNA	LOC	42 19 171 43	63
WAIPUNA	LOC	42 19 171 43	64
WAIPUNA	LOC	42 19 171 43	70
WAIPUNA RIVER	STRM	42 17 171 39	63
WAIPUNA RIVER	STRM	42 17 171 39	64
WAIPUNA RIVER, LEFT BRANCH	STRM	42 21 171 44	70
WAIPUNA RIVER, RIGHT BRANCH	STRM	42 21 171 44	70
WAIPUNA STREAM	STRM	35 28 174 12	5
WAIPUNA STREAM	STRM	39 17 176 39	39
WAIPUNA STREAM	STRM	39 17 176 39	40
WAIPUNGA RIVER	STRM	39 06 176 41	40
WAIPUPU STREAM	STRM	37 36 175 46	19
WAIPUPU STREAM	STRM	37 36 175 46	20
WAIPURA (TRIG)	HILL	38 36 177 59	32

WAIPURU	LOC	39 55 175 42	46
WAIPUTATAWA (TRIG)	HILL	38 05 177 13	23
WAIRAKA POINT	PNT	41 02 174 52	52
WAIRAKA POINT	PNT	41 02 174 52	55
WAIRAKAI (TRIG)	HILL	40 00 176 30	43
WAIRAKAI (TRIG)	HILL	40 00 176 30	47
WAIRAKAIA STREAM	STRM	38 47 177 55	32
WAIRAKAIA STREAM	STRM	38 47 177 55	33
WAIRAKATOKE STREAM	STRM	39 21 176 02	37
WAIRAKAU	LOC	37 35 175 46	19
WAIRAKAU	LOC	37 35 175 46	20
WAIRAKAU STREAM	STRM	37 57 175 35	19
WAIRAKE STREAM	STRM	37 54 174 46	18
WAIRAKEI	LOC	38 38 176 05	28
WAIRAKEI	LOC	38 38 176 05	29
WAIRAKEI STREAM	STRM	38 38 176 06	28
WAIRAKEI STREAM	STRM	38 38 176 06	29
WAIRAKEI VILLAGE	LOC	38 37 176 06	28
WAIRAKEI VILLAGE	LOC	38 37 176 06	29
WAIRAKI RIVER	STRM	45 56 167 41	106
WAIRAKI (TRIG)	HILL	45 56 167 42	106
WAIRAMARAMA	LOC	37 25 174 52	14
WAIRAMARAMA (TRIG)	HILL	37 25 174 51	14
WAIRANGI	HSTD	41 02 173 45	60
WAIRANGI	HSTD	41 02 173 45	61
WAIRAPUKAO	LOC	38 32 176 34	30
WAIRARAPA, LAKE	LAKE	41 13 175 15	53
WAIRARI STREAM	STRM	37 46 176 21	20
WAIRARI STREAM	STRM	37 46 176 21	21
WAIRATA	LOC	38 17 177 21	31
WAIRATA STREAM	STRM	38 19 177 19	31
WAIRAU BAR	LOC	41 30 174 03	60
WAIRAU LAGOON	LAGN	39 03 177 30	33
WAIRAU PA	PA	41 28 173 59	54
WAIRAU PA	PA	41 28 173 59	60
WAIRAU RIVER	STRM	35 36 173 25	6
WAIRAU RIVER	STRM	36 09 174 23	7
WAIRAU RIVER	STRM	36 09 174 23	8
WAIRAU RIVER	STRM	41 30 174 03	60
WAIRAU VALLEY	LOC	41 34 173 32	59
WAIRAUMOANA	BAY	38 47 177 01	30
WAIRAURAHIRI RIVER	STRM	46 16 167 13	105
WAIREIA	LOC	35 25 173 22	3
WAIREIA	LOC	35 25 173 22	6
WAIREIA CREEK	STRM	35 26 173 22	3
WAIREIA CREEK	STRM	35 26 173 22	6
WAIREKA	LOC	38 16 176 12	21
WAIREKA	LOC	38 16 176 12	29
WAIREKA RIVER	STRM	43 36 172 04	81
WAIREKA RIVER	STRM	43 36 172 04	85
WAIREPA	LOC	46 16 169 38	111
WAIREPA	LOC	46 16 169 38	113
WAIREPO CREEK	STRM	44 21 169 51	91
WAIREPO CREEK	STRM	46 22 169 22	113
WAIRERE	LOC	35 23 173 35	3
WAIRERE	LOC	35 23 173 35	4
WAIRERE	LOC	35 23 173 35	6
WAIRERE	LOC	36 05 174 19	7
WAIRERE	LOC	36 05 174 19	8
WAIRERE BAY	BAY	37 39 176 25	21
WAIRERE BAY	BAY	37 39 176 25	22
WAIRERE STREAM	STRM	35 22 173 35	3
WAIRERE STREAM	STRM	35 22 173 35	4
WAIRERE STREAM	STRM	35 22 173 35	6
WAIRERE STREAM	STRM	39 51 175 23	45
WAIRERE STREAM	STRM	39 51 175 23	46
WAIRERE STREAM	STRM	46 10 167 15	105
WAIRERE (TRIG)	HILL	41 13 174 15	54
WAIRERE (TRIG)	HILL	41 13 174 15	60
WAIRERE (TRIG)	HILL	41 13 174 15	61
WAIRIO	LOC	46 00 168 02	106
WAIRIO	LOC	46 00 168 02	107
WAIRIO HILL	HILL	46 00 167 58	106
WAIRIO HILL	HILL	46 00 167 58	107
WAIRIO STREAM	STRM	46 07 167 58	106
WAIRIO STREAM	STRM	46 07 167 58	107
WAIROA	LOC	37 43 176 05	20
WAIROA	LOC	37 43 176 05	21
WAIROA	TOWN	39 03 177 25	33
WAIROA	TOWN	39 03 177 25	41
WAIROA BAY	BAY	35 15 174 04	4
WAIROA BAY	BAY	35 11 174 05	4
WAIROA BAY	BAY	35 11 174 05	5
WAIROA BAY	BAY	35 15 174 04	5
WAIROA BAY	BAY	36 56 175 08	13
WAIROA BAY	BAY	36 56 175 08	14
WAIROA BAY	BAY	36 56 175 08	15
WAIROA PA	LOC	37 41 176 05	20
WAIROA PA	LOC	37 41 176 05	21
WAIROA RESERVOIR	LAKE	37 05 175 08	13
WAIROA RESERVOIR	LAKE	37 05 175 08	14
WAIROA RESERVOIR	LAKE	37 05 175 08	15
WAIROA RIVER	STRM	36 11 174 02	7
WAIROA RIVER	STRM	36 57 175 05	13
WAIROA RIVER	STRM	36 57 175 05	14
WAIROA RIVER	STRM	36 57 175 05	15
WAIROA RIVER	STRM	37 42 176 06	20
WAIROA RIVER	STRM	37 49 178 23	25
WAIROA RIVER	STRM	39 04 177 25	33
WAIROA RIVER	STRM	39 04 177 25	41
WAIROA RIVER	STRM	40 37 172 35	56
WAIROA RIVER	STRM	40 37 172 35	57
WAIROA RIVER	STRM	41 21 173 07	58
WAIROA RIVER	STRM	41 21 173 07	59
WAIROA RIVER, LEFT BRANCH	STRM	41 29 173 05	58
WAIROA RIVER, LEFT BRANCH	STRM	41 29 173 05	59
WAIROA RIVER, RIGHT BRANCH	STRM	41 29 173 05	58
WAIROA RIVER, RIGHT BRANCH	STRM	41 29 173 05	59
WAIROA STREAM	STRM	35 27 173 18	6
WAIROA STREAM	STRM	37 30 175 52	17
WAIROA STREAM	STRM	37 50 175 51	20
WAIROA (TRIG)	HILL	39 03 177 22	41
WAIRORO STREAM	STRM	35 27 173 50	4
WAIRORO STREAM	STRM	35 27 173 50	6
WAIROU STREAM	STRM	38 33 178 11	32
WAIRUA RIVER	STRM	35 47 174 03	5
WAIRUA RIVER	STRM	35 47 174 03	7
WAIRUA STREAM	STRM	38 13 176 25	21
WAIRUA STREAM	STRM	38 13 176 25	29
WAIRUNA	LOC	46 10 169 19	110
WAIRUNA	LOC	46 10 169 19	112
WAIRUNA	LOC	46 10 169 19	113
WAIRUNA PEAK (TRIG)	HILL	46 09 169 13	110
WAIRUNA PEAK (TRIG)	HILL	46 09 169 13	112
WAIRUNA STREAM	STRM	46 04 169 18	110
WAIRUNA STREAM	STRM	46 04 169 18	112
WAIRUNA STREAM	STRM	46 04 169 18	113
WAIRUNGA	LOC	45 31 170 42	102
WAITA BEACH (TRIG)	HILL	43 48 169 06	78
WAITA RIVER	STRM	43 47 169 07	78
WAITAANGA	LOC	38 50 174 50	26
WAITAANGA SADDLE	SAD	38 52 174 49	26
WAITAANGA STREAM	STRM	38 54 174 52	26
WAITAHA	LOC	43 02 170 45	74
WAITAHA RIVER	STRM	42 57 170 40	68
WAITAHA RIVER	STRM	42 57 170 40	74
WAITAHA RIVER	STRM	43 08 170 50	75
WAITAHA STREAM	STRM	35 14 173 06	3
WAITAHA STREAM	STRM	39 19 173 46	34
WAITAHA STREAM	STRM	39 10 177 06	41
WAITAHAIA RIVER	STRM	38 01 178 04	25
WAITAHANUI	LOC	38 48 176 05	28
WAITAHANUI	LOC	38 48 176 05	29
WAITAHANUI	LOC	38 48 176 05	38
WAITAHANUI RIVER	STRM	38 47 176 05	28
WAITAHANUI RIVER	STRM	38 47 176 05	29
WAITAHANUI STREAM	STRM	37 50 176 36	21
WAITAHANUI STREAM	STRM	37 50 176 36	22
WAITAHEKE STREAM	STRM	38 07 175 08	18
WAITAHI BLUFF (TRIG)	CLIF	43 09 170 14	74
WAITAHI HILL (TRIG)	HILL	44 06 171 06	87
WAITAHORA	LOC	40 19 176 11	50
WAITAHORA STREAM	STRM	34 27 172 49	2
WAITAHU	LOC	42 05 171 51	63
WAITAHU	LOC	42 05 171 51	64
WAITAHU RIVER	STRM	42 04 171 49	63
WAITAHU RIVER	STRM	42 04 171 49	64
WAITAHU SADDLE	SAD	42 05 172 08	64
WAITAHUNA	LOC	45 59 169 45	111
WAITAHUNA	LOC	45 59 169 45	113
WAITAHUNA GULLY	LOC	46 00 169 47	111
WAITAHUNA GULLY	LOC	46 00 169 47	113
WAITAHUNA HILL (TRIG)	HILL	45 55 169 54	111
WAITAHUNA RIVER	STRM	46 09 169 35	111
WAITAHUNA RIVER	STRM	46 09 169 35	113
WAITAIA	LOC	36 46 175 45	16
WAITAIA BAY	BAY	36 46 175 45	16
WAITAIA STREAM	STRM	38 43 175 39	28
WAITAIA STREAM	STRM	38 43 175 39	38
WAITAIA (TRIG)	HILL	36 44 175 45	16
WAITAKARURU	LOC	37 14 175 23	13
WAITAKARURU	LOC	37 14 175 23	15
WAITAKARURU RIVER	STRM	37 14 175 23	15
WAITAKARURU STREAM	STRM	37 40 175 32	19
WAITAKERE	LOC	36 51 174 33	10
WAITAKERE	LOC	36 51 174 33	11
WAITAKERE	LOC	36 51 174 33	12
WAITAKERE RANGES	MTNS	36 59 174 32	12
WAITAKERE RESERVOIR	LAKE	36 55 174 31	10
WAITAKERE RESERVOIR	LAKE	36 55 174 31	11
WAITAKERE RESERVOIR	LAKE	36 55 174 31	12
WAITAKERE RIVER	STRM	36 54 174 27	10
WAITAKERE RIVER	STRM	36 54 174 27	11
WAITAKERE RIVER	STRM	36 54 174 27	12
WAITAKERE RIVER	STRM	41 44 171 27	63
WAITAKI	LOC	44 56 171 06	93
WAITAKI, LAKE	LAKE	44 41 170 23	92
WAITAKI, LAKE	LOC	44 42 170 25	92
WAITAKI RIVER	STRM	44 57 171 09	93
WAITAKI (TRIG)	HILL	44 57 171 01	93
WAITAKOTORUA STREAM	STRM	40 25 175 57	49
WAITANE	LOC	46 11 168 38	110
WAITANE	LOC	46 11 168 38	112
WAITANGATA STREAM	STRM	38 48 175 03	26
WAITANGATA STREAM	STRM	38 48 175 03	27
WAITANGI	LOC	35 16 174 05	4
WAITANGI	LOC	35 16 174 05	5
WAITANGI	HSTD	38 21 177 56	32
WAITANGI	LOC	44 36 170 18	92
WAITANGI RIVER	STRM	35 16 174 03	4
WAITANGI RIVER	STRM	35 16 174 03	5
WAITANGI RIVER	STRM	35 40 174 28	5
WAITANGI RIVER	STRM	35 40 174 28	7
WAITANGI RIVER	STRM	35 40 174 28	8
WAITANGI STREAM	STRM	37 14 174 44	12
WAITANGI STREAM	STRM	37 14 174 44	14
WAITANGI STREAM	STRM	39 29 175 34	37
WAITANGI (TRIG)	HILL	36 35 174 29	10
WAITANGI (TRIG)	HILL	36 35 174 29	11
WAITANGIROTO RIVER	STRM	43 09 170 14	74
WAITANGIRUA STREAM	STRM	38 12 177 40	31
WAITANGITAONA RIVER	STRM	43 15 170 17	74
WAITANGITAONA RIVER	STRM	43 09 170 14	74
WAITANGURU	LOC	38 23 174 52	26
WAITANHUNA WEST	LOC	46 00 169 37	111
WAITANHUNA WEST	LOC	46 00 169 37	113
WAITAO	LOC	37 43 176 14	20
WAITAO	LOC	37 43 176 14	21
WAITAO STREAM	STRM	37 43 176 13	20
WAITAO STREAM	STRM	37 43 176 13	21
WAITAPI CREEK	STRM	43 23 169 56	76
WAITAPU	LOC	35 28 173 23	6
WAITAPU	LOC	40 50 172 48	57
WAITAPU BAY	BAY	35 03 173 46	4
WAITAPU STREAM	STRM	35 45 173 33	6
WAITAPU STREAM	STRM	36 15 174 36	8
WAITAPU STREAM	STRM	36 15 174 36	11
WAITAPU STREAM	STRM	40 02 175 32	46
WAITAPU STREAM	STRM	46 05 167 16	105
WAITAPU (TRIG)	HILL	40 02 175 32	45
WAITAPU (TRIG)	HILL	40 02 175 32	46
WAITAPU (TRIG)	HILL	40 24 175 57	49
WAITARA	POPL	39 00 174 14	34
WAITARA RIVER	STRM	38 59 174 14	34
WAITARA STREAM	STRM	37 10 174 35	12
WAITARA STREAM	STRM	37 10 174 35	14
WAITARA STREAM	STRM	39 09 176 40	40
WAITARAITI (TRIG)	HILL	38 55 174 45	26
WAITARERE	LOC	40 33 175 12	48
WAITARIA BAY	BAY	41 10 174 02	54
WAITARIA BAY	HSTD	41 09 174 02	54
WAITARIA BAY	HSTD	41 09 174 02	60
WAITARIA BAY	BAY	41 10 174 02	60
WAITARIA BAY	BAY	41 10 174 02	61
WAITARIA BAY	HSTD	41 09 174 02	61
WAITARIA STREAM	STRM	39 11 177 01	40
WAITARIA STREAM	STRM	39 11 177 01	41
WAITARUKE	LOC	35 05 173 43	4
WAITARUNA STREAM	STRM	38 25 176 42	30
WAITATA BAY	BAY	40 58 173 55	54
WAITATA BAY	BAY	40 58 173 55	60
WAITATA BAY	BAY	40 58 173 55	61
WAITATAPIA STREAM	STRM	40 52 175 14	48
WAITATI	LOC	45 45 170 35	103
WAITATI RIVER	STRM	45 45 170 34	103
WAITAWA	LOC	44 17 171 11	87
WAITAWA STREAM	STRM	37 29 175 25	15
WAITAWA (TRIG)	HILL	35 15 173 24	3
WAITAWHAI STREAM	STRM	39 51 176 58	42
WAITAWHAI STREAM	STRM	39 51 176 58	43
WAITAWHERO SADDLE	SAD	39 09 176 11	39
WAITAWHETA	LOC	37 27 175 47	17
WAITAWHETA RIVER	STRM	37 26 175 43	17
WAITAWHITI STREAM	STRM	40 40 176 00	49
WAITEIKA STATION	HSTD	38 00 174 53	18
WAITEITEI	LOC	36 17 174 34	11
WAITEKAURI	LOC	37 23 175 46	17
WAITEKAURI RIVER	STRM	37 25 175 47	17
WAITEKOHE STREAM	STRM	37 35 175 57	20
WAITEKURI RIVER	STRM	36 45 175 36	13
WAITEKURI RIVER	STRM	36 45 175 36	16
WAITEMATA HARBOUR	HARB	36 50 174 41	11
WAITEMATA HARBOUR	HARB	36 50 174 41	12
WAITENGAUE STREAM	STRM	37 30 175 53	17
WAITEPEKA	LOC	46 17 169 40	111
WAITEPEKA	LOC	46 17 169 40	113
WAITEPEKA RIVER	STRM	46 20 169 45	111
WAITEPEKA RIVER	STRM	46 20 169 45	113
WAITERIMU	LOC	37 28 175 17	15
WAITETE BAY	BAY	36 40 175 26	13
WAITETE BAY	BAY	36 40 175 26	16
WAITETI	LOC	38 04 176 12	20
WAITETI	LOC	38 04 176 12	21
WAITETI	LOC	38 24 175 12	27
WAITETI STREAM	STRM	38 05 175 37	19
WAITETI STREAM	STRM	38 04 176 13	20
WAITETI STREAM	STRM	38 04 176 13	21
WAITETOKO	LOC	38 55 175 56	28
WAITETOKO	LOC	38 55 175 56	29
WAITETOKO	LOC	38 55 175 56	38
WAITETOKO STREAM	STRM	38 55 175 55	37
WAITETOKO STREAM	STRM	38 55 175 55	38
WAITETUNA	LOC	37 51 175 02	18
WAITETUNA RIVER	STRM	37 48 174 58	18
WAITETUNA STREAM	STRM	41 17 175 40	51
WAITETUNA STREAM	STRM	41 17 175 40	53
WAITETUNA STREAM	STRM	41 36 175 20	53
WAITEWAEWAE RIVER	STRM	40 49 175 18	48
WAITEWAEWAE (TRIG)	PEAK	40 45 175 18	48
WAITEWHENA STREAM	STRM	38 47 175 00	26
WAITEWHENA STREAM	STRM	38 47 175 00	27
WAITI	LOC	37 30 175 27	15
WAITI STREAM	STRM	37 30 175 27	15
WAITIKI LANDING	LOC	34 31 172 50	2
WAITIKI STREAM	STRM	34 31 172 50	2
WAITIO STREAM	STRM	39 36 176 43	42
WAITIO STREAM	STRM	39 36 176 43	43
WAITIO STREAM	STRM	39 36 176 43	47
WAITIRI	LOC	45 03 169 03	99
WAITIRI (TRIG)	HILL	39 22 174 34	35
WAITIRI (TRIG)	HILL	39 22 174 34	44
WAITOA	LOC	37 36 175 38	19
WAITOA RIVER	STRM	37 29 175 33	15
WAITOA RIVER	STRM	37 34 175 38	19
WAITOHI	LOC	40 15 175 26	45
WAITOHI	LOC	40 15 175 26	46
WAITOHI	LOC	44 13 171 11	87
WAITOHI DOWNS	HSTD	42 49 172 33	71
WAITOHI PEAKS	HSTD	42 51 172 33	71
WAITOHI RIVER	STRM	42 53 172 46	71
WAITOHI RIVER	STRM	42 53 172 46	72
WAITOHI STREAM	STRM	44 02 170 56	87
WAITOHU STREAM	STRM	40 44 175 07	48
WAITOKI	LOC	36 38 174 33	11
WAITOKI	LOC	36 38 174 33	12
WAITOKI	LOC	37 28 175 39	15
WAITOKI	LOC	37 28 175 39	17
WAITOKI STREAM	STRM	36 38 174 33	10
WAITOKI STREAM	STRM	36 38 174 33	11
WAITOKI STREAM	STRM	36 38 174 33	12
WAITOKI STREAM	STRM	37 28 175 39	15
WAITOKI STREAM	STRM	37 28 175 39	17
WAITOMO CAVES	CAVE	38 16 175 07	18
WAITOMO CAVES	CAVE	38 16 175 07	27
WAITOMO STREAM	STRM	38 11 175 12	18
WAITOMO VALLEY	LOC	38 14 175 07	18
WAITORE (TRIG)	HILL	38 59 176 59	40
WAITORE (TRIG)	HILL	38 59 176 59	41
WAITOTARA	POPL	39 49 174 44	44
WAITOTARA RIVER	STRM	39 51 174 41	44
WAITOTOKI STREAM	STRM	35 16 173 12	3
WAITOTOROA STREAM	STRM	39 18 173 45	34
WAITUHI	LOC	38 35 177 54	32
WAITUHI SADDLE	SAD	38 52 175 33	27
WAITUHI SADDLE	SAD	38 52 175 33	28
WAITUHI SADDLE	SAD	38 52 175 33	38
WAITUI BAY	BAY	41 00 174 11	54
WAITUI BAY	BAY	41 00 174 11	60
WAITUI BAY	BAY	41 00 174 11	61
WAITUI STREAM	STRM	41 01 172 49	57
WAITUI STREAM	STRM	41 01 172 49	58
WAITUI (TRIG)	HILL	39 08 174 20	34
WAITUI (TRIG)	HILL	39 08 174 20	35
WAITUNA	LOC	44 42 171 01	93
WAITUNA	LOC	46 24 168 38	112
WAITUNA BAY	BAY	46 47 167 43	114
WAITUNA CREEK	STRM	46 34 168 33	109
WAITUNA LAGOON	LAGN	46 34 168 36	112
WAITUNA STREAM	STRM	38 20 175 50	28
WAITUNA STREAM	STRM	38 20 175 50	29
WAITUNA STREAM	STRM	40 05 175 29	45
WAITUNA STREAM	STRM	40 05 175 29	46
WAITUNA WEST	LOC	40 03 175 38	46
WAITUTAKI STREAM	STRM	39 32 176 22	39
WAITUTU RIVER	STRM	46 15 167 04	105
WAIUKU	LOC	37 15 174 44	12
WAIUKU	LOC	37 15 174 44	14
WAIUKU RIVER	STRM	37 09 174 42	12
WAIUKU RIVER	STRM	37 09 174 42	14
WAIURA LAGOON	LAKE	44 19 168 08	88
WAIURA LAGOON	LAKE	44 19 168 08	89
WAIUTA	LOC	42 18 171 49	63
WAIUTA	LOC	42 18 171 49	64
WAI-WAIATA STREAM	STRM	45 34 167 31	105
WAIWAKA	LOC	40 41 175 42	49
WAIWAKARUKU (TRIG)	HILL	35 20 173 25	3
WAIWAWA RIVER	STRM	36 54 175 42	15
WAIWAWA RIVER	STRM	36 54 175 42	16
WAIWAWA RIVER	STRM	36 54 175 42	17
WAIWERA	LOC	36 33 174 42	11
WAIWERA	LOC	40 33 175 40	49
WAIWERA CREEK	STRM	44 52 169 26	91
WAIWERA RIVER	STRM	36 33 174 43	11
WAIWERA RIVER	STRM	46 09 169 34	111
WAIWERA RIVER	STRM	46 09 169 34	113
WAIWERA SOUTH	LOC	46 13 169 29	111
WAIWERA SOUTH	LOC	46 13 169 29	113
WAIWERANUI STREAM	STRM	39 13 173 47	34
WAIWHAKAIHO RIVER	STRM	39 02 174 06	34
WAIWHAKANGAU STREAM	STRM	37 56 176 00	20
WAIWHAKAPA STREAM	STRM	38 09 176 36	21
WAIWHAKAPA STREAM	STRM	38 09 176 36	22
WAIWHAKAPOUA STREAM	STRM	39 33 176 02	39
WAIWHANGO RIVER	STRM	36 44 175 28	13
WAIWHANGO RIVER	STRM	36 44 175 28	16
WAIWHERO CREEK	STRM	41 10 172 55	58
WAIWHERO STREAM	STRM	38 17 177 32	31
WAIWHERO STREAM	STRM	40 01 176 41	43
WAIWHERO STREAM	STRM	40 01 176 41	47
WAIWHIU	LOC	36 22 174 37	11
WAIWHIU STREAM	STRM	36 18 174 35	11
WAIWIRI ISLAND	ISLD	35 12 174 20	5
WAKAATEA (TRIG)	PEAK	39 12 176 42	40
WAKAMARAMA RANGE	MTNS	40 48 172 27	56
WAKAMARINA RIVER	STRM	41 17 173 40	60
WAKAMOEKAU CREEK	STRM	40 54 175 37	48
WAKAMOEKAU CREEK	STRM	40 54 175 37	49
WAKAMOEKAU CREEK	STRM	40 54 175 37	51
WAKANUI	LOC	43 58 171 49	84
WAKANUI CREEK	STRM	44 02 171 52	84
WAKAPATU	LOC	46 22 167 49	108
WAKAPUAKA	LOC	41 12 173 22	59
WAKAPUAKA RIVER	STRM	41 11 173 25	59
WAKAPUTA POINT	PNT	46 23 167 47	108
WAKARARA	LOC	39 47 176 15	47
WAKARARA RANGE	MTNS	39 41 176 19	47
WAKAROA POINT	PNT	43 37 172 56	82
WAKAROA POINT	PNT	43 37 172 56	83
WAKATIPU, LAKE	LAKE	45 06 168 31	95
WAKATIPU, LAKE	LAKE	45 06 168 31	98
WAKATIPU, LAKE	LAKE	45 06 168 31	99
WAKEFIELD	POPL	41 24 173 03	58
WAKEFIELD	POPL	41 24 173 03	59
WAKEFIELD, MOUNT	MTN	43 42 170 07	77
WAKEFIELD, MOUNT	MTN	43 42 170 07	86
WALCOTT, MOUNT	MTN	42 52 171 25	69
WALDRONVILLE	LOC	45 55 170 24	103
WALES, MOUNT	MTN	45 38 166 40	104
WALKER CREEK	STRM	45 06 167 58	97
WALKER CREEK	STRM	45 06 167 58	98
WALKER, MOUNT (TRIG)	MTN	44 00 170 59	87
WALKER PASS	PASS	42 54 171 43	70
WALKER RIVER	STRM	45 50 167 29	105
WALKERS HILL (TRIG)	HILL	46 57 167 48	114
WALKERS STREAM	STRM	41 33 173 33	59
WALL MOUNTAINS	MTNS	45 35 167 15	105
WALL (TRIG)	HILL	39 00 175 16	36
WALLACE CREEK	STRM	42 41 171 27	69
WALLACE HEAD	HEAD	46 38 169 19	112
WALLACE HEAD	HEAD	46 38 169 19	113
WALLACE PEAK	PEAK	42 36 172 48	71
WALLACE PEAK	PEAK	42 36 172 48	72
WALLACETOWN	LOC	46 20 168 17	109
WALLACEVILLE	SBRB	41 08 175 04	52
WALLACEVILLE	SBRB	41 08 175 04	55
WALLER, MOUNT (TRIG)	HILL	41 49 171 53	63
WALLER, MOUNT (TRIG)	HILL	41 49 171 53	64
WALLINGFORD	LOC	40 12 176 36	43
WALLINGFORD	LOC	40 12 176 36	47
WALMSLEY STREAM	STRM	37 22 175 52	17
WALTER, MOUNT	MTN	43 29 170 19	74
WALTER, MOUNT	MTN	43 29 170 19	77
WALTER PEAK	HSTD	45 07 168 32	95
WALTER PEAK	HSTD	45 07 168 32	99
WALTER PEAK (TRIG)	PEAK	45 08 168 34	95
WALTER PEAK (TRIG)	PEAK	45 08 168 34	99
WALTON	LOC	37 44 175 42	19
WANAKA	POPL	44 42 169 08	90
WANAKA, LAKE	LAKE	44 28 169 09	90
WANBROW, CAPE	CAPE	45 07 170 59	102
WANDLE RIVER	STRM	42 35 173 06	72
WANGALOA	LOC	46 17 169 56	111
WANGALOA	LOC	46 17 169 56	113
WANGALOA CREEK	STRM	46 15 170 00	111
WANGALOA CREEK	STRM	46 15 170 00	113
WANGANUI	TOWN	39 56 175 03	45
WANGANUI BLUFF	CLIF	43 02 170 25	74
WANGANUI EAST	SBRB	39 55 175 04	45
WANGANUI RIVER	STRM	39 57 174 59	45
WANGANUI RIVER	STRM	43 02 170 26	74
WANGANUI RIVER	STRM	43 13 170 47	75
WANGANUI (TRIG)	HILL	43 02 170 26	74
WANGAPEKA RIVER	STRM	41 20 172 47	58
WANGAPEKA RIVER, NORTH BRANCH	STRM	41 28 172 29	62
WANGAPEKA RIVER, SOUTH BRANCH	STRM	41 28 172 29	62
WANGAPEKA SADDLE	SAD	41 25 172 25	62
WANGARANGI STREAM	STRM	38 30 178 04	32
WANSTEAD	LOC	40 08 176 32	43
WANSTEAD	LOC	40 08 176 32	47
WANTWOOD (TRIG)	HILL	41 38 173 25	59
WAOTU	LOC	38 09 175 41	19
WAPITI, LAKE	LAKE	45 04 167 27	94
WAPITI, LAKE	LAKE	45 04 167 27	97
WAPITI RIVER	STRM	45 00 167 34	94
WAPITI RIVER	STRM	45 00 167 34	97
WARBECK STREAM	STRM	42 00 172 20	65
WARD	LOC	41 50 174 08	67
WARD HILL	HILL	43 43 169 27	76
WARD HILL	HILL	43 43 169 27	78
WARD HILL	HILL	43 43 169 27	79
WARD ISLAND	ISLD	41 18 174 52	52
WARD ISLAND	ISLD	41 18 174 52	55
WARD, MOUNT	MTN	43 52 169 50	76
WARD, MOUNT	MTN	43 52 169 50	79
WARD, MOUNT	MTN	45 37 167 11	105
WARD, MOUNT (TRIG)	HILL	42 46 173 11	72
WARD, MOUNT (TRIG)	HILL	42 46 173 11	73
WARD STREAM	STRM	41 59 173 26	66
WARDER NECK	SAD	42 18 173 23	66
WARDER (TRIG)	MTN	42 17 173 22	66
WARDS PASS	PASS	41 37 173 07	58
WARDS PASS	PASS	41 37 173 07	59
WARDS PASS	PASS	42 06 173 12	66
WARDS PASS STREAM	STRM	41 37 173 10	59
WARDS PEAK (TRIG)	PEAK	41 39 173 47	60
WARDS STREAM	STRM	41 34 173 48	60
WARDVILLE	LOC	37 43 175 47	19
WARDVILLE	LOC	37 43 175 47	20
WAREA	LOC	39 14 173 49	34
WAREA RIVER	STRM	39 14 173 46	34
WAREWARE	TRIG	39 13 173 47	34
WARKWORTH	POPL	36 24 174 40	11
WARNER, MOUNT	MTN	43 10 171 03	75
WARO	LOC	35 35 174 18	5
WARO	LOC	35 35 174 18	7
WARO	LOC	35 35 174 18	8
WARREN, MOUNT	MTN	44 00 169 00	78
WARREN SPUR (TRIG)	MTN	43 59 168 59	78
WARRINGTON	LOC	45 43 170 35	103
WARRIOR, THE	MTN	43 21 170 51	75

WART, THE	MTN	44 06 168 54	78
WART, THE (TRIG)	HILL	42 44 173 09	72
WART, THE (TRIG)	HILL	42 44 173 09	73
WARWICK JUNCTION	LOC	42 08 172 14	64
WARWICK RIVER	STRM	42 06 172 12	64
WASH CREEK	STRM	45 29 168 03	98
WASH STREAM, THE	STRM	46 10 169 38	111
WASH STREAM, THE	STRM	46 10 169 38	113
WASHDYKE	LOC	44 21 171 14	93
WASHDYKE LAGOON	LAGN	44 22 171 15	93
WASHDYKE STREAM	STRM	42 05 173 56	67
WASHDYKE STREAM	STRM	43 53 170 33	77
WASHDYKE STREAM	STRM	43 53 170 33	86
WASHPEN CREEK	STRM	43 08 172 41	82
WASHPEN STREAM	STRM	42 54 172 43	71
WASHPOOL CREEK	STRM	45 29 169 19	100
WASHPOOL CREEK	STRM	45 44 168 46	110
WASHPOOL CREEK	STRM	46 17 169 57	111
WASHPOOL CREEK	STRM	46 17 169 57	113
WASHPOOL STREAM	STRM	45 35 170 17	101
WASHPOOL STREAM	STRM	46 08 169 28	111
WASHPOOL STREAM	STRM	46 08 169 28	113
WASHPOOL (TRIG)	HILL	39 40 176 43	42
WASHPOOL (TRIG)	HILL	39 40 176 43	43
WATCHMAN ROCK	ROCK	37 03 175 55	16
WATCHMAN ROCK	ROCK	37 03 175 55	17
WATERFALL	HSTD	41 45 174 02	67
WATERFALL CREEK	STRM	41 28 173 10	59
WATERFALL CREEK	STRM	43 32 171 27	75
WATERFALL CREEK	STRM	44 16 169 27	78
WATERFALL CREEK	STRM	44 16 169 27	79
WATERFALL CREEK	STRM	43 32 171 27	80
WATERFALL CREEK	STRM	46 02 168 46	110
WATERFALL CREEK	STRM	46 02 168 46	112
WATERFALL CREEK	STRM	46 59 167 53	114
WATERFALL STREAM	STRM	42 42 172 00	70
WATERFALLS STREAM	STRM	39 24 176 32	39
WATERFALLS STREAM	STRM	39 24 176 32	40
WATERFALLS STREAM	STRM	39 24 176 32	42
WATERLOO	SBRB	41 13 174 56	52
WATERLOO	SBRB	41 13 174 56	55
WATERLOO BURN	STRM	45 45 168 01	106
WATERLOO BURN	STRM	45 45 168 01	107
WATERLOO PEAK	PEAK	45 36 167 58	106
WATERLOO PEAK	PEAK	45 36 167 58	107
WATERTON	LOC	44 03 171 44	84
WATKIN CREEK	STRM	45 33 170 43	102
WATKIN, MOUNT (TRIG)	HILL	45 34 170 34	102
WATKINS	MTN	44 30 168 22	88
WATKINS	MTN	44 30 168 22	89
WATNEY, MOUNT (TRIG)	MTN	44 03 168 50	78
WATSON BLUFF (TRIG)	HILL	44 04 168 20	88
WATSON CREEK	STRM	42 01 172 31	65
WATSON CREEK	STRM	44 05 168 20	88
WATSON, MOUNT	MTN	45 36 167 13	105
WATSON, MOUNT	MTN	42 01 172 35	65
WATSON STREAM	STRM	44 12 169 38	79
WATTA (TRIG)	HILL	40 35 175 53	49
WATTLE BAY	LOC	37 03 174 35	12
WATTLE BAY	LOC	37 03 174 35	14
WATTLE DOWNS	LOC	37 03 174 54	12
WATTLE DOWNS	LOC	37 03 174 54	14
WATTS ROCK (TRIG)	PEAK	45 10 169 05	99
WAVE (TRIG)	HILL	41 32 175 14	53
WAVERLEY	POPL	39 46 174 38	44
WAVERLEY	SBRB	45 53 170 32	103
WAWA	LOC	38 20 175 55	28
WAWA	LOC	38 20 175 55	29
WAYBY	LOC	36 20 174 32	10
WAYBY	LOC	36 20 174 32	11
WAYBY VALLEY	LOC	36 19 174 34	11
WAYNES	LOC	45 22 170 37	102
WEAVERS CROSSING	LOC	37 34 175 08	14
WEAVERS CROSSING	LOC	37 34 175 08	15
WEBB, MOUNT (TRIG)	MTN	44 26 168 05	88
WEBB, MOUNT (TRIG)	MTN	44 26 168 05	89
WEBB STREAM	STRM	40 43 172 22	56
WEBER	LOC	40 24 176 19	50
WEBSTER, MOUNT	MTN	44 00 169 10	78
WEDDERBURN	LOC	45 02 170 01	101
WEDGE PEAK	PEAK	45 02 168 34	95
WEDGE PEAK	PEAK	45 02 168 34	99
WEDGE POINT	PNT	41 16 174 00	54
WEDGE POINT	PNT	41 16 174 00	60
WEDGE POINT	PNT	41 16 174 00	61
WEDNESDAY PEAK (TRIG)	MTN	46 09 166 51	104
WEEDONS	LOC	43 34 172 26	81
WEEDONS	LOC	43 34 172 26	85
WEIR CREEK	STRM	42 58 170 52	68
WEITI RIVER	STRM	36 39 174 44	11
WEITI RIVER	STRM	36 39 174 44	12
WEITI STREAM	STRM	36 38 174 39	11
WEITI STREAM	STRM	36 38 174 39	12
WEITI STREAM	STRM	36 50 175 40	16
WEKA BROOK	STRM	42 03 173 21	66
WEKA BROOK	STRM	42 30 173 18	72
WEKA BROOK	STRM	42 30 173 18	73
WEKA BURN	STRM	45 59 167 36	106
WEKA ISLAND	ISLD	46 06 166 42	104
WEKA ISLAND	ISLD	47 03 168 13	115
WEKA PASS	LOC	43 00 172 43	71
WEKA SADDLE	SAD	41 26 173 17	59
WEKAKURA CREEK	STRM	41 01 172 07	56
WEKAKURA CREEK	STRM	41 01 172 07	62
WEKAKURA POINT	PNT	40 55 172 06	56
WEKANUI (TRIG)	HILL	38 38 176 46	30
WEKARUA ISLAND	ISLD	34 57 173 39	4
WEKARUA ISLAND	ISLD	36 51 175 25	13
WEKARUA ISLAND	ISLD	36 51 175 25	16
WEKAWEKA	LOC	35 34 173 32	6
WELCOME BAY	SBRB	37 44 176 12	20
WELCOME BAY	SBRB	37 44 176 12	21
WELCOME BAY	BAY	46 05 166 36	104
WELCOME POINT	PNT	45 09 167 49	94
WELCOME POINT	PNT	45 09 167 49	97
WELCOME POINT	PNT	45 09 167 49	98
WELD CONE (TRIG)	HILL	41 51 174 10	67
WELD, MOUNT	MTN	42 06 172 51	65
WELD PASS	PASS	41 36 174 03	60
WELDS HILL	HSTD	41 47 173 51	67
WELDS HILL (TRIG)	HILL	41 51 173 46	67
WELLINGTON	METR	41 17 174 46	52
WELLINGTON	METR	41 17 174 46	55
WELLINGTON HEAD	HEAD	36 10 175 17	9
WELLS CREEK	STRM	43 45, 169 10	78
WELLSFORD	POPL	36 18 174 31	10
WELLSFORD	POPL	36 18 174 31	11
WELLSHOT STREAM	STRM	44 05 170 48	87
WELSHMAN CREEK	STRM	41 50 171 56	64
WELSHMANS	LOC	42 33 171 13	68
WELSHMANS	LOC	42 33 171 13	69
WELSHMANS CREEK	STRM	45 27 168 59	99
WELSHMANS CREEK	STRM	45 31 169 02	99
WELSHMANS CREEK	STRM	45 21 170 18	101
WENDON	LOC	45 53 168 49	110
WENDON, MOUNT (TRIG)	HILL	45 49 169 00	110
WENDON STREAM	STRM	45 51 168 47	110
WENTWORTH RIVER	STRM	37 13 175 52	17
WERA, MOUNT	MTN	45 15 167 17	96
WERAROA	LOC	40 38 175 16	48
WERAROA STREAM	STRM	38 16 177 51	32
WERAROA (TRIG)	HILL	38 38 175 36	27
WERAROA (TRIG)	HILL	38 38 175 36	28
WERAWERAONGA STREAM	STRM	39 46 174 44	44
WEREKINO STREAM	STRM	39 11 173 49	34
WEREWERE POINT	PNT	36 13 174 09	7
WEST ARM	BAY	45 30 167 22	96
WEST BRANCH HUNTER RIVER	STRM	44 02 169 37	79
WEST BRANCH (LITTLE VALLEY CREEK)	STRM	45 20 169 30	100
WEST CAPE	CAPE	45 54 166 26	104
WEST DOME	HSTD	45 38 168 14	107
WEST DOME (TRIG)	PEAK	45 35 168 13	98
WEST END	SBRB	40 22 175 36	48
WEST END	SBRB	40 22 175 36	49
WEST EWEBURN DAM	DAM	45 00 170 05	92
WEST EWEBURN DAM	DAM	45 00 170 05	101
WEST EYRETON	LOC	43 21 172 23	81
WEST EYRETON	LOC	43 21 172 23	85
WEST HARBOUR	LOC	36 49 174 37	11
WEST HARBOUR	LOC	36 49 174 37	12
WEST HEAD	HEAD	41 13 174 19	54
WEST HEAD	HEAD	41 13 174 19	61
WEST HEAD	HEAD	43 41 173 04	82
WEST HEAD	HEAD	43 41 173 04	83
WEST ISLAND	ISLD	34 11 172 02	2
WEST MATHIAS RIVER	STRM	43 11 171 08	75
WEST MELTON	LOC	43 32 172 22	81
WEST MELTON	LOC	43 32 172 22	85
WEST PEAK	PEAK	40 42 175 29	48
WEST PEAK	PEAK	40 42 175 29	49
WEST PEAK	PEAK	46 03 167 09	105
WEST PEAK (TRIG)	HILL	43 42 173 01	83
WEST PEAK (TRIG)	PEAK	46 05 168 35	107
WEST PLAINS	LOC	46 22 168 19	109
WEST POINT	PNT	46 46 168 28	109
WEST POINT	PNT	46 46 168 28	115
WEST TAIERI (TRIG)	HILL	45 54 170 09	103
WEST WANAKA	HSTD	44 37 169 00	90
WESTERFIELD	LOC	43 50 171 37	84
WESTERN BAY	BAY	38 44 175 50	28
WESTERN BAY	BAY	38 44 175 50	38
WESTERN HUTT RIVER	STRM	41 02 175 13	53
WESTERN PASSAGE	STRA	46 02 166 30	104
WESTERN VALLEY	LOC	43 45 172 48	83
WESTLAND, MOUNT	MTN	43 16 170 52	75
WESTLAND NATIONAL PARK	PARK	43 18 170 11	74
WESTLAND NATIONAL PARK	PARK	43 32 170 05	76
WESTLAND NATIONAL PARK	PARK	43 32 170 05	77
WESTMERE	LOC	37 35 175 09	14
WESTMERE	LOC	37 35 175 09	15
WESTMERE	LOC	39 54 175 00	45
WESTON	LOC	45 05 170 55	102
WESTOWN	SBRB	39 04 174 03	34
WESTPORT	TOWN	41 45 171 36	63
WESTPORT	TOWN	41 45 171 36	64
WESTSHORE	SBRB	39 28 176 53	40
WESTSHORE	SBRB	39 28 176 53	41
WESTSHORE	SBRB	39 28 176 53	42
WESTWOOD	LOC	45 56 170 22	103
WET GULLY	STRM	45 06 169 11	100
WET JACKET ARM	BAY	45 40 166 45	104
WETA, MOUNT	MTN	44 43 170 14	92
WETA (TRIG)	HILL	35 03 173 51	4
WETHER BURN	STRM	45 06 169 57	101
WETHER HILL	HILL	45 48 168 20	107
WETHER HILL (TRIG)	HILL	45 52 167 55	106
WETHER HILL (TRIG)	HILL	45 52 167 55	107
WETHER HILL (TRIG)	HILL	41 40 173 07	66
WETHER HILL (TRIG)	HILL	41 43 173 27	66
WETHER RANGE	MTNS	44 36 169 45	91
WETHERAL	LOC	43 22 172 36	82
WETHERAL	LOC	43 22 172 36	83
WETHERAL	LOC	43 22 172 36	85
WETHERSTON	LOC	45 54 169 42	111
WEYDON BURN	STRM	45 36 168 09	98
WEYMOUTH	SBRB	37 03 174 52	12
WEYMOUTH	SBRB	37 03 174 52	14
WHAHARANGI (TRIG)	HILL	39 29 175 05	36
WHAINGAINGA (TRIG)	HILL	38 32 174 57	26
WHAINGAPUNA (TRIG)	PEAK	40 01 176 02	46
WHAITI STREAM	STRM	42 49 171 43	70
WHAKAAHU (TRIG)	HILL	38 27 175 49	28
WHAKAAHU (TRIG)	HILL	38 27 175 49	29
WHAKAANGI (TRIG)	HILL	34 57 173 33	3
WHAKAANGI (TRIG)	HILL	34 57 173 33	4
WHAKAANGIANGI (TRIG)	HILL	37 46 178 16	25
WHAKAARI (WHITE ISLAND)	ISLD	37 31 177 11	23
WHAKAAURANGA STREAM	STRM	38 25 178 06	32
WHAKAHAU (TRIG)	MTN	38 40 176 54	30
WHAKAHAUPAPA STREAM	STRM	37 54 176 34	21
WHAKAHAUPAPA STREAM	STRM	37 54 176 34	22
WHAKAHORO	LOC	39 06 175 04	36
WHAKAHU STREAM	STRM	39 10 176 30	39
WHAKAHU STREAM	STRM	39 10 176 30	40
WHAKAIHUWHAKA	LOC	39 46 175 10	45
WHAKAIKAI RIVER	STRM	43 01 170 30	74
WHAKAIPO BAY	BAY	38 42 175 57	28
WHAKAIPO BAY	BAY	38 42 175 57	29
WHAKAIPO BAY	BAY	38 42 175 57	38
WHAKAIRONGA STREAM	STRM	38 11 175 52	20
WHAKAKAIWHARA POINT	PNT	36 54 175 06	13
WHAKAKAIWHARA POINT	PNT	36 54 175 06	14
WHAKAKAIWHARA POINT	PNT	36 54 175 06	15
WHAKAKI	LOC	39 03 177 36	33
WHAKAKI LAGOON	LAGN	39 03 177 33	33
WHAKAKI RIVER	STRM	36 15 174 19	10
WHAKAMAHI LAGOON	LAGN	39 04 177 24	41
WHAKAMAI (TRIG)	HILL	38 57 177 23	41
WHAKAMARAMA	LOC	37 44 175 59	20
WHAKAMARIA STREAM	STRM	38 11 177 41	24
WHAKAMARIA STREAM	STRM	38 11 177 41	31
WHAKAMARINO, LAKE	LAKE	38 49 177 09	31
WHAKAMARO STREAM	STRM	38 55 175 09	27
WHAKAMARU	HILL	38 24 175 53	28
WHAKAMARU	LOC	38 26 175 48	28
WHAKAMARU	LOC	38 26 175 48	29
WHAKAMARU	HILL	38 24 175 53	29
WHAKAMARU, LAKE	LAKE	38 26 175 53	28
WHAKAMARU, LAKE	LAKE	38 26 175 53	29
WHAKAMARUMARU (TRIG)	PEAK	39 14 176 01	38
WHAKAMARUMARU (TRIG)	PEAK	39 14 176 01	39
WHAKAMOA REEF	REEF	43 54 172 53	83
WHAKAMOEHAU	HILL	37 19 175 47	17
WHAKAMOENGA POINT	PNT	38 44 176 00	28
WHAKAMOENGA POINT	PNT	38 44 176 00	29
WHAKAMOENGA POINT	PNT	38 44 176 00	38
WHAKAMU (TRIG)	HILL	37 55 178 19	25
WHAKANAKENEKE RIVER	STRM	35 19 173 38	4
WHAKANEKENEKE STREAM	STRM	35 18 173 44	4
WHAKANGAROMANGA STREAM	STRM	39 43 175 03	45
WHAKAOMA (TRIG)	HILL	35 19 173 35	3
WHAKAOMA (TRIG)	HILL	35 19 173 35	4
WHAKAPAPA RIVER	STRM	38 56 175 25	36
WHAKAPAPA RIVER	STRM	38 56 175 25	37
WHAKAPAPA (TRIG)	PEAK	40 49 175 33	48
WHAKAPAPA (TRIG)	PEAK	40 49 175 33	49
WHAKAPAPA (TRIG)	PEAK	40 49 175 33	51
WHAKAPAPA VILLAGE	LOC	39 12 175 33	36
WHAKAPAPA VILLAGE	LOC	39 12 175 33	37
WHAKAPAPA VILLAGE	LOC	39 12 175 33	38
WHAKAPAPAITI STREAM	STRM	39 08 175 29	36
WHAKAPAPAITI STREAM	STRM	39 08 175 29	37
WHAKAPAPANUI STREAM	STRM	39 08 175 29	36
WHAKAPAPANUI STREAM	STRM	39 08 175 29	37
WHAKAPAPANUI STREAM	STRM	39 08 175 29	38
WHAKAPARA	LOC	35 33 174 17	5
WHAKAPARA RIVER	STRM	35 32 174 17	5
WHAKAPIRAU	LOC	36 10 174 14	7
WHAKAPIRAU	LOC	36 10 174 14	8
WHAKAPIRAU CREEK	STRM	36 11 174 17	7
WHAKAPIRAU CREEK	STRM	36 11 174 17	8
WHAKAPOAI POINT	PNT	40 56 172 06	56
WHAKAPOHAI RIVER	STRM	43 43 169 15	78
WHAKAPOURANGI	LOC	37 54 178 15	25
WHAKAPUNAKE (TRIG)	MTN	38 48 177 36	31
WHAKAPUNAKE (TRIG)	MTN	38 48 177 36	33
WHAKAPUNI	HSTD	41 23 175 30	53
WHAKAPUNUI STREAM	STRM	41 23 175 31	51
WHAKAPUNUI STREAM	STRM	41 23 175 31	53
WHAKARAE PA	LOC	38 17 177 07	31
WHAKARAPA STREAM	STRM	35 23 173 23	3
WHAKARAPA STREAM	STRM	35 23 173 23	6
WHAKARARA (TRIG)	HILL	35 03 173 53	4
WHAKARAU	HSTD	38 23 177 38	31
WHAKARAUTAWA STREAM	STRM	38 04 175 08	18
WHAKAREORO (TRIG)	HILL	35 39 174 30	5
WHAKAREORO (TRIG)	HILL	35 39 174 30	8
WHAKAREWAREWA	SBRB	38 10 176 15	20
WHAKAREWAREWA	SBRB	38 10 176 15	21
WHAKAREWAREWA STATE FOREST PARK	PARK	38 12 176 18	20
WHAKAREWAREWA STATE FOREST PARK	PARK	38 12 176 18	21
WHAKARONGO	LOC	40 20 175 40	49
WHAKARONGOTAIAROA	HILL	39 24 174 54	35
WHAKARORA STREAM	STRM	40 55 176 04	49
WHAKARORA STREAM	STRM	40 55 176 04	51
WHAKARORA (TRIG)	HILL	40 51 176 00	49
WHAKARORA (TRIG)	HILL	40 51 176 00	51
WHAKARUA STREAM	STRM	41 13 175 34	51
WHAKARUA STREAM	STRM	41 13 175 34	53
WHAKARUANGANGANA (TRIG)	HILL	35 27 173 45	4
WHAKARUANGANGANA (TRIG)	HILL	35 27 173 45	6
WHAKATAHINE RIVER	STRM	41 03 175 50	51
WHAKATAKA (TRIG)	MTN	38 42 176 59	30
WHAKATAKAHE HEAD	HEAD	39 06 177 51	33
WHAKATAKI	LOC	40 52 176 13	50
WHAKATAKI RIVER	STRM	40 52 176 13	50
WHAKATANE	TOWN	37 58 176 59	22
WHAKATANE	TOWN	37 58 176 59	23
WHAKATANE RIVER	STRM	37 57 177 00	22
WHAKATANE RIVER	STRM	37 57 177 00	23
WHAKATANE WEST	RSTN	38 00 176 56	22
WHAKATANE WEST	RSTN	38 00 176 56	23
WHAKATATARA (TRIG)	HILL	38 28 177 04	30
WHAKATAUTUNA POINT	PNT	36 10 175 30	9
WHAKATEREPAPANUI ISLAND	ISLD	40 45 174 00	61
WHAKATETE BAY	LOC	37 06 175 31	13
WHAKATETE BAY	LOC	37 06 175 31	15
WHAKATETE BAY	LOC	37 06 175 31	16
WHAKATETEREKIA STREAM	STRM	35 13 173 41	4
WHAKATIKI RIVER	STRM	41 07 175 03	52
WHAKATIKI RIVER	STRM	41 07 175 03	55
WHAKATINA	LOC	39 23 175 01	36
WHAKATIWAI	LOC	37 05 175 18	13
WHAKATIWAI	LOC	37 05 175 18	15
WHAKATIWAI STREAM	STRM	37 05 175 18	13
WHAKATIWAI STREAM	STRM	37 05 175 18	15
WHAKATU	LOC	39 36 176 54	42
WHAKATU	LOC	39 36 176 54	43
WHAKAUAHI (TRIG)	HILL	39 28 174 50	35
WHAKAUAHI (TRIG)	HILL	39 28 174 50	44
WHAKAUMU (TRIG)	HILL	38 10 178 08	25
WHAKAUMU (TRIG)	HILL	38 10 178 08	32
WHAKAUMU (TRIG)	HILL	38 58 177 34	33
WHAKAUREKOU RIVER	STRM	39 39 176 03	47
WHAKAURU STREAM	STRM	38 12 175 51	20
WHAKAURU STREAM	STRM	38 12 175 51	29
WHAKAWHITIRA	LOC	37 50 178 20	25
WHAKOAU STREAM	STRM	38 05 178 03	25
WHALAN STREAM	STRM	44 35 170 13	92
WHALE BAY	BAY	35 10 174 07	4
WHALE BAY	BAY	35 10 174 07	5
WHALE HILL (TRIG)	HILL	43 04 171 56	80
WHALE HILL (TRIG)	HILL	43 04 171 56	81
WHALE ISLAND	ISLD	34 47 173 23	3
WHALE ROCK	ROCK	36 42 175 55	16
WHALE STREAM	STRM	43 57 170 08	77
WHALE STREAM	STRM	43 57 170 08	86
WHALES BACK	HSTD	42 30 173 11	72
WHALES BACK	HSTD	42 30 173 11	73
WHALES BACK SADDLE	SAD	42 29 173 12	72
WHALES BACK SADDLE	SAD	42 29 173 12	73
WHALES BACK (TRIG)	HILL	42 28 173 14	72
WHALES BACK (TRIG)	HILL	42 28 173 14	73
WHANAKE (TRIG)	HILL	36 38 175 34	13
WHANAKE (TRIG)	HILL	36 38 175 34	16
WHANAKE (TRIG)	HILL	38 01 175 29	19
WHANAKI RIVER	STRM	36 21 174 26	10
WHANAKI RIVER	STRM	36 21 174 26	11
WHANANAKI	LOC	35 31 174 25	5
WHANANAKI SOUTH	LOC	35 31 174 27	5
WHANARUA BAY	BAY	37 41 177 47	24
WHANAWHANA	HSTD	39 33 176 26	39
WHANAWHANA	HSTD	39 33 176 26	40
WHANGAAHEI	LOC	36 37 175 28	13
WHANGAAHEI	LOC	36 37 175 28	16
WHANGAE	LOC	35 21 174 01	4
WHANGAE	LOC	35 21 174 01	5
WHANGAE BRIDGE	LOC	35 20 174 06	4
WHANGAE BRIDGE	LOC	35 20 174 06	5
WHANGAEHU	LOC	40 01 175 10	45
WHANGAEHU	LOC	40 56 175 46	49
WHANGAEHU	LOC	40 56 175 46	51
WHANGAEHU RIVER	STRM	40 03 175 06	45
WHANGAEHU RIVER	STRM	40 59 175 41	51
WHANGAEHU RIVER	STRM	41 14 175 30	51
WHANGAEHU RIVER	STRM	41 14 175 30	53
WHANGAI RANGE	MTNS	40 11 176 25	47
WHANGAI STREAM	STRM	40 13 176 20	47
WHANGAI (TRIG)	HILL	40 19 176 22	50
WHANGAIHE BAY	BAY	35 00 173 49	4
WHANGAIMOANA	LOC	41 24 175 10	52
WHANGAIMOANA	LOC	41 24 175 10	53
WHANGAIMOANA	LOC	41 24 175 10	55
WHANGAIMOANA STREAM	STRM	41 25 175 10	53
WHANGAIPETEKI STREAM	STRM	37 58 175 37	19
WHANGAIREHE STREAM	STRM	39 11 175 17	36
WHANGAITERENGA STREAM	STRM	37 05 175 39	15
WHANGAITERENGA STREAM	STRM	37 05 175 39	16
WHANGAMAIRE STREAM	STRM	37 06 174 52	12
WHANGAMAIRE STREAM	STRM	37 06 174 52	14
WHANGAMARINO	LOC	37 21 175 07	14
WHANGAMARINO	LOC	37 21 175 07	15
WHANGAMARINO RIVER	STRM	37 18 175 04	14
WHANGAMARINO RIVER	STRM	37 18 175 04	15
WHANGAMATA	LOC	37 13 175 52	17
WHANGAMATA BAY	BAY	38 40 175 54	28
WHANGAMATA BAY	BAY	38 40 175 54	29
WHANGAMATA BAY	BAY	38 40 175 54	38
WHANGAMATA HARBOUR	HARB	37 12 175 53	17
WHANGAMATA STREAM	STRM	38 40 175 55	28
WHANGAMATA STREAM	STRM	38 40 175 55	29
WHANGAMOA	HSTD	41 09 173 32	59
WHANGAMOA HEAD	HEAD	41 06 173 31	59
WHANGAMOA HEAD (TRIG)	HILL	41 06 173 31	59
WHANGAMOA RIVER	STRM	41 06 173 32	59
WHANGAMOA SADDLE	SAD	41 13 173 26	59
WHANGAMOMONA	LOC	39 09 174 44	35
WHANGAMOMONA RIVER	STRM	39 16 174 53	35
WHANGAMOMONA SADDLE	SAD	39 09 174 42	35
WHANGAMUMU HARBOUR	HARB	35 15 174 18	5
WHANGAMUMU POINT	PNT	35 15 174 20	5
WHANGANUI	LOC	38 47 175 44	28
WHANGANUI	LOC	38 47 175 44	38
WHANGANUI INLET	BAY	40 36 172 33	57
WHANGANUI ISLAND	ISLD	36 47 175 27	13
WHANGANUI ISLAND	ISLD	36 47 175 27	16
WHANGANUI STREAM	STRM	38 47 175 44	28
WHANGANUI STREAM	STRM	38 47 175 44	38
WHANGAOKENO ISLAND (EAST ISLAND)	ISLD	37 41 178 35	25
WHANGAPARAOA	POPL	36 38 174 46	11
WHANGAPARAOA	POPL	36 38 174 46	12
WHANGAPARAOA	LOC	37 34 178 00	24
WHANGAPARAOA	LOC	37 34 178 00	25
WHANGAPARAOA BAY	BAY	36 35 174 45	11
WHANGAPARAOA BAY	BAY	36 35 174 45	12
WHANGAPARAOA BAY	BAY	37 35 177 57	24
WHANGAPARAOA BAY	BAY	37 35 177 57	25
WHANGAPARAOA PASSAGE	STRA	36 36 174 52	11
WHANGAPARAOA PASSAGE	STRA	36 36 174 52	12
WHANGAPARAOA PENINSULA	PEN	36 37 174 48	11
WHANGAPARAOA PENINSULA	PEN	36 37 174 48	12
WHANGAPARAOA RIVER	STRM	37 34 178 00	25
WHANGAPARAPARA	LOC	36 15 175 24	9
WHANGAPARAPARA HARBOUR	HARB	36 15 175 24	9
WHANGAPARAPARA (TRIG)	HILL	36 14 175 23	9
WHANGAPE	LOC	35 21 173 13	3
WHANGAPE HARBOUR	HARB	35 23 173 13	3
WHANGAPE, LAKE	LAKE	37 28 175 03	14
WHANGAPOROTO	LOC	38 55 175 26	27
WHANGAPOUA	LOC	36 43 175 37	16
WHANGAPOUA BEACH	BCH	36 08 175 25	9
WHANGAPOUA CREEK	STRM	36 09 175 24	9
WHANGAPOUA HARBOUR	HARB	36 45 175 38	16
WHANGAPOURI CREEK	STRM	37 06 174 55	12
WHANGAPOURI CREEK	STRM	37 06 174 55	14
WHANGARA	LOC	38 34 178 14	32
WHANGARA ISLAND	ISLD	38 34 178 14	32
WHANGARARA ISLAND	ISLD	36 15 175 22	9
WHANGARATA	LOC	37 16 174 59	12
WHANGARATA	LOC	37 16 174 59	14
WHANGAREI	TOWN	35 43 174 19	5
WHANGAREI	TOWN	35 43 174 19	7
WHANGAREI	TOWN	35 43 174 19	8
WHANGAREI HARBOUR	HARB	35 48 174 24	7
WHANGAREI HARBOUR	HARB	35 48 174 24	8
WHANGAREI HEADS	LOC	35 49 174 30	8
WHANGARIPO	LOC	36 18 174 39	11
WHANGARIPO STREAM	STRM	36 17 174 35	11
WHANGAROA	LOC	35 03 173 45	4
WHANGAROA BAY	BAY	34 59 173 45	4
WHANGAROA HARBOUR	HARB	35 04 173 44	4
WHANGARURU	LOC	35 21 174 19	5
WHANGARURU HARBOUR	HARB	35 21 174 20	5
WHANGARURU NORTH	LOC	35 21 174 21	5
WHANGARURU SOUTH	LOC	35 23 174 21	5
WHANGATEAU	LOC	36 19 174 46	11
WHANGATEAU HARBOUR	HARB	36 19 174 46	11
WHANGATUPERE BAY	BAY	34 50 173 27	3
WHANGAWAHIA (TRIG)	HILL	36 10 175 27	9
WHANGAWEHI STREAM	STRM	39 06 177 57	33
WHANUI (TRIG)	HILL	35 43 174 27	5
WHANUI (TRIG)	HILL	35 43 174 27	8
WHARANGI (TRIG)	HILL	39 02 176 34	39
WHARANGI (TRIG)	HILL	39 02 176 34	40
WHARANUI	LOC	41 55 174 06	67
WHARARIKI (TRIG)	HILL	39 32 174 38	35
WHARARIKI (TRIG)	HILL	39 32 174 38	44
WHARATEA	HSTD	40 49 173 55	61
WHARE	TRIG	40 24 175 24	48
WHARE CREEK	STRM	45 38 167 41	106
WHARE FLAT	LOC	45 49 170 26	103
WHARE STREAM	STRM	41 50 173 26	66
WHAREAMA	LOC	40 58 176 03	51
WHAREAMA RIVER	STRM	41 01 176 06	51
WHAREANA BAY	BAY	34 28 173 00	2
WHAREATEA	LOC	40 49 173 56	54
WHAREATEA RIVER	STRM	41 43 171 43	63
WHAREATEA RIVER	STRM	41 43 171 43	64
WHAREHANGA (TRIG)	HILL	38 51 175 04	26
WHAREHANGA (TRIG)	HILL	38 51 175 04	27
WHAREHINE	LOC	36 19 174 24	10
WHAREHINE	LOC	36 19 174 24	11
WHAREHINU (TRIG)	MTN	37 48 177 55	24
WHAREHUANUI	LOC	44 57 168 46	90
WHAREHUANUI	LOC	44 57 168 46	95
WHAREHUANUI	LOC	44 57 168 46	99
WHAREHUIA	LOC	39 19 174 20	34
WHAREHUIA	LOC	39 19 174 20	35
WHAREHUIA	LOC	39 19 174 20	44
WHAREIHUNGARU STREAM	STRM	39 52 175 29	45

WHAREIHUNGARU STREAM	STRM	39 52 175 29	46
WHAREKAHIKA RIVER	STRM	37 35 178 17	25
WHAREKAKA	LOC	38 20 178 17	32
WHAREKAKA STREAM	STRM	38 30 176 10	29
WHAREKAUHAU	LOC	41 23 175 05	52
WHAREKAUHAU	LOC	41 23 175 05	55
WHAREKAUHAU STREAM	STRM	41 22 175 04	52
WHAREKAUHAU STREAM	STRM	41 22 175 04	55
WHAREKAUNGA STREAM	STRM	38 26 176 20	29
WHAREKAWA	LOC	37 04 175 18	13
WHAREKAWA	LOC	37 04 175 18	15
WHAREKAWA	LOC	37 08 175 51	17
WHAREKAWA HARBOUR	HARB	37 07 175 53	17
WHAREKAWA RIVER	STRM	37 08 175 52	17
WHAREKIA (TRIG)	MTN	37 53 178 06	25
WHAREKIRAUPONGA STREAM	STRM	37 15 175 52	17
WHAREKIRI	HSTD	38 31 178 07	32
WHAREKIRI STREAM	STRM	38 28 175 29	27
WHAREKIRI STREAM	STRM	42 08 173 52	67
WHAREKIRI (TRIG)	HILL	38 06 178 11	25
WHAREKOHE	LOC	35 45 174 08	5
WHAREKOHE	LOC	35 45 174 08	7
WHAREKOPAE	LOC	38 33 177 30	31
WHAREKOPAE RIVER	STRM	38 27 177 46	31
WHAREKOPAE RIVER	STRM	38 27 177 46	32
WHAREKOPAE (TRIG)	HILL	38 29 177 35	31
WHAREKURA POINT	PNT	37 44 177 41	24
WHAREKURI	POPL	44 42 170 26	92
WHAREKURI CREEK	STRM	44 40 170 22	92
WHAREMATA (TRIG)	HILL	39 47 175 21	45
WHAREONGAONGA (TRIG)	HILL	38 52 177 55	33
WHAREOPAIA (TRIG)	HILL	38 25 178 16	32
WHAREORA	LOC	35 41 174 23	5
WHAREORA	LOC	35 41 174 23	7
WHAREORA	LOC	35 41 174 23	8
WHAREORINO (TRIG)	HILL	38 25 174 42	26
WHAREOTAMANUI (TRIG)	HILL	38 53 177 49	33
WHAREOTARITA (TRIG)	HILL	39 52 175 21	45
WHAREPAIHA	LOC	38 24 176 20	29
WHAREPAPA	LOC	36 43 174 26	10
WHAREPAPA	LOC	36 43 174 26	11
WHAREPAPA	HSTD	41 22 175 05	52
WHAREPAPA	HSTD	41 22 175 05	55
WHAREPAPA RIVER	STRM	41 23 175 05	52
WHAREPAPA RIVER	STRM	41 23 175 05	55
WHAREPAPA SOUTH	LOC	38 09 175 32	19
WHAREPAPA (TRIG)	HILL	38 23 176 17	29
WHAREPOA	LOC	37 16 175 38	15
WHAREPONGA	LOC	37 58 178 22	25
WHAREPUHUNGA	LOC	38 13 175 29	19
WHAREPUHUNGA (TRIG)	HILL	38 14 175 37	19
WHAREPUHUNGA (TRIG)	HILL	38 14 175 37	28
WHARERANGI (TRIG)	HILL	39 28 176 49	40
WHARERANGI (TRIG)	HILL	39 28 176 49	41
WHARERANGI (TRIG)	HILL	39 28 176 49	42
WHARERANGIORA (TRIG)	PEAK	38 55 176 47	40
WHARERE STREAM	STRM	37 49 176 29	21
WHARERE STREAM	STRM	37 49 176 29	22
WHAREROA STREAM	STRM	38 52 175 47	28
WHAREROA STREAM	STRM	38 52 175 47	38
WHAREROA STREAM	STRM	40 14 175 47	46
WHARETI STREAM	STRM	38 45 177 31	31
WHARETI STREAM	STRM	38 45 177 31	33
WHARETOA	LOC	46 03 169 30	111
WHARETOA	LOC	46 03 169 30	113
WHAREWAKA	SBRB	38 44 176 05	28
WHAREWAKA	SBRB	38 44 176 05	29
WHAREWAKA	SBRB	38 44 176 05	38
WHAREWAKA POINT	PNT	38 44 176 04	28
WHAREWAKA POINT	PNT	38 44 176 04	29
WHAREWAKA POINT	PNT	38 44 176 04	38
WHARF STREAM	STRM	41 57 173 52	67
WHARITE (TRIG)	PEAK	40 15 175 51	46
WHARUA	LOC	44 41 170 31	92
WHARUARUA (TRIG)	HILL	35 06 173 42	4
WHATAIPU (TRIG)	HILL	37 56 174 54	18
WHATANIHI	HSTD	41 14 173 51	54
WHATANIHI	HSTD	41 14 173 51	60
WHATANIHI	HSTD	41 14 173 51	61
WHATANUI ROCKS	ROCK	35 31 173 21	6
WHATARANGI	HSTD	41 29 175 13	53
WHATARANGI (TRIG)	HILL	41 28 175 15	53
WHATAROA	LOC	43 16 170 22	74
WHATAROA BASE SOUTH (TRIG)	HILL	43 14 170 23	74
WHATAROA RIVER	STRM	43 07 170 16	74
WHATAROA SADDLE	SAD	43 30 170 24	74
WHATAROA SADDLE	SAD	43 30 170 24	77
WHATAROA STREAM	STRM	37 54 176 15	20
WHATAROA STREAM	STRM	37 54 176 15	21
WHATAROA (TRIG)	HILL	43 08 170 20	74
WHATAROA (TRIG)	HILL	37 22 175 12	15
WHATATUTU	LOC	38 23 177 50	32
WHATAUMU STREAM	STRM	39 35 175 07	36
WHATAWHATA	LOC	37 48 175 09	18
WHATIPU	LOC	37 02 174 30	12
WHATIPU STREAM	STRM	37 03 174 30	12
WHATITIRI	LOC	35 47 174 10	5
WHATITIRI	LOC	35 47 174 10	7
WHATNO, MOUNT (TRIG)	MTN	42 56 172 17	71
WHATORO	LOC	35 45 173 41	6
WHATUPUKE ISLAND	ISLD	35 54 174 45	8
WHATUWHIWHI	LOC	34 53 173 25	3
WHAU POINT	PNT	35 38 174 32	5
WHAU POINT	PNT	35 38 174 32	8
WHAU RIVER	STRM	36 51 174 41	11
WHAU RIVER	STRM	36 51 174 41	12
WHAWANUI RIVER	STRM	41 34 175 24	53
WHAWHARUA	LOC	38 15 175 14	18
WHAWHARUA	LOC	38 15 175 14	19
WHAWHARUA	LOC	38 15 175 14	27
WHEADONS CREEK	STRM	41 18 173 49	54
WHEADONS CREEK	STRM	41 18 173 49	60
WHEADONS CREEK	STRM	41 18 173 49	61
WHEAO RIVER	STRM	38 34 176 38	30
WHEAO STREAM	STRM	38 29 177 50	32
WHEATSHEAF CORNER	LOC	43 36 172 31	81
WHEATSHEAF CORNER	LOC	43 36 172 31	82
WHEATSHEAF CORNER	LOC	43 36 172 31	83
WHEATSHEAF CORNER	LOC	43 36 172 31	85
WHEATSTONE	LOC	44 01 171 45	84
WHEEL CREEK	STRM	42 04 172 11	64
WHEELER CREEK	STRM	42 01 172 23	65
WHEKI VALLEY	LOC	35 48 174 07	5
WHEKI VALLEY	LOC	35 48 174 07	7
WHELAN CREEK	STRM	43 24 169 51	76
WHENUAHOU	LOC	40 05 176 18	47
WHENUAKITE	LOC	36 55 175 47	16
WHENUAKITE	LOC	36 55 175 47	17
WHENUAKITE RIVER	STRM	36 54 175 43	16
WHENUAKITE RIVER	STRM	36 54 175 43	17

WHENUAKURA ISLAND	ISLD	37 13 175 54	17
WHENUAKURA RIVER	STRM	39 47 174 31	44
WHENUANUI	LOC	36 05 174 03	7
WHENUAPAI	LOC	36 47 174 38	11
WHENUAPAI	LOC	36 47 174 38	12
WHERONUI STREAM	STRM	35 22 174 14	5
WHETU (TRIG)	HILL	40 33 175 41	49
WHETUKURA	LOC	40 09 176 18	47
WHETURAU (TRIG)	HILL	38 17 177 50	32
WHIRINAKI	LOC	35 29 173 28	6
WHIRINAKI RIVER	STRM	35 27 173 28	6
WHIRINAKI RIVER	STRM	38 26 176 42	30
WHIRINAKI STREAM	STRM	38 20 176 12	21
WHIRINAKI STREAM	STRM	38 20 176 12	29
WHIRINAKI (TRIG)	HILL	39 15 175 02	36
WHIRITOA	LOC	37 17 175 54	17
WHIRITOA STREAM	STRM	37 18 175 55	17
WHIRIWHIRI	LOC	37 17 174 42	14
WHIRLING WATER	STRM	43 08 170 45	74
WHISKY GULLY	STRM	45 55 169 16	110
WHISTLER RIVER	STRM	43 11 172 09	81
WHITBOURN SADDLE	SAD	44 27 168 34	88
WHITBOURN SADDLE	SAD	44 27 168 34	90
WHITCOMBE, MOUNT	MTN	43 13 170 55	75
WHITCOMBE PASS	PASS	43 14 170 58	75
WHITCOMBE RIVER	STRM	42 59 171 00	75
WHITE BLUFFS	CLIF	41 34 174 09	60
WHITE BURN	STRM	45 14 168 19	95
WHITE BURN	STRM	45 14 168 19	98
WHITE CLIFFS	CLIF	38 51 174 34	26
WHITE COL	SAD	43 00 171 24	75
WHITE COL	SAD	43 00 171 24	80
WHITE CREEK	STRM	46 08 167 33	105
WHITE CREEK	STRM	46 08 167 33	106
WHITE CREEK	STRM	46 08 167 33	108
WHITE HEAD	HEAD	46 31 169 42	113
WHITE HERON LAGOON	LAKE	43 11 170 26	74
WHITE HILL	MTN	45 41 167 47	106
WHITE HILL	HILL	45 46 168 18	107
WHITE HILL (TRIG)	HILL	45 49 167 35	105
WHITE HILL (TRIG)	HILL	45 49 167 35	106
WHITE HILL (TRIG)	PEAK	46 06 167 32	105
WHITE HILL (TRIG)	PEAK	46 06 167 32	106
WHITE HILL (TRIG)	PEAK	46 06 167 32	108
WHITE ISLAND	ISLD	45 56 170 30	103
WHITE ISLAND	ISLD	46 45 168 28	115
WHITE ISLAND (WHAKAARI)	ISLD	37 31 177 11	23
WHITE KNIGHT	PEAK	42 11 171 29	63
WHITE, MOUNT (TRIG)	MTN	43 01 171 58	80
WHITE, MOUNT (TRIG)	MTN	43 01 171 58	81
WHITE PEAK	PEAK	45 53 167 15	105
WHITE PINE BUSH	LOC	38 00 176 57	22
WHITE PINE BUSH	LOC	38 00 176 57	23
WHITE POINT	PNT	45 05 168 28	95
WHITE POINT	PNT	45 05 168 28	98
WHITE RIVER	STRM	42 58 171 27	69
WHITE ROCK	ROCK	41 34 175 24	53
WHITE ROCK	HSTD	41 34 175 24	53
WHITE ROCK	LOC	43 10 172 27	81
WHITE ROCK	ROCK	47 08 168 00	114
WHITE ROCK	ROCK	47 08 168 00	115
WHITE ROCK POINT	PNT	46 42 167 55	108
WHITE ROCK POINT	PNT	46 42 167 55	109
WHITE ROCK POINT	PNT	46 42 167 55	114
WHITE ROCK POINT	PNT	46 42 167 55	115
WHITE ROCK RIVER	STRM	44 22 170 56	93
WHITE ROCKS	ROCK	41 05 174 22	54
WHITE ROCKS	ROCK	41 05 174 22	61
WHITE ROCKS	ROCK	47 07 168 06	115
WHITE, THE	MTN	44 25 169 02	90
WHITECLIFFS	LOC	43 28 171 54	80
WHITECLIFFS	LOC	43 28 171 54	81
WHITECOOMB (TRIG)	PEAK	45 36 169 05	99
WHITECOOMB CREEK	STRM	45 30 169 05	99
WHITECRAIG	LOC	45 08 170 54	102
WHITEHALL	LOC	37 52 175 35	19
WHITEHORN PASS	PASS	42 57 171 24	69
WHITEMANS VALLEY	LOC	41 05 175 10	52
WHITEMANS VALLEY	LOC	41 05 175 10	53
WHITEMANS VALLEY	LOC	41 05 175 10	55
WHITERIGG	LOC	46 04 168 57	110
WHITERIGG	LOC	46 04 168 57	112
WHITES GULLY	STRM	42 25 173 33	73
WHITESTONE RIVER	STRM	45 32 167 45	97
WHITESTONE RIVER	STRM	45 32 167 45	98
WHITEWATER RIVER	STRM	43 15 171 44	80
WHITEWATER RIVER	STRM	44 57 167 21	94
WHITEWATER RIVER	STRM	44 57 167 21	96
WHITFORD	LOC	36 57 174 57	12
WHITFORD	LOC	36 57 174 57	14
WHITIANGA	POPL	36 49 175 42	16
WHITIANGA	LOC	37 50 177 36	24
WHITIANGA BAY	BAY	37 50 177 36	24
WHITIANGA HARBOUR	HARB	36 52 175 41	16
WHITIKAHU	LOC	37 37 175 21	19
WHITIKAU	LOC	38 09 177 30	24
WHITIKAU STREAM	STRM	38 05 177 35	24
WHITIKAU STREAM	STRM	39 03 175 50	37
WHITIKAU STREAM	STRM	39 03 175 50	38
WHITIPIRORUA POINT	PNT	37 09 175 53	17
WHITLOW (TRIG)	HILL	41 11 172 50	58
WHITSTONE	LOC	45 04 170 55	102
WHITTENS CREEK	STRM	45 18 168 54	95
WHITTENS CREEK	STRM	45 18 168 54	99
WHYMPER GLACIER	GLCR	43 28 170 22	74
WHYMPER GLACIER	GLCR	43 28 170 22	77
WHYMPER SADDLE	SAD	43 30 170 23	74
WHYMPER SADDLE	SAD	43 30 170 23	77
WICK MOUNTAINS	MTNS	44 47 167 53	89
WICK MOUNTAINS	MTNS	44 47 167 53	94
WICKLIFFE BAY	BAY	45 50 170 44	103
WIDGEON, LAKE	LAKE	45 55 166 55	104
WIDGEON, LAKE	LAKE	45 55 166 55	105
WIG (TRIG)	HILL	40 42 176 19	50
WILBERFORCE RIVER	STRM	43 21 171 28	75
WILBERFORCE RIVER	STRM	43 21 171 28	80
WILBERG MOUNT (TRIG)	MTN	43 11 170 36	74
WILBERG RANGE	MTNS	43 14 170 37	74
WILBERG RIVER	STRM	43 16 170 34	74
WILCZEK PEAK	PEAK	43 26 170 21	74
WILCZEK PEAK	PEAK	43 26 170 21	77
WILD CATTLE HILL (TRIG)	HILL	43 40 172 51	82
WILD CATTLE HILL (TRIG)	HILL	43 40 172 51	83
WILD DOG CREEK	STRM	45 17 170 20	101
WILD MANS BROTHER RANGE	MTNS	43 27 171 05	75
WILD MANS HILL	MTN	43 25 171 03	75
WILD NATIVES RIVER	STRM	44 53 167 32	94
WILD NATIVES RIVER	STRM	44 53 167 32	97
WILD PUP STREAM	STRM	41 49 173 22	66
WILDER SETTLEMENT	LOC	40 15 176 30	50

WILLAWA POINT	PNT	41 58 174 03	67
WILLIAM, MOUNT	HILL	37 13 175 01	12
WILLIAM, MOUNT	HILL	37 13 175 01	13
WILLIAM, MOUNT	HILL	37 13 175 01	14
WILLIAM, MOUNT	MTN	42 58 171 38	69
WILLIAM, MOUNT	MTN	42 58 171 38	70
WILLIAM, MOUNT (TRIG)	MTN	41 46 171 50	63
WILLIAM, MOUNT (TRIG)	MTN	41 46 171 50	64
WILLIAM STREAM	STRM	42 04 173 26	66
WILLIAM, PORT	HARB	46 50 168 05	109
WILLIAMS, MOUNT	MTN	43 07 171 11	75
WILLIAMS, MOUNT	MTN	43 50 169 53	76
WILLIAMS, MOUNT	MTN	43 50 169 53	79
WILLIAMSON RIVER	STRM	44 23 168 24	88
WILLIAMSON RIVER	STRM	44 23 168 24	89
WILLOW BRIDGE	LOC	44 46 171 07	93
WILLOWBANK	LOC	46 02 169 01	110
WILLOWBANK	LOC	46 02 169 01	112
WILLOWBY	LOC	43 59 171 41	84
WILLOWFLAT	HSTD	39 00 176 57	40
WILLOWFLAT	HSTD	39 00 176 57	41
WILLS PASS	PASS	44 02 169 32	79
WILLS RIVER	STRM	44 03 169 23	79
WILLSHER BAY	BAY	46 24 169 47	113
WILMER, MOUNT	MTN	42 23 172 41	71
WILMONT, LAKE	LAKE	44 23 168 13	88
WILMONT, LAKE	LAKE	44 23 168 13	89
WILMONT SADDLE	SAD	44 23 168 50	90
WILMOT, MOUNT (TRIG)	MTN	45 31 167 11	96
WILMOT PASS	PASS	45 31 167 11	96
WILMUR, MOUNT	MTN	44 47 167 48	94
WILSON CREEK	STRM	44 05 169 22	78
WILSON HILL (TRIG)	HILL	43 15 172 00	81
WILSON, LAKE	LAKE	44 43 168 11	89
WILSON, MOUNT	MTN	42 56 171 40	70
WILSON, MOUNT (TRIG)	MTN	42 43 171 52	70
WILSON, MOUNT (TRIG)	MTN	42 40 173 22	72
WILSON, MOUNT (TRIG)	MTN	42 40 173 22	73
WILSON RIVER	STRM	46 11 166 39	104
WILSON SADDLE	SAD	42 56 170 54	68
WILSON SWAMP	SWMP	43 24 170 00	76
WILSON SWAMP	SWMP	43 24 170 00	77
WILSONS CROSSING	LOC	46 15 168 20	107
WILSONS CROSSING	LOC	46 15 168 20	109
WILSONS POINT	PNT	47 17 167 36	114
WILSONS SIDING	LOC	43 22 172 36	82
WILSONS SIDING	LOC	43 22 172 36	83
WILSONS SIDING	LOC	43 22 172 36	85
WILSONVILLE	LOC	35 36 174 16	5
WILSONVILLE	LOC	35 36 174 16	7
WILSONVILLE	LOC	35 36 174 16	8
WILTON	SBRB	41 16 174 45	52
WILTON	SBRB	41 16 174 45	55
WILTSDOWN	LOC	38 10 175 48	19
WILTSDOWN	LOC	38 10 175 48	20
WIMBLEDON	LOC	40 26 176 30	50
WIN VALLEY STREAM	STRM	41 17 172 55	58
WINCHESTER	LOC	44 11 171 17	84
WINCHESTER	LOC	44 11 171 17	87
WINCHMORE	LOC	43 50 171 43	84
WINDBAG, THE	STRM	43 44 169 24	78
WINDEMERE, LAKE	LAKE	43 09 170 14	74
WINDERMERE	LOC	43 59 171 37	84
WINDING CREEK	STRM	43 11 171 50	80
WINDING CREEK	STRM	45 45 168 55	110
WINDLEY CREEK	STRM	45 23 168 25	98
WINDLEY RIVER	STRM	45 33 168 09	98
WINDON BURN	STRM	45 10 168 10	98
WINDROW CREEK	STRM	43 52 169 16	78
WINDSOR	LOC	45 00 170 48	93
WINDSOR	LOC	45 00 170 48	102
WINDSOR PARK	LOC	45 01 170 53	93
WINDSOR PARK	LOC	45 01 170 53	102
WINDSOR POINT	PNT	46 12 166 38	104
WINDWARD RIVER	STRM	45 09 167 10	96
WINDWHISTLE	LOC	43 31 171 43	80
WINDY HILL	LOC	35 56 173 59	7
WINDY HILL (TRIG)	HILL	35 55 173 59	7
WINDY HILL (TRIG)	HILL	36 18 175 32	9
WINDY KNOB (TRIG)	PEAK	42 38 172 37	71
WINDY PEAK (TRIG)	HILL	41 17 175 31	51
WINDY PEAK (TRIG)	HILL	41 17 175 31	53
WINDY POINT	PNT	41 24 174 59	52
WINDY POINT	PNT	41 24 174 59	55
WINDY RIVER COL	SAD	45 44 167 48	106
WINDY (TRIG)	HILL	40 54 176 10	50
WINGATE	SBRB	41 12 174 57	52
WINGATE	SBRB	41 12 174 57	55
WINGATUI	POPL	45 52 170 23	103
WINI (TRIG)	HILL	38 31 175 25	27
WINIATA	LOC	39 42 175 49	46
WINSCOMBE	LOC	44 08 170 50	87
WINSLOW	LOC	43 57 171 40	84
WINTERBURN STREAM	STRM	42 20 173 12	72
WINTERBURN STREAM	STRM	42 20 173 12	73
WINTERSLOW, MOUNT (TRIG)	MTN	43 35 171 24	75
WINTERSLOW, MOUNT (TRIG)	MTN	43 35 171 24	80
WINTERSLOW, MOUNT (TRIG)	MTN	43 35 171 24	84
WINTERSLOW RANGE	MTNS	43 35 171 28	75
WINTERSLOW RANGE	MTNS	43 35 171 28	80
WINTERSLOW RANGE	MTNS	43 35 171 28	84
WINTERTON RIVER	STRM	41 57 173 32	66
WINTON	POPL	46 09 168 19	107
WINTON HILL	HILL	46 07 168 24	107
WINTON PEAK	PEAK	45 07 168 02	97
WINTON PEAK	PEAK	45 07 168 02	98
WINTON STREAM	STRM	46 13 168 17	107
WIRE SADDLE	SAD	44 54 168 28	89
WIRE SADDLE	SAD	44 54 168 28	95
WIRITOA, LAKE	LAKE	39 59 175 05	45
WIROA ISLAND	ISLD	37 01 174 49	12
WIROA ISLAND	ISLD	37 01 174 49	14
WISE, MOUNT	MTN	42 07 171 38	63
WISE, MOUNT	MTN	42 07 171 38	64
WISELY, LAKE	LAKE	45 13 167 25	96
WISELY, LAKE	LAKE	45 13 167 25	97
WISH (TRIG)	HILL	41 30 175 15	53
WISP HILL (TRIG)	HILL	46 23 169 25	113
WISP RANGE	MTNS	46 22 169 25	113
WITHER PEAK	PEAK	45 11 168 32	95
WITHER PEAK	PEAK	45 11 168 32	99
WIWIKI, CAPE	CAPE	35 09 174 08	4
WIWIKI, CAPE	CAPE	35 09 174 08	5
WIX STREAM	STRM	42 37 172 01	70
WOLF RIVER	STRM	44 29 167 51	89
WOLSELEY, MOUNT	MTN	43 26 170 31	74
WOLSELEY, MOUNT	MTN	43 26 170 31	77
WOMENS ISLAND	ISLD	46 49 168 15	109
WOMENS ISLAND	ISLD	46 49 168 15	115
WONDERLAND STREAM	STRM	44 16 168 58	78

WOOD BURN	STRM	45 26 168 04	97
WOOD BURN	STRM	45 26 168 04	98
WOOD HILL (TRIG)	HILL	45 35 167 53	97
WOOD HILL (TRIG)	HILL	45 35 167 53	98
WOOD HILL (TRIG)	HILL	45 35 167 53	106
WOODBANK	HSTD	42 32 172 46	71
WOODBURY	LOC	44 02 171 12	87
WOODCHESTER	HSTD	42 36 173 13	72
WOODCHESTER	HSTD	42 36 173 13	73
WOODCOCKS	LOC	36 27 174 34	10
WOODCOCKS	LOC	36 27 174 34	11
WOODCUTTERS PEAK	PEAK	44 52 167 29	94
WOODED GULLY	STRM	43 13 172 20	81
WOODED ISLAND	ISLD	36 36 174 53	11
WOODED ISLAND	ISLD	36 36 174 53	12
WOODEND	LOC	43 19 172 40	82
WOODEND	LOC	43 19 172 40	83
WOODEND	LOC	43 19 172 40	85
WOODEND	LOC	46 28 168 24	109
WOODEND BEACH	LOC	43 20 172 42	82
WOODEND BEACH	LOC	43 20 172 42	83
WOODHEN COVE	BAY	45 38 166 33	104
WOODHEN CREEK	STRM	44 10 168 29	88
WOODHEN HILL	PEAK	45 36 167 55	106
WOODHEN POND	LAKE	44 11 168 28	88
WOODHILL	LOC	36 45 174 26	10
WOODHILL	LOC	36 45 174 26	11
WOODLANDS	LOC	37 32 175 54	17
WOODLANDS	LOC	38 02 177 16	23
WOODLANDS	LOC	46 23 168 33	109
WOODLAW	LOC	46 02 168 02	106
WOODLAW	LOC	46 02 168 02	107
WOODLAW (TRIG)	HILL	46 01 167 54	106
WOODLAW (TRIG)	HILL	46 01 167 54	107
WOODLEIGH	LOC	37 32 174 54	14
WOODPECKER BAY	BAY	42 01 171 23	63
WOODROW BURN	STRM	45 10 167 29	97
WOODSIDE	LOC	41 04 175 24	53
WOODSIDE	LOC	45 52 170 10	103
WOODSIDE CREEK	STRM	41 56 174 06	67
WOODSTOCK	LOC	41 16 172 50	58
WOODSTOCK	LOC	42 46 171 00	68
WOODSTOCK	LOC	42 46 171 00	69
WOODVILLE	POPL	40 21 175 52	49
WOODY HILL (TRIG)	HILL	37 02 175 48	16
WOODY HILL (TRIG)	HILL	37 02 175 48	17
WOOLHOUSE CREEK	STRM	42 51 170 50	68
WOOLLEY RIVER	STRM	42 11 172 13	64
WOOLLEYS BAY	LOC	35 34 174 29	5
WOOLLEYS BAY	BAY	35 34 174 29	5
WOOLLEYS BAY	LOC	35 34 174 29	8
WOOLSACK, THE (TRIG)	HILL	44 00 168 55	78
WOOLSHED CREEK	STRM	43 41 171 21	75
WOOLSHED CREEK	STRM	43 41 171 21	80
WOOLSHED CREEK	STRM	43 41 171 21	84
WOOLSHED HILL (TRIG)	PEAK	42 58 171 47	70
WOOLSHED STREAM	STRM	41 52 172 55	65
WOOLSHED STREAM	STRM	42 50 172 19	71
WOOLSHED (TRIG)	HILL	43 09 172 48	82
WOOLSTON	SBRB	43 33 172 41	82
WOOLSTON	SBRB	43 33 172 41	83
WOOLSTON	SBRB	43 33 172 41	85
WOOLWASH CREEK	STRM	39 24 176 10	39
WOORE, MOUNT (TRIG)	HILL	40 49 173 51	54
WOORE, MOUNT (TRIG)	HILL	40 49 173 51	61
WORKMAN (TRIG)	HILL	37 07 175 13	13
WORKMAN (TRIG)	HILL	37 07 175 13	15
WORSER BAY	BAY	41 19 174 50	52
WORSER BAY	BAY	41 19 174 50	55
WORSLEY ARM	BAY	44 57 167 52	94
WORSLEY ARM	BAY	44 57 167 52	97
WORSLEY ARM	BAY	44 57 167 52	98
WORSLEY PASS	PASS	42 51 171 45	70
WORSLEY PASS	PASS	44 54 167 40	94
WORSLEY PASS	PASS	44 54 167 40	97
WORSLEY STREAM	STRM	44 57 167 50	94
WORSLEY STREAM	STRM	44 57 167 50	97
WREYS BUSH	LOC	46 00 168 06	106
WREYS BUSH	LOC	46 00 168 06	107
WRIGHT COL	SAD	44 37 168 25	89
WRIGHTS BUSH	LOC	46 18 168 12	109
WRIGHTS CREEK	STRM	45 21 168 52	95
WRIGHTS CREEK	STRM	45 21 168 52	99
WYE CREEK	STRM	45 08 168 45	95
WYE CREEK	STRM	45 08 168 45	99
WYE CREEK (SOUTH BRANCH)	STRM	45 08 168 46	95
WYE CREEK (SOUTH BRANCH)	STRM	45 08 168 46	99
WYE RIVER	STRM	41 39 173 19	66
WYLDE BROWN, MOUNT	MTN	43 08 170 57	75
WYNDHAM	POPL	46 20 168 51	112
WYNN, MOUNT (TRIG)	MTN	41 57 172 03	64
WZANIA, MOUNT	MTN	44 08 168 54	78

X

XENICUS, MOUNT (TRIG)	MTN	44 43 168 11	89

Y

YALDHURST	LOC	43 31 172 30	81
YALDHURST	LOC	43 31 172 30	82
YALDHURST	LOC	43 31 172 30	83
YALDHURST	LOC	43 31 172 30	85
YANKS HILL (TRIG)	MTN	42 16 172 36	65
YARRA RIVER	STRM	42 20 173 00	66
YARRA SADDLE	SAD	42 18 172 59	66
YARROW STREAM	STRM	39 40 176 34	42
YARROW STREAM	STRM	39 40 176 34	43
YARROW STREAM	STRM	39 40 176 34	47
YASHMAK CREEK	STRM	44 21 168 32	88
YASHMAK CREEK	STRM	44 21 168 32	90
YATES POINT	PNT	44 30 167 49	94
YEO CREEK	STRM	42 45 171 48	70
YEO STREAM	STRM	42 06 173 15	66
YORK BAY	LOC	41 16 174 35	52
YORK BAY	LOC	41 16 174 35	55
YORK, MOUNT	HILL	45 34 167 44	97
YORKIES SADDLE	SAD	43 29 171 50	80
YOUNG HILL CREEK	STRM	45 07 169 28	100
YOUNG NICKS HEAD	HEAD	38 46 177 58	32
YOUNG NICKS HEAD	HEAD	38 46 177 58	33
YOUNG PEAK	PEAK	44 07 169 05	78
YOUNG, MOUNT	MTN	43 08 171 04	75
YOUNG, MOUNT	MTN	36 12 175 23	9
YOUNG RANGE	MTNS	44 10 169 25	78
YOUNG RANGE	MTNS	44 10 169 25	79
YOUNG RIVER	STRM	44 12 169 14	78

Za-Islands

■ Z

Name	Type	Coords	Pg
ZALAS CREEK	STRM	43 15 170 14	74
ZAMPA (TRIG)	MTN	42 21 172 27	71
ZEILIAN CREEK	STRM	43 54 169 31	76
ZEILIAN CREEK	STRM	43 54 169 31	79
ZETLAND, MOUNT	PEAK	41 24 172 16	62
ZIGZAG (TRIG)	HILL	43 39 172 55	82
ZIGZAG (TRIG)	HILL	43 39 172 55	83
ZIT SADDLE	SAD	42 59 171 11	68
ZIT SADDLE	SAD	42 59 171 11	69
ZORA CREEK	STRM	43 48 169 50	76
ZORA CREEK	STRM	43 48 169 50	79
ZORA GLACIER	GLCR	43 45 169 49	76
ZORA GLACIER	GLCR	43 45 169 49	79

ANTIPODES ISLANDS

Name	Type	Coords	Pg
ALBATROSS POINT	PNT	49 43 178 47	116
BOLLONS	ISLD	49 39 178 49	116
CAVE POINT	PNT	49 41 178 44	116
GALLOWAY, MOUNT	HILL	49 41 178 47	116
LEEWARD	ISLD	49 42 178 49	116
NORTH CAPE	CAPE	49 40 178 48	116
REEF POINT	PNT	49 40 178 49	116
RINGDOVE BAY	BAY	49 43 178 47	116
STACK BAY	BAY	49 42 178 44	116
WINDWARD ISLANDS	ISLS	49 41 178 43	116

AUCKLAND ISLANDS

Name	Type	Coords	Pg
ADAM ROCKS	ROCK	50 51 165 54	118
ADAMS	ISLD	50 53 166 03	118
ASTROLABE POINT	PNT	50 54 165 57	118
AUCKLAND	ISLD	50 42 166 06	118
BENNETT, CAPE	CAPE	50 50 166 15	118
BIVOUAC HILL	HILL	50 36 166 07	118
BLACK HEAD	HEAD	50 31 166 08	118
BRISTOW POINT	PNT	50 46 165 53	118
CARNLEY HARBOUR	BAY	50 51 166 07	118
CASTLE POINT	PNT	50 54 166 06	118
CAVERN PEAK	HILL	50 45 166 07	118
CHAMBRES INLET	BAY	50 37 166 12	118
CIRCULAR HEAD	HEAD	50 48 166 02	118
CLOUDY PEAK	HILL	50 35 166 09	118
CROZIER POINT	PNT	50 33 166 18	118
DEEP INLET	BAY	50 45 166 12	118
DICK, MOUNT	HILL	50 54 166 02	118
DISAPPOINTMENT	ISLD	50 36 165 59	118
DUNDAS	ISLD	50 35 166 20	118
D'URVILLE, MOUNT	HILL	50 49 166 09	118
EASTON, MOUNT	HILL	50 38 166 06	118
ENDERBY	ISLD	50 30 166 18	118
EREBUS COVE	BAY	50 33 166 14	118
EWING	ISLD	50 32 166 19	118
FALLA PENINSULA	PEN	50 42 166 11	118
FARR, CAPE	CAPE	50 52 166 14	118
FLEMING PLATEAU	PLAT	50 48 165 57	118
GILROY HEAD	HEAD	50 53 166 07	118
GRAFTON POINT	PNT	50 51 166 04	118
GREEN	ISLD	50 34 166 22	118

Name	Type	Coords	Pg
HASKELL BAY	BAY	50 35 166 15	118
HINEMOA, LAKE	LAKE	50 39 166 09	118
HOGSBACK	HILL	50 37 166 12	118
HOOKER	HILL	50 33 166 09	118
INVERCAULD ROCK	ROCK	50 34 166 02	118
KEKENO POINT	PNT	50 35 166 18	118
LANTERN ROCKS	ROCK	50 53 165 57	118
LOGAN POINT	PNT	50 52 165 55	118
LOVITT, CAPE	CAPE	50 48 165 53	118
MASKED	ISLD	50 51 166 02	118
MCCLURE HEAD	HEAD	50 49 166 01	118
MCLENNAN INLET	BAY	50 48 166 13	118
MEGGS HILL	HILL	50 34 166 14	118
MUSGRAVE INLET	BAY	50 40 166 11	118
MUSGRAVE PENINSULA	PEN	50 50 166 03	118
NORMAN INLET	BAY	50 44 166 11	118
NORTH ARM	BAY	50 46 166 02	118
NORTH POINT	PNT	50 31 166 11	118
NORTH WEST CAPE	CAPE	50 32 166 04	118
OMEGA PEAK	HILL	50 41 166 06	118
PINNACLE ROCKS	ROCK	50 36 165 57	118
PORT ROSS	BAY	50 32 166 14	118
RAYNAL, MOUNT	HILL	50 44 166 03	118
ROSE	ISLD	50 31 166 15	118
SHAG ROCK	ROCK	50 43 166 13	118
SIGNBOARD POINT	PNT	50 41 166 12	118
SMITH HARBOUR	BAY	50 41 166 11	118
SOUTH CAPE	CAPE	50 56 166 05	118
SOUTH WEST CAPE	CAPE	50 50 165 58	118
SPEIGHT, LAKE	LAKE	50 49 165 59	118
SUGAR LOAF ROCKS	ROCK	50 36 166 02	118
TAGUA BAY	BAY	50 49 166 05	118
THE DOME	HILL	50 52 166 06	118
THOMSON, CAPE	CAPE	50 55 166 08	118
TOWER OF BABEL	HILL	50 48 165 58	118
TURBOTT, LAKE	LAKE	50 54 166 03	118
TUTANEKAI, LAKE	LAKE	50 38 166 15	118
VICTORIA PASSAGE	STRA	50 51 165 50	118
WATERFALL INLET	BAY	50 49 166 13	118
WESTERN ARM	BAY	50 52 166 00	118
YULE	ISLD	50 32 166 19	118

BOUNTY ISLANDS

Name	Type	Coords	Pg
CENTRE GROUP	ISLS	47 46 179 02	116
EAST GROUP	ISLS	47 46 179 03	116
MAIN GROUP	ISLS	47 45 179 01	116

CAMPBELL ISLAND

Name	Type	Coords	Pg
COURREJOLLES POINT	PNT	52 29 169 08	118
DENT	ISLD	52 32 169 04	118
DUMAS, MOUNT	HILL	52 34 169 06	118
EAST CAPE	CAPE	52 33 169 16	118
EREBUS POINT	PNT	52 34 169 16	118
FAYE, MOUNT	HILL	52 30 169 11	118
HONEY, MOUNT	HILL	52 34 169 16	118
HOOKER STREAM	STRM	52 29 169 12	118
JACQUEMART	ISLD	52 37 169 08	118
LYALL, MOUNT	HILL	52 32 169 10	118
MOUBRAY HILL	HILL	52 33 169 16	118
NORTH CAPE	CAPE	52 28 169 14	118

Name	Type	Coords	Pg
NORTH EAST HARBOUR	BAY	52 31 169 14	118
NORTH WEST BAY	BAY	52 33 169 06	118
PARIS, MOUNT	HILL	52 34 169 03	118
PERSEVERANCE HARBOUR	BAY	52 33 169 12	118
SMOOTHWATER BAY	BAY	52 33 169 15	118
SOUTH EAST HARBOUR	BAY	52 36 169 11	118
SOUTH POINT	PNT	52 35 169 15	118

CHATHAM ISLANDS

Name	Type	Coords	Pg
BIG BUSH	LOC	43 53 176 33	117
CATTLE POINT	PNT	43 47 176 33	117
CHATHAM	ISLD	43 52 176 30	117
DURHAM, POINT	PNT	44 01 176 42	117
FANCY ROCK	ROCK	44 23 176 09	117
FLOWER POT	LOC	44 15 176 15	117
FOURNIER, CAPE	CAPE	44 03 176 20	117
GAP, POINT	PNT	44 04 176 40	117
GILLESPIE CREEK	STRM	44 01 176 24	117
HANSON BAY	BAY	43 54 176 20	117
HEAPHY SHOAL	SHL	43 58 176 37	117
HOURUAKOPARA	ISLD	44 06 176 32	117
HURO, LAKE	LAKE	43 57 176 31	117
HUTT, PORT (WHANGAROA HARBOUR)	HARB	43 49 176 42	117
ISLAND REEF	REEF	43 50 176 43	117
KAHUITARA	PNT	44 16 176 10	117
KAINGARAHU, LAKE	LAKE	43 50 176 23	117
KAINGAROA HARBOUR	BAY	43 44 176 16	117
KAIRAE, LAKE	LAKE	43 51 176 24	117
KAREWA POINT	PNT	43 49 176 27	117
L'EVEQUE, CAPE	CAPE	44 08 176 38	117
LONG BEACH	BCH	43 52 176 34	117
MAINUI, LAKE	LAKE	43 51 176 24	117
MAKARA RIVER	STRM	43 59 176 26	117
MANGAHOU CREEK	STRM	43 59 176 26	117
MANGERE	ISLD	44 16 176 18	117
MANUKAU REEF	REEF	44 02 176 20	117
MARAKAPIA, LAKE	LAKE	43 51 176 34	117
MATAKITAKI	HILL	43 49 176 51	117
MAUNGANUI BEACH	BCH	43 46 176 45	117
MIHITOROA POINT	PNT	43 46 176 31	117
MOTUTAPU	PNT	44 14 176 14	117
MUNNING, POINT	PNT	43 44 176 13	117
NAIRN RIVER	STRM	43 57 176 33	117
NAPPER POINT	PNT	43 49 176 41	117
OKAWA POINT	PNT	43 47 176 15	117
OLD MAN REEF	REEF	44 01 176 21	117
OWENGA	LOC	44 02 176 22	117
PARITU	PNT	43 49 176 38	117
PATERIKI, LAKE	LAKE	43 45 176 19	117
PATTISSON, CAPE	CAPE	43 45 176 49	117
PETRE BAY	BAY	43 54 176 37	117
PITT	ISLD	44 17 176 13	117
PITT STRAIT	STRA	44 06 176 18	117
RABBIT	ISLD	44 15 176 15	117
RAKEINUI LAKE	LAKE	44 06 176 35	117
RANGATIRA	ISLD	44 21 176 11	117
RANGIAURIA	PNT	44 20 176 16	117
RANGITAI, LAKE	LAKE	43 46 176 21	117
RED BLUFF	CLIF	43 54 176 33	117
RENWEEKS REEF	REEF	44 04 176 22	117

Name	Type	Coords	Pg
ROTOEKA, LAKE	LAKE	43 47 176 36	117
ROTOKAWAU, LAKE	LAKE	43 45 176 36	117
TAIAU, LAKE	LAKE	43 52 176 25	117
TAUPEKA POINT	PNT	43 44 176 30	117
TE ONE	LOC	43 56 176 32	117
TE RANGATAPU, LAKE	LAKE	44 07 176 36	117
TE WAPU, LAKE	LAKE	43 45 176 15	117
TE WHANGA LAGOON	LAGN	43 50 176 27	117
TENNANTS LAKE	LAKE	43 50 176 35	117
THE CASTLE	ISLD	44 18 176 21	117
THE FORT	ISLD	44 17 176 20	117
THE PYRAMID	ISLD	44 26 176 15	117
THE SISTERS	ISLD	43 34 176 49	117
TUTUIRI CREEK	STRM	43 45 176 40	117
UREPURIRI	PNT	43 51 176 48	117
WHAIHERE BAY	BAY	44 16 176 15	117
WAIKAUIA, LAKE	LAKE	43 43 176 38	117
WAIKAWA	ISLD	43 45 176 15	117
WAITANGI	TOWN	43 57 176 33	117
WAITANGI WEST	LOC	43 48 176 50	117
WHANGAROA HARBOUR (PORT HUTT)	HARB	43 49 176 42	117
WHAREKAURI	LOC	43 43 176 35	117
WHAREMANU, LAKE	LAKE	43 45 176 25	117
YOUNG, CAPE	CAPE	43 42 176 38	117

KERMADEC ISLANDS

Name	Type	Coords	Pg
BLUE LAKE	LAKE	29 15 177 54	116
CHEESEMAN	ISLD	30 32 178 35	116
CURTIS	ISLD	30 32 178 36	116
D'ARCY POINT	PNT	29 18 177 55	116
DENHAM BAY	BAY	29 16 177 57	116
GREEN LAKE	LAKE	29 16 177 55	116
HASZARD	ISLD	30 14 178 25	116
HASZARD, MOUNT	HILL	30 14 178 24	116
HERALD ISLET	ISLS	29 15 177 51	116
HUTCHISON BLUFF	CLIF	29 15 177 58	116
L'ESPERANCE ROCK	ROCK	31 21 178 50	116
MACAULEY	ISLD	30 14 178 24	116
MEYER ISLANDS	ISLS	29 15 177 57	116
NAPIER	ISLD	29 14 177 52	116
NASH POINT	PNT	29 17 177 53	116
NUGENT	ISLD	29 14 177 52	116
RAOUL	ISLD	29 16 177 55	116
RAYNER POINT	PNT	29 15 177 53	116
SMITH BLUFF	CLIF	29 18 177 57	116
STELLA PASSAGE	STRA	30 32 178 36	116
WEST BLUFF	CLIF	30 14 178 24	116

SNARES ISLANDS

Name	Type	Coords	Pg
ALERT STACK	ISLD	48 02 166 34	116
BROUGHTON	ISLD	48 02 166 36	116
DAPTION ROCKS	ROCK	48 00 166 36	116
NORTH EAST	ISLD	48 01 166 36	116
NORTH PROMONTORY	PNT	48 00 166 36	116
SOUTH PROMONTORY	PNT	48 02 166 37	116
VANCOUVER ROCK	ROCK	48 03 166 31	116
WESTERN CHAIN	ISLS	48 03 166 30	116